Learning and Practicing Econometrics

William E. Griffiths
University of New England
Armidale, Australia

R. Carter Hill
Louisiana State University

George G. Judge
University of California, Berkeley

D1394001

JOHN WILEY & SONS, INC.
New York   Chichester   Brisbane   Toronto   Singapore

The cover features a newly issued 10 DM bill containing a portrait of
Carl Friedrich Gauss (1777–1855) and a graphic illustrating the
normal distribution. Gauss, who is ranked as one of the three or four
greatest mathematicians of all time, and one of the fathers of
statistics, fulfilled the role of establishing and popularizing the
normal probability distribution. Gauss shares with Legendre the
development of the method of least squares and used this principle in
1801, with a few observations, to predict the location of a missing
planet. The linear regression model, one of the basic statisitical
models covered in this book, owes so much to Gauss that probably it
should be called the Gauss linear model.

Acquisitions Editor	Whitney Blake
Marketing Manager	Carolyn Henderson
Production Supervisor	Sandra Russell
Designer	Laura Nicholls
Digital Production Supervisor	Ann Louise Stevens
Manufacturing Manager	Lorraine Fumoso/Andrea Price
Copy Editing Supervisor	Deborah Herbert
Illustration Coordinator	Edward Starr

This book was set in Times Roman by Digital Production

Coventry University

Library of Congress Cataloging-in-Publication Data:

Griffiths, William E.
   Learning and practicing econometrics / William E. Griffiths, R.
Carter Hill, George G. Judge.
   Includes bibliographical references and index.

   1. Econometrics.   I. Hill, R. Carter.   II. Judge, George G.
III. Title.
HB139.G75   1992
330'.01'5195—dc20   92-22788
                                                CIP

Printed in Singapore

10 9 8 7 6 5 4 3 2 1

To
my wife, JoAnn Griffiths
my wife, Melissa Waters
my sister, Pauline Judge Cannon

Preface

APPROACH OF THIS BOOK

The objective of this book is to integrate, at an elementary level, economic and statistical models and econometric methods, in a way that puts some economics into econometrics and that parallels the process followed in empirical economic research.

Introductory and intermediate economic textbooks contain economic models that provide a basis for tracing through the allocative and distributive impacts that result from alternative choices. Conventional econometric and statistical textbooks present a wide range of statistical-sampling models and methods for estimating and testing hypotheses about the corresponding unknown parameters. They occasionally identify the statistical model with a quasi-real-world problem but, all too often, the relationship between the economic and statistical models is unclear and the student is left with the question: Where do statistical models come from? To motivate students in their study of econometrics, and to provide a better training ground for a practicing economist, we seek a greater integration of economics and inferential statistics than that provided in most traditional introductory econometrics books. Our hope is that students will also learn some economics by actually applying the tools of statistical inference within an econometric format. By starting with the economic model, the student should acquire an operational knowledge of the applicability of a range of statistical tools and gain some insights into the research process.

The intersection of economics, econometrics, and economic data defines the field of applied econometrics. What gives this field richness is the possibility of using real economic variables (observables) to obtain information about real unknown economic parameters so that we may effectively deal with real decision problems. In the search and learning process, the economic theory base is paramount. Economic models provide a basis for describing the sampling process by which the underlying data are thought to be generated and, thus, form the basis for specifying the statistical model and identifying effective information-processing (decision) rules, interpreting the results, and devising a basis for choice or action. It is important for introductory material to be written within this framework, for that is how good empirical economic research is carried out.

In the analysis of economic problems, there often exists much prior information about the unknown economic parameters, an idea about the uses to which the information is to be put, and a desire to be able to evaluate the consequences of pursuing alternative courses of action. In addition, economic data are usually scarce, and we do not have the luxury of an infinite sample or an infinite number of repeated samples. Consequently, in addition to the traditional sampling theory approach to inference, we make it possible to introduce the student to inference procedures that take account, within a decision framework, of whatever data and prior or nonsample information that we have.

CHAPTER FORMAT

Based on these foundation stones, in this book we observe the following guidelines:

1. As a format, we *(i)* start each chapter with a particular economic problem(s), *(ii)* identify the relevant economic framework and specify the corresponding economic model, *(iii)* use this information in specifying the statistical-sampling model, *(iv)* identify data consistent with the specified statistical model and note any unique characteristics it has, *(v)* consider alternative methods of estimation and inference and select an efficient information-processing rule, *(vi)* present the empirical results, *(vii)* discuss the statistical and economic implications, and *(viii)* identify other economic models for which the statistical model and estimation rule may be used.

2. We make it possible for the student to understand and use both sampling theory and Bayesian methods of inference to interweave economic theory, inferential statistics, and practice.

3. We make the computer an important foundation and a tool in the teaching and learning process.

This book has an elementary focus and is intended for undergraduates or graduates who have had basic elementary courses in statistics and mathematics and introductory and/or intermediate courses in economics. It is assumed that students have had little or no exposure to the simple and general linear (regression) statistical model. Two chapters are provided for instructors who wish to introduce Bayesian techniques to students who have studied regression analysis from only a sampling theory viewpoint.

This book is not intended as examples-of-applications for students who have completed an intermediate level econometrics course by using the equivalent of a text such as *Introduction to the Theory and Practice of Econometrics* (Judge et al., Wiley 1988). Instead, the book focuses on developing new econometric tools as the student faces various economic problems and takes on the task of learning about them from samples of economic data. Thus, in contrast to conventional econometric texts, we start with the economic problem and conceptual model and then specify the appropriate statistical model. This approach gives the student a feeling for the importance of the economic model in the research process and a basis for selecting the appropriate econometric tool when he or she is confronted with analyzing the data associated with an economic problem. It is hoped that this approach not only will let the student *gain an understanding of econometrics* but that it will help to build an *operational knowledge of economics*.

Economic questions or problems are linked, when possible, to discussions in popular introductory and intermediate economics texts, and are chosen because of their convenience as vehicles to deal with economic data that require, for analysis purposes, increasingly more difficult econometric techniques. Given the economic questions, the emphasis is on the relationship between the economic and statistical models, on how to choose estimation (information-processing) rules consistent with the underlying sampling model, on the computer implementation of the techniques to obtain empirical results, and on the interpretation of the resulting statistics and how to make use of them within a decision context.

ANCILLARY MATERIALS

Computer Handbooks relating to the problems discussed in each of the chapters of the book, and that use SHAZAM and SAS software packages, have been prepared and are available to make the computer an integral part of the teaching–learning process.

In particular, the SAS and SHAZAM computer manuals (1) provide computer code to produce all the empirical results in the book, and explain the computer output; (2) provide sufficient background in each chapter to carry out the empirical and Monte Carlo exercises; and (3) include in some chapter appendices with programs for the more advanced topics. The *Computer Handbooks* provide convenient instructed procedures for learning each of the software packages.

A comprehensive *Instructor's Manual* has been prepared that (1) contains material to aid the instructor in presenting the concepts to be emphasized in each chapter; (2) provides answers to all analytical, empirical and Monte Carlo exercises; and (3) provides computer programs for all empirical exercises.

Possible ways in which the instructor and students may extend the statistical models presented are identified with relevant sections in the chapters of the first and second editions of *Introduction to the Theory and Practice of Econometrics*. An extensive set of exercises is included in each chapter with a range of economic data sets.

SUGGESTED COURSE FORMATS

This book is designed so that it can be used in a one- or two-quarter/semester context. For example, consider the following:

1. Students who have a limited statistical background may focus on a review of basic statistical concepts and the analysis and interrelation of observable economic variables through variants of the simple and general linear (regression) model. This route would involve Chapters 1 to 11.

2. Students wanting a review of sampling theory inference and an introduction to Bayesian inference and the simple regression model may cover Chapters 1 to 8 and Chapters 24 and 25.

3. Students with a good background in statistics may review Chapters 1 to 8 and focus on the general linear statistical model, Chapters 9 to 11, and a selection of what-if questions for single and multiple equation models, that is, Chapters 12 to 23 and Chapter 26. To facilitate this strategy, summary-reviews are provided at the end of Parts I (Chapters 2 to 4) and II (Chapters 5 to 8).

Each instructor will, of course, wish to emphasize different aspects of the econometric story, and the book is designed to accommodate this objective. Table P.1 suggests some of the topic-roads that may be followed through the book. In Table P.1 it is assumed that instructors will work their way down the chapters in the core column (starting at the appropriate point for their students) and then will branch out to the topics in the right-hand column when and where they see fit. The arrows from the left-hand column suggest the earliest point at which the topics on the right should be covered. Instructors interested in obtaining for their classes a customized book containing only a subset of chapters should contact John Wiley & Sons, Inc. Economics Editor.

Starting with Chapter 10 the book is also organized to provide either an introductory or fairly complete coverage of each topic. For example, in regard to heteroskedasticity or autocorrelation, the student may discover why these departures in error characteristics may cause a problem and then may stop anywhere along the estimation and inference way leading to the estimated generalized least squares estimator and its asymptotic properties.

Table P.1   Some Alternative Paths Through the Chapters of the Book

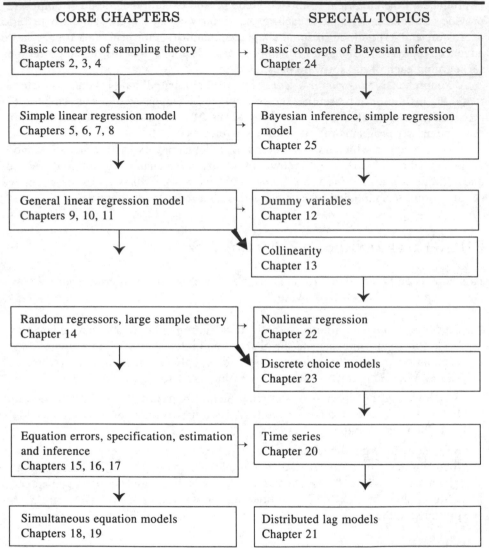

CORE CHAPTERS	SPECIAL TOPICS
Basic concepts of sampling theory Chapters 2, 3, 4	Basic concepts of Bayesian inference Chapter 24
Simple linear regression model Chapters 5, 6, 7, 8	Bayesian inference, simple regression model Chapter 25
General linear regression model Chapters 9, 10, 11	Dummy variables Chapter 12
	Collinearity Chapter 13
Random regressors, large sample theory Chapter 14	Nonlinear regression Chapter 22
	Discrete choice models Chapter 23
Equation errors, specification, estimation and inference Chapters 15, 16, 17	Time series Chapter 20
Simultaneous equation models Chapters 18, 19	Distributed lag models Chapter 21

USE OF LINEAR ALGEBRA

Appendices containing linear algebra specifications and operations are introduced in the early chapters of the book. However, the book is written so that it is possible for the student to cover the concepts and topics introduced in the first eight chapters without using linear algebra. This means a simple scalar notation may be used in covering the early chapters while the student gains a basic understanding of linear algebra operations and specifications that are important, starting with Chapter 9. Appendices are also introduced in the early chapters that provide a review and application of integral and differential calculus as it relates to the interpretation and analysis of economic-statistical models.

ACKNOWLEDGEMENTS

For us, the authors, this has been a joint venture, and the order of the names has nothing more than alphabetic significance. We developed the conviction early on in writing this introductory book that one changes the way students think about the econometric world one word-equation at a time. We hope that the process that has evolved has resulted in a meaningful mix of words, symbols, and ideas.

Many individuals helped to shape the contents of this book, including many colleagues who helped to identify some of our errors of commission or omission. We thank the following reviewers: M. M. Ali, University of Kentucky; R. T. Ballie, Michigan State University; C. W. Mischoff, SUNY Binghamton; A. Bhargava, University of Wisconsin—Whitewater; A. S. Caniglia, Franklin & Marshall College; F. X. Diebold, Federal Reserve Bank of Philadelphia; R. L. Dixon, University of Arkansas; G. E. Metcalf, Princeton University; W. Parke, University of North Carolina—Chapel Hill; J. F. Quinn, Boston College; G. Solon, University of Michigan; H. Stokes, University of Illinois—Chicago; M. E. Storer, University of Missouri—St. Louis; R. A. Stout, Knox College; D. Sullivan, Princeton University; R. E. Townsend, University of Maine; P. Trivedi, Indiana University; K. West, University of Wisconsin—Madison; Frank Wolak, Stanford University; G. D. Wozniak, University of Tulsa; F. C. Wycoff, Pomona College.

For a book of this nature a skilled person to do the word-equation processing is a necessity. In this context, Dana Keil provided an interface with Wiley in the preparation of the manuscript disks and was a valuable colleague in preparing the many drafts for each chapter.

Others who helped by reading or doing some of the rough word processing for various chapters include Duangkamon Chotikapanich, Diane Dancer, H. Hessenius, Tae-Hwy Lee, S. Nano, S. Yoo, and M. Youman.

William E. Griffiths
R. Carter Hill
George G. Judge

Contents

Part VIII   *Econometric Topics II*   **709**

Chapter 1

Why Is Econometrics Necessary?

New Key Words and Concepts

Economic Problems	Economic Model
Economic Relationship	Statistical Model
Sample Information	Controlled Experiment
Nonexperimental Data	Statistical Inference
Unknown Parameters	Learning and Research Format

Economics is a social *science*. Its subject matter is society, and the behavior of institutions and individuals of which it is composed. It is called a science to reflect the fact that, as a discipline, knowledge is built via the scientific method. This simply means that theories about phenomena in the economic domain are subjected to scrutiny that is both logical and empirical. The deductive logic by which a theory is developed is carefully checked. Then the implications or predictions of the theory are tested by observing whether real-world experience is consistent with them. The latter step is carried out by using scientific methods to generate and interpret (analyze) *data*.

"Pure" scientific inquiry is one of the things that economists do. Economists engaged in pure research are found in universities, private "think tanks," government agencies and, to some extent, in economic research units within private corporations. These economists devote themselves to developing theories and to refining economic logic. Many research economists, however, both build theories *and* then test these theories by analyzing data. Also, economists who build economic theories must be aware of the outcome of data analyses, and how these outcomes relate to the theories on which they are working. Thus, in the daily lives of many research economists, the analysis of *data* is a *major* preoccupation.

What kind of questions are of concern to both economists who build theories and to those who engage in data analyses? One has to do only a casual reading of the daily newspaper or a sampling of a national news program to see that economic questions are pervasive. In fact, the number of questions underlying decisions or choices regarding our own economic welfare or that of others is seemingly infinite. Consider these examples:

What is the impact of the federal budget deficit on the level of interest rates and the rate of inflation?

Is there a relationship between the level of interest rates and the level of the Dow-Jones Stock Index?

How do recent mergers and leveraged buy-outs of corporations affect the returns to stockholders?

How does the trade deficit affect the level of employment and the bargaining position of labor unions?

What is the relationship between the quantity of money, say M-1, and the level of economic activity?

If the Federal Reserve increases the discount rate, will this cause stagflation?

How will changes in the tax law affect the distribution of income?

Does the level of economic well-being have an impact on crime patterns across cities?

What is the impact of changing the capital gains tax on the level of investment?

If the rent control law is repealed, what will be the impact on apartment and house prices in Berkeley, California, next year?

Should I invest in long-term government bonds or short-term treasury bills?

Economists have some things to say about all of these questions. Thus, economists are often called on by those in decision-making positions, in government and the private sector, to provide economic input into a decision process. Although some of the input may be general in nature, economists are most frequently called on to answer questions beginning with the phrase, "How much." Answers to questions like these can be obtained *only* by *analyzing data*. Let us be more specific and consider the following examples:

1. The President of the United States contemplates an increase in the income tax to pay for new social programs. The Council of Economic Advisors is asked: How much will unemployment, inflation, and real gross national product change if income taxes are increased enough to raise $100 billion in tax revenues? To answer the President's question the Council of Economic Advisors must have an economic theory about how taxes are related to unemployment, inflation, and GNP (these theories have been discussed in your macroeconomics courses). But a *theory is not enough*. To put numerical magnitudes into the answer, historical data on the relationships between these (and other) economic variables must be analyzed. Magic, mysticism, and revelation have their places, but in the economic decision process they appear to have limited usefulness.

2. The Public Service Commission (PSC) in each state regulates public utilities, the companies that provide electricity, water, local phone service, and so on. These firms are regulated because they are "natural" monopolies and, if not regulated, will charge a higher price and produce a smaller output than a competitive industry, resulting in an inefficient allocation of resources. The regulated firms are permitted to charge a price that yields revenue sufficient to cover "legitimate" costs of providing service and to earn a "fair" rate of return for the stockholders. As costs of providing service rise, the PSC asks both staff and consulting economists to determine "how much" of a price increase will be required to generate adequate revenue for the firm. The answer depends, of course, on the numerical magnitude of the price response or elasticity of demand for the good in question, say, electricity. The economists questioned must collect and analyze data on the price of electricity and the quantities of electricity consumed to obtain an *estimate* of the price response (elasticity) on which to base their answers to the PSC.

3. Businesses, both large and small, engage in advertising their products. Large businesses devise sophisticated marketing strategies that include advertising in alternative media and at the retail level, plus coupons, sales, and other price adjustment schemes. The question that naturally arises is "how much" do sales increase as the result of a specific marketing strategy, such as the widespread distribution of a "50 cents off" coupon? The answer to the question is important for making business decisions about how much and what type of advertising to engage in. What is needed is an estimate of the responsiveness of product sales, for example, to coupon discounts of varying amounts, or a "coupon"-price elasticity of demand. The way to obtain such an estimate is to analyze data on sales of the product and to observe the effects of a coupon distribution.

Two points should be noticed about the three examples just given. First, though the questions discussed are "ordinary" ones for economists to be asked, the phenomena in each one are *very* complicated. In the first example the answers involve the understanding not only of the complete U. S. economy but also the international reactions to the policy changes. Important issues are: How can all these related factors be taken into account? What about those that will affect the outcome of the policy decision but over which we have no control and which we cannot predict? The second and third examples involve price elasticities of demand and thus, implicitly, the demand curves for the products in question. Once again it could be asked: What about all those factors that enter into the demand for a product, like the prices of related goods, consumer income, and so on? How can we account for these factors? Do they matter? Taking into account the factors, and interrelationships, that play a role in determining economic variables is a difficult but essential part of the economic learning process. It is a task that we address throughout this book.

A second observation is that in each of the examples a decision is involved. The decision made will lead to consequences that are favorable or unfavorable. Although we cannot be sure that it will be true *every time*, it is reasonable to assume that better decisions are made, on average, if decision makers are provided with better, more accurate (i.e., closer to the truth) answers to their questions. For example, suppose the Council of Economic Advisors underestimates the effect a tax increase will have on unemployment. If, based in part on this misinformation, the tax increase is passed, and then the unemployment rate rises more than anticipated, there are social (and political) costs that must be borne that were not anticipated. These additional costs may mean that the policy decision was a poor one based on social cost/benefit calculus.

In this light we see that the analysis of economic data is extremely important. Estimates of key multipliers or elasticities that are too high or too low can lead to poor decisions and undesirable outcomes. As a consequence, *great stress is placed on the proper analysis and interpretation of economic data.*

In each of these three examples a policy decision is contemplated, with an analysis of economic data serving as *one input* into the decision process. The tools and methods of using data to test economic theories are *also* used to obtain answers to these and other "how much" questions. The techniques for analyzing data that you learn in this book will serve you in roles as both a researcher and an economic analyst/advisor. In mastering this material, you will make an important step in the transition from economics student to "working economist."

Keeping in mind the above discussion of the world of the economist and econometrician, in the sections that follow we consider the role of the economic and statistical models in an econometric analysis and suggest a format for learning from economic data. The methods of carrying out the analysis of economic data, *Econometrics*, is the subject of this book.

1.1   Economics and the Role of the Economic Model

Economics has a major preoccupation with the implications of scarcity. Our wants seem to be unbounded and resources, human and otherwise, are limited. As a basis for understanding the implications of scarcity and perhaps solving this conflict situation, we have over time developed a general theory of choice to explain the production, allocation, and distribution decisions within a market-oriented economy, in which consumers attempt to maximize utility and firms try to maximize profits. In the courses you have taken, you have learned that these forces suggest relationships between economic variables. For example, when thinking about the level of consumption of a particular commodity, it is natural to think about consumption levels being related to the price of the commodity, the prices of substitute and complementary products, and the level of income; in production we think about the level of output of a commodity as being technically related to the use of factor-resource inputs, and the forthcoming supply of the commodity as being some function of its price, the price of commodities that compete in the production process, and the prices of the factors-inputs. In macroeconomics it is natural to think that aggregate consumption is related to the level of aggregate income, that changes in investment are related to the level of interest rates both current and expected, and that the level of aggregate income is related to aggregate consumption and investment plus government expenditures.

Not only do we think that we know something about these and other relationships among economic variables, but we also believe, given an optimizing objective, that we know something about the direction of some of the relationships. For example,

as the price of a commodity increases, we believe its rate of consumption will decrease;

as the price of a substitute commodity increases, the rate of consumption for a normal good will increase;

there is a positive technical relation between inputs and outputs;

there is a positive relationship between the price of a commodity and the quantity supplied;

changes in interest rates are negatively related to changes in investment; and

for the consumption–income relation, the marginal propensity to consume is positive and around 0.8.

These types of propositions provide a way of identifying and thinking about relationships among economic variables and a way for making qualitative predictions about outcomes under changing conditions. These propositions also reflect hypotheses about the direction of the relationship between economic variables or about whether a relationship actually exists. For example, one hypothesis might be that there is no relationship between the price of a commodity and the corresponding level of consumption. Alternatively, our hypothesis might relate to a positive or negative relationship between price and quantity. Such knowledge or hypotheses may be formalized and codified in terms of paradigms that we call economic models. The economic model reflects the known or conjectural relationship among economic variables (prices, quantities, income, etc.) and provides a basis for classifying the variables and identifying relevant and hopefully testable hypotheses.

1.1.1   Expressing the Relationship

In terms of the above examples, we need a formal way to express whatever information we have in terms of relations among economic variables. For the aggregate consumption (c) and income (y) variables we may write

$$c = f(y)$$

which says aggregate consumption is *some* function of income. If we focus on an individual commodity, for example, a Honda Accord, we might express our conjecture or hypothesis as

$$q^d = f(p, p_s, p_c, y)$$

which says that the quantity of Honda Accords demanded, q^d, is *some* function of the price of Honda Accords p, the price of cars that are substitutes p_s, the price of items that are complements p_c, and the level of income y.

Alternatively, if we were considering an agricultural commodity such as beef, we might conjecture that the supply of beef may be expressed as

$$q^s = f(p, p_c, p_f)$$

where q^s is the quantity supplied, p is the price of beef, p_c is the price of competitive products in production (for example, the price of hogs), and p_f is the price of factors or inputs (for example, the price of corn) used in the production process. Note that current, past, and future (expected) values of the prices may be relevant in specifying the economic supply response model. As another example, consider the input–output process in production. One possibility is to express this as a production function

$$z = f(f_1, f_2, \ldots, f_m)$$

which says that output z is described by a technical process that is a function of the level and mix of the m factors of production or inputs, $f_1, f_2, \ldots, f_m$.

Each of the above equations or set of equations is a specific economic model that describes how we visualize the way in which the economic variables are interrelated. Economic models of this type *guide our economic analysis* and permit us to reach certain conclusions, under different scenarios, about what is happening in the economy. The economic model must also say something about the timing of the variables: Should price appear in the supply relation with a time lag and should future expected profits appear in the investment relation? The economic model describes how we visualize (hypothesize) that the observed values of the economic variables came about. To explain the behavior of observable economic variables, we start with the economic model that reflects, as we understand them, the underlying relationships between the economic variables. In this context we should realize that just like the number system, economic models are invented and not discovered. As Haavelmo, the father of econometrics, put it, "It is not to be forgotten that they (theoretical economic models) are all our own inventions in a search for an understanding of real life; they are not hidden truths to be discovered."

It should be clear that economic models provide a range of conjectures and hypotheses and result in a number of questions concerning relationships among economic variables. They do not tell us anything about whether the hypotheses or predicted outcomes are true or false. They only say that, given the assumptions, if we correctly make use of the rules of logic, certain conclusions follow. Since our underlying assumptions may be in conflict with reality, uncertainty usually exists concerning the specification of the economic model as it relates to the appropriate set of economic variables, and to their timing. Even so, the theoretical economic model goes a long way toward helping us to identify the systematic component of an economic relation and to make order out of seeming disorder.

1.1.2   What Is the Direction of the Relationship?

Finally, it is important to note that for most economic decision or choice problems, it is not enough to know that certain economic variables are interrelated. In addition, we wish to know the direction of the relationship and the magnitudes involved. That is, we must be able to answer the *how much* question or, at least, to say something about the *probability of how much.*

As an example, consider the problem faced by the Central Bank. In a period when price increases are beginning to indicate an increase in the inflation rate, the Central Bank must make a decision about whether to dampen the rate of growth of the economy by raising the interest rate it charges its member banks when they borrow money, or whether to reduce the supply of money. These actions reduce the supply of lendable funds and increase the interest rates faced by would-be investors, who may be firms seeking funds for capital expansion or individuals who wish to buy consumer durables like automobiles and refrigerators. As the quantity of the durable goods demanded declines, this reduces aggregate demand and slows the rate of inflation. While these relationships are suggested by economic theory and reflected in our economic model, the real question faced by the Central bankers is: *How much* do we have to reduce the money supply to reduce the rate of inflation by one percent? The answer will depend on the responsiveness of firms and individuals to increases in the interest rates and to the effects of reduced investment on Gross National Product. The key elasticities and multipliers, such as those that depend on the marginal propensity to consume, must be known if an appropriate decision is to be made.

As another example, the U. S. Department of Agriculture has a complicated set of policies that are designed to stabilize the prices of farm goods and to reduce the risk of farming. One of these policies is to "support" prices of specific goods, like corn, sugar, and milk, by creating a price floor. As you have learned in your economics classes, the existence of price floors sometimes leads to excess supply in the marketplace. As the Department of Agriculture officials ponder their programs, one question they must ask is: If we raise the support price for milk by 25 cents, *how much* will the excess supply of milk increase? This question is relevant for the officials who must determine the economic cost of the program and must decide what to do with all the milk that U.S. consumers do not purchase. To answer the question, the unknown price elasticities of supply and demand for milk must be determined.

Thus, the economic models that express relationships between economic variables also involve questions concerning the signs and magnitudes of *unknown parameters* like the price elasticities and multipliers noted above. Therefore, our economic model that expresses the demand for Honda Accords should be specified as

$$q^d = f\left(p, p_s, p_c, y; \beta_1, \beta_2, ..., \beta_M\right)$$

where $\beta_1, \beta_2, ..., \beta_M$ reflect the unknown and unsigned parameters connecting the price and income variables and the quantity variable q^d. It is these unknown and unobservable parameters that are directly or indirectly related to elasticities and multipliers that underlie economic decisions and actions. The question then before us is how do we capture these unknown parameters and make measurement in economics operational?

1.2 The Statistical Model and Sample Information

One way to gain information about the unknown parameters of economic relationships is to conduct or to observe the outcome of an experiment. Within this context, an economic model provides a basis for describing the process by which the experimental observation or observed values of economic variables, such as prices and outputs, are determined. In an idealized setting we could think of each economic model as describing how we might design an experiment that could be used as a basis for obtaining economic observations or sample information that then could be used to provide insights about the unknown economic parameters. If, for example, we wanted information concerning the unknown price and income elasticities in a demand relation, the economic model will help us (*i*) specify the relevant price and income variables and (*ii*) make it clear, in a controlled experiment setting, how the prices and incomes will have to vary to provide sample observations so the influence of price and quantity may be estimated. Alternatively, in economics where many of the experiments are uncontrolled and in a sense designed and carried out by society, the economic model helps us identify the relevant variables, along with the appropriate timing (current, lagged, or expected) and provides a basis for an economic interpretation of the results. Haavelmo, the 1989 Nobel Prize winner in economics, summed all this up about five decades ago as follows: "When we set up a system of theoretical relationships and use economic names for the otherwise purely theoretical variables involved, we have in mind some *actual experiment* or some *design of experiment*, which we could at least imagine arranging, in order to measure those quantities in real economic life that we think might obey the laws imposed on their theoretical namesakes."

To use controlled experimental or uncontrolled nonexperimentally generated sample observations to learn something about the unknown parameters in our economic model, we need to specify a corresponding *statistical model* that is very specific about the process by which the data (the sample observations) were generated, or at least the sampling process by which we *think* they were generated. In this statistical model we must realize that economic relations are not exact. Thus, for example, each demand function, supply function, and production function contains both a predictable systematic component and an unobserved and unpredictable random error component, *e*. In a demand relation tastes may not have been controlled for, an important economic variable may have been omitted or, perhaps, human behavior has a random component. In the supply relation for an agricultural commodity, weather may not have been taken into account. In a consumption function, measurements on the wealth variable may not be available. This means that, in general, we can specify our model as

$$y = f(x_1, x_2, ..., x_K, \beta_1, \beta_2, ..., \beta_M, e)$$

where $f(x_1, x_2, ..., x_K, \beta_1, \beta_2, ..., \beta_M)$ is the systematic part and e is the nonsystematic, *random*, error component that we know is present but cannot observe.

To make this a complete statistical model, we need to be very specific about the process by which the errors were generated. For example, if we view the errors as outcomes of unobserved random variables, then we need to be specific about the means and variances of these random variables and perhaps the distributions from which they were drawn. *Giving the errors a random interpretation converts our economic model into a statistical-probability model and gives us a basis for statistical inference, that is, a basis for estimating unknown parameters and testing hypotheses about them.*

To complete the specification of the statistical model, we must also say something about the functional form or algebraic relationship among our economic variables. For example, are the right-hand side variables x_i transformed into y in a linear or nonlinear way? For many of the statistical models considered in the chapters ahead, we will assume that the relationship is linear. If we had a sample of T observations, then we might specify our statistical model for the tth observation as

$$y_t = \beta_1 + x_{t2}\beta_2 + ... + x_{tK}\beta_K + e_t$$

where we note that if e_t is a random variable so is y_t. For example, with a production function we might think that the input x–output y relationship could be linear

$$y_t = \beta_1 + x_t\beta_2 + e_t$$

or nonlinear with the alternative algebraic forms

$$y_t = \beta_1 + x_t\beta_2 + x_t^2\beta_3 + e_t \quad \text{or} \quad \ln y_t = \beta_1 + (\ln x_t)\beta_2 + e_t$$

Each of these functional forms represents a hypothesis about the form of the relationship, and our interest might center on trying to determine which hypothesis is compatible with the data. The relevant form will vary from problem to problem.

We now have the following ingredients:

(i)   An economic model that helps us identify the relevant economic variables and economic parameters and gives us a basis for making economic conclusions.

(ii) A statistical model that specifies a sampling process by which the sample data are generated and identifies the unknown parameters that describe the underlying probability system.

(iii) Observed values of the economic variables that were generated in line with the sampling process specified in the statistical model.

The question before us is: How do we use the information contained in (i), (ii), and (iii) to obtain information about the unknown economic parameters that we need as a basis for decision making and choice? In this context our objective is to increase the content of the systematic (explained) part $f(x_1, x_2, ..., x_K, \beta_1, \beta_2, ..., \beta_M)$ and to reduce the content of the unexplained errors e. One can trace the evolution of science by what has happened over time to these two components.

We have noted that in an idealized setting we could think of each economic model describing an experimental design. This design would reflect the sampling plan leading to the economic sample information that would then be used to provide insights about the unknown parameters in the statistical model. One example of this is a price and quantity experiment in a supermarket. Another example is the experimental data produced by agricultural experiments on plants and animals. This type of controlled experimental economic data is sometimes available, and in one or more of the coming chapters we will use data that come from a designed experiment to analyze an economic problem. However, we must realize that much of the economic data that we will be using is nonexperimentally generated. In fact, much of it is collected for administrative purposes and thus may not be compatible with our needs for economic research. Thus, to a large extent we are passive observers of the process by which the data we use are obtained. Our data on economic variables come from experiments conducted by society, and we must find ways to make use of this information in our economic and statistical models. Consequently, there is usually no possibility of producing the data beforehand in a laboratory or controlled experiment that is consistent with our economic and statistical models. This means we work under a nonexperimental model-building restriction with economic data that are scarce and costly to obtain. Consequently, we must be very efficient in using whatever sample and nonsample information is available. This quest for efficiency in learning from sample information leads us to our next topic—inferential statistics.

1.3   Statistical Inference

In discussing the role of the economic and statistical models, we have focused on the relationships among observable economic variables such as prices, consumption, and investment, and the desire to obtain information about the corresponding unknown and unobservable parameters, such as elasticities and marginal products. Information about these unknown economic parameters helps us understand the underlying economic relationships and puts us in a position to discriminate among alternative hypotheses (theories), to draw economic policy implications, or to predict, and possibly control, the outcomes of important economic variables. Given this objective and a sample of data that is collected or generated consistent with the sampling process described by the statistical model, the problem before us is to devise some procedure for using the information in a sample of economic data for purposes of parameter estimation and inference. By inference we mean we want to use the information in a sample of data to "infer" something about the real world. For example, as the price of a commodity increases, how much does the quantity consumed decrease? Does aggregate output increase in a linear or nonlinear way with increases in the quantity of labor?

Fortunately, statistical theory provides well-defined procedures or rules for using a sample of data to obtain point (single-valued) estimates of such parameters as elasticities and marginal productivities, for assessing the corresponding reliability of the estimates, and for testing hypotheses. Point estimates and their corresponding reliability can be expressed through interval estimates. Also we can check the compatibility of the data with our conjectures through tests of hypotheses such as (i) whether the price elasticity of demand for electricity was inelastic (less than one) or (ii) whether an increase in the level of consumption of pasta sauce was due to advertising or a change of tastes.

Also, since there may be several alternative ways (rules) for how we use a set of data, statistical theory provides a basis for comparing estimation rules. For example, is the estimation rule an unbiased rule, that is, on the average does it hit the target, or is the reliability of one estimation rule superior to another? Also, if we associate a loss with not knowing the true parameter and having to make decisions, does one estimation rule minimize average loss or minimize the maximum possible loss? Since sample information is scarce and costly, statistical theory suggests procedures that permit us to combine and use both sample and other types of nonsample information (an input coefficient is positive, the marginal propensity to consume lies between zero and one) in the process of estimating and making inferences about unknown parameters. To summarize, statistical theory lets us use our sample information to move from the theoretical parameters in the economic and statistical models to their empirical counterparts, and to make probability statements concerning possible outcomes.

It is the complete bag of tools (economic theory, the economic model, the statistical model, the sample information, and statistical theory) that defines econometrics and gives us the basis for measurement in economics, and the possibility of understanding, predicting, and having some control over economic processes and institutions.

1.4   A Format for Learning from Economic Data

Let us see if we can now pull all of these ideas together and find out what they mean for the practice of econometrics.

 (i) It all starts with a problem—a lack of information or uncertainty regarding an outcome or a question that involves "what if...".

 (ii) Economic theory gives us a way of thinking about the problem: What economic variables are involved and what is the possible direction of the relationship(s)? How would we make use of new information if we had it—for example, how would we make use of a production function to determine the "best" mix of factors, the optimum level of output, or the demand for an input?

(iii) This information is then arranged in terms of a working economic model that lists our underlying assumptions and forms the basis for our experimental abstraction. Hypotheses of interest are specified.

(iv) The working economic model leads to the statistical model that describes the process by which the sample observations and equation errors are viewed as having been generated, the classification of the variables, and the functional form of the relationship.

(v) Sample observations are generated or collected that are consistent with the economic model and the random component of the statistical model.

(vi) Given the statistical model and sample observations, an estimation rule is selected or developed that has good statistical properties such as unbiasedness and/or has low variability or high precision.

(vii) Point and interval estimates of the unknown parameters are obtained with the help of a statistical software package and a computer; appropriate hypothesis tests are performed.

(viii) The statistical and economic consequences and the implications of the empirical results are analyzed and evaluated. For example, were all of the right-hand-side explanatory variables statistically significant? Were the assumptions about the random equation errors correct? Was the correct functional form used? What economic resource allocation and distribution results are implied, and what are their policy-choice implications?

(ix) If consistency between the economic and statistical models and the sample data was not achieved, what are the potential trouble spots and what are the suggestions for future analysis and evaluation? For example, were the data inadequate to support the questions asked, were the variables in the economic model classified correctly, did the variables appear with the correct leads and lags, and should the statistical model have involved nonlinearities in both the variables and the parameters?

This is the format we will follow as we work our way through the chapters ahead, and this is a format that will serve you well in your econometric work as you try to learn from a sample of economic data. It is a format that will also serve you well in writing up your econometric results and in evaluating the applied econometric work of others.

1.5 Organization of the Book

The book is organized so as to emphasize why and how econometrics is useful in economic analysis. The choice and coverage of economic and statistical topics is not comprehensive. Economic questions or problems are chosen because of their convenience as vehicles to introduce and deal with economic data that require, for analysis purposes, increasingly more difficult econometric techniques. Given the economic questions, the emphasis will be on the relationship between the economic and statistical models, on how to choose estimation or information processing rules consistent with the underlying sampling model, on the computer implementation of the techniques to obtain empirical results, and on the interpretation of the resulting statistics and how to make use of them within a decision context.

To be consistent with the bulk of statistics taught, most of the book will emphasize the sampling theory approach to inference in economics. In general, we are concerned with making inferences about unknown numerical constants or parameters. The sampling theory approach to this problem makes use of the information provided by data that results from statistical investigations. Bayesian inference, which is discussed in two chapters in Part IX of the book, will be considered as a means for accumulating or taking account of both sample and nonsample information and for using the quantitative information within a decision context.

In specifying and analyzing an array of economic and statistical models we have organized the book in 10 parts. In Part I (Chapters 2, 3 and 4), to ensure that there is a foundation for understanding statistical inference and its corresponding implications for econometric analysis, we focus on a review of probability and the basic concepts of inferential statistics. Economic examples involving a mean-variance (location-scale) linear statistical model are used to provide an understanding of the importance and use of these concepts. Some information on the geometry and interpretation of derivatives and definitions as well as rules for operations with vectors and matrices are given in the appendices to Chapter 3. A review and summary of Part I is given after Chapter 4.

In Part II (Chapters 5, 6, 7 and 8) the basic simple linear statistical model involving one right-hand-side explanatory variable is used in conjunction with the sampling theory approach to inference to obtain point and interval estimates of the unknown parameters and to evaluate alternative linear hypotheses for a range of economic models and data. The presentation is carried through in both a scalar and linear algebra notation. Discussions of partial derivatives and the inverse of a matrix are given as appendices to Chapter 5. A review and summary of Part II that serves as a lead-in to Chapter 9 is given after Chapter 8.

In Part III (Chapters 9, 10 and 11) the general linear statistical model involving two or more right-hand-side (explanatory) variables is specified, and estimation and inference procedures are developed. The possibility of combining sample and nonsample information for purposes of estimation and inference is considered, and an applied analysis is carried through that involves data from a controlled experiment. The problems of variable selection and the choice of functional form are also considered, and a discussion of the use of partial derivatives in econometric analysis is given in an appendix to Chapter 10.

In Part IV (Chapters 12, 13 and 14) models and techniques that accommodate some special characteristics of economic data are investigated. These chapters consider, for example, how to cope with the problems of estimation and inference when a sample of data must be represented by general linear statistical models that have varying parameters or collinear right-hand-side variables or a random regressor. Instrumental variable and method of moments estimators are developed, and the large sample properties of estimators and test statistics are reviewed.

Part V (Chapters 15, 16 and 17) is concerned with estimation and inference from (*i*) a single sample of data in a statistical model with heteroskedastic and/or autocorrelated errors and (*ii*) two or more samples of data with related error structures. The generalized least-squares estimator is developed, and the concept of asymptotic (large sample) properties of this estimator are discussed.

In Part VI (Chapters 18 and 19) linear statistical models involving right- and left-hand economic variables that are jointly (endogenously) determined are specified and analyzed. The concepts of least-squares bias and identification are introduced, and alternative procedures for estimating equations in a simultaneous system of relations are discussed.

In Part VII (Chapters 20 and 21) the focus is on univariate, bivariate, and multivariate time series models and the special problems of model specification, estimation, and inference that arise when analyzing time series data. Finite and infinite distributed lag models are presented, and the topics of vector autoregression, units root tests, and cointegration are discussed.

In Part VIII (Chapters 22 and 23) it is recognized that statistical models consistent with the sampling process for certain economic data may involve variables that contain variables that are discrete rather than continuous and statistical models that are nonlinear in the parameters.

In Part IX (Chapters 24 and 25) the Bayesian approach to inference is considered and applied in the analysis of economic data sets for the mean-variance and simple linear statistical models. Part X (Chapter 26), the final chapter of the book, contains some thoughts on sources and the nature and quality of economic data, and a format that may be useful in writing up the results of econometric research.

We have arranged the chapters of this book in what we consider a building-block fashion. Obviously, the sequence in which the chapters are covered can be tailored to fit the desires of the instructor and the needs of the student. Several alternative routes for traveling through the book are discussed in the preface. Given this overview of the econometric process, let us turn to the problems of estimation and inference for an observed sample of economic data.

1.6   A Suggestion for Further Reading

To get an idea of the steps involved in the search for quantitative economic knowledge and some of the special economic data problems, read Chapter 1 in the following textbook:

JUDGE, G. G., R. C. HILL, W. E. GRIFFITHS, H. LÜTKEPOHL AND T. C. LEE (1988) *Introduction to the Theory and Practice of Econometrics*, 2nd Edition, New York: John Wiley and Sons.

To give some intellectual perspective to the work of econometricians, it would be useful to have a cursory look at the following book:

BERNDT, E. R. (1990) *The Practice of Econometrics*, Reading, MA: Addison-Wesley.
This book also contains biographical sketches of a sample of econometricians.

If you do not have access to the Berndt book it may be useful to have a look at such early papers as:

ANDO, A. AND F. MODIGLIANA (1963) "The Life Cycle Hypothesis for Saving: Aggregate Implications and Tests," *American Econometric Review*, 56:55–84.

CHENERY, H. B. AND L. S. TAYLOR (1968) "Development Patterns Among Countries Over Time," *Review of Economics and Statistics*, 50:391–416.

GRILICHES, Z. (1960) "Hybrid Corn and the Economics of Innovation," *Science*, 132:275–280.

LIPSEY, R. E. (1960) "The Relation Between Unemployment and the Rate of Change of Money Wage Rates in the United Kingdom, 1862–1957: A Further Analysis," *Economica*, 27:1–31.

PHILLIPS, A. W. (1955) "The Relation Between Unemployment and the Rate of Change of Money Wage Rates in the United Kingdom, 1862–1957," *Economica*, 25:283–299.

SOLOW, R. M. (1957) "Technical Change and the Aggregate Production Function," *Review of Economics and Statistics*, 39:312–320.

Part I

The Foundations of Estimation and Inference

Part I of this book comprises three chapters and several appendices that present and summarize the statistical and mathematical foundations for econometrics. The concept of a random variable is introduced in Chapter 2, and probability distributions and various mathematical expectations (mean, variance, and covariance) are discussed. Included in Chapter 2 is a short appendix on summation operations as well as an appendix on the geometric interpretation of the integral of a function. Estimators for the mean and variance of a normal population are developed in Chapter 3. The sampling distributions and properties of the estimators are derived and several real-world examples are given. There are two appendices to Chapter 3; the first discusses the geometry and interpretation of the first and second derivative of a function; and the second appendix expresses the model and assumptions used in the chapter in vector and matrix terms. Procedures for constructing interval estimators and testing hypotheses about unknown parameters are presented in Chapter 4. Several examples are considered. Part I ends with a very complete summary of Chapters 2, 3, and 4, which may be used for review purposes.

Chapter 2

Some Basic Ideas: Statistical Concepts for Economists

New Key Words and Concepts

Sampling	**Random Variable**
Probability Density Functions	**Mathematical Expectation**
Mean	**Variance**
Covariance	**Correlation**
Normal Distribution	

We observed in Chapter 1 that economists are social scientists who make use of the scientific method in (*i*) developing and testing economic theories and (*ii*) providing economic information for policy analyses and decisions. Both of these activities involve the analysis of data about economic variables. In this chapter we review the foundations of inference necessary for developing the methods for carrying out an analysis of and learning from a sample of economic data.

2.1 Where Do Economic Data Come from: The Differences Between Experimental and Nonexperimental Data

We have made the point that economics is a social science that follows the scientific method. In this sense it is the same as a physical science, like physics or chemistry. There is, however, another division of the sciences besides social/physical that provides a sharp contrast between economics and some other disciplines. This division is between sciences that are *experimental* and those that are *nonexperimental*. This categorization reflects the different ways that data are obtained by the member disciplines and it has a great impact on how data are used to investigate questions and to make inferences about the real world.

2.1.1 Experimental Data

An example of an experimental science is chemistry. The data that chemists analyze come from a carefully specified theoretical model and corresponding controlled experimental settings. The typical chemistry experiment may involve the meticulous measuring of ingredients into a beaker or test tube, which is subsequently stirred, heated, and cooled to produce a "substance" that is weighed, X-rayed, and otherwise measured.

All measurements and experimental conditions are carefully recorded and punched into a computer.

All the measurements recorded from a *single* run of an experiment constitute one *observation* on a variety of chemical factors or *variables*. To have a way to designate these outcomes, let us denote the measured and *controlled* factors in the experiment, including controlled conditions like temperature, humidity, and pressure as $x_{t1}, x_{t2}, \ldots,$ x_{tK}; where the subscript t denotes the "run or observation number" of the experiment, and the second subscript $(1, 2, \ldots, K)$ indicates the specific experimental ingredient or controlled condition. These controlled factors will be called *control* or *explanatory variables* as the settings they take help determine the characteristics of the *experimental outcome*. The experimental outcome itself will be measured in a variety of ways (i.e., weight, volume, hardness), and we will denote the M outcomes of the tth experimental run as $y_{t1}, y_{t2}, \ldots, y_{tM}$. The observed and measured results of the experiment will be called *outcome variables* as their values are thought to depend on the settings of the explanatory variables. We can write this postulated one-way relationship as

$$y_{tm} = f_m\left(x_{t1}, x_{t2}, \ldots, x_{tK}\right) \tag{2.1.1a}$$

where $f_m(\cdot)$ indicates that y_{tm} is "some unknown function" of the explanatory variables, that is, the relation 2.1.1a indicates that the experimental outcome y_{tm} "depends on" or "is some function of" the values of the explanatory variables.

It should be noted that despite the fact that the outcomes y_{tm} are generated under a controlled environment, the relation 2.1.1a is not an exact one. In every experiment there are *unpredictable* or *random* components that affect y_{tm}; these components we will represent by "e_{tm}," denoting random errors. Consequently the relation 2.1.1a will be written

$$y_{tm} = f_m\left(x_{t1}, x_{t2}, \ldots, x_{tK}\right) + e_{tm} \tag{2.1.1b}$$

where e_{tm} is an uncontrolled and unpredictable component of the experiment. Since the outcome y_{tm} includes the uncontrolled, random, component e_{tm}, it too is random and not completely predictable.

In the social sciences, and economics in particular, an example of a controlled setting in which experimental data are obtained is a supermarket. There the prices of products are fixed, promotional campaigns are employed, and the levels of sales are observed. In Table 2.1 are data on the weekly unit sales (y) of a certain "target" brand of canned tuna, the actual price of the canned tuna (x_1), and the actual price of a competitive brand (x_2). In this experimental setting we may write the relationship to be investigated as

$$y_t = f\left(x_{t1}, x_{t2}\right) + e_t \tag{2.1.2}$$

One of the advantages of a controlled experiment is that it is reproducible and can be repeated by independent researchers as a check on experimental procedures. A second advantage of controlled experiments is that runs of the experiment can be repeated with different settings for the control-explanatory variables carefully chosen so that the relation between an outcome variable (y_{tm}) and each separate explanatory variable (x_{tk}) can be isolated and accurately estimated. In the context of the experimental data in Table 2.1, involving weekly sales of canned tuna, its price, and the price of a competitive brand, we may be interested in the what-if question: If I change the explanatory variable product price by 10 cents, how much will this change the outcome variable, cans of tuna sold? Proper *experimental design* is a key factor in constructing the procedure by which the sample data are generated and in determining the usability of the resulting experimental data.

Table 2.1 Market Research Data[a]

y	x_1	x_2
133	0.68	0.85
27	0.67	0.85
35	0.70	0.85
46	0.71	0.67
42	0.68	0.67
52	0.71	0.67
400	0.67	0.67
253	0.67	0.85
37	0.88	0.63
26	0.93	0.79
353	0.70	0.93
125	0.74	0.93
35	0.95	0.93
32	0.93	0.93
49	0.94	0.93
28	0.94	0.80
84	0.81	0.87
94	0.87	0.97
26	0.97	0.97
45	0.97	0.97

[a]Supermarket weekly unit sales of a target brand of canned tuna (y), actual price of target brand (x_1), actual price of a competitive brand (x_2).
(These data are provided by Nielsen Marketing Research.)

2.1.2   Nonexperimental Data

There is a sharp distinction between experimental data, like that in Table 2.1, and nonexperimental data. The discipline of economics is, for the most part, a nonexperimental science. Although economic models reflect a fictitious experimental design involving hypothetical stimulus-response experiments, the primary source of economic data is from the *observation of real-world outcomes*. For example, demand curves indicate quantities demanded by consumers in price-taking situations. This suggests the hypothetical experiment of varying the price, while other factors such as income and prices of related goods are held constant, and observing how much consumers purchase. Alternatively, one can visualize society as having carried out the experiment. In this case we *observe* the quantities of the goods that are consumed for alternative prices. In a macroeconomic setting outcomes are from hypothetical experiments involving variables like tax rates, levels of government spending, investment, GNP, inflation, and unemployment. The research economist cannot, of course, *control or determine the settings for any of these variables*. However, an economic model provides a framework for us to think of a hypothetical controlled experiment by which the data we observe *could* have been generated. Despite our limited ability to execute controlled experiments, economists are interested in studying relationships similar in form to equation 2.1.1, using data we have observed, for economic variables. As for controlled experiments, the resulting economic relationships are not exact, and each contains a random component. Thus the outcomes we observe for economic variables are random and not completely predictable.

If most economic data do not come from controlled experiments designed by the researcher but instead from experiments conducted by society, how do we go about obtaining observations on economic variables? Fortunately, in developed countries, government agencies at all levels collect data for administrative and other purposes. In the United States at the federal level some of the data are disseminated in regular published sources such as the *Survey of Current Business* or the *Economic Report of the President*. Data of this type are usually on economic aggregates and serve as one basis for macroeconomic analysis. Other sources of macroeconomic data are computerized data banks constructed (and sold) by Data Resources, Inc., Chase Econometric Associates, The National Bureau of Economic Research, and other organizations. Microeconomic data are collected as part of the U. S. Census. Massive surveys, such as the U. S. National Longitudinal Surveys, are available that contain economic, sociological, and other variables on individuals. Specific information about sources for various types of data is discussed in Section 1 of Chapter 26. Although many data sources exist, for the most part (*i*) the data are "observed" and not the result of a controlled experiment, and (*ii*) the data may have been collected for purposes other than economic analysis. Thus the data may not contain observations on variables that a particular investigator wants, the variables may not vary over a range that will permit an effect to be isolated, or, in the case of survey data, the variables may be based on questions that the investigator may have preferred to ask in a different way. As a result, one of the challenges of economic research is to *obtain* data that are consistent with the theoretical variables in the economic model and that are useful in analyzing an economic problem.

At this point, several qualifying comments are in order. First, in some branches of economics (agricultural economics, experimental economics, public utility economics) the data generated from at least partially controlled experiments can be obtained. An example using production function experimental data is given in Chapter 11. Experimental data, however, are limited and usually are not applicable to a study of general economic questions. Second, economists *occasionally* design and carry out surveys of individuals and firms as a way of obtaining data that are specifically useful to them for a research project. As noted in Chapter 26, negative income tax experiments commissioned by the Ford Foundation are one example in this area. This type of activity, too, however, is very expensive and limited.

An example of some "typical" economic data that might be used to investigate various economic relationships is found in Table 2.2. The variables are standard macroeconomic measures as reported in the *Economic Report of the President*, 1990.

The "experiment" that created these data is neither controlled nor repeatable. In fact, we can describe these data as resulting from an experiment carried out by "society" and in which the researcher is a passive observer. Not only do we have no control over the experiment but we also have only a limited vision of its totality. *Econometrics is, in part, a collection of statistical models and methods that are designed to deal with data on economic variables that are highly interrelated and observed over time, individuals, or space.* It is an exercise in nonexperimental model building.

2.2 Sampling, Variability, and Randomness

Given this overview concerning economic data, let us turn to some of the basic concepts underlying inferential statistics and, thus, econometrics. The essential characteristic of an experiment, whether or not it is controlled, is that its outcome is never known beforehand. Consider the example of experimental (supermarket) data generation given in Table 2.1. In a controlled experiment all aspects of the experimental design thought

Table 2.2 Macroeconomic Data

Year	GNP	Consumption	Investment	Population	Unemployment Rate	Housing Starts	New Home Mortage Rate	Prime Rate	Money Supply	GNP Deflator
T	Y	C	I	Pop	U	HS	M	R	M1	P
1963	1873.30	1108.40	307.10	189242	5.50	1603.20	5.89	4.50	153.40	32.40
1964	1973.30	1170.60	325.90	191889	5.00	1528.80	5.82	4.50	160.40	32.90
1965	2087.60	1236.40	367.00	194303	4.40	1472.80	5.81	4.54	167.90	33.80
1966	2208.30	1298.90	390.50	196560	3.70	1164.90	6.25	5.63	172.10	35.00
1967	2271.40	1337.70	374.40	198712	3.70	1291.60	6.46	5.61	183.30	35.90
1968	2365.60	1405.90	391.80	200706	3.50	1507.60	6.97	6.30	197.50	37.70
1969	2423.30	1456.70	410.30	202677	3.40	1466.80	7.80	7.96	204.00	39.80
1970	2416.20	1492.00	381.50	205052	4.80	1433.60	8.45	7.91	214.50	42.00
1971	2484.80	1538.80	419.30	207661	5.80	2052.20	7.74	5.72	228.40	44.40
1972	2608.50	1621.90	465.40	209896	5.50	2356.60	7.60	5.25	249.40	46.50
1973	2744.10	1689.60	520.80	211909	4.80	2045.30	7.96	8.03	263.00	49.50
1974	2729.30	1674.00	481.30	213854	5.50	1337.70	8.92	10.81	274.40	54.00
1975	2695.00	1711.90	383.30	215973	8.30	1160.40	9.00	7.86	287.60	59.30
1976	2826.70	1803.90	453.50	218035	7.60	1537.50	9.00	6.84	306.50	63.10
1977	2958.60	1883.90	521.30	220239	6.90	1987.11	9.02	6.83	331.40	67.30
1978	3115.20	1961.00	576.90	222585	6.00	2020.30	9.56	9.06	358.70	72.20
1979	3192.40	2004.40	575.20	225055	5.80	1745.10	10.78	12.67	386.10	78.60
1980	3187.10	2000.40	509.30	227757	7.00	1292.20	12.66	15.27	412.20	85.70
1981	3248.80	2024.20	545.50	230138	7.50	1084.20	14.70	18.87	439.10	94.00
1982	3166.00	2050.70	447.30	232520	9.50	1062.20	15.14	14.86	476.40	100.00
1983	3279.10	2146.00	504.00	234799	9.50	1703.00	12.57	10.79	522.10	103.90
1984	3501.40	2249.30	658.40	237001	7.40	1749.50	12.38	12.04	551.90	107.70
1985	3618.70	2354.80	637.00	239279	7.10	1741.80	11.55	9.93	620.50	110.90
1986	3717.90	2446.40	639.60	241625	6.90	1805.40	10.17	8.33	725.90	113.80
1987	3853.70	2513.70	674.00	243934	6.10	1620.50	9.31	8.21	752.30	117.40
1988	4024.40	2598.40	715.80	246329	5.40	1488.10	9.19	9.32	790.30	121.30
1989	4142.60	2668.50	724.50	248777	5.20	1374.30	10.13	10.87	797.60	126.30

Source: Economic Report of the President, 1990. Tables C-2, C-31, C-32, C-53, C-71, C-67, C-3; Y, C, I are in billions of dollars, M1 is in billions of 1982 dollars, and population is in thousands.

to be relevant, and capable of being controlled, are noted. In the context of relation 2.1.1 we assign or fix the values of the explanatory variables $x_{t1}, x_{t2}, \ldots, x_{tK}$ *before* the experiment is carried out. However, before the various runs of the experiment are made, the values that the dependent or outcome variables will take are unknown. Variables like this, whose precise values or outcomes are not known until an experiment is performed, are called *random variables*, and it is the study of these variables, and their properties, that is a main concern of this book. Experiments yield outcomes that are *random* in the sense that their outcomes are not known a priori nor can they be exactly predicted. As an example, the data on economic variables in Table 2.2 are not known ahead of time and are not exactly predictable. Thus these economic variables are random variables.

If two or more *identical* runs of a controlled experiment are made, that is, with settings of the explanatory variables kept the same, the experimental outcomes y_{tm} will almost certainly still be different. This occurs even in a controlled experiment, since not *all* factors affecting the outcome are really controlled. Ingredients of the experiment may be measured with small errors. Also, the process that transforms inputs into outputs itself may vary a bit from run to run, introducing random variation in the output. In the social sciences perhaps there is a component of randomness in human behavior. This may also reflect the fact that the theory under which the experiment is designed is incomplete and that there is information used by economic agents that is unaccounted for and/or unobserved. All of these factors suggest that "identical" controlled experiments, if repeated, will produce different values of the outcome or dependent variables. If you examine the last two rows of data in Table 2.1, you can see that, despite identical settings on prices for two consecutive weeks, unit sales of tuna vary substantially.

Most economic data are generated from nature's ongoing experiment involving individuals, households, business firms, and governments as they act to maximize objectives such as utility and profit. Microeconomic data, for example, arise from *observation* of individual economic agents. In studying the microeconomy at the firm level, we can *record* the values of a single firm's costs, employment, and output during regular calendar periods and thereby produce a *time series* of data. Alternatively, at any one point in time, we may record the values of the economic variables for a number of different firms, creating a *cross section* of data.

Suppose a cross section of sample size $T = 20$ business firms is selected from a large industry and their costs and output are recorded for the year 1989. If *another* $T = 20$ firms were selected, a different set of costs and outputs would be obtained. It should not surprise you that when these two sets of data are analyzed, using techniques described later in this book, the estimates of marginal and average costs of production are *different*. The act of selecting a *sample* of *economic agents* to examine from a larger population introduces randomness in the form of uncontrolled and unpredictable variation, called *sampling variation*. Sampling variation refers to the variation in outcomes that occurs as we move from one sample to another.

2.3   Types of Economic Variables

In this section we describe the types of variables economists work with and then examine ways of summarizing the characteristics of one or more economic variables.

2.3.1 Discrete and Continuous Variables

Economic variables are classified as continuous or discrete. A variable that can take only a finite number of values, or states, and that can be counted by using the positive integers is called *discrete*. Examples of discrete economic variables are the following:

1. The number of children in a household: 0, 1, 2, . . .
2. The number of shopping trips an individual takes to a particular shopping mall per week: 0, 1, 2, . . .

These economic variables take only a limited number of values, and it makes sense to *count* them in whole numbers. Discrete variables are also commonly used in economics to record qualitative, or nonnumerical, characteristics of an economic agent. In this role they are called *discrete*, *dummy*, or *qualitative random variables*. For example, if we are studying household behavior, we may want to record the gender of the head of the household. One way to do this is to let the random variable, D, take the value 1 if the head of household is female and 0 if male. That is, the random variable is defined as

$$D = \begin{cases} 1 & \text{if head of household is female} \\ 0 & \text{if head of household is male} \end{cases}$$

Any qualitative characteristic that has two states (e.g., a yes-or-no, or buy-or-not-buy type of variable) can be characterized by a discrete random variable. The actual *values* the discrete random variable takes do not matter mathematically, but the choice of the values 0 and 1 is convenient for a variety of reasons. In macroeconomics the political party of the U. S. President is an example of a variable that can be represented by a discrete random variable. In this context Republican or Democrat may be represented by a variable that is 1 if the President is Republican, at a particular point in time, or 0 if Democrat. If we observed the political party of the U. S. President over time, we could record the *values* that the discrete random variable actually took. Such values are *data*.

In contrast to situations in which discrete random variables can be used, there are many times when it is not convenient to think of random variables as having a countable number of possible outcome values or states. A continuous random variable can take *any* real value (not just whole numbers) in an interval of the real number line. An example is gross national product (GNP). In 1987 the U. S. *value* of GNP was 3853.7 billion (1982) dollars. For practical purposes the GNP *variable* can take any value in the interval zero to infinity and, thus, is a continuous random variable. Admittedly, the GNP is measured in dollars and *can* be counted in whole dollars, but the value is so large that counting individual dollars serves no purpose. It is more convenient simply to assume that the number can be any real number larger than, or equal to, zero. Other examples of continuous random economic variables are all the usual macroeconomic variables, like money supply, interest rates, the federal deficit, and government spending; microeconomic examples are prices, household income, and expenditures on specific products. The time-series data recorded in Table 2.2 are the *values* of real GNP, and the values of other macroeconomic variables.

2.3.2.   Univariate, Bivariate, and Multivariate Variables

Economic variables are characterized not only by whether they are discrete or continuous, but also by the *number* of variables that are observed at the same time. Consider a survey of $T = 20$ households in which a single question is asked, "What is the gross income of this household?" Denote the household response by y_t, the subscript t being the number of the household among those questioned, or the observation number, with $t = 1, 2, ...,$ 20. Then the variable y_t is a single or *univariate* economic variable, indicating that it is only one variable.

In fact, of course, when a survey of households is carried out, *many* questions are asked. If there are M questions, we may record and identify each of the responses as the values of discrete and continuous random variables $(y_{t1}, y_{t2}, ..., y_{tM})$. This is an observation on a *multivariate* random variable, where information on multiple economic variables are recorded together. If $M = 2$, so that data on two random economic variables are recorded together (y_{t1}, y_{t2}), then the observation is a *bivariate* one.

The names univariate, bivariate, and multivariate are terms that describe the number of economic (random) variables that are *observed or analyzed* together. The names apply to both micro- and macroeconomic data. If we think of tabled data, such as those in Tables 2.1 and 2.2, then each row of the table represents a single observation. Examining one column (the observations on a single variable) is a univariate analysis, examining two columns is a bivariate analysis, and examining more than two columns is a multivariate analysis.

2.3.3 Summarizing the Characteristics of Economic Data

Given a sample of economic data, what do we do with it? The major emphasis of this book is directed toward procedures for learning from a sample of data. For example, this may involve using a sample of data to estimate unknown economic constants, or *parameters*, like the marginal propensity to consume or save and to make inferences or judgments about important economic questions. That is, we can use data to test economic theories and to answer questions about the signs and magnitudes of unknown economic parameters. This is a useful input to decision or choice problems. Before using data as a basis for inference, we may want to examine the sample of data and summarize or simply *describe* it, that is, identify its primary characteristics and get a "picture" of it in our minds. Consequently, in this section, we will describe some *descriptive statistics* that are used for this purpose. Later on in this chapter the emphasis will shift to *using* the data for estimation and to making inferences about economic questions.

Given a set of time-series or cross-sectional observations on a single economic variable, such as output or price (i.e., univariate observations), how can we summarize its characteristics? It is customary, for reasons that will become increasingly clear as progress is made through this chapter, to examine the following two aspects of data on an economic variable: (*i*) a measure of the *center* (central tendency) or *location* of the data, and (*ii*) a measure of the spread, dispersion, or *scale* of the data.

2.3.3a Finding the Center of the Data   The most common measure for the center or location of data on an economic variable is the *arithmetic mean* of the sample. If x_t is one of $t = 1, 2, ..., T$ observations on an economic variable X, then the arithmetic mean of the sample data is

$$\bar{x} = \frac{\sum_{t=1}^{T} x_t}{T} = \frac{x_1 + x_2 + ... + x_T}{T} \tag{2.3.1}$$

where "Σ" indicates the summation operation. Rules for using the summation operation are given in Appendix 2A at the end of this chapter. The symbol $\bar{x}$ is read "x-bar" and is used to represent the sample mean in many books. The arithmetic mean is the *average value* of the observations x_t. Two other commonly used measures of data location are the *median* and the *mode*. The median of the data is the value of the middle observation (or the average of the middle two if the number of observations is even) *after* the values have been ordered from smallest to largest. The mode is the most frequently occurring value, if a variable is discrete.

As an example of finding the center of data, consider the macroeconomic data in Table 2.2 and let us focus on the prime interest rate variable, R. The arithmetic mean of the sample values r_t is

$$\bar{r} = \frac{\sum_{t=1}^{T} r_t}{T} = \frac{238.51}{27} = 8.83$$

The sorted, or ranked, data from lowest to highest, is

4.50, 4.50, 4.54, 5.25, 5.61, 5.63, 5.72, 6.30, 6.83, 6.84, 7.86, 7.91, 7.96, *8.03*, 8.22, 8.33, 9.06, 9.32, 9.93, 10.79, 10.81, 10.87, 12.04, 12.67, 14.86, 15.27, 18.87

and the median is 8.03, which is the fourteenth and "middle" value of the $T = 27$ observations.

The arithmetic sample mean and median provide information about the "central value" of the interest rate R over the sample period 1963–1989. The median of a sample depends only on the order of the sample value magnitudes and not on the specific values. For example, the median of the sample of interest rate values is unaffected if the largest sample value were 28.0, or 108.0, rather than 18.87. The arithmetic mean, on the other hand, as it is the average of all sample values, is sensitive to extreme magnitudes. The mode is not useful for continuous variables, since each data value will usually appear only once.

2.3.3b Finding the Dispersion of the Data

The dispersion, or sample variability, of the data (how spread out it is) can be measured by the *range* of the data, which is the difference between its minimum and maximum value. The most common measure of dispersion, however, is the *sample variance* of the data. This measure tells us how the sample data varies or is spread out *about the arithmetic sample mean*. The sample variance of data on a variable X, denoted s_X^2, is the average squared distance between x_t, the observed values of the variable X, and the arithmetic sample mean $\bar{x}$. Algebraically,

$$s_X^2 = \frac{\sum_{t=1}^{T} \left(x_t - \bar{x} \right)^2}{T - 1} \tag{2.3.2}$$

The numerator of s_X^2 is the sum of the squared deviations between the observed values x_t and the sample mean $\bar{x}$. Why the divisor used to compute the "average squared deviation" is $(T - 1)$ rather than T (as used in calculating the sample mean) will be discussed in Section 3.6 of Chapter 3.

The square root of the sample variance is called the *sample standard deviation* of X and is denoted s_X. That is

$$s_X = \sqrt{s_X^2} \tag{2.3.3}$$

As a measure of dispersion the sample standard deviation has the advantage of being in the same units of measure as X. *Large values of s_X and s_X^2 indicate more dispersion of the values of X about the arithmetic sample mean*, and small values of s_X and s_X^2 indicate that the values of X are clustered about the sample mean.

For the interest rate R in Table 2.2, the range of the data, which is the difference between the minimum value 4.50 and the maximum value 18.87, is 14.37. The sample variance is

$$s_R^2 = \frac{\sum_{t=1}^{T}(r_t - \bar{r})^2}{T-1} = \frac{334.29}{26} = 12.86$$

and the sample standard deviation is

$$s_R = \sqrt{s_R^2} = 3.59$$

Isolated in this way, the values of s_R and s_R^2 are not easily interpreted. What if, however, you were told that values of a different interest rate variable, R^*, over the same sample period had sample mean $\bar{r}^* = 8.50$ and sample variance $s_{R^*}^2 = 7.19$. You would immediately conclude that the R^* rate exhibited less variation about its mean (which is similar to the mean of R, 8.83) than the prime rate R. In other words, the sample values of R^* were more clustered about their mean than the values of R about its mean.

Of course, the magnitudes of the values of the variables, and their unit of measure, affects their sample variability. For example, the sample variance of real GNP (Y) in Table 2.2 is $s_Y^2 = 398,619$. Comparing the variability of Y to R based on sample variance is futile given their differing magnitudes. To alleviate the difference in magnitudes and measurement units, the *coefficient of variation* of a variable X is defined as

$$CV_X = \frac{s_X}{\bar{x}} \times 100 \tag{2.3.4}$$

It is the standard deviation of a variable's values as a percentage of the sample mean. Dividing the standard deviation by the sample mean accounts for the "size" of the variable's values and removes the effect of units of measure. For the prime rate (R) and real GNP (Y) we find that

$$CV_R = \frac{s_R}{\bar{r}} = \frac{3.59}{8.83} \times 100 = 40.59\%$$

$$CV_Y = \frac{s_Y}{\bar{y}} = \frac{631.36}{2915.31} = 21.66\%$$

Thus the prime rate has a larger coefficient of variation than real GNP, indicating that it is *relatively* more variable about its sample mean, despite the fact that $s_Y^2 > s_R^2$.

Further insights can be gained from graphical presentations of the data, discussed in the following section.

2.3.3c *Depicting the Data*   If a picture is worth a thousand words, then the same is certainly true for a graph. Seeing a "picture" of the observations on an economic variable is extremely useful and helps explain why the summary statistics on location and dispersion are informative. Data on a single economic variable may be depicted by using a *histogram* or a *relative frequency distribution*.

A histogram is a *bar chart* with each bar representing the *number* of values of the variable that fall into convenient intervals. For example, given the data on the interest rate R in Table 2.2, the intervals (4.5, 7.5), (7.5, 10.5), (10.5, 13.5), (13.5, 16.5), and (16.5, 19.5) cover the range of the data and are of equal width. If we construct a bar chart with the widths of each bar being the defined intervals and the heights of the bars indicating the number of values that fall in each interval, then we have a histogram, as in Figure 2.1.

By examining the histogram we can see "where the data fall." The range of R roughly defines the width of the histogram. The sample mean and median, which give measures of the center of the data, fall in the interval (7.5, 10.5).

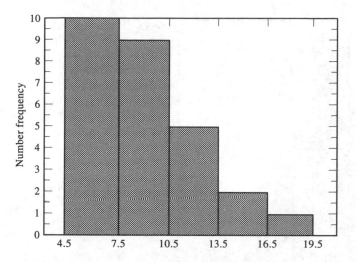

Figure 2.1   Histogram of prime interest rate data, 1963–1989.

The sample variance s_R^2 measures how spread out the data are about the central value $\bar{r}$. If the data are all clustered about the sample mean, then variance and standard deviation of R are smaller. If the data are very spread out, then the sample variance of R is larger.

If the frequencies (actual counts) of observations on the vertical axis of a histogram are divided by the number of observations available, T, then the resulting figure is a *relative frequency distribution*. Obviously it has exactly the same shape as the histogram, but the bar heights are *percentages* of the actual data observations falling in the intervals rather than the actual number. In Figure 2.2 are two relative frequency distributions (artificially generated) for 2000 data points with the same sample mean (8.83) but different variances (1.0 and 0.25). The effect of the small variance, panel *b*, is to "pull" a greater percentage of the data close to the sample mean. For example, when the variance is 0.25, panel *b*, 95% of the data fall within 1 unit of the sample mean. When the sample variance is 1.0, panel *a*, only 67.5% of the data fall within 1 unit of the sample mean.

2.3.3d   *Summarizing Bivariate Outcomes*

The measures we have examined are used to summarize or to describe outcome data on single economic variables. What if the economic outcomes are bivariate or multivariate? Certainly univariate summary statistics can be computed for the values of each variable, but univariate summary statistics do not capture or describe any *relationships* between economic variables. One way to depict *bivariate* data that can identify an association between two random variables is the *scatter diagram*. This is simply a two-dimensional plot of observations on economic variables. In Figure 2.3 we use the data in Table 2.2 and plot scatter diagrams on two pairs of variables. In Figure 2.3*a* the new home mortgage rate is plotted on the horizontal axis and the number of housing starts is plotted on the vertical axis. Figure 2.3*b* contains a plot of the new home mortgage rate and the prime interest rate. Casual observation of these two data scatter plots reveals a strong positive association between the two interest rates in panel *b*, but a less clear picture of association between housing starts and the new home mortgage rate in panel *a*. We begin the process of learning how to study relationships between variables like these in the following sections.

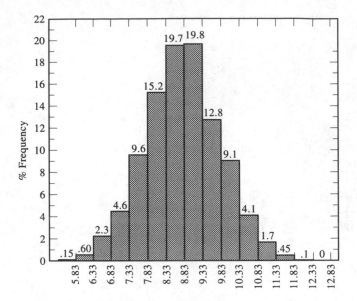

Figure 2.2a   Relative frequency distribution when variance is 1.0.

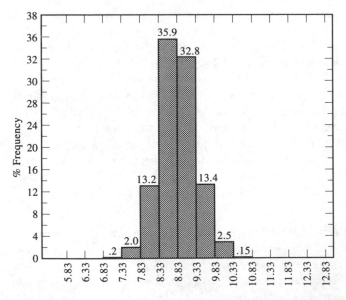

Figure 2.2b   Relative frequency distribution when variance is 0.25.

2.4   A Description of the Data-Generation Process

To this point we have used general terms to describe where economic data come from. We must now describe the process more *precisely* and develop a vocabulary that will serve as a basis for discussion of statistical inference. The ideas we present in the rest of this chapter are statistical definitions and concepts that are the foundation for the

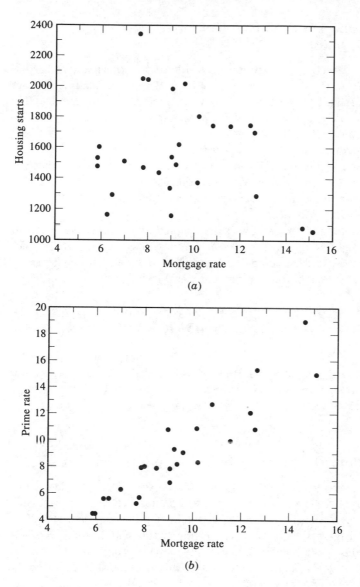

Figure 2.3   Data scatter diagrams for two pairs of macroeconomic variables.

remainder of this book. Thus, because of the potential payoff, there is an incentive for the reader to make an investment in this material now.

Throughout this book we assume that economic data are the outcome of a hypothetical *experiment*, which may be experimental (controlled) or nonexperimental (uncontrolled). The macroeconomic data in Table 2.2 are the *outcome* of a largely uncontrolled social experiment, and the actual values of these variables are never known until they are observed. Consequently, the variables—GNP, personal consumption and the rest—are *random variables*. Given this assumption, to study economic variables, and the relationships between them, we must study the characteristics of random variables and relationships between them.

2.4.1 Continuous and Discrete Random Variables and Their Values

In general, a variable for which values are not known until an experiment is carried out is a *random variable*. In the rest of this chapter we will carefully distinguish between a random variable and the *values* that a random variable takes. For example, GNP is a random variable. *We will denote random variables by uppercase letters*; hence, let Y represent GNP. From Table 2.2 we know that in 1987 real GNP took the *value* $3853.7 billion. *We will let lowercase letters be the observed values of random variables*. Thus, Y = GNP is a random variable that can take any value until it is observed in a particular year, and $y = 3853.7$ is a value (an actual number) that Y has taken or can take. The random variable Y = GNP is a continuous random variable, and the outcome values y can be any nonnegative number; hence, $y \geq 0$.

An example of a *discrete* random variable is the league (American or National) of the winner of the U. S. Major League Baseball World Series. The league of the winner is unknown from year to year, until the completion of the World Series, and consequently it, too, is a random variable. We define the random variable L as

$$L = \begin{cases} 1 & \text{American League wins World Series} \\ 0 & \text{National League wins World Series} \end{cases}$$

The random variable L is a *discrete* random variable as it can only take the values $l = 0, 1$. In fact, L is a dummy variable as its numeric values describe qualitative, not quantitative, characteristics. In the 1990 World Series the Cincinnati Reds (National League) defeated the Oakland Athletics (American League), so that the value of L for 1990 is $l = 0$.

2.4.2 The Probability Distribution of a Single Random Variable

In Table 2.2 we have a time-series of observations on a set of random variables. The numbers recorded are time-dated *values* of the random variables. As we have discussed, we can *describe* the values of these variables by using descriptive summary statistics, histograms, and scatter diagrams. This, however, is not an adequate basis for statistical inference. Statistical inference is based on the ability to make *probability statements about random variables*. To make such statements we need information concerning the *probability distribution* of a random variable, a concept we will now define.

When the values of a random variable are listed with their chances of occurring, the resulting table of outcomes is called a *probability function* or a *probability density function*, or simply a *density function*. The word "density" is included to provide the physical interpretation of probability as a weight or mass. That is, the probability density function spreads the total of 1 unit of "probability mass" over the set of possible values that a random variable can take. Consider a discrete random variable X = the number of heads obtained in a single flip of a coin. The probability density function, say $f(x)$, for this random variable is

x	$f(x)$
0	.5
1	.5

Think about the meaning of the statement "The probability that X takes the value 1 is .5." It implies that the two values 0 and 1 have an equal chance of occurring and, if we flipped the coin *a very large number of times*, the value $x = 1$ would occur 50% of the time. We can denote this as $P[X = 1] = f(1) = 0.5$, where $P[X = 1]$ denotes the probability of the event that the random variable $X = 1$. For discrete random variables the values of the probability density function *are* the probabilities that a random variable takes the associated values.

It is often convenient to have a graphical representation of probability density functions. In Figure 2.4 the probability density function for the discrete random variable X is depicted. Sometimes the probability density function of a discrete random variable can be represented by a mathematical formula, as the following example illustrates.

Example 2.1

Consider the discrete random variable that only takes two values, 1 and 0. The probability of a 1 occurring is p and the probability of a 0 occurring is $1-p$. An example of this random variable is the number of heads (i.e., whether or not one occurs) on a coin toss with $p = 0.5$.   ■

In Example 2.1, if X is the random variable, its probability density function can be written in tabular form as

x	$f(x)$
0	$1-p$
1	p

Alternatively we can express $f(x)$ as

$$f(x) = p^x (1-p)^{1-x}, \qquad \text{for } x = 0, 1$$

This formula can be used to calculate probabilities for this discrete random variable as

$$P[X = 1] = f(1) = p^1 (1-p)^{1-1} = p$$
$$P[X = 0] = f(0) = p^0 (1-p)^{1-0} = 1-p$$

where we have used the mathematical convention that $p^0 = 1$.

Alternatively, the random variable $Y = \text{GNP}$ is a continuous random variable that can take any nonnegative value; thus, $y \geq 0$. The probability that Y takes any single value

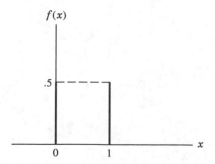

Figure 2.4   Probability density function of the discrete random variable X.

is zero. That is, $P[Y = 140.36] = 0$. The intuition behind this fact is that a continuous random variable can take an *uncountably infinite* number of values, and thus the chance of any one value occurring is 0. Nevertheless, there is a total probability mass of 1 that is spread, or distributed, over the set of values that Y can take. The probability density function for the continuous random variable Y is a function $f(y)$, which is the *equation of a curve*, whose graph might be represented as in Figure 2.5. For continuous random variables, like Y, the *area* under the probability density function corresponds to probability mass. (In contrast, the probability density function of a discrete random variable is a formula for computing the probability of a specific value occurring.) Thus the total area under a probability density function is 1 and the probability that Y *takes* a value in the interval $[a,b]$, or $P[a \le Y \le b]$, is the area under the probability density function between the values $y = a$ and $y = b$. This is shown in Figure 2.5 by the shaded area.

In calculus the *integral* of a function defines the area under it; hence, we will use this fact to write

$$P[a \le Y \le b] = \int_a^b f(y) \, dy$$

You will not be asked to carry out the mathematical process of finding the integral in this book, but if you continue your study of statistics and/or econometrics, the mathematical tools of integral calculus will be important ones for you to acquire. To provide an intuitive basis for the operation, a geometric interpretation of the integral is given in Appendix 2B at the end of this chapter.

Even if you cannot find the probability of an event involving a continuous random variable via integration of the probability density function, you may be able to use plane geometry to achieve the same objective, as the following example illustrates.

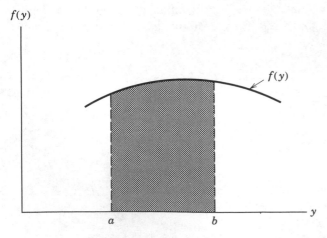

Figure 2.5   Probability as an area under a probability density function.

Example 2.2

A very useful continuous random variable is the *uniform* random variable. *U* is a uniform random variable on the interval [*a*, *b*] if its probability density function is

$$f(u) = \begin{cases} 1/(b-a) & \text{if } a \leq u \leq b \\ 0 & \text{otherwise} \end{cases}$$

The graph of this probability density function is given in Figure 2.6. Suppose the values of *a* and *b* are *a* = 0 and *b* = 1. Then $P[.1 \leq U \leq .3] = .2$, since that is the area under *f*(*u*) between the limits .1 and .3.   ∎

2.4.3   Using Joint Probability Density Functions to Make Probability Statements Involving Several Random Variables

Frequently we will want to make simultaneous probability statements about more than one random variable. For example, in Table 2.2 we have recorded values of the unemployment rate *U* and the inflation rate *P*. Both of these variables are random variables. It is easy to imagine a governmental official asking his or her economic advisers: What is the chance that inflation will be less than 5% *and* the unemployment rate less than 6% next year? The politician is asking for the probability that the random variable *P* takes a value $p \leq 5$ and, *at the same time*, the random variable *U* takes a value $u \leq 6$.

To answer probability questions involving two or more random variables, we must know their *joint probability density function*. For the continuous random variables *U* and *P*, this will be a function *f*(*u*, *p*), which might look something like Figure 2.7.

This joint probability density function has the total probability mass of one unit as the total *volume* under its surface. The probability that the bivariate variable (*u*, *p*) has $u \leq 6$ and $p \leq 5$, written $P[U \leq 6, P \leq 5]$, corresponds to the *volume* under *f*(*u*, *p*) above the rectangle (in the base of the figure) defining the event. If the joint probability density function were known (which it is not) the probability of the event in question could be calculated by using integral calculus or numerical methods on a computer.

The idea of a joint probability density function extends to more than two random variables. For example, if $X_1, X_2, \ldots, X_n$ are all random variables, then their joint probability density function will be written $f(x_1, x_2, \ldots, x_n)$, and if it is known it can be used to calculate probabilities involving $X_1, X_2, \ldots, X_n$.

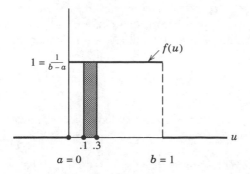

Figure 2.6   Probability density function of a uniform random variable.

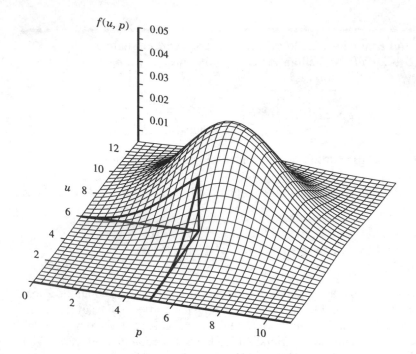

Figure 2.7   A joint probability density function.

2.4.4   Independent Random Variables

Making probability statements about more than one random variable is simplified if the random variables involved are unrelated, or *statistically independent* of one another. *Two random variables are statistically independent, or independently distributed, if knowing the value that one will take does not reveal anything about what value the other may take.* A simple example is what happens when two coins are tossed simultaneously. The fact that one coin lands "heads" reveals nothing about the outcome for the other coin. Thus if the discrete random variable X_1 is the number of heads showing on a toss of the first coin, and X_2 is the number of heads occurring on the second coin, then X_1 and X_2 are independent random variables. An example of independent economic variables might be the expenditures on beef by two randomly chosen individuals. An example of dependent economic variables might be the inflation and unemployment rates.

When random variables are statistically independent, their joint probability density function factors into the *product of their individual probability density functions*, and vice versa. That is, if X_1 and X_2 are statistically independent random variables, then their *joint* probability density function $f(x_1, x_2)$ factors into the *product* of their individual probability density functions $f_1(x_1)$ and $f_2(x_2)$. Therefore, if X_1 and X_2 are independent random variables, then

$$f(x_1, x_2) = f_1(x_1)f_2(x_2)$$

for each and every pair of values x_1 and x_2.

Thus, for example, the joint probability density function $f(x_1, x_2)$ for two independent discrete random variables X_1 and X_2 described in and following example 2.1 (each with $p = 0.5$) is

$$f(x_1, x_2) = f(x_1) \cdot f(x_2)$$
$$= p^{x_1}(1-p)^{1-x_1} p^{x_2}(1-p)^{1-x_2}$$
$$= .5^{x_1}(1-.5)^{1-x_1} .5^{x_2}(1-.5)^{1-x_2}$$

Then the probability of obtaining a head on the first coin and a tail on the second coin is

$$P[X_1 = 1, X_2 = 0] = f(1, 0)$$
$$= f(1) \cdot f(0)$$
$$= (.5)(1)(1)(.5) = .25$$

To consider more than two independent random variables, let $X_1, \ldots, X_n$ be independent random variables with joint probability density function $f(x_1, \ldots, x_n)$ and individual probability density functions $f_1(x_1), f_2(x_2), \ldots, f_n(x_n)$. The independence of $X_1, \ldots, X_n$ allows the joint probability density function to be factored and written as

$$f(x_1, \ldots, x_n) = f_1(x_1) \cdot f_2(x_2) \cdot \ldots \cdot f_n(x_n)$$

2.4.5   Obtaining Probability Density Functions for Individual Random Variables from Joint Probability Density Functions

We have seen that when random variables are statistically independent their joint probability density function can be factored into the product of the probability density functions of the individual random variables. But what if the random variables are *not* independent? Can individual probability density functions be obtained from joint ones? The answer is yes, and we will demonstrate this with an example. Suppose there is a *population* (not a sample) of 1000 individuals whom we wish to categorize by their gender (male or female) and political affiliation (Democrat, Republican, or other). Suppose the population breakdown is given in Table 2.3. Given this population of 1000 persons, consider the experiment of drawing an individual at random. Define two discrete random variables G (gender) and P (political affiliation) as

$$G = \begin{cases} 1 & \text{individual is male} \\ 0 & \text{individual is female} \end{cases}$$

$$P = \begin{cases} 0 & \text{individual is Democrat} \\ 1 & \text{individual is Republican} \\ 2 & \text{individual has other affiliation} \end{cases}$$

Given that the experiment is random, then the *joint* probability distribution of G and P is obtained by dividing the entries of Table 2.3 by 1000, to obtain the results shown in Table 2.4.

The joint probability density function is a function of the values g and p and can be used to compute the probabilities of joint events involving the random drawing of

Table 2.3   Population Breakdown by Gender and Political Affiliation

	Male	Female	Political Totals
Democrat	200	270	470
Republican	300	100	400
Other	60	70	130
Gender totals	560	440	1000

individuals from the population. Thus the probability of drawing a female Republican is .10, or $f(0, 1) = .10$.

Given this joint probability density function, we can obtain the probability distributions of G and P. From the totals in Table 2.3 we can see that the population contains 560 men and 440 women. Thus the probability of randomly drawing a male is .56 and is .44 for a female. In Table 2.4 these values are given in the bottom margin in the row labeled $f(g)$, which is the probability density function of G alone, and is sometimes called the *marginal* distribution of G, since it is obtained from the joint distribution $f(g, p)$ and is found in the margin of the table. The probability of drawing a male $f(1) = .56$ is found by summing down the first column of the joint probability Table 2.4, corresponding to $g = 1$, over *all* the values of P. Similarly $f(0) = .44$, the probability of randomly choosing a female from the population, is found by summing the second column of the joint probability table over all values of p. Mathematically

$$f(1) = \sum_p f(1, p) = .56$$

$$f(0) = \sum_p f(0, p) = .44$$

or, generally,

$$f(g) = \sum_p f(g, p) \qquad \text{for } g = 0, 1$$

where $\sum_p$ means sum over all values that the random variable P can take, as noted in Appendix 2A. This operation is sometimes called "summing out" the unwanted variable in the table of joint probabilities.

The same operations can be carried out to obtain the individual, or marginal, probability density function for P as

$$h(0) = \sum_g f(g, 0) = .47$$

$$h(1) = \sum_g f(g, 1) = .40$$

$$h(2) = \sum_g f(g, 2) = .13$$

or

$$h(p) = \sum_g f(g, p) \qquad \text{for } p = 0, 1, 2$$

Table 2.4   Joint Probability Density Function $f(g, p)$ of G and P

		G		
		1	0	$h(p)$
	0	.20	.27	.47
P	1	.30	.10	.40
	2	.06	.07	.13
	$f(g)$	.56	.44	

The same process works when there are more than two discrete random variables. If $X_1, \ldots, X_n$ are discrete random variables with joint probability density function $f(x_1, \ldots, x_n)$, then the marginal probability density function of X_1 *alone* is

$$f_1(x_1) = \sum_{x_2} \sum_{x_3} \cdots \sum_{x_n} f(x_1, \ldots, x_n)$$

We have summed out the variables $X_2, \ldots, X_n$ using multiple summation, which is discussed in Appendix 2A. To obtain the marginal probability density function of any single random variable, sum out the other $n-1$ random variables. If the random variables are continuous the same idea works, with integrals replacing the summation signs.

2.4.6   Conditional Probabilities and Conditional Probability Density Functions

Many times the chances of an event occurring are *conditional* on the occurrence of another event. For example, you may hear a weather forecaster on the morning news state that "If the cold front reaches here today, then the chances of rain are 80%, but otherwise the chance of rain is low." The forecaster is giving the probability of rain *conditioned* by the event that the cold front arrives. As another example, consider the population of individuals represented by Table 2.3. Suppose we wish to focus on female voters, and ask the question: What is the probability that a randomly selected woman (from this population) is a Republican? Thus we are asking for the probability that the random variable $P = 1$ given (or conditional upon) that $G = 0$. From Table 2.3 we calculate that the probability of selecting a Republican, given that we sample *only* from the female population, is 0.227 (= 100/440). Similarly the conditional probabilities of drawing a Democrat or other political affiliation from the female population are 0.614 and 0.159, respectively.

For *discrete* random variables like gender (G) and political affiliation (P), these conditional probabilities can be calculated easily from the joint probability density function $f(g, p)$ and marginal probability density function of the *conditioning* random variable $f(g)$. Specifically, the probability that the random variable P takes the value p *given* that $G = g$, is written $P[P = p|G = g]$. This conditional probability is given by the *conditional probability density function* $f(p|g)$:

$$f(p \mid g) = P[P = p \mid G = g] = \frac{f(g, p)}{f(g)} \tag{2.4.1}$$

That is, the conditional probability that $P = p$ given $G = g$ is the joint probability that $P = p$ *and* $G = g$ *divided* by the probability of the conditioning event. Applying this rule to obtain $f(p|0)$, we find that

$$
\begin{array}{ll}
\underline{p} & \qquad\quad \underline{f(p|0)} \\[4pt]
0 & f(0, 0)/f(0) = .27/.44 = .614 \\[2pt]
1 & f(0, 1)/f(0) = .10/.44 = .227 \\[2pt]
2 & f(0, 2)/f(0) = .07/.44 = .159
\end{array}
\tag{2.4.2}
$$

For discrete random variables the conditional probability density function gives the probabilities of one event conditional on another. If the random variables are continuous, then the conditional probability density function is constructed in the same way but yields the equation of a curve that can be used to calculate probabilities as areas (or volumes) beneath it.

The idea of conditional probability provides a useful way to characterize the statistical independence of two random variables. Suppose that knowing the gender of an individual from a population tells us *nothing* about the probability that a randomly chosen individual is a Democrat, a Republican, or an Independent. That is, suppose that the conditional probability of a woman being Democrat, Republican, or Independent is the same as the unconditional, or marginal, probability; or

$$f(p|g) = h(p) \quad \text{for } g = 0, 1$$

If the conditional probabilities of $P = 0, 1, 2$ given $g = 0, 1$ are all the same as the marginal (unconditional) probabilities for P, then there is no information about political affiliation in the knowledge of gender, and the two random variables are *statistically independent*. In that instance

$$f(p|g) = h(p) = \frac{f(g, p)}{f(g)} \tag{2.4.3}$$

so the joint probability density function of the two random variables factors into the product of the marginal probability functions:

$$f(g, p) = f(g)h(p) \tag{2.4.4}$$

The result in equation 2.4.4 is a general one regarding statistically independent random variables and was introduced in Section 2.4.4.

2.5 The Expected Value of a Random Variable: The Mean

When we discussed descriptive statistics in Section 2.3.3, we used location and dispersion characteristics to describe a sample of data. Likewise, an important characteristic of a random variable is its *mathematical expectation* or *expected value*, which is also called the *mean* of the random variable. *The expected value of a random variable X is the average value of the random variable in an infinite number of repetitions of the experiment (samples), and it is denoted E[X].* As an example, let X be the number of heads occurring in the toss of a single, well-balanced coin. The values that X can take are $x = 0$, 1. *If this experiment is repeated a very large number of times, the average value of X will be 0.5.* Note that $E[X] = 0.5$ *is not* the value we expect to obtain on a single toss, since the value 0.5 cannot even occur. It is the *long run average value we expect after making repeated trials of an experiment.*

Although $E[X]$ is easy to determine intuitively in the example of the coin toss, it will not always be so obvious. The mathematical representation of the expected value of a discrete random variable X, which can take the values $x_1, x_2,...,x_T$ with probability density values $f(x_1), f(x_2),..., f(x_T)$, is

$$E[X] = x_1 f(x_1) + x_2 f(x_2) + ... + x_T f(x_T)$$

$$= \sum_{i=1}^{T} x_i f(x_i)$$

$$= \sum_{x} x f(x) \tag{2.5.1}$$

The notation Σ_x means "sum over all values that X can take." Equation 2.5.1 shows that for a discrete random variable its *mathematical expectation or mean value is a "weighted" average of the values of the random variable, with the weights being probabilities attached to each value.*

Example 2.3

Let the random variable X be the number of heads in *two* tosses of a coin. The values that X can take are $x = 0, 1, 2$. The probability density function of X is

x	$f(x)$
0	.25
1	.50
2	.25

The graphical representation of $f(x)$ is given in Figure 2.8. The expected value of X is

$$E[X] = \sum_x xf(x)$$
$$= 0(.25) + 1(.50) + 2(.25) = 1$$

Thus the average value of X that would occur in an infinite number of repetitions of the experiment of flipping a coin twice is $E[X] = 1$. Note that the value $x = 1$ is at the center of the probability density function and is in fact the "center of the mass" $f(x)$. The mean or expected value of the random variable X represents the "center of the distribution" in this very special sense.   ■

To calculate the expected value of a continuous random variable Y, we once again will "add up" all the values of the random variable weighted by the values of the probability density function $f(y)$. The only problem now is that we must add up an *infinite*

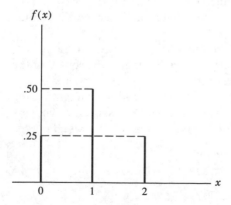

Figure 2.8   The probability density function of X = number of heads in two tosses of a coin.

number of weighted values and $f(y)$ must be known. The way to actually do this is to use integration, which can be represented as

$$E[Y] = \int_{-\infty}^{\infty} yf(y)\, dy \qquad (2.5.2)$$

Although you may or may not know how this is done mathematically, we can visualize the process by recalling that integration finds areas under curves. In Appendix 2B the geometry of integration is reviewed. All equation 2.5.2 means is that we must find the area under the "curve" or function $g(y) = yf(y)$, as the following example illustrates.

Example 2.4

In Example 2.2 we considered the uniform random variable U. Suppose that the distribution parameters $a = 0$ and $b = 3$ so that $f(u) = 1/(b - a) = 1/3$ for $0 \le u \le 3$. Then the expected value of U is

$$E[U] = \int_{0}^{3} uf(u)\, du$$

This integral is the area under the curve $g(u) = uf(u) = (1/3)u$ for values of u between 0 and 3. In Figure 2.9 $f(u)$ and $g(u)$ are graphed. The area of the shaded triangle in Figure 2.9*b* is $E[U] = 1.5$. The interpretation of the expected value as the center of the probability mass is still correct. There is just as much probability area under $f(u)$ to the left of $u = 1.5$ as there is to the right, as is shown in Figure 2.9*a*. In general, the expected value of a uniform random variable is $E[u] = (a + b)/2$. See Exercise 2.10. Note that the *parameters a* and *b* that define the distribution of the uniform random variable are used to calculate the *mean* of the uniform random variable.   ■

2.6 The Expected Value of a Function of a Random Variable: The Variance

The mean of a random variable tells us about the average value of the random variable. What can we use to tell us about the dispersion, spread, or range of values that the random variable can take? To answer this question we must explore how to take the mathematical expectation of a function of a random variable, and then we must define the *variance* of a random variable.

To do this we need to return to Example 2.3, but now let us find the mathematical expectation of $g(X) = X^2$, where $g(X)$ is a new random variable that is the square of the random variable X. The solution is straightforward if you remember that the expected value of a random variable is a weighted average of its values, with the weights being the values of its probability density function. Since X is random, its square, the variable X^2, is also a random variable. The values of X^2 and the probability weights are

x	x^2	$f(x)$	$f(x^2)$
0	0	.25	.25
1	1	.50	.50
2	4	.25	.25

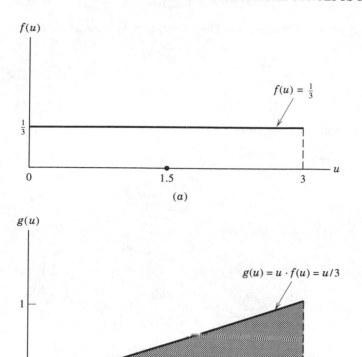

Figure 2.9   (a) The probability density function $f(u)$ for the uniform random variable. (b) The function $g(u)$ for the uniform random variable.

As you can see the appropriate weights for X^2 are simply $f(x)$, so

$$E[g(X)] = E[X^2] = 0f(0) + 1f(1) + 4f(2)$$
$$= 0 + .50 + 1 = 1.50$$

This procedure is correct in general as well, so if X is a discrete random variable and $g(X)$ is a function of it, then

$$E[g(X)] = \sum_x g(x)f(x) \tag{2.6.1}$$

The idea of how to determine the expected value of a function of a continuous random variable Y, say $g(y)$, is exactly the same as in the discrete case. The terms $g(y)$ must be weighted by $f(y)$ and then all those products summed. The integral representation of $E[g(y)]$ when Y is continuous is

$$E[g(y)] = \int_{-\infty}^{\infty} g(y)f(y)\, dy \tag{2.6.2}$$

2.6.1   Some Properties of Mathematical Expectation

There are some properties of mathematical expectation that work for discrete and continuous random variables and follow from equations 2.6.1 and 2.6.2. We will show that the properties are true for the discrete case. The summation operations used are reviewed in Appendix 2A.

1. If c is a constant,

$$E[c] = c \qquad (2.6.3a)$$

To see this let $g(x) = c$ and use equation 2.6.1.

$$E[c] = E[g(x)] = \sum_x cf(x) = c\sum_x f(x) = c$$

since

$$\sum_x f(x) = \text{ total probability mass } = 1$$

2. If c is a constant and X is a random variable, then

$$E[cX] = cE[X] \qquad (2.6.3b)$$

That is, constants can *always* be factored out of expectations. To show this let $g(X) = cX$. Then,

$$E[cX] = E[g(X)] = \sum_x cxf(x) = c\sum_x xf(x) = cE[X]$$

using equation 2.6.1.

3. If a and c are constants

$$E[a + cX] = a + cE[X] \qquad (2.6.3c)$$

To show this let $g(X) = a + cX$, so

$$\begin{aligned} E[a + cX] = E[g(x)] &= \sum_x (a + cX)fx \\ &= \sum_x af(x) + \sum_x cxf(x) \\ &= a\sum_x f(x) + c\sum_x xf(x) \\ &= a + cE[X] \end{aligned}$$

In Section 2.8 we show that the expected value of *any* sum is always the sum of the expected values.

2.6.2   The Variance of a Random Variable

Given the properties of mathematical expectation, we may define the *variance of a discrete or continuous random variable* X as the expected value of $g(X) = [X - E(X)]^2$. Like the mean, the variance of a random variable is an important characteristic of its probability distribution, to which we give the symbol σ^2 or "sigma squared." Algebraically,

$$\text{var}(X) = \sigma^2 = E\left[(X - E(X))^2\right] \qquad (2.6.4)$$

Examining $g(X)$ closely we observe that it is the squared difference between the random variable X and its mean value $E[X]$. Furthermore, since X is random, $g(X)$ is random. However, the mean of a random variable $E[X]$ is just a number or constant. Recall that the expected value of a function of a random variable, like $g(X)$, is the weighted average of the values $g(x)$ weighted by the probability density function values $f(x)$. Thus the variance of a random variable is the weighted average of the squared differences (or distances) between the *values* x of the random variable X and the mean (center of the probability mass) of the random variable. The larger the variance of a random variable, the greater the average squared distance between the values of the random variable and its mean, or the more "spread out" the values of the random variable are. Equivalently, the larger the variance of a random variable, the greater the range or spread of the population values about the population mean.

To illustrate, let us consider Example 2.3 again.

Example 2.3 (continued)

We have determined that $E[X] = 1$. To compute the variance of X we must compute

$$\text{var}(X) = E\big[X - E(X)\big]^2 = \sum_x (x-1)^2 f(x)$$

x	$(x-1)^2$	$f(x)$
0	1	.25
1	0	.50
2	1	.25

Therefore,

$$\sigma^2 = \sum_x (x-1)^2 f(x) = 1(.25) + 0(.50) + 1(.25) = .50 \qquad \blacksquare$$

There is an alternative, but equivalent, expression for the variance of a random variable that is sometimes used, namely

$$\sigma^2 = E\big[X^2\big] - \big[E(X)\big]^2 \qquad (2.6.5)$$

To show that equation 2.6.5 is an equivalent expression for the variance of X, use equation 2.6.1 to write out the expectation in equation 2.6.4 as

$$\sigma^2 = E\big[X - E(X)\big]^2 = E\big[g(X)\big]$$
$$= \sum_x \big(x - E(X)\big)^2 f(x)$$
$$= \sum_x \Big(x^2 - 2xE(X) + \big[E(X)\big]^2\Big) f(x)$$

Take the sum of the three separate terms, and remember that the expectation $E(X)$ is a constant and can be factored out of a sum, to obtain

$$\sigma^2 = \sum_x x^2 f(x) - 2E(X)\sum_x xf(x) + \left[E(X)\right]^2 \sum_x f(x)$$

$$= E\left[X^2\right] - 2\left[E(X)\right]^2 + \left[E(X)\right]^2$$

$$= E\left[X^2\right] - \left[E(X)\right]^2$$

Another useful property of variances is the following. If a and c are constants, let $Z = a + cX$. Then Z is a random variable and its variance is

$$\mathrm{var}(Z) = E\left[Z - E(Z)\right]^2$$

$$= E\left[a + cX - E(a + cX)\right]^2$$

$$= E\left[a + cX - a - cE(X)\right]^2$$

$$= E\left[c\left(X - E(X)\right)\right]^2$$

$$= c^2 E\left[X - E(X)\right]^2$$

$$= c^2 \,\mathrm{var}(X) \tag{2.6.6}$$

What this says is that if you

(i)   add a constant to a random variable it does not affect its variance, or dispersion. This follows since adding a constant to a random variable *shifts* the location of its probability density function but leaves its shape, and dispersion, unaffected.

(ii) and if you multiply a random variable by a constant, the variance is multiplied by the square of the constant.

Given a random variable, the square root of the variance is called the *standard deviation*, and it is denoted by σ. It too measures the spread or dispersion of a distribution and has the advantage of being in the same units of measure as the random variable.

2.7 The Expected Value of a Function of Several Random Variables: Covariance and Correlation

In economics we are *usually* interested in exploring relationships between economic variables. One question that is frequently asked is: How closely do two price variables move together or track one another? An answer to this important question is provided by the *covariance* (and *correlation*) between these two random variables. The covariance literally indicates the amount of covariation exhibited by the two random variables. As with the mean and variance of single random variables, the covariance is a mathematical expectation. If X_1 and X_2 are random variables, then their covariance is

$$\mathrm{cov}(X_1, X_2) = E\left[\left(X_1 - E[X_1]\right)\left(X_2 - E[X_2]\right)\right] \tag{2.7.1}$$

This expectation is more complicated than the ones we have taken thus far because it involves two random variables. However, there are expressions analogous to equations 2.6.1 and 2.6.2 that we can use. For example, if X_1 and X_2 are discrete random variables, $g(X_1, X_2)$ is a function of the random variables, and $f(X_1, X_2)$ is their joint probability density function, then

$$E\big[g(X_1, X_2)\big] = \sum_{x_1} \sum_{x_2} g(x_1, x_2) f(x_1, x_2)$$ (2.7.2)

Thus

$$\text{cov}(X_1, X_2) = E\big[X_1 - E(X_1)\big]\big[X_2 - E(X_2)\big]$$
$$= \sum_{x_1} \sum_{x_2} \big[x_1 - E(X_1)\big]\big[x_2 - E(X_2)\big] f(x_1, x_2)$$ (2.7.3)

If X_1 and X_2 are continuous random variables, then the definition of covariance is similar, with integrals replacing the summation signs.

The *sign* of the covariance between two random variables indicates whether their association is positive (direct) or negative (inverse). Examining the definition 2.7.1, the covariance between X_1 and X_2 is seen to be the expected, or average, value of the random product $[X_1 - E(X_1)][X_2 - E(X_2)]$. In Figure 2.10 are plotted typical pairs of randomly drawn values (x_1, x_2) of two continuous random variables, X_1 and X_2. In quadrant I of Figure 2.10 the values (x_1, x_2) are greater than their means, $[E(X_1), E(X_2)]$, and thus the product $[x_1 - E(X_1)][x_2 - E(X_2)]$ is positive. In quadrant III the values of the random variables are both less than the mean values, and the product is also positive. In quadrants II and IV the product is negative. For the values of the random variables depicted in Figure 2.10, the greater proportion of values fall in quadrants I and III, and thus *on the average* the product is positive and cov $(X_1, X_2) > 0$. From Figure 2.10 we

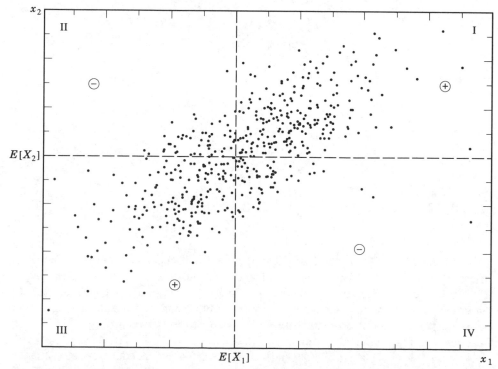

Figure 2.10   Data scatter of joint values of random variables with a positive covariance.

see that values of two random variables with positive covariance tend to be positively (or directly) related.

By examining the data scatter in Figure 2.11, we determine that the greater proportion of values (x_1, x_2) fall in quadrants II and IV, where the product $[x_1 - E(X_1)][x_2 - E(X_2)]$ is negative, and thus on average the product is negative and $cov(X_1, X_2) < 0$. The values of two random variables with negative covariance tend to be negatively (or inversely) related. Zero covariance implies that there is neither positive nor negative association between pairs of values.

The magnitude of covariance is difficult to interpret because it depends on the units of measurement of the random variables. The meaning of "covariation" is revealed more clearly if we divide the covariance between X_1 and X_2 by their respective standard deviations. The resulting ratio is defined as the *correlation* between the random variables X_1 and X_2 and is often denoted by the Greek letter rho, ρ. Thus

$$\rho = \frac{\text{cov}(X_1, X_2)}{\sqrt{\text{var}(X_1)}\sqrt{\text{var}(X_2)}} \tag{2.7.4}$$

As with the covariance, the correlation ρ between two random variables measures the degree of *linear* association between them. However, unlike the covariance, the correlation must lie between -1 and 1. To illustrate this, suppose X_1 is a *perfect* linear function of X_2, or $X_1 = a + cX_2$ where a and c are constants and $c \neq 0$. Then

$$\begin{aligned}
\text{cov}(X_1, X_2) &= E[X_1 - E(X_1)][X_2 - E(X_2)] \\
&= E[(a + cX_2) - E(a + cX_2)][X_2 - E(X_2)] \\
&= E[a - a + cX_2 - cE(X_2)][X_2 - E(X_2)] \\
&= cE[X_2 - E(X_2)]^2 \\
&= c\,\text{var}(X_2)
\end{aligned}$$

and $\text{var}(X_1) = c^2\,\text{var}(X_2)$, so

$$\begin{aligned}
\rho &= \frac{\text{cov}(X_1, X_2)}{\sqrt{\text{var}(X_1)}\sqrt{\text{var}(X_2)}} \\
&= \frac{c\,\text{var}(X_2)}{\sqrt{c^2\,\text{var}(X_2)}} \\
&= \begin{cases} 1 & c > 0 \\ -1 & c < 0 \end{cases}
\end{aligned}$$

Thus the correlation between X_1 and X_2 is 1 or -1 if X_1 is a perfect positive or negative linear function of X_2. If there is *no linear* association between X_1 and X_2, then $\text{cov}(X_1, X_2) = 0$ and $\rho = 0$. For other values of correlation the magnitude of $|\rho|$ indicates the "strength" of the association between the values of the random variable. The larger the value of $|\rho|$ the more nearly exact the linear association between the values. This is illustrated in Figure 2.16 (Section 2.8).

A consequence of statistical independence between two independent random variables is that the *covariance* and *correlation* between them is zero. We can use equation 2.7.2 to show what happens to the covariance if X_1 and X_2 are independent random variables

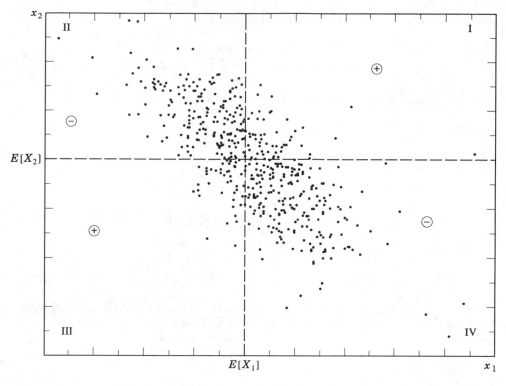

Figure 2.11   Data scatter of joint values of random variables with a negative covariance.

$$\text{cov}(X_1, X_2) = E\big[X_1 \quad E(X_1)\big]\big[X_2 \quad E(X_2)\big]$$

$$= \sum_{x_1}\sum_{x_2}\big(x_1 - E(X_1)\big)\big(x_2 - E(X_2)\big)f(x_1, x_2)$$

[use 2.7.2]

$$= \sum_{x_1}\sum_{x_2}\big(x_1 - E(X_1)\big)\big(x_2 - E(X_2)\big)f_1(x_1)f_2(x_2)$$

[use independence to factor $f(x_1, x_2) = f_1(x_1)f_2(x_2)$]

$$= \sum_{x_1}\big(x_1 - E(X_1)\big)f_1(x_1)\sum_{x_2}\big(x_2 - E(X_2)\big)f_2(x_2)$$

[factor]

$$= 0$$

The covariance between the independent random variables X_1 and X_2 is zero, indicating that there is *no linear association* between them. The converse of this relationship is *not* true. That is, just because the covariance or correlation between two random variables is zero *does not* mean that they are necessarily independent. *Zero covariance means that there is no exact linear association between the random variables.* However, there may be more complicated nonlinear associations, like $X_1^2 + X_2^2 = 1$.

In Section 2.3.3 we discussed the descriptive statistics arithmetic mean, sample variance, and sample standard deviation that may be used to describe a sample of data. Bivariate data were summarized only by a data scatter, as in Figure 2.3. Now we will define the sample covariance and sample correlation between pairs of data values of two random variables X and Y. If (x_t, y_t), $t = 1, \ldots, T$, are observed sample values of random variables X and Y, then their sample covariance is

$$s_{XY} = \sum_{t=1}^{T} \frac{(x_t - \bar{x})(y_t - \bar{y})}{T-1} \tag{2.7.5}$$

where $\bar{x}$ and $\bar{y}$ are sample means. The sample correlation coefficient is

$$r_{XY} = \frac{s_{XY}}{s_X s_Y} = \frac{\sum_{t=1}^{T}(x_t - \bar{x})(y_t - \bar{y})/(T-1)}{\sqrt{\dfrac{\Sigma(x_t - \bar{x})^2}{T-1}}\sqrt{\dfrac{\Sigma(y_t - \bar{y})^2}{T-1}}}$$

$$= \frac{\sum_{t=1}^{T}(x_t - \bar{x})(y_t - \bar{y})}{\sqrt{\sum_{t=1}^{T}(x_t - \bar{x})^2}\sqrt{\sum_{t=1}^{T}(y_t - \bar{y})^2}} \tag{2.7.6}$$

These values are interpreted in the same way as the actual covariance and correlation between random variables; however, these sample analogues only describe a characteristic of the sample data scatter. See Exercise 2.19 for practice calculating sample covariances and correlations.

2.7.1 The Mean of a Weighted Sum of Random Variables

In equation 2.7.2 we presented the rule for finding the expected value of a function of two discrete random variables. Let the function $g(X_1, X_2)$ be a weighted sum of X_1 and X_2, that is,

$$g(X_1, X_2) = c_1 X_1 + c_2 X_2$$

where c_1 and c_2 are constant. Now use equation 2.7.2 to find the expectation

$$
\begin{aligned}
E[g(X_1, X_2)] &= E[c_1 X_1 + c_2 X_2] \\
&= \sum_{x_1}\sum_{x_2} g(x_1, x_2) f(x_1, x_2) \\
&= \sum_{x_1}\sum_{x_2} [c_1 x_1 + c_2 x_2] f(x_1, x_2) \\
&= \sum_{x_1}\sum_{x_2} c_1 x_1 f(x_1, x_2) + \sum_{x_1}\sum_{x_2} c_2 x_2 f(x_1, x_2)
\end{aligned}
$$

(sums can be broken into parts)

$$= \sum_{x_1} c_1 x_1 \sum_{x_2} f(x_1, x_2) + \sum_{x_2} c_2 x_2 \sum_{x_1} f(x_1, x_2)$$

$\left(\text{since } c_i x_i \text{ is constant with respect to } x_j\right)$

$$= c_1 \sum_{x_1} x_1 f(x_1) + c_2 \sum_{x_2} x_2 f(x_2)$$

$\left(\text{since } \sum_{x_j} f(x_i, x_j) = f(x_i)\right)$

$$= c_1 E[X_1] + c_2 E[X_2]$$

That is

$$E[c_1 X_1 + c_2 X_2] = c_1 E[X_1] + c_2 E[X_2]$$

This rule says that the expected value of a weighted sum of two random variables is the weighted sum of their expected value. This rule works for any number of random variables whether they are *discrete or continuous*:

$$E[c_1 X_1 + c_2 X_2 + \ldots + c_n X_n] = c_1 E[X_1] + c_2 E[X_2] + \ldots + c_n E[X_n] \tag{2.7.7}$$

Note that if all the $c_i = 1$, then the rule says that the expected value of the sum of a set of random variables is the sum of their expected values, or

$$E[X_1 + X_2 + \ldots + X_n] = E[X_1] + E[X_2] + \ldots + E[X_n] \tag{2.7.8}$$

See Exercise 2.15 for hints about how to show that this result is true for discrete random variables. In fact the rule can be extended to sums of *functions* of random variables, as

$$E[g_1(X_1, \ldots, X_n) + g_2(X_1, \ldots, X_n) + \ldots + g_n(X_1, \ldots, X_n)]$$
$$= E[g_1(X_1, \ldots, X_n)] + E[g_2(X_1, \ldots, X_n)] + \ldots + E[g_n(X_1, \ldots, X_n)] \tag{2.7.9}$$

where the $g_i(X_1, \ldots, X_n)$ are functions of the random variables. In general, *the expected value of any sum is the sum of the expected values.*

2.7.2   The Variance of a Weighted Sum of Random Variables

We can use equation 2.7.7 to find the variance of a weighted sum of two discrete or continuous random variables. If we let the weighted sum in equation 2.7.7 be represented by a *new* random variable

$$Z = g(X_1, X_2) = c_1 X_1 + c_2 X_2$$

then

$$E[Z] = E[c_1 X_1] + E[c_2 X_2] = c_1 E[X_1] + c_2 E[X_2]$$

since the expected value of a sum is the sum of the expected values and constants can be factored out. To find the variance of Z, we use the definition of the variance of a random variable, equation 2.6.4.

$$\begin{aligned}
\text{var}(Z) &= E[Z - E[Z]]^2 \\
&= E\{(c_1 X_1 + c_2 X_2) - (c_1 E[X_1] + c_2 E[X_2])\}^2 \\
&= E\{c_1(X_1 - E[X_1]) + c_2(X_2 - E[X_2])\}^2 \\
&= E\{c_1^2(X_1 - E[X_1])^2 + c_2^2(X_2 - E[X_2])^2 + 2c_1 c_2(X_1 - E[X_1])(X_2 - E[X_2])\} \\
&= c_1^2 E[X_1 - E[X_1]]^2 + c_2^2 E[X_2 - E[X_2]]^2 + 2c_1 c_2 E[(X_1 - E[X_1])(X_2 - E[X_2])]
\end{aligned}$$

(since the expected value of a sum is the sum of the expected values)

$$= c_1^2 \, \text{var}(X_1) + c_2^2 \, \text{var}(X_2) + 2c_1 c_2 \, \text{cov}(X_1, X_2)$$

That is, the variance of a weighted sum of two random variables is

$$\text{var}(c_1 X_1 + c_2 X_2) = c_1^2 \, \text{var}(X_1) + c_2^2 \, \text{var}(X_2) + 2c_1 c_2 \, \text{cov}(X_1, X_2) \qquad (2.7.10)$$

An important special case occurs when X_1 and X_2 are independent random variables. In that case the covariance between X_1 and X_2 is zero and the rule is

If X_1 and X_2 are *independent* random variables then

$$\text{var}(c_1 X_1 + c_2 X_2) = c_1^2 \, \text{var}(X_1) + c_2^2 \, \text{var}(X_2) \ .$$

The rule for the variance of a weighted sum of random variables extends to *more than* 2 random variables. If $X_1,\ldots, X_n$ are random variables and $c_1,\ldots, c_n$ constants then

$$\text{var}(c_1 X_1 + c_2 X_2 + \ldots + c_n X_n) = c_1^2 \, \text{var}(X_1) + c_2^2 \, \text{var}(X_2) +$$
$$\ldots + c_n^2 \, \text{var}(X_n) + \sum \sum_{i \neq j} c_i c_j \, \text{cov}(X_i, X_j) \qquad (2.7.11)$$

where the symbol $\Sigma\Sigma_{i \neq j}$ means "take the double sum for all pairs of subscripts such that i is not equal to j." For example, if $n = 3$

$$\text{var}(c_1 X_1 + c_2 X_2 + c_3 X_3) = c_1^2 \, \text{var}(X_1) + c_2^2 \, \text{var}(X_2) + c_3^2 \, \text{var}(X_3)$$
$$+ c_1 c_2 \, \text{cov}(X_1, X_2) + c_1 c_3 \, \text{cov}(X_1, X_3)$$
$$+ c_2 c_1 \, \text{cov}(X_2, X_1) + c_2 c_3 \, \text{cov}(X_2, X_3)$$
$$+ c_3 c_1 \, \text{cov}(X_3, X_1) + c_3 c_2 \, \text{cov}(X_3, X_2)$$

If $X_1,\ldots, X_n$ are all *independent* random variables, then the covariance terms are zero and the rule becomes:

If $X_1, X_2,\ldots, X_n$ are independent random variables, then

$$\text{var}(c_1 X_1 + c_2 X_2 + \ldots + c_n X_n) = \sum_{i=1}^{n} c_i^2 \, \text{var}(X_i)$$

If $c_1 = c_2 = \ldots = c_n = 1$, we see that the variance of the sum of random variables is the sum of their variances when the random variables are all independent, or their covariances are zero.

2.8 Examples of Probability Density Functions

In the previous sections we discussed random variables and their probability density functions in a general way. In real economic contexts some *specific* probability density functions have been found to be very useful. In this section we examine two important and frequently used probability distributions: the normal and the bivariate normal (which is the joint probability density function of two normal random variables).

2.8.1 The Normal Distribution

Here we discuss the properties of normally distributed random variables. The normal probability density function is the most important of all density functions. Random variables that have this probability density function are called "normal" random variables. If X is a normal random variable with mean β and variance σ^2, symbolized as $X \sim N(\beta, \sigma^2)$ and read "X is a normally distributed random variable with mean β and variance σ^2," then its probability density function is given by the following mathematical expression:

$$f(x) = \frac{1}{\sqrt{2\pi\sigma^2}} \exp\left[\frac{-\frac{1}{2}(x-\beta)^2}{\sigma^2}\right], \quad -\infty < x < \infty \tag{2.8.1}$$

where $\exp[a]$ denotes the exponential function e^a. The mean β and variance σ^2 are the parameters of this distribution and determine its location and dispersion. The range of this continuous random variable is minus infinity to plus infinity. Pictures of the normal probability density functions are given in Figure 2.12 for various values of its mean and variance.

The normal probability density function is a symmetric bell-shaped curve centered at β, its mean value. Note from Figure 2.12 that normal distributions with the same mean β but different variances σ^2 are more or less spread out about the mean depending on the magnitude of the variance. For example, the larger the variance, the more disperse and spread out the values. Distributions with the same variance but different means are identical in shape but located at different points along the x axis.

Like all continuous random variables, probabilities involving normal random variables are found as areas under probability density functions. Unfortunately, these areas are not easy to calculate directly unless you have a computer program that will do the work. Alternatively, we can make use of the relation between a normal random variable and its "standardized" equivalent. A *standard normal random variable* is one that has a normal probability density function with mean 0 and variance 1. If $X \sim N(\beta, \sigma^2)$, then

$$Z = (X-\beta)/\sigma \sim N(0, 1) \tag{2.8.2}$$

Dividing by the standard deviation σ is appropriate, since it has the same units of measure as the random variable X. Since $Z = (X/\sigma) - (\beta/\sigma)$, it is easy to use the rules for mean and variance that we have derived to verify that the mean and variance of Z are 0 and 1, respectively:

$$E[Z] = \frac{1}{\sigma}E[X] - \frac{\beta}{\sigma} = \frac{\beta}{\sigma} - \frac{\beta}{\sigma} = 0$$

$$\mathrm{var}(Z) = \left(\frac{1}{\sigma}\right)^2 \mathrm{var}(X) = \sigma^2/\sigma^2 = 1$$

The standard normal random variable is important for theoretical and practical reasons. Theoretically the standard normal random variable is related to the chi-square random variable, the t random variable, and the F random variable, all of which are discussed in Chapter 4. The relationship between the standard normal random variable Z and the normal random variable X is very useful, since any probability statement involving X can be recast as a probability statement involving Z, and probabilities (areas under the probability density function) for Z are found in Table 1 at the back of this book. In general,

$$P[X \geq a] = P\left[\frac{X-\beta}{\sigma} \geq \frac{a-\beta}{\sigma}\right] = P\left[Z \geq \frac{a-\beta}{\sigma}\right]$$

and

$$P[a \leq X \leq b] = P\left[\frac{a-\beta}{\sigma} \leq \frac{X-\beta}{\sigma} \leq \frac{b-\beta}{\sigma}\right] = P\left[\frac{a-\beta}{\sigma} \leq Z \leq \frac{b-\beta}{\sigma}\right]$$

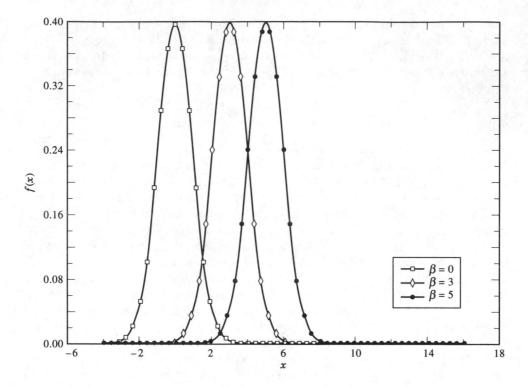

Figure 2.12a   Normal probability density functions: mean β and variance one.

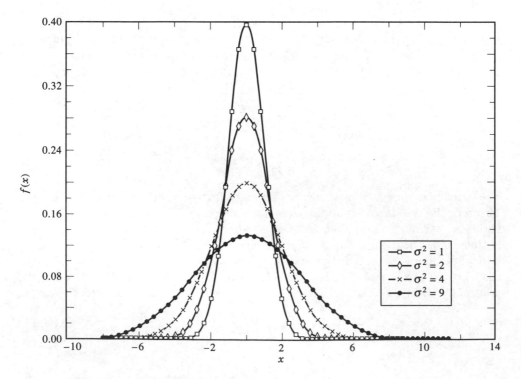

Figure 2.12b   The normal probability density functions: mean zero and variances σ^2.

For example, suppose $X \sim N(3, 9)$. To calculate $P[4 \leq X \leq 6]$ we can write

$$P\left[\frac{4-3}{\sqrt{9}} \leq \frac{X-3}{\sqrt{9}} \leq \frac{6-3}{\sqrt{9}}\right] = P[.33 \leq Z \leq 1]$$

$$= .3413 - .1293 = .212$$

The standard normal probability density function is depicted in Figure 2.13. On it are marked the positions of one, two, and three standard deviations. From Table 1 at the back of the book we see that 68.2% of the probability mass of a standard normal random variable falls within one standard deviation, on either side, of the mean value (zero), 95.4% of the probability falls within two standard deviations, and 99.7% of the probability falls within three standard deviations.

An interesting and useful fact about the normal distribution is that a weighted sum of normal random variables has a normal distribution. That is,

If $X_1 \sim N(\beta_1, \sigma_1^2)$, $X_2 \sim N(\beta_2, \sigma_2^2), \ldots, X_n \sim N(\beta_n, \sigma_n^2)$, and $c_1, \ldots, c_n$ are constants, then
$$Z = c_1 X_1 + c_2 X_2 + \ldots + c_n X_n \sim N\big(E(Z), \text{var}(Z)\big)$$

The rules 2.7.7 and 2.7.11 can be used to calculate the mean and variance of Z in the usual way. We will use this rule countless times in the remainder of this book.

2.8.2   The Central Limit Theorem

The reason that the normal distribution is an important distribution in statistics is in part due to the *Central Limit Theorem*. We state one version of this remarkable theorem here:

Central Limit Theorem. If $X_1, \ldots, X_T$ are independent and identically distributed random variables with mean β and variance σ^2 and

$$\overline{X} = \frac{1}{T}\big(X_1 + X_2 + \ldots + X_T\big) = \sum_{i=1}^{T} X_i/T$$

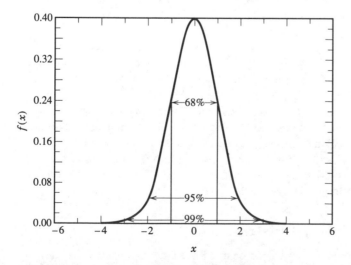

Figure 2.13   Standard normal probability density function.

then

$$Z = \frac{\bar{X} - E[\bar{X}]}{\left[\text{var}(\bar{X})\right]^{\frac{1}{2}}} = \frac{\bar{X} - \beta}{\sigma/\sqrt{T}}$$

has a probability distribution that approaches the standard normal, $N(0, 1)$, as $T \to \infty$.

This theorem says that the average value of T independent random variables from *any* probability distribution (as long as it has a mean and a variance) will have approximately a standard normal distribution after subtracting its mean and dividing by its standard deviation, if the sample size T is sufficiently large.

We will carry out a simulation, or Monte Carlo, experiment on the computer to demonstrate the Central Limit Theorem. Let the continuous random variable X have the probability density function

$$f(x) = \begin{cases} 2x & 0 < x < 1 \\ 0 & \text{otherwise} \end{cases}$$

The mean of X is $E[X] = 2/3$ and its variance is $\text{var}(X) = 1/18$. These results are obtained in Appendix 2B. The Central Limit Theorem says that if $X_1, X_2, \ldots, X_T$ are independent and identically distributed with this distribution, then the standardized variable

$$Z = \frac{\bar{X} - E[X]}{\sqrt{\dfrac{\text{var}(X)}{T}}} = \frac{\bar{X} - 2/3}{\sqrt{\dfrac{1/18}{T}}}$$

where $\bar{X} = (X_1 + X_2 + \ldots + X_T)/T$ is the mean of the X_is, and has a distribution that approaches the standard normal as $T \to \infty$.

In the simulation experiment we will create $N = 1000$ samples of size $T = 1$, $T = 2$, $T = 5$, and $T = 10$ from this "triangular" distribution, using a random-number generator on the computer. See the computer handbook for details of how this is done. For each sample and sample size, we create the standardized variable Z. The 1000 values of Z should exhibit a distribution that is "more like" a $N(0, 1)$ as T gets larger, according to the Central Limit Theorem. The relative frequency distributions for the 1000 values of Z for each sample size are presented in Figure 2.14. Figure 2.14a ($T = 1$) is the relative frequency distribution of standardized values from the distribution $f(x)$. Note that it is triangular in shape. In Figures 2.14b, 2.14c, and 2.14d are standardized values of the sample means based on samples of sizes $T = 2, 5, 10$. Clearly the distributions quickly become "bell-shaped" with centers located at zero. Furthermore, the sample standard deviations of the standardized means are very close to 1. Comparing the percentage of values that fall in each interval to those of a $N(0, 1)$ random variable (see Figure 2.11 and Table 1 at the end of this book), it is clear that by the time $T = 5$ the standardized variable Z has a distribution that is extremely close to the standard normal. Convergence is "quick" for the sample mean of this triangularly distributed random variable. For distributions with more irregular shapes, convergence may require larger sample sizes, but the Central Limit Theorem assures us that the standardized sample mean will converge in distribution to the standard normal.

2.8.3   The Bivariate Normal Distribution

In Section 2.8.2 we examined random variables that have a normal probability density function. There is a special joint probability density function for two random variables,

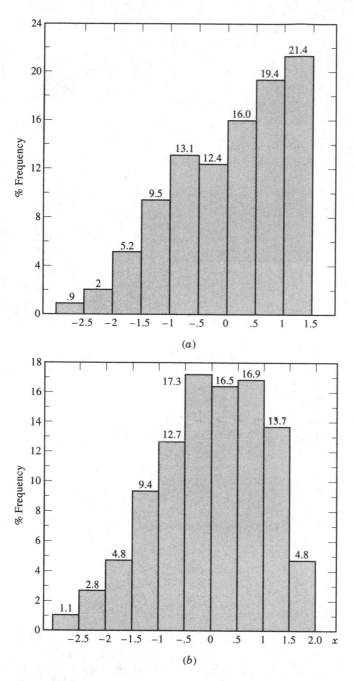

Figure 2.14 Relative frequency distributions for standardized sample means based on samples of different sizes: (*a*) $T = 1$; (*b*) $T = 2$.

say X_1 and X_2, called the *bivariate normal distribution* that is a generalization of the univariate normal probability density function. The mathematical formula for the joint probability density function $f(x_1, x_2)$ is complicated, and we will not give it here. The distribution is represented graphically in Figure 2.15 for standardized normal random variables with the correlation $\rho = 0.6$. If X_1 and X_2 have a joint normal probability density function, then each of the individual random variables has a normal distribution, say

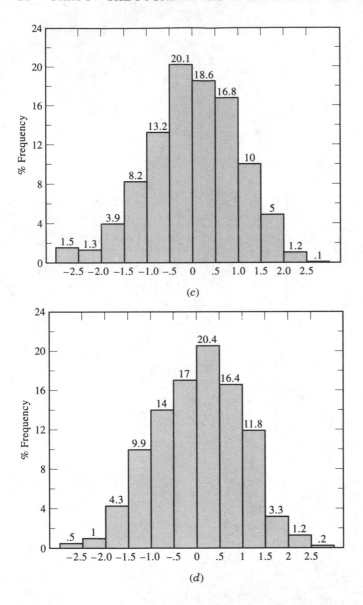

Figure 2.14 (continued)   Relative frequency distributions for standardized sample means based on samples of different sizes: (c) $T = 5$; (d) $T = 10$.

$X_1 \sim N(\beta_1, \sigma_1^2)$ and $X_2 \sim N(\beta_2, \sigma_2^2)$. Furthermore, the shape of the bivariate normal distribution $f(x_1, x_2)$ is completely determined by the means and variances of X_1 and X_2 *and* the covariance (or equivalently the correlation) between them, which are the five parameters of the distribution.

Like all joint probability density functions, the bivariate normal probability density function can be used to find probabilities of events involving X_1 and X_2. For example, the probability that X_1 and X_2 both take values between zero and one would be calculated by computing the volume under $f(x_1, x_2)$ when $0 \leq x_1 \leq 1$ and $0 \leq x_2 \leq 1$.

Since the shape of the bivariate normal probability density function is controlled in part by the correlation between X_1 and X_2, it is informative to look at a scatter diagram of bivariate observations (x_1, x_2) from distributions with fixed means (β_1 and β_2) and

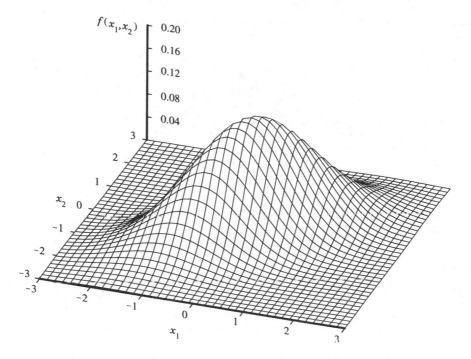

Figure 2.15   The bivariate normal probability density function

variances (σ_1^2 and σ_2^2) but different covariances and correlations. In Figure 2.16 we present data scatters (500 pairs of values) from $f(x_1, x_2)$ where $\beta_1 = \beta_2 = 0$, $\sigma_1^2 = \sigma_2^2 = 1$ and $\rho - 0, .3, .7$, and .95, respectively. Note that as ρ gets larger the positive *linear* association between the values of X_1 and X_2 becomes stronger, in the sense that for larger values of ρ, the values of X_1 and X_2 tend to fall along a straight line with a positive slope. When $\rho = 0$ there is no linear association between the values of X_1 and X_2.

In much of the rest of this book we will be concerned with sets of two or more random variables that are *jointly* normal. These will be called *multivariate* normal random variables, and we will explore their properties as need arises.

2.9   Summary

In this book we are concerned with the process of learning from a sample of data, and thus we started this chapter with a discussion of the nature and characteristics of economic data. In Section 2.2 we recognized that the outcomes we observe are not known a priori, nor can they be exactly predicted, and thus they are random variables. Given that economic variables are random variables, in Section 2.3 we define both discrete and continuous random variables, and in Section 2.4 we considered how to represent a single random variable in the form of a probability distribution and to represent several random variables in the form of a joint probability density function.

In Section 2.5 the average or mean value of a random variable X in an infinite number of experimental repetitions is defined to be the mathematical expectation or expected value of X, denoted $E[X]$. The mean is a location parameter for the random variable. In Section 2.6 we considered the variance of a random variable, which measures its dispersion, and defined it as $E[X - E(X)]^2$. When we are concerned with several random variables, we must consider the expected value of functions of several random

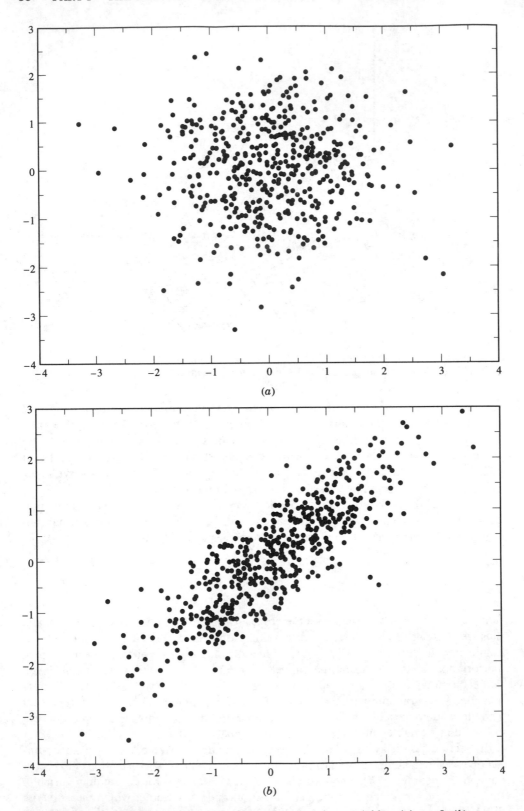

Figure 2.16   Data scatters from the bivariate normal random variables: (*a*) $\rho = 0$; (*b*) $\rho = $ .03; (*c*) $\rho = .7$; (*d*) $\rho = .95$.

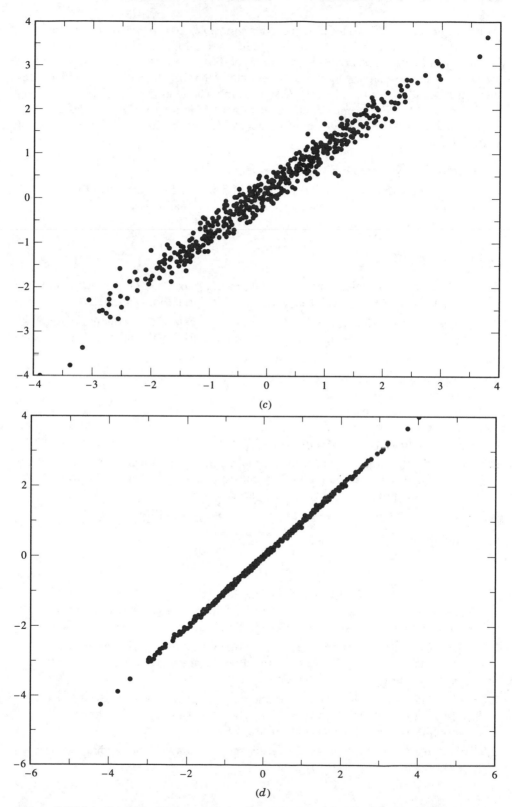

Figure 2.16 (continued)   Data scatters from the bivariate normal random variables: (*a*) $\rho = 0$; (*b*) $\rho = .03$; (*c*) $\rho = .7$; (*d*) $\rho = .95$.

variables. In Section 2.7 this led us to the terms *covariance* and *correlation*, which provide a basis for describing the association between two random variables.

Finally in Section 2.8 we discussed the properties of normal random variables, the frequently used normal and the bivariate normal probability distributions, and a statement of a beautiful result called the Central Limit Theorem.

Given these basic concepts about experiments, random variables, probability density functions, and expected values of random variables, in Chapter 3 we make use of these tools and

(i) specify a very simple linear statistical model and

(ii) consider how to estimate from a sample of data (random variables) the underlying unknown location (mean) and scale (variance) parameters.

2.10   Exercises

2.1   Calculate the arithmetic mean, median, mode, range, sample variance, and sample standard deviation for each economic variable in Table 2.2.

2.2   Construct a relative frequency distribution for each of the economic variables in Table 2.2. On each figure locate the sample arithmetic mean and median.

2.3   Using the data in Table 2.1, construct scatter plots of each pair of variables.

2.4   Use the macroeconomic data in Table 2.2 to construct scatter plots of
(a) GNP and consumption
(b) GNP and investment
(c) money supply and inflation rate
(d) inflation rate and unemployment rate

2.5   Let X be a discrete random variable that is the value shown on a single roll of a fair die. Represent the probability density function $f(x)$ in tabular form. What is the probability that $X = 4$? That $X = 4$ or $X = 5$?

2.6   Let X be a continuous random variable whose probability density function is

$$f(x) = \begin{cases} 2x & 0 \leq x \leq 1 \\ 0 & \text{otherwise} \end{cases}$$

(a) Sketch the probability density function $f(x)$.
(b) Geometrically calculate the probability that X falls between 0 and 1/2.
(c) Geometrically calculate the probability that X falls between 1/4 and 3/4.

2.7   Suppose X_1 and X_2 are independent continuous random variables each of which has the probability density function $f(x)$ in Exercise 2.6. What is their *joint* probability density function $f(x_1, x_2)$?

2.8   The random variables gender (G) and political affiliation (P) have (hypothetical) joint probability density function $f(g, p)$ in Table 2.4. Are the random variables G and P independent? If not, why not?

2.9   Find the mean and variance of the discrete random variable X that has probability density function (Example 2.1)

$$f(x) = p^x (1 - p)^{1-x}, \qquad \text{for } x = 0, 1$$

2.10 Use a geometric argument to show that the expected value, or mean of a uniform random variable (Examples 2.2 and 2.4) is $(a + b)/2$.

2.11 Consider the discrete random variable X in Example 2.3. Find the expected value of the function $g(X) = 3X + 2$ using equation 2.6.1.

2.12 Consider the discrete random variable X in Example 2.3. Find the variance of the function $g(X) = 3X + 2$. Explain the meaning of this result.

2.13 The joint probability density function of two discrete random variables X and Y is given by the following table:

		Y		
		1	3	9
X	2	$\frac{1}{8}$	$\frac{1}{24}$	$\frac{1}{12}$
	4	$\frac{1}{4}$	$\frac{1}{4}$	0
	6	$\frac{1}{8}$	$\frac{1}{24}$	$\frac{1}{12}$

(a) Find the marginal probability density function of Y.
(b) Find the conditional probability density function of Y given that $X = 2$.
(c) Find the covariance of X and Y.
(d) Are X and Y independent?

2.14 A fair die is rolled 2 times. Let X_1 and X_2 denote the number of points showing on the first and second rolls, respectively. Let $U = X_1 + X_2$ and $V = X_1 - X_2$.
(a) Find the mean and variance of V.
(b) Find the covariance of U and V.
(c) Show that U and V are not independent.

2.15 Verify the result in equation 2.7.8 using the following generalization of equation 2.6.2. If $X_1,\ldots, X_n$ are discrete random variables and $g(X_1,\ldots, X_n)$ is a function of $X_1,\ldots, X_n$, then

$$E\big[g(X_1,\ldots, X_n)\big] = \sum_{x_1}\sum_{x_2}\cdots\sum_{x_n} g(x_1,\ldots, x_n)f(x_1,\ldots, x_n)$$

Now let $g(X_1,\ldots, X_n) = X_1 + X_2 +\ldots+ X_n$ and break the sum into n parts and show that each equals $E[X_i]$.

2.16 Let $X_1,\ldots, X_n$ be independent discrete $(0, 1)$ random variables with probability density functions

$$f(x) = p^x(1-p)^{1-x}$$

The random variable $B = X_1 + X_2 +\ldots+ X_n$ has a binomial distribution with parameters n and p. The values of B are $b = 0,\ldots, n$ and represent the number of "successes" (i. e., $X_i = 1$) in n independent trials of an experiment, each with probability p of success. Calculate the mean and variance of B.

2.17 Let $X_1,\ldots, X_n$ be independent discrete $(0, 1)$ random variables with probability density functions

$$f(x) = p^x(1-p)^{1-x}, \qquad x = 0, 1$$

The random variable $B = X_1 +\ldots+ X_n$ has a binomial distribution. The random variable $Y = B/n$ is the proportion of successes in n trials of an experiment. Find the mean and variance of Y.

2.18 Let X_1 and X_2 be *independent* discrete random variables with joint probability density function $f(x_1, x_2)$. Show that

$$E[X_1 X_2] = E[X_1] E[X_2]$$

2.19 Compute the sample covariance and sample correlation for each of the pairs of variables listed in Exercise 2.4. Are the variables' values positively or negatively associated? Does this make "economic" sense?

2.20 Table 2.5 contains data on 32 light water reactor power plants constructed in the United States [*Source:* D. R. Cox and E. J. Snell, *Applied Statistics, Principles and Examples*, 1981, London: Chapman-Hall, p. 82].
(a) Classify each variable as continuous or discrete. Justify your choice.
(b) Find the mean and variance of cost (*C*) and power plant capacity (*S*) and the correlation between them. Does the sign of the correlation coefficient seem reasonable? Explain.
(c) Plot cost versus plant capacity.

2.21 In the study of finance an important model is the *capital asset pricing model* (CAPM), which is concerned with the risk of a security's return. Financial economists define a security's systematic risk (risk that is related to the market's risk) as

$$\beta = \frac{\text{cov}(x, m)}{\text{var}(m)}$$

where x = the rate of return on a security—the risk-free rate—and m = the rate of return on the market portfolio—the risk-free rate.

Loosely speaking, firms with $\beta > 1$ may be thought as "aggressive" stocks, since their security's systematic risk is greater than that of the market portfolio. Similarly, stocks with $\beta < 1$ may be thought of as more "conservative" than the market.

In Table 2.6 are 5 years of monthly data on excess returns (*x*) for two firms and the market (*m*). [*Source:* R. Butler, J. McDonald, R. Nelson, and S. White, "Robust and Partially Adaptive Estimation of Regression Models," *Review of Economics and Statistics*, 72(2), May 1990, 321–327.]
(a) Plot the excess returns of American Can (x_1) and Martin Marietta (x_2) against the CRSP Index (*m*).
(b) Calculate the sample mean and variance of x_1, x_2, and *m*.
(c) Calculate the sample correlation coefficient for each pair of variables.
(d) Use the results in (b) and (c) to calculate the β-values for each of the securities. (*Hint:* Use the sample correlation coefficient to calculate the sample covariance.)

2.11 References

The material we have considered in this chapter is presented in many elementary and intermediate statistics texts. One useful source is Beals (1972, Chapters 1–6). A useful resource at an elementary level is Brennan and Carroll (1987, Chapters 14 and 15). Part I of this book also discusses mathematics that is useful for beginning econometrics students. A more advanced treatment may be found in Judge et al. (1988, Chapter 2).

BEALS, R. E. (1972) *Statistics for Economists: An Introduction*, Chicago: Rand McNally & Co..

BRENNAN, M. J. and T. M. CARROLL (1987) *Preface to Quantitative Economics and Econometrics*, 4th Edition, Cincinnati, OH: South-Western Publishing Co.

JUDGE, G. G., R. C. HILL, W. E. GRIFFITHS, H. LÜTKEPOHL, and T. C. LEE (1988) *Introduction to the Theory and Practice of Econometrics*, 2nd Edition, New York: John Wiley and Sons.

Table 2.5 Data on 32 LWR Power Plants in the United States

C	D	T_1	T_2	S	PR	NE	CT	BW	N	PT
460.05	68.58	14	46	687	0	1	0	0	14	0
452.99	67.33	10	73	1065	0	0	1	0	1	0
443.22	67.33	10	85	1065	1	0	1	0	1	0
652.32	68.00	11	67	1065	0	1	1	0	12	0
642.23	68.00	11	78	1065	1	1	1	0	12	0
345.39	67.92	13	51	514	0	1	1	0	3	0
272.37	68.17	12	50	822	0	0	0	0	5	0
317.21	68.42	14	59	457	0	0	0	0	1	0
457.12	68.42	15	55	822	1	0	0	0	5	0
690.19	68.33	12	71	792	0	1	1	1	2	0
350.63	68.58	12	64	560	0	0	0	0	3	0
402.59	68.75	13	47	790	0	1	0	0	6	0
412.18	68.42	15	62	530	0	0	1	0	2	0
495.58	68.92	17	52	1050	0	0	0	0	7	0
394.36	68.92	13	65	850	0	0	0	1	16	0
423.32	68.42	11	67	778	0	0	0	0	3	0
712.27	69.50	18	60	845	0	1	0	0	17	0
289.66	68.42	15	76	530	1	0	1	0	2	0
881.24	69.17	15	67	1090	0	0	0	0	1	0
490.88	68.92	16	59	1050	1	0	0	0	8	0
567.79	68.75	11	70	913	0	0	1	1	15	0
665.99	70.92	22	57	828	1	1	0	0	20	0
621.45	69.67	16	59	786	0	0	1	0	18	0
608.80	70.08	19	58	821	1	0	0	0	3	0
473.64	70.42	19	44	538	0	0	1	0	19	0
697.14	71.08	20	57	1130	0	0	1	0	21	0
207.51	67.25	13	63	745	0	0	0	0	8	1
288.48	67.17	9	48	821	0	0	1	0	7	1
284.88	67.83	12	63	886	0	0	0	1	11	1
280.36	67.83	12	71	886	1	0	0	1	11	1
217.38	67.25	13	72	745	1	0	0	0	8	1
270.71	67.83	7	80	886	1	0	0	1	11	1

C	Cost in dollars $\times\ 10^{-6}$, adjusted to 1976 base
D	Date construction permit issued
T_1	Time between application for and issue of permit
T_2	Time between issue of operating license and construction permit
S	Power plant net capacity (MWe)
PR	Prior existence of an LWR on same site (= 1)
NE	Plant constructed in northeast region of USA (= 1)
CT	Use of cooling tower (= 1)
BW	Nuclear steam supply system manufactured by Babcock-Weber (= 1)
N	Cumulative number of power plants constructed by each architect-engineer
PT	Partial turnkey plant (= 1)

Table 2.6 Data: Excess Returns

Date	American Can (x_1)	Martin Marietta (x_2)	Value Weighted CRSP Index (m)
Jan. 1982	−.0596	−.1365	−.0300
Feb. 1982	−.1700	−.0769	−.0584
Mar. 1982	.0276	−.0575	−.0181
Apr. 1982	.0058	.0526	.0306
May 1982	−.0106	−.0449	−.0397
Jun. 1982	.0450	−.0859	−.0295
Jul. 1982	−.0243	−.0742	−.0316
Aug. 1982	.1135	.6879	.1176
Sep. 1982	−.0331	−.0770	.0075
Oct. 1982	.0468	.0850	.1098
Nov. 1982	−.0223	.0030	.0408
Dec. 1982	−.0026	.0754	.0095
Jan. 1983	.0166	−.0412	.0301
Feb. 1983	.0343	−.0850	.1098
Mar. 1983	.0443	.2319	.0269
Apr. 1983	.1477	.1087	.0655
May 1983	.1728	.0375	−.0030
Jun. 1983	−.0372	.0958	.0325
Jul. 1983	−.0451	.0174	−.0374
Aug. 1983	−.0257	−.0724	.0049
Sep. 1983	.0509	.0750	.0105
Oct. 1983	.0035	−.0588	−.0257
Nov. 1983	.1334	−.0620	.0186
Dec. 1983	−.0458	−.0378	−.0155
Jan. 1984	.1199	.0169	−.0165
Feb. 1984	−.0766	−.0799	−.0440
Mar. 1984	−.0511	−.0147	.0094
Apr. 1984	−.0194	.0106	−.0028
May 1984	−.0687	−.0421	−.0591
Jun. 1984	.0928	−.0036	.0158
Jul. 1984	−.0704	.0876	−.0238
Aug. 1984	.0905	.1025	.1031
Sep. 1984	.0232	−.0499	−.0065
Oct. 1984	−.0054	.1953	−.0067
Nov. 1984	.0082	−.0714	−.0167
Dec. 1984	.0242	.0469	.0188
Jan. 1985	.0153	.1311	.0733
Feb. 1985	.0016	.0461	.0105
Mar. 1985	.0280	−.0328	−.0070
Apr. 1985	.0088	−.0096	−.0099
May 1985	.0734	.1272	.0521
Jun. 1985	.0315	−.0077	.0117
Jul. 1985	−.0276	.0165	−.0099
Aug. 1985	.0162	−.0150	−.0102
Sep. 1985	−.0975	−.1479	−.0428
Oct. 1985	.0563	−.0065	.0376
Nov. 1985	.1368	.0390	.0628
Dec. 1985	−.0690	.0223	.0391
Jan. 1986	.1044	−.0690	.0002
Feb. 1986	.1636	.1338	.0688
Mar. 1986	−.0190	.1458	.0486
Apr. 1986	−.0746	.0063	−.0174
May 1986	.0433	.0692	.0460
Jun. 1986	.0306	−.0239	.0100
Jul. 1986	.0636	−.0568	−.0594
Aug. 1986	.0917	.0814	.0680
Sep. 1986	−.0796	−.0889	−.0839
Oct. 1986	.0778	−.0887	.0481
Nov. 1986	−.0353	.1037	.0136
Dec. 1986	−.0137	−.1163	−.0322

APPENDIX 2A   Summation Operations

Throughout this book we will denote certain sums of variables by using the shorthand notation of a *summation operator*. The summation operator will be denoted by the Greek letter sigma, Σ.

2A.1   The Notation

If $x_1, x_2, \ldots, x_n$ are values of a variable X whose sum we wish to denote, we may do so as

$$\sum_{i=1}^{n} x_i = x_1 + x_2 + \ldots + x_n \qquad (2A.1)$$

The expression $\sum_{i=1}^{n} x_i$ is read, "the sum of x_i, for i equal 1 to n." The letter "i" is the index of summation and ranges between the lower and upper limits (indicated below and above Σ) in increments of one. Thus, for example,

$$\sum_{i=3}^{5} x_i = x_3 + x_4 + x_5$$

The index of summation may be the variable to be summed. For example,

$$\sum_{i=1}^{5} i = 1 + 2 + 3 + 4 + 5$$

2A.2   Some Summation Rules

We will use the following algebraic properties of sums repeatedly.

1. If a is a constant (such as $a = 3$) then

$$\sum_{i=1}^{n} ax_i = a \sum_{i=1}^{n} x_i \qquad (2A.2)$$

Proof:

$$\sum_{i=1}^{n} ax_i = ax_1 + ax_2 + \ldots + ax_n$$

$$= a(x_1 + x_2 + \ldots + x_n)$$

$$= a \sum_{i=1}^{n} x_i$$

2. If X and Y are two variables, then

$$\sum_{i=1}^{n} (x_i + y_i) = \sum_{i=1}^{n} x_i + \sum_{i=1}^{n} y_i \qquad (2A.3)$$

Proof:

$$\sum_{i=1}^{n}(x_i + y_i) = (x_1 + y_1) + (x_2 + y_2) + \ldots + (x_n + y_n)$$

$$= (x_1 + x_2 + \ldots + x_n) + (y_1 + y_2 + \ldots + y_n)$$

$$= \sum_{i=1}^{n} x_i + \sum_{i=1}^{n} y_i$$

3. If X and Y are two variables, and a and b are constants, then

$$\sum_{i=1}^{n}(ax_i + by_i) = a\sum_{i=1}^{n} x_i + b\sum_{i=1}^{n} y_i \qquad (2A.4)$$

4. If $\bar{x}$ is the arithmetic mean of n values of a variable X, denoted by

$$\bar{x} = \frac{\sum_{i=1}^{n} x_i}{n} = \frac{x_1 + x_2 + \ldots + x_n}{n} \qquad (2A.5)$$

then

$$\sum_{i=1}^{n}(x_i - \bar{x}) = 0 \qquad (2A.6)$$

Proof:

$$\sum_{i=1}^{n}(x_i - \bar{x}) = (x_1 - \bar{x}) + (x_2 - \bar{x}) + \ldots + (x_n - \bar{x})$$

$$= (x_1 + x_2 + \ldots + x_n) - \underbrace{(\bar{x} + \bar{x} + \ldots + \bar{x})}_{n \text{ terms}}$$

$$= \sum_{i=1}^{n} x_i - n\bar{x}$$

but

$$n\bar{x} = n \cdot \frac{\sum_{i=1}^{n} x_i}{n} = \sum_{i=1}^{n} x_i$$

therefore,

$$\sum_{i=1}^{n}(x_i - \bar{x}) = \sum_{i=1}^{n} x_i - \sum_{i=1}^{n} x_i = 0$$

5.

$$\sum_{i=1}^{n}(x_i - \bar{x})^2 = \sum_{i=1}^{n} x_i^2 - n\bar{x}^2 \qquad (2A.7)$$

Proof:

$$\sum_{i=1}^{n}(x_i - \bar{x})^2 = \sum_{i=1}^{n}(x_i - \bar{x})(x_i - \bar{x}) = \sum_{i=1}^{n}\left[x_i(x_i - \bar{x}) - \bar{x}(x_i - \bar{x})\right]$$

$$= \sum_{i=1}^{n}x_i(x_i - \bar{x}) - \bar{x}\sum_{i=1}^{n}(x_i - \bar{x}) = \sum_{i=1}^{n}x_i(x_i - \bar{x}) \qquad \text{(using equation 2A.6)}$$

$$= \sum_{i=1}^{n}(x_i^2 - x_i\bar{x}) = \sum_{i=1}^{n}x_i^2 - \bar{x}\sum_{i=1}^{n}x_i = \sum_{i=1}^{n}x_i^2 - \bar{x}(n\bar{x}) \qquad \text{(using equation 2A.5)}$$

$$= \sum_{i=1}^{n}x_i^2 - n\bar{x}^2$$

2A.3   Some Additional Notation

Many times when the summation operator is used, some shorthand notation is used to indicate the range of summation. For example, if the variable X can take the values x_1, $x_2, \ldots, x_n$, and $f(x)$ is a function of X, such as $f(x) = x^2$, then the sum

$$\sum_{i=1}^{n}x_i f(x_i) = x_1 f(x_1) + x_2 f(x_2) + \ldots + x_n f(x_n)$$

may be written more simply as

$$\sum_i x_i f(x_i) \quad \text{(``Sum over all possible values of the index } i\text{'')}$$

or

$$\sum_x x f(x) \quad \text{(``Sum over all possible values of } X\text{'')}$$

2A.4   Multiple Summation

Several summation signs may be used in the same expression. For example, let the variable Y take the values $y_1, \ldots, y_n$ and the variable X take values $x_1, \ldots, x_m$. Let the function $f(x, y)$ be a function of X and Y, such as

$$f(x, y) = x + y$$

Then the *double summation* of this function is

$$\sum_{i=1}^{m}\sum_{j=1}^{n}f(x_i, y_j) = \sum_{i=1}^{m}\sum_{j=1}^{n}(x_i + y_j)$$

To evaluate such expressions work from the inner-most sum outward. First set $i = 1$ and sum over all j, and so on. Thus

$$\sum_{i=1}^{m}\sum_{j=1}^{n}f(x_i, y_j) = \sum_{i=1}^{m}\sum_{j=1}^{n}(x_i + y_j)$$

$$= (x_1 + y_1) + (x_1 + y_2) + \ldots + (x_1 + y_n)$$

$$+ (x_2 + y_1) + (x_2 + y_2) + \ldots + (x_2 + y_n)$$

$$\vdots$$

$$+ (x_m + y_1) + (x_m + y_2) + \ldots + (x_m + y_n)$$

The *order* of multiple summation does not matter, thus

$$\sum_{i=1}^{m}\sum_{j=1}^{n}f(x_i, y_j) = \sum_{j=1}^{n}\sum_{i=1}^{m}f(x_i, y_j)$$

The notation is often simplified to

$$\sum_{i}\sum_{j}f(x_i, y_j)$$

or

$$\sum_{x}\sum_{y}f(x, y)$$

but the meaning remains the same. Sums of higher order work in the same way.

APPENDIX 2B   The Geometry of Integration

The probability that a continuous random variable X takes a value in the interval $[a, b]$ is the *area* under its probability density function, $f(x)$, between those limits, as shown in Figure 2.5. Thus, the ability to find areas under curves is an important skill when studying probability. In this appendix we show how the integral of a function can be used to calculate areas under curves, and thus probabilities. Furthermore, since the mathematical expectation of a continuous random variable is defined as an integral, it, too, can be found by calculating the area under a curve, as we will demonstrate.

Consider the continuous random variable X with probability density function, $f(x)$, given by

$$f(x) = \begin{cases} 2x & 0 \le x \le 1 \\ 0 & \text{otherwise} \end{cases} \tag{2B.1}$$

and depicted in Figure 2B.1.

To calculate the probability that the value of X falls in the interval $[a, b]$, we must calculate the shaded area in Figure 2B.1. Using the geometry of triangles, we calculate

$$P[a \le X \le b] = \Delta 0bc - \Delta 0ad$$

$$= \left(\frac{1}{2}b\right)(2b) - \frac{1}{2}a(2a)$$

$$= b^2 - a^2 = (b-a)(b+a)$$

Let us take a more general approach that will lead us to the integral. Divide the interval

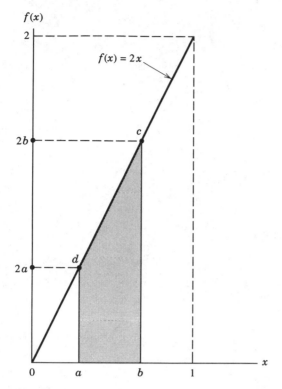

Figure 2B.1   The probability density function $f(x) = 2x$, $0 \le x \le 1$.

$[a, b]$ into n subintervals of width $\Delta x = (b - a)/n$ by inserting the points

$$x_1 = a + \Delta x$$
$$x_2 = a + 2(\Delta x)$$
$$\vdots$$
$$x_i = a + i(\Delta x)$$
$$\vdots$$
$$x_{n-1} = a + (n-1)(\Delta x)$$

between $x_0 = a$ and $x_n = b$, as shown in Figure 2B.2.
   The areas of the inscribed rectangles are

$$A_1 = f(x_0)\Delta x = (2a)(\Delta x)$$
$$A_2 = f(x_1)\Delta x = 2(a + \Delta x)(\Delta x)$$
$$A_i = f(x_{i-1})\Delta x = 2[a + (i-1)\Delta x](\Delta x)$$
$$A_n = f(x_{n-1})\Delta x = 2[a + (n-1)\Delta x](\Delta x)$$

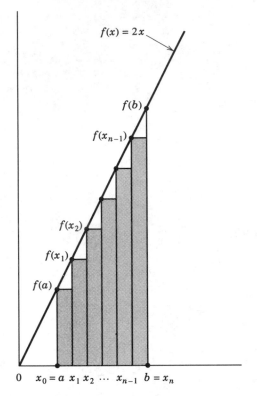

Figure 2B.2   Area under $f(x) = 2x$, $a \le x \le b$.

Their sum is

$$S_n = A_1 + A_2 + \ldots + A_n$$

$$= \sum_{i=1}^{n} f(x_{i-1}) \Delta x$$

$$= \sum_{i=1}^{n} 2[a + (i-1)\Delta x] \Delta x$$

$$= 2a\Delta x \sum_{i=1}^{n} 1 + 2(\Delta x)^2 \sum_{i=1}^{n} (i-1)$$

But

$$\sum_{i=1}^{n} 1 = 1 + 1 + \ldots + 1 = n$$

$$\sum_{i=1}^{n} (i-1) = 0 + 1 + \ldots + (n-1) = \sum_{i=1}^{n-1} i = \frac{(n-1)(n)}{2}$$

$$\left(\text{from } \sum_{i=1}^{k} i = k(k+1)/2 \right)$$

Thus, by substituting those results and $\Delta x = (b - a)/n$, we have

$$S_n = 2a(b-a)(n/n) + \frac{2(b-a)^2}{n^2} \cdot \frac{(n-1)n}{2}$$

$$= 2a(b-a) + (b-a)^2 \cdot \frac{n-1}{n} \qquad (2B.2)$$

This sum S_n will be an approximation to the area under the curve and will understate the area since we have inscribed the rectangles. Clearly the sum S_n will become a better approximation the more rectangles we use, or equivalently the larger the number of subintervals n. *The area under the graph is defined to be the limit of S_n as $n \to \infty$.*

The only place n appears in S_n is in the fraction

$$\frac{n-1}{n} = 1 - \frac{1}{n}$$

and $1/n \to 0$ as $n \to \infty$. So

$$\lim_{n \to \infty} \frac{n-1}{n} = 1$$

Therefore,

$$P[a \le X \le b] = \lim_{n \to \infty} S_n = \lim_{n \to \infty} \sum_{i=1}^{n} f(x_i) \Delta x$$

$$= 2a(b-a) + (b-a)^2$$

$$= (b-a)(b+a)$$

$$= b^2 - a^2 \qquad (2B.3)$$

which is identical to the solution we obtained using the geometry of triangles.

The limit in equation 2B.3 is the area of the region under the graph $f(x)$, and above the x axis, between the limits $x = a$ and $x = b$. This number is called the *definite integral* of $f(x)$ between $x = a$ and $x = b$ and is written

$$\int_a^b f(x)dx = \int_a^b 2x \cdot dx = b^2 - a^2 \qquad (2B.4)$$

The symbol $\int$ is called the *integral sign*, and it can be thought of as a "stylized" summation process, specifically the limit of a sum. The values b and a in equation 2B.4 are called the *upper* and *lower limits* of integration, respectively, and "dx" replaces Δx to remind us that $\Delta x = (b - a)/n$ becomes infinitesimally small as $n \to \infty$.

To summarize, if X is a continuous random variable with probability density function $f(x)$, then

$$P[a \le X \le b] = \int_a^b f(x)dx \qquad (2B.5)$$

where $\int_a^b f(x)dx$ is the definite integral of the function $f(x)$ between lower limit a and upper limit b. The definite integral is the area under $f(x)$ between $x = a$ and $x = b$.

The definite integral can also be used to calculate the mathematical expectation of a continuous random variable, which is defined to be

$$E(X) = \int_{-\infty}^{\infty} xf(x)dx \qquad (2B.6)$$

where the limits of integration $-\infty$ to ∞ represent a shorthand way of saying "over the whole domain of $f(x)$."

Let us use the ideas we have developed to compute $E[X]$ for the continuous random variable X with probability density function 2B.1. We must find the area under $g(x) = xf(x) = 2x^2$ between the limits $x = 0$ and $x = 1$, as depicted in Figure 2B.3. We divide the interval $[0, 1]$ into n parts of length $\Delta x = 1/n$ by inserting the values

$$x_1 = \Delta x$$
$$x_2 = 2\Delta x$$
$$\vdots$$
$$x_i = i(\Delta x)$$
$$\vdots$$
$$x_{n-1} = (n-1)(\Delta x)$$

The inscribed rectangles have areas

$$A_1 = g(x_0) \cdot \Delta x = 0$$
$$A_2 = g(x_1) \cdot \Delta x = 2(\Delta x)^2 \cdot \Delta x$$
$$\vdots$$
$$A_i = g(x_{i-1}) \cdot \Delta x = 2\left[(i-1)(\Delta x)\right]^2 \Delta x$$
$$\vdots$$
$$A_n = g(x_{n-1})\Delta x = 2\left[(n-1)(\Delta x)\right]^2 \Delta x$$

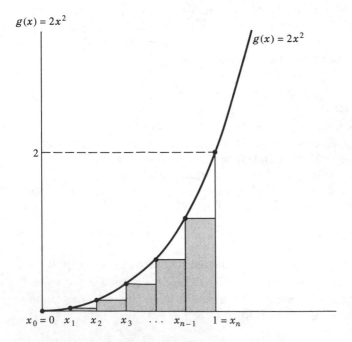

Figure 2B.3   Area under $g(x) = 2x^2$, $0 \le x \le 1$.

and sum

$$S_n = A_1 + A_2 + \ldots + A_n = \sum_{i=1}^{n} g(x_{i-1}) \cdot \Delta x$$

$$= 2 \sum_{i=1}^{n} [(i-1)\Delta x]^2 \cdot \Delta x$$

$$= 2(\Delta x)^3 \left(0^2 + 1^2 + \ldots + (n-1)^2 \right)$$

but

$$\sum_{i=1}^{k} i^2 - \frac{k(k+1)(2k+1)}{6}$$

so

$$S_n = 2 \left(\frac{1}{n} \right)^3 \frac{(n-1)(n)(2n-1)}{6}$$

$$= \frac{1}{3} \left(1 - \frac{1}{n} \right) \left(2 - \frac{1}{n} \right)$$

Then the limiting area is

$$A = \lim_{n \to \infty} S_n = \lim_{n \to \infty} \frac{1}{3} \left(1 - \frac{1}{n} \right) \left(2 - \frac{1}{n} \right) = \frac{2}{3}$$

Consequently,

$$E[X] = \int_{-\infty}^{\infty} x \cdot f(x) dx = \int_{0}^{1} 2x^2 dx = \frac{2}{3}$$

Similarly,

$$E[X^2] = \int_{-\infty}^{\infty} x^2 \cdot f(x) dx = \int_{0}^{1} 2x^3 dx = \frac{1}{2}$$

using

$$\sum_{i=1}^{k} i^3 = \left[\frac{n(n+1)}{2} \right]^2$$

Therefore the variance of X can be computed using equation 2.6.5 as

$$\text{var}(X) = E[X^2] - [E(X)]^2$$

$$= \frac{1}{2} - \left(\frac{2}{3} \right)^2 = \frac{1}{18}$$

Chapter 3

Statistical Inference I: Estimating the Mean and Variance of a Population

New Key Words and Concepts

Economic Model	**Statistical Model**
Population Mean	**Least Squares Estimator**
Unbiased Estimator	**Consistent Estimator**
Best Linear Unbiased Estimator	

3.1 Introduction

In Chapter 2 we described how data arise from experiments. We noted that in economics the experiments are generally uncontrolled and the data are observed, rather than generated from a controlled experimental design. Since the *values* of economic variables we wish to explain are unknown until they are actually observed, economic variables are *random variables*. In Sections 2.4 to 2.8 we reviewed the properties of random variables and their probability density functions. *That material forms the basis for this chapter, and for that matter all the work in this book.*

In Chapter 2 we also noted that economic data can be *described* and *summarized* by measures of location and dispersion and that these results can be depicted by using various graphical techniques. Although describing and summarizing data on economic variables can be useful, our objective is to *explain* the behavior of economic variables and the relationship between them. A glance at Table 2.2 reveals the fact that the values of economic variables *change* from one observation to another. These changes are unpredictable and uncontrollable.

Can we explain *how much*, on average, they change?

Can we *predict*, on average, what their values might be in future periods?

Can we determine if the amount of change in one economic variable is *related to*, on average, the amount of change in another?

These are questions of *statistical inference*, a branch of statistics that will allow us to use a sample of data to examine relationships within and conjectures about a population of subjects. The ability to carry out statistical inference is an important one. Think about the importance of the "how much" questions raised in Chapter 1.

Within an economic context, the first step in statistical inference is to construct an *economic model* that forms the basis for understanding the behavior of an economic variable. An economic *model* is a simplified representation of reality. Modeling is important to all sciences because the real-world phenomena studied are usually viewed, at least initially, as enormously complicated. Useful economic models are a compromise between realism and tractability. The hope is to capture the essence of the real world phenomena while eliminating unnecessary detail. Using economic models that are simplified representations of reality, it is often possible to draw conclusions about the real world that could not be obtained by simply examining the data directly.

An economic model encountered early in principles of economics courses is the *consumption function*. The consumption function $C = f(Y)$ is a macroeconomic model relating consumer expenditure on economic goods and services (C) to a measure of national income (Y). Graphically, the consumption function is usually depicted as a linear relationship, as in Figure 3.1, with algebraic representation

$$C = a + bY \qquad (3.1.1)$$

where the constant a is autonomous consumption and b is the marginal propensity to consume. This economic model is a very simple abstraction of the complicated real-world relationship between consumption and income. It simply posits that the level of consumption goes up, linearly, when income goes up. *Nevertheless*, this simple model, when combined with simple assumptions about investment, savings, taxes, and government expenditures, has led to many conclusions about the effects of economics policies on the level of economic activity.

The model in Figure 3.1 and equation 3.1.1 is an economic model but not a *statistical model* because it does not recognize the random component of consumption expenditures. Introducing this random specification converts the economic model into a statistical model and provides a basis for *statistical inference*.

In this chapter we begin studying statistical inference. At the outset we are not going to study *relationships* like the consumption function; they will be taken up in Chapter 5. Instead we will focus on the simplest of all economic and statistical models; one that

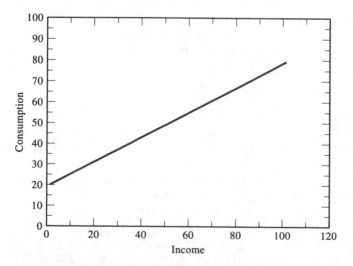

Figure 3.1 A consumption function.

involves a *single* observable economic variable. However, the simple model we use in this chapter, and the next, is a fertile training ground, in which we introduce concepts that will be used in later chapters. There are two appendices to this chapter. The first appendix describes the *derivative* of a function. The second develops the model presented in this chapter by using vector and matrix notation.

3.2   An Economic and Statistical Model for the Mean of a Population

The consumption variable discussed in Section 3.1 was aggregate consumption of final goods and services. Underlying aggregate consumption is the consumption of goods and services by individuals and households. We will focus on a microeconomic variable, household expenditure on food, as the primary example in this chapter. In particular, we pose the question: How much does a typical household spend on food during a week? The answer to this question is important, for example, to the Chief Executive Officers (CEOs) of supermarket chains, who plan new stores, and to officials at the local, state, and national levels who engage in welfare analysis.

3.2.1   The Economic Model

The process of inference begins with the specification of an *economic model*. We will begin with the simplest of all possible economic models for household expenditure on food. It is clear that the food expenditure by any household depends on a number of factors, such as household income, the number of members in the household, and so on. In this chapter we are not going to try to explain variations in food expenditure due to changes in those factors. That will be done in Chapters 5 and beyond. For the purposes of this chapter we are going to *condition* our analysis by considering *only* households with three members (size 3) *and* with the same level of income, $25,000. Households with these characteristics define the population we are interested in. Thus we focus on the economic variable *weekly food expenditure by households of size 3 with income $25,000/year*. Our economic model will assume that the weekly food expenditure by each household is an autonomous and fixed constant. However, we know that if we actually observe a sample of household expenditures on food, expenditures will vary from household to household. At this point, consistent with our economic model, we will assume that household differences result from varying tastes and preferences that are random and thus unpredictable.

3.2.2   The Statistical Model

A *statistical model* describes the sampling process that we visualize was used to produce the sample data. Consequently, it must take into account the method of obtaining the sample *and* what economic theory has to tell us about the characteristics of the economic variable in question. In our food expenditure example, the amount of economics we will use is minimal. We assume that food expenditures differ among households of size 3 and income of $25,000 because of differences in tastes and preferences. Also, we assume that the data will be obtained via a random sampling process. That is, households will be chosen for interview at random from the population we have defined; this is our conceptual "experiment" and our experimental design.

Within this context let Y represent the expenditure on food reported by a surveyed household. *Before* the sample data are actually collected, the value of Y is not known, except that we know it has to be a nonnegative number. Consequently, this unpredictable outcome Y is a *random variable*. After the sample is collected we have a real number, like $46.79, which we will denote by y and call it the *value of the random variable Y*. We will assume that the mathematical expectation, or expected value, of the random variable Y is

$$E[Y] = \beta \qquad (3.2.1)$$

where the Greek letter beta (β) denotes the mean value of the random variable Y. Since Y represents the amount of expenditure by *any* household in the population, its mean β *is* the mean or average expenditure in the population. We will call β the *population mean*. If we knew the value of β it would represent the answer to the question of how much, on average, households of size 3 with incomes of $25,000 spend on food per week. But β is not known and we signify its importance by calling it an *unknown population parameter*, or just a *parameter*. One of our objectives in this chapter is to learn how to use a sample of data to make inferences, or judgments, about the unknown population parameter β.

The other characteristic of the random variable Y that is of interest is its variability, which we measure by its variance, defined as

$$\text{var}(Y) = E\left[Y - E(Y)\right]^2$$
$$= E\left[Y - \beta\right]^2 = \sigma^2 \qquad (3.2.2)$$

The quantity σ^2 (read "sigma-squared") is also an unknown population parameter. Recall from Chapter 2 that *the variance of a random variable is the average squared distance that the values of the random variable are from β, their mean*. As such it informs us how much expenditures vary within the population and thus how different the sample values of Y can be.

Throughout this book we will denote the mean and variance of a random variable by writing

$$Y \sim \left(\beta, \sigma^2\right)$$

where "~" means "is distributed as," with the first of the two enclosed elements being the mean and the second the variance. So far, of course, we have not said what type of probability distribution we think Y has.

Suppose that the sample we collect will consist of T randomly selected households. Then Y_i, $i = 1, \ldots, T$, represents the potential expenditure of the ith sampled household. The index "i" is often used for *cross-sectional* data, collected at one point in time, and can be thought of as representing "individual" observations. Before the sample is drawn, $Y_1, \ldots, Y_T$ are T random variables whose values are to be drawn from the same population. Thus, the random variables Y_i all have the same mean β and variance σ^2. Furthermore, we will assume that all the random variables Y_i have the same probability density function $f(y_i)$.

Since the T households to be surveyed will be selected "randomly," we will assume that the random variables Y_i are all statistically independent. This means, for example, that if we knew the expenditure of one of our sampled households is $49.56, it tells us nothing about the expenditure of any other household. Thus, so far, we have assumed that the random variables Y_i that represent the possible values of household expenditure on food in a yet-to-be-taken sample of size T are *statistically independent* and all have identical probability density functions with mean β and variance σ^2. We say $Y_1, \ldots, Y_T$ constitute a *random sample* in the statistical sense.

Our objective in this chapter is to use a random sample of data to learn about the population parameters β and σ^2. Since the population mean expenditure β is an important object of our study, we will isolate it in the following way. By making use of the random variable Y, let us define a random variable e_i as

$$e_i = Y_i - E[Y_i] = Y_i - \beta \tag{3.2.3}$$

Unlike Y_i, e_i *is an unobservable random variable, since the true population mean β is unknown*. The random variable e_i represents the effects of all those unexplained factors that cause a household's food expenditure to differ from the population mean β. Note that in the food expenditure example e_i does *not* include the effect of household size or income, since these factors are held constant or conditioned upon. It represents unexplained tastes and preferences, the random component of human behavior, *plus* the effects of any other variables on food expenditure. Note that we use a lowercase letter (e_i) to denote this unobservable random variable since it will never be confused with any observable values. For the present we will continue to distinguish between the random variables Y_i and their observed value, y_i. For expository convenience this convention will be dropped entirely in Chapters 5 and beyond.

Rearranging equation 3.2.3 we can write

$$Y_i = \beta + e_i, \qquad i = 1,\ldots,T \tag{3.2.4a}$$

Given the way e_i is defined, it follows that the mean of e_i is

$$E[e_i] = E[Y_i - \beta] = 0$$

and its variance is

$$\text{var}(e_i) = E\{e_i - E[e_i]\}^2 = E[e_i]^2 = \sigma^2$$

This follows since $e_i = Y_i - \beta$, and β is a constant and does not vary. So $\text{var}(e_i) = \text{var}(Y_i) = \sigma^2$. Consequently we can use the shorthand expression

$$e_i \sim (0, \sigma^2) \tag{3.2.4b}$$

Furthermore, since we assume that the random variables Y_i are a random sample, they are independent. Consequently, the random errors e_i are independent and thus also uncorrelated: $\text{cov}(e_i, e_j) = 0$. Equation 3.2.4 is a *statistical* model. It represents one view of the sampling process by which the observations on household expenditure for food are obtained and it is consistent with our naive economic theory. The expenditure Y_i is equal to the population mean value β (an unknown constant and the mean weekly food expenditure) *plus* a random component e_i that represents all the factors that affect the individual household expenditures Y_i and cause them to be different from the mean value β. Thus the random variable e_i is the sum of all those unique characteristics that make households different from one another. The random component e_i is usually called a *random disturbance* or *error term*.

In the context of the statistical model it is sometimes reasonable to assume that the random disturbances e_i have a *normal* distribution with mean 0 and variance σ^2, or

$$e_i \sim N(0, \sigma^2) \tag{3.2.4c}$$

One justification for this assumption is the following. As we have noted, the random disturbance e_i contains all those factors that explain why an individual household's expenditure on food differs from the population mean. Consequently, e_i is the sum of a large number of factors. *If* those factors are independent of one another and if none of the factors is large relative to the rest, then it can be shown that e_i does in fact have a normal distribution by the Central Limit Theorem. We assume that the random disturbances e_i *are* normally distributed random variables with the above explanation as one possible justification. Since the random disturbances are assumed to be normally distributed, so is Y_i in equation 3.2.4. This result follows since adding a constant to a normal random variable serves only to shift the center of the distribution and changes nothing else; so

$$Y_i \sim N(\beta, \sigma^2) \tag{3.2.5}$$

The probability density functions for e_i and Y_i are pictured in Figure 3.2.

Thus, for the purposes of statistical inference about the population, we are *assuming* that the household expenditures on food, given household size and income, can be represented by a *normal* distribution with mean β and variance σ^2.

3.3 Estimating the Mean of a Normal Population

Having specified the economic and statistical model, now we can proceed to collect the data and begin the process of analyzing it to obtain estimates of the unknown parameters β and σ^2. Denote *the observed sample values of* Y_i as y_i. In Table 3.1 we provide a sample of size $T = 40$ of weekly household expenditures on food. These are the sample data $y_1, y_2,\ldots, y_{40}$, and $y_1 = 49.48$, $y_2 = 55.33,\ldots, y_{40} = 51.85$.

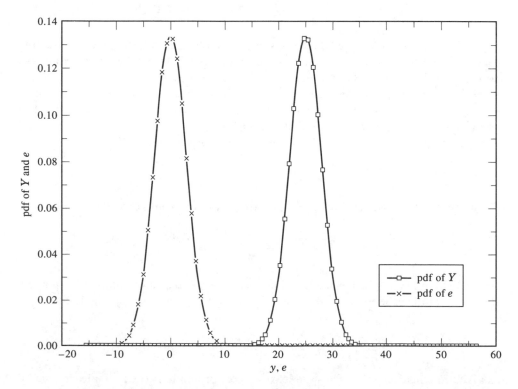

Figure 3.2 The probability density functions of e_i and Y_i.

Table 3.1 **Weekly Expenditures on Food by** $T = 40$ **Randomly Selected Households of Size 3 and \$25,000 Income**

49.98	55.33	50.39	46.83
47.43	48.47	52.73	52.32
50.35	47.57	49.52	51.56
55.17	52.65	51.43	45.96
50.86	52.37	50.10	49.74
49.07	48.91	58.06	51.26
51.52	51.10	52.92	53.07
49.35	54.85	54.14	47.75
50.88	49.44	53.02	53.50
49.65	52.39	49.81	51.85

The first question is: How can we use the sample of economic data in Table 3.1 to estimate the population mean β? Recall that $E[Y_i] = \beta$ and that the mathematical expectation is the "center" of the probability density function of Y_i. The data in Table 3.1 were obtained by randomly selecting households, and should reflect the characteristics of the population. It is appealing to think that the center of the sample data will yield a good estimate of the population mean β. But what rule should we use to find the center of the data?

One way to find the center of a sample is to use the *principle of least squares*. Under this principle the center of the sample values $y_1, y_2, \ldots, y_T$ is the value of β that minimizes

$$S = \sum_{i=1}^{T} (y_i - \beta)^2 \tag{3.3.1}$$

where S is the sum of squared deviations of the data values from β. Given the sample data, the value of β minimizing the sum of squares equation 3.3.1 is called the *least squares estimate* of β. We will denote this estimate as b. The motivation for the least squares principle is the following: Suppose the T sample values $y_1, y_2, \ldots, y_T$ are arrayed on a number line. We wish to choose a value for β that is in the center of the sample of data. If the data points y_i were stores along a street that you wished to visit *one* at a time, where would *you* want to park your car? The Euclidean distance between y_i and β is

$$d_i = \sqrt{(y_i - \beta)^2}$$

To minimize total distance between β and all the y_is you would choose β to minimize

$$D = \sum_{i=1}^{T} d_i = \sum_{i=1}^{T} \sqrt{(y_i - \beta)^2}$$

The radical in D complicates matters, but we can obtain the same solution for placing β if we minimize the total *squared* distances between β and the y_is, which is

$$S = \sum_{i=1}^{T} d_i^2 = \sum_{i=1}^{T} (y_i - \beta)^2$$

as given in equation 3.3.1. Thus the least squares principle is really the least squared *distance* principle.

Since the values y_i are known, the sum of squares S is a function of the unknown parameter β. Multiplying $S = \Sigma(y_i - \beta)^2$ out we obtain

$$S = \sum_{i=1}^{T} y_i^2 - 2\beta \sum_{i=1}^{T} y_i + T\beta^2$$

$$= a_0 - 2a_1\beta + a_2\beta^2 \qquad (3.3.2)$$

where $a_0 = \Sigma y_i^2$, $a_1 = \Sigma y_i$, and $a_2 = T$. Equation 3.3.2 is a quadratic equation in terms of β whose graph is a parabola, which is shown in Figure 3.3 for a range of values for β and the data in Table 3.1. The "least squares estimate of β" is given by the value b that minimizes S.

The minimum of this function occurs where its slope is zero. From calculus (reviewed in Appendix 3A) we know that the minimum of this function occurs when the rate of change, the first derivative, is zero, and its second derivative is positive. Thus to find b we will differentiate S with respect to β, set the derivative to zero, and solve. The derivative of S, using the rules in Appendix 3A.2, is

$$\frac{dS}{d\beta} = -2a_1 + 2a_2\beta \qquad (3.3.3)$$

The value of β that makes $dS/d\beta$ zero is the least squares estimate of β, which we denote as b. That is, if we set $dS/d\beta = 0$, we obtain

$$-2a_1 + 2a_2 b = 0$$

Solving for b, this yields the least squares estimate of β

$$b = \frac{a_1}{a_2} = \frac{\sum_{i=1}^{T} y_i}{T} \qquad (3.3.4)$$

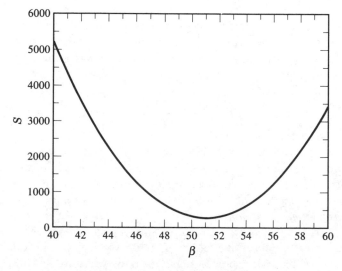

Figure 3.3 The sum of the squares parabola.

We see that b, the least squares estimate of β, is the arithmetic or sample mean, and it is this value that minimizes the sum of squares S. What we are calling b you may have called $\bar{y}$, the sample mean, in a previous statistics course.

For the sample of food expenditure data in Table 3.1

$$b = \frac{\sum_{i=1}^{T} y_i}{T} = \frac{2043.30}{40} = \$51.08$$

Thus our estimate of the population's mean weekly expenditure on food is $51.08, and this corresponds to the minimum value of the sum of squares parabola in Figure 3.3. Given our current economic model, this value *explains* household expenditure on food. Our model, given in equation 3.4.1, says that when a household's weekly food expenditure is observed, it is equal to the population mean consumption β, which we now estimate to be $51.08, plus a random error that reflects household tastes and preferences *and* any other factors that affect household expenditure except number of members and income.

Technically, for b to minimize S we must show that the second derivative of S is positive. See Appendix 3A.4. The second derivative of S is

$$\frac{d^2 S}{d\beta^2} = 2a_2 = 2T = 80 > 0$$

Thus, the value b does minimize S and is the least squares estimate of β.

3.4   Discussion of the Estimation Rule

For the data in Table 3.1 the value of $b = \$51.08$. Since this estimate came from a sample of data, a critical question is: How good an estimate is $b = \$51.08$ of the true population mean? That is, how close is b to β? The problem with this question is clear. To answer it the true value of β must be known! And if β were known we would not be working so hard to estimate it!! So the question of how good an estimate is cannot be answered. We can make some progress, however, if we back up to the time *before* we actually collected the data. At this presample time the values of Y_i (the random variables) are not known, and equation 3.3.4 is a rule or formula, called an *estimator*, that tells us how to use the data when they are finally collected. The least squares rule tells us, *no matter what the values of Y_i turn out to be*, calculate

$$b = \sum_{i=1}^{T} Y_i / T \qquad (3.4.1a)$$

In equation 3.4.1a we have used Y_i instead of y_i to indicate that, *prior to the sample*, the observations on the economic variable Y_i are *random*. Since b is a function of the Y_i, the estimator b *is random too!* Before we collect the data, b is a random variable (or a random estimation rule) that depends on the outcomes or values of the random variables $Y_1, Y_2,..., Y_T$. *Different samples of data will yield different values for b.* This random estimation rule is the *least squares estimator* of the mean of a population.

The least squares estimator's variability is due to the fact that its value depends on what the sample values $y_1, y_2,..., y_T$ turn out to be. For that reason the variability of the estimation rule b is called *sampling variability*. This literally means that the variation in b arises from the process of drawing a random sample. Consequently, the distribution of the random variable b is called a *sampling distribution* and its characteristics called *sampling properties*.

Although we cannot ask whether $b = \$51.08$ is a good estimate, *we can ask whether the estimator*

$$b = \sum_{i=1}^{T} Y_i / T$$

is a good rule to use. Since the least squares estimator is a continuous random variable, we can use the probability density function of b, its sampling distribution, to calculate probabilities that it will fall in given intervals when repeated samples are drawn. Two characteristics of the probability density function of the random variable b that are of interest are its mean $E[b]$ and its variance var(b).

Since

$$b = \sum_{i=1}^{T} Y_i / T = \frac{1}{T}Y_1 + \frac{1}{T}Y_2 + ... + \frac{1}{T}Y_T \tag{3.4.1b}$$

determining the sampling properties of b involves finding the probability density function, mean, and variance of a weighted sum of independent random variables Y_i that are normal with mean β and variance σ^2.

3.4.1   The Mean of b

In Section 2.7.1 we developed rules for determining the expected value of a weighted sum of random variables. The rule is that the expected value of a sum of random variables is the sum of their expected values, and multiplicative constants can be factored out. Thus

$$\begin{aligned}
E[b] &= E\left[\frac{1}{T}Y_1\right] + E\left[\frac{1}{T}Y_2\right] + ... + E\left[\frac{1}{T}Y_T\right] \\
&= \frac{1}{T}E[Y_1] + \frac{1}{T}E[Y_2] + ... + \frac{1}{T}E[Y_T] \\
&= \frac{1}{T}\beta + \frac{1}{T}\beta + ... + \frac{1}{T}\beta \\
&= \beta
\end{aligned} \tag{3.4.2}$$

The mathematical expectation, or mean, of the least squares estimator b *is* the true population parameter β that we are trying to estimate. What does this mean? Since the estimator b is random, its mean is the average value of b that would occur if the experiment of drawing and obtaining an estimate from a random sample of T values of Y were to be repeated *many* times. Another way of saying this result is that if the experiment were repeated many times, "on average" the least squares estimator yields the true population mean β. Estimators with this property are called *unbiased estimators*. Under the assumptions we have made, the least squares estimator is unbiased. Hence, although we don't know whether $b = \$51.08$ is a good estimate of mean population expenditure on food or not, we know that the rule that gave us this number is right on average.

The fact that the least squares estimator hits the target on average is comforting. However, given a real problem, we are likely to be more interested in the probability of getting an estimate that is "close" to the true parameter value given the one, and usually only one, sample that we may have to work with. An estimator can be unbiased, but still unreliable, if large overestimates are offset by equally large underestimates. When random samples of size T are drawn and the least squares estimates of the population mean β are calculated, we will observe that the estimates vary from sample to sample since they are based on different sample values. This variation in the estimates is a reflection of the *repeated sampling variability*, or just *sampling variability*, of the least squares estimation rule. To assess the amount of sampling variability of the estimator, we can determine its *variance*, which we will do now.

3.4.2   The Variance of b

To calculate the variance of the random variable b, we need to find the variance of a weighted sum of random variables. The method for doing this is developed in Section 2.7.2; see equation 2.7.11. The rule is that the variance of a sum of random variables is the sum of the variances *if* the random variables are not correlated (i.e., have zero covariances). We can apply this rule because the random variables Y_i that help make up b are obtained by a random sampling procedure and hence are statistically independent and thus uncorrelated. Furthermore, we have assumed that all the Y_is have identical variances, σ^2. So using equation 3.4.1

$$
\begin{aligned}
\operatorname{var}(b) &= \operatorname{var}\left(\frac{1}{T}Y_1 + \frac{1}{T}Y_2 + \ldots + \frac{1}{T}Y_T\right) \\
&= \operatorname{var}\left(\frac{1}{T}Y_1\right) + \operatorname{var}\left(\frac{1}{T}Y_2\right) + \ldots + \operatorname{var}\left(\frac{1}{T}Y_T\right) \\
&= \frac{1}{T^2}\operatorname{var}(Y_1) + \frac{1}{T^2}\operatorname{var}(Y_2) + \ldots + \frac{1}{T^2}\operatorname{var}(Y_T) \quad\quad (3.4.3) \\
&= \frac{1}{T^2}\sigma^2 + \frac{1}{T^2}\sigma^2 + \ldots + \frac{1}{T^2}\sigma^2 \\
&= \sigma^2\left(T\big/T^2\right) = \sigma^2/T
\end{aligned}
$$

The variance of the least squares estimator decreases as the sample size T increases. This simply means that the more data one has from a population, the more accurate the estimation of its mean is likely to be. Also, the smaller the variance of the population (and the random errors) σ^2, the more precisely the mean of the population can be estimated.

3.4.3   The Probability (Sampling) Distribution of b in Repeated Samples

Finally, we can determine the repeated sampling distribution of the random variable b. From equation 3.4.1 we know that b is a weighted average of *independent* normal random variables. As we saw in Section 2.8.1, a random variable that is such a weighted sum has a normal probability density function itself with mean β and variance σ^2/T. Consequently, we can summarize what we know about the least squares estimator by saying: Under the assumptions we have made about the linear statistical model for the mean of a normal population, the least squares estimator b of β is distributed $N(\beta, \sigma^2/T)$. What does this mean?

First, given the assumptions of our statistical model, we have shown that the least squares estimator b is random; it is a rule that we use no matter what the sample values of Y turn out to be.

Second, we have shown that the mean of b is β, the true population parameter we are trying to estimate. Thus, *on average*, the least squares rule gives us the correct value.

Third, the variance of b is σ^2/T. Remember that the variance of *any* random variable indicates how spread out or dispersed the values of the random variable are about its mean. The variance of b is interesting in this regard. Since $\mathrm{var}(b) = \sigma^2/T$, the larger the sample size T, the smaller the sampling variability (or the greater the precision) of b about its mean, which is β. Thus, if T is very large, b will randomly vary about its mean β, but will not be too far away from β! This is great because our goal was to get a "good" estimate of the population mean β, which we can take to mean "coming close" to the true value.

Finally, we have asserted that the least squares estimator b has a normal probability distribution. This powerful result depends on the random variables Y_i, and the random errors e_i, being normal. Recall that this assumption has been justified by noting that the random errors e_i represent the many individual factors that make food expenditure by one household differ from the expenditures of other households. If these factors are numerous, and none is too large, then the random errors e_i are normal by the Central Limit Theorem.

Let us put all this together. In Figure 3.4 we have plotted three (hypothetical) probability density functions of b that are normal with a mean of β and a variance σ^2/T. In each case the only difference is the sample size T and $T_3 > T_2 > T_1$. Note what happens

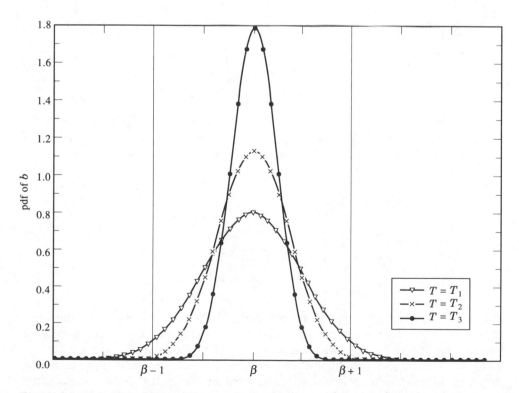

Figure 3.4 Probability density functions for the least squares estimator based on different sample sizes $T_3 > T_2 > T_1$.

as the sample size gets larger. The spread or variance of the probability density function gets smaller. More of the probability mass (total of one) is concentrated about the true parameter value.

When unknown parameters are estimated, a reasonable objective is to obtain an estimate that is *close* to the true parameter value with a high probability. Suppose that we are willing to define "close" as being within $1 of the true parameter value; the interval in which b is within $1 of β is indicated in Figure 3.4 by two vertical lines. From Figure 3.4 it is clear that the probability of the least squares estimation rule yielding an estimate that is close (within $1) increases as the sample size gets larger. In fact as $T \to \infty$ the probability mass of the estimator b "collapses" right on the population mean β. This property of the least squares estimator is called *consistency*. More precisely, suppose ε is an arbitrary small positive number. Then the estimator b is a *consistent estimator* of β if the probability that the value of b falls in the interval $[\beta - \varepsilon, \beta + \varepsilon]$ can be made as close to 1 as desired by choosing the sample size T large enough. To get a better feel for what this result means, let us suppose for the moment that our sample of $T = 40$ households comes from a population in which the household expenditure on food is normally distributed with an unknown mean β, but a *known* variance of $\sigma^2 = 10$. Then the least squares estimator b will be distributed as $N(\beta, \sigma^2/T = 10/40 = .25)$. Now we can calculate the probability that the least squares estimator will yield an estimate of β within $1 of the true value, or

$$P[\beta - 1 \le b \le \beta + 1]$$

To calculate this probability we can use the results in Section 2.8.1 to convert the problem into one involving a "standard normal" random variable Z that will have a $N(0, 1)$ probability density function. We do so by subtracting from b its mean β and dividing by its standard deviation $\sigma/\sqrt{T}$. That is, since $b \sim N(\beta, \sigma^2/T)$, the standardized variable

$$Z = \frac{b - \beta}{\sqrt{\sigma^2/T}} = \frac{b - \beta}{\sigma/\sqrt{T}} \qquad (3.4.4)$$

has the standard normal $N(0, 1)$ probability density function. In Table 1 at the end of this book you will find tables for computing the probabilities that Z falls in intervals from 0 to a particular value z. So we proceed as follows:

$$P[\beta - 1 \le b \le \beta + 1] = P\left[\frac{-1}{\sigma/\sqrt{T}} \le \frac{b - \beta}{\sigma/\sqrt{T}} \le \frac{1}{\sigma/\sqrt{T}}\right]$$

$$= P\left[\frac{-1}{\sqrt{.25}} \le Z \le \frac{1}{\sqrt{.25}}\right]$$

$$= P[-2 \le Z \le 2]$$

Since $Z \sim N(0, 1)$ we can compute this probability from Table 1 at the end of this book to be .9544. That is, if the population variance of food expenditure is 10, then based on a sample of size $T = 40$ the least squares estimator will provide an estimate within $1 of the true mean expenditure 95% of the time. This is a very reassuring fact. You may want to investigate the probability statement we could make if the sample size $T = 80$ or $T = 200$, and verify that as $T \to \infty$ the probability that b falls in the interval $\beta \pm 1$ approaches *one*.

Given the time and energy we have spent deriving the least squares estimator b and studying its properties, you probably have guessed that it is a very good, if not the best, way to estimate the mean of a normal population. In fact it turns out that we can show that b has the smallest variance of any unbiased estimation rule, and thus it has the *best* chance, of *any* unbiased estimator, to yield an estimate that is "close" to the true parameter value. As we show in Section 3.4.4, when learning from a sample of data taken from a normal population, the *least squares estimator or rule is the best unbiased estimator.*

3.4.4   Best Linear Unbiased Estimation

We have adopted the statistical model

$$Y_i = \beta + e_i \qquad i = 1, \ldots, T$$

to represent how observations on food expenditure by randomly selected households are created. The random errors e_i are independent $N(0, \sigma^2)$ random errors that represent factors causing the ith household's expenditure Y_i to differ from the population mean expenditure β. The least squares estimation rule

$$b = \sum_{i=1}^{T} Y_i / T$$

has been shown to be unbiased ($E[b] = \beta$), have a variance $\mathrm{var}(b) = \sigma^2/T$, and have a normal distribution, $b \sim N(\beta, \sigma^2/T)$. These properties are illustrated using a simulation or Monte Carlo sampling experiment in Section 3.6.

Now the least squares estimation rule is just one of a very large number of rules for estimating β that one could use. In this section we show that of all *similar* rules that are unbiased, the least squares rule is the *best* one to use given the assumptions we have made about how the sample of data is created. First, let us define the "type" of rule the least squares estimator is so that it can be compared to similar rules.

The least squares estimator is a weighted average of the Y_i

$$
\begin{aligned}
b &= \sum_{i=1}^{T} Y_i / T = \frac{1}{T} Y_1 + \frac{1}{T} Y_2 + \ldots + \frac{1}{T} Y_T \\
&= a_1 Y_1 + a_2 Y_2 + \ldots + a_T Y_T \\
&= \sum_{i=1}^{T} a_i Y_i
\end{aligned}
\qquad (3.4.5)
$$

where the weights are $a_i = 1/T$. Another word for weighted average is *linear combination*, and the least squares estimator is called a *linear* estimator. Any estimation rule that is written like equation 3.4.5 is called a linear estimator. For example, suppose the weights a_i^* are constants different from $a_i = 1/T$. Then we can define *another* linear estimator of β as

$$b^* = \sum_{i=1}^{T} a_i^* Y_i \qquad (3.4.6)$$

The least squares estimator is a *linear unbiased* estimator: it is this general type of estimation rule to which we will compare it. The estimator b^* is a linear estimator, but it is not necessarily unbiased. We can restrict it to be linear unbiased by placing conditions on the weights a_i^*. To ensure that b^* is *different* from b, let us define

$$a_i^* = a_i + c_i = \frac{1}{T} + c_i \tag{3.4.7}$$

so the constants c_i are simply the difference between any values a_i^* we might choose and $1/T$. Thus

$$
\begin{aligned}
b^* &= \sum_{i=1}^{T} a_i^* Y_i = \sum_{i=1}^{T} \left(\frac{1}{T} + c_i \right) Y_i \\
&= \sum_{i=1}^{T} \frac{1}{T} Y_i + \sum_{i=1}^{T} c_i Y_i \\
&= b + \sum_{i=1}^{T} c_i Y_i
\end{aligned} \tag{3.4.8}
$$

The expected value of b^* is

$$
\begin{aligned}
E[b^*] &= E\left[b + \sum_{i=1}^{T} c_i Y_i \right] \\
&= \beta + \sum_{i=1}^{T} c_i E[Y_i] \\
&= \beta + \beta \sum_{i=1}^{T} c_i
\end{aligned} \tag{3.4.9}
$$

Clearly b^* is not unbiased unless the constants c_i sum to zero. That is, b^* is linear unbiased only if $\Sigma_{i=1}^{T} c_i = 0$. Thus we will compare b to b^*, which represents any *other* linear unbiased estimator, when the condition $\Sigma_{i=1}^{T} c_i = 0$ holds.

Given that we are comparing b to b^*, and both are linear unbiased rules when $\Sigma c_i = 0$, we will define the estimator with the smallest variance to be *best*. We know that $\text{var}(b) = \sigma^2/T$ and

$$
\begin{aligned}
\text{var}(b^*) &= \text{var}\left(\sum_{i=1}^{T} a_i^* Y_i \right) = \text{var}\left(\sum_{i=1}^{T} \left(\frac{1}{T} + c_i \right) Y_i \right) \\
&= \sum_{i=1}^{T} \left(\frac{1}{T} + c_i \right)^2 \text{var}(Y_i) \\
&= \sigma^2 \sum_{i=1}^{T} \left(\frac{1}{T} + c_i \right)^2 \\
&= \sigma^2 \sum_{i=1}^{T} \left(\frac{1}{T^2} + \frac{2}{T} c_i + c_i^2 \right) \\
&= \sigma^2 \left(\frac{1}{T} + \frac{2}{T} \sum_{i=1}^{T} c_i + \sum_{i=1}^{T} c_i^2 \right) \\
&= \sigma^2 / T + \sigma^2 \sum_{i=1}^{T} c_i^2 \qquad \left(\text{since } \sum_{i=1}^{T} c_i = 0 \right) \\
&= \text{var}(b) + \sigma^2 \sum_{i=1}^{T} c_i^2
\end{aligned} \tag{3.4.10}
$$

Thus the variance of b^* must be *greater* than the variance of b since $\Sigma_{i=1}^{T} c_i^2 = 0$ no matter what the values of the c_i (unless all the c_i are zero, in which case $b^* = b$, which doesn't count).

What we have shown, for the linear statistical model $Y_i = \beta + e_i$ with $E(e_i) = 0$, var (e_i) $= \sigma^2$ and $cov(e_i, e_j) = 0$ is that if b is compared to any other linear and unbiased estimator b^*, then b has a smaller variance and is the best linear unbiased estimator (BLUE) of the population mean. This important result does *not* depend on the random errors e_i having a normal distribution, only that $e_i \sim (0, \sigma^2)$ and that the random errors are uncorrelated with one another. Using the assumption of normality, it is possible to make the even stronger claim that b is the *best unbiased* estimator. The proof of this fact is given in Judge et al. (1988, pp.74–75). The stronger claim means that b has the smallest variance of all unbiased estimators of β, whether they are linear or nonlinear. This stronger result depends on the population being a normal one. If the population, and random errors e_i, are not normal, then we can say only that b is the best *linear* unbiased estimator.

But why does having the smallest variance make b best? The answer to that question is very important and is based on the objective of the experiment of drawing a sample of data. We wished to answer the question: How much does a typical household spend on food per week? Given our economic and statistical model, the answer to the question is provided by the unknown parameter β. Thus, our objective is to get "as good (precise) an estimate of β as possible." Reasonably enough, we can interpret that to mean to get an *estimate* of β that is close to the true value. Suppose we consider using the two estimation rules b and b^*, both of which are linear and unbiased estimators of β and have normal distributions, but for which var(b^*) > var(b). Now suppose we define getting an estimate that is *close* to β as getting an estimate within \$1 of the true mean expenditure. In Figure 3.5 we depict the probability distributions of b based on all $T = 20$ sample observations, and the estimator b^* given by

$$b^* = \sum_{i=1}^{T} a_i^* Y_i = \sum_{i=1}^{10} Y_i / 10$$

This estimator uses only the first 10 sample values, so $a_1^* = \ldots = a_{10}^* = 1/10$ and $a_{11}^* = \ldots = a_{20}^* = 0$. The probability that b is within \$1 of β is 95% (approximately), and the probability that b^* is within \$1 of β is 64%. Thus b, the linear unbiased

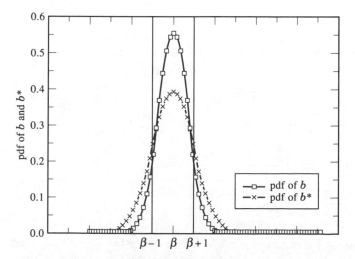

Figure 3.5 Probability distributions of b and b^*.

estimator with the *smaller variance*, has a higher probability of getting *close* to the true value of β. This will be true for any other linear unbiased estimator of β one could create.

3.5   Estimating the Variance of a Normal Population

One parameter of the statistical model

$$Y_i = \beta + e_i \qquad i = 1, \ldots, T \tag{3.5.1}$$

remains to be estimated. We have assumed that the random errors $e_i \sim N(0, \sigma^2)$ and that $Y_i \sim N(\beta, \sigma^2)$ where β is the location parameter, or mean, and the parameter σ^2 is variance. The parameter σ^2 tells us the amount of variation (variance) in household food expenditures Y_i about their mean, $E[Y_i] = \beta$. Since $\mathrm{var}(b) = \sigma^2/T$, the variance σ^2, along with the sample size T, also determines the sampling variation (variance) of the least squares estimator of the population mean.

While knowledge of σ^2 is important, we *cannot* estimate it by using the least squares principle. The sum of squares function

$$S = \sum_{i=1}^{T} \left(y_i - \beta \right)^2$$

does not contain σ^2 and thus does not provide a basis for its estimation. Instead, we use heuristic procedures to develop an estimation rule. Remember, we have assumed that $E[e_i] = 0$, so that $\mathrm{var}(e_i) = \sigma^2 = E[e_i^2]$. That is, the variance σ^2 is the expected value of the squared random errors. Recall that the "expectation" of a random variable is an average of all the values that the random variable takes in an infinitely large number of trials of the underlying experiment. Suppose for a moment that we actually *knew* the values of the random disturbances $e_1, e_2, \ldots, e_T$. Then it would be reasonable to average their squared values in order to obtain an estimate of σ^2. That is, we could estimate σ^2 using the rule

$$\tilde{\sigma}^2 = \frac{e_1^2 + e_2^2 + \ldots + e_T^2}{T} \tag{3.5.2}$$

The symbol "~" over σ^2 is called a "tilde" and indicates that $\tilde{\sigma}^2$ is an estimator, or estimate, of σ^2, depending on the context.

Since $e_i = Y_i - \beta$ and β is unknown, the random errors e_i are not observable. We can, however, form an "estimator" of e_i by replacing β with the least squares estimator. We define the *least squares residual* as

$$\hat{e}_i = Y_i - b \tag{3.5.3}$$

Replacing e_i^2 with $\hat{e}_i^2$ we have the estimator of σ^2

$$\tilde{\sigma}^2 = \frac{\hat{e}_1^2 + \hat{e}_2^2 + \ldots + \hat{e}_T^2}{T}$$

$$= \sum_{i=1}^{T} \hat{e}_i^2 / T \tag{3.5.4}$$

This estimator is an intuitively pleasing one, since it follows from the idea of expected values. However, we need to determine the sampling properties of this estimation rule.

What is its sampling distribution? What are its mean and variance? To answer these questions we need to develop the chi-square distribution.

3.5.1 The Chi-Square Probability Distribution

In the last section, in defining an estimator for σ^2, we made use of the independent $N(0, \sigma^2)$ random variables $e_1, e_2, ..., e_T$. Consequently, (e_i/σ) are independent $N(0, 1)$ random variables. Chi-square random variables arise when standard normal, $N(0, 1)$, random variables are squared. Let $Z_1, Z_2, ..., Z_m$ denote m independent $N(0, 1)$ random variables. Then

$$V - Z_1^2 + Z_2^2 + ... + Z_m^2 \qquad (3.5.5)$$

has a *chi-square distribution with m degrees of freedom*. We denote this result as $V \sim \chi_{(m)}^2$. The degrees-of-freedom parameter m indicates the number of *independent* $N(0, 1)$ random variables that have been squared and summed to form V. Furthermore, the single parameter m completely determines the properties of V. In particular the mean and variance of V are

$$E[V] = m \qquad (3.5.6a)$$

$$\text{var}(V) = 2m \qquad (3.5.6b)$$

In Figure 3.6 we depict the probability density function for chi-square random variables with various degrees of freedom. Note that since V is formed from *squared* $N(0, 1)$ random variables its values v are nonnegative, $v \geq 0$, and the distribution has a long tail, or, in statistical parlance, is *skewed* to the right. As the degrees of freedom parameter m gets larger, however, the probability density function becomes more symmetric and "bell-shaped." In fact as $m \to \infty$ the chi-square distribution converges to, or essentially becomes, a normal distribution.

In order to calculate probabilities involving chi-square random variables, a specialized computer program is required. Alternatively, at the end of this book we present Table 3 containing various percentiles of the chi-square distribution that are useful for hypothesis testing and interval estimation.

3.5.2 The Probability Distribution of $\tilde{\sigma}^2$

The probability distribution of the estimator $\tilde{\sigma}^2$ is a multiple of a chi-square distribution. We know that the random errors $e_i = Y_i - \beta \sim N(0, \sigma^2)$ and consequently $(e_i/\sigma) \sim N(0, 1)$. Thus each (e_i/σ) is a standard normal random variable and $(e_i/\sigma)^2$ is a χ^2 random variable with one degree of freedom, $\chi_{(1)}^2$. Since the random errors are independent, the sum

$$\left(\frac{e_1}{\sigma}\right)^2 + \left(\frac{e_2}{\sigma}\right)^2 + ... + \left(\frac{e_T}{\sigma}\right)^2 = \sum_{i=1}^{T}\left(\frac{e_i}{\sigma}\right)^2 \sim \chi_{(T)}^2 \qquad (3.5.7)$$

using equation 3.5.5.

The estimator $\tilde{\sigma}^2$ in equation 3.5.4 replaces e_i^2 with $\hat{e}_i^2$, and unlike the random errors e_i the least squares residuals $\hat{e}_i$ are *not* all independent. If we know any $(T - 1)$ of the residuals $\hat{e}_i$, the remaining one may be calculated using the fact that $\Sigma_{i=1}^{T}\hat{e}_i = 0$ (Exercise 3.5). Furthermore, it can be shown [Judge et al., 1988, pp. 81–82] that $\Sigma_{i=1}^{T}(\hat{e}_i/\sigma)^2$ is equivalent to the sum of $(T - 1)$ independent, squared

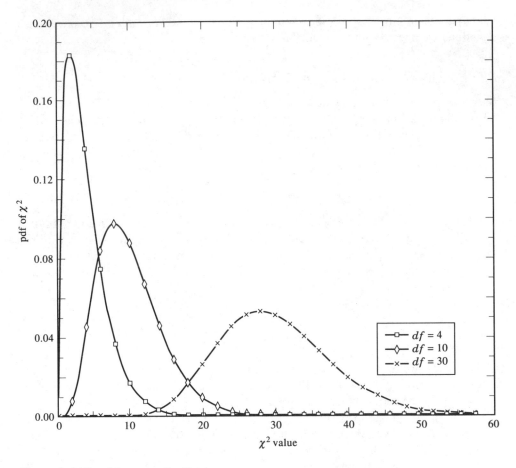

Figure 3.6 The chi-square distribution.

$N(0, 1)$ random variables and thus has a $\chi^2_{(T-1)}$ distribution. Consequently

$$\sum_{i=1}^{T}\left(\frac{\hat{e}_i}{\sigma}\right)^2 = \frac{T\tilde{\sigma}^2}{\sigma^2} \sim \chi^2_{(T-1)} \tag{3.5.8}$$

which means that

$$\tilde{\sigma}^2 \sim \frac{\sigma^2}{T}\chi^2_{(T-1)} \tag{3.5.9}$$

Using equation 3.5.9 and the rules of mean and variance, we see that

$$E\left[\tilde{\sigma}^2\right] = \frac{\sigma^2}{T}E\left[\chi^2_{(T-1)}\right] = \frac{\sigma^2(T-1)}{T} \tag{3.5.10}$$

$$\text{var}\left(\tilde{\sigma}^2\right) = \frac{\sigma^4}{T^2}\text{var}\left(\chi^2_{(T-1)}\right) = \frac{\sigma^4}{T^2}2(T-1) \tag{3.5.11}$$

Note that the estimator $\tilde{\sigma}^2$ is biased. That is,

$$E\left[\tilde{\sigma}^2\right] \neq \sigma^2$$

However, using equation 3.5.10 we can easily develop an *unbiased* estimator. Let us define

$$\hat{\sigma}^2 = \frac{T\tilde{\sigma}^2}{T-1} = \frac{\sum_{i=1}^{T} \hat{e}_i^2}{T-1} \tag{3.5.12}$$

The mean and variance of $\hat{\sigma}^2$ are

$$E[\hat{\sigma}^2] = E\left[\frac{T\tilde{\sigma}^2}{T-1}\right] = \frac{T}{T-1} E[\tilde{\sigma}^2]$$

$$= \frac{T}{T-1} \frac{\sigma^2(T-1)}{T} = \sigma^2 \tag{3.5.13}$$

$$\text{var}(\hat{\sigma}^2) = \left(\frac{T}{T-1}\right)^2 \text{var}(\tilde{\sigma}^2) = \frac{T^2}{(T-1)^2} \frac{\sigma^4}{T^2} 2(T-1)$$

$$= \frac{2\sigma^4}{T-1} \tag{3.5.14}$$

Furthermore, using equation 3.5.8,

$$\sum_{i=1}^{T} \left(\frac{\hat{e}_i}{\sigma}\right)^2 = \frac{(T-1)\hat{\sigma}^2}{\sigma^2} \sim \chi^2_{(T-1)} \tag{3.5.15}$$

which means that

$$\hat{\sigma}^2 \sim \frac{\sigma^2}{T-1} \chi^2_{(T-1)} \tag{3.5.16}$$

To summarize, the estimator $\hat{\sigma}^2$ given in equation 3.5.1 is an unbiased estimator of σ^2, with variance $2\sigma^4/(T-1)$ and a distribution that is proportional to a $\chi^2_{(T-1)}$.

Since we have shown that the least squares estimator b is the *best unbiased* estimator of β, it is natural to ask whether similar results hold for $\hat{\sigma}^2$. The answer to that question is yes! The estimator $\hat{\sigma}^2$ is the best unbiased estimator for σ^2, the variance of a normal population. Discussion of this result can be found in Judge et al. (1988, pp. 79–83). Using $\hat{\sigma}^2$ we can also obtain an unbiased estimator of the variance of the least squares estimator b, which is

$$\hat{\text{var}}(b) = \hat{\sigma}^2 / T \tag{3.5.17}$$

The square root of this estimator is called the "standard error" of b, which we will denote as

$$\text{se}(b) = \sqrt{\hat{\text{var}}(b)} = \hat{\sigma} / \sqrt{T} \tag{3.5.18}$$

Now let us put this theory to practice. For the statistical model 3.5.1, representing household food expenditures, we have a sample of data given in Table 3.1. The least squares estimate of the population mean is $b = \$51.08$. In Table 3.2 are the sample values of household expenditure and the corresponding least squares estimates (residuals) $\hat{e}_i = y_i - b$. Using the least squares residuals and the estimator $\hat{\sigma}^2$ in equation 3.5.12 we can estimate the population variance as

Table 3.2 Household Food Expenditure and Least Squares Residuals

Household	Y_i	$\hat{e}_i$	Household	Y_i	$\hat{e}_i$
1	49.98	−1.10	21	49.07	−2.01
2	55.33	4.25	22	48.91	−2.17
3	50.39	−0.69	23	58.06	6.98
4	46.83	−4.25	24	51.26	0.18
5	47.43	−3.65	25	51.52	0.44
6	48.47	−2.61	26	51.10	0.02
7	52.73	1.65	27	52.92	1.84
8	52.32	1.24	28	53.07	1.99
9	50.35	−0.73	29	49.35	−1.73
10	47.57	−3.51	30	54.85	3.77
11	49.52	−1.56	31	54.14	3.06
12	51.56	0.48	32	47.75	−3.33
13	55.17	4.09	33	50.88	−0.20
14	52.65	1.57	34	49.44	−1.64
15	51.43	0.35	35	53.02	1.94
16	45.96	−5.12	36	53.50	2.42
17	50.86	−0.22	37	49.65	−1.43
18	52.37	1.29	38	52.39	1.31
19	50.10	−0.98	39	49.81	−1.27
20	49.74	−1.34	40	51.85	0.77

$$\hat{\sigma}^2 = \frac{\sum_{i=1}^{T} \hat{e}_i^2}{T-1} = \frac{248.74}{39} = 6.38 \qquad (3.5.19)$$

Thus, based on a sample of $T = 40$ households, we estimate the population mean food expenditure β to be $b = \$51.08$ and the population variance σ^2 to be 6.38. That is, we *estimate* the distribution of food expenditure to be $Y_i \sim N(51.08, 6.38)$.

Using the estimated population variance we can also estimate the variance of the least squares estimator as

$$\hat{var}(b) = \hat{\sigma}^2 / T = 6.38 / 40 = .159 \qquad (3.5.20)$$

Therefore, we estimate the distribution of the least squares estimator b to be $b \sim N(51.08, .159)$.

3.5.3   Another Way to Obtain Estimators

To obtain an estimator for the mean β of a normal population, we used the least squares principle. This principle cannot *always* be used to obtain estimators. The variance parameter σ^2, for example, does not appear in the sum of squares function, and we were forced to develop the estimator $\hat{\sigma}^2$ on the basis of analogies. There is a principle that we can use to estimate both β and σ^2 given our statistical model, and that is the *likelihood principle*.

In our model household food expenditure, Y_i is expressed as

$$Y_i = \beta + e_i \qquad i = 1,\ldots, T$$

where β is the mean household food expenditure and the independent random errors

$e_i \sim N(0, \sigma^2)$. The errors e_i are independent since our sample will consist of randomly selected households and all are drawn from the same $N(0, \sigma^2)$ distribution. Food expenditures Y_i are also independent random variables and are drawn from a $N(\beta, \sigma^2)$ distribution. In Section 2.4.4 we saw that the joint probability density function of independent random variables can be formed by *multiplying* their individual probability density functions. Thus, for the joint probability density function of $Y_1, \ldots, Y_T$, the sample of household food expenditures is

$$f(y_1, \ldots, y_T) = f(y_1) \cdot f(y_2) \cdot \cdots f(y_T)$$

Since each of the random variables $Y_i \sim N(\beta, \sigma^2)$, their probability density functions are

$$f(y) = \frac{1}{\sqrt{2\pi\sigma^2}} \exp\left\{-\frac{(y-\beta)^2}{2\sigma^2}\right\}$$

$$= (2\pi)^{-\frac{1}{2}} (\sigma^2)^{-\frac{1}{2}} \exp\left\{-\frac{(y-\beta)^2}{2\sigma^2}\right\}$$

Thus the joint probability density function of the T independent random variables $Y_1, \ldots, Y_T$ is

$$f(y_1, \ldots, y_T | \beta, \sigma^2) = (2\pi)^{-\frac{T}{2}} (\sigma^2)^{-\frac{T}{2}} \exp\left\{-\sum_{i=1}^{T} \frac{(y_1 - \beta)^2}{2\sigma^2}\right\} \qquad (3.5.21)$$

On the left-hand side of equation 3.5.2 1, we have used "conditional" notation to indicate that the joint probability density function is a function of the values $y_1, \ldots, y_T$ *given* the values of the parameters β and σ^2. That is, to use equation 3.5.21 to calculate probabilities, the parameters β and σ^2 must be given.

The likelihood principle of parameter estimation rests on the fact that we can *observe* sample values $y_1, \ldots, y_T$ but *not* the parameters β and σ^2. Therefore we *could* treat the mathematical function in equation 3.5.21 as a function of the unknowns β and σ^2 *given* the observed sample values $y_1, \ldots, y_T$. Recall that if $Y_1, \ldots, Y_T$ are *discrete* random variables, then their joint probability density function yields *probabilities* that the random variables jointly take sets of values. If parameters such as β and σ^2 change, then the probabilities change. Thus, if $Y_1, \ldots, Y_T$ were discrete and observed, we could choose as estimates of β and σ^2 the values that maximize equation 3.5.21, the probability of obtaining the sample that was actually drawn. That, in a nutshell, is the likelihood principle of parameter estimation. It is called the "likelihood" principle because when the Y_i are continuous, their joint probability density function does not actually give probabilities (see Section 2.4.3), but estimates of the unknown parameters are still obtained by maximizing equation 3.5.21, which is called the *likelihood function* to avoid confusion. The resulting estimates are called *maximum likelihood estimates*.

Note that equation 3.5.21 contains both parameters β and σ^2. Thus, we can estimate both parameters by choosing values for them that maximize $f(y_1, \ldots, y_T | \beta, \sigma^2)$. If we make use of calculus, the values of β and σ^2 that maximize equation 3.5.21 are

$$\tilde{\beta} = \sum_{i=1}^{T} y_i / T \qquad (3.5.22a)$$

$$\tilde{\sigma}^2 = \sum_{i=1}^{T} \frac{\left(y_i - \tilde{\beta}\right)^2}{T} \qquad (3.5.22b)$$

From our statistical model the maximum likelihood estimate of β, $\tilde{\beta}$, happens to be the same as the least squares estimate. The estimate of the population variance $\tilde{\sigma}^2$ is the rule we developed intuitively in equation 3.5.4 and showed in equation 3.5.10 to be a biased estimator of σ^2. Thus, in this case maximum likelihood estimation results in an unbiased estimator of β and a biased estimator for σ^2.

The likelihood principle of estimation is an important one and is used in a variety of statistical models to obtain what are called maximum likelihood estimators. See Judge et al. (1988, Chapter 12) for a discussion of the properties of maximum likelihood estimators.

3.6   A Sampling Experiment

To provide a feel for the sampling properties of the least squares estimator of the mean and the unbiased variance estimator $\hat{\sigma}^2$, we will carry out a *sampling experiment*, also called a *Monte Carlo* or *simulation* experiment. The idea is this. We will "create" a sample of T observations using the statistical model for the mean of a normal population given in equation 3.2.4 and with parameters β and σ^2 set to values that *we choose*. The estimates for the mean and variance of this artificially constructed sample are calculated and recorded. Since the mean, variance, and probability distribution of the estimators of the mean and variance are *repeated sample* characteristics, we will repeat the sample construction process a large number of times, say $N = 1000$, and then examine the 1000 least squares estimates of β and σ^2 to see if they conform to our theoretically derived properties.

Recall the statistical model we have specified to represent the process by which household expenditure data are determined. The expenditure of the ith household is given by

$$Y_i = \beta + e_i \qquad i = 1,\ldots,T \qquad (3.6.1)$$

and the normal random error e_i is independent of all other errors and has mean 0 and variance σ^2. In order to create an *artificial sample* we must specify the sample size T, the population mean β, and the population variance σ^2. That part is easy as we can set these values to be anything we like. So let $T = 10$, $\beta = 20$, and $\sigma^2 = 10$. Thus we are specifying, for the purpose of the sampling experiment, that $e_i \sim N(0, 10)$ and $Y_i \sim N(20, 10)$. According to our statistical theory the least squares estimator b of β using data from such a population *should have* a normal distribution with mean $\beta = 20$ and variance $\sigma^2/T = 10/10 = 1$, that is

$$b \sim N\left(\beta = 20, \; \sigma^2/T = 1\right)$$

The only remaining puzzle in executing the simulation or sampling experiment is how to create independent random errors from a normal distribution with a mean of zero and variance 10. The problem of how to do this has been solved by computer scientists, and computer packages routinely incorporate a *normal random number generator*. These "generators" are actually functions that can create series of independent standard normal [$N(0, 1)$] random errors. If Z_i is a standard normal random error then

$$e_i = \sigma \cdot Z_i = \sqrt{10} \cdot Z_i$$

has a $N(0, \sigma^2)$ distribution, and

$$Y_i = \beta + e_i = 20 + e_i$$
$$= 20 + \sqrt{10}Z_i$$

Adding a $N(0, 10)$ random error to the population mean expenditure, $\beta = 20$ represents how we visualize expenditure values from a $N(20, 10)$ population being created. In Table 3.3 we show one sample of $T = 10$ values of z_i, e_i, and y_i.

We have constructed values of Y_i from the desired population by choosing values for β and σ^2 (which are *unknown* in a real problem) and by using a normal random number generator.

Given this one sample we can now *pretend* that β is unknown and see how close the least squares estimate, based on the sample of data, is to the true parameter value. By using the artificial sample of data in Table 3.3, we find that the least squares estimate of β is

$$b = \frac{\Sigma y_i}{T} = 206.921/10 - 20.692$$

Comparing this value to the true value we see that the estimation error for this sample is $b - \beta = 20.692 - 20 = 0.692$.

Now, instead of *one* artificial sample let us create $N = 1000$. The least squares estimates of the population mean β for the first 10 samples are given in Table 3.4. Note that the least squares estimates of $\beta = 20$ change from sample to sample. In sample number one the least squares estimate of β is 20.692, whereas in the eighth the estimate is 21.501. The fact that the least squares estimate varies from sample to sample reflects the fact that the least squares *estimator* (the estimation rule) is a random variable whose value is unknown until an experiment is performed and a sample of data is collected.

Since the least squares estimator is a random variable, it has a probability or sampling distribution, which we know is normal. We can verify this fact by examining the 1000 estimates of β we have obtained from the simulation experiment.

In Figure 3.7 we have the relative frequency distribution (defined in Chapter 2) of the $N = 1000$ values of the standardized variable

$$Z_i = \frac{b_i - \beta}{\sqrt{\sigma^2/T}}$$

which has a $N(0, 1)$ distribution if the b_i values have a $N(\beta, \sigma^2/T)$ distribution. Compare the percentages of standardized Z_i values in the given intervals to the $N(0, 1)$ distribution in Figure 2.12 and you see that the percentages are very close.

Table 3.3 One Artificial Sample from a $N(20, 10)$ Population

i	z_i	e_i	y_i
1	0.193	0.610	20.610
2	−0.504	−1.594	18.406
3	−2.318	−7.331	12.669
4	0.257	0.813	20.813
5	1.784	5.641	25.641
6	1.627	5.145	25.145
7	0.708	2.238	22.238
8	2.252	7.120	27.120
9	−0.462	−1.460	18.540
10	−1.348	−4.261	15.739

Table 3.4 Least Squares Estimates of the Population Mean for 10 Samples of Size $T = 10$

Sample	b_i
1	20.692
2	21.326
3	20.318
4	20.717
5	22.043
6	19.586
7	19.651
8	21.501
9	19.575
10	19.304

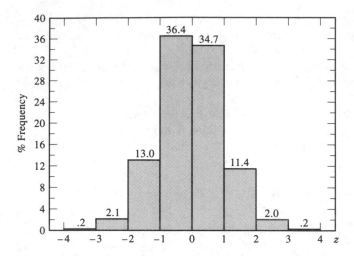

Figure 3.7 Relative frequency histogram for standardized least squares estimates of the population mean.

The average value of all $N = 1000$ values of b_i is

$$\bar{b} = \sum_{n=1}^{N} b_n / 1000 = 19.976$$

Thus, in 1000 repeated samples the average value of the least squares estimates is 19.976, which is very close to the true mathematical expectation $E(b) = \beta = 20$. After all, *mathematical expectation, or the expected value, is the average value of a random variable in a large number of repeated trials of an experiment*. Thus, even though the least squares estimates of β vary from sample to sample, their value is, on average, equal to the true value. Although $\bar{b}$ is not exactly β, the difference is small and due to the fact that results from "only" $N = 1000$ samples were averaged. The use of a larger number of samples would have produced an average closer to the true value.

Furthermore, the sample variance of the 1000 estimates b_n is

$$\bar{s}_{b_n}^2 = \sum_{n=1}^{N} \left(b_n - \bar{b} \right)^2 \Big/ 999 = 0.919$$

compared to the true sampling variability of 1.0.

Our sampling experiment results closely conform to the theoretically derived properties of the least squares estimator. We have used the simulation experiment to illustrate the analytically derived properties of the least squares estimator. We will use this device many times in this book to illustrate statistical properties, and in some cases, to get an idea of estimator performance when properties cannot be derived.

Using that same experiment we can demonstrate the properties of $\hat{\sigma}^2$. For the first 10 Monte Carlo samples, the estimates of β and σ^2 are given in Table 3.5.

Recall that in the experiment the true population variance was chosen to be $\sigma^2 = 10$. We see from Table 3.5 that the estimates $\hat{\sigma}^2$ vary considerably from sample to sample. However, the average value of all $N = 1000$ estimates of σ^2 is

$$\bar{\hat{\sigma}}^2 = \sum_{n=1}^{N=1000} \hat{\sigma}_n^2 / N = 10.207$$

Table 3.5 Estimates of β and σ^2 for
10 Samples of Size $T = 10$

sample n	b_n	$\hat{\sigma}_n^2$
1	20.692	20.757
2	21.326	6.376
3	20.318	20.819
4	20.717	17.638
5	22.043	10.427
6	19.586	11.336
7	19.651	16.044
8	21.501	11.638
9	19.575	7.559
10	19.304	4.861

and their sample variance is

$$s_{\hat{\sigma}_n^2}^2 = \sum_{n=1}^{N=1000} \left(\hat{\sigma}_n^2 - \overline{\hat{\sigma}}^2\right)^2 \bigg/ (N-1) = 20.817$$

These values are close to $E[\hat{\sigma}^2] = \sigma^2 = 10$ and var($\hat{\sigma}^2$) = $2\sigma^4/(T-1) = 22.222$. The simulated values are not as "close" to the true values for the variance parameter σ^2 as they were for the mean parameter β, since the variance estimator is subject to more sampling variation. If we were to draw a larger number of samples N, the accuracy of the sampling experiment would increase.

3.7 Some Other Examples

The statistical model for the mean β of a random economic variable Y_i that is normally distributed can be represented as

$$Y_i = \beta + e_i \qquad i = 1,\ldots, T \tag{3.7.1a}$$

$$e_i \sim N\left(0, \sigma^2\right) \tag{3.7.1b}$$

$$E(e_i e_j) = \text{cov}(e_i, e_j) = 0 \qquad i \neq j \tag{3.7.1c}$$

In equation 3.7.1a the observable random variable Y_i is represented as equal to β, the population mean, plus an unobservable random error e_i that accounts for all factors causing Y_i to differ from its mean. The random error e_i is assumed normally and independently distributed with mean zero and a variance σ^2. Thus, $Y_i \sim N(\beta, \sigma^2)$ and independently as well. In this chapter we have used this model to study food consumption of households with three members and $25,000 income, and in particular have estimated the population mean household expenditure and expenditure variance. We have determined the statistical properties of the least squares estimator of the population mean β. *Assuming that the model 3.7.1 is correct, we have shown that b is the best linear unbiased estimator of β.*

The model in equation 3.7.1 is of course a general one. Any economic variable that can be expressed as its mean plus a random disturbance e_i that is normally and independently distributed with mean zero and variance σ^2 can be analyzed in *exactly* the same way. In this section we explore two other examples in which the model 3.7.1 can be employed.

3.7.1 Rational Expectations

The behavioral assumption of *rational expectations* is important to modern economic theory. This assumption is that at any time, given all available current information, an individual's expectations about macroeconomic random variables are "unbiased," that is, correct on average. Thus, for example, if conditions leading to inflation are observed, the inflation is anticipated and individuals take measures to protect themselves against it. The rational expectations hypothesis asserts that individuals correctly forecast, on average, the rate of inflation given the information they have.

Let us investigate the rational expectations hypothesis and *estimate* the amount of average expectation error, or bias, when individuals forecast inflation. In Table 3.6 we present data on expected inflation, actual inflation, and expectation error for the years 1978–1988. The data on expected inflation rate come from the arithmetic mean survey response to the question: How much do you expect prices to go up in the next 12 months? The survey is conducted monthly (since January 1978) and the figure reported in Table 3.6 is the mean survey response in December of the previous year. The actual annual inflation rate is constructed from the GNP deflator in Table 2.2 by taking the percentage change from one year to the next. The expectation error is the difference between the expected and actual inflation rate.

As a starting point we treat the expectation error as observations on a random variable Y_i that fits the statistical model assumptions in equation 3.7.1. That is, the error in inflationary expectations Y_i equals the population mean expectation error β plus a random disturbance e_i that accounts for all factors causing expectation errors to be different from β, their population mean value. It is assumed that $Y_i \sim N(\beta, \sigma^2)$ and independently, so $e_i \sim N(0, \sigma^2)$ and independently. Using the data in Table 3.6 we can estimate the mean and variance of Y_i, using the estimators b in equation 3.4.1 and $\hat{\sigma}^2$ in equation 3.5.12, as

$$b = \sum_{i=1}^{T} y_i \, / \, T = \frac{6.650}{11} = .605 \tag{3.7.2a}$$

$$\hat{\sigma}^2 = \sum_{i=1}^{T} (y_i - b)^2 \, / \, (T-1) = \frac{31.130}{10} = 3.113 \tag{3.7.2b}$$

Thus we *estimate* the distribution of inflationary expectation errors to be $Y_i \sim N(.605, 3.113)$ and since the estimator $b \sim N(\beta, \sigma^2/T)$, we *estimate* its variance to be

$$\hat{\text{var}}(b) = \hat{\sigma}^2 \, / \, T = \frac{3.113}{11} = .283 \tag{3.7.3}$$

Thus, based on our sample of data we estimate that on average the population *overanticipates* the amount of inflation by .60 points. Or, we estimate that inflationary expectations are positively (upwardly) biased by about half a percentage point.

A follow-up question of immediate interest to economists concerns the rational expectations hypothesis. If expectations are rational, then the population average or mean expectation error β *should be zero*. That is, if rational expectations hold, then $Y_i \sim N(0, \sigma^2)$. Do our empirical results support or refute rational expectations? An answer to this question will be given in Chapter 4 when *hypothesis tests* are introduced. There procedures for using a sample of data to test the rational expectations hypothesis $\beta = 0$ will be developed and applied.

Table 3.6 Inflationary Expectations Data

Year	Expected	Actual	Error
1978	7.9	7.28	0.62
1979	10.8	8.86	1.94
1980	10.1	9.03	1.07
1981	5.7	9.68	−3.98
1982	5.1	6.38	−1.28
1983	5.0	3.90	1.10
1984	4.8	3.66	1.14
1985	5.0	2.97	2.03
1986	4.1	2.61	1.49
1987	4.0	3.16	0.84
1988	5.0	3.32	1.68

Source: Expectations data from University of Michigan
Survey Research Center.

3.7.2   Sales of Canned Tuna

Grocery store chains (e.g., Kroger, A&P) are large corporations in an extremely competitive industry. Every product and facet of operation is continually scrutinized for ways to increase sales, reduce costs, and increase profits. Sales figures for each and every item in a store are carefully monitored, and explanations for variations are sought. As economists we recognize that the sales and quantity demanded of any product are determined by its price, the prices of related products, consumer income, the size of the population, and tastes and preferences. That is, the sales are affected by the usual factors explaining demand.

Let us focus on one standard grocery product, canned tuna. Grocery store chain executives recognize that regional differences exist across the United States and monitor sales at several levels of aggregation. First, the sales of each *store* are recorded. Within any city there may be several stores owned by each chain and thus the store data can be aggregated, or summed, to yield total *chain* sales in a particular city. Then city sales are aggregated to form regional figures and these combined to obtain national sales. In Table 3.7 are *weekly* data on the number of cans of tuna sold by one large grocery store chain in a large Midwestern city. The data are "real" and provided by Nielsen Marketing Research. The data are proprietary and thus the chain identity, location, and so on cannot be revealed.

As noted, the chain executives may be interested in explaining the weekly variation in sales, which is substantial. In Chapters 5 to 9 we will study how the variation in an economic variable, like weekly sales, can be explained by, or related to, the variation in explanatory variables, like price, price of related goods, and advertisements. For the present, however, let us focus on a more restricted question: What is the mean sales of canned tuna by this chain, in this city, per week? If we let Y_i = weekly tuna sales, we might adopt the statistical model 3.7.1 and represent weekly sales as independent random variables $Y_i \sim N(\beta, \sigma^2)$. If we did so, *and if the model 3.7.1 is correct*, then we know how to estimate the mean weekly sales β and the variance σ^2.

Unfortunately the model 3.7.1 is not correct for the weekly sales of tuna. In Figure 3.8*a* we plot the relative frequency distribution of weekly sales of tuna, which is clearly nonnormal. Many times it will be necessary to *transform* the data in order to satisfy the assumptions of a statistical model. For marketing data of the sort we are examining, the (natural) logarithmic transformation of sales is satisfactory. The economic implications of this choice are examined in Chapter 8. For the present we simply note

Table 3.7 Total Chain Tuna Sales (cans per week)

Week	Sales	Week	Sales	Week	Sales	Week	Sales
1	21050	14	15742	27	28583	40	39952
2	31097	15	16786	28	30915	41	36068
3	29278	16	26992	29	24160	42	46755
4	26389	17	27405	30	13482	43	31613
5	24542	18	22702	31	20078	44	22832
6	29120	19	20075	32	24430	45	17496
7	37154	20	23203	33	36706	46	16294
8	30290	21	19566	34	42696	47	16651
9	37187	22	23144	35	25105	48	49964
10	31046	23	18570	36	19309	49	42372
11	34379	24	24588	37	55784	50	25867
12	20556	25	18625	38	55103	51	25814
13	16479	26	12551	39	50710	52	18893

that the distribution of tuna sales is "skewed" to the right and that the logarithmic transformation "shrinks" the large values more than small ones. In Figure 3.8*b* the histogram of logarithmic sales is shown and, as expected, its distribution is more symmetric.

Thus, for the tuna sales data a correctly specified statistical model may involve the observable variable $Y_t = \ln(\text{weekly tuna sales})$, where we have used the subscript "t" to denote the fact that we have observed a *time-series* of data. The statistical model is then

$$Y_t = \beta + e_t \tag{3.7.4a}$$

$$e_t \sim N(0, \sigma^2) \tag{3.7.4b}$$

$$\text{cov}(e_t, e_s) = 0 \quad t \neq s \tag{3.7.4c}$$

The population parameters β and σ^2 are now the mean and variance of the logarithm of weekly tuna sales. If the assumptions 3.7.4b and 3.7.4c are correct (see Exercises 3.7 and 3.8), then we may correctly use the estimators b and $\hat{\sigma}^2$, which yield

$$b = \sum_{t=1}^{T} y_t / T = 10.1735 \tag{3.7.5a}$$

$$\hat{\sigma}^2 = .1329 \tag{3.7.5b}$$

The estimate $b = 10.1735$ is of the mean of the logarithm of weekly tuna sales. The question of how to use this value to estimate the mean of weekly tuna sales is explored in Exercise 3.13.

3.8   A Summary and Critique

In this chapter we have presented a statistical model that can be used to estimate the mean and variance of a normal population. Specifically, if $Y_1, \ldots, Y_T$ is a random sample of data from a normal population with mean β and variance σ^2, then the linear statistical model for the population mean is

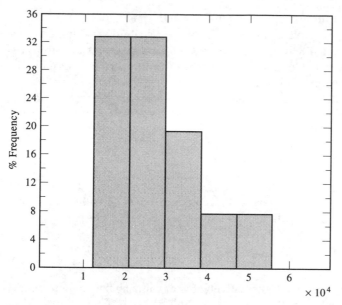

Figure 3.8a Relative frequency distribution of weekly sales of tuna.

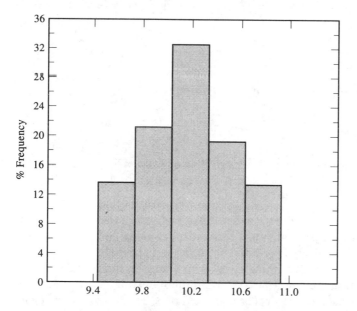

Figure 3.8b Relative frequency distribution of log (weekly sales of tuna).

$$Y_i = \beta + e_i \qquad (3.8.1a)$$

$$e_i \sim N\left(0, \sigma^2\right) \qquad (3.8.1b)$$

$$\mathrm{cov}\left(e_i, e_j\right) = 0 \quad i \neq j \qquad (3.8.1c)$$

In equation 3.8.1a the random variable Y_i is decomposed into its mean $E[Y_i] = \beta$, which is not random, and a random component e_i that represents, in this model, all the random factors that cause Y_i to differ from its mean value. In equation 3.8.1b we assume that the random errors e_i have a normal probability distribution with mean zero and a variance σ^2. In equation 3.8.1c we assume that the random errors have zero covariance and thus are not correlated. Since the e_i are also assumed to be normally distributed, the random errors are also independent.

Given the model 3.8.1 we have developed estimation rules, or estimators, for the unknown population parameters β and σ^2. We have used the least squares principle to estimate β as

$$b = \sum_{i=1}^{T} Y_i / T \qquad (3.8.2)$$

Under the assumptions 3.8.1, b is the best unbiased estimator of β, and it has a sampling distribution that is normal, with mean β and variance σ^2/T. That is,

$$b \sim N\!\left(\beta, \sigma^2/T\right) \qquad (3.8.3)$$

We also showed that b may be obtained, alternatively, by maximizing the joint probability density function of the random sample, or the likelihood function. As such it is called the maximum likelihood estimator of β.

The estimator $\hat{\sigma}^2$ of the population variance σ^2 is based on the least squares residuals $\hat{e}_i = Y_i - b$

$$\hat{\sigma}^2 = \sum_{i=1}^{T} \hat{e}_i^2 / (T-1) \qquad (3.8.4)$$

Use of the divisor $(T - 1)$ makes this estimator unbiased and

$$\frac{(T-1)\hat{\sigma}^2}{\sigma^2} \sim \chi^2_{(T-1)} \qquad (3.8.5)$$

Given the estimator $\hat{\sigma}^2$, we may estimate the variance of b as

$$\hat{\mathrm{var}}(b) = \hat{\sigma}^2 / T \qquad (3.8.6)$$

The properties of the estimation rules b and $\hat{\sigma}^2$ summarized in the previous paragraph were derived under the assumption that the statistical model 3.8.1 was correct. One might ask: What are the properties of b and $\hat{\sigma}^2$ if the statistical model 3.8.1 is *not* correct? The correct response is "something else," which may be undesirable. In particular the least squares estimator b may not be best, or unbiased, or have the distribution $N(\beta, \sigma^2/T)$; and the estimator $\hat{\sigma}^2$ may not be unbiased nor be a multiple of a chi-square random variable.

Each time the model 3.8.1 is adopted, it is crucially important that the logic of the assumptions be examined in light of the problem at hand.

Let us reexamine the model 3.8.1 in the context of economic variables:

1. The model 3.8.1 implies $E[Y_i] = \beta$. That is, the mean or expected value of each random observation Y_i is identical and equal to the constant parameter β. Equivalently, this implies that the random errors $e_i = Y_i - \beta$ have expectation zero. Recall that e_i represents all factors explaining why Y_i differs from its mean. In the context of the model 3.8.1 this assumption means that there are *no* significant factors that cause systematic variation in $E[Y_i]$. If there are impor-

tant factors that "explain" variation in Y_i, then this assumption is incorrect. If $E[e_i] \neq 0$, then the least squares estimator b is not unbiased and does not have the distribution $N(\beta, \sigma^2/T)$.

2. The random errors e_i, and the observations Y_i, all have the same variance. This means that each observation, or experimental outcome, has the same amount of information, and uncertainty, about the mean of the population. If some observations had smaller variances than others, then they have a higher probability of falling near the population mean. The low variance observations, if any, should therefore be given more weight in the process of estimating the mean of the population. The assumption that the error variances are all equal implies that all observations should be treated "equally," as is done in the case of the least squares estimator. Furthermore, if $\text{var}(Y_i) = \text{var}(e_i) \neq \sigma^2$ for all observations then $\text{var}(b) \neq \sigma^2/T$.

3. The random variables Y_i and random errors e_i are assumed to have normal probability distributions. Since Y_i and e_i differ by only a constant β, this assumption implies that both random variables represent the sum of many independent factors, none of which is larger relative to the others. If there *are* dominant factors that "explain" Y_i, then Y_i and e_i are not likely to be normal. If Y_i and e_i are *not* normal, then the least squares estimator b does not have a normal distribution and $(T - 1)\hat{\sigma}^2/\sigma^2$ does not have a chi-square distribution.

4. Assumption 3.8.1c implies that there is no linear association between the random errors e_i or between the random outcomes Y_i. Thus by assumption, both $\text{cov}(e_i, e_j) = 0$ and $\text{cov}(Y_i, Y_j) = 0$. Also, since both errors and outcomes follow normal distributions, the assumption of zero covariance implies statistical Independence. Thus, knowledge of any value Y_i does not affect the probability density functions of the other random outcomes. If the zero covariance assumption is not met, this means that there is a linear association between the random variables. In this event the least squares estimator b of the population mean β is unbiased but not the best, most efficient estimation rule. Also, the estimator $\hat{\sigma}^2$ is not unbiased and does not have the assumed distribution.

These observations make the point that the estimation rules we have developed operate as expected only if the assumptions of the model are correct. Thus, it is extremely important to examine logically the model assumptions prior to analysis. Procedures for hypothesis testing and interval estimation discussed in the next chapter are valid only with a properly specified statistical model.

3.9 Exercises

3.1 Consider the variable U (unemployment) in Table 2.2. Assume that $U \sim N(\beta, \sigma^2)$ and that the observations satisfy the assumptions 3.7.4.
   (a) Sketch the sum of squares parabola S given in equation 3.3.1.
   (b) Obtain the least squares estimate b of β.
   (c) Calculate the sum of squared residuals $\Sigma_{i=1}^{T} \hat{e}_i^2$.
   (d) Calculate $\hat{\sigma}^2$.
   (e) What is your estimate of $\text{var}(b)$?

3.2 Substitute $b = \Sigma_{i=1}^{T} y_i / T$ into equation 3.3.3 for β, and show that $dS/d\beta = 0$. Why is this important?

3.3   Suppose $Y_1, \ldots, Y_T$ is a random sample of data from a $N(\beta, \sigma^2)$ population. An alternative to the least squares estimator of β is the "easy" estimator

$$b_E = \frac{Y_1 + Y_T}{2}$$

(a) Show that b_E is a linear estimator.
(b) Show that b_E is an unbiased estimator.
(c) Find the variance of b_E.

3.4   Let Y_1, Y_2, Y_3 be a random sample from a $N(\beta, \sigma^2)$ population. An alternative to the least squares estimator is the "weighted" estimator, which weights observations unequally,

$$b_W = \frac{1}{2}Y_1 + \frac{1}{3}Y_2 + \frac{1}{6}Y_3$$

(a) Show that b_W is a linear estimator.
(b) Show that b_W is an unbiased estimator.
(c) Find the variance of b_W.
(d) What is the variance of the least squares estimator b of β?
(e) Is b_W as good an estimator as b?
(f) If $\sigma^2 = 9$, calculate the probability that each estimator is within 1 unit (on either side) of β.

3.5   Given the linear statistical model of the mean in equation 3.8.1, show that the least squares residuals $\hat{e}_i = y_i - b$, where b is the least squares estimate of β, always sum to zero. That is, show that

$$\sum_{i=1}^{T} \hat{e}_i = \sum_{i=1}^{T} (y_i - b) = 0$$

3.6   This is a question about model misspecification. Suppose $Y_1, \ldots, Y_T$ is a random sample of observations on household food expenditure by households of size 3. Unlike the example in Section 3.2, suppose we do *not* limit ourselves to households with the same income. In this case it is easy to argue that the mean expenditure by any household $E[Y_i]$ is not the same constant for all households but also depends on household income (X_i). That is

$$E[Y_i] = \beta_1 + \beta_2 X_i$$

where β_1 is autonomous consumption of food and β_2 is the marginal propensity to consume food. Thus an appropriate statistical model (fully explored in Chapter 5) is

$$Y_i = E[Y_i] + e_i$$
$$= \beta_1 + \beta_2 X_i + e_i$$

where e_i now represents all factors explaining household food expenditures *except* household size (which we have held fixed) and income, which is now *in* the model.

Suppose we *erroneously* adopt the linear statistical model for the mean given in equation 3.8.1, which ignores the fact that $E[Y_i]$ is *not* constant for all observations.

(a) What is b an estimator of?

(b) Show that the least squares estimator b

$$b = \sum_{i=1}^{T} Y_i / T$$

is a *biased* estimator of autonomous food consumption, β_1.

(c) Find the variance of b.

3.7   Suppose Y_1, Y_2, Y_3 is a sample of observations from a $N(\beta, \sigma^2)$ population but that Y_1, Y_2, and Y_3 are *not* independent. In fact, suppose

$$\text{cov}(Y_1, Y_2) = \text{cov}(Y_2, Y_3) = \text{cov}(Y_1, Y_3) = .5\sigma^2$$

(a) Show that the least squares estimator $b = \sum_{i=1}^{T} Y_i / 3$ is an unbiased estimator of β.

(b) Find the variance of the least squares estimator. (*Hint:* It is *not* var$(b) = \sigma^2/T$).

(c) Does σ^2/T understate or overstate the actual variance?

3.8   Suppose Y_1, Y_2, Y_3 is a sample of observations, and each random outcome is independent of the others and has a normal distribution with mean β but var$(Y_i) \neq \sigma^2$. Suppose var$(Y_1) = \sigma^2$, var$(Y_2) = 4\sigma^2$, var$(Y_3) = 9\sigma^2$.

(a) Show that the least squares estimator $b = \sum_{i=1}^{3} y_i / 3$ is an unbiased estimator of β.

(b) Find the variance of the least squares estimator. (*Hint:* It is *not* var$(b) = \sigma^2/T$.)

(c) Consider the weighted estimator

$$b_W = \frac{36}{49} Y_1 + \frac{9}{49} Y_2 + \frac{4}{49} Y_3$$

Show that

(i) b_W is unbiased.

(ii) var$(b_W) <$ var(b)

3.9   In Section 3.4.3 the probability or sampling distribution of b is shown to be $N(\beta, \sigma^2/T)$ under the model assumptions 3.8.1. Suppose $\sigma^2 = 10$. Calculate the probability that the least squares estimator yields an estimate within $\beta \pm 1$ if the sample size is (*i*) $T = 5$, (*ii*) $T = 10$, (*iii*) $T = 20$, (*iv*) $T = 80$.

3.10 The statistical model 3.8.1 ensures that the probability or sampling distribution of the least squares estimator b is $N(\beta, \sigma^2/T)$. This result allows us to make probability calculations as in Exercise 3.9 and Section 3.4.3. However, what happens if the random outcomes $Y_i \sim (\beta, \sigma^2)$ but their distribution is not known? Clearly, the distribution of b is not known, and probability statements cannot be made in the usual way. However, the Central Limit Theorem of Section 2.8.2a *can* be used to make probability statements if the sample size T is sufficiently large. The Central Limit Theorem says that if $Y_1,..., Y_T$ are independent and identically distributed with mean β and variance σ^2 then

$$Z = \frac{b - \beta}{\sigma / \sqrt{T}}$$

has a distribution that *approaches* $N(0, 1)$ as the sample size $T \to \infty$. That is, the distribution of b approaches $N(\beta, \sigma^2/T)$ as $T \to \infty$.

In this exercise you will carry out a Monte Carlo experiment that illustrates the Central Limit Theorem. To generate the y_i values, let $\beta = 5$ and let the random errors e_i follow a *uniform* distribution with mean 0 and variance $\sigma^2 = 2$. Specifically, the probability density function of the random disturbance will be

$$f(e) = \begin{cases} \dfrac{1}{2\sqrt{6}} & -\sqrt{6} \le e \le \sqrt{6} \\ 0 & \text{otherwise} \end{cases}$$

The computer manuals that accompany this book will show you how to generate 500 samples of the e_is with $T = 5$ observations each. By adding 5 to each of these values, 500 samples of size 5 from a uniformly distributed population with mean 5 and variance 2 are generated.

(a) Estimate β using the least squares estimator b for all 500 samples. If b_i is the least squares estimate for the ith sample, compute

$$\bar{b} = \sum_{i=1}^{500} b_i / 500$$

Compare $\bar{b}$ to $E[b] = \beta$.

(b) Calculate the sampling variability of the least squares estimator as

$$s^2 = \sum_{i=1}^{500} \left(b_i - \bar{b}\right)^2 \Big/ (500 - 1)$$

Compare s^2 to $\text{var}(b) = \sigma^2/T$.

(c) Estimate σ^2 using $\hat{\sigma}^2$ for each sample. If $\hat{\sigma}_i$ is the estimate from the ith sample, calculate

$$\bar{\hat{\sigma}}^2 = \sum_{i=1}^{500} \hat{\sigma}_i^2 / 500$$

Compare $\bar{\hat{\sigma}}^2$ to $E[\hat{\sigma}^2] = \sigma^2$.

(d) For each of the 500 samples construct the standardized variables

$$z_i = \frac{b_i - \beta}{\sigma/\sqrt{T}}$$

where you use the true values $\beta = 5$ and $\sigma = \sqrt{2}$. Construct a percentage histogram for the 500 values of z_i and compute the percentages that fall in the intervals $[-4, -3]$, $[-3, -2]$, $[-2, -1]$, $[-1, -0]$ and the same intervals on the positive side. Compare these frequencies to the probabilities for a $N(0, 1)$ random variable falling in those same intervals.

(e) Repeat (a)–(d) using sample sizes of $T = 10$ and $T = 20$.

(f) What do you conclude about how well the Central Limit Theorem works in this case?

3.11 Repeat Exercise 3.10 (a)–(e) using *normal* random errors, that is $e_i \sim N(0, \sigma^2 = 2)$. Compare and contrast your results to those in Exercise 3.10.

3.12 In Section 3.8 the assumptions of the linear statistical model 3.8.1 were critiqued in the context of economic data. Reexamine the examples used in the chapter in light of that discussion.
  (a) In the household food expenditure example begun in Section 3.2, discuss each of the model assumptions and concerns you may have about their correctness.
  (b) Examine the rational expectations model in Section 3.7.1 and discuss each of the model assumptions.
  (c) Discuss the assumption of the linear statistical model for the mean of the weekly sales of tuna in Section 3.7.2. Plot the least squares residuals $\hat{e}_i$ against the week. Do these residuals appear uncorrelated? Why might weekly tuna sales be correlated over time?

3.13 If $\ln Y \sim N(\beta, \sigma^2)$, or $\ln Y_i = \beta + e_i$, $e_i \sim N(0, \sigma^2)$, it is natural to estimate β by $b = \Sigma_{i=1}^{T} \ln y_i / T$. But what then do we use to estimate the mean of Y? It can be shown that

$$E[Y] = e^{\beta} e^{\sigma^2/2}$$

Thus an estimator of $E[Y]$ is

$$\hat{E}[Y] = e^{b} e^{\hat{\sigma}^2/2}$$

Use this rule to estimate the mean of Y for the weekly tuna sales data discussed in Section 7.2.

3.14 In Exercise 2.20, Table 2.5 contains data on $T = 32$ nuclear power plants constructed in the United States. Assume that the reactor cost C can be represented by the statistical model 3.8.1.
  (a) Obtain estimates of β and σ^2 using the data on C in Table 2.5.
  (b) What is the *estimate* of var(b)?
  (c) Discuss the appropriateness of the assumptions in equation 3.8.1 for modeling these data.

3.15 In Exercise 2.21, Table 2.6 contains data on excess security returns for two firms and a market portfolio. Assume that the data on each of these variables is generated by a statistical model *like* equation 3.8.1. Each variable may, however, have a different mean and variance.
  (a) Obtain estimates of the mean and variance of each of the variables in Table 2.6.
  (b) Discuss the appropriateness of the assumptions 3.8.1 for these types of variables.

3.10 References

The material in this chapter may be supplemented by consulting the following works.

JUDGE, G. G., R. C. HILL, W. E. GRIFFITHS, H. LÜTKEPOHL, and T. C. LEE (1988) *Introduction to the Theory and Practice of Econometrics*, 2nd Edition, New York: John Wiley & Sons, Inc., Chapter 3.

KMENTA, J. (1986) *Elements of Econometrics*, 2nd Edition, New York: MacMillan Publishing Co., Chapters 1–4.

BEALS, R. (1972) *Statistics for Economists: An Introduction*, Chicago: Rand McNally & Co., Chapters 6 and 7.

Elements of matrix algebra and calculus are reviewed in the following text.

BRENNAN, M. J. and T. M. CARROLL (1987) *Preface to Quantitative Economics and Econometrics*, 4th Edition, Cincinnati, OH: South-Western Publishing Co., Chapters 1–10.

APPENDIX 3A   The Derivative: Geometry and Interpretation

3A.1   The First Derivative of a Function

The slope m of a straight line is the ratio of the change in vertical distance (rise) to the change in horizontal distance (run) as a point moves along the line in either direction, as illustrated in Figure 3A.1.

Algebraically the slope is defined

$$m = \frac{y_2 - y_1}{x_2 - x_1} = \frac{\Delta y}{\Delta x} \tag{3A.1}$$

The slope of a straight line is *constant*; the rate at which y changes as x changes is constant over the length of the line.

However, for curves, graphs of functions $y = f(x)$, other than straight lines, the slope is *not* constant and must be determined at each point.

Suppose that (x_1, y_1) and (x_2, y_2) are two points on the curve $y = f(x)$. See Figure 3A.2. The slope of the line segment (called a secant) joining (x_1, y_1) and (x_2, y_2) is given by equation 3A.1. Suppose that the point (x_1, y_1) remains fixed and we slide the point (x_2, y_2) *along the curve* $f(x)$ toward (x_1, y_1). The slope of the line segment will vary from point to point. However, for most smooth curves, as (x_2, y_2) moves closer and closer to the point (x_1, y_1), the slope of the secant will change less and less and will approach a constant limiting value. When this occurs, this limiting value is said to be the *slope of the tangent* to the curve at (x_1, y_1), or the *slope of the curve* $f(x)$ at (x_1, y_1). The slope of the curve $f(x)$ is the *first derivative* of the function $f(x)$, with respect to x, at the point (x_1, y_1). The first derivative is defined as

$$\frac{dy}{dx} = \lim_{\Delta x \to 0} \frac{\Delta y}{\Delta x} \tag{3A.2}$$

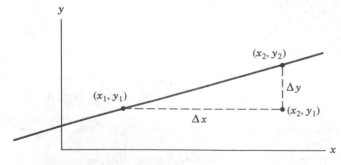

Figure 3A.1 The slope of a straight line.

$y = f(x)$

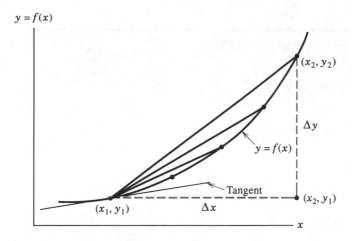

Figure 3A.2 The slope of a curve.

The notation dy/dx is the first derivative, or the derivative, of $y = f(x)$.

To actually calculate a derivative using the definition 3A.2 it is customary to let the stationary point be $(x_1, y_1) = (x, y)$ and the moving point $(x_2, y_2) = (x + \Delta x, y + \Delta y)$. Then the first derivative of $f(x)$ at (x, y) is

$$\frac{dy}{dx} = \lim_{\Delta x \to 0} \frac{\Delta y}{\Delta x} = \lim_{\Delta x \to 0} \frac{y_2 - y_1}{\Delta x}$$
$$= \lim_{\Delta x \to 0} \frac{f(x + \Delta x) - f(x)}{\Delta x}$$

(3A.3)

The derivative dy/dx will, in general, be a function of x, which must be evaluated at specific points in order to obtain the slope of the function at those points. Consider the following two examples.

Example 3A.1

Find the first derivative of $y = f(x) = 4x + 1$.

$$\frac{dy}{dx} = \lim_{\Delta x \to 0} \frac{f(x + \Delta x) - f(x)}{\Delta x} = \lim_{\Delta x \to 0} \frac{4(x + \Delta x) + 1 - (4x + 1)}{\Delta x}$$
$$= \lim_{\Delta x \to 0} \frac{4\Delta x}{\Delta x}$$
$$= \lim_{\Delta x \to 0} 4 = 4$$

The slope of the straight line $y = 4x + 1$ is $dy/dx = 4$. The rate of change of the function is constant since it is a straight line. For each 1 unit increase in x the value of y increases by 4 units.

Example 3A.2

Find the first derivative of $y = x^2 - 8x + 16$.

$$\frac{dy}{dx} = \lim_{\Delta x \to 0} \frac{f(x + \Delta x) - f(x)}{\Delta x}$$

$$= \lim_{\Delta x \to 0} \frac{\left[(x + \Delta x)^2 - 8(x + \Delta x) + 16 - \left(x^2 - 8x + 16\right)\right]}{\Delta x}$$

$$= \lim_{\Delta x \to 0} \frac{\left[x^2 + 2x(\Delta x) + (\Delta x)^2 - 8x - 8\Delta x + 16 - x^2 + 8x - 16\right]}{\Delta x}$$

$$= \lim_{\Delta x \to 0} \frac{2x(\Delta x) + (\Delta x)^2 - 8\Delta x}{\Delta x}$$

$$= \lim_{\Delta x \to 0} 2x + \Delta x - 8$$

$$= 2x - 8$$

The first derivative of the function $y = f(x) = x^2 - 8x + 16$ is $dy/dx = 2x - 8$. Note that the derivative is a function of x and that the derivative is different at every value of x, as illustrated in Table 3A.1. The curve is graphed in Figure 3A.3. ∎

From Table 3A.1 we see that the slope of the function is negative for $x < 4$, the slope is zero at $x = 4$, and the slope is positive for $x > 4$. To interpret these facts, recall that the derivative of a function at a point is the slope of the tangent *at that point*. The slope of the tangent is the rate of change of the function, how much $y = f(x)$ is changing as x changes. Thus at $x = 0$, the derivative -16 indicates that y is *falling* as x increases and that the *rate* of change is 16 units in y per unit in x. At $x = 2$ the rate of change of the function is diminished, and at $x = 4$ the rate of change of the function is $dy/dx = 0$. At $x = 4$ the slope of the tangent is zero. For values of $x > 4$ the derivative is positive, which indicates that the function $f(x)$ is increasing in x. As x increases the rate of change of the function increases without bound.

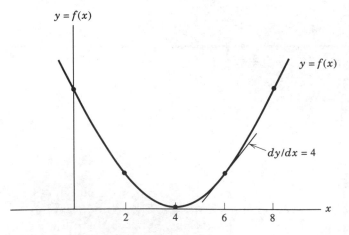

Figure 3A.3 The function $y = x^2 - 8x + 16$.

Table 3A.1 The derivative of
$y = f(x) = x^2 - 8x + 16$

x	$y = f(x)$	dy/dx
0	16	-8
2	4	-4
4	0	0
6	4	4
8	16	8

3A.2   Rules for Calculating Derivatives

Clearly it would *not* be fun to calculate the derivative using the limit definition every time a different function was considered. Luckily, for general functions there are some rules that can be used to calculate the derivative.

1. The derivative of a constant is zero. If $y = f(x) = c$ where c is a constant,

$$\frac{dy}{dx} = 0$$

2. If $y = x^n$

$$\frac{dy}{dx} = nx^{n-1}$$

3. If c is a constant and $u = f(x)$ is a function of x and $y = cu$, then

$$\frac{dy}{dx} = c\frac{du}{dx}$$

    (That is, constants can be factored out of functions prior to calculating the derivative.)

4. If c is a constant and $y = cx^n$

$$\frac{dy}{dx} = cnx^{n-1} \qquad \text{(using rule 3)}$$

5. If $y = u + v$ where $u = f(x)$ and $v = g(x)$ are functions of x, then

$$\frac{dy}{dx} = \frac{du}{dx} + \frac{dv}{dx}$$

    (The derivative of a sum of functions is the sum of the derivatives. This rule extends to more than two terms in a sum.)

6. If $y = uv$, where $u = f(x)$ and $v = g(x)$ are functions of x, then

$$\frac{dy}{dx} = u\frac{dv}{dx} + v\frac{du}{dx}$$

Example 3A.3

Using these rules, calculate the derivative of the function in Example 3A.2

$$y = x^2 - 8x + 16$$

$$\frac{dy}{dx} = \frac{d(x^2 - 8x + 16)}{dx}$$

$$= \frac{d(x^2)}{dx} - 8\frac{d(x^1)}{dx} + \frac{d(16)}{dx}$$

$$= 2x^1 - 8x^0 + 0$$

$$= 2x - 8$$

∎

3A.3   Second Derivatives

Since the derivative dy/dx of $y = f(x)$ is a function of x itself, we can define the derivative of the first derivative of $f(x)$, or *second derivative* of $f(x)$, as

$$\frac{d^2 y}{dx^2} = \frac{d[dy/dx]}{dx} \tag{3A.4}$$

The second derivative of a function is interpreted as the rate of change of the first derivative and indicates whether the function in increasing or decreasing at an increasing, constant, or decreasing rate.

Example 3A.4

Find the second derivative of $y = 4x + 1$. Using the rules of differentiation

$$dy/dx = \frac{d(4x+1)}{dx} = \frac{d(4x)}{dx} + \frac{d(1)}{dx} = 4$$

and

$$\frac{d^2 y}{dx^2} = \frac{d[dy/dx]}{dx} = \frac{d(4)}{dx} = 0$$

The function $y = f(x)$ is a straight line, thus its first derivative is constant. Thus, the rate of change of the first derivative is zero, and the function increases at a constant rate.

∎

Example 3A.5

Find the second derivative of $y = x^2 - 8x + 16$.

$$\frac{dy}{dx} = \frac{d\left(x^2 - 8x + 16\right)}{dx} = 2x - 8$$

$$\frac{d^2 y}{dx^2} = \frac{d[2x - 8]}{dx} = 2$$

The second derivative of $y = f(x)$ is *positive*, which indicates that the first derivative is increasing. (See Example 3A.2.) Thus for $x < 4$, the function decreases at a decreasing rate; at $x > 4$ the function increases at an increasing rate. ∎

3A.4   Maxima and Minima

Using first and second derivatives we can define relative, or local, maxima and minima of functions. The function $y = f(x)$ has a relative or local maximum at $x = a$ if $f(a)$ is greater than any other value of $f(x)$ in an interval around $x = a$; the function $y = f(x)$ has a relative or local minimum at $x = a$ if $f(a)$ is smaller than any other value of $f(x)$ in an interval around $x = a$. We may summarize the conditions for a local maximum or minimum of a function $y = f(x)$ at $x = a$ as follows:

If $y = f(x)$ and dy/dx are nice (continuous) functions at $x = a$, and if $dy/dx = 0$ at $x = a$, then

1. If $d^2y/dx^2 < 0$ at $x = a$, then $f(a)$ is a local maximum.
2. If $d^2y/dx^2 > 0$ at $x = a$, then $f(a)$ is a local minimum.

Example 3A.6

Find the local maxima or minima of the function $y = x^2 - 8x + 16$. (See Examples 3A.2 and 3A.5.) Local maxima or minima occur where the first derivative is zero; therefore obtain the first derivative, set it to zero, and solve for values of x where $dy/dx = 0$.

$$\frac{dy}{dx} = 2x - 8$$

$$\frac{dy}{dx} = 0 \Rightarrow 2x - 8 = 0 \Rightarrow x = 4$$

Thus, at $x = 4$ the slope of the function is zero, and we may have a local maximum or minimum.

$$\frac{d^2 y}{dx^2} = 2 > 0$$

Since $d^2y/dx^2 > 0$ the function is increasing at an increasing rate at $x = 4$ (and everywhere else) and thus $f(4) = 0$ is a *local minimum* of $y = f(x)$. ∎

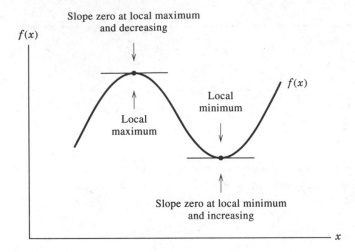

Figure 3A.4 Local maxima and minima.

Two notes regarding this example: First, $y = f(x)$ achieves its global or absolute minimum at $x = 4$ as well as its local minimum. Second, if $dy/dx = 0$ at a point $x = a$ where $d^2y/dx^2 = 0$, then the "test" for local maxima and minima using first and second derivatives does not apply.

APPENDIX 3B   Representing the Sampling Process Using a New Notation

In this appendix we develop a concise notation for the linear statistical model introduced in this chapter. Let us summarize the statistical model and its assumptions. The statistical model is

$$Y_i = \beta + e_i, \qquad i = 1,\ldots,T \tag{3B.1}$$

where Y_i is the weekly expenditure on food by a yet-to-be and randomly chosen sample household of size 3 and with income \$25,000. The parameter β is the population mean or average expenditure. The random error e_i accounts for all the factors that cause the ith household's expenditure to differ from the population mean β. We have assumed that the random errors e_i are independent and identically distributed normal random variables with mean zero and variance σ^2. Since the errors are independent, the covariance between every pair of errors, e_i and e_j, is zero. Thus, the random variables Y_i are independent and identically distributed normal random variables with mean β, variance σ^2, and the covariances between them are zero. Based on a sample of data, we wish to make inferences about the unknown population parameters β and σ^2. Thus, in addition to equation 3B.1 the statistical model also contains the information

$$e_i \sim N\left(0, \sigma^2\right) \tag{3B.2}$$

$$Y_i \sim N\left(\beta, \sigma^2\right) \tag{3B.3}$$

3B.1   Model Specification Using Vectors

To represent a sample of observations in a concise way, we develop notation in this section that uses vector and matrix algebra. Since the use of matrix algebra may be new to you, we will develop these ideas slowly. An investment now in matrix algebra will pay large dividends to you in this course and possibly many others.

Equations 3B.1–3B.3 represent a statistical model for a sample of data. Equation 3B.1 can be written as the T equations

$$Y_1 = \beta + e_1$$
$$Y_2 = \beta + e_2$$
$$\vdots$$
$$Y_T = \beta + e_T$$
$$(3B.4)$$

To simplify the writing of these equations we stack all the Y_is into a column called **Y**.

$$\mathbf{Y} = \begin{bmatrix} Y_1 \\ Y_2 \\ \vdots \\ Y_T \end{bmatrix} \qquad (3B.5)$$

Y is a *column vector* whose elements are the random variables Y_i. It has T rows and is said to have dimension "T by 1," which is written $(T \times 1)$. Now take all the elements on the right-hand side of equation 3B.4 and stack them into a $(T \times 1)$ column vector.

$$\begin{bmatrix} \beta + e_1 \\ \beta + e_2 \\ \vdots \\ \beta + e_T \end{bmatrix} \qquad (3B.6)$$

The column vector in equation 3B.6 can be neatly expressed by defining two new $(T \times 1)$ column vectors **x** and **e** as

$$\mathbf{x} = \begin{bmatrix} 1 \\ 1 \\ \vdots \\ 1 \end{bmatrix}_{(T\times1)} \qquad \mathbf{e} = \begin{bmatrix} e_1 \\ e_2 \\ \vdots \\ e_T \end{bmatrix}_{(T\times1)} \qquad (3B.7)$$

The column vector **x** is a $(T \times 1)$ vector of ones and **e** is a $(T \times 1)$ vector containing the random disturbances e_i. With these definitions we can write expression 3B.4 as

$$\begin{bmatrix} Y_1 \\ Y_2 \\ \vdots \\ Y_T \end{bmatrix} = \begin{bmatrix} 1 \\ 1 \\ \vdots \\ 1 \end{bmatrix} \beta + \begin{bmatrix} e_1 \\ e_2 \\ \vdots \\ e_T \end{bmatrix} \qquad (3B.8)$$

or

$$\mathbf{Y} = \mathbf{x}\beta + \mathbf{e} \qquad\qquad (3B.9)$$

To explain why equation 3B.9 represents equation 3B.4, we must define what is meant by vector equality, vector addition, and scalar multiplication of a vector.

3B.2 Rules for Vector Addition and Scalar Multiplication

Two vectors are equal if they have the same number of rows, or same dimensions, and are equal element by element. For example, the two (3×1) column vectors $\mathbf{v}$ and $\mathbf{w}$

$$\mathbf{v} = \begin{bmatrix} v_1 \\ v_2 \\ v_3 \end{bmatrix} \qquad \mathbf{w} = \begin{bmatrix} w_1 \\ w_2 \\ w_3 \end{bmatrix}$$

are equal if and only if $v_1 = w_1$, $v_2 = w_2$, and $v_3 = w_3$. If $\mathbf{v}$ and $\mathbf{w}$ are equal we can write $\mathbf{v} = \mathbf{w}$.

To add two column vectors, $\mathbf{v}$ and $\mathbf{w}$, they must have the same dimensions, or number of rows. Their sum is a new column vector $\mathbf{c}$, whose elements are the sum of the corresponding elements of $\mathbf{v}$ and $\mathbf{w}$. For example, if

$$\mathbf{v} = \begin{bmatrix} 2 \\ -1 \\ 3 \end{bmatrix} \qquad \mathbf{w} = \begin{bmatrix} 8 \\ 9 \\ 5 \end{bmatrix}$$

then

$$\mathbf{c} = \mathbf{v} + \mathbf{w} = \begin{bmatrix} 10 \\ 8 \\ 8 \end{bmatrix}$$

The usual laws of addition hold for vectors, so that if $\mathbf{v}$, $\mathbf{w}$, and $\mathbf{c}$ are vectors of the same dimension, then

$$\mathbf{v} + \mathbf{w} = \mathbf{w} + \mathbf{v}$$
$$(\mathbf{v} + \mathbf{w}) + \mathbf{c} = \mathbf{v} + (\mathbf{w} + \mathbf{c})$$

If a is a number, or *scalar*, and $\mathbf{v}$ is a column vector, then the product of a times $\mathbf{v}$ is called a *scalar multiplication*. The product is a new column vector that is a times each element of $\mathbf{v}$. For example, if $a = 2$ and $\mathbf{v}$ is as given above, then

$$\mathbf{c} = a\mathbf{v} = \mathbf{v}a = 2\begin{bmatrix} 2 \\ -1 \\ 3 \end{bmatrix} = \begin{bmatrix} 4 \\ -2 \\ 6 \end{bmatrix}$$

3B.3 Model Specification Using Vectors (Continued)

Now examine equation 3B.9. Using the definition of scalar multiplication we see that

$$\mathbf{x}\beta = \begin{bmatrix} 1 \\ 1 \\ \vdots \\ 1 \end{bmatrix}\beta = \begin{bmatrix} \beta \\ \beta \\ \vdots \\ \beta \end{bmatrix}$$

Then

$$\mathbf{x}\beta + \mathbf{e} = \begin{bmatrix} \beta \\ \beta \\ \vdots \\ \beta \end{bmatrix} + \begin{bmatrix} e_1 \\ e_2 \\ \vdots \\ e_T \end{bmatrix} = \begin{bmatrix} \beta + e_1 \\ \beta + e_2 \\ \vdots \\ \beta + e_T \end{bmatrix}$$

which is the same as equation 3B.6. Then, the equality in equation 3B.9 means that

$$\begin{bmatrix} Y_1 \\ Y_2 \\ \vdots \\ Y_T \end{bmatrix} = \begin{bmatrix} \beta + e_1 \\ \beta + e_2 \\ \vdots \\ \beta + e_T \end{bmatrix}$$

or

$$Y_i = \beta + e_i, \qquad i = 1,\ldots,T$$

Equation 3B.9 is a *linear statistical model for the mean of a population*. In this formulation we want to make inferences about the unknown parameter β, which is the mean of the population.

3B.4 The Expectation of a Vector

Using vector notation we can write the model assumptions in an equally concise form. We will adopt the convention that the mathematical expectation of a vector is simply the vector of expected values of all its elements. Then

$$E[\mathbf{Y}] = \begin{bmatrix} E(Y_1) \\ E(Y_2) \\ \vdots \\ E(Y_T) \end{bmatrix} = E\begin{bmatrix} \beta + e_1 \\ \beta + e_2 \\ \vdots \\ \beta + e_T \end{bmatrix} = \begin{bmatrix} \beta \\ \beta \\ \vdots \\ \beta \end{bmatrix} = \begin{bmatrix} 1 \\ 1 \\ \vdots \\ 1 \end{bmatrix}\beta = \mathbf{x}\beta \qquad (3B.10)$$

since $E[\beta] = \beta$, because β is a constant, and

$$E[\mathbf{e}] = \begin{bmatrix} E(e_1) \\ E(e_2) \\ \vdots \\ E(e_T) \end{bmatrix} = \begin{bmatrix} 0 \\ 0 \\ \vdots \\ 0 \end{bmatrix} = \mathbf{0} \tag{3B.11}$$

where $\mathbf{0}$ is a $(T \times 1)$ column vector of zeros. Equation 3B.11, $E[\mathbf{e}] = \mathbf{0}$, embodies the assumption that $E[e_i] = 0$, $i = 1,\ldots,T$. Thus for the statistical model $\mathbf{Y} = \mathbf{x}\beta + \mathbf{e}$, where $E[\mathbf{e}] = \mathbf{0}$, it follows that $E[\mathbf{Y}] = \mathbf{x}\beta$. That is, the mean or expected value of the random vector $\mathbf{Y}$ is $\mathbf{x}\beta$.

To more completely define the statistical model $\mathbf{Y} = \mathbf{x}\beta + \mathbf{e}$, recall that the variance of the random error e_i is

$$\operatorname{var}(e_i) = E\big[e_i - E(e_i)\big]^2 = E\big[e_i^2\big] = \sigma^2$$

Also, the covariance between e_i and e_j is

$$\begin{aligned} \operatorname{cov}(e_i \ e_j) &= E\big[e_i - E(e_i)\big]\big[e_j - E(e_j)\big] \\ &= E\big[e_i e_j\big] \\ &= E\big[e_i\big]E\big[e_j\big] = 0 \end{aligned}$$

The last step follows since we have assumed that the random errors are independent. The mathematical expectation of the product of two random variables is the product of their expectations *only* if the random variables are statistically independent. To provide you with a compact, shorthand way of expressing the variances and covariances of the random vector $\mathbf{e}$, we take time now to introduce some basic matrix definitions and operations.

3B.5 Matrix Definitions: Equality, Sums, Scalar Multiplication, Transpose, and Multiplication

To represent these variance and covariance assumptions in matrix and vector notation, we need the following definitions:

Definition: A *matrix* is a rectangular array of elements arranged in rows and columns as in

$$A = \begin{bmatrix} a_{11} & a_{12} & \cdots & a_{1n} \\ a_{21} & a_{22} & & a_{2n} \\ \vdots & & \ddots & \\ a_{m1} & a_{m2} & \cdots & a_{mn} \end{bmatrix}$$

The matrix A has m rows and n columns and is said to be of order or dimension "m by n," which is written $(m \times n)$. The element in the ith row and jth column is denoted a_{ij}. A matrix that has a single column is a *column vector*, whereas a matrix with a single row is a *row vector*.

Matrix definitions of equality, addition, and scalar multiplication are similar to the vector definitions and we state them for completeness.

Definition: Two matrices, A and B, are equal if they are of the same dimensions and equal element by element.

Definition: The *sum* of two matrices A and B requires that A and B have the same dimensions and is defined to be a new matrix whose elements are the sum of corresponding elements of A and B. Thus $C = A + B$ implies that $c_{ij} = a_{ij} + b_{ij}$ for all i and j. For example, if

$$A = \begin{bmatrix} 2 & 3 \\ -1 & 7 \end{bmatrix}, \quad B = \begin{bmatrix} 8 & 1 \\ 9 & 6 \end{bmatrix}$$

then

$$C = A + B = \begin{bmatrix} 10 & 4 \\ 8 & 13 \end{bmatrix}$$

It is also true that $A + B = B + A$ and $(A + B) + C = A + (B + C)$.

Definition: If λ is a number (or a *scalar*), and A is a matrix, then the product of λ times A is called a scalar multiplication. The product is a new matrix that is λ times each element of A. That is, if $B = \lambda A = A\lambda$, then $b_{ij} = \lambda a_{ij}$ for all i and j. For example, if A is the matrix given above and $\lambda = 2$, then

$$C = \lambda A = A\lambda = 2\begin{bmatrix} 2 & 3 \\ -1 & 7 \end{bmatrix} = \begin{bmatrix} 4 & 6 \\ -2 & 14 \end{bmatrix}$$

Definition: The *transpose* of a matrix or vector is formed by interchanging the rows and columns. The transpose of an $(m \times n)$ matrix is $(n \times m)$. That is, if

$$A = \begin{bmatrix} a_{11} & a_{12} & a_{13} \\ a_{21} & a_{22} & a_{23} \end{bmatrix}$$

then the transpose of A is denoted A' and is

$$A' = \begin{bmatrix} a_{11} & a_{21} \\ a_{12} & a_{22} \\ a_{13} & a_{23} \end{bmatrix}$$

Some useful properties of transposes are $(A')' = A$ and $(A + B)' = A' + B'$.

Definition: If A is of order $(m \times n)$ and B is of order $(n \times p)$, then the *product AB* is an $(m \times p)$ matrix whose ijth element is formed by multiplying corresponding elements in the ith *row* of A and jth *column* of B, and summing the resulting products. To illustrate, let A and B be

$$A = \begin{bmatrix} a_{11} & a_{12} & a_{13} \\ a_{21} & a_{22} & a_{23} \end{bmatrix}_{(2 \times 3)}, \quad B = \begin{bmatrix} b_{11} & b_{12} \\ b_{21} & b_{22} \\ b_{31} & b_{32} \end{bmatrix}_{(3 \times 2)}$$

Their product C will be a (2×2) matrix

$$AB = C = \begin{bmatrix} c_{11} & c_{12} \\ c_{21} & c_{22} \end{bmatrix}$$

The element c_{11} is formed by taking the *first row* of A and the *first column* of B to obtain

$$c_{11} = a_{11}b_{11} + a_{12}b_{21} + a_{13}b_{31}$$

The element c_{21} is formed by taking the *second row* of A and the *first column* of B to obtain

$$c_{21} = a_{21}b_{11} + a_{22}b_{21} + a_{23}b_{31}$$

In general

$$c_{ij} = \sum_{k=1}^{n} a_{ik}b_{kj}$$

In order for matrix multiplication to be possible the number of *columns* of the first matrix (n) must be equal to the number of *rows* in the second matrix. Such matrices are said to be *conformable* for multiplication.

To illustrate matrix multiplication, let

$$A = \begin{bmatrix} 2 & 3 & -1 \\ -1 & 7 & 0 \end{bmatrix}, \qquad B = \begin{bmatrix} 6 & 1 \\ -2 & 9 \\ 3 & -4 \end{bmatrix}$$

Then

$$AB = \begin{bmatrix} (2)(6)+(3)(-2)+(-1)(3) & (2)(1)+(3)(9)+(-1)(-4) \\ (-1)(6)+(7)(-2)+(0)(3) & (-1)(1)+(7)(9)+(0)(-4) \end{bmatrix}$$

$$= \begin{bmatrix} 12-6-3 & 2+27+4 \\ -6-14+0 & -1+63+0 \end{bmatrix}$$

$$= \begin{bmatrix} 3 & 33 \\ -20 & 62 \end{bmatrix} = C$$

Matrix multiplication is unlike algebraic multiplication since, in general, $AB \neq BA$. See Exercise B3.2. But it is true that $A(BC) = (AB)C$ and $A(B + C) = AB + AC$. Also $(AB)' = B'A'$, $(ABC)' = C'B'A'$, etc.

3B.6 Model Assumptions Using Vectors and Matrices

We have specified the linear statistical model for the mean of a population as

$$\mathbf{Y} = \mathbf{x}\beta + \mathbf{e}$$

and assumed that the $(T \times 1)$ column vector of random disturbances $\mathbf{e}$ has mean

$$E[\mathbf{e}] = \mathbf{0}$$

Now we will use matrix notation to summarize our assumptions about the variances and covariances of the random errors.

Consider the matrix formed by multiplying the column vector $\mathbf{e}$ times its transpose, which is a row vector,

$$\mathbf{ee}' = \begin{bmatrix} e_1 \\ e_2 \\ \vdots \\ e_T \end{bmatrix}_{(T \times 1)} \begin{bmatrix} e_1 & e_2 & \cdots & e_T \end{bmatrix}_{(1 \times T)}$$

$$= \begin{bmatrix} e_1^2 & e_1 e_2 & \cdots & e_1 e_T \\ e_2 e_1 & e_2^2 & & e_2 e_T \\ \vdots & & \ddots & \vdots \\ e_T e_1 & e_T e_2 & \cdots & e_T^2 \end{bmatrix}_{(T \times T)}$$

It is a mathematical convention that the expected value of a matrix is the matrix of expected values of its elements. Thus, we take the mathematical expectation of the $(T \times T)$ matrix $\mathbf{ee}'$ by taking the expected value of each element to obtain

$$E[\mathbf{ee}'] = \begin{bmatrix} E(e_1^2) & E(e_1 e_2) & \cdots & E(e_1 e_T) \\ E(e_2 e_1) & E(e_2^2) & & E(e_2 e_T) \\ \vdots & & \ddots & \vdots \\ E(e_T e_1) & E(e_T e_2) & \cdots & E(e_T^2) \end{bmatrix}$$

$$= \begin{bmatrix} \mathrm{var}(e_1) & \mathrm{cov}(e_1, e_2) & \cdots & \mathrm{cov}(e_1, e_T) \\ \mathrm{cov}(e_2, e_1) & \mathrm{var}(e_2) & & \mathrm{cov}(e_2, e_T) \\ \vdots & & \ddots & \vdots \\ \mathrm{cov}(e_T, e_1) & \mathrm{cov}(e_T, e_2) & \cdots & \mathrm{var}(e_T) \end{bmatrix} \tag{3B.12}$$

$$= \begin{bmatrix} \sigma^2 & 0 & \cdots & 0 \\ 0 & \sigma^2 & & 0 \\ \vdots & & \ddots & \vdots \\ 0 & 0 & \cdots & \sigma^2 \end{bmatrix}_{T \times T}$$

The terms σ^2 on the diagonal of this square matrix are the variances of the random errors. The zeros in the remaining spaces are the covariances between the random errors. The matrix 3B.12 is called the "variance–covariance" matrix of the random vector $\mathbf{e}$ (or just the "covariance" matrix for short) and denoted $\mathrm{cov}(\mathbf{e})$.

Equation 3B.12 can be simplified by using the definition of scalar multiplication and factoring the constant σ^2 out to obtain

$$\mathrm{cov}(\mathbf{e}) = E[\mathbf{ee}'] = \sigma^2 \begin{bmatrix} 1 & 0 & 0 & \cdots & 0 \\ 0 & 1 & 0 & \cdots & 0 \\ 0 & 0 & 1 & \cdots & 0 \\ \vdots & \vdots & \vdots & \ddots & \vdots \\ 0 & 0 & 0 & \cdots & 1 \end{bmatrix} \tag{3B.13}$$

$$= \sigma^2 I_T$$

In the last expression in equation 3B.13 the symbol I_T denotes a $(T \times T)$ matrix with ones on the diagonal and zeros elsewhere, and is called a *Tth order identity matrix*. The matrix I_T is called the "identity" matrix since if A is any $(T \times T)$ matrix, multiplication of A by I_T is "identically" A. That is, $A = AI_T = I_T A$. Equation 3B.13 summarizes the assumptions that all the errors e_i have the same variance σ^2 and all covariances between errors are zero.

The final piece of information we must include is that the random errors e_i are normal random variables. For a single error we have signified this by writing $e_i \sim N(0, \sigma^2)$, where 0 is the mean and σ^2 the variance. We will follow the same convention for the $(T \times 1)$ vector of random variables $\mathbf{e}$ and write

$$\mathbf{e} \sim N\left(\mathbf{0}, \sigma^2 I_T\right)$$

which means that the $(T \times 1)$ vector of normal random errors $\mathbf{e}$ has expected or mean vector $\mathbf{0}$ [a $(T \times 1)$ vector of zeros], variance–covariance matrix $\text{cov}(\mathbf{e}) = \sigma^2 I_T$, and each of the random errors has a normal probability density function.

Consequently, we can compactly represent the linear statistical model for the mean expenditure on food from a normal population as

$$\mathbf{Y} = \mathbf{x}\beta + \mathbf{e} \qquad (3B.14a)$$

where the error assumptions of the model are

$$\mathbf{e} \sim N\left(\mathbf{0}, \sigma^2 I_T\right) \qquad (3B.14b)$$

The one remaining point is: What about the assumption that the random errors are independent? That assumption is actually implicit in equation 3B.14b. Normal random variables have the very special property that if the covariance between them is zero, *then* they are statistically independent. This is *not* true for other random variables.

We may summarize the meaning of equations 3B.14 as follows:

(i)   The $(T \times 1)$ observable random vector $\mathbf{Y}$ has mean $\mathbf{x}\beta$, since

(ii) the $(T \times 1)$ unobservable random error vector $\mathbf{e}$ has mean $\mathbf{0}$;

(iii) the variance of each individual random error e_i is σ^2;

(iv) the covariance between any pair of random errors e_i and e_j is 0;

(v)   the random errors e_i are independent normal random variables, with mean zero and variance σ^2, and

(vi) the random variables Y_i are independent normal random variables with mean β and variance σ^2.

The equations 3B.14 represent our statistical model and all its assumptions. It has been specified to explain how we visualize that the sample of values on household food expenditure will be obtained in the sampling process. In the next section we consider the problem of how to use a sample of data to estimate the unknown parameter β, the mean of the population from which the sample is drawn.

3B.7 The Least Squares Estimator of β in Vector Notation

To put the least squares estimator b of β in vector notation, refer to the vectors $\mathbf{x}$ in equation 3B.7 and $\mathbf{Y}$ in equation 3B.5 and write out $\mathbf{x}'\mathbf{x}$ and $\mathbf{x}'\mathbf{Y}$.

$$\mathbf{x}'\mathbf{x} = \begin{bmatrix} 1 & 1 & \cdots & 1 \end{bmatrix} \begin{bmatrix} 1 \\ 1 \\ \vdots \\ 1 \end{bmatrix} = 1 + 1 + \ldots + 1 = T$$

$$\mathbf{x}'\mathbf{Y} = \begin{bmatrix} 1 & 1 & \cdots & 1 \end{bmatrix} \begin{bmatrix} Y_1 \\ Y_2 \\ \vdots \\ Y_T \end{bmatrix} = Y_1 + Y_2 + \ldots + Y_T$$

$$= \sum_{i=1}^{T} Y_i$$

Consequently

$$b = \sum_{i=1}^{T} Y_i / T = \mathbf{x}'\mathbf{Y} / \mathbf{x}'\mathbf{x}$$

$$= \frac{1}{\mathbf{x}'\mathbf{x}} \cdot \mathbf{x}'\mathbf{Y} \tag{3B.15}$$

$$= \left(\mathbf{x}'\mathbf{x}\right)^{-1} \mathbf{x}'\mathbf{Y}$$

where $a^{-1} = 1/a$ is the reciprocal, or inverse, of a. This matrix representation of b may have no special appeal to you at this moment, but it will, and you will use this formula repeatedly in the remainder of this book.

We obtain the mean and variance of b as

$$E[b] = E\left[\left(\mathbf{x}'\mathbf{x}\right)^{-1} \mathbf{x}'\mathbf{Y}\right]$$

$$= \left(\mathbf{x}'\mathbf{x}\right)^{-1} \mathbf{x}' E[\mathbf{Y}] \text{ since } \mathbf{x} \text{ is not random } \left(\mathbf{x}'\mathbf{x}\right)^{-1} \mathbf{x}' \text{ is a constant}$$

$$= \left(\mathbf{x}'\mathbf{x}\right)^{-1} \mathbf{x}'\mathbf{x}\beta \quad \text{since } E[\mathbf{Y}] = \mathbf{x}\beta \tag{3B.16}$$

$$= \frac{1}{T} T\beta = \beta$$

and

$$\text{var}(b) = \sigma^2 / T = \sigma^2 \left(\mathbf{x}'\mathbf{x}\right)^{-1} \tag{3B.17}$$

3B.8   The Estimator of σ^2 in Vector Notation

The sum of squared errors S, given in equation 3.3.1, that served as a basis for least squares estimation can be written in vector notation as

$$S = \sum_{i=1}^{T} (Y_i - \beta)^2$$

$$= (\mathbf{Y} - \mathbf{x}\beta)' (\mathbf{Y} - \mathbf{x}\beta) \tag{3B.18}$$

The estimator $\hat{\sigma}^2$ of σ^2 is

$$\hat{\sigma}^2 = \frac{\sum_{i=1}^{T} \hat{e}_i^2}{T-1} = \frac{\sum_{i=1}^{T} (Y_i - b)^2}{T-1} \tag{3B.19}$$

using $\hat{e}_i = Y_i - b$. Consequently $\hat{\sigma}^2$ can be written, analogous to (3B.18),

$$\hat{\sigma}^2 = \frac{(\mathbf{Y} - \mathbf{x}b)'(\mathbf{Y} - \mathbf{x}b)}{T-1} \tag{3B.20}$$

3B.9   Matrix Exercises

B3.1. Let

$$\mathbf{a} = \begin{bmatrix} 9 \\ 7 \\ 3 \end{bmatrix} \qquad \mathbf{c} = \begin{bmatrix} -2 \\ 3 \\ 1 \end{bmatrix} \qquad \mathbf{x} = \begin{bmatrix} 1 \\ 1 \\ 1 \end{bmatrix} \qquad \mathbf{y} = \begin{bmatrix} 13 \\ 10 \\ 7 \end{bmatrix}$$

$$X = \begin{bmatrix} 1 & 2 \\ 1 & 3 \\ 1 & 5 \end{bmatrix} \qquad A = \begin{bmatrix} 1 & 3 & 9 \\ 3 & 1 & 7 \\ 9 & 7 & 1 \end{bmatrix} \qquad I = \begin{bmatrix} 1 & 0 & 0 \\ 0 & 1 & 0 \\ 0 & 0 & 1 \end{bmatrix}$$

Evaluate the following vector and matrix expressions:
(a) (*i*) $\mathbf{a} + \mathbf{c}$; (*ii*) $\mathbf{c} + \mathbf{a}$
(b) (*i*) $(\mathbf{a} + \mathbf{c}) + \mathbf{x}$; (*ii*) $\mathbf{a} + (\mathbf{c} + \mathbf{x})$
(c) $3\mathbf{a}$
(d) (*i*) $\mathbf{a}'\mathbf{c}$; (*ii*) $\mathbf{c}'\mathbf{a}$
(e) (*i*) $\mathbf{x}'\mathbf{y}$; $\mathbf{x}'\mathbf{x}$; (*ii*) $(\mathbf{x}'\mathbf{x})^{-1}\mathbf{x}'\mathbf{y}$
(f) (*i*) $X\mathbf{a}$; (*ii*) $\mathbf{a}'X'$; (*iii*) $A\mathbf{c}$; (*iv*) $A\mathbf{x}$; (*v*) $\mathbf{x}'A$
(g) (*i*) $X'A$; (*ii*) AX
(h) $3X$
(i) (*i*) $X'X$; (*ii*) $X'\mathbf{y}$
(j) (*i*) $I\mathbf{a}$; (*ii*) IX; (*iii*) IA; (*iv*) AI
(k) (*i*) $\mathbf{x}'I\mathbf{y}$; (*ii*) $\mathbf{x}'\mathbf{x}$

B3.2. Let the matrices A, B, and C be given by

$$A = \begin{bmatrix} 3 & 1 \\ 7 & 2 \end{bmatrix}, \qquad B = \begin{bmatrix} -1 & 4 \\ -1 & 0 \end{bmatrix}, \qquad C = \begin{bmatrix} 1 & 0 \\ 1 & 2 \end{bmatrix}$$

Show the following
(a) $AB \neq BA$
(b) $A(BC) = (AB)C$
(c) $A(B + C) = AB + AC$
(d) $(AB)' = B'A'$
(e) $(ABC)' = C'B'A'$

B3.3. Show that the sum of squares 3.3.2 can be written in vector notation as

$$\sum_{i=1}^{T}(y_i - \beta)^2 = (\mathbf{y} - \mathbf{x}\beta)'(\mathbf{y} - \mathbf{x}\beta)$$

$$= \mathbf{y}'\mathbf{y} - 2\beta\mathbf{x}'\mathbf{y} + \beta^2\mathbf{x}'\mathbf{x}$$

Verify that b_w in Exercise 3.8 arises by applying the least squares formula 3B.15 with observations weighted by their standard deviations, that is,

$$\mathbf{x} = \begin{bmatrix} 1/\sigma \\ 1/2\sigma \\ 1/3\sigma \end{bmatrix} \qquad \mathbf{y} = \begin{bmatrix} Y_1/\sigma \\ Y_2/2\sigma \\ Y_3/3\sigma \end{bmatrix}$$

Chapter 4

Statistical Inference II: Interval Estimation and Hypothesis Tests for the Mean of a Normal Population

New Key Words and Concepts

Confidence Interval Estimates	**Hypothesis Tests**
Type I and Type II Error	***p*-values**
***t*-statistic**	***F*-statistic**
Chi-square Distribution	**Prediction**
Two-Sample Problem	

4.1 Introduction

In Chapter 3 we considered the problem of estimating the unknown mean and variance of a normal population using a randomly drawn sample of data. We developed estimation rules, or *estimators*, for the unknown population parameters within the framework of a *linear statistical model*, $y_i = \beta + e_i$, $i = 1, \ldots, T$, where β is the unknown population mean and the independent random errors e_i have a $N(0, \sigma^2)$ distribution. The linear statistical model represents our assumptions about the nature of the sampling process and how the T sample observations on the outcome variable y, are related to the unknown population parameters. The estimators $b = \Sigma_{i=1}^{T} Y_i / T$, for β, and $\hat{\sigma}^2 = \Sigma_{i=1}^{T} (Y_i - b)^2 / (T-1)$ for σ^2, are random variables, since their values depend on the sample values of y_i that are collected. The probability density functions of the estimators b and $\hat{\sigma}^2$ are called *sampling distributions*. In Chapter 3 we showed that $b \sim N(\beta, \sigma^2 / T)$ and $(T-1)\hat{\sigma}^2 / \sigma^2 \sim \chi^2_{(T-1)}$.

In this chapter we build on these results and show how to

(i) use an estimator of β as a basis for making *predictions* about the outcome variable y;

(ii) construct an interval estimation rule for the β, the population mean;

(iii) test hypotheses (conjectures) about the unknown population mean β; and

(iv) test whether or not to pool, or combine, two samples of data into one.

We use the least squares estimator of the population mean, and its sampling distribution, as a basis for appropriate interval estimation and hypothesis testing procedures. To introduce these ideas we begin by assuming that the variance of the normal population is *known*. Once an interval estimator and hypothesis test is developed for the known σ^2 case, we proceed to the more realistic situation where the population variance is unknown.

4.2 An Interval Estimator for the Mean of a Normal Population: Known σ^2

To develop interval estimation and hypothesis tests we continue to use, as an example, a statistical model designed to explain, or represent, weekly expenditure on food by households of a given size and with a given income. More specifically, we assume that the weekly food expenditure by a randomly chosen household of size 3 with income $25,000, Y_i, equals the population mean value β, plus a random error e_i, which represents all factors causing the household expenditure to differ from the population mean. We also assume that these random errors e_i are independent normal random variables with mean zero and variance σ^2. That is,

$$Y_i = \beta + e_i \qquad i = 1, \ldots, T \tag{4.2.1a}$$

and the equation errors e_i are independently and identically distributed normal random variables,

$$e_i \sim N(0, \sigma^2) \tag{4.2.1b}$$

We assume, consequently, that the random variable weekly household food expenditure $Y_i \sim N(\beta, \sigma^2)$, and that households will be randomly selected so that each household's expenditure Y_i is independent of all others. For the present we assume that the population variance σ^2 is *known*, and thus does not have to be estimated.

In the model 4.2.1 the least squares estimator of β is

$$b = \sum_{i=1}^{T} Y_i / T \tag{4.2.2a}$$

This point estimator b is unbiased

$$E[b] = \beta \tag{4.2.2b}$$

has variance

$$\text{var}(b) = E\left[(b - \beta)^2\right] = \sigma^2 / T \tag{4.2.2c}$$

and has a normal distribution

$$b \sim N(\beta, \sigma^2 / T) \tag{4.2.2d}$$

Also, we have shown in Chapter 3 that of all linear unbiased estimators of β, the least squares estimator b is the *best*, where "best" means that it has the smallest sampling variance. In fact, the least squares estimator is the best of all unbiased rules, whether linear or not when the e_i are normally distributed. We now use these distribution results to construct an *interval estimator* of the population mean β.

Since $b \sim N(\beta, \sigma^2/T)$ it follows that $(b - \beta) \sim N(0, \sigma^2/T)$. Consequently, we can construct the standardized normal random variable by dividing the random variable $(b - \beta)$ by its standard deviation, $\sigma/\sqrt{T}$,

$$Z = \frac{b - \beta}{\sqrt{\sigma^2/T}} = \frac{b - \beta}{\sigma/\sqrt{T}} \qquad (4.2.3)$$

The standard normal random variable Z has mean zero, variance one, and is normally distributed. That is, $Z \sim N(0, 1)$. Let z_c be a "critical value" for the $N(0, 1)$ probability density function such that $\alpha = .05$ of the probability mass is in the tails of the distribution, with $\alpha/2 = .025$ in each tail. From the table of standard normal probabilities, Table 1 at the end of the book, $z_c = 1.96$ when $\alpha = .05$. This critical value is illustrated in Figure 4.1 and has the properties that

$$P[Z \geq 1.96] = P[Z \leq -1.96] = 0.025 \qquad (4.2.4a)$$

and

$$P[-1.96 \leq Z \leq 1.96] = 1 - .05 = .95 \qquad (4.2.4b)$$

If we substitute the standardized normal random variable in equation 4.2.3 into equation 4.2.4 we obtain

$$P\left[-1.96 \leq \frac{b - \beta}{\sigma/\sqrt{T}} \leq 1.96\right] = .95$$

Multiplying the inequality within the brackets by $\sigma/\sqrt{T}$ yields

$$P\left[-1.96\,\sigma/\sqrt{T} \leq b - \beta \leq 1.96\,\sigma/\sqrt{T}\right] = .95$$

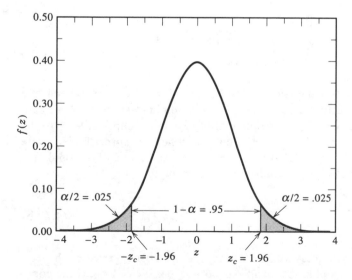

Figure 4.1 $\alpha = .05$ critical values for the $N(0, 1)$ distribution.

Subtracting b from each term in the inequality produces

$$P\left[-b-1.96\,\sigma/\sqrt{T} \le -\beta \le -b+1.96\,\sigma/\sqrt{T}\right]=.95$$

Multiplying the inequality by -1 reverses the direction of the inequality and gives us

$$P\left[b-1.96\,\sigma/\sqrt{T} \le \beta \le b+1.96\,\sigma/\sqrt{T}\right]=.95$$

or, in general,

$$P\left[b-z_c\,\frac{\sigma}{\sqrt{T}} \le \beta \le b+z_c\,\frac{\sigma}{\sqrt{T}}\right]=1-\alpha \qquad (4.2.5)$$

where z_c is the appropriate critical value for α percent of tail probability. In equation 4.2.5 we have defined a *random interval estimator*, $b \pm z_c\sigma/\sqrt{T}$, that has, in repeated sampling, a $(1 - \alpha)$ percent chance of containing the true population parameter β. The random interval estimator has endpoints that are random because, prior to the collection of the sample, b is a random variable. The probability statement in equation 4.2.5 means that if we draw random samples of size T repeatedly from the population, and compute the intervals $b \pm z_c\sigma/\sqrt{T}$, then $(1 - \alpha)$ *percent of them* will contain the true population mean parameter β.

We can increase or decrease the probability that the random interval $b \pm z_c\sigma/\sqrt{T}$ contains the true population mean β, in repeated sampling, by varying the critical value z_c. Note that, to increase the probability that the interval contains the parameter β, the critical value z_c must be made larger. A larger critical value z_c produces a wider interval.

By using the sample of data, as in Table 3.1 on weekly food expenditures by $T = 40$ randomly selected households of size 3 with income \$25,000, we estimated the population mean expenditure to be $b = \$51.08$. This single value is called a *point estimate* of β, and it represents our best guess, given the sample data, at the parameter value. Assume, for the purpose of illustration, that we know the population variance is $\sigma^2 = 10$. Consequently the population standard deviation is $\sigma = \sqrt{10} = 3.162$. Given the information from this sample of data, we can construct a 95% *confidence interval estimate*, which is also frequently called just a *confidence interval*, for the population mean expenditure β, as

$$b \pm z_c\,\sigma/\sqrt{T} = \$51.08 \pm 1.96(3.16)/\sqrt{40}$$
$$= \left[\$50.10,\,\$52.06\right] \qquad (4.2.5a)$$

If the value of $\sigma^2 = 10$, our interval estimate for the population mean food expenditure is [\$50.10, \$52.06]. Is the true population mean β contained in this interval? We cannot say because β is not known. But in the context of repeated sampling, 95% of the *intervals* constructed this way will contain β. Thus, we would be surprised if β were not in the interval estimate. To be 99% sure, using Table 1 at the end of the book, the critical value $z_c = 2.58$ and the interval must be wider, namely

$$b \pm z_c\,\sigma/\sqrt{T} = \$51.08 \pm 2.58(3.16)/\sqrt{40}$$
$$= \left[\$49.79,\,\$52.37\right] \qquad (4.2.5b)$$

Confidence intervals are extremely useful when reporting statistical results. The least squares point estimate of the population mean expenditure β is $b = \$51.08$. If the population variance is $\sigma^2 = 10$, then the *estimated* distribution of weekly food expenditures is $Y_i \sim N(\$51.08, 10)$. This estimated distribution can be used to make probability statements about food expenditure, but it conveys nothing about the sampling variance of b, which equals $\sigma^2/T = .25$ in this case. For the purpose of informing an audience of both the best estimate of the population mean and some indication of its sampling precision, an interval estimate is a convenient tool. The 95% interval estimate [\$50.10, \$52.06] shows the range of values centered at the best guess for β, which is $b = \$51.08$, and serves as one measure of the uncertainty about β that remains after the sample of data is analyzed.

4.2.1   Predicting the Value of a Normal Random Variable

The linear statistical model given in equation 4.2.1 is a statement of our assumptions about how a sample of data on food expenditure by households of size 3 and \$25,000 income is generated. That is, it is a model of a *data generation process*. We have estimated the population parameters β and σ^2 and have determined the sampling properties of the estimation rules. The model 4.2.1 and estimator 4.2.2 can also be used to answer the question: What do you predict the *value* of expenditure will be for a household that is not included in the sample? This question demands that we estimate or *predict* the actual value that a random variable will take.

Let us denote the household expenditure random variable that we want to predict as Y_0. In order to legitimately use data from the data generation process assumptions in equation 4.2.1 to help predict the value that Y_0 will take, we must assume that it is the food expenditure by a household from the same population of households, and thus that it is generated by the same process. That is, Y_0 is given by

$$Y_0 = \beta + e_0 \qquad (4.2.6a)$$

and

$$e_0 \sim N(0, \sigma^2) \qquad (4.2.6b)$$

where e_0 is independent of $e_1, e_2, \ldots, e_T$ and thus of $Y_1, Y_2, \ldots, Y_T$. Examining equation 4.2.6 we see that Y_0 is composed of an unknown fixed part β, which we can estimate, and an unobservable random part e_0, which we cannot estimate without knowing the value that Y_0 takes. Thus, a reasonable way to predict the value that Y_0 will take is to replace β by its estimate b and to replace e_0 by its most likely (and mean) value, namely zero. Thus, we predict Y_0 to be

$$\hat{Y}_0 = b \qquad (4.2.7)$$

This simply says that in the absence of any other information we predict the value of food expenditure by a randomly chosen household to be the estimated population mean. Using the data in Table 3.1 on weekly food expenditures by $T = 40$ randomly selected households of size 3 and income \$25,000, the estimated population mean expenditure is $b = \$51.08$. Thus, in the absence of any other information, we predict the consumption of another randomly drawn household to be $\hat{Y}_0 = \$51.08$.

We know that this prediction *rule* is random, since the least squares estimation rule b depends on a random sample of data and is a random variable. Consequently, we can investigate its sampling properties. First, define the *prediction error* in using $\hat{Y}_0$ to predict Y_0 as

$$\hat{e}_0 = Y_0 - \hat{Y}_0 \qquad (4.2.8)$$

Thus, $\hat{e}_0$ is the difference between the actual and predicted values of population household food expenditure. Substitute $\beta + e_0$ for Y_0 and b for $\hat{Y}_0$ to obtain

$$\hat{e}_0 = \beta + e_0 - b \tag{4.2.9}$$

Then, using the prediction rule 4.2.7, the expected prediction error is

$$E[\hat{e}_0] = E[\beta] + E[e_0] - E[b]$$
$$= \beta + 0 - \beta = 0$$

Since the expected prediction error is zero, $\hat{Y}_0$ is said to be an *unbiased predictor* of Y_0.

We can measure the variability of this prediction error by determining the variance of $\hat{e}_0$. In equation 4.2.9 we see that $\hat{e}_0$ is composed of three terms. The parameter β is a constant and has zero variance. The terms e_0 and b are independent, so that

$$\text{var}(\hat{e}_0) = \text{var}(e_0) + \text{var}(b)$$
$$= \sigma^2 + \sigma^2 / T = \sigma^2 \left(1 + \frac{1}{T}\right) \tag{4.2.10}$$

Note that the prediction error $\hat{e}_0$ has variability greater than that of the least squares estimator. The logic of this result follows from the fact that $Y_0 = \beta + e_0$, and when predicting Y_0 uncertainty arises from two sources. First, the population mean β is unknown and is estimated using the least squares rule b; the uncertainty from estimating β is measured by $\text{var}(b) = \sigma^2/T$. Second, there is additional uncertainty in predicting Y_0 as, *even if β were known exactly*, it varies randomly about the population mean, with error $e_0 = Y_0 - \beta$. The uncertainty introduced by the fact that Y_0 is random is measured by $\text{var}(e_0) = \text{var}(Y_0) = \sigma^2$. The prediction error has variability that is the simple sum of the variances of b and e_0 since the sample data used to estimate β are independent of Y_0.

Furthermore, in Section 2.8.1 of Chapter 2, we noted the useful fact that a weighted sum of normal random variables is normal itself. Using that fact (see Exercise 4.5), we can show that the prediction error $\hat{e}_0$ is a normal random variable. Thus we can summarize the properties of the prediction rule $\hat{Y}_0 = b$ by characterizing its prediction error $\hat{e}_0$ as

$$\hat{e}_0 = Y_0 - \hat{Y}_0 \sim N\left(0, \sigma^2 \left(1 + \frac{1}{T}\right)\right) \tag{4.2.11}$$

Using equation 4.2.11 we can also construct prediction intervals for Y_0. Specifically, if σ^2 is known, then we have the standard normal random variable

$$Z = \frac{\hat{e}_0 - E[\hat{e}_0]}{\sqrt{\text{var}(\hat{e}_0)}} = \frac{\hat{e}_0}{\sqrt{\sigma^2 \left(1 + \frac{1}{T}\right)}} \sim N(0, 1) \tag{4.2.12}$$

Consequently, if z_c is the upper-$\alpha/2$ percentile of the $N(0, 1)$ distribution

$$\text{Pr}[-z_c \le Z \le z_c] = 1 - \alpha$$

$$= \text{Pr}\left[-z_c \le \frac{Y_0 - b}{\sigma\sqrt{1 + \frac{1}{T}}} \le z_c\right] = 1 - \alpha$$

$$= \text{Pr}\left[b - z_c \sigma\sqrt{1 + \frac{1}{T}} \le Y_0 \le b + z_c \sigma\sqrt{1 + \frac{1}{T}}\right] = 1 - \alpha$$

The *random interval estimator* for Y_0

$$b \pm z_c \sigma \sqrt{1 + \frac{1}{T}} \tag{4.2.13}$$

will contain household expenditure Y_0 with probability $1 - \alpha$.

Using the data in Table 3.1 and assuming that the population variance is known to be $\sigma^2 = 10$, the 95% and 99% prediction intervals for food expenditure by a randomly drawn household are

$$1 - \alpha = .95: \quad b \pm z_c \sigma \sqrt{1 + 1/T} = 51.08 \pm (1.96)(3.16)\sqrt{1 + 1/40}$$
$$= [44.95, 57.20] \tag{4.2.14}$$

$$1 - \alpha = .99: \quad b \pm z_c \sigma \sqrt{1 + 1/T} = 51.08 \pm (2.58)(3.16)\sqrt{1 + 1/40}$$
$$= [43.02, 59.14] \tag{4.2.15}$$

Note that these prediction intervals are *wider* than the corresponding interval estimates for β given in equations 4.2.5a,b. This is due to the variability of Y_0 about its mean.

4.3 Hypothesis Tests About the Mean of a Normal Population When the Population Variance, σ^2, is Known

Besides wanting to obtain point and interval estimates of an unknown population mean, economists also empirically test conjectures, or hypotheses, about unknown population parameters. For example, suppose public policy establishes welfare payments based on population averages, and payments currently assume that the mean population expenditure for food is $\beta = \$50$/per week. It is reasonable for public officials to want to check whether data support this assumption about the population mean. We can treat $\beta = \$50$ as a hypothesis to be tested. Hypotheses are always paired with a logical alternative that will be accepted if the hypothesis itself is rejected. We denote the primary (or "null") and alternative hypotheses as

$$H_0 : \beta = 50 \tag{4.3.1}$$

$$H_1 : \beta \neq 50 \tag{4.3.2}$$

This means that for testing purposes we have paired the primary hypothesis H_0: $\beta = 50$ with the alternative that H_1: $\beta \neq 50$.

A statistical test of the null hypothesis is carried out by examining whether or not the information about the value of β contained in a sample of data supports, or appears to be consistent with, the null hypothesis. The sample information about β is summarized by the least squares estimator b, and the foundation of a statistical test of the null hypothesis is the sampling theory result that, under the assumptions of the normal linear statistical model, $b \sim N(\beta, \sigma^2/T)$. This sampling theory result allows us to say, for example, that *if the null hypothesis, H_0: $\beta = 50$, is true, then $b \sim N(50, \sigma^2/T)$*. This probability density function is depicted in Figure 4.2 under the assumption that $\sigma^2 = 10$, sample size $T = 40$, and var$(b) = \sigma^2/T = 10/40 = .25$.

We can use the probability density function of b, which holds when the null hypothesis is true, as a basis for determining whether or not the data support the null hypothesis.

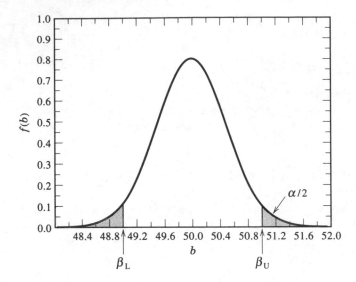

Figure 4.2 Probability density function of the least squares estimator b if H_0: $\beta = 50$ is true.

If the data provide an estimate that is *unlikely* to have come from the distribution of the least squares estimator when the null hypothesis is true, then we conclude that the data *do not* support or are not compatible with the null hypothesis. In Figure 4.2 we identify two values of the least squares estimator, β_U and β_L, such that it is *unlikely* (that is, the probability is *small*) that we observe values of $b \geq \beta_U$ or $b \leq \beta_L$, if the null hypothesis is true.

In a statistical test the investigators *define* what is meant by "unlikely" by selecting, *prior to the test*, the probability that b falls in the shaded tail area of its probability density function, shown in Figure 4.2. The tail area has probability content that is often denoted by "α," and α, called the *level of significance* of the test, is usually chosen to be .01 or .05. The values of β_U and β_L are chosen so that

$$P[b \geq \beta_U] = P[b \leq \beta_L] = \alpha/2$$

The logic of the statistical test of the null hypothesis, H_0: $\beta = 50$, is as follows:

1. If the sample data yields an estimate $b \geq \beta_U$ or $b \leq \beta_L$, we reason that
    (a) The probability that we would obtain, by chance, such a value from the distribution $N(50, 0.25)$ is small (α).
    (b) The estimator $b \sim N(\beta = 50, \sigma^2/T = 0.25)$ *if the null hypothesis H_0: $\beta = 50$ is correct.*
    (c) Therefore it is unlikely (that is, the probability is small) that the null hypothesis is true, and we *reject* the null hypothesis in favor of the alternative hypothesis, H_1: $\beta \neq 50$.
2. If the sample of data yields an estimate $\beta_L \leq b \leq \beta_U$, then
    (a) The probability that we would obtain such a value from the distribution $N(50, .25)$ is $1 - \alpha$, a large value.
    (b) The estimator $b \sim N(\beta = 50, \sigma^2/T = .25)$ if the hypothesis is true.
    (c) Therefore the information in the sample data about the population mean is consistent (not inconsistent) with the null hypothesis and *we do not reject it.*

To summarize the steps of the statistical test: Given the null and alternative hypotheses

$$H_0 : \beta = \beta_0$$
$$H_1 : \beta \neq \beta_0$$

where β_0 is some value of β. Select values β_U and β_L such that $P[b \geq \beta_U] = P[b \leq \beta_L]$ $= \alpha/2$ *if the hypothesis is true.* Then (1) reject the null hypothesis H_0: $\beta = \beta_0$ if $b \geq \beta_U$ or $b \leq \beta_L$. (2) Do not reject the null hypothesis H_0: $\beta = \beta_0$ if $\beta_L \leq b \leq \beta_U$.

A comment is in order about how the conclusion of the test is stated. We have said that if $b \geq \beta_L$ or $b \leq \beta_U$ we *reject* the null hypothesis and if $\beta_L \leq b \leq \beta_U$ we *do not reject* the null hypothesis. The phrases "reject" and "do not reject" are chosen with some care. When a null hypothesis is rejected, it means that the sample information does not support the null hypothesis, and thus we conclude that it is unlikely to be true; this is a definitive statement. On the other hand, when a null hypothesis is not rejected, this simply means that the sample evidence is consistent with the null hypothesis. *This does not mean that we conclude that the null hypothesis is true.* You can *never prove* that a statistical hypothesis is true by using a statistical test. The value of the population mean we have estimated to be $b = \$51.08$ is consistent with *many* conjectures about the true parameter value. If the null hypothesis H_0: $\beta = 50$ is not rejected then we would also not reject H_0: $\beta = 50.50$, H_0: $\beta = 51.00$ and many others. *Failing to reject a null hypothesis does not mean that it is true!*

In practice, rather than determining the critical values β_L and β_U in each problem (see Exercise 4.6), a standardized normal *test statistic* may be employed.

If the null hypothesis H_0: $\beta = 50$ is true, then $b \sim N(\beta = 50, \sigma^2/T = 0.25)$. We can construct a standardized normal random variable(see equation 4.2.3) if the null hypothesis is true, as

$$Z = \frac{b - \beta}{\sigma / \sqrt{T}} = \frac{b - 50}{\sqrt{.25}} \tag{4.3.3}$$

The random variable Z has the standard normal distribution $N(0, 1)$ if the null hypothesis is true. We may define unlikely values of b by selecting the values β_U and β_L such that $P[b \geq \beta_U] = P[b \leq \beta_L] = \alpha/2$, and carry out the test as described above. It is generally more convenient, however, to state unlikely values of b in terms of the standard normal distribution. In Figure 4.1 the standard normal $N(0, 1)$ is depicted. The value z_c is such that $P[Z \geq z_c] = P[Z \leq -z_c] = \alpha/2$.

The values of z_c that correspond to different values of α can be found in Table 1 at the back of the book. If $\alpha = .05$ then $z_c = 1.96$; if $\alpha = .01$ then $z_c = 2.58$. The random variable Z can be used as a *test statistic* since its distribution is known to be $N(0, 1)$ if the null hypothesis is true. If b is the least squares estimate of β based on a sample of data, use it to calculate a *value* z of the test statistic Z in equation 4.3.3. Then

1. If $z \geq z_c$ or $z \leq -z_c$ (or $|z| \geq z_c$, where $|z|$ is the absolute value of z), then
    (a) The probability that we would obtain such a value z by chance from the distribution $N(0, 1)$ is small (α).
    (b) The standardized random variable $Z \sim N(0, 1)$ if the null hypothesis is true.
    (c) It is unlikely that the null hypothesis is true, and we reject the null hypothesis in favor of the alternative.

Or

2.   If $|z| < z_c$ then

   (a) The probability that we would obtain such a value from a $N(0, 1)$ distribution is $1 - \alpha$, a large value.

   (b) The standardized random variable $Z \sim N(0, 1)$ if the null hypothesis is true.

   (c) The information in the sample data is consistent with $Z \sim N(0, 1)$ and *we do not* reject the null hypothesis.

Given the null and alternative hypotheses

$$H_0 : \beta = \beta_0$$
$$H_1 : \beta \neq \beta_0$$

The steps of testing a hypothesis about the mean of a normal population when σ^2 is known are: (a) Select critical values z_c from the standard normal $N(0, 1)$ distribution such that $P[Z \geq z_c] = P[Z \leq -z_c] = \alpha/2$; (b) use the least squares estimate b of β to calculate the value z of $Z = (b - \beta_0)/\sqrt{\sigma^2/T}$; and (c) reject the null hypothesis H_0: $\beta = \beta_0$ if $|z| \geq z_c$ or (d) do not reject the null hypothesis if $|z| < z_c$.

As an example of this test procedure, let us test the null hypothesis H_0: $\beta = 50$ using the food expenditure data. The estimated value of the population mean is $b = \$51.08$, and the calculated value of the test statistic Z is

$$z = \frac{b - \beta}{\sigma/\sqrt{T}} = \frac{51.08 - 50}{\sqrt{0.25}} = 2.16$$

If we choose the level of significance of the test to be $\alpha = 0.05$ then $z_c = 1.96$. Since $z = 2.16 \geq z_c = 1.96$ we reject the hypothesis that the population mean weekly expenditure on food is \$50. We conclude that the average food expenditure by the test households is different from the hypothesized mean of \$50.

If we choose the level of significance of the test to be $\alpha = .01$, then $z_c = 2.58$. Since $z \leq z_c = 2.58$, we *do not* reject the null hypothesis at this level of significance. Since different conclusions are reached depending on the value of α that is chosen, one thing you will need to think about is: What are the statistical and economic implications of choosing $\alpha = .05$ or $\alpha = .01$?

4.3.1 Types of Decision Errors and *p*-Values

4.3.1a Type I and Type II Error   Whenever a decision is made, there is the chance that it will be the wrong decision. The same is true for decisions based on a statistical test. Consider the contingency layout in Table 4.1.

When the null hypothesis is *true* there is still an α percent chance of rejecting it. This "Type I" error of rejecting a true null hypothesis occurs when unlikely values of the test statistic Z are obtained. Recall that if the null hypothesis is true the probability it will be (incorrectly) rejected is $P[Z \geq z_c] + P[Z \leq -z_c] = \alpha/2 + \alpha/2 = \alpha$, the level of significance of the test. Thus the probability of a Type I error is α. Thus the question at the end of the previous section can now be answered. By choosing $\alpha = .05$ or $\alpha = .01$ we determine the probability that the statistical test will incorrectly reject a true null hypothesis. The value of α should be chosen with the *cost* of a Type I error in mind. If the cost of rejecting a true null hypothesis is very large, then the level of significance α should be set to a small value.

Table 4.1   Statistical Test Contingencies

		States of the World	
		$H_0: \beta = 50$ true	$H_0: \beta = 50$ false
Action	**Reject H_0**	Type I error	Correct decision
	Do not reject H_0	Correct decision	Type II error

When the null hypothesis is false and it is not rejected, then a Type II error has been committed. While we can fix the probability of a Type I error by selecting the value α, the same control of Type II error is not possible. In Figure 4.1 we depict the standard normal density function of the test statistic Z in equation 4.3.3 that holds if the null hypothesis $H_0: \beta = 50$ is true. Suppose, however, that the null hypothesis is *false* and in fact $\beta = \$50.50$. Then what is the distribution of Z? If $\beta = \$50.50$ then $b \sim N(50.50, \sigma^2/T = .25)$, and $Z = (b - 50)/\sqrt{.25} \sim N(1, 1)$, since the expected value of Z is

$$E[Z] = E\left[\frac{b - 50}{\sqrt{.25}}\right] = \frac{1}{.50}\left(E[b] - 50\right)$$

$$= \frac{1}{.50}(50.50 - 50) = 1$$

The distribution of Z when $\beta = \$50.50$ is depicted in Figure 4.3. If $\beta = 50.50$ then the null hypothesis is false, but our test decision rule is *not* to reject the null hypothesis if $|z| \le z_c$. If $\alpha = .05$, that probability is $P[-1.96 \le Z \le 1.96] = .83$, which is depicted by the shaded area in Figure 4.3. If $\beta = 50.50$ then the probability of a Type II error is .83, a rather large value. Other values of β produce other probabilities of Type II errors.

Thus, if the null hypothesis is false, we can calculate the probability of a Type II error; but *only if we know the true value of β!* Of course we don't know the true value of β, but we can say some things about the probability of a Type II error:

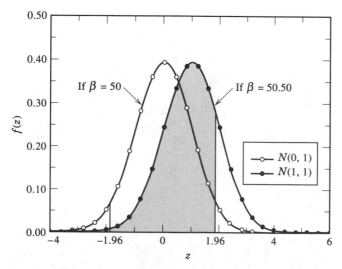

Figure 4.3 The distribution of Z when $\beta = 50$ and $\beta = 50.50$.

(*i*) The probabilities of Type I and Type II error are inversely related. The lower the chance of a Type I error, the larger the chance of a Type II error.

(*ii*) The *closer* the true value of β is to the hypothesized value, the *greater* the probability of a Type II error.

(*iii*) Despite our inability to control the probabilities of both types of decision error, the test we have described is a very good test procedure. In fact, it is the *best* way to test a hypothesis about the mean of a normal population, in the sense that given the probability of a Type I error, the test minimizes the probability of a Type II error.

4.3.1b Using p-values   It is an increasingly common practice, when reporting the outcome of a statistical test, to state the value of the test statistic along with its "probability-value," or "*p*-value." *The p-value of a standard normal test statistic value is the probability that the N(0, 1) test statistic Z takes a value larger than the test statistic value z or smaller than −z.* For example, corresponding to the test of equation 4.3.1, the *p*-value of $z = 2.16$ is .0308, and this result is depicted in Figure 4.4. The *p*-value provides a convenient way to determine the outcome of a statistical test based on any specified level of Type I error α. The rule is:

The null hypothesis H_0: $\beta = \beta_0$ is rejected if the *p*-value is less than or equal to α, the level of Type I error.

The reasoning of the rule is made clear by examining Figure 4.4. If the *p*-value is less than or equal to α, then $|z|$ is greater than or equal to z_c, and the data do not support the null hypothesis and the null hypothesis is rejected. Thus by knowing that the *p*-value of $z = 2.16$ is .0308, we can determine immediately that the hypothesis will be rejected at $\alpha = .05$ but will not be rejected at $\alpha = .01$. Testing a hypothesis by using a *p*-value will always lead to the same conclusion as the "regular" test procedure given the level of significance α.

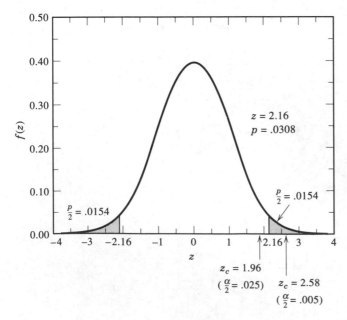

Figure 4.4 The *p*-value of a Z test statistic value $z = 2.16$.

To calculate the p-value of $z = 2.16$ we proceed as follows:

$$p\text{- value } (z = 2.16) = \Pr[Z \leq -2.16 \text{ or } Z \geq 2.16]$$
$$= 2\Pr[Z \geq 2.16]$$
$$= 2[1 - \Pr[Z < 2.16]]$$
$$= 2[1 - .9846]$$
$$= 2[.0154] = .0308$$

The calculation of $\Pr[Z < 2.16]$ can be carried out in two ways. By using the probability values for standard normal random variables that are tabulated in Table 1 at the end of the book we find that

$$\Pr[0 \leq Z \leq 2.16] = .4846$$

So $\Pr[Z < 2.16] = .9846$. Alternatively, many computer software programs have built into them functions that evaluate the cumulative distribution function of the standard normal random variable z:

$$F(z) = \Pr[Z \leq z] = \int_{-\infty}^{z} \frac{1}{\sqrt{2\pi}} e^{-x^2/2} dx$$

These programs will yield $F(2.16) = .9846$ directly.

In the general case, where z is the value of the standard normal test statistic Z,

$$p\text{- value}(z) = 2\left(1 - F(|z|)\right)$$

where $|z|$ is the absolute value of the test statistic.

4.3.2   One-Tailed Tests

In equations 4.3.1 and 4.3.2 the null and alternative hypotheses are stated as "the population mean *equals* \$50" and "the population mean is *not equal to* \$50," respectively. This "point" null hypothesis is rejected if the least squares estimate b is significantly *larger or smaller* than \$50, or if the test statistic Z is significantly larger or smaller than zero. Although this is certainly an appropriate way to state our conjecture, it is sometimes possible to state the null and alternative hypotheses in a more precise manner. For example, suppose a public official will deem a pilot welfare program a success, and recommend its implementation, if the average weekly household food expenditure of \$50 in a test group is in line with expenditures by the rest of the population. More specifically, however, the official is not worried about the possibility that the test households are spending too much, but will recommend that the welfare program be scrapped if the population mean expenditure β is significantly greater than the \$50 average expenditure by the test group.

How should the null and alternative hypotheses be framed? The null hypothesis represents the state of affairs that will be maintained till proven otherwise. In this case the maintained hypothesis is that the program is good and that the population mean β is less than or equal to the test group average expenditure of \$50 per week. The public official does *not* want to reject the program if it is doing some good and wants to make the probability of this error small. Thus the null hypothesis will be stated in an inequality form as

$$H_0 : \beta \leq 50 \qquad \text{(do not scrap program)} \qquad (4.3.4)$$

against the alternative that

$$H_1 : \beta > 50 \qquad \text{(scrap program)} \qquad (4.3.5)$$

The null hypothesis, that the project is successful, will be rejected if the sample evidence clearly favors H_1 rather than H_0. Given inequality hypotheses, the test statistic is formed using the "borderline" value of the population mean, $\beta = 50$. This value of β is the "least favorable" value of β toward the null hypothesis. It is used in the construction of the test statistic so that the test is as objective as possible. The test statistic, assuming $\sigma^2 = 10$ and $T = 40$,

$$Z = \frac{b - \beta}{\sigma / \sqrt{T}} = \frac{b - 50}{0.25}$$

will tend to become *large* if the alternative hypothesis is correct, since the mean of b is the true population mean, and thus we reject the null hypothesis $H_0 : \beta \leq 50$ if the value of the test statistic $z \geq z_c$, where $P[Z \geq z_c] = \alpha$. Tests of inequality hypotheses like inequality 4.3.4 are called *one-tailed tests*, since the hypothesis is rejected only if the value of the test statistic is too large, in this case, and not if it is a large negative. Note that the level of Type I error is α and represented by the shaded area in the right-tail of the distribution of the test statistic Z. The critical value z_c for this test is shown in Figure 4.5.

The null hypothesis will be rejected only if the value of the test statistic is too large, which corresponds to the alternative hypothesis that $\beta > 50$. If the level of significance of this test is to be $\alpha = .05$, then the critical value of the test statistic z_c is chosen so that 5% of the probability mass is in the *right tail* of the probability density function of the test statistic z. From Table 1 at the back of the book, this value is $z_c = 1.65$. Since the value of the test statistic is $z = 2.16$, which we have already computed, we reject the hypothesis that $\beta \leq 50$ and accept the alternative that $\beta > 50$. If $\alpha = .025$ is chosen, the critical value $z_c = 1.96$ and the null hypothesis is also rejected. Based on this evidence the public official may conclude that the welfare project has not brought the test

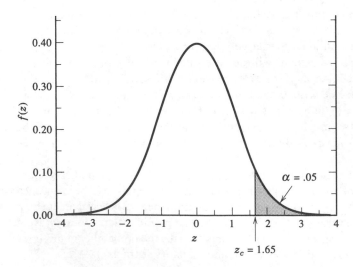

Figure 4.5 Rejection region for a one-tailed test.

population's expenditure on food in line with the overall population's and does not recommend its wider implementation.

4.4 Statistical Inference About the Mean of a Normal Population When the Variance is Unknown: The *t*-Distribution

In Sections 4.2 and 4.3 we developed procedures for constructing interval estimates and testing hypotheses about the mean of a normal population when the variance of the population, the parameter σ^2, is known. Usually, however, σ^2 is unknown, and the test procedures and statistics of the previous section must be modified.

4.4.1 The *t*-Distribution

The statistic that forms the basis for interval estimation and hypothesis testing when σ^2 is known is the standardized $N(0, 1)$ random variable

$$Z = \frac{b - \beta}{\sigma / \sqrt{T}} \tag{4.4.1}$$

When σ^2 is unknown, it is natural to replace it with its unbiased estimator $\hat{\sigma}^2$ (see Section 3.6 of Chapter 3). However, when we do so $(b - \beta)/(\hat{\sigma}/\sqrt{T})$ is the ratio of two random variables b and $\hat{\sigma}^2$, and this ratio no longer has a standard normal distribution. Consequently, the $N(0, 1)$ distribution does not provide a basis for inference. The correct probability distribution of the statistic $(b - \beta)/(\hat{\sigma}/\sqrt{T})$ was worked out by W. S. Gossett, an employee of the Guiness Brewery, who, in 1919, published his work under the pseudonym "Student." Gossett called the statistic "*t*" and, hence, its distribution is called "Student's" *t*-distribution. The *t*-statistic is actually a clever combination of the Z statistic in equation 4.4.1 and the independent chi-square random variable $W = (T-1)\hat{\sigma}^2/\sigma^2 \sim \chi^2_{(T-1)}$ developed in equation 3.6.13. Specifically, the ratio $(b - \beta)/(\hat{\sigma}/\sqrt{T})$ is formed as follows

$$
\begin{aligned}
t &= \frac{Z}{\sqrt{W/(T-1)}} \\[2mm]
&= \frac{\dfrac{b - \beta}{\sigma/\sqrt{T}}}{\sqrt{\dfrac{(T-1)\hat{\sigma}^2}{\sigma^2} \Big/ (T-1)}} = \frac{\dfrac{b-\beta}{\sigma/\sqrt{T}}}{\dfrac{\hat{\sigma}}{\sigma}} \\[2mm]
&= \frac{b - \beta}{\hat{\sigma}/\sqrt{T}} \sim t_{(T-1)}
\end{aligned}
\tag{4.4.2}
$$

The notation $t_{(T-1)}$ denotes Student's *t*-distribution with $T - 1$ "degrees of freedom." The degrees of freedom parameter is important, since it determines the shape of the *t*-distribution. In general, a *t* random variable with m degrees of freedom, $t_{(m)}$ is formed by dividing a standard normal $N(0, 1)$ random variable by the square root of an independent $\chi^2_{(m)}$ random variable that has been divided by its degrees of freedom. That is,

$$t = \frac{N(0,1)}{\sqrt{\chi^2_{(m)}/m}} \sim t_{(m)} \qquad (4.4.3)$$

if numerator and denominator are independent random variables.

The probability density function of a t random variable is determined by the degrees of freedom parameter m. In Figure 4.6 the t probability density function for $m = 3$ degrees of freedom is graphed with the density function of a $N(0, 1)$ random variable. Note that the t probability density function is less "peaked" and there is more probability mass in the tails of the distribution. The probability density function of a t random variable is symmetric, with mean 0 and variance $k = m/(m - 2)$. As the degrees of freedom parameter becomes large, $m \to \infty$, and the probability density function of $t_{(m)}$ approaches that of a standard normal $N(0, 1)$ random variable. Critical values of the t-distribution that are useful for hypothesis tests and confidence interval statements are given in Table 2 at the end of this book.

For future reference we note that the t-distribution is directly related to another important distribution that is widely used in statistical tests, the F-distribution. Specifically, from equation 4.4.2 we know that the $t_{(T-1)}$ random variable is

$$t = \frac{Z}{\sqrt{W/(T-1)}}$$

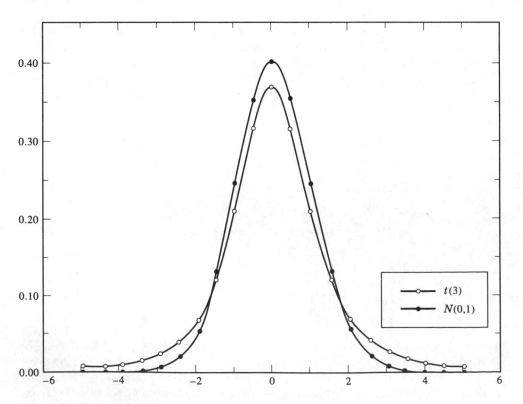

Figure 4.6 The standard normal and $t_{(3)}$ probability density functions.

where Z is a standard normal random variable and W is an independent $\chi^2_{(T-1)}$ random variable. Then the $t_{(T-1)}$ random variable *squared* is

$$t^2_{(T-1)} = \frac{Z^2}{W/(T-1)} = \frac{\chi^2_{(1)}}{\chi^2_{(T-1)}/(T-1)}$$

The numerator of t^2 is a $\chi^2_{(1)}$ random variable as it is the square of a $N(0, 1)$ random variable. An F random variable is the ratio of two independent chi-square random variables that are divided by their degrees of freedom. Thus

$$t^2_{(T-1)} = F_{1,(T-1)}$$

where $F_{1,(T-1)}$ denotes an F random variable with 1 degree of freedom in the numerator chi-square random variable and $(T-1)$ degrees of freedom in the denominator chi-square random variable. You will encounter the F distribution many times in the chapters to come, and in Chapter 10 an appendix is devoted to this topic.

4.4.2   Interval Estimation

When the error variance σ^2 is unknown, the t random variable that is useful for statistical inference about the mean of a normal population is that given in equation 4.4.2 as

$$t_{(T-1)} = \frac{b-\beta}{\hat{\sigma}/\sqrt{T}}$$

Given these results, we can use the t-distribution, instead of the standard normal distribution, to form an interval estimator for β and to form the probability statement

$$P\left[-t_c \leq \frac{b-\beta}{\hat{\sigma}/\sqrt{T}} \leq t_c\right] = 1-\alpha$$

or, following the steps leading to equation 4.2.5 in the case where σ^2 was known,

$$P\left[b-t_c\frac{\hat{\sigma}}{\sqrt{T}} \leq \beta \leq b+t_c\frac{\hat{\sigma}}{\sqrt{T}}\right] = 1-\alpha \tag{4.4.4}$$

The $(1 - \alpha)$ percent interval estimator for β is

$$b \pm t_c\frac{\hat{\sigma}}{\sqrt{T}} \tag{4.4.5}$$

Unlike the situation in Section 4.2, where only the center of the interval estimator $b \pm z_c\sigma/\sqrt{T}$ was random, *when σ^2 is unknown both the center and width of the interval estimator in equation 4.4.5 are random.*

Let us apply these results to our food expenditure example. In Section 4.2 we constructed a confidence interval for the population mean food expenditure under the assumption that the variance σ^2 was known to be 10. The 95% confidence interval $b \pm z_c\ \sigma/\sqrt{T} = 51.08 \pm 1.96\sqrt{10}/\sqrt{40}$ was [\$50.10, \$52.06]. If σ^2 is unknown and estimated by $\hat{\sigma}^2 = 6.38$ (equation 3.6.9), then equation 4.4.5 is used to obtain the interval estimate. The critical value t_c should come from a t-distribution with $m = T - 1 = 39$ degrees of freedom. The closest available value from Table 2 at the end of the book is for a t-distribution for $m = 40$ degrees of freedom. This value is $t_c = 2.021$ and will be very close to the correct critical value. Some specialized computer programs, such as SHAZAM or SAS, have algorithms for computing the correct critical value, which in this case is $t_c = 2.023$. We will use this value in our calculations. See Exercise 4.7 to explore the consequences of using the approximate value. The 95% confidence interval estimate for the population mean food expenditure is

$$b \pm t_c \hat{\sigma} \sqrt{T} = \$51.08 \pm 2.023 \sqrt{6.38} / \sqrt{40} \quad \text{or} \quad [\$50.27, \$51.89]$$

Recall that our confidence is in the *procedure*, not these numbers, and to be *more* confident the interval would have to be wider. As in the known-σ^2 case, the statement we can make is that, in a repeated sampling sense, where many intervals are computed, we expect $(1 - \alpha)$ percent to contain the parameter β.

Note that this confidence interval is narrower than the one constructed assuming the variance σ^2 was known despite the fact that the critical value t_c is always greater than z_c. In this example $\hat{\sigma}^2$ is much smaller than the value we assumed for σ^2. In other samples $\hat{\sigma}^2$ may be larger or smaller than the true, but unknown, variance σ^2.

4.4.3 Hypothesis Testing

When σ^2 is unknown, hypothesis tests about the mean of a population are also based on the t-distribution. To test the hypothesis $H_0: \beta = \beta_0$ against $H_1: \beta \neq \beta_0$, we use the test statistic

$$t = \frac{b - \beta_0}{\hat{\sigma} / \sqrt{T}} \tag{4.4.6}$$

If you compare this test statistic to the standardized normal random variable in equation 4.3.3 you will see that $\hat{\sigma}$ has replaced σ. The test statistic t has a t probability density function with $(T - 1)$ degrees of freedom *if* the hypothesis $\beta = \beta_0$ is *true*. The null hypothesis is rejected if $|t| > t_c$.

If a public official wants to test the null hypothesis $H_0: \beta = 50$ against the alternative $H_1: \beta \neq 50$, assuming σ^2 is unknown, the appropriate test statistic is the t random variable that is given in equation 4.4.6 as

$$t = \frac{b - \beta_0}{\hat{\sigma} / \sqrt{T}} = \frac{51.08 - 50}{.399} = 2.707$$

By using the $\alpha = .05$ critical value for a t-distribution with 39 degrees of freedom ($t_c = 2.023$), we reject the hypothesis that the population mean weekly food expenditure is \$50. To test the inequality hypothesis $H_0: \beta \leq 50$ against $H_1: \beta > 50$, we compare the value of the test statistic to the upper $\alpha = .05$ percentile of the $t_{(39)}$ distribution, which is 1.685, and reject the hypothesis that the population mean is less than or equal to 50.

Computing the p-value of a t-statistic requires specialized computer software, since tables of commonly used critical values are not sufficiently detailed. Many programs, however, contain the cumulative distribution function for the t-random variable with m degrees of freedom, $F(t, m)$. For situations where these programs are available, the p-value of the t-statistic is

$$p - \text{value}(t) = 2(1 - F(|t|, m))$$

For example,

$$p - \text{value}(2.70) = 2(1 - F(2.70, 39)) = .01$$

That is, .01 of the probability mass under the $t_{(39)}$ probability density function lies in the tails where $|t| \geq 2.70$. This indicates that the hypothesis H_0: $\beta = 50$ should be rejected at any level of Type I error $\alpha \geq .01$.

4.5 A Sampling Experiment

To illustrate the sampling properties of the interval estimators and hypothesis tests that we have discussed, we continue the sampling experiment begun in Section 3.5.4. Recall that the statistical model on which the Monte Carlo experiment is based is

$$Y_i = \beta + e_i = 20 + e_i, \qquad i = 1,\dots, T = 10 \qquad (4.5.1a)$$

$$e_i \sim N\left(0, \sigma^2 = 10\right) \qquad (4.5.1b)$$

In the experiment we create $N = 1000$ samples of size $T = 10$ using the model and parameter values in equation 4.5.1 and obtain estimates b and $\hat{\sigma}^2$ for each. We can use the same experiment to investigate interval estimators and hypothesis tests.

4.5.1 Sampling Properties of Interval Estimators

Let us consider interval estimation of β. If σ^2 is known the appropriate interval estimator is

$$b \pm z_c\, \sigma/\sqrt{T} \qquad (4.5.2a)$$

and if σ^2 is unknown the interval estimator of β is

$$b \pm t_c\, \hat{\sigma}/\sqrt{T} \qquad (4.5.2b)$$

For $T = 10$, the critical value of the t-statistic comes from the $t_{(T-1)} = t_{(9)}$ distribution and is $t_c(\alpha = .05) = 2.262$ or $t_c(\alpha = .01) = 3.250$. In Table 4.2 the 95% confidence interval estimates for the first 10 samples are reported for both the known and unknown σ^2 cases. In Table 4.2, note that 9 of the 10 intervals for the case where $\sigma^2 = 10$ is known contain the true population mean $\beta = 20$, whereas all 10 of the intervals based on estimates of σ^2 contain $\beta = 20$. In 1000 samples the 95% confidence interval, for the known σ^2

Table 4.2 95% Confidence Intervals for 10 Monte Carlo Samples

Sample	$b \pm z_c\left(\sigma/\sqrt{T}\right)$	$b \pm t_c\left(\hat{\sigma}/\sqrt{T}\right)$
1	[18.73, 22.65]	[17.43, 23.95]
2	[19.36, 23.28]	[19.52, 23.13]
3	[18.35, 22.27]	[17.05, 23.58]
4	[18.75, 22.67]	[17.71, 23.72]
5	[20.08, 24.00]	[19.73, 24.35]
6	[17.62, 21.54]	[17.17, 21.99]
7	[17.69, 21.61]	[16.78, 22.51]
8	[19.54, 23.46]	[19.06, 23.94]
9	[17.61, 21.53]	[17.60, 21.54]
10	[17.34, 21.26]	[17.72, 20.88]

case, contains the true parameter 95.4% of the time, and the 99% confidence interval contains it 99.2% of the time. When σ^2 is not assumed known, 96.5% of the 95% confidence intervals and 99.4% of the 99% confidence intervals contain $\beta = 20$. These proportions would approach .95 and .99, respectively, if the number of samples were increased.

4.5.2   Sampling Properties of Hypothesis Tests

To test the null hypothesis $H_0: \beta = \beta_0$ against the alternative $H_1: \beta \neq \beta_0$ when σ^2 is known the test statistic is

$$Z = \frac{b - \beta_0}{\sigma / \sqrt{T}} \sim N(0, 1) \qquad \text{if } H_0: \beta = \beta_0 \text{ is true} \qquad (4.5.3a)$$

and if σ^2 is unknown the test statistic is

$$t = \frac{b - \beta_0}{\hat{\sigma} / \sqrt{T}} \sim t_{(T-1)} \qquad \text{if } H_0: \beta = \beta_0 \text{ is true} \qquad (4.5.3b)$$

In Table 4.3 are the test statistics and their p-values for the tests when $\beta_0 = 20$, and thus the null hypothesis is true. Note that only sample number 5, with σ^2 known, leads to rejection of the null hypothesis at the $\alpha = .05$ level of significance. This is the same sample, in Table 4.2, that did not produce a 95% confidence interval estimate containing the true parameter. Furthermore, in the $N = 1000$ samples 4.6% of the Z-tests and 3.5% of the t-tests led to rejection of the null hypothesis at the $\alpha = .05$ level of test significance. These are the same percentages in which the corresponding confidence intervals did not contain, or "cover," the true parameter value $\beta = 20$. This result is not an accident. In Exercise 4.3 you are asked to show that a test of the null hypothesis that $\beta = \beta_0$, against the two-sided alternative that $\beta \neq \beta_0$, *rejects* that hypothesis at the α level of significance *only* if the $(1 - \alpha)$ percent confidence interval *does not* cover the value β_0. In other words, a z- or t-test will not reject a null hypothesis of $\beta = \beta_0$ if β_0 is contained in the corresponding confidence interval.

Table 4.3   Test Statistics and p-values for 10 Monte Carlo Samples

Sample	z	p-value z	t	p-value t
1	0.692	0.488	0.480	0.642
2	1.326	0.184	1.661	0.131
3	0.318	0.750	0.220	0.830
4	0.717	0.473	0.540	0.602
5	2.043	0.041	2.000	0.076
6	−0.413	0.678	−0.388	0.706
7	−0.348	0.727	−0.275	0.789
8	1.501	0.133	1.391	0.197
9	−0.424	0.671	−0.487	0.637
10	−0.695	0.486	−0.998	0.344

4.6 Other Examples

4.6.1 Rational Expectations

In Section 3.7.1 we considered the rational expectations hypothesis. In developing the statistical model we assumed that the random variable Y, which is equal to expected inflation minus actual inflation, is distributed $N(\beta, \sigma^2)$. Also assuming that the data in Table 3.6 represent a random sample from that population we obtained the estimates $b = .605$ of inflationary overexpectations and $\hat{\sigma}^2 = 3.113$ of the error variance. As noted in Section 3.7.1 of Chapter 3, we are concerned with testing the null hypothesis H_0: $\beta = 0$ against the alternative H_1: $\beta \neq 0$. We can test this hypothesis using the test statistic

$$t = \frac{b - \beta_0}{\hat{\sigma}/\sqrt{T}}$$

If the null hypothesis is true, the test statistic t has a t-distribution with $T - 1$ degrees of freedom. The $\alpha = .05$ critical value is $t_c = 2.262$. Given our sample of data, the value of the test statistic is

$$t = \frac{b - \beta_0}{\hat{\sigma}/\sqrt{T}} = \frac{.605 - 0}{\sqrt{3.113/11}} = \frac{.605}{.532} = 1.136$$

Since this value is less than the critical value, we do not reject the null hypothesis and conclude that our data are compatible (not inconsistent) with the rational expectations hypothesis. The p-value for this t-statistic is

$$2\left(1 - \Pr\left[t_{(\tau-1)} \leq 1.1316\right]\right) = .282$$

which indicates that the null hypothesis H_0: $\beta = 0$ (that the population mean inflationary overexpectation is zero) will *not* be rejected at usual levels of Type I error, like $\alpha = .01$, .05, or .10.

We can construct a 95% interval estimate for the mean inflationary overexpectation as

$$b \pm t_c \hat{\sigma}/\sqrt{T} = .605 \pm 2.262(.532)$$

$$= \left[-.599, 1.808\right]$$

The 95% interval estimate "covers" the value $\beta = 0$. This outcome is consistent with the failure to reject the null hypothesis. See Exercise 4.3.

4.6.2 Sales of Canned Tuna

In Section 3.7.2 we considered the weekly sales of canned tuna to be a random variable, the natural logarithm of which was assumed to follow a $N(\beta, \sigma^2)$ distribution. That is $Y = \ln(\text{chain tuna sales}) \sim N(\beta, \sigma^2)$. Based on the sample of data in Table 3.7, we estimated the mean β and variance σ^2 to be

$$b = 10.1735$$

$$\hat{\sigma}^2 = .1329$$

The chain manager can be provided a 95% interval estimate for β as

$$b \pm t_c \; \hat{\sigma} / \sqrt{T} = 10.1735 \pm 1.96 \sqrt{\frac{.1329}{52}}$$

or [10.07, 10.27]. To convert these values to sales we calculate the antilogs as [$e^{10.07} =$ 23624, $e^{10.27} = 28854$] to obtain the interval estimate of weekly sales of canned tuna as [23624, 28854]. Recall what this interval estimate *does not tell us. It does not tell us that there is a 95% chance that sales will fall in that interval.* The true mean β is either in this interval or it is not. However, since the *procedure* we use produces intervals that cover, or contain, the true parameter 95 times out of 100, we should be surprised if β were not in the interval estimate. The probability that the *procedure used* will create an interval estimate containing the mean β of the *logarithm* of sales is .95.

4.6.3   A Two-Sample Problem

The techniques we have developed in this chapter can be applied in a wide variety of circumstances. One common problem is to investigate whether two populations have the same mean parameter. For example, a grocery store chain executive may be interested in knowing whether two stores in the chain have identical mean weekly sales of tuna. We will assume that the natural logarithm of each store's weekly sales of tuna follows a normal distribution with possibly different mean values but a *common variance*. That is,

$$Y_1 = \ln(\text{store 1 tuna sales}) \sim N(\beta_1, \sigma^2) \tag{4.6.1a}$$

$$Y_2 = \ln(\text{store 2 tuna sales}) \sim N(\beta_2, \sigma^2) \tag{4.6.1b}$$

The null and alternative hypotheses we wish to test are

$$\begin{aligned} H_0 &: \beta_1 = \beta_2 \\ H_1 &: \beta_1 \neq \beta_2 \end{aligned} \tag{4.6.2}$$

The null hypothesis states that the two stores' mean weekly sales (actually logarithms of sales) are equal. Let us assume that we have a sample of T weeks of sales data from each store: $Y_{11}, Y_{12}, \ldots, Y_{1T}$ (store 1) and $Y_{21}, Y_{22}, \ldots, Y_{2T}$ (store 2), and that the weekly sales of each store are independent not only of each other but from week to week. Thus, $Y_{1i} \sim N(\beta_1, \sigma^2)$ and independently of $Y_{2i} \sim N(\beta_2, \sigma^2)$. Written in the form of two linear models

$$\begin{aligned} Y_{1i} &= \beta_1 + e_{1i} \qquad Y_{2i} = \beta_2 + e_{2i} \\ e_{1i} &\sim N(0, \sigma^2) \quad e_{2i} \sim N(0, \sigma^2) \\ \text{cov}(e_{1i}, e_{1j}) &= 0 \; \text{cov}(e_{2i}, e_{2j}) = 0 \qquad i \neq j \\ \text{cov}(e_{1i}, e_{2j}) &= 0 \end{aligned} \tag{4.6.3}$$

The least squares, and maximum likelihood, estimators of β_1 and β_2 are

$$b_1 = \sum_{i=1}^{T} Y_{1i} / T \sim N(\beta_1, \sigma^2 / T) \tag{4.6.4a}$$

$$b_2 = \sum_{i=1}^{T} Y_{2i} / T \sim N\left(\beta_2, \sigma^2 / T\right) \tag{4.6.4b}$$

The common variance σ^2 of the two populations can be estimated using the "pooled" estimator

$$\hat{\sigma}^2 = \frac{\sum_{i=1}^{T}\left[\left(Y_{1i} - b_1\right)^2 + \left(Y_{2i} - b_2\right)^2\right]}{2(T-1)} \tag{4.6.5}$$

This estimator is the sum of squared errors from the two samples divided by the *total* number of degrees of freedom in the two samples. The degrees of freedom are $2T - 2$ since two population means were estimated using the data. To form an appropriate test statistic, we must have a statistic with a known distribution when the null hypothesis is true. Consider the random variable

$$d = b_1 - b_2 = \sum_{i=1}^{T} \frac{Y_{1i}}{T} - \sum_{i=1}^{T} \frac{Y_{2i}}{T}$$

which is the difference between the maximum likelihood estimators for the two population means. The mean and variance of d are

$$E[d] = E[b_1] - E[b_2] = \beta_1 - \beta_2 \tag{4.6.6a}$$

$$\text{var}(d) = \text{var}(b_1) + \text{var}(b_2) = \frac{\sigma^2}{T} + \frac{\sigma^2}{T} = \frac{2\sigma^2}{T} \tag{4.6.6b}$$

The latter result holds since b_1 and b_2 are independent, which means that the variance of the sum is the sum of the variances. See Chapter 2, Section 2.7.2. Furthermore, since d is the weighted sum of independent normal random variables, it is normally distributed itself. That is,

$$d \sim N\left(\beta_1 - \beta_2, 2\sigma^2 / T\right) \tag{4.6.6c}$$

Consequently, we can construct a standard normal random variable as

$$Z = \frac{d - \left(\beta_1 - \beta_2\right)}{\left(2\sigma^2 / T\right)^{1/2}} \sim N(0, 1) \tag{4.6.7}$$

Since the population variance σ^2 is not known, Z cannot be used as a basis for a statistical test. To construct a t-random variable we will use the fact that the random variable

$$W = \frac{2(T-1)\hat{\sigma}^2}{\sigma^2} \sim \chi^2_{(2(T-1))} \tag{4.6.8}$$

is distributed independently of Z. The degrees of freedom are $2(T - 1)$ since $\hat{\sigma}^2$ here is the pooled estimator given in equation 4.6.5. Recall that a t random variable is formed by dividing Z by the square root of the chi-square random variable W, which has been divided by its degrees of freedom, $m = 2(T - 1)$. That is,

$$t = \frac{N(0,1)}{\sqrt{\chi^2_{(m)} \big/ m}} = \frac{\dfrac{d-(\beta_1 - \beta_2)}{(2\sigma^2/T)^{1/2}}}{\sqrt{\dfrac{2(T-1)\hat{\sigma}^2}{\sigma^2} \bigg/ 2(T-1)}} = \frac{d-(\beta_1 - \beta_2)}{(2\hat{\sigma}^2/T)^{1/2}} \sim t_{(2(T-1))} \qquad (4.6.9)$$

To test the null hypothesis H_0: $\beta_1 = \beta_2$ against the alternative H_1: $\beta_1 \neq \beta_2$ we observe that if the null hypothesis is true, that is $\beta_1 = \beta_2$, then

$$t = \frac{d}{(2\hat{\sigma}^2/T)^{1/2}} \sim t_{(2(T-1))}$$

We reject the null hypothesis if $|t| \geq t_c$, where t_c is a critical value from the $t_{(2(T-1))}$ distribution.

Let us carry out this test based on $T = 20$ weeks of actual store level data on weekly tuna sales of two stores in the same chain in a large midwestern city. The sales are given in Table 4.4. Using these data, we estimate values of b_1, b_2, and σ^2 as

$$b_1 = \sum_{i=1}^{T} \frac{y_{1i}}{T} = 6.18006$$

$$b_2 = \sum_{i=1}^{T} \frac{y_{2i}}{T} = 6.78461$$

$$\hat{\sigma}^2 = \sum_{i=1}^{T} \frac{(y_{1i} - b_1)^2 + (y_{2i} - b_2)^2}{2(T-1)} = .06885$$

Table 4.4 Weekly Log-Sales of Tuna for Two Stores

Week	Store 1	Store 2
1	6.15698	6.62274
2	6.10702	7.09506
3	6.28413	7.19068
4	6.29711	6.81235
5	6.08677	6.80128
6	6.16331	6.51767
7	6.57368	7.21671
8	6.46459	7.00307
9	6.39693	7.23634
10	6.15910	6.99485
11	6.38856	7.13090
12	5.92158	6.60123
13	5.97126	6.25958
14	5.94017	6.24804
15	5.93754	6.47080
16	6.08904	6.95940
17	6.32615	6.87626
18	6.13556	6.55678
19	6.15910	6.31173
20	6.04263	6.78672

The value of the t-statistic in equation 4.6.10 is

$$t = \frac{d}{\sqrt{\dfrac{2\hat{\sigma}^2}{T}}} = \frac{6.18006 - 6.78461}{\sqrt{\dfrac{2(.06885)}{20}}} = -7.28$$

The $\alpha = .05$ critical value of the $t_{(38)}$ distribution is 2.024, which we calculate using SHAZAM or SAS. Thus, we reject the hypothesis that these two stores' weekly tuna sales come from a population with the same mean, and we therefore cannot pool the samples of data for estimation purposes. In passing, we note that the straightforward test procedure used in this example depends crucially on the two population variances being equal. Procedures for testing whether or not the populations have identical variances are discussed in Chapter 15.

The test statistic in equation 4.6.9 was derived under the assumption that the two sample sizes are equal. If the sample sizes are not the same, then the t-statistic is

$$t = \frac{d - \left(\beta_1 - \beta_2\right)}{\hat{\sigma}_p \sqrt{\dfrac{1}{T_1} + \dfrac{1}{T_2}}} \sim t_{(T_1 + T_2 - 2)} \tag{4.6.10}$$

where T_1 and T_2 are the sample sizes and the pooled estimator of the populations' variance is

$$\hat{\sigma}_p^2 = \frac{\displaystyle\sum_{i=1}^{T_1}\left(Y_{1i} - b_1\right)^2 + \sum_{i=1}^{T_2}\left(Y_{2i} - b_2\right)^2}{T_1 + T_2 - 2}$$

4.7 Summary

In this chapter we have introduced procedures for constructing confidence intervals and carrying out tests of hypotheses. The statistical model on which our work was based is

$$Y_i = \beta + e_i \qquad i = 1, \ldots, T \tag{4.7.1a}$$

$$e_i \sim N\left(0, \sigma^2\right) \tag{4.7.1b}$$

and

$$\mathrm{cov}\left(e_i, e_j\right) = 0 \quad i \neq j \tag{4.7.1c}$$

Given this model the least squares (and maximum likelihood) estimator of the population mean is

$$b = \sum_{i=1}^{T} Y_i / T \sim N\left(\beta, \sigma^2\right) \tag{4.7.2a}$$

and the unbiased estimator of σ^2 is

$$\hat{\sigma}^2 = \sum_{i=1}^{T}\left(Y_i - b\right)^2 \Big/ T - 1 \sim \frac{\sigma^2}{T-1} \chi_{(T-1)}^2 \tag{4.7.2b}$$

Using these results we can construct standardized random variables that have known distributions

$$Z = \frac{b-\beta}{\sigma/\sqrt{T}} \sim N(0, 1) \qquad (4.7.3a)$$

and

$$t = \frac{b-\beta}{\hat{\sigma}/\sqrt{T}} \sim t_{(T-1)} \qquad (4.7.3b)$$

where $t_{(T-1)}$ denotes Student's t-distribution with $T-1$ degrees of freedom.

Interval *estimators* with $(1 - \alpha)$ probability of containing the true parameter β are

$$\sigma^2 \text{ known:} \qquad b \pm z_c \left(\sigma/\sqrt{T} \right) \qquad (4.7.4a)$$

$$\sigma^2 \text{ unknown:} \qquad b \pm t_c \left(\hat{\sigma}/\sqrt{T} \right) \qquad (4.7.4b)$$

where z_c and t_c are critical values from the $N(0, 1)$ and $t_{(T-1)}$ distributions, respectively, such that $\Pr[|z| \geq z_c] = \Pr[|t| \geq t_c] = \alpha$. We want to emphasize that when *estimates* (numbers) replace the estimators (random variables) b and $\hat{\sigma}$ in expression 4.7.4, then the resulting interval *estimate* (two numbers) *does not* have a $(1 - \alpha)\%$ chance of containing β.

To test the null hypothesis

$$H_0 : \beta = \beta_0 \qquad (4.7.5a)$$

against the alternative

$$H_1 : \beta \neq \beta_0 \qquad (4.7.5b)$$

we use the test statistics

$$\sigma^2 \text{ known:} \qquad Z = \frac{b-\beta_0}{\sigma/\sqrt{T}} \qquad (4.7.6a)$$

$$\sigma^2 \text{ unknown:} \qquad t = \frac{b-\beta_0}{\hat{\sigma}/\sqrt{T}} \qquad (4.7.6b)$$

If the null hypothesis $\beta = \beta_0$ is *true*, then $Z \sim N(0, 1)$ and $t \sim t_{(T-1)}$ from equation 4.7.3. If we reject H_0: $\beta = \beta_0$ in favor of H_1: $\beta \neq \beta_0$ when $|z| \geq z_c$ (σ^2 known), or $|t| \geq t_c$ (σ^2 unknown) we will make the Type I error of rejecting a true hypothesis only $\alpha\%$ of the time. While following this testing procedure, and fixing the probability of a Type I error at α, we are simultaneously maximizing the probability of rejecting a false hypothesis.

All of the interval estimation and hypothesis testing results we have stated depend on our statement of the statistical model in equation 4.7.1 being correct (Section 3.8 of Chapter 3). If any of the stated assumptions are *not correct* then the random variables b, $\hat{\sigma}^2$, Z, and t *do not* have the distributions stated in equations 4.7.2 and 4.7.3. Thus, confidence interval statements and hypothesis test conclusions, and the inferences that follow, may well be incorrect.

As we noted already, the hypothesis tests and interval estimation procedures that we developed in this chapter are based on the assumption of a normal population, or equivalently, that the errors e_i (see equation 4.7.1b) are normal. If this assumption holds true, then all the tests and procedures we have suggested are correct for any sample size, large or small.

Even if the population, and errors e_i, are *not* normal, however, the tests and procedures we have described can be used in *large* samples if the other model assumptions hold. This is possible because of the Central Limit Theorem we introduced in Chapter 2, which says that the *sample mean* has a distribution that is *approximately* distributed as $N(\beta, \sigma^2/T)$ when the sample size T is large. In Chapter 14 other results that hold in large samples are examined.

4.8 Exercises

4.1   Construct 95% and 99% confidence intervals for the mean U. S. unemployment rate β_u using the data in Table 2.2. Test the null hypothesis H_0: $\beta_u = 4\%$ against the alternative H_1: $\beta_u \neq 4\%$.

4.2   Repeat the sampling experiment in Section 4.5 using uniform random numbers, as described in Exercise 3.10. Are we justified in using normal test and interval estimation procedures in this case?

4.3   Show that if the $(1 - \alpha)$ confidence interval estimate $b \pm t_c \, \hat{\sigma}/\sqrt{T}$ contains the value β_0 then the t-test of the null hypothesis H_0: $\beta = \beta_0$ against the alternative H_1: $\beta \neq \beta_0$ will *not* be rejected at the α level of significance.

4.4   Following the example in Section 4.6.2, suppose that we are interested in whether weekly tuna sales will be less than 15,000 cans. The natural logarithm of 15,000 is 9.6158. Test the null hypothesis that the mean of the logarithm of weekly sales is less than 9.6158.

4.5   Show that the prediction error $\hat{e}_0 = Y_0 - \hat{Y}_0$ in equation 4.2.8 is a weighted sum of the independent normal random variables $e_1, e_2, \ldots, e_T$ and e_0.

4.6   Given that $Y_1, \ldots, Y_T$ is a random sample from a $N(\beta, \sigma^2)$ population we may test the null hypothesis H_0: $\beta = \beta_0$ against the alternative H_1: $\beta \neq \beta_0$ by using the test statistic $Z = (b - \beta_0)/(\sigma/\sqrt{T})$, which has a standard normal distribution if the null hypothesis is true. The null hypothesis is rejected if $|Z| \geq z_c$, where z_c is a critical value from the $N(0, 1)$ distribution. Determine what the critical values β_L and β_U (see Figure 4.2) would be if we chose to use the testing rule: Reject the null hypothesis when $b \geq \beta_U$ or $b \leq \beta_L$.

4.7   Following the example in Section 4.4.2, suppose that the correct critical value $t_c = 2.023$ for a 95% confidence interval for the $t_{(39)}$ distribution were not known. Construct "95%" interval estimates using the critical values from the $t_{(30)}$ and $t_{(40)}$ distributions, which can be found in Table 2 at the end of the book. If these values are used, are the resulting intervals actually 95% confidence intervals? If you wished to report the more "conservative" result, which would you use?

4.8   Carry through the sampling experiment discussed in Section 4.5 and discuss how your results differ from theoretical expectations.

4.9   A vending machine is designed to pour 7.0 oz. of Cajun Cola into 8-oz. cups. A technician takes $T_1 = 4$ sample cups yielding the following measurements: 6.92 oz., 7.34 oz., 7.26 oz., and 6.88 oz. If we assume the poured amounts follow a normal distribution, (*i*) test the hypothesis that the true average amount of cola poured is 7 oz., against the alternative that the average amount is not 7 oz. at $\alpha = .05$ level of significance. (*ii*) Construct a 95% interval estimate for the mean amount of cola dispensed.

4.10 Refer to Exercise 4.9. The Cajun Cola vending machine is adjusted and a sample of $T_2 = 5$ cups is taken yielding the measurements: 7.33 oz., 7.93 oz., 7.65 oz., 7.49 oz., 7.10 oz. If the adjustment is known to affect the mean amount poured, but not the variance of the amount of cola poured, test the hypothesis that the adjustment had no effect on the mean amount of Cajun Cola dispensed at the $\alpha = .01$ level of significance.

4.11 At the Bayou Bean Coffee store the daily demand for coffee is normally distributed. A random sample of $T = 5$ days showed the amounts demanded (pounds/day) to be 29, 22, 32, 19, and 28. Construct a 99% interval estimate for the mean daily demand for coffee.

4.12 The number of miles that a jogger can get on a pair of jogging shoes is a normally distributed random variable. A random sample of $T = 6$ joggers who use Kanga-leapers running shoes got 850, 1565, 1020, 1380, 1215, and 1170 miles, respectively. Kanga-leapers management wants to advertise that their shoes can be used for *at least* 1000 miles on the average. (*i*) Do these data support such a claim at the $\alpha = .01$ level of significance? (*ii*) Construct a 95% interval estimate for the mean number of miles the shoes are good for.

4.13 At Bubba's Burger Barn the number of burgers sold per day is normally distributed. On the basis of a random sample of $T = 20$ days the *sample* mean number of burgers sold is 80.21 and the *sample* standard deviation is 15.56. Test the hypothesis, at the $\alpha = .05$ level, that the population mean is (*i*) 78 burgers per day, (*ii*) at least 78 burgers per day.

4.14 Assume that the random variable $X \sim N(\beta, \sigma^2 = 200^2)$. Find the probability of a Type II error when testing the null hypothesis $H_0\colon \beta = 1000$ at the $\alpha = .05$ level *if* the *true* population mean is $\beta = 1200$.

4.15 Lolita works for a consumer protection group whose concern is to protect consumers against fraud. She is currently interested in whether Cajun Cola properly fills its one-liter bottles. She wishes to test the null hypothesis that the mean amount poured by filling machines is less than or equal to 1000 ml against the alternative that the mean amount poured is greater than 1000 ml. The contents of a randomly chosen bottle of Cajun Cola is normally distributed with a variance of 16 ml. If a sample of $T = 25$ bottles has *average* contents of 1001.6 ml, what should she conclude at the $\alpha = .05$ level?

4.16 Tofu World, a vegetarian restaurant, wishes to test the hypothesis that its male customers' average weight equals the population average of 165 lb. A random sample of $T = 6$ customers yields weights of 154, 196, 180, 162, 173, and 190 lb. If we assume the population of customers has weights that are normally distributed, (*i*) test the null hypothesis that Tofu's customers' mean weight is 165 lb. against the alternative that it isn't, at $\alpha = .05$ level of significance. (*ii*) Calculate the *p*-value of the test.

4.17 To evaluate various pension and superannuation schemes the Ideal-Product Corporation must determine the mean age of its workforce. Assume that age is normally distributed. Since the company has several thousand employees, a sample is to be taken. Given the standard deviation of ages is 21 years, how large should the sample be to ensure that the 95% interval estimate of mean age is no more than 4 years wide? Will this desired level of precision necessarily be obtained? Would the desired precision be obtained if 21 years was only a preliminary *estimate* of the standard deviation?

4.18 The Matchless Match Company claims that their boxes of matches contain at least 50 matches on average. The Company operates a monitoring policy in which samples of 40 boxes are taken periodically to see if their claim is justified. Suppose the following sample is taken:

48	47	49	49	49	47	49	48	49	49
50	51	48	49	48	51	50	50	53	49
51	48	47	49	48	50	51	48	52	51
47	50	49	53	49	48	51	51	51	49

(a) If the company uses a 5% significance level, will they decide their claim is justified?

(b) Suppose that a sample of only 10 had been taken (the first row of observations), would the same conclusion have been reached?

(c) What reservations, if any, do you have about the test procedure in (b)?

4.19 Suppose that a random variable Y is such that $Y \sim N(34.8, 280)$. In addition, suppose that you are unaware that $E(Y) = \beta = 34.8$, and that you wish to use a random sample of 45 observations to test

$$H_0 : \beta = 30 \qquad \text{against} \quad H_1 : \beta > 30$$

(a) If you use a 5% significance level, what is the probability of making a Type II error?

(b) What is the probability of discerning that the mean is greater than 30?

(c) What is the probability of a Type I error?

4.20 The daily sales of a shop have had mean $3200 per day, with standard deviation of $400, for some time. The management is to initiate an extensive advertising campaign and then see if there is an improvement in sales during the next 20 shopping days. Assume that daily sales are normally distributed.

(a) If the average daily sales for the period after the campaign was $3356.00, what should the management conclude about the advertising campaign? (Assume that the management does not want to falsely conclude that the advertising was successful more frequently than 10% of times.) Clearly state your null and alternative hypotheses and show your work.

(b) If the sample standard deviation of daily sales for the period after the advertising campaign was equal to $290, should the management conclude that the variability of daily sales has changed? (Assume that the management does not want to falsely conclude that the variance has changed more than 10% of times.) Clearly state your null and alternative hypotheses and show your work.

(c) If the sample mean and sample standard deviations are as given in (a) and (b), should the management conclude that the advertising campaign was successful in increasing daily sales? (Assume that the management does not want to falsely conclude that the campaign was successful more than 5% of times.) Clearly state your hypotheses and show your work.

4.21 Miracle Manufacturing is considering a new procedure for assembling units. The mean assembly time using the old procedure is 14 minutes. Management wishes to know whether or not the mean assembly time for the new procedure is less than that for the old one. For a sample of 64 assembly times, the sample mean and sample standard deviation are found to be 13.2 minutes and 4.0 minutes, respectively. Is the new assembly time shorter? (Assume that the management does not want to falsely conclude that the new assembly time is shorter more often than 1% of times.) Clearly state your hypotheses and assumptions. Show your work.

4.22 Table 2.5, in Exercise 2.20, contains data on the cost of constructing nuclear power plants (C). Assume that the cost data satisfies the assumptions of the linear statistical model in equation 4.2.1.

(a) Construct a 95% confidence interval estimate for β, the mean construction cost.

(b) Test the null hypothesis that the population mean construction cost β is 600 against the alternative that it is not 600 at the $\alpha = .01$ level of significance.

(c) In Section 4.2.1 we developed procedures for predicting a value from a normal population when σ^2 was known. Predict the cost of a new nuclear power plant, assuming the statistical model 4.2.1 is correct. Construct a 95% *prediction interval estimate* for Y_0. (*Hint:* You need to use a t-distribution.)

(d) The last six observations are on "partial turnkey plants," as indicated by the variable $PT = 1$. Test the hypothesis that the mean cost for these 6 plants is identical to the mean cost for the remaining plants at the $\alpha = .05$ level of significance. What key assumption does this test depend on?

(e) In parts (a)–(c) of this question we assumed that the model 4.2.1 correctly represented how the nuclear cost data were generated. Critically evaluate those assumptions in this context.

4.23 Table 2.6, in Exercise 2.21, contains data on the excess returns of two securities and a market portfolio. Assume that the data on *each* variable arises from a linear statistical model 4.2.1.

(a) Test, at the $\alpha = .05$ level of significance, the null hypothesis that each variable has mean zero, against the alternative that the mean is not zero. Describe the economic consequence of the null hypothesis, if true.

(b) Construct a 95% confidence interval estimate for the mean of *each* variable.

(c) Test, at the $\alpha = .05$ level of significance, the null hypothesis that the mean excess returns for the securities are equal against the alternative that they are not equal. What key assumption is the test based on?

(d) Critically evaluate the appropriateness of the linear statistical model for the three variables in Table 2.6.

4.9   References

Many statistics and econometrics books cover the material discussed in this chapter. For elementary treatments see the following works:

BEALS, R. (1972) *Statistics for Economists: An Introduction*, Chicago: Rand McNally & Co.,Chapter 8.

BRENNAN, M. J. and T. M. CARROLL (1987) *Preface to Quantitative Economics and Econometrics*, 4th Edition, Cincinnati, OH: South-Western Publishing Co., Chapter 16.

MADSEN, R. W. and M. L. MOESCHBERGER (1983) *Introductory Statistics for Business and Economics*, Englewood Cliffs, NJ: Prentice-Hall, Inc., Chapters 7 and 8.

More advanced treatments may be found in these texts:

JUDGE, G.G., *et al.* (1988) *Introduction to the Theory and Practice of Econometrics*, 2nd Edition, New York: John Wiley & Sons, Inc., Chapter 3.

KMENTA, J. (1986) *Elements of Econometrics*, 2nd Edition, New York: Macmillan Publishing Co., Chapters 4–6.

Appendix to Part I

Review-Summary of Chapters 2 to 4

Chapter 2

2.1 (Section 2.1) Economic data are outcomes of controlled and uncontrolled experiments. Observations on an economic variable are the experimental outcomes $y_1, y_2, \ldots, y_T$, that are observed and measured.

2.2 (Section 2.2) Economic variables are experimental outcomes whose precise values are not known a priori nor can they be predicted. Such variables are called *random variables*.

2.3 (Section 2.2) Observations on single economic units (a household, firm, state, etc.) recorded over time at regular intervals are a *time-series* of data. At a single point in time, observations on many economic units are *cross-sectional* data. Data on many economic units observed over time are a *panel* of data.

2.4 (Section 2.3.1) Economic random variables may be *discrete* or *continuous*. Discrete random variables take only a countable number of values. Continuous random variables can take any value in an interval of the real number line.

2.5 (Section 2.3.2) Economic random variables may be T recorded values of a single variable y_t, or *univariate*. Two random variables recorded together (y_{t1}, y_{t2}) are *bivariate*. Many random variables recorded together $(y_{t1}, y_{t2}, \ldots, y_{tm})$ are *multivariate*.

2.6 (Section 2.3.3) Descriptive statistics are used to describe or depict a sample of economic data. If X is an economic random variable with observed values x_t, $t = 1, \ldots, T$, then

(*i*) the arithmetic mean is

$$\bar{x} = \sum_{t=1}^{T} x_t \, / \, T \tag{S.2.1}$$

(*Note:* Summation operations are reviewed in Appendix 2A of Chapter 2.)

(*ii*) the sample variance is

$$s_x^2 = \sum_{t=1}^{T}(x_t - \bar{x})^2 \big/ (T-1) \tag{S.2.2}$$

(*iii*) the sample standard deviation is

$$s_x = \sqrt{s_x^2} \tag{S.2.3}$$

(*iv*) the coefficient of variation is

$$cv_x = (s_x / \bar{x}) \times 100 \tag{S.2.4}$$

Bar charts, histograms and relative frequency distributions can be used to depict observations on single economic random variables. Bivariate observations may be viewed in scatter diagrams.

2.7 (Section 2.4.1)   As noted in (2.2) the outcome values for random variables are not known until an experiment is carried out. In Chapters 2–4 we denote a random variable as X and its outcome value as x, and recognize that, depending on the range of values it can take, a random variable may be discrete or continuous.

2.8 (Sections 2.4.2–2.4.3)   Let $f(x)$ denote the probability density function of a *discrete* random variable X. Then, $f(x)$ is the probability that X takes the value x,

$$P[X = x] = f(x) \tag{S.2.5}$$

If Y is a continuous random variable, its probability density function $f(y)$ is the equation of a curve. The probability that Y takes a value in the interval $[a, b]$ is the area under the curve $f(y)$ between $y = a$ and $y = b$,

$$P[a \leq Y \leq b] = \int_a^b f(y)dy \tag{S.2.6}$$

(*Note:* Integrals are discussed in Appendix 2B of Chapter 2.)

If $Y_1, Y_2, \ldots, Y_m$ are random variables, then their *joint* probability density function $f(y_1, \ldots, y_m)$ can be used to make probability statements. If the random variables are continuous, then $f(\cdot)$ is the equation of a surface and probability is *volume* under the surface.

2.9 (Section 2.4.4)   Two random variables X_1 and X_2 are *statistically independent* if and only if their joint probability density function $f(x_1, x_2)$ factors into the product of their individual probability density functions $f_1(x_1)$ and $f_2(x_2)$. That is, X_1 and X_2 are independent if and only if

$$f(x_1, x_2) = f_1(x_1)f_2(x_2) \tag{S.2.7}$$

2.10 (Section 2.4.5)   Individual, or *marginal*, probability density functions may be obtained from joint probability density functions. If X_1 and X_2 are discrete random variables with joint probability density function $f(x_1, x_2)$, then

$$f_1(x_1) = \sum_{x_2} f(x_1, x_2)$$
$$f_2(x_2) = \sum_{x_1} f(x_1, x_2) \tag{S.2.8}$$

where Σ_{x_2} means sum over all values that X_2 can take. Given the discrete random variables $X_1,..., X_n$ with joint probability density function $f(x_1,..., x_n)$, then the marginal probability density function for X_1 is

$$f_1(x_1) = \sum_{x_2} \sum_{x_3} \cdots \sum_{x_n} f(x_1,..., x_n) \qquad \text{(S.2.9)}$$

Procedures for continuous random variables are similar, with integrals replacing the summations.

2.11 (Section 2.4.6)   If X and Y are discrete random variables, the *conditional probability* that $X = x$, *given* that $Y = y$, is the joint probability that $X = x$ and $Y = y$ divided by the probability of the conditioning event $Y = y$. That is,

$$P[X = x | Y = y] = f(x|y) = f(x, y)/f(y) \qquad \text{(S.2.10)}$$

where $f(x|y)$ is the conditional probability density function.

If X and Y are independent random variables, then knowing the value of y conveys no information about the probability that X takes any particular value, thus

$$P[X = x | Y = y] = P[X = x]$$

and the conditional probability density function of X given $Y = y$ is the marginal probability density function of X alone,

$$f(x|y) = f(x) \qquad \text{(S.2.11)}$$

The converse is also true.

2.12 (Section 2.5)   The *mathematical expectation, mean,* or *expected value* of a random variable X, $E[X]$, is the average value of the random variable in an infinite number of repetitions of an experiment. If X is a random variable with probability density function $f(x)$, then

$$E[X] = \begin{cases} \displaystyle\sum_x xf(x) & \text{if } X \text{ is discrete} \\ \displaystyle\int_{-\infty}^{\infty} xf(x)dx & \text{if } X \text{ is continuous} \end{cases} \qquad \text{(S.2.12)}$$

2.13 (Section 2.6)   If X is a random variable and $g(X)$ is a function of it, then

$$E[g(X)] = \begin{cases} \displaystyle\sum_x g(x)f(x) & \text{if } X \text{ is discrete} \\ \displaystyle\int_{-\infty}^{\infty} g(x)f(x)dx & \text{if } X \text{ is continuous} \end{cases} \qquad \text{(S.2.13)}$$

Some convenient properties of mathematical expectation that hold for discrete and continuous random variables are:

(*i*) if c is a constant

$$E[c] = c \qquad \text{(S.2.14a)}$$

(*ii*) if c is a constant and X is a random variable

$$E[cX] = cE[X] \tag{S.2.14b}$$

(*iii*) if a and c are constants

$$E[a + cX] = a + cE[X] \tag{S.2.14c}$$

2.14 (Section 2.6)   The *variance* of a random variable X

$$\text{var}(X) = \sigma^2 = E[X - E(X)]^2 = E[X^2] - [E(X)]^2 \tag{S.2.15}$$

is the average squared distance of the values of the random variable from its mean. The larger the variance of X the greater the range or spread of the values X about its mean. The standard deviation of X is

$$\sigma = \sqrt{\sigma^2} = \sqrt{\text{var}(X)}$$

If a and c are constants, and $Z = a + cX$, then

$$\text{var}(Z) = c^2 \, \text{var}(X) \tag{S.2.16}$$

2.15 (Section 2.7)   If X_1 and X_2 are random variables their *covariance*

$$\text{cov}(X_1, X_2) = E\big[\big(X_1 - E(X_1)\big)\big(X_2 - E(X_2)\big)\big] \tag{S.2.17}$$

measures their linear association. The sign of the covariance indicates whether their *linear* association is direct or inverse. If $\text{cov}(X_1, X_2) = 0$, there is no linear association.

The *correlation* between two random variables X_1 and X_2

$$\rho = \frac{\text{cov}(X_1, X_2)}{\sqrt{\text{var}(X_1)}\sqrt{\text{var}(X_2)}} \tag{S.2.18}$$

also measures the degree of *linear* association between X_1 and X_2. The value ρ must fall between -1 and $+1$. If

$$\rho = \begin{cases} 1 & \text{there is a perfect direct linear association between } X_1 \text{ and } X_2 \\ 0 & \text{there is no linear association between } X_1 \text{ and } X_2 \\ -1 & \text{there is a perfect inverse linear association between } X_1 \text{ and } X_2 \end{cases}$$

For two random variables X and Y, the *sample* covariance and the correlation coefficient are descriptive statistics used with bivariate data scatters. The sample covariance is

$$s_{xy} = \sum_{t=1}^{T} \frac{(x_t - \bar{x})(y_t - \bar{y})}{T - 1} \tag{S.2.19}$$

and the sample correlation coefficient is

$$r_{xy} = \frac{s_{xy}}{s_x s_y} = \frac{\sum_{t=1}^{T}(x_t - \bar{x})(y_t - \bar{y})}{\sqrt{\sum_{t=1}^{T}(x_t - \bar{x})^2}\sqrt{\sum_{t=1}^{T}(y_t - \bar{y})^2}} \tag{S.2.20}$$

2.17 (Sections 2.7.1–2.7.2)   There are convenient rules for finding the mean and variance of linear combinations of random variables. If $c_1, c_2,..., c_n$ are constants and $X_1, X_2,..., X_n$ are random variables, then

$$E[c_1 X_1 + c_2 X_2] = c_1 E[X_1] + c_2 E[X_2] \tag{S.2.21a}$$

$$E[c_1 X_1 + c_2 X_2 +...+c_n X_n] = c_1 E[X_1] + c_2 E[X_2] +...+c_n E[X_n] \tag{S.2.21b}$$

$$E[X_1 + X_2 +...+X_n] = E[X_1] + E[X_2] +...+E[X_n] \tag{S.2.21c}$$

$$\text{var}(c_1 X_1 + c_2 X_2) = c_1^2 \, \text{var}(X_1) + c_2^2 \, \text{var}(X_2) + 2c_1 c_2 \, \text{cov}(X_1, X_2) \tag{S.2.21d}$$

$$\text{var}(c_1 X_1 + c_2 X_2) = c_1^2 \, \text{var}(X_1) + c_2^2 \, \text{var}(X_2)$$
if X_1 and X_2 are independent or uncorrelated
$$\tag{S.2.21e}$$

$$\text{var}(c_1 X_1 + c_2 X_2 +...+c_n X_n) = c_1^2 \, \text{var}(X_1) + c_2^2 \, \text{var}(X_2) +...+c_n^2 \, \text{var}(X_n)$$

$$+ \sum_{i \neq j} c_i c_j \, \text{cov}(X_i, X_j) \tag{S.2.21f}$$

$$\text{var}(c_1 X_1 + c_2 X_2 +...+c_n X_n) = c_1^2 \, \text{var}(X_1) + c_2^2 \, \text{var}(X_2) +...+c_n^2 \, \text{var}(X_n)$$
if $X_1,..., X_n$ are independent or uncorrelated

$$\tag{S.2.21g}$$

2.17 (Section 2.8.1)   The continuous random variable X is a normal random variable with mean $E[X] = \beta$ and variance $\text{var}(X) = \sigma^2$, and $X \sim N(\beta, \sigma^2)$, if its probability density function is

$$f(x) = \frac{1}{\sqrt{2\pi\sigma^2}} \exp\left[-\frac{(x-\beta)^2}{2\sigma^2}\right], \quad -\infty < x < \infty \tag{S.2.22}$$

The standard normal random variable $Z = (X - \beta)/\sigma$ is normally distributed with a mean of zero and a variance of one. We denote this result as

$$Z = \frac{X - \beta}{\sigma} \sim N(0, 1) \tag{S.2.23}$$

If $c_1,..., c_n$ are constants and $X_i \sim N(\beta_i, \sigma_i^2)$, $i = 1,..., n$, then

$$Z = c_1 X_1 + c_2 X_2 +...+c_n X_n \sim N(E(Z), \text{var}(Z)) \tag{S.2.24}$$

2.18 (Section 2.8.2)   *Central Limit Theorem*: If $X_1, X_2,..., X_T$ are independent and identically distributed random variables with mean β and variance σ^2, and

$$\overline{X} = \sum_{i=1}^{T} X_i / T$$

then

$$Z = \frac{\overline{X} - \beta}{\sigma / \sqrt{T}}$$

has a distribution that approaches standard normal, $N(0, 1)$, as $T \to \infty$.

Chapter 3

3.1 (Section 3.1)   An *economic model* is a representation of hypothesized relationships between economic variables. *Statistical models* recognize the random nature of economic variables and seek to describe the process by which economic data are generated.

3.2 (Section 3.2)   Let Y be a normally distributed economic random variable with mean $E[Y] = \beta$ and variance $\text{var}(Y) = E[Y - \beta]^2 = \sigma^2$; or $Y \sim N(\beta, \sigma^2)$. Let $Y_1,..., Y_T$ be a *random sample* of observations from the population where the Y_i are independent and identically distributed as $N(\beta, \sigma^2)$.

The linear statistical model for the mean is

$$Y_i = \beta + e_i \qquad i = 1,..., T \qquad \text{(S.3.1)}$$

where the random variable

$$e_i = Y_i - E[Y_i] = Y_i - \beta \qquad \text{(S.3.2)}$$

is the *unobservable* difference between the observable random variable Y_i and its unknown mean β, and

$$e_i \sim N(0, \sigma^2) \qquad \text{(S.3.3)}$$

3.3 (Section 3.3)   To estimate the population mean β, we may use the *least squares criterion*: given a sample of values $y_1,..., y_T$, we choose, as an estimate of β, the value of β that minimizes the sum of squares function

$$S = \sum_{i=1}^{T}(y_i - \beta)^2 \qquad \text{(S.3.4)}$$

The minimizing value of β is the *least squares estimate* of the population mean

$$b = \sum_{i=1}^{T} y_i / T \qquad \text{(S.3.5)}$$

The value b satisfies the necessary and sufficient conditions for a local minimum of the sum of squares function; that is

$$\frac{dS}{d\beta} = 0 \quad \text{and} \quad \frac{d^2S}{d\beta^2} > 0 \qquad \text{(S.3.6)}$$

Derivatives and local minima (and maxima) are discussed in Appendix 3A of Chapter 3.

3.4 (Section 3.4)   Prior to collection of the data the least squares estimator (estimation rule)

$$b = \sum_{i=1}^{T} Y_i / T \qquad \text{(S.3.7)}$$

is a random variable since its value depends on the random outcomes $Y_1,..., Y_T$.

Different samples of size T from the population will produce different values of b. The *repeated sampling*, or just *sampling*, properties of b are:

(*i*) $E[b] = \beta$ \qquad (b is unbiased) \hfill (S.3.8a)

(*ii*) $\text{var}(b) = \sigma^2 / T$ \hfill (S.3.8b)

(*iii*) $b \sim N(\beta, \sigma^2 / T)$ \hfill (S.3.8c)

(*iv*) $Z = \dfrac{b - \beta}{\sigma / \sqrt{T}} \sim N(0, 1)$ \hfill (S.3.8d)

(*v*) $\lim\limits_{T \to \infty} P[|b - \beta| < \varepsilon] = 1$ \qquad for any $\varepsilon > 0$ \qquad (b is consistent) \hfill (S.3.8e)

(*vi*) b is the best linear unbiased estimator (BLUE) of β.

The meaning of (*vi*) is that if $b^* = \Sigma_{i=1}^{T} a_i^* Y_i$ is any other unbiased linear estimator of β, then $\text{var}(b^*) \geq \text{var}(b)$. In fact, if Y is normally distributed, b is the *best unbiased estimator* of β.

3.5 (Section 3.5.1)   A *chi-square* random variable with m degrees of freedom is obtained when m independent standard normal random variables are squared and summed. That is, if $Z_1, \ldots, Z_m$ are statistically independent $N(0, 1)$ random variables then, $Z_i^2 \sim \chi_{(1)}^2$ and

$$W = Z_1^2 + Z_2^2 + \ldots + Z_m^2 \sim \chi_{(m)}^2 \tag{S.3.9}$$

The mean and variance of W are

$$\begin{aligned} E[W] &= m \\ \text{var}(W) &= 2m \end{aligned} \tag{S.3.10}$$

3.6 (Section 3.5.2)   If we define the *least squares residual* as

$$\hat{e}_i = Y_i - b \tag{S.3.11}$$

then the best unbiased estimator of σ^2 is

$$\hat{\sigma}^2 = \frac{\sum\limits_{i=1}^{T} \hat{e}_i^2}{T - 1} \tag{S.3.12}$$

The properties of the estimator $\hat{\sigma}^2$ are obtained from the distributional result that

$$W = \frac{(T-1)\hat{\sigma}^2}{\sigma^2} \sim \chi_{(T-1)}^2 \tag{S.3.13}$$

Consequently, since $\hat{\sigma}^2 = \sigma^2 W / (T - 1)$,

$$\begin{aligned} E[\hat{\sigma}^2] &= \sigma^2 \\ \text{var}(\hat{\sigma}^2) &= 2\sigma^4 / (T - 1) \end{aligned} \tag{S.3.14}$$

The estimator of σ^2 can be used to form an estimator of the variance of b:

$$\hat{\text{var}}(b) = \hat{\sigma}^2 / T \tag{S.3.15}$$

It is also true that the least squares estimator b and $\hat{\sigma}^2$ are statistically independent.

3.7 (Section 3.5.3)   Given that $Y_i \sim N(\beta, \sigma^2)$, the joint probability density function of the random sample $Y_1, Y_2, \ldots, Y_T$ is

$$f\left(y_1, \ldots, y_T | \beta, \sigma^2\right) = (2\pi)^{-T/2} \left(\sigma^2\right)^{-T/2} \exp\left\{ -\frac{\sum_{i=1}^{T} (y_i - \beta)^2}{2\sigma^2} \right\} \qquad \text{(S.3.16)}$$

$$= l\left(\beta, \sigma^2 | y_1, \ldots, y_T\right)$$

The last equality in equation S.3.16 defines the *likelihood function*, which is the joint probability density function of the sample, interpreted as a function of the unknown parameters β and σ^2, and conditional on the sample values $y_1, \ldots, y_T$ actually drawn. The values of β and σ^2 that maximize the likelihood function are maximum likelihood estimates and the resulting maximum likelihood estimators are

$$\tilde{\beta} = \sum_{i=1}^{T} Y_i / T = b$$

$$\tilde{\sigma}^2 = \sum_{i=1}^{T} \hat{e}_i^2 / T = \left(\frac{T-1}{T}\right)\hat{\sigma}^2 \qquad \text{(S.3.17)}$$

Writing the statistical models S.3.2 and S.3.3 and the estimators in vector-matrix notation and corresponding vector-matrix operations are discussed in Appendix 3B of Chapter 3.

Chapter 4

4.1 (Section 4.2)   The linear statistical model for the mean of a normal population is

$$Y_i = \beta + e_i \qquad i = 1, \ldots, T$$

$$e_i \sim N\left(0, \sigma^2\right) \qquad \qquad \text{(S.4.1)}$$

$$\operatorname{cov}\left(e_i, e_j\right) = 0 \quad i \neq j$$

For this model the least squares estimator of β is

$$b = \sum_{i=1}^{T} Y_i / T \sim N\left(\beta, \sigma^2 / T\right) \qquad \text{(S.4.2)}$$

4.2 (Section 4.2)   If the error variance σ^2 is *known*, the standardized normal random variable

$$Z = \frac{b - \beta}{\sigma / \sqrt{T}} \sim N(0, 1) \qquad \text{(S.4.3)}$$

If z_c is a critical value from the $N(0, 1)$ distribution such that

$$P\left[Z \geq z_c\right] = \alpha/2 \qquad \text{(S.4.4)}$$

then

$$P\left[-z_c \leq Z \leq z_c\right] = 1 - \alpha \qquad \text{(S.4.5)}$$

The $(1 - \alpha) \times 100\%$ interval estimator for β is

$$b \pm z_c \sigma/\sqrt{T} \qquad \text{(S.4.6)}$$

since

$$P\left[b - z_c \sigma/\sqrt{T} \leq \beta \leq b + z_c \sigma/\sqrt{T}\right] = 1 - \alpha \qquad \text{(S.4.7)}$$

In repeated trials of selecting random samples of size T from the $N(\beta, \sigma^2)$ population, $(1 - \alpha) \times 100\%$ of the intervals constructed using expression S.4.6 will contain β.

4.3 (Section 4.2.1)   Let Y_0 be an outcome from the $N(\beta, \sigma^2)$ population that we wish to predict using an independent random sample $Y_1, Y_2,..., Y_T$. Then Y_0 is

$$
\begin{aligned}
Y_0 &= \beta + e_0 \\
e_0 &\sim N\left(0, \sigma^2\right) \\
\mathrm{cov}\left(e_0, e_i\right) &= 0 \quad i = 1,..., T
\end{aligned}
\qquad \text{(S.4.8)}
$$

A predictor of Y_0 is $\hat{Y}_0 = b$. The prediction error is

$$\hat{e}_0 = Y_0 - \hat{Y}_0 \qquad \text{(S.4.9)}$$

and

$$\hat{e}_0 \sim N\left(0, \sigma^2\left(1 + 1/T\right)\right) \qquad \text{(S.4.10)}$$

A $(1 - \alpha) \times 100\%$ prediction interval for Y_0, assuming σ^2 is known, is

$$b \pm z_c \sigma\sqrt{1 + \frac{1}{T}} \qquad \text{(S.4.11)}$$

which is based on

$$P\left[b - z_c \sigma\sqrt{1 + \frac{1}{T}} \leq Y_0 \leq b + z_c \sigma\sqrt{1 + \frac{1}{T}}\right] = 1 - \alpha \qquad \text{(S.4.12)}$$

4.4 (Section 4.3)   To test the null hypothesis

$$H_0 : \beta = \beta_0 \qquad \text{(S.4.13a)}$$

against the alternative

$$H_1 : \beta \neq \beta_0 \qquad \text{(S.4.13b)}$$

if the population variance σ^2 is known, the test statistic is

$$Z = \frac{b - \beta_0}{\sigma / \sqrt{T}} \tag{S.4.14}$$

If the null hypothesis H_0: $\beta = \beta_0$ is *true*, then $Z \sim N(0, 1)$. If z is a value of the test statistic based on a sample of data then

$$\begin{aligned} H_0 : \beta = \beta_0 &\qquad \text{is rejected if } |z| \geq z_c \\ H_0 : \beta = \beta_0 &\qquad \text{is not rejected if } |z| < z_c \end{aligned} \tag{S.4.15}$$

4.5 (Section 4.3.1a)   Rejection of a null hypothesis when it is true is called a Type I error. When testing equation S.4.13 using equation S.4.15

$$P[\text{Type I error}] = P\big[|z| \geq z_c \,|\, H_0 : \beta = \beta_0 \text{ is true}\big] = \alpha \tag{S.4.16}$$

The failure to reject a false null hypothesis is a Type II error.

$$P[\text{Type II error}] = P\big[|z| < z_c \,|\, H_0 : \beta = \beta_0 \text{ is false}\big] \tag{S.4.17}$$

The probability of a Type II error depends on the true value of β, and thus cannot be determined explicitly.

4.6 (Section 4.3.1b)   The p-value of a test statistic value z is the probability of obtaining a value larger than z or smaller than $-z$. That is

$$p\text{-value}\,(z) = P[Z \geq z \text{ or } Z \leq -z] \tag{S.4.18}$$

The p-value of a test statistic can be used to determine the outcome of the test in expression S.4.15.

$$\text{If } p\text{-value}\,(z) \leq \alpha, \text{ reject } H_0 : \beta = \beta_0$$

$$\text{If } p\text{-value}\,(z) > \alpha, \text{ do not reject } H_0 : \beta = \beta_0$$

4.7 (Section 4.3.2)   A *one-tailed test* can be used to test the one-sided null and alternative hypotheses

$$\begin{aligned} H_0 : \beta &\leq \beta_0 \\ H_1 : \beta &> \beta_0 \end{aligned} \tag{S.4.19}$$

If the error variance σ^2 is known, the test statistic Z in equation S.4.14 may be used as a basis for the test. For this one-tailed test let the critical value z_c be such that

$$P[Z \geq z_c] = \alpha \tag{S.4.20}$$

Then

$$\begin{aligned} H_0 : \beta \leq \beta_0 &\text{ is rejected if } z \geq z_c \\ H_0 : \beta \leq \beta_0 &\text{ is not rejected if } z < z_c \end{aligned} \tag{S.4.21}$$

4.8 (Section 4.4.1)   When the error variance σ^2 is *not* known statistical inference about the mean of a normal population is based on "Student's" t-distribution. A t random variable with m degrees of freedom is denoted $t_{(m)}$ and is formed as

$$t = \frac{N(0, 1)}{\sqrt{\chi^2_{(m)} / m}} \sim t_{(m)} \tag{S.4.22}$$

where the numerator and denominator are independent random variables. In inferences about the mean of a normal population the relevant random variables are

$$Z = \frac{b - \beta}{\sigma / \sqrt{T}} \sim N(0, 1) \qquad \text{(S.4.23a)}$$

$$W = \frac{(T-1)\hat{\sigma}^2}{\sigma^2} \sim \chi^2_{(T-1)} \qquad \text{(S.4.23b)}$$

and

$$t = \frac{b - \beta}{\hat{\sigma} / \sqrt{T}} \sim t_{(T-1)} \qquad \text{(S.4.24)}$$

A squared $t_{(T-1)}$ random variable is the ratio of two independent chi-square random variables, which are divided by their degrees of freedom.

$$t^2_{(T-1)} = \frac{\chi^2_{(1)}}{\chi^2_{(T-1)} / (T-1)} \sim F_{1, T-1} \qquad \text{(S.4.25)}$$

The result is an F random variable with 1 degree of freedom in the numerator chi-square and $(T-1)$ degrees of freedom in the denominator chi-square random variable.

4.9 (Section 4.4.2)   A $(1-a) \times 100\%$ interval estimator for the mean β of a normal population, with unknown variance σ^2, is

$$b \pm t_c \hat{\sigma} / \sqrt{T} \qquad \text{(S.4.26)}$$

where t_c is the critical value from the $t_{(T-1)}$ distribution such that

$$P[t \geq t_c] = \alpha / 2 \qquad \text{(S.4.27)}$$

The interval estimator is based on the probability statement

$$P\left[b - t_c \hat{\sigma} / \sqrt{T} \leq \beta \leq b + t_c \hat{\sigma} / \sqrt{T}\right] = 1 - \alpha \qquad \text{(S.4.28)}$$

4.10 (Section 4.4.3)   When σ^2 is unknown, hypothesis tests about the mean of a normal population are based on the t-distribution. To test H_0: $\beta = \beta_0$ against H_1: $\beta \neq \beta_0$ we use the test statistic

$$t = \frac{b - \beta_0}{\hat{\sigma} / \sqrt{T}} \qquad \text{(S.4.29)}$$

The test statistic $t \sim t_{(T-1)}$ if the null hypothesis is true. The null hypothesis is rejected if $|t| \geq t_c$.

4.11 (Section 4.6.3)   Consider two normal populations with a common variance, σ^2, and means β_1 and β_2 that may be different. Let Y_{1i} and Y_{2i}, $i = 1, \ldots, T$, be independent random samples from the two populations. To test the null hypothesis H_0: $\beta_1 = \beta_2$ against the alternative H_1: $\beta_1 \neq \beta_2$ use the test statistic

$$t = \frac{b_1 - b_2}{\left(2\hat{\sigma}^2 / T\right)^{1/2}} \qquad \text{(S.4.30)}$$

where $b_1 = \Sigma_{i=1}^{T} Y_{1i} / T$ and $b_2 = \Sigma_{i=1}^{T} Y_{2i} / T$ are the least squares estimators of the respective population means and $\hat{\sigma}^2$ is a "pooled" estimator of the common population variance

$$\hat{\sigma}^2 = \frac{\sum_{i=1}^{T} \left[(Y_{1i} - b_1)^2 + (Y_{2i} - b_2)^2 \right]}{2(T-1)} \tag{S.4.31}$$

If the null hypothesis is true then $t \sim t_{(2(T-1))}$. Consequently

$$\begin{aligned} H_0: \beta_1 = \beta_2 \text{ is rejected if } |t| \geq t_c \\ H_0: \beta_1 = \beta_2 \text{ is not rejected if } |t| < t_c \end{aligned} \tag{S.4.32}$$

where t_c is a critical value from the $t_{(2(T-1))}$ distribution such that

$$P\left[t_{(2(T-1))} \geq t_c \right] = \alpha / 2 \tag{S.4.33}$$

If the two sample sizes are T_1 and T_2, then the t-statistic is

$$t = \frac{b_1 - b_2}{\hat{\sigma}_p \sqrt{\dfrac{1}{T_1} + \dfrac{1}{T_2}}} \tag{S.4.34}$$

where

$$\hat{\sigma}_p = \frac{\sum_{i=1}^{T_1} (Y_{1i} - b_1)^2 + \sum_{i=1}^{T_2} (Y_{2i} - b_2)^2}{T_1 + T_2 - 2} \tag{S.4.35}$$

If the null hypothesis $H_0: \beta_1 = \beta_2$ is true, then $t \sim t_{(T_1 + T_2 - 2)}$.

Part II

The Simple Linear Statistical Model

In Part I we reviewed the basic concepts of statistical inference and analyzed a linear statistical model that involved a sample of observations for a single observable economic variable and unknown β (location) and σ^2 (scale) parameters. Building on these results, in Part II we focus on the specification of economic and statistical models that reflect a relationship between two economic variables, and develop estimation and inference procedures that may be used with a sample of data to learn about the corresponding unknown parameters. As in Part I we start our knowledge search with an economic model, which forms the basis for specifying the statistical model. Procedures are then developed for obtaining point and interval estimates of the unknown parameters and for performing tests of relevant hypotheses. Part II concludes with a discussion of appropriate functional forms, a measure of goodness-of-fit, and an application of the tools developed in Part II for estimating the unknown parameters of an aggregate consumption function. A summary that may be used for review purposes is given after Chapter 8.

Chapter 5

Simple Regression: Economic and Statistical Model Specification and Estimation

New Key Words and Concepts

Economic Model
Statistical Model
Least Squares Estimator
Elasticity
Inverse Matrix

Household Expenditure Function
Estimation Rule
Maximum-Likelihood Estimators
Sampling Process
Partial Derivatives

In Chapters 2 to 4 we reviewed the basic concepts of statistical inference and indicated how these concepts could be used to summarize the information contained in a sample of economic data in terms of parameter estimates for the mean (location parameter) and variance (scale parameter). In this chapter we move from studying one economic variable to studying two economic variables, and we focus on a major objective of economic analysis, to identify *relationships between economic variables*. Economic theory suggests many relationships between economic variables. For example, in introductory economics you considered demand and supply curves where the quantity demanded and supplied of a commodity depends on its market price. In terms of production you visualized the output of a commodity as a function of the level of input (e.g., labor). Aggregate investment in the economy was specified to depend on the interest rate and aggregate consumption to depend on the level of disposable income. Each of these specifications involves a relationship with unknown parameters. In this chapter we pursue the question of how to use the information contained in samples of economic data to learn about the unknown parameters of such relationships. Our interest centers on questions like: If one variable (e.g., price) changes in a certain way, *by how much* will another variable (e.g., quantity) change? Also, given that we know the value of one variable, can we *forecast* or *predict* the corresponding outcome value of another?

Although the tools we will develop have general applicability, to give the discussion realism and a tie-in with observable economic variables, let us pursue these questions in terms of the relationship between average weekly household expenditure on food and household income. To consider this question we must extend the economic and statistical models of Chapter 3 in which only households of size 3 with an annual income of $25,000 were considered. The population of interest is now *all* households of size 3. Thus, we may want to know if household income goes up by, say, $100 per week, by how much will average weekly expenditure on food rise? Or, could expenditure on food *fall* as income rises? A possible forecasting question is: What would be the average weekly expenditure on food for a family with a weekly income of $800? The answers to such questions provide valuable information. For example, suppose that we are concerned with long-run planning for a supermarket chain. If the supermarket anticipates that household income in its surrounding neighborhood will increase over the next year, then it wants to know if, and by how much, it should enlarge its food sections. Should it expand its facilities? Should it hire more butchers? If the chain had one supermarket in a high-income neighborhood and another in a low-income neighborhood, then forecasts of expenditure on food for different income levels give an indication of how large the food sections should be at the different supermarkets. Note how this kind of information is an improvement, for choice or decision purposes, over the information collected and analyzed in Chapters 3 and 4. In these chapters we only had information on the average expenditure on food by households of size 3 and income of $25,000, that is, our results were conditional on this situation. Knowing average expenditure and perhaps the number of households in a neighborhood gives *some* indication of how big to make the food sections. However, we can improve on this information if we also know the neighborhood levels of household income and the relationship between income and expenditure on food. Furthermore, on an aggregate or economy level this information might be useful to predict what might happen as levels of income change, that is, the information may be useful for economic policy purposes.

In this chapter we describe general techniques for analyzing the relationship between two economic variables. To give an economic focus we consider the problem of estimating a household expenditure function for food. We are interested in understanding and describing how expenditure depends on income. The first step in sorting out this question and in obtaining this information is to provide an economic model for the relationship. After this we will specify a corresponding statistical model and face up to the problem of using a sample of data to estimate the unknown parameters of the expenditure function. *Although in the discussion we use a specific relation, the procedures that we develop have application to a wide range of economic problems and questions that are the focus of most economic texts.*

The major questions posed in this chapter are the following:

Given an economic model involving a relationship between two economic variables, how do we go about specifying the corresponding statistical model?

Given the statistical model and a sample of data on two economic variables, how do we use this information to obtain estimates of the unknown and unobservable parameters of the relationship connecting these variables?

5.1   The Economic Model

In developing an economic model that specifies how expenditure relates to income, if we label household expenditure on food as y and the corresponding household income as x, then we may express a relationship between them in general form as

$$y = f(x)$$

This relation specifies that y is *some* function of x. For the commodity food, economic principles suggest a positive relation between expenditure and income. That is, as income increases, so too does expenditure on food. We can represent these increases by using the familiar indifference curve framework that forms the choice basis for a household in microeconomic theory. To confirm your understanding of the logic of household choices, you may want to refer to the relevant chapter in the book you used for your introductory or intermediate economics course(s). Suppose that a consumer must choose between the two commodities, food and nonfood. Using the indifference curves and budget lines (incomes) in Figure 5.1a, a household is in equilibrium at the point F where the budget line 1 just touches indifference curve I. At this point the household is consuming 3 units of food and 3 units of all nonfood goods. Under constant prices, an increase in income is represented by a shift in the budget line from 1 to 2, and by a new equilibrium point E on indifference curve II, where 5 and 5 units of food and all other goods, respectively, are now being consumed. Thus, an increase in income has led to an increase in the quantity of food consumed from 3 to 5 units. Given that prices remain constant (parallel budget lines), expenditure on food (price × quantity) will also increase. For individual food components, the indifference curves will be positioned differently and, for some components, as income increases the quantity consumed will fall. When only income is varied, the equilibrium points F, E, and S trace out an income–consumption curve. Correspondingly, in Figure 5.1b we have drawn the Engel curve that reflects the amount of food that a household will purchase per unit of time at various levels of total income (TI).

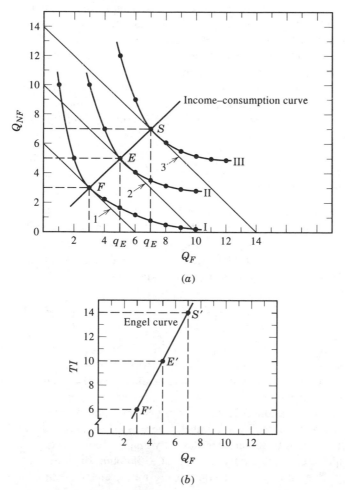

Figure 5.1 The effect of an increase in total income on household consumption.

Our task is to measure or to quantify the change in food expenditure that occurs when we move from q_F to q_E, given a change in income. To do so we need to be more precise about the relationship between expenditure (y) and income (x). Is it linear? Or does expenditure increase at an increasing rate, or at a decreasing rate? In practice, we never know the exact functional form for the relation $y = f(x)$, although we often can use economic theory or the information contained in the data to help us choose a reasonable one. At this point, for simplicity, we assume that it is reasonable to model the relationship as a linear one in terms of y and x. Thus we may specify our economic model, as illustrated in Figure 5.2, with the algebraic form

$$y = \beta_1 + x\beta_2 \qquad (5.1.1)$$

In this equation β_1 is the intercept term, or the level of household expenditure on food when income is zero, and β_2 is the slope or rate of change of the function and shows by how much expenditure on food increases as household income increases. As indicated in Appendix 3B of Chapter 3, β_2 is equal to the derivative dy/dx. Note that knowledge of the *unknown parameters* β_1 and β_2 would help us to answer the questions we posed in the introduction. If household weekly income increases by \$100, and x is measured in \$100 units, then β_2 tells us directly by how much food expenditure will rise. If we wanted to forecast food expenditure for a household with a weekly income of \$800, then we can do so by setting $x = 8$ and using the equation $\beta_1 + 8\beta_2$. Thus, our two major objectives of learning about β_2, and using the equation for prediction, can be summarized by saying: We require estimates of the two parameters β_1 and β_2.

Sometimes, in addition to being interested in β_2, the amount by which y changes when x changes by one unit, we are also interested in the percentage change in y brought about by a 1% change in x. In our example, this quantity is the percentage change in food expenditure that results from a 1% increase in income. In economics we call it the *elasticity* of expenditure on food with respect to a change in income. As explained in Appendix 5A, symbolically it is written as

$$\eta = \frac{\text{percent change in } y}{\text{percent change in } x} = \frac{\Delta y / y}{\Delta x / x} = \frac{\Delta y}{\Delta x} \cdot \frac{x}{y} \qquad (5.1.2)$$

The notation ($\Delta y / \Delta x$) represents the change in expenditure Δy for a given change in income Δx. When it is written this way, the elasticity η is often referred to as an *arc* elasticity. In this book we will be more concerned with *point* elasticities. To obtain a point elasticity we replace ($\Delta y / \Delta x$) by the derivative (dy/dx), which yields the instantaneous rate of change. Thus, our expression for the point elasticity of expenditure is

$$\eta_y = \frac{dy}{dx} \cdot \frac{x}{y} = \beta_2 \frac{x}{y} \qquad (5.1.3)$$

The notation η_y is used to denote the elasticity of *expenditure* with respect to income; soon we shall introduce another elasticity, the elasticity of *quantity* with respect to income, which we will denote by η_q. First, however, note that the elasticity of expenditure in equation 5.1.3 depends on the slope coefficient β_2 and on the levels of income and expenditure, x and y. Thus, in terms of Figure 5.2, the elasticity at the point A, where x/y is relatively large, is greater than the elasticity at point B, where x/y is relatively small.

For the expenditure–income relationship, another elasticity that is often of economic interest is the elasticity of quantity demanded with respect to income, or, more simply, "the income elasticity of demand." Such elasticities are important, for example, in framing growth strategies in developing countries, and they are often used for clas-

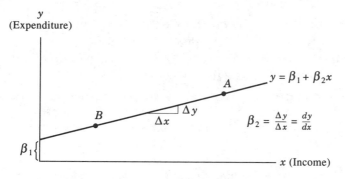

Figure 5.2 The economic model: a linear relationship between expenditure on food and income.

sifying commodities as luxuries or necessities; a commodity with an income elasticity of demand greater than one is a luxury, whereas a necessity has an income elasticity less than one. If q is the weekly quantity of food purchased by a household, then the income elasticity of demand is given by

$$\eta_q = \frac{dq}{dx} \cdot \frac{x}{q} \qquad (5.1.4)$$

In Appendix 5A we show that this elasticity is equal to the expenditure elasticity η_y.

Because knowledge of β_1 and β_2 gives us information about economic behavior, it is important to learn how to use a sample of data to obtain point estimates of these parameters. Also, since we use just one sample of data to estimate β_1 and β_2, another problem we must face is how to assess the reliability of our estimates and to make inferences about the true but always unknown values of β_1 and β_2. The next steps in this learning process are to specify a statistical model involving the unknown parameters and to collect or generate the relevant data.

5.2   The Statistical Model and Data

5.2.1   Introducing the Error Term

The economic model $y = \beta_1 + x\beta_2$ that we specified in Section 5.1 is an abstraction from reality. If we took a random sample of households and recorded average weekly expenditure on food (y) and average weekly income (x) for each of these households, then it would be unrealistic to expect each observed pair (y, x) to lie exactly on the straight line pictured in Figure 5.2. Furthermore, there are likely to be many factors other than income that influence a household's expenditure on food. When moving from the economic model to the statistical model, we know the statistical relation is not exact and allow for this fact by adding an unknown and unobservable random variable e to our economic model as we did in Section 3.2 of Chapter 3. We write

$$y = \beta_1 + x\beta_2 + e \qquad (5.2.1)$$

where we emphasize that the new variable e cannot be observed and is viewed as a random error in the equation. The random error term serves three main purposes.

1. It is introduced to capture the combined effect of all other influences on the expenditure of food (other than the influence of income). At this point we

assume that these other effects are unobservable, otherwise we would attempt to include them explicitly in the model, as we have done for income.

2. It captures any approximation error that arises because the linear functional form we have assumed may be only an approximation to reality.

3. It captures any elements of random behavior present in each individual. Knowledge of all variables that influence an individual's food expenditure may not be sufficient to predict that expenditure. There may be an unpredictable random component.

The reader may very well question the assumption that all other variables that influence expenditure on food are unobservable. What about the price of food, household size, and the age and sex composition of the household? Because the information that we will be collecting is from a random sample of households taken at a given point in time (known as *cross-sectional data*), it is reasonable to assume that the price faced by all households is the same. Price is constant over the whole sample. Thus, changes in expenditure cannot be attributed to price changes, and there is no need to include price in the model. However, household size and composition are a different matter. If we had data on these variables it would be prudent to include them in the expenditure function, along with income, rather than lumping them in the error *e* with all other factors. For now, we will not follow this path so that we can restrict this chapter to the study of a simple relationship between two variables. In Chapter 9 we examine the consequences of and procedures for introducing additional explanatory variables.

5.2.2 Introducing Observations

A second change that we make to the linear expenditure equation when going from the economic model to the statistical model is to add a subscript to each of the variables. Since we will be collecting household observations on y and x, the subscript t is introduced to describe the tth observation on each of the variables. We use y_t to denote expenditure on food for the tth household, x_t for income of the tth household, and the unobservable random variable e_t for all other influences on expenditure for the tth household. Our new model, *the statistical model*, is written as

$$y_t = \beta_1 + x_t \beta_2 + e_t \qquad (5.2.2)$$

In general terms we call y_t the *dependent* or *outcome variable* and x_t the *explanatory variable*. That is, the level of food expenditure y_t is related to or partially explained by the level of income x_t. Note that in this chapter and those to follow, we eliminate the notational distinction between random variables (e.g., Y) and their observed values (e.g., y) that was used in Chapters 2, 3 and 4.

To make the statistical model in equation 5.2.2 complete, some kind of mechanism for modeling e_t is required. We will assume that e_t is a random variable that can be represented by a probability or sampling distribution. Thus, when we select a sample of households and observe y_t and x_t for each household, we view each unobservable error e_t as the outcome of a random experiment or, in other words, a drawing from the probability distribution for e_t. Because y_t depends directly on e_t, food expenditure y_t is also a random variable. Observing expenditure for a sampled household is equivalent to the outcome obtained from a random drawing from the probability distribution for y_t. Thus, our statistical model seeks to describe the sampling process by which the outcome data are generated. We must therefore be definite about the probability characteristics underlying the sampling processes for y_t and e_t.

5.2.3   The Sampling Process

The sampling process underlying the observed y_t is directly related to the assumptions made about the random variables e_t and y_t and their probability distributions. As in Chapter 3, we first assume that e_t has a zero mean; that is

$$E[e_t] = 0 \qquad (5.2.3)$$

Thus, when we sample a number of households, some households will have positive errors and others will have negative errors. If we continue to sample long enough, the errors from all the households will have a mean equal to zero. In terms of the other influences on expenditure that the error e_t represents, these factors will have a negative influence on some households and a positive influence on other households, but if we observe enough households, the average effect will be zero.

Let us examine the implication of the assumption $E[e_t] = 0$ for the mean of y_t. We assume that x_t is fixed, or nonrandom, so from Chapter 2 we know that $E[x_t] = x_t$; then, for the purpose of taking expectations, β_1, β_2, and x_t are all treated as constants. Thus,

$$\begin{aligned} E[y_t] &= E[\beta_1 + x_t\beta_2 + e_t] = \beta_1 + x_t\beta_2 + E[e_t] \\ &= \beta_1 + x_t\beta_2 \end{aligned} \qquad (5.2.4)$$

From equations 5.2.2 and 5.2.4 we can write each observed level of expenditure as the sum of two components, the mean component and the error component:

$$y_t = E[y_t] + e_t \qquad (5.2.5)$$

For our *statistical model*, the linear equation in Figure 5.2 takes on a new meaning. It is no longer a linear relationship between *observed* expenditure and income; instead, as we have written in equation 5.2.4, it represents a linear relationship between *mean* expenditure $E[y_t]$ and income x_t. Each observed expenditure value will fall above or below the linear equation depending on whether its corresponding realized e_t is positive or negative. In equation 3.2.4 of Chapter 3 we also obtained the result $y_t = E[y_t] + e_t$, but in that chapter mean expenditure of households of a given size and income was treated as a constant, $E[y_t] = \beta$. By writing $E[y_t] = \beta_1 + x_t\beta_2$, as we have done in equation 5.2.4, we are recognizing that mean expenditure on food depends on the level of income. Thus, relative to Chapter 3, instead of e_t representing the difference between observed expenditure for a single household income y_t and the mean β, the error e_t now represents the difference between observed expenditure y_t and the mean relationship between expenditure and income, $E[y_t] = \beta_1 + x_t\beta_2$. The two models are compared in Figure 5.3, assuming we have sampled just four households of size 3 and using the income level observations (x_1, x_2, x_3, x_4) with expenditures (y_1, y_2, y_3, y_4). In Chapter 3 the mean model was used to model expenditures for incomes fixed at \$25,000. In Figure 5.3a the mean model is used to model expenditures for four different income levels. Using the model of Chapter 3, the constant mean is given by the horizontal line at β and the realized error terms (e_1, e_2, e_3, e_4) are equal to the corresponding differences between the observed expenditures and β. Changes in the y_t are identical to changes in the e_t, and thus the e_t can be viewed as representing all influences on y_t, including that of income. Using the model of the mean, there is no recognition that big negative errors are primarily a result of low incomes and that big positive errors are primarily a result of high incomes. Such recognition is made when we turn to the model of this chapter, where mean expenditure increases as income increases. In this case we have a new set of error terms that do not include changes in y_t that are attributable to changes in income. We can think of changes in y_t that are attributable to changes in x_t as being given by the line $E[y_t] = \beta_1 + x_t\beta_2$, and changes in y_t that are attributable to changes in other factors as being given by the e_t.

Again as in Chapter 3, in addition to the zero mean, we will also assume that the e_t have a constant variance σ^2 from drawing to drawing and that they are uncorrelated. Let us examine each of these assumptions about the e_t and the corresponding ones for the y_t. The constant variance assumption for the e_t is written as

$$\text{var}(e_t) = E[e_t^2] = \sigma^2 \tag{5.2.6a}$$

This assumption is equivalent to saying that big e_t are not more likely to occur when x_t is big, or vice versa. The e_t will tend to be distributed evenly around the line at all levels of income. The corresponding assumption for the y_t is

$$\text{var}(y_t) = E\left[\left(y_t - E[y_t]\right)^2\right] = E\left[\left(y_t - \beta_1 - x_t\beta_2\right)^2\right] = E[e_t^2] = \sigma^2 \tag{5.2.6b}$$

Thus, the variance of y_t is σ^2, the same as the variance of e_t.

The other assumption is that the error terms for two different observations (two different households) are uncorrelated. Using the notation e_t and e_s to denote the error terms from two different households, we write this assumption as

$$\text{cov}(e_t, e_s) = E\left[\left(e_t - E[e_t]\right)\left(e_s - E[e_s]\right)\right] = E[e_t e_s] = 0 \qquad t \neq s \tag{5.2.7a}$$

The two errors will be uncorrelated if they are independent. Independence arises naturally when we take a *random* sample of cross-sectional data. That is, the choice of one household does not influence the choice of other households. From equation 5.2.7a, we can show that the covariance between two values y_t and y_s is zero, the same as the covariance between the corresponding errors e_t and e_s. Specifically,

$$\text{cov}(y_t, y_s) = E\left[\left(y_t - E[y_t]\right)\left(y_s - E[y_s]\right)\right] = E\left[\left(y_t - \beta_1 - x_t\beta_2\right)\left(y_s - \beta_1 - x_s\beta_2\right)\right] = E[e_t e_s] = 0$$
$$\tag{5.2.7b}$$

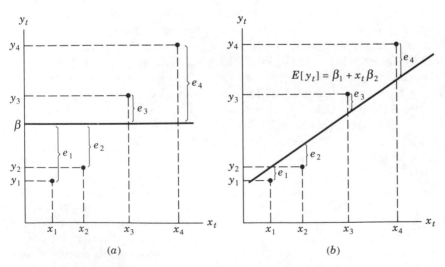

(a)   (b)

Figure 5.3 A comparison of the expenditure models in Chapters 3 and 5. (a) Constant mean model of Chapter 3. (b) Model for Chapter 5, where the mean depends on level of income.

Thus, as in Figure 3.2 of Chapter 3, if we give y_t and e_t a probability density function representation, what we have shown is that the probability density functions for y_t and e_t have the same shape, but they are centered at different points. This fact is illustrated in Figure 5.4 where, assuming normality, we have drawn a normal probability density function for e_t centered at its mean 0, and a corresponding normal probability density function for y_t centered at its mean $\beta_1 + x_t\beta_2$. Note that each y_t will have the same shaped density function, but that the mean will change depending on the level of x_t.

We are now in a position to summarize our statistical model. It is given by

$$y_t = E[y_t] + e_t = \beta_1 + x_t\beta_2 + e_t \tag{5.2.8}$$

where the x_t are nonstochastic (fixed in repeated samples) and not all identical,

$$E[e_t] = 0 \tag{5.2.9}$$

$$E[y_t] = \beta_1 + x_t\beta_2 \tag{5.2.10}$$

$$\text{var}(e_t) = \text{var}(y_t) = \sigma^2 \tag{5.2.11}$$

and

$$\text{cov}(e_t, e_s) = \text{cov}(y_t, y_s) = 0 \qquad (t \neq s) \tag{5.2.12}$$

A way of writing the results in equations 5.2.9, 5.2.10, and 5.2.11 in compact form is

$$e_t \quad (0, \sigma^2) \quad \text{and} \quad y_t \sim (\beta_1 + x_t\beta_2, \sigma^2) \tag{5.2.13}$$

which in words says, for example, y_t is a random variable that has a mean $\beta_1 + x_t\beta_2$ and variance σ^2. If e_t and y_t are normally distributed random variables then we write

$$e_t \sim N(0, \sigma^2) \quad \text{and} \quad y_t \sim N(\beta_1 + x_t\beta_2, \sigma^2) \tag{5.2.14}$$

This relationship is depicted in a three-dimensional diagram in Figure 5.5. A particular value of y, say y_1, consists of two parts; the first part is given by the line $\beta_1 + x_t\beta_2$ at the point x_1. It represents the amount of expenditure "expected," given a household's income. The second part, e_1, is unexpected or at least not explained by income. As we have noted, it is a combination of *all* the other factors that affect expenditure except income. These unexplained factors or errors are represented by the probability density function that is centered at $E[y_1] = \beta_1 + x_1\beta_2$. The outcome y_1 is obtained by adding to

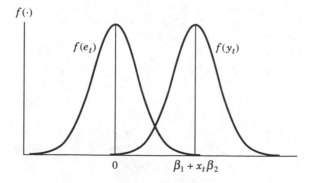

Figure 5.4 Probability density functions for e_t and y_t.

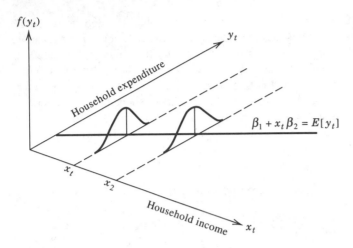

Figure 5.5 The probability density function for y_t at two levels of income.

$E[y_1]$ a drawing e_1 from this probability distribution. The model of the mean in Chapter 3 is based on one "slice" of this figure, that is, the distribution of expenditure given a single level of income.

5.2.4.   An Example of an "Artificial" Sampling Process

To improve your understanding of the role of the statistical model in the generation of sample observations, consider the following example, which involves the generation of artificial or simulated data: Suppose for your class that you are the one who is asked to design an experiment that will provide some artificial sample observations y_t that your colleagues must use in their statistical analysis. In the context of Section 3.6 of Chapter 3 and the discussion of this chapter to this point, how would you do it? That is, how would you go about using a computer to *simulate* a data generation process? To generate values of y_t, what pieces of information would you need if, in line with equation 5.2.8, you let $y_t = \beta_1 + \beta_2 x_t + e_t$ be the data generation process? First, assuming this relationship is the correct one, you would need to know the coefficients β_1 and β_2. For the purpose of the simulated experiment, these values will simply be assigned. Next you would need to know the characteristics of the random errors e_t. For example, it may be appropriate to assume that the errors are independent and identical drawings from a normal distribution with a mean zero and variance σ^2. Once the error assumption choice has been made, the e_t can be obtained by using the appropriate "random number" generator that is included in most computer software packages. Also, since interest centers on the relationship between y_t and x_t, you would need to design your simulated experiment so that you could observe the different outcome values for y_t for the different values of the variable x_t that you may choose. With this information you would be in a position to create or generate some artificial sample observations y_t.

Suppose that you designed your experiment by choosing the following: $\beta_1 = 3$, $\beta_2 = 0.8$, $e_t \sim N(0, 1)$, and $x_t = \{64, 81, 100, 121, 144, 169, 196, 225\}$. In this instance the systematic component or mean of each sample value y_t is $3 + 0.8x_t$. To obtain the observed y_t you add to each $3 + 0.8x_t$ an error component e_t that is drawn from a normal distribution with a mean of zero and variance of one, or in symbols

$$y_t = 3 + 0.8x_t + e_t$$

Table 5.1   The Results of a Sampling Experiment

x_t	$3 + 0.8x_t$		Drawings for e_t from $e_t \sim N(0, 1)$		y_t
64	$3 + (0.8)64 = 54.2$	+	0.4529	=	54.6529
81	$3 + (0.8)81 = 67.8$	+	−1.5912	=	66.2088
100	$3 + (0.8)100 = 83.0$	+	1.6100	=	84.6100
121	$3 + (0.8)121 = 99.8$	+	0.5319	=	100.3319
144	$3 + (0.8)144 = 118.2$	+	−0.2955	=	117.9045
169	$3 + (0.8)169 = 138.2$	+	−0.5374	=	137.6626
196	$3 + (0.8)196 = 159.8$	+	−0.3045	=	159.4955
225	$3 + (0.8)225 = 183.0$	+	0.5974	=	183.5974

Under this sampling scheme for one set of x_t, and using a table of random numbers to generate the e_t, or a corresponding random number generator on a computer, one set of possible sample values for y_t is given in Table 5.1.

If you wanted to generate 16 sample values of y_t as an experiment for your colleagues, you could repeat the x_t values and use a table of random numbers or a random number generator on a computer to take 8 more independent drawings for e_t from a $N(0, 1)$ distribution. If you wanted to produce 20 samples of y_t of size 8, you would repeat the original experiment 20 times.

In any event this is the *imagined* sampling process that underlies the sample observations in our statistical model. The statistical model is in a linear additive form and both the y_t and e_t are random variables. The outcome of the experiment y_t has mean $3 + 0.8x_t$ and a sampling variability that is the same as e_t. That is

$$y_t \sim N\big([3+0.8x_t], 1\big) \quad \text{and} \quad e_t = \big(y_t - [3+0.8x_t]\big) \sim N(0, 1)$$

In practice, when we specify a statistical model to explain the relationship between the two variables y_t and x_t, we are specifying the imagined sampling process by which the observations are generated. The difference between reality and our simulated experiment is that, in reality, we do not know the values of the parameters β_1, β_2, and σ^2; nor can we observe the values of the errors e_t. Our objective is to use the outcomes of an experiment, which are the observed values (sample observations) (y_t, x_t), to make inferences about β_1, β_2, and σ^2. When we change the statistical model, we change the imagined sampling process by which the observations are generated. In the chapters to follow, the statistical model will be changed to describe the nature of the sampling process for different economic data sets. From now on when you see a statistical model, you should think about what it implies in terms of an experiment and how you would go about simulating the sample observations. Sample observations come from somewhere. What the statistical model does is to describe the envisioned data generation (sampling) process. Without it we do not have a basis for estimation and inference concerning the unknown parameters.

5.2.5 A Sample of Economic Data

Now that we have specified a statistical model for household expenditure on food, data on food expenditure and income are needed so that we can learn about the parameters β_1 and β_2. We will use data from a random sample of 40 households. These data are

Table 5.2 Average Weekly Expenditure on Food and Average Weekly Income in Dollars for 40 Households of Size 3

Observation Number	Household Expenditure on Food y_t	Household Income x_t	Observation Number	Household Expenditure on Food y_t	Household Income x_t
1	9.46	25.83	21	17.77	71.98
2	10.56	34.31	22	22.44	72.00
3	14.81	42.50	23	22.87	72.23
4	21.71	46.75	24	26.52	72.23
5	22.79	48.29	25	21.00	73.44
6	18.19	48.77	26	37.52	74.25
7	22.00	49.65	27	21.69	74.77
8	18.12	51.94	28	27.40	76.33
9	23.13	54.33	29	30.69	81.02
10	19.00	54.87	30	19.56	81.85
11	19.46	56.46	31	30.58	82.56
12	17.83	58.83	32	41.12	83.33
13	32.81	59.13	33	15.38	83.40
14	22.13	60.73	34	17.87	91.81
15	23.46	61.12	35	25.54	91.81
16	16.81	63.10	36	39.00	92.96
17	21.35	65.96	37	20.44	95.17
18	14.87	66.40	38	30.10	101.40
19	33.00	70.42	39	20.90	114.13
20	25.19	70.48	40	48.71	115.46

typical of those obtained by conducting a survey. Observations on average weekly expenditure on food (in dollars) and average weekly total expenditure (in dollars) for each of the households are given in Table 5.2. Also, our data are only part of a larger random sample; we have chosen to use only those households that have three family members. Using observations that come from households of the same size means there is no variation in food expenditure that can be attributed to variation in household size; it gives us a better chance of accurately estimating the influence of income on food expenditure. In line with our statistical model, which is summarized in equation 5.2.13 and the sampling experiment of Section 5.2.4, we assume that our 40 observations on expenditure for food, $y_1, y_2, \ldots, y_{40}$, can be viewed as independent and identically distributed drawings from a probability distribution with mean $\beta_1 + x_t\beta_2$ and variance σ^2. The 40 income observations $x_1, x_2, \ldots, x_{40}$, are also given in Table 5.2.

5.3 Estimating the Parameters for the Expenditure Relationship

Given a theoretical model for explaining how the sample of household expenditure data is generated, the problem now is how to use our sample information on y and x to estimate the unknown parameters (β_1 and β_2) that represent the unknown intercept and slope coefficients for the household expenditure–income relationship. In other words, we are faced with the 40 data points $(y_1, x_1), (y_2, x_2), \ldots, (y_{40}, x_{40})$ pictured in the *scatter diagram* in Figure 5.6, and our problem is to estimate the location or position of the mean expenditure line $E[y_t] = \beta_1 + x_t\beta_2$. We would expect the position of this line to be somewhere in the middle of all the data points. Such a position would mean some e_t are positive and some e_t are negative, in line with our assumptions about the model. However, where

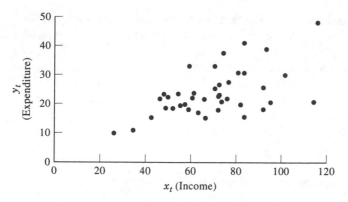

Figure 5.6 Scatter diagram for observations on food expenditure and income.

is it located exactly? Or, what would be our best guess about its location? One way to guess would be simply to draw a line that you think would represent all the points. The problem with this method is that different people would draw different lines, and the lack of a formal criterion makes it difficult to assess the accuracy of the method. Another method is to draw a line from the smallest income point to the largest income point. This approach does provide a formal rule. However, it may not be a very good rule because it ignores information on the exact position of the remaining 38 observations. It would be better if we could devise a rule that uses all the information from all the data points.

5.3.1   The Least Squares Estimation Rule

To estimate β_1 and β_2 we need a rule that tells us how to make use of the sample observations. Many rules are, of course, possible. Out of the possibilities, the rule that we will use to make use of the sample information is called the *least squares* rule. With this rule we fit a line or choose a line so that the sum of the squares of the vertical distances from each point to the line is as small as possible. Let us elaborate on this concept. We need to choose a line that best fits the data points in some sense. Choosing a line is equivalent to choosing values for β_1 and β_2. Indeed, our problem is that β_1 and β_2 are unknown (the true line or underlying model consistent with the way the data were generated is unknown), and we need a rule for how to use the sample of data to estimate them. For some particular choice of β_1 and β_2, say β_1^0 and β_2^0, we will have a fitted or estimated line

$$y_t^0 = \beta_1^0 + x_t \beta_2^0 \qquad (5.3.1)$$

The vertical distances from each point to this line we call residuals or the "residual errors" for *this line*. They are given by

$$e_t^0 = y_t - y_t^0 = y_t - \beta_1^0 - x_t \beta_2^0 \qquad t = 1, 2, \ldots, T \qquad (5.3.2)$$

The residuals are the errors depicted in Figure 5.3, except that they correspond to our fitted line and not to the true underlying model. The sum of squares of the vertical distances for all points or the sum of squared residuals or sum of squared error line is

$$\sum_{t=1}^{T} \left(e_t^0 \right)^2 = \sum_{t=1}^{T} \left(y_t - y_t^0 \right)^2 = \sum_{t=1}^{T} \left(y_t - \beta_1^0 - x_t \beta_2^0 \right)^2$$

Now suppose we pick another line $y_t^1 = \beta_1^1 + x_t \beta_2^1$. The residuals for this line, namely $e_t^1 = y_t - y_t^1 = y_t - \beta_1^1 - x_t \beta_2^1$, will likely be different from those given in equation 5.3.2) for the first line. Also, the sum of squared residuals $\Sigma_{i=1}^{T}(y_t - \beta_1^1 - x_t \beta_2^1)^2$ will likely be different from that given in equation 5.3.3. Thus, different choices for β_1 and β_2 will give different estimated lines (see Figure 5.7) and, for each estimated line, the sum of the squares of the vertical distances from each point to the line (the sum of squared residuals) will be different. The least squares criterion says let us choose the line that makes this sum of squared distances as small as possible. In other words, let us choose values (estimates) for β_1 and β_2 such that the sum of squared residuals is minimized.

How do we perform this task? *Given the sample observations* on y and x, we want to find values for the unknown parameters β_1 and β_2 that minimize

$$S(\beta_1, \beta_2) = \Sigma(y_t - \beta_1 - x_t \beta_2)^2 \qquad (5.3.4a)$$

Here and elsewhere in this chapter we use Σ as shorthand notation for $\Sigma_{t=1}^{T}$. *Since the points (y_t, x_t) have been observed*, we view the sum of squares S as a function of the unknowns β_1 and β_2. Expanding this function yields

$$
\begin{aligned}
S(\beta_1, \beta_2) &= \Sigma\left(y_t^2 + \beta_1^2 + x_t^2 \beta_2^2 - 2y_t \beta_1 - 2x_t y_t \beta_2 + 2x_t \beta_1 \beta_2\right) \\
&= \Sigma y_t^2 + \beta_1^2 T + \beta_2^2 \Sigma x_t^2 - 2\beta_1 \Sigma y_t - 2\beta_2 \Sigma x_t y_t + 2\beta_1 \beta_2 \Sigma x_t
\end{aligned}
\qquad (5.3.4b)
$$

For our particular data set where

$$T = 40 \qquad \Sigma x_t = 2792 \qquad \Sigma y_t = 943.78$$
$$\Sigma x_t y_t = 69435.0404 \quad \Sigma x_t^2 = 210206.2302 \quad \Sigma y_t^2 = 24875.065$$

we have

$$S(\beta_1, \beta_2) = 24875.07 + 40\beta_1^2 + 210206.23\beta_2^2 - 1887.56\beta_1 - 138870.08\beta_2 + 5584\beta_1 \beta_2$$

$$(5.3.5)$$

This function, which is quadratic in terms of the unknown parameters β_1 and β_2, is "bowl-shaped," like the one depicted in Figure 5.8.

Our task is to find, out of all the possible values for β_1 and β_2, the point (b_1, b_2) at which the function (the residual or error sum of squares) is a minimum. This minimization problem is a common one in calculus, and the minimizing point is at the "bottom of the bowl," where the slopes $\partial S/\partial \beta_1$ and $\partial S/\partial \beta_2$ are zero. This minimization

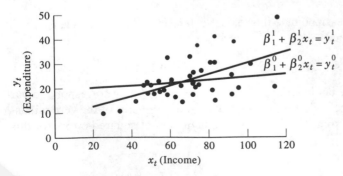

 ~ure 5.7 Two estimated lines for the food expenditure and income data.

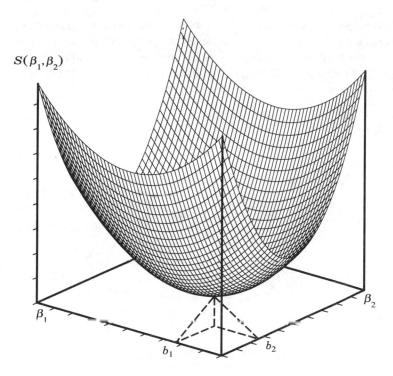

Figure 5.8 A quadratic function and the minimizing values b_1 and b_2.

process is discussed in detail in Appendix 5B at the end of this chapter, and you may wish to invest a bit of time there to obtain an intuitive feel for the minimum–maximum process with two variables.

Returning to the more general expression in equation 5.3.4b, and making use of the rules of partial differentiation discussed in Appendix 5B, the partial derivatives $\partial S/\partial \beta_1$ and $\partial S/\partial \beta_2$ are given by the linear equations

$$\frac{\partial S}{\partial \beta_1} = 2T\beta_1 - 2\Sigma y_t + 2\Sigma x_t \beta_2 \qquad (5.3.6a)$$

$$\frac{\partial S}{\partial \beta_2} = 2\Sigma x_t^2 \beta_2 - 2\Sigma x_t y_t + 2\Sigma x_t \beta_1 \qquad (5.3.6b)$$

The point at which these derivatives (slopes) are zero is the minimizing point (b_1, b_2). Thus, to obtain this point we set equations 5.3.6a and 5.3.6b to zero and we replace β_1 and β_2 by b_1 and b_2, respectively. Carrying out this step yields

$$2\left(\Sigma y_t - Tb_1 - \Sigma x_t b_2\right) = 0 \qquad (5.3.7a)$$

$$2\left(\Sigma x_t y_t - \Sigma x_t b_1 - \Sigma x_t^2 b_2\right) = 0 \qquad (5.3.7b)$$

Rearranging equation 5.3.7 leads to

$$Tb_1 + \Sigma x_t b_2 = \Sigma y_t \qquad (5.3.8a)$$

$$\Sigma x_t b_1 + \Sigma x_t^2 b_2 = \Sigma x_t y_t \qquad (5.3.8b)$$

These two equations comprise a set of two linear equations in two unknowns b_1 and b_2 and are sometimes called the *normal equations*. We can find the estimates that our least squares rule has produced by solving these two linear equations for b_1 and b_2. Let us proceed in this direction. Multiplying both sides of equation 5.3.8a by Σx_t and both sides of equation 5.3.8b by T yields

$$T\Sigma x_t b_1 + (\Sigma x_t)^2 b_2 = \Sigma x_t \Sigma y_t \qquad (5.3.9a)$$

$$T\Sigma x_t b_1 + T\Sigma x_t^2 b_2 = T\Sigma x_t y_t \qquad (5.3.9b)$$

Subtracting equation 5.3.9a from equation 5.3.9b gives

$$\left[T\Sigma x_t^2 - (\Sigma x_t)^2 \right] b_2 = T\Sigma x_t y_t - \Sigma x_t \Sigma y_t$$

with

$$b_2 = \frac{T\Sigma x_t y_t - \Sigma x_t \Sigma y_t}{T\Sigma x_t^2 - (\Sigma x_t)^2} \qquad (5.3.10a)$$

or by making use of identities developed in Exercise 5.3,

$$b_2 = \frac{\Sigma(y_t - \bar{y})(x_t - \bar{x})}{\Sigma(x_t - \bar{x})^2} \qquad (5.3.10b)$$

where $\bar{y} = \Sigma y_t/T$ and $\bar{x} = \Sigma x_t/T$ are the sample means of the observations on y and x. Sometimes the expression 5.3.10b is used to denote the *least squares estimator* b_2. In solving for b_1, we note that dividing both sides of equation 5.3.8a by T yields

$$b_1 = \bar{y} - b_2 \bar{x} \qquad (5.3.10c)$$

Having used equation 5.3.10a to compute b_2, we can estimate b_1 by using equation 5.3.10c. Thus, if we use the least squares rule to estimate β_1 and β_2 or to estimate the mean equation $E[y_t] = \beta_1 + x_t\beta_2$, we are led to the pair of expressions 5.3.10. This pair of expressions, when viewed as an estimation rule, is called the *least squares estimators* for β_1 and β_2. The values for b_1 and b_2 that are obtained by using specific data in the formulas 5.3.10 are called the *least squares estimates*.

5.3.2   Estimates for the Household Expenditure Function

We have used the least squares rule to derive the pair of scalar expressions 5.3.10 for the least squares estimator. To illustrate the use of these expressions, we will use both equations to calculate the values of b_1 and b_2 for the household expenditure data given in Table 5.2. From equation 5.3.10a we have

$$b_2 = \frac{T\Sigma x_t y_t - \Sigma x_t \Sigma y_t}{T\Sigma x_t^2 - (\Sigma x_t)^2} = \frac{(40)(69435.04) - (2792)(943.78)}{(40)(210206.23) - (2792)^2} \qquad (5.3.11a)$$

$$= 0.2323$$

and from equation 5.3.10b

$$b_1 = \bar{y} - b_2 \bar{x} = 23.5945 - (0.232253)(69.8) = 7.3832 \qquad (5.3.11b)$$

Once the values for b_1 and b_2 have been computed it is customary to report these results in terms of the estimated relationship between y_t and x_t. Thus, we write our *estimated* or fitted relationship between mean household expenditure on food and income as

$$\hat{y}_t = 7.3832 + 0.2323x_t \qquad (5.3.12)$$

This line is graphed in Figure 5.9. One of its characteristics is that it passes through the point $(\bar{x}, \bar{y})$ defined by the sample means $\bar{y} = 23.595$ and $\bar{x} = 69.800$. (See Exercise 5.4.)

Let us interpret the results and see how they can be used. First, the value $b_2 = 0.2323$ is an estimate of β_2, the amount by which average weekly expenditure on food increases, for a household of size 3, when average weekly income increases by $1. Thus, we estimate that if weekly income goes up by $100, expenditure on food will increase by approximately $23. A supermarket chain with information on likely changes in income, and in the number of households, could estimate how much more food it is likely to sell, namely, $23 per household per week for every $100 increase in income.

The income elasticity of demand for food is also of interest. From equation 5.1.3 an estimate of this value is

$$\eta_y = b_2 \frac{x}{y} = 0.23 \frac{x}{y} \qquad (5.3.13)$$

When elasticities depend on the levels of the relevant variables (expenditure and income in this case), it is common to report an elasticity at the means of these variables. Following this practice we have

$$\eta_y = 0.2323 \frac{\bar{x}}{\bar{y}} = 0.2323 \times \frac{69.800}{23.595} = 0.687 \qquad (5.3.14)$$

Thus, we estimate that a 1% change in household income will lead to approximately a 0.7% increase in household consumption of (or expenditure on) food when $x = \bar{x}$ and $y = \bar{y}$. On the basis of these results we have some information on how food consumption changes as income levels and the distribution of income change. For more information on the use of this result see Exercise 5.6.

Strictly speaking, the intercept estimate $b_1 = 7.382$ is an estimate of the weekly amount spent on food for a family with zero income. In general, however, one needs to be careful when interpreting intercept estimates. If we do not have any observations in the region

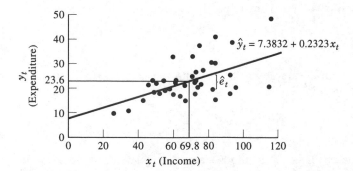

Figure 5.9 The estimated relationship between expenditures on food and income.

where income is zero, our estimated relationship may not be a good approximation to reality in that region. Thus, although our estimated model suggests that a household with zero income will spend $7.38 per week on food, it might be dangerous to place too much faith in this estimate.

Finally, we note how our estimated equation can be used for prediction or forecasting purposes. Suppose that we wanted to predict weekly food expenditure for a household of size 3 with an average weekly income of $100. This prediction is carried out by substituting $x = 100$ into our estimated equation to obtain

$$\hat{y} = 7.3832 + 0.2323x = 7.3832 + (0.2323)(100) = \$30.61 \qquad (5.3.15)$$

Thus, on average, we would expect a household of size 3 with a weekly income of $100 to spend $30.61 per week on food.

5.3.3   A Discussion of the Estimation Rule

With the linear statistical model

$$y_t = \beta_1 + x_t \beta_2 + e_t, \qquad e_t \sim \left(0, \sigma^2\right) \qquad (5.2.2)$$

and a corresponding sample of data (y_t, x_t), we have used the criterion of choosing estimates b_1 and b_2 for β_1 and β_2 that minimize the sum of squares $S(\beta_1, \beta_2) = \Sigma(y_t - \beta_1 - \beta_2 x_t)^2 = \Sigma e_t^2$. This approach led in Section 5.3.1 to the following set of simultaneous linear equations

$$\begin{aligned} Tb_1 + \Sigma x_t b_2 &= \Sigma y_t \\ \Sigma x_t b_1 + \Sigma x_t^2 b_2 &= \Sigma x_t y_t \end{aligned} \qquad (5.3.8)$$

and the solutions

$$b_2 = \frac{T\Sigma x_t y_t - \Sigma x_t \Sigma y_t}{T\Sigma x_t^2 - \left(\Sigma x_t\right)^2} \qquad (5.3.10a)$$

$$b_2 = \frac{\Sigma \left(y_t - \bar{y}\right)\left(x_t - \bar{x}\right)}{\Sigma \left(x_t - \bar{x}\right)^2} \qquad (5.3.10b)$$

$$b_1 = \bar{y} - b_2 \bar{x} \qquad (5.3.10c)$$

that indicate how the sample observations y_t and x_t are to be used to obtain estimates of β_1 and β_2.

This result should be contrasted to that developed in Section 3.3 of Chapter 3 where the statistical model was

$$y_t = \beta + e_t, \qquad e_t \sim \left(0, \sigma^2\right)$$

In this case, with a corresponding sample of data, y_t, and the least squares criterion, we were led to the estimation rule

$$b = \sum_t y_t / T = \bar{y}$$

Thus, in this chapter we have repeated the methods learned in Chapter 3 when we were estimating just the scalar location parameter β. The only change is that now we are considering a statistical model with two unknown parameters β_1 and β_2.

5.3.4   The Maximum-Likelihood Estimation Rule

If the equation errors e_t and the observations y_t are assumed to be normally distributed random variables, we can, as we did in Section 3.5.3 of Chapter 3, write the joint density function for the sample $y_1, y_2, \ldots, y_T$ given $x_1, x_2, \ldots, x_T, \beta_1, \beta_2, \sigma^2$. It is given by

$$f\left(y_1, y_2, \ldots, y_T \middle| x_1, x_2, \ldots, x_T, \beta_1, \beta_2, \sigma^2\right) = \left(2\pi\sigma^2\right)^{-\frac{T}{2}} \exp\left[-\frac{\Sigma\left(y_t - \beta_1 - x_t\beta_2\right)^2}{2\sigma^2}\right]$$

$$= \frac{1}{\left(2\pi\sigma^2\right)^{\frac{T}{2}} \exp\left[\dfrac{\Sigma\left(y_t - \beta_1 - x_t\beta_2\right)^2}{2\sigma^2}\right]}$$

$$(5.3.16)$$

Under this formulation, which makes use of the information that y_t and e_t are normal random variables, we can proceed as we did in Chapter 3 to use the criterion of choosing estimates for β_1 and β_2 that maximize the probability of obtaining the sample of data that we have observed. For this criterion, we maximize equation 5.3.16 by choosing values for β_1 and β_2 that make the residual or error sum of squares in the exponent $\Sigma\left(y_t - \beta_1 - x_t\beta_2\right)^2$ a minimum. This means we make the denominator in equation 5.3.16 as small as possible. Thus, the maximum-likelihood rule, which says choose the estimator that maximizes equation 5.3.16, leads to the same result (estimator) as the least squares rule, which says minimize $\Sigma\left(y_t - \beta_1 - x_t\beta_2\right)^2$. Whenever you can specify and write down the joint density function for the sample, as we did in equation 5.3.16, you can then go on to obtain the corresponding maximum-likelihood estimator. In this case the least squares and maximum-likelihood estimators for β_1 and β_2 are the same as they are for many of the statistical models in this book. However, in other statistical models these estimators can differ. For the cases where they are identical, we will stay with the simpler, more intuitive least squares rules.

5.3.5   Other Economic–Statistical Models

We have focused in this chapter on a statistical model that provides a basis for estimating the unknown parameters for a household expenditure–income relationship. Fortunately, the statistical model can be used as a basis for estimation and inference for a variety of economic relationships. Examples include a demand relationship involving price and quantity data for a particular commodity; a production function reflecting the relationship for a sample of data involving the output of a product and the input of a factor; an aggregate consumption function involving a sample of data for aggregate consumption and income; an aggregate investment function involving a sample of data representing the level of investment and the rate of interest; and a supply function involving data relative to quantity supplied and the price when the production decision was taken. Economic theory is rich with possible relationships between economic variables, and thus there are a large number of possibilities for making use of our linear statistical model. With each economic model we must, of course, ask questions as to the appropriate assumptions concerning the error process in the statistical model; for example, in estimating a demand relationship, can we assume that the errors are independent from drawing to drawing or come from distributions that have identical variances (scale parameters)? Also, what is the correct functional form; is it linear or is it nonlinear with a constant elasticity? And finally, is the statistical model realistic in describing the sampling process underlying the data generation? Have the relevant explanatory variables been included? These questions will be taken up as we progress through the coming chapters.

5.3.6   What Have We Learned?

We started with the objective of learning about a simple economic relationship from a sample of data involving two economic variables—household expenditure and household income. To model the data we specified a simple linear statistical model that we hoped would reflect the sampling process by which the data were generated. The statistical model we specified involved two coefficients β_1 and β_2 and the variance parameter σ^2. We then faced the question of how to use the sample observations to estimate these unknown parameters realizing that, if we could understand the relationship (obtain "good" estimates of β_1 and β_2), then we would be in a position, given the level of household income, to make predictions about the most probable outcomes for household expenditures y. We made use of the criterion that sought to find β_1 and β_2, for our data, so as to minimize the equation residual error sum of squares. This criterion led to the least squares rule and the estimates b_1 and b_2. Thus in this estimation process, we used the data, the least squares rule, and the estimates b_1 and b_2 to learn about the unknown parameters β_1 and β_2. The least squares estimation rule is applicable to a wide range of economic–statistical models.

The important concepts we have covered in this chapter may be summarized as follows:

1. For many decision problems it is necessary to have information on the relationship among economic variables.

2. Economic theory provides a basis for expressing the potential relationships.

3. Statistical models such as $y_t = \beta_1 + x_t\beta_2 + e_t$ and $e_t \sim (0, \sigma^2)$ or $e_t \sim N(0, \sigma^2)$ provide a basis for specifying the sampling process that we use to visualize how economic data are generated and a basis for identifying the corresponding useful unknown and unobservable parameters.

4. To use the sample data to provide some information about the unknown parameters, we must have some rule that specifies how the data are to be used.

5. Given the data, the criterion of choosing values for the unknown parameters that minimize the equation residual or error sum of squares leads to the least squares rule or estimator 5.3.10, which indicates how the sample of observations is to be used to obtain estimates of β_1 and β_2.

6. To obtain least squares estimates, a system of linear simultaneous equations must be solved. As we discover in Section 5.4, linear algebra provides a simple way to express the system of equations, and the computer provides a basis for obtaining empirical solutions.

7. The resulting estimated parameters and the estimated model $\hat{y}_t = b_1 + x_tb_2$ provide a basis for predicting y_t for different values of x_t and for analyzing different if-then propositions.

8. The estimation procedure has application to a wide range of economic–statistical models.

9. The next time you see an economic relationship with given coefficient values, you should know that the parameters have been estimated by some variant of the procedures used in this chapter.

5.4   A Restatement of the Results
Using a Shorthand-Linear Algebra Notation

5.4.1   The Statistical Model

It is convenient and useful in the chapters ahead to be able to write our statistical model and the underlying assumptions in compact form as we did in Appendix 3B of Chapter 3. As preparation for this section, you may wish to review the linear algebra formulation for the mean–variance statistical model that is presented in Appendix 3B. If you make a small investment now in this section and Appendix 5C, it will permit you to get rid of the cumbersome summation notation, eliminate the need for you to remember a set of identities, and let you concentrate on the concepts involved and understand the basis of your results.

Working in this direction, suppose that we have a sample of T households. Thus, for our subscript t that denotes the tth household, we have $t = 1, 2,..., T$. To model the complete set of T observations, we rewrite the statistical model 5.2.8 T times. That is,

$$y_1 = \beta_1 + x_1\beta_2 + e_1$$
$$y_2 = \beta_1 + x_2\beta_2 + e_2$$
$$\vdots$$
$$y_T = \beta_1 + x_T\beta_2 + e_T$$

(5.4.1)

By using a notation of Appendix 3B, involving matrices and vectors, these equations may be written as

$$\begin{bmatrix} y_1 \\ y_2 \\ \vdots \\ y_T \end{bmatrix} = \begin{bmatrix} 1 \\ 1 \\ \vdots \\ 1 \end{bmatrix}\beta_1 + \begin{bmatrix} x_1 \\ x_2 \\ \vdots \\ x_T \end{bmatrix}\beta_2 + \begin{bmatrix} e_1 \\ e_2 \\ \vdots \\ e_T \end{bmatrix}$$

(5.4.2a)

or

$$\begin{bmatrix} y_1 \\ y_2 \\ \vdots \\ y_T \end{bmatrix} = \begin{bmatrix} 1 & x_1 \\ 1 & x_2 \\ \vdots & \vdots \\ 1 & x_T \end{bmatrix}\begin{bmatrix} \beta_1 \\ \beta_2 \end{bmatrix} + \begin{bmatrix} e_1 \\ e_2 \\ \vdots \\ e_T \end{bmatrix}$$

(5.4.2b)

To write 5.2.4a in compact form, we make use of the following T-dimensional vectors:

$$\mathbf{y} = \begin{bmatrix} y_1 \\ y_2 \\ \vdots \\ y_T \end{bmatrix} \quad \mathbf{x}_1 = \begin{bmatrix} 1 \\ 1 \\ \vdots \\ 1 \end{bmatrix} \quad \mathbf{x}_2 = \begin{bmatrix} x_1 \\ x_2 \\ \vdots \\ x_T \end{bmatrix} \quad \mathbf{e} = \begin{bmatrix} e_1 \\ e_2 \\ \vdots \\ e_T \end{bmatrix}$$

Thus, $\mathbf{y}$ is a T-dimensional vector of observations on household expenditure on food, $\mathbf{x}_2$ is a T-dimensional vector of observations on household income, $\mathbf{x}_1$ is a T-dimensional vector whose elements are all equal to 1, and $\mathbf{e}$ is a T-dimensional vector of error terms, one for each household. Note that we observe **y** and **x**$_2$, but not **e**. With these definitions we can rewrite equation 5.4.2a as

$$\mathbf{y} = \mathbf{x}_1\beta_1 + \mathbf{x}_2\beta_2 + \mathbf{e} \qquad (5.4.3)$$

where **y**, **x**$_1$, **x**$_2$ and **e** are $(T \times 1)$ vectors and β_1 and β_2 are unknown, unobserved parameters.

An even more compact notation can be developed by combining the vectors **x**$_1$ and **x**$_2$ into a $(T \times 2)$ matrix X and by writing the two unknown parameters β_1 and β_2 as a (2×1) vector β. That is,

$$X = (\mathbf{x}_1 \;\; \mathbf{x}_2) = \begin{bmatrix} 1 & x_1 \\ 1 & x_2 \\ \vdots & \vdots \\ 1 & x_T \end{bmatrix} \quad \text{and} \quad \beta = \begin{bmatrix} \beta_1 \\ \beta_2 \end{bmatrix}$$

We can think of each of the coefficients or parameters in β as being linked with a corresponding column of the X matrix. The coefficient β_2 is the coefficient of income, the second variable or column in X. The coefficient β_1 is the intercept coefficient and is the coefficient of the first "variable" or column in X; this "variable" is actually a constant, a column of ones. Using this notation, we can write

$$\mathbf{x}_1\beta_1 + \mathbf{x}_2\beta_2 = \begin{bmatrix} \mathbf{x}_1 & \mathbf{x}_2 \end{bmatrix}\begin{bmatrix} \beta_1 \\ \beta_2 \end{bmatrix} = X\beta \qquad (5.4.4)$$

and so, from equation 5.4.3, our statistical model in a simple form can be written as

$$\mathbf{y} = X\beta + \mathbf{e} \qquad (5.4.5)$$

This equation is an equivalent and compact way, as you should demonstrate, of writing the T equations in equation 5.4.1 or the eight equations in Table 5.1. It is this simple linear algebra formulation of the linear statistical model that we will refer to throughout a large part of this text. As an example of the elements in **y**, X, and β, we have the sampling experiment given in Table 5.1

$$X = \begin{bmatrix} 1 & 64 \\ 1 & 81 \\ 1 & 100 \\ 1 & 121 \\ 1 & 144 \\ 1 & 169 \\ 1 & 196 \\ 1 & 225 \end{bmatrix}, \quad \mathbf{y} = \begin{bmatrix} 54.6529 \\ 66.2088 \\ 84.6100 \\ 100.3319 \\ 117.9045 \\ 137.6626 \\ 159.4955 \\ 183.5974 \end{bmatrix} \quad \text{and} \quad \beta = \begin{bmatrix} 3.0 \\ 0.8 \end{bmatrix}$$

5.4.1a The Statistical Assumptions for y and e

Given the statistical model in the form of equation 5.4.5 the next task is to write the statistical assumptions in equations 5.2.9–5.2.14 in compact linear algebra notation as we did in Appendix 3B of Chapter 3. The mean vectors for **e** and **y** are obtained by taking the expectation of every element in **e** and **y**, respectively. Thus, the matrix algebra representations of equations 5.2.9 and 5.2.10 are

$$E[\mathbf{e}] = \mathbf{0} \qquad \text{and} \qquad E[\mathbf{y}] = X\boldsymbol{\beta} \qquad (5.4.6)$$

To confirm the last result, you should write out each element in the matrix product $X\boldsymbol{\beta}$.

Equations 5.2.11 and 5.2.12 are written in matrix algebra notation by forming the *covariance matrices* for **e** and **y**. Recall that the covariance matrix for **e**, for example, is a $(T \times T)$ matrix that contains the variances of each of the elements in **e** on the diagonal and the covariances between pairs of elements in **e** off the diagonal. It turns out that the covariance matrices for **e** and **y** are identical. From equation 5.2.11 we know that every element in **e** and every element in **y** has a variance of σ^2; from equation 5.2.12 we see that every pair of elements in **e** and every pair of elements in **y** is random and has a covariance of zero. Thus, for **e** we have

$$\text{cov}(\mathbf{e}) = \begin{bmatrix} \text{var}(e_1) & \text{cov}(e_1, e_2) & \cdots & \text{cov}(e_1, e_T) \\ \text{cov}(e_2, e_1) & \text{var}(e_2) & \cdots & \text{cov}(e_2, e_T) \\ \vdots & \vdots & \ddots & \vdots \\ \text{cov}(e_T, e_1) & \text{cov}(e_T, e_2) & \cdots & \text{var}(e_T) \end{bmatrix}$$

$$\qquad (5.4.7)$$

$$= \begin{bmatrix} \sigma^2 & 0 & \cdots & 0 \\ 0 & \sigma^2 & \cdots & 0 \\ \vdots & \vdots & \ddots & \vdots \\ 0 & 0 & \cdots & \sigma^2 \end{bmatrix} = \sigma^2 I_T$$

Similarly, $\text{cov}(\mathbf{y}) = \sigma^2 I_T$. We can derive these results by writing the covariance matrices for the vectors **e** and **y** in terms of the expectation and transpose operations used in Appendix 3B. Specifically,

$$\text{cov}(\mathbf{e}) = E\left[(\mathbf{e} - E[\mathbf{e}])(\mathbf{e} - E[\mathbf{e}])'\right] = E[\mathbf{e}\mathbf{e}'] = E\left[\begin{bmatrix} e_1 \\ e_2 \\ \vdots \\ e_T \end{bmatrix}\begin{bmatrix} e_1 & e_2 & \cdots & e_T \end{bmatrix}\right]$$

$$= E\begin{bmatrix} e_1^2 & e_1 e_2 & \cdots & e_1 e_T \\ e_2 e_1 & e_2^2 & \cdots & e_2 e_T \\ \vdots & \vdots & \ddots & \vdots \\ e_T e_1 & e_T e_2 & \cdots & e_T^2 \end{bmatrix} = \begin{bmatrix} \text{var}(e_1) & \text{cov}(e_1, e_2) & \cdots & \text{cov}(e_1, e_T) \\ \text{cov}(e_2, e_1) & \text{var}(e_2) & \cdots & \text{cov}(e_2, e_T) \\ \vdots & \vdots & \ddots & \vdots \\ \text{cov}(e_T, e_1) & \text{cov}(e_T, e_2) & \cdots & \text{var}(e_T) \end{bmatrix}$$

$$= \begin{bmatrix} \sigma^2 & 0 & \cdots & 0 \\ 0 & \sigma^2 & \cdots & 0 \\ \vdots & \vdots & \ddots & \vdots \\ 0 & 0 & \cdots & \sigma^2 \end{bmatrix} = \sigma^2 I_T$$

$$(5.4.8)$$

and

$$\begin{aligned}\text{cov}(\mathbf{y}) &= E\big[(\mathbf{y}-E[\mathbf{y}])(\mathbf{y}-E[\mathbf{y}])'\big]\\ &= E\big[(\mathbf{y}-X\boldsymbol{\beta})(\mathbf{y}-X\boldsymbol{\beta})'\big] \\ &= E\big[\mathbf{ee}'\big]=\sigma^2 I_T\end{aligned}\tag{5.4.9}$$

Thus, the compact way of writing assumptions 5.2.11 and 5.2.12 is

$$E\big[(\mathbf{y}-X\boldsymbol{\beta})(\mathbf{y}-X\boldsymbol{\beta})'\big]=E\big[\mathbf{ee}'\big]=\sigma^2 I_T\tag{5.4.10}$$

When using scalar notation e_t, we needed separate equations for stating the constant variance assumption and the zero covariance assumption. With matrix notation just one equation equation 5.4.10 is needed to state both assumptions. Also, we can combine equations 5.4.6 and 5.4.10 and write

$$\mathbf{e}\sim\left(\mathbf{0},\sigma^2 I_T\right)\quad\text{and}\quad \mathbf{y}\sim\left(X\boldsymbol{\beta},\sigma^2 I_T\right)\tag{5.4.11}$$

If $\mathbf{e}$ and $\mathbf{y}$ are *normally* distributed we write

$$\mathbf{e}\sim N\left(\mathbf{0},\sigma^2 I_T\right)\quad\text{and}\quad \mathbf{y}\sim N\left(X\boldsymbol{\beta},\sigma^2 I_T\right)\tag{5.4.12}$$

In words, we say that $\mathbf{e}$ and $\mathbf{y}$ are normally distributed random vectors with means $\mathbf{0}$ and $X\boldsymbol{\beta}$ and covariance matrix $\sigma^2 I_T$.

Next, it is worthwhile to examine how to express the least squares estimator in linear algebra notation. Linear algebra proves to be a very useful tool when using the computer to solve linear systems of equations, and also later in the book when we consider models with more than one explanatory variable.

5.4.2   The Least Squares Estimator

To make things easier both now and in the future, it is convenient to use linear or matrix algebra that was introduced in Appendix 3B of Chapter 3 and Section 5.4.1 to solve the normal equations 5.3.8. The first step in this direction is to rewrite equation 5.3.8 as

$$\begin{bmatrix} T & \Sigma x_t \\ \Sigma x_t & \Sigma x_t^2 \end{bmatrix}\begin{bmatrix} b_1 \\ b_2 \end{bmatrix}=\begin{bmatrix} \Sigma y_t \\ \Sigma x_t y_t \end{bmatrix}\tag{5.4.13}$$

From the definition of X below equation 5.4.3, where we let $X=\begin{bmatrix}\mathbf{x}_1 & \mathbf{x}_2\end{bmatrix}$, it follows that $X'X$ is the following (2×2) matrix:

$$X'X=\begin{bmatrix} 1 & 1 & \cdots & 1 \\ x_1 & x_2 & \cdots & x_T \end{bmatrix}\begin{bmatrix} 1 & x_1 \\ 1 & x_2 \\ \vdots & \vdots \\ 1 & x_T \end{bmatrix}=\begin{bmatrix} T & \Sigma x_t \\ \Sigma x_t & \Sigma x_t^2 \end{bmatrix}\tag{5.4.14}$$

where X' is the transpose (interchange rows and columns) of X. Likewise $X'\mathbf{y}$ is the following two-dimensional vector:

$$X'\mathbf{y}=\begin{bmatrix} 1 & 1 & \cdots & 1 \\ x_1 & x_2 & \cdots & x_T \end{bmatrix}\begin{bmatrix} y_1 \\ y_2 \\ \vdots \\ y_T \end{bmatrix}=\begin{bmatrix} \Sigma y_t \\ \Sigma x_t y_t \end{bmatrix}\tag{5.4.15}$$

The least squares estimates b_1 and b_2 we write as components of a vector

$$\mathbf{b} = \begin{bmatrix} b_1 \\ b_2 \end{bmatrix}$$

Using these results, the set of linear equations 5.4.13 can be written as

$$X'X\mathbf{b} = X'\mathbf{y} \tag{5.4.16}$$

The next step is to solve this linear algebra representation of a set of linear equations for the unknown vector $\mathbf{b}$. If $X'X$ in equation 5.4.16 were a scalar, we could solve this equation by multiplying each side by $1/X'X$. However, since $X'X$ is not a scalar but a (2×2) matrix, we achieve this step by premultiplying (on the left) both sides of equation 5.4.16 by $(X'X)^{-1}$, the inverse of the matrix $X'X$. This procedure yields

$$\left(X'X\right)^{-1} X'X\mathbf{b} = \left(X'X\right)^{-1} X'\mathbf{y}$$

or

$$\mathbf{b} = \left(X'X\right)^{-1} X'\mathbf{y} \tag{5.4.17}$$

since $(X'X)^{-1}X'X\mathbf{b} = I_2\mathbf{b} = \mathbf{b}$. This expression is a matrix representation of the solution of a system of linear simultaneous equations. The result is a formula for computing the least squares estimates b_1 and b_2 for the unknown parameters β_1 and β_2. Consequently, $\mathbf{b}$ in equation 5.4.17 is the *matrix formula for* the least squares estimator for β, and it is equivalent to the pair of formulas 5.3.10. Before we can use this formula, we need to learn how to compute the inverse matrix $(X'X)^{-1}$. For those who are not familiar with the inverse of a matrix, this piece of machinery is introduced in Appendix 5C of this chapter. Those with knowledge of the inverse operation may want to use this for a quick review. Others who do not need a time out should go directly to Section 5.4.3. As discussed in the *Computer Handbook*, the computer makes the computation of an inverse matrix, of the dimensions we will encounter, a very easy operation.

The least squares rule 5.4.1 should be contrasted to that developed in Appendix 3B of Chapter 3 where the statistical model was

$$\mathbf{y} = \mathbf{x}\beta + \mathbf{e} \qquad \mathbf{e} \sim N\left(\mathbf{0}, \sigma^2 I_T\right) \tag{5.4.18}$$

and where $\mathbf{x} = (1, 1, \ldots, 1)'$. In this case, with a corresponding sample of data and the least squares criterion, we were led to the estimation rule

$$\begin{aligned} b &= \left(\mathbf{x}'\mathbf{x}\right)^{-1} \mathbf{x}'\mathbf{y} = \mathbf{x}'\mathbf{y}/\mathbf{x}'\mathbf{x} \\ &= \mathbf{x}'\mathbf{y}/T = \sum_t y_t /T = \bar{y} \end{aligned} \tag{5.4.19}$$

where $\mathbf{x}'\mathbf{x}$ and $\mathbf{x}'\mathbf{y}$ are scalars. The only change, when we considered the two-parameter case, was that $\mathbf{x}'\mathbf{x}$ was no longer a scalar and we considered operations with a matrix that could be performed by a computer.

5.4.3   Estimates of β_1 and β_2

To use the matrix expression $\mathbf{b} = (X'X)^{-1}X'\mathbf{y}$ for estimating β_1 and β_2, we first need to find $(X'X)^{-1}$. Making use of the data in Table 5.2, the corresponding sums of squares in equation 5.3.11 and the inverse rule given in equation 5C.9 in Appendix 5C, we have

$$
(X'X)^{-1} = \begin{bmatrix} T & \Sigma x_t \\ \Sigma x_t & \Sigma x_t^2 \end{bmatrix}^{-1} = \frac{1}{T\Sigma x_t^2 - (\Sigma x_t)^2} \begin{bmatrix} \Sigma x_t^2 & -\Sigma x_t \\ -\Sigma x_t & T \end{bmatrix}
$$

$$
= \begin{bmatrix} 40 & 2792 \\ 2792 & 210206.2 \end{bmatrix}^{-1} = \frac{1}{40(210206.2)-(2792)^2} \begin{bmatrix} 210206.2 & -2792 \\ -2792 & 40 \end{bmatrix}
$$

$$
= \begin{bmatrix} 0.3429222 & -0.0045548 \\ -0.0045548 & 0.0000653 \end{bmatrix}
$$

(5.4.20)

To verify this is the correct inverse you should show that

$$
(X'X)^{-1}(X'X) = \frac{1}{T\Sigma x_t^2 - (\Sigma x_t)^2} \begin{bmatrix} \Sigma x_t^2 & -\Sigma x_t \\ -\Sigma x_t & T \end{bmatrix} \begin{bmatrix} T & \Sigma x_t \\ \Sigma x_t & \Sigma x_t^2 \end{bmatrix} = \begin{bmatrix} 1 & 0 \\ 0 & 1 \end{bmatrix}
$$

Then, using the formula $b = (X'X)^{-1}X'y$ produces the least squares estimates

$$
b = (X'X)^{-1} X'y = \begin{bmatrix} 40 & 2792 \\ 2792 & 210206.2 \end{bmatrix}^{-1} \begin{bmatrix} 943.78 \\ 69435.04 \end{bmatrix} = \begin{bmatrix} 0.3429222 & -0.0045548 \\ -0.0045548 & 0.0000653 \end{bmatrix} \begin{bmatrix} 943.78 \\ 69435.04 \end{bmatrix}
$$

$$
= \begin{bmatrix} (0.3429222)(943.78)+(-0.0045548)(69435.04) \\ (-0.0045548)(943.78)+(0.0000653)(69435.04) \end{bmatrix} = \begin{bmatrix} 7.38 \\ 0.23 \end{bmatrix} = \begin{bmatrix} b_1 \\ b_2 \end{bmatrix}
$$

(5.4.21)

Thus, both formulas lead to identical results. If we had written the answers in terms of more decimal places, they would actually show a slight discrepancy in the results. This discrepancy is caused by rounding error—not carrying through the calculations with enough significant digits. In practice, when the calculations are done by a computer, little or no discrepancy arises. The student is encouraged to attempt Exercise 5.12 to prove, in general, that both formulas are the same.

5.5 Exercises

5.1 (a) Contrast the sampling characteristics of the statistical model, $y_t = \beta + e_t$; $e_t \sim N(0, \sigma_1^2)$, of Chapter 3 and the statistical model, $y_t = \beta_1 + x_t\beta_2 + e_t$; $e_t \sim N(0, \sigma_2^2)$, of Chapter 5.
   (b) Contrast $E[y_t] = E[\beta + e_t]$ and $E[y_t] = E[\beta_1 + x_t\beta_2 + e_t]$.
   (c) What would you expect to be the relationship between the var(y_t) from the first model and var(y_t) from the second model and why?

5.2 Consider the following five observations on $y_t = \{5, 2, 3, 2, -2\}$ and $x_t = \{3, 2, 1, -1, 0\}$.
   (a) Find $\Sigma_{t=1}^{5} x_t^2$, $\Sigma_{t=1}^{5} x_t y_t$, $\Sigma_{t=1}^{5} x_t$, and $\Sigma_{t=1}^{5} y_t$.
   (b) Find

$$
b_2 = \frac{5\Sigma x_t y_t - \Sigma x_t \Sigma y_t}{5\Sigma x_t^2 - (\Sigma x_t)^2}
$$

and
$$b_1 = \bar{y} - b_2 \bar{x}$$

(c) Give an interpretation to the quantities you have calculated.

(d) Also use the deviation formula 5.3.10a to estimate b_2.

5.3   Prove that

$$b_1 = \frac{\Sigma x_t^2 \Sigma y_t - \Sigma x_t \Sigma x_t y_t}{T \Sigma x_t^2 - (\Sigma x_t)^2} = \bar{y} - b_2 \bar{x}$$

$$b_2 = \frac{T \Sigma x_t y_t - \Sigma x_t \Sigma y_t}{T \Sigma x_t^2 - (\Sigma x_t)^2} = \frac{\Sigma (x_t - \bar{x})(y_t - \bar{y})}{\Sigma (x_t - \bar{x})^2}$$

5.4   (a) Show that the least squares line $\hat{y}_t = b_1 + x_t b_2$ passes through the point $(\bar{y}, \bar{x})$.

(b) Show that $\bar{\hat{y}} = \bar{y}$ where $\bar{\hat{y}} = \dfrac{\Sigma \hat{y}_t}{T}$.

5.5   Consider the income elasticity of demand for food given in equation 5.3.13

$$\eta - 0.23 \frac{x}{y}$$

and the least squares line from which it was derived

$$\hat{y}_t = 7.38 + 0.23 x_t$$

(a) Show that the income elasticity of demand is less than 1 for all (x,y) points that lie on the estimated line.

(b) Consider the more general expenditure–income relationship $\hat{y}_t = b_1 + x_t b_2$, where it is assumed $b_2 > 0$. Under what conditions on b_1 will the income elasticity of demand be greater than 1? When will it be less than 1? (Consider only points that lie on the line $\hat{y}_t = b_1 + x_t b_2$.)

5.6   Consider the problem of estimating a production function that expresses the relationship between the level of output of a commodity and the level of input of a factor and assume that you have the input–output data given in Table 5.3.

(a) Assume that the data can be described by the statistical model, $y_t = \beta_1 + x_t \beta_2 + e_t$, where the random variable $e_t \sim (0, \sigma^2)$. Use the least squares rule to estimate β_1 and β_2.

(b) Give an economic interpretation to the estimated parameters.

(c) Use the results of part (a) to plot the production function.

(d) If the cost of feed is 6 cents per pound, derive the total cost and marginal cost functions.

(e) Show how to use the total cost function (which relates total cost to output) to obtain estimates of the parameters of the production function connecting feed inputs and poultry meat outputs.

5.7   Assume that a new hamburger outlet in Moscow that we label as the Moscow Makkers is unsure of its pricing policy. Consequently, each week they change the hamburger price slightly using specials of various kinds. The quantities sold and their corresponding prices are as shown in Table 5.4

(a) Assume the statistical model $\ln q_t = \beta_1 + \beta_2 \ln p_t + e_t$, where $e_t \sim N(0, \sigma^2)$. Discuss the characteristics of the statistical model and the interpretation of β_2. (*Hint:* See Appendix 8A, Examples 5 and 8.)

Table 5.3 A Sample of Observations from a Controlled Experiment Involving Poultry Meat Outputs and Feed Inputs

Input x	Output y
1.00	0.58
2.00	1.10
3.00	1.20
4.00	1.30
5.00	1.95
6.00	2.55
7.00	2.60
8.00	2.90
9.00	3.45
10.00	3.50
11.00	3.60
12.00	4.10
13.00	4.35
14.00	4.40
15.00	4.50

(b) Find $y_t = \ln q_t$ and $x_t = \ln p_t$, for $t = 1, 2,\ldots, 12$. Report these quantities correct to 4 decimal places.
(c) Find $\Sigma y_t x_t$, Σx_t^2, Σy_t^2, Σx_t and Σy_t.
(d) Find least squares estimates b_1 and b_2 of β_1 and β_2 and interpret.
(e) Should the Makkers increase or decrease price if they want to increase total receipts?

5.8 In the macroeconomics literature there are two competing theories concerning consumption behavior. According to Keynes, aggregate consumption is determined by aggregate income. Alternatively, the classical economists believed that consumption should be inversely related to interest rates [See Sheffrin et al. (1988, pp. 56–61) for a discussion of these propositions]. Using

Table 5.4 A Sample of Quantity and Price Observations

Week	Number of Hamburgers Sold (q_t)	Price (p_t)
1	892	1.23
2	1012	1.15
3	1060	1.10
4	987	1.20
5	680	1.35
6	739	1.25
7	809	1.28
8	1275	0.99
9	946	1.22
10	874	1.25
11	720	1.30
12	1096	1.05

the data given in Table 5.5 for the sample of years 1955 to 1986 [see Sheffrin et al. (1988. p. 57) or *The Economic Report of the President*]

(a) Set up the economic and statistical model for each hypothesis.

(b) Estimate the unknown parameters for each model.

(c) Based on these data and your econometric results, what are your conclusions relative to the validity of the two hypotheses?

5.9 Suppose for the food expenditure–income data in Table 5.2 you knew that the intercept β_1 was equal to zero, that is, $\beta_1 = 0$. How would you proceed to estimate β_2 and what is its estimated value?

5.10 Using the statistical model $\mathbf{y} = X\beta + \mathbf{e}$ and $\mathbf{e} \sim N(0, \sigma^2 I_T)$ and the data in Table 5.3

(a) Set up and compute the $X'X$ matrix and the $X'\mathbf{y}$ vector.

(b) Compute the inverse of $X'X$.

(c) Compute a least squares estimate of β and compare with the results in Exercise 5.6.

Table 5.5 A Sample of Consumption, Income and the Interest Rate Data 1955–1986

Year	Consumption Expenditures (billions 1982$)	Disposable Personal Income (billions 1982$)	Real Interest Rate
1955	873.8	944.5	3.43
1956	899.8	989.4	1.86
1957	919.7	1,012.1	0.33
1958	932.9	1,028.8	1.06
1959	979.4	1,067.2	3.57
1960	1,005.1	1,091.1	2.81
1961	1,025.2	1,123.2	3.34
1962	1,069.0	1,170.2	3.21
1963	1,108.4	1,207.3	3.05
1964	1,170.6	1,291.0	3.09
1965	1,236.4	1,365.7	2.77
1966	1,298.9	1,431.3	2.27
1967	1,337.7	1,493.2	2.63
1968	1,405.9	1,551.3	1.98
1969	1,456.7	1,599.8	1.66
1970	1,492.0	1,668.1	2.12
1971	1,538.8	1,728.4	3.09
1972	1,621.9	1,797.4	3.91
1973	1,689.6	1,916.3	1.21
1974	1,674.0	1,896.6	-2.40
1975	1,711.9	1,931.7	0.31
1976	1,803.0	2,001.0	2.66
1977	1,883.8	2,066.6	1.57
1978	1,961.0	2,167.4	1.07
1979	2,004.4	2,212.6	-1.63
1980	2,000.4	2,214.3	-1.58
1981	2,024.2	2,248.6	3.80
1982	2,050.7	2,261.5	7.66
1983	2,146.0	2,331.9	8.82
1984	2,246.3	2,470.6	8.45
1985	2,324.5	2,528.0	7.80
1986	2,418.6	2,603.7	7.10

5.11 Using the data given in Exercise 5.2 and the statistical model $\mathbf{y} = X\boldsymbol{\beta} + \mathbf{e}$ and $\mathbf{e} \sim N\left(\mathbf{0}, \sigma^2 I_T\right)$, where

$$X = \begin{bmatrix} 1 & 3 \\ 1 & 2 \\ 1 & 1 \\ 1 & -1 \\ 1 & 0 \end{bmatrix} \quad \text{and} \quad \mathbf{y} = \begin{bmatrix} 5 \\ 2 \\ 3 \\ 2 \\ -2 \end{bmatrix}$$

(a) Find $X'X$, $X'\mathbf{y}$ and $(X'X)^{-1}$.
(b) Find $\mathbf{b} = (X'X)^{-1}X'\mathbf{y}$.
(c) Give an interpretation of the quantities you have calculated.

5.12 Prove that

$$\mathbf{b} = \left(X'X\right)^{-1} X'\mathbf{y} = \begin{bmatrix} \dfrac{\Sigma x_t^2 \Sigma y_t - \Sigma x_t \Sigma x_t y_t}{T\Sigma x_t^2 - \left(\Sigma x_t\right)^2} \\[2ex] \dfrac{T\Sigma x_t y_t - \Sigma x_t y_t}{T\Sigma x_t^2 - \left(\Sigma x_t\right)^2} \end{bmatrix}$$

5.6 References

Some of the concepts we have discussed in this chapter are more completely covered in

JUDGE, G. G., R. C. HILL, W. E. GRIFFITHS, H. LÜTKEPOHL and T. C. LEE (1988) *Introduction to the Theory and Practice of Econometrics*, New York: John Wiley & Sons, Inc., pp. 159–174.

Often it is good to read the same material in different books. In this case for other coverage see:

KMENTA, JAN (1986) *Elements of Econometrics*, New York: Macmillan Publishing Co., pp. 203–254.

PINDYCK, R.S. and D. RUBINFELD (1990) *Econometric Models and Economic Forecasts*, New York: McGraw-Hill Book Co., Chapter 3.

For discussions of the household expenditure–income model see one of the following books:

LIPSEY, R.G., P.O. STEINER and D.D. PURVIS (1987) *Economics*, New York: Harper & Row, pp. 148-155.

SAMUELSON, P.A. and W.D. NORDHAUS (1985) *Economics*, New York: McGraw-Hill Book Co., pp. 422-429.

SHEFFRIN, S.M., D.A. WILTON and D.M. PRESCOTT (1988) *Macroeconomics: Theory and Policy*, Cincinnati, OH: South-Western Publishing Co., pp. 56–61.

APPENDIX 5A   Elasticities

Suppose that a change in an explanatory variable Δx leads to a change in an outcome variable equal to Δy. Then the percentage change in x is given by $(\Delta x/x)100$ and the percentage change in y is given by $(\Delta y/y)100$. In this case the elasticity of y with respect to x is defined as

$$\eta = \frac{(\Delta y/y)100}{(\Delta x/x)100} = \frac{\Delta y/y}{\Delta x/x} = \frac{\Delta y}{\Delta x} \cdot \frac{x}{y} \tag{5A.1}$$

This expression was given in Equation 5.1.2 for the elasticity of expenditure on food with respect to a change in income. It is relevant when we are considering an *arc* elasticity, which is the elasticity between two points (x_1, y_1) and (x_2, y_2), where $\Delta x = x_2 - x_1$ and $\Delta y = y_2 - y_1$. The expression $\Delta y/\Delta x$ represents the *slope between two points,* and the derivative dy/dx represents the slope of the curve $y = f(x)$ at a *single point.* Similarly, equation 5A.1 defines the elasticity between two points, and the elasticity at a single point is given by

$$\eta = \frac{dy}{dx} \cdot \frac{x}{y} \tag{5A.2}$$

Thus, the elasticity of y with respect to x at a given point (x, y) is obtained by multiplying the derivative dy/dx by the ratio (x/y).

For the linear model studied in Chapter 5, where expenditure on food y is related to income x through the linear function

$$y = \beta_1 + \beta_2 x$$

the *elasticity of food expenditure with respect to income* is given by (see equation 5.1.3)

$$\eta_y = \frac{dy}{dx} \cdot \frac{x}{y} = \beta_2 \frac{x}{y} \tag{5A.3}$$

In Figure 5.2 we demonstrated how the ratio x/y increases as x increases. This result implies that the elasticity of food expenditure is higher for high-income households than it is for low-income households.

In equation 5.1.4 we noted that the *elasticity for the quantity of food demanded q with respect to income x* is defined as

$$\eta_q = \frac{dq}{dx} \cdot \frac{x}{q} \tag{5A.4}$$

and that a shorter way of referring to this elasticity is as the "income elasticity of demand for food." It is straightforward to show that this elasticity is identical to the elasticity of expenditure η_y. To do so, we note that, given the price of food p, expenditure y is equal to the product of price and quantity, $y = pq$, and we manipulate equation 5A.4 as follows:

$$\eta_q = p \frac{dq}{dx} \cdot \frac{x}{pq} = p \frac{d(pq)}{dx} \cdot \frac{x}{y} = \frac{dy}{dx} \cdot \frac{x}{y} = \eta_y \tag{5A.5}$$

Thus

$$\eta_q = \beta_2 \frac{x}{y} \tag{5A.6}$$

If interest centers on the income elasticity of demand, this elasticity can be computed without knowledge of separate values of p and q; all that is required is the expenditure ($y = pq$).

Because the elasticity of y with respect to x depends on the derivative dy/dx, the nature of the function $y = f(x)$ has a big bearing on the nature of the expression for the elasticity. In particular, it determines whether the elasticity is constant or whether it depends in some way on x and/or y. Equation 5A.3 gives the expression for the elasticity when y and x are linearly related. Other examples will be given in Appendix 8A of Chapter 8.

APPENDIX 5B   The Minimum or Maximum of a Multivariate Function; The Partial Derivative

In Appendix 3A we investigated the use of the derivative with the univariate function $y = f(x)$. In Chapter 5 in developing the least squares estimator for the unknowns in the statistical model $y_t = \beta_1 + x_t\beta_2 + e_t$, we found we needed a mechanism for finding the minimum error sum of squares for the multivariate function 5.3.4a:

$$S(\beta_1, \beta_2) = \Sigma(y_t - \beta_1 - x_t\beta_2)^2 \tag{5B.1}$$

involving the unknown parameters β_1 and β_2. Since for a given sample of data, y_t and x_t are known, the unknowns β_1 and β_2 are treated as variables. This function generated the bowl-shaped function $S(\beta_1, \beta_2)$ that appears in Figure 5.8. Given the data to obtain least squares estimates, we needed to determine values $\beta_1 = b_1$ and $\beta_2 = b_2$ where the function reaches a minimum at the bottom of the bowl. To do this we need to expand the ideas of Appendix 3A and consider a procedure called partial derivatives. This is necessary since we need a procedure that describes how $S(\beta_1, \beta_2)$ changes when there is a change in *each* of the variables β_1 and β_2. The partial derivative provides one way of measuring such changes.

5B.1   Partial Derivatives

To introduce the idea of a partial derivative that will be useful in helping us determine the values of β_1 and β_2 that minimize the quadratic function 5.3.4, let us consider an economic example with which you are probably familiar. Let's suppose we have a demand equation where quantity demanded q is a function of price p and income i. That is

$$q = f(p, i) \tag{5B.2}$$

We now ask the question: How will quantity demanded respond if price changes and income is held constant? Let Δp be the change in price and let income be fixed at i_0. The resulting change in quantity demanded is given by

$$\Delta q = f(p + \Delta p, i_0) - f(p, i_0) \tag{5B.3}$$

For example, if

$$q = \beta_1 + \beta_2 p + \beta_3 p^2 + \beta_4 i \tag{5B.4}$$

then

$$\Delta q = \beta_1 + \beta_2(p + \Delta p) + \beta_3(p + \Delta p)^2 + \beta_4 i_0 - \beta_1 - \beta_2 p - \beta_3 p^2 - \beta_4 i_0$$
$$= \beta_2 \Delta p + 2\beta_3 p\Delta p + \beta_3(\Delta p)^2 \tag{5B.5}$$

In this case the change in q per unit change in p is given by

$$\frac{\Delta q}{\Delta p} = \beta_2 p + 2\beta_3 p + \beta_3 \Delta p \qquad (5\text{B}.6)$$

The partial derivative of q with respect to p, at the point (p, i, q), is defined as

$$\frac{\partial q}{\partial p} = \lim_{\Delta p \to 0} \left(\frac{\Delta q}{\Delta p} \right) = \lim_{\Delta p \to 0} \frac{f(p + \Delta p, i) - f(p, i)}{\Delta p} \qquad (5\text{B}.7)$$

The symbol "∂" is used rather than "d" to indicate that other variables (income in this case) are being held constant. We interpret the partial derivative $\partial q / \partial p$ as the rate of response of q with respect to a change in p, given all other variables are held constant. Like the derivative defined in Appendix 3A, it measures the instantaneous rate of response at a particular point. For the function in equation 5B.4, the partial derivative of q with respect to p is given by

$$\frac{\partial q}{\partial p} = \lim_{\Delta p \to 0} \frac{\Delta q}{\Delta p} = \lim_{\Delta p \to 0} (\beta_2 + 2\beta_3 p + \beta_3 \Delta p)$$
$$= \beta_2 + 2\beta_3 p \qquad (5\text{B}.8)$$

We think of the change in price Δp as being small relative to the magnitude of p.

The partial derivative also represents the slope of a curve or the slope of a tangent to a curve. To find the relevant curve, consider the three-dimensional diagram in Figure 5B.1. The plane $ABCi_0$ represents the space of all values of q and p for the fixed income value i_0. Let AB be the curve defined by the intersection of the plane $ABCi_0$ with the function $q = f(p, i)$. Thus, AB is the curve $q = f(p, i_0)$ that shows how q varies when p varies and i is fixed at i_0. The tangent to AB at the point P is given by $T_1 T_2$. The partial derivative $\partial q / \partial p$, at the point P, is equal to the slope of this tangent. In general this derivative will depend on both p and i.

The rules for obtaining partial derivatives are similar to those for obtaining derivatives. We follow the same procedure, but we treat all explanatory variables, other than

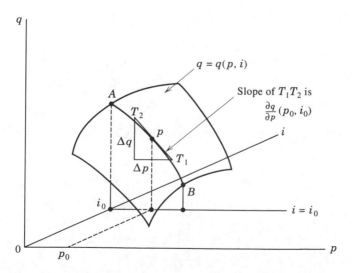

Figure 5B.1 Three dimensional diagram of partial derivative.

the one with which we are directly concerned, as constants. For example, in equation 5B.4, when partially differentiating with respect to p, the term $\beta_4 i$ is treated as a constant and hence has a derivative equal to zero. Thus, direct application of our rules to equation 5B.4 leads to the result in equation 5B.8, namely

$$\frac{\partial q}{\partial p} = \beta_2 + 2\beta_3 p \qquad (5B.9)$$

We can also take the partial derivative of q with respect to i. This derivative tells us the rate of response of q to a change in i when p is held fixed. It is obtained by differentiating q with respect to i and treating p as a constant. From equation 5B.4

$$\frac{\partial q}{\partial i} = \beta_4 \qquad (5B.10)$$

Since this derivative does not depend on p or i, a one-unit increase in income will result in a change in demand of β_4 units, irrespective of the levels of p and i.

To represent the partial derivative $\partial q / \partial i$ geometrically, we consider the curve $q = f(p_0, i)$ that is defined by the intersection of the function $q = f(p, i)$ with the plane containing all points (i, q), for a given price p_0. The derivative $\partial q / \partial i$ is the slope of a tangent to this curve. Note that, for some value p_0, the curve $q = f(p_0, i)$ will also pass through the point P in Figure 5B.1. Thus, we can also evaluate $\partial q / \partial i$ at the point P; it will be given by the slope of a tangent to a curve that goes in a direction that is at right angles to the direction of the curve AB.

5B.2   The Minimum (and Maximum) of a Multivariate Function

Let us now apply what we have learned to the least squares problem of finding the values for the unknown parameters β_1 and β_2 that minimize equation 5.3.4

$$S(\beta_1, \beta_2) = \Sigma(y_t - \beta_1 - x_t \beta_2)^2 \qquad (5B.11a)$$

In this function β_1 and β_2 play the role of the variables p and i in our demand example. Expanding this function yields

$$\begin{aligned} S(\beta_1, \beta_2) &= \Sigma(y_t^2 + \beta_1^2 + x_t^2 \beta_2^2 - 2y_t \beta_1 - 2x_t y_t \beta_2 + 2x_t \beta_1 \beta_2) \\ &= \Sigma y_t^2 + \beta_1^2 T + \beta_2^2 \Sigma x_t^2 - 2\beta_1 \Sigma y_t - 2\beta_2 \Sigma x_t y_t + 2\beta_1 \beta_2 \Sigma x_t \end{aligned}$$
$$(5B.11b)$$

For the quadratic function 5B.11b, the partial derivatives $\partial S / \partial \beta_1$ and $\partial S / \partial \beta_2$ are given by the linear equations

$$\frac{\partial S}{\partial \beta_1} = 2T\beta_1 - 2\Sigma y_t + 2\Sigma x_t \beta_2 \qquad (5B.12a)$$

$$\frac{\partial S}{\partial \beta_2} = 2\Sigma x_t^2 \beta_2 - 2\Sigma x_t y_t + 2\Sigma x_t \beta_1 \qquad (5B.12b)$$

In Appendix 3A we discovered that the derivative dy/dx equals zero at the point where the function $y = f(x)$ achieves a maximum or minimum value. This result extends naturally to functions of more than one variable.

Consider the bowl-shaped function $S(\beta_1, \beta_2)$ that appears in Figure 5.8. This function (the error sum of squares) reaches a minimum at the bottom of the bowl where $\beta_1 = b_1$ and $\beta_2 = b_2$. At this minimum both partial derivatives, or the slopes of the function in both directions, will be equal to zero. That is

$$\frac{\partial S}{\partial \beta_1} = 0 \qquad \text{and} \qquad \frac{\partial S}{\partial \beta_2} = 0$$

To find the minimizing values $\beta_1 = b_1$ and $\beta_2 = b_2$, we proceed as follows:

1. Set the expressions for the two partial derivatives equal to zero. Replacing β_1 and β_2 by the optimizing values b_1 and b_2, this yields

$$2\left(\Sigma y_t - Tb_1 - \Sigma x_t b_2\right) = 0 \qquad (5B.13a)$$

$$2\left(\Sigma x_t y_t - \Sigma x_t b_1 - \Sigma x_t^2 b_2\right) = 0 \qquad (5B.13b)$$

or

$$Tb_1 + \Sigma x_t b_2 = \Sigma y_t \qquad (5B.14a)$$

$$\Sigma x_t b_1 + \Sigma x_t^2 b_2 = \Sigma x_t y_t \qquad (5B.14b)$$

This step yields two simultaneous linear equations whose unknowns are the minimizing values b_1 and b_2.

2. Solve, by procedures noted in the text, the two simultaneous equations for the squared error minimizing values $\beta_1 = b_1$ and $\beta_2 = b_2$.

Other examples of the use of partial derivatives to find the minima or maxima of a multivariate function will be given in Appendix 10A of Chapter 10.

APPENDIX 5C   The Inverse of a Matrix

Consider the simple linear equation

$$2z = 4 \qquad (5C.1)$$

To solve this equation for z you would divide both sides by 2 to obtain

$$\frac{2}{2}z = \frac{4}{2} \qquad or \qquad z = 2 \qquad (5C.2a)$$

This operation is, of course, exactly the same as multiplying both sides of the equation by 2^{-1}. Viewing the procedure in this way, we have

$$2^{-1} \cdot 2z = 2^{-1} \cdot 4 \qquad or \qquad z = 2 \qquad (5C.2b)$$

In general terms, for the solution to the equation $az = d$ we have

$$a^{-1}az = a^{-1}d \qquad or \qquad z = a^{-1}d = \frac{d}{a} \qquad (5C.2c)$$

The operation in equation 5C.2 can be generalized to solve a system of K linear equations in K unknowns, written in general notation as

$$Az = d \qquad (5C.3)$$

where A is a $(K \times K)$ known matrix, d is a $(K \times 1)$ known vector, and z is a $(K \times 1)$ vector whose solution we seek. To solve equation 5C.3 we premultiply both sides of the equation by a matrix A^{-1} that is called the inverse of A. Thus, we have

$$A^{-1}Az = A^{-1}d \qquad (5C.4)$$

Now the inverse matrix A^{-1} is constructed so that

$$A^{-1}A = AA^{-1} = I_K \qquad (5C.5)$$

That is, pre- (on the left) or post- (on the right) multiplying the matrix A by its inverse yields the identity matrix of order K. Using this result, equation 5C.4 becomes

$$I_K z = A^{-1}d \qquad \text{or} \qquad z = A^{-1}d \qquad (5C.6)$$

Thus, the solution vector z is obtained by premultiplying d by the matrix A^{-1}.

This result can be applied to equation 5.4.16 to obtain a solution for our least squares estimates. In this instance $A = X'X$, $d = X'y$, and $z = b$, so the least squares estimates are given by

$$b = (X'X)^{-1} X'y \qquad (5C.7)$$

The missing ingredient in this discussion is a method for constructing the inverse of a matrix. How do we find A^{-1} or $(X'X)^{-1}$? Most of the time we let a computer do it for us. Finding an inverse is a computationally tedious task, one of the kinds of tasks for which computers are particularly well suited. However, we will give details on how to find an inverse for a (2×2) matrix and how to find the inverse of a diagonal matrix. Both of these cases are relatively straightforward.

Let A be the following (2×2) matrix

$$A = \begin{bmatrix} a_{11} & a_{12} \\ a_{21} & a_{22} \end{bmatrix} \qquad (5C.8)$$

Then the matrix A^{-1} that has the property $A^{-1}A = AA^{-1} = I_2$ is given by

$$A^{-1} = \frac{1}{a_{11}a_{22} - a_{12}a_{21}} \begin{bmatrix} a_{22} & -a_{12} \\ -a_{21} & a_{11} \end{bmatrix} \qquad (5C.9)$$

providing that $a_{11}a_{22} - a_{12}a_{21} \neq 0$. The expression $a_{11}a_{22} - a_{12}a_{21}$ is the *determinant* of A. If $a_{11}a_{22} - a_{12}a_{21} = 0$ then A is said to be *singular* and its inverse does not exist. Trying to find the inverse of a singular matrix is like trying to find the inverse of zero in scalar notation. If A is not singular, it is called a *nonsingular* matrix. The reader should verify that multiplication of A in equation 5C.8 by A^{-1} in equation 5C.9 yields the identity matrix of order 2.

As an example, let

$$A = \begin{bmatrix} 4 & 1 \\ 3 & 2 \end{bmatrix}$$

Then, applying the result in equation 5C.9, we have

$$A^{-1} = \frac{1}{8-3}\begin{bmatrix} 2 & -1 \\ -3 & 4 \end{bmatrix} = \frac{1}{5}\begin{bmatrix} 2 & -1 \\ -3 & 4 \end{bmatrix} = \begin{bmatrix} 0.4 & -0.2 \\ -0.6 & 0.8 \end{bmatrix}$$

Note that

$$\begin{bmatrix} 0.4 & -0.2 \\ -0.6 & 0.8 \end{bmatrix}\begin{bmatrix} 4 & 1 \\ 3 & 2 \end{bmatrix} = \begin{bmatrix} 1.6-0.6 & 0.4-0.4 \\ -2.4+2.4 & -0.6+1.6 \end{bmatrix} = \begin{bmatrix} 1 & 0 \\ 0 & 1 \end{bmatrix}$$

Consider a *diagonal matrix*; that is, a square matrix whose off-diagonal elements are zero. Providing none of the diagonal elements is also zero, the inverse of a diagonal matrix is obtained by replacing the diagonal elements by their inverses (reciprocals). For example, suppose that

$$A = \begin{bmatrix} 2 & 0 & 0 & 0 \\ 0 & 4 & 0 & 0 \\ 0 & 0 & 1 & 0 \\ 0 & 0 & 0 & .5 \end{bmatrix} \quad \text{then} \quad A^{-1} = \begin{bmatrix} .5 & 0 & 0 & 0 \\ 0 & .25 & 0 & 0 \\ 0 & 0 & 1 & 0 \\ 0 & 0 & 0 & 2 \end{bmatrix}$$

If one or more of the diagonal elements of A are zero, then A is singular.

The following definitions and results on matrix inverses are often useful. We state these results without proofs. Students can obtain a feel for some of these results by attempting Exercise 5C.1.

1. A matrix A has an inverse if and only if it is square and nonsingular.
2. If A^{-1} exists, then it is unique.
3. $(A^{-1})^{-1} = A$
4. If A and B are square nonsingular matrices, then $(AB)^{-1} = B^{-1}A^{-1}$.
5. $(A')^{-1} = (A^{-1})'$

We are now in a position to return to the problem of computing the least squares estimates in Section 5.4.3.

Exercise

5C.1   Consider the following matrices:

$$A = \begin{bmatrix} 2 & 1 \\ 2 & 2 \end{bmatrix} \quad B = \begin{bmatrix} 3 & -1 \\ 1 & 1 \end{bmatrix} \quad C = \begin{bmatrix} 1 & -1 \\ 0 & 2 \end{bmatrix}$$

(a) Find A^{-1}, B^{-1}, AB, and $B^{-1}A^{-1}$.
(b) Find $(AB)^{-1}$ and compare with $B^{-1}A^{-1}$.
(c) Find $(B^{-1})^{-1}$ and compare with B.
(d) Find ABC and A', B', and C'.
(e) Find $C'B'A'$ and compare with $(ABC)'$.
(f) Find $(A')^{-1}$ and compare with $(A^{-1})'$.

Chapter 6

Inference in the Simple Regression Model: Estimator Sampling Characteristics and Properties

New Key Words and Concepts

Linear Estimator
Mean Parameter Vector
Variance–Covariance Matrix
Unbiased Estimator
Monte Carlo Sampling Experiment

Normally Distributed Vector of
 Random Variables
Properties of Estimators
Variance Estimator

In Chapter 5 we specified an economic model that led to the statistical model

$$y_t = \beta_1 + x_t \beta_2 + e_t$$

where e_t and y_t were independently and identically distributed normal random variables that we expressed in compact form as $e_t \sim N(0, \sigma^2)$ and $y_t \sim N(\beta_1 + x_t \beta_2, \sigma^2)$.

Based on this statistical model, in Chapter 5 we obtained just one sample of 40 households. There are, of course, many other households that could have been chosen. Other samples of 40 households would yield other expenditure outcomes y_t and other pairs of estimates b_1 and b_2. Consequently, the random variables y_t and b_1 and b_2 vary from sample to sample. Alternatively, it is important to note that since the least squares estimators b_1 and b_2 are based on the random observations y_t, the least squares estimators b_1 and b_2 are also random variables. The resulting random (stochastic) nature of the least squares estimation rule raises several fundamental questions.

1. If the least squares estimators b_1 and b_2 are random variables, what do we know about their corresponding means, variances, covariances, and probability distributions?

2. The least squares rule is only *one* way of using the data to obtain estimates of β_1 and β_2. How does the least squares rule compare with other rules that might be used, and indeed what basis should be used for comparing this sampling performance of estimation rules (estimators)? For example, is there another estimation rule that, on average, produces estimates that are closer to β_1 and β_2 than the least squares rule?

3. How good are the estimates b_1 and b_2? That is, how close is our pair of estimates b_1 and b_2 (from just a single sample) likely to be to their population counterparts β_1 and β_2?

4. In the food expenditure example, we have hypothesized that β_1 and β_2 are positive. How do we go about statistically testing these hypotheses?

Questions of this type, which are investigated in Chapters 6 and 7, are fundamental in inferential statistics. If you can master the application of a few basic concepts, then you are well on your way to understanding the sampling theory approach to inference and how economists use data to answer questions about economic phenomena. The machinery that we will need to answer such questions was introduced in Chapters 3 and 4, where it was recognized that an estimator is a random variable with a probability distribution. Of interest now are the random variables b_1 and b_2. The values these random variables take on are the estimates obtained by taking alternative samples of 40 households. Since an estimator is a random variable, here, and elsewhere, *if someone proposes an estimation rule for a particular statistical model, your next question should be: What are its sampling characteristics and how good is it?*

6.1   The Least Squares Estimators as Random Variables

The least squares rule for making use of the sample information is

$$b_1 = \frac{\Sigma x_t^2 \Sigma y_t - \Sigma x_t \Sigma x_t y_t}{T \Sigma x_t^2 - (\Sigma x_t)^2} = \overline{y} - b_2 \overline{x}$$

$$b_2 = \frac{T \Sigma x_t y_t - \Sigma x_t \Sigma y_t}{T \Sigma x_t^2 - (\Sigma x_t)^2} = \frac{\Sigma(x_t - \overline{x})(y_t - \overline{y})}{\Sigma(x_t - \overline{x})^2}$$

$$(6.1.1)$$

where x_t is assumed fixed in repeated samples. Since the x_t are fixed, this means b_1 and b_2 may be written as $b_1 = \Sigma a_t y_t$ and $b_2 = c_t y_t$, where a_t and c_t are constants. Thus, b_1 and b_2 are *linear* functions of the random variable y_t, and since function of random variables are random too, the linear least squares estimators b_1 and b_2 are random variables.

Since linear functions of independent normal random variables are also normal random variables (Section 2.8.1 of Chapter 2), one consequence of the linearity of b_1 and b_2 is that when y_t is a normally distributed random variable, then b_1 and b_2 will be normally distributed random variables. This implies that the least squares rules b_1 and b_2 are normally distributed random variables with particular means and variances (sampling variability). *Even if the distribution of y_t is unknown, a Central Limit Theorem like that discussed in Section 2.8.2 of Chapter 2 permits us to state that the least squares estimator will be approximately normally distributed for sample sizes usually employed in practice.* Consequently, we now have a basis for understanding the sampling characteristics of the least squares estimation rule and for evaluating its sampling performance.

In equation 6.1.1 we noted that $x_t = \{x_1 \quad x_2 \quad \cdots \quad x_T\}$ is fixed from sample to sample. Before going on to the sampling characteristics of our estimation rule, we need to consider, in the context of the household expenditure example, how x_t changes (or does not change) in repeated samples. In the previous paragraph we argued that b_1 and b_2 were random because they depend on y_t and that y_t is a random variable because the observed outcomes (household expenditures on food) will depend on what households are sampled. It is of course also true that x_t, the household incomes, will depend on what households are being sampled. Hence, we could argue that b_1 and b_2 are random variables because they depend on x_t and y_t, *both* of which are random. However, we will, for the present, assume that x_t is not random but is instead fixed or constant in repeated samples. In effect we are assuming that we can perform controlled experiments using an experimental design for x_t that remains the same when we produce repeated samples of data. The implication of this assumption is that we know the income levels of the households to be sampled, but not their levels of expenditure on food. Thus, when we conceptualize repetition of the sampling process, the taking of more and more samples of size 40, the expenditure outcomes y_t can vary from sample to sample, but each sample is assumed to have the same set of x_t; only households with the same income levels are sampled. The consequences of relaxing this assumption are examined in Chapter 14.

6.2 Sampling Properties of the Least Squares Rule for Estimating β

The parameters of interest β_1 and β_2 describe the data generation process (the food expenditure–income relationship) for the whole population of households. When we sample just 40 households and use the values b_1 and b_2 from these household data as estimates for β_1 and β_2, we naturally would like to know how close b_1 and b_2 are to β_1 and β_2. We cannot answer this sampling precision question exactly. Indeed, if we could, we would know β_1 and β_2 and there would be no need to obtain estimates. What we *can* do is to estimate how much the estimates b_1 and b_2 can vary from sample to sample if we take a large number of samples each of size 40 with the same set of x_t. To illustrate how such knowledge can help, suppose we estimate the sampling variability of b_1 and b_2 and it tells us that it is possible for the estimates b_1 and b_2 to vary a lot from sample to sample. In that event we would not feel confident that our values b_1 and b_2, obtained from our *one* sample of size 40, are close to β_1 and β_2. We would say there is a high probability that b_1 and b_2, resulting from a particular sample, could be quite different from β_1 and β_2. On the other hand, if our estimate of sampling variability suggests that b_1 and b_2 do not vary much from sample to sample, and if we know that the different sample values for b_1 and b_2 average out to β_1 and β_2, we would be confident that the values of b_1 and b_2 from our one sample are quite close to β_1 and β_2. We would conclude that there is a high probability that b_1 and b_2 could be close to β_1 and β_2. Thus, although we cannot say, for example, exactly how close one estimate of b_2 is to β_2, we can do so in a probabilistic sense, and we do so by examining how much b_2 can vary from sample to sample, and by examining the average value of b_2 over a large number of samples.

Fortunately, we do not have to go out knocking on doors and collecting large numbers of samples of size 40 to estimate how much the estimates of b_1 and b_2 can vary from sample to sample. *Before any samples are taken,* we can examine the "sampling properties" or characteristics of *the rule* that we use to obtain estimates. For a particular estimation rule, these sampling properties tell us about the performance of that rule if many sets of experimental data were available and the same rule was applied to each sample.

The rule that we have used to obtain the least squares estimates is given in equation 6.2.1. When we have one sample of data, the y_t and x_t from that sample are treated as given fixed numbers. In these circumstances the necessary computations discussed in Chapter 5 can be carried out and the resulting b_1 and b_2 are viewed as *estimates*. The term *estimator* is relevant *before* we take a sample, when the y_t and x_t are, as yet, unobserved. At this time the set of y_t are random variables since the outcomes will depend on the households that are randomly drawn. Because b_1 and b_2 depend on the random variable y_t through the formula or rule in equation 6.2.1, they too are random variables whose value will depend on the households that are randomly drawn. Indeed, it is for this reason we get different estimates in repeated samples. Thus, the expression 6.2.1 can be treated as an estimate—a computed value taken from an observed sample (y_t, x_t). Alternatively, it can be treated as a rule or an estimator that could be applied to *repeated* samples of data from the same experimental design. When we view b_1 and b_2 as estimators, they are random variables and as such *each will have a probability distribution with a mean and a variance as well as a covariance between the random variables b_1 and b_2.* It is these probability distributions and their characteristics (the means, variances, and covariances), that tell us, if we use the least squares rule, how much least squares *estimates* for β_1 and β_2 can vary.

Let us proceed, therefore, to summarize what we can say about the means, variances, and covariance of the least squares estimator for β_1 and β_2. The derivations for these results are given in Section 6.6.

6.2.1   Means of b_1 and b_2

To get the means of the random variables b_1 and b_2, or, in other words, the *average* of all the least squares estimates that would be obtained in a large number of *repeated* samples, we use the expected value results of Chapter 2 and take expectations of both sides of equation 6.1.1 and find that

$$E[b_1] = \beta_1 \tag{6.2.1a}$$

and

$$E[b_2] = \beta_2 \tag{6.2.1b}$$

Thus, the means for b_1 and b_2 are the underlying parameters β_1 and β_2. When $E[b_1] = \beta_1$ and $E[b_2] = \beta_2$, this means that we have an *unbiased estimator* for β_1 and β_2, and this statement can be made *even before any samples are drawn*. Unbiasedness means the least squares rule produces estimates b_1 and b_2 that will *on average* hit the targets β_1 and β_2 and *does not* mean that the estimates of β_1 and β_2 *from one sample of data* are equal to the true parameters. *What is unbiased is the rule or estimator and not the estimates that come from a particular sample.* While the estimator is unbiased, any single estimate from one particular sample could still miss the mark rather badly. To discover by *how much* an estimate could differ from β_1 and β_2 and how good our least squares estimator is in this respect, we present the variances and covariance for b_1 and b_2.

6.2.2   Variances and Covariances for b_1 and b_2

Given the means of b_1 and b_2, we now present the sampling variances for the random variables b_1 and b_2 and the covariance between b_1 and b_2. They are defined as

$$\mathrm{var}(b_1) = E\left[\left(b_1 - E[b_1]\right)^2\right]$$
$$\mathrm{var}(b_2) = E\left[\left(b_2 - E[b_2]\right)^2\right] \tag{6.2.2}$$
$$\mathrm{cov}(b_1, b_2) = E\left[\left(b_1 - E[b_1]\right)\left(b_2 - E[b_2]\right)\right]$$

Since $E[b_1] = \beta_1$ and $E[b_2] = \beta_2$, we can rewrite these definitions as

$$\text{var}(b_1) = E\left[(b_1 - \beta_1)^2\right]$$
$$\text{var}(b_2) = E\left[(b_2 - \beta_2)^2\right] \qquad\qquad (6.2.3)$$
$$\text{cov}(b_1, b_2) = E\left[(b_1 - \beta_1)(b_2 - \beta_2)\right]$$

Before presenting expressions for these variances and covariance, let us recall how, following Section 3.4.2 of Chapter 3, the variance concept helps us measure how far b_1 and b_2 can differ from β_1 and β_2. In Figure 6.1a we have graphed a possible probability density function for b_2. Because b_2 is unbiased, this probability density function is centered around β_2. Let b_2^* be a possible estimate or value produced by the estimator b_2. The variance of b_2 can be viewed in the following way. We take the squared distance between every possible value of b_2^* and the parameter β_2; that is, $(b_2^* - \beta_2)^2$. This function is graphed in Figure 6.1b. Each of these squared distances is weighted by $f(b_2^*)$, the corresponding value of the probability density function at the point b_2^*. This weighting procedure (multiplying the functions in Figures 6.1a and 6.1b together) yields the curve in Figure 6.1c. The variance of b_2 can be viewed as a *weighted average* of the squared distances $(b_2^* - \beta_2)^2$ with weights given by the probability density function values $f(b_2^*)$. Thus, if values b_2^* that are quite distant from β_2 have a high probability of occurring, large values of $(b_2^* - \beta_2)^2$ will be weighted relatively heavily, and the variance will be large. On the other hand, if values of b_2^* that are distant from β_2 have a low probability of occurring, their squared distances $(b_2^* - \beta_2)^2$ will be weighted lightly and the variance will be small. In Figure 6.1c the integral

$$\text{var}(b_2) = \int_{-\infty}^{\infty} (b_2 - \beta_2)^2 \, f(b_2) db_2$$
$$= E\left[(b_2 - \beta_2)^2\right]$$

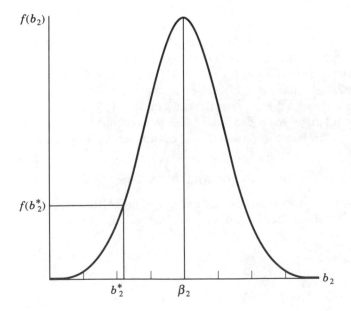

Figure 6.1a The probability density for b_2.

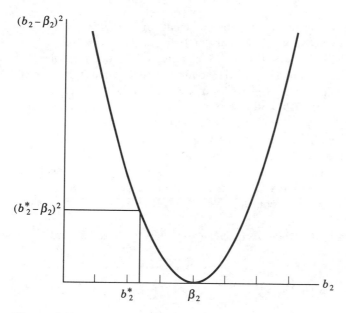

Figure 6.1b The function $(b_2 - \beta_2)^2$.

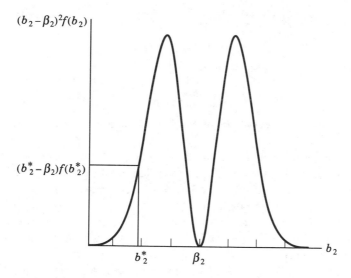

Figure 6.1c The function $(b_2 - \beta_2)^2 f(b_2)$.

giving the variance is the area under the curve $\left(b_2 - \beta_2\right)^2 f\!\left(b_2^*\right)$. This area will be relatively small when $f\!\left(b_2^*\right)$ is concentrated around β_2 and relatively large when $f\!\left(b_2^*\right)$ is more spread out.

As explained in Section 3.4.2 of Chapter 3, the variance of an estimator measures the precision of the estimator in the sense that it tells us, in a probabilistic sense, how much, in a repeated sampling sense, the estimates from that estimator can vary from sample to sample. As such, we often refer to it as the *sampling* variance or sampling precision. The lower the variance of an estimator, the greater the *sampling precision* of that estimator. We say that one estimator is *more precise* than another estimator if its sampling variance is less than that of the other estimator. The exact way in which the variance enables us to make probability statements about sampling differences such as $(b_2 - \beta_2)$ depends on the nature of the probability density function for b_2. Later in this chapter we will see the way in which the normal distribution can be used.

The covariance term $E[(b_1 - \beta_1)(b_2 - \beta_2)]$ describes how, as random variables, the estimates b_1 and b_2 are related. A positive covariance implies that, when b_1 is an overestimate of β_1, it is likely that b_2 will also overestimate β_2. Similarly, when b_1 is an underestimate of β_1, it is likely that b_2 will also underestimate β_2. On the other hand, with a negative covariance, if b_1 is an overestimate of β_1, then b_2 is likely to be an underestimate of β_2. A zero covariance implies that b_1 and b_2 are uncorrelated—the value of one has no linear association with the value of the other. We shall discover that, in the two-variable model studied in this chapter, where $\bar{x}$ is positive, b_1 and b_2 are negatively correlated—their covariance is negative. Thus, in a repeated sample context, a sample that yields a high estimate for the intercept is likely to yield a low estimate for the slope parameter and vice versa.

With this background the individual variances and covariances for b_1 and b_2 are given by

$$\text{var}(b_1) = \sigma^2 \left[\frac{\Sigma x_t^2}{T\Sigma(x_t - \bar{x})^2} \right] \tag{6.2.4a}$$

$$\text{var}(b_2) = \frac{\sigma^2}{\Sigma(x_t - \bar{x})^2} \tag{6.2.4b}$$

$$\text{cov}(b_1, b_2) = \sigma^2 \left[\frac{-\bar{x}}{\Sigma(x_t - \bar{x})^2} \right] \tag{6.2.4c}$$

The derivations for these expressions are given in Section 6.6. What can we learn from these expressions?

First, the larger the value of σ^2 the greater will be the variances of the estimators. A relatively large value of σ^2 means that the errors e_t can be relatively large, and hence that the observations y_t can lie a long way from the line (the mean regression function $E[y_t] = \beta_1 + x_t\beta_2$) that we are trying to estimate. The further the y_t lie from the line, the less likely we are to obtain good estimates of that line. Thus, the larger the value of σ^2, the less precise is our least squares estimator. The lower precision is captured by larger variances, $\text{var}(b_1)$ and $\text{var}(b_2)$.

The second observation to make is that $\text{var}(b_2)$ will be smaller, the larger the value of $\Sigma(x_t - \bar{x})^2$. This statement is also true for $\text{var}(b_1)$, but it is less evident because Σx_t^2 appears in the numerator of equation 6.2.4a. Since $\Sigma(x_t - \bar{x})^2$ measures the variation in incomes around the sample mean income $\bar{x}$, we are saying that the greater the variation in incomes, the greater the precision of b_1 and b_2. This result is illustrated in Figure 6.2. In Figure 6.2a, where all incomes are clustered close to their mean and $\Sigma(x_t - \bar{x})^2$ is relatively small, it is difficult to tell where the underlying mean regression function $E[y_t] = \beta_1 + x_t\beta_2$ might lie. The least squares line could go in almost any direction through the mean values ($\bar{y}$, $\bar{x}$). Under these circumstances we do not feel confident that we can estimate β_1 and β_2 accurately; this lack of confidence is captured through large values of $\text{var}(b_1)$ and $\text{var}(b_2)$. In Figure 6.2b, where incomes are more dispersed and $\Sigma(x_t - \bar{x})^2$ is relatively large, we have a much clearer idea of the position of the underlying model and of where the least squares line would go; our increased confidence is captured through smaller values of $\text{var}(b_1)$ and $\text{var}(b_2)$. Finally, observe that because the number of terms in the summation $\Sigma(x_t - \bar{x})^2$ increases as sample size increases, an increase in sample size generally leads to an increase in precision. With respect to the covariance term, we note that, providing $\bar{x}$ is positive, as indeed it is in our example, cov $(b_1, b_2) < 0$. Thus, overestimates of β_1 tend to occur with underestimates of β_2 and vice versa. To get some intuitive feel for this result, note that the fitted line always passes through the sample means ($\bar{y}$, $\bar{x}$). Also, $\bar{x}$ is fixed in repeated samples and $\bar{y}$, because it is a sample average, will vary very little in repeated samples. Thus, if the fitted line always passes through approximately the same central point ($\bar{y}$, $\bar{x}$), changing the intercept in one direction must change the slope in the other direction and vice versa. Since the fitted line goes through ($\bar{y}$, $\bar{x}$) underestimates and overestimates of b_1 have a great deal of leverage on b_2.

6.2.3 The Least Squares Variances and Covariance for the Household Expenditure Relationship

Using the data on expenditure and income that we introduced in Chapter 5 with the expressions 6.2.4, we have

$$\text{var}(b_1) = .3429\sigma^2$$
$$\text{var}(b_2) = .000065\sigma^2$$
$$\text{cov}(b_1, b_2) = -.0046\sigma^2 \tag{6.2.5}$$

For an interpretation of the results in equation 6.2.5 it may be useful to reread Section 6.2.2.

At this point, we have no basis for saying anything about the magnitude of the unknown scale parameter σ^2. However, we will soon discover that we can estimate σ^2 from just one sample of data, and hence obtain an *estimate* for the variances and covariance for b_1 and b_2 from this sample. Thus, we can find an *estimate* or measure of how much the elements of b_1 and b_2 can vary in repeated samples without having to collect these repeated samples.

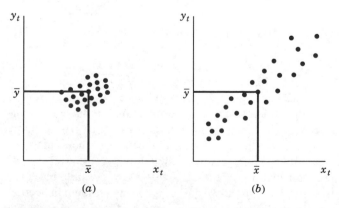

Figure 6.2 The influence of variation in the explanatory variable on precision of estimation. (*a*) Low variation, low precision. (*b*) High variation, high precision.

6.2.4 A Review

Before facing the problem of estimating σ^2, let us summarize what we have learned and see if we can say anything else about our least squares estimator. Thus far we have learned that if outcome data y_t are generated that are consistent with our statistical model, $y_t = \beta_1 + x_t\beta_2 + e_t$, where $e_t \sim (0, \sigma^2)$ and $y_t \sim (\beta_1 + x_t\beta_2, \sigma^2)$, the least squares rule 6.2.1 for b_1 and b_2

1. Is a linear function of the random variable y_t.

2. Has a sampling or probability distribution.

3. Is an unbiased estimation rule since the means of the random variables b_1 and b_2 are $E[b_1] = \beta_1$ and $E[b_2] = \beta_2$. This means that, although the least squares rule may in a repeated sampling context miss the mark for a particular sample, it is *on the average* a correct basis for estimating β_1 and β_2.

4. Has a sampling precision or sampling variability that is measured by the variances and covariance given in expressions 6.2.4.

In other words, we started with the statistical model specification $y_t \sim (\beta_1 + x_t\beta_2, \sigma^2)$ and $e_t \sim (0, \sigma^2)$ and the least squares rule b_1 and b_2, and we argued that the random variables

$$b_1 \sim \left(\beta_1, \sigma^2 \left[\frac{\Sigma x_t^2}{T\Sigma(x_t - \bar{x})^2} \right] \right) \tag{6.2.6a}$$

and

$$b_2 \sim \left(\beta_2, \frac{\sigma^2}{\Sigma(x_t - \bar{x})^2} \right) \tag{6.2.6b}$$

If we had assumed the e_t was a normal random variable, b_1 and b_2 in equation 6.2.6 would also have been normally distributed random variables.

Since the least squares estimator is only one possible linear unbiased estimator, if we are going to have much confidence in this rule, we need to know how good it is relative to all other possible linear unbiased rules. As we will see in Section 6.6.3, *the least squares rule is best in its class relative to other linear unbiased rules.*

6.3 Estimating the Variance Parameter σ^2

Having available a basis for assessing, in a repeated sample context, the sampling performance of the least squares rule, let us return to the problem of estimating the variances of b_1 and b_2 and the covariance (b_1, b_2). In the previous section we presented the sampling expressions 6.2.4 for the least squares estimator that contained the unknown variance (scale) parameter σ^2. If the sampling expressions are to give us some idea in practice of how much b_1 and b_2 can vary in repeated samples (their sampling variability), we need an estimate of σ^2. Thus, just as we developed a rule for estimating β_1 and β_2, we need an estimator or rule for estimating σ^2. As a possible basis for an estimator, one alternative is to consider, just as we did for the mean problem in Section 3.6, the sum of squares of the errors e_t. Since we have assumed that $E[e_t^2] = \sigma^2$, we know that

$$E\left[\Sigma e_t^2\right] = E\left[e_1^2 + e_2^2 + \ldots + e_T^2\right]$$
$$= E\left[e_1^2\right] + E\left[e_2^2\right] + \ldots + E\left[e_T^2\right]$$
$$= \sigma^2 + \sigma^2 + \ldots + \sigma^2 \tag{6.3.1}$$
$$= T\sigma^2$$

Thus,

$$E\left[\frac{\Sigma e_t^2}{T}\right] = \sigma^2 \tag{6.3.2}$$

and so $\Sigma e_t^2 / T$ is an unbiased estimator for σ^2. However, this estimator is not a feasible one, since the errors e_t are unobserved and unobservable.

6.3.1   A Feasible Unbiased Estimator of σ^2

Since the true errors e_t are not observable, perhaps we can estimate e_t and then make use of the information from the estimates. In Chapter 3 we noted that e_t is equal to the difference between y_t and its mean $E[y_t]$. Thus for our statistical model $y_t = \beta_1 + x_t\beta_2 + e_t$ and $e_t \sim (0, \sigma^2)$, we have

$$e_t = y_t - E[y_t] = y_t - (\beta_1 + x_t\beta_2) \tag{6.3.3}$$

A reasonable way to estimate e_t is to take this expression and to replace the unknown mean $E[y_t] = \beta_1 + x_t\beta_2$ by an estimate. One estimate for $E[y_t]$ is the least squares result that we derived in Section 5.3.2, namely,

$$\hat{y}_t = b_1 + x_t b_2 \tag{6.3.4}$$

Thus, as an estimate for e_t, we have

$$\hat{e}_t = y_t - \hat{y}_t = y_t - (b_1 + x_t b_2) \tag{6.3.5}$$

Returning to the estimator $\Sigma e_t^2 / T$ that we suggested below equation 6.3.2, a feasible alternative that now seems reasonable is $\Sigma \hat{e}_t^2 / T$. It was shown, however, in Chapter 3, that this estimator is biased. To obtain an unbiased estimator in Chapter 3 we changed the divisor of $\Sigma \hat{e}_t^2$ from T to $(T - 1)$. The difference occurred because of the number of parameters being estimated in the mean function. In Chapter 3 we had just one parameter β that was the mean of the random variable y_t. In this chapter there are two parameters in the mean function, β_1 and β_2. To obtain an unbiased estimator for σ^2 the divisor T is reduced by the number of parameters being estimated in the mean function. Thus, for our two-parameter (β_1, β_2) statistical model we have, as an unbiased estimator for σ^2,

$$\hat{\sigma}^2 = \frac{\Sigma \hat{e}_t^2}{T - 2} \tag{6.3.6}$$

Since the estimator $\hat{\sigma}^2$ is a function of random variables, it is also a random variable. For this estimation rule to be unbiased implies the estimator (random variable) $\hat{\sigma}^2$ has a mean equal to σ^2. That is,

$$E\left[\hat{\sigma}^2\right] = E\left[\frac{\Sigma \hat{e}_t^2}{T - 2}\right] = \sigma^2 \tag{6.3.7}$$

Also, since this estimator of σ^2 is a random variable, it seems natural to consider the sampling distribution for $\hat{\sigma}^2$, and its sampling variance. For a discussion of the sampling characteristics of $\hat{\sigma}^2$ and for a detailed proof that this estimator is unbiased, see Judge et al. (1988, pp. 207 and 226). For now let us just use the material in Sections 3.6.1 and 3.6.2 of Chapter 3 to note that, *if the e_t are normal random variables*, then

$$\hat{\sigma}^2 \sim \frac{\sigma^2}{T-2}\chi^2_{(T-2)} \tag{6.3.8}$$

or in words, $\hat{\sigma}^2$ is distributed as a constant times a chi-square random variable with $(T-2)$ degrees of freedom. Consequently, following Section 3.6.2, this means that

$$E[\hat{\sigma}^2] = \frac{\sigma^2}{T-2}E[\chi^2_{(T-2)}] = \frac{\sigma^2}{T-2}(T-2) = \sigma^2 \tag{6.3.9a}$$

$$\text{var}(\hat{\sigma}^2) = \frac{\sigma^4}{(T-2)^2}\text{var}(\chi^2_{(T-2)}) = \frac{\sigma^4}{(T-2)^2}2(T-2) = \frac{2\sigma^4}{T-2} \tag{6.3.9b}$$

6.4   An Estimate of the Variances of b_1 and b_2 and the Covariance (b_1, b_2)

Now that we have an unbiased estimation rule for σ^2, let us apply the estimator in equation 6.3.9 to our expenditure–income data. Our estimate in this case is

$$\hat{\sigma}^2 = \frac{\Sigma\hat{e}_t^2}{T-2} = \frac{1708.4}{38} = 46.853 \tag{6.4.1}$$

Consequently, making use of equations 6.2.5 and 6.4.1 the estimated variances of b_1 and b_2 and the covariance between b_1 and b_2 are

$$\hat{\text{var}}(b_1) = 46.853(.3429) = 16.0669$$
$$\hat{\text{var}}(b_2) = 46.853(.0000653) = .0031$$
$$\hat{\text{cov}}(b_1, b_2) = 46.853(-.00455) = -.2134 \tag{6.4.2}$$

where the $\hat{\text{var}}(b_i)$ are estimates of the sampling variability of b_1 and b_2, and $\hat{\text{cov}}(b_1, b_2)$ is the estimated covariance. What do these magnitudes imply in terms of the spread or dispersion of the probability density functions for b_1 and b_2? Or, in other words, given that we have these estimated variance values for b_1 and b_2, what do they tell us about how much b_1 and b_2 can vary in repeated samples? To answer this question we need to know something, or assume something, about the probability density function for the e_t. In the next section we make use of the computer and carry out our own sampling experiment to demonstrate how much b_1 and b_2 can vary in repeated samples when the e_t are normally distributed. In Chapter 7 we learn how the estimated sampling variances can be used to draw inferences about the unknown parameters β_1 and β_2.

6.5 A Monte Carlo Experiment to Demonstrate the Sampling Performance of the Least Squares Estimator

In Chapter 5 we specified the general linear statistical model $y_t = \beta_1 + x_t\beta_2 + e_t$ and $e_t \sim N(0, \sigma^2)$. On the basis of this particular specification, we developed rules that yielded estimates of the unknown parameters β_1, β_2, and σ^2. By evaluating the rules (estimators), within a sampling theory context, we found that they satisfied certain statistical properties, such as unbiasedness. In this section, to highlight the sampling theory approach to inference and to illustrate the results that we have derived, we design a simulation experiment as we did in Section 5.2.4 and use the computer to carry out what is known as a Monte Carlo sampling experiment. If you understand this Monte Carlo sampling experiment, you will be well on your way to understanding the sampling theory approach to inference and how to interpret (and how not to interpret) econometric results. Does the theory that we have been through in this chapter really work? Let's check it out.

We begin by summarizing what we have learned so far about the expenditure–income relationship. The model is given by

$$y_t = \beta_1 + x_t\beta_2 + e_t \tag{6.5.1}$$

where *we will now assume the e_t are normally distributed random variables* with mean $E[e_t] = 0$ and variance $E[e_t^2] = \sigma^2$, that is, $e_t \sim N(0, \sigma^2)$. For our estimates of the unknown parameters we have obtained

$$b_1 - 7.3832 \qquad \hat{\text{var}}(b_1) = 16.0669$$

$$b_2 = 0.2323 \qquad \hat{\text{var}}(b_2) = 0.00306$$

$$\hat{\sigma}^2 = 46.853$$

Now, in terms of designing a simulation experiment to investigate the sampling properties of the least squares estimators, *let us assume that these values are not estimates but are instead the true underlying parameters of our statistical model.* Thus, we will act as if the true statistical model is

$$y_t = 7.3832 + 0.2323x_t + e_t \qquad \text{where} \quad E[e_t^2] = 46.853 \tag{6.5.2}$$

and var(b_1) = 16.0669 and var(b_2) = 0.00306. Of course, in reality, we never really know the values of the unknown parameters; the best we can do is estimate them. Introducing the assumption of normally distributed e_t, we can now extend the simulation model in equation 6.5.2 and write

$$e_t \sim N(0, 46.853) \tag{6.5.3a}$$

and

$$y_t \sim N(7.3832 + 0.2323x_t, 46.853) \tag{6.5.3b}$$

Given these distributional results, if we use the least squares estimator, we know that

$$b_1 \sim N(7.3832, 16.0669) \tag{6.5.4a}$$

$$b_2 \sim N(0.2323, 0.00306) \tag{6.5.4b}$$

Now suppose that we simulate 1000 samples, each of size 40, and each with the same 40 income levels $(x_1, x_2, \ldots, x_T)$ specified originally in Table 5.2. Thus, the experiment is designed so that the same households are being resampled independently over time. Each of these i samples, $i = 1, 2, \ldots, 1000$, will have a different set of random errors and hence a different set of expenditures y_t. The estimates b_1 and b_2 and the estimate $\hat{\sigma}^2$ will also be different in each sample. Consequently, this sampling experiment should help to illustrate how much b_1, b_2, and $\hat{\sigma}^2$ can vary from sample to sample. First of all let us see what our theory says about this matter. If we collect 1000 samples, because the estimators b_1, b_2 and $\hat{\sigma}^2$ are unbiased, we would expect the 1000 values we obtain for these estimators to average out fairly closely to the true underlying parameters, β_1, β_2, and σ^2, respectively. We can get an idea of how much b_1 and b_2 can vary by working out the proportion of estimates that fall inside or outside particular ranges. For example, from Chapter 2 we know that we can use the normal distribution to compute

$$P\big(6 < b_1 < 12\big) = P\left(\frac{6 - 7.3832}{\sqrt{16.0669}} < \frac{b_1 - \beta_1}{\sqrt{\mathrm{var}(b_1)}} < \frac{12 - 7.3832}{\sqrt{16.0669}}\right)$$

$$= P(-0.345 < Z < 1.152) \tag{6.5.5}$$

$$= 0.510$$

where $Z = (b_1 - \beta_1)/\sqrt{\mathrm{var}(b_1)}$ is a standard normal random variable with mean zero and variance 1. This result tells us we would expect b_1 to lie between 6 and 12 for approximately 510 of our 1000 samples, or that it would lie outside this range in approximately 490 of the 1000 samples. Similarly, suppose we are interested in the proportion of times b_2 could lie outside the range (.1, .3); we can find that

$$P\big(.1 < b_2 < .3\big) = P\left(\frac{.1 - .2323}{\sqrt{.00306}} < \frac{b_2 - \beta_2}{\sqrt{\mathrm{var}(b_2)}} < \frac{.3 - .1519}{\sqrt{.00306}}\right)$$

$$= P(-2.392 < Z < 1.224) \tag{6.5.6}$$

$$= 0.881$$

Approximately 119 of the 1000 samples should yield values of b_2 outside the range (.1, .3).

What other information could we get from the 1000 samples? Because we have 1000 "observations" on b_1 and b_2, we could use these observations to estimate the variances of b_1 and b_2. If our theory is correct, these estimated variances should agree fairly closely with the true variances that we have been able to compute because of our assumed knowledge about σ^2 and x_t. Finally, each sample will provide us with estimates $\hat{\mathrm{var}}(b_1)$ and $\hat{\mathrm{var}}(b_2)$. These estimates should be unbiased, which means their averages should come out close to the assumed true values for $\mathrm{var}(b_1)$ and $\mathrm{var}(b_2)$.

How then do we obtain our 1000 samples? Since we have specified parameter values for the usually unknown parameters β_1, β_2 and σ^2, we can simulate the sampling process on a computer. Such a simulation is called a *Monte Carlo experiment* or a *sampling experiment*. To carry out a Monte Carlo experiment we begin, as we did in Section 5.2.4, by calculating the mean or systematic portion of our expenditure function $E[y_t] = \beta_1 + x_t\beta_2$. Then we use a computer-based random number generator to draw 40 independent observations from a normal distribution with mean zero and variance σ^2. These observations comprise our outcomes for the errors e_t. Having obtained e_t in this way we can obtain sample observations y_t from $y_t = E[y_t] + e_t = \beta_1 + x_t\beta_2 + e_t$. For β_1, β_2, and σ^2 that are required for this process we use the values in equation 6.5.2, the ones we are using as the true parameters. Given y_t and x_t, we can then turn around and estimate β_1, β_2, and σ^2 using our estimation rules b_1 and b_2 (equation 6.2.1) and $\hat{\sigma}^2 = \Sigma\hat{e}_t^2 / (T-2)$, respectively. Also, estimates $\hat{var}(b_1)$ and $\hat{var}(b_2)$ can be obtained. The whole procedure is repeated 1000 times so that we have 1000 samples of 40 observations and 1000 sets of estimates. What we do in a Monte Carlo sampling experiment is to simulate the sampling theory (repeated sampling) approach to inference. You might want to remind yourself that in this instance you can predict the results of the experiment even before it is run. Later on we will find several instances when this is not possible, and the Monte Carlo type information is all we have as a gauge of estimator sampling performance.

6.5.1   The Sampling Results

In this section the results from the foregoing simulated sampling experiment are reported. An idea of the sampling variability of the estimates can be obtained from Table 6.1, where estimates of β_1, β_2, σ^2, var(b_1), and var(b_2) are reported for the first 20 samples. The true parameter values are given in parentheses. In some instances the variability is quite striking. For example, for all 1000 samples, the sample estimates for $\beta_2 = .2323$ vary over the range .0232 to .4119, and the sample estimates of $\sigma^2 = 46.853$ vary over the range 21.73 to 87.082. As predicted by the negative covariance between b_1 and b_2, overestimates of b_1 generally appear with underestimates of b_2 (samples 2, 4, 6, 7, 8, 13, 15, 17) and underestimates of b_1 appear with overestimates of b_2 (samples 5, 9, 10, 12, 16, 20).

Table 6.1   Point Estimates of β_1, β_2, σ^2, var(b_1), and var(b_2) for 20 Samples of Size 40

Sample Number	b_1 (7.383)	b_2 (.2323)	$\hat{\sigma}^2$ (46.853)	$\hat{var}(b_1)$ (16.07)	$\hat{var}(b_2)$ (.00306)
1	8.505	.2399	73.41	25.17	.00479
2	10.348	.2114	60.59	20.78	.00395
3	6.613	.2353	30.46	10.45	.00199
4	13.812	.1383	55.35	18.98	.00361
5	4.824	.2815	50.79	17.42	.00331
6	9.086	.1748	70.79	24.27	.00462
7	11.897	.1597	36.32	12.45	.00237
8	12.168	.1608	66.89	22.94	.00437
9	2.596	.2977	49.07	16.83	.00320
10	5.763	.2737	54.14	18.57	.00353
11	8.312	.2042	36.09	12.38	.00235
12	3.482	.2816	54.96	18.85	.00359
13	10.498	.1889	51.79	17.76	.00338
14	9.930	.1921	49.75	17.06	.00325
15	10.876	.2027	51.53	17.67	.00336
16	3.533	.2629	48.22	16.53	.00315
17	11.764	.1707	43.34	14.86	.00283
18	7.152	.2449	42.49	14.57	.00277
19	5.688	.2613	51.19	17.55	.00334
20	2.132	.3047	39.26	13.46	.00256

The average values of the estimates of β_i and σ^2 over the 1000 samples (the empirical analogues of the expected values) are

$$\bar{b}_1 = \frac{1}{1000}\sum_{n=1}^{1000} b_{1n} = 7.3412 \qquad \bar{b}_2 = \frac{1}{1000}\sum_{n=1}^{1000} b_{2n} = 0.2321 \qquad \bar{\sigma}^2 = \frac{1}{1000}\sum_{n=1}^{1000} \hat{\sigma}_n^2 = 46.586$$

(6.5.7)

Note that these values are quite close to $\beta_1 = 7.3832$, $\beta_2 = .2323$, and $\sigma^2 = 46.853$. The empirical frequency distribution of b_2 for all 1000 samples given in Figure 6.3 reflects the variability in the estimates from sample to sample and, as expected, approaches that of a normal distribution. For b_2 the number of estimates of β_2 that fell outside the range (.1, .3) was 136, compared to an expected number of 119. For b_1, 492 estimates of β_1 fell outside the range (6, 12), compared to an expected number of 490.

The *empirical* variances for b_1 and b_2 estimated from the 1000 samples were

$$\text{vâr}^*(b_1) = \frac{1}{999}\sum_{n=1}^{1000}(b_{1n} - \bar{b}_1)^2 = 17.184 \qquad (6.5.8a)$$

$$\text{vâr}^*(b_2) = \frac{1}{999}\sum_{n=1}^{1000}(b_{2n} - \bar{b}_2)^2 = .00325 \qquad (6.5.8b)$$

These values compare well with the true variances that are given in equation 6.5.4. They are $\text{var}(b_1) = 16.067$ and $\text{var}(b_2) = .00306$. The *average* values of the variance estimates obtained from each of the 1000 samples also correspond closely to $\text{var}(b_1)$ and $\text{var}(b_2)$. They are

$$\overline{\text{vâr}}(b_1) = \frac{1}{1000}\sum_{n=1}^{1000} \text{vâr}_n(b_1) = 15.975 \qquad (6.5.9a)$$

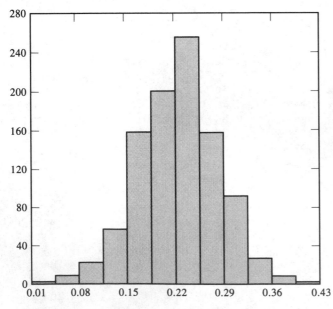

Figure 6.3 Frequency distribution of the estimates for β_2 from 1000 samples of size 40.

and

$$\bar{\text{var}}(b_2) = \frac{1}{1000}\sum_{n=1}^{1000}\hat{\text{var}}_n(b_2) = .00304 \tag{6.5.9b}$$

What have we learned from the sampling experiment? One thing that stands out is the variability in the point estimates from sample to sample (see Table 6.1). Another thing is that in spite of the variability of the estimates, *on the average* they are close to the true parameters (the unbiased property for b_1, b_2, and $\hat{\sigma}^2$ suggested that this would be true). Also the empirical distributions of the estimates for b_1 and b_2 are approximately normal distributions. If we increased the number of samples, the approximation of the empirical distribution to that of the theoretical (normal) distribution would become better and better.

Another important concept illustrated by our Monte Carlo experiment is what we mean by the variance of an estimator. How b_1 and b_2 may vary in repeated samples is described by the variance estimates in equation 6.5.6. The 1000 estimates were used to compute the variance estimates. However, one of the amazing consequences of our theory is that we do not need to obtain repeated samples to work out how the estimates may vary in repeated samples. The estimated variances, obtained from just one sample, provide this information.

Monte Carlo experimentation is a useful tool for investigating and illustrating the sampling performance (properties) of estimators. However, in a real-world, practical situation, where the parameter values are unknown, and where we only have *one* sample of data from which to make judgments, alternative techniques must be found. That is why it was desirable to find analytical expressions for the variances of our estimators and to estimate such expressions from one sample of data. Also, we might be interested in using one sample of data to test hypotheses concerning whether or not β_1 or β_2 are equal to prescribed values. These questions will be analyzed in Chapter 7.

6.6   Some Basic Derivations

Some readers may wish to understand more fully the unbiased claim for the least squares estimator and the basis for the variance and covariance expressions in equation 6.2.4. To make this straightforward and simple, we make use of the linear algebra notation developed in Section 5.4 of Chapter 5. In this section we respecified the scalar formulation $y_t = \beta_1 + x_t\beta_2 + e_t$ of the linear statistical model as

$$\mathbf{y} = \mathbf{x}_1\beta_1 + \mathbf{x}_2\beta_2 + \mathbf{e} = \begin{bmatrix} \mathbf{x}_1 & \mathbf{x}_2 \end{bmatrix}\begin{bmatrix} \beta_1 \\ \beta_2 \end{bmatrix} + \mathbf{e}$$
$$= X\boldsymbol{\beta} + \mathbf{e} \tag{6.6.1}$$

where

$$\mathbf{x}_1 = \begin{bmatrix} 1 \\ 1 \\ \vdots \\ 1 \end{bmatrix}, \qquad \mathbf{x}_2 = \begin{bmatrix} x_1 \\ x_2 \\ \vdots \\ x_T \end{bmatrix}, \qquad \mathbf{e} = \begin{bmatrix} e_1 \\ e_2 \\ \vdots \\ e_T \end{bmatrix} \qquad \text{and} \qquad \mathbf{y} = \begin{bmatrix} y_1 \\ y_2 \\ \vdots \\ y_T \end{bmatrix}$$

The vectors $\mathbf{e}$ and $\mathbf{y}$ contain independently and identically distributed random variables, which we expressed in compact form as $\mathbf{e} \sim (\mathbf{0}, \sigma^2 I_T)$ and $\mathbf{y} \sim (X\boldsymbol{\beta}, \sigma^2 I_T)$. With this statistical model we used the least squares estimation rule

$$\mathbf{b} = \begin{bmatrix} b_1 \\ b_2 \end{bmatrix} = \left(X'X\right)^{-1} X'\mathbf{y} \qquad (6.6.2a)$$

to obtain sample estimates (b_1 and b_2) of the unknown parameters β_1 and β_2. The inverse operation $(X'X)^{-1}$ was discussed in Appendix 5C of Chapter 5. In this section we make use of the linear algebra notation to investigate questions concerning the "quality" of the least squares estimator and how to make inferences about the unknown parameter vector β. Since the matrix X in equation 6.6.1 is assumed fixed in repeated samples, we may express the least squares estimator as

$$\mathbf{b} = \left(X'X\right)^{-1} X'\mathbf{y} = A\mathbf{y} \qquad (6.6.2b)$$

where $A = (X'X)^{-1}X'$ is a nonstochastic matrix. Writing the least squares estimator as $\mathbf{b} = A\mathbf{y}$ emphasizes that $\mathbf{b}$ is a *linear* function of the *random* vector $\mathbf{y}$. Because $\mathbf{y}$ is random, $\mathbf{b}$ is random and the least squares estimators b_1 and b_2 are *random* variables.

6.6.1 Mean of **b**

Consider the problem of finding the mean and covariance matrix for $\mathbf{b}$ assuming that $\mathbf{y}$ and $\mathbf{e}$ are random vectors, but X is fixed or constant in repeated samples. First, making use of the elementary operations of linear algebra that we have learned, we rewrite $\mathbf{b}$ in terms of β in the following way:

$$\begin{aligned} \mathbf{b} &= \left(X'X\right)^{-1} X'\mathbf{y} = \left(X'X\right)^{-1} X'(X\beta + \mathbf{e}) \qquad \text{from (6.6.1)} \\ &= \left(X'X\right)^{-1} X'X\beta + \left(X'X\right)^{-1} X'\mathbf{e} = I_K \beta + \left(X'X\right)^{-1} X'\mathbf{e} \qquad (6.6.3) \\ &= \beta + \left(X'X\right)^{-1} X'\mathbf{e} \end{aligned}$$

To get the mean of the random vector $\mathbf{b}$, or, in other words, the *average* of all the least squares estimates that would be obtained in a large number of *repeated* samples, we use the expected value results of Chapter 2 and take expectations of both sides of equation 6.2.2a. Thus, we have

$$E[\mathbf{b}] = E[\beta] + E\left[\left(X'X\right)^{-1} X'\mathbf{e}\right] \qquad (6.6.4)$$

Because the unknown parameter vector β and the design matrix X are not random (they are constant from sample to sample) and $\mathbf{e}$ has by assumption mean zero, equation 6.6.4 becomes

$$E[\mathbf{b}] = \beta + \left(X'X\right)^{-1} X'E[\mathbf{e}] = \beta + \left(X'X\right)^{-1} X'\mathbf{0} = \beta \qquad (6.6.5)$$

Thus, since the mean vector for $\mathbf{b}$ is the underlying parameter vector β, we can say that $\mathbf{b}$ is an *unbiased estimator* for β.

6.6.2 Covariance Matrix for **b**

The covariance matrix for the random vector

$$\begin{bmatrix} b_1 \\ b_2 \end{bmatrix} = \mathbf{b}$$

is a (2×2) matrix that contains the sampling variances for the random variables b_1 and b_2 on the diagonal and the covariance between b_1 and b_2 off the diagonal. To illustrate this we begin with the definition of the covariance matrix, which is

$$\text{cov}(\mathbf{b}) = E\big[(\mathbf{b} - E[\mathbf{b}])(\mathbf{b} - E[\mathbf{b}])'\big]$$

Since $E[\mathbf{b}] = \beta$, we can rewrite this definition as

$$\text{cov}(\mathbf{b}) = E\big[(\mathbf{b} - \beta)(\mathbf{b} - \beta)'\big] = E\left[\begin{bmatrix}(b_1 - \beta_1)\\(b_2 - \beta_2)\end{bmatrix}\big[(b_1 - \beta_1),(b_2 - \beta_2)\big]\right]$$

$$= \begin{bmatrix} E\big[(b_1 - \beta_1)^2\big] & E\big[(b_1 - \beta_1)(b_2 - \beta_2)\big] \\ E\big[(b_1 - \beta_1)(b_2 - \beta_2)\big] & E\big[(b_2 - \beta_2)^2\big] \end{bmatrix} \tag{6.6.6}$$

$$= \begin{bmatrix} \text{var}(b_1) & \text{cov}(b_1,b_2) \\ \text{cov}(b_1,b_2) & \text{var}(b_2) \end{bmatrix}$$

In deriving an expression for cov(**b**), we begin by using the result in equation 6.6.3 that states

$$\mathbf{b} = \beta + (X'X)^{-1} X'\mathbf{e} \tag{6.6.7a}$$

or

$$\mathbf{b} - \beta = (X'X)^{-1} X'\mathbf{e} \tag{6.6.7b}$$

Also, the transpose of this vector (converting from a column to a row vector) is given by

$$(\mathbf{b} - \beta)' = \mathbf{e}'X(X'X)^{-1} \tag{6.6.8}$$

To derive equation 6.6.8 from equation 6.6.7 we use a matrix algebra result that $(ABC)' = C'B'A'$, where A, B, and C are conformable matrices (have dimensions so they can be multiplied). In our case $A = (X'X)^{-1}$, $B = X'$, and $C = \mathbf{e}$. We also need the result that the transpose of the symmetric matrix $(X'X)^{-1}$ is again $(X'X)^{-1}$. To gain more insight into these results, redo Exercise 5C.1. Substituting equations 6.6.7 and 6.6.8 into equation 6.6.6 yields

$$\text{cov}(\mathbf{b}) = E\big[(\mathbf{b} - \beta)(\mathbf{b} - \beta)'\big]$$

$$= E\big[(X'X)^{-1} X'\mathbf{e}\mathbf{e}'X(X'X)^{-1}\big] \tag{6.6.9}$$

$$= (X'X)^{-1} X'E[\mathbf{e}\mathbf{e}']X(X'X)^{-1}$$

Because X is fixed from sample to sample, it is legal to bring the expectations operator into the middle of expression 6.6.9. Recalling that the covariance matrix for **e** is $E[\mathbf{e}\mathbf{e}'] = \sigma^2 I_T$, equation 6.6.9 becomes

$$\text{cov}(\mathbf{b}) = \left(X'X\right)^{-1} X'\sigma^2 I_T X\left(X'X\right)^{-1} = \sigma^2 \left(X'X\right)^{-1} X'X\left(X'X\right)^{-1}$$

$$= \sigma^2 \left(X'X\right)^{-1} I_K = \sigma^2 \left(X'X\right)^{-1} \qquad (6.6.10)$$

$$= \sigma^2 \begin{bmatrix} x_1'x_1 & x_1'x_2 \\ x_2'x_1 & x_2'x_2 \end{bmatrix}^{-1} = \begin{bmatrix} \text{var}\, b_1 & \text{cov}(b_1, b_2) \\ \text{cov}(b_2, b_1) & \text{var}\, b_2 \end{bmatrix}$$

where σ^2 is taken to the left because it is a scalar. Thus, before any samples are drawn, we can say that the least squares estimator has mean $E[\mathbf{b}] = \beta$ and covariance matrix $\text{cov}(\mathbf{b}) = \sigma^2(X'X)^{-1}$. We summarize these mean and covariance results in shorthand notation as

$$\mathbf{b} \sim \left[\beta, \sigma^2 \left(X'X\right)^{-1}\right] \qquad (6.6.11)$$

Understanding this and the preceding sections of this chapter is crucial to establishing an operational grasp of the sampling theory approach to inference. At this point you may wish to reread Section 3.4 and the earlier sections of this chapter and compare them step by step with the evaluations given in this section. If you can grasp the repeated sampling framework that formed the basis for determining the mean and covariance matrix for the random vector $\mathbf{b} = [b_1, b_2]'$, then you have begun to understand the sampling theory approach to inference and what information econometric (statistical) methods can and cannot yield.

Given the covariance matrix $\sigma^2(X'X)^{-1}$, and the inverse operations rule 5C.9 from Appendix 5C, we may express equation 6.6.10 as

$$\text{cov}(\mathbf{b}) = \sigma^2 \left(X'X\right)^{-1} = \frac{\sigma^2}{T\Sigma x_t^2 - \left(\Sigma x_t\right)^2} \begin{bmatrix} \Sigma x_t^2 & -\Sigma x_t \\ -\Sigma x_t & T \end{bmatrix} \qquad (6.6.12)$$

Using the result $T\Sigma x_t^2 - \left(\Sigma x_t\right)^2 = T\Sigma(x_t - \bar{x})^2$, developed in Appendix 2A.2, the individual variances and covariances are given by

$$\text{cov}(\mathbf{b}) = \sigma^2 \left(X'X\right)^{-1} = \sigma^2 \begin{bmatrix} \dfrac{\Sigma x_t^2}{T\Sigma(x_t - \bar{x})^2} & \dfrac{-\bar{x}}{\Sigma(x_t - \bar{x})^2} \\ \dfrac{-\bar{x}}{\Sigma(x_t - \bar{x})^2} & \dfrac{1}{\Sigma(x_t - \bar{x})^2} \end{bmatrix} \qquad (6.6.13)$$

This result is the same as expression 6.2.4.

For the household expenditure problem, the least squares covariance matrix is

$$\text{cov}(\mathbf{b}) = \sigma^2 \left(X'X\right)^{-1} = \sigma^2 \begin{bmatrix} \mathbf{x}_1'\mathbf{x}_1 & \mathbf{x}_1'\mathbf{x}_2 \\ \mathbf{x}_2'\mathbf{x}_1 & \mathbf{x}_2'\mathbf{x}_2 \end{bmatrix}^{-1}$$

$$= \sigma^2 \begin{bmatrix} T & \Sigma x_t \\ \Sigma x_t & \Sigma x_t^2 \end{bmatrix}^{-1} = \sigma^2 \begin{bmatrix} 40 & 2792 \\ 2792 & 210206.2 \end{bmatrix}^{-1} \qquad (6.6.14)$$

$$= \sigma^2 \begin{bmatrix} 0.342922 & -0.0045548 \\ -0.0045548 & 0.0000653 \end{bmatrix}$$

6.6.3   How Good is the Least Squares Rule?

Starting with the statistical model $\mathbf{y} = X\boldsymbol{\beta} + \mathbf{e}$ and $\mathbf{e} \sim (\mathbf{0}, \sigma^2 I_T)$, we derived the least squares rule $\mathbf{b} = (X'X)^{-1}X'\mathbf{y}$, and we showed that the random vector $\mathbf{b} \sim [\boldsymbol{\beta}, \sigma^2(X'X)^{-1}]$.

Since the least squares estimator is only one possible linear unbiased estimator, if we are going to have much confidence in this rule, we need to know how good it is relative to all other possible linear unbiased rules. To make progress in this direction, we must compare its sampling performance with others in the class of linear unbiased rules or estimators.

As we have already noted, a linear estimator for $\boldsymbol{\beta}$ is an estimator that is a linear function of $\mathbf{y}$ and can be written as $\overline{\boldsymbol{\beta}} = A\mathbf{y}$, where A is a fixed matrix. The least squares estimator $\mathbf{b} = (X'X)^{-1}X'\mathbf{y} = A\mathbf{y}$ is a linear estimator where $A = (X'X)^{-1}X'$. Linear estimators are often convenient because they are computationally simple. Fortunately, a result known as the Gauss-Markov Theorem assures us, for our statistical model, that *out of the class of linear unbiased estimators* ($\overline{\boldsymbol{\beta}} = A\mathbf{y}$ and $E[\overline{\boldsymbol{\beta}}] = \boldsymbol{\beta}$) *the least squares estimator is best, where best implies minimum sampling variability*. In our multiparameter context, minimum sampling variability means that $\text{var}(b_i) \leq \text{var}(b_i^*)$ for $i = 1, 2$ and $\text{var}(c_1 b_1 + c_2 b_2) \leq \text{var}(c_1 b_1^* + c_2 b_2^*)$ for all c_1, c_2 and any competing estimator b_i^*. Thus we may say $\text{var}(\mathbf{c}'\mathbf{b}) \leq \text{var}(\mathbf{c}'\mathbf{b}^*)$ for all $\mathbf{c}$ (all linear combinations of $\mathbf{b}$) and any competing estimator $\mathbf{b}^*$. Thus, we have the important result that *the least squares rule is the best in its class relative to other linear unbiased estimators*. This means that, for our statistical model, if we are content to work with linear unbiased rules, then the least squares rule is king. The Gauss-Markov proof, sketched in Chapter 3, provides the logic underlying this result. Those interested in a more detailed proof of this important result should see Judge *et. al.* (1988, pp. 202–205). It is interesting to note that if we start with a criterion that minimizes the residual (error) sum of squares $S(\beta_1, \beta_2) = (\mathbf{y} - X\boldsymbol{\beta})'(\mathbf{y} - X\boldsymbol{\beta})$, we are led to an estimator (rule) that has excellent sampling properties, that is, it is unbiased and efficient (high relative sampling precision).

6.6.4   Estimating σ^2

In developing an estimator of σ^2 in Section 6.3, we made use of the least squares residual

$$\hat{e}_t = y_t - \hat{y}_t = y_t - (b_1 + x_t b_2) \tag{6.6.15}$$

The corresponding *vector of least squares residuals* can be written as

$$\hat{\mathbf{e}} = \mathbf{y} - \hat{\mathbf{y}} = \mathbf{y} - X\mathbf{b} \tag{6.6.16}$$

where

$$\hat{\mathbf{y}} = X\mathbf{b}, \quad \hat{\mathbf{e}} = \begin{bmatrix} \hat{e}_1 \\ \hat{e}_2 \\ \vdots \\ \hat{e}_T \end{bmatrix} \quad \text{and} \quad \hat{\mathbf{y}} = \begin{bmatrix} \hat{y}_1 \\ \hat{y}_2 \\ \vdots \\ \hat{y}_T \end{bmatrix} \tag{6.6.17}$$

Thus, for our two-parameter statistical model we have, as an unbiased estimator for σ^2,

$$
\begin{aligned}
\hat{\sigma}^2 &= \frac{\hat{\mathbf{e}}'\hat{\mathbf{e}}}{T-2} = \frac{(\mathbf{y}-X\mathbf{b})'(\mathbf{y}-X\mathbf{b})}{T-2} = \frac{\Sigma\hat{e}_t^2}{T-2} \\
&= \frac{\mathbf{y}'\mathbf{y} - 2\mathbf{b}'X'\mathbf{y} + \mathbf{b}'X'X\mathbf{b}}{T-2} \\
&= \frac{\mathbf{y}'\mathbf{y} - 2\mathbf{b}'X'\mathbf{y} + \mathbf{b}'(X'X)(X'X)^{-1}X'\mathbf{y}}{T-2} \\
&= \frac{\mathbf{y}'\mathbf{y} - \mathbf{b}'X'\mathbf{y}}{T-2}
\end{aligned} \tag{6.6.18}
$$

6.6.5   A Maximum Likelihood Estimator of σ^2

In Chapters 3 and 5 we discussed how to use the joint density function for the sample to obtain a maximum likelihood estimator for β. Since the likelihood function also contains σ^2, we can use this concept to derive an estimator for σ^2. In line with Chapter 3, if we assume normal errors, the joint density function for the sample $\mathbf{y}$ is

$$
f(\mathbf{y}|X, \boldsymbol{\beta}, \sigma^2) = (2\pi\sigma^2)^{-\frac{T}{2}} \exp\left[-\frac{(\mathbf{y}-X\boldsymbol{\beta})'(\mathbf{y}-X\boldsymbol{\beta})}{2\sigma^2}\right] \tag{6.6.19}
$$

Note that $(\mathbf{y}-X\boldsymbol{\beta})'(\mathbf{y}-X\boldsymbol{\beta}) = \sum_{t=1}^{T}(y_t - \beta_1 - x_t\beta_2)^2$ and so equation 6.6.19 is identical to equation 5.3.16 and this is just another way of writing the same thing. The maximum likelihood estimator for σ^2 is that value for σ^2 that maximizes equation 6.6.19 or, alternatively, the value that maximizes the logarithm of equation 6.6.19. The function $\ln f$ reaches a maximum at the same value of σ^2 that f reaches a maximum, and so it does not matter whether we use $\ln f$ or f to find the maximum likelihood estimator for σ^2. In this case the evaluation is easier if we use $\ln f$, which is given by

$$
\ln f(\mathbf{y}|X, \boldsymbol{\beta}, \sigma^2) = -\frac{T}{2}\ln(2\pi) - \frac{T}{2}\ln\sigma^2 - \frac{(\mathbf{y}-X\boldsymbol{\beta})'(\mathbf{y}-X\boldsymbol{\beta})}{2\sigma^2} \tag{6.6.20}
$$

A maximum likelihood estimator for σ^2 is obtained by maximizing equation 6.6.20, the natural logarithm of equation 6.6.19. Following Appendix 5B, to obtain the maximizing value we set the derivative of equation 6.6.20, with respect to σ^2, equal to zero and obtain

$$
\frac{\partial \ln f(\mathbf{y}|X, \boldsymbol{\beta}, \sigma^2)}{\partial\sigma^2} = -\frac{T}{2\tilde{\sigma}^2} + \frac{1}{2(\tilde{\sigma}^2)^2}(\mathbf{y}-X\mathbf{b})'(\mathbf{y}-X\mathbf{b}) = 0 \tag{6.6.21}
$$

where $\tilde{\sigma}^2$ and $\mathbf{b}$ are the maximum likelihood estimators for σ^2 and β. Solving equation 6.6.21 yields

$$
\tilde{\sigma}^2 = \frac{(\mathbf{y}-X\mathbf{b})'(\mathbf{y}-X\mathbf{b})}{T} = \frac{\hat{\mathbf{e}}'\hat{\mathbf{e}}}{T} \tag{6.6.22}
$$

This is the maximum likelihood estimator for σ^2. It can be viewed as an alternative estimator to the unbiased estimator of σ^2 given in equation 6.3.8. In the case of $\tilde{\sigma}^2$, the maximum likelihood estimator for σ^2, the expected value is

$$E\left[\tilde{\sigma}^2\right] = E\left[\frac{\hat{e}'\hat{e}}{T}\right] = \frac{T-2}{T} E\left[\frac{\hat{e}'\hat{e}}{T-2}\right] = \frac{T-2}{T} E\left[\hat{\sigma}^2\right] = \frac{(T-2)\sigma^2}{T} \quad (6.6.23)$$

Since $(T-2)/T$ is less than unity, this means that $\tilde{\sigma}^2$ is a biased estimator of σ^2 and will on average underestimate σ^2. For completeness we note from equation 6.3.9 that var($\tilde{\sigma}^2$) is

$$\mathrm{var}\left(\tilde{\sigma}^2\right) = \frac{\sigma^4}{T^2}\mathrm{var}\left(\chi^2_{(T-2)}\right) = \frac{\sigma^4\,2(T-2)}{T^2} = \frac{2\sigma^4(T-2)}{T^2} \quad (6.6.24)$$

which means the biased estimator $\tilde{\sigma}^2$ has, relative to equation 6.3.9b, a smaller sampling variability than the unbiased estimator $\hat{\sigma}^2$.

6.6.6 Summary

In this section we have been concerned with the properties of the least squares estimator for β that is given by $\mathbf{b} = (X'X)^{-1}X'\mathbf{y} = \mathbf{b} = \left[b_1, b_2\right]$. We have learned that

1. The least squares estimator $\mathbf{b}$ is a random vector with its components b_1 and b_2 being random variables.
2. $\mathbf{b}$ is a linear function of the random observation vector $\mathbf{y}$.
3. If $\mathbf{y}$ is a vector of the normally distributed random variables, then $\mathbf{b}$ is a vector of normally distributed random variables b_1 and b_2.
4. The mean of the random vector $\mathbf{b}$ is $E[\mathbf{b}] = \beta$, and thus the least squares estimator has the statistical property of unbiasedness.
5. If we compare the sampling variability of the least squares estimator with that of other linear unbiased estimators, we find that it is best—best in the sense of having a minimum sampling variability from sample to sample.
6. To obtain an empirical estimate of the sampling variability of $\mathbf{b}$, we need a rule for estimating σ^2. An unbiased estimator of σ^2 is

$$\hat{\sigma}^2 = \hat{e}'\hat{e}/(T-2) = (\mathbf{y} - X\mathbf{b})'(\mathbf{y} - X\mathbf{b})/(T-2).$$

7. An unbiased estimator of the covariance matrix expression for $\mathbf{b}$ is $\hat{\sigma}^2\left(X'X\right)^{-1}$.

6.7 Exercises

6.1 Write down your understanding of what is meant by sampling performance of an estimation rule or estimator.

6.2 Since we usually have only one sample of data, why should we be interested in the sampling properties of an estimator?

6.3 If the random error e_t is distributed normally with mean zero and variance σ^2, i.e. $e_t \sim N(0, \sigma^2)$, how are e_t/σ, and e_t^2/σ^2 distributed?

6.4 Given the simple linear statistical model $y_t = \beta_1 + x_t\beta_2 + e_t$, and the least squares estimator for β_1 and β_2, we can estimate the $E[y_t]$, for any value of x_t, as $\hat{E}\left[y_t\right] = b_1 = x_t b_2$. Using the results in Section 2.7 of Chapter 2 find the mean and variance of $\hat{E}\left[y_t\right]$.

6.5 Consider Exercise 5.6 and the data in Table 5.3. Given the least squares estimator for β_1 and β_2 in Exercise 5.6a

(a) Compute $\hat{e}_t = y_t - \hat{y}_t = y_t - (b_1 + x_t b_2)$ and use the least squares estimator $\hat{\sigma}^2 = \Sigma \hat{e}_t^2 / (T - 2)$ to compute an estimate of σ^2.

(b) What does your estimate for σ^2 imply about observations generated from the production function?

(c) Compute an estimate of the variance and covariance expressions for b_1 and b_2.

(d) Give a statistical interpretation of your results and discuss any economic implications.

6.6   Consider the data on number of hamburgers sold and price given in Exercise 5.7. Estimate the variances of the least squares estimators b_1 and b_2. What is the estimated covariance between b_1 and b_2? What can you infer from the sign of the estimated covariance?

6.7   The gross income and tax paid by a cross section of 30 companies in 1988 and 1989 is given in Table 6.2.

(a) Use these data to estimate the relationship

$$\text{tax}_t = \beta_1 + \beta_2 \text{income}_t + e_t$$

for each of the years 1988 and 1989.

(b) Give interpretations of the two estimates of β_2.

(c) Find the average income for each year and predict the tax paid for each average income. Compare the average and marginal tax rates.

(d) Consider the estimate for β_2 for 1989 and the corresponding estimated variance $\hat{\text{var}}(b_2)$. Pretend that $\hat{\text{var}}(b_2)$ is the same as the true variance $\text{var}(b_2)$, and assume that b_2 is normally distributed. Find the probability that the sampling error $|b_2 - \beta_2|$ is (i) less than .04, and (ii) less than .01.

(e) Pool the observations from the two years of data and use the resulting 40 observations to estimate one tax–income relationship. Compare the estimates for β_1 and β_2, and the estimated variances $\hat{\text{var}}(b_1)$ and $\hat{\text{var}}(b_2)$, with those from the separate equations. What implicit assumptions are you making when you pool the two sets of observations?

6.8.   Making use of the computer handbook and the computer, design and analyze a Monte Carlo experiment like that given in Section 6.5. Compare your empirical results with their theoretical counterparts.

Students who worked their way through Section 6.6 should have a go at the following exercises.

6.9   If the random vector **e** is distributed normally with mean vector **0** and covariance matrix $\sigma^2 I_T$, that is, $\mathbf{e} \sim N(\mathbf{0}, \sigma^2 I_T)$, how are the quadratic forms

$$\frac{e_t^2}{\sigma^2} \text{ and } \frac{1}{\sigma^2} \mathbf{e}'\mathbf{e} = \frac{1}{\sigma^2} \mathbf{e}'I_T\mathbf{e},$$

distributed?

6.10   Since in the simple regression model $\mathbf{y} = X\beta + \mathbf{e}$, where X is a $(T \times 2)$ matrix, we cannot observe **e** and must work with

$$\hat{\mathbf{e}} = \mathbf{y} - X\mathbf{b} = \mathbf{y} - X(X'X)^{-1}X'\mathbf{y} = \left(I_T - X(X'X)^{-1}X'\right)\mathbf{y}$$

$$= \left(I_T - X(X'X)^{-1}X'\right)(X\beta + \mathbf{e}) = \left(I_T - X(X'X)^{-1}X'\right)\mathbf{e}$$

Table 6.2 Gross Income and Tax for 30 Companies (Millions of Dollars)

1988		1989	
Income	Tax	Income	Tax
9.215	1.643	9.518	2.125
2.047	0.413	2.068	0.565
9.989	1.752	9.992	2.221
8.321	1.408	8.515	1.905
4.588	0.838	4.389	0.943
4.736	0.748	5.015	1.051
3.596	0.577	3.811	0.819
4.830	0.752	4.939	1.015
4.508	0.761	4.539	1.096
7.506	1.331	7.806	1.654
4.052	0.548	4.583	0.836
6.015	1.121	6.345	1.602
7.775	1.316	8.227	1.877
3.105	0.503	3.129	0.698
2.215	0.514	2.691	0.246
5.676	1.057	6.015	1.146
5.554	0.942	5.702	1.221
5.360	0.803	5.150	0.920
10.394	1.902	10.579	2.150
3.473	0.513	3.341	0.570
4.022	0.868	4.400	0.917
6.119	1.067	6.682	1.157
3.362	0.559	3.487	0.678
7.203	1.318	7.557	1.637
3.874	0.580	3.929	0.515
7.259	1.138	7.636	1.721
2.130	0.414	2.169	0.433
7.528	1.331	7.862	1.461
9.578	1.662	9.997	2.166
2.015	0.351	2.259	0.447

show that

$$\frac{1}{\sigma^2}\hat{e}'\hat{e} = e'\left(I_T - X(X'X)^{-1}X'\right)\left(I_T - X(X'X)^{-1}X'\right)e$$

$$= \frac{1}{\sigma^2}e'\left(I_T - X(X'X)^{-1}X'\right)e$$

is distributed as a $\chi^2_{(T-2)}$ random variable.

6.11 Consider, as an alternative to the least squares estimator, the linear estimator $\bar{\beta} = \left[(X'X)^{-1}X' + C\right]y$ where C is some $2 \times T$ matrix that is conformable with $(X'X)^{-1}X'$.

(a) Is $\bar{\beta}$ an unbiased estimator?

(b) If not, how would you make it unbiased?

(c) What is the variance–covariance expression for the unbiased version of $\bar{\beta}$, that is, the estimator $\bar{\beta}$ with the conditions developed in (b)?

   (d) Contrast the variance-covariance matrix for $\bar{\beta}$ with the variance–covariance expression for **b**.
   (e) Under (d), how would you reach a conclusion as to which is "best" in terms of sampling variability?

6.12 Consider the linear model $y_t = x_{t1}\beta_1 + x_{t2}\beta_2 + e_t$, where the e_t are independent normal random variables with mean zero and variance σ^2. Suppose that we have only the following 4 observations:

y_t	x_{t1}	x_{t2}
2	1	0
−1	0	1
4	1	1
0	1	−1

Note that this is a special model without an intercept or constant term.
   (a) Define **y**, X, and β such that the model can be written in matrix algebra form.
   (b) Find $X'X$, $X'\mathbf{y}$ and $\mathbf{y}'\mathbf{y}$.
   (c) Find b_1 and b_2.
   (d) Compute $\hat{\mathbf{e}} = \mathbf{y} - X\mathbf{b} = \mathbf{y} - \hat{\mathbf{y}}$ and use the estimator $\hat{\mathbf{e}}'\hat{\mathbf{e}}/(T-2)$ to compute an estimate of the variance σ^2.
   (e) Find estimated variances for b_1 and b_2.
   (f) Find an estimate of the covariance between b_1 and b_2.
   (g) What is the true covariance between b_1 and b_2?

6.8 References

For a more complete write up of the theoretical background for the material in this chapter see:

JUDGE, G. G., R. C. HILL, W. E. GRIFFITHS, H. L. LÜTKEPOHl and T. C. LEE (1988) *Introduction to the Theory and Practice of Econometrics*, New York: John Wiley & Sons, Inc., pp. 164–171, 221–226.

For another treatment of topics covered in this chapter see:

KMENTA, JAN (1986) *Elements of Econometrics*, New York: Macmillan Publishing Co., pp. 203–254.

PINDYCK, R. S. and D. RUBINFELD (1990) *Econometric Models and Economic Forecasts*, New York: McGraw-Hill Book Co., Chapter 3.

Chapter 7

Inference in the Simple Regression Model: Interval Estimation, Hypothesis Testing, and Prediction

New Key Words and Concepts

Interval Estimation

Prediction Equation

Best Unbiased Predictor

Random Interval

Hypothesis Testing

Confidence Interval

Conditional Mean Forecasting

In Chapters 5 and 6 we focused on the relationship between two economic variables and specified a statistical model, $y_t = \beta_1 + x_t\beta_2 + e_t$; $e_t \sim (0, \sigma^2)$, that described the sampling process by which we visualized the data as having been generated. Since the statistical model involved unknown parameters β_1 and β_2 and σ^2, we

1. Used the least squares concept to develop a rule or estimators, b_1 and b_2, for estimating β_1 and β_2.

2. Noted that, since b_1 and b_2 were linear functions of the random sample observations y_t, the estimator was also random and b_1 and b_2 were random variables.

3. Found that b_1 and b_2 had means $E[b_1] = \beta_1$ and $E[b_2] = \beta_2$ and thus the least squares estimator is an unbiased estimation rule.

4. Noted that the estimates b_1 and b_2 could vary from sample to sample and some of the estimates could miss the mark quite badly, that is, b_1 and b_2 could be quite different from the true parameters.

5. Investigated this sampling variability in terms of the variances and covariance of the random variables b_1 and b_2.

6. Found that the variances and covariance involved the unknown parameter σ^2.

7. Developed as an estimator of σ^2 the unbiased estimation rule

$$\hat{\sigma}^2 = \Sigma\hat{e}_t^2 / (T-2)$$

and used this estimation rule to obtain an estimate of the variances and covariance of b_1 and b_2.

8. Noted that out of the class of linear unbiased estimation rules for our statistical model, the least squares estimators b_1 and b_2 are best in the sense of having a minimum sampling variability.

By using a simple linear statistical model, the least squares rule, and a sample of household expenditure-income data, we have been able to obtain what are known as *point* estimates of the unknown parameters β_1 and β_2. Point estimates are single numbers that, given the data and in the least squares sense, represent our best guesses for β_1 and β_2. To obtain these least squares estimates, and derive some of their properties, we only needed to assume that the random variable e_t has a mean 0 and a variance σ^2. We made no assumption about the shape of the distribution for e_t until we discussed the maximum likelihood estimator and developed the sampling characteristics of the random variable $\hat{\sigma}^2$. In these contexts we assumed that e_t was normally distributed; this assumption allowed us to develop maximum likelihood estimators for β_1, β_2, and σ^2 and in the case of the least squares estimator $\hat{\sigma}^2$ to conclude that $(T-2)\hat{\sigma}^2 / \sigma^2$ was distributed as a chi-square random variable with $(T-2)$ degrees of freedom. In the Monte Carlo experiment we were able to artificially generate data from the normal distribution so that we could examine the variability of the least squares estimates.

   In this chapter *we retain the assumption that e_t is normally distributed*. The challenge before us is to make use of the machinery developed in Chapter 6 to discover how to get some additional information out of the data and how to use this information for making probability statements that result in *interval estimates* and hypothesis tests for β_1 and β_2.

7.1   Interval Estimation

We discussed in Section 3.2 of Chapter 3 why the random errors may have a normal distribution. Also we have noted that when e_t is normally distributed, so too are our least squares estimators b_1 and b_2. Within this context we can summarize what we know about b_1 and b_2 using the notation

$$b_1 \sim N\big[\beta_1, \text{var}(b_1)\big] \qquad\qquad b_2 \sim N\big[\beta_2, \text{var}(b_2)\big] \tag{7.1.1}$$

where

$$\text{var}(b_1) = \frac{\sigma^2 \Sigma x_t^2}{T\Sigma(x_t - \bar{x})^2} \qquad\qquad \text{var}(b_2) = \frac{\sigma^2}{\Sigma(x_t - \bar{x})^2} \tag{7.1.2}$$

and

$$\text{cov}(b_1, b_2) = -\frac{\sigma^2 \bar{x}}{\Sigma(x_t - \bar{x})^2} \tag{7.1.3}$$

Given this normal distribution framework the next step is to develop a procedure so that we can use this information for making probability statements relative to interval estimation and hypothesis testing. The procedures developed in Section 4.2 of Chapter 4 in connection with an interval estimator for the mean of a population provide us with a conceptual basis for analyzing this problem. We begin with interval estimation under the special case where σ^2 is known. We then analyze the case, usually found in practice, where σ^2 is unknown.

7.1.1 σ^2 Known

To provide a basis for interval estimation we focus first on the estimate b_2 when the variance (scale) parameter σ^2 is known. If σ^2 is known, then we see from equation 7.1.2 that var(b_2) is known. Therefore, from equation 7.1.2, it follows that

$$\frac{b_2 - \beta_2}{\sqrt{\operatorname{var}(b_2)}} \sim N(0, 1) \tag{7.1.4}$$

That is, $(b_2 - \beta_2) / \sqrt{\operatorname{var}(b_2)}$ is distributed as a standard normal random variable with zero mean and variance one. Along the lines of Section 2.8.1 of Chapter 2, from tabulated values of the $N(0, 1)$ probability density function, we can pick critical values z_c and $-z_c$ such that $P(Z > z_c) = P(Z < -z_c) = \alpha/2$, where $Z \sim N(0, 1)$ and α is a chosen probability level. Then we can write

$$P\left[-z_c \leq Z \leq z_c\right] = 1 - \alpha \tag{7.1.5}$$

and

$$P\left[-z_c \leq \frac{b_2 - \beta_2}{\sqrt{\operatorname{var}(b_2)}} \leq z_c\right] = 1 - \alpha \tag{7.1.6}$$

Suppose $\alpha = .05$, then $z_c = 1.96$ and equation 7.1.6 becomes

$$P\left[-1.96 \leq \frac{b_2 - \beta_2}{\sqrt{\operatorname{var}(b_2)}} \leq 1.96\right] = 0.95 \tag{7.1.7}$$

That is, if we take repeated samples of data then, on average, 95 times out of 100, $(b_2 - \beta_2) / \sqrt{\operatorname{var}(b_2)}$ will lie in the interval $(-1.96, 1.96)$. If we know σ^2 and hence var(b_2), we can use equation 7.1.6 to derive a $100(1 - \alpha)\%$ confidence interval for β_2. Specifically, by making use of equation 7.1.6 we can write

$$P\left[b_2 - z_c \sqrt{\operatorname{var}(b_2)} \leq \beta_2 \leq b_2 + z_c \sqrt{\operatorname{var}(b_2)}\right] = 1 - \alpha \tag{7.1.8}$$

For $\alpha = .05$ and $z_c = 1.96$ this statement becomes

$$P\left[b_2 - 1.96\sqrt{\operatorname{var}(b_2)} \leq \beta_2 \leq b_2 + 1.96\sqrt{\operatorname{var}(b_2)}\right] = 0.95 \tag{7.1.9}$$

The interpretation we place on equation 7.1.9 is as follows: *Before* we sample there is a .95 probability of obtaining a value b_2 such that the interval $b_2 \pm 1.96\sqrt{\operatorname{var}(b_2)}$ contains β_2. Equation 7.1.9 is a probability statement about the endpoints of a *random* interval. Having obtained a sample, and a particular value b_2, we say that a 95% confidence interval or interval estimate is given by

$$b_2 \pm 1.96\sqrt{\operatorname{var}(b_2)} \tag{7.1.10}$$

Of course, for a particular sample of data the interval estimate 7.1.10 may or may not contain the true parameter β_2.

7.1.2   Unknown σ^2

In practice, σ^2 and hence var(b_2) is not known and thus it is not feasible to obtain intervals like those of equation 7.1.10. However, we can replace var(b_2) in equation 7.1.3 by its unbiased estimator $\text{vâr}(b_2)$, which makes use of an unbiased estimator of σ^2. In this case we would consider instead the random variable

$$t = \frac{b_2 - \beta_2}{\sqrt{\text{vâr}(b_2)}} \sim t_{(T-2)}$$

(7.1.11a)

which, because of the random variable in the denominator, no longer has a standard normal distribution. Fortunately, however, as in Section 4.4 of Chapter 4, we can prove that equation 7.1.11a has a t distribution by using the result that the ratio of a normal random variable divided by the square root of a $\chi^2_{(T-2)}$ random variable divided by its degrees of freedom results in a random variable t that has a Student t probability distribution with $(T-2)$ degrees of freedom. In this case the standard normal random variable is

$$\frac{b_2 - \beta_2}{\sigma \big/ \sqrt{\Sigma(x_t - \bar{x})^2}}$$

and the square root of the $\chi^2_{(T-2)}$ random variable divided by its degrees of freedom is

$$\sqrt{\frac{(T-2)\hat{\sigma}^2 / \sigma^2}{T-2}}$$

Thus to derive the result in equation 7.1.11a we have

$$t = \frac{\dfrac{b_2 - \beta_2}{\sigma \big/ \sqrt{\Sigma(x_t - \bar{x})^2}}}{\sqrt{\dfrac{(T-2)\hat{\sigma}^2 / \sigma^2}{T-2}}} = \frac{b_2 - \beta_2}{\hat{\sigma} \big/ \sqrt{\Sigma(x_t - \bar{x})^2}} = \frac{b_2 - \beta_2}{\sqrt{\text{vâr}(b_2)}}$$

(7.1.11b)

In contrast to Chapter 4, we have $(T-2)$ rather than $(T-1)$ degrees of freedom because we are estimating two parameters β_1 and β_2 in the mean expenditure function.

So that we can make use of this t distribution, critical values t_c have been tabulated for various degrees of freedom and various confidence or probability (α) levels and are contained in Table 2 in the Appendix of this book. Thus, we can write

$$P\left[-t_c \le t_{(T-2)} \le t_c\right] = 1 - \alpha$$

(7.1.12)

where t_c is such that $P[t_{(T-2)} > t_c] = P[t_{(T-2)} < -t_c] = \alpha/2$.

Put another way

$$P\left[-t_c \le \frac{b_2 - \beta_2}{\sqrt{\text{vâr}(b_2)}} \le t_c\right] = 1 - \alpha$$

(7.1.13)

or

$$P\left[b_2 - t_c\sqrt{\hat{\text{var}}(b_2)} \le \beta_2 \le b_2 + t_c\sqrt{\hat{\text{var}}(b_2)}\right] = 1-\alpha \qquad (7.1.14)$$

For our household expenditure–income problem where $T = 40$ and the degrees of freedom are $T - 2 = 38$, if we let $\alpha = .05$, this statement becomes

$$P\left[b_2 - 2.024\sqrt{\hat{\text{var}}(b_2)} \le \beta_2 \le b_2 + 2.024\sqrt{\hat{\text{var}}(b_2)}\right] = 0.95 \qquad (7.1.15)$$

The value $t_c = 2.024$, which is relevant for $\alpha = .05$ and 38 degrees of freedom, does not appear in the t table at the end of the book. However, it can be approximated by considering the values for 30 and 40 degrees of freedom in the t table. Alternatively, it can be computed exactly using SHAZAM, SAS, or some other software package. The interpretation we give to equation 7.1.15 is as follows. *Before* we collect a sample there is a 0.95 probability of obtaining estimates b_2 and $\hat{\text{var}}(b_2)$ such that the interval $\left(b_2 - 2.024\sqrt{\hat{\text{var}}(b_2)}, b_2 + 2.024\sqrt{\hat{\text{var}}(b_2)}\right)$ contains β_2. If we use equation 7.1.15 to compute interval estimates for β_2 over repeated samples, 95% of the time these intervals will contain β_2. As in the standard normal case, we are making probability statements about the endpoints of a random interval. However, in this case each endpoint depends on two random variables, b_2 and $\hat{\text{var}}(b_2)$.

A 95% confidence interval for a particular sample is obtained by using estimates b_2 and $\hat{\text{var}}(b_2)$ from that sample. For our household expenditure-income problem where $b_2 = .2323$ and $\hat{\text{var}}(b_2) = .00306$, the 95% interval estimate is

$$.2323 \pm 2.024\sqrt{.00306}$$

or

$$\left(.12 \le \beta_2 \le .34\right) \qquad (7.1.16)$$

Thus, our sample information about β_2 now consists of a point estimate of .2323 and a 95% interval estimate of (.12, .34). In general, we desire narrow intervals because they imply precise estimates, and thus convey a good deal of information. Note well that in giving a statistical interpretation, if we use the sampling theory approach to inference, we *cannot* say that the probability is .95 that β_2 falls in the interval (.12, .34). Even though in your heart this is the statement you would like to make, in your applied work *do not fall in this trap* when you present and discuss interval estimates. *In a repeated sampling context, it is the confidence intervals that work 95% of the time.* That is, in a repeated sampling context, we would expect 95% of the interval estimates to contain the unknown parameter. After we have computed a single interval, we cannot make probability statements about that interval.

For our household expenditure–income problem where $b_1 = 7.3832$ and $\hat{\text{var}}(b_1) = 16.0669$, the 95% interval estimate corresponding to equation 7.1.15 is

$$7.3832 \pm 2.024\sqrt{16.0669}$$

or

$$\left(-0.73 \le \beta_1 \le 15.50\right) \qquad (7.1.17)$$

Thus, the interval estimate for β_1 includes the possibility of negative values and reflects the high degree of sampling variability that we noted in Chapter 6. Since there are no data when income is near zero, perhaps it is asking too much to hope for a reliable estimate of β_1.

7.1.3   Some Monte Carlo Results

To give an idea of the sampling variability of random intervals, interval estimates for β_1 and β_2 for the first 10 samples of data from the Monte Carlo experiment presented in Section 6.5 are given in Table 7.1. In developing the interval estimates, the confidence level of $\alpha = .05$ was used.

A quick look at the interval estimates in Table 7.1 reveals how much they vary in width and end points. For example, in sample 6 the interval estimates are relatively wide. In sample 10 they are relatively narrow. In all 10 samples the intervals contain the true parameters. However, as suggested by theory, for the 1000 Monte Carlo samples, β_1 was contained in 94.1% of the intervals and β_2 was also contained in 94.1% of the intervals. The Monte Carlo experiment helps us to understand and interpret inferences relating to interval estimation. However, we should remember that in practice we usually have a single sample of data and just one point and interval estimate.

7.2   Hypothesis Testing

Interval estimation or confidence intervals are major techniques for making statistical inferences from the data. Another area, related to the evaluation of confidence intervals is that of hypothesis testing. Many decision problems require some basis for deciding whether or not a parameter is a specified value. For example, for decision purposes it makes a good deal of difference whether or not $\beta_2 \neq 0$. If $\beta_2 = 0$, then income has no effect on the level of household expenditure on food, and there would be no need for a supermarket chain to worry about income changes in the future planning of its food sections. To test the point null hypothesis $H_0: \beta_2 = 0$ against the alternative $H_1: \beta_2 \neq 0$, we examine whether or not the estimate b_2 from our sample of data is compatible with the null hypothesis. From equation 7.1.11 we know that

$$t = \frac{b_2 - \beta_2}{\sqrt{\hat{\text{var}}(b_2)}} \sim t_{(T-2)}$$

Consequently, *if the null hypothesis* $\beta_2 = 0$ *is correct*

$$t = \frac{b_2}{\sqrt{\hat{\text{var}}(b_2)}} \sim t_{(T-2)} \tag{7.2.1}$$

Table 7.1   Point and Interval Estimates for β_1 and β_2 for 10 Samples of Data for the Monte Carlo Experiment Presented in Section 6.5

Sample Number	$\beta_1 = 7.3832$ Point	Interval		$\beta_2 = .2323$ Point	Interval	
1	8.505	−1.650	18.660	0.2399	0.0998	0.3800
2	10.348	1.121	19.574	0.2114	0.0841	0.3387
3	6.613	0.071	13.154	0.2353	0.1451	0.3256
4	13.812	4.994	22.629	0.1383	0.0166	0.2599
5	4.824	−3.623	13.271	0.2815	0.1649	0.3980
6	9.086	−0.886	19.058	0.1748	0.0373	0.3124
7	11.897	4.755	19.040	0.1597	0.0611	0.2582
8	12.168	2.474	21.862	0.1608	0.0271	0.2946
9	2.596	−5.707	10.898	0.2977	0.1832	0.4122
10	5.763	−2.958	14.484	0.2737	0.1534	0.3940

If the sample value of t that we compute from equation 7.2.1 is unlikely to have come from a $t_{(T-2)}$-distribution, then we question the assumption on which equation 7.2.1 is based. That is, we question whether H_0: $\beta_2 = 0$ could be true. Such "questioning" is made more rigorous by setting a significance level (Type I error probability) and a corresponding critical value, as we discussed in Section 4.3 of Chapter 4. If α is the significance level of the test and t_c is the critical value such that $P[|t_{(T-2)}| > t_c] = \alpha$, then we use the test mechanism that rejects the null hypothesis H_0: $\beta_2 = 0$, if $|t| > t_c$.

For our sample of data, equation 7.2.1 yields

$$t = \frac{b_2}{\sqrt{\text{vâr}(b_2)}} = \frac{.2323}{\sqrt{.00306}} = 4.20 \tag{7.2.2}$$

As mentioned for equation 7.1.15, the critical value for $t_{(38)}$ at the .05 level of significance is 2.024. Again we note this value can be approximated from the t table at the back of the book or computed exactly by using SHAZAM, SAS, or some other software package. In terms of the $t_{(38)}$ distribution, the p-value, which is the probability of exceeding the computed value $t = 4.20$, is $p = .00016$. Thus, in this case we would reject the hypothesis that $\beta_2 = 0$ and conclude that income does influence food expenditure. In other words we find the null hypothesis is not compatible with our data and go with our estimate $b_2 = .2323$. Under the null hypothesis $\beta_2 = 0$, another way to think about this problem is in terms of which the statistical model, $y_t = \beta_1 + e_t$ or $y_t = \beta_1 + x_t\beta_2 + e_t$, more appropriately describes the data-generation process. In our case the outcome of the hypothesis test lends support to the conjecture that the statistical model that includes income is compatible with the underlying data-generation process.

Let us look now at the test statistic for the null hypothesis that $\beta_1 = 0$. Here we have

$$t = \frac{b_1}{\sqrt{\text{vâr}(b_1)}} = \frac{7.3832}{4.0084} = 1.8419 \tag{7.2.3}$$

which has a p-value, $p = .0733$. Thus, as you might have expected from the corresponding interval estimate we obtained in equation 7.1.1, the critical value for t of 2.024, at the .05 level, is greater than the outcome in equation 7.2.3. Consequently, we cannot reject the hypothesis that the data may be consistent with $\beta_1 = 0$. These two testing results should help bring out the symmetry of interval estimation and hypothesis testing.

7.2.1   A More General Null Hypothesis

For testing the more general null hypothesis H_0: $\beta_2 = \beta_2^0$ against the alternative H_1: $\beta_2 \neq \beta_2^0$, where β_2^0 is a specific value for β_2 other than zero, we compute

$$t = \frac{b_2 - \beta_2^0}{\sqrt{\text{vâr}(b_2)}} \tag{7.2.4}$$

and reject H_0 if $|t| > t_c$. For example, if our null hypothesis is that $\beta_2^0 = .25$, then for the household consumption–income data,

$$t = \frac{b_2 - \beta_2^0}{\sqrt{\text{vâr}(b_2)}} = \frac{.2323 - .2500}{\sqrt{.00306}} = -\frac{.0177}{.0553} = -.3200 \tag{7.2.5}$$

and the p-value is $p = .7507$. Thus at the 5% level we cannot reject the hypothesis that our data are compatible with $\beta_2 = .2500$.

To see the close tie between interval estimation and hypothesis testing, note that we *fail to reject* H_0 when

$$-t_c < t < t_c \tag{7.2.5a}$$

or when

$$-t_c < \frac{b_2 - \beta_2^0}{\sqrt{\hat{\text{var}}(b_2)}} < t_c \tag{7.2.5b}$$

or when

$$b_2 - t_c \sqrt{\hat{\text{var}}(b_2)} < \beta_2^0 < b_2 + t_c \sqrt{\hat{\text{var}}(b_2)} \tag{7.2.6}$$

The endpoints of this interval are identical to the endpoints of the confidence interval that we derived in equation 7.1.14. Thus, we reject the hypothesis H_0: $\beta_2 = \beta_2^0$, at the α significance level, when β_2^0 lies outside the corresponding $100(1 - \alpha)\%$ confidence interval. In our household expenditure–income example, $\beta_2^0 = 0$ does not lie within the 95% confidence interval (.12, .34), and so, using this approach, we again reject H_0: $\beta_2 = 0$ at the 5% level of significance. *In fact we will reject any null hypothesis where β_2^0 is not contained in the confidence interval (.12, .34).*

At this stage you should be thinking about other economic-statistical problems and how you would make use of the information obtained from interval estimates and hypothesis tests. Sometimes a single-tailed test, which involves inequalities in the null and alternative hypotheses, may be more appropriate than the two-tailed test discussed here. Examples of single-tailed tests appear in Chapters 4, 8 and 10.

Before closing this section, let us note that sometimes a single hypothesis or interval estimate can involve two parameters, for example, H_0: $\beta_1 + \beta_2 = k$, for some constant k. This topic will be covered in Chapter 10. However, to get you thinking about this problem, let us move a little in this direction. Remember that if b_1 and b_2 are normally distributed random variables then the sum of two normally distributed variables is normal. Thus, we can say that

$$(b_1 + b_2) \sim N\big(\beta_1 + \beta_2,\ \text{var}(b_1 + b_2)\big) \tag{7.2.7}$$

where $\text{var}(b_1 + b_2) = \text{var}(b_1) + \text{var}(b_2) + 2\,\text{cov}(b_1, b_2)$. If σ^2 is unknown and we use an unbiased estimator of $\text{var}(b_1 + b_2)$, then

$$\frac{(b_1 + b_2) - (\beta_1 + \beta_2)}{\sqrt{\hat{\text{var}}(b_1 + b_2)}} \sim t_{(T-2)} \tag{7.2.8}$$

This expression forms the basis for interval estimation or hypothesis tests for the sum $\beta_1 + \beta_2$ The difference $\beta_1 - \beta_2$ and other linear combinations can be handled in a similar way.

7.3 Predicting Expenditure

In Section 4.2.1 of Chapter 4 we introduced the problem of predicting the outcome of a random variable. In this connection one objective in obtaining estimates of the unknown parameters β_1 and β_2 in a relationship $y_t = \beta_1 + x_t \beta_2 + e_t$ is to be able to make informed predictions about the outcomes for the random variable y_t. If we can understand the relationship between two economic variables, we can use our knowledge of this relationship to predict the outcome of many variables of economic interest. In our case we are interested in predicting household expenditure on food for a given level of household income. Such information would be useful to a supermarket chain wishing to establish how much food might be purchased in different neighborhoods with different income levels. Suppose that we are interested in predicting household expenditure on food for a household of a family of three with an average weekly income of x_0 dollars. We think of this household as a new one, not one that has previously been sampled. Using our model that explains the level of expenditure on food we can say that the expenditure that we wish to predict, y_0, is given by

$$y_0 = \beta_1 + x_0\beta_2 + e_0 \tag{7.3.1}$$

where $e_0 \sim N(0, \sigma^2)$ and $y_0 \sim N(\beta_1 + x_0\beta_2, \sigma^2)$. Thus, y_0 consists of two components, mean or average expenditure from households with an income of x_0, given by $E[y_0] = \beta_1 + x_0\beta_2$, and the out-of-sample household error, e_0.

7.3.1   The Predictor

The exact value for y_0 is unknown because β_1, β_2, and e_0 are unknown. However, we have the least squares estimators b_1 and b_2 as estimators for β_1 and β_2; and since e_0 is an unobservable random error with zero mean and is not correlated with any other errors, our best predictor for e_0 is 0. Thus, as a predictor for y_0, we take equation 7.3.1 with β_1 and β_2 replaced by b_1 and b_2, and e_0 replaced by zero. Specifically, we form the prediction equation or make use of the estimator or predictor

$$\hat{y}_0 = b_1 + x_0 b_2 \tag{7.3.2}$$

When assessing the sampling properties of a random variable-predictor $\hat{y}_0$, it is conventional to examine the mean and variance of the prediction error. This is in contrast to the assessment of the sampling properties of an estimator, where the mean and variance of the estimator itself are examined. Thus, making use of equation 7.3.2, the prediction error from using $\hat{y}_0$ as the predictor of y_0 is

$$\hat{y}_0 - y_0 = (b_1 - \beta_1) + x_0(b_2 - \beta_2) - e_0 \tag{7.3.3}$$

where e_0 is unknown and unobservable. Since the prediction error $\hat{y}_0 - y_0$ is a random variable, we need to find its mean and variance.

7.3.2   Sampling Properties

What are the properties of this predictor-estimator of y_0? The predictor $\hat{y}_0$ is called an *unbiased predictor* if the mean of the prediction error is zero. Unbiasedness is satisfied in this case because the mean prediction error is given by

$$E[\hat{y}_0 - y_0] = E[b_1 - \beta_1] + x_0 E[b_2 - \beta_2] - E[e_0]$$
$$= 0 + 0 - 0 = 0 \tag{7.3.4}$$

In fact it can be shown that $\hat{y}_0 = b_1 + x_0 b_2$ is a *best* linear unbiased predictor.

Note that $\hat{y}_0$ can differ from y_0 because

(i) the estimates b_1 and b_2 will differ from their mean values β_1 and β_2 and

(ii) the future disturbance e_0 may differ from its implicit predictor, which is its mean value of 0.

Consequently, these two components contribute to the variance of the prediction error.

As an expression for the variance of the prediction error, it can be shown that (see Appendix 7A and Exercise 7.17)

$$\text{var}(\hat{y}_0 - y_0) = \sigma^2 \left[1 + \frac{1}{T} + \frac{(x_0 - \bar{x})^2}{\Sigma(x_t - \bar{x})^2} \right] \tag{7.3.5}$$

This result implies that, the farther the income level x_0 is from the mean of the sample incomes $\bar{x}$, the larger the variance of the prediction error. In line with the discussion in Chapter 6, the greater the variance the less reliable the prediction. In other words, our predictions for income levels close to the sample mean $\bar{x}$ are more reliable than our predictions for income levels quite different from $\bar{x}$. This outcome is a reasonable one. We would not expect to predict very accurately for income levels about which we have little previous information. Also, even small errors in estimating β_1 and β_2 can lead to big forecast errors as $(x_0 - \bar{x})$ gets large.

The variance of the prediction error cannot be computed in equation 7.3.5 because it depends on the unknown error variance σ^2. Instead, we can estimate the prediction error variance by replacing σ^2 by its unbiased estimator $\hat{\sigma}^2$. Thus, an estimator of $\text{var}(\hat{y}_0 - y_0)$ is given by

$$\hat{\text{var}}(\hat{y}_0 - y_0) = \hat{\sigma}^2 \left[1 + \frac{1}{T} + \frac{(x_0 - \bar{x})^2}{\Sigma(x_t - \bar{x})^2} \right] \tag{7.3.6}$$

This is an unbiased estimator that can be used to obtain an interval prediction or to make a hypothesis test.

7.3.3   An Application

The next step is to apply these results to our data on household food expenditure and income. Given estimates b_1 and b_2 for the household expenditure–income sample, we have, in line with equation 7.3.2, the prediction equation

$$\hat{y}_0 = 7.3832 + 0.2323x_0 \tag{7.3.7}$$

This prediction equation can be used for a given level of household income x_0 to predict the level of household expenditure y_0. If we set weekly household income at $x_0 = 60$ dollars, the predicted household expenditure level is

$$\hat{y}_0 = 7.3832 + 0.2323(60) = 21.32 \tag{7.3.8}$$

The corresponding estimate of the sampling variability attached to the prediction error $\hat{e}_0 = \hat{y}_0 - y_0$ is from equation 7.3.6

$$\hat{\text{var}}(\hat{y}_0 - y_0) = 46.853 \left[1 + \frac{1}{40} + \frac{(60 - 69.8)^2}{15324.6} \right]$$

$$= 48.318 \tag{7.3.9}$$

Because our sample size is relatively large, and because $x_0 = 60$ is close to the sample mean of $\bar{x} = 69.8$, the estimated prediction error variance is only slightly greater than the estimated variance of σ^2.

7.3.4   Interval Prediction

When dealing with estimation, we learned how to use the least squares estimator to obtain *point* estimates for β_1 and β_2, and we learned how to use the least squares estimator *and* its estimated variances to obtain *interval* estimates for β_1 and β_2. These interval estimates took the form of $100(1 - \alpha)\%$ confidence intervals. We have just seen how we can use the least squares line or prediction equation to obtain a *point* prediction, and also how we can estimate the variance of the prediction error. As we did in Section 4.2.1 of Chapter 4, it is now possible to use both these pieces of information, along with an assumption that the errors are normally distributed, to obtain a prediction confidence interval.

From equation 7.3.4 and the normality assumption, we have $(\hat{y}_0 - y_0) \sim N[0, \mathrm{var}(\hat{y}_0 - y_0)]$, consequently,

$$\frac{\hat{y}_0 - y_0}{\sqrt{\mathrm{var}(\hat{y}_0 - y_0)}} \sim N(0,1) \tag{7.3.10}$$

is a standard normal random variable. In line with Section 7.1.2, replacing $\mathrm{var}(\hat{y}_0 - y_0)$ by its estimator $\hat{\mathrm{var}}(\hat{y}_0 - y_0)$ yields the t random variable

$$\frac{\hat{y}_0 - y_0}{\sqrt{\hat{\mathrm{var}}(\hat{y}_0 - y_0)}} \sim t_{(T-2)} \tag{7.3.11}$$

Suppose now that we are interested in a 95% interval prediction. Let t_c be the value such that $P[t_{(T-2)} > t_c] = .025$. For $T - 2 = 38$ degrees of freedom the critical value for $t_{(38)}$ is $t_c = 2.024$. Thus, we write

$$P\left[-t_c \leq t_{(T-2)} \leq t_c\right] = .95$$

$$P\left[-t_c \leq \frac{\hat{y}_0 - y_0}{\sqrt{\hat{\mathrm{var}}(\hat{y}_0 - y_0)}} \leq t_c\right] = .95$$

$$P\left[\hat{y}_0 - t_c \sqrt{\hat{\mathrm{var}}(\hat{y}_0 - y_0)} \leq y_0 \leq \hat{y}_0 + t_c \sqrt{\hat{\mathrm{var}}(\hat{y}_0 - y_0)}\right] = .95 \tag{7.3.12}$$

A 95% confidence interval for y_0 is given by

$$\hat{y}_0 \pm t_c \sqrt{\hat{\mathrm{var}}(\hat{y}_0 - y_0)} \tag{7.3.13}$$

The relationship between point and interval predictions for different values of x_0 is illustrated in Figure 7.1. A point prediction is always given by the least squares line $\hat{y}_0 = b_1 + x_0 b_2$. A prediction confidence interval takes the form of two bands around the least squares line. In line with equation 7.3.5, the farther x_0 departs from $\bar{x}$, the greater the distance between each of these bands and the least squares line, reflecting the fact that $\hat{\mathrm{var}}(\hat{y}_0 - y_0)$ increases as $(x_0 - \bar{x})^2$ increases.

Using the values from our data, the confidence interval in equation 7.3.13 becomes

$$21.32 \pm 2.024\sqrt{48.318}$$

or

$$\left(7.25 \leq y_0 \leq 35.39\right) \tag{7.3.14}$$

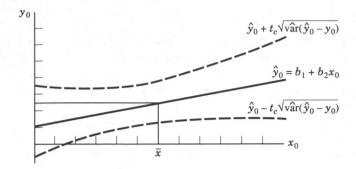

Figure 7.1 Point and interval prediction.

Our prediction interval suggests that a household unit with an average weekly income of \$60 will spend somewhere between \$7.25 and \$35.39 per week on food. Such a wide interval means that our point prediction of \$21.32 per week may not be reliable. It is possible that a large proportion of the variation in household expenditures on food is attributable to factors other than income, and so, without knowledge of these factors, prediction based only on income is relatively imprecise.

7.3.5 Hypothesis Testing with a New Observation

Suppose that, having used observations from 40 households to estimate our expenditure function for food, we obtain an observation (y_0, x_0) from a household in another city. The supermarket chain will be interested in whether the results it has obtained for one city can carry over to another city. Is the observation y_0 from the second city compatible with those from the sample city in the sense that it could have been generated by the same model with the same parameters β_1 and β_2? We can test this hypothesis by examining whether or not y_0 lies in the confidence interval given in equtaion 7.3.13. A value outside the interval suggests that the second city's households have a different expenditure function; a value inside the interval implies that y_0 is compatible with the sample city's expenditure function.

7.3.6 Conditional Mean Forecasting

In some instances, such as for the manager of a food chain, interest may center on the conditional mean forecasting problem, where the focus is on the mean $E[y_0] = \beta_1 + x_0\beta_2$, rather than the individual observation $y_0 = \beta_1 + x_0\beta_2 + e_0$. For example, suppose we are interested in predicting the household expenditures for all families of a particular income level. In this case the same predictor is appropriate, namely $\hat{y}_0 = b_1 + x_0 b_2$, but the mean and variance of $\hat{y}_0$ rather than $(\hat{y}_0 - y_0)$ are relevant. For the mean we have

$$E[\hat{y}_0] = E[b_1 + x_0 b_2] = \beta_1 + x_0\beta_2 \tag{7.3.15}$$

Thus, $\hat{y}_0 = b_1 + x_0 b_2$ is an unbiased estimator of $E[y_0] = \beta_1 + x_0\beta_2$. In line with equation 7.3.3, $\hat{y}_0 - E[\hat{y}_0] = (b_1 - \beta_1) + x_0(b_2 - \beta_2)$ and the variance of the estimator $\hat{y}_0$ is

$$\mathrm{var}(\hat{y}_0) = E[\hat{y}_0 - E[\hat{y}_0]]^2$$

$$= \sigma^2 \left[\frac{1}{T} + \frac{(x_0 - \bar{x})^2}{\Sigma(x_t - \bar{x})^2} \right] \tag{7.3.16}$$

This result differs from equation 7.3.5 by the error variability σ^2. In this case the sampling variability of $\hat{y}_0$ depends only on the sampling variability of the least squares estimator and the choice of x_0. Note that $\beta_1 + x_0\beta_2$ is just *one* possible linear combination that could be of interest. More will be said about this in Chapter 10.

7.3.7   Section Summary

Let us summarize what we have discovered in this section. The least squares predictor $\hat{y}_0 = b_1 + x_0 b_2$, given by equation 7.3.2, is a best unbiased linear predictor of $y_0 = \beta_1 + x_0\beta_2 + e_0$. The estimated sampling variability of its prediction error is given by equation 7.3.6. The prediction precision depends on the variance of e_0, and through the sampling variability of b_1 and b_2, the sample size, and the distance of x_0 from $\bar{x}$. Prediction far from $\bar{x}$ or outside the range of the x_t used in estimation leads to large prediction or forecast sampling variance. We can use the information in equations 7.3.2 and 7.3.6, along with an assumption of normally distributed errors, to obtain prediction intervals or to test a hypothesis about the compatibility of the sample observations and a new observation.

7.4   Summary of Chapter

Building on Chapters 5 and 6, where we developed point estimators for β_1 and β_2 and σ^2 and discussed their sampling characteristics, in this chapter we made use of the additional information that b_1 and b_2, the least squares estimators for β_1 and β_2, are normally distributed random variables where

$$b_1 \sim N\big(\beta_1, \text{var}(b_1)\big)$$

and

$$b_2 \sim N\big(\beta_2, \text{var}(b_2)\big)$$

Making use of this information we developed interval estimators and a hypothesis testing mechanism for β_1 and β_2 and investigated the problem of prediction or forecasting from the standpoint of estimation and inference. Let's review each of these new concepts.

1. The random variables $(b_1 - \beta_1)\big/\sqrt{\hat{\text{var}}(b_1)}$ and $(b_2 - \beta_2)\big/\sqrt{\hat{\text{var}}(b_2)}$ are distributed as t random variables with $(T - 2)$ degrees of freedom.

2. An interval estimator for b_1 or b_2 may be expressed, for $i = 1, 2$, as

$$P\Big[b_i - t_c \sqrt{\hat{\text{var}}(b_i)} \le \beta_i \le b_i + t_c \sqrt{\hat{\text{var}}(b_i)}\Big] = 1 - \alpha$$

where t_c is the critical value for t with $(T - 2)$ degrees of freedom and a $(1 - \alpha)$ 100% level of confidence.

3. The interpretation in (2) is that, in a repeated sample framework, we should expect $(1 - \alpha)100\%$ of these random intervals to contain the true parameter β_i.

4. The random variables $(b_i - \beta_i)\big/\sqrt{\hat{\text{var}}(b_i)} \sim t_{(T-2)}$, for $i = 1, 2$, may be used to test hypotheses concerning the β_i.

5. If the critical value of the test statistic t_c at the α level of statistical significance exceeds, in absolute value, the test value from our sample of data, then we cannot reject the point null hypothesis.

6. In prediction the point predictor-estimator $\hat{y}_0 = b_1 + x_0 b_2$ is a best linear unbiased predictor.

7. The estimator or predictor $\hat{y}_0$ has mean $E[b_1 + x_0 b_2] = \beta_1 + x_0 \beta_2$, the mean of its prediction error is zero, and the variance of the prediction error is

$$\text{var}(\hat{y}_0 - y_0) = \sigma^2 \left[1 + \frac{1}{T} + \frac{(x_0 - \bar{x})^2}{\Sigma(x_t - \bar{x})^2} \right]$$

8. In conditional mean forecasting interest centers on the mean $E[y_0] = \beta_1 + x_0 \beta_2$ and the variance

$$E[\hat{y}_0 - E[\hat{y}_0]]^2 = \sigma^2 \left(\frac{1}{T} + \frac{(x_0 - \bar{x})^2}{\Sigma(x_t - \bar{x})^2} \right).$$

9. Since $\hat{y}_0$ is a normally distributed random variable, this means $(\hat{y}_0 - y_0)/\sqrt{\hat{\text{var}}(\hat{y}_0 - y_0)}$ is distributed as a t random variable with $(T - 2)$ degrees of freedom.

10. $P\left[\hat{y}_0 - t_c \sqrt{\hat{\text{var}}(\hat{y}_0 - y_0)} \leq y_0 \leq \hat{y}_0 + t_c \sqrt{\hat{\text{var}}(\hat{y}_0 - y_0)}\right] = (1 - \alpha)$ may be used to provide an interval prediction for y_0.

11. The t statistic specified in 9 and 10 may be used to test a hypothesis with a new observation from outside the sample.

We now have the machinery for both estimation and inference as it applies to estimating economic relations with the simple regression model. If you understand point and interval estimation and hypothesis testing for this simple linear statistical model, then you should have little trouble with the *general* linear statistical model that will be considered starting with Chapter 9. Before going on to Chapter 9, we take up in Chapter 8 a few unfinished matters for the simple linear statistical (regression) model and carry through an application that makes use of time series data.

7.5 Exercises

7.1 What do you understand as the sampling theory approach to inference as it relates to interval estimation and hypothesis testing?

7.2 What is the statistical difference between an estimator and an estimate?

7.3 For the estimators b_1 and b_2, why are b_1 and b_2 considered random variables and what is the implication of this for interval estimation and hypothesis testing?

7.4 Under what situation are we permitted to say, in Exercise 7.3, that b_1 and b_2 are normally distributed random variables?

7.5 Why are we interested in being able to make a normally distributed random variable statement in Exercise 7.4?

7.6 What are the different ingredients in the standard normal and t distributions; what is the difference in the characteristics of these two distributions; and what happens to the t distribution as the sample size increases?

7.7 Contrast the inferences resulting from interval estimation and hypothesis testing.

7.8 Write down an interval estimator for β_1 and interpret.

7.9 Write down the test statistic for the hypothesis $\beta_1 = 0$; assume that the test value is less than the critical value and interpret.

7.10 Specify and contrast the predictors-estimators and the sampling variability for predicting y_0, and for predicting the mean of y_0.

7.11 Discuss the sampling theory interpretation of the prediction error and its variance.

7.12 Using the data for the production function discussed in Exercise 5.6 and the linear functional form of Exercise 5.6a and an $\alpha = .05$ level
   (a) (i) find interval estimates for β_1 and β_2 and interpret, (ii) test the hypothesis that $\beta_1 = 0$ and interpret, (iii) test the hypothesis that $\beta_2 = 0$ and interpret, (iv) test the hypothesis that the marginal product of the input is 0.35 and interpret.
   (b) Develop point and interval predictors for each input level and construct a figure such as Figure 7.1.
   (c) Compute and compare the sampling variability that is attached to the prediction error for input levels 8 and 16. Discuss the sampling theory interpretation of the variance of the prediction error.

7.13 Using the Monte Carlo experiment discussed in Sections 6.5 and 7.1.3, with $\alpha = .05$,
   (a) Compute 100 interval estimates for β_2 and interpret.
   (b) Compute 100 tests of the hypothesis that $\beta_2 = 0.2323$; make a frequency diagram of the test values and interpret your results.
   (c) Let $x_0 = 70$, compute the predicted value of y_0 for 100 samples, determine the mean and variance of $(\hat{y}_0 - y_0)$ for the 100 samples, and compare them with the true mean and variance. Make a frequency distribution of the 100 predicted values of y_0 and interpret.

7.14 In the macroeconomics literature there are two competing theories concerning consumption behavior. According to Keynes, aggregate consumption is determined by aggregate income. Alternatively, the classical economists feel that consumption should be inversely related to interest rates [see Sheffrin et al. (1988, pp. 56–61) for a discussion of these propositions]. Using the data given in Table 5.4 of Chapter 5, for the sample of years 1955 to 1986:
   (a) Set up the economic and statistical model for each hypothesis.
   (b) Estimate the unknown parameters for each model and make the relevant tests of hypotheses.
   (c) Based on these data and your econometric results, what are your conclusions relative to the validity of the two hypotheses?
   (d) For the Keynes hypothesis, compute and interpret an interval estimate for the marginal propensity to consume.

7.15 Using the data and your answers from Exercise 5.7 and Exercise 6.6, test the point null hypothesis that the elasticity of demand for hamburgers is equal to -1. Predict the number of hamburgers that will be sold when the price is $2.

7.16 A life insurance company wishes to examine the relationship between the amount of life insurance held by a family and family income. From a random sample of 20 households, the company collected the following observations:

Table 7.2

Family	Life Insurance ($ thousands)	Income ($ thousands)	Family	Life Insurance ($ thousands)	Income ($ thousands)
1	90	25	11	230	57
2	165	40	12	262	72
3	220	60	13	570	140
4	145	30	14	100	23
5	114	29	15	210	55
6	175	41	16	243	58
7	145	37	17	335	87
8	192	46	18	299	72
9	395	105	19	305	80
10	339	81	20	205	48

(a) Estimate a linear relationship between life insurance (y) and income (x).

(b) Discuss the relationship you estimated in (a). In particular:

   (i)   What is your estimate of the resulting change in the amount of life insurance when income increases by $1000?

   (ii) What is the standard error of the estimate in (i) and how do you use this standard error for interval estimation and hypothesis testing?

   (iii) One member of the management board claims that, for every $1000 increase in income, the amount of life insurance held will go up by $5000. Does your estimated relationship support this claim? Use a 5% significance level.

(c) Test the hypothesis that the amount of life insurance held is proportional to income.

(d) Predict the amount of life insurance held by a family with an income of $100,000.

(e) Ten years hence, it is found that a family with an income of $100,000 has life insurance totaling $440,000. Is there any evidence to suggest that your estimated relationship is no longer relevant?

7.17 Prove within the context of Appendix 7A that

$$\mathbf{x}_0'\left(X'X\right)^{-1}\mathbf{x}_0 = \frac{1}{T} + \frac{\left(x_0 - \bar{x}\right)^2}{\Sigma\left(x_t - \bar{x}\right)^2}$$

See equations 7.3.5, 7.3.16, 7A.7, and 7A.11 for the relevance of this result.

7.6 References

For a more complete discussion of the theoretical basis for the concepts discussed in this chapter see:

JUDGE, G. G., R. C. HILL, W. E. GRIFFITHS, H. LÜTKEPOHL, and T. C. LEE (1988) *Introduction to the Theory and Practice of Econometrics*, New York: John Wiley & Sons, Inc., pp. 240–264.

For a discussion of the Keynes and classical hypotheses concerning aggregate consumption see:

SHEFFRIN, S. M., D. A. WILTON, and D. M. PRESCOTT (1988) *Macroeconomics: Theory and Policy*, Cincinnati, OH: South-Western Publishing Co., pp. 56–61.

APPENDIX 7A Linear Algebra Specifications and Derivations in Prediction

Using our model that explains the level of expenditure on food, we can say that the expenditure that we wish to predict, y_0, is given by

$$y_0 = \beta_1 + x_0\beta_2 + e_0$$

$$= \begin{pmatrix} 1 & x_0 \end{pmatrix}\begin{bmatrix} \beta_1 \\ \beta_2 \end{bmatrix} + e_0$$

$$= \mathbf{x}_0'\boldsymbol{\beta} + e_0 \qquad (7A.1)$$

where $\mathbf{x}_0' = \begin{pmatrix} 1 & x_0 \end{pmatrix}$, $e_0 \sim N(0, \sigma^2)$, and $y_0 \sim N(\beta_1 + x_0\beta_2, \sigma^2)$. Specifically, we form the prediction equation or make use of the estimator or predictor

$$\hat{y}_0 = b_1 + x_0 b_2$$

$$= \begin{pmatrix} 1 & x_0 \end{pmatrix}\begin{pmatrix} b_1 \\ b_2 \end{pmatrix}$$

$$= \mathbf{x}_0'\mathbf{b} \qquad (7A.2)$$

Making use of equation 7.3.2, we obtain the prediction error from using $\hat{y}_0$ as the predictor of y_0 as

$$\hat{y}_0 - y_0 = (b_1 - \beta_1) + x_0(b_2 - \beta_2) - e_0$$

$$= \begin{pmatrix} 1 & x_0 \end{pmatrix}\begin{pmatrix} b_1 - \beta_1 \\ b_2 - \beta_2 \end{pmatrix} - e_0$$

$$= \mathbf{x}_0'(\mathbf{b} - \boldsymbol{\beta}) - e_0 \qquad (7A.3)$$

where e_0 is unknown and unobservable.

7A.1 Sampling Properties

The mean prediction error is given by

$$E[\hat{y}_0 - y_0] = \mathbf{x}_0' E[\mathbf{b} - \boldsymbol{\beta}] - E[e_0]$$

$$= \mathbf{x}_0'\mathbf{0} - 0 = 0 \qquad (7A.4)$$

To derive an expression for the variance of the prediction error, we can write, from equation 7A.3,

$$\hat{y}_0 - y_0 = \mathbf{x}_0'(\mathbf{b} - \boldsymbol{\beta}) - e_0 = (\mathbf{b} - \boldsymbol{\beta})'\mathbf{x}_0 - e_0 \qquad (7A.5)$$

and

$$(\hat{y}_0 - y_0)^2 = \mathbf{x}_0'(\mathbf{b} - \boldsymbol{\beta})(\mathbf{b} - \boldsymbol{\beta})'\mathbf{x}_0 + e_0^2 - 2e_0(\mathbf{b} - \boldsymbol{\beta})'\mathbf{x}_0 \qquad (7A.6)$$

Thus, the variance of the prediction error is given by

$$
\begin{aligned}
\operatorname{var}(\hat{y}_0 - y_0)^2 &= E\left[(\hat{y}_0 - y_0)^2\right] \\
&= \mathbf{x}_0' E\left[(\mathbf{b} - \boldsymbol{\beta})(\mathbf{b} - \boldsymbol{\beta})'\right]\mathbf{x}_0 + E\left[e_0^2\right] - 2E\left[e_0(\mathbf{b} - \boldsymbol{\beta})' \mathbf{x}_0\right] \\
&= \mathbf{x}_0'\left[\operatorname{cov}(\mathbf{b})\right]\mathbf{x}_0 + \sigma^2 - 0 = \sigma^2 \mathbf{x}_0'\left(X'X\right)^{-1}\mathbf{x}_0 + \sigma^2 \\
&= \sigma^2\left[\mathbf{x}_0'\left(X'X\right)^{-1}\mathbf{x}_0 + 1\right]
\end{aligned}
\tag{7A.7}
$$

The term $E\left[e_0(\mathbf{b} - \boldsymbol{\beta})'\right]$ is equal to zero because the *future* disturbance e_0 is assumed uncorrelated with the least squares estimator $\mathbf{b}$ that depends only on *past* observations. The variance of the prediction error is made up of the following components:

(i) the component $\mathbf{x}_0'\left[\operatorname{cov}(\mathbf{b})\right]\mathbf{x}_0 = \sigma^2 \mathbf{x}_0'\left(X'X\right)^{-1}\mathbf{x}_0$, which depends on the covariance matrix for $\mathbf{b}$ and arises because $\mathbf{b}$ differs from $\boldsymbol{\beta}$, and

(ii) the component σ^2, which is the variance of the future error term and arises because this error will differ from its predicted value of zero.

If in equation 7.3.7 we replace $(X'X)^{-1}$ and $\mathbf{x}_0$ by their individual elements, it can be shown (see Exercise 7.17) that equation 7A.7 is equivalent to

$$
\operatorname{var}(\hat{y}_0 - y_0) = \sigma^2\left[1 + \frac{1}{T} + \frac{(x_0 - \bar{x})^2}{\Sigma(x_t - \bar{x})^2}\right]
\tag{7A.8}
$$

and

$$
\begin{aligned}
\widehat{\operatorname{var}}(\hat{y}_0 - y_0) &= \hat{\sigma}^2\left[1 + \mathbf{x}_0'\left(X'X\right)^{-1}\mathbf{x}_0\right] \\
&= \hat{\sigma}^2\left[1 + \frac{1}{T} + \frac{(x_0 - \bar{x})^2}{\Sigma(x_t - \bar{x})^2}\right]
\end{aligned}
\tag{7A.9}
$$

In conditional mean forecasting, for the mean we have

$$
E\left[\hat{y}_0\right] = E\left[b_1 + x_0 b_2\right] = \beta_1 + x_0 \beta_2 = \mathbf{x}_0'\boldsymbol{\beta}
\tag{7A.10}
$$

Thus $\hat{y}_0 = \mathbf{x}_0'\mathbf{b}$ is an unbiased estimator of $E\left[y_0\right] = \mathbf{x}_0'\boldsymbol{\beta}$ where $\mathbf{x}_0 = \begin{bmatrix} 1 & x_0 \end{bmatrix}'$. In line with equation 7A.5, $\hat{y}_0 - E\left[\hat{y}_0\right] = \mathbf{x}_0'(\mathbf{b} - \boldsymbol{\beta}) = (\mathbf{b} - \boldsymbol{\beta})'\mathbf{x}_0$ and the variance of the estimator $\hat{y}_0 = \mathbf{x}_0'\mathbf{b}$ is

$$
\begin{aligned}
\operatorname{var}(\hat{y}_0) &= E\left[\hat{y}_0 - E[\hat{y}_0]\right]^2 \\
&= E\left[\mathbf{x}_0'(\mathbf{b} - \boldsymbol{\beta})(\mathbf{b} - \boldsymbol{\beta})'\mathbf{x}_0\right] \\
&= \mathbf{x}_0' E\left[(\mathbf{b} - \boldsymbol{\beta})(\mathbf{b} - \boldsymbol{\beta})'\right]\mathbf{x}_0 \\
&= \sigma^2 \mathbf{x}_0'\left(X'X\right)^{-1}\mathbf{x}_0
\end{aligned}
\tag{7A.11}
$$

Chapter 8

The Simple Linear Statistical Model: Choosing the Functional Form, Reporting Results, and Carrying Through an Econometric Analysis

New Key Words and Concepts

Correlation
Measure of Goodness of Fit
Linear and Nonlinear
 Functional Forms
Government Expenditure
Tax Multipliers

Model for Economic Aggregate
 Consumption
Marginal Propensity to Consume
Empirical Results
Time Series Data

In the last three chapters we have considered the simple linear econometric-statistical model $y_t = \beta_1 + x_t\beta_2 + e_t$, where $e_t \sim (0, \sigma^2)$, and have developed procedures for estimating the unknown parameters and for drawing inferences in the form of interval estimates and hypothesis tests. To complete the analysis of this statistical model, in this chapter we will consider

(*i*)   a basis for gauging how well we are able to track the outcome variable y_t,

(*ii*) how to report the results of a statistical analysis, and

(*iii*) the alternative functional forms that are available for representing the relationship between y_t and x_t.

Finally, to integrate and make use of the tools of this and the preceding chapters, we carry through an analysis of an aggregate consumption function and discuss some of the possible economic problems for which the simple linear statistical model may be appropriate.

8.1   Explaining Variation in the Dependent Variable

The two major reasons for analyzing the model

$$y_t = \beta_1 + x_t\beta_2 + e_t \tag{8.1.1}$$

are to gather information on how expenditure on food (y_t) changes as income (x_t) changes, and to devise a method for predicting expenditure on food for a given level of income. These two objectives come under the broad headings of estimation and prediction. Closely allied with the prediction problem is the desire to explain as much of the variation in food expenditure (the dependent variable y_t) as possible. In using statistical model 8.1.1, we introduced the "explanatory" variable x_t in the hope of doing a better job of tracking the random variable y_t; better, that is, than using the model of the mean ($y_t = \beta + e_t$) introduced in Chapter 3. When one uses the model of the mean, the best predictor for y_t for *any* household is $\bar{y}$, the sample mean. There was no basis for explaining why the difference ($y_t - \bar{y}$) was, for example, a large positive quantity for some households and a large negative quantity for other households. Now, by using the statistical model 8.1.1, we can write the difference ($y_t - \bar{y}$) in terms of two components, a component of the difference that is attributable to income (x_t), and an unexplained component of the difference that is attributable to the error. Thus, we may write

$$y_t - \bar{y} = (\hat{y}_t - \bar{y}) + (y_t - \hat{y}_t)$$
$$= (\hat{y}_t - \bar{y}) + \hat{e}_t \tag{8.1.2a}$$

which in words is

total deviation = component explained by x + component unexplained

$$\tag{8.1.2b}$$

where $\hat{y}_t = b_1 + x_t b_2$ is the predicted level of expenditure for income level x_t, using estimates of β_1 and β_2. Equation 8.1.2 is illustrated in Figure 8.1. Note that $\hat{e}_t = y_t - \hat{y}_t$ is what we defined in Chapter 6 as a least squares residual. If our goal is accurate prediction, we would like the component explained by x, which is ($\hat{y}_t - \bar{y}$), to be large relative to the error component ($y_t - \hat{y}_t$). A large unexplained or unpredictable component would mean our prediction could be way off. In this section we are concerned with developing a measure of the proportion of variation in y_t that is explained by x_t. If this proportion is close to one, our model has predicted (tracked the sample observation y_t) well over the sample period. A small proportion implies that other predictable and unpredictable factors may contribute to a large part of the variation in y_t.

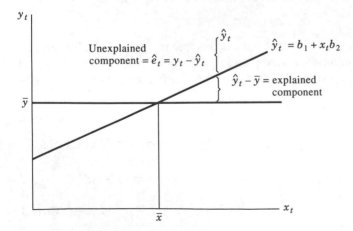

Figure 8.1 Explained and unexplained components of y_t.

The explained and unexplained components given in equation 8.1.2 will, of course, exist for each of our 40 observations. What we would like is *one* measure of the relative contribution of income toward explaining variation in y_t over all 40 observations. To get such a measure, we proceed as follows. Squaring both sides of equation 8.1.2 yields

$$\left(y_t - \bar{y}\right)^2 = \left(\hat{y}_t - \bar{y}\right)^2 + \hat{e}_t^2 + 2\left(\hat{y}_t - \bar{y}\right)\hat{e}_t$$

Summing over all observations, we have

$$\Sigma\left(y_t - \bar{y}\right)^2 = \Sigma\left(\hat{y}_t - \bar{y}\right)^2 + \Sigma\hat{e}_t^2 \tag{8.1.3a}$$

where a proof that $\Sigma(\hat{y}_t - \bar{y})\hat{e}_t = 0$ is left as an exercise (Exercise 8.1). Making these substitutions for our household consumption–income problem, we obtain

$$2607.04 = 826.64 + 1780.4 \tag{8.1.3b}$$

In equation 8.1.3 the terms are defined as follows:

$\Sigma(y_t - \bar{y})^2$ = total sum of squares (a measure of *total variation* in y_t about the sample mean).

$\Sigma(\hat{y}_t - \bar{y})^2$ = explained sum of squares or explained variation (that part of total variation in y about the sample mean explained by x).

$\Sigma\hat{e}_t^2$ = error or residual sum of squares or unexplained error variation (that part of total variation in y about the sample mean not explained by x).

Given these definitions, a measure of the *proportion of variation* in y explained by x is

$$R^2 = \frac{\Sigma\left(\hat{y}_t - \bar{y}\right)^2}{\Sigma\left(y_t - \bar{y}\right)^2} = \frac{\Sigma\left(y_t - \bar{y}\right)^2}{\Sigma\left(y_t - \bar{y}\right)^2} - \frac{\Sigma\hat{e}_t^2}{\Sigma\left(y_t - \bar{y}\right)^2} = 1 - \frac{\Sigma\hat{e}_t^2}{\Sigma\left(y_t - \bar{y}\right)^2} \tag{8.1.4}$$

where R^2 is called the *coefficient of determination*. The closer R^2 is to one, the better the job we have done in tracking y_t with $\hat{y}_t = b_1 + x_t b_2$ and the greater is the predictive ability (precision) of our model over the sample observations. For those who have been using the linear algebra notation, we can also write R^2 as

$$R^2 = 1 - \frac{\hat{e}'\hat{e}}{y'y - T\bar{y}^2} \tag{8.1.5}$$

where $\hat{e}'\hat{e} = \Sigma\hat{e}_t^2$ and $y'y - T\bar{y}^2 = \Sigma\left(y_t - \bar{y}\right)^2$.

For our household expenditure–income relationship based on the data in Table 5.2

$$R^2 = 1 - \frac{1780.4}{24875.07 - 40(23.5945)^2} = \frac{1780.4}{2607.0} = 0.317 \tag{8.1.6}$$

Thus, through the inclusion of the income variable, we have been able to explain 31.7% of the variation in food expenditure about the sample mean. Since it leaves 68.3% of the variation in y_t unexplained, the value $R^2 = 0.317$ is not a high one. It is nevertheless characteristic of many cross-sectional studies—studies that use data collected from a number of economic units, such as households, at a given point in time. With aggregate time-series data (data collected over time), larger R^2 values are more common. A low R^2 means that the predictive ability of a model is low, and hence explains the wide prediction interval in Section 7.3, but it does not necessarily mean that the coefficients β_1 and β_2 cannot be reliably estimated; the point and interval estimates for β_1 and β_2 are still proper reflections of our sample knowledge about them.

One final interpretive note should be made. A useful way to think about R^2 is that it is the square of the sample correlation coefficient between the two random variables y_t and $\hat{y}_t$. That is,

$$r_{\hat{y}y}^2 = \frac{\left[\Sigma(y_t - \bar{y})(\hat{y}_t - \bar{y})\right]^2}{\Sigma(y_t - \bar{y})^2 \, \Sigma(\hat{y}_t - \bar{y})^2} = R^2 \tag{8.1.7}$$

Consequently, the R^2 can be thought of as a measure of linear association between y_t and $\hat{y}_t$, as well as a measure of the proportion of the variation in y_t that is explained by the estimated equation. In other words, it is useful as a measure of how well the within sample predictions $\hat{y}_t$ match the realizations y_t. Sometimes it is referred to as a measure of goodness of fit. However, as we will see in the chapters to come, its potential for misuse is great and, when it is misused, the corresponding statistical and economic implications are rarely easy to draw.

8.2   Reporting–Summarizing Results

It is convenient at this point to stop and report, in a summary form, what we have learned thus far in general about parameter estimation and inference and in particular about the food expenditure–income relationship. A standard way of reporting the empirical results is

$$\hat{y}_t = 7.3832 + 0.2323x_t, \quad R^2 = 0.317$$
$$(4.008) \quad (0.0553) \tag{8.2.1}$$

The estimates $b_1 = 7.3832$ and $b_2 = 0.2323$ and the R^2 are self-explanatory. What may require some explanation is the numbers in parentheses underneath the estimated coefficients. These numbers are the square roots of the corresponding estimated variances. They are known as *standard errors*. Thus,

$$\text{standard error}\left(b_1\right) = \text{se}\left(b_1\right) = \sqrt{\text{vâr}\left(b_1\right)} = 4.008$$
$$\text{standard error}\left(b_2\right) = \text{se}\left(b_2\right) = \sqrt{\text{vâr}\left(b_2\right)} = 0.0553$$

Apart from tabulated critical values, equation 8.2.1 contains all the information that is required to construct interval estimates for β_1 or β_2 or to test hypotheses about β_1 or β_2.

Another conventional way to report results is to replace the standard errors with the "t-values" that arise when testing H_0: $\beta_1 = 0$ against H_1: $\beta_1 \neq 0$ and H_0: $\beta_2 = 0$ against H_1: $\beta_2 \neq 0$. These t values are given by

$$t = \frac{b_1}{\sqrt{\text{vâr}\left(b_1\right)}} = \frac{7.3832}{4.008} = 1.84$$

and

$$t = \frac{b_2}{\sqrt{\text{vâr}\left(b_2\right)}} = \frac{0.2323}{0.0553} = 4.20$$

Thus, our equation may be reported as

$$\hat{y}_t = 7.3832 + 0.2323 x_t \qquad R^2 = 0.317$$
$$(1.84) \quad (4.20) \tag{8.2.2}$$

Reporting the results in this way implicitly assumes that the null hypothesis H_0: $\beta_2 = 0$ is an important one; if $\beta_2 = 0$, then x does not influence y. It is less likely that the hypothesis H_0: $\beta_1 = 0$ is an important one. Nevertheless, it is conventional to also include the t-value for this hypothesis. In some analyses both the standard errors and t-values are reported in parentheses below the coefficients. However, you should note, given the t-statistics, that the standard errors are easily reconstructed by dividing the coefficient estimates by the corresponding t-statistics. Given the t-statistics it is sometimes useful to report the p-values, which are the probabilities of exceeding the computed t-value.

8.2.1   Computer Output

Output from most econometric computer programs contains at least the coefficient estimates, their standard errors, and corresponding t- and p-values, usually written in columns as in Table 8.1. In terms of p-values, in Table 8.1, $p[|t_{(38)}| > 1.84] = 0.074$ and $P[|t_{(38)}| > 4.20] = 0.000$. In the first case we do not reject H_0: $\beta_1 = 0$ at the $\alpha = .05$ level because $.074 > .05$. In the second case we reject H_0: $\beta_2 = 0$ because $.000 < .05$.

Another part of the computer output is what is known as the *analysis of variance* table (Table 8.2). This table gives the total variation in y, the variation explained by x and the unexplained variation. It also gives the ratio of the explained to the unexplained, which provides a test of the "significance" of the overall relationship. In this chapter, where there is only one explanatory variable, this ratio is equivalent to the t-test for H_0: $\beta_2 = 0$. In fact, as was discussed in Chapters 2 and 4, the ratio, which is an F-test statistic, is equal to the *square* of the t-test statistic value. We will return to this ratio or F-test in Chapter 10 when we consider a statistical model that has more than one explanatory x variable. However, let us illustrate for the estimated food expenditure–income relationship the information that is typically provided by an analysis of variance table.

The entries in the "variation" column are the explained sum of squares, the unexplained or error sum of squares, and the total sum of squares, respectively. The "degrees of freedom" entries are 1, $(T - 2)$, and $(T - 1)$. Each "mean square" is obtained by dividing each variation source by its corresponding number of degrees of freedom. Thus, $826.64 = 826.64/1$ and $46.85 = 1780.4/38$. Finally, as discussed in Section 4.4 of Chapter 4, the F-value is the ratio of the two mean squares, $17.64 = 826.64/46.85$. Note that F-value $= (t$-value$)^2$; that is, $17.64 = (4.20)^2$. A more detailed explanation of the F-test that leads to the value of 17.64 and its use in hypothesis testing will be given in Chapter 10. For our purposes in this chapter, it is sufficient to note that the t-test for H_0: $\beta_2 = 0$ serves the same purpose.

Table 8.1   Summary of Least Squares Results

Variable	Coefficient	Standard Error	t-Value (zero null)	p-Value
Constant	7.3832	4.0080	1.84	0.07330
Income	0.2323	0.0553	4.20	0.00016

Table 8.2   Analysis of Variance Table

Source of Variation	Degrees of Freedom	Mean Square	Explained/ Unexplained
Explained	826.64	1	826.64	17.64
Unexplained	1780.4	38	46.85	
Total	2607.0	39	66.847	

	In General		
Explained	$\Sigma(\hat{y}_t - \bar{y})^2$	1	$\Sigma(\hat{y}_t - \bar{y})^2 / 1$
Unexplained	$\Sigma(y_t - \hat{y})^2$	$T-2$	$\Sigma(y_t - \hat{y})^2 / (T-2) = \hat{\sigma}^2$
Total	$\Sigma(y_t - \bar{y})^2$	$T-1$	$\Sigma(y_t - \bar{y})^2 / (T-1)$

8.3   Questions Relative to the Algebraic Form of the Household Expenditure–Income Relationship

In this and the preceding three chapters we have studied situations in which a household expenditure variable is thought to be a linear function of a household income variable. Our task has been, within the context of a linear statistical model, to use a sample of economic data to estimate the coefficients of that *linear* function. We should emphasize that the theoretical model (equation 5.2.1) is an attempt to describe, within a probability context, how one variable is related to another and, as such, it is an attempt at economic model building. Specifying the algebraic form and the underlying error assumptions are necessary steps in going from an economic model to its statistical (econometric) model counterpart.

The statistical model we analyzed was specified to be linear in the expenditure–income variables. Perhaps it is now time to ask another what-if question: What if the functional form describing the expenditure–income relationship is not linear in the natural units of the variables? Economic principles suggest that as income increases, consumption expenditures increase, but that these increases may come at a decreasing rate. In other words, the linear (constant) relationship between expenditure and income may be in conflict with economic principles and thus with the data. In this section we examine a number of alternative functional forms. Many of them are consistent with a nonlinear relationship between expenditure and income. For a proper understanding of the characteristics of these functional forms, it is desirable to refer to Appendix 8A as you go through this section.

The linear in the variables and linear in the parameters specification that we used may have led you to believe that our statistical model was a restrictive one. Such is the case, but our model is not as restrictive as you might at first think. There is a rich variety of functional forms that can be used within this framework. For example, in the household expenditure–income problem, we could have used instead of the linear in variables and linear in the parameters form

$$y_t = \beta_1 + x_t \beta_2 + e_t \tag{8.3.1}$$

an alternative functional form,

$$y_t = \beta_1 + \left(\frac{1}{x_t}\right)\beta_2 + e_t$$

$$= \beta_1 + x_t^{-1}\beta_2 + e_t \tag{8.3.2}$$

that is nonlinear in the explanatory variable x_t. This function is graphed in Figure 8.2a, assuming that $\beta_1 > 0$ and $\beta_2 < 0$. Note that, for the expenditure–income problem, the use of equation 8.3.2 means that expenditure y_t approaches β_1 as the level of income x_t becomes very large. Another property is that when $x_t < -\beta_2/\beta_1$, expenditure on food is negative. A property such as this is clearly unrealistic and so, if this function was used, we would regard only that part above the x axis as an approximation to the expenditure–income relationship.

Following Appendix 8A, *to find how expenditure changes as income changes,* we examine the derivative

$$\frac{dy_t}{dx_t} = -\frac{\beta_2}{x_t^2}$$

(8.3.3)

The reason for assuming that $\beta_2 < 0$ with this reciprocal functional form is now clear. We expect expenditure to increase as income increases; that is, we expect $dy_t/dx_t > 0$. To make the derivative positive, we need β_2 to be negative. Also, the presence of x_t^2 in the denominator in equation 8.3.3 means that the increase in expenditure for a given increase in income will get smaller and smaller as income increases (expenditure increases at a decreasing rate). For large x_t, dy_t/dx_t will be almost zero. Based on results on elasticities developed in Appendices 5A and 8A, the corresponding income elasticity of food consumption for equation 8.3.2 is

$$\frac{dy_t}{dx_t}\frac{x_t}{y_t} = -\frac{\beta_2}{x_t^2}\frac{x_t}{y_t} = -\beta_2\frac{1}{x_t y_t}$$

The functional form of equation 8.3.2, *although nonlinear in the variables, is linear in the parameters β_1 and β_2.* Thus, our least-squares rule b_1 and b_2 can still be used.

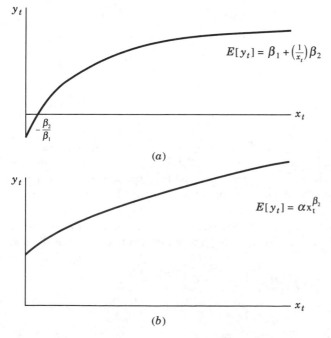

Figure 8.2   Two alternative nonlinear functions for explaining household expenditure.

All the inference and prediction procedures we have outlined in the last three chapters are still valid. Instead of x_t for the right-hand-side variable we use x_t^{-1}.

The two functional forms 8.3.1 and 8.3.2 are two very different ways of modeling the data and lead to estimates of the unknown parameters that have very different economic implications. In the case of food, the functional form 8.3.2 indicates that as income increases, household consumption of food increases at a decreasing rate and reaches an upper bound β_1. Consequently, this functional form does not contradict what we know about human behavior and the capacity for food consumption.

The functional form 8.3.2 reflects a parametric model that is nonlinear in terms of the variables but linear in terms of the parameters. One possible expenditure–income relationship, which is nonlinear in the parameters α and β_2, is the statistical model

$$y_t = \alpha x_t^{\beta_2} \exp\{e_t\} \tag{8.3.4a}$$

This function is graphed in Figure 8.2b, assuming that $\beta_2 < 1$. One nice feature of this model is that it can be rewritten in a linear form, that is, it can be rewritten as the linear model,

$$\ln y_t = \ln \alpha + \beta_2 \ln x_t + e_t$$
$$= \beta_1 + \beta_2 \ln x_t + e_t \tag{8.3.4b}$$

Here the nonlinear relationship between the parameters α and β_2 is transformed to a relationship that is linear in the parameters β_1 and β_2; again, the least squares estimation rule may be used. You should ask yourself how you would set inputs for the computer program in order to use the least squares rule.

To see what equations 8.3.4a and 8.3.4b imply about how expenditures increase as income increases (the marginal effect), we use the rules discussed in Appendix 3A and differentiate both sides of equation 8.3.4b with respect to x_t. From Example 5 in Appendix 8A, we have

$$\frac{d(\ln y_t)}{dy_t} \frac{dy_t}{dx_t} = \beta_2 \frac{d(\ln x_t)}{dx_t}$$
$$\frac{1}{y_t} \frac{dy_t}{dx_t} = \frac{\beta_2}{x_t}$$
$$\frac{dy_t}{dx_t} = \beta_2 \frac{y_t}{x_t} \tag{8.3.5}$$

If $\beta_2 < 1$, then, for all points that lie on the function, (y_t/x_t) declines as x_t increases (see Figure 8.2b). Thus, as with the function in equation 8.3.2, expenditure increases at a decreasing rate as income increases. No maximum value for expenditure exists in this case, however. Given equation 8.3.6, the income elasticity $(dy_t / dx_t)(x_t / y_t) = \beta_2$ and thus is *constant* over all values of x_t and y_t.

Two other nonlinear alternatives that are consistent with the linear-additive nature of our statistical model are the linear-log (semilog) and log-linear (exponential) forms. The semilog form

$$\exp\{y_t\} = \exp\{\beta_1\} x_t^{\beta_2} \exp\{e_t\} \tag{8.3.6a}$$

can be rewritten as the linear model

$$y_t = \beta_1 + \beta_2 \ln x_t + e_t \tag{8.3.6b}$$

where the marginal effect is

$$\frac{dy_t}{dx_t} = \beta_2 \frac{1}{x_t}$$

and the income elasticity is

$$\frac{dy_t}{dx_t} \frac{x_t}{y_t} = \beta_2 \frac{1}{y_t}$$

The exponential form

$$y_t = \exp\{\beta_1 + x_t\beta_2 + e_t\} \tag{8.3.7a}$$

may be rewritten in the linear-additive form

$$\ln y_t = \beta_1 + x_t\beta_2 + e_t \tag{8.3.7b}$$

The corresponding marginal effect is

$$\frac{dy_t}{dx_t} = \beta_2 \exp\{\beta_1 + x_t\beta_2 + e_t\} = \beta_2 y_t$$

and the elasticity is

$$\frac{dy_t}{dx_t} \frac{x_t}{y_t} = \beta_2 x_t$$

As another alternative the log-inverse function is often used to model sales response y_t to advertising x_t. The log-inverse function $\ln y_t = \beta_1 - (\beta_2 / x_t) + e_t$ is S shaped and implies increasing returns at low levels of advertising and diminishing returns at high levels. The inflection point $\beta_2/2$ identifies the minimum level of advertising necessary to achieve diminishing returns and thus the minimum profitable level. The sales response function becomes asymptotic to $\exp\{\beta_1\}$, which is the intercept of the advertising–sales response function. This function is graphed in Figure 8.3 and included in Table 8.3.

To provide a basis of comparison, the alternative nonlinear-linear additive functional forms are presented in Table 8.3.

We will investigate, in some of the exercises at the end of the chapter, some of the implications of these alternative functional forms for our household expenditure–income and other economic data. At this point the reader should be aware of the

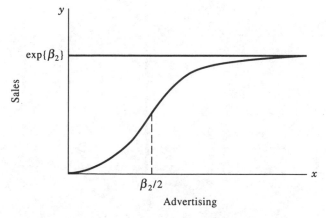

Figure 8.3 Log-inverse function sometimes used to model sales response to advertising.

Table 8.3 Some Conventional Functional Forms

Type	Nonlinear Form	Statistical Model (linear and additive form)	Impact at Margin $\frac{dy_t}{dx_t}$	Elasticity $\frac{dy_t}{dx_t}\frac{x_t}{y_t}$
Linear		$y_t = \beta_1 + x_t\beta_2 + e_t$	β_2	$\beta_2 \frac{x_t}{y_t}$
Reciprocal		$y_t = \beta_1 + \frac{1}{x_t}\beta_2 + e_t$	$-\beta_2 \frac{1}{x_t^2}$	$-\beta_2 \frac{1}{x_t y_t}$
Log-log	$y_t = \alpha_1 x_t^{\beta_2} \exp\{e_t\}$	$\ln y_t = \beta_1 + \beta_2 \ln x_t + e_t$	$\beta_2 \frac{y_t}{x_t}$	β_2
Log-linear (exponential)	$y_t = \exp\{\beta_1 + x_t\beta_2 + e_t\}$	$\ln y_t = \beta_1 + x_t\beta_2 + e_t$	$\beta_2 y_t$	$\beta_2 x_t$
Linear-log (semilog)	$\exp\{y_t\} = \exp\{\beta_1 + e_t\}x_t^{\beta_2}$	$y_t = \beta_1 + \beta_2 \ln x_t + e_t$	$\beta_2 \frac{1}{x_t}$	$\beta_2 \frac{1}{y_t}$
Log-inverse	$y_t = \exp\left\{\beta_1 - \frac{1}{x_t}\beta_2 + e_t\right\}$	$\ln y_t = \beta_1 - \frac{1}{x_t}\beta_2 + e_t$	$\beta_2 \frac{y_t}{x_t^2}$	$\beta_2 \frac{1}{x_t}$

flexibility that exists in regard to formulations that may be nonlinear in terms of the variables and the parameters.

8.4   Analysis of Another Estimation and Inference Problem

In Chapters 5–8 we have been concerned with estimating the unknown parameters of a relationship between two economic variables. As a basis for identifying and interpreting the appropriate econometric tools we considered food expenditure of individual households and how this expenditure depends on the level of household income. In this section, in order to summarize what we have learned in terms of estimation and inference, we are again concerned with methods for learning about the parameters of relationships between two economic variables, but we do so within the context of an aggregate economic relationship that is estimated using time-series data.

To estimate a function describing the dependence of household expenditure on income we used a random sample of *household data*, collected at a given point in time. Such data are called *cross-sectional data*. In this section we are concerned with an economic model for aggregate consumption (consumption for a whole economy). In particular, we are interested in how consumption changes as a result of changes in aggregate disposable income. We examine how these changes take place *over time* and use aggregate economic data observed over a sample of years. As noted in Chapter 20, time-series data are data on an economic unit (in our particular example, a complete economy), collected at different points in time. The sampling characteristics of time-series data may differ substantially from those of cross-sectional data; the econometric consequences of these differences occupy some of the chapters ahead.

To put the economic problem in context we begin by noting that, in macroeconomics, it is customary to separate an economy's aggregate expenditure (Y) into four categories: consumption (C), investment (I), government expenditure (G), and net foreign expenditure, or exports less imports ($X - M$). The familiar national income identity

$$Y \equiv C + I + G + (X - M)$$

is used to represent the four components. It is useful to make this categorization because different economic groups or agents are responsible for each type of expenditure and hence the determinants of each type of expenditure are likely to be different. If we can model the aggregate consumption behavior of households, or the aggregate investment behavior of firms, then we can go a long way toward predicting how these quantities will change as a result of changes in government policy. For example, it would be useful to know if and by how much a reduction in taxes would increase consumption; how does the effect of a temporary change in taxes differ from the effect of a permanent change in taxes? Also, if the government pursues a monetary policy that leads to an increase in interest rates, by how much will investment change? Will there be any change in consumption? We can attempt to answer these questions by specifying models or equations that describe the relationships between consumption and investment and their determinants and, given an appropriate sample of data, by using econometric techniques to estimate the equations.

The relationship of interest in this section is a consumption function, an equation that relates aggregate consumption expenditure to its determinants. This is just one more economic example, and you should keep in mind that *the techniques used have much wider applicability; they are relevant for estimation and inference in a wide range of economic problems.*

8.4.1   Economic Model for Aggregate Consumption

One simple way to model aggregate consumption is to specify that it is linearly related to disposable income; that is,

$$C = \beta_1 + \beta_2 Y_D \qquad (8.4.1)$$

where C represents aggregate consumption, Y_D represents disposable income (income less taxes or $Y_D = Y - T$, and β_1 and β_2 are the unknown parameters of the consumption function. The parameter β_1 is autonomous consumption, the quantity consumed when disposable income is zero. The other parameter β_2 is the marginal propensity to consume; it gives the change in consumption that occurs when disposable income changes by one unit. This rate of change can be written as the derivative

$$\frac{dC}{dY_D} = \beta_2 \qquad (8.4.2)$$

The marginal propensity to consume is an important parameter because it has a direct bearing on the multiplier or income-generating effects of government policy. To illustrate this effect, we substitute the consumption function $C = \beta_1 + \beta_2 Y_D$ or $C = \beta_1 + \beta_2(Y - T)$ into the national income identity. The result is

$$Y = \beta_1 + \beta_2 (Y - T) + I + G + (X - M) \qquad (8.4.3)$$

Solving this equation for Y we have

$$Y = \frac{\beta_1}{1 - \beta_2} - \frac{\beta_2 T}{1 - \beta_2} + \frac{I}{1 - \beta_2} + \frac{G}{1 - \beta_2} + \frac{(X - M)}{1 - \beta_2} \qquad (8.4.4)$$

From equation 8.4.4 we see that an increase in government expenditure G by one unit increases national income Y by $1/(1 - \beta_2)$ units. The term $1/(1 - \beta_2)$ is the government expenditure multiplier. Similarly, an increase in taxes T by one unit will decrease national income by $\beta_2/(1 - \beta_2)$ units. The term $-\beta_2/(1 - \beta_2)$ is the tax multiplier.

Because both multipliers depend on the unknown parameter β_2, it is important to learn something about the magnitude of β_2. Another problem is that of predicting future values of consumption for given levels of national income. For this prediction problem we need information on the autonomous consumption parameter β_1 as well as the marginal propensity to consume β_2. Thus, our objective in this section is to estimate, and make inferences, about the unknown parameters β_1 and β_2. The first step toward achieving this objective is to specify a statistical model that corresponds to equation 8.4.1 and that is consistent with an observed sample of data on C and Y_D. We will then need to choose appropriate statistical techniques to analyze the data and to provide information about β_1 and β_2 in terms of point estimates and the sampling characteristics of estimators for β_1 and β_2. The techniques that we use are based on results from Chapters 5 to 7. The least squares estimator introduced in Chapter 5 is used to provide point estimates for β_1 and β_2; corresponding interval estimates (Chapters 6 and 7) are used as an indication of the reliability of the point estimates.

8.4.2 Statistical Model and Data

To convert the economic model for the consumption function in equation 8.4.1 to a statistical model that we can use for estimation and inference, we make three changes. We change the notation to make it conform more to our statistical conventions; we add a subscript t to denote the tth observation; and we recognize that consumption will be made up of two components, the "systematic" component that depends on income, and a random unpredictable component that we capture with the error component e_t. After making these changes, we specify our statistical model as

$$y_t = \beta_1 + \beta_2 x_t + e_t \qquad (8.4.5)$$

where y_t denotes aggregate consumption in period t, x_t denotes disposable income in period t, and e_t is the equation error. By including the equation error, we are recognizing that it is impossible for equation 8.4.1 to hold exactly for all observations that we collect. The term e_t captures a multitude of effects. For example, there will be variables other than disposable income that influence consumption, the linear equation is likely to be only an approximation to reality, and it is probable that there is some unpredictable randomness in human behavior. In a given time period t, all these influences are combined to yield one value for the error e_t. If we knew precisely what functional form was relevant, and if we could specify and observe all relevant variables that influence consumption, then equation 8.4.5 should be modified accordingly. In practice, however, we cannot hope to do so, and we need to recognize that all economic and statistical models are simplified representations of reality.

To make the statistical model complete, we must specify the characteristics of the random errors e_t. If we have T observations on consumption y_t and income x_t, then there will be T realized errors. In line with Chapter 7, to describe the sampling process by which the y_t are generated, we continue to assume that these T unobservable values of e_t represent independent drawings from a normal distribution with mean zero and variance σ^2. Thus, in line with previous chapters, we write

$$e_t \sim N\left(0, \sigma^2\right) \qquad (8.4.6)$$

Because the drawings are assumed independent, the covariance between any pair of errors is zero, $E[e_t e_s] = 0$ for $t \neq s$. In later chapters we will examine the consequences of relaxing these assumptions about the errors and consider the particular stochastic characteristics of time-series errors. Another assumption that we make is that x_t and e_t are uncorrelated. That is, the combined effect of all other variables that we are collecting together in the error term is uncorrelated with income. The implications of relaxing this assumption are also examined later in the book.

For an empirical example of a consumption function, we will use 10 observations on disposable personal income and personal consumption expenditures for the U.S. economy for the period 1969–1978. These data are measured on a per capita basis and are expressed in terms of 1982 dollars. They can be found on p. 317 of *Economic Report of the President, 1991* and are reproduced in Table 8.4.

Because we have only chosen 10 observations, we should not be too optimistic about obtaining precise estimates for β_1 and β_2. A sample of size 10 is not large. On the other hand, one of the difficulties associated with using a long time-series of data to estimate a consumption function is that the parameters of the consumption function (the level of autonomous consumption β_1 and the marginal propensity to consume β_2) might change over time. A change in the underlying structure of the economy may mean a change in the nature of the consumption function. By choosing a small sample size, we decrease the chance of major changes in the parameters over the sample period. Other procedures for coping with parameters that may vary over time are discussed in Chapter 12.

It is customary to define an aggregate consumption function in *real* rather than *money* terms. For this reason the effects of inflation were eliminated from the data by expressing

Table 8.4 **U.S. Data on Consumption and Income**

Year	Per Capita Disposable Personal Income in 1982 Dollars	Per Capita Consumption in 1982 Dollars
69	7891	7185
70	8134	7275
71	8322	7409
72	8562	7726
73	9042	7972
74	8867	7826
75	8944	7926
76	9175	8272
77	9381	8551
78	9735	8808

all consumption and income values in constant (1982) dollar terms. Also, it is possible that the level of population may exert an influence on consumption separate from that exerted by income. To eliminate this possible population effect the data were expressed in per capita terms.

8.4.3 Estimation and Inference

The estimation and inference procedures that were introduced in Chapters 5 to 7 were considered desirable ones because of their properties in repeated samples. We were concerned with the *sampling characteristics* of point and interval estimators and of hypothesis testing procedures. We turn now to the results produced by these *sampling theory* procedures.

8.4.3a Statistical Model and Estimates   As a starting point in the sampling theory approach to learning about β_1 and β_2 in the statistical model $y_t = \beta_1 + x_t\beta_2 + e_t$, we have the consumption–income data given in Table 8.4. Given these data, to obtain point estimates of β_1 and β_2 we apply the least squares rule equation 5.3.10. This rule yields, via the computer,

$$\begin{bmatrix} b_1 \\ b_2 \end{bmatrix} = \begin{bmatrix} -128.9411 \\ 0.91126 \end{bmatrix} \tag{8.4.7}$$

Our estimate of the marginal propensity to consume is 0.91 and that for autonomous consumption is −128.94. We say more about these values later.

8.4.3b Sampling Variability   To gauge the reliability of the estimates, we need an estimate of the variances for b_1 and b_2. The first step in this direction is to obtain an estimate of the error variance σ^2. Using the unbiased estimator introduced in Chapter 6 we have

$$\hat{\sigma}^2 = \frac{\Sigma \hat{e}_t^2}{T-2} = \frac{87312.93}{8} = 10,914.12 \tag{8.4.8}$$

The estimated variances for b_1 and b_2 and covariance for (b_1, b_2) can now be computed using equation 6.4.2 and displayed as

$$
\begin{bmatrix}
\text{v\^ar}(b_1) & \text{c\^ov}(b_1, b_2) \\
\text{c\^ov}(b_1, b_2) & \text{v\^ar}(b_1)
\end{bmatrix}
=
\begin{bmatrix}
\hat{\sigma}^2\left(\dfrac{\Sigma x_t^2}{T(\Sigma x_t - \bar{x})^2}\right) & \hat{\sigma}^2\left(\dfrac{-\bar{x}}{\Sigma(x_t - \bar{x})^2}\right) \\[3mm]
\hat{\sigma}^2\left(\dfrac{-\bar{x}}{\Sigma(x_t - \bar{x})^2}\right) & \dfrac{\hat{\sigma}^2}{\Sigma(x_t - \bar{x})^2}
\end{bmatrix}
$$

$$
= 10914.12
\begin{bmatrix}
26.02321 & -0.29440 \times 10^{-2} \\
-0.29440 \times 10^{-2} & 0.33435 \times 10^{-6}
\end{bmatrix}
$$

$$
=
\begin{bmatrix}
284020.3 & -32.132 \\
-32.132 & 0.0036491
\end{bmatrix}
$$

(8.4.9)

Those who are using the linear algebra notation developed in Section 6.6 will recognize equation 8.4.9 as $\text{c\^ov}(\mathbf{b}) = \hat{\sigma}^2 (X'X)^{-1}$. The square roots of the variances of b_1 and b_2 (diagonal elements of equation 8.4.9) are the standard errors for b_1 and b_2. Later, we will want to use these standard errors for testing hypotheses about β_1 and β_2 and for constructing confidence intervals that give us an idea of how precisely we have estimated β_1 and β_2. We have

$$
\text{se}(b_1) = \sqrt{284020.3} = 532.94 \tag{8.4.10a}
$$

and

$$
\text{se}(b_2) = \sqrt{0.0036491} = 0.060408 \tag{8.4.10b}
$$

The estimated covariance between b_1 and b_2 is given by $\text{c\^ov}(b_1, b_2) = -32.132$. The negative value indicates that, in any sample where β_2 is overestimated, it is likely that β_1 will be underestimated, and vice versa.

To find out how well the model fits the data or, in other words, how well the model predicts over the sample period, we use the goodness-of-fit statistic R^2. Our computations for this measure yield

$$
R^2 = 1 - \frac{\Sigma \hat{e}_t^2}{\Sigma(y_t - \bar{y})^2} = 1 - \frac{87312.93}{2570942} = 0.966 \tag{8.4.11}
$$

This value tells us that 96.6% of the variation in per capita consumption has been explained by the variation in per capita disposable income. In this regard the economic-statistical model chosen has performed well.

The information that we have collected so far can be summarized using a format introduced in Section 8.2. Our estimated equation is given by

$$
\hat{y}_t = -128.94 + 0.9113 x_t \qquad R^2 = 0.966
$$
$$
\quad\;\;(532.94)\quad(0.0604) \tag{8.4.12}
$$

where the numbers in parenthesis below the estimated coefficients are the corresponding standard errors.

8.4.3c Interval Estimation and Hypothesis Testing
The estimates in equation 8.4.12 can be used in conjunction with their standard errors to construct interval estimates for each of the parameters. For a 95% interval estimate, the appropri-

ate critical value from the t-distribution with 8 degrees of freedom is $t_c = 2.306$. Thus, a 95% interval estimate for β_1 is

$$b_1 - t_c \operatorname{se}(b_1) \le \beta_1 \le b_1 + t_c \operatorname{se}(b_1)$$

or

$$-128.94 - (2.306)(532.94) \le \beta_1 \le -128.94 + (2.306)(532.94)$$

or

$$-1358 \le \beta_1 \le 1100 \tag{8.4.13}$$

Our interval estimate for β_1 suggests that autonomous consumption could be as high as \$1100 and as low as −\$1358. For a 95% interval estimate for β_2 we obtain

$$b_2 - t_c \operatorname{se}(b_2) \le \beta_2 \le b_2 + t_c \operatorname{se}(b_2)$$

or

$$0.9113 - (2.306)(0.0604) \le \beta_2 \le 0.9113 + (2.306)(0.0604)$$

or

$$0.772 \le \beta_2 \le 1.051 \tag{8.4.14}$$

This interval suggests a range for the marginal propensity to consume between 0.772 and 1.051.

Let us now consider a hypothesis test about the marginal propensity to consume. Further comments on our point and interval estimates and the information they convey will be made after we consider this test. Suppose that it is critical for the government to learn whether or not the government expenditure multiplier is greater than 10. From the advice of its economists, the government presumes that the multiplier is less than 10, but it would like to know if there is strong evidence to the contrary before implementing a specific policy. A multiplier $1/(1 - \beta_2) = 10$ arises when the marginal propensity to consume $\beta_2 = 0.9$. Thus, a pair of hypotheses relevant for the government's question is

$$H_0 : \beta_2 \le 0.9 \quad H_1 : \beta_2 > 0.9 \tag{8.4.15}$$

From the results in Chapter 7 we know that

$$t = \frac{b_2 - \beta_2}{\operatorname{se}(b_2)} \sim t_{(T-2)} \tag{8.4.16}$$

Assuming that H_0 is true, and using the least favorable value for β_2 under H_0, the calculated value for the t statistic in equation 8.4.16 is

$$t = \frac{0.91126 - 0.9}{0.060408} = 0.186 \tag{8.4.17}$$

At a 5% significance level the critical value for this one-tailed test is $t_c = 1.86$. Since $t = 0.186 < 1.86 = t_c$, we conclude that there is insufficient evidence in the sample to contradict H_0. An equivalent way to make a test decision is to compute the p-value that is given by $P[t_{(8)} > .186] = 0.428$. Since $0.429 > 0.05$, we do not reject H_0. Thus the government will stick with its presumption that $\beta_2 \le 0.9$, and that the multiplier is less than 10.

8.4.3d Interpreting the Results   Let us look more closely at our point estimate $b_1 = -128.94$ and interval estimate $\left(-1358 \le \beta_1 \le 1100 \right)$ for autonomous consumption. First, what have we learned about autonomous consumption? The negative value of approximately -129 dollars is nonsensical; consumption cannot be negative, even at a zero level of income. Can we give an explanation for this seemingly weird estimate? One possibility is that we have a bad model. There could be some relevant explanatory variables, other than per capita income, that we have omitted from the function. We might have the wrong functional form. Our stochastic assumptions about the equation errors might be inappropriate. However, *even within the framework of the model we are using*, there are two possible explanations for a negative value. The first explanation is that the estimate might be imprecise or unreliable. The interval estimate $(-1358, 1100)$ is a wide one that includes a considerable range of positive values. Thus, it is quite likely that autonomous consumption is indeed positive but, because of sampling error, our one sample has produced a negative point estimate. If we use information from the sample alone, and not information from our economic principles, it is difficult to say whether β_1 is negative or positive.

The second possible explanation for a negative estimate for β_1 is that the model may be only a reasonable approximation in the region for which we have data. If there are no years when income is approximately zero, then perhaps it is asking too much to have the data tell us what the level of consumption will be at a zero income level. Under these circumstances we treat β_1 as a parameter that helps determine the position of the estimated line in the region of the data, and as such it is important for prediction, but we do not attempt to give β_1 an economic interpretation.

The point estimate of approximately 0.91 for the marginal propensity to consume is a reasonable one, but the interval estimate of $(0.772, 1.051)$ is not very informative. The lower limit of this interval leads to a multiplier of 4.4; the upper limit of 1.051 is greater than 1 and hence is not a feasible value. If we excluded from the interval the infeasible range from 1 to 1.051, then the multiplier from an upper limit of 1 is infinite! A research report that said the multiplier lies between 4.4 and infinity would not be an informative one.

The fact that both our interval estimates include infeasible parameter ranges raises an interesting question. Since we know that negative values of β_1 are impossible, and values of β_2 greater than 1 are impossible, is it meaningful to present interval estimates that include such infeasible values? With β_1 we have the additional complication that the *point* estimate is an infeasible value. When we use sampling theory procedures that make no provision for including prior inequality information, there is no way of avoiding the infeasible point and interval estimates that arise from our sample of data. In Chapters 24 and 25 we consider another way of using the data to construct point and interval estimates that includes information and yields results consistent with our economic principles.

The purpose of this econometric analysis was to suggest *(i)* how one goes about learning from a sample of data, or in other words, *(ii)* how an economic and statistical model, sample data, and sampling theory procedures may be used as a basis for estimation and inference. In the next section we consider several other traditional economic-statistical models.

8.5   Other Economic-Statistical Models

We have focused in this chapter on a statistical model that provides a basis for estimating the unknown parameters for a household expenditure–income relationship and for an aggregate consumption function. Fortunately, this statistical model can be used as a basis for estimation and inference for a variety of economic relationships. Examples can be taken from almost every two-dimensional diagram that appears in introductory and intermediate economics books. One of the first that may come to mind is a partial equilibrium demand relation connecting the quantity consumed and price. Most text books model this in the linear form

$$y_t^d = \beta_1 + x_t \beta_2 + e_t \qquad (8.5.1a)$$

where y_t^d is the quantity consumed in the tth period and x_t is the corresponding price. Alternatively, if this linear in the variables world does not seem appropriate, the double log function

$$y_t^d = \beta_1 x_t^{\beta_2} \exp\{e_t\} \qquad (8.5.1b)$$

or

$$\ln y_t^d = \ln \beta_1 + \beta_2 \ln x_t + e_t \qquad (8.5.1c)$$

is often used in applied work, as indicated in Section 8.3 and Appendix 8A, and yields a constant price elasticity of demand equal to β_2.

In economics textbooks the other side of the scissors is the supply relation, which is often modeled as

$$y_t^s = \beta_1 + x_t \beta_2 + e_t \qquad (8.5.2)$$

where y_t^s is the quantity produced and x_t is the corresponding price. Alternatively, we may have a supply relation where the production decision is based on the price in a previous time period and thus lagged price $x_{(t-1)}$ is the right-hand-side variable in equation 8.5.2. We will have much more to say about the modeling of these demand and supply relationships in Chapter 18, when we look at the implications of the price and quantity variables being jointly or interdependently determined.

Another basic economic relation that can be reflected by the simple linear statistical model is the production function (input–output relation). To permit a decreasing marginal product, this relation is often modeled as

$$y_t = \beta_1 x_t^{\beta_2} \exp\{e_t\} \qquad (8.5.3a)$$

or

$$\ln y_t = \ln \beta_1 + \beta_2 \ln x_t + e_t \qquad (8.5.3b)$$

where y_t is output and x_t is the primary resource input. Given a decreasing marginal product, $\beta_2 < 1$, and prices for the output and the input, the optimum level of input and output can then be determined.

Of course, the mirror of the production function is the cost function, and here our statistical model can be used along with the data as a basis for estimating the parameters of the total, average, and marginal cost functions. In this context the total cost function might be modeled as

$$y_t = \beta_1 + x_t^2 \beta_2 + e_t \qquad (8.5.4a)$$

where y_t is total cost and x_t is the corresponding quantity produced. This total cost function leads to the following average cost function

$$\frac{y_t}{x_t} = \beta_1 \frac{1}{x_t} + x_t \beta_2 + \frac{e_t}{x_t} \qquad (8.5.4b)$$

and marginal cost function

$$\frac{dy_t}{dx_t} = 2 x_t \beta_2 \qquad (8.5.4c)$$

The result in equation 8.5.4b suggests that the model

$$\frac{y_t}{x_t} = \beta_1 \frac{1}{x_t} + x_t \beta_2 + e_t \frac{1}{x_t} \tag{8.5.4d}$$

might serve as the statistical model if we estimated the average cost directly from a sample of cost-quantity data. Alternatively, we might begin with an alternative statistical model for average cost such as the reciprocal function

$$y_t = \beta_1 + \frac{1}{x_t} \beta_2 + e_t \tag{8.5.5a}$$

where y_t is now average cost. This would then yield a total cost function

$$y_t x_t = x_t \beta_1 + \beta_2 + x_t e_t \tag{8.5.5b}$$

as the relevant statistical model.

Examples of textbook diagrams in the macroeconomics area involve such well-known aggregate functions as consumption and investment where aggregate consumption, aggregate income, aggregate investment, and the interest rate are the relevant economic variables and data.

One important relationship in the macro literature is the Phillips curve that was suggested by A. W. Phillips in 1958. This important relationship conjectures a systematic relationship between changes in the wage rate and changes in the level of unemployment. Let's see if we can build an economic and statistical model for this hypothesis. If we let w_t be the wage rate in time t, we may represent the proportional or percentage change in the wage rate as

$$\dot{w}_t = \frac{w_t - w_{t-1}}{w_{t-1}} \tag{8.5.6}$$

If we assume that $\dot{w}_t$ is proportional to the excess demand for labor d_t, we may write

$$\dot{w}_t = \gamma d_t \tag{8.5.7}$$

where γ is some constant. Since the unemployment rate u_t is inversely related to the excess demand for labor, we could write this using our reciprocal function as

$$d_t = a + c \frac{1}{u_t} \tag{8.5.8}$$

Given equation 8.5.7 we may then specify $\dot{w}_t$ as

$$\dot{w}_t = \gamma \left(a + c \frac{1}{u_t} \right)$$
$$= \gamma a + \gamma c \frac{1}{u_t} \tag{8.5.9}$$

where $\dot{w}_t$ is linearly related to the nonlinear-reciprocal variable u_t. An appropriate linear statistical model may then be

$$y_t = \beta_1 + x_t \beta_2 + e_t \tag{8.5.10}$$

where $y_t = \dot{w}_t = (w_t - w_{t-1})/w_{t-1}$, $x_t = 1/u_t$, and e_t is a normal random equation error.

Economic theory is rich with possible relationships between economic variables, and thus there are a large number of possibilities for making use of our linear statistical model. With each economic model we must, of course, ask questions as to the appropriate assumptions concerning the error process in the statistical model. For example, in estimating a demand relationship, can we assume that the errors are independent and/or identical from drawing to drawing? Also, what is the correct functional form:Is it linear or is it nonlinear with a constant elasticity? And finally, is the statistical model realistic in describing the sampling process underlying the data generation? These are all questions that are taken up later in the book. Of immediate interest in the next chapter is whether we might conclude that relevant explanatory variables are omitted if we restrict ourselves to the simple $y = f(x, \beta) + e$ linear statistical model with only one explanatory variable. For example, in a demand relationship both price and income should be included as explanatory variables for determining the level of consumption. In a production function there are usually two or more inputs. In the Phillips curve inflation expectations and productivity are usually important. This means we will frequently need a more general statistical model to capture the characteristics of economic data and it is to this task that we turn in Chapter 9.

8.6   Critique of Concepts

We started in Chapter 5 with the objective of learning about a simple economic relationship from a sample of data involving two economic variables—household expenditure and household income. In order to model the data, we specified a simple linear statistical model that we hoped would reflect the sampling process by which the data were generated. The statistical model we specified involved two coefficients β_1 and β_2 and the variance parameter σ^2. We then faced the question of how to use the sample observations to estimate these unknown parameters realizing that, if we could obtain "good" estimates of β_1 and β_2, then we would be in a position, given the level of household income, to make predictions about the most probable outcomes for household expenditures y. We made use of the criterion that sought to find β_1 and β_2, for our data, so as to minimize the equation residual (error) sum of squares. This led to the least squares estimator or rule that we were able to demonstrate was unbiased; we also established that within the class of linear unbiased rules the least squares estimator had minimum sampling variability. Using this rule we then obtained estimates of β_1 and β_2 and their sampling variability. Under the assumption that the e_t were normally distributed random variables, we were able to obtain the sampling distribution for the random variables b_1 and b_2 and to develop interval estimates and make hypothesis tests. Procedures for prediction and forecasting were developed and a measure of goodness-of-fit R^2 was specified. To summarize what we had learned about the process of estimation and inference, we specified and analyzed an economic–statistical model for aggregate consumption. Chapter 8, the last chapter in Part II, ended with a discussion of alternative possible algebraic forms for the economic-statistical relation and a consideration of the range of economic problems that might be considered when using this simple statistical model. At this point we are painfully aware that a statistical model involving a single x variable and a linear in the parameters and variables specification may be only a first approximation in the process of obtaining information from a sample of economic data.

The formulations and problems discussed in Chapters 5 to 8 (Part II) provide a brief introduction to the first of a large number of what-if situations that you will confront as you learn about and practice econometrics. In general a large number of advancements in knowledge are brought about by someone looking at a situation and asking the question "what if ...?" This is certainly true in econometrics, since there are many ways to specify a sampling process by which economic data may be generated. Thus, in a sense, every assumption underlying our statistical model is questionable. Economic models reflect various data generation schemes and thus provide one basis for raising this question. If you will add this what-if tool in your analysis of problems, not only will you be rewarded in many instances for having asked the right question but your associates will also think you very clever.

8.7 Exercises

8.1. Prove that

$$\Sigma(\hat{y}_t - \bar{y})\hat{e}_t = 0$$

See equation 8.1.3a.

8.2. Consider the problem of estimating a production function that expresses the relationship between the level of output of a commodity and the level of input of a factor and assume that you have the input–output data that we used in Chapter 5 and that is given in Table 8.5.

(a) Assume first that the data can be described by the statistical model $y_t = \beta_1 + x_t\beta_2 + e_t$, where the random variable $e_t \sim (0, \sigma^2)$. Set up the sums of squares and cross products corresponding to the data and with these results, use the least-squares rule to estimate β_1, β_2, and σ^2 and determine R^2.

(b) Assume that the data can be described by the functional form $y_t = \alpha x_t^{\beta_2}$. Write the statistical model $y_t = \alpha x_t^{\beta_2} \exp\{e_t\}$ in a linear form and use the least squares rule to estimate $\beta_1 = \ln \alpha$ and β_2 and determine R^2.

(c) Use the results of parts (a) and (b) to plot the respective production functions. For each functional form, predict the output from eight units of input. Estimate the corresponding prediction error for the statistical model in part (a).

(d) Assume the feed cost P_x is 6 cents per pound and the price of poultry P_y is 30 cents per pound. Use the estimated production function obtained in part (b) to determine the optimum level of feed inputs and poultry food outputs and discuss the economic principle used in your result.

(e) The total cost function indicates how cost of production increases as output increases. Based on the results from part (b) derive the total cost function ($T_c = P_x x$), and using the food outputs given in (d), determine the optimum level of output.

(f) If you had only sample observations on the food outputs and total feed costs, is there any way, assuming the functional form in (b), to get an estimate of the parameter β_2 in the production function connecting feed inputs and food outputs?

(g) How would you make a choice between the two algebraic forms in (a) and (b)?

8.3. Using the data in Table 8.4, consider a functional form different from that employed in Section 8.4 and estimate the corresponding consumption expenditures–disposable personal income relationship.

(a) Give the economic logic behind your functional form choice.

(b) How would you choose between the two alternative models?

Table 8.5 **A Sample of Observations from a Controlled Experiment Involving Poultry Meat Outputs, Feed Inputs, and Total Feed Costs**

Input	Output	Total Feed Costs
x	y	z
1.00	0.58	0.06
2.00	1.10	0.12
3.00	1.20	0.18
4.00	1.30	0.24
5.00	1.95	0.30
6.00	2.55	0.36
7.00	2.60	0.42
8.00	2.90	0.48
9.00	3.45	0.54
10.00	3.50	0.60
11.00	3.60	0.66
12.00	4.10	0.72
13.00	4.35	0.78
14.00	4.40	0.84
15.00	4.50	0.90

8.4. The version of the so-called Phillips curve that was introduced in Section 8.5 says that the rate of change of money wages is a function of the reciprocal of the unemployment rate. Specifically, let

w_t = money wage rate in year t

u_t = unemployment rate in year t

$\dot{w}_t = \left(\dfrac{w_t - w_{t-1}}{w_{t-1}} \right) \times 100$ = percentage rate of change in the wage rate

The Phillips curve is given by

$$\dot{w}_t = \beta_1 + \beta_2 \left(\frac{1}{u_t} \right) + e_t$$

where it is hypothesized that $\beta_1 < 0$ and $\beta_2 > 0$. Use the country data given in Table 8.6 to

(a) Find least squares estimates for β_1 and β_2.
(b) Test whether there is any relationship between $\dot{w}$ and $(1/u)$.
(c) Draw a graph of the estimated relationship with u on the horizontal axis and $\dot{w}$ on the vertical axis.
(d) Find an estimate for the "natural rate of unemployment" (the natural rate of unemployment is the rate for which $\dot{w} = 0$).
(e) Find estimates for $d\dot{w}/du$ when $u = 1$ and when $u = 3$.
(f) When does a change in the unemployment rate have the greatest impact on the rate of change in wages? When does it have the smallest?
(g) What is the economic meaning of β_1?
(h) Find 95% interval estimates for β_1 and β_2.

Table 8.6 **Data on w_t and u_t for the Period 1949 to 1966**

Year	w_t	u_t
1949	1.62	1.0
1950	1.65	1.4
1951	1.79	1.1
1952	1.94	1.5
1953	2.03	1.5
1954	2.12	1.2
1955	2.26	1.0
1956	2.44	1.1
1957	2.57	1.3
1958	2.66	1.8
1959	2.73	1.9
1960	2.80	1.5
1961	2.92	1.4
1962	3.02	1.8
1963	3.13	1.1
1964	3.28	1.5
1965	3.43	1.3
1966	3.58	1.4

8.5. (a) Write up the research results for Exercise 8.4. As noted in Section 26.3 of Chapter 26, your write-up should include the economic model, the statistical model, the sample observations, the estimation methods, the empirical results, the statistical implications, and the economic implications.

   (b) Suppose you did not have the sample of data given in Table 8.6. Locate the sources and develop the nominal wage change $\dot{w}_t$ and unemployment rate u observations for the period 1974–1983 for the U. S. economy.

   (c) Carry through an econometric analysis of the data obtained under (b).

8.6. The catering company Thirst Quenchers has a contract to supply soda at the University of California football games. They suspect that the major factor influencing the quantity of soda consumed is the maximum temperature on the day of each game. The last three football seasons have yielded the data in Table 8.7.

   (a) Estimate a linear equation that relates the quantity of soda sold to the maximum temperature. Construct 95% interval estimates for each of the parameters. Comment on the results.

   (b) Is there evidence to suggest that the temperature does influence the quantity consumed?

   (c) At the 18 games from which the data were collected, there was always enough soda available to meet demand. Suppose that Thirst Quenchers decides to stock 1100 gallons for the next game. What is the probability that they will run out of soda if the maximum temperature is (*i*) 70° and (*ii*) 75°? (To work out these probabilities assume that the coefficient vector β and the error variance σ^2 have been estimated without sampling error.)

   (d) Suppose that Thirst Quenchers can always accurately predict the maximum temperature on the day of the game. Suppose also that their decision rule is to stock 30 gallons more soda than their predicted requirements. Find the probability that they will run out of soda when the maximum temperature is (*i*) 70° and (*ii*) 80°. (Allow for sampling error in the estimation of β but assume that the error variance σ^2 has been estimated without sampling error.)

Table 8.7 Data for Exercise 8.6

Game	Soda Sold (gallons)	Max. Temp. °F	Game	Soda Sold (gallons)	Max. Temp °F
1	1250	81	10	1410	84
2	890	60	11	987	69
3	1093	73	12	1198	77
4	1546	86	13	1429	85
5	635	58	14	1147	74
6	937	68	15	1200	74
7	1142	75	16	904	62
8	1120	76	17	1342	83
9	1067	72	18	1005	70

8.8 References

For a more complete discussion of the theoretical basis for the concepts introduced in Part II, see:

JUDGE, G .G., R. C. HILL, W. E. GRIFFITHS, H. LÜTKEPOHL AND T. C. LEE (1988) *Introduction to the Theory and Practice of Econometrics*, New York: John Wiley & Sons, Inc., pp. 159–274.

For a discussion of the economic basis and implications of the Phillips curve and other aggregate economic relations, see a macroeconomics textbook such as:

SHEFFRIN, S. M., D. A. WILTON AND D. M. PRESCOTT (1988) *Macroeconomics: Theory and Policy*, Cincinnati, OH: South-Western Publishing Co., pp. 231–246.

APPENDIX 8A   The Derivative Revisited

We have considered in Section 8.3 of Chapter 8 alternative functional forms for modeling the way an outcome variable y depends on an explanatory variable x. Since in economics rates of change are important, the choice of a functional form should always involve a consideration of the nature of the corresponding derivative dy/dx. Our knowledge of economics often suggests how an outcome variable y will change in response to a change in x. Since this knowledge is described by the derivative dy/dx, it is important to choose a function that has a derivative compatible with our knowledge. For example, if the change in y is likely to be constant, a linear function is appropriate. If the change depends on x, then a quadratic function or a function involving logarithms might be appropriate.

In Appendix 3A of Chapter 3 the derivative of a function $y = f(x)$ at the point (x, y) was defined as

$$\frac{dy}{dx} = \lim_{\Delta x \to 0} \frac{f(x + \Delta x) - f(x)}{\Delta x} \tag{8A.1}$$

Geometrically, this derivative represents the slope of the curve $y = f(x)$ at the point (x, y). It is the rate of response of y to a change in x at that point. Its units of measurement are units of y per unit of x. Except where $y = f(x)$ is a straight line, the derivative dy/dx depends on x. That is, the slope of the function, or the rate of response, changes as x changes. Consequently, if we pick a point (x, y) and think of the derivative at this point as describing the change in y that results from a change in x at this point, we must think in terms of a change in x that is small relative to the magnitude of x. Various rules for obtaining derivatives were also described in Appendix 3A. In this appendix we review and extend these rules and relate them to the question of functional form, by considering a number of examples.

Example 1

In equation 5.1.1 of Chapter 5, we related expenditure on food (y) to income (x) through the equation

$$y = \beta_1 + \beta_2 x \tag{8A.2}$$

Using the rules in Appendix 3A, the derivative of this function is given by

$$\frac{dy}{dx} = \beta_2 \tag{8A.3}$$

In this case the relationship between y and x is a straight line; as a consequence, the derivative (or slope or marginal propensity to spend on food) is a constant, namely β_2. A one-unit increase in income leads to a change in food expenditure of β_2 units. The fact that β_2 is a constant means that the change in food expenditure is the same (β_2) irrespective of the level of income. ■

Example 2

Consider the linear demand equation

$$q = \beta_1 + \beta_2 p \tag{8A.4}$$

where quantity demanded (q) is a function of price (p). This example is similar to the first in the sense that the derivative $dq/dp = \beta_2$ is a constant. A one-unit increase in price leads to a change in quantity demanded of β_2 units. One difference is that we would expect β_2 to be negative; an increase in price leads to a decrease in quantity demanded.

Let us consider the definition of total revenue (tr), which corresponds to the demand in equation 8A.4. It is given by

$$tr = pq = \beta_1 p + \beta_2 p^2 \tag{8A.5}$$

Marginal revenue (mr), which describes how total revenue changes in response to a price change, is given by the derivative

$$mr = \frac{d(tr)}{dp} = \beta_1 + 2\beta_2 p \tag{8A.6}$$

Given the expected signs, $\beta_1 > 0$ and $\beta_2 < 0$, marginal revenue will be positive when p is small and negative when p is large. That is, when price is low, increasing price increases total revenue (demand is inelastic). When price is high, increasing price decreases total revenue (demand is elastic). Elasticities were considered in Appendix 5A and will be considered later on in this appendix. You may be more familiar with mr in terms of quantity. If so, you may want to write the demand function as $p = \alpha_1 + \alpha_2 q$ and tr as $tr = \alpha_1 + \alpha_2 q^2$ and obtain mr and give it a quantity interpretation. ■

ider the one-input production function

$$y = \alpha x^{\beta} \tag{8A.7}$$

where y denotes output and x denotes the input. The response of output to a change in the level of the input is known as the marginal product (mp) of that input. It is given by the derivative

$$mp = \frac{dy}{dx} = \alpha\beta x^{\beta-1} \tag{8A.8}$$

This example is one where it is sometimes more convenient to include y in the expression for the derivative. Specifically, using equation 8A.7,

$$mp = \frac{dy}{dx} = \alpha\beta x^{\beta-1} = \frac{\alpha\beta x^{\beta}}{x} = \frac{\beta y}{x} \tag{8A.9}$$

The theory of the firm tells us that a marginal product should be positive but a decreasing function of the input x. From equation 8A.9, it is clear that mp is positive if $\beta > 0$. To discover when mp is a decreasing function of x we take the derivative $d(mp)/dx$, which tells us how mp changes when x changes. From equation 8A.8, it is given by

$$\frac{d(mp)}{dx} = \frac{d^2 y}{dx^2} = \alpha\beta(\beta-1)x^{\beta-2} \tag{8A.10}$$

For an increase in x to lead to a decrease in the marginal product we require $d(mp)/dx$ to be negative. That is, we need $\beta < 1$. Thus, we have established that, for the production function in (8A.7) to satisfy conditions prescribed by the theory of the firm, we need the condition $0 < \beta < 1$.   ∎

Example 4

In many instances to describe an economic relation it is necessary to use functions that contain the logarithms of x and/or y. As an example, suppose that quantity demanded y depends on the logarithm of price x through the equation

$$y = \beta_1 + \beta_2 \ln x \tag{8A.11}$$

To evaluate how quantity demanded changes in response to a change in x, we need the derivative dy/dx. It is given by

$$\frac{dy}{dx} = \beta_2 \frac{d(\ln x)}{dx} \tag{8A.12}$$

Thus, to evaluate this derivative, we need a new rule, one for differentiating a logarithm. This rule is given by

$$\frac{d(\ln x)}{dx} = \frac{1}{x} \tag{8A.13}$$

Using this result, the response of quantity demanded to a change in price is given by

$$\frac{dy}{dx} = \frac{\beta_2}{x} \tag{8A.14}$$

This result suggests that the higher the price, the less will be the response of quantity demanded to a given change in price.   ∎

Example 5

Another common economic-statistical model is one that involves the logarithm of y on the left side of the equation. It is useful to introduce another rule of differentiation to cope with this type of equation. Suppose we have

$$\ln y = \beta_1 + \beta_2 \ln x \tag{8A.15}$$

Note that this equation can be derived from equation 8A.7 by taking logarithms of equation 8A.7 and setting $\beta_1 = \ln \alpha$ and $\beta_2 = \beta$. We seek the derivative dy/dx. We know from equation 8A.9 that the result is $\beta_2 y/x$, but it is instructive, and useful later on, to derive the result from equation 8A.15. Differentiating both sides of equation 8A.15 with respect to x yields

$$\frac{d(\ln y)}{dx} = \frac{d(\beta_1 + \beta_2 \ln x)}{dx} \tag{8A.16}$$

The derivative of the right side of this equation is β_2/x and was obtained in equation 8A.14. For the left side we use the "chain" rule given by

$$\frac{d[f(y)]}{dx} = \frac{d[f(y)]}{dy}\frac{dy}{dx} \tag{8A.17}$$

Application of this rule to equation 8A.16 leads to

$$\frac{d(\ln y)}{dx} = \frac{d(\ln y)}{dy}\frac{dy}{dx} = \frac{1}{y}\frac{dy}{dx} \tag{8A.18}$$

Thus,

$$\frac{1}{y}\frac{dy}{dx} = \frac{\beta_2}{x}$$

or

$$\frac{dy}{dx} = \beta_2 \frac{y}{x} \tag{8A.19}$$

In this case the response of y to changes in x increases as the ratio y/x increases.   ∎

Example 6

In the theory of the firm, the total cost function relates total cost (tc) to output (q) of the firm. A common cost function is the cubic

$$tc = \beta_1 + \beta_2 q + \beta_3 q^2 + \beta_4 q^3 \tag{8A.20}$$

Marginal cost is defined as the response or change in total cost that occurs as output is increased. In other words, marginal cost (mc) is equal to the derivative of the total cost function with respect to output. Applying our rules for differentiation we have

$$mc = \frac{d(tc)}{dq} = \beta_2 + 2\beta_3 q + 3\beta_4 q^2 \qquad (8A.21)$$

In this case the derivative (marginal cost) is a quadratic function of q. In line with theory, we would expect the quadratic to be U-shaped with marginal cost decreasing for small values of q and increasing for large values of q. ∎

8A.1   Functional Form and Elasticity

In economics we are not only concerned with the *magnitude* of the rate of response of an outcome variable y to changes in an explanatory variable x. Also of interest is the *percentage* rate of response of y from a given percentage change in x, and from your introductory economics you know that this percentage change is called an *elasticity*.

Because the elasticity of y with respect to x depends on the derivative dy/dx, the *nature of the algebraic form of the function $y = f(x)$* has a big bearing on the nature of the expression for the elasticity. In particular, it determines whether the elasticity is constant or whether it depends in some way on x and/or y. The expression for the elasticity when y and x are linearly related was discussed in Appendix 5A of Chapter 5. Other examples follow.

Example 7

The elasticity of demand for a commodity q with respect to its price p, for the linear demand equation $q = \beta_1 + \beta_2 p$ (see Example 1) is

$$\eta = \frac{dq}{dp}\frac{p}{q} = \beta_2 \frac{p}{q} \qquad (8A.22)$$

Since β_2 is negative (increasing price leads to a decline in demand), the elasticity η will also be negative. When the elasticity is less than minus one ($\eta < -1$), we say demand is elastic; demand is referred to as inelastic when $\eta > -1$. In Example 2 we suggested that marginal revenue, defined by

$$mr = \beta_1 + 2\beta_2 p \qquad (8A.23)$$

will be negative when demand is elastic and positive when demand is inelastic. Let us prove this result. Suppose that demand is elastic. Thus, we can write

$$\frac{\beta_2 p}{q} < -1 \quad \text{or} \quad \beta_2 p < -q \quad \text{or} \quad \beta_2 p < -\beta_1 - \beta_2 p \quad \text{or} \quad \beta_1 + 2\beta_2 p < 0$$

$$(8A.24)$$

That is, $mr < 0$. For an inelastic demand the converse follows. ∎

Example 8

In Examples 3 and 5 we considered the function

$$y = \alpha x^{\beta} \tag{8A.25}$$

which, after taking logarithms, can be written as

$$\ln y = \ln \alpha + \beta \ln x = \beta_1 + \beta_2 \ln x \tag{8A.26}$$

where $\beta_1 = \ln \alpha$ and $\beta_2 = \beta$. Using either equation 8A.9 or 8A.19 the elasticity of y with respect to x from this function is given by

$$\eta = \frac{dy}{dx}\frac{x}{y} = \beta\frac{y}{x}\frac{x}{y} = \beta \tag{8A.27}$$

That is, the elasticity is a constant and equal to the parameter β; it does not depend on x or y. Consequently, *functions where the logarithm of the outcome variable is linearly related to the logarithm of the explanatory variable are known as constant elasticity functions.* In the context of a production function where y is output, β is the elasticity of production with respect to the input x. In the context of a demand equation where y is quantity, β is the elasticity of demand with respect to price x.

Using the tools developed in this appendix and Appendix 5A we should find it straightforward to show that for the model in Example 4, where $y = \beta_1 + \beta_2 \ln x$, the elasticity of y with respect to x is given by $\eta = \beta_2/y$. ∎

Appendix to Part II

Review-Summary of Chapters 5–8

This appendix to Part II is intended as a summary of the material just covered and as a lead-in to Chapter 9 and Part III. The results are summarized in both the scalar notation of Part II and the linear algebra notation that will be used starting with Chapter 9.

In Part II we considered economic and statistical models that may, given a sample of data, be used as a basis for investigating the possible relationship between two economic variables. In this process the outcome variable y, say, household food consumption, was specified to be a linear function, $y = \beta_1 + \beta_2 x$, of an explanatory variable x, say, household income. The corresponding statistical model that reflects the sampling process, by which the sample outcome value y_t was generated, was specified (Section 5.2) as

$$y_t = \beta_1 + \beta_2 x_t + e_t; \qquad t = 1, 2, \ldots, T$$

where y_t and e_t are random variables and x_t is a fixed, nonstochastic (not random) explanatory variable. The means and variances of the random variables y_t and e_t that are assumed to be normally distributed may be represented as follows:

$$y_t \sim N\!\left(\beta_1 + \beta_2 x_t,\, \sigma^2\right)$$
$$e_t \sim N\!\left(0,\, \sigma^2\right)$$

Making use of Section 5.4, for the complete set of sample observations $t = 1, 2, \ldots, T$,

$$
\begin{bmatrix} y_1 \\ y_2 \\ \vdots \\ y_T \end{bmatrix}
=
\begin{bmatrix} 1 \\ 1 \\ \vdots \\ 1 \end{bmatrix} \beta_1
+
\begin{bmatrix} x_1 \\ x_2 \\ \vdots \\ x_T \end{bmatrix} \beta_2
+
\begin{bmatrix} e_1 \\ e_2 \\ \vdots \\ e_T \end{bmatrix}
$$

the statistical model may be written compactly as

$$
\mathbf{y} = \mathbf{x}_1 \beta_1 + \mathbf{x}_2 \beta_2 + \mathbf{e} = \begin{bmatrix} \mathbf{x}_1 & \mathbf{x}_2 \end{bmatrix} \begin{bmatrix} \beta_1 \\ \beta_2 \end{bmatrix} = X\boldsymbol{\beta} + \mathbf{e}
$$

and

$$
\mathbf{e} \sim N\!\left(\mathbf{0},\, \sigma^2 I_T\right)
$$

where $\mathbf{y}$, $\mathbf{x}_1$, $\mathbf{x}_2$, $\mathbf{e}$, and $\mathbf{0}$ are $(T \times 1)$ vectors, X is a $(T \times 2)$ known matrix, and I_T is a Tth order identity matrix. The covariance matrix (Appendix 3B)

$$\text{cov}(\mathbf{e}) = \begin{bmatrix} \text{var}(e_1) & \text{cov}(e_1 e_2) & \cdots & \text{cov}(e_1 e_T) \\ \text{cov}(e_2 e_1) & \text{var}(e_2) & \cdots & \text{cov}(e_2 e_T) \\ \vdots & \vdots & \ddots & \vdots \\ \text{cov}(e_T e_1) & \text{cov}(e_T e_2) & \cdots & \text{var}(e_T) \end{bmatrix} = \begin{bmatrix} \sigma^2 & 0 & \cdots & 0 \\ 0 & \sigma^2 & \cdots & 0 \\ \vdots & \vdots & \ddots & \vdots \\ 0 & 0 & \cdots & \sigma^2 \end{bmatrix} = \sigma^2 I_T$$

reflects the independent and identical random process assumed for the unobserved and unobservable error variable $\mathbf{e}$.

The unknown parameters in the statistical model are β_1, β_2, and σ^2. To estimate the unknown parameters $[\beta_1 \ \beta_2]' = \beta$, use is made of the least squares criterion (Sections 5.3.1 and 5.4.2), which seeks to minimize the error sum of squares,

$$\Sigma e_t^2 = \mathbf{e}'\mathbf{e} = (\mathbf{y} - X\beta)'(\mathbf{y} - X\beta)$$

and results in the following set of linear (normal) equations (Sections 5.3 and 5.4)

$$Tb_1 + \Sigma x_t b_2 = \Sigma y_t$$
$$\Sigma x_t b_1 + \Sigma x_t^2 b_2 = \Sigma x_t y_t$$

or

$$\begin{bmatrix} T & \Sigma x_t \\ \Sigma x_t & \Sigma x_t^2 \end{bmatrix} \begin{bmatrix} b_1 \\ b_2 \end{bmatrix} = \begin{bmatrix} \Sigma y_t \\ \Sigma x_t y_t \end{bmatrix}$$

or

$$X'X\mathbf{b} = X'\mathbf{y}$$

A solution to this system of linear equations yields the following least squares estimator (Section 5.4)

$$\mathbf{b} = \begin{bmatrix} b_1 \\ b_2 \end{bmatrix} = (X'X)^{-1} X'\mathbf{y} = \begin{bmatrix} T & \Sigma x_t \\ \Sigma x_t & \Sigma x_t^2 \end{bmatrix}^{-1} \begin{bmatrix} \Sigma y_t \\ \Sigma x_t y_t \end{bmatrix}$$

which is a random variable and has sampling variability (Section 6.6.2) that is measured by its covariance matrix

$$\text{cov}(\mathbf{b}) = E\left[(\mathbf{b} - \beta)(\mathbf{b} - \beta)'\right] = E\left[(X'X)^{-1} X'\mathbf{ee}'X(X'X)^{-1}\right] = \sigma^2 (X'X)^{-1}$$

$$= \begin{bmatrix} \text{var}(b_1) & \text{cov}(b_1, b_2) \\ \text{cov}(b_1, b_2) & \text{var}(b_2) \end{bmatrix} = \sigma^2 \begin{bmatrix} \dfrac{\Sigma x_t^2}{T\Sigma(x_t - \bar{x})^2} & \dfrac{-\bar{x}}{\Sigma(x_t - \bar{x})^2} \\ \dfrac{-\bar{x}}{\Sigma(x_t - \bar{x})^2} & \dfrac{1}{\Sigma(x_t - \bar{x})^2} \end{bmatrix}$$

The inverse matrix operation

$$(X'X)^{-1} = \begin{bmatrix} T & \Sigma x_t \\ \Sigma x_t & \Sigma x_t^2 \end{bmatrix}^{-1} = \frac{1}{T\Sigma x_t^2 - (\Sigma x_t)^2} \begin{bmatrix} \Sigma x_t^2 & -\Sigma x_t \\ -\Sigma x_t & T \end{bmatrix}$$

is discussed in Appendix 5C. The least squares estimator has mean

$$E[\mathbf{b}] = E\left[\left(X'X\right)^{-1} X'(X\boldsymbol{\beta} + \mathbf{e})\right] = \boldsymbol{\beta}$$

and thus is an unbiased estimator. It is in fact the best (minimum sampling variability) unbiased estimator (Section 6.6.3).

The estimator of the scale parameter σ^2 (Section 6.6.3 and 6.6.4)

$$\hat{\sigma}^2 = \frac{\Sigma \hat{e}_t^2}{T-2} = \frac{(\mathbf{y} - X\mathbf{b})'(\mathbf{y} - X\mathbf{b})}{T-2}$$

is also a random variable and has mean

$$E\left[\hat{\sigma}^2\right] = \sigma^2$$

and is thus an unbiased estimator of σ^2. Since the least squares estimator $\mathbf{b} = (X'X)^{-1}X'\mathbf{y} = A\mathbf{y}$ is a linear function of the normal random vector $\mathbf{y}$, it is a random vector that is distributed as follows (Appendix 7A):

$$\mathbf{b} \sim N\left(\boldsymbol{\beta}, \sigma^2 \left(X'X\right)^{-1}\right)$$

where the individual components of this matrix result are given by

$$b_1 \sim N\left(\beta_1, \operatorname{var}(b_1) = \frac{\sigma^2 \Sigma x_t^2}{T\Sigma\left(x_t - \bar{x}\right)^2}\right) \qquad \text{and} \qquad b_2 \sim N\left(\beta_2, \operatorname{var}(b_2) = \frac{\sigma^2}{\Sigma\left(x_t - \bar{x}\right)^2}\right)$$

The distribution of the random variable $\hat{\sigma}^2$ is (Section 6.3.1)

$$\frac{(T-2)}{\sigma^2}\hat{\sigma}^2 \sim \chi^2_{(T-2)}$$

where $\chi^2_{(T-2)}$ is a chi-square random variable with $(T-2)$ degrees of freedom. Furthermore, the ratio

$$t = \frac{\left(b_i - \beta_i\right)}{\sqrt{\hat{\operatorname{var}}(b_i)}} \sim t_{(T-2)}$$

for $i = 1, 2$, is distributed as a Student-t random variable with $(T-2)$ degrees of freedom. This result is used to develop

(i) interval estimates for the individual parameters (Section 7.1.2)

$$P\left[b_i - t_c \sqrt{\hat{\operatorname{var}}(b_i)} \le \beta_i \le b_i + t_c \sqrt{\hat{\operatorname{var}}(b_i)}\right] = 1 - \alpha$$

where t_c is the critical value such that $P\left[t_{(T-2)} > t_c\right] = P\left[t_{(T-2)} < -t_c\right] = \alpha/2$ and α is the level of statistical significance.

(ii) hypothesis tests where, if the null hypothesis $\beta_i = \beta_i^0$ is correct, then (Section 7.2)

$$t = \frac{b_i - \beta_i^0}{\sqrt{\hat{var}(b_i)}} \sim t_{(T-2)}$$

In the test mechanism normally used, the null hypothesis is rejected if $|t| > t_c$.

If the objective is to predict an outside sample outcome y_0 by the process (Section 7.3)

$$y_0 = \beta 1 + \beta_2 x_0 + e_0 = \begin{bmatrix} 1 & x_0 \end{bmatrix} \begin{bmatrix} \beta_1 \\ \beta_2 \end{bmatrix} + e_0 = \mathbf{x}_0' \beta + e_0$$

then the predictor

$$\hat{y}_0 = b_1 + b_2 x_0$$

is an unbiased predictor and the sampling variability of its prediction error is

$$\text{var}(\hat{y}_0 - y_0) = \sigma^2 \left[1 + \mathbf{x}_0' (X'X)^{-1} \mathbf{x}_0 \right] = \sigma^2 \left[1 + \frac{1}{T} + \frac{(x_0 - \bar{x})^2}{\Sigma(x_t - \bar{x})^2} \right]$$

Therefore,

$$(\hat{y}_0 - y_0) \sim N\left(0, \sigma^2 \left[1 + \mathbf{x}_0' (X'X)^{-1} \mathbf{x}_0 \right] \right)$$

Consequently, the corresponding prediction interval for y_0 is

$$P\left[\hat{y}_0 - t_c \sqrt{\hat{var}(\hat{y}_0 - y_0)} < y_0 < \hat{y}_0 + t_c \sqrt{\hat{var}(\hat{y}_0 - y_0)} \right] = 1 - \alpha$$

The coefficient of determinism, which is the measure of the proportion of variation in y explained by x, is

$$R^2 = 1 - \frac{\Sigma \hat{e}_t^2}{\Sigma(y_t - \bar{y})^2} = 1 - \frac{\hat{\mathbf{e}}' \hat{\mathbf{e}}}{\mathbf{y}'\mathbf{y} - T\bar{y}^2}$$

Many possibilities exist for extending the linear in the variables specification $y_t = \beta_1 + \beta_2 x_t + e_t$ (Section 8.3). Some alternatives are

$$\ln y_t = \ln \beta_1 + \beta_2 \ln x_t + e_t \qquad \text{or} \qquad y_t = \beta_1 + \beta_2 x_t^2 + e_t \qquad \text{or} \qquad y_t = \beta_1 + \beta_2 \frac{1}{x_t} + e_t$$

Part III

General Linear Statistical Model

In Part II we specified and analyzed a linear statistical model that relates a sample of observations for a dependent or outcome variable to one explanatory variable. The least squares rule was used to estimate the unknown coefficient vector that describes this relationship and an unbiased estimator of the error variance (scale parameter) σ^2 was suggested. The least squares rule was shown in the case of normal errors to be a *best unbiased* estimator of β. Interval estimators and hypothesis tests for β and σ^2 were investigated and applied. Alternative functional forms for the relationship were specified and the characteristics of each was analyzed.

In Part III we extend the simple linear statistical model of Part II to a general form involving two or more explanatory variables and three or more elements of the corresponding unknown coefficient vector β. Point and interval estimators for the unknowns β and σ^2 are developed and a general linear hypothesis-testing mechanism is demonstrated. To indicate the applicability of this general linear model, estimation and inference procedures are developed for three economic problems.

Chapter 9

A General Linear Statistical Model: Model Specification and Estimation

Key Words and Concepts

General Linear Statistical Model
Properties of Least Squares
Covariance Matrix of Least Squares
  Estimator
Omitted Variable Bias

Least Squares Estimator
Unbiased Estimator of Error Variance
Regressor Matrix Misspecification
Coefficient of Determination
Reporting Results

In Part II (Chapters 5–8) we considered a *simple* linear statistical (regression) model, with the adjective "simple" being used to describe a linear statistical model where an observed random variable y is a function of a *single* explanatory variable x. As an example of such a model, we developed and analyzed a relationship where food expenditure is modeled as a function of income. We concluded Chapter 8 by noting that there are many economic relationships where more explanatory variables than one are likely to influence the outcome variable y. For example, in a demand equation, the quantity demanded of a commodity is likely to depend on the price of that commodity, the prices of substitute and complimentary commodities, and income. Output in a production function will typically be a function of more than one input. Aggregate money demand will, among other things, be a function of aggregate income and the interest rate. Investment will depend on the interest rate and changes in income. The list of examples of economic models is a long one.

When we turn an economic model with more than one explanatory variable into its corresponding linear statistical model, where the outcome variable is a function of more than one explanatory variable, it becomes a *general linear statistical model* or the *multiple regression model*. In this chapter we begin a study of this general statistical model. What we discover is that most of the results that we developed for the simple statistical model in Chapters 5 to 8 carry over or extend naturally to the general case. For example, the unknown parameter vector β, which describes the relationship between the variables, can be estimated with the same least squares rule. The same compact matrix expression for the least squares estimator and its covariance matrix are valid. The least squares residuals can be used to estimate σ^2, the variance of the error term. This estimated variance can be used, in turn, to estimate the covariance matrix of the least squares estimator. Inferences about the coefficient vector, in the form of interval estimates and hypothesis tests, are based on distributional assumptions about the error term and the estimated covariance matrix of the least squares estimator. These are some of the important things ahead in the next few chapters. One important new development that we encounter in

Chapter 10 is the use of the F distribution to simultaneously test a null hypothesis involving two or more hypotheses about the parameters in the linear statistical model.

Another feature of this and subsequent chapters is that the use of matrix algebra becomes more extensive. Thus far in the book it has been possible to avoid the sections on linear algebra and still retain an understanding and appreciation of estimation and inference in the linear regression model. From now on it will become increasingly difficult to do so. For this reason you may wish to reread Sections 5.4 and 6.6 in Chapters 5 and 6 before proceeding.

As a vehicle for introducing and analyzing the multiple regression model, it is convenient to use the framework of a specific economic model; this was the strategy we adopted in Chapters 5 to 8 where our example was the food expenditure–income relationship. In this chapter and the next we consider a model used to explain receipts for a fast-food hamburger chain in the San Francisco Bay Area. We begin with an outline of this model and the questions that we hope it will answer.

9.1 Model Specification and the Data

9.1.1 The Economic Model

Each week the management of a Bay Area hamburger chain must decide how much money should be spent on advertising their products and what specials (lower prices) should be introduced for that week. It is a large chain that usually spends thousands of dollars each week on advertising, both on television and in newspapers. Of particular interest to management is how total receipts change as the level of advertising expenditure changes. Does an increase in advertising expenditure lead to an increase in total receipts? If so, is the increase in total receipts sufficient to justify the increased advertising expenditure? Management is also interested in the best pricing strategy. The products sold by each hamburger outlet are identical and the prices of most of these products are kept constant from week to week. However, one or two products are usually targeted each week by reducing their prices and sometimes also by concentrating advertising on these products. Moreover, new products (or slight variations on old ones) are often introduced at selected prices. Of relevance in this case is the question of whether reducing prices leads to an increase or decrease in total receipts. If a reduction in price leads only to a small increase in the quantity sold, total receipts will fall (demand is price inelastic); a price reduction that leads to a large increase in quantity sold will produce an increase in total receipts (demand is price elastic).

How does management answer these questions about the dependence of total receipts on advertising expenditure and price? Imagine that you are an economic consultant, retained by the hamburger chain, to provide the answers. The first step in your search for quantitative knowledge is to set up an economic model. For this purpose, it may seem reasonable to hypothesize that total receipts tr are linearly related to price p and advertising expenditure a. Thus, you set up the economic model

$$tr = \beta_1 + \beta_2 p + \beta_3 a \qquad (9.1.1)$$

where tr represents receipts for a given week, p represents price in that week, and a is the level of advertising expenditure during that week. Both tr and a are measured in terms of thousands of dollars. How we measure price is not so clear, however. The hamburger outlets sell a number of products such as burgers, fries and shakes, and each product has its own price. What we need for the model in equation 9.1.1 is some kind of average price for all products, and details on how this average price changes from week to week. Such an average would typically be a weighted average, with quantities used as weights, and the construction of a weekly series of this type is an index number problem. Fortunately, it is a problem that management has already tackled. They can provide you, the economist, with a single weekly price series that describes the overall state of prices for each week. The units for this series are dollars and cents.

The remaining items in equation 9.1.1 are the unknown parameters β_1, β_2 and, β_3 that describe the dependence of receipts (tr) on price (p) and advertising (a). Our job is to learn about these unknown parameters. The response parameter β_2 is interpreted as follows:

$$\beta_2 = \begin{bmatrix} \text{the change in } tr \text{ (in thousands of dollars)} \\ \text{when } p \text{ is increased by one unit (one dollar),} \\ \text{and } a \text{ is held constant} \end{bmatrix} = \frac{\partial tr}{\partial p}$$

The notation $\partial tr/\partial p$ represents the partial derivative of tr with respect to p. In general a partial derivative describes how one variable changes (tr in this case) when another variable changes (p in this case) *and all other variables are held constant*. Details of how to obtain partial derivatives were given in Appendix 5A in Chapter 5 and further examples appear in Appendix 10A in Chapter 10. At this point is is sufficient to recognize that $\partial tr/\partial p$ describes the *response* of tr to a change in p. It is for this reason β_2 is called a *response coefficient*. The sign of β_2 could be positive or negative. If an increase in price leads to an increase in receipts, then $\beta_2 > 0$, and the demand for the chain's products is price inelastic. Conversely, a price elastic demand exists if an increase in price leads to a decline in receipts, in which case $\beta_2 < 0$. Thus, knowledge of the *sign* of β_2 provides important information on the elasticity and on whether it is likely to be preferable to increase or decrease price. Knowledge of the *magnitude* of β_2 gives an idea of the extent of the change in receipts for a given price change.

The other response parameter β_3 describes the response of receipts to a change in the level of advertising expenditure. That is,

$$\beta_3 = \begin{bmatrix} \text{the change in } tr \text{ (in thousands of dollars)} \\ \text{when } a \text{ is increased by one unit (one thousand dollars),} \\ \text{and } p \text{ is held constant} \end{bmatrix} = \frac{\partial tr}{\partial a}$$

We would expect the sign of β_3 to be positive. That is, an increase in advertising expenditure will always lead to an increase in total receipts. Whether or not the increase in total receipts is sufficient to justify the added advertising expenditure, and the added cost of producing more hamburgers, is another question. With $\beta_3 < 1$, an increase of $1000 in advertising expenditure will yield an increase in total receipts that is less than $1000. For $\beta_3 > 1$, it will be greater. Thus, in terms of the chain's advertising policy, knowledge of β_3 is very important.

The remaining parameter is the intercept parameter β_1. The strict mathematical interpretation of β_1 is the level of receipts when price and advertising expenditure are zero. Since we will never have data where p and a are zero, it is unrealistic to think our model will be a good approximation to reality in that region, and so the strict mathematical interpretation is not realistic. Thus, in this case (and it is also true for many other models) we are not interested in the parameter β_1 for its own sake, but it is an important ingredient for estimation of the equation as a whole.

How far along the road as an economic consultant have you come? We have set up an economic model to describe the relationship between receipts, price, and advertising expenditure, and, from that model, we have identified the unknown parameters β_1, β_2 and β_3, that will help answer the questions of interest to the hamburger chain's management. We have turned management's general questions about pricing and advertising policies into questions that require us to make use of a sample of data to estimate and draw inferences about the unknown parameters β_1, β_2, and β_3. The next step along the road to learning about β_1, β_2, and β_3 is to convert the economic model into a statistical model.

9.1.2   The Statistical Model

In Chapter 5 when we considered a model for describing the generation of observations on household food expenditure, we recognized that all observations on food expenditure and on income would not lie exactly on a straight line relationship between the two variables. Consequently, it was necessary to modify the *economic* model by adding to it a *random error term*. The introduction of the error term, and the associated assumptions about its sampling distribution, turned the economic model into a *statistical* model. The statistical model provided a more realistic description of the stochastic relationship between the variables as well as a framework for developing and assessing *estimators* and the precision of *estimates* that they produced.

The same strategy is followed in this section where we have total receipts as a *linear* function of price and advertising expenditure. Observations on these variables will not coincide *exactly* with the relationship $tr = \beta_1 + \beta_2 p + \beta_3 a$. To recognize this fact, and to recognize that there are many factors influencing tr other than p and a, we introduce, as we did in Chapters 3 and 5, a random error term e so that the model becomes $tr = \beta_1 + \beta_2 p + \beta_3 a + e$. Using a subscript t to denote the tth observation, our *statistical model* can be written as

$$tr_t = \beta_1 + \beta_2 p_t + \beta_3 a_t + e_t \tag{9.1.2}$$

where the error term e_t is a random variable with a probability distribution. Consequently, in a given time period t, the dependent variable tr is a random variable; an observed value of this random variable can be viewed as a random drawing from a probability distribution that depends on, or is conditioned on, the values of p and a.

The statistical model in equation 9.1.2 is one example (special case) of a *general linear statistical model* and is frequently termed a *multiple regression model*. Let us digress for a moment and summarize how the concepts developed thus far relate to the general case. In a general linear statistical model a dependent outcome variable y_t is related to (or depends on) a number of *explanatory variables* $x_{t2}, x_{t3}, \ldots, x_{tK}$ through a linear equation that can be written as

$$y_t = \beta_1 + \beta_2 x_{t2} + \beta_3 x_{t3} + \ldots + \beta_K x_{tK} + e_t \tag{9.1.3}$$

The explanatory variables $x_{t2}, x_{t3}, \ldots, x_{tK}$ are also called *regressor variables* or, more simply, *regressors*. The unknown parameters $\beta_2, \beta_3, \ldots, \beta_K$ are response coefficients whereas β_1 is an intercept parameter. In general terms, a given response coefficient, say β_k, shows the response in y_t that results from a change in x_{tk}. That is

$$\beta_k = \frac{\partial y_t}{\partial x_{tk}} \tag{9.1.4}$$

The intercept parameter is, theoretically, the average value of the dependent variable when all explanatory variables are zero. As we have noted, however, in many practical examples the function may not be a good approximation to reality in this region.

The subscript notation in the general model in equation 9.1.3 is worthy of further explanation. There are K unknown parameters β_1, β_2,..., β_K and $(K - 1)$ explanatory variables x_{t2}, x_{t3},..., x_{tK}. The numbering of the explanatory variables has been chosen to correspond with that of the parameters. We can think of the "first explanatory variable" x_{t1} as the variable that corresponds to β_1; it is equal to 1 for all observations, and, hence, the general equation can instead be written as

$$y_t = \beta_1 x_{t1} + \beta_2 x_{t2} + \beta_3 x_{t3} + ... + \beta_K x_{tK} + e_t \qquad (9.1.5)$$

When $x_{t1} = 1$, the meaning of the equation is the same irrespective of whether x_{t1} is explicitly or implicitly included.

The equation for total receipts can be viewed as a special case of equation 9.1.3 where $K = 3$, $y_t = tr_t$, $x_{t1} = 1$, $x_{t2} = p_t$, and $x_{t3} = a_t$. Thus we rewrite equation 9.1.2 as

$$y_t = \beta_1 x_{t1} + \beta_2 x_{t2} + \beta_3 x_{t3} + e_t \qquad (9.1.6)$$

In this chapter and the next one we will introduce estimation, hypothesis testing, and other statistical procedures in terms of this model. The results generally will hold true for models with more explanatory variables ($K > 3$).

To make the statistical model in equation 9.1.6 complete, further assumptions about the probability distribution of the random errors (the e_ts) need to be made. These assumptions are important because they have a bearing on the estimation procedure employed to estimate the β_ks and on methods for interval estimation and hypothesis testing. The assumptions that we introduce for e_t are similar to those introduced for the model for estimating a population mean in Chapter 3 and the simple linear model in Chapter 5. That is,

1. $E[e_t] = 0$. Each random error is drawn from a probability distribution with zero mean. Some errors will be positive, some will be negative; over a large number of observations they will average out to zero.

2. $\text{var}(e_t) = E[e_t^2] = \sigma^2$. Each random error is drawn from a probability distribution with variance σ^2. The variance σ^2 is unknown, but it is the same for each observation. Some errors are not more likely to be bigger than others.

3. $\text{cov}(e_t, e_s) = E[e_t e_s] = 0$. The covariance between the two random errors corresponding to two different observations is zero. The size of an error for one observation has no bearing on the likely size of an error for another observation. Thus, any pair of errors is uncorrelated.

Because each observation on the dependent variable y_t depends on the random error term e_t, each y_t is also a random variable that can be viewed as a drawing from a probability distribution. Furthermore, the statistical properties of y_t follow from those of e_t. These properties are

1. $E[y_t] = \beta_1 x_{t1} + \beta_2 x_{t2} + \beta_3 x_{t3}$. The mean of y_t depends on the corresponding values of the explanatory variables. In other words, the mean of the probability distribution for y_t changes with each observation and it is given by the *mean function* or *regression function* $E[y_t] = \beta_1 x_{t1} + \beta_2 x_{t2} + \beta_3 x_{t3}$.

2. $\text{var}(y_t) = \sigma^2$. The variance of the probability distribution from which y_t is drawn does not change with each observation. Some observations on y_t are not more likely to be further from the mean function than others.

3. $\text{cov}(y_t, y_s) = 0$. Any two observations on the dependent variable are uncorrelated. For example, if one observation is above the mean function, a subsequent observation is not more or less likely to be above the mean function.

These assumptions may be compactly summarized by saying the e_t and y_t are uncorrelated and that

$$e_t \sim \left(0, \sigma^2\right) \quad \text{and} \quad y_t \sim \left(\beta_1 x_{t1} + \beta_2 x_{t2} + \beta_3 x_{t3}, \sigma^2\right)$$

If, in addition, we assume that e_t and y_t are normally distributed, we write

$$e_t \sim N\left(0, \sigma^2\right) \quad \text{and} \quad y_t \sim N\left(\beta_1 x_{t1} + \beta_2 x_{t2} + \beta_3 x_{t3}, \sigma^2\right)$$

The benefits of being able to assume that the errors are normally distributed have been shown in Chapters 4 and 7 and will emerge as we travel through this chapter and Chapters 10 and 11.

In addition to the above three assumptions about the error term (and, hence, about the dependent variable), we make two assumptions about the explanatory variables. The first is that the explanatory variables are fixed or nonstochastic and thus are not random variables. In other words, they *are not* viewed as drawings from a probability distribution; we can always say in advance what are or will be the values of x_{t2} and x_{t3}. This assumption is realistic for our hamburger chain, where a decision about prices and advertising is made each week and values for these variables are set accordingly.

The second assumption about the explanatory variables is that one is not an exact linear function of the other. That is, it is not possible to write

$$x_{t3} = c_1 + c_2 x_{t2} \tag{9.1.7}$$

for some values of c_1 and c_2. When we have $(K - 1)$ explanatory variables, we assume that it is not possible to write

$$x_{tK} = c_1 + c_2 x_{t2} + c_3 x_{t3} + \ldots + c_{K-1} x_{t,K-1} \tag{9.1.8}$$

for some values of $c_1, c_2, c_3, \ldots, c_{K-1}$. Note that this assumption is equivalent to assuming that each variable does have some additional information content not contained in the other variables. No variable is redundant. If equation 9.1.7 did hold, then x_{t2} and x_{t3} would always move together and it would be impossible to work out the separate effects of x_{t2} and x_{t3} on y_t. That is, we could not obtain separate estimates for β_2 and β_3. More details of these circumstances and the associated problem will be discussed in Chapter 13 under the heading "Multicollinearity."

9.1.2a The Statistical Model in Matrix Notation

To work with the general linear statistical model, it simplifies matters if we make use of the linear algebra notation that was introduced for the mean-variance model in Appendix 3B in Chapter 3 and for the linear model with one explanatory variable (two coefficients) in Section 5.4. This linear algebra notation can be extended in a natural way to our current model with two explanatory variables and three coefficients. Indeed, the advantage of using linear algebra notation is that the same notation can be used irrespective of the number of explanatory variables. The dimensions of the matrices used to represent the set of explanatory variables and the set of unknown parameters change, but the notation itself does not. Thus, in what follows, matrices and vectors that have a row or column dimension of 3 will have a corresponding dimension of K in the general case.

We begin by considering the general model given in equation 9.1.3, where we have K coefficients and $(K - 1)$ explanatory variables. The complete set of T observations for this general equation can be written out in full as

$$
\begin{aligned}
y_1 &= \beta_1 + \beta_2 x_{12} + \beta_3 x_{13} + \ldots + \beta_K x_{1K} + e_1 \\
y_2 &= \beta_1 + \beta_2 x_{22} + \beta_3 x_{23} + \ldots + \beta_K x_{2K} + e_2 \\
&\vdots \\
y_T &= \beta_1 + \beta_2 x_{T2} + \beta_3 x_{T3} + \ldots + \beta_K x_{TK} + e_T
\end{aligned}
\tag{9.1.9}
$$

In matrix algebra notation these equations can be written as

$$
\begin{bmatrix} y_1 \\ y_2 \\ \vdots \\ y_T \end{bmatrix}
=
\begin{bmatrix}
1 & x_{12} & x_{13} & \cdots & x_{1K} \\
1 & x_{22} & x_{23} & \cdots & x_{2K} \\
\vdots & \vdots & \vdots & & \vdots \\
1 & x_{T2} & x_{T3} & \cdots & x_{TK}
\end{bmatrix}
\begin{bmatrix} \beta_1 \\ \beta_2 \\ \vdots \\ \beta_K \end{bmatrix}
+
\begin{bmatrix} e_1 \\ e_2 \\ \vdots \\ e_T \end{bmatrix}
\tag{9.1.10}
$$

The matrices in this equation will be represented with the following notation

$$
\mathbf{y} = \begin{bmatrix} y_1 \\ y_2 \\ \vdots \\ y_T \end{bmatrix}
\qquad
X = \begin{bmatrix}
1 & x_{12} & x_{13} & \cdots & x_{1K} \\
1 & x_{22} & x_{23} & \cdots & x_{2K} \\
\vdots & \vdots & \vdots & & \vdots \\
1 & x_{12} & x_{T3} & \cdots & x_{TK}
\end{bmatrix}
\qquad
\boldsymbol{\beta} = \begin{bmatrix} \beta_1 \\ \beta_2 \\ \vdots \\ \beta_K \end{bmatrix}
\qquad
\mathbf{e} = \begin{bmatrix} e_1 \\ e_2 \\ \vdots \\ e_T \end{bmatrix}
$$

$$
T \times 1 \qquad\qquad T \times K \qquad\qquad\qquad K \times 1 \qquad\qquad T \times 1
$$

$$
\tag{9.1.11}
$$

Thus, $\mathbf{y}$ is a vector containing all the observations on the dependent variable, X is a matrix containing all the observations on all the explanatory variables including the constant term, $\boldsymbol{\beta}$ is a vector of unknown coefficients that we wish to estimate, and $\mathbf{e}$ is a vector containing the error terms for all observations. In compact notation our model therefore becomes

$$
\mathbf{y} = X\boldsymbol{\beta} + \mathbf{e}
\tag{9.1.12}
$$

Sometimes it is convenient to write the model in another way, where each explanatory variable is separate and the observations for each explanatory variable are in separate vectors. In this case we define

$$
\mathbf{x}_1 = \begin{bmatrix} 1 \\ 1 \\ \vdots \\ 1 \end{bmatrix}
\qquad
\mathbf{x}_2 = \begin{bmatrix} x_{12} \\ x_{22} \\ \vdots \\ x_{T2} \end{bmatrix}
\qquad
\mathbf{x}_3 = \begin{bmatrix} x_{13} \\ x_{23} \\ \vdots \\ x_{T3} \end{bmatrix} \cdots
\qquad
\mathbf{x}_K = \begin{bmatrix} x_{1K} \\ x_{2K} \\ \vdots \\ x_{TK} \end{bmatrix}
\tag{9.1.13}
$$

and the model becomes

$$
\mathbf{y} = \mathbf{x}_1 \beta_1 + \mathbf{x}_2 \beta_2 + \mathbf{x}_3 \beta_3 + \ldots + \mathbf{x}_K \beta_K + \mathbf{e}
\tag{9.1.14}
$$

Note that $\mathbf{x}_1$, the vector of ones, plays the same role as the vector $\mathbf{x}_1$ that was used in Chapters 5 to 8 where we had only one explanatory variable.

To write the receipts–price–advertising relationship $tr_t = \beta_1 + \beta_2 p_t + \beta_3 a_t + e_t$ in the general form $\mathbf{y} = X\boldsymbol{\beta} + \mathbf{e}$, we note that $K = 3$ and define $\mathbf{y}$, X, and $\boldsymbol{\beta}$ as follows

$$
\mathbf{y} = \begin{bmatrix} y_1 \\ y_2 \\ \vdots \\ y_T \end{bmatrix} = \begin{bmatrix} tr_1 \\ tr_2 \\ \vdots \\ tr_T \end{bmatrix} \qquad X = \begin{bmatrix} x_{11} & x_{12} & x_{13} \\ x_{21} & x_{22} & x_{23} \\ \vdots & \vdots & \vdots \\ x_{T1} & x_{T2} & x_{T3} \end{bmatrix} = \begin{bmatrix} 1 & p_1 & a_1 \\ 1 & p_2 & a_2 \\ \vdots & \vdots & \vdots \\ 1 & p_T & a_T \end{bmatrix} \qquad \boldsymbol{\beta} = \begin{bmatrix} \beta_1 \\ \beta_2 \\ \beta_3 \end{bmatrix}
$$

$$
T \times 1 \qquad\qquad\qquad T \times 3 \qquad\qquad\qquad\qquad\qquad 3 \times 1
$$

$$(9.1.15)$$

Alternatively, the model could be written as

$$
\mathbf{y} = \mathbf{x}_1 \beta_1 + \mathbf{x}_2 \beta_2 + \mathbf{x}_3 \beta_3 + \mathbf{e} \tag{9.1.16}
$$

where

$$
\mathbf{x}_1 = \begin{bmatrix} x_{11} \\ x_{21} \\ \vdots \\ x_{T1} \end{bmatrix} = \begin{bmatrix} 1 \\ 1 \\ \vdots \\ 1 \end{bmatrix} \qquad \mathbf{x}_2 = \begin{bmatrix} x_{12} \\ x_{22} \\ \vdots \\ x_{T2} \end{bmatrix} = \begin{bmatrix} p_1 \\ p_2 \\ \vdots \\ p_T \end{bmatrix} \quad \text{and} \quad \mathbf{x}_3 = \begin{bmatrix} x_{13} \\ x_{23} \\ \vdots \\ x_{T3} \end{bmatrix} = \begin{bmatrix} a_1 \\ a_2 \\ \vdots \\ a_T \end{bmatrix}
$$

$$(9.1.17)$$

Hence, in this instance, $\mathbf{y}$ contains the observations on receipts; X contains the constant term $\mathbf{x}_1$ and the observations on price $\mathbf{x}_2$ and advertising expenditure $\mathbf{x}_3$.

The last step in developing the statistical model is to specify in compact notation the assumptions about the random error vector $\mathbf{e}$. In line with Chapters 3 and 5 we have

$$
E[\mathbf{e}] = \mathbf{0} \quad\text{and}\quad \text{cov}(\mathbf{e}) = E[\mathbf{e}\mathbf{e}'] = \sigma^2 I_T \tag{9.1.18a}
$$

or

$$
\mathbf{e} \sim \left(\mathbf{0}, \sigma^2 I_T\right) \tag{9.1.18b}
$$

Correspondingly

$$
E[\mathbf{y}] = E[X\boldsymbol{\beta} + \mathbf{e}] = X\boldsymbol{\beta} \tag{9.1.19a}
$$

$$
E\left[(\mathbf{y} - X\boldsymbol{\beta})(\mathbf{y} - X\boldsymbol{\beta})'\right] = E[\mathbf{e}\mathbf{e}'] = \sigma^2 I_T \tag{9.1.19b}
$$

and

$$
\mathbf{y} \sim \left(X\boldsymbol{\beta}, \sigma^2 I_T\right) \tag{9.1.19c}
$$

If, in addition, we assume that the elements in $\mathbf{e}$ are normally distributed, we write

$$
\mathbf{e} \sim N\left(\mathbf{0}, \sigma^2 I_T\right) \tag{9.1.20a}
$$

and

$$
\mathbf{y} \sim N\left(X\boldsymbol{\beta}, \sigma^2 I_T\right) \tag{9.1.20b}
$$

Thus, the specification $\mathbf{y} = X\boldsymbol{\beta} + \mathbf{e}$ where $\mathbf{e} \sim \left(\mathbf{0}, \sigma^2 I_T\right)$, or $\mathbf{e} \sim N\left(\mathbf{0}, \sigma^2 I_T\right)$, defines the statistical model and describes the sampling process from which we assume our sample observations $\mathbf{y}$ are generated.

9.1.2b Data   Given this statistical model, the next step is to use a sample of data, which are assumed generated by this model, to estimate the unknown coefficient vector β. The hamburger chain's management has given us data on the observed values of receipts *y*, the average price *p*, and advertising expenditure *a* that were used for each week of last year. These 52 observations are given in Table 9.1.

9.2   Estimation

Having specified a statistical model and identified the data we wish to use, our next task is to estimate the unknown parameters of the model. As we have indicated, such estimates contain useful information on how total receipts are affected by price and advertising expenditure and provide a basis for decision making. In this regard we will examine

1. The least squares estimator (rule) for the parameter vector β.
2. An unbiased estimator for σ^2.
3. The sampling properties and an unbiased estimator for the covariance matrix of the least squares estimator.
4. A goodness-of-fit measure.

Table 9.1 Weekly Observations on Receipts, Price and Advertising Expenditure for the Hamburger Chain

Week	Receipts (*tr*) $1000 Units	Price (*p*) $	Advertising (*a*) $1000 Units	Week	Receipts (*tr*) $1000 Units	Price (*p*) $	Advertising (*a*) $1000 Units
1	123.1	1.92	12.4	27	124.2	2.12	8.8
2	124.3	2.15	9.9	28	98.4	2.13	3.2
3	89.3	1.67	2.4	29	114.8	1.89	5.4
4	141.3	1.68	13.8	30	142.5	1.50	17.3
5	112.8	1.75	3.5	31	122.6	1.93	11.2
6	108.1	1.55	1.8	32	127.7	2.27	11.2
7	143.9	1.54	17.8	33	113.0	1.66	7.9
8	124.2	2.10	9.8	34	144.2	1.73	17.0
9	110.1	2.44	8.3	35	109.2	1.59	3.3
10	111.7	2.47	9.8	36	106.8	2.29	7.1
11	123.8	1.86	12.6	37	145.0	1.86	15.3
12	123.5	1.93	11.5	38	124.0	1.91	12.7
13	110.2	2.47	7.4	39	106.7	2.34	6.1
14	100.9	2.11	6.1	40	153.2	2.13	19.6
15	123.3	2.10	9.5	41	120.1	2.05	6.3
16	115.7	1.73	8.8	42	119.3	1.89	9.0
17	116.6	1.86	4.9	43	150.6	2.12	18.7
18	153.5	2.19	18.8	44	92.2	1.87	2.2
19	149.2	1.90	18.9	45	130.5	2.09	16.0
20	89.0	1.67	2.3	46	112.5	1.76	4.5
21	132.6	2.43	14.1	47	111.8	1.77	4.3
22	97.5	2.13	2.9	48	120.1	1.94	9.3
23	106.1	2.33	5.9	49	107.4	2.37	8.3
24	115.3	1.75	7.6	50	128.6	2.10	15.4
25	98.5	2.05	5.3	51	124.6	2.29	9.2
26	135.1	2.35	16.8	52	127.2	2.36	10.2

9.2.1 Least Squares Estimation of the Coefficient Vector β

To find an estimator or rule for estimating the unknown coefficients in the vector β, we follow the least squares procedure that was first introduced in Chapter 3 and that was used in Chapter 5 for the simple linear model. A given estimate for β gives an estimate of the mean function

$$E[y_t] = \beta_1 + x_{t2}\beta_2 + x_{t3}\beta_3 \qquad (9.2.1)$$

We would like to choose an estimate such that the sum of squared differences between each observation y_t and the estimate of the mean function $E[y_t]$ is a minimum. Under this criterion, our least squares estimate for β is that value of β that minimizes

$$S(\beta_1, \beta_2, \beta_3) = \sum_{t=1}^{T}(y_t - E[y_t])^2$$

$$= \sum_{t=1}^{T}(y_t - \beta_1 - \beta_2 x_{t2} - \beta_3 x_{t3})^2 \qquad (9.2.2)$$

To find the least squares estimates b_1, b_2, and b_3 that are the minimizing values of equation 9.2.2, we follow the same procedure that was outlined in Chapter 5. The first step is to partially differentiate equation 9.2.2 with respect to β_1, β_2, β_3, and to set the first-order partial derivatives to zero. We can think of the function S in equation 9.2.2 as a bowl; the minimum of S is at the bottom of the bowl. Also, at the bottom of the bowl the slopes or partial derivatives $\partial S/\partial \beta_1$, $\partial S/\partial \beta_2$, and $\partial S/\partial \beta_3$ are all zero. The minimizing values for β_1, β_2, and β_3 are, therefore, those values that make the slopes equal to zero. Thus, to obtain the minimizing values, we set the first-order partial derivatives equal to zero and solve the resulting linear equations for β_1, β_2, and β_3. *Before* we set the derivatives equal to zero, we use the notation β_1, β_2, and β_3 to indicate that the value of the sum of squares function, and the values of the derivatives, depend on the βs. *After* we set the derivatives equal to zero, we use the notation b_1, b_2, and b_3 to indicate that we are now considering only one set of values for the βs, that set where S is a minimum and the first-order derivatives are equal to zero. Details for obtaining a minimum or a maximum from a multivariate function were given in Appendix 5A in Chapter 5.

Expanding equation 9.2.2 gives the quadratic equation

$$S(\beta_1, \beta_2, \beta_3) = \Sigma y_t^2 + T\beta_1^2 + \Sigma x_{t2}^2 \beta_2^2 + \Sigma x_{t3}^2 \beta_3^2 - 2\beta_1 \Sigma y_t - 2\beta_2 \Sigma x_{t2} y_t - 2\beta_3 \Sigma x_{t3} y_t$$
$$+ 2\beta_1 \beta_2 \Sigma x_{t2} + 2\beta_1 \beta_3 \Sigma x_{t3} + 2\beta_2 \beta_3 \Sigma x_{t2} x_{t3}$$

Partially differentiating this function with respect to β_1, β_2, and β_3 gives

$$\frac{\partial S}{\partial \beta_1} = 2T\beta_1 + 2\beta_2 \Sigma x_{t2} + 2\beta_3 \Sigma x_{t3} - 2\Sigma y_t$$

$$\frac{\partial S}{\partial \beta_2} = 2\beta_1 \Sigma x_{t2} + 2\beta_2 \Sigma x_{t2}^2 + 2\beta_3 \Sigma x_{t2} x_{t3} - 2\Sigma x_{t2} y_t$$

$$\frac{\partial S}{\partial \beta_3} = 2\beta_1 \Sigma x_{t3} + 2\beta_2 \Sigma x_{t2} x_{t3} + 2\beta_3 \Sigma x_{t3}^2 - 2\Sigma x_{t3} y_t$$

Setting these partial derivatives equal to zero, dividing by 2, and rearranging yields

$$Tb_1 + \Sigma x_{t2} b_2 + \Sigma x_{t3} b_3 = \Sigma y_t$$

$$\Sigma x_{t2} b_1 + \Sigma x_{t2}^2 b_2 + \Sigma x_{t2} x_{t3} b_3 = \Sigma x_{t2} y_t$$

$$\Sigma x_{t3} b_1 + \Sigma x_{t2} x_{t3} b_2 + \Sigma x_{t3}^2 b_3 = \Sigma x_{t3} y_t$$

The least squares estimator for b_1, b_2, and b_3 is given by the solution of this set of three *linear simultaneous equations* in the unknowns b_1, b_2, and b_3. These equations are known as the *normal equations*, and the easiest way to solve them is by using the matrix algebra procedures developed in Section 5.4 and Appendix 5C in Chapter 5. Specifically, we can rewrite the equations as

$$\begin{bmatrix} T & \Sigma x_{t2} & \Sigma x_{t3} \\ \Sigma x_{t2} & \Sigma x_{t2}^2 & \Sigma x_{t2} x_{t3} \\ \Sigma x_{t3} & \Sigma x_{t2} x_{t3} & \Sigma x_{t3}^2 \end{bmatrix} \begin{bmatrix} b_1 \\ b_2 \\ b_3 \end{bmatrix} = \begin{bmatrix} \Sigma y_t \\ \Sigma x_{t2} y_t \\ \Sigma x_{t3} y_t \end{bmatrix} \tag{9.2.3}$$

With the definitions for X and $\mathbf{y}$ given in equation 9.1.16, it is straightforward to show that, in matrix notation, equation 9.2.3 becomes

$$X'X\mathbf{b} = X'\mathbf{y} \tag{9.2.4}$$

This result is identical to the expression for the normal equations that was obtained in equation 5.4.16 in Chapter 5. The only difference is in the dimension of the vectors and matrices. Since we now have three unknown coefficients, $\mathbf{b}$ is (3×1), $X'X$ is (3×3), and $X'\mathbf{y}$ is (3×1). In Chapter 5 the corresponding dimensions were (2×1), (2×2), and (2×1), respectively.

To solve equation 9.2.4 we use the formula for the least squares estimator that we get by premultiplying both sides of equation 9.2.4 by $(X'X)^{-1}$. This matrix is the inverse of $X'X$; the inverse operation was developed in Appendix 5C in Chapter 5 and is handily performed by a computer. Carrying out the multiplication yields

$$\left(X'X\right)^{-1} X'X\mathbf{b} = \left(X'X\right)^{-1} X'\mathbf{y}$$

or

$$\mathbf{b} = \left(X'X\right)^{-1} X'\mathbf{y} \tag{9.2.5}$$

Again, this is the same formula as we obtained in Chapter 5, only the dimensions of the matrices are different. There is an important consequence of the increase in dimensions, however. In Chapter 5, where $\mathbf{b}$ was (2×1) with components b_1 and b_2, we obtained explicit expressions for these components, namely (see equation 5.3.10),

$$\mathbf{b} = \left(X'X\right)^{-1} X'\mathbf{y} = \begin{bmatrix} b_1 \\ b_2 \end{bmatrix} = \begin{bmatrix} \bar{y} - b_2 \bar{x} \\ \dfrac{T\Sigma x_t y_t - \Sigma x_t \Sigma y_t}{T\Sigma x_t^2 - \left(\Sigma x_t\right)^2} \end{bmatrix}$$

These expressions are no longer relevant when $K \geq 3$. The estimate b_2, for example, will depend on both the explanatory variables p_t and a_t. To obtain the relevant explicit expressions for b_1, b_2, and b_3 we could use equation 9.2.5 and follow the same steps as we did in Chapter 5. However, there is little if any practical usefulness from doing so. A better alternative is to obtain estimates b_1, b_2, and b_3 by using an appropriate computer package to compute the matrix expression in equation 9.2.5. Thus, for the two-dimensional (one explanatory variable) model we have given explicit algebraic expressions for the components of **b**, and it is worth your while to remember these expressions. For models with two or more explanatory variables, however, it is better for you to remember the matrix expression $\mathbf{b} = (X'X)^{-1}X'\mathbf{y}$ and to view this expression as the formula implemented by the computer for its computations. In the general case where β is an unknown K-dimensional vector of parameters, $X'X$ is of dimension $(K \times K)$, and $X'\mathbf{y}$ is $(K \times 1)$, the least squares estimator $\mathbf{b} = (X'X)^{-1}X'\mathbf{y}$ becomes

$$
\begin{bmatrix} b_1 \\ b_2 \\ \vdots \\ b_K \end{bmatrix} =
\begin{bmatrix}
\Sigma x_{t1}^2 & \Sigma x_{t1} x_{t2} & \cdots & \Sigma x_{t1} x_{tK} \\
\Sigma x_{t1} x_{t2} & \Sigma x_{t2}^2 & \cdots & \Sigma x_{t2} x_{tK} \\
\vdots & \vdots & & \vdots \\
\Sigma x_{t1} x_{tK} & \Sigma x_{t2} x_{tK} & \cdots & \Sigma x_{tK}^2
\end{bmatrix}^{-1}
\begin{bmatrix} \Sigma x_{t1} y_t \\ \Sigma x_{t2} y_t \\ \vdots \\ \Sigma x_{tK} y_t \end{bmatrix}
$$

We think of $\mathbf{b} = (X'X)^{-1}X'\mathbf{y}$ as *a rule that describes how the data* **y** *are to be used*, for whatever values of **y** occur; we call it an *estimator*. After we collect the data $(X,$ **y**$)$, and the matrices X and **y** contain numbers, not just symbols, then we can compute a *value* for the estimator. This value is called an *estimate*. You should remember that the estimation rule is an *estimator*; the numerical values obtained by using data are estimates. For our set of data on receipts, price, and advertising expenditure, the components of the matrices in equation 9.2.5 are given by

$$
X'X = \begin{bmatrix}
\Sigma x_{t1}^2 & \Sigma x_{t1} x_{t2} & \Sigma x_{t1} x_{t3} \\
\Sigma x_{t1} x_{t2} & \Sigma x_{t2}^2 & \Sigma x_{t2} x_{t3} \\
\Sigma x_{t1} x_{t3} & \Sigma x_{t2} x_{t3} & \Sigma x_{t3}^2
\end{bmatrix} =
\begin{bmatrix}
T & \Sigma x_{t2} & \Sigma x_{t3} \\
\Sigma x_{t2} & \Sigma x_{t2}^2 & \Sigma x_{t2} x_{t3} \\
\Sigma x_{t3} & \Sigma x_{t2} x_{t3} & \Sigma x_{t3}^2
\end{bmatrix}
$$

$$
= \begin{bmatrix}
52.00 & 104.0900 & 502.400 \\
104.09 & 212.0153 & 1012.755 \\
502.40 & 1012.7550 & 6189.660
\end{bmatrix}
\tag{9.2.6}
$$

and

$$
X'\mathbf{y} = \begin{bmatrix} \Sigma x_{t1} y_t \\ \Sigma x_{t2} y_t \\ \Sigma x_{t3} y_t \end{bmatrix} = \begin{bmatrix} \Sigma y_t \\ \Sigma x_{t2} y_t \\ \Sigma x_{t3} y_t \end{bmatrix} = \begin{bmatrix} 6256.80 \\ 12521.30 \\ 64389.39 \end{bmatrix}
\tag{9.2.7}
$$

A computer was used to obtain these matrices and the following least squares estimates.

$$
\mathbf{b} = \begin{bmatrix} b_1 \\ b_2 \\ b_3 \end{bmatrix} = \begin{bmatrix}
52.00 & 104.090 & 502.400 \\
104.09 & 212.015 & 1012.755 \\
502.40 & 1012.755 & 6189.660
\end{bmatrix}^{-1}
\begin{bmatrix} 6256.80 \\ 12521.30 \\ 64389.39 \end{bmatrix}
$$

$$
= \begin{bmatrix}
1.140756 & -0.539170 & -0.004373 \\
-0.539170 & 0.276429 & -0.001466 \\
-0.004373 & -0.001466 & 0.000756
\end{bmatrix}
\begin{bmatrix} 6256.80 \\ 12521.30 \\ 64389.39 \end{bmatrix}
$$

$$
= \begin{bmatrix} 104.79 \\ -6.642 \\ 2.984 \end{bmatrix}
\tag{9.2.8}
$$

The mean function that we are estimating is given by

$$E[y_t] = \beta_1 + \beta_2 x_{t2} + \beta_3 x_{t3} \tag{9.2.9}$$

In general terms the estimated mean function (or fitted regression line) is represented by

$$\hat{y}_t = b_1 + b_2 x_{t2} + b_3 x_{t3} \tag{9.2.10}$$

For our particular data set we have

$$\hat{y}_t = 104.79 - 6.642 x_{t2} + 2.984 x_{t3} \tag{9.2.11}$$

Or, in terms of the original economic variables,

$$\hat{tr}_t = 104.79 - 6.642 p_t + 2.984 a_t \tag{9.2.12}$$

Based on these results, what can we say to the management group of the hamburger chain? First, the negative coefficient of p_t suggests that demand is price elastic and that an increase in price of $1 will lead to a fall in weekly receipts of $6642. It might be of more interest to management to state this result in the opposite way, namely, that a reduction in price of $1 will lead to an increase in receipts of $6642. If such is the case, a management strategy of price reduction through the offering of specials would be a successful one.

Turning to the influence of advertising, our results suggest that an increase in advertising expenditure of $1000 will lead to an increase in total receipts of $2984. We can use this information, along with the costs of producing the additional hamburgers, to determine whether an increase in advertising expenditures is worthwhile.

The estimated equation can also be used for prediction. Suppose management is interested in predicting total receipts for a price of $2 and an advertising expenditure of $10,000. This prediction is given by

$$\hat{tr}_t = 104.785 - 6.6419(2) + 2.9843(10)$$
$$= 121.34$$

Thus, the predicted value of total receipts for the specified values of p and a is approximately $121,340.

From a practical standpoint we need to qualify this conclusion somewhat. It is ridiculous to suggest that a continual reduction in price will continue to lead to an increase in total receipts. If we reduced the price to zero, total receipts would necessarily be zero! Thus, our linear relationship is unlikely to be a good approximation to reality for all possible levels of advertising expenditure and price. It is more reasonable to think of it as being realistic within the range of our data which is $1.8 \le a_t \le 19.6$ and $1.50 \le p_t \le 2.47$. This question of the appropriate functional form will be taken up further in Chapter 10. For the moment, however, we note that giving the interpretation of $b_2 = -6.642$ in terms of the effect of a price change as large as $1 could be misleading.

9.2.2 Estimation of the Error Variance σ^2

Thus far in this chapter we have learned how to obtain least squares estimates for the coefficients in a general linear statistical model. The principles and the matrix formula for this task were the same as those given in Chapter 5 for the single explanatory variable case—only the dimensions of the matrices changed. For our example dealing with a Bay Area hamburger chain, where we imagine we have been retained as an economic consultant to estimate the dependence of total receipts on price and advertising expenditure, we estimated the relationship

$$\hat{tr}_t = 104.79 - 6.642p_t + 2.984a_t \qquad (9.2.13)$$

We learned how the *point estimates* $b_2 = -6.642$ and $b_3 = 2.984$ tell us something about how receipts are likely to change as a consequence of changes in price and advertising expenditure. The next logical step is to ask: How reliable are the estimates $b_2 = -6.642$ and $b_3 = 2.984$? Can we be confident that they are close to the true parameters β_2 and β_3 that describe the underlying process that we assumed generated the sample observations? Or, in other words, have we estimated β_2 and β_3 with low sampling variability and high precision?

To answer this question we need an estimate of the sampling variability of b_2 and b_3. A large sampling variability implies *alternative 52-week samples* could yield estimates b_2 and b_3 that are quite different from β_2 and β_3. With low sampling variability the estimates would not vary much in alternative or repeated samples. Given that the least squares estimator is unbiased, a low sampling variability implies the estimates are more reliable; β_2 and β_3 are estimated with more precision. The statistical measure of the sampling variability of the least squares estimator **b** is its covariance matrix. In Chapter 6 we found that this covariance matrix is given by $\sigma^2(X'X)^{-1}$, and that an estimate of it is given by $\hat{\sigma}^2(X'X)^{-1}$. These two results are also valid for the more general model that is currently under consideration. What is of immediate interest in this section is how to estimate the error variance σ^2. In Section 9.2.3 that follows, we use the estimated error variance $\hat{\sigma}^2$ to form the estimated covariance matrix $\hat{\sigma}^2(X'X)^{-1}$.

To find an estimator for σ^2 we follow the same steps that were outlined in Sections 6.3 and 6.6.4 of Chapter 6. The least squares residuals are computed from

$$\hat{e}_t = y_t - \hat{y}_t = y_t - \left(b_1 + x_{t2}b_2 + x_{t3}b_3\right) \qquad (9.2.14)$$

or, in matrix notation,

$$\hat{e} = y - \hat{y} = y - Xb \qquad (9.2.15)$$

An unbiased estimator of σ^2 is given by

$$\hat{\sigma}^2 = \frac{\Sigma\hat{e}_t^2}{T-K} = \frac{\hat{e}'\hat{e}}{T-K} = \frac{(y-Xb)'(y-Xb)}{T-K} \qquad (9.2.16)$$

where K is the number of coefficients being estimated; K is also the dimension of β or the number of columns in X. Note that in Chapter 6, where there was one explanatory variable and two coefficients, $K = 2$. In the hamburger chain example we have $K = 3$. The estimate for our sample of data in Table 9.1 is

$$\hat{\sigma}^2 = \frac{\hat{e}'\hat{e}}{T-K} = \frac{1805.168}{52-3} = 36.84 \qquad (9.2.17)$$

One major purpose of obtaining this estimate is to enable us to get an estimated covariance matrix for the least squares estimator **b**. Nevertheless, it is helpful to see what kind of interpretation we can place on this estimate; what does it say in terms of the variability of the error term?

From equation 9.2.17, the estimated standard deviation of the errors is approximately 6. That is, $\hat{\sigma} \approx 6$. To interpret this value, we must make some assumption about the probability distribution of e_t. If we can assume the e_t are normally distributed, then we know that 95% of the errors will fall within 1.96 standard deviations of their zero mean. If we treat 1.96 as being approximately 2, then the estimate $\hat{\sigma} = 6$ suggests that 95% of the errors will lie between -12 and $+12$. In other words, we should not be surprised if total receipts were as much as $12,000 above or below the value that would be given by the mean function. Thus, although the value $\hat{\sigma}^2 = 36$ does not convey much information by itself, in conjunction with an assumption about the error distribution, we can work out what it implies about the range of the errors, and hence what it implies about the range of y around the mean function $\beta_1 + x_{t2}\beta_2 + x_{t3}\beta_3$.

Let us turn now to the properties of the least squares estimator and, in particular, to its estimated covariance matrix.

9.2.3 Sampling Properties of the Least Squares Estimator

Because the least squares estimator $\mathbf{b} = (X'X)^{-1}X'\mathbf{y}$ is a function of the random vector $\mathbf{y}$, it too is a random vector that, in a repeated sample context, takes on different values in diffcrent samples. An examination of the sampling properties of the least squares estimator tells us something about whether it is a desirable estimator and how to assess the reliability of the estimates it produces. In Chapter 6 we found that the least squares estimator was unbiased and that it had a covariance matrix given by $\sigma^2(X'X)^{-1}$. That is,

$$E[\mathbf{b}] = \boldsymbol{\beta} \quad \text{and} \quad \text{cov}(\mathbf{b}) = E\left[(\mathbf{b}-\boldsymbol{\beta})(\mathbf{b}-\boldsymbol{\beta})'\right] = \sigma^2\left(X'X\right)^{-1}$$
(9.2.18)

Our proofs were given in terms of the model $\mathbf{y} = X\boldsymbol{\beta} + \mathbf{e}$ where $\boldsymbol{\beta}$ was of dimension (2×1) and X was $(T \times 2)$. However, it should be clear that the samc proofs will be valid for the more general case where $\boldsymbol{\beta}$ is $(K \times 1)$ and X is $(T \times K)$. Changing the matrix dimensions does not alter any of the steps used to derive the results in equation 9.2.18. Students who need reassurance on this point should reread Section 6.6. In Section 6.6.3 of Chapter 6 we also noted that $\mathbf{b}$ is a linear function of the random vector $\mathbf{y}$ because it can be written as $\mathbf{b} = A\mathbf{y}$ where $A = (X'X)^{-1}X'$ is a nonrandom matrix. We went on to say that $\mathbf{b}$ is the *best linear unbiased estimator* for $\boldsymbol{\beta}$ in the sense that there is no other linear unbiased estimator that has a sampling variability less than that of $\mathbf{b}$. This result remains true for the *general* linear statistical model that we are considering in this chapter. *The dimensions of the problem have changed, but the sampling properties have not.*

If we are able to assume that the errors are *normally distributed*, then $\mathbf{y}$ too will be a normally distributed random variable; in turn, because it is a linear function of $\mathbf{y}$, the least squares estimator $\mathbf{b}$ will also be normally distributed. Under these circumstances we summarize the probability distribution of $\mathbf{b}$ by writing

$$\mathbf{b} \sim N\left[\boldsymbol{\beta}, \sigma^2\left(X'X\right)^{-1}\right]$$

The normality assumption also means that $\mathbf{b}$ becomes the *best unbiased estimator* for $\boldsymbol{\beta}$, not just the best *linear* unbiased estimator. When the errors are not normally distributed, there may exist an unbiased nonlinear estimator that has a smaller sampling variability than the least squares estimator. With normally distributed errors we know that no superior nonlinear unbiased estimator exists.

Another consequence of making a distributional assumption about the errors is that it permits us to use the maximum likelihood criterion for choosing estimators for β and σ^2. This criterion was discussed briefly for the simple linear model in Chapters 5 and 6. As in Chapter 5, when the errors are normally distributed, application of the maximum likelihood criterion leads to the same rule for estimating β as does the least squares criterion. That is, when $\mathbf{y}$ is a normal random vector, $\mathbf{b} = (X'X)^{-1}X'\mathbf{y}$ is both the least squares and the maximum likelihood estimator for β. As we will discuss in Chapter 14, maximum likelihood estimators have certain desirable properties. The maximum likelihood estimator for σ^2 is different from the one we suggested in equation 9.2.16. It is given by

$$\tilde{\sigma}^2 = \frac{(\mathbf{y} - X\mathbf{b})'(\mathbf{y} - X\mathbf{b})}{T} = \left(\frac{T}{T-K}\right)\hat{\sigma}^2$$

In general, we prefer the estimator $\hat{\sigma}^2$ to the maximum likelihood estimator $\tilde{\sigma}^2$ because of its property of unbiasedness. Those interested in a more complete discussion of the maximum likelihood rules for the general linear statistical model should read Judge et al. (1988, pp. 222–225).

9.2.3a The Least Squares Covariance Matrix

Before leaving this section on the properties of the least squares estimator, it is useful to examine the covariance matrix of the estimator in more detail. It is the estimated covariance matrix that gives us sampling information about the point estimate $\mathbf{b}$. A proper understanding of the covariance matrix for $\mathbf{b}$, and the elements it contains, is made easier if we write out its various representations. For $K = 3$, as it is in the example in this chapter, we have

$$\text{cov}(\mathbf{b}) = E\left[(\mathbf{b} - \beta)(\mathbf{b} - \beta)'\right]$$

$$= \begin{bmatrix} \text{var}(b_1) & \text{cov}(b_1, b_2) & \text{cov}(b_1, b_3) \\ \text{cov}(b_1, b_2) & \text{var}(b_2) & \text{cov}(b_2, b_3) \\ \text{cov}(b_1, b_3) & \text{cov}(b_2, b_3) & \text{var}(b_3) \end{bmatrix}$$

$$= \begin{bmatrix} E(b_1 - \beta_1)^2 & E(b_1 - \beta_1)(b_2 - \beta_2) & E(b_1 - \beta_1)(b_3 - \beta_3) \\ E(b_1 - \beta_1)(b_2 - \beta_2) & E(b_2 - \beta_2)^2 & E(b_2 - \beta_2)(b_3 - \beta_3) \\ E(b_1 - \beta_1)(b_3 - \beta_3) & E(b_2 - \beta_2)(b_3 - \beta_3) & E(b_3 - \beta_3)^2 \end{bmatrix}$$

$$= \sigma^2 (X'X)^{-1} = \sigma^2 \begin{bmatrix} T & \Sigma x_{t2} & \Sigma x_{t3} \\ \Sigma x_{t2} & \Sigma x_{t2}^2 & \Sigma x_{t2} x_{t3} \\ \Sigma x_{t3} & \Sigma x_{t2} x_{t3} & \Sigma x_{t3}^2 \end{bmatrix}^{-1} \tag{9.2.19}$$

Using the estimate $\hat{\sigma}^2 = 36.84$ found in equation 9.2.17 and the matrix $(X'X)^{-1}$ found in equation 9.2.8, the estimated covariance matrix for $\mathbf{b}$ for our receipts–price–advertising relationship is

$$\hat{\text{cov}}(\mathbf{b}) = \hat{\sigma}^2 (X'X)^{-1}$$

$$= 36.84 \begin{bmatrix} 1.140756 & -0.5391702 & -0.00437318 \\ -0.5391702 & 0.2764296 & -0.00146637 \\ -0.0043732 & -0.0014664 & 0.00075645 \end{bmatrix}$$

$$= \begin{bmatrix} 42.026 & -19.863 & -0.16111 \\ -19.863 & 10.184 & -0.05402 \\ -0.16111 & -0.05402 & 0.02787 \end{bmatrix} \tag{9.2.20}$$

Thus, we have

$$\hat{\text{var}}(b_1) = 42.026 \qquad \hat{\text{cov}}(b_1, b_2) = -19.863$$

$$\hat{\text{var}}(b_2) = 10.184 \qquad \hat{\text{cov}}(b_1, b_3) = -0.16111$$

$$\hat{\text{var}}(b_3) = 0.02787 \qquad \hat{\text{cov}}(b_2, b_3) = -0.05402$$

Just as we used the estimated error variance to say something about the likely range of the errors, these estimated variances can be used to say something about the likely range of the least squares estimates in a repeated-sampling context. For example, the estimated standard deviation for b_2 is given by the square root of 10.184, which is approximately 3.2. If the errors and hence b_2 are normally distributed, then, in repeated samples, we would expect 95% of the estimates b_2 to be within two standard deviations of the mean β_2. In our particular sample, 6.4 is the estimate of two standard deviations; hence, we estimate that 95% of the b_2 values would lie within 6.4 of the mean β_2. Another way of viewing this result is to say that, in our one particular sample, where we have an estimate of $b_2 = -6.642$, we should not be surprised if the difference between this estimate and the underlying parameter β_2 is as great as 6.4. It is in this sense that the estimated covariance matrix for β tells us something about the reliability of the least squares estimates. If the difference between b_2 and β_2 can be large, b_2 is not regarded as reliable; if the difference between b_2 and β_2 is likely to be small, we treat b_2 as reliable. Whether a particular difference is "large" or "small" will depend on the context of the problem and the use to which the estimates are to be put, but closely allied with this question is the problem of interval estimation that we take up in Chapter 10. Also in Chapter 10, we learn how the estimated variances and covariances can be used to test hypotheses about the parameters and to draw other inferences such as interval estimation and hypothesis testing for linear combinations of the parameters.

9.2.4   Coefficient of Determination

When dealing with the simple linear model in Chapter 8, we introduced a measure of the proportion of variation in the dependent variable that is explained by variation in the explanatory variable. This measure was called the coefficient of determination and was defined by

$$R^2 = \frac{\text{variation in } y \text{ attributable to explanatory variable}}{\text{total variation in } y} = \frac{\Sigma(\hat{y}_t - \bar{y})^2}{\Sigma(y_t - \bar{y})^2}$$

$$= 1 - \frac{\text{error variation}}{\text{total variation in } y} = 1 - \frac{\Sigma\hat{e}_t^2}{\Sigma(y_t - \bar{y})^2} = 1 - \frac{\hat{e}'\hat{e}}{y'y - T\bar{y}^2} \tag{9.2.21}$$

In the general linear statistical model (the concern of this chapter), the same measure is relevant and the same formulas are valid, but now we talk of the proportion of variation in the dependent variable explained by *all* of the explanatory variables in the linear model. Thus, for our receipts–price–advertising example we have

$$R^2 = 1 - \frac{\Sigma\hat{e}_t^2}{\Sigma(y_t - \bar{y})^2} = 1 - \frac{1805.168}{13581.35} = 0.867 \tag{9.2.22}$$

The interpretation we give this result is to say that 86.7% of the variation in total receipts is explained by the variation in price and by the variation in the level of advertising expenditure. We should be quite happy with this result. It means that, *in our sample*, only 13.3% of the variation in receipts is left unexplained and is due to variation in the error term or to variation in other variables that implicitly form part of the error term.

As mentioned in Chapter 8, the coefficient of determination is also viewed as a measure of the predictive ability of the model over the sample period or as a measure of how well the estimated regression fits the data. It can be shown that R^2 is equal to the squared sample correlation coefficient between the $\hat{y}_t$ and the y_t. Since the $\hat{y}_t$ represent predictions of receipts for the prices and advertising expenditures in the sample, the correlation between these predicted values and the observed y_t gives a measure of predictive ability within the sample. Also, if R^2 is high, and hence the correspondence between $\hat{y}_t$ and y_t is high, the estimated regression is said to be a "good fit." If the correspondence between $\hat{y}_t$ and y_t is low, as it is when R^2 is low, the estimated regression is said to be a "poor fit."

Sometimes R^2 (or a modification of it called adjusted R^2 or $\overline{R}^2$) is used as a device for model selection, or selection of the appropriate set of explanatory variables. Its use and misuse for this purpose will be discussed in Chapter 10. Here we think of R^2 as a descriptive device for telling us about the "fit" of the model in terms of the proportion of variation in the dependent variable explained by the explanatory variables and in terms of the predictive ability of the model over the sample period.

One final note is in order. If the model does not contain a constant term (there is no intercept and the matrix X does not contain a column of ones), then the measure R^2 given in equation 9.2.21 is no longer appropriate. The reason it is no longer appropriate is that, without a constant

$$\Sigma\left(y_t - \overline{y}\right)^2 \neq \Sigma\left(\hat{y}_t - \overline{y}\right)^2 + \Sigma\hat{e}_t^2 \qquad (9.2.23)$$

or

total variation $\neq$ variation explained by regression + error variation

Under these circumstances it does not make sense to talk of the proportion of total variation that is explained by the regression. Two alternatives are possible. One is to not report an R^2 value if the model does not contain a constant. The other is to measure variation around zero instead of around the sample mean $\overline{y}$. In this latter instance we have

$$R_*^2 = 1 - \frac{\Sigma\hat{e}_t^2}{\Sigma y_t^2}$$

9.3 Reporting–Summarizing Results

A convenient way to report a summary of the various results developed in this chapter is to write down the estimated equation, with standard errors of coefficients written in parentheses below the estimated coefficients, and with the R^2-value written next to the equation. This was the approach that was adopted for the simple linear model in Section 8.2. Extending this approach to the model estimated in this chapter, we begin by calculating the standard errors given by the square roots of the diagonal elements of $\hat{\sigma}^2(X'X)^{-1}$. That is,

$$\text{standard error}(b_1) = \text{se}(b_1) = \sqrt{\hat{\text{var}}(b_1)} = \sqrt{42.026} = 6.483$$

$$\text{standard error}(b_2) = \text{se}(b_2) = \sqrt{\hat{\text{var}}(b_2)} = \sqrt{10.184} = 3.191$$

$$\text{standard error}(b_3) = \text{se}(b_3) = \sqrt{\hat{\text{var}}(b_3)} = \sqrt{0.02787} = 0.1669$$

A summary of the results can then be reported as

$$\hat{y}_t = 104.79 - 6.642x_{t2} + 2.984x_{t3} \qquad R^2 = 0.862$$
$$\quad (6.48) \quad (3.191) \quad (0.167) \qquad \text{(st. errors)} \qquad\qquad (9.3.1)$$

From this summary we can read off the estimated effects of changes in the explanatory variables on the dependent variable, we can predict values of the dependent variable for given values of the explanatory variables, we can test hypotheses about the individual coefficients and, to give an idea of the reliability of our estimates, we can construct confidence intervals for the individual coefficients. How we perform all of these tasks will become clear in Chapter 10 where we generalize the hypothesis testing and interval estimation procedures that were introduced in Chapter 7 for the simple linear statistical model. In Section 10.5 in particular we give more details on how the reporting–summary procedure can be utilized. A summary of the main results covered so far for the general linear statistical model follows.

9.4   Summary of New Concepts

In this chapter we have reformulated the linear statistical model to allow for the inclusion of more than one explanatory variable and analyzed this more general model. The main points that we have covered thus far are as follows:

1. There are many economic models where an outcome or dependent variable is a function of a number of explanatory variables. A linear statistical model where there is more than one explanatory variable is called a general linear statistical model.

2. A general linear statistical model with $(K-1)$ explanatory variables plus a constant term, and K unknown coefficients, can be written as

$$y_t = \beta_1 + x_{t2}\beta_2 + x_{t3}\beta_3 + \ldots + x_{tK}\beta_K + e_t$$

or

$$\mathbf{y} = X\boldsymbol{\beta} + \mathbf{e}$$

where $\mathbf{y}$ is a T-dimensional vector of observations on the dependent variable, X is a $(T \times K)$ matrix of observations on the explanatory variables, $\mathbf{e}$ is a T-dimensional error vector, and $\boldsymbol{\beta}$ is a $(K \times 1)$ vector of unknown coefficients to be estimated. This expression is identical to the matrix expression for the simple linear model; only the dimensions of X and $\boldsymbol{\beta}$ are different.

3. We continue with the random error assumptions employed earlier, namely,

$$\mathbf{e} \sim \left(\mathbf{0}, \sigma^2 I_T\right)$$

An additional assumption we introduce is that none of the explanatory variables can be written as a linear function of any of the others. Later in the book we learn that this assumption implies the absence of exact multicollinearity.

4. To find an estimator for the unknown vector of parameters $\boldsymbol{\beta}$, we apply the least squares principle. This principle leads to the estimator

$$\mathbf{b} = \left(X'X\right)^{-1} X'\mathbf{y}$$

This is the same formula as used for the simple regression model; only the dimensions of $\mathbf{b}$ and X are different.

5. We do not derive individual formulas for the components of **b**; instead, we let the computer calculate the inverse matrix $(X'X)^{-1}$ and the expression $(X'X)^{-1}X'\mathbf{y}$.

6. The estimator $\mathbf{b} = (X'X)^{-1}X'\mathbf{y}$ has desirable sampling properties. It is a linear function of **y**. It is an unbiased estimator for β. It has a smaller sampling variability than any other linear unbiased estimator for β.

7. An unbiased estimator of the error variance σ^2 is given by the residual or error sum of squares divided by $(T - K)$. That is

$$\hat{\sigma}^2 = \frac{\hat{\mathbf{e}}'\hat{\mathbf{e}}}{T - K} \qquad \text{where} \qquad \hat{\mathbf{e}} = \mathbf{y} - X\mathbf{b}$$

8. The expression for the covariance matrix of the least squares estimator is

$$\text{cov}(\mathbf{b}) = \sigma^2 (X'X)^{-1}$$

and an estimate of this matrix is given by

$$\hat{\text{cov}}(\mathbf{b}) = \hat{\sigma}^2 (X'X)^{-1}$$

9. The proportion of variation in the dependent variable explained by the estimated function is given by the coefficient of determination:

$$R^2 = 1 - \frac{\hat{\mathbf{e}}'\hat{\mathbf{e}}}{\mathbf{y}'\mathbf{y} - T\bar{y}^2}$$

10. One way to report the results developed in this chapter is in the form

$$\hat{y}_t = \underset{\text{se}(b_1)}{b_1} + \underset{\text{se}(b_2)}{b_2 x_{t2}} + \ldots + \underset{\text{se}(b_K)}{b_K x_{tK}}$$

where the $\text{se}(b_k)$ are "standard errors" given by the square roots of the diagonal elements of $\hat{\sigma}^2(X'X)^{-1}$.

Now that we have developed a *general* linear statistical model where the matrix X can contain a general number of explanatory variables, the range of economic models that will fit within this framework has been greatly expanded. Any economic model where an outcome variable y depends on a number of explanatory variables is a candidate for this framework.

The specification of a linear statistical model with more than one explanatory (regressor) variable brings with it uncertainty concerning whether we have chosen the correct set of regressors. In the sample introduced in Section 9.1, and in applied work in general, the possibility of over- or underspecifying the number of regressor variables appearing in the X matrix is a real one. Overspecifying means we have included irrelevant regressors that have no influence on the outcomes for y. Underspecifying means we have omitted relevant variables that do influence y. Given that there could be uncertainty concerning what the relevant variables are, it is natural to pursue the question: What are the statistical implications of incorrectly specifying the X matrix? We take up this question in the next section. Then, given some insights on this question, in Chapters 10 and 11 we turn to the problems of interval estimation and hypothesis testing and consider the following questions: Which regressor variables should be included? What is the correct functional form for relating the X regressors to the outcome variable y?

9.5   Statistical Implications of Misspecifying the Set of Regressors

Economic theory usually provides a basis for choosing the variables to include in the design matrix X of an economic or statistical model. However, economic theory often provides only a general guideline; in most instances there is uncertainty relative to the variables to include or exclude. For example, economic theory may suggest a primary set of variables that should be included, but there may be a secondary, possibly extraneous, set of variables that may or may not have a systematic impact on the economic or dependent variable y whose behavior is explained by the economic and statistical model.

Uncertainty about the number and form of variables that should appear in the design matrix is a common problem that will repeatedly occupy us in the chapters ahead. If a model is constructed to explain the sales of a product by a supermarket, or the per capita or aggregate demand for a commodity, it is certain that the price of the product is relevant, but which competing and complementary products' prices should be included? There is often a substantial question about which product prices have a significant impact on the sales of another product. Alternatively, in a model of aggregate consumption there is usually uncertainty relative to *how many lagged (previous) values of income should be included*. This question, which will be pursued in the context of distributed lag models in Chapter 21, is equivalent to asking how long the effects of a change in income on consumption may be delayed or carried over. Again, it results in uncertainty regarding the correct specification of the design matrix X, either by including too few or including too many explanatory variables. Questions like these, regarding the dynamic behavior of the economy, are very difficult to answer, since *it may be too much to ask that the data both provide estimates of the unknown parameters and help to determine the correct content of the design matrix X.*

9.5.1   Economic Model

To motivate the problem of specifying the matrix of explanatory variables, it is useful to examine the economic model

$$C_t = \beta_1 + \delta S_t + \gamma_1 E_{1t} + \gamma_2 E_{2t} + \gamma_3 E_{3t} + \beta_2 Y_t \qquad (9.5.1)$$

which is an economic model for beer expenditure (C) by a cross section of $t = 1, 2,\ldots,$ T individuals. Economic theory strongly suggests that income (Y) be included in this model as an explanatory variable. The remaining variables represent characteristics of the individuals, gender (S) and levels of educational attainment (E_1, E_2, E_3) that may or may not have a systematic effect on expenditure on beer. How we measure such variables is a question taken up in Chapter 12. Of relevance now is the fact that we may have some sociological suspicions that these factors do affect beer expenditure, but the argument for their inclusion is not nearly as strong as for the inclusion of income. Thus we ask: What are the consequences of including these variables in the economic and statistical model if they have no effect on beer expenditure?

Alternatively we may have judged a priori that neither gender nor level of educational attainment have a systematic effect on beer expenditure and considered only the basic relationship

$$C_t = \beta_1 + \beta_2 Y_t \qquad (9.5.2)$$

What if gender and level of educational attainment *do* systematically affect an individual's expenditure on beer and we omit them from the economic and statistical models? What are the consequences of incorrectly omitting these relevant variables? Incorrect choices where relevant variables are omitted or irrelevant variables are included are called *variable specification errors*.

In the following sections we examine the statistical consequences of variable specification error and present a sampling experiment to reflect the bias-variance trade-off from over- and underspecifying the number of explanatory variables.

9.5.2 Representing Competing Statistical Models

To make specific the consequences of misspecifying the X matrix, let us use the beer expenditure example introduced at the beginning of this section. Given economic model 9.5.1, consider the following two competing statistical models:

$$\text{Model 1:} \qquad \mathbf{y} = X_1\boldsymbol{\beta}_1 + X_2\boldsymbol{\beta}_2 + \mathbf{e}_1 = X\boldsymbol{\beta} + \mathbf{e}_1 \qquad (9.5.3)$$

and

$$\text{Model 2:} \qquad \mathbf{y} = X_1\boldsymbol{\beta}_1 + \mathbf{e}_2 \qquad (9.5.4)$$

where X_1 contains the intercept and income (Y) variables, X_2 contains the gender (S) and education (E_1, E_2, E_3) variables. The corresponding parameter vectors are $\boldsymbol{\beta}_1 = (\beta_1\ \beta_2)'$, $\boldsymbol{\beta}_2 = (\delta\ \gamma_1\ \gamma_2\ \gamma_3)$, $\mathbf{e}_1 \sim (\mathbf{0}, \sigma_1^2 I_T)$, and $\mathbf{e}_2 = X_2\boldsymbol{\beta}_2 + \mathbf{e}_1 \sim (\mathbf{0}, \sigma_2^2 I_T)$. We have added subscripts to the errors to indicate that they correspond to different model specifications. Also, note that when we omit the variables in X_2 from the model specification we are equivalently assuming that the parameters $\boldsymbol{\beta}_2 = \mathbf{0}$! *Deleting variables from a model is equivalent to assuming that they have no systematic effect on the dependent or outcome variable and thus that their associated parameters are zero.* Thus, Model 2 is a restricted version of Model 1. In the following section we assume in turn that each model is correct and discuss the bias and sampling variability of the corresponding least squares estimators of Model 1 and Model 2.

9.5.3   Bias and Sampling Variability of the Least Squares Estimator Under Model Misspecification

If we apply the least squares estimation rule to Model 1 or Model 2, the resulting sampling properties depend on whether or not we have correctly specified the model.

1. *If the variables in X_2 are not extraneous, then Model 1 is the correct specification.* In this case the least squares estimator of Model 1 has all the desirable properties discussed in the previous chapters, namely, it is the best (minimum variance) unbiased estimator of $\boldsymbol{\beta}$.

Suppose, however, we incorrectly adopt Model 2. That is, we incorrectly assume that the X_2 variables are extraneous and that $\boldsymbol{\beta}_2 = 0$. What are the statistical properties of the least squares estimator of $\boldsymbol{\beta}_1$ when the incorrectly specified Model 2 is estimated by least squares? If Model 1 is correct, then the error term in Model 2 is $\mathbf{e}_2 = X_2\boldsymbol{\beta}_2 + \mathbf{e}_1$. The effects of omitted variables are captured by and included in the model error term. In this case the mean of the error term $\mathbf{e}_2$ is not zero, which is a violation of one of the standard model assumptions, since $E[\mathbf{e}_2] = E[X_2\boldsymbol{\beta}_2 + \mathbf{e}_1] = X_2\boldsymbol{\beta}_2 \neq \mathbf{0}$. The corresponding least squares estimator of $\boldsymbol{\beta}_1$ is

$$
\begin{aligned}
\mathbf{b}_1 &= \left(X_1'X_1\right)^{-1} X_1'\mathbf{y} \\
&= \left(X_1'X_1\right)^{-1} X_1'\left(X_1\boldsymbol{\beta}_1 + X_2\boldsymbol{\beta}_2 + \mathbf{e}_1\right) \qquad \text{(since Model 1 is correct)} \\
&= \boldsymbol{\beta}_1 + \left(X_1'X_1\right)^{-1} X_1'X_2\boldsymbol{\beta}_2 + \left(X_1'X_1\right)^{-1} X_1'\mathbf{e}_1
\end{aligned}
$$

$$\qquad (9.5.5)$$

Since $\beta_2 \neq \mathbf{0}$ unless $X_1'X_2 = 0$, the expected value of $\mathbf{b}_1$ is

$$E[\mathbf{b}_1] = \beta_1 + \left(X_1'X_1\right)^{-1} X_1'X_2\beta_2 \neq \beta_1 \qquad (9.5.6)$$

We summarize this result as follows:

2. If Model 1 is correct ($\beta_2 \neq \mathbf{0}$) and Model 2 is estimated by least squares, the least squares estimator is biased, unless the variables in X_1 and X_2 happen to be "orthogonal," or have zero cross-product.

3. *If the variables in X_2 are extraneous, then Model 2 is the correct specification.* In this instance the least squares estimator of β_1 in Model 2 has a minimum variance unbiased property.

Alternatively, suppose we incorrectly adopt Model 1 when the X_2 variables are extraneous and $\beta_2 = \mathbf{0}$. The consequences of this misspecification are, in one sense, not as severe as incorrectly omitting a relevant variable. Adopting Model 1 when Model 2 is correct does not lead to the standard assumptions about the error term $\mathbf{e}_1$ being incorrect. Model 1 is "appropriate" by this definition, although we will be unnecessarily using information in the data to estimate the parameters β_2, which are in fact zero. The least squares estimator $\mathbf{b} = (X'X)^{-1}X'\mathbf{y}$, where $X = [X_1\ X_2]$, is an unbiased estimator of β, since

$$E[\mathbf{b}] = \beta = \begin{bmatrix} \beta_1 \\ \mathbf{0} \end{bmatrix} \qquad (9.5.7)$$

This leads us to conclude:

4. If $\beta_2 = \mathbf{0}$ and we use Model 1 then the least squares estimator is unbiased.

Of course, bias is just one aspect of estimator sampling performance. Another factor we must examine and identify is the *effect of regressor misspecification on sampling variability.* In this case

5. If $\beta_2 = \mathbf{0}$ and we use Model 1, then the least squares estimator is unbiased, but it is *inefficient* relative to the least squares estimator from the correctly specified Model 2. This inefficiency necessarily follows because we know the least squares estimator for the correctly specified Model 2 has minimum variance.

6. Finally, if $\beta_2 \neq \mathbf{0}$ and we adopt Model 2, then the least squares estimator of β_1 has smaller sampling variability than the least squares estimator of β_1 for the correctly specified Model 1, but it is *biased.*

In terms of the beer expenditure model equation 9.5.1 we have the following results: If Model 1 is estimated by least squares, the least squares estimator is the best unbiased estimator of the parameters, if Model 1 is the correct specification; that is, if gender and educational attainment have a systematic effect on beer expenditures, then it is correct to include these variables into the economic and statistical model. On the other hand, if gender and level of educational attainment have no systematic effect on expenditures, that is, Model 2 is correct, and Model 1 is estimated by least squares, then the least squares estimator of the parameters (β_1) of Model 1 are unbiased but not efficient. The inefficiency arises because there is information about β_2 that has *not* been employed, namely that $\beta_2 = \mathbf{0}$. As we will find in Chapter 11, *making use of correct information does not introduce bias and does reduce sampling variability.* Thus estimation of Model 1 when Model 2 is true yields parameter estimators that are not as precise as could be obtained by correctly estimating Model 2. Also, of course, estimation of Model 1 will yield estimates of $K = 6$ parameters even though $\delta = \gamma_1 = \gamma_2 = \gamma_3 = 0$.

Estimation of Model 2 by least squares is, as we find in Chapter 11, equivalent to the application of restricted least squares to Model 1 with the restrictions $\delta = \gamma_1 = \gamma_2 = \gamma_3 = 0$ imposed. If gender and level of educational attainment have no systematic effect on beer expenditures, then the restrictions are correct, Model 2 is correctly specified, and the least squares estimator is the best unbiased estimation rule for the parameters β_1. If the restrictions are incorrect, then estimation of Model 2 by least squares yields a biased estimator of β_1, with reduced sampling variability.

To summarize the effects of misspecifying the design matrix X:

1. If the design matrix X omits relevant explanatory or control variables, then the least squares estimator is biased but has smaller sampling variability than the unbiased rule.

2. If the design matrix X includes irrelevant explanatory or control variables, then the least squares estimator is unbiased but does not have sampling variances that are as small as could be obtained by estimating the correctly specified model by least squares.

9.5.4   A Sampling Experiment

In Section 9.5.3 we explored the bias-variance implications of misspecifying the right-hand-side explanatory variables. To make these results a little more real, let's consider a sampling experiment where we know the correct model and want to discern the bias-variance impact of over- and underspecifying the number of right-hand-side variables.

As a basis for the sampling experiment, assume you are setting up a controlled experiment to estimate the parameters of the following demand relation:

$$q_t = \beta_1 + \beta_2 p_t + \beta_3 y_t + \beta_4 ps_t \qquad (9.5.8)$$

where q_t is quantity, p_t is price, y_t is income, and ps_t is the price of a presumed substitute good. Since this is a controlled experiment, the right-hand-side variables are fixed by the experiment and are thus nonstochastic.

In developing the sampling experiment, we consider the following statistical model:

$$\begin{aligned} q_t &= \beta_1 + \beta_2 p_t + \beta_3 y_t + \beta_4 ps_t + e_t \\ &= \beta_1 x_{1t} + \beta_2 x_{2t} + \beta_3 x_{3t} + \beta_4 x_{4t} + e_t \end{aligned} \qquad (9.5.9)$$

where the independent random variable $e_t \sim N(0, \sigma^2)$. The sampling process described by the statistical model suggests the least squares rule is appropriate for estimating the unknown parameters. To give us an idea of performance under correct and misspecified right-hand-side variables, we use the following parameter values in our sampling experiment:

$$\begin{aligned} \beta_1 &= 15 & \beta_2 &= -1.6 & \beta_3 &= 0.7 \\ \beta_4 &= 0 & \sigma^2 &= 16 \end{aligned}$$

and we use the values for **p**, **y**, and **ps** given in Table 9.2. Based on these values for the X matrix, 1000 samples of size 20 were generated.

Since in the statistical model 9.5.9 the parameter $\beta_4 = 0$, the correct statistical model is

$$\begin{aligned} q_t &= \beta_1 + \beta_2 p_t + \beta_3 y_t + e_t \\ &= 15 - 1.6 p_t + 0.7 y_t + e_t \\ &= 15 x_{1t} - 1.6 x_{2t} + 0.7 x_{3t} + e_t \end{aligned} \qquad (9.5.10)$$

Table 9.2   Treatment Values Chosen
for **p**, **y**, and **ps**

p	y	ps
5.40	32.45	5.85
5.18	34.29	5.23
5.18	34.29	5.23
5.01	29.61	5.51
5.55	31.45	6.10
4.86	29.98	5.67
5.45	32.04	5.09
5.15	32.91	5.90
5.63	37.36	6.02
5.53	35.94	5.22
5.75	30.93	6.56
6.47	33.56	6.91
6.20	35.87	6.17
6.13	36.69	6.35
5.67	36.74	6.42
6.43	41.28	6.41
6.65	40.27	6.49
7.19	42.78	6.46
6.49	35.81	7.58
7.42	43.22	7.58
7.20	42.26	7.18

with

$$e_t \sim N(0, 16)$$

(9.5.11)

The variances of the least squares estimator for the correctly specified model are given by the diagonal elements of $\sigma^2(X'X)^{-1}$, where $X = \begin{bmatrix} \mathbf{x}_1 & \mathbf{p} & \mathbf{y} \end{bmatrix}$. These variances are

$$\text{var}(b_1) = 60.14 \qquad \text{var}(b_2) = 5.44 \qquad \text{var}(b_3) = 0.17 \qquad (9.5.12)$$

9.5.4a Results of the Sampling Experiment   What we hope to gain from this sampling experiment are some insights into the effects of omitting a variable that should be included in the model, and including an extraneous variable in the model. The correctly specified model contains the variables x_1, x_2 and x_3. The omitted variable model contains the variables x_1 and x_2. The overspecified model contains the variables x_1, x_2, x_3 and x_4. Consequently, the three alternative models are

$$q_t = \beta_1 x_{1t} + \beta_2 x_{2t} + \beta_3 x_{3t} + e_t \qquad \text{(correct model)}$$
$$q_t = \beta_1 x_{1t} + \beta_2 x_{2t} + e_t \qquad \text{(omitted variable model)}$$
$$q_t = \beta_1 x_{1t} + \beta_2 x_{2t} + \beta_3 x_{3t} + \beta_4 x_{4t} + e_t \qquad \text{(extraneous variable model)}$$

For these three models the sampling experiment results are summarized in Table 9.3.

   Let's use these sampling experiment results to see if the conclusions on model misspecification that are summarized in Section 9.5.4 are borne out. The results in Table 9.3 based on 1000 samples of data suggest the following:

1.   If the model contains the correct right-hand-side variables (row one of Table 9.3), the means and variances of the estimates are close to their true parameters, a result that we have known since Chapters 3 and 6.

Table 9.3 Sampling Experiment Results for Correct, Under-, and Overspecified Models

Model	Mean from 1000 Samples				Bias from 1000 Samples				Variance from 1000 Samples			
	b_1	b_2	b_3	b_4	b_1	b_2	b_3	b_4	b_1	b_2	b_3	b_4
Correct (x_1, x_2, x_3)	15.11	−1.66	0.70	0	0.11	−0.06	0	0	55.42	5.22	0.16	0
Underspecified (x_1, x_2)	19.88	1.77	0	0	4.88	3.37	−0.70	0	48.02	1.33	0	0
Overspecified (x_1, x_2, x_3, x_4)	14.92	−1.75	0.71	0.08	−0.08	−0.15	0.01	0.08	85.90	13.00	0.21	5.68

2. If a relevant right-hand-side variable is excluded, in this instance x_3, then the estimator is biased but has improved sampling precision. This is exactly the result that the underspecified row of Table 9.3 reflects. Note the larger average bias of the estimates of β_1 and β_2 and note that the sampling precision of b_1 and b_2 have improved relative to that of the correct model. The average of the estimates for β_2 changed in sign from −1.6 to 1.77. Thus, if you incorrectly omit income from the demand equation, it is highly likely that you will infer that the relationship between quantity demanded and price is positive rather than negative.

3. If the right-hand-side variables are overspecified (an extraneous variable is included), the bias of the least squares estimator approaches zero, but the sampling variances are inflated. Note that for b_1 the sampling variance increases from 55.42 to 85.90.

These results help to confirm the statistical implications of misspecifying the right-hand-side X matrix and suggest, in terms of model misspecification, the bias and variance trade-offs. You should note that for an omitted variable, there was significant bias in terms of estimating β_1 and β_2, but the sampling variability was decreased relative to equation 9.5.12. Alternatively, when an additional (extraneous) variable was included, the sampling variance increased relative to equation 9.5.12 and the bias was approximately zero.

When choosing an estimator or model, some may be willing to give up a bit of bias if they can attain increased sampling precision. Given this possible trade-off, one basis that is often used in problems of variable selection is the mean squared error criterion. The mean-squared error (MSE) criterion for a single element of the β parameter vector is

$$E\left[(b_i - \beta_i)^2\right] = E\left[\left(E[b_i] - \beta_i\right)^2\right] + E\left[\left(b_i - E[b_i]\right)^2\right]$$

$$= (\text{Bias})^2 + \text{Variance} \qquad (9.5.13)$$

In the omitted variable case in the sampling experiment, the mean-squared error of b_1 = $(4.88)^2 + 48.02 = 71.83$. For the extraneous variable, the mean-squared error of b_1 = $(0.08)^2 + 85.90 = 85.91$. Thus, using the MSE criterion for this situation, the (bias)^2 + variance is smaller for the omitted variable (restricted least squares) case. Note, however, both are worse than the mean-squared error of b_1 for the correct specification, which is $b_1 = (0.11)^2 + 55.42 = 55.43$. If our parametric sampling model involving β and σ^2 had been different, then of course the MSE results might have been different.

Since for most economic-econometric models we have uncertainty as to the correct set of economic variables and their corresponding magnitudes, an important question involves how to go about the variable selection (model) search to identify the "correct" X matrix. This is one of the most difficult problems in econometrics and inferential statistics. In the next chapter we will consider this question within the context of hypothesis testing and make some comments about conventional model search procedures.

9.6 Exercises

9.1   Consider the multiple regression model

$$y_t = x_{t1}\beta_1 + x_{t2}\beta_2 + x_{t3}\beta_3 + e_t$$

with the nine observations on y_t, x_{t1}, x_{t2}, and x_{t3} given in Table 9.4.

(a) What are the elements in $\mathbf{y}$ and X when the model is written in the matrix notation $\mathbf{y} = X\boldsymbol{\beta} + \mathbf{e}$? (*Note:* This is a special model where the first column in X is no longer a column of ones.)

(b) Use a hand calculator to find the following:

(i) $X'X$, $X'\mathbf{y}$, and $(X'X)^{-1}$ (*Note:* In this case $X'X$ is called a diagonal matrix. The inverse of a diagonal matrix is equal to the inverse of the diagonals.)

(ii)   the least squares estimator $\mathbf{b}$

(iii)   the least squares residual vector $\hat{\mathbf{e}}$

(iv)   the variance estimate $\hat{\sigma}^2$

(v)   the estimated covariance matrix $\hat{\sigma}^2 (X'X)^{-1}$

(vi)   the standard errors for b_1, b_2 and b_3

(vii)   the coefficient of determination R^2

(c) Use a computer to verify the results you obtained in (b).

9.2   The international hamburger chain known colloquially as Makkers has recently opened a franchise in Moscow. There has been little experience with such establishments in Moscow and so there is considerable uncertainty about the optimal price for hamburgers and the optimal advertising expenditure. During the first 20 weeks of its operation, the Moscow Makkers experimented with alternative prices for its hamburgers and with the level of advertising expenditure, and collected the data on number of hamburgers sold, price, and advertising expenditure given in Table 9.5. Makkers' economist decided to model the quantity of

Table 9.4 Data for Exercise 9.1

y_t	x_{t1}	x_{t2}	x_{t3}
1	1	0	−1
−1	−1	1	0
2	1	0	0
0	0	1	0
4	1	2	0
2	0	3	0
2	0	0	1
0	1	−1	1
2	0	0	1

hamburgers sold (q) as the following function of price in rubles (p) and the level of advertising expenditure in hundreds of rubles (a).

$$q_t = \beta_1 + \beta_2 p_t + \beta_3 a_t + \beta_4 a_t^2 + e_t$$

(a) What quantities appear in $\mathbf{y}$ and X when this model is written in the matrix algebra notation $\mathbf{y} = X\beta + \mathbf{e}$?

(b) The coefficient β_2 shows the response of quantity of hamburgers sold to a change in price. It is given by the partial derivative $\partial q/\partial p$. Similarly, the response of quantity to a change in advertising expenditure is given by the partial derivative $\partial q/\partial a$. However, in this case the response is not simply equal to a constant coefficient but depends on a, the level of advertising. Specifically,

$$\frac{\partial q}{\partial a} = \beta_3 + 2\beta_4 a$$

What signs do you expect for the parameters β_2, β_3, and β_4?

(c) Find least squares for β_1, β_2, β_3, and β_4. Report these estimates and their standard errors in the conventional way. Do the signs of your estimates agree with your expectations?

(d) Suppose that the average cost of producing hamburgers is 1 ruble and that this cost is constant (does not depend on number of hamburgers sold). Makkers' weekly profit from hamburger sales is given by

$$\text{profit} = pq - q - 100a$$

Table 9.5 Number of Hamburgers, Price, and Advertising Expenditure for Moscow Makkers

Week	Hamburgers	Price (rubles)	Advertising (hundreds of rubles)
1	425	4.92	4.79
2	467	5.50	3.61
3	296	5.54	5.49
4	626	5.11	2.78
5	165	5.62	5.74
6	515	5.24	1.34
7	270	4.15	5.81
8	689	4.02	3.39
9	413	5.77	3.74
10	561	4.57	3.59
11	307	5.67	5.19
12	508	5.92	3.27
13	299	5.97	4.69
14	531	5.59	3.79
15	445	5.50	4.29
16	412	5.86	2.71
17	845	4.09	2.21
18	471	5.08	3.09
19	439	5.36	4.65
20	520	5.22	1.97

The term $100a$ arises because advertising expenditure is measured in hundreds of rubles. Use your estimated demand function to write profit as a function of p and a only.

(e) Find the profit-maximizing price of hamburgers when advertising expenditure is 280 rubles. (*Hint:* Make use of the equation obtained by setting the partial derivative $\partial(\text{profit})/\partial p$ equal to zero. The way in which partial derivations are used for obtaining maximizing values is considered in Appendix 10A.)

(f) Find the profit-maximizing level of advertising expenditure when the price of hamburgers is 5 rubles. (*Hint:* Make use of the equation obtained by setting the partial derivative $\partial(\text{profit})/\partial a$ equal to zero.)

(g) Find the optimal p when $a = 2.13$. Find the optimal a when $p = 5.32$. What settings for p and a do you think Makkers' economist will recommend?

9.3 In the Keynesian theory of liquidity preference the transactions, precautionary and speculative motives for holding money lead to a function where the demand for money depends on income and the interest rate. Suppose that we can write the demand for money as the linear function

$$m_t - \beta_1 + \beta_2 y_t + \beta_3 i_t + e_t$$

where

m_t represents money in the form currency and demand deposits (commonly called M1),

y_t is gross national product, and

i_t is the interest rate on 6-month U.S. Treasury Bills.

Observations on these variables in the U.S. economy for the period 1960 to 1983 appear in Table 9.6. Money m and gross national product y are in billions of dollars; the interest rate i is a percentage.

(a) What signs would you expect on β_2 and β_3? Why?

(b) Find the least squares estimates of the coefficients β_1, β_2, and β_3. Do these estimates have the expected signs? Give an interpretation to each of the estimates.

(c) Predict money demanded for (*i*) a gross national product of 1000 billion dollars and an interest rate of 12%, (*ii*) a gross national product of 2000 billion dollars and an interest rate of 6%.

(d) The elasticity of demand for money with respect to income is defined as

$$\frac{\partial m_t}{\partial y_t} \cdot \frac{y_t}{m_t} = \beta_2 \frac{y_t}{m_t}$$

Find the elasticity of demand for money with respect to income at the point in part (c)(*i*) and at the point in part (c)(*ii*). Interpret these elasticities. Can you explain the different values?

(e) Repeat part (d) for the elasticity of demand with respect to the interest rate.

(f) Compute the estimated covariance matrix for b_1, b_2, and b_3. What is the standard error for b_2? What is the estimated covariance between b_2 and b_3? What is meant by this covariance?

(g) What is the value for the coefficient of determination? What information does it give?

Table 9.6 Data for Money Demand Equation

Year	y ($ billions)	m ($ billions)	i (%)	Year	y ($ billions)	m ($ billions)	i (%)
1960	506.5	141.8	3.247	1972	1185.9	251.9	4.466
1961	524.6	146.5	2.605	1973	1326.4	265.8	7.178
1962	565.0	149.2	2.908	1974	1434.2	277.5	7.926
1963	596.7	154.7	3.253	1975	1549.2	291.1	6.122
1964	637.7	161.8	3.686	1976	1718.0	310.4	5.266
1965	691.1	169.5	4.055	1977	1918.3	335.5	5.510
1966	756.0	173.7	5.082	1978	2163.9	363.2	7.572
1967	799.6	185.1	4.630	1979	2417.8	389.0	10.017
1968	873.4	199.4	5.470	1980	2631.7	414.1	11.374
1969	944.0	205.8	6.853	1981	2954.1	440.6	13.776
1970	992.7	216.5	6.562	1982	3073.0	478.2	11.084
1971	1077.6	230.7	4.511	1983	3309.5	521.1	8.750

Source: Economic Report of the President, Department of Commerce, Bureau of Economic Analysis.

9.4 Suppose that, instead of the linear demand for money function in Exercise 9.3, you hypothesize the log-linear demand function

$$\ln m_t = \alpha_1 + \alpha_2 \ln y_t + \alpha_3 \ln i_t + e_t$$

(a) Find least squares estimates of α_1, α_2, α_3 and the corresponding estimated covariance matrix. Interpret the estimated αs.

(b) Compare the predictions of m_t from this model with those obtained from the linear model in Exercise 9.3(c).

(c) Find expressions for $\partial m_t/\partial y_t$ and $\partial m_t/\partial i_t$ and evaluate these expressions at the sample means of the data. How do these values compare with those obtained for $\partial m_t/\partial y_t$ and $\partial m_t/\partial i_t$ in Exercise 9.3?

9.5 Consider the following consumption function, where consumption (c_t) is a linear function of gross national product (y_t) and lagged consumption (c_{t-1})

$$c_t = \beta_1 + \beta_2 y_t + \beta_3 c_{t-1} + e_t$$

In this function β_2 is called the short-run marginal propensity to consume. The long-run marginal propensity to consume is given by the change in consumption from a one-unit change in income, after a new equilibrium has been reached. To find equilibrium c as a function of y, we set $c_{t-1} = c_t$ and solve for c_t in terms of y_t. The long-run marginal propensity to consume is the coefficient of y_t in this new equation.

(a) Use the U.S. data in Table 9.7 to find least squares estimates of β_1, β_2, and β_3. Report these estimates and their standard errors in the usual way.

(b) What are the estimated short-run and long-run marginal propensities to consume?

(c) Given that $c_{1985} = 2313$, and that $y_{1986} = y_{1987} = y_{1988} = y_{1989} = y_{1990} = 3800$, use your estimated equation to predict consumption for the years 1986–1990. Do these predictions suggest how long it might take for consumption to reach equilibrium?

9.6 Data on per capita consumption of beef, the price of beef, the price of lamb, the price of pork, and per capita disposable income for Australia, for the

Table 9.7 GNP (y) and Consumption (c) for the U.S. Economy (billions of 1982 dollars)

Year	y	c	Year	y	c
1955	1494.9	873.8	1971	2484.8	1538.7
1956	1525.7	899.8	1972	2608.5	1621.8
1957	1551.1	919.7	1973	2744.0	1689.6
1958	1539.3	932.9	1974	2729.3	1674.0
1959	1629.1	979.3	1975	2695.0	1711.9
1960	1665.2	1005.1	1976	2826.7	1803.9
1961	1708.7	1025.1	1977	2958.7	1883.7
1962	1799.4	1069.0	1978	3115.2	1960.9
1963	1873.3	1108.3	1979	3192.3	2004.4
1964	1973.3	1170.6	1980	3187.2	2000.4
1965	2087.6	1236.3	1981	3248.7	2024.2
1966	2208.4	1298.9	1982	3166.0	2050.7
1967	2271.3	1337.7	1983	3277.6	2145.9
1968	2365.6	1405.8	1984	3492.0	2239.9
1969	2423.3	1456.6	1985	3570.0	2313.0
1970	2416.2	1492.0			

Source: Economic Report of the President, Department of Commerce, Bureau of Economic Analysis.

period 1949 to 1965, are given in Table 9.8. All prices and income have been deflated with 1953 as the base year. Consider the log-linear demand curve

$$\ln qb_t = \beta_1 + \beta_2 \ln pb_t + \beta_3 \ln pl_t + \beta_4 \ln pp_t + \beta_5 \ln y_t + e_t$$

where
  qb_t is per capita consumption of beef in year t (pounds),
  pb_t is the price of beef in year t (pence per pound),
  pl_t is the price of lamb in year t (pence per pound),
  pp_t is the price of pork in year t (pence per pound), and
  y_t is per capita disposable income in year t (Australian currency pounds).

(a) What signs do you expect on each of the coefficients?
(b) Estimate $\beta = (\beta_1, \beta_2, \beta_3, \beta_4)'$ using least squares. Interpret the results. Do they seem reasonable?
(c) Compute the estimated covariance matrix for the least squares estimator and the standard errors. Also compute R^2.
(d) Reproduce each observation twice so that, instead of having a sample of size $T = 17$, you have a sample of size $T = 51$. Repeat parts (b) and (c) with this increased sample and note any changes in the results. Can you explain these changes? Do you think this procedure of reproducing the observations is a valid one?

9.7 Consider the following total cost function, where y_t represents total cost for the tth firm and x_t represents quantity of output.

$$y_t = \beta_1 + \beta_2 x_t + \beta_3 x_t^2 + \beta_4 x_t^3 + e_t$$

Data on a sample of 28 firms in the clothing industry are given in Table 9.9.
(a) If this model were to be written in the form $\mathbf{y} = X\beta + \mathbf{e}$, what would be the dimensions of $\mathbf{y}$ and X and what elements would these matrices contain?

Table 9.8   Data for Demand for Beef in Australia

Year	qb	y	pb	pl	pp
1949	121.3	355	25.68	20.01	45.74
1950	124.3	380	26.30	18.74	53.00
1951	131.6	426	30.19	22.45	57.90
1952	118.9	353	33.13	27.11	56.56
1953	119.7	354	31.61	20.69	55.25
1954	114.6	361	30.15	18.89	55.69
1955	116.5	380	32.23	19.16	50.62
1956	119.1	391	31.80	20.10	52.36
1957	128.9	380	30.76	20.60	53.96
1958	125.1	368	32.08	19.46	51.78
1959	117.6	385	33.34	17.90	51.01
1960	98.4	403	36.66	17.86	54.64
1961	85.4	406	39.71	19.14	53.04
1962	93.3	411	37.79	18.03	49.47
1963	100.4	427	38.38	18.82	53.70
1964	104.9	459	39.10	19.04	55.22
1965	98.8	469	39.84	20.63	56.03

Source: Commonwealth Bureau of Census and Statistics, *Quarterly Summary of Australian Statistics,* and Bureau of Agricultural Economics, *Beef Situation.*

(b) Write down the marginal cost function corresponding to the above total cost function. What sign would you expect for β_4?

(c) Write down the average cost function that corresponds to the above total cost function.

(d) Use the total cost function to find least squares estimates of β_1, β_2, β_3, and β_4. Graph the total, average, and marginal cost functions implied by these estimates.

(e) At what output price is it profitable for firms to produce? How many firms in the sample are producing unprofitable outputs?

Table 9.9   Total Cost and Output for 28 Firms in the Clothing Industry

Firm	Total Cost	Output	Firm	Total Cost	Output
1	493	8.20	15	196	3.17
2	410	7.39	16	238	2.36
3	451	7.68	17	269	2.33
4	723	9.88	18	256	2.76
5	329	5.65	19	605	8.97
6	432	7.10	20	246	2.77
7	294	5.17	21	222	3.14
8	270	3.34	22	204	2.47
9	311	5.63	23	356	6.77
10	194	1.39	24	378	7.00
11	640	9.30	25	177	1.69
12	217	2.21	26	263	4.41
13	272	2.88	27	549	8.60
14	401	6.94	28	267	4.71

(f) Find estimates of β_1, β_2, β_3, and β_4 by applying least squares to the average cost function you derived in (c). Are the standard errors of the estimates greater or less than those that were obtained in (d) when the total cost function was used? Is it possible to make any conjectures about which set of estimates might be "best"?

9.8 Consider the following aggregate production function for the U.S. manufacturing sector

$$Y_t = f(K_t, L_t, E_t, M_t; \beta)$$

where Y_t is gross output in time t, K_t is capital, L_t is labor, E_t is energy, M_t is other intermediate materials, and β is a vector of unknown parameters. The data underlying these variables are given in index form in Table 9.10. Assume the statistical model $Y_t = \alpha K_t^{\beta_2} L_t^{\beta_3} E_t^{\beta_4} M_t^{\beta_5} \exp\{e_t\}$ where $e_t \sim N(0, \sigma^2)$.
(a) Estimate the unknown parameters of the production function, and find the corresponding standard errors.
(b) Discuss the economic and statistical implications of these results.

9.9 With the use of the *Computer Handbook* and the sampling experiment presented in Section 9.5, use 100 samples of data and analyze and interpret the results.

Table 9.10 Quantity Indexes of Capital, Labor, Energy, Other Intermediate Products, Gross Output for U.S. Manufacturing

Time period	K	L	E	M	Y
1	1.0000	1.0000	1.0000	1.0000	1.0000
2	1.1410	0.9750	0.9293	0.8857	0.9694
3	1.2394	0.9273	1.0199	0.9409	0.9376
4	1.2845	0.9868	1.0842	1.0763	1.1187
5	1.3204	1.0813	1.1814	1.1371	1.3154
6	1.4007	1.1340	1.1896	1.1741	1.1073
7	1.4687	1.2076	1.2862	1.3036	1.4108
8	1.5269	1.1375	1.2993	1.1814	1.1035
9	1.5809	1.1996	1.3397	1.3231	1.3091
10	1.6293	1.2370	1.4119	1.3501	1.4721
11	1.7214	1.2399	1.5247	1.3571	1.4161
12	1.8062	1.1686	1.4466	1.2540	1.3853
13	1.8207	1.2513	1.5417	1.4125	1.4803
14	1.8151	1.2636	1.5683	1.4078	1.4334
15	1.8373	1.2422	1.5915	1.3974	1.5050
16	1.8493	1.2994	1.6569	1.4861	1.5032
17	1.8738	1.3219	1.7628	1.5958	1.6719
18	1.9122	1.3563	1.7672	1.6499	1.6904
19	1.9821	1.4346	1.8170	1.7933	1.6787
20	2.1064	1.5361	1.9253	1.9000	1.9165
21	2.2781	1.5558	2.0388	1.9516	1.9019
22	2.4149	1.6033	2.0900	2.0838	1.9689
23	2.5264	1.6471	2.1989	2.1066	2.1945
24	2.6557	1.5789	2.3950	2.0323	1.8787
25	2.7495	1.5285	2.3080	2.1885	2.1233

9.10 (a) Use equation 9.5.6 to compute the true bias of the least squares estimator for the omitted variable model in Section 9.5.4a and compare it with the estimated bias in Table 9.3.

(b) If you knew price and income were positively correlated, show how to tell the direction of the bias in the least squares estimate of price, when income is incorrectly omitted.

9.11 Reconsider Exercise 9.2 and the statistical model

$$q_t = \beta_1 + \beta_2 p_t + \beta_3 a_t + \beta_4 a_t^2 + e_t$$

Compare your estimates and standard errors from this model with those from each of the following two models:

$$q_t = \beta_1 + \beta_2 p_t + e_{t1}$$

$$q_t = \beta_1 + \beta_2 p_t + \beta_3 a_t + \beta_4 a_t^2 + \beta_5 p_t^2 + \beta_6 a_t p_t + e_{t2}$$

Comment on the results.

9.7   References

The material covered in this chapter can also be found in a number of other textbooks. An example of a book at a higher level that gives a more complete coverage is

JUDGE, G. G., R. C. HILL, W. E. GRIFFITHS, H. LÜTKEPOHL and T. C. LEE (1988) *Introduction to the Theory and Practice of Econometrics*, New York: John Wiley & Sons, Inc., pp. 159–225.

A discussion of the macroeconomic functions in the exercises concerning the demand for money and the consumption function can be found in

SHEFFRIN, S. M., D. A. WILTON and D. M. PRESCOTT (1988) *Macroeconomics: Theory and Policy*, Cincinnati, OH: South-Western Publishing Co., pp. 158–166, 504–529, 603–634.

A discussion of the microeconomic functions that we encountered, including revenue, price and quantity for demand analysis, and involving cost and output for a cost function, can be found in

MANSFIELD, E. (1985) *Microeconomics: Theory and Applications*, 5th Edition, New York: W. W. Norton, & Co., Inc., pp. 49–150, 183–230.

Chapter 10

Inference in the General Linear Statistical Model

New Key Words and Concepts

Properties of Least Squares Estimator
Interval Estimation
One-Sided Hypothesis Tests
Testing the Significance of
    One or More Coefficients

F-Distribution
F-Test
Regressor Selection
Testing for Functional Form

There are three main reasons why, as economists, we might be interested in the general linear statistical model $\mathbf{y} = X\beta + \mathbf{e}$ that was introduced in Chapter 9. We can write these reasons in terms of the following questions:

1. How is the outcome or dependent variable y influenced by changes in the explanatory variables $x_2, x_3,..., x_K$? That is, what are the likely magnitudes of the elements in the unknown coefficient vector β?

2. How do we test hypotheses about the magnitudes of such influences or about combinations of the individual coefficients in the vector β?

3. Is there a mechanism we can use to predict the outcome of the dependent variable y for given values of the explanatory variables?

In Chapter 9 we used economic and statistical models for a Bay Area hamburger chain as a basis for handling the first of these three questions. For the general linear statistical model, we learned how to use the least squares estimator $\mathbf{b} = (X'X)^{-1}X'\mathbf{y}$ to find *point* estimates of the elements in β. We also developed a basis for estimating the sampling variability or precision of the least squares estimator. The remaining task for the first question is to develop interval estimates for the elements in β by combining the information provided by the point estimates with the information from the estimated sampling variability. Through their sampling characteristics, interval estimates tell us something about the *reliability* of the point estimates. To complete the picture we also need to tackle questions 2 and 3 on hypothesis testing and prediction. Developing the methodology for these tasks is the objective of this chapter and Chapter 11.

Note that we are going over familiar ground. In Chapters 4 and 7 we dealt with these questions in terms of simple linear models. Our current purpose is to extend the material in Chapters 4 and 7 to the general linear statistical model. We learned in Chapter 9 that, for the least squares estimator and its estimated covariance matrix, this extension is straightforward; the formulas and the sampling properties are essentially the same, only the dimensions (of the matrices) change. Some of the material in this chapter will again be a straightforward extension of concepts covered for the simple linear model. Other material will be new. In particular, we introduce the F-distribution for testing hypotheses that involve more than one parameter. Also, studying the general linear statistical model with more than one explanatory variable brings with it the problem of choice of explanatory variables. This problem, along with the problem of choosing a functional form, are considered. The highlights of the chapter are as follows.

1. The sampling properties of the least squares estimator are summarized since these properties form the basis of the inference procedures to come (Section 10.1).

2. In Sections 10.2, 10.3, and 10.4 we are concerned with interval estimation and hypothesis testing for a *single* coefficient. The procedures are all based on the result that the random variable $t = \left(b_k - \beta_k\right) / \sqrt{\hat{\text{var}}\left(b_k\right)}$ has a t-distribution.

3. How to report results so that interval estimates and hypothesis test results are evident is outlined in Section 10.5.

4. Testing the "significance of an estimated relationship" appears in Section 10.6.

5. Using the t-test for testing a single linear combination of coefficients is considered in Section 10.7.

6. The F-test for testing more than one linear hypothesis about β is discussed in Section 10.8, and the conceptual basis for this test is developed in Appendix 10B.

7. Criteria for choosing explanatory variables, for assessing whether a model is misspecified, and for choosing between alternative functional forms are discussed in Sections 10.9 and 10.10.

8. A more formal matrix development of general linear hypothesis testing is given in Appendix 10C.

10.1 Sampling Properties of the Least Squares Estimator

The properties of the least squares estimator for the general linear statistical model were described in Chapter 9. However, it is worth summarizing them again because they form the basis of much of the methodology in this chapter. Our general model is given by

$$\mathbf{y} = X\boldsymbol{\beta} + \mathbf{e} \tag{10.1.1}$$

where $\mathbf{y}$ is a $(T \times 1)$ vector containing observations on the dependent variable, X is a $(T \times K)$ matrix containing observations on $(K - 1)$ explanatory variables and a constant term, $\boldsymbol{\beta}$ is a $(K \times 1)$ vector of unknown coefficients to be estimated, and $\mathbf{e}$ is a $(T \times 1)$ vector of random error terms. In Chapter 9 no specific probability distribution was assumed for the random errors in $\mathbf{e}$, although at times we discussed the implications of normally distributed errors. In this chapter we assume throughout that the errors are *normally distributed*; this assumption is needed for our results on interval estimation and hypothesis testing to hold true. Also, we retain the earlier assumptions of a zero mean vector ($E[\mathbf{e}] = \mathbf{0}$) and a "scalar-times-identity" covariance matrix ($E[\mathbf{ee}'] = \sigma^2 I_T$). We summarize this information about the probability distribution of $\mathbf{e}$ by writing that the es are drawings from the following probability distribution:

$$\mathbf{e} \sim N\left(\mathbf{0}, \sigma^2 I_T\right) \tag{10.1.2a}$$

Because $\mathbf{y}$ is a random vector that is a linear function of $\mathbf{e}$, the distributional assumption about $\mathbf{e}$ in equation 10.1.2a implies the following distributional assumption about $\mathbf{y}$:

$$\mathbf{y} \sim N\left(X\boldsymbol{\beta},\, \sigma^2 I_T\right) \tag{10.1.2b}$$

Given these assumptions we know that the least squares and maximum likelihood estimator

$$\mathbf{b} = \left(X'X\right)^{-1} X'\mathbf{y} \tag{10.1.3}$$

is the minimum variance (best) unbiased estimator for $\boldsymbol{\beta}$. Because of the additional assumption of normally distributed errors, it is best from within the class of all unbiased estimators, not just from those that are linear. To find the probability distribution for $\mathbf{b}$ we note that, because $\mathbf{y}$ is a normally distributed random vector, and $\mathbf{b}$ is a linear function of $\mathbf{y}$, $\mathbf{b}$ is a normally distributed random vector. Furthermore, its mean vector and covariance matrix are given by

$$E[\mathbf{b}] = \boldsymbol{\beta} \quad \text{and} \quad \text{cov}(\mathbf{b}) = E\left[(\mathbf{b}-\boldsymbol{\beta})(\mathbf{b}-\boldsymbol{\beta})'\right] = \sigma^2 \left(X'X\right)^{-1} \tag{10.1.4}$$

These results about the least squares estimator can be summarized as

$$\mathbf{b} \sim N\left[\boldsymbol{\beta},\, \sigma^2 \left(X'X\right)^{-1}\right] \tag{10.1.5}$$

To find an estimator for $\text{cov}(\mathbf{b}) = \sigma^2(X'X)^{-1}$, we need an estimator for the error variance σ^2. We found in Chapter 9 that an unbiased estimator for σ^2 is found by first computing the least squares residuals

$$\hat{\mathbf{e}} = \mathbf{y} - X\mathbf{b} \tag{10.1.6}$$

and then dividing the sum of squares of residuals by $(T - K)$. That is,

$$\hat{\sigma}^2 = \frac{\hat{\mathbf{e}}'\hat{\mathbf{e}}}{T-K} = \frac{(\mathbf{y}-X\mathbf{b})'(\mathbf{y}-X\mathbf{b})}{T-K} \tag{10.1.7}$$

An unbiased estimator of the covariance matrix for $\mathbf{b}$ can then be computed from

$$\hat{\text{cov}}(\mathbf{b}) = \hat{\sigma}^2 \left(X'X\right)^{-1} \tag{10.1.8}$$

It is important for what follows to remember that $\hat{\text{cov}}(\mathbf{b})$ contains estimates of the variances of $b_1, b_2, \ldots, b_K$ on the diagonal. Corresponding estimates of the covariances appear as off-diagonal elements. Numerical values for these estimated variances and covariances are given by the corresponding elements in $\hat{\sigma}^2(X'X)^{-1}$. For example, we estimated the receipts–price–advertising relationship in Chapter 9 as

$$\hat{tr} = b_1 + b_2 p_t + b_3 a_t$$
$$= 104.79 - 6.642 p_t + 2.984 a_t \tag{10.1.9}$$

and the estimated covariance matrix was given by equations 9.2.19 and 9.2.20:

$$\text{cov}(\mathbf{b}) = \begin{bmatrix} \hat{\text{var}}(b_1) & \hat{\text{cov}}(b_1, b_2) & \hat{\text{cov}}(b_1, b_3) \\ \hat{\text{cov}}(b_1, b_2) & \hat{\text{var}}(b_2) & \hat{\text{cov}}(b_2, b_3) \\ \hat{\text{cov}}(b_1, b_3) & \hat{\text{cov}}(b_2, b_3) & \hat{\text{var}}(b_3) \end{bmatrix} = \hat{\sigma}^2 (X'X)^{-1}$$

$$= \begin{bmatrix} 42.026 & -19.863 & -0.16111 \\ -19.863 & 10.184 & -0.05402 \\ -0.16111 & -0.05402 & 0.02787 \end{bmatrix} \qquad (10.1.10)$$

In Chapter 7 where β was of dimension 2, we obtained specific results for the individual coefficients of β_1 and β_2. In the more general framework of this chapter we have

$$b_k \sim N\big[\beta_k, \text{var}(b_k)\big] \qquad (10.1.11a)$$

and

$$z = \frac{b_k - \beta_k}{\sqrt{\text{var}(b_k)}} \sim N(0, 1), \quad \text{for } k = 1, 2, \ldots, K \qquad (10.1.11b)$$

That is, each element in the vector $\mathbf{b}$ has a normal distribution with mean and variance given by the corresponding elements in β and cov($\mathbf{b}$), respectively. Furthermore, by subtracting its mean and dividing by the square root of its variance (standard deviation), we can transform the normal random variable b_k into the standard normal variable z, which has mean zero and a variance of unity. This result, given in equation 10.1.11b, may be used for interval estimation and hypothesis testing for β_k if σ^2 and, hence, var(b_k) are known. In the absence of a known σ^2, we replace var(b_k) by $\hat{\text{var}}(b_k)$ and use the t-distribution instead of the normal distribution. Thus, for unknown σ^2, we use the t random variable

$$t = \frac{b_k - \beta_k}{\sqrt{\hat{\text{var}}(b_k)}} \sim t_{(T-K)} \qquad (10.1.12)$$

To derive this t random variable we use the standard normal random variable z defined in equation 10.1.11b and another random variable, $w = (T-K)\hat{\sigma}^2 / \sigma^2$, that is a chi-squared random variable with $(T-K)$ degrees of freedom. Following equations 4.4.2 and 4.4.3 of Chapter 4, and given that z and w are independent, the t random variable is defined as the ratio of the standard normal random variable z to the square root of the chi-squared random variable w, divided by its degrees of freedom. That is,

$$t = \frac{z}{\sqrt{w/(T-K)}} = \frac{(b_k - \beta_k)/\sqrt{\text{var}(b_k)}}{\sqrt{\hat{\sigma}^2/\sigma^2}} = \frac{(b_k - \beta_k)/\sqrt{\sigma^2 c_{kk}}}{\sqrt{\hat{\sigma}^2/\sigma^2}}$$

$$= \frac{b_k - \beta_k}{\sqrt{\hat{\sigma}^2 c_{kk}}} = \frac{b_k - \beta_k}{\sqrt{\hat{\text{var}}(b_k)}}$$

where c_{kk} is the kth diagonal element of $(X'X)^{-1}$.

One difference between this result and that in Chapter 7 (see equation 7.1.11) is the degrees of freedom of the t random variable. In Chapter 7 where there were 2 coefficients to be estimated (the dimension of β was 2), the number of degrees of freedom was

$(T - 2)$. In Chapters 9 and 10 there are K unknown coefficients in the general model and *the number of degrees of freedom is* $(T - K)$.

Our first task is to examine how the result in equation 10.1.12 can be used for hypothesis testing and interval estimation. The procedures are identical to those described in Chapter 7, only the degrees of freedom change. The discussion will therefore be brief.

10.2   Interval Estimation

Returning to the equation used to describe how the hamburger chain's receipts depend on price and advertising expenditure, we have, from Chapter 9

$$T = 52 \qquad K = 3$$
$$b_1 = 104.79 \quad se(b_1) = \sqrt{\hat{var}(b_1)} = 6.483$$
$$b_2 = -6.642 \quad se(b_2) = \sqrt{\hat{var}(b_2)} = 3.191$$
$$b_3 = 2.984 \quad se(b_3) = \sqrt{\hat{var}(b_3)} = 0.1669$$

We will use this information, and the result on the t-distribution in equation 10.1.12, to construct interval estimates and hypothesis tests for

β_2 = the response of receipts to a price change

β_3 = the response of receipts to a change in advertising expenditure

Extending the methodology introduced in Sections 4.4.2 and 7.1.2, to construct a 95% confidence interval for β_2, we make use of the t-distribution and begin by writing

$$P\left[-2.01 \le t_{(49)} \le 2.01\right] = 0.95 \tag{10.2.1}$$

In words, there is a .95 probability that a t random variable with 49 degrees of freedom will lie between −2.01 and 2.01. The degrees of freedom are given by $(T - K) = (52 - 3) = 49$. The critical value $t_c = 2.01$ does not appear in the tabulated values for the t-distribution found in Table 2 at the end of the book. However, it can be found by interpolating these values or, as described in the *Computer Handbook*, by using an appropriate computer package. Since $(b_2 - \beta_2)/se(b_2)$ is a $t_{(49)}$ random variable, we can make this substitution into equation 10.2.1 to yield

$$P\left[-2.01 \le \frac{b_2 - \beta_2}{se(b_2)} \le 2.01\right] = .95 \tag{10.2.2}$$

This equation tells us about the reliability of the point estimate b_2 in the sense that, before we sample, there is a 0.95 probability of getting values b_2 and $se(b_2)$ such that the sampling error $|b_2 - \beta_2|$, divided by $se(b_2)$, is less than 2.01.

Alternatively, we write equation 10.2.2 as

$$P\left[b_2 - 2.01se(b_2) \le \beta_2 \le b_2 + 2.01se(b_2)\right] = 0.95 \tag{10.2.3}$$

The interpretation we place on this equation is to say that, in a repeated-sample context, 95% of the interval endpoints $b_2 \pm 2.01se(b_2)$ will be such that β_2 lies in the range $b_2 - 2.01se(b_2)$ to $b_2 + 2.01se(b_2)$. In other words, there is a 0.95 probability of getting a sample that yields an interval $[b_2 - 2.01\mathrm{se}(b_2), b_2 + 2.01\mathrm{se}(b_2)]$ that contains β_2.

A 95% confidence interval for our particular sample is obtained from equation 10.2.3 by replacing b_2 and $\mathrm{se}(b_2)$ by their estimates $b_2 = -6.642$ and $\mathrm{se}(b_2) = 3.191$. Thus, our 95% interval estimate for β_2 is given by

$$-13.06 \le \beta_2 \le -0.23 \qquad (10.2.4)$$

The *interval estimation procedure* that works 95% of the time suggests that decreasing price by \$1 will lead to an increase in receipts somewhere between \$230 and \$13,060. Since this is a wide interval, it is likely that the hamburger chain's management will not find it very informative. Another way of describing this situation is to say that the point estimate of $b_2 = -6.642$ is not very reliable; its standard error (sampling variability) is relatively large.

In general, if an interval estimate is uninformative because it is too wide, there is nothing immediate that can be done. A wide uninformative confidence interval for a parameter (say β_2) arises because the estimated sampling variability of the least squares estimator b_2 is large. In the computation of a confidence interval, a large sampling variability is reflected by a large standard error. A narrower interval can be obtained only by reducing the sampling variability of the estimator. However, since we are using an estimator that, based on the sample information, is best (has minimum sampling variability for an unbiased estimator), such a reduction is impossible within the bounds of the model and data that are available. To reduce sampling variability we need to collect more data or introduce some kind of nonsample information on the coefficients. The question of using both sample and nonsample information within a sampling theory context is taken up in Chapter 11.

Returning to the receipts–price–advertising relationship, if we follow a similar procedure for β_2, we find the 95% interval estimate for β_3, the response of receipts to advertising, as

$$2.65 \le \beta_3 \le 3.32 \qquad (10.2.5)$$

This interval is relatively narrow and informative. In the context of the 95% interval estimation procedure, we have estimated that an increase in advertising expenditure of \$1000 leads to an increase in total receipts that is somewhere between \$2650 and \$3320. In a repeated sampling sense, intervals computed in this way contain the true parameter β_3 in 95% of the cases.

10.3   One-Sided Hypothesis Testing for a Single Coefficient

In Chapter 9 we noted that two important considerations for the management of the hamburger chain were whether demand was price elastic or inelastic and whether the additional receipts from additional advertising expenditure would cover the costs of the advertising. We were able to frame these questions in terms of the magnitudes of the unknown parameters β_2 and β_3. Now we are in a position to put the questions in terms of testable hypotheses, and to ask whether such hypotheses are compatible with the data.

With respect to demand elasticity we have

$\beta_2 \ge 0$: a decrease in price leads to a decrease in total receipts (in economic terminology we say that demand is price inelastic)

$\beta_2 < 0$: a decrease in price leads to an increase in total receipts (we say that demand is price elastic)

If we are not prepared to accept that demand is elastic unless there is strong evidence from the data to support this claim, it is appropriate to take the assumption of an inelastic demand as our null hypothesis. That is,

$$H_0 : \beta_2 \geq 0 \text{ (demand is inelastic)}$$

$$H_1 : \beta_2 < 0 \text{ (demand is elastic)}$$

Inequality hypotheses of this type were first encountered in equations 4.3.4 and 4.3.5 of Chapter 4. To test such hypotheses, a one-sided or one-tailed test is used. We compute a value for the t-statistic assuming β_2 is equal to the value at the boundary between H_0 and H_1. This is the point where $\beta_2 = 0$. This point is least favorable to the null hypothesis. That is, it is that point in H_0 that is closest to H_1. Using equation 10.1.12 to compute a t-value under this assumption yields

$$t = \frac{b_2 - \beta_2}{se(b_2)} = \frac{-6.642 - 0}{3.191} = -2.08 \tag{10.3.1}$$

Being negative, this value obviously favors the alternative hypothesis. But is it sufficiently negative to suggest H_0 is "unlikely" to be true? If we define "unlikely" in terms of a 5% significance level, we answer this question by finding a critical value t_c such that $P[t_{(49)} < t_c] = 0.05$. Then, we reject H_0 if $t < t_c$. Using an approximation from the t-tables (or an appropriate computer program), we have $t_c = -1.68$. Since $t = -2.08 < t_c = -1.68$, we reject $H_0 : \beta_2 \geq 0$ and conclude that $H_1 : \beta_2 < 0$ (demand is elastic) is more compatible with the data. The sample evidence supports the proposition that a reduction in price will bring about an increase in total receipts.

An alternative to comparing the computed value -2.08 to the critical value $t_c = -1.68$ is to compute the p-value that is given by $P[t_{(49)} < -2.08]$ and to reject H_0 if this p-value is less than 0.05. Using appropriate computer software (see the *Computer Handbook* for details), we find that $P[t_{(49)} < -2.08] = 0.021$. Since $0.021 < 0.05$, the same conclusion is reached.

The other hypothesis of interest relates to whether an increase in advertising expenditure will bring an increase in total receipts that is sufficient to cover the increased cost of advertising. In terms of the parameter β_3 we have

$H_0 : \beta_3 \leq 1$ (increase in receipts is less than or equal to additional advertising expense)

$H_1 : \beta_3 > 1$ (increase in receipts is greater than the additional advertising expense)

Like the previous one, this is a one-tailed test with inequality hypotheses for both the null and the alternative. We compute a value for the t-statistic for the endpoint in the null hypothesis, $\beta_3 = 1$. Thus, we have

$$t = \frac{b_3 - \beta_3}{se(b_3)} = \frac{2.984 - 1}{0.1669} = 11.89 \tag{10.3.2}$$

In this case we reject H_0 if $t > t_c = 1.68$. Since 11.89 is much greater than 1.68, we do indeed reject H_0 and accept the alternative $\beta_3 > 1$ as more compatible with the data. Also, the p-value in this instance is essentially zero (less than 10^{-12}). Thus, we have *statistical evidence* that an increase in advertising expenditure will be justified by the increase in receipts. Of course, to totally justify the increase in advertising expenditure, we also need to consider the cost of producing the extra hamburgers that have led to the increase in receipts.

Because both of the foregoing tests are one-sided tests, a critical value from just one side of the t-distribution is considered in each instance. For β_2 the critical value of -1.68 from the left side of the distribution was considered; for β_3 the critical value of 1.68 from the right side of the distribution was considered. We turn now to examples of two-sided tests where critical values from both sides of the t-distribution are used.

10.4   Testing a Zero Null Hypothesis for a Single Coefficient

Consider the following general linear statistical model with $(K-1)$ explanatory variables and K coefficients to be estimated

$$y_t = \beta_1 + x_{t2}\beta_2 + x_{t3}\beta_3 + \ldots + x_{tK}\beta_K + e_t \qquad (10.4.1)$$

When we set up this model we do so because we believe that all the $(K-1)$ explanatory variables have some bearing on, or influence the outcome of, the dependent variable y. If we are to confirm this belief, we need to examine whether it is supported by the data. That is, we need to ask whether the data provide any evidence to suggest that y is related to each of the explanatory variables. If a given explanatory variable, say x_k, has no bearing on y, then $\beta_k = 0$. Thus, to find whether the data contain any evidence suggesting y is related to x_k we can test the null hypothesis

$$H_0 : \beta_k = 0$$

against the alternative

$$H_1 : \beta_k \neq 0$$

Hypotheses of this type were tested in Section 7.2. To carry out the test we compute a value for

$$t = \frac{b_k - \beta_k}{\sqrt{\hat{\mathrm{var}}(b_k)}} = \frac{b_k - \beta_k}{\mathrm{se}(b_k)} \qquad (10.4.2)$$

under the assumption H_0: $\beta_k = 0$ is true, and reject H_0 if this computed value is greater than t_c (the critical value from the right side of the distribution), or less than $-t_c$ (the critical value from the left side of the distribution). Thus, in contrast to the tests in Section 10.3, we are considering two-sided or two-tailed tests; the two-sided nature of the test arises because we are testing a point null hypothesis against an alternative where β_k can be either side of the point. The procedure of testing H_0: $\beta_k = 0$ against H_1: $\beta_k \neq 0$ is sometimes referred to as testing whether b_k is "significantly different" from zero.

In the receipts–price–advertising relationship we test whether receipts are related to price by testing

$$H_0 : \beta_2 = 0 \quad \text{against} \quad H_1 : \beta_2 \neq 0$$

Under H_0, the computed value of the t-statistic is given by

$$t = \frac{-6.642 - 0}{3.191} = -2.08 \qquad (10.4.3)$$

With 49 degrees of freedom and a 5% significance level, the critical values that lead to an area (probability) of 0.025 in each tail of the distribution are $t_c = 2.01$ and $-t_c = -2.01$. Since $-2.08 < -2.01$, we reject H_0: $\beta_2 = 0$ and conclude that there is evidence from the data to suggest receipts depend on price. Note that the computed value in this instance is identical to that obtained in Section 10.3 when we were testing $H_0: \beta_2 < 0$, but the critical values are different. Also, the p-value in this case is given by $P[|t_{(49)}| > 2.08] = 2 \times 0.021 = 0.042$. Using this procedure we reject H_0 because $0.042 < 0.05$.

For testing whether receipts are related to advertising expenditure, we test $H_0: \beta_3 = 0$ against the alternative $H_1: \beta_3 \neq 0$. In this case

$$t = \frac{2.984 - 0}{0.1669} = 17.88$$

(10.4.4)

Because $17.88 > t_c = 2.01$, the data support the conjecture that receipts are related to advertising expenditure.

10.4.1   Testing Significance and Selecting Regressors

When there is uncertainty about whether or not a particular regressor should be included in our model, the significance test developed in Section 10.4 provides one way of assessing the relevance of that regressor. As a consequence, many applied researchers use significance testing for exploratory data analysis. The approach taken is to begin with a hypothesized model and to assess the adequacy of that model by checking whether the chosen regressors are compatible with the data, in the sense that their estimated coefficients are significant. If agreement with the data is judged to be "bad," because of insignificant coefficient estimates, a search is started for an alternative set of regressors that fits the data better. You should be aware that, unfortunately, there are no current statistical inference procedures that provide guidance on how to carry out such a search. Such searching is subjective and leads us to an estimated model about which it is difficult to draw inferences. To see the problems, consider testing a null hypothesis of the form

$$H_0 : \beta_k = 0 \quad \text{against} \quad H_1 : \beta_k \neq 0$$

We are using β_k to denote the coefficient of any one of the regressors, say the kth regressor, in the general linear model in equation 10.4.1. Rejection of H_0 implies that the corresponding regressor variable x_{tk} is a relevant one in the sense that it appears to exert an influence on the dependent variable y_t, and hence its inclusion in the model is justified.

If we do not reject H_0, what do we conclude? A failure to reject H_0 could mean $H_0: \beta_k = 0$ is true. If indeed H_0 is true, then x_{tk} is an irrelevant or extraneous variable and, as we discovered in Section 9.5 of Chapter 9, we can obtain more efficient estimates of the remaining coefficients by omitting x_{tk} from the model. Another possible reason for not rejecting H_0 is that our data are not good enough to disprove $\beta_k = 0$. Even if $\beta_k \neq 0$, it can be difficult to establish the truth of H_1 if our data are too poor. For example, given that β_k describes the effect on y_t of changes in x_{tk}, if our data are such that x_{tk} changes very little, then it is clearly expecting too much of our data to have them produce a precise estimate of the effect of such changes. If we cannot get a precise estimate of β_k, we will not reject $H_0: \beta_k = 0$. Further details concerning the consequences and identification of poor data are considered in Chapter 13.

Thus, a failure to reject H_0 can mean either

(i) H_0 is true, or

(ii) our data are not sufficiently good to reject H_0 even although it is false.

If (i) is the reason for not rejecting H_0, then the obvious strategy is to drop x_{tk} from the model to improve the efficiency of the remaining coefficient estimates. However, if (ii) represents the reason for not rejecting H_0, then dropping x_{tk} from the model means we are omitting a relevant variable; in Section 9.5 we saw that the consequences of such an action are biased estimates of the remaining coefficients. Consequently, if a coefficient estimate in a model is insignificant (H_0 is not rejected), we must decide whether the corresponding variable is irrelevant, or whether our data are too poor to accurately measure its effect.

There is another issue. As discussed in Section 9.5 of Chapter 9, we are often uncertain as to what explanatory (regressor) variables should be included in our model. Facing this uncertainty, one possible strategy is to estimate a model that includes all possibly relevant variables and to drop all those variables whose estimated coefficients are not significant. As we have seen, one difficulty with this strategy is that we may be throwing out relevant variables whose coefficients are insignificant because of poor data. Another difficulty is that, *in the reestimated equation, standard errors, confidence intervals, and hypothesis tests are not valid.* They are valid only if the adopted strategy *always* produces the correct model. This will not be true because any hypothesis testing strategy, by its nature, produces Type I and Type II errors.

Coefficient estimates in a model that has been chosen from the outcomes of one or more hypothesis tests are called *preliminary-test* (or *pretest*) *estimates*. Derivation of the sampling properties of preliminary-test estimators is a difficult task. Consequently, when pretest estimates are reported, the fact that they are *pretest* estimates is usually ignored. Reported standard errors and confidence intervals are only valid if the preliminary testing had not taken place. Hence, they are likely to overstate the preciseness of the coefficient estimates. Also, the possible omission of relevant variables means that the pretest estimator will be biased.

What are the implications of these results for the selection of regressors? They mean that, in practice, our theory and logic, along with statistical evidence, play a prominent role in such selection. *Mechanical selection of regressors on the basis of statistical criteria only is not recommended and, in all cases, we should be aware of the consequences of preliminary testing.* These comments are equally relevant for other "statistical methods" of variable selection that are discussed in Section 10.9.

10.5   Inference and the Reporting of Results

In Chapter 9 we reported the estimated relationship between receipts, price and advertising expenditure as

$$\hat{tr} = 104.79 - 6.642 p_t + 2.984 a_t$$

$$(6.48)\quad (3.191)\quad (0.167)\quad \text{(s.e.)} \qquad\qquad (10.5.1)$$

where the numbers in parentheses are the corresponding standard errors. Now that we have completed sections on interval estimation and hypothesis testing, the usefulness of reporting the results in this way should be clear. For the construction of an interval estimate, we need the least squares estimate, its standard error, and a critical value from the t-distribution. For a 95% confidence interval and at least moderate degrees of freedom, the critical t-value is approximately 2. Thus, from the information in equation 10.5.1, an approximate 95% confidence interval can be obtained by mentally calculating the points two standard errors either side of the least squares estimate. Similarly, the t-value used to test a null hypothesis of the form $H_0: \beta_k = 0$ is simply given by the ratio of the least squares estimate to its standard error that appears underneath. It too can be calculated mentally by simple inspection of equation 10.5.1. Sometimes results are reported with t-values in parentheses, rather than standard errors. In this case we have

Table 10.1 Summary of Least Squares Results

Variable	Coefficient	Standard Error	*t*-Value	*p*-Value
Constant	104.79	6.48	16.17	0.000
Price	−6.642	3.191	2.081	0.042
Advertising	2.984	0.167	17.868	0.000

$$\hat{tr} = 104.79 - 6.642 p_t + 2.984 a_t$$

$$(16.17) \ (-2.081) \ (17.868) \quad (t) \tag{10.5.2}$$

Thus, from any estimated equation that has been reported in the conventional way, you should be able to immediately read off, or calculate, point and interval estimates for all the coefficients. In addition, if the ratio of an estimate to its standard error is absolutely greater than 2 (approximately), you know that a null hypothesis of the form $H_0: \beta_k = 0$ would be rejected. Furthermore, from an interval estimate we can tell whether any hypothesis of the form $H_0: \beta_k = r$ would be accepted or rejected. If r is within the interval, H_0 is accepted, otherwise H_0 is rejected. Remembering these quick "inspection techniques" will help you make "on the spot" assessments of reported results.

In Table 10.1 the information in equations 10.5.1 and 10.5.2 is presented in the way that it usually appears on computer output. The format is identical to that given in Table 8.1 of Chapter 8.

10.6   Testing a Zero Null Hypothesis for All Response Coefficients

In Section 10.4 we developed a *t*-test for testing whether the dependent variable *y* is related to a particular explanatory variable x_k. In this section we extend this procedure to a joint test of the relevance of all the included explanatory variables. Consider again the general linear statistical model with $(K - 1)$ explanatory variables and K unknown coefficients

$$y_t = \beta_1 + x_{t2}\beta_2 + x_{t3}\beta_3 + \ldots + x_{tK}\beta_K + e_t \tag{10.6.1}$$

One potential advantage of this model over the mean model studied in Chapters 3 and 4, and given by

$$y_t = \beta_1 + e_t \tag{10.6.2}$$

is that the set of explanatory variables $(x_2, x_3, \ldots, x_K)$ will explain a substantial proportion of the variation in *y*. The variables $(x_2, x_3, \ldots, x_K)$ are included in equation 10.6.1 with this purpose in mind. Thus, it is desirable if we can show, statistically, that the data support the presence of $(x_2, x_3, \ldots, x_K)$. Otherwise, the model reduces to that in equation 10.6.2, which is not a viable *explanatory* model, but a way of summarizing the information in terms of mean and variance parameters. To examine whether we have a viable explanatory model, we set up the following hypotheses:

$$H_0: \beta_2 = \beta_3 = \ldots = \beta_K = 0$$

$$H_1: \textit{at least one of the } \beta_k \textit{ is nonzero} \tag{10.6.3}$$

If the null hypothesis H_0 is true, none of the explanatory variables influence *y*, and the model becomes that given in equation 10.6.2. If the alternative hypothesis H_1 is true, then at least one of the explanatory variables should be included in the model. The coefficients in H_0 are the response coefficients that describe the response of y to changes in the explanatory variables. The remaining coefficient β_1, which does not appear in H_0, is the intercept coefficient. Since we are testing whether or not we have a viable explanatory model, the test for equation 10.6.3 is sometimes referred to as a test of the significance of the regression relationship.

To develop a test and associated test statistic for testing H_0 against H_1, we begin by introducing some matrix algebra notation. Using the subscript "s" to denote "slopes," we define the $(K-1)$ dimensional vector β_s as that vector that contains all the response coefficients; the least squares estimator for these coefficients is denoted by $\mathbf{b}_s$ and its estimated covariance matrix by $\hat{\text{cov}}(\mathbf{b}_s)$. Thus, we have

$$
\beta_s = \begin{bmatrix} \beta_2 \\ \beta_3 \\ \vdots \\ \beta_K \end{bmatrix} \quad \mathbf{b}_s = \begin{bmatrix} b_2 \\ b_3 \\ \vdots \\ b_K \end{bmatrix} \quad \hat{\text{cov}}(\mathbf{b}_s) = \begin{bmatrix} \hat{\text{var}}(b_2) & \hat{\text{cov}}(b_2, b_3) & \cdots & \hat{\text{cov}}(b_2, b_K) \\ \hat{\text{cov}}(b_2, b_3) & \hat{\text{var}}(b_3) & \cdots & \hat{\text{cov}}(b_3, b_K) \\ \vdots & \vdots & \ddots & \vdots \\ \hat{\text{cov}}(b_2, b_K) & \hat{\text{cov}}(b_3, b_K) & \cdots & \hat{\text{var}}(b_K) \end{bmatrix}
$$

$$(10.6.4)$$

Using equation 10.6.4, the null and alternative hypotheses in equation 10.6.3 can be rewritten as

$$H_0 : \beta_s = \mathbf{0} \quad \text{and} \quad H_1 : \beta_s \neq \mathbf{0} \tag{10.6.5}$$

To introduce a test for H_0 against H_1, we begin by reconsidering how we would handle this problem if just *one* coefficient was involved (β_s was a scalar). If β_2 was the coefficient of interest, then, from Section 10.4, we would set up the t random variable

$$t = \frac{b_2 - \beta_2}{\sqrt{\hat{\text{var}}(b_2)}} \sim t_{(T-K)} \tag{10.6.6}$$

This random variable cannot be used for testing H_0: $\beta_s = \mathbf{0}$ because (*i*) replacing $b_2 - \beta_2$ by $\mathbf{b}_s - \beta_s$ would mean that the numerator in equation 10.6.6 is no longer a scalar value, but a vector of values, and (*ii*) replacing $\hat{\text{var}}(b_2)$ by $\hat{\text{cov}}(\mathbf{b}_s)$ would mean the denominator in equation 10.6.6 is equal to the square root of a matrix; it is not possible to get the square root of the $[(K-1) \times (K-1)]$ matrix $\hat{\text{cov}}(\mathbf{b}_s)$ or to "divide by" such a matrix.

We can escape from this dilemma by squaring the t random variable in equation 10.6.6 and developing a more general test statistic based on t^2. Following this suggestion we have

$$t^2 = \frac{(b_2 - \beta_2)^2}{\hat{\text{var}}(b_2)} = (b_2 - \beta_2)' \left[\hat{\text{var}}(b_2) \right]^{-1} (b_2 - \beta_2) \tag{10.6.7}$$

Because $(b_2 - \beta_2)$ is a scalar, $(b_2 - \beta_2)' = (b_2 - \beta_2)$. Including the transpose is convenient for our generalization for β_s. Specifically, equation 10.6.7 is in a form where replacing $(b_2 - \beta_2)$ by $(\mathbf{b}_s - \beta_s)$ and $\hat{\text{var}}(b_2)$ by $\hat{\text{cov}}(\mathbf{b}_s)$ yields a scalar random variable that can be used as the basis for a test statistic. Making these substitutions, and dividing by $(K-1)$, the number of elements in β_s, yields an F random variable with $(K-1)$ and $(T-K)$ degrees of freedom. That is,

$$F = \frac{(\mathbf{b}_s - \beta_s)' \left[\hat{\text{cov}}(\mathbf{b}_s) \right]^{-1} (\mathbf{b}_s - \beta_s)}{K-1} \sim F_{[(K-1),(T-K)]} \tag{10.6.8}$$

Whereas the t random variable can be viewed as a measure of the difference between b_2 and β_2, weighted by the estimated variance $\hat{var}(b_2)$, the F random variable can be viewed as the *average* difference between the $(K-1)$ components of $\mathbf{b}_s$ and those of $\boldsymbol{\beta}_s$, weighted by the estimated covariance matrix $\hat{cov}(\mathbf{b}_s)$. Details about the F random variable in general, and its derivation, are given in Appendix 10B. In the context of equation 10.6.3, *the F random variable is a generalization of the t random variable for the multiple parameter case involving the simultaneous testing of more than one restriction in a null hypothesis.*

To test the null hypothesis $H_0: \boldsymbol{\beta}_s = \mathbf{0}$ we compute a value for F in equation 10.6.8 under the assumption that the null hypothesis is true. That is, we compute

$$F = \frac{\mathbf{b}_s'\left[\hat{cov}(\mathbf{b}_s)\right]^{-1}\mathbf{b}_s}{K-1} \tag{10.6.9}$$

If this value could reasonably have come from an $F_{[(K-1),(T-K)]}$ distribution, we conclude that there is no evidence to suggest that H_0 is false. If the value is unlikely to be a realization from the F-distribution, the data do not support H_0, and so we conclude that the assumption $H_0: \boldsymbol{\beta}_s = \mathbf{0}$ is incorrect and reject H_0. The decision about what are reasonable values and what are unlikely values is made by choosing a significance level and the corresponding critical value F_c. In addition to the significance level, the critical value F_c depends on the degrees of freedom $(K-1)$ and $(T-K)$. If $F < F_c$, we conclude that the value F is a likely value that could have occurred when H_0 is true; we do not reject H_0. If $F \geq F_c$, we treat F as unlikely to occur if H_0 is true; we reject H_0. *Only the upper tail constitutes the rejection region because small values of $\mathbf{b}_s$ provide evidence in support of H_0.*

To test the significance of the regression used to explain the hamburger chain's total receipts, we need to test whether the coefficients of price and of advertising expenditure are both zero. Thus, in the model

$$tr = \beta_1 + \beta_2 p_t + \beta_3 a_t + e_t \tag{10.6.10}$$

we need to test

$$H_0: \beta_2 = \beta_3 = 0 \quad \text{or} \quad H_0: \boldsymbol{\beta}_s = \begin{bmatrix} \beta_2 \\ \beta_3 \end{bmatrix} = \mathbf{0} \tag{10.6.11a}$$

against the alternative

$$H_1: \beta_2 \text{ or } \beta_3 \text{ or both are nonzero} \quad \text{or} \quad H_1: \boldsymbol{\beta}_s = \begin{bmatrix} \beta_2 \\ \beta_3 \end{bmatrix} \neq \mathbf{0} \tag{10.6.11b}$$

Using equations 9.2.8 and 9.2.20, the value of the test statistic in equation 10.6.9 is given by

$$F = \frac{\begin{bmatrix} -6.6419 & 2.9843 \end{bmatrix} \begin{bmatrix} 10.184 & -0.05402 \\ -0.05402 & 0.02787 \end{bmatrix}^{-1} \begin{bmatrix} -6.6419 \\ 2.9843 \end{bmatrix}}{2}$$

$$= 159.83$$

The 5% critical value for the F statistic with $(2, 49)$ degrees of freedom is $F_c = 3.19$. Since $159.83 > 3.19$, we reject H_0 and conclude that the estimated relationship is a significant one. Our sample of data suggests that price or advertising expenditure or both have an influence on total receipts. Note that this conclusion is consistent with

Table 10.2   Analysis of Variance Table for Testing H_0: $\beta_2 = \beta_3 = 0$

Source of Variation		Degrees of Freedom	Mean Square	F
Explained	11776.18	$K - 1 = 2$	11776.18/2 = 5888.09	5888.09/36.34 = 159.83
Unexplained	1805.17	$T - K = 49$	1805.17/ = 36.34	
Total	13581.35	$T - 1 = 51$		

conclusions reached by using separate t-tests for testing the significance of price (equation 10.4.3) and the significance of advertising expenditure (equation 10.4.4).

10.6.1   The Analysis of Variance Table

Most computer software packages automatically compute the F statistic given in equation 10.6.9 and report it as part of an "analysis of variance table." This table was presented in Section 8.2.1 for the simple linear model where there is just one explanatory variable and, hence, only one response coefficient is involved when testing the significance of the regression relationship $[(K - 1) = 1]$. Here we consider the analysis of variance table for the general linear model.

It can be shown (see Exercise 10.4) that

$$F = \frac{\mathbf{b}_s' \left[\hat{\mathrm{cov}}(\mathbf{b}_s) \right]^{-1} \mathbf{b}_s}{K - 1} = \frac{\text{explained variation} / (K - 1)}{\text{unexplained variation} / (T - K)} \qquad (10.6.12)$$

What equation 10.6.12 tells us is that an examination of the explained and unexplained variation in the model provides an alternative method for computing the F statistic. In our example, we have, from equation 9.2.22,

$$\text{explained variation} = \text{total variation} - \text{unexplained (error) variation}$$
$$= 13581.35 - 1805.17 = 11776.18$$
$$\text{unexplained variation} = 1805.17$$

Table 10.2 shows how these quantities appear in the analysis of variance table and how the value of the F statistic is computed from them. The numerator and the denominator on the right side of equation 10.6.12 appear in the column headed "Mean Square", where each source of variation has been divided by its degrees of freedom. The F-value is given by the ratio of the mean squares. As before, the test is carried through by comparing the computed value 159.83 with the critical value for (2, 49) degrees of freedom, $F_c = 3.19$. Since $159.83 > 3.19$, we reject H_0.

10.6.2   Using t- and F-Tests for Zero Coefficients

We conclude this section on using the F-statistic to test a zero null hypothesis on all response coefficients by tying together a few loose ends on the relationship between t- and F-tests. First consider the simple linear model $y_t = \beta_1 + \beta_2 x_{t2} + e_t$ where $K = 2$. In this instance the vector β_s is really just the scalar β_2 and the problem of testing H_0: $\beta_s = \mathbf{0}$ reduces to testing H_0: $\beta_2 = 0$. For testing this hypothesis, either the t-test or the F-test can be used; in fact, they are identical tests in the sense that they both produce the same result. To see the equivalence note that equations 10.6.7 and 10.6.8 are identical when $K = 2$. That is,

$$t^2 = (b_2 - \beta_2)' \left[\text{vâr}(b_2) \right]^{-1} (b_2 - \beta_2) \sim F_{[1,(T-K)]} \qquad (10.6.13)$$

In fact, this result can be used to test a zero null hypothesis for a single coefficient, irrespective of whether or not $K = 2$. In general, the square of a t random variable with $(T - K)$ degrees of freedom is equal to an F random variable that has 1 degree of freedom for its first parameter and $(T - K)$ degrees of freedom for its second parameter

$$t^2_{(T-K)} = F_{[1,(T-K)]} \qquad (10.6.14)$$

Illustrating this result with the hamburger example and equation 10.4.3, we find the computed value of t^2 as

$$F = t^2 = \frac{(b_2 - \beta_2)^2}{\text{vâr}(b_2)} = \left(\frac{6.642 - 0}{3.191} \right)^2 = (-2.08)^2 = 4.33$$
$$(10.6.15)$$

Since $t^2 \sim F_{[1,(T-K)]}$, we compare 4.33 with the 5% critical value from an $F_{[1,49]}$-distribution, which is $F_c = 4.04$. Given that $4.33 > F_c = 4.04$, we reject the null hypothesis and conclude that the data support the hypothesis that $\beta_2 \neq 0$. The point to notice is that both the computed F value (4.33) and the critical $F_{[1,49]}$ value (4.04) are respectively equal to the squares of the computed t value (−2.08) and the critical $t_{(49)}$ value (2.01). The tests are therefore equivalent. If we test a hypothesis such as H_0: $\beta_2 = 0$ by calculating a value for t^2 and comparing it with a critical value from the $F_{[1,(T-K)]}$-distribution, we get exactly the same test outcome as we get by using the calculated value for t, and a critical value from the $t_{(T-K)}$-distribution. You may confirm this fact by comparing squares of the critical values from the t-distribution with critical values from the F-distribution with 1 degree of freedom in the numerator.

Given this equivalence, and that the F-distribution can be used for more general hypotheses, you may very well ask why the t-distribution is considered at all. The answer is that the t-distribution is needed for one-sided tests like those in Section 10.3. Since $F = t^2$, the F-distribution does not discriminate between positive and negative t values, which are needed to delineate the critical region in a one-sided t-test.

Another question that also might have been provoked by the development in this section is: Why use the F-distribution to perform a simultaneous test of H_0: $\beta_2 = \beta_3 = 0$? Why not just use separate t-tests on each of the null hypotheses H_0: $\beta_2 = 0$ and H_0: $\beta_3 = 0$? The answer relates to the correlation between the test outcomes. The F test that tests both hypotheses simultaneously makes allowance for the fact that the least squares estimators b_2 and b_3 are correlated. When separate t-tests are performed, the test outcomes will be correlated, but, because each t-test is treated in isolation from the other, no allowance is made for this correlation. As a consequence, a 5% significance level used for the simultaneous F-test is not equivalent to separate t tests that each use a 5% significance level. Conflicting results can occur. For example, it is possible for individual t-tests to accept a number of zero hypotheses when the F-test that simultaneously tests the same zero hypotheses rejects them. This circumstance is illustrated in Figure 10.1. The ellipse in this figure contains all pairs of values β_2^0 and β_3^0 where a joint null hypothesis of the form

$$H_0 : \boldsymbol{\beta}_s = \begin{pmatrix} \beta_2 \\ \beta_3 \end{pmatrix} = \begin{pmatrix} \beta_2^0 \\ \beta_3^0 \end{pmatrix}$$

would be accepted. Note that the origin, where $\beta_2 = \beta_3 = 0$, is not constrained within the ellipse. Thus, the null hypothesis H_0: $\boldsymbol{\beta}_s = \mathbf{0}$ would be rejected. Nevertheless, it is

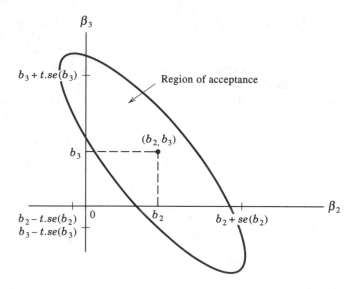

Figure 10.1 The relationship between individual and joint tests of hypotheses.

possible for each of the separate interval estimates $[b_2 - t_c.se(b_2), b_2 + t_c.se(b_2)]$ and $[b_3 - t_c.se(b_3), b_3 + t_c.se(b_3)]$ to contain zero, as illustrated in the figure. Under these circumstances the separate null hypotheses $H_0: \beta_2 = 0$ and $H_0: \beta_3 = 0$ would not be rejected.

The F-test for simultaneously testing a null hypothesis made up of a number of zero hypotheses was developed as a generalization of the t-test for testing a single null hypothesis. In the remainder of this chapter we consider t- and F-tests for more general hypotheses than involve linear functions of the coefficients.

10.7   Testing a Single Linear Combination of Coefficients

It is frequently useful to test more general linear hypotheses about the coefficient vector β than those we have considered thus far. To provide an empirical context for extending our framework to accommodate more general hypotheses, it is convenient to modify the receipts–price–advertising relationship for our Bay Area hamburger chain.

10.7.1   An Extended Model

The hypothesized relationship between total receipts, price, and advertising that we have been using in Chapter 9, and thus far in this chapter, is given by

$$tr_t = \beta_1 + \beta_2 p_t + \beta_3 a_t + e_t \tag{10.7.1}$$

and its estimated counterpart is

$$\hat{tr}_t = 104.79 - 6.642 p_t + 2.984 a_t \tag{10.7.2}$$

One aspect of this model that is worth questioning is whether the *linear* relationship between receipts, price, and advertising expenditure is likely to be a good approximation to reality. The linear model implies that increasing advertising expenditure will continue to increase total receipts at the same rate irrespective of the existing levels of receipts and advertising expenditure. That is, the response coefficient β_3 [or the partial derivative $\partial(tr)/\partial a$], that measures the response of tr to a change in a, is constant; it does not depend on a. This may be an unrealistic assumption. As the level of advertising expenditure increases, we would expect diminishing returns to set in. That is, the increase in receipts that results from an advertising expenditure increase of $1000 is likely to decline as the total amount spent on advertising grows. One way of modeling a relationship where the change in receipts depends on a is to write the response coefficient β_3 as a function of a. That is, we write the model as

$$tr_t = \beta_1 + \beta_2 p_t + \beta_{3t} a_t + e_t \qquad (10.7.3)$$

where

$$\beta_{3t} = \beta_3 + \beta_4 a_t \qquad (10.7.4)$$

In equation 10.7.3 the subscript t has been added to β_3 to recognize that it will depend on weekly advertising expenditure a_t. In equation 10.7.4, β_{3t} is written as a linear function of a_t, with this linear function described by *two new parameters* β_3 and β_4. We can view β_{3t} as an example of a systematically varying parameter; models with such parameters are studied in more detail in Chapter 12.

Substituting equation 10.7.4 into equation 10.7.3 yields the new equation

$$tr_t = \beta_1 + \beta_2 p_t + \beta_3 a_t + \beta_4 a_t^2 + e_t \qquad (10.7.5)$$

Thus, adding the term $\beta_4 a_t^2$ to our original specification yields a model where the response of revenue to advertising depends on the level of advertising. This response of tr to a is measured by the partial derivative

$$\frac{\partial(tr_t)}{\partial a_t} = \beta_3 + 2\beta_4 a_t \qquad (10.7.6)$$

When a_t increases, tr_t increases at the rate of $(\beta_3 + 2\beta_4 a_t)$ units. To determine the expected signs for β_3 and β_4, we note that we would expect the response of revenue to advertising to be positive when $a_t = 0$. That is, we expect that $\beta_3 > 0$. Also, to achieve diminishing returns the response must decline as a_t increases. That is, we expect $\beta_4 < 0$. For further details and examples of partial derivatives see Appendix 10A.

10.7.2   Estimating the Extended Model

Having proposed an extended model that we feel might be more realistic, our next step is to estimate it. In terms of our general notation for the general linear statistical model, we can write equation 10.7.5 as

$$y_t = \beta_1 + \beta_2 x_{t2} + \beta_3 x_{t3} + \beta_4 x_{t4} + e_t \qquad (10.7.7)$$

where

$$y_t = tr_t \qquad x_{t2} = p_t \qquad x_{t3} = a_t \qquad x_{t4} = a_t^2$$

The (52×4) matrix X that contains all of the observations on the explanatory variables is of the form

$$X = \begin{bmatrix} 1 & p_1 & a_1 & a_1^2 \\ 1 & p_2 & a_2 & a_2^2 \\ \vdots & \vdots & \vdots & \vdots \\ 1 & p_{52} & a_{52} & a_{52}^2 \end{bmatrix} \qquad (10.7.8)$$

Application of the least squares rule $\mathbf{b} = (X'X)^{-1}X'\mathbf{y}$ to the data in Table 9.1 with X defined as in equation 10.7.8 yields the following estimated equation, with standard errors in parentheses:

$$\hat{t}r_t = 104.81 - 6.582p_t + 2.948a_t + 0.0017a_t^2$$
$$\quad\quad (6.58) \quad (3.459) \quad\quad (0.786) \quad (0.0361) \quad\quad (\text{s.e.})$$
$$T = 52 \quad R^2 = 0.867 \quad \hat{\sigma}^2 = 37.606 \quad\quad\quad\quad (10.7.9)$$

What can we say about the addition of a_t^2 to the equation? The first thing to notice is that its coefficient is positive, not negative as was expected. Second, its t-value for the hypotheses $H_0\colon \beta_4 = 0$ is given by $t = 0.0017/0.0361 = 0.048$. This very low value indicates that β_4 has been estimated imprecisely. A 95% confidence interval for β_4 will be a relatively wide one that includes both a negative and a positive range. Specifically, the 95% interval estimate for β_4 is

$$0.0017 - (2.01)(0.0361) \le \beta_4 \le 0.0017 + (2.01)(0.0361)$$

or

$$-0.071 \le \beta_4 \le 0.074 \quad\quad\quad\quad (10.7.10)$$

Because the estimate for β_4 is imprecise, as reflected by the uninformative interval estimate in equation 10.7.10, another 26 weeks of data were collected. These data are presented in Table 10.3. The ranges of p_t and a_t are wider in this data set and, as we will see in Chapter 13, the greater the variation in the explanatory variables, the more precise the least squares estimator. This fact, coupled with the fact that we now have a total of 78 observations, rather than 52, gives us a better chance of obtaining a more precise estimate of β_4.

Combining the additional data in Table 10.3 with the previous data in Table 9.1 yields the following least squares estimated equation (standard errors in parentheses):

$$\hat{t}r_t = 110.46 - 10.198p_t + 3.361a_t - 0.0268a_t^2$$
$$\quad\quad (3.74) \quad (1.582) \quad\quad (0.422) \quad (0.0159) \quad\quad (\text{s.e.})$$
$$T = 78 \quad R^2 = 0.879 \quad \hat{\sigma}^2 = 35.031 \quad\quad\quad\quad (10.7.11)$$

Table 10.3 An Additional 26 Weeks of Data on Revenue, Price, and Advertising

Week	tr	p	a	Week	tr	p	a
53	129.9	2.87	16.0	66	108.6	1.61	4.8
54	101.5	2.05	4.0	67	158.8	2.66	27.7
55	136.3	2.55	19.6	68	147.2	1.74	20.6
56	97.6	3.49	10.2	69	146.3	3.21	25.4
57	118.9	3.45	17.5	70	121.2	1.50	10.2
58	130.5	3.45	18.3	71	107.0	1.78	4.9
59	128.5	2.58	18.2	72	121.2	2.43	12.1
60	138.3	2.87	22.1	73	125.4	2.04	12.3
61	103.6	1.76	4.1	74	141.9	2.99	19.7
62	151.8	2.97	24.9	75	120.0	2.83	14.3
63	128.5	2.77	14.7	76	101.9	2.47	4.8
64	128.5	2.64	18.6	77	130.4	2.04	11.6
65	143.7	1.50	20.9	78	139.9	1.87	19.8

A comparison of the standard errors in this equation with those in equation 10.7.9 indicates that the inclusion of the additional 26 observations has greatly improved the precision of our estimates. In particular, the estimated coefficient of a_t^2 now has the expected sign. The corresponding t-value of $t = -0.0268/0.0159 = -1.68$ still implies the 95% confidence interval for β_4 includes a range of positive values for β_4. However, because the improvement in precision is quite substantial, we proceed with further analysis on the basis of this equation.

10.7.3   Testing the Optimality of Advertising Expenditure

From equations 10.7.6 and 10.7.9, the estimated response of receipts to a one-unit change in advertising expenditure is given by

$$\frac{\partial(\hat{tr}_t)}{\partial a_t} = b_3 + 2b_4 a_t = 3.361 - 2(0.026755)a_t$$

$$= 3.361 - 0.0535a_t \qquad (10.7.12)$$

In our sample of 78 observations a_t ranges from a low of 1.8 to a high of 27.7. Using these values in equation 10.7.12 we estimate that $\partial(\hat{tr}_t)/\partial a_t = 3.265$ when $a_t = 1.8$ and $\partial(\hat{tr}_t)/\partial a_t = 1.879$ when $a_t = 27.7$. That is, when $a_t = 1.8$, increasing a_t increases total receipts at the rate of 3.265 units. Since we are working in one thousand dollar units, we are saying that when advertising expenditure is $1800, increasing this expenditure increases total receipts at the rate of $3265 per $1000 increase in a_t. When $a_t = 27.7$, increasing a_t leads to an increase in total receipts at the rate of $1879 per $1000 increase in a_t.

To find the optimal level of advertising expenditure we need to find that value of a where the increase in total receipts from a change in a (marginal revenue) is equal to the increase in costs associated with an increase in a (marginal cost). The costs will include the cost of advertising itself as well as the costs associated with producing more hamburgers, fries, shakes, and so on. For the purpose of this example we will ignore additional production costs and assume that the only costs from additional advertising are the costs of the advertising itself. Under these circumstances, if these results indicate the existence of diminishing returns to advertising expenditure, it will pay the hamburger chain to increase advertising expenditure to the point where the increase in receipts is equal to the increase in advertising cost. That is, advertising expenditure should be such that the last one unit of advertising expenditure (one thousand dollars in this case) yields an increase in receipts of one unit. In terms of equation 10.7.6, we require

$$\frac{\partial tr_t}{\partial a_t} = \beta_3 + 2\beta_4 a_t = 1 \qquad (10.7.13)$$

One of the executives in the hamburger chain claims, on the basis of her experience, that the optimal advertising expenditure is $40,000. Thus, she is claiming that equation 10.7.13 holds when $a = 40$. That is,

$$\beta_3 + 2\beta_4 \times 40 = 1$$

or

$$\beta_3 + 80\beta_4 = 1 \qquad (10.7.14)$$

Suppose that you would like to test whether the executive's assessment of the optimal advertising policy is correct. In other words, you wish to test the validity of equation 10.7.14; the null and alternative hypotheses are

$$H_0: \beta_3 + 80\beta_4 = 1 \quad \text{and} \quad H_1: \beta_3 + 80\beta_4 \neq 1 \tag{10.7.15}$$

The null hypothesis in equation 10.7.15 is described as a hypothesis on a single linear combination of the elements in β. Using equation 10.7.12, an estimate of the marginal returns to advertising when $a_t = 40$ is given by

$$3.361 - 0.0535 \times 40 = 1.221$$

To test H_0 against H_1 we ask whether the difference between the estimated value 1.221 and the hypothesized value of 1 could be due to chance, or whether the difference is sufficiently great to suggest the executive is wrong.

To carry out the test we use the fact that

$$t = \frac{(b_3 + 80b_4) - (\beta_3 + 80\beta_4)}{\sqrt{\hat{\text{var}}(b_3 + 80b_4)}} \sim t_{(T-K)} \tag{10.7.16}$$

where, using results in Chapter 2 on the variance of a linear function of random variables,

$$\hat{\text{var}}(b_3 + 80b_4) = \hat{\text{var}}(b_3) + (80)^2 \hat{\text{var}}(b_4) + (2)(80)\hat{\text{cov}}(b_3, b_4)$$
$$= 0.17784 + (6400)(0.0002524) + (160)(-0.0064346)$$
$$= 0.76366$$

Computing a value for t in equation 10.7.16 under the assumption that the null hypothesis $H_0: \beta_3 + 80\beta_4 = 1$ is true yields

$$t = \frac{1.221 - 1}{\sqrt{0.7637}} = \frac{1.221 - 1}{0.8739} = 0.252$$

For a 5% significance level and $(T - K) = 78 - 4 = 74$ degrees of freedom the critical value for the $t_{(74)}$ distribution is $t_c = 1.99$. Since $t = 0.252 < 1.99 = t_c$, there is no sample evidence to suggest the executive's claim about the optimal advertising expenditure is incorrect.

In general, there are many different kinds of linear hypotheses that arise from the vast array of economic and statistical models that are utilized in practice. Other examples, in the context of demand and production theory, are given in Chapter 11. In each case a t random variable, comparable to that in equation 10.7.16, can be used to test the single linear combination of coefficients that is of interest. A general linear hypothesis framework for representing linear combinations of coefficients is developed in Appendix 10C.

Given that the square of a $t_{(T-K)}$ random variable is equal to an $F_{[1,(T-K)]}$ random variable, single linear combinations of the elements in β can also be tested using an F-test with one degree of freedom in the numerator. *To simultaneously test more than one linear combination of the coefficients, an F-test is required.* In practice, the value of a relevant t- or F-statistic is usually computed automatically by whatever econometric computer software is being employed; it is simply a matter of specifying the appropriate hypothesis. In the next section we give an example of an F-test used for testing two linear combinations. A more formal development of the testing procedure appears in Appendix 10C.

10.8   Testing More Than One Linear Combination of Coefficients

Let us suppose that, in addition to the claim that optimal advertising expenditure is $40,000, the hamburger chain's executive believes that setting advertising expenditure at $40,000 and price at $2 will, on average, produce total receipts equal to $175,000. To examine this claim we begin by noting that average weekly receipts when $a_t = 40$ and $p_t = 2$ are given by

$$E[tr_t] = \beta_1 + \beta_2 p_t + \beta_3 a_t + \beta_4 a_t^2$$
$$= \beta_1 + 2\beta_2 + 40\beta_3 + 1600\beta_4 \qquad (10.8.1)$$

Thus, the executive's hypothesis about average receipts can be written as

$$\beta_1 + 2\beta_2 + 40\beta_3 + 1600\beta_4 = 175 \qquad (10.8.2)$$

To *simultaneously test* this equality, and the equality that holds when $a_t = 40$ is the optimal level of advertising expenditure, we set up the following hypotheses:

$$H_0 : \begin{cases} \beta_1 + 2\beta_2 + 40\beta_3 + 1600\beta_4 = 175 \\ \beta_3 + 80\beta_4 = 1 \end{cases} \qquad (10.8.3a)$$

$$H_1 : \text{at least one of the equalities under } H_0 \text{ is false} \qquad (10.8.3b)$$

The equalities in H_0 can be described as hypotheses about two linear combinations of the elements in β. We want to jointly test whether these equalities are compatible with the sample of data.

The appropriate test for testing H_0 against H_1 is an F-test that is a generalization of the F-test developed in Section 10.6. In that section we were interested in testing a zero hypothesis for all response coefficients; here we are concerned with testing *general linear hypotheses* about β. Details of the more general test are given later, in Appendix 10C, and, in a different form, in Section 11.6. At this point it is sufficient to note that specification of the linear equalities in H_0 is usually all that is required to make most econometric computer programs compute a value of the F-statistic. Under H_0, that is, assuming that the null hypothesis is true, the F-statistic has an F-distribution with numerator degrees of freedom equal to J, the number of equalities in H_0, and with denominator degrees of freedom equal to $T - K$.

Using a computer program and our data set to compute the F-value for testing equation 10.8.3a against equation 10.8.3b yields $F = 1.753$. The 5% critical value from an F-distribution with (2, 74) degrees of freedom is $F_c = 3.12$. This value can be obtained as an approximation from Table 4 at the end of this book, or by using an appropriate computer program. Since $F = 1.753 < 3.12 = F_c$, we conclude that there is no evidence in the data to suggest that the executive's claim is incorrect. In other words, the executive's conjecture is compatible with the sample of data.

10.9   Selecting Regressor Variables and Model Misspecification

In Section 9.5 of Chapter 9 and Section 10.4.1 of this chapter, we raised the question of uncertainty concerning the set of variables that should be included in the matrix of

explanatory or regressor variables X. In Section 9.5 we examined the statistical consequences of misspecifying X. In Section 10.4.1 we indicated that applied workers choose
explanatory variables through a judicious combination of (*i*) a priori judgement from
knowledge of economic theory and (*ii*) testing hypotheses of the form H_0: $\beta_k = 0$ for
variables whose inclusion is in doubt. Because of the implications of preliminary-test
estimation and omitted variable bias, we warned against mechanical application of rules
such as: Delete all variables whose coefficient estimates are not significantly different from zero.

*Selecting the appropriate set of regressors, and an appropriate model, are difficult
problems for which no satisfactory solution exists.* It is therefore impossible to give a
prescription that should be followed at all times. There is no clear-cut definitive method
for deciding on the "best" set of variables. So that you will be informed, it may be useful
at this point to describe some of the variable and model selection criteria that can be
used and the statistical consequences that follow. In practice researchers generally use
some *subjective* combination of these criteria. The degree of subjectivity and the lack
of information on the sampling properties of various rules prevent us from saying how
much weight should be placed on each criterion. We can, however, be definite about
the following two points:

1. We must in some way make use of nonsample information in the form of
    economic principles and other logic, as well as the information in our sample
    of data.

2. Blind mechanical application of one particular criterion, or many criteria, is not
    a satisfactory strategy. All of the criteria suffer from the defects of preliminary-
    test estimation.

With this background, let us summarize and comment on a number of criteria that
are often used for selection of regressors, and sometimes for assessing model adequacy.

1. Economic theory and logic and compatibility with a priori expectations. As we
have mentioned, economic theory and logic should play a prominent and vital role in
the selection of the model and the regressors within that model. Suppose that we estimate a model that has been selected in this way and we find that some of the signs of
the coefficients do not agree with our a priori expectations. For example, suppose that
the estimated coefficient of price in a demand equation has a positive sign. How we
proceed will depend on what we judge to be the reason for the wrong sign. We must
ask questions such as: Have we specified the model correctly? Could the wrong sign
be caused by omitted variable(s)? Is it possible that our model is correct, but our data
are too poor to obtain a precise estimate of the offending coefficient?

2. Use of t- and F-tests. As discussed in Section 10.4.1, one method for assessing
the relevance of a particular variable is by testing hypotheses such as H_0: $\beta_k = 0$. If H_0
is rejected we should ask: Is x_{tk} irrelevant? Are our data too poor for us to accurately
estimate the effect of x_{tk}? Is there some misspecification problem that is invalidating
the test? If we are interested in the relevance of a group of variables (say three), rather
than just a single variable, we can use an F-test to test hypotheses of the form H_0: β_k
$= \beta_l = \beta_m = 0$.

3. Using the coefficient of determination R^2. Since the coefficient of determination R^2 tells us the proportion of variation in the dependent variable explained by the
regressor variables, one way of choosing between two competing models is to choose
the one with the larger R^2. This procedure gives us the model with the greater explanatory

power. Some words of caution are in order, however. Using R^2 to compare models is invalid where

   (i)   the models have different dependent variables,
  (ii)   the models have different numbers of regressors, and
 (iii)   one of the models does not have a constant term.

Since we are comparing the ability of models to explain variations in the dependent variable, it does not make sense to make such a comparison if the dependent variables are different. Note that, for this purpose, y_t and $\ln y_t$ are different dependent variables. Using R^2 to compare models that have a different number of regressors is not valid because adding a regressor always increases R^2 even if that regressor is irrelevant. The problems associated with the definition of R^2 in models without a constant term were discussed in Section 9.2.4. It can also be misleading to use R^2 for model selection when the explanatory variables are trending stochastic regressors. This problem is discussed in Chapter 21 under the heading of "spurious regressions."

   4. Choose the model with the largest adjusted coefficient of determination $\overline{R}^2$ that is defined by

$$\overline{R}_i^2 = 1 - \frac{\text{SSE}_i / (T - K_i)}{\text{SST}/(T - 1)}$$

where SST is the total sum of squares of the dependent variable y about its arithmetic mean, SSE_i is the sum of squared errors from the ith model, and K_i is the number of coefficients in that model. This adjusted R^2, which is described as "R-bar-squared," does not always increase when additional regressors are added. Consequently, it is often used to compare models with differing numbers of regressors. However, it can be shown that the addition of a regressor, say x_{tk}, will increase $\overline{R}^2$ if and only if the t-value for the hypothesis H_0: $\beta_k = 0$ is greater than one in absolute value. In this sense, using $\overline{R}^2$ can be viewed as testing the significance of β_k with a critical value $t_c = \pm 1$. It is worth noting that $\overline{R}^2$ can be negative.

   5. Choose the model that minimizes the Akaike information criterion (AIC), given by

$$\text{AIC}_i = \ln\left(\frac{\text{SSE}_i}{T}\right) + \frac{2K_i}{T}$$

Like $\overline{R}_i^2$, this measure involves a trade-off between minimizing the sum of squared errors SSE_i and limiting any increase in the number of regressors.

   6. The J test. For criteria such as R^2, $\overline{R}^2$, and AIC an observed difference between two values does not necessarily mean one model is preferable; it may be due to chance. The J test can be used to test whether one model has better explanatory power than another in the following way. We estimate one model, say model A, and use it to compute predictions of the dependent variable over the sample period. Those predictions are then included as an additional explanatory variable in the other model (model B). If the coefficient of the "prediction variable" turns out to be significant when model B is estimated, this suggests that there is information in model A that can significantly improve the explanatory power of model B. We are therefore led to ask whether model B is adequate. Also, the models can be reversed so that we can test whether information in model B can improve the explanatory power of model A.

7. The RESET test. With this test the squares and possibly the cubes of the predictions from a model are included in that model as additional explanatory variables, and the model is reestimated. Either a t- or an F-test is used to test whether the coefficients of the prediction variables are singly, or collectively, significantly different from zero. Significance of the coefficients is *intended to be indicative* of some kind of specification error such as omitted variables or incorrect functional form.

As we mentioned at the beginning of this section, model specification in general, and the inclusion of the appropriate set of regressor variables in particular, is a difficult and unsolved problem. The criteria we have described can give some indication of when a model is misspecified, or when one set of regressors is preferable to another set, and hence they may be some guide to the model specification process when our theory is lacking. However, when evaluating empirical results produced by *any sort of model selection methodology*, extreme caution should be exercised. The two-step estimation rules consisting of (*i*) screening models using the data and one or more model selection procedures and (*ii*) applying least squares to the model finally selected, have virtually unknown sampling properties. Furthermore, the statistics printed out by your computer program at the end of step (*ii*) are incorrect. The F-statistic, t-statistics, and estimated standard errors are all misleading since they ignore the fact that step (*i*) ever took place!!! The fact is that the empirical results *look better* than they actually are, since the usual least squares formulas *understate the standard errors* of the actual two-step estimation procedure, where supposed extraneous variables have been eliminated. Consequently, if the data are subjected to a large battery of tests and criteria, there is a high probability of choosing a model that "looks good" but is not consistent with the true data-generation process. When you draw conclusions from such a good-looking model, you should be aware of the shaky foundation on which they rest. For this reason, extensive model selection exercises are referred to as *data mining*. For further details of model selection rules, their motivation and problems with pretest estimation see Judge et al. (1988, Chapter 20).

10.10   Choice of Functional Form

A question related to variable selection is that of choosing the functional form appropriate for a particular economic relation. Economic theory, while useful in helping us identify economic variables that may be relevant in a particular problem setting, gives very little guidance as to the corresponding functional form.

In the examples covered thus far we have encountered models with many different kinds of functional forms, all of which can be written in terms of a general statistical model that is linear in the parameters. Examples are linear models, log-linear models, and a model quadratic in the variables. Many other possibilities in the case of the simple regression model were described in Chapter 8. A natural question to ask is: How should a choice between the various alternatives be made?

The first consideration in this regard should always be to choose a functional form whose characteristics reflect the economic nature of the relationship. Should the elasticities be constant over the whole range of the explanatory variables? Should the marginal responses (first-order partial derivatives) be constant over the whole range of explanatory variables? In the case of a production function, should we allow for diminishing returns to some variables? These types of questions were discussed in Chapter 8 and at various other places along the way. What questions are relevant will depend on what economic relationship is being considered, but it must be remembered that issues like these are paramount.

Sometimes, however, economic logic is not sufficiently adequate to prescribe a particular kind of functional form. Under these circumstances it might be desirable to see which functional form is most supported by the data. We looked at one example of this strategy when in Section 10.7 we investigated whether a quadratic function might be a better representation of the receipts–price–advertising relationship for the hamburger chain. We tested whether the additional quadratic variable a_t^2 was relevant by testing whether its coefficient could be zero. In this section we examine another test for functional form, one for examining whether a linear or a log-linear function might be more appropriate.

10.10.1   Testing a Linear Versus a Log-Linear Model

Let us return to the receipts–price–advertising relationship for the hamburger chain and suppose that we are undecided between the log-linear model

$$\ln(tr_t) = \gamma_1 + \gamma_2 \ln p_t + \gamma_3 \ln a_t + e_t \tag{10.10.1}$$

and the linear model

$$tr_t = \beta_1 + \beta_2 p_t + \beta_3 a_t + e_t \tag{10.10.2}$$

We have mentioned on two occasions that the linear model could not be regarded as realistic for all possible prices and advertising expenditures; it must be viewed as an approximation over a limited range of data. Let us examine whether the data suggest that the log-linear model is preferable.

One approach that might be considered for this problem is to examine the unexplained variation for each equation, as measured by their sums of squared errors, and choose the equation with the smallest unexplained variation. Some of the variable selection procedures of Section 10.9 are based on minimizing some function of the sum of squared errors. However, this procedure is not legitimate because the dependent variables are different. In one case we are explaining variation in $\ln(tr)$ and in the other we are explaining variation in tr. It is not possible to choose on the basis of a comparison between the sum of squared errors where $\ln(tr)$ is the dependent variable and the sum of squared errors where tr is the dependent variable. This fact is even more evident when we note that the sum of squared errors for the linear model depends on the units of measurement for tr, but that for the log-linear model does not. As shown in Exercise 10.16, we can always improve the sum of squared errors for the linear model by measuring total receipts in terms of million dollar units instead of thousand dollar units. As an alternative we could try the coefficient of determination R^2, which is a unit-free measure of the proportion of variation in the dependent variable explained by the relationship. However, because the dependent variables are different in each instance, it too is not a useful basis for comparison; we are talking about the proportion of variation in different things.

One way to solve this problem is to use a test suggested by Box and Cox (1964) that involves an alternative, unit-free, transformed tr as the dependent variable in the linear equation. Specifically, if we divide each observation tr_t by the geometric mean of all the tr_t, then the sum of squared errors from the linear equation that uses the transformed tr is in comparable units to the sum of squared errors from the log-linear equation. Let's carry through with this idea. The geometric mean of the $y_t = tr_t$ is given by

$$\bar{y}_G = \left(y_1 \times y_2 \times \ldots \times y_T\right)^{1/T} \tag{10.10.3}$$

A handy way to compute this quantity is by noting that

$$\ln \bar{y}_G = \frac{1}{T} \sum_{t=1}^{T} \ln y_t$$

and thus

$$\bar{y}_G = \exp\left\{\frac{1}{T}\sum_{t=1}^{T}\ln y_t\right\}$$ (10.10.4)

If we let SSE_L be the sum of squared errors from the original linear model in natural units, and SSE_{LL} be the sum of squared errors from the log-linear model, and we apply least squares to the linear model with $(y_t / \bar{y}_G)$ as the dependent variable, then the resulting sum of squared errors will be $SSE_L / \bar{y}_G^2$. As demonstrated in Exercise 10.16, this quantity is unit-free and, hence, can be directly compared with SSE_{LL} to see which model is better supported by the data. Of course, it may turn out that $SSE_L / \bar{y}_G^2$ and SSE_{LL} are very similar in magnitude. If so, the difference could be due to chance, not because one model is necessarily a better description of the data. Fortunately, a test statistic is available for testing whether $SSE_L / \bar{y}_G^2$ and SSE_{LL} are "significantly different." Box and Cox (1964) have shown, under a null hypothesis that *the two models are empirically equivalent,* that

$$l = \frac{T}{2}\left|\ln\left(\frac{SSE_L / \bar{y}_G^2}{SSE_{LL}}\right)\right| \sim \chi_{(1)}^2$$ (10.10.5)

Thus, we compute a value for l assuming that both models are equally satisfactory (the data cannot discriminate between them), and we reject this assumption if l exceeds an appropriate critical value from the $\chi_{(1)}^2$ distribution. With a 5% significance level, 3.84 is the critical value. If the null hypothesis is rejected, then the linear model is preferred if $SSE_L / \bar{y}_G^2$ is smaller and the log-linear model is preferred if SSE_{LL} is smaller. Note that taking the absolute value in equation 10.10.5 means that interchanging the numerator and denominator does not change the value for l. Thus, the null hypothesis is rejected if the linear model is "much better" *or* if the log-linear model is "much better."

If we apply this test to the 52 observations that appear in Table 9.1, we find that

$$SSE_L = 1805.2 \quad \bar{y}_G = 119.24 \quad SSE_{LL} = 0.16842$$

Thus, the value of the test statistic is

$$l = \frac{T}{2}\left|\ln\left(\frac{1805.2/(119.24)^2}{0.16842}\right)\right|$$

$$= 26\left|\ln\left(\frac{0.12696}{0.16842}\right)\right|$$

$$= 7.35$$ (10.10.6)

Since $7.35 > 3.84$, we reject H_0 at the 5% significance level and conclude the two models are not observationally equivalent. Since $SSE_L / \bar{y}_G^2 = 0.12696 < SSE_{LL} = 0.16842$, we conclude that the linear model fits the data better than the log-linear model.

In this section we have restricted ourselves to a choice between the log-linear and linear functional forms. Since for many problems these two alternatives may not be appropriate, it is important to realize that by applying a transformation to some or all of the variables in a relationship, it is possible to create a family of functions where linear and log-linear specifications are only *two* members of the family. A procedure, called the Box-Cox transformation, reflects a specification where the data are used to determine the "appropriate" functional form. In the Box-Cox procedure the variables are transformed as follows:

$$z^{(\lambda)} = \begin{cases} \dfrac{z^{\lambda}-1}{\lambda} & \text{if } \lambda \neq 0 \\ \ln z & \text{if } \lambda = 0 \end{cases}$$

where λ is an unknown parameter to be "determined by the data." If $\lambda = 1$, for the x and y variables, the linear functional form results and when $\lambda = 0$ a log-linear form results. Other values of λ suggest alternative functional forms (see Judge et al., pp. 555–563).

10.11 Summary and Critique

This chapter is concerned with inference in the general linear statistical model $\mathbf{y} = X\boldsymbol{\beta} + \mathbf{e}$ where the matrix X contains two or more explanatory variables. Specifically, we have examined interval estimation and hypothesis testing for the elements in $\boldsymbol{\beta}$. We have also recognized that, in practice, uncertainty about the specification of X exists, and we have examined methods for assessing alternative specifications. The main results of the chapter are as follows:

1. For the inference results in this chapter to hold true we need to be able to make the additional assumption that the errors are normally distributed. That is $\mathbf{e} \sim N(\mathbf{0}, \sigma^2 I_T)$.

2. For interval estimation or hypothesis testing that involves a single element from the vector $\boldsymbol{\beta}$, say β_k, we use the fact that

$$t = \frac{b_k - \beta_k}{\sqrt{\hat{\text{var}}(b_k)}} \sim t_{(T-K)}$$

where b_k is the kth element from the least squares estimator $\mathbf{b} = (X'X)^{-1}X'\mathbf{y}$ and $\hat{\text{var}}(b_k)$ is the kth diagonal element of the estimated covariance matrix $\hat{\text{cov}}(\mathbf{b}) = \hat{\sigma}^2 (X'X)^{-1}$.

3. When results are reported in the form

$$\hat{y}_t = \quad b_1 \quad\quad +b_2 x_{t2} \quad +b_3 x_{t3}$$
$$\left[\text{se}(b_1)\right]\ \left[\text{se}(b_2)\right]\ \left[\text{se}(b_3)\right]$$
$$\text{or} \quad\quad \left[t(b_1)\right]\ \left[t(b_2)\right]\ \left[t(b_3)\right]$$

we can, by simple inspection, form approximate 95% confidence intervals for β_1, β_2, and β_3 and determine whether null hypotheses of the form H_0: $\beta_k = 0$ are rejected. If a null hypothesis of the form H_0: $\beta_k = 0$ is not rejected, there is no evidence in the data to establish that x_k influences the dependent variable y. This lack of evidence could be because H_0 is true, but it also could be a consequence of poor data. These facts should be kept in mind and used in conjunction with our nonsample information when significance tests of the form H_0: $\beta_k = 0$ are used to decide what regressors should be included.

4. The t-test is needed for testing one-sided hypotheses about single elements in $\boldsymbol{\beta}$, but, for testing a two-sided hypothesis about a single element in $\boldsymbol{\beta}$, such as a zero hypothesis, either a t-test or an F-test can be used; both yield the same outcome. For a zero null hypothesis on more than one element in $\boldsymbol{\beta}$, the F-test is required and can be viewed as a generalization of the t-test.

5. The value of the F-statistic required for testing whether all response coefficients could equal zero is automatically calculated in the analysis of variance table produced on most computer output. The two expressions for the "overall" F-statistic are

$$F = \frac{\mathbf{b}_s' \left[c\hat{o}v(\mathbf{b}_s) \right]^{-1} \mathbf{b}_s}{K-1} = \frac{\text{explained variation}/(K-1)}{\text{unexplained variation}/(T-K)}$$

6. Both the t- and F-tests are useful for testing more general linear hypotheses about β. Such hypotheses involve linear combinations of the elements in β. The t-test is used for a single linear combination; the F-test can be used for jointly testing one or more linear combinations and is identical to the t-test if just one linear combination is involved.

7. All the tests described in this chapter can be routinely carried out by commonly used econometric computer software; all that is required is specification of the linear hypotheses. Because of the ease with which values of the test statistics can be calculated, it is not necessary for the practitioner to remember and apply specific formulas. An understanding of the procedure is all that is required. For this reason, in Section 10.8 we did not give an expression for the F-statistic used to test a set of general linear hypotheses. The reader should be able to apply this test without explicit knowledge of the statistic. Those readers who are content with this amount of information can, at this point, move directly to Chapter 11, where a formulation of the F-statistic in terms of sums of squared errors is developed. Readers who would like a greater appreciation and a greater depth of understanding of the F test can proceed to the general linear hypotheses development of the statistic in Appendix 10C.

8. Selecting the appropriate set of explanatory variables for a model is a difficult problem for which no easy solution exists. Variable choice is usually based on some combination of a priori knowledge and information obtained from the data. Many data-based criteria exist for choosing variables and assessing model misspecification. While such criteria can provide useful information, their repeated mechanistic application is not recommended. Furthermore, we must be cautious when assessing the reliability of an estimated model produced by some model-selection process.

9. A test for discriminating between linear and log-linear models is one example of a test for alternative model specification.

10.12   Exercises

10.1 In Exercise 9.1 the model

$$y_t = x_{t1}\beta_1 + x_{t2}\beta_2 + x_{t3}\beta_3 + e_t$$

was estimated using the data in Table 9.4. Using a hand calculator, test the following hypotheses
(a) H_0: $\beta_2 = 0$ against H_1: $\beta_2 \neq 0$
(b) H_0: $\beta_1 = \beta_2 = 0$ against H_1: β_1 or β_2 or both are nonzero
(c) H_0: $\beta_2 = \beta_3 = 0$ against H_1: β_2 or β_3 or both are nonzero
(d) H_0: $\beta_1 = \beta_2 = \beta_3 = 0$ against H_1: at least β_1, β_2, or β_3 is nonzero

10.2 Consider the model

$$y_t = \beta_1 + x_{t2}\beta_2 + x_{t3}\beta_3 + e_t$$

and suppose that application of least squares to 20 observations on these variables yields the following results

$$\mathbf{b} = \begin{bmatrix} 0.96587 \\ 0.69914 \\ 1.7769 \end{bmatrix} \quad \hat{cov}(\mathbf{b}) = \hat{\sigma}^2 (X'X)^{-1} = \begin{bmatrix} 0.21812 & 0.019195 & -0.050301 \\ 0.019195 & 0.048526 & -0.031223 \\ -0.050301 & -0.031223 & 0.037120 \end{bmatrix}$$

$$\hat{\sigma}^2 = 2.5193 \qquad R^2 = 0.9466$$

(a) Find the total variation, unexplained variation, and explained variation for this model.
(b) Find 95% interval estimates for β_2 and β_3.
(c) Use a t-test to test the hypothesis H_0: $\beta_2 \geq 1$ against the alternative H_1: $\beta_2 < 1$.
(d) Use your answers in part (a) to test the hypothesis that $\beta_2 = \beta_3 = 0$.
(e) Write the hypotheses $\beta_2 = \beta_3 = 0$ in the form $\boldsymbol{\beta}_s = \mathbf{0}$ and find $\hat{cov}(\mathbf{b}_s)$. Use this information to test the hypothesis. Does your answer agree with that in part (d)?

10.3 In Exercises 9.3 and 9.4 the following linear and log-linear equations for the demand for money were estimated

$$m_t = \beta_1 + \beta_2 y_t + \beta_3 i_t + e_t$$
$$\ln m_t = \alpha_1 + \alpha_2 \ln y_t + a_3 \ln i_t + e_t$$

Use the results you obtained in Exercises 9.3 and 9.4 to solve the following problems:
(a) Find 95% interval estimates for β_2, β_3, α_2, and α_3.
(b) Test each of the null hypotheses H_0: $\beta_2 = \beta_3 = 0$ and H_0: $\alpha_2 = \alpha_3 = 0$.
(c) Is there any evidence in the data to suggest that the linear or the log-linear model is more appropriate?

10.4 This exercise provides a proof of the result given in equation 10.6.12 concerning the analysis of variance table for testing whether all response coefficients are zero. Consider the linear model

$$\mathbf{y} = \mathbf{x}_1\beta_1 + \mathbf{x}_2\beta_2 + \mathbf{x}_3\beta_3 + \mathbf{e}$$
$$= \mathbf{x}_1\beta_1 + X_s\boldsymbol{\beta}_s + \mathbf{e}$$

where $\mathbf{x}_1 = (1, 1,\ldots, 1)'$, $X_s = (\mathbf{x}_2, \mathbf{x}_3)$ and $\boldsymbol{\beta}_s = (\beta_2, \beta_3)'$.
(a) Given that $X = (\mathbf{x}_1, X_s)$ and that

$$X'X = \begin{bmatrix} T & \mathbf{x}_1'X_s \\ X_s'\mathbf{x}_1 & X_s'X_s \end{bmatrix}$$

use matrix multiplication to show that $(X'X)(X'X)^{-1} = I$ where

$$(X'X)^{-1} = \begin{bmatrix} \frac{1}{T}\left[1 + \mathbf{x}_1'X_s (X_s'DX_s)^{-1} X_s'\mathbf{x}_1 / T\right] & -\mathbf{x}_1'X_s (X_s'DX_s)^{-1} / T \\ -(X_s'DX_s)^{-1} X_s'\mathbf{x}_1 / T & (X_s'DX_s)^{-1} \end{bmatrix}$$

and $D = I_T - \mathbf{x}_1\mathbf{x}_1' / T$.

(b) Use (a) to show that the least squares estimator for β_s is

$$\mathbf{b}_s = \left(X_s' D X_s\right)^{-1} X_s' D \mathbf{y}_s$$

and that its covariance matrix is given by

$$\mathrm{cov}(\mathbf{b}_s) = \sigma^2 \left(X_s' D X_s\right)^{-1}$$

(c) Prove that $D\mathbf{x}_1 = \mathbf{0}$.

(d) Given that $\mathbf{x}_1' \hat{\mathbf{e}} = 0$, where $\hat{\mathbf{e}}$ is the vector of least squares residuals, prove that $D\hat{\mathbf{e}} = \hat{\mathbf{e}}$.

(e) Use (c) and (d) to prove that

$$\hat{\mathbf{e}} = \mathbf{y} - X\mathbf{b} = \mathbf{y} - \mathbf{x}_1 b_1 - X_s \mathbf{b}_s = D\mathbf{y} - DX_s \mathbf{b}_s$$

(f) Prove that $DD = D$ and that $D = D'$.

(g) Use (b), (e) and (f) to prove that

$$\hat{\mathbf{e}}' \hat{\mathbf{e}} = \mathbf{y}' D\mathbf{y} - \mathbf{b}_s' X_s' DX_s \mathbf{b}_s$$

(h) Prove that

$$\sum_{t=1}^{T} (y_t - \bar{y})^2 = \mathbf{y}' D\mathbf{y}$$

(i) Use all the above results to show that

$$\frac{\mathbf{b}_s' \left[\hat{\mathrm{cov}}(\mathbf{b}_s)\right]^{-1} \mathbf{b}_s}{K - 1} = \frac{\left(\sum_{t=1}^{T} (y_t - \bar{y})^2 - \hat{\mathbf{e}}' \hat{\mathbf{e}}\right) \Big/ (K - 1)}{\hat{\mathbf{e}}' \hat{\mathbf{e}} \big/ (T - K)}$$

10.5 Consider Exercise 9.7 where the cubic cost function

$$y_t = \beta_1 + \beta_2 x_t + \beta_3 x_t^2 + \beta_4 x_t^3 + e_t$$

was estimated.

(a) Find 95% interval estimates for the parameters β_2, β_3, and β_4.

(b) Test whether the data suggest that a linear function will suffice.

(c) Test whether the data suggest that a quadratic function will suffice.

(d) What parameter restrictions imply a linear average cost function? Test these restrictions.

(e) Test whether a log-linear cost function of the form

$$\ln y_t = \alpha_1 + \alpha_2 \ln x_t + e_t$$

would be preferable to the cubic. Is the log-linear cost function reasonable from an economic standpoint?

10.6 Consider Exercise 9.2, where the economist from Moscow Makkers estimated the equation

$$q_t = \beta_1 + \beta_2 p_t + \beta_3 a_t + \beta_4 a_t^2 + e_t$$

(a) Find 95% interval estimates for the parameters β_2, β_3, and β_4.

(b) Test the hypothesis that price has no influence on quantity demanded.

(c) Test the hypothesis that advertising expenditure has no influence on quantity demanded.

10.7 In Section 10.7.1 we questioned whether the linear relationship between receipts, price, and advertising expenditure is likely to be realistic and suggested instead a model that contained the square of advertising expenditure as an additional term. This additional term was designed to capture possible diminishing returns to advertising expenditure. A similar argument can be made with respect to the response of receipts to price changes. Our estimates suggested that demand is price elastic. Is it reasonable to think demand will always be price elastic irrespective of the price? That is, as we continually lower the price, will receipts continue to increase? Bay Area residents are discerning diners; it is unlikely that they will consume the necessary number of burgers to keep receipts increasing.

With these thoughts in mind, consider the alternative statistical model

$$tr_t = \beta_1 + \beta_2 p_t + \beta_3 a_t + \beta_4 p_t^2 + \beta_5 a_t^2 + \beta_6 a_t p_t + e_t$$

that is a general quadratic function of p_t and a_t; that is, it includes p_t^2, a_t^2, and the interaction term $a_t p_t$.

(a) Find expressions for the response of total receipts to price and the response of total receipts to advertising expenditure. That is, find the partial derivatives $\partial tr_t / \partial p_t$ and $\partial tr_t / \partial a_t$. (For further information on partial derivatives see Appendix 10A.)

(b) From an economic standpoint, what signs would you expect on each of the coefficients?

(c) Using the 52 observations in Table 9.1, find least squares estimates of the coefficients and report the estimated equation in the conventional way. Comment on the estimated equation from both an economic and a statistical standpoint.

(d) Show that advertising expenditure will be optimal for $p = 1$ and $a = 40$ if

$$\beta_3 + 80\beta_5 + \beta_6 = 1$$

Test whether this relationship between the βs is compatible with the sample of data.

(e) In Section 10.8 we investigated an executive's claim that setting $a_t = 40$ and $p_t = 2$ would yield $E[tr_t] = 175$. In the context of the model being considered in this exercise, find the relationship between the βs that must hold for this claim to be true. Test the compatibility of this relationship with the sample of data.

(f) Perform a *joint* test of the hypotheses in parts (d) and (e).

(g) Test the null hypothesis H_0: $\beta_4 = \beta_5 = \beta_6 = 0$. What is the relevance of this hypothesis?

10.8 Answer Exercise 10.7 using the 78 observations obtained by combining the data in Table 9.1 with the data in Table 10.3.

10.9 Suppose that, from a sample of 63 observations, the least squares estimates **b** and the corresponding estimated covariance matrix $\hat{cov}(\mathbf{b})$ are given by

$$\mathbf{b} = \begin{bmatrix} 2 \\ 3 \\ -1 \end{bmatrix} \qquad \hat{cov}(\mathbf{b}) = \begin{bmatrix} 3 & -2 & 1 \\ -2 & 4 & 0 \\ 1 & 0 & 3 \end{bmatrix}$$

Test each of the following hypotheses:

(a) $\beta_2 = 0$
(b) $\beta_1 + 2\beta_2 = 5$
(c) $\beta_1 - \beta_2 + \beta_3 = 4$

10.10. Consider the following per capita meat demand equation

$$\ln q_t^c = \beta_1 + \beta_2 \ln p_t + \beta_3 \ln y_t + e_t$$

where q_t^c is the per capita quantity consumed in period t, p_t is the price in period t, and y_t is the per capita disposable income in period t, and it is assumed $e_t \sim N(0, \sigma^2)$. A sample of data on quantities, prices, and incomes for 30 time periods appears in Table 10.4.

(a) Estimate the demand equation and interpret the price and income elasticities.
(b) Using an $\alpha = .05$ level of statistical significance, (i) test the hypothesis that the price elasticity is unity, that is, $\beta_2 = -1$, (ii) test the hypothesis that the price elasticity $\beta_2 = -1$ and the income elasticity $\beta_3 = 1$.
(c) Using the $\alpha = .05$ significance level, what is your intuition relative to how you might compute a joint confidence interval for β_2 and β_3?
(d) Assume the following linear form for the demand relation:

$$q_t^c = \alpha_1 + \alpha_2 p_t + \alpha_3 y_t + e_t, \qquad \text{where } e_t \sim N(0, \sigma^2)$$

(i) Using the data from Table 10.4, estimate α_1, α_2 and α_3 and find 95% interval estimates.
(ii) Compute the price and income elasticities at the means.
(iii) Holding income constant at its mean, develop and graph average, marginal and total revenue relations.
(iv) What is the price elasticity when total revenue is a maximum and marginal revenue is zero?

10.11. Use the air transportation data in Table 11.6 to estimate the production function

$$\ln Y_t = \beta_1 + \beta_2 \ln K_t + \beta_3 \ln L_t + \beta_4 t + e_t$$

Note that the variable t (of which β_4 is the coefficient) is a time trend that takes the values $1, 2, \ldots, 32$. A time trend is often included in production functions estimated with time series data as a proxy for technological change.
(a) How do you interpret the estimates?
(b) Do they all have the expected signs?

Table 10.4 Data for Exercise 10.10

Time Period	q	p	y	Time Period	q	p	y
1	11.632	10.763	487.648	16	14.096	14.219	462.621
2	12.029	13.033	364.877	17	4.118	6.769	312.659
3	8.916	9.244	541.037	18	10.489	7.769	400.848
4	33.908	4.605	760.343	19	6.231	9.804	392.215
5	4.561	13.045	421.746	20	6.458	11.063	377.724
6	17.594	7.706	578.214	21	8.736	6.535	343.552
7	18.842	7.405	561.734	22	5.158	11.063	301.599
8	11.637	7.519	301.470	23	16.618	4.016	294.112
9	7.645	8.764	379.636	24	11.342	4.759	365.032
10	7.881	13.511	478.855	25	2.903	5.483	256.125
11	9.614	4.943	433.741	26	3.138	7.890	184.798
12	9.067	8.360	525.702	27	15.315	8.460	359.084
13	14.070	5.721	513.067	28	22.240	6.195	629.378
14	15.474	7.225	408.666	29	10.012	6.743	306.527
15	3.041	6.617	192.061	30	3.982	11.977	347.488

(c) Based on the estimates and their standard errors, are there any estimates that appear unreliable or convey little information?

(d) Test the hypothesis, at the $\alpha = .05$ level of significance, that $\beta_4 = 0$; interpret.

10.12. To demonstrate the use of some variable selection procedures discussed in this chapter, consider the following statistical model and regressor matrix

$$\mathbf{y} = X\boldsymbol{\beta} + \mathbf{e} = 10\mathbf{x}_1 + 0.4\mathbf{x}_2 + 0.6\mathbf{x}_3 + 0.0\mathbf{x}_4 + 0.0\mathbf{x}_5 + 0.0\mathbf{x}_6 + \mathbf{e}$$

where $\mathbf{e} \sim N(\mathbf{0}, .0625I_{20})$. Assume the (20×6) regressor matrix is

$$
X = \begin{bmatrix}
1 & 0.693 & 0.693 & 0.610 & 1.327 & -2.947 \\
1 & 1.733 & 0.693 & -1.714 & 2.413 & 0.788 \\
1 & 0.693 & 1.386 & 0.082 & 3.728 & -0.813 \\
1 & 1.733 & 1.386 & -0.776 & -0.757 & 1.968 \\
1 & 0.693 & 1.792 & 1.182 & -0.819 & 3.106 \\
1 & 2.340 & 0.693 & 3.681 & 2.013 & -3.176 \\
1 & 1.733 & 1.792 & -1.307 & 0.464 & -2.407 \\
1 & 2.340 & 1.386 & 0.440 & -2.493 & 0.136 \\
1 & 2.340 & 1.792 & 1.395 & -1.637 & 3.427 \\
1 & 0.693 & 0.693 & 0.281 & 0.504 & 0.687 \\
1 & 0.693 & 1.386 & -1.929 & -0.344 & -2.609 \\
1 & 1.733 & 0.693 & 1.985 & -0.212 & -0.741 \\
1 & 1.733 & 1.386 & -2.500 & -0.875 & 0.264 \\
1 & 0.693 & 1.792 & 0.335 & 2.137 & 0.631 \\
1 & 2.340 & 0.693 & 0.464 & 1.550 & -1.169 \\
1 & 1.733 & 1.792 & 4.110 & -1.664 & 1.585 \\
1 & 2.340 & 1.386 & -2.254 & -0.285 & -0.131 \\
1 & 2.340 & 1.792 & -1.906 & 1.162 & 0.903 \\
1 & 1.733 & 1.386 & 0.125 & 0.399 & -1.838 \\
1 & 0.693 & 0.693 & -2.935 & -2.600 & -2.634
\end{bmatrix}
$$

Using this regressor matrix, five artificial samples of y values were created by following the procedures described in the *Computer Handbook*. The five vectors of y values are

$\mathbf{y}_1 =$	$\mathbf{y}_2 =$	$\mathbf{y}_3 =$	$\mathbf{y}_4 =$	$\mathbf{y}_5 =$
10.7413	10.3190	11.2184	10.8103	10.4659
10.9830	11.0625	11.5291	11.6286	11.1073
10.5292	11.2412	11.1243	11.5497	11.1383
11.5891	11.2126	11.5101	11.2277	11.3616
11.7983	12.0107	11.3689	11.2438	11.5067
11.7585	11.3858	11.0993	11.1450	11.5190
11.9453	11.4619	11.9737	11.6020	11.9679
12.3305	12.1091	12.0109	11.2821	11.4187
11.8957	11.7076	11.9894	11.8623	12.1972
10.3561	11.1209	11.1712	10.7528	10.3621
11.1672	11.4532	11.5586	11.1047	11.2126
11.1655	10.9391	11.2851	10.9497	11.1790
11.6820	12.0581	11.4785	11.0640	11.6859
11.4135	11.1557	11.3825	11.5900	11.2743
11.2097	10.7298	11.1437	11.5725	11.3872
11.9817	11.8400	11.9701	11.8679	11.5297
12.3242	11.9796	11.5033	12.2664	11.6401
12.0297	12.0892	11.8325	12.2556	12.1048
11.3930	11.8572	11.0494	11.8257	11.3121
10.8940	10.6770	10.6809	10.9019	10.3359

For each sample of data choose the "best model" using the $\overline{R}^2$ and AIC criteria from the alternative specifications

$$y = f_1(x_1, x_2, x_3) + e_1$$
$$y = f_2(x_1, x_2, x_3, x_4) + e_2$$
$$y = f_3(x_1, x_2, x_3, x_5) + e_3$$
$$y = f_4(x_1, x_2, x_3, x_6) + e_4$$
$$y = f_5(x_1, x_2, x_3, x_4, x_5) + e_5$$
$$y = f_6(x_1, x_2, x_3, x_4, x_6) + e_6$$
$$y = f_7(x_1, x_2, x_3, x_5, x_6) + e_7$$

Assume all the f_i are linear functions. Comment on your results.

10.13. Reconsider Exercise 10.12 and the additional function

$$y = f_8(x_1, x_2, x_3, x_4, x_5, x_6) + e_8$$

For each of the five samples, what model would be selected if we adopt the strategy of estimating f_8 and discarding variables whose estimated coefficients are insignificant? Comment on the outcomes.

10.14. Using the input–output sample of data in Table 5.3 of Exercise 5.6 in Chapter 5, compare and contrast the following statistical models:

$$y_t = \beta_1 + x_t\beta_2 + e_{1t}; \quad e_{1t} \sim N(0, \sigma_1^2 I_T)$$
$$\ln y_t = \ln\beta_1 + \beta_2 \ln x_t + e_{2t}; \quad e_{2t} \sim N(0, \sigma_2^2 I_T)$$
$$y_t = \beta_1 + x_t\beta_2 + x_t^2\beta_3 + e_{3t}; \quad e_{3t} \sim N(0, \sigma_3^2 I_T)$$

Reach a decision in each of the pairwise comparisons.

10.15. Using information provided in the *Computer Handbook* and the statistical model described in Exercise 10.12, develop 100 samples of y. Given the sample observations, use the AIC criterion to make a choice, from among the alternative specifications listed in Exercise 10.12, of the correct model in each case. Tabulate and discuss the frequency of each model choice and in general the statistical implications of using this criterion.

10.16. Suppose that the units of the dependent variable y are changed by multiplying it by a constant to form a new dependent variable $y^* = ky$. Prove that:
(a) The sum of squared errors from the least squares estimation of a statistical model with y^* as the dependent variable is k^2 times greater than that where y is the dependent variable.
(b) If the dependent variables are $\ln y^*$ and $\ln y$, the sums of squared errors are identical.
(c) If $\overline{y}_G$ is the geometric mean of y and $\overline{y}_G^*$ is the geometric mean of the y^*, then

$$\frac{y}{\overline{y}_G} = \frac{y^*}{\overline{y}_G^*}$$

10.13   References

A more extensive development of hypothesis testing in the general linear statistical model can be found in

JUDGE, G. G., R. C. HILL, W. E. GRIFFITHS, H. LÜTKEPOHL and T. C. LEE (1988) *Introduction to the Theory and Practice of Econometrics*, 2nd Edition, New York: John Wiley & Sons, Inc., pp. 252-262, 555–563, 838–851.

Further details on specification testing can be found in

BERA, A. K. and M. MCALEER (1989) "Nested and Non-nested Procedures for Testing Linear and Log-linear Models," *Sankhya*, 51, pp. 212–224.

BOX, G .E. P. and D. R. COX (1964) "An Analysis of Transformations," *Journal of the Royal Statistical Society*, Series B, 26, pp. 211–243.

DORAN, H. E. (1989) *Applied Regression Analysis in Econometrics*, New York: Marcel Dekker, Chapter 14.

Further details on demand functions and demand analysis can be found in microeconomic texts such as

MANSFIELD, E. (1985) *Microeconomics: Theory and Applications*, 5th Edition, New York: W. W. Norton & Co., Inc., pp. 49–150.

APPENDIX 10A   Partial Derivatives Revisited

Partial derivatives for multivariate functions were discussed in Appendix 5B of Chapter 5. In that appendix we focused on finding optimizing (minimum least squares) values for β_1 and β_2 in the simple regression model. These were the values (b_1, b_2) that minimized the function $S(\beta_1, \beta_2)$. Starting with Chapter 9 we have been considering the general linear statistical model, involving K right-hand-side (X) variables. It is now appropriate to consider the use of partial derivatives in this context. In doing so we first consider for our general linear statistical model the problem of finding values ($\beta_1 = b_1$, $\beta_2 = b_2, \ldots, \beta_K = b_K$) that minimize the squared errors given by the function $S(\beta_1, \beta_2, \ldots, \beta_K)$. Next, we consider the concept of an elasticity when a multivariate function is involved. Finally, we consider an economic problem where partial derivatives are used to determine, in the case of a firm, a profit-maximizing outcome.

10A.1   The Least Squares Rule

Under the least squares rule, we seek to determine, for the general linear statistical model discussed in Chapter 9, the minimizing values for the function

$$S(\beta_1, \beta_2, \ldots, \beta_K) = \Sigma\left(y_t - x_{t1}\beta_1 - x_{t2}\beta_2 - \ldots - x_{tK}\beta_K\right)^2 \qquad (10A.1)$$

That is, we wish to determine the values ($\beta_1 = b_1$, $\beta_2 = b_2, \ldots, \beta_K = b_K$) that make the error sum of squares in equation 10A.1 a minimum.

In Appendix 3A.3 of Chapter 3 we found that the derivative dy/dx equals zero for all points where the function $y = f(x)$ achieves a maximum or minimum. In Appendix 5B of Chapter 5 we found that for the bivariate function $S(\beta_1, \beta_2)$ a minimum was achieved when

$$\frac{\partial S}{\partial \beta_1} = 0 \quad \text{and} \quad \frac{\partial S}{\partial \beta_2} = 0 \qquad (10A.2)$$

Thus, to find the minimizing values $\beta_1 = b_1$ and $\beta_2 = b_2$, we had to find the point at which the partial derivatives of S with respect to β_1 and β_2 were equal to zero. These results for the bivariate function extend naturally to our multivariate function $S(\beta_1, \beta_2, \ldots, \beta_K)$. For our multivariate case equation 10A.1, the first step is to find expressions for the partial derivatives of equation 10A.1 and to set them equal to zero. This step yields

$$\frac{\partial S}{\partial \beta_1} = 2\left(\Sigma x_{t1} y_t - \Sigma x_{t1}^2 b_1 - \Sigma x_{t1} x_{t2} b_2 - \ldots - \Sigma x_{t1} x_{tK} b_K\right) = 0$$

$$\frac{\partial S}{\partial \beta_2} = 2\left(\Sigma x_{t2} y_t - \Sigma x_{t2} x_{t1} b_1 - \Sigma x_{t2}^2 b_2 - \ldots - \Sigma x_{t2} x_{tK} b_K\right) = 0$$

$$\vdots$$

$$\frac{\partial S}{\partial \beta_K} = 2\left(\Sigma x_{tK} y_t - \Sigma x_{tK} x_{t1} b_1 - \Sigma x_{tK} x_{t2} b_2 - \ldots - \Sigma x_{tK}^2 b_K\right) = 0 \tag{10A.3}$$

This means the expressions within the parentheses must equal zero and, hence, we have the set of K simultaneous equations

$$\Sigma x_{t1}^2 b_1 + \Sigma x_{t1} x_{t2} b_2 + \ldots + \Sigma x_{t1} x_{tK} b_K = \Sigma x_{t1} y_t$$

$$\Sigma x_{t2} x_{t1} b_1 + \Sigma x_{t2}^2 b_2 + \ldots + \Sigma x_{t2} x_{tK} b_K = \Sigma x_{t2} y_t$$

$$\vdots$$

$$\Sigma x_{tK} x_{t1} b_1 + \Sigma x_{tK} x_{t2} b_2 + \ldots + \Sigma x_{tK}^2 b_K = \Sigma x_{tK} y_t \tag{10A.4}$$

that must be solved for the minimizing values $b_1, b_2, \ldots, b_K$. The set of equations 10A.4 can then, using matrix notation, be written in the compact form

$$X'X\mathbf{b} = X'\mathbf{y} \tag{10A.5}$$

or

$$\mathbf{b} = \left(X'X\right)^{-1} X'\mathbf{y}$$

10A.2 Elasticities

Building on the discussion of elasticities in Appendix 5A of Chapter 5 and Appendix 8A of Chapter 8, we show that elasticities can also be defined in terms of partial derivatives. For functions of one variable such as $y = f(x)$, the elasticity of y with respect to x may be defined as

$$\eta = \frac{dy}{dx} \frac{x}{y} \tag{10A.6}$$

The elasticity describes the percentage rate of response of y to a percentage change in x at a given point (x, y). When we have a function of more than one variable, the elasticity is written in terms of a partial derivative, signifying that other variables are held constant. Thus, for the demand function $q = f(p, i)$ where quantity q is a function of price p and income i, the elasticity of quantity demanded with respect to price is given by

$$\eta = \frac{\partial q}{\partial p} \frac{p}{q} \tag{10A.7}$$

For example, if

$$q = \beta_1 + \beta_2 p + \beta_3 p^2 + \beta_4 i \qquad (10A.8)$$

then the partial derivative of q with respect to p is

$$\frac{\partial q}{\partial p} = \beta_2 + 2\beta_3 p \qquad (10A.9)$$

From equation 10A.7 the elasticity is

$$\eta = \frac{\beta_2 p + 2\beta_3 p^2}{q} \qquad (10A.10)$$

Similarly, the elasticity of demand with respect to income in this example is

$$\eta = \frac{\partial q}{\partial i}\frac{i}{q} = \frac{\beta_4 i}{q} \qquad (10A.11)$$

Both these elasticities depend on p and q or i and q.
Let us consider some more examples.

Example 1

In Chapter 9 the total receipts (tr) from a hamburger chain are related to price (p) and advertising expenditure (a) through the linear equation

$$tr = \beta_1 + \beta_2 p + \beta_3 a \qquad (10A.12)$$

The response of total receipts to a change in price, with advertising expenditure held fixed, is given by

$$\frac{\partial (tr)}{\partial p} = \beta_2 \qquad (10A.13)$$

Similarly,

$$\frac{\partial (tr)}{\partial a} = \beta_3 \qquad (10A.14)$$

Because both these partial derivatives are constant, total receipts change at a constant rate for both changes in price and changes in advertising expenditure. The corresponding elasticities, the first being the elasticity of total revenue with respect to price and the second being the elasticity of total revenue with respect to advertising expenditure, are given by

$$\frac{\partial (tr)}{\partial p}\frac{p}{tr} = \frac{\beta_2 p}{tr} \qquad \frac{\partial (tr)}{\partial a}\frac{a}{tr} = \frac{\beta_3 p}{tr} \qquad (10A.15)$$

These elasticities vary depending on the ratios (p/tr) and (a/tr), respectively.   ■

Example 2

In Exercise 10.7 the model in equation 10A.12 is extended to the quadratic equation

$$tr = \beta_1 + \beta_2 p + \beta_3 a + \beta_4 p^2 + \beta_5 a^2 + \beta_6 ap \qquad (10A.16)$$

Here the partial derivatives, first with respect to price and then with respect to advertising expenditure are given by

$$\frac{\partial(tr)}{\partial p} = \beta_2 + 2\beta_4 p + \beta_6 a \qquad \frac{\partial(tr)}{\partial a} = \beta_3 + 2\beta_5 a + \beta_6 p \qquad (10A.17)$$

Unlike in Example 1, both these partial derivatives depend on p and a, indicating that the response of total receipts to changes in p or a will depend on the levels of these variables. Elasticities can be found by multiplying the expressions in equation 10A.17 by (p/tr) and (a/tr), respectively. ∎

Example 3

Consider the function

$$y = \alpha x_2^{\beta_2} x_3^{\beta_3} \qquad (10A.18)$$

which can be written in terms of logarithms as

$$\ln y = \ln \alpha + \beta_2 \ln x_2 + \beta_3 \ln x_3 \qquad (10A.19)$$

We will find the partial derivative $\partial y/\partial x_2$ in two ways, first by differentiating equation 10A.18 and then by differentiating equation 10A.19. From equation 10A.18

$$\frac{\partial y}{\partial x_2} = \beta_2 \alpha x_2^{\beta_2 - 1} x_3^{\beta_3} = \frac{\beta_2 \alpha x_2^{\beta_2} x_3^{\beta_3}}{x_2} = \frac{\beta_2 y}{x_2} \qquad (10A.20)$$

Using equation 10A.19 and the rule in equation 8A.18, we obtain, from the left-hand side,

$$\frac{\partial(\ln y)}{\partial x_2} = \frac{\partial(\ln y)}{\partial y}\frac{\partial y}{\partial x_2} = \frac{1}{y}\frac{\partial y}{\partial x_2} \qquad (10A.21)$$

From the right-hand side

$$\frac{\partial[\beta_1 + \beta_2 \ln x_2 + \beta_3 \ln x_3]}{\partial x_2} = \frac{\beta_2}{x_2} \qquad (10A.22)$$

Thus

$$\frac{1}{y}\frac{\partial y}{\partial x_2} = \frac{\beta_2}{x_2}$$

or

$$\frac{\partial y}{\partial x_2} = \frac{\beta_2 y}{x_2} \qquad (10A.23)$$

Similarly,

$$\frac{\partial y}{\partial x_3} = \frac{\beta_3 y}{x_3} \tag{10A.24}$$

The model in equation 10A.18 or 10A.19, and the partial derivatives in equations 10A.23 and 10A.24, have wide applicability. In Chapter 11 this type of equation is used to model both the demand for beer and a production function that uses experimental data. One special feature of the model is that it has constant elasticities that are given by β_2 and β_3. Specifically,

$$\frac{\partial y}{\partial x_2}\frac{x_2}{y} = \frac{\beta_2 y}{x_2}\frac{x_2}{y} = \beta_2 \tag{10A.25}$$

and

$$\frac{\partial y}{\partial x_3}\frac{x_3}{y} = \frac{\beta_3 y}{x_3}\frac{x_3}{y} = \beta_3 \tag{10A.26}$$

This result is a generalization of that for a function of only one variable given in Example 8 of Appendix 8A of Chapter 8.   ∎

10A.3   Maxima and Minima

In Section 10A.1 of this appendix we considered the problem of obtaining a minimizing value for the multivariate function $S(\beta_1, \beta_2,..., \beta_K)$. In this section we consider how to make use of the tools developed in Appendices 5A and 8A to investigate the profit-maximizing behavior of a firm.

Example 4

Suppose that the demand curve for a firm's product is given by

$$q = \beta_1 + \beta_2 p + \beta_3 n \tag{10A.27}$$

where q is quantity demanded, p is price, and n is the number of TV advertisements. Suppose, also, that the cost c of producing a quantity q is given by

$$c_q = \alpha_1 + \alpha_2 q \tag{10A.28}$$

The cost of TV advertising is

$$c_a = \gamma_0 + \gamma_1 n + \gamma_2 n^2 \tag{10A.29}$$

Profit is given by

profit = total revenue − total cost

$$= pq - c_q - c_a$$

$$= pq - (\alpha_1 + \alpha_2 q) - (\gamma_0 + \gamma_1 n + \gamma_2 n^2)$$

$$= \beta_1 p + \beta_2 p^2 + \beta_3 np - \alpha_1 - \alpha_2\beta_1 - \alpha_2\beta_2 p - \alpha_2\beta_3 n - \gamma_0 - \gamma_1 n - \gamma_2 n^2$$

$$= -(\alpha_1 + \alpha_2\beta_1 + \gamma_0) + (\beta_1 - \alpha_2\beta_2)p - (\alpha_2\beta_3 + \gamma_1)n + \beta_2 p^2 - \gamma_2 n^2 + \beta_3 np$$

$$\tag{10A.30}$$

The firm would like to choose the price p and the number of TV advertisements n that will maximize its profits. We can solve this problem by following the steps outlined in Section 10A.1. First, we obtain expressions for the partial derivatives of profit with respect to price and number of advertisements. That is,

$$\frac{\partial(\text{profit})}{\partial p} = \beta_1 - \alpha_2\beta_2 + 2\beta_2 p + \beta_3 n \tag{10A.31}$$

$$\frac{\partial(\text{profit})}{\partial n} = -(\gamma_1 + \alpha_2\beta_3) + \beta_3 p - 2\gamma_2 n \tag{10A.32}$$

The second step is to form two simultaneous equations whose unknowns are the minimizing values of n and p. The equations are formed by setting the partial derivatives equal to zero. That is,

$$2\beta_2 p + \beta_3 n = \alpha_2\beta_2 - \beta_1 \tag{10A.33}$$

$$\beta_3 p - 2\gamma_2 n = \gamma_1 + \alpha_2\beta_3 \tag{10A.34}$$

Solving these two equations for the profit-maximizing values of n and p (step 3) yields

$$p = \frac{2\gamma_2(\alpha_2\beta_2 - \beta_1) + \beta_3(\gamma_1 + \alpha_2\beta_3)}{4\beta_2\gamma_2 + \beta_3^2} \tag{10A.35}$$

$$n = \frac{-\beta_1\beta_3 - 2\beta_2\gamma_1 - \alpha_2\beta_2\beta_3}{4\beta_2\gamma_2 + \beta_3^2} \tag{10A.36}$$

With knowledge of the parameters of the demand curve, and each of the cost functions, the firm can use equations 10A.35 and 10A.36 to find that price and the number of TV advertisements that will maximize profits.   ■

Example 5

A further example along the lines of Example 4 can be found in Chapter 11 where, given a production function that relates output to inputs, profit-maximizing levels of the inputs are found. For an application of partial derivatives for this problem, see equations 11.8.17a and 11.8.17b and the surrounding discussion.   ■

APPENDIX 10B   The *F* Random Variable

An *F* random variable is defined as the ratio of two independent chi-square random variables, each divided by its degrees of freedom. Let w_1 and w_2 be such chi-square random variables, with m_1 and m_2 degrees of freedom, respectively. That is,

$$w_1 \sim \chi^2_{(m_1)} \qquad w_2 \sim \chi^2_{(m_2)} \tag{10B.1}$$

Then, we write

$$F = \frac{w_1 / m_1}{w_2 / m_2} \sim F_{(m_1, m_2)} \tag{10B.2}$$

In words, F is a random variable with an F-distribution with (m_1, m_2) degrees of freedom. The shape and properties of the F-distribution are determined by two parameters, the numerator degrees of freedom m_1, and the denominator degrees of freedom m_2. An example of an F-distribution appears in Figure 10B.1. Note that the range of the F-distribution is $(0, \infty)$. Most of the probability appears in the left side of the distribution and it has a long tail to the right.

The F-distribution is an important sampling distribution that can be used to test a variety of hypotheses relevant in economics and statistics. In the tests that we consider, large values of F, calculated assuming the null hypothesis is true, represent evidence against the null hypothesis. Small values represent evidence in support of H_0. Thus, we reject a null hypothesis if the calculated value exceeds a critical value F_c; the rejection region appears only in the right side of the distribution, not the left. For a 5% significance level, F_c is such that $P[F > F_c] = .05$. Critical values F_c have been tabulated for alternative values of the degrees of freedom m_1 and m_2 and appear at the end of this book. Alternatively, using p-values, we reject H_0 if the probability of an F random variable exceeding the calculated value is less than .05.

Let us consider some examples. From equation 10.1.11b we know that

$$z = \frac{b_2 - \beta_2}{\sqrt{\text{var}(b_2)}} = \frac{b_2 - \beta_2}{\sqrt{\sigma^2 c_{22}}} \sim N(0, 1) \tag{10B.3}$$

where $\text{var}(b_2) = \sigma^2 c_{22}$ and c_{22} is the second diagonal element of $(X'X)^{-1}$. In Section 3.6 we learned that the square of a standard normal random variable is a chi-square random variable with 1 degree of freedom. Thus, for our first example, we let

$$w_1 = z^2 = \frac{(b_2 - \beta_2)^2}{\sigma^2 c_{22}} \sim \chi^2_{(1)} \tag{10B.4}$$

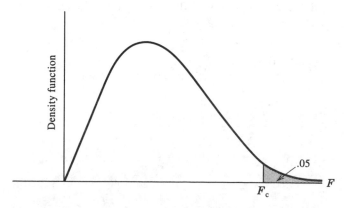

Figure 10B.1 The density function of an F random variable.

Furthermore, in Section 10.1 we discovered that

$$w_2 = \frac{(T-K)\hat{\sigma}^2}{\sigma^2} \sim \chi^2_{(T-K)}$$

(10B.5)

It can also be shown that w_1 and w_2 are independent. Substituting these results into the definition of an F random variable in equation 10B.2 provides a means for eliminating the unknown variance σ^2 and producing a test statistic that depends on the estimate $\hat{\sigma}^2$, not on σ^2. Specifically,

$$
\begin{aligned}
F = \frac{w_1/1}{w_2/(T-K)} &= \frac{(b_2-\beta_2)^2/\sigma^2 c_{22}}{\hat{\sigma}^2/\sigma^2} \\
&= \frac{(b_2-\beta_2)^2}{\hat{\sigma}^2 c_{22}} \\
&= \frac{(b_2-\beta_2)^2}{\hat{var}(b_2)} \sim F_{[1,(T-K)]}
\end{aligned}
$$

(10B.6)

This random variable can be recognized as the square of the t random variable $t = (b_2-\beta_2)\big/\sqrt{\hat{var}(b_2)}$ that was defined in equation 10.1.12. In fact, as explained in Section 10.6.2, the square of a t random variable with $(T-K)$ degrees of freedom is equal to an F random variable with $[1,(T-K)]$ degrees of freedom; either the t test or the F-test can be used to test hypotheses about β_2.

As a second example, consider $\mathbf{b}_s$, the vector of least squares estimates of the "slope coefficients" that was defined in Section 10.6. This vector has a $(K-1)$ dimensional normal distribution written as

$$\mathbf{b}_s \sim N\big[\boldsymbol{\beta}_s, \text{cov}(\mathbf{b}_s)\big] \quad \text{or} \quad \mathbf{b}_s \sim \big[\boldsymbol{\beta}_s, \sigma^2 M\big]$$

(10B.7)

where M is the matrix $(X'X)^{-1}$ with its first row and first column deleted. Given equation 10B.7 it can be shown that

$$w_1 = (\mathbf{b}_s-\boldsymbol{\beta}_s)'\big[\text{cov}(\mathbf{b}_s)\big]^{-1}(\mathbf{b}_s-\boldsymbol{\beta}_s) = \frac{(\mathbf{b}_s-\boldsymbol{\beta}_s)' M^{-1}(\mathbf{b}_s-\boldsymbol{\beta}_s)}{\sigma^2} \sim \chi^2_{(K-1)}$$

(10B.8)

Combining this result with w_2 defined in equation 10B.5, recognizing independence of w_1 and w_2, and substituting into equation 10B.2 yields

$$
\begin{aligned}
F = \frac{w_1/(K-1)}{w_2/(T-K)} &= \frac{(\mathbf{b}_s-\boldsymbol{\beta}_s)' M^{-1}(\mathbf{b}_s-\boldsymbol{\beta}_s)\big/(K-1)\sigma^2}{\hat{\sigma}^2/\sigma^2} \\
&= \frac{(\mathbf{b}_s-\boldsymbol{\beta}_s)'(\hat{\sigma}^2 M)^{-1}(\mathbf{b}_s-\boldsymbol{\beta}_s)}{K-1} \\
&= \frac{(\mathbf{b}_s-\boldsymbol{\beta}_s)'\big[\hat{cov}(\mathbf{b}_s)\big]^{-1}(\mathbf{b}_s-\boldsymbol{\beta}_s)}{K-1} \sim F_{[(K-1),(T-K)]}
\end{aligned}
$$

(10B.9)

This is the random variable given in equation 10.6.8 for testing $H_0: \boldsymbol{\beta}_s = \mathbf{0}$ against the alternative $H_1: \boldsymbol{\beta}_s \neq \mathbf{0}$.

For the third and final example, consider the general problem of testing J linear restrictions of the form H_0: $R\beta = \mathbf{r}$ against the alternative H_1: $R\beta \neq \mathbf{r}$. This problem is considered in Appendix 10C. In this case

$$R\mathbf{b} \sim N\left[R\beta,\ \sigma^2 R(X'X)^{-1} R'\right] \tag{10B.10}$$

and

$$w_1 = \frac{(R\mathbf{b} - R\beta)'\left[R(X'X)^{-1} R'\right]^{-1}(R\mathbf{b} - R\beta)}{\sigma^2} \sim \chi^2_{(J)} \tag{10B.11}$$

Again, w_1 and w_2 are independent, and this time substitution into equation 10B.2 yields

$$F = \frac{w_1/J}{w_2/(T-K)} = \frac{(R\mathbf{b} - R\beta)'\left[R(X'X)^{-1} R'\right]^{-1}(R\mathbf{b} - R\beta)\big/ J\sigma^2}{\hat{\sigma}^2/\sigma^2}$$

$$= \frac{(R\mathbf{b} - R\beta)'\left[R(X'X)^{-1} R'\right]^{-1}(R\mathbf{b} - R\beta)}{J\hat{\sigma}^2} \sim F_{[J,(T-K)]} \tag{10B.12}$$

As discussed in Appendix 10C, to test H_0: $R\beta = \mathbf{r}$ against the alternative H_1: $R\beta \neq \mathbf{r}$, we replace $R\beta$ by $\mathbf{r}$ and compute a value for equation 10B.12.

APPENDIX 10C   Testing General Linear Hypotheses

10C.1   The t-Test

To introduce a general framework for testing linear hypotheses, let us return to the linear version of the receipts–price–advertising relationship

$$tr_t = \beta_1 + \beta_2 p_t + \beta_3 a_t + e_t \tag{10C.1}$$

and consider testing

$$H_0: \beta_2 = 0 \quad \text{against} \quad H_1: \beta_2 \neq 0 \tag{10C.2}$$

Our objective is to write these hypotheses and the associated random variable

$$t = \frac{b_2 - \beta_2}{\sqrt{\hat{\mathrm{var}}(b_2)}} \tag{10C.3}$$

in a general notation that is relevant for all linear hypotheses. We begin by defining (*i*) a matrix R that in this special case is a (1×3) row vector, and (*ii*) a scalar r, such that

$$R = \begin{bmatrix} 0 & 1 & 0 \end{bmatrix} \quad \text{and} \quad r = 0 \tag{10C.4}$$

Using these definitions we can write

$$R\beta = \begin{bmatrix} 0 & 1 & 0 \end{bmatrix} \begin{bmatrix} \beta_1 \\ \beta_2 \\ \beta_3 \end{bmatrix} = \beta_2 \tag{10C.5}$$

Hence, the null and alternative hypotheses in equation 10C.2 can be written instead as

$$H_0: R\beta = r \quad \text{and} \quad H_1: R\beta \neq r \tag{10C.6}$$

The purpose of the row vector R is to *select* the appropriate element (β_2 in this case) from the vector β. The notation $R\beta = r$ will prove to be useful general notation that can be used for any linear hypothesis.

If we want to select the least squares estimate b_2 from the vector of least squares estimates $\mathbf{b}$, we can similarly write

$$R\mathbf{b} = \begin{bmatrix} 0 & 1 & 0 \end{bmatrix} \begin{bmatrix} b_1 \\ b_2 \\ b_3 \end{bmatrix} = b_2 \tag{10C.7}$$

This device can also be used to select the variance of b_2 (or its estimate) from the covariance matrix of the whole vector $\mathbf{b}$. Specifically, premultiplying $\hat{\text{cov}}(\mathbf{b})$ by R, and postmultiplying by R', will select $\hat{\text{var}}(b_2)$ from the matrix $\hat{\text{cov}}(\mathbf{b})$. This result is demonstrated as follows

$$\hat{\text{var}}(b_2) = \hat{\text{var}}(R\mathbf{b}) = R\,\hat{\text{cov}}(\mathbf{b})R'$$

$$= \begin{bmatrix} 0 & 1 & 0 \end{bmatrix} \begin{bmatrix} \hat{\text{var}}(b_1) & \hat{\text{cov}}(b_1, b_2) & \hat{\text{cov}}(b_1, b_3) \\ \hat{\text{cov}}(b_1, b_2) & \hat{\text{var}}(b_2) & \hat{\text{cov}}(b_2, b_3) \\ \hat{\text{cov}}(b_1, b_3) & \hat{\text{cov}}(b_2, b_3) & \hat{\text{var}}(b_3) \end{bmatrix} \begin{bmatrix} 0 \\ 1 \\ 0 \end{bmatrix}$$

$$= \begin{bmatrix} \hat{\text{cov}}(b_1, b_2) & \hat{\text{var}}(b_2) & \hat{\text{cov}}(b_2, b_3) \end{bmatrix} \begin{bmatrix} 0 \\ 1 \\ 0 \end{bmatrix}$$

$$= \hat{\text{var}}(b_2) \tag{10C.8}$$

Collecting the results in equations 10C.5, 10C.7, and 10C.8, the t random variable for testing $H_0: \beta_2 = 0$ (or $R\beta = r$) against the alternative $H_1: \beta_2 \neq 0$ (or $R\beta \neq r$) can be written as

$$t = \frac{b_2 - \beta_2}{\sqrt{\hat{\text{var}}(b_2)}} = \frac{R\mathbf{b} - R\beta}{\sqrt{R\,\hat{\text{cov}}(\mathbf{b})R'}} = \frac{R\mathbf{b} - R\beta}{\sqrt{R\hat{\sigma}^2\left(X'X\right)^{-1}R'}} = \frac{R\mathbf{b} - R\beta}{\hat{\sigma}\sqrt{R\left(X'X\right)^{-1}R'}} \tag{10C.9}$$

Furthermore, instead of writing $b_2 \sim N[\beta_2, \text{var}(b_2)]$, we could write

$$R\mathbf{b} \sim N\left[R\beta, \sigma^2 R\left(X'X\right)^{-1}R'\right] \tag{10C.10}$$

Under the assumption that $H_0: R\beta = r$ is true, equation 10C.9 becomes

$$t = \frac{b_2}{\sqrt{\hat{\text{var}}(b_2)}} = \frac{R\mathbf{b} - r}{\hat{\sigma}\sqrt{R\left(X'X\right)^{-1}R'}} \tag{10C.11}$$

The right side of this test statistic is in a general form that is relevant for testing any single linear hypothesis about the elements in β. To demonstrate its generality, let us reconsider the model and hypotheses discussed in Section 10.7, namely,

$$tr_t = \beta_1 + \beta_2 p_t + \beta_3 a_t + \beta_4 a_t^2 + e_t \qquad (10C.12)$$

and

$$H_0: \beta_3 + 80\beta_4 = 1 \qquad \text{against} \qquad H_1: \beta_3 + 80\beta_4 \neq 1 \qquad (10C.13)$$

We wish to write H_0 in the form $R\beta = r$ and to write the test statistic

$$t = \frac{b_3 + 80b_4 - 1}{\sqrt{\hat{\text{var}}(b_3 + 80b_4)}} \qquad (10C.14)$$

in the form given by the right side of equation 10C.11. For this purpose we define

$$R = (0 \quad 0 \quad 1 \quad 80) \qquad \text{and} \qquad r = 1 \qquad (10C.15)$$

so that

$$R\beta = (0 \quad 0 \quad 1 \quad 80)\begin{pmatrix} \beta_1 \\ \beta_2 \\ \beta_3 \\ \beta_4 \end{pmatrix} = \beta_3 + 80\beta_4 \quad \text{and} \quad Rb = (0 \quad 0 \quad 1 \quad 80)\begin{pmatrix} b_1 \\ b_2 \\ b_3 \\ b_4 \end{pmatrix} = b_3 + 80b_4$$

$$(10C.16)$$

Thus, H_0: $\beta_3 + 80\beta_4 = 1$ can be written as H_0: $R\beta = r$, and for the numerator in equation 10C.14 we have

$$b_3 + 80b_4 - 1 = Rb - r \qquad (10C.17)$$

For the denominator in equation 10C.14, we calculate the variance of $(b_3 + 80b_4)$ in the following way

$$\hat{\text{var}}(b_3 + 80b_4) = \hat{\text{var}}(Rb) = R\hat{\text{cov}}(b)R'$$

$$= \hat{\text{var}}(b_3) + (80)^2 \hat{\text{var}}(b_4) + (2)(80)\hat{\text{cov}}(b_3, b_4) \qquad (10C.18)$$

In words, through the term $R\hat{\text{cov}}(b)R'$, the row vector R has the effect of selecting, weighting and summing the relevant elements from the covariance matrix $\hat{\text{cov}}(b)$. Substituting equations 10C.17 and 10C.18 into equation 10C.14, and using the result $\hat{\text{cov}}(b) = \hat{\sigma}^2 (X'X)^{-1}$, yields

$$t = \frac{b_3 + 80b_4 - 1}{\sqrt{\hat{\text{var}}(b_3 + 80b_4)}} = \frac{Rb - r}{\hat{\sigma}\sqrt{R(X'X)^{-1}R'}} \qquad (10C.19)$$

Results in equations 10C.11 and 10C.19 suggest that *by appropriately choosing R and r, any single linear hypothesis about the coefficient vector β can be written in a general form* given by the right side of these equations.

10C.2 The *F*-Test

We can go further than the result on the *t*-test and show that the *F*-statistic for jointly testing any number of linear hypotheses can also be written in a general form by appropriately defining a $(J \times K)$ matrix R and a $(J \times 1)$ vector $\mathbf{r}$, where J is the number of linear hypotheses. We will give the general form of this F-statistic and then consider examples to show how special cases fit within the general framework.

We are concerned with simultaneously testing J linear combinations or hypotheses about the elements in $\boldsymbol{\beta}$, where the null and alternative hypotheses can be written as

$$H_0 : R\boldsymbol{\beta} = \mathbf{r} \quad \text{and} \quad H_1 : R\boldsymbol{\beta} \neq \mathbf{r} \tag{10C.20}$$

Each row in the $(J \times K)$ matrix R defines a linear combination of the elements in $\boldsymbol{\beta}$, and $\mathbf{r}$ is a $(J \times 1)$ vector of the values hypothesized for the J linear combinations. If the null hypothesis H_0 is true, it can be shown that (see Appendix 10B on the F random variable)

$$F = \frac{(R\mathbf{b} - \mathbf{r})' \left[R\,\hat{\text{cov}}(\mathbf{b}) R' \right]^{-1} (R\mathbf{b} - \mathbf{r})}{J} = \frac{(R\mathbf{b} - \mathbf{r})' \left[R(X'X)^{-1} R' \right]^{-1} (R\mathbf{b} - \mathbf{r})}{J\hat{\sigma}^2} \sim F_{[J,(T-K)]} \tag{10C.21}$$

We reject H_0 if $F > F_c$, where, for a given significance level, F_c is the critical value from an $F_{[J,(T-K)]}$ distribution.

10C.2a   Testing a Zero Null Hypothesis for All Response Coefficients

The first example we consider is that given in Section 10.6. In that section we were concerned with testing

$$H_0 : \beta_2 = \beta_3 = 0 \quad \text{against} \quad H_1 : \text{either } \beta_2 \text{ or } \beta_3 \text{ or both are nonzero} \tag{10C.22}$$

in the statistical model $tr_t = \beta_1 + \beta_2 p_t + \beta_3 a_t + e_t$. In this case, we wrote the null and alternative hypotheses as

$$H_0 : \boldsymbol{\beta}_s = \begin{pmatrix} \beta_2 \\ \beta_3 \end{pmatrix} = \mathbf{0} \quad \text{and} \quad H_1 : \boldsymbol{\beta}_s = \begin{pmatrix} \beta_2 \\ \beta_3 \end{pmatrix} \neq \mathbf{0} \tag{10C.23}$$

and we used the test statistic

$$F = \frac{\mathbf{b}_s' \left[\hat{\text{cov}}(\mathbf{b}_s) \right]^{-1} \mathbf{b}_s}{K - 1} \tag{10C.24}$$

To write these hypotheses and the test statistic in the general form, we define

$$R = \begin{bmatrix} 0 & 1 & 0 \\ 0 & 0 & 1 \end{bmatrix} \quad \text{and} \quad \mathbf{r} = \begin{bmatrix} 0 \\ 0 \end{bmatrix} \tag{10C.25}$$

From these definitions we have

$$R\boldsymbol{\beta} = \begin{bmatrix} 0 & 1 & 0 \\ 0 & 0 & 1 \end{bmatrix} \begin{bmatrix} \beta_1 \\ \beta_2 \\ \beta_3 \end{bmatrix} = \begin{bmatrix} \beta_2 \\ \beta_3 \end{bmatrix} = \boldsymbol{\beta}_s \tag{10C.26}$$

Hence, using these definitions, the hypotheses $H_0 : R\boldsymbol{\beta} = \mathbf{r}$ and $H_1 : R\boldsymbol{\beta} \neq \mathbf{r}$ are equivalent to $H_0 : \boldsymbol{\beta}_s = \mathbf{0}$ and $H_1 : \boldsymbol{\beta}_s \neq \mathbf{0}$.

To show the equivalence of the test statistics in equations 10C.21 and 10C.24, we note that $R\mathbf{b} = \mathbf{b}_s$ follows by replacing the βs in equation 10C.26 with bs. Also,

$$R\hat{\text{cov}}(\mathbf{b})R' = \begin{bmatrix} 0 & 1 & 0 \\ 0 & 0 & 1 \end{bmatrix} \begin{bmatrix} \hat{\text{var}}(b_1) & \hat{\text{cov}}(b_1, b_2) & \hat{\text{cov}}(b_1, b_3) \\ \hat{\text{cov}}(b_1, b_2) & \hat{\text{var}}(b_2) & \hat{\text{cov}}(b_2, b_3) \\ \hat{\text{cov}}(b_1, b_3) & \hat{\text{cov}}(b_2, b_3) & \hat{\text{var}}(b_3) \end{bmatrix} \begin{bmatrix} 0 & 0 \\ 1 & 0 \\ 0 & 1 \end{bmatrix}$$

$$= \begin{bmatrix} \hat{\text{var}}(b_2) & \hat{\text{cov}}(b_2, b_3) \\ \hat{\text{cov}}(b_2, b_3) & \hat{\text{var}}(b_3) \end{bmatrix} = \hat{\text{cov}}(\mathbf{b}_s)$$

$$(10C.27)$$

As before, the matrix R can be viewed as a "selection matrix" that chooses the appropriate elements from β, $\mathbf{b}$, and $\hat{\text{cov}}(\mathbf{b})$. Collecting these various results together and noting that $J = K - 1 = 2$, it follows that

$$F = \frac{(R\mathbf{b} - \mathbf{r})'\left[R\hat{\text{cov}}(\mathbf{b})R'\right]^{-1}(R\mathbf{b} - \mathbf{r})}{J} = \frac{\mathbf{b}_s'\left[\hat{\text{cov}}(\mathbf{b}_s)\right]^{-1}\mathbf{b}_s}{K - 1} \qquad (10C.28)$$

10C.2b   Testing Two Hypotheses Concerning Price and Advertising Expenditure

The second example that we reconsider is that given in Section 10.8. In that section we were concerned with the statistical model

$$tr_t = \beta_1 + \beta_2 p_t + \beta_3 a_t + \beta_4 a_t^2 + e_t \qquad (10C.29)$$

and with testing

$$H_0 : \begin{cases} \beta_1 + 2\beta_2 + 40\beta_3 + 1600\beta_4 = 175 \\ \beta_3 + 80\beta_4 = 1 \end{cases} \quad \text{against} \quad H_1 : \begin{cases} \text{at least one of the equalities} \\ \text{under } H_0 \text{ is false} \end{cases}$$

These two hypotheses can be written as H_0; $R\beta = \mathbf{r}$ and H_1: $R\beta \neq \mathbf{r}$ by defining

$$R = \begin{bmatrix} 1 & 2 & 40 & 1600 \\ 0 & 0 & 1 & 80 \end{bmatrix} \quad \text{and} \quad \mathbf{r} = \begin{bmatrix} 175 \\ 1 \end{bmatrix} \qquad (10C.30)$$

Let us compute values for the various components of the F-statistic given in equation 10C.21. Bringing all these components together should then yield the F-value of 1.753 that was used in Section 10.8. We have

$$R\mathbf{b} - \mathbf{r} = \begin{bmatrix} 1 & 2 & 40 & 1600 \\ 0 & 0 & 1 & 80 \end{bmatrix} \begin{bmatrix} 110.46 \\ -10.198 \\ 3.361 \\ -0.0268 \end{bmatrix} - \begin{bmatrix} 175 \\ 1 \end{bmatrix}$$

$$= \begin{bmatrix} 181.7003 \\ 1.2206 \end{bmatrix} - \begin{bmatrix} 175 \\ 1 \end{bmatrix} = \begin{bmatrix} 6.7003 \\ 0.2206 \end{bmatrix} \qquad (10C.31)$$

Also,

$$
\left[R\left(X'X\right)^{-1} R' \right]^{-1} = \begin{bmatrix} 3.9040 & 0.28724 \\ 0.28724 & 0.02180 \end{bmatrix}^{-1} = \begin{bmatrix} 8.3785 & -110.392 \\ -110.392 & 1500.35 \end{bmatrix}
$$

Therefore, the F-value is given by

$$
\begin{aligned}
F &= \frac{\left(R\mathbf{b} - \mathbf{r}\right)' \left[R\left(X'X\right)^{-1} R' \right]^{-1} \left(R\mathbf{b} - \mathbf{r}\right)}{J\hat{\sigma}^2} \\[2mm]
&= \frac{\left(6.700 \quad 0.221\right) \begin{bmatrix} 8.3785 & -110.392 \\ -110.392 & 1500.35 \end{bmatrix} \begin{bmatrix} 6.700 \\ 0.221 \end{bmatrix}}{2 \times 35.031} \\[2mm]
&= \frac{122.82}{70.06} = 1.753
\end{aligned}
$$

We have demonstrated how the value of the F-statistic given in Section 10.8 is computed. As is explained in that section, such computation is typically carried out automatically by a computer. The details we have provided give a conceptual basis for the procedure, as well as a greater appreciation of the mechanics.

10C.2c The Relationship Between the t- and F-Tests

As a third "example," we consider the relationship between the t- and F-tests when the null hypothesis comprises just one linear combination of the elements in β. That is, $J = 1$. In Sections 10.6.2 and 10.7.3 we indicated that the square of a t random variable is identical to an F random variable with one degree of freedom in the numerator. Hence, the F-distribution can also be used to test a single linear equality hypothesis. To see the equivalence in the general case, we square equation 10C.19 yielding

$$
t^2 = \frac{\left(R\mathbf{b} - \mathbf{r}\right)^2}{\hat{\sigma}^2 R\left(X'X\right)^{-1} R'} = \frac{\left(R\mathbf{b} - \mathbf{r}\right)' \left[R\left(X'X\right)^{-1} R' \right]^{-1} \left(R\mathbf{b} - \mathbf{r}\right)}{\hat{\sigma}^2}
$$

It is clear that this result is a special case of the general expression for the F-statistic in equation 10C.21 for when $J = 1$.

10C.2d Looking Ahead

In Chapter 11 we introduce a restricted least squares estimator that is computed under the assumption that the restrictions $H_0 : R\beta = \mathbf{r}$ are true. This estimator leads to another method for computing a value for the F-statistic used for testing H_0. The basis for this new method is a comparison of the sum of squared errors from the restricted and unrestricted least squares estimators. Two new empirical applications are also considered in Chapter 11.

Chapter 11

Combining Sample and Nonsample Information and Further Applications of the General Linear Statistical Model

New Key Words and Concepts

Nonsample Information	General Linear Equality Restrictions
Restricted Least Squares Estimation	Estimating via Reparameterization
F-Test	Testing with Error Sums of Squares
Prediction	Production Function Specification
Estimation, Inference	

This chapter continues our concern with economic problems and models that lead to the general linear statistical model $\mathbf{y} = X\boldsymbol{\beta} + \mathbf{e}$ where $\mathbf{e} \sim N(\mathbf{0}, \sigma^2 I_T)$. As an extension to previous analysis, we examine how to estimate the elements in $\boldsymbol{\beta}$ such that our estimates satisfy certain linear restrictions. These restrictions take the form of relationships among the elements in $\boldsymbol{\beta}$, with these relationships being suggested by economic principles or some other source of nonsample information. For example, if all prices and income in a demand equation increase by the same proportion, we do not expect quantity demanded to change. If a production function exhibits constant returns to scale, its coefficients should reflect this characteristic. When such nonsample information exists, it seems intuitively reasonable that our estimation procedures should use both this nonsample information *and* the sample information that is provided by the data. The conventional sampling theory procedures we have used to this point have focused on how to use just sample information. If nonsample information exists, we need a way for combining both sources of information. The restricted least squares estimation procedure that we develop provides such a way. Other procedures for combining sample and nonsample information, and that come under the general heading of Bayesian methodology, are taken up in Chapters 24 and 25. To reinforce and make operational the tools contained in Chapters 9 to 11, this chapter ends with a production function application that makes use of data from a controlled experiment.

The contents of the chapter can be summarized as follows. Restricted estimation procedures for combining sample and nonsample information are introduced using a linear statistical model designed to explain the demand for beer. Hypothesis testing procedures for checking the compatibility of the sample and nonsample information are described and related to the testing procedures introduced in Chapter 10. The material on prediction that was developed in Chapter 8 for the simple linear model is extended. The chapter closes with a statistical and economic analysis of a production function involving two inputs. Emphasis is directed to how the estimated parameters of the production function can be used in a decision context. A general formal development of the restricted least squares estimator is given in Appendix 11A.

11.1   An Economic Model and Nonsample Information

The economic model considered in this section is a model designed to explain the demand for beer. From the theory of consumer choice in microeconomics, we know that the demand for a good will depend on the price of that good, on the prices of other goods, particularly substitutes and complements, and on income. For beer, it is reasonable to relate the quantity demanded (q) to the price of beer (p_B), the price of other liquor (p_L), the price of all other remaining goods and services (p_R), and income (m). Mathematically, we write this relationship as

$$q = f(p_B, p_L, p_R, m) \qquad (11.1.1)$$

However, before much progress toward quantifying this relationship can be made, we need to specify a particular functional form for f. Using ln to denote the natural logarithm, we observe that a commonly used functional form for a demand relation is the log-linear one

$$\ln q = \beta_1 + \beta_2 \ln p_B + \beta_3 \ln p_L + \beta_4 \ln p_R + \beta_5 \ln m \qquad (11.1.2)$$

This model is a convenient one because it precludes infeasible negative prices, quantities, and income, and because the coefficients β_2, β_3, β_4, and β_5 are in the form of elasticities. (See Example 3 in Appendix 10A.) In addition to being convenient, it is hoped that the model will be an adequate one to explain beer consumption for a randomly selected household in a large U.S. city.

Our first objective is to estimate the parameters $\beta_1, \beta_2, \ldots, \beta_5$. Except for the intercept parameter, all these parameters are elasticities, and we can write these elasticities as partial derivatives. Specifically, using results in Appendix 10A (see also Exercise 11.1), we can write

β_2 = direct price elasticity of demand for beer = $\dfrac{\partial q}{\partial p_B} \cdot \dfrac{p_B}{q}$

β_3 = cross-price elasticity of demand for beer with respect to a change in the

price of other liquor = $\dfrac{\partial q}{\partial p_L} \cdot \dfrac{p_L}{q}$

β_4 = cross-price of elasticity of demand for beer with respect to a change in the

price of remaining goods and services = $\dfrac{\partial q}{\partial p_R} \cdot \dfrac{p_R}{q}$

β_5 = income elasticity of demand for beer = $\dfrac{\partial q}{\partial m} \cdot \dfrac{m}{q}$

A relevant piece of nonsample information can be derived for the beer demand model by noting that, if all prices and income go up by the same proportion, we would expect there to be no change in quantity demanded. For example, a doubling of all prices and income should not change the quantity of beer consumed. This seems a reasonable result and it is one that is shown to hold true in household demand theory. Let us impose this result on our demand model and see what happens. Having all prices and income change by the same proportion is equivalent to multiplying each price and income by some constant. Denoting this constant by λ, and multiplying each of the variables in equation 11.1.2 by λ, yields

$$\ln q = \beta_1 + \beta_2 \ln(\lambda p_B) + \beta_3 \ln(\lambda p_L) + \beta_4 \ln(\lambda p_R) + \beta_5 \ln(\lambda m)$$

$$= \beta_1 + \beta_2 \ln p_B + \beta_3 \ln p_L + \beta_4 \ln p_R + \beta_5 \ln m + (\beta_2 + \beta_3 + \beta_4 + \beta_5) \ln \lambda$$

$$(11.1.3)$$

Comparing equation 11.1.2 with equation 11.1.3 shows that multiplying each price and income by λ will give a change in $\ln q$ equal to $(\beta_2 + \beta_3 + \beta_4 + \beta_5) \ln \lambda$. Thus, for there to be no change in $\ln q$ when all prices and income go up by the same proportion, we require

$$\beta_2 + \beta_3 + \beta_4 + \beta_5 = 0 \qquad (11.1.4)$$

Thus we can say something about how quantity demanded should not change when prices and income change by the same proportion, and this information can be written in terms of a specific restriction on the parameters of the demand model. We call such a restriction nonsample information. If we believe that this nonsample information makes sense, and hence that the parameter restriction in equation 11.1.4 holds true, then it seems desirable to be able to obtain estimates (say b_2^*, b_3^*, b_4^* and b_5^*) such that $b_2^* + b_3^* + b_4^* + b_5^* = 0$. The question of how to obtain such estimates is addressed in Sections 11.3 and 11.6. Before turning to these sections we use our economic model as a basis for specifying a corresponding statistical model, provide some sample data, and examine the estimates from using sample information only.

11.2   Statistical Model and Estimation with Sample Information

Along the lines of our previous economic and statistical models, to turn equation 11.1.2 into a statistical model we introduce a random error term, make assumptions about the probability distribution of the error term and include a subscript t to denote the tth observation. Thus, we write the statistical model as

$$\ln q_t = \beta_1 + \beta_2 \ln p_{Bt} + \beta_3 \ln p_{Lt} + \beta_4 \ln p_{Rt} + \beta_5 \ln m_t + e_t \qquad (11.2.1)$$

and we will assume that the errors are independent, identically distributed normal random variables with zero mean and variance σ^2. In matrix notation the model becomes

$$\mathbf{y} = X\boldsymbol{\beta} + \mathbf{e} \qquad \text{and} \qquad \mathbf{e} \sim N(\mathbf{0}, \sigma^2 I_T) \qquad (11.2.2)$$

where

$$\mathbf{y} = \begin{bmatrix} \ln q_1 \\ \ln q_2 \\ \vdots \\ \ln q_T \end{bmatrix} \qquad X = \begin{bmatrix} 1 & \ln p_{B1} & \ln p_{L1} & \ln p_{R1} & \ln m_1 \\ 1 & \ln p_{B2} & \ln p_{L2} & \ln p_{R2} & \ln m_2 \\ \vdots & \vdots & \vdots & \vdots & \vdots \\ 1 & \ln p_{BT} & \ln p_{LT} & \ln p_{RT} & \ln m_T \end{bmatrix} \qquad \boldsymbol{\beta} = \begin{bmatrix} \beta_1 \\ \beta_2 \\ \beta_3 \\ \beta_4 \\ \beta_5 \end{bmatrix} \qquad \text{and} \qquad \mathbf{e} = \begin{bmatrix} e_1 \\ e_2 \\ \vdots \\ e_T \end{bmatrix}$$

The sample information consists of 30 years of annual data collected from a randomly selected U. S. household. These data appear in Table 11.1. The price series p_B, p_L, and p_R were constructed by taking weighted averages of the nominal (undeflated) prices for the different kinds of beer, "other liquor," and "remaining goods and services." Consumption of beer seems to have declined slightly over the 30-year period, with the price of beer, the price of other liquor, and income all steadily increasing. The price of remaining goods and services increased gradually too, but in a more erratic fashion. Let us examine how well consumption of beer can be explained by the price and income variables, and what we can say about the various elasticities, before and after introducing the nonsample information.

11.2.1 Estimation with Sample Information

Before introducing an estimation procedure for combining the sample and nonsample information, let us examine the results from direct application of the least squares rule to equation 11.2.1. By using the data in Table 11.1, we find that the estimated equation and corresponding standard errors are

$$\ln \hat{q}_t = -3.243 - 1.020 \ln p_{Bt} - 0.583 \ln p_{Lt} + 0.210 \ln p_{Rt} + 0.923 \ln m_t$$

$$\quad (3.743) \quad (0.239) \qquad (0.560) \qquad (0.080) \qquad (0.416)$$

$$R^2 = 0.825 \qquad\qquad SSE = 0.08992$$

$$(11.2.3)$$

Table 11.1   Price, Quantity and Income Data for
Beer Demand Model

q (liters)	p_B ($)	p_L ($)	p_R ($)	m ($)
81.7	1.78	6.95	1.11	25088
56.9	2.27	7.32	0.67	26561
64.1	2.21	6.96	0.83	25510
65.4	2.15	7.18	0.75	27158
64.1	2.26	7.46	1.06	27162
58.1	2.49	7.47	1.10	27583
61.7	2.52	7.88	1.09	28235
65.3	2.46	7.88	1.18	29413
57.8	2.54	7.97	0.88	28713
63.5	2.72	7.96	1.30	30000
65.9	2.60	8.09	1.17	30533
48.3	2.87	8.24	0.94	30373
55.6	3.00	7.96	0.91	31107
47.9	3.23	8.34	1.10	31126
57.0	3.11	8.10	1.50	32506
51.6	3.11	8.43	1.17	32408
54.2	3.09	8.72	1.18	33423
51.7	3.34	8.87	1.37	33904
55.9	3.31	8.82	1.52	34528
52.1	3.42	8.59	1.15	36019
52.5	3.61	8.83	1.39	34807
44.3	3.55	8.86	1.60	35943
57.7	3.72	8.97	1.73	37323
51.6	3.72	9.13	1.35	36682
53.8	3.70	8.98	1.37	38054
50.0	3.81	9.25	1.41	36707
46.3	3.86	9.33	1.62	38411
46.8	3.99	9.47	1.69	38823
51.7	3.89	9.49	1.71	38361
49.9	4.07	9.52	1.69	41593

What can we say about these results, from both an economic and a statistical stand-point? From microeconomic theory of the household, we would expect the direct price elasticity (β_2) to be negative and the cross-price elasticities (β_3 and β_4) to be positive; the income elasticity could be positive or negative depending on whether beer is a "normal" or an "inferior" good. The intercept parameter has no direct economic meaning and could be of any sign. Taking these points into consideration, we see that all the estimated coefficients have appropriate signs, except for the cross-price elasticity with respect to the competitive good liquor. One might also question the magnitude of the income elasticity. This value is approximately one. Would we expect (say) a 10% increase in income to yield a 10% increase in beer consumption?

When we consider the results from a statistical standpoint, we examine t-values and interval as well as point estimates. Ignoring the intercept, we can see from inspection that, with the exception of the coefficient of $\ln p_L$, the ratio of each coefficient to its standard error is greater than 2. Thus, the only 95% interval estimate that will include zero is that for the coefficient of $\ln p_L$. With $t_c = 2.06$, the relevant value for 95% intervals, and 25 degrees of freedom, the 95% interval estimates are

$$\text{for } \beta_2: \ [-1.512, -0.528]$$

$$\text{for } \beta_3: \ [-1.737, 0.571]$$

$$\text{for } \beta_4: \ [0.045, 0.375]$$

$$\text{for } \beta_5: \ [0.066, 1.780]$$

Notice the additional information these intervals convey. In particular, (*i*) the income elasticity β_5 could be much less (or much more) than the point estimate suggested, and (*ii*) the cross-elasticity β_3 could be positive even although its point estimate was negative. Finally, with 82.5% of the variation in $\ln q$ being explained, the fitted equation does a good job of tracking the data.

11.3   Estimation with Sample and Nonsample Information

Previously we suggested that the condition $\beta_2 + \beta_3 + \beta_4 + \beta_5 = 0$ should logically hold true. From our empirical results in equation 11.2.3 we find that $b_2 + b_3 + b_4 + b_5 = -0.47$. That is, our empirical results are not exactly consistent with our nonsample information. This, by itself, is not sufficient evidence to suggest the nonsample information is invalid; the least squares estimates (b_2, b_3, b_4, b_5) are subject to sampling error, meaning that their sum is unlikely to be zero even when $\beta_2 + \beta_3 + \beta_4 + \beta_5 = 0$. This consequence raises the following question. How do we include the nonsample information in equation 11.1.4 into the estimation procedure, and how does its inclusion change our results? There are two ways of introducing nonsample information in the form of parameter restrictions. One is to *estimate a reparameterized version of the model* obtained by substituting the restrictions into the equation. The other is to develop a *general restricted estimation formula* that is derived from a constrained least squares rule. Both methods yield the same results. They are different computational procedures for achieving the same answer. The nature of the reparameterized model will depend on the particular restrictions being imposed; the general restricted least squares estimation formula can be applied to any set of linear restrictions. We consider reparameterization in this section and the general constrained least squares formula in Appendix 11A.

To derive the reparameterized model, we begin by rewriting equation 11.1.4, the nonsample parameter restriction $\beta_2 + \beta_3 + \beta_4 + \beta_5 = 0$, as

$$\beta_4 = -\beta_2 - \beta_3 - \beta_5 \qquad (11.3.1)$$

Substituting this expression into the original equation 11.2.1 gives

$$
\begin{aligned}
\ln q_t &= \beta_1 + \beta_2 \ln p_{Bt} + \beta_3 \ln p_{Lt} + \left(-\beta_2 - \beta_3 - \beta_5\right)\ln p_{Rt} + \beta_5 \ln m_t + e_t \\
&= \beta_1 + \beta_2\left(\ln p_{Bt} - \ln p_{Rt}\right) + \beta_3\left(\ln p_{Lt} - \ln p_{Rt}\right) + \beta_5\left(\ln m_t - \ln p_{Rt}\right) + e_t \\
&= \beta_1 + \beta_2 \ln\!\left(\frac{p_{Bt}}{p_{Rt}}\right) + \beta_3 \ln\!\left(\frac{p_{Lt}}{p_{Rt}}\right) + \beta_5 \ln\!\left(\frac{m_t}{p_{Rt}}\right) + e_t
\end{aligned}
$$

$$(11.3.2)$$

We have used the parameter restriction to eliminate the parameter β_4 and in so doing we have constructed the new variables $\ln(p_{Bt}/p_{Rt})$, $\ln(p_{Lt}/p_{Rt})$, and $\ln(m_t/p_{Rt})$. The last line in equation 11.3.2 represents our reparameterized model. To get restricted least squares estimates that satisfy the parameter restriction, we can simply apply the least squares rule directly to this equation. The estimated equation and corresponding standard errors that we obtain are

$$
\ln \hat{q}_t = \underset{(3.714)}{-4.798} \underset{(0.166)}{-1.299}\ln\!\left(\frac{p_{Bt}}{p_{Rt}}\right) + \underset{(0.284)}{0.187}\ln\!\left(\frac{p_{Lt}}{p_{Rt}}\right) + \underset{(0.427)}{0.946}\ln\!\left(\frac{m_t}{p_{Rt}}\right)
$$

$$R^2 = 0.808 \qquad\qquad\qquad \text{SSE} = 0.098901 \quad (11.3.3)$$

Using the empirical counterpart of equation 11.3.1, and the notation b_k^* to denote the restricted estimate or estimator for the coefficient β_k, the restricted estimate of the eliminated coefficient β_4 can be calculated as

$$
\begin{aligned}
b_4^* &= -b_2^* - b_3^* - b_5^* \\
&= -(-1.2994) - 0.1868 - 0.9458 \\
&= 0.1668
\end{aligned}
$$

To compute the standard error for b_4^*, we first compute $\hat{\mathrm{var}}(b_4^*)$ using the formula for the variance of a weighted sum of random variables, equation 2.7.11:

$$
\begin{aligned}
\hat{\mathrm{var}}(b_4^*) &= \hat{\mathrm{var}}(b_2^*) + \hat{\mathrm{var}}(b_3^*) + \hat{\mathrm{var}}(b_5^*) + 2\hat{\mathrm{cov}}(b_2^*, b_3^*) + 2\hat{\mathrm{cov}}(b_2^*, b_5^*) + 2\hat{\mathrm{cov}}(b_3^*, b_5^*) \\
&= 0.027469 + 0.080874 + 0.18237 + (2)(0.028849) + (2)(-0.055881) + (2)(-0.11535) \\
&= 0.005949
\end{aligned}
$$

The values used for this calculation are taken from the estimated covariance matrix that is a by-product of the least squares computer output. The standard error is given by

$$
\mathrm{se}(b_4^*) = \sqrt{0.005949} = 0.077
$$

Including nonsample information via reparameterization of the model provides insights into restricted estimation and is useful if flexible computer programs are not available. However, in practice, restricted least squares estimates are seldom computed via reparameterization. As is illustrated in the *Computer Handbook*, a simple instruction that specifies any restriction(s) is usually sufficient for a computer program to produce the restricted estimates and their standard errors. Most programs use a general restricted-estimation formula that makes use of the notation $R\beta = \mathbf{r}$. This notation is a general way of writing nonsample information that takes the form of any set of linear restrictions on the parameters; it was introduced in Appendix 10C. Details of how to write $\beta_2 + \beta_3 + \beta_4 + \beta_5 = 0$ in the form $R\beta = \mathbf{r}$, as well as other examples, and the general restricted-estimation formula, appear in Appendix 11A.

11.4   A Comparison of Restricted and Unrestricted Least Squares

We are now in a position to compare the restricted least squares results that make use of the sample and nonsample information and the unrestricted least squares results that make use only of the sample information. For convenience, we have reproduced them in Table 11.2.

Perhaps the most noticeable change in the results is the change in the estimate for β_3, from -0.583 to 0.187. The positive sign of the restricted estimate is more in line with our a priori views about the cross-price elasticity with respect to liquor. However, its magnitude may still be smaller than we would suspect; it is only slightly greater than 0.167, the cross-price elasticity with respect to the remaining goods and services. Nevertheless, if we compare the interval estimates for β_3 and β_4 that appear below, we find that the a priori view that β_3 is much greater than β_4 is still a possibility. For computing these 95% confidence intervals, we first note that, because the introduction of one restriction has meant that one parameter could be eliminated, *introducing one restriction increases the degrees of freedom by one.* Hence, there are 26 degrees of freedom, and for a critical value, we have $t_c = 2.056$. Using this value and the information in Table 11.2 leads us to the 95% confidence intervals

$$\text{for } \beta_3: \quad [-0.397, 0.771]$$

$$\text{for } \beta_4: \quad [0.009, 0.325]$$

The relatively large standard error for β_3 has produced a confidence interval that is much wider than that for β_4. A reasonable general question to ask is whether restricted estimates, obtained through the inclusion of nonsample information, are any better than unrestricted estimates. In other words, how do the sampling properties of the restricted estimator compare with those of the unrestricted estimator. The first point to note is that *the true variances of the restricted estimator will always be less than those of the*

Table 11.2   Unrestricted and Restricted Least Squares Estimates and Their Standard Errors (in Parentheses)

Parameter	Unrestricted		Restricted	
β_1	-3.243	(3.743)	-4.798	(3.714)
β_2	-1.020	(0.239)	-1.299	(0.166)
β_3	-0.583	(0.560)	0.187	(0.284)
β_4	0.210	(0.080)	0.167	(0.077)
β_5	0.923	(0.416)	0.946	(0.427)
R^2	0.825		0.808	

unrestricted estimator. At first glance this result might seem to contradict an earlier result that we learned, namely, that the (unrestricted) least squares estimator is *best* in terms of minimum variance. However, we can resolve this apparent contradiction by recognizing that, by "best," we meant *best out of all those estimators that were a function only of the sample information.* Here we have used both sample and nonsample information; it is reasonable to expect that the additional information will lead to more precise estimation. With one exception the standard errors in Table 11.2 support this conclusion; those for the restricted estimates are less than their counterparts for the unrestricted estimates, except for β_5. How can we explain the result for β_5? *What we must remember is that standard errors are only estimates obtained from one sample of data.* The true variances refer to the way estimates vary in repeated samples and in this context it must be true that $\text{var}(b_5^*) < \text{var}(b_5)$. However, in terms of estimated variances, it does not necessarily follow that, in a single sample, $\hat{\text{var}}(b_5^*) < \hat{\text{var}}(b_5)$. This result occurs because different estimates of σ^2 are used in restricted and unrestricted estimation. We can underestimate $\text{var}(b_5)$ or overestimate $\text{var}(b_5^*)$, or both.

A second important result about the restricted estimator is that *it is unbiased if the restrictions are true, but it is biased if the restrictions are not correct.* In our example the restricted estimator will be unbiased if quantity demanded does *not* change with equiproportionate changes in all prices and income, otherwise it will be biased. Thus, although introducing any restriction will reduce variance, if such a restriction has no justification and is incorrect, it will yield biased results and possibly nullify any advantages from the reduced variance. There is a trade-off between increasing bias and reducing variance. Clearly, it would be advantageous to be able to test whether one or more restrictions might be true. This question is addressed in Sections 11.5 and 11.6.

The foregoing results on the sampling properties of restricted and unrestricted least squares estimators are consistent with those that we considered for another example of restricted estimation in Section 9.5 of Chapter 9. In that section we examined the effect of omitting regressors on the sampling properties of the least squares estimator of the remaining coefficients. Omitting regressors is a simple example of restricted estimation; it is equivalent to imposing zero restrictions on the coefficients of the omitted variables. If the omitted variables are truly extraneous (in other words the restrictions are true), then the restricted least squares estimator that omits these variables is unbiased and more efficient. If the omitted variables are not extraneous (their coefficients are nonzero), then their omission means the restricted least squares estimator is biased, even although it has lower variance.

Returning to the beer demand model, we see that a comparison of the coefficients of determination (R^2s) for the restricted and unrestricted least squares equations yields a higher value for the unrestricted set of estimates (0.825 compared to 0.808). When we compute restricted least squares estimates, we are minimizing the residual or error sum of squares, subject to one or more restrictions. The minimum from any restricted minimization problem will always be greater than the minimum from the corresponding unrestricted minimization problem. Hence, the unexplained variation (or minimum) from restricted least squares is greater than the unexplained variation (or minimum) from unrestricted least squares. This in turn implies that the R^2 (proportion of variation explained by the estimated equation) is greater for unrestricted least squares. Thus, restricted least squares yields an estimated equation that does not track the sample observations as well as unrestricted least squares, but it can produce more reasonable parameter estimates because of the inclusion of nonsample information.

Before turning to how we might test whether the sample and nonsample information are compatible, let us consider another question that probably occurred to you when we used substitution to eliminate β_4 from the equation. Why β_4? Why not one of the other parameters? Any of the parameters (except the intercept that did not feature in the restriction) could have been substituted out. In each case a different reparameterized model would have been obtained, but *the restricted least squares estimates would turn out to be identical*. We chose β_4 because of an interpretation that it is possible to put on equation 11.3.2. We can view this equation as one where the price of beer, the price of liquor, and income have been *deflated by a general price index* for all remaining goods and services. Thus, the variables (p_B/p_R) and (p_L/p_R) are real rather than money prices and (m/p_R) is a measure of real income. We are saying that changes in beer consumption depend on changes in real prices and real income. In general, when estimating the unknown coefficients of demand equations, it is common practice to deflate prices and income by some kind of general price index. Deflation is one way of recognizing that equiproportionate changes in all prices and income do not lead to a change in quantity demanded.

11.5   Testing the Restriction from the Nonsample Information

Suppose there exists some uncertainty about whether the nonsample information is valid. One way of gathering more evidence on this question is to ask, through a hypothesis test, whether the nonsample information is compatible with the sample data. If it is, then we would feel happier imposing restrictions implied by the nonsample information on the estimation process. If it is not, then the restricted least squares estimator may be biased.

In Sections 10.7 and 10.8 of Chapter 10, we saw how t- and F-tests can be used to test hypotheses that involve linear functions of the coefficients. We discovered that the t-test is relevant when a hypothesis involves just one linear function of the coefficients, and that the F-test is relevant for hypotheses involving one or more linear functions; with one linear function the t- and F-tests are equivalent test procedures. Since the nonsample information $\beta_2 + \beta_3 + \beta_4 + \beta_5 = 0$ takes the form of a linear function or restriction, it can be tested using the procedures developed in Chapter 10. Specifically, a t-test (Section 10.7) or an F-test (Section 10.8) can be used to test this restriction.

We begin this section by presenting the results from the t-test. Then, we indicate how the F-test can be written in a form that involves results from both restricted and unrestricted estimation. This form provides additional insights into the testing procedure as well as a formula that will prove to be useful in other contexts.

11.5.1   The t-Test

We are concerned with testing the null hypothesis

$$H_0 : \beta_2 + \beta_3 + \beta_4 + \beta_5 = 0 \qquad (11.5.1a)$$

against the alternative

$$H_1 : \beta_2 + \beta_3 + \beta_4 + \beta_5 \neq 0 \qquad (11.5.1b)$$

Following Section 10.7, one strategy for performing this test is to begin by computing the least squares estimate of the left side in equation 11.5.1a, namely,

$$b_2 + b_3 + b_4 + b_5 = -1.0204 - 0.5829 + 0.2095 + 0.9229 = -0.4709 \quad (11.5.2)$$

We then ask whether the difference between the value -0.4709 and the hypothesized value of zero could be attributable to sampling error, or whether the data suggest that the hypothesized value of zero is incorrect. This question is answered by computing the value of the t-statistic

$$t = \frac{b_2 + b_3 + b_4 + b_5}{\sqrt{\text{vâr}(b_2 + b_3 + b_4 + b_5)}} \tag{11.5.3}$$

and comparing this computed value with the appropriate critical value. Carrying out the necessary computations (see Exercise 11.2), we find that

$$\text{vâr}(b_2 + b_3 + b_4 + b_5) = 0.0888 \tag{11.5.4}$$

and, hence, that

$$t = \frac{-0.4709}{\sqrt{0.0888}} = -1.58 \qquad p\text{-value} = 0.126 \tag{11.5.5}$$

Since $-t_c < -1.58 < t_c$, where $t_c = 2.06$ is the 5% critical value for 25 degrees of freedom, we do not reject H_0. The same conclusion is reached by noting that the p-value is greater than .05. The evidence from the sample does not contradict our nonsample information that $\beta_2 + \beta_3 + \beta_4 + \beta_5 = 0$, and we do not reject the null hypothesis.

11.5.2   The F-Test

The same hypothesis (equation 11.5.1) can be tested using the F-test introduced in Chapter 10. It is now convenient to introduce a new expression for the F-statistic used for this test.

In Section 11.4 we discussed restricted least squares estimation, where the restriction came from the nonsample information $\beta_2 + \beta_3 + \beta_4 + \beta_5 = 0$. In this discussion we mentioned that the error sum of squares from unrestricted least squares estimation, SSE_U, will always be less than the error sum of squares from restricted estimation, SSE_R. This inequality holds true because SSE_U is the unrestricted least squares minimum, obtained by minimizing the sum of squared errors without any restrictions, and SSE_R is the restricted least squares minimum, obtained by minimizing the sum of squared errors subject to the linear restriction provided by the nonsample information. The restricted minimum is always greater than the unrestricted minimum. Denoting the vector of restricted least squares estimates by $\mathbf{b}*$, and the corresponding residuals (or estimated errors) by $\hat{\mathbf{e}}*$, we have

$$\text{SSE}_U = \hat{\mathbf{e}}'\hat{\mathbf{e}} = (\mathbf{y} - X\mathbf{b})'(\mathbf{y} - X\mathbf{b}) \tag{11.5.6a}$$

$$\text{SSE}_R = \hat{\mathbf{e}}*'\hat{\mathbf{e}}* = (\mathbf{y} - X\mathbf{b}*)'(\mathbf{y} - X\mathbf{b}*) \tag{11.5.6b}$$

If SSE_R is "not much" greater than SSE_U, then imposition of the restriction has cost little in terms of the reduction in explained variation and, hence, there is little evidence in the data to suggest that the restriction does not hold. On the other hand, a restricted least squares minimum that is much larger than the unrestricted minimum suggests that the restriction is not compatible with the data. From these observations it seems reasonable that a test for the validity of the restriction can be based on the difference ($\text{SSE}_R - \text{SSE}_U$). Indeed, it can be shown in this instance that, when the null hypothesis is true,

$$F = \frac{\text{SSE}_R - \text{SSE}_U}{\text{SSE}_U / (T - K)} \sim F_{[1, (T-K)]} \tag{11.5.7}$$

If the difference $SSE_R - SSE_U$ is large, a large value for F is computed. When this value exceeds the critical value from an F-distribution with $[1, (T - K)]$ degrees of freedom, the null hypothesis is rejected.

For the restriction $\beta_2 + \beta_3 + \beta_4 + \beta_5 = 0$ in the beer demand model we use the results in equations 11.2.3 and 11.3.3 and obtain

$$F = \frac{0.098901 - 0.08992}{0.08992/25} = 2.50 \qquad p\text{-value} = 0.126 \qquad (11.5.8)$$

With a 5% significance level and $(1, 25)$ degrees of freedom, the critical value for this test is $F_c = 4.24$. Thus, because $F = 2.50 < F_c = 4.24$, we do not reject H_0, and we conclude that the data are compatible with the proposition that all price elasticities and the income elasticity sum to zero.

To see that this test procedure is identical to the t test procedure in Section 11.5.1, note that the computed F-value (2.50) is equal to the square of the computed t value (-1.58) in equation 11.5.5, and that the critical F-value (4.24) is equal to the square of the critical t-value (2.06). Also, the p-values are identical.

The F-statistic in equation 11.5.7, and its equivalence with a t-statistic, *are valid only when the nonsample information comprises one linear restriction on the coefficients.* When there is more than one linear restriction, the formula 11.5.7 is modified slightly and there is no longer an equivalent t-test. In Section 11.6 we give the expression and an application for the general case of testing any number of linear restrictions. In Appendix 11A this formulation of the F-statistic is tied together with that introduced in Section 10.8 and Appendix 10C.

11.6   Restricted Estimation and Hypothesis Testing with More Than One Restriction

As an example of estimation and hypothesis testing for nonsample information that involves more than one linear restriction, we again consider the demand for beer model that is given by

$$\ln q_t = \beta_1 + \beta_2 \ln p_{Bt} + \beta_3 \ln p_{Lt} + \beta_4 \ln p_{Rt} + \beta_5 \ln m_t + e_t \qquad (11.6.1)$$

We will be concerned with three linear restrictions on the coefficients in this model. One is the condition that all elasticities sum to zero; we have already discussed this restriction at length. The other restrictions are that (*i*) the two cross-price elasticities are equal, and (*ii*) the income elasticity is equal to unity. We can write these restrictions as

$$\beta_2 + \beta_3 + \beta_4 + \beta_5 = 0 \qquad (11.6.2a)$$

$$\beta_3 = \beta_4 \quad \text{or} \quad \beta_3 - \beta_4 = 0 \qquad (11.6.2b)$$

$$\beta_5 = 1 \qquad (11.6.2c)$$

We are assuming that we have nonsample information, perhaps from another study, that suggests that these three restrictions are true.

11.6.1   Restricted Estimation

As illustrated in the *Computer Handbook*, with most econometric computer programs it is a straightforward matter to obtain restricted least squares estimates that satisfy restrictions such as those in equation 11.6.2. A list of the restrictions and an appropriate command is all that is needed to produce the estimates. Computer programs make use of the restrictions written in the general linear form $R\beta = \mathbf{r}$ and employ a general restricted-estimation formula. Details are provided in Appendix 11A. In our example the least squares estimates that satisfy equation 11.6.2, and their corresponding standard errors, are given by

$$\ln q_t = -5.279 - 1.318 \ln p_{Bt} + 0.159 \ln p_{Lt} + 0.159 \ln p_{Rt} + 1.000 \ln m_t$$

$$ (0.012) \quad (0.096) \qquad (0.048) \qquad (0.048) \qquad (0.000) \quad \text{(s.e.)}$$

$$R^2 = 0.808 \qquad\qquad \text{SSE} = 0.09899$$

$$(11.6.3)$$

The implications of estimates similar in magnitude to these were discussed at length in Sections 11.2 and 11.3. However, it is instructive to compare the standard errors we obtained here with those presented in Table 11.2, where just one restriction was imposed. This comparison is made in Table 11.3. We notice that in all cases the standard errors have decreased dramatically, reflecting the increased efficiency of estimation. Providing that the restrictions are correct, and thus the restricted estimator is not biased, we have a much more reliable set of estimates. The corresponding interval estimates will be much narrower. An extreme case is the zero standard error for b_5^*; this result occurs because we are assuming that $\beta_5 = 1$ is known with certainty.

We can also compute the estimates in equation 11.6.3 by eliminating three parameters of the model by direct substitution, and then estimating the resulting reparameterized version of the model. This strategy can be followed if a restricted least squares command is not available on your computer program. In Exercise 11.6 you are asked to show that the reparameterized model can be written as

$$\ln\left(\frac{q_t p_{Bt}}{m_t}\right) = \beta_1 + \beta_3 \ln\left(\frac{p_{Lt} p_{Rt}}{p_{Bt}^2}\right) + e_t \qquad (11.6.4)$$

The existence of three restrictions means that it is possible to eliminate three of the five parameters, leaving β_1 and β_3. Application of the least squares rule to equation 11.6.4 yields

$$\ln\left(\frac{q_t p_{Bt}}{m_t}\right) = -5.279 + 0.159 \ln\left(\frac{p_{Lt} p_{Rt}}{p_{Bt}^2}\right)$$

$$\phantom{\ln\left(\frac{q_t p_{Bt}}{m_t}\right) =} (0.012) \quad (0.048) \qquad\qquad \text{(s.e.)}$$

These results are consistent with those presented in equation 11.6.3. The remaining parameter estimates and their standard errors are obtained directly from the parameter restrictions. That is

$$b_4^* = b_3^* = 0.159 \qquad \text{se}(b_4^*) = \text{se}(b_3^*) = 0.048$$

$$b_5^* = 1 \qquad\qquad\qquad \text{se}(b_5^*) = \text{se}(1) = 0$$

$$b_2^* = -b_3^* - b_4^* - b_5^*$$

$$ = -2b_3^* - 1$$

$$ = -2(0.159) - 1$$

$$ = -1.318$$

$$\text{var}(b_2^*) = 4\,\text{var}(b_3^*) \qquad \text{se}(b_2^*) = 2\,\text{se}(b_3^*) = 2(0.048) = 0.096$$

Table 11.3   A Comparison of Standard Errors from Restricted Estimation

	$se(b_1^*)$	$se(b_2^*)$	$se(b_3^*)$	$se(b_4^*)$	$se(b_5^*)$
1 restriction	3.714	0.166	0.284	0.077	0.427
3 restrictions	0.012	0.096	0.048	0.048	0.000

Note that all these values agree with those in equation 11.6.3.

11.6.2   Testing the Restrictions

When the nonsample information involves more than one linear restriction, the relevant F-statistic for testing the compatibility of the sample and nonsample information is given by

$$F = \frac{(SSE_R - SSE_U)/J}{SSE_U/(T-K)} \tag{11.6.5}$$

where J is the number of linear restrictions. This expression is a more general form of equation 11.5.7; we get equation 11.5.7 from equation 11.6.5 by setting $J = 1$. As before, SSE_R and SSE_U are the sums of squared errors from restricted and unrestricted least squares estimation, respectively.

Under the null hypothesis that all J restrictions are true, the F-statistic in equation 11.6.5 has an $F_{[J,(T-K)]}$ distribution. The null hypothesis is rejected if the computed F-value exceeds an appropriate critical value from this distribution.

In our example the joint null hypothesis is

$$H_0: \begin{cases} \beta_2 + \beta_3 + \beta_4 + \beta_5 = 0 \\ \beta_3 - \beta_4 = 0 \\ \beta_5 = 1 \end{cases} \tag{11.6.6a}$$

and the alternative is

$$H_1: \text{At least one of the restrictions in } H_0 \text{ is false.} \tag{11.6.6b}$$

The sums of squared errors from equations 11.2.3 and 11.6.3 are $SSE_U = 0.08992$ and $SSE_R = 0.09899$. Using these values as well as $J = 3$ and $(T - K) = 25$ yields

$$F = \frac{(0.09899 - 0.08992)/3}{0.08992/25} = 0.84 \qquad p\text{-value} = 0.485 \tag{11.6.6c}$$

The 5% critical value from the F-distribution with (3, 25) degrees of freedom is $F_c = 2.76$. Since $F = 0.84 < F_c = 2.76$, we conclude that the three restrictions are compatible with our sample of data. There is no sample evidence to suggest that the restrictions are false.

The F-statistic in equation 11.6.5 is identical to that developed in Appendix 10C and given in equation 10C.21. Both formulas will yield the same result. This equivalence is discussed further in Appendix 11A.

11.6.3 The Analysis of Variance Test Revisited

In Chapters 8 and 10 (Sections 8.2 and 10.6), we indicated how most computer programs, as part of their least squares output, produce an "analysis of variance" table. This analysis of variance table separates the total variation in the dependent variable into two components, the explained variation and the unexplained variation, and gives the result of an F-test for simultaneously testing whether all response coefficients are zero. This F-test is a special case of the general F-test for testing any set of linear restrictions on the coefficients and, consequently, it can be considered within the framework suggested by equation 11.6.5. Let us explore this framework by using the beer demand model

$$y_t = \ln q_t = \beta_1 + \beta_2 \ln p_{Bt} + \beta_3 \ln p_{Lt} + \beta_4 \ln p_{Rt} + \beta_5 \ln m_t + e_t \quad (11.6.7)$$

When simultaneously testing whether all response coefficients are zero, our joint null hypothesis is

$$H_0 : \beta_2 = \beta_3 = \beta_4 = \beta_5 = 0 \quad (11.6.8)$$

The restricted (reparameterized) model obtained by assuming H_0 is true is

$$y_t = \beta_1 + e_t \quad (11.6.9)$$

The sum of squared errors from the restricted model SSE_R is given by the sum of squared errors from least squares estimation of this model. Now, the least squares estimator for β_1 in this model is the sample mean $\bar{y}$, implying that

$$SSE_R = \sum_{t=1}^{T} (y_t - b_1)^2 = \sum_{t=1}^{T} (y_t - \bar{y})^2$$
$$= \text{"total variation" in the dependent variable} \quad (11.6.10)$$

The sum of squared errors from least squares estimation of the unrestricted model in equation 11.6.7 gives us SSE_U, or, in other words, the "unexplained variation" in the dependent variable.

Making these substitutions into expression 11.6.5, and recognizing that the number of restrictions is $J = K - 1$, gives

$$F = \frac{(SSE_R - SSE_U)/J}{SSE_U/(T-K)}$$
$$= \frac{(\text{total variation} - \text{unexplained variation})/(K-1)}{\text{unexplained variation}/(T-K)}$$
$$= \frac{\text{explained variation}/(K-1)}{\text{unexplained variation}/(T-K)} \quad (11.6.11)$$

This is the formula used to compute the F-value given in the analysis of variance tables in Sections 8.2 and 10.6. In the demand for beer example being considered in this chapter, the value of the F-statistic is

$$F = \frac{0.42505/4}{0.08992/25} = 29.544$$

With a 5% significance level and (4, 25) degrees of freedom, the critical F-value is F_c = 2.76. Since 29.54 > 2.76, we reject H_0 and conclude that not all response coefficients are zero.

11.6.4 A Summary Statement

Nonsample information in the form of linear restrictions on the coefficients is frequently available in economics. If it is available, using restricted least squares to include this information in the estimation procedure will lead to more precise estimates, providing the restrictions are correct. If there is doubt about the validity of the restrictions, an F-test (or a t-test if there is only one restriction) can be used to test the compatibility of the sample data and the restrictions. Both the F-statistic and the restricted least squares estimates can be obtained from most computer programs simply by using an appropriate command and listing the restrictions. One convenient way to express the F-statistic is in terms of restricted and unrestricted sums of squared errors. A more formal development of the testing procedure was given in Appendix 10C. Similarly, a more formal development of the restricted least squares procedure is presented in the appendix to this chapter, Appendix 11A.

11.7 Prediction

The prediction problem for a linear statistical model with one explanatory variable was covered in depth in Chapter 7. See Section 7.3 and Appendix 7A. The results in these sections extend naturally to the more general model that has more than one explanatory variable. Let us summarize these results.

Consider a linear statistical model with an intercept term and four explanatory variables x_2, x_3, x_4, and x_5. That is

$$y_t = \beta_1 + x_{t2}\beta_2 + x_{t3}\beta_3 + x_{t4}\beta_4 + x_{t5}\beta_5 + e_t \tag{11.7.1}$$

where the e_t are independent $N(0, \sigma^2)$ random variables. We can think of this model as the beer demand model where the log of quantity demanded depends on the logs of the three prices and the log of income. Given a set of values for the explanatory variables, namely, $\mathbf{x}_0 = \begin{pmatrix} 1 & x_{02} & x_{03} & x_{04} & x_{05} \end{pmatrix}'$, the prediction problem is to predict the random variable y_0 whose outcome is given by

$$\begin{aligned} y_0 &= \beta_1 + x_{02}\beta_2 + x_{03}\beta_3 + x_{04}\beta_4 + x_{05}\beta_5 + e_0 \\ &= \mathbf{x}_0'\boldsymbol{\beta} + e_0 \end{aligned} \tag{11.7.2}$$

The best linear unbiased predictor for y_0 is given by

$$\hat{y}_0 = \mathbf{x}_0'\mathbf{b} \tag{11.7.3}$$

where $\mathbf{b} = (X'X)^{-1}X'\mathbf{y}$ is the least squares estimator. When predicting y_0, we can be in error because $\mathbf{b}$ is an estimate of $\boldsymbol{\beta}$ and because e_0 may differ from zero. These two components lead to a variance of *prediction error* that is given by

$$\mathrm{var}(\hat{y}_0 - y_0) = \sigma^2 \left[1 + \mathbf{x}_0'(X'X)^{-1}\mathbf{x}_0 \right] \tag{11.7.4}$$

Replacing σ^2 by $\hat{\sigma}^2$ in this expression yields an estimator for the prediction error variance. For hypothesis testing and interval prediction, we can use the result

$$\frac{\hat{y}_0 - y_0}{\sqrt{\text{vâr}(\hat{y}_0 - y_0)}} \sim t_{(T-K)} \tag{11.7.5}$$

Details and examples of how to use the results in equations 11.7.3–11.7.5 are given in Section 7.3 of Chapter 7. For the beer demand model, let us suppose we wish to predict the log of quantity for a beer price of $p_B = 3.00$, a liquor price of $p_L = 8.00$, a remaining goods price of $p_R = 1.00$, and an income of $m = 30,000$. Thus, we have

$$\begin{aligned} \mathbf{x}_0 &= \begin{pmatrix} 1 & \ln 3 & \ln 8 & \ln 1 & \ln 30,000 \end{pmatrix}' \\ &= \begin{pmatrix} 1 & 1.09861 & 2.07944 & 0.0 & 10.30895 \end{pmatrix}' \end{aligned}$$

Our unrestricted set of parameter estimates for β is

$$\mathbf{b} = \begin{pmatrix} -3.2432 & -1.0204 & -0.58293 & 0.20954 & 0.92286 \end{pmatrix}'$$

Using this information our predicted value for $\ln q_0$ is

$$\hat{y}_0 = \ln \hat{q}_0 = \mathbf{x}_0' \mathbf{b} = 3.9373 \tag{11.7.6}$$

From equation 11.7.4, and using an estimate of σ^2, the estimated variance of the prediction error is given by

$$\begin{aligned} \text{vâr}(\hat{y}_0 - y_0) &= 0.0035968(1 + 0.20198) \\ &= 0.004323 \end{aligned} \tag{11.7.7}$$

From equation 11.7.6 we can predict quantity, rather than the log of quantity, as

$$\hat{q}_0 = e^{3.9373} = 51.3 \text{ liters}$$

Furthermore, a 95% prediction interval for y_0 is given by

$$\left[\hat{y}_0 - t_c \sqrt{\text{vâr}(\hat{y}_0 - y_0)}, \; \hat{y}_0 + t_c \sqrt{\text{vâr}(\hat{y}_0 - y_0)} \right]$$
$$\left[3.9373 - 2.06\sqrt{0.004323}, \; 3.9373 + 2.06\sqrt{0.004323} \right]$$

or

$$\text{for } y_0 : \begin{bmatrix} 3.802, & 4.073 \end{bmatrix}$$

The corresponding prediction interval for beer consumption is

$$\text{for } q_0 : \begin{bmatrix} 44.8, & 58.7 \end{bmatrix}$$

Thus, the methodology for prediction in the linear model with one explanatory variable readily extends to the more general model with any number of right-hand-side variables. The conditional mean forecasting problem that was discussed in Section 7.3.6 and Appendix 7A can be similarly extended to the general linear statistical model.

11.8 An Econometric Application Using Experimental Data

In this section, we use the general linear statistical model and the estimation and inference procedures developed in Chapters 9 and 10, and earlier in this chapter, to carry through a statistical and economic analysis of a firm decision problem. The example is designed to reinforce previously introduced statistical techniques and to illustrate how econometric results can be utilized.

11.8.1   Economic Model and Data Generation

To give some real-world content to firm theory and the related problem of estimating the unknown parameters of a production function, consider the following situation: In corn production, nitrogen (n) and phosphate (p) are two of the major nutrients (inputs) determining the amount of corn (output) that can be grown on an acre of land. Given the output and input prices, in order for the corn producer to make decisions about the proper mix of the inputs (nutrients n and p), and the optimum level of output, information about the underlying production function for corn is needed.

11.8.1a The Economic Model   To provide a basis for thinking about and answering firm decision questions, economists have developed an abstract model of production. In this model the technical relationship between inputs and outputs is summarized by a production function that indicates the maximum output attainable from various combinations of inputs. It is usually assumed that these inputs are continuously variable and substitutable in production. In this section we consider the case of a firm producing one output (corn) from two inputs (n and p). The production function may be expressed as

$$q = f(n, p; \boldsymbol{\beta}) \tag{11.8.1}$$

where q is the level of corn output per acre, n, p are the pounds of the two inputs nitrogen and phosphate that are used, and β is a vector of parameters that governs the rates at which n and p are transformed into output. The function $f(\cdot)$ that summarizes the efficient production possibilities open to the corn-producing firm is usually assumed to be nicely behaved, that is, single-valued, continuous, and differentiable. One functional form that is widely used in economic analysis, and one that may be appropriate in corn production, is the Cobb-Douglas production function, named after its proposers, Cobb and Douglas. For two inputs, this function has the form

$$q = \alpha n^{\beta_2} p^{\beta_3}$$

or

$$\begin{aligned} \ln q &= \ln \alpha + \beta_2 \ln n + \beta_3 \ln p \\ &= \beta_1 + \beta_2 \ln n + \beta_3 \ln p \end{aligned} \tag{11.8.2}$$

where ln denotes the natural logarithm, $\beta_1 = \ln \alpha$, and β_2 and β_3 describe the technical process whereby the inputs n and p are converted into corn output. For the corn producer, representing a firm with two inputs and one output, the problem is to choose q, n, and p so as to maximize profits π, subject to the production function linking inputs and outputs. Given that this problem requires knowledge of the unknown parameters $\beta_1 = \ln \alpha$, β_2, and β_3, the problem faced by the applied econometrician is how to go about getting this type of information.

11.8.1b The Statistical Model   In corn production there are many inputs other than n and p. In the economic model, factors such as capital, labor, and quality of land, have been assumed controlled and held constant. Although most factors are controlled, there are some things such as soil quality and rainfall that cannot be controlled. Taking into account these uncontrollable factors, the economic model in equation 11.8.2

may be rewritten as the statistical model

$$\ln q_t = \ln \alpha + \beta_2 \ln n_t + \beta_3 \ln p_t + e_t \qquad (11.8.3)$$

where e_t is a normal random variable representing experimental sampling error, which we assume has mean zero and is, from plot to plot, independently and identically distributed. Compactly, we express these stochastic assumptions by saying $e_t \sim N(0, \sigma^2)$ and the e_t are independent.

Letting $\ln q_t = y_t$, $\ln \alpha = \beta_1$, $\ln n_t = x_{t2}$, and $\ln p_t = x_{t3}$, we can specify the production function 11.8.3 as the linear statistical model $y_t = \beta_1 + \beta_2 x_{t2} + \beta_3 x_{t3} + e_t$; $t = 1, 2,..., T$, which we write in vector form as

$$\mathbf{y} = \mathbf{x}_1 \beta_1 + \mathbf{x}_2 \beta_2 + \mathbf{x}_3 \beta_3 + \mathbf{e} \quad \text{and} \quad \mathbf{e} \sim N\left(\mathbf{0}, \sigma^2 I_T\right) \qquad (11.8.4)$$

Thus, y_t is the logarithm of the yield of corn in bushels for the tth plot, β_1, β_2, and β_3 are unknown coefficients in the production function to be estimated, and x_{t2} and x_{t3} are the logarithms of the tth levels or treatments for the two explanatory variables n and p.

11.8.1c The Experimental Design

Given the economic and statistical models, one way to gain additional information is to conduct an experiment. Underlying the experiment is an experimental design that specifies the treatments, which in our case are the various combinations of nitrogen and phosphate to be used on test plots devoted to raising corn. Consistent with our economic and statistical models, one possible layout for the experimental design is given in Table 11.4.

In controlled experiments, in keeping with the uncorrelated error assumption of the statistical model, treatments are typically assigned at random to the various experimental plots. In Table 11.4 an experimental plot is represented by X, and usually there are two or more plots for each treatment (combination of n and p). Given our experimental design for generating the corn output and observations for various treatments (combinations of n and p), the next step is to conduct the experiment. Fortunately for us, for the use of nitrogen and phosphate in corn production, experiments have been conducted by agricultural experiment stations located at various land grant universities in the United States. One of these experiments, consistent with the experimental design of Table 11.4, resulted in the set of data given in Table 11.5.

Table 11.4   The Layout of an Experiment Involving Various Combinations of Nitrogen and Phosphate in Corn Production

		Pounds Nitrogen per Acre							
		40	80	120	160	200	240	280	320
	40	XX	XX		XX		XX		XX
	80		XX		XX			XX	
Pounds	120	XX		XX		XX		XX	XX
Phosphate	160		XX		XX		XX		
per Acre	200	XX		XX		XX			XX
	240				XX		XX	XX	
	280		XX				XX		
	320	XX			XX		XX		XX	XX

Table 11.5 Experimental Data for Corn Output per Acre
in Bushels q, and Inputs of n and p in Pounds per Acre

n	p	q	ln n	ln p	ln q
40	40	32.06	3.6889	3.6889	3.4675
40	120	45.01	3.6889	4.7875	3.8069
40	200	42.80	3.6889	5.2983	3.7564
40	320	59.85	3.6889	5.7683	4.0918
80	40	36.40	4.3820	3.6889	3.5946
80	80	33.61	4.3820	4.3820	3.5149
80	160	62.06	4.3820	5.0752	4.1281
80	280	85.92	4.3820	5.6348	4.4534
120	120	54.77	4.7875	4.7875	4.0031
120	200	66.00	4.7875	5.2983	4.1896
120	320	94.28	4.7875	5.7683	4.5463
160	40	38.20	5.0752	3.6889	3.6430
160	80	61.82	5.0752	4.3820	4.1242
160	160	87.56	5.0752	5.0752	4.4723
160	240	77.97	5.0752	5.4806	4.3563
200	120	81.16	5.2983	4.7875	4.3965
200	200	80.92	5.2983	5.2983	4.3934
200	320	115.43	5.2983	5.7683	4.7487
240	40	39.35	5.4806	3.6889	3.6726
240	160	89.94	5.4806	5.0752	4.4991
240	240	90.26	5.4806	5.4806	4.5027
240	280	100.10	5.4806	5.6348	4.6062
280	80	67.97	5.6348	4.3820	4.2190
280	120	59.77	5.6348	4.7875	4.0904
280	240	115.02	5.6348	5.4806	4.7451
280	320	112.48	5.6348	5.7683	4.7228
320	40	54.19	5.7683	3.6889	3.9925
320	120	118.14	5.7683	4.7875	4.7719
320	200	134.45	5.7683	5.2983	4.9012
320	320	125.27	5.7683	5.7683	4.8305

11.8.2 Estimating the Unknown
Parameters of the Production Function

In line with the economic and statistical models for the corn production function, we
now use the 30 experimentally generated observations in Table 11.5 to obtain (*i*) an
estimate of the unknown production function parameter vector β, (*ii*) an estimate of
the error variance σ^2, (*iii*) estimates of the sampling variability of the estimated components of β, and (*iv*) a goodness-of-fit statistic R^2.

11.8.2a An Estimate of β   Using the statistical model $\mathbf{y} = X\beta + \mathbf{e}$, the data given
in Table 11.5, and the least squares estimation rule discussed in Chapters 5 and 9, result
in the following estimates for the unknown coefficients of the production function:

$$\mathbf{b} = \left(X'X\right)^{-1} X'\mathbf{y} = \begin{bmatrix} 3.25809 & -0.33835 & -0.30884 \\ -0.33835 & 0.07340 & -0.00598 \\ -0.30884 & -0.00598 & 0.06844 \end{bmatrix} \begin{bmatrix} 127.2411 \\ 643.0617 \\ 636.3578 \end{bmatrix} = \begin{bmatrix} 0.45010 \\ 0.34703 \\ 0.41449 \end{bmatrix}$$

(11.8.5)

Because of the log-linear nature of the Cobb-Douglas function, the estimates b_2 and b_3 are production elasticities. Given the point estimates of the elements in β, we may write the estimated production function in logarithmic form as

$$\hat{\mathbf{y}} = 0.45010\mathbf{x}_1 + 0.34703\mathbf{x}_2 + 0.41449\mathbf{x}_3 \quad \text{or} \quad \hat{q} = 1.568n^{0.34703}p^{0.41449}$$

$$(11.8.6)$$

An unbiased estimator of the error variance σ^2 is

$$\hat{\sigma}^2 = \frac{(\mathbf{y} - X\mathbf{b})'(\mathbf{y} - X\mathbf{b})}{T - K} = \frac{0.64499}{30 - 3} = \frac{0.64499}{27} = 0.02389 \qquad (11.8.7)$$

Making use of this estimated variance $\hat{\sigma}^2$, the estimated covariance matrix of $\mathbf{b}$ is

$$
\hat{\text{cov}}(\mathbf{b}) = \hat{\sigma}^2 \left(X'X \right)^{-1} = 0.02389 \begin{bmatrix} 3.25809 & -0.33835 & -0.30884 \\ -0.33835 & 0.07340 & -0.00598 \\ -0.30884 & -0.00598 & 0.06844 \end{bmatrix}
$$

$$
= \begin{bmatrix} 0.07784 & -0.00808 & -0.00738 \\ -0.00808 & 0.00175 & -0.00014 \\ -0.00738 & -0.00014 & 0.00164 \end{bmatrix} \qquad (11.8.8)
$$

The standard errors (se) of the coefficient estimates b_1, b_2, and b_3, given by $\sqrt{\hat{\text{var}}(b_i)}$, are $se(b_1) = .27899$, $se(b_2) = .041876$, and $se(b_3) = .040437$. Note that the estimates of the sampling variabilities for b_2 and b_3 are quite small relative to the magnitudes of b_2 and b_3, and this implies that the unknowns β_2 and β_3 have been estimated with a reasonable degree of precision.

Finally, the goodness-of-fit statistic R^2 for our problem is

$$R^2 = 1 - \frac{\Sigma \hat{e}_t^2}{\Sigma(y_t - \bar{y})^2} = 1 - \frac{0.64504}{5.1705} = 0.8752 \qquad (11.8.9)$$

This result implies that, in this sample, a good portion of the variability of $\ln q = y$ about its mean is associated with the inputs n and p. It also gives us the feeling that the Cobb-Douglas functional form may provide a good basis for describing the relationship that is consistent with the experimental data.

The information that we have thus far on the point estimates of β_1, β_2, β_3 and σ^2 and the sampling variabilities may be summarized, using the format employed in previous chapters, as

$$
\begin{aligned}
\hat{y}_t &= 0.45010 + 0.34703x_{t2} + 0.41449x_{t3} \\
&\quad (0.27899) \quad (0.04187) \quad\ (0.04044) \quad \text{(s.e.)}
\end{aligned}
$$

$$\hat{\sigma}^2 = 0.02389 \quad R^2 = 0.8752 \qquad (11.8.10)$$

11.8.2b Tests of Hypotheses
First let us consider the following null and alternative individual hypotheses that ask whether nitrogen and phosphate have an effect on corn output:

$$H_0: \beta_2 = 0 \quad H_1: \beta_2 \geq 0 \quad \text{and} \quad H_0: \beta_3 = 0 \quad H_1: \beta_3 \geq 0 \quad (11.8.11)$$

The procedure for testing such hypotheses is similar to that outlined in Section 10.3. Since we would expect β_2 and β_3 to be nonnegative, we use only the positive tail of the $t_{(27)}$ distribution. Thus, with a $\alpha = .05$ level of significance, $t_c = 1.703$. For our estimated production function, assuming H_0 is true, we have the results

$$\frac{b_2 - \beta_2}{\sqrt{\text{vâr}(b_2)}} = \frac{b_2}{\text{se}(b_2)} = \frac{0.34703}{0.04187} = 8.288 > t_c = 1.703 \qquad p\text{-value} = 0.000$$

$$\frac{b_3 - \beta_3}{\sqrt{\text{vâr}(b_3)}} = \frac{b_3}{\text{se}(b_3)} = \frac{0.41449}{0.04044} = 10.250 > t_c = 1.703 \qquad p\text{-value} = 0.000$$

$$(11.8.12)$$

These results lead us to conclude that we have strong evidence against the null hypothesis and that the use and mix of the nutrients does affect the level of corn output.

Other items we might want to check relate to the sum or equality of the elasticities of production. In regard to equality of the elasticities, our null and alternative hypotheses are

$$H_0 : \beta_2 - \beta_3 = 0 \quad \text{and} \quad H_1 : \beta_2 - \beta_3 \neq 0$$

Along the lines of Sections 10.6 and 11.5.1, this null yields the test statistic and result

$$t = \frac{b_2 - b_3}{\sqrt{\text{vâr}(b_2 - b_3)}}$$

$$= \frac{0.34706 - 0.41449}{\sqrt{.00175 + .00164 - 2(-0.00014)}}$$

$$= \frac{0.34706 - 0.41449}{0.0606} = -1.11 \qquad p\text{-value} = 0.276 \qquad (11.8.13)$$

In the denominator of equation 11.8.13 we have used the result $\text{vâr}(b_2 - b_3) = \text{vâr}(b_2) + \text{vâr}(b_3) - 2\text{côv}(b_2, b_3)$. Using a two-tailed test, with $\alpha/2 = .025$ and df = 27, $t = -1.11$ is smaller than the critical value $t_c = 2.052$ and greater than $-t_c = -2.052$. Consequently, we cannot reject the null hypothesis that the production elasticities are equal.

Alternatively, we may be interested in determining if we are operating under decreasing returns to scale. This depends on whether or not the sum of elasticities, $\beta_2 + \beta_3$, is less than one. Setting up a null hypothesis of constant or increasing returns to scale and an alternative of decreasing returns to scale, we have

$$H_0 : \beta_2 + \beta_3 \geq 1$$

and

$$H_1 : \beta_2 + \beta_3 < 1$$

The hypothesis $H_0: \beta_2 + \beta_3 = 1$, which is least favorable to the null, leads to the following test statistic and result

$$t = \frac{b_2 + b_3 - 1}{\sqrt{\text{vâr}(b_2) + \text{vâr}(b_3) + 2\text{côv}(b_2, b_3)}} = \frac{0.34706 + 0.41449 - 1.0}{\sqrt{.00175 + .00164 + 2(-0.00014)}}$$

$$= \frac{0.34706 + 0.41449 - 1.0}{0.0557} = -4.28 \qquad p\text{-value} = 0.000$$

$$(11.8.14)$$

Under the one-tailed t-test, the realized value of the test statistic is -4.28 and is less than $t_c = -1.703$. Thus, we reject the null hypothesis of $\beta_2 + \beta_3 \geq 1$ as not being compatible with our data and take this as evidence that $\beta_2 + \beta_3 < 1$ (decreasing returns to scale).

11.8.2c Testing a Joint Hypothesis About β_2 and β_3   Following Sections 10.6 and 11.6.3, we know that one of the tests usually made is the point null hypothesis that all coefficients except the intercept coefficient are zero. This null hypothesis may be set up as

$$H_0 : \boldsymbol{\beta}_s = \begin{pmatrix} \beta_2 \\ \beta_3 \end{pmatrix} = \begin{pmatrix} 0 \\ 0 \end{pmatrix}$$

The corresponding test statistic value is

$$F = \frac{\mathbf{b}_s' \left[\mathrm{c\hat{o}v}(\mathbf{b}_s) \right]^{-1} \mathbf{b}_s}{K-1} = \frac{\begin{bmatrix} .34706 & .41449 \end{bmatrix} \begin{bmatrix} 574.34 & 50.15 \\ 50.15 & 615.95 \end{bmatrix} \begin{bmatrix} .34706 \\ .41449 \end{bmatrix}}{2} = 94.71$$

$$(11.8.15)$$

Since at the 5% level of significance ($\alpha = .05$), the critical F-value for 2 and 27 degrees of freedom is 5.49, and thus less than the value of the test statistic 94.71, we reject the null hypothesis that $\beta_2 = \beta_3 = 0$. This same result can be obtained from the analysis of variance table on the computer output.

11.8.2d Predictions for Corn Output   We may also use the estimated production function 11.8.6 to predict the output of corn from a particular combination of n and p. For example, with inputs of 100 pounds of n and 100 pounds of p, the predicted output of corn is

$$\hat{y}_0 = \ln \hat{q} = 0.4501 + 0.34703 \ln(100) + 0.41449 \ln(100)$$
$$= 0.4501 + 0.34703(4.605) + 0.41449(4.605)$$
$$= 3.957$$
$$\hat{q}_0 = e^{3.957} = 52.3 \text{ bushels per acre}$$

$$(11.8.16)$$

By choosing various combinations of outputs we can identify various points on the production surface consistent with the estimated production function. The resulting production surface is of the form given in Figure 11.1.

11.8.3   An Economic Analysis of the Estimated Production Function

Statistical information is useful if it helps us make the right decisions. Thus, given a statistical analysis of the observations on corn output (q) and the nitrogen (n) and phosphate (p) inputs, our next task is to make use of this information for decision purposes. The estimated coefficients b_2 and b_3 are *elasticities of production*. Therefore, it is estimated that a 10% increase in n (nitrogen) will bring about a 3.47% increase in corn production. Likewise, it is estimated that a 10% increase in p (phosphate) will bring about a 4.14% increase in corn output. The sum of these constant elasticities $0.34706 + 0.41449 = 0.76155$, is considerably less than one and suggests, along with our test result equation 11.8.14, that corn production takes place under decreasing returns to

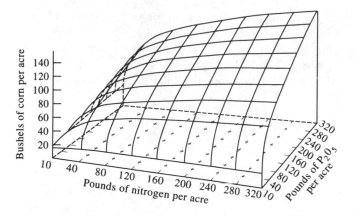

Figure 11.1 Predicted production surface for corn from a log-linear production function.

scale relative to fertilizer inputs. Decreasing returns to scale is a necessary ingredient for a profit-maximizing solution.

For the corn producer, representing a firm with two inputs and one output, the problem is to choose q, n, and p so as to maximize profits π, subject to the production function linking inputs and outputs. The problem may be formally specified as max $\pi = w_0 q - w_1 n - w_2 p = r - c$, subject to the production function $q = \alpha n^{\beta_2} p^{\beta_3}$, where w_0 is the price of corn, w_1 and w_2 are the prices of nitrogen and phosphate, respectively, $r = w_0 q$ is revenue, and $c = w_1 n + w_2 p$ is the total cost of producing q. Assuming perfect competition, the prices w_0, w_1, and w_2 are treated as constants by the firm. Thus, for profit maximization, the marginal (first-order) conditions

$$\frac{\partial \pi}{\partial n} = w_0 \frac{\partial q}{\partial n} - w_1 = 0 \quad \text{and} \quad \frac{\partial \pi}{\partial p} = w_0 \frac{\partial q}{\partial p} - w_2 = 0 \qquad (11.8.17a)$$

must hold true. Further details concerning partial derivatives and the first-order conditions for maximization can be found in Appendices 5B and 10A. Rewriting equation 11.8.17a, we have

$$w_0 \frac{\partial q}{\partial n} = w_1 \quad \text{and} \quad w_0 \frac{\partial q}{\partial p} = w_2 \qquad (11.8.17b)$$

The left-hand sides of equations 11.8.17b represent the marginal value products of nitrogen and phosphorous, respectively. Thus, equation 11.8.17b says that marginal value product must be equal to input price. These equations, along with the production function 11.8.2, can be solved simultaneously to yield optimum input levels n and p and optimum corn output q.

11.8.3a The Estimated Marginal Products
The marginal physical product equations for the estimated production function $q = \alpha n^{\beta_2} p^{\beta_3} = 1.568 n^{.34703} p^{.41449}$ are

$$\text{MP}_n \equiv \frac{\partial q}{\partial n} = \alpha \beta_2 n^{\beta_2 - 1} p^{\beta_3} = \frac{\beta_2 \alpha n^{\beta_2} p^{\beta_3}}{n} = \frac{\beta_2 q}{n} = .34703 \frac{q}{n} > 0$$

$$\text{MP}_p \equiv \frac{\partial q}{\partial p} = .41449 \frac{q}{p} > 0$$

$$(11.8.18)$$

The marginal physical product equations give estimates of the rate of change of yield for changes of the inputs n and p.

Given the estimated marginal products, we could consider, for example, the optimum application of nitrogen when the level of phosphate is fixed at a given level say, 80 pounds per acre. From equation 11.8.17b the profit-maximizing level is attained when

$$w_0 \frac{\partial q}{\partial n} = w_1$$

which, using equation 11.8.18, implies

$$w_0 \beta_2 \alpha n^{\beta_2 - 1} p^{\beta_3} = w_1$$

Solving this last equation for n yields

$$n = \left[\beta_2 \alpha p^{\beta_3} \left(\frac{w_0}{w_1} \right) \right]^{\frac{1}{1 - \beta_2}}$$

Using point estimates of α, β_2 and β_3, a fixed level of phosphate of 80 pounds, a corn price of $w_0 = \$2.00$ per bushel and a nitrogen price of $w_1 = \$0.20$ per pound, we find that the optimum n is

$$n = \left[(.34703)(1.538)(80)^{.41449} (2/.2) \right]^{1.5315} = 216.27 \text{ pounds of nitrogen}$$

$$(11.8.19)$$

11.8.3b Estimated Least Cost Output
In input equilibrium the ratio of marginal product to input price must be the same for each input. Thus, in equilibrium,

$$\frac{\text{MP}_p}{w_2} = \frac{\text{MP}_n}{w_1} \quad \text{or} \quad \frac{\partial q / \partial p}{\partial q / \partial n} = \frac{\text{MP}_p}{\text{MP}_n} = \frac{\beta_3}{\beta_2} \frac{n}{p} = \frac{w_2}{w_1} \quad \text{or} \quad n = \left(\frac{w_2 \beta_2}{w_1 \beta_3} \right) p$$

$$(11.8.20)$$

This equation, which defines the least-cost mix of n and p for any level of output, is known as the expansion path; it is the line joining all points of tangency between price ratio lines and isoquants. When we use, for example, a nitrogen cost of $w_1 = \$0.20$ per pound and a phosphate cost of $w_2 = \$0.14$ per pound, the equation for the optimum mix of inputs is

$$n = \left[\frac{(0.14)(.34703)}{(0.20)(.41449)} \right] p = (.7)(.837) p = 0.586 p$$

$$(11.8.21)$$

Thus, the nitrogen–phosphate ratio is constant and equal to 0.586 for all profit maximizing levels of corn output.

11.8.3c Determining the Optimum Output
Finally, given prices, we consider the equilibrium output and input mix solution. For the corn producer, this decision involves an optimum solution for both corn output per acre and the combination of the inputs n and p. To indicate the reach of the results, let us find the equilibrium solution for a corn price $w_0 = \$2.00$ per bushel, a nitrogen price $w_1 = \$0.35$ per pound, and a phosphate price $w_2 = \$0.30$ per pound.

In line with the objective of maximizing profit (π), subject to the production function, the first-order equilibrium conditions given in equation 11.8.17 and the production function can be solved simultaneously for n, p, and q. With equations 11.8.17 and 11.8.18 used to specify the first-order conditions, these conditions, along with the production function, can be written as

$$q = \alpha n^{\beta_2} p^{\beta_3} \qquad w_0 \beta_2 \frac{q}{n} = w_1 \qquad w_0 \beta_3 \frac{q}{p} = w_2$$

Rearranging, taking logs, and inserting the relevant values results in the following set of linear equations

$$\ln q - .34706 \ln \quad n - .41449 \ln \ p \ = \ln 1.568$$

$$\ln q \qquad - \ln \quad n \qquad \qquad = \ln\left(\frac{w_1}{w_0 \beta_2}\right) = \ln\left(\frac{.35}{2(.34703)}\right)$$

$$\ln q \qquad - \ln \qquad \qquad p = \ln\left(\frac{w_2}{w_0 \beta_3}\right) = \ln\left(\frac{.30}{2(.41449)}\right)$$

or

$$\begin{bmatrix} 1 & -.34703 & -.41449 \\ 1 & -1.0 & 0 \\ 1 & 0 & -1.0 \end{bmatrix} \begin{bmatrix} \ln q \\ \ln n \\ \ln p \end{bmatrix} = \begin{bmatrix} .4501 \\ -.6846 \\ -1.0164 \end{bmatrix} \qquad (11.8.22)$$

Solving simultaneously yields the result

$$\begin{aligned} \ln q &= 4.6504 & \qquad q &= 104.63 \text{ bushels} \\ \ln n &= 5.3350 & \quad \text{or} \quad n &= 207.4 \text{ pounds} \\ \ln p &= 5.6668 & \qquad p &= 289.12 \text{ pounds} \end{aligned}$$

This completes our economic analysis of the estimated corn production function. We could go on to demonstrate input demand and cost functions. However, what we have already done should be suggestive of how to turn economic and statistical theory into practice.

11.8.3d Other Types of Production Functions   In estimating the corn production function we used data that were experimentally generated, where other factors that influenced output were held constant. This type of technical relation has some shortcomings when it comes to making recommendations that are optimal for an individual firm. Continuing our focus on agriculture, the individual firm may, for example, operate with varying amounts of labor, capital and fertility of the soil and be involved in both crop and livestock production. To capture these various effects, alternative production functions that usually involve aggregate resource categories need to be considered. For example, let us consider a fixed plant and assume we have T observations on a firm or industry over time, or alternatively, for a point in time, T cross-sectional observations on a number of firms. If we consider an agricultural firm producing one or more crops, then we might consider the aggregate resource categories and specify the production function as

$$q_{tc} = f\left(x_{t1}, x_{t2}, x_{t3}, x_{t4}, x_{t5} \mid \boldsymbol{\beta}\right) + e_t$$

where q_{tc} is the dollar value of the income from crop sales, x_{t1} is the acres of cropland, x_{t2} is the labor used in crop production, x_{t3} is the dollar value of machine services, x_{t4} is the dollar value of fertilizer, and x_{t5} is the dollar value of seed, insecticides, and so on.

Alternatively, we might be interested in an aggregate production function for the automobile or rail industry or the U.S. manufacturing sector. For example, if we have observational data in billions of dollars on gross output y for the U.S. manufacturing sector and the four inputs capital (K), labor (L), energy (E), and other intermediate materials (M), we might specify our economic model as

$$y_t = f\left(K_t, L_t, E_t, M_t \mid \boldsymbol{\beta}\right)$$

Given observations on these firm level or industry aggregates, our next step would be to specify an appropriate functional form, identify the stochastic assumptions appropriate for describing the error process e_t, and to proceed with estimation or inference. From an economic standpoint these type of aggregate production functions never provide information about specific disaggregated input categories. The results are used for diagnostic purposes such as discerning the relative efficiency of the broad input categories within and between firms and industries. Questions such as input and substitution elasticities, returns to scale, technical change (neutral or capital using) and the share of total cost going to various inputs may be evaluated.

11.9 Critique of the Knowledge Search and Concepts

In Section 11.8 we started with the problem of how to determine the economic optimum level and combinations of two inputs to use in producing a commodity. In particular, we looked at the problem of determining the optimum levels of nitrogen n and phosphate p in corn production. The theory of the firm gave us a way to think about this problem and caused us to cast it in the form of a production function. As a starting point, we assumed that the equation errors for the production function were independently and identically distributed random variables and specified an algebraic form of the production function that was linear in logs. Fortunately, experimental data were available that reflected corn output data for a range of mixes of inputs n and p. Given the statistical model and the experimental data, we made use of the least squares rule to estimate the unknown parameters of the production function and to obtain an estimate of the sampling precision of our result. This put us in a position to do interval estimation and test hypotheses concerning the characteristics of the unknown technical coefficients.

Given the estimated parameters, we then went on to consider economic implications of our results such as: What is the economic interpretation of the estimated parameters b_1, b_2, and b_3? What are the marginal productivities? And, under certain input and output prices, what is the optimum level of corn production and fertilizer use?

The linear statistical model may also be used to describe the underlying sampling process for many other economic data sets and other economic relationships. The revenue–price–advertising relationship in Chapters 9 and 10 and the demand for beer equation in Chapter 11 are two examples. Other examples include a supply relation involving factor and product prices, a consumption function involving income, lagged income and wealth, or an investment function involving interest rates and past and current profits. In these cases we could envision the experiment generating the data as being carried on by society. Our task is then to observe and make use of the data thereby produced. Consequently, with either experimentally or passively generated observational data, we now have the basis for specifying general linear statistical models and for the corresponding estimation and inference procedures that give quantitative economic life to a wide range of economic relationships.

By now you should be thinking, for each economic problem that you covered in your introductory and possibly intermediate economic courses, about the following search and learning format. As an example of each step, we indicate what that step involved for the production function example of Section 11.8.

1. The general economic problem (for example, optimum resource use within the context of the theory of the firm).
2. The specific economic problem (the production function and economic optima).
3. Choosing the statistical model (two treatment variables, normal independently and identically distributed errors, and a log-linear functional form).
4. Collecting or experimentally generating the economic data (an experimental design was specified and the data were experimentally produced).
5. Estimation procedure (the least squares estimator).
6. Empirical results (obtaining point and interval estimates of unknown coefficients and making tests of hypotheses).
7. Economic implications (using the empirical results as a basis for economic analysis and choice).
8. Identify and possibly resolve some additional questions (for example, have we used the correct functional form and/or error process or possibly included all of the relevant right-hand-side variables and nonsample information).

The questions introduced in no. 8 may require more general economic and statistical models and lead us to other questions concerning estimation and inference, and to another chapter.

11.10   Exercises

11.1 Consider the log-linear demand model

$$\ln q = \beta_1 + \beta_2 \ln p_B + \beta_3 \ln p_L + \beta_4 \ln p_R + \beta_5 \ln m$$

The elasticity of demand for q with respect to p_L can be written as

$$\frac{\partial q}{\partial p_L} \frac{p_L}{q}$$

Show that this elasticity is equal to β_3. *Hint:* Differentiate both sides of the equation with respect to p_L. To differentiate the left-hand side, use the result

$$\frac{\partial(\ln q)}{\partial p_L} = \frac{\partial(\ln q)}{\partial q} \frac{\partial q}{\partial p_L}$$

11.2 Consider equation 11.5.4 in the text. Show that

$$\hat{\text{var}}(b_2 + b_3 + b_4 + b_5) = \sum_{i=2}^{5} \text{var}(b_i) + 2\sum_{i=2}^{4} \sum_{j=i+1}^{5} \text{cov}(b_i, b_j) = 0.0888$$

given that the lower left triangle of the estimated covariance matrix for **b** = $(b_1, b_2, b_3, b_4, b_5)'$ is given by

$$\hat{cov}(\mathbf{b}) = \begin{bmatrix} 14.010 & & & & \\ 0.63591 & 0.057141 & & & \\ 0.46000 & -0.058721 & 0.31377 & & \\ 0.12403 & 0.004369 & -0.007871 & 0.006351 & \\ -1.5131 & -0.055405 & -0.10199 & -0.010922 & 0.17265 \end{bmatrix}$$

11.3 In Exercise 9.1 the model

$$y_t = x_{t1}\beta_1 + x_{t2}\beta_2 + x_{t3}\beta_3 + e_t$$

was estimated using the data in Table 9.4.
(a) Use a hand calculator to reestimate this model under the assumption that $\beta_1 = \beta_2 = \beta_3$.
(b) Find the restricted sum of squared errors from this reestimated model.
(c) Test the restrictions $\beta_1 = \beta_2 = \beta_3$.
(d) Compare the standard errors of the restricted and unrestricted least squares estimates of β_1.

11.4 (a) For the model

$$y_t = \beta_1 + \beta_2 x_{t2} + \beta_3 x_{t3} + \beta_4 x_{t4} + e_t$$

substitute each of the following restrictions into the original equation and rewrite the equation in a form where least squares applied to the new equation will yield restricted estimates.
(i) $\beta_3 = 0$
(ii) $\beta_2 + \beta_3 + \beta_4 = 1$
(iii) $\beta_2 = 3\beta_3$ and $\beta_1 = \beta_4$
(iv) $\beta_2 - \beta_3 = 2$, $\beta_4 = 6$, and $\beta_1 = 3\beta_2$
(b) Define R and $\mathbf{r}$ for each set of restrictions in Exercise 11.4a such that each of these sets of restrictions can be written in the form $R\beta = \mathbf{r}$.

11.5 Consider the restricted least squares estimator in equation 11A.13 of the appendix. Given the following expression for $(X'X)^{-1}$, verify the results for $(X'X)^{-1}R'$ and $R(X'X)^{-1}R'$ given in equations 11A.15 and 11A.16.

$$(X'X)^{-1} = \begin{bmatrix} 3895.147 & 176.798 & 127.891 & 34.484 & -420.690 \\ 176.798 & 15.887 & -16.326 & 1.215 & -15.404 \\ 127.891 & -16.326 & 87.235 & -2.188 & -28.357 \\ 34.484 & 1.215 & -2.188 & 1.766 & -3.036 \\ -420.690 & -15.404 & -28.357 & -3.036 & 48.002 \end{bmatrix}$$

11.6 Consider the demand for beer model

$$\ln q_t = \beta_1 + \beta_2 \ln p_{Bt} + \beta_3 \ln p_{Lt} + \beta_4 \ln p_{Rt} + \beta_5 \ln m_t + e_t$$

where

$$\beta_2 + \beta_3 + \beta_4 + \beta_5 = 0$$
$$\beta_3 = \beta_4$$
$$\beta_5 = 1$$

Use these three restrictions on the elements of β to eliminate the parameters β_2, β_4, and β_5 from the model and show that the resulting model can be written as

$$\ln\left(\frac{q_t P_{Bt}}{m_t}\right) = \beta_1 + \beta_3 \ln\left(\frac{P_{Lt} P_{Rt}}{P_{Bt}^2}\right) + e_t$$

11.7 Consider the model

$$y_t = \beta_1 + x_{t2}\beta_2 + x_{t3}\beta_3 + e_t$$

and suppose that application of least squares to 20 observations on these variables yields the following results

$$\mathbf{b} = \begin{bmatrix} 0.96587 \\ 0.69914 \\ 1.7769 \end{bmatrix} \quad \hat{\text{cov}}(\mathbf{b}) = \hat{\sigma}^2 (X'X)^{-1} = \begin{bmatrix} 0.21812 & 0.019195 & -0.050301 \\ 0.019195 & 0.048526 & -0.031223 \\ -0.050301 & -0.031223 & 0.037120 \end{bmatrix}$$

$$\hat{\sigma}^2 = 2.5193 \qquad R^2 = 0.9466$$

(a) Use a t-test to test the hypothesis H_0: $\beta_2 = \beta_3$ against the alternative H_1: $\beta_2 \neq \beta_3$.

(b) Test the hypotheses that $\beta_1 = \beta_2 = \beta_3 = 1$.

(c) Predict a value y_0 for the dependent variable given the explanatory variable values $\mathbf{x}'_0 = (1, 0, 2)$.

(d) Find the estimated variance of the prediction error and a 95% prediction interval using the same vector $\mathbf{x}_0$.

11.8 Suppose that you reestimate the model in Exercise 11.7 with the restriction $\beta_2 = \beta_3$ imposed and you obtain the following results:

$$\mathbf{b} = \begin{bmatrix} 1.4716 \\ 1.2795 \\ 1.2795 \end{bmatrix} \quad \hat{\text{cov}}(\mathbf{b}*) = \begin{bmatrix} 0.25604 & -0.025159 & -0.025159 \\ -0.025159 & 0.007702 & -0.025159 \\ -0.025159 & -0.025159 & 0.007702 \end{bmatrix}$$

$$\hat{\sigma}^2 = 3.4771 \qquad R^2 = 0.9219$$

(a) Compare the standard errors from these values with the standard errors for the unrestricted estimates. Are there any surprises?

(b) Test the hypothesis H_0: $\beta_2 = \beta_3$ against the alternative H_1: $\beta_2 \neq \beta_3$ by comparing the restricted and unrestricted sum of squared errors. Does your answer agree with that in Exercise 11.7(a)?

(c) Find the predicted value $\hat{y}_0^* = \mathbf{x}'_0 \mathbf{b}*$.

(d) Find the variance of the prediction error $(\hat{y}_0^* - y_0)$.

(e) Has imposition of the restriction improved the estimated variance of the prediction error?

11.9 In Exercise 9.3 the following linear equation for the demand for money was estimated

$$m_t = \beta_1 + \beta_2 y_t + \beta_3 i_t + e_t$$

Suppose that, in a future year, we observe

$$m_0 = 600 \quad y_0 = 3000 \quad \text{and} \quad i_0 = 10$$

Using the results you obtained in Exercise 9.3, investigate whether there is any evidence to suggest that the linear function that was previously estimated is no longer adequate for this future observation?

11.10 Consider the results and data for Exercise 9.6 where a log-linear equation for the demand for beef was estimated using 17 observations. This equation was

$$\ln qb_t = \beta_1 + \beta_2 \ln pb_t + \beta_3 \ln pl_t + \beta_4 \ln pp_t + \beta_5 \ln y_t + e_t$$

(a) Test the following hypotheses
   (i) $\beta_2 + \beta_3 + \beta_4 + \beta_5 = 0$
   (ii) $\beta_3 = \beta_4$
   (iii) $\beta_2 + \beta_3 + \beta_4 + \beta_5 = 0$ and $\beta_3 = \beta_4$
(b) Find three sets of restricted least squares estimates, one for each of the hypotheses in part (a). Comment on these estimates and their standard errors.

11.11 Suppose, in Exercise 11.10, that you are given nonsample information that $\beta_2 = -1$, and that $\beta_4 = -\beta_5$.
(a) Use substitution to eliminate β_2 and β_4 from the model and rewrite the equation in a form that lends itself to restricted least squares estimation of β_1, β_3, and β_5. Find restricted least squares estimates for β_1, β_3, and β_5.
(b) Show that the estimates obtained in (a) are identical to those obtained using the formula for direct restricted estimation.
(c) Test the joint hypothesis that $\beta_2 = -1$ and $\beta_4 = -\beta_5$.

11.12(a) Consider the restriction $\beta_3 + 80\beta_4 = 1$ that was tested in relation to the receipts–price–advertising relationship of Chapter 10. See equations 10.7.15 and 10.7.16.
   (i) Using all 78 observations, reestimate the model with the restriction imposed. Compare the restricted and unrestricted least squares estimates and their standard errors.
   (ii) Test the restriction using the restricted and unrestricted sum of squared errors; compare the test result with that in Chapter 10.
(b) Repeat Exercise 11.12a, but with the two restrictions that appear in equation 10.8.3a, namely,

$$\beta_1 + 2\beta_2 + 40\beta_3 + 1600\beta_4 = 175 \quad \text{and} \quad \beta_3 + 80\beta_4 = 1$$

11.13. Using the experimental data given in Table 11.5, estimate the unknown parameters for the following production function

$$q_t = \beta_1 + \beta_2 n_t + \beta_3 p_t + \beta_4 n_t^{0.5} + \beta_5 p_t^{0.5} + \beta_6 n_t p_t + e_t$$

(a) Do the signs of the estimated coefficients agree with your a priori expectation?
(b) Find 95% interval estimates for each of the response coefficients and comment on the reliability of the point estimates.
(c) Predict output for nitrogen and phosphorous levels equal to 200. Given $n = p = 200$ and the predicted output level, find the elasticities of production with respect to each of the inputs.
(d) Treating the n, p, and q values in (c) as fixed, test the hypothesis that the elasticity of production with respect to nitrogen is equal to 0.45.
(e) Given $p = 200$, find an expression for MP_n. Graph this function and compare it with a graph of the corresponding MP_n function for the log-linear production function reported in Section 11.8.

11.14. Repeat Exercise 11.13 using the quadratic production function

$$q_t = \beta_1 + \beta_2 n_t + \beta_3 p_t + \beta_4 n_t^2 + \beta_5 p_t^2 + \beta_6 n_t p_t + e_t$$

11.15. Consider the aggregate production function $q_t = aK_t^{\alpha} L_t^{\gamma}$, where the industry output q is assumed to be a function of the level of the inputs capital K and labor L. Consistent with this economic model, consider the following annual observations $\mathbf{y}$, that you may assume were generated from the statistical model

$$\mathbf{y} = X\boldsymbol{\beta} + \mathbf{e} = \beta_1 \mathbf{x}_1 + \beta_2 \mathbf{x}_2 + \beta_3 \mathbf{x}_3 + \mathbf{e}$$

where $\mathbf{e} \sim N(\mathbf{0}, \sigma^2 I_T)$, $\mathbf{y}$ is ln $\mathbf{q}$, $\mathbf{x}_2$ is ln $\mathbf{K}$, $\mathbf{x}_3$ is ln $\mathbf{L}$, $\beta_1 = \ln a$, $\beta_2 = \alpha$, and $\beta_3 = \gamma$.

$$
\mathbf{y} =
\begin{bmatrix}
10.7413 \\
10.9830 \\
10.5292 \\
11.5891 \\
11.7983 \\
11.7586 \\
11.9454 \\
12.3305 \\
11.8958 \\
10.3561 \\
11.1673 \\
11.1656 \\
11.6819 \\
11.4135 \\
11.2097 \\
11.9817 \\
12.3243 \\
12.0298 \\
11.3930 \\
10.8940
\end{bmatrix}
\qquad
\begin{matrix}
\mathbf{x}_1 & \mathbf{x}_2 & \mathbf{x}_3 \\
\end{matrix}
\\
X =
\begin{bmatrix}
1 & 0.693 & 0.693 \\
1 & 1.733 & 0.693 \\
1 & 0.693 & 1.386 \\
1 & 1.733 & 1.386 \\
1 & 0.693 & 1.792 \\
1 & 2.340 & 0.693 \\
1 & 1.733 & 1.792 \\
1 & 2.340 & 1.386 \\
1 & 2.340 & 1.792 \\
1 & 0.693 & 0.693 \\
1 & 0.693 & 1.386 \\
1 & 1.733 & 0.693 \\
1 & 1.733 & 1.386 \\
1 & 0.693 & 1.792 \\
1 & 2.340 & 0.693 \\
1 & 1.733 & 1.792 \\
1 & 2.340 & 1.386 \\
1 & 2.340 & 1.792 \\
1 & 1.733 & 1.386 \\
1 & 0.693 & 0.693
\end{bmatrix}
$$

(a) Use these data with the design matrix X to compute least squares estimates of β_1, β_2, and β_3, and use an unbiased estimator of σ^2 to obtain an estimate of the error variance.

(b) Give an economic interpretation to β_2, β_3, and $\beta_2 + \beta_3$.

(c) Compute the estimated covariance matrix and give a statistical interpretation.

(d) Using a level of statistical significance of $\alpha = .05$, compute and interpret interval estimates for β_2, β_3, and $\beta_2 + \beta_3$.

(e) Using values of 2.000 and 1.000 for x_2 and x_3, predict the outcome for y and, using $\alpha = .05$, compute an interval estimate and interpret.

(f) Using a level of statistical significance of $\alpha = .05$, test
   (i) the hypothesis $\beta_2 = \beta_3$
   (ii) the joint hypothesis $\beta_2 + \beta_3 = 1$ and $\beta_3 = .3$

(g) If output $y_t = 10$, derive the isoquant reflecting the possible combinations of K and L for this output.

(h) Given the input prices are $P_K = 2$ and $P_L = 3$, solve the following problems:
   (*i*) Use the estimated production function to find the optimal ratio of L to K.
   (*ii*) Use the result in (*i*) to eliminate K from the production function and hence find the demand for L as a function of output.
   (*iii*) Use a procedure similar to that in (*ii*) to find the demand for K as a function of output.
   (*iv*) Use the results in (*ii*) and (*iii*), and the fact that total cost = $P_L \cdot L + P_K \cdot K$, to find total cost as a function of output.

(i) Make a graph of the estimated total cost function.

(j) If the output price is $P_q = 4$ and capital is held constant at $\ln K = x_2 = 1.2$, compute the optimum (profit maximizing) values of q and L.

(k) How would you make use of these results in evaluating the economic performance of the industry?

(l) Suppose you knew that $\beta_2 + \beta_3 = 1$ (constant returns to scale), estimate the production function under this restriction and compare the estimated covariance matrix with that obtained under Exercise 11.15a.

11.16 Consider a production function where output (Y) depends on two inputs, capital (K) and labor (L). The optimal levels of K and L for a *given output* are given by the point where the "cost line" is tangential to the isoquant. The optimal levels of K and L for *different outputs* are given by the expansion path that is the locus of points where the cost lines are tangential to the isoquants. This scenario is depicted in Figure 11.2.

In Figure 11.2*a* the production function is such that the expansion path is a straight line; the optimal input *ratio L/K* depends on the relative input prices, but it does not depend on Y (it does not change as we move outward on the expansion path). In Figure 11.2*b* the production function is such that the expansion path is curved; the input ratio *L/K* depends on both the relative

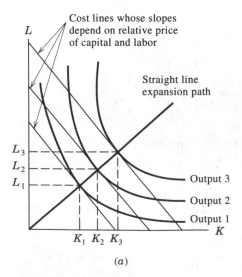

(a)

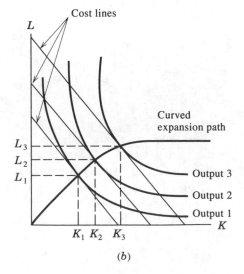

(b)

Figure 11.2 Optimal levels of capital (K_1, K_2, K_3) and labor (L_1, L_2, L_3) for three different output levels and a given input price ratio. (*a*) Straight-line expansion path. (*b*) Curved expansion path.

input prices and on output. The drawing in Figure 11.2b suggests L/K will decline as Y increases.

Given this background, we wish to find how the labor/capital ratio depends on the relative price of labor and capital and on output for the U.S. Air Transport Industry. Observations on indices of these variables for the period 1948–79 appear in Table 11.6. We set up the model

$$\ln\left(\frac{L_t}{K_t}\right) = \beta_1 + \beta_2 \ln\left(\frac{W_t}{R_t}\right) + \beta_3 \ln(Y_t) + e_t$$

Table 11.6   Capital, Labor, Output and Price Indices for the U. S. Air Transportation Industry

Year	Y	R	K	W	L
1948	1.214	0.1454	0.612	0.243	1.415
1949	1.354	0.2181	0.559	0.260	1.384
1950	1.569	0.3157	0.573	0.278	1.388
1951	1.948	0.3940	0.564	0.297	1.550
1952	2.265	0.3559	0.574	0.310	1.802
1953	2.731	0.3593	0.711	0.322	1.926
1954	3.025	0.4025	0.776	0.335	1.964
1955	3.562	0.3961	0.827	0.350	2.116
1956	3.979	0.3822	0.800	0.361	2.435
1957	4.420	0.3045	0.921	0.379	2.707
1958	4.563	0.3284	1.067	0.391	2.706
1959	5.385	0.3856	1.083	0.426	2.846
1960	5.554	0.3193	1.481	0.441	3.089
1961	5.465	0.3079	1.736	0.460	3.122
1962	5.825	0.3783	1.926	0.485	3.184
1963	6.876	0.4180	2.041	0.506	3.263
1964	7.823	0.5163	1.997	0.538	3.412
1965	9.120	0.5879	2.257	0.564	3.623
1966	10.512	0.5369	2.742	0.586	4.074
1967	13.020	0.4443	3.564	0.622	4.710
1968	15.261	0.3052	4.767	0.666	5.217
1969	16.313	0.2332	6.511	0.731	5.569
1970	16.002	0.1883	7.627	0.831	5.495
1971	15.876	0.2023	8.673	0.906	5.334
1972	16.662	0.2506	8.331	1.000	5.345
1973	17.014	0.2668	8.557	1.056	5.662
1974	19.305	0.2664	9.508	1.131	5.729
1975	18.721	0.2301	9.062	1.247	5.722
1976	19.250	0.3452	8.262	1.375	5.762
1977	20.647	0.4508	7.474	1.544	5.877
1978	22.726	0.5877	7.104	1.703	6.108
1979	23.619	0.5346	6.874	1.779	6.852

Source: Jorgenson, D., F. Gallop, and B. Fraumeni (1988) *Productivity and U.S. Economic Growth*, Amsterdam: North Holland.

where

L_t is an index of labor input in year t,
K_t is an index of capital services in year t,
W_t is an index of the price of labor in year t,
R_t is an index of the price of capital in year t, and
Y_t is an index of output in year t.

(a) What variables appear in the vector **y** and the matrix X when the model is written in the form $\mathbf{y} = X\beta + \mathbf{e}$?

(b) What signs do you expect on the coefficients β_2 and β_3? How does the sign on β_3 relate to the shape of the expansion path for the air transportation production function?

(c) Find least squares estimates of β_1, β_2, and β_3. Interpret the estimates. Do these estimates have the expected signs?

(d) Compute standard errors for the estimates b_1, b_2, and b_3.

(e) Construct a 95% confidence interval for β_3. Based on this confidence interval, do you think the expansion path could be a straight line?

(f) Test the joint hypothesis that $\beta_2 = 1$ and $\beta_3 = 0$. What is the significance of this test in terms of the nature of the production function?

(g) What proportion of variation in $\ln(L_t/K_t)$ is explained by movements in $\ln(W_t/K_t)$ and $\ln(Y_t)$?

11.11   References

A more extensive development of the linear statistical model in general and restricted estimation and hypothesis testing in particular can be found in

JUDGE,G. G., R. C. HILL, W. E. GRIFFITHS, H. LÜTKEPOHL and T. C. LEE (1988) *Introduction to the Theory and Practice of Econometrics*, New York: John Wiley & Sons, Inc., pp. 178–274.

In terms of the economic analysis section of this chapter, you may feel you need or want further reading on demand functions and analysis, as well as firm theory and the economic analysis of production functions. If so, then have a look at the designated sections of one or more of the following:

BEATTIE, B. R. and C. R. TAYLOR (1985) *The Economics of Production*, New York: John Wiley & Sons, Inc., pp. 9–73.

BINGER, B. R., and E. HOFFMAN (1988) *Microeconomics with Calculus*, Glenview, IL: Scott, Foresman and Company, pp. 230–276

GOULD, J. P., and C. E. FERGUSON (1980) *Microeconomic Theory*, Homewood, IL: Richard D. Irwin, Inc., Chapters 5 and 6.

HEADY, E. O., and J. L. DILLON (1961) *Agricultural Production Functions*, Ames, IA: Iowa State University Press, pp. 73–108, 475–512.

INTRILIGATOR, M. O. (1978), *Econometric Models, Techniques and Applications*, Englewood Cliffs, NJ: Prentice-Hall, Inc., pp. 251–291.

MANSFIELD, E. (1985) *Microeconomics: Theory and Applications*, 5th edition, New York: W. W. Norton & Co., Inc., pp.49-150.

PINDYCK, R., and D. RUBINFELD (1988), *Microeconomics*, New York: Macmillan Publishing Co., pp. 193–245.

VARIAN, HAL (1984) *Microeconomic Analysis*, New York: W.W. Norton & Co., Inc., pp. 171–181.

APPENDIX 11A   The Restricted Least Squares Estimator for Combining Sample and Nonsample Information

In Sections 11.3 and 11.6 of this chapter, we described nonsample information that took the form of linear restrictions on the elements of the coefficient vector β, and we indicated that a restricted estimation procedure that combines the sample information with the nonsample information can be implemented on most computer programs by listing the restrictions that make up the nonsample information. In this appendix we describe in detail the restricted least squares estimator whose values are calculated by most computer programs.

To begin, recall that, in Appendix 10C of Chapter 10, we wrote J linear restrictions on the elements of β in the form

$$R\beta = r \tag{11A.1}$$

where the $(J \times K)$ matrix R and the $(J \times 1)$ vector $\mathbf{r}$ defined the J restrictions. In Section 10C we were concerned with testing these linear restrictions. We now turn from the testing problem to the estimation problem. The purpose of this appendix is to present and to apply a general matrix expression for the restricted least squares estimator that combines the sample information $(\mathbf{y}, X)$ with the nonsample information that takes the form of the linear restrictions in equation 11A.1.

As an example, reconsider the single restriction $\beta_2 + \beta_3 + \beta_4 + \beta_5 = 0$ that we considered in Sections 11.1 and 11.3. In this instance we have $J = 1$ and the restriction or nonsample information can be written as

$$
(0 \quad 1 \quad 1 \quad 1 \quad 1) \begin{pmatrix} \beta_1 \\ \beta_2 \\ \beta_3 \\ \beta_4 \\ \beta_5 \end{pmatrix} = 0 \tag{11A.2}
$$

Thus, here, we define R and $\mathbf{r}$ as

$$
\begin{array}{cc}
R = (0 \quad 1 \quad 1 \quad 1 \quad 1) & \mathbf{r} = 0 \\
1 \times 5 & 1 \times 1
\end{array} \tag{11A.3}
$$

Different linear combinations can be described by changing the definitions of R and $\mathbf{r}$.

To obtain a general formula for least squares estimates that use the sample information *and* satisfy the nonsample restrictions, we find that value of β that minimizes the sum of squared errors, subject to the linear equality restrictions in equation 11A.1. That is, given the model $\mathbf{y} = X\beta + \mathbf{e}$, the problem is to find that value of β that minimizes the sum of squared errors

$$(\mathbf{y} - X\beta)' (\mathbf{y} - X\beta) \tag{11A.4}$$

subject to the linear restrictions

$$R\beta = r \tag{11A.5}$$

Note that we are still using the same least squares principle, but we have the side condition that the estimates must satisfy equation 11A.5. The solution to this problem is obtained by setting up what is known as the Lagrangian function

$$L = (\mathbf{y} - X\boldsymbol{\beta})'(\mathbf{y} - X\boldsymbol{\beta}) + 2\boldsymbol{\lambda}'(\mathbf{r} - R\boldsymbol{\beta}) \tag{11A.6}$$

where $\boldsymbol{\lambda}$ is a $(J \times 1)$ vector of "Lagrange multipliers." You may have encountered such multipliers in maximum or minimum problems in economics. Solving the equations that result from setting first derivatives of the Lagrangian function equal to zero yields the restricted least squares estimator. We shall not go through this optimizing procedure; instead, we present the result. Details can be found in Judge et al. (1988, p. 236). The concept being used is the same as that used in microeconomic theory courses when a household maximizes utility subject to a budget constraint or when a firm maximizes profit subject to the production function. The solution to the restricted minimization problem is the restricted least squares estimator

$$\mathbf{b}^* = \mathbf{b} + (X'X)^{-1} R'\left[R(X'X)^{-1} R'\right]^{-1} (\mathbf{r} - R\mathbf{b}) \tag{11A.7}$$

where $\mathbf{b} = (X'X)^{-1}X'\mathbf{y}$ is the unrestricted least squares estimator that uses only sample information. The restricted estimator $\mathbf{b}^*$ has the property that $R\mathbf{b}^* = \mathbf{r}$, for any sample of data $(\mathbf{y}, X)$. The expression in equation 11A.7 looks somewhat daunting, but it need not. It is a matter of constructing the appropriate matrices and having the computer multiply them together in the correct order.

In the beer demand example with the single restriction that the elasticities sum to zero, R and $\mathbf{r}$ are defined in equation 11A.3, and we have

$$\mathbf{b} = \begin{bmatrix} -3.2432 \\ -1.0204 \\ -0.5829 \\ 0.2095 \\ 0.9229 \end{bmatrix} \quad (X'X)^{-1} R' = \begin{bmatrix} -81.5181 \\ -14.6285 \\ 40.3642 \\ -2.2445 \\ 1.2042 \end{bmatrix}$$

$$R(X'X)^{-1} R' = 24.6954 \qquad R\mathbf{b} = -0.4709$$

Substituting these values into equation 11A.7 and using $\mathbf{r} = \mathbf{0}$ yields

$$\mathbf{b}^* = \begin{bmatrix} -3.2432 \\ -1.0204 \\ -0.5829 \\ 0.2095 \\ 0.9229 \end{bmatrix} + \begin{bmatrix} -81.5181 \\ -14.6285 \\ 40.3642 \\ -2.2445 \\ 1.2042 \end{bmatrix} (24.6954)^{-1} (0.4709) = \begin{bmatrix} -4.798 \\ -1.299 \\ 0.187 \\ 0.167 \\ 0.946 \end{bmatrix} \tag{11A.8}$$

As expected, these estimates are identical to those given in Table 11.2. For standard errors we need the square roots of the diagonal elements of $\hat{\text{cov}}(\mathbf{b}^*)$. This estimated covariance matrix is derived in Judge et al. (1988, pp. 238–239); it is given by

$$\hat{\text{cov}}(\mathbf{b}^*) = \hat{\sigma}_*^2 (X'X)^{-1} \left\{ I_K - R'\left[R(X'X)^{-1} R'\right]^{-1} R(X'X)^{-1} \right\} \tag{11A.9}$$

with

$$\hat{\sigma}_*^2 = \frac{(\mathbf{y} - X\mathbf{b}^*)'(\mathbf{y} - X\mathbf{b}^*)}{T - K + J} \tag{11A.10}$$

The divisor in equation 11A.10 has been increased from $(T - K)$ to $(T - K + J)$. In general, this increase is equal to the number of restrictions. In our example, $J = 1$, and, as we can see from equation 11.3.2, there is effectively one less parameter to estimate. The new divisor gives an unbiased estimator for σ^2 and is equal to the number of degrees of freedom in the restricted model. The computation of equations 11A.9 and 11A.10 also yields standard errors identical to those in Table 11.2.

As a second example, consider the three linear restrictions given in equation 11.6.2, namely,

$$\beta_2 + \beta_3 + \beta_4 + \beta_5 = 0$$
$$\beta_3 - \beta_4 = 0$$
$$\beta_5 = 1 \qquad (11A.11)$$

Writing these restrictions together in the general linear equality form $R\beta = r$, we have

$$\begin{bmatrix} 0 & 1 & 1 & 1 & 1 \\ 0 & 0 & 1 & -1 & 0 \\ 0 & 0 & 0 & 0 & 1 \end{bmatrix} \begin{bmatrix} \beta_1 \\ \beta_2 \\ \beta_3 \\ \beta_4 \\ \beta_5 \end{bmatrix} = \begin{bmatrix} 0 \\ 0 \\ 1 \end{bmatrix}$$

Thus, in this case, R is a (3×5) matrix and $\mathbf{r}$ is a (3×1) vector, defined respectively as

$$R = \begin{bmatrix} 0 & 1 & 1 & 1 & 1 \\ 0 & 0 & 1 & -1 & 0 \\ 0 & 0 & 0 & 0 & 1 \end{bmatrix} \quad \text{and} \quad \mathbf{r} = \begin{bmatrix} 0 \\ 0 \\ 1 \end{bmatrix} \qquad (11A.12)$$

Computing the various components on the right-hand side of the expression for the restricted least squares estimator

$$\mathbf{b}^* = \mathbf{b} + \left(X'X\right)^{-1} R' \left[R\left(X'X\right)^{-1} R'\right]^{-1} (\mathbf{r} - R\mathbf{b}) \qquad (11A.13)$$

we have

$$R\mathbf{b} = \begin{bmatrix} 0 & 1 & 1 & 1 & 1 \\ 0 & 0 & 1 & -1 & 0 \\ 0 & 0 & 0 & 0 & 1 \end{bmatrix} \begin{bmatrix} -3.2432 \\ -1.0204 \\ -0.5829 \\ 0.2095 \\ 0.9229 \end{bmatrix} = \begin{bmatrix} -0.4709 \\ -0.7925 \\ 0.9229 \end{bmatrix} \qquad (11A.14)$$

$$\left(X'X\right)^{-1} R' = \begin{bmatrix} -81.518 & 93.407 & -420.690 \\ -14.629 & -17.541 & -15.404 \\ 40.364 & 89.424 & -28.357 \\ -2.245 & -3.954 & -3.036 \\ 1.204 & -25.320 & 48.002 \end{bmatrix} \qquad (11A.15)$$

$$R(X'X)^{-1}R' = \begin{bmatrix} 24.695 & 42.609 & 1.204 \\ 42.609 & 93.378 & -25.320 \\ 1.204 & -25.320 & 48.002 \end{bmatrix} \qquad (11\text{A}.16)$$

To verify these results you should attempt Exercise 11.5.

Carrying the computations further we have

$$\mathbf{r} - R\mathbf{b} = \begin{bmatrix} 0.4709 \\ 0.7925 \\ 0.0771 \end{bmatrix} \qquad (11\text{A}.17)$$

$$\left[R(X'X)^{-1}R' \right]^{-1} = \begin{bmatrix} 0.7716 & -0.4170 & -0.2393 \\ -0.4170 & 0.2378 & 0.1359 \\ -0.2393 & 0.1359 & 0.0985 \end{bmatrix} \qquad (11\text{A}.18)$$

and

$$\mathbf{b}^* = \begin{bmatrix} -3.2432 \\ -1.0204 \\ -0.5829 \\ 0.2095 \\ 0.9229 \end{bmatrix} + \begin{bmatrix} -2.0360 \\ -0.2974 \\ 0.7418 \\ -0.0507 \\ 0.0771 \end{bmatrix} = \begin{bmatrix} -5.279 \\ -1.318 \\ 0.159 \\ 0.159 \\ 1.000 \end{bmatrix} \qquad (11\text{A}.19)$$

As expected, these estimates satisfy the equation $R\mathbf{b}^* = \mathbf{r}$; the elasticities sum to zero, the cross-price elasticities are equal, and the income elasticity is equal to one. Furthermore, the results are identical to those presented earlier in equation 11.6.3. The standard errors are given by the square roots of the diagonal elements of the expression for $\hat{\text{cov}}(\mathbf{b}^*)$ given in equation 11A.9. The estimated error variance is

$$\hat{\sigma}_*^2 = \frac{(\mathbf{y} - X\mathbf{b}^*)'(\mathbf{y} - X\mathbf{b}^*)}{T - K + J} = \frac{0.09899}{28} = 0.0035354$$

Let us recapitulate. We began this chapter by introducing nonsample information in the form of linear restrictions on $\boldsymbol{\beta}$, and we showed how these linear restrictions can be included in the estimation procedure by reparameterizing the model. We also indicated that most computer programs do not require reparameterization to obtain restricted estimates; the appropriate command plus a list of the restrictions is usually sufficient. In this appendix we have shown *how the computer calculates the restricted least squares estimates*.

11A.1   The Two Formulations of the *F*-Statistic

Also considered earlier in this chapter was a reformulation of the *F*-statistic introduced in Chapter 10, with this reformulation being written in terms of the sums of squared errors from restricted and unrestricted least squares estimation. We round off this appendix by reconsidering the examples used to illustrate the new form of the *F*-statistic. Our reconsideration will be in terms of the previous formula developed in Appendix 10C. Both formulations are useful and intuitively instructive. The sum of squared errors formulation is convenient when comparing the computer output results from restricted and unrestricted models; the calculations necessary to compute the F-value from this output can be done on a hand calculator. The formulation in Appendix 10C is the formula used by most computer programs when the instruction to test a set of linear restrictions is given.

The form of the F–statistic developed in Appendix 10C is given by

$$F = \frac{(Rb - r)' \left[R(X'X)^{-1} R' \right]^{-1} (Rb - r)}{J\hat{\sigma}^2}$$

(11A.20)

Under the assumption that the null hypothesis H_0: $R\beta = r$ is true, F has an $F_{[J,(T-K)]}$ distribution.

In the beer demand model, for the restriction defined by

$$R = \begin{bmatrix} 0 & 1 & 1 & 1 & 1 \end{bmatrix} \quad \text{and} \quad r = 0$$

we have

$$Rb = -0.4709 \qquad \hat{\sigma}^2 = 0.0035968 \qquad R(X'X)^{-1} R' = 24.6954 \qquad \text{and} \qquad J = 1$$

Collecting these various results and substituting them into equation 11A.20 yields

$$F = \frac{(-0.4709)(24.6954)^{-1}(-0.4709)}{0.0035968} = 2.496$$

As expected, this value is identical to that in equation 11.5.8 and thus leads to the same test conclusion.

For the restrictions defined by

$$R = \begin{bmatrix} 0 & 1 & 1 & 1 & 1 \\ 0 & 0 & 1 & -1 & 0 \\ 0 & 0 & 0 & 0 & 1 \end{bmatrix} \quad \text{and} \quad r = \begin{bmatrix} 0 \\ 0 \\ 1 \end{bmatrix}$$

we have

$$F = \frac{(Rb - r)' \left[R(X'X)^{-1} R' \right]^{-1} (Rb - r)}{J\hat{\sigma}^2}$$

$$= \frac{\begin{bmatrix} 0.4709 & 0.7925 & 0.0771 \end{bmatrix} \begin{bmatrix} 0.7716 & -0.4170 & -0.2393 \\ -0.4170 & 0.2378 & 0.1359 \\ -0.2393 & 0.1359 & 0.0985 \end{bmatrix} \begin{bmatrix} 0.4709 \\ 0.7925 \\ 0.0711 \end{bmatrix}}{3 \times 0.0035968}$$

$$= 0.841$$

Again, this value is identical to that computed in equation 11.6.6c, where the sum of squared errors formulation of the test statistic was used. Thus, the two formulations are equivalent. That is,

$$\frac{(Rb - r)' \left[R(X'X)^{-1} R' \right]^{-1} (Rb - r)}{J\hat{\sigma}^2} = \frac{(\text{SSE}_R - \text{SSE}_U)/J}{\text{SSE}_U/(T - K)}$$

(11A.21)

A proof of this result can be found in Judge et al. (1988, pp. 257–258).

Part IV

Econometric Topics I

In Parts I, II and III we examined statistical models for the mean of an economic variable and we progressed through such models that contain one, two and many (K) parameters. For each model we developed estimation and testing rules and examined their sampling properties.

In Part IV we discuss three topics related to the simple and multiple regression models of Parts II and III. In Chapter 12 we consider the possibility that one or more of the parameters in the regression model may change during the sample period. Dichotomous 0–1 variables, called *dummy variables*, are used to capture such parameter shifts. Dummy variables may also be used to capture the effects of qualitative explanatory factors, like the race or gender of a person, or a person's geographic location.

Chapter 13 discusses the problems frequently caused by the passive role economists usually play in the data-generation process. The explanatory and control variables may not take values exhibiting sufficient independent variation to permit precise least squares estimation of a model's parameters. This is the "collinearity" problem, and in Chapter 13 we illustrate its effects on the least squares estimator and suggest diagnostic procedures. The introduction of nonsample information, in the form of linear restrictions on a model's parameters, is considered as one way to ameliorate the problem.

The final chapter in Part IV, Chapter 14, deals with another problem encountered by economists in empirical work. On many occasions it is more realistic to assume that the explanatory variables are random variables rather than nonstochastic and fixed in repeated samples. The consequences of random regressors are considered in Chapter 14, along with new estimation rules that are useful in this context. Instrumental variable and method of moments estimators' sampling properties are developed for large samples. The large sample properties of estimators and test statistics are called "asymptotic properties" and play an important role in modern econometric theory and practice.

Chapter 12

Dummy Variables and Varying Coefficient Models

New Key Words and Concepts

Qualitative Variables   Binary Variables

Dichotomous Variables   Interaction Variables

Coefficient Variability   Dummy Variable Trap

12.1 Introduction

In this chapter we discuss statistical models in which the parameters may vary from one observation to another. This is in contrast to the models that we have considered in Chapters 1 to 11, in which the economic and statistical models have had fixed coefficients that are identical for all sample observations. We recognize that coefficients may vary within the sample, and that this variability may be associated with qualitative characteristics such as gender, race, or geographical region of residence. These characteristics are represented by discrete or dummy variables. We also consider the possibility that coefficient variability is conditioned on continuous variables. These types of models will also enable us to introduce *qualitative* factors into our econometric analyses. Using dummy variables we may also be able to pool or combine different samples of data into one sample. We introduce this idea here and more fully explore it in Chapter 17.

12.2 Varying Intercept Parameters: Dummy Variables

To make matters specific, let us consider the problem of estimating the relationship between U. S. consumption and income during the period 1929–1970. Let C_t denote the real per capita personal consumption in year t and Y_t denote real per capita disposable income in year t. Initially we may specify the economic model as

$$C_t = \beta_1 + \beta_2 Y_t \qquad t = 1929,\ldots,1970 \qquad (12.2.1)$$

A moment's reflection will indicate a difficulty with this specification. During part of this period the world was waging war, and we know that personal consumption expenditures were drastically reduced during the years of confrontation; the relationship between consumption and income was altered during these years. To account for this change, and recognize the fact that some years of the sample period were war years, we develop a way to incorporate nonquantitative, or *qualitative*, factors into an economic model.

One way to capture qualitative characteristics within economic models is to use *dummy variables*. These are often called *binary* or *dichotomous* variables as they take just two values, usually 1 or 0, to indicate the presence or absence of a characteristic. That is, a dummy variable D is

$$D = \begin{cases} 1 & \text{if the characteristic is present} \\ 0 & \text{if the characteristic is not present} \end{cases} \qquad (12.2.2)$$

To incorporate this idea into the consumption model, let us define the war period for the United States as 1941–1946 and construct the dummy variable D as

$$D_t = \begin{cases} 1 & \text{if } t = 1941,\ldots, 1946 \\ 0 & \text{otherwise} \end{cases} \qquad (12.2.3)$$

Thus the dummy variable D is 1 during the war period and 0 during nonwar years.

The next step in the model formulation is critical. A decision must be made about *how* the qualitative factor of war affected the relationship between consumer expenditure and disposable income. Let us assume that the effect of the war was felt in the *level* of autonomous consumption, which is represented in the economic model 12.2.1 by the intercept parameter β_1. What we are now suggesting is that this parameter is *not* fixed at the same value for all the sample observations. We will make this assumption explicit in the economic model by writing it as

$$C_t = \beta_{1t} + \beta_2 Y_t \qquad t = 1929,\ldots, 1970 \qquad (12.2.4)$$

The change we have made is to recognize explicitly that the intercept parameter may change from observation to observation, by attaching the subscript "t" to the intercept parameter. Furthermore, economic logic provides us with a conceptual model of how the intercept parameter changes. We expect it to be one value during the war years and another value (presumably higher) in all other years. Following this logic, we use the dummy variable D_t in a "model" for the intercept parameter. Specifically, let

$$\beta_{1t} = \beta_1 + \delta D_t \qquad (12.2.5)$$

Assuming consumption is less during the war years, the parameter δ is the reduction in autonomous consumption during the war years. We can incorporate this assumption into equation 12.2.4 by substituting for β_{1t} to obtain

$$C_t = \beta_1 + \delta D_t + \beta_2 Y_t \qquad t = 1929,\ldots, 1970 \qquad (12.2.6)$$

The effect of the inclusion of a dummy variable D_t into the economic model is best seen by examining the economic model during the war and non-war years.

$$C_t = \begin{cases} (\beta_1 + \delta) + \beta_2 Y_t & \text{when } D_t = 1 \\ \beta_1 + \beta_2 Y_t & \text{when } D_t = 0 \end{cases}$$

We see that by adding the dummy variable D_t to the model the value of the intercept parameter is different for the war and nonwar years. During the war years, when $D_t = 1$, the intercept of the regression function is $(\beta_1 + \delta)$. During the nonwar years the regression function intercept is simply β_1. This difference is depicted in Figure 12.1.

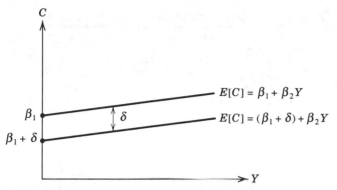

Figure 12.1 An intercept dummy variable.

Adding the dummy variable D_t to the economic model creates a *parallel shift* in the consumption relationship by the amount δ. The interpretation of the parameter δ is that it is the change in autonomous consumption during the war years. *A dummy variable like D_t that is incorporated into a regression model to capture a shift in the intercept as the result of some qualitative factor is called an "intercept dummy variable."* In this application we expect the level of consumption to decline, and anticipate that δ will be negative.

Recognizing the random nature of C_t, the statistical model for the consumption relationship is specified as

$$C_t = \beta_1 + \delta D_t + \beta_2 Y_t + e_t, \qquad t = 1929,\ldots, 1970 \qquad (12.2.7)$$

If e_t in equation 12.2.7 obeys the assumptions of the classical normal linear regression model, we may estimate the model parameters via least squares as usual. The least squares estimator's properties are not affected by the fact that one of the explanatory variables consists only of zeros and ones. The parameter δ is treated like the other parameters in the model. We can construct an interval estimate for it or we can test its "significance" which, in effect, will be a test of whether the war had a "significant effect" on autonomous consumption. If $\delta = 0$ then the war years have no effect on the amount of autonomous consumption.

To further illustrate these ideas, let us examine the data. In Table 12.1 are data on U. S. per capita consumption and disposable income in 1958 dollars. Using these data we estimate the model in equation 12.2.7 by least squares and obtain the following results (*t*-statistics in parentheses)

$$\hat{C}_t = 101.36 - 204.95 D_t + 0.86 Y_t \qquad R^2 = .99$$
$$(3.98) \ (-10.91) \quad (58.73) \qquad\qquad\qquad (12.2.8)$$

Note that, as anticipated, the estimated value of the parameter δ is negative. Based on the reported *t*-statistic we also see that the null hypothesis that the war years had no effect on autonomous consumption, H_0: $\delta = 0$, is rejected in favor of the alternative H_1: $\delta \neq 0$ at the .01 level of significance. The fitted regression lines for the war and nonwar years, and the data scatter, are shown in Figure 12.2. The data points for the war years are indicated and are clearly "below" the fitted regression for the nonwar years. We conclude that during the war years the level of consumption spending dropped in a significant way. That is, there was a "structural change" in the economy during the war period that manifested itself, in one way, by a change in the relationship between disposable income and consumption.

Table 12.1 U.S. Real Per Capita Income and Consumption

Year	C	Y	Year	C	Y
1929	1145	1236	1950	1520	1646
1930	1059	1128	1951	1509	1657
1931	1016	1077	1952	1525	1678
1932	919	9210	1953	1572	1726
1933	897	8930	1954	1575	1714
1934	934	9520	1955	1659	1795
1935	985	1035	1956	1673	1839
1936	1080	1158	1957	1683	1844
1937	1110	1187	1958	1666	1831
1938	1097	1105	1959	1735	1881
1939	1131	1190	1960	1749	1883
1940	1178	1259	1961	1755	1909
1941	1240	1427	1962	1813	1968
1942	1197	1582	1963	1865	2013
1943	1213	1629	1964	1945	2123
1944	1238	1673	1965	2044	2235
1945	1308	1642	1966	2123	2331
1946	1439	1606	1967	2160	2398
1947	1431	1513	1968	2248	2480
1948	1438	1567	1969	2301	2517
1949	1451	1547	1970	2323	2579

Source: Economic Report of the President, 1972.

12.3 Varying Response Parameters and Dummy Variables

Instead of assuming that the effect of the war was to cause a change in the level of autonomous consumption, let us assume that the change was in the marginal propensity to consume (mpc), represented in the consumption relation 12.2.1 by the parameter β_2. Dummy variables can be used to permit changes in response coefficients that are associated with changes in qualitative characteristics. To do so we alter the basic consumption relation and index β_2 as follows:

$$C_t = \beta_1 + \beta_{2t} Y_t \quad t = 1929,\ldots,1970 \qquad (12.3.1)$$

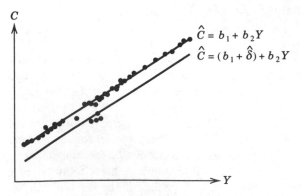

Figure 12.2 The estimated consumption function for the war and nonwar years.

Note that we have added the subscript "t" to the coefficient of income, indicating that it is a *time varying parameter*. For illustrative purposes we have assumed that the intercept parameter is fixed. If our assumption is that the marginal propensity to consume is one value during the war period and another value during peace, we may specify

$$\beta_{2t} = \beta_2 + \gamma D_t \qquad (12.3.2)$$

where the parameter γ is the difference in the slope of the consumption relation between the war and nonwar years. We may incorporate this assumption into equation 12.3.1 by substituting for β_{2t} to obtain

$$C_t = \beta_1 + \beta_2 Y_t + \gamma(Y_t D_t) \qquad t = 1929,\ldots, 1970 \qquad (12.3.3)$$

The effect of assuming that the marginal propensity to consume is time varying is to include another variable in the economic model. The new variable $(Y_t D_t)$ is the product of income and the dummy variable and is called an "interaction variable" in much economic literature, as it captures the interaction effect of war and income on consumption. The interaction variable takes a value equal to income during the war period, when $D_t = 1$, and zero during nonwar years. The effect of the inclusion of the interaction variable into the economic model is best seen by examining the economic model during the war and nonwar years.

$$C_t = \begin{cases} \beta_1 + (\beta_2 + \gamma)Y_t & \text{when } D_t = 1 \\ \beta_1 + \beta_2 Y_t & \text{when } D_t = 0 \end{cases} \qquad (12.3.4)$$

During the war years the marginal propensity to consume is $(\beta_2 + \gamma)$; it is β_2 in peacetime. We would anticipate that γ, the difference between the war and nonwar marginal propensities to consume, is less than zero. This situation is depicted in Figure 12.3a. Adding an error term to equation 12.3.3, and assuming that the assumptions of the classical normal linear statistical model hold, the intercept and slope parameters may be estimated by least squares. A test of the hypothesis that the marginal propensity to consume did not change during the war period can be carried out by testing the null hypothesis H_0: $\gamma = 0$.

If we assume that the war affected both autonomous consumption and the marginal propensity to consume, both effects may be incorporated into a single model. The resulting statistical model is

$$C_t = \beta_1 + \delta D_t + \beta_2 Y_t + \gamma(Y_t D_t) + e_t \qquad t = 1929,\ldots, 1970 \qquad (12.3.5)$$

See Exercise 12.1 for more on this model and its application. In Figure 12.3b we depict the consumption relation with reduced intercept and slope during the war period.

12.4   Extending the Use of Dummy Variables

Many times a qualitative characteristic has more than two states. For example, suppose we are considering individual purchasing behavior for some product and plan to use a cross section of data to explore the issue. What is of interest in this case are some of the characteristics of an individual that may affect purchasing habits for a specific product, like beer. For a cross section of data in a specific market area, the prices of the product and its substitutes and complements are the same for all individuals in the market, so prices will not enter the economic model. Factors that may affect the amount consumed include income and socioeconomic characteristics of the individual, such as age, gender, race, geographic region of residence, type of residence (apartment, townhouse, trailer, or a house), marital status, level of educational attainment (high school diploma, a college degree, or a graduate degree), and so on.

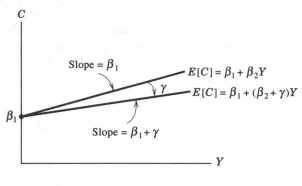

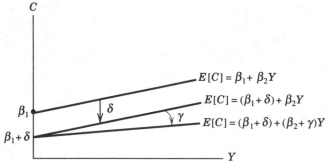

Figure 12.3 *(a)* A response parameter dummy variable. *(b)* A response parameter and intercept dummy variable.

The variables consumer expenditure, income, and age are quantitative and *continuous* variables. The remaining variables are not the same. Variables like gender, race, type of residence, and marital status are *qualitative* variables. There is no numerical value that these variables naturally take. The level of educational attainment may be measured by a continuous variable like "years of schooling," but often surveys do not ask such specific questions. Instead, boxes are provided that represent levels of education.

Simple dummy variables can be defined for the gender of the individual, or marital status, which take only two states. For example, we may define a variable to capture an individual's gender as

$$S = \begin{cases} 1 & \text{if the individual is female} \\ 0 & \text{if the individual is male} \end{cases}$$

This variable is commonly known as a "sex dummy," with the subsequent ribaldry that economists define sex as a dummy variable.

Qualitative factors like type of residence, level of educational attainment, and race have more than two possible categories. In these situations a dummy variable may be defined for each of the possible states. For example, we may define the dummy variables

$$\text{APART} = \begin{cases} 1 & \text{if an individual lives in an apartment} \\ 0 & \text{otherwise} \end{cases}$$

$$\text{TOWN} = \begin{cases} 1 & \text{if an individual lives in a townhouse} \\ 0 & \text{otherwise} \end{cases}$$

$$\text{TRAIL} = \begin{cases} 1 & \text{if an individual lives in a trailer} \\ 0 & \text{otherwise} \end{cases}$$

and so on, to capture the effects of residence type. If education is measured by a question noting the highest level of schooling completed, we may define

$$E_1 = \begin{cases} 1 & \text{if individual has a high school education} \\ 0 & \text{otherwise} \end{cases}$$

$$E_2 = \begin{cases} 1 & \text{if individual has a college education} \\ 0 & \text{otherwise} \end{cases}$$

$$E_3 = \begin{cases} 1 & \text{if individual has a graduate degree} \\ 0 & \text{otherwise} \end{cases}$$

12.5 The Dummy Variable Trap and Model Interpretation

One note of warning on the use of dummy variables. It may seem appropriate to define additional dummy variables to capture the effects of each state that a qualitative characteristic may assume and to include them all in the statistical model. To do so, however, would be a mistake that is often described as falling into the "dummy variable trap."

To illustrate the problem, reconsider the war–nonwar consumption example in Section 12.2. Let $H_t = 1 - D_t$ be a dummy variable that denotes the nonwar years. You may be tempted to include this variable in equation 12.2.4 to capture the effect of the nonwar years on autonomous consumption, but this would be an error. If H_t is added as an explanatory variable, in addition to D_t, the resulting X matrix does not have linearly independent columns. The dummy variables D_t and H_t sum to one, which is the value of the intercept variable. This is a violation of a basic assumption of the linear statistical model, as pointed out in Chapter 9, equation 9.1.7. It is explored further in Exercise 12.3. It is also clear intuitively that H_t is not needed. By introducing D_t we have been able to distinguish the war and nonwar years in equation 12.2.7; no further distinction is necessary. Consequently, one cannot include an intercept and two dummy variables, one for each qualitative state being considered. To do so is described as falling into the dummy variable "trap." It is also called the situation of "exact collinearity," a term that we define in the following chapter. Whatever its name, the consequence of a design matrix X that does not have linearly independent columns is that the least squares criterion breaks down, and unique estimates for all the model parameters cannot be obtained.

To avoid the dummy variable "trap" in the beer expenditure example of Section 12.4, we define one less dummy variable than the number of categories that exist for each characteristic. Otherwise the dummy variables will sum to one and be linearly dependent with the intercept variable. Thus for residence type, we have omitted the dummy variable for house dwellers; for educational attainment, we have omitted the dummy variable for those with less than a high school degree.

For illustrative purposes, let us assume that the basic economic model that relates beer expenditure (per year) (BE) to annual income (Y) for the ith individual is

$$BE_i = \beta_1 + \beta_2 Y_i \quad i = 1, \dots, T \tag{12.5.1}$$

Furthermore, to keep matters simple, we just consider the qualitative factors gender and level of educational attainment as possibly having an effect on beer expenditure, and assume that these factors affect only the autonomous level of beer consumption measured by β_1, the intercept parameter. (See Exercise 12.4 for extensions.) The assumption that the intercept varies according to individual characteristics is made explicit by writing

$$BE_i = \beta_{1i} + \beta_2 Y_i \quad i = 1, \ldots, T \qquad (12.5.2)$$

We have added the subscript "i" to the intercept parameter to indicate that it may change from individual to individual. If we assume that the intercept changes with each qualitative characteristic we may specify

$$\beta_{1i} = \beta_1 + \delta S_i + \gamma_1 E_{1i} + \gamma_2 E_{2i} + \gamma_3 E_{3i} \qquad (12.5.3)$$

where δ and γ_1, γ_2, and γ_3 are parameters that reflect the effects of the qualitative characteristics on the intercept parameter, or level of the expenditure relationship. Incorporating equation 12.5.3 into the expenditure relationship by substitution, we obtain

$$BE_i = \beta_1 + \delta S_i + \gamma_1 E_{1i} + \gamma_2 E_{2i} + \gamma_3 E_{3i} + \beta_2 Y_i \qquad (12.5.4)$$

The effect of the various qualitative states on the expenditure relationship may be seen by enumerating them

$$BE_i = \beta_1 + \beta_2 Y_i \qquad \text{for male with less than HS} \qquad (12.5.5a)$$

$$BE_i = \beta_1 + \gamma_1 + \beta_2 Y_i \qquad \text{for male with HS degree} \qquad (12.5.5b)$$

$$BE_i = \beta_1 + \gamma_2 + \beta_2 Y_i \qquad \text{for male with college degree} \qquad (12.5.5c)$$

$$BE_i = \beta_1 + \gamma_3 + \beta_2 Y_i \qquad \text{for male with graduate degree} \qquad (12.5.5d)$$

$$BE_i = \beta_1 + \delta + \beta_2 Y_i \qquad \text{for female with less than HS} \qquad (12.5.5e)$$

$$BE_i = \beta_1 + \delta + \gamma_1 + \beta_2 Y_i \qquad \text{for female with HS degree} \qquad (12.5.5f)$$

$$BE_i = \beta_1 + \delta + \gamma_2 + \beta_2 Y_i \qquad \text{for female with college degree} \qquad (12.5.5g)$$

$$BE_i = \beta_1 + \delta + \gamma_3 + \beta_2 Y_i \qquad \text{for female with graduate degree} \qquad (12.5.5h)$$

In equation 12.5.5a the "base case" is represented by males with less than a high school education. Equation 12.5.5 completely enumerates the eight cases of gender and education level, with each case having a *different* intercept parameter. Only one dummy variable for gender and three for educational attainment were necessary for this complete enumeration. If an additional dummy variable for males had been introduced, or for individuals with less than a high school degree, we would fall into the dummy variable trap.

With such a specification of an economic model, we can address questions such as: Is there a significant difference between the purchasing practices of men and women? Does the level of education have an effect on the level of expenditure? If the statistical model corresponding to equation 12.5.4 satisfies the usual assumptions of the linear statistical model, then the parameters of the model can be estimated by least squares and the various effects tested for statistical significance. For example, we may test whether there is a significant difference in the behavior of men and women by testing the null hypothesis H_0: $\delta = 0$ using a t-test. To test whether the effect of a college education on expenditure on beer is the same as the effect of a graduate education we test the null hypothesis H_0: $\gamma_2 - \gamma_3 = 0$ using a t- or F-test.

12.6   Testing the Significance of Qualitative Characteristics

One question that will naturally arise is whether the combined qualitative factors have a significant effect on individual beer expenditures. To examine this question we may test the joint null hypothesis H_0: $\delta = \gamma_1 = \gamma_2 = \gamma_3 = 0$. The appropriate test statistic may be easily computed in this instance by comparing the sums of squared errors obtained by applying least squares to the complete model that includes all the dummy variables (corresponding to equation 12.5.4) and to the restricted model (corresponding to equation 12.5.2) that is correct if the null hypothesis is true. The restricted model includes only income and an intercept variable on the right-hand side of the equation. The test statistic is (see Chapter 11, Section 11.6)

$$u = \frac{(\text{SSE}_R - \text{SSE}_U)/J}{\text{SSE}_U/(T-K)} \tag{12.6.1}$$

where SSE_R and SSE_U are the sums of squares of the least squares residuals from the restricted and unrestricted models, respectively, $J = 4$ is the number of hypotheses being tested jointly, T is the sample size, and $K = 6$ is the number of parameters estimated in the unrestricted model. If the null hypothesis is true, then the test statistic u has an F-distribution with J and $(T - K)$ degrees of freedom. The test is carried out by comparing the calculated value of the test statistic u to a critical value F_c for the appropriate F-distribution and rejecting the null hypothesis if $u \geq F_c$. The test may also be formulated by using the restricted least squares estimator. See Exercise 12.5.

The model 12.5.4 does not permit us to answer questions regarding potentially different educational effects for men and women. For example, in equation 12.5.5 the parameter γ_1 reflects the difference in beer expenditure between high school graduates and those without a high school degree whether they are male *or* female. Similarly, γ_2 is the difference in expenditure between college and high school graduates whether they are male or female. It is possible that this restriction is unrealistic. Perhaps the effect on expenditure of a college education for a male is different from the effect of a college education for a female. To answer that question we must allow for an *interaction effect* between gender and level of education. This idea is pursued in Exercise 12.6.

In addition to testing the hypothesis that education has a differential impact on beer expenditure depending on the gender of the individual, it is straightforward to examine whether men's and women's beer expenditure functions are *completely different*. That is, not only may the education effects be different for men and women, but the effect of income on beer expenditure, or the effect of any other variable considered, may differ as well. *In this case all of the parameters in an economic model for beer expenditure by men may be different from corresponding parameters in an economic model for beer expenditure by women.* Continuing with the beer expenditure model, assume that the structural parameters of the beer expenditure equation are completely different for males and females. A statistical model incorporating this flexibility is

$$BE_i = \beta_{1i} + \gamma_{1i}E_{1i} + \gamma_{2i}E_{2i} + \gamma_{3i}E_{3i} + \beta_{2i}Y_i + e_i \tag{12.6.2}$$

We have now specified that the parameters on the levels of educational attainment and income may change from individual to individual. To make such changes dependent on the gender of the individual, we express each parameter as

$$\beta_{ji} = \beta_j + \delta_j S_i \qquad j = 1, 2 \tag{12.6.3a}$$

$$\gamma_{ki} = \gamma_k + \theta_k S_i \qquad k = 1, 2, 3 \tag{12.6.3b}$$

In equations 12.6.3 the parameter δ_1 is the difference between male and female intercepts, and δ_2 is the difference between the income slope parameter for males and the income slope parameter for females. Similarly, the parameters θ_k are the differences in effects of levels of education associated with gender differences. Inserting equations 12.6.3 into the statistical model 12.6.2, we obtain

$$BE_i = \beta_1 + \delta_1 S_i + \gamma_1 E_{1i} + \theta_1 (E_{1i} S_i) + \gamma_2 E_{2i} + \theta_2 (E_{2i} S_i)$$
$$+ \gamma_3 E_{3i} + \theta_3 (E_{3i} S_i) + \beta_2 Y_i + \delta_2 (Y_i S_i) + e_i \qquad (12.6.4)$$

The corresponding mean regression functions are

$$E[BE_i] = \begin{cases} (\beta_1 + \delta_1) + (\gamma_1 + \theta_1)E_{1i} + (\gamma_2 + \theta_2)E_{2i} + (\gamma_3 + \theta_3)E_{3i} + (\beta_2 + \delta_2)Y_i & \text{female} \\ \beta_1 + \gamma_1 E_{1i} + \gamma_2 E_{2i} + \gamma_3 E_{3i} + \beta_2 Y_i & \text{male} \end{cases}$$
$$(12.6.5)$$

Examining the mean regression functions in equation 12.6.5, we see that each and every corresponding parameter is different for males and females. The parameters δ_1 and δ_2 are the gender differences for the intercept and coefficient of income parameters, respectively. The parameters θ_1, θ_2, and θ_3 are the differences that gender makes on the effect of educational attainment on beer expenditure. For example, the parameter θ_2 is the difference between the intercept values (recall that the education variables are themselves dummy variables) for college-educated males and college-educated females. If $\theta_2 \neq 0$ then the effect of college education upon the autonomous consumption of beer is different for males and females.

If the statistical model in equation 12.6.4 obeys the assumptions of the classical normal linear statistical model, then the parameters may be estimated by least squares. The properties of the least squares estimator are not affected by the fact that some of the explanatory variables are dummy variables, interactions between dummy and continuous variables, and interactions between dummy variables. Interval estimates of individual parameters may be constructed and individual and joint hypotheses about the structural parameters can be tested by using the t- and F-statistics developed for these purposes.

Within the context of the model 12.6.4, we may ask whether the behavioral characteristics of men and women are the same with regard to expenditures on beer. This means we are asking if $\delta_1 = \delta_2 = \theta_1 = \theta_2 = \theta_3 = 0$. This hypothesis is an important one, for if it is true, males and females may be "pooled" and treated as identical within the context of the statistical model

$$BE_i = \beta_1 + \gamma_1 E_{1i} + \gamma_2 E_{2i} + \gamma_3 E_{3i} + \beta_2 Y_i + e_i \qquad (12.6.6)$$

To test the joint null hypothesis that there are no behavioral differences between men and women with respect to beer expenditure, we specify the null and alternative hypotheses as

$$H_0 : \delta_1 = 0, \ \delta_2 = 0, \ \theta_1 = 0, \ \theta_2 = 0, \ \theta_3 = 0$$
$$H_1 : \text{at least one of the parameters is not zero} \qquad (12.6.7)$$

The appropriate test statistic is equation 12.6.1 with $J = 5$ and T the total number of men and women in the cross-section of data. The restricted sum of squared errors is the sum of squared errors from the model assuming that the null hypothesis is in fact true, namely equation 12.6.6. The unrestricted sum of squared errors is the sum of squared errors from the complete model given in equation 12.6.4. It is interesting that in this case, in which *all* of the parameters are allowed to differ on the basis of a qualitative factor, it can be shown that

$$\text{SSE}_U = \text{SSE}_M + \text{SSE}_F \tag{12.6.8}$$

where SSE_M is the sum of squared errors when the model 12.6.6 is estimated by least squares using only the data for males, and SSE_F is the sum of squared errors using only the data for females. The sum $\text{SSE}_M + \text{SSE}_F$ is the unrestricted sum of squared errors for the full model in equation 12.6.4. Since we have allowed *all* the economic parameters to differ for men and women, equation 12.6.4 is equivalent to specifying two separate structural equations explaining their behavior.

12.6.1 An Example

Relative to the statistical model given in equation 12.6.4, consider the data in Table 12.2, which represent observations on beer expenditure, gender, educational level, income, and age of $T = 40$ randomly chosen adults. Using this sample of data, we estimate the $K = 10$ parameters of the unrestricted, full model in equation 12.6.4 by least squares and report the results in Table 12.3 as Model 1. The least squares estimates of the restricted model, equation 12.6.6, appear in Table 12.3 as Model 2. By using these results and the test statistic 12.6.1, we can test the null hypothesis 12.6.7, that there are no behavioral differences between males and females:

$$u = \frac{\left(\text{SSE}_R - \text{SSE}_U\right)/J}{\text{SSE}_U /(T - K)} = \frac{(741486 - 411677)/5}{411677/30}$$
$$= 4.8068$$

The $\alpha = .05$ critical value of an $F_{5,30}$ random variable is $F_c = 2.53$. Since $u \geq F_c$, we reject the null hypothesis and conclude that there are behavioral differences with regard to expenditure on beer by males and females.

In Table 12.3 we report separate estimates of the restricted model for males (Model 3) and females (Model 4). Note that these results confirm equation 12.6.8, as the sum of the separate sums of squared errors yielding the following sum of squared errors in the unrestricted model:

$$\text{SSE}_U = 411677 = \text{SSE}_M + \text{SSE}_F$$
$$= 273413 + 138264$$

Note also that the parameter estimates, for corresponding variables, using data on males only Model (3), are identical to those in the full, unrestricted model Model (1). Also, parameter estimates of the restricted model using the female data only Model (4) equal the sum of corresponding estimates in the full model Model (1) and the coefficient estimates on the gender-interaction variables. For example, using the data on females alone, we estimate that .0013 of each additional dollar of income is spent on beer. This estimate of the marginal propensity to purchase beer by women $(\beta_2 + \delta_2)$, equals the male propensity (β_2), estimated in the full model to be .0023, plus the incremental effect of gender (δ_2) which is estimated to be -0.0010.

12.7 Systematically Varying Parameter Models

In Sections 12.3 and 12.4 we examined how to allow the parameters of a statistical model to vary, depending on the value of one or more zero–one or qualitative variables. This

Table 12.2 Beer Expenditure and Related Variables
for 40 Individuals

BE	S	E_1	E_2	E_3	Y	Age
109	1	0	0	0	15000	25
0	1	0	0	0	30000	45
0	1	0	0	0	12000	20
108	1	0	0	0	20000	28
220	1	1	0	0	15000	25
189	1	1	0	0	30000	35
64	1	1	0	0	12000	40
262	1	1	0	0	12000	22
64	1	1	0	0	28000	30
35	1	1	0	0	22000	21
94	1	1	0	0	44000	40
71	1	0	1	0	10000	21
403	1	0	1	0	222000	45
41	1	0	1	0	32000	36
10	1	0	1	0	45000	36
110	1	0	1	0	55000	40
239	1	0	1	0	29000	23
63	1	0	1	0	39000	32
0	1	0	1	0	70000	52
106	1	0	0	1	55000	30
0	1	0	0	1	90000	45
141	0	0	0	0	6000	32
299	0	0	0	0	18000	20
148	0	0	0	0	55000	55
424	0	1	0	0	10000	18
242	0	1	0	0	23000	30
119	0	1	0	0	35000	45
338	0	1	0	0	38000	40
135	0	1	0	0	45000	50
590	0	1	0	0	85000	32
324	0	1	0	0	22000	30
87	0	1	0	0	25000	51
395	0	0	1	0	29000	22
513	0	0	1	0	132000	40
56	0	0	1	0	35000	30
400	0	0	1	0	80000	36
384	0	0	1	0	55000	27
262	0	0	1	0	30000	24
336	0	0	1	0	27000	21
281	0	0	0	1	80000	45

idea can be extended to allow parameters to vary in a way related to continuous economic variables. To illustrate let us return to the basic statistical model that relates individual beer expenditure (BE) to income (Y), corresponding to the economic model in equation 12.5.1, which is

$$BE_i = \beta_1 + \beta_2 Y_i + e_i \qquad i = 1,\dots, T \qquad (12.7.1)$$

We will not include education, gender, or any other variables in the model in order to keep things simple. Let us now focus on the idea that *age*, a continuous variable

Table 12.3 Beer Expenditure Modeling Results

Variable	Model 1 Unrestricted		Model 2 Restricted		Model 3 Males		Model 4 Females	
	Est.	t-Stat.	Est.	t-Stat.	Est.	t-Stat.	Est.	t-Stat.
Const	134.89	1.86	77.42	1.36	134.89	1.56	28.28	.60
S	−106.61	−1.13						
E_1	65.39	.82	84.91	1.27	65.39	.69	72.87	1.25
$E_1 \cdot S$	7.48	.07						
E_2	71.62	.83	41.39	.58	71.62	.70	4.18	.07
$E_2 \cdot S$	−67.44	−.58						
E_3	−39.54	−.27	−74.90	−.70	−39.54	−.23	−73.10	−.86
$E_3 \cdot S$	−33.56	−.19						
Y	0.0023	2.34*	0.0017	2.53*	0.0023	1.96	0.0013	2.63*
$Y \cdot S$	−0.0010	−.82						
SSE	411677		741486		273413		138264	
$T - K$	30		35		14		16	

Note: * indicates significance at $\alpha = .05$ level.

measured in years, may affect the relationship between income and beer expenditure. In particular, suppose we wish to incorporate the idea that as a person's age increases he or she may spend more or less of any additional amount of income on beer. That is, we wish to permit the parameter β_2 to change depending upon the age (A) of the individual. As in the previous sections we make this assumption explicit by writing

$$BE_i = \beta_1 + \beta_{2i} Y_i + e_i \quad i = 1, \dots, T \tag{12.7.2}$$

We have added the subscript "i" to the parameter β_2 to indicate that it may change from individual to individual. Our model of how β_{2i} changes is

$$\beta_{2i} = \beta_2 + \delta_2 A_i \tag{12.7.3}$$

The parameter δ_2 reflects the change that age has on the coefficient of income in the expenditure model. Incorporate equation 12.7.3 into the expenditure model by substitution to obtain

$$BE_i = \beta_1 + \beta_2 Y_i + \delta_2 (Y_i A_i) + e_i \tag{12.7.4}$$

The effect of assuming that the coefficient of income varies is to introduce an *interaction* variable into the statistical model. The parameter δ_2 measures the effect of age on

Table 12.4 Beer Expenditure Modeling Results (continued)

Variable	Model 5		Model 6		Model 7	
	Est.	t-Stat.	Est.	t-Stat.	Est.	t-Stat.
Const	128.98	3.73*	58.97	1.68	161.47	1.34
Y	0.0015	2.44*	0.0113	4.23*	0.0091	2.47*
A					−2.98	−.89
$Y \cdot A$			−0.0002	−3.75*	−.0002	−1.85
SSE	819286		593333		580609	
$T - K$	38		37		36	

Note: * indicates significance at $\alpha = .05$ level.

the marginal propensity to consume for beer as seen by examining the partial derivative

$$\frac{\partial[BE_i]}{\partial Y_i} = \beta_2 + \delta_2 A_i \qquad (12.7.5)$$

If the parameter δ_2 is negative, then as the age of the individual increases, the amount of extra beer consumption resulting from an increase in income diminishes. Other examples of this effect appear in Section 10.7 and Exercise 10.7 of Chapter 10.

To illustrate, we continue the beer expenditure example by using the data in Table 12.2. In Table 12.4 the least squares estimates of the unknown parameters of equations 12.7.1, 12.7.4, and 12.7.8 are reported as Models 5, 6, and 7, respectively. First, let us test the hypothesis that age affects an individual's propensity to spend on beer. We do so by testing the null hypothesis H_0: $\delta_2 = 0$, against H_1: $\delta_2 \neq 0$, in the statistical model 12.7.4 that contains the income–age interaction variable, $Y \times A$. Based on the reported t-value, we reject the null hypothesis and conclude that age alters (diminishes) the propensity to spend on beer from additional income.

The level of autonomous expenditure on beer (that is not related to income) is given by the intercept parameter β_1. If we assume that it too is affected by the age of the individual, then the basic model is rewritten

$$BE_i = \beta_{1i} + \beta_{2i} Y_i + e_i \qquad (12.7.6)$$

and the intercept parameter is modeled as

$$\beta_{1i} = \beta_1 + \delta_1 A_i \qquad (12.7.7)$$

Incorporating both equations 12.7.3 and 12.7.7 into the expenditure relation in equation 12.7.6 yields

$$BE_i = \beta_1 + \delta_1 A_i + \beta_2 Y_i + \delta_2 (Y_i A_i) + e_i \qquad (12.7.8)$$

The partial derivative of beer expenditure with respect to age is

$$\frac{\partial[BE_i]}{\partial A_i} = \delta_1 + \delta_2 Y_i$$

In this instance the effect of a change in age on beer consumption depends on income level. If δ_1 and δ_2 are both negative, then as age increases, beer expenditure will decline, and the decline will be greater for individuals with higher incomes. Thus, incorporating the assumption that age affects the level of consumption expenditure results in age appearing as a separate variable on the right-hand side of the equation.

We can test the hypothesis that age has *no* effect on the relationship between income and expenditure on beer by testing the joint null and alternative hypotheses

$$H_0 : \delta_1 = 0,\ \delta_2 = 0$$
$$H_1 : \text{at least one of the } \delta_k \text{ is not zero}$$

Given a set of data, this hypothesis is easily tested by using the test statistic u in equation 12.6.1, with the unrestricted sum of squared errors coming from the "full" model in equation 12.7.8 and the restricted sum of squared errors coming from the model in which the null hypothesis is assumed true, which is the basic model in equation 12.7.1. Estimates of the model in equation 12.7.8 are given in Table 12.4 and are used in Exercise 12.7.

12.8 Summary

In this chapter we have considered linear regression models whose parameters may not be the same for all observations in a sample. Using a statistical model that assumes fixed coefficients—when the parameters actually vary over individuals, space, or time—is an example of model misspecification. We have examined *varying parameter* economic models and focused on how this feature can be incorporated into a simple regression model, and how estimation and inference can be carried through. We have examined how dummy variables are incorporated into a regression model to permit parameters to differ for groups of observations with distinct qualitative characteristics, such as gender, race, or occupation. Inclusion of dummy variables, and interactions between dummy variables, permits parallel shifts in a regression function by changing a model's intercept. When dummy variables are interacted with continuous explanatory variables, the result is a change in the slope of the regression function. We have also seen that an intercept or a response coefficient may be conditioned on continuous variables, the result being the inclusion of the conditioning variable into the model as well as the product of two continuous variables.

In the cases we have considered, the parameter variation was taken to be a nonrandom function of one or more explanatory variables. The resulting models are often *systematically varying parameter* models. It is possible, however, to specify the parameter variation as consisting of a systematic *and* a random component. The resulting models are called *random coefficient* models and are introduced in Exercise 12.8. In Appendix 17B of Chapter 17 we consider systematically varying and random coefficients (or error components) models that may be used when pooling time series and cross-sectional data.

12.9 Exercises

12.1 (a) Write down the basic consumption function, relating consumption to income, with *time varying* intercept and response parameters. Substitute equations 12.2.5 and 12.3.2 into the economic model, and add an error term to obtain a statistical model that permits both response and intercept to change during war years.

(b) Use the data in Table 12.1 and estimate the parameters of the statistical model 12.3.5 by least squares. Sketch the consumption relation for war and nonwar years, and compare the resulting sketch to Figure 12.3*b*.

(c) Let $P_t = 1 - D_t$ define a dummy variable that is 1 during nonwar years and 0 during war years. Estimate by least squares the model

$$C_t = \delta_1 P_t + \delta_2 D_t + \beta_1 (P_t Y_t) + \beta_2 (D_t Y_t) + e_t$$

Note that this model does *not* contain an overall constant term. Compare the resulting estimates to those in (b).

(d) Use the data in Table 12.1 to estimate *separate* consumption relations

$$C_t = \beta_1 + \beta_2 Y_t + e_t$$

for the war and nonwar periods. Compare the resulting estimates *and* standard errors to those obtained in parts (b) and (c). Explain any differences you observe.

12.2 Use the data in Table 12.1 to estimate the economic model given in equation 12.3.3 and comment on the results.

12.3 Use the data in Table 12.1 to construct the design matrix X that contains *(i)* an intercept variable, *(ii)* income, *(iii)* the dummy variable D_t in equation 12.2.3, and *(iv)* the dummy variable $H_t = 1 - D_t$. Identify the linearly dependent columns.

12.4 Within the context of the expenditure relationship 12.5.2, assume that the intercept parameter is affected by gender, level of educational attainment, *and* residence type, as defined in Section 12.4.
   (a) Modify equations 12.5.3 and 12.5.4 appropriately.
   (b) What is the expenditure relationship for a female with a college degree who lives in a townhouse?
   (c) Formulate the joint null and alternative hypotheses that would be used to test whether gender, educational attainment, or residence type, jointly, have an effect on beer expenditure.

12.5 In Section 12.6 the joint null hypothesis that gender and level of educational attainment have no effect on beer expenditure is discussed.
   (a) Given the economic model 12.5.4, write down the corresponding statistical model *with appropriate assumptions*.
   (b) Write down, in specific terms, the null hypothesis in the form H_0: $R\beta = \mathbf{r}$, as discussed in Chapter 11.

12.6 Consider the economic model in equation 12.5.4. Modify it further by permitting the effect of education to vary by the gender of the individual. To illustrate, attach a subscript "i" to the parameter γ_2 on the education dummy variable E_2. Then write

$$\gamma_{2i} = \theta_1 + \theta_2 S_i$$

and substitute into equation 12.5.4. Interpret the parameters θ_1 and θ_2.

12.7 In Section 12.7 the effect of income on beer expenditure was permitted to vary by the age of the individual.
   (a) Test the hypothesis that age does not affect beer expenditure through *either* the slope or the intercept parameter. Specifically, using the results in Table 12.4, test the null hypothesis that $\delta_1 = \delta_2 = 0$ in equation 12.7.8.
   (b) Modify equation 12.7.3 to permit a "life-cycle" effect in which the marginal effect of income on beer expenditure increases with age, up to a point, and then falls. Do so by adding a quadratic term to equation 12.7.3. Substitute the resulting model into the expenditure relationship equation 12.7.1. What sign do you anticipate on the quadratic term?
   (c) Assume that the effect of age on the response of the beer expenditure relation 12.7.3 differs according to the *gender* of the individual. Develop a model that incorporates this possibility and discuss how the conjecture could be tested.

12.8 Consider the simple beer expenditure model

$$BE_i = \beta_{1i} + \beta_{2i} Y_i + e_i \qquad (12.7.6)$$

The intercept and slope parameters have an "i" subscript to indicate that they may vary over the sample of individuals. Suppose, however, we consider the possibility that each individual in the *population* has a *different* beer expenditure function, with parameters that vary randomly around a population average. That is, we model the parameter variation as

$$\beta_{1i} = \overline{\beta}_1 + u_{1i}$$
$$\beta_{2i} = \overline{\beta}_2 + u_{2i}$$

where $\bar{\beta}_1$ and $\bar{\beta}_2$ are the population average response coefficients and u_{1i} and u_{2i} are independent random errors reflecting individual differences from the population average. If we assume $u_{1i} \sim N(0, \sigma_1^2)$ and $u_{2i} \sim N(0, \sigma_2^2)$ what are the consequences, for estimation, of this random coefficient assumption? Proceed by substituting β_{1i} and β_{2i} into the model, separating the systematic and random components, and examining the properties of the resulting error term. Specifically, is least squares an appropriate estimation technique? If not, why not?

12.9 Consider the beer expenditure model

$$BE_i = \beta_{1i} + \beta_{2i} Y_i + e_i$$

as discussed in Section 12.5. Assume that the intercept and slope parameters vary with the gender of the individual, so

$$\beta_{1i} = \delta_1 + \delta_2 S_i$$
$$\beta_{2i} = \theta_1 + \theta_2 S_i$$

(a) Substitute these expressions for the parameter variation into the model. What are the regression functions $E[BE_i]$ for males and females?
(b) Using the data in Table 12.2, estimate the parameters of the statistical model in (a) using least squares applied to the entire data set (all $T = 40$ observations).
(c) Using the data in Table 12.2, apply least squares to estimate the simple expenditure model

$$BE_i = \beta_1 + \beta_2 Y_i + e_i$$

first using only the data on males, and then using only the data on females. Compare and contrast the results to those obtained in (b). Explain the reason for any differences.
(d) Define a new dummy variable $H_i = 1 - S_i$. Model the parameter variation as

$$\beta_{1i} = \alpha_1 H_i + \alpha_2 S_i$$
$$\beta_{2i} = \gamma_1 H_i + \gamma_2 S_i$$

Substitute these expressions into the expenditure model. What are the regression functions $E[BE_i]$ for males and females? Compare the results in part (a).
(e) Estimate the statistical model in (d) by least squares, using the data in Table 12.2, and compare and contrast the results to those obtained in (b) and (c).

12.10 In Table 12.5 are data on the weekly sales of a major brand of canned tuna by a supermarket chain in a large midwestern U. S. city during a recent calendar year. The variables are

Sal1   = unit sales of brand no. 1 canned tuna
Apr1   = price per can of brand no. 1 canned tuna
Apr2, 3 = price per can of brands nos. 2 and 3 of canned tuna
Disp   = a dummy variable that takes the value 1 if there is a store display for brand no. 1 during the week but no newspaper ad; 0 otherwise
DispAd = a dummy variable that takes the value 1 if there is a store display *and* a newspaper ad during the week; 0 otherwise

(a) Estimate, by least squares, the semilogarithmic model

$$\ln(\text{Sal1}) = \beta_1 + \beta_2 \text{Apr1} + \beta_3 \text{Apr2} + \beta_4 \text{Apr3} + \beta_5 \text{Disp} + \beta_6 \text{DispAd} + e$$

Table 12.5   Sales of Canned Tuna

Sal1	Apr1	Apr2	Apr3	Disp	DispAd
6439	0.66	0.82	0.79	1	0
3329	0.62	0.80	0.59	1	0
3415	0.62	0.77	0.63	0	0
2909	0.62	0.66	0.81	0	0
2598	0.63	0.65	0.81	0	0
3773	0.69	0.63	0.80	0	0
20383	0.63	0.65	0.78	0	1
11761	0.65	0.78	0.80	1	0
2614	0.77	0.62	0.77	1	0
2496	0.81	0.69	0.68	1	0
20811	0.68	0.85	0.70	0	1
8339	0.71	0.86	0.80	1	0
2793	0.84	0.86	0.80	1	0
2416	0.82	0.86	0.82	0	0
2837	0.84	0.86	0.81	0	0
2110	0.82	0.77	0.83	0	0
6422	0.78	0.82	0.81	1	0
4539	0.81	0.91	0.85	1	0
2493	0.89	0.91	0.82	0	0
2262	0.85	0.89	0.76	0	0
2145	0.85	0.89	0.77	0	0
11996	0.71	0.90	0.84	0	1
5847	0.78	0.92	0.83	1	0
2257	0.85	0.43	0.84	1	0
2461	0.87	0.82	0.83	0	0
2075	0.86	0.93	0.84	1	0
14044	0.77	0.90	0.82	0	1
4521	0.80	0.75	0.78	0	0
2052	0.85	0.76	0.80	0	0
1762	0.85	0.89	0.78	0	0
2375	0.87	0.91	0.78	0	0
3256	0.88	0.85	0.88	0	0
3280	0.83	0.78	0.90	0	0
27254	0.69	0.93	0.87	0	1
14129	0.69	0.92	0.90	1	0
2906	0.90	0.91	0.87	1	0
17630	0.69	0.68	0.69	0	1
9431	0.73	0.69	0.73	1	0
32820	0.61	0.73	0.87	0	1
12635	0.67	0.90	0.89	1	0
2509	0.89	0.91	0.69	1	0
2184	0.89	0.59	0.71	1	0
12485	0.70	0.65	0.87	0	1
6560	0.75	0.90	0.69	1	0
2647	0.92	0.91	0.74	1	0
2949	0.91	0.92	0.89	1	0
3016	0.91	0.91	0.90	1	0
2370	0.91	0.91	0.59	0	0
2006	0.91	0.76	0.62	0	0
2556	0.90	0.77	0.86	0	0
13808	0.69	0.76	0.88	0	1
6668	0.82	0.77	0.86	1	0

Source: Nielsen Marketing Research.

(b) Discuss and interpret the estimates of β_2, β_3, and β_4.

(c) Are the signs and *relative* magnitudes of the estimates of β_5 and β_6 consistent with economic logic? (*Note:* To interpret the dummy variables within this semilogarithmic equation, you may wish to consult "Estimation with Correctly Interpreted Dummy Variables in Semi-logarithmic Equations," by Peter Kennedy, *American Economic Review*, 71, 1981, p. 801.)

(d) Test, at the $\alpha = .05$ level of significance, each of the following hypotheses:

    (i) H_0: $\beta_5 = 0$ H_1: $\beta_5 \neq 0$

    (ii) H_0: $\beta_6 = 0$ H_1: $\beta_6 \neq 0$

    (iii) H_0: $\beta_5 = \beta_6 = 0$ H_1: β_5 or $\beta_6 \neq 0$

    (iv) H_0: $\beta_6 \geq \beta_5$ H_1: $\beta_6 < \beta_5$

Discuss the relevance of these hypothesis tests for the supermarket chain's executives.

12.11 In Table 12.6 are investment data, for the years 1935 to 1954, by two major U. S. corporations, Westinghouse and General Electric. The variables, for each firm, are

i = gross investment in plant and equipment (1947 $)

v = value of the firm = value of common and perferred stock (1947 $)

k = stock of capital (1947 $)

(a) For each corporation (separately) use least squares to estimate the investment functions

$$i = \beta_1 + \beta_2 v + \beta_3 k + e$$

(b) These two firms engage in similar activities, and we conjecture that the coefficients of v and k are identical for the two firms, but that the intercept parameters *may* be different for the firms' investment functions. Use

Table 12.6   Investment Data

	Westinghouse			General Electric	
i	v	k	i	v	k
12.93	191.50	1.80	33.10	1170.60	97.80
25.90	516.00	0.80	45.00	2015.80	104.40
35.05	729.00	7.40	77.20	2803.30	118.00
22.89	560.40	18.10	44.60	2039.70	156.20
18.84	519.90	23.50	48.10	2256.20	172.60
28.57	628.50	26.50	74.40	2132.20	186.60
48.51	537.10	36.20	113.00	1834.10	220.90
43.34	561.20	60.80	91.90	1588.00	287.80
37.02	617.20	84.40	61.30	1749.40	319.90
37.81	626.70	91.20	56.80	1687.20	321.30
39.27	737.20	92.40	93.60	2007.70	319.60
53.46	760.50	86.00	159.90	2208.30	346.00
55.56	581.40	111.10	147.20	1656.70	456.40
49.56	662.30	130.60	146.30	1604.40	543.40
32.04	583.80	141.80	98.30	1431.80	618.30
32.24	635.20	136.70	93.50	1610.50	647.40
54.38	723.80	129.70	135.20	1819.40	671.30
71.78	864.10	145.50	157.30	2079.70	726.10
90.08	1193.50	174.80	179.50	2371.60	800.30
68.60	1188.90	213.50	189.60	2759.90	888.90

a dummy variable to allow for differing firm intercepts, but *common* coefficients of v and k, and estimate the resulting model. What do you conclude about our conjecture?

(c) Use an intercept dummy and interaction variables to test whether or not the Westinghouse investment function is identical to the General Electric investment function. State and discuss your conclusion.

12.10   References

There are many text books with more examples of dummy variable use. Two are
GUJARATI, D. M. (1988) *Basic Econometrics*, 2nd Edition, New York: McGraw-Hill, Inc., Chapter 14.
JOHNSTON, J. (1984) *Econometric Methods*, 3rd Edition, New York: McGraw-Hill, Inc., Chapter 6.3.

Chapter 13

Collinear Economic Variables

New Key Words and Concepts

Multicollinearity   Linearly Dependent Columns of the X
Auxiliary Regressions   Matrix

To a large extent observed economic data are used for estimating economic relationships, and thus are nonexperimental or passively generated. Often they are simply "collected" for administrative or other purposes. Consequently, the outcome data are not the result of a planned experiment, where an experimental design is specified for the explanatory variables X. For example, in controlled experiments, such as in the production function example of Chapter 11, the right-hand-side variables in the statistical model can be assigned values, through an experimental design, in such a way that their individual effects can be identified and estimated with precision. When, as in economics, data are the result of an uncontrolled experiment that is carried out by nature and society, many of the economic variables *move together* in systematic ways. When this happens the variables are said to be *collinear*, and the problem is labeled *collinearity*, or *multicollinearity* when several variables are involved. When such data are observed, there is no guarantee that the data will be "rich in information," nor that it will be possible to isolate the economic relationship or parameters of interest. The incidence of, and the statistical consequences for, estimation and inference when using poor, ill-conditioned, or collinear data are examined in this chapter and some strategies for dealing with these problems are suggested.

13.1 The Economic Setting

The problem of "collinearity," or "multicollinearity," arises in nonexperimental data when society's experimental design for the explanatory variables is such that their individual effects cannot be isolated and the corresponding parameter magnitudes cannot be determined with the desired degree of precision. In this section we give some examples of common economic models in which we can expect data on explanatory variables to move in systematic ways and thus exhibit what we define as collinearity.

As a first example, consider an economic model designed to explain the weekly sales of a specific item by a supermarket. The factors that affect the sales of the item include, among other things, the price of the product, the prices of competitive and complementary goods, and the extent of marketing or advertising efforts devoted to the product. When the experimental design is determined by the uncontrolled operation of the market, one group of variables that may move together in a systematic way are the prices of the product and its competitors. Under this situation, it would not be a surprise to find in a sample of data that when one price is going up all the prices are going up, and when one price is falling all are falling. These systematic, collinear relationships between the prices are the type that are a potential problem.

Alternatively, within this example, there is another group of explanatory variables in which relationship patterns may be found. Marketing and advertising campaigns are often concerted efforts in which several strategies or devices are coordinated to occur at the same time. A product may be advertised by using coupons, store displays, and newspaper ads concurrently. If we used dummy variables to indicate the presence or absence of any of these types of marketing strategies, we may find that the dummy variables generally take the value 1 during the same weeks, and the value 0 in the same weeks. Marketing strategies based on using these tools together ensure that there will be systematic relationships between the variables used to indicate their presence. Once again this is a potential source of difficulty if one of the objectives of the modeling effort is to measure the individual effects of coupons, store displays, and newspaper ads.

As a second example consider an aggregate consumption function in which we express consumption in a given time period as a function of income in the current and preceding time periods, plus perhaps some other factors. A rationale for including income in earlier time periods may be that changes in income affect consumption expenditures in a systematic way only after a delay of one, two, or more periods, that is, the total impact is distributed over several future periods. It is clear that the dynamics of macroeconomic relationships are crucially important for the proper timing of fiscal and monetary policy and thus are important to measure. Income at the aggregate level is a strongly *trended* variable over time. It follows a cycle related to the business cycle. Because of this pattern we find that income in the current and preceding periods, taken as separate variables, are highly correlated. In fact most macroeconomic aggregates exhibit broad systematic patterns. When several of these variables, or their lagged values, appear on the right-hand side of an economic model, we can anticipate that the resulting variables will be highly correlated, and thus they may cause statistical problems if our objective is to isolate individual time effects of income.

A related phenomenon occurs in models designed to explain capital expenditures by manufacturing industries. In each quarter we observe a certain amount of expenditure on plant and equipment by business firms. Even within a single industry these expenditures represent the initiation and continuance of a wide variety of investment projects. Because of the nature of the budgetary process in any institutional setting, private or public, current capital expenditures are the result of decisions made one, two or more years earlier. An economic model designed to explain current capital expenditure will naturally include, as explanatory variables, capital appropriations made during each of the previous eight or more quarters. Quarterly capital appropriations are strongly trended and cyclical in nature, and consequently any lagged values of this variable are highly correlated. Thus it is logical to anticipate collinear data for the X variables in the statistical model explaining capital expenditures as a function of lagged capital appropriations. This example is representative of an important class of models that use *finite* distributed lags, as will be considered in detail in Chapter 21.

As a final example, consider a production relationship explaining output over time as a function of the amounts of various quantities of inputs employed. In aggregate, or in a cross section of firms, there are certain factors of production (inputs), such as labor and capital, that are *used in relatively fixed proportions*. As production increases, the amounts of two, or more, such inputs reflect proportionate increases. Proportionate relationships between variables are the very sort of systematic relationships that epitomize "collinearity." It is clear, a priori, that any effort to measure the individual or separate effects (marginal products) of various mixes of inputs from these data will be difficult.

In the following section we define exactly the type of systematic relationships between variables that are called collinear. Before proceeding, however, we note that it is not just *relationships between variables* in a sample of data that make it difficult to isolate the separate effects of individual explanatory variables in an economic or statistical model. A related problem exists when the values of an explanatory variable do not vary or change much within the sample of data. When an explanatory variable exhibits little variation then it is difficult to detect or isolate what impact the variable has within the model. This problem also falls within the context of "collinearity."

13.2 The Nature of Collinear Data

In order to be specific about the problems caused by collinearity, we examine the aggregate economic data used by Klein and Goldberger (1955) that is reproduced in Table 13.1. These time series data are U. S. domestic consumption (c), wage income (w), nonwage-nonfarm income (p), and farm income (a) for the years 1928 to 1950, with the war years 1942 to 1944 deleted. The economic relationship we wish to investigate is the relationship between consumption and the three components of income. We *expect* the components of income to move together, over time, due to linkages within the economy. Thus, we can anticipate that we may encounter problems associated with using collinear economic variables on the right-hand side of a statistical model. The statistical model employed by Klein and Goldberger is

$$c_t = \beta_1 + \beta_2 w_t + \beta_3 p_t + \beta_4 a_t + e_t \tag{13.2.1}$$

Table 13.1 The Klein-Goldberger Data

Year	c	w	p	a
1928	58.2	39.21	17.73	4.39
1929	62.2	42.31	20.29	4.60
1930	58.6	40.37	18.83	3.25
1931	56.6	39.15	17.44	2.61
1932	51.6	34.00	14.76	1.67
1933	51.1	33.59	13.39	2.44
1934	54.0	36.88	13.93	2.39
1935	57.2	39.27	14.67	5.00
1936	62.8	45.51	17.20	3.93
1937	65.0	46.06	17.15	5.48
1938	63.9	44.16	15.92	4.37
1939	67.5	47.68	17.59	4.51
1940	71.3	50.79	18.49	4.90
1941	76.6	57.78	19.18	6.37
1945	86.3	78.97	19.12	8.42
1946	95.7	73.54	19.76	9.27
1947	98.3	71.92	17.55	8.87
1948	100.3	74.01	19.17	9.30
1949	103.2	75.51	20.20	6.95
1950	108.9	80.97	22.12	7.15

and it is assumed that the error term satisfies the properties of the classical linear statistical model. The least squares estimates are

$$\hat{c}_t = 8.133 \quad + \quad 1.059 w_t \quad + \quad 0.452 p_t \quad + \quad 0.121 a_t$$

(0.91)	(6.10)	(0.69)	(0.11)	t – value
8.92	0.17	0.66	1.09	Std Error
(−10.78, 27.04)	(0.69, 1.43)	(−0.94, 1.84)	(−2.18, 2.43)	95% Interval Est

$$(13.2.2)$$

The R^2 for the estimated model is .95 and the F-statistic for the overall significance of the model is 107.37, which is large relative to the $\alpha = .01$ critical value of the F-distribution $F_{(3,16)} = 5.29$.

The effects of collinearity are readily observed. First, the estimate of the incremental effect of wage income on consumption, 1.059, is large, in that it implies that a $1 increase in wage income leads to more than a $1 increase in consumption expenditure. Second, the effects of nonwage-nonfarm and farm income do not appear to be individually significant, although theoretically they should be important variables in explaining consumption behavior. The lack of individual significance occurs despite the overall significance of the statistical model and the high R^2. The imprecision of the least squares estimates is clearly seen by examining the interval estimates. Klein and Goldberger (1955) state that interrelationships "among the different components of income mask separate contributions of each component toward the explanation of spending behavior."

13.3   The Statistical Model

Denote, as usual, the linear statistical model as

$$\mathbf{y} = X\boldsymbol{\beta} + \mathbf{e} \qquad (13.3.1)$$

where we will assume the random disturbances $\mathbf{e}$ have zero means, $E[\mathbf{e}] = \mathbf{0}$, and covariance matrix $\text{cov}(\mathbf{e}) = \sigma^2 I_T$. Represent the $(T \times K)$ matrix X as $X = (\mathbf{x}_1, \mathbf{x}_2, ..., \mathbf{x}_K)$, where $\mathbf{x}_i$ is the ith column of X and represents the T observations on the corresponding explanatory variable. *Exact or perfect collinearity* exists when there is an *exact* linear relationship among the explanatory variables (columns of X). That is, one or more relations of the form

$$\mathbf{x}_1 c_1 + \mathbf{x}_2 c_2 + ... + \mathbf{x}_K c_K = \mathbf{0} \qquad (13.3.2)$$

exist, where the constants c_i are not all zero. For example, if $\mathbf{x}_2 = \mathbf{x}_3 + 2\mathbf{x}_4$ then the variables $\mathbf{x}_2$, $\mathbf{x}_3$, and $\mathbf{x}_4$ are exactly linearly related. When equation 13.3.2 holds true, the variables are linearly dependent and the number of linearly independent columns of the matrix X is less than K. Following the discussion in Chapter 9, the $(K \times K)$ matrix $X'X$ is singular and the inverse matrix $(X'X)^{-1}$ does not exist. See Exercise 13.1.

In practice, for economic variables, relationships like equation 13.3.2 will usually not hold *exactly*. When linear relationships between economic variables do not hold exactly, but only approximately, the data are said to be collinear, or multicollinear. If equation 13.3.2 *holds only approximately*, then X has K linearly independent columns, the cross-product matrix $X'X$ is nonsingular, and the matrix $(X'X)^{-1}$ exists, *but near singularity of the X'X matrix causes the elements of the inverse matrix to be very large*.

Systematic linear relationships or near linear relationships between explanatory variables have unfortunate statistical consequences that we identify in the following section.

13.4   The Statistical Consequences of Collinearity

The consequences of collinear relationships among explanatory variables in a statistical model may be summarized as follows:

1. *Whenever there are one or more exact linear relationships among the explanatory variables, represented by the columns of the X matrix, then the condition of exact collinearity, or exact multicollinearity, exists, the X′X matrix is singular, and the least squares estimator* $\mathbf{b} = (X'X)^{-1}X'\mathbf{y}$ *is not defined.* Thus we *cannot* obtain estimates of β using the least squares estimation rule.

When the data on right-hand-side variables exhibit *nearly exact* linear dependencies, or collinearity, the following statistical consequences result:

2. When nearly exact linear dependencies among the explanatory variables exist, some elements of $(X'X)^{-1}$ may be large. Since the covariance matrix of the least squares estimator is $\text{cov}(\mathbf{b}) = \sigma^2(X'X)^{-1}$, this means that the sampling variances, standard errors, and covariances of the least squares estimator may be large. Large standard errors for the least squares estimators imply that sampling variability is high, that interval estimates are wide, and that the information provided by the sample data about the unknown parameters is relatively imprecise.

3. When estimator standard errors are large, it is likely that the usual *t*-tests will lead to the conclusion that parameter values are not significantly different from zero. This outcome occurs despite possibly high R^2 or "*F*-values" indicating "significant" explanatory power of the model for this combination of variables. The problem is that *collinear variables do not provide enough information to estimate their separate effects*, even though economic theory, and their total effect, may indicate their importance in the relationship.

4. Estimators may be very sensitive to the addition or deletion of a few observations, or the deletion of an apparently insignificant variable.

5. Despite the difficulties in isolating the effects of individual variables from such a sample, accurate forecasts may still be possible if the nature of the collinear relationship remains the same within the new (future) sample observations. For example, in an aggregate production function where the inputs labor and capital are nearly collinear, accurate forecasts of output may be possible for a particular ratio of inputs but not for various mixes of inputs.

In the next section we define multicollinearity precisely and then summarize its consequences.

13.5   Identifying Multicollinearity

Given the discussion of the previous section, and given a sample of data, we can identify several ways to detect, in advance, collinear relationships between variables and the effects they are likely to have.

1. Sample correlation coefficients between pairs of explanatory variables can indicate linear associations between them. Since the design matrix X is treated as fixed, the sample correlations are strictly descriptive measures of linear association. A commonly used rule of thumb is that a correlation coefficient between two explanatory variables greater than 0.8 or 0.9 indicates a strong linear association and a potentially harmful collinear relationship.

The sample correlation matrix for the explanatory variables in the Klein–Goldberger model is given in Table 13.2. In the sample of data, the correlation coefficient of 0.91 indicates a strong linear association between wage income and farm income, and thus a potential problem.

2. The use of sample correlations is an "easy" way to identify collinearity, but unfortunately this tool does not give any insights into collinear relationships involving *three* or more variables. For the multivariate case we need another diagnostic tool.

When exact linear relationships like equation 13.3.2 exist, it is possible to solve for one of the variables involved. Let us suppose that the constant $c_K \neq 0$ so that we can solve equation 13.3.2 for $\mathbf{x}_K$ as

$$
\begin{aligned}
\mathbf{x}_K &= \mathbf{x}_1\left(-c_1/c_K\right)+\ldots+\mathbf{x}_{K-1}\left(-c_{K-1}/c_K\right) \\
&= \mathbf{x}_1 a_1 + \mathbf{x}_2 a_2 + \ldots + \mathbf{x}_{K-1} a_{K-1}
\end{aligned} \tag{13.5.1}
$$

For every exact relationship like equation 13.3.2 we can solve for one of the variables as in equation 13.5.1.

In practice, exact multicollinearity rarely occurs. Instead collinearity relationships are not exact and hold only approximately. One convenient way to represent an inexact relationship among the columns of X is to specify that equation 13.5.1 holds true, but with an error. That is,

$$
\mathbf{x}_K = \mathbf{x}_1 a_1 + \mathbf{x}_2 a_2 + \ldots + \mathbf{x}_{K-1} a_{K-1} + \mathbf{v} \tag{13.5.2}
$$

where $\mathbf{v}$ is a vector of constants that makes the left- and right-hand sides of the equation equal. It is *not* a "random error" in the sense of the linear statistical model, even though equation 13.5.2 *looks like* a regression equation. Relations like equation 13.5.2, where one right-hand-side economic variable is written as a linear function of the other right-hand-side variables plus the difference (or error) $\mathbf{v}$, are called "auxiliary regressions," since they have the form of a regression model but are only descriptive of the collinearity relationship that exists.

Examination of equation 13.5.2 makes it clear that the better the "fit" of the auxiliary regression the more nearly the relationship 13.5.1 holds, and the more severe the collinearity.

The auxiliary regression also provides a direct way to demonstrate some of the statistical consequences of collinear variables when using the least squares estimator, since it can be shown that the variance of the least squares estimator of β_K is

$$
\text{var}(b_K) = \frac{\sigma^2}{\sum_{t=1}^{T} \hat{v}_t^2} \tag{13.5.3}
$$

Table 13.2 Correlation Matrix for Klein–Goldberger Data

	w	*p*	*a*
w	1.000		
p	0.718	1.000	
a	0.915	0.630	1.000

where $\hat{v}_t^2$ is the squared least squares residual obtained by fitting the auxiliary regression 13.5.2 by least squares, as if it were a real statistical model. This is illustrated in Exercise 13.5. Intuitively, the precision of estimation of a single parameter is the ratio of the uncertainty in the model (σ^2) to the amount of variability in the Kth explanatory variable that is *not* explained by the other $(K - 1)$ explanatory variables $\left(\Sigma\hat{v}_t^2\right)$. This relationship shows explicitly that the smaller the sum of squared errors from auxiliary regressions like equation 13.5.2, relative to the error variance σ^2, the larger the sampling variance of the associated least squares parameter estimator. See Exercises 13.2 and 13.3 for more on this.

Auxiliary regressions of the form of equation 13.5.2 can be estimated for each of the independent variables. If the R^2 is high, or the sum of squared errors is low, then a collinear relationship is indicated. It is important to examine the R^2 *and* the sum of squared errors of the auxiliary regressions, since collinearity actually appears in two guises. The first is the "common" way of thinking about collinear variables in which a linear dependence between the variables is stressed. A high auxiliary regression R^2 indicates this type of problem.

The other way in which nonexperimental data can cause problems appears as a *lack of variation* in the values of a control variable about its mean. This is not usually thought of as a "collinearity" problem but it is, since in this case there is a linear dependence between the control variable and the intercept variable, which is a column of ones. The auxiliary regression R^2 may not be high, since the other control variables are not involved in the collinear relationship. The key factor is the sum of squared least squares residuals from the auxiliary regression. If the variable exhibits little variation, for instance, as measured by the coefficient of variation, to begin with, the least squares residuals from the auxiliary regression will vary even less.

13.6   Possible Solutions for Collinear Data

The problem of multicollinearity is that the experimental design is such that the data do not contain enough "information" about the individual effects of control variables to permit us to estimate the parameters of the statistical model precisely. One solution is to obtain more information and include it in the analysis.

One form the new information can take is more, and better, sample data. Unfortunately, in economics this is not always possible. Cross-sectional data are expensive to obtain and, with time series data, not only must one wait for the data to appear, but if the structure of the economy changes, as the analysis is spread over a longer time period, then we face the varying parameter problem discussed in Chapter 12. Alternatively, if new data are obtained via the same passive observational process as the original sample of data, then the new observations may suffer the same collinear relationships and provide little in the way of new, independent information. Under these circumstances the new data will help little to improve the precision of the least squares estimates.

13.6.1   Using Nonsample Information

An alternative to introducing new sample information is to add structure by introducing *nonsample* information in the form of restrictions on the parameters. The idea of introducing nonsample information in the form of *linear* restrictions on the parameters, of the form $R\beta = \mathbf{r}$, was introduced in Chapter 11. Recall that the matrix R defines the information on β in the form of a known $(J \times K)$ matrix that has J linearly independent rows. The vector $\mathbf{r}$ is a known $(J \times 1)$ column of constants. This information is then combined with the sample information by using the restricted least squares estimator

$$\mathbf{b*} = \mathbf{b} + (X'X)^{-1} R' \left[R(X'X)^{-1} R' \right]^{-1} (\mathbf{r} - R\mathbf{b}) \qquad (13.6.1)$$

To illustrate, let us consider restrictions imposed by Klein and Goldberger on the parameter values of their consumption relation. They were willing to assume that the effect of wage income on consumption (β_2) is greater than the effect of nonwage-non-farm income (β_3) and farm income (β_4). Specifically, based on prior empirical work, they specify

$$\beta_3 = 0.75\beta_2, \qquad \beta_4 = 0.625\beta_2$$

or

$$R\boldsymbol{\beta} = \begin{bmatrix} 0 & -0.75 & 1 & 0 \\ 0 & -0.625 & 0 & 1 \end{bmatrix} \begin{bmatrix} \beta_1 \\ \beta_2 \\ \beta_3 \\ \beta_4 \end{bmatrix} = \begin{bmatrix} 0 \\ 0 \end{bmatrix} = \mathbf{r} \qquad (13.6.2)$$

The effects of these restrictions are summarized in Table 13.3.

In Table 13.3 the unrestricted least squares estimates are reported as Model 1. Model 2 results from the imposition of only the first restriction, model 3 from the imposition of only the second restriction, and Model 4 from both restrictions. Note that the effect of the restrictions is to lower the standard errors of each of the estimated coefficients, and, of course, to yield estimates that satisfy the constraints. The F-statistic reported is the usual F-statistic for the test of the null hypothesis $H_0: R\boldsymbol{\beta} = \mathbf{r}$, which is distributed $F_{(J, T-K)}$ if the null hypothesis is true. The $\alpha = .05$ critical value for the individual null hypotheses $\beta_3 = .75\beta_2$ and $\beta_4 = .625\beta_2$ is $F_{(1, 16)} = 4.49$ and for the joint null hypotheses, stated in Equation 13.6.2, it is $F_{(2, 16)} = 3.63$. Given the small values of the computed F-statistic, the restrictions (linear hypotheses) imposed are deemed consistent with the data.

We have shown that using nonsample information in the form of linear constraints on the parameter values reduces estimator sampling variability. However, the restricted estimator is *biased* unless the restrictions are *exactly* true. Thus it is important to use good nonsample information, so that the reduced sampling variability is not bought at a price of large estimator biases.

Table 13.3 Effect of Exact Restrictions on Klein–Goldberger Model (Standard Errors in Parentheses Based on Restricted SSE)

Parameter/Model	1	2	3	4
Constant	8.133	4.600	8.486	5.605
	(8.92)	(4.75)	(8.68)	(3.68)
w	1.059	1.010	0.989	0.966
	(0.17)	(0.14)	(0.08)	(0.05)
p	0.452	0.758	0.491	0.725
	(0.66)	(0.10)	(0.63)	(0.04)
a	0.121	0.245	0.618	0.604
	(1.09)	(1.03)	(0.05)	(12.38)
F-statistic	—	0.22	0.21	0.17

13.7 Collinearity Summary

In this chapter we have defined the problem of collinear economic variables, or multicollinearity, and examined how it affects the least squares estimator. Collinearity among variables of interest is always present to some degree in passively generated economic data. Rarely are economists able to plan their experiments so that they can isolate the individual effects that are of interest. The tools we have presented are basic ones for identifying and possibly mitigating the impacts of collinear variables in the design matrix X. More sophisticated procedures exist and are discussed in Judge et al. (1988, Chapter 21) and the references contained therein. Other introductory discussions of collinearity may be found in Gujarati (1988, Chapter 10) and Maddala (1992, Chapter 7).

It is worth reiterating that collinearity is *not* a violation of any basic assumption of the linear statistical model. The least squares estimator is *still* the best linear unbiased estimate. The problem is that the best linear unbiased estimator *may* be too imprecise to yield useful results. If estimates are adequately precise, then the degree of collinearity is not severe enough to warrant remedial measures.

It is also important to remember that using nonsample information can cure the collinearity problem by improving estimator precision. However, if the nonsample information is *not correct*, then the restricted estimator is *biased*, and the size of the bias is unobservable! Thus there exists the difficulty of trading one problem off for another.

13.8 Exercises

13.1 In the context of the simple linear regression model

$$y_t = \beta_1 + x_t\beta_2 + e_t, \qquad t = 1,\ldots,10$$

where $x_t = 1 + a$, $t = 1,\ldots,5$ and $x_t = 1 - a$, $t = 6,\ldots,10$
(a) Write down the (10×2) matrix X.
(b) Calculate $X'X$.
(c) Use the formula for finding the inverse of a (2×2) matrix,

$$\begin{bmatrix} a & c \\ b & d \end{bmatrix}^{-1} = \frac{1}{ad - bc}\begin{bmatrix} d & -c \\ -b & a \end{bmatrix}$$

to calculate $(X'X)^{-1}$.
(d) Verify that $(X'X)^{-1}$ is the inverse of $X'X$.
(e) Calculate $(X'X)^{-1}$ for $a = 10, 5, 1, .1$, and 0.
(f) How does this relate to the problem of collinearity?

13.2 By using the data in Table 2.2 of Chapter 2, estimate by least squares a model explaining housing starts (HS) as a function of GNP, the unemployment rate (U), the new home mortgage rate (M), the prime rate (R), and the money supply ($M1$).
(a) Do you expect that collinearity may be a problem? If so, why?
(b) Examine the simple correlation coefficients between the explanatory variables and comment on them.
(c) Obtain the auxiliary regressions for all the explanatory variables and comment on them, as they relate to collinearity.

13.3   To demonstrate the effects of collinearity consider the following experiment. Modify the design matrix X, given below, by constructing a fourth variable that is

$$\mathbf{x}_4 = 3\mathbf{x}_2 + 4\mathbf{x}_3 + c\mathbf{v}$$

where $\mathbf{x}_i$ is the ith column of X and $\mathbf{v}$ is a vector of "normal random numbers," from a $N(0, 1)$ distribution, that appears adjacent to X. The scalar c is a constant. Augment the matrix X with the variable X_4, letting the scalar c take the values 10, 1, 0.1, 0.001, and 0.0, respectively. What happens to the collinearity in the augmented X matrix as $c \to 0$? For each value of c construct and examine the determinant of $X'X$ and the elements of $(X'X)^{-1}$.

$$
X =
\begin{bmatrix}
1.0 & .693 & .693 \\
1.0 & 1.733 & .693 \\
1.0 & .693 & 1.386 \\
1.0 & 1.733 & 1.386 \\
1.0 & .693 & 1.792 \\
1.0 & 2.340 & .693 \\
1.0 & 1.733 & 1.792 \\
1.0 & 2.340 & 1.386 \\
1.0 & 2.340 & 1.792 \\
1.0 & .693 & .693 \\
1.0 & .693 & 1.386 \\
1.0 & 1.733 & .693 \\
1.0 & 1.733 & 1.386 \\
1.0 & .693 & 1.792 \\
1.0 & 2.340 & .693 \\
1.0 & 1.733 & 1.792 \\
1.0 & 2.340 & 1.386 \\
1.0 & 2.340 & 1.792 \\
1.0 & 1.733 & 1.386 \\
1.0 & .693 & .693
\end{bmatrix}
\quad
\mathbf{v} =
\begin{bmatrix}
0.1930 \\
-0.5041 \\
-2.3183 \\
0.2572 \\
1.7837 \\
1.6270 \\
0.7078 \\
2.2516 \\
-0.4618 \\
-1.3475 \\
0.2338 \\
0.2262 \\
0.6286 \\
0.2443 \\
-0.5685 \\
0.8531 \\
2.2266 \\
0.0742 \\
-0.5271 \\
0.8041
\end{bmatrix}
$$

13.4   Repeat Exercise 13.3, using

$$\mathbf{x}_4 = \bar{x}_3 \cdot \mathbf{x}_1 + c\mathbf{v}$$

where $\bar{x}_3$ is the arithmetic mean of $\mathbf{x}_3$ and $\mathbf{x}_1$ is a column of ones. What is happening to the variability of $\mathbf{x}_4$ about its arithmetic mean as $c \to 0$?

13.5   Use the Klein–Goldberger data in Table 13.1 to estimate auxiliary regressions of w, p, and a on each other *and* an intercept. Verify that equation 13.5.3 gives the estimated variance of the least squares estimator for each parameter when the estimated error variance is used for the true error variance.

13.6   In Table 2.5 of Chapter 2 (Exercise 2.20), there are data on construction costs of 32 nuclear power plants in the United States. Consider the statistical model

$$\log(C) = \beta_1 + \beta_2 D + \beta_3 \log(T_1) + \beta_4 \log(T_2) + \beta_5 \log(S) + \beta_6 Pr + \beta_7 NE$$
$$+ \beta_8 CT + \beta_9 BW + \beta_{10} \log(N) + \beta_{11} PT + e$$

(a)   Estimate the model parameters by least squares.
(b)   Do you find evidence that multicollinearity is a problem? If so, explain why. If not, why not?

13.7   In Table 12.5 of Chapter 12 (Exercise 12.10), we introduced data on the weekly unit sales of a major brand of canned tuna by a large supermarket in the Midwest region of the United States. Table 13.4 contains some additional variables:

Apr4, 5: The price per can of two additional competitive brands of tuna.

Rpr1–5: The "regular" price of each of the five brands of canned tuna. (Thus Apr1–5 are "discounted" prices.)

NoAd: A dummy variable that is 1 if no promotion for brand no. 1 of canned tuna appears during the week.

Ad: A dummy variable that is 1 if *only* a newspaper ad appears during the week.

(a) Using the data in Tables 12.5 and 13.4 and least squares, estimate the linear model

$$\log(\text{Sal1}) = f(\text{Apr1} - 5, \text{Rpr1} - 5)$$

Examine this model for the presence of multicollinearity.

(b) Include the variables Ad, Disp, and Dispad to the right-hand side of the model in (a). Explain the results.

(c) Delete Ad from the model used in part (b). Discuss the results.

13.8 Table 13.5 contains a data set used by Longley to examine the accuracy of computer software available in the mid-1960s.

(a) Use least squares to estimate the model

$$\text{total employment} = f(\text{Year, GNP Deflator, GNP, Armed Forces})$$

(b) Do you find evidence of multicollinearity? Explain.

(c) Delete one or two observations and reestimate the model. What changes do you observe?

13.9 In Chapter 11 production functions were considered of the form $Q = f(L, K)$, where Q is the output measure and L and K are labor and capital inputs, respectively. A popular functional form is the Cobb-Douglas equation.

(a) Use the data in Table 13.6 to estimate the Cobb-Douglas production function. Is there evidence of multicollinearity?

(b) A generalization of the Cobb Douglas production function is the "translog" production function:

$$\log(Q) = \beta_1 + \beta_2 \log(L) + \beta_3 \log(K) + \beta_4 \left[\log(L) \cdot \log(K)\right] + \beta_5 \left[\log(L)\right]^2 + \beta_6 \left[\log(K)\right]^2 + e$$

Use the data in Table 13.6 to estimate this production function. Is there a multicollinearity problem when estimating this equation? Explain.

13.10 In Chapter 6 we considered the simple linear regression model

$$y_t = \beta_1 + \beta_2 x_t + e_t$$

and showed that the variance of the least squares estimator b_2 is

$$\text{var}(b_2) = \frac{\sigma^2}{\displaystyle\sum_{t=1}^{T}(x_t - \bar{x})^2}$$

Suppose two alternative experimental designs with $T = 5$ observations were offered to you for use:

$$\mathbf{x}_a = \{4.8 \quad 4.9 \quad 5.0 \quad 5.1 \quad 5.2\}$$
$$\mathbf{x}_b = \{1.0 \quad 3.0 \quad 5.0 \quad 7.0 \quad 9.0\}$$

Table 13.4 More Data on Sales of Canned Tuna

Apr4	Apr5	Rpr1	Rpr2	Rpr3	Rpr4	Rpr5	Noad	Ad
0.70	0.59	0.82	0.85	0.80	0.71	0.59	0	0
0.68	0.59	0.74	0.83	0.90	0.70	0.59	0	0
0.59	0.59	0.73	0.83	0.87	0.72	0.59	1	0
0.59	0.59	0.73	0.86	0.81	0.71	0.59	1	0
0.68	0.59	0.72	0.87	0.81	0.71	0.59	1	0
0.69	0.59	0.74	0.89	0.81	0.70	0.59	1	0
0.67	0.59	0.81	0.86	0.79	0.69	0.59	0	0
0.59	0.59	0.83	0.82	0.81	0.72	0.59	0	0
0.59	0.59	0.77	0.86	0.81	0.71	0.59	0	0
0.59	0.59	0.81	0.86	0.89	0.69	0.59	0	0
0.68	0.59	0.86	0.87	0.87	0.69	0.59	0	0
0.69	0.59	0.85	0.89	0.82	0.70	0.59	0	0
0.70	0.59	0.84	0.88	0.82	0.70	0.59	0	0
0.69	0.59	0.83	0.88	0.83	0.70	0.59	1	0
0.69	0.59	0.85	0.89	0.82	0.70	0.59	1	0
0.60	0.59	0.83	0.88	0.84	0.69	0.59	1	0
0.60	0.59	0.85	0.89	0.82	0.70	0.59	0	0
0.60	0.59	0.85	0.93	0.85	0.70	0.59	0	0
0.60	0.59	0.89	0.93	0.84	0.70	0.59	1	0
0.69	0.59	0.85	0.91	0.91	0.69	0.59	1	0
0.69	0.59	0.85	0.91	0.91	0.69	0.59	1	0
0.69	0.59	0.86	0.92	0.85	0.70	0.59	0	0
0.69	0.59	0.88	0.94	0.85	0.70	0.59	0	0
0.69	0.59	0.86	0.95	0.84	0.70	0.59	0	0
0.69	0.59	0.87	0.93	0.83	0.70	0.59	1	0
0.69	0.59	0.88	0.95	0.84	0.70	0.59	0	0
0.67	0.59	0.93	0.92	0.82	0.68	0.59	0	0
0.60	0.59	0.89	0.96	0.78	0.71	0.59	1	0
0.60	0.59	0.85	0.93	0.83	0.70	0.59	1	0
0.69	0.59	0.86	0.92	0.93	0.69	0.59	1	0
0.72	0.59	0.87	0.92	0.92	0.72	0.59	1	0
0.77	0.59	0.88	0.93	0.88	0.78	0.59	1	0
0.67	0.59	0.89	0.98	0.90	0.73	0.59	1	0
0.67	0.58	1.00	0.95	0.88	0.73	0.59	0	0
0.78	0.58	0.98	0.94	0.91	0.78	0.59	0	0
0.76	0.58	0.93	0.94	0.93	0.78	0.59	0	0
0.68	0.58	0.98	0.99	0.96	0.77	0.59	0	0
0.68	0.58	0.96	0.99	0.95	0.77	0.59	0	0
0.71	0.58	0.97	0.97	0.90	0.75	0.58	0	0
0.58	0.58	0.94	0.95	0.91	0.76	0.58	0	0
0.59	0.58	0.91	0.95	0.95	0.77	0.58	0	0
0.76	0.58	0.91	0.98	0.96	0.79	0.58	0	0
0.77	0.58	0.98	0.97	0.90	0.79	0.58	0	0
0.77	0.58	0.96	0.93	0.97	0.79	0.58	0	0
0.79	0.58	0.95	0.95	0.95	0.81	0.58	0	0
0.79	0.58	0.93	0.96	0.92	0.80	0.58	0	0
0.79	0.58	0.93	0.95	0.92	0.81	0.58	0	0
0.71	0.58	0.93	0.94	0.95	0.76	0.58	1	0
0.61	0.58	0.93	0.96	0.94	0.78	0.58	1	0
0.61	0.58	0.92	0.97	0.89	0.77	0.58	1	0
0.60	0.58	0.99	0.96	0.92	0.76	0.58	0	0
0.61	0.58	0.96	0.96	0.93	0.75	0.58	0	0

Source: Nielsen Marketing Research.

Table 13.5 The Longley Data

Year	GNP Deflator	GNP (millions $)	Armed Forces	Total Employment
1947	83.00	234289	1590	60323
1948	88.50	259426	1456	61122
1949	88.20	258054	1616	60171
1950	89.50	284599	1650	61187
1951	96.20	328975	3099	63221
1952	98.10	346999	3594	63639
1953	99.00	365385	3547	64989
1954	100.00	363112	3350	63761
1955	101.20	397469	3048	66019
1956	104.60	419180	2857	67857
1957	108.40	442769	2798	68169
1958	110.80	444546	2637	66513
1959	112.60	482704	2552	68655
1960	114.20	502601	2514	69564
1961	115.70	518173	2572	69331
1962	116.90	554894	2827	70551

Source: J. W. Longley., "An Appraisal of Least Squares Programs for the Electronic Computer from the Point of View of the User," *Journal of the American Statistical Association*, 62, 1967, pp. 819–841.

(a) Other things being the same, which set of x values would you prefer to use? Why?

(b) How does your answer in (a) relate to the problem of multicollinearity?

13.11 Consider the following regression model, in which the data are in deviation from the mean form. That is, $y_t = Y_t - \bar{Y}$, $x_{t2} = X_{t2} - \bar{X}_2$, and $x_{t3} = X_{t3} - \bar{X}_3$.

$$y_t = \beta_2 x_{t2} + \beta_3 x_{t3} + e_t$$

It can be shown that the variances of the least squares estimators b_2 and b_3 and their covariance are

$$\text{var}(b_2) = \frac{\sigma^2}{\sum_{t=1}^{T} x_{t2}^2 \left(1 - r_{23}^2\right)}$$

$$\text{var}(b_3) = \frac{\sigma^2}{\sum_{t=1}^{T} x_{t3}^2 \left(1 - r_{23}^2\right)}$$

$$\text{cov}(b_2, b_3) = \frac{-r_{23}^2 \sigma^2}{\left(1 - r_{23}^2\right) \sqrt{\Sigma x_{t2}^2 \, \Sigma x_{t3}^2}}$$

where r_{23}^2 is the square of the sample correlation coefficient between x_{t2} and x_{t3},

$$r_{23}^2 = \frac{\left(\Sigma x_{t2} x_{t3}\right)^2}{\Sigma x_{t2}^2 \, \Sigma x_{t3}^2}$$

Table 13.6   Production Data

log(Q)	log(L)	log(K)
−1.35900	−1.47841	−0.22065
−1.69500	−1.35480	−1.39030
0.19300	−0.19723	−0.26007
−0.64900	−0.26527	−0.67139
−0.16500	−0.70320	−0.27707
−0.27000	−0.71949	−0.85567
−0.47300	−0.38861	−0.79407
0.03100	−0.29035	−0.20212
−0.56300	−0.31883	−0.16842
−0.12500	−0.36384	−0.04291
−2.21800	−0.78089	−2.47694
−3.63300	−0.01918	−3.86323
−5.58600	−6.21461	−1.22078
−0.77300	−0.84630	−1.28374
−1.31500	−1.46534	−0.60514
−1.67800	−0.40947	−2.04794
−3.87900	−0.46045	−4.07454
−2.30100	−2.83022	−0.09872
−1.37700	−0.20949	−1.50058
−2.27000	−0.27707	−1.93102
−2.53900	−2.99573	−1.82635
−5.15000	−0.19480	−5.11600
−0.32400	−0.72774	−0.17913
−0.25300	−0.38273	−0.65201
−1.53000	−2.15417	−0.07257
−0.61400	−0.82098	−0.70320
−1.15100	−0.78526	−1.68740
−2.08900	−1.07294	−2.38597
−0.95100	−1.02722	−0.72361
−1.27500	−1.82016	−0.06828

(a) If $r_{23} = 0$ what do the covariance and variances become? How does this relate to the collinearity problem?

(b) For each of the values $r_{23} = .1, .2, .3,..., .9, .99$, calculate the *ratio* of var(b_2) to the "base" value derived in (a). What does this exercise reveal about collinearity?

(c) As r_{23}^2 values increase in part (b), what would happen to the 95% confidence interval estimates for β_2 and β_3? What happens to cov(b_2, b_3)?

13.9 References

GUJARATI, D. (1988) *Basic Econometrics*, 2nd Edition, New York: McGraw-Hill, Inc.

JUDGE, G. G., R. C. HILL, W. E. GRIFFITHS, H. LÜTKEPOHL and T.C. LEE (1988) *Introduction to the Theory and Practice of Econometrics*, 2nd Edition, New York: John Wiley & Sons, Inc.

KLEIN, L. R. and A. S. GOLDBERGER (1955) *An Econometric Model of the United States, 1929–1952*, Amsterdam: North-Holland.

MADDALA, G. S. (1992) *Introduction to Econometrics*, 2nd Edition, New York: Macmillan Publishing Co.

Chapter 14

Large Sample Theory and Models with Random Regressors

New Key Words and Concepts

Consistency

Contemporaneous Correlation

Errors in Variables

Wald, Lagrange Multiplier and
  Likelihood Ratio Tests

Method of Moments Estimators

Hausman Specification Test

Probability Limit

Measurement Error

Large Sample or Asymptotic
  Distributions

Large Sample Efficiency

Instruments and Instrumental
  Variable Estimation

In the preceding chapters we made a number of assumptions about the various ingredients in the linear statistical model $\mathbf{y} = X\beta + \mathbf{e}$. We assumed that the error vector $\mathbf{e}$ is a $(T \times 1)$ random vector with mean $\mathbf{0}$ and covariance matrix $\sigma^2 I_T$. Furthermore, we assumed that the $(T \times K)$ matrix of explanatory variables X is nonstochastic. This last assumption meant that when we investigated the sampling properties of the least squares estimator $\mathbf{b} = (X'X)^{-1}X'\mathbf{y}$, we could do so within the context of a matrix X that is fixed in repeated samples.

Sampling properties such as the mean and covariance matrix for $\mathbf{b}$ tell us something about the characteristics of a large number of estimates for β that would be obtained from a large number of repeated samples. When we say X is fixed in repeated samples, we picture each of the repeated samples as having the same X matrix (the same values of the explanatory variables), but a different vector of errors $\mathbf{e}$ and, hence, a different vector of dependent variable values $\mathbf{y}$. For example, in the food expenditure–income example of Chapters 5 to 8, the assumption that X (consisting of income and a column of ones) is nonstochastic implies that the household incomes are known before the households are sampled; the assumption that X is fixed in repeated samples implies that, if we did take hypothetical repeated samples, the sampled households in each of the repeated samples would have the same set of income values.

Given the assumption of a nonstochastic X, and the assumptions about the error vector $\mathbf{e}$, we discovered that the least squares estimator is the best possible estimator (minimum variance) from the class of all linear unbiased estimators. With the additional assumption that $\mathbf{e}$ is normally distributed, we discovered that the least squares estimator is the best possible estimator from the class of all unbiased estimators. Furthermore, the normality assumption permitted us to use t- and F-statistics for testing linear hypotheses about the coefficient vector β. We also used the t-distribution for constructing confidence intervals.

The starting point for this chapter is to emphasize that, given the assumptions made thus far, the properties of minimum variance and unbiasedness are *exact* properties; the *t*- and *F*-statistics used for hypothesis testing and interval estimation have, respectively, *exact t*- and *F*-distributions. Unfortunately, we are not always in the happy situation of being able to derive exact properties of estimators; nor can we always suggest estimators with exact properties or test statistics whose exact probability distributions are known. Under these circumstances we must be content with approximate properties of estimators, and with test statistics whose approximate probability distributions are known. How do we find such approximations? The usual approach is to examine results *as the sample size T approaches infinity*. Of course, we never have infinite samples, but examining properties and distributions as *T* approaches infinity gives us results that approximately hold when sample size is large. Results obtained by letting sample size approach infinity come under the general heading of *large sample* or *asymptotic theory*.

We have already encountered two large sample results. We have seen (in Chapters 2 and 4) that if we have a random sample from a nonnormal distribution with finite variance, the Central Limit Theorem tells us that we can use the sample mean and its approximate normal distribution to test hypotheses and to construct interval estimates for the mean of the nonnormal distribution. A similar result is true for the least squares estimator of the coefficient vector β in the linear statistical model with nonnormal errors. Both these results are approximate ones that hold true when sample size is large. The second large sample result that we encountered was that of consistency. In Chapter 3 we learned that the sample mean is a consistent estimator of the population mean in the sense that its probability distribution collapses around the population mean as the sample size approaches infinity.

As we travel through the remainder of the book, we will discover that there are many circumstances where we must rely on the approximations generated by large sample theory. One particular circumstance that we introduce in this chapter is one where X is stochastic and, hence, cannot be viewed as being fixed in repeated samples. We describe this situation as one with random regressors (explanatory variables). In the food expenditure–income example, the random regressor assumption implies the incomes of the sample households are not known before sampling. Also, when we conceptualize repeated samples, we do not think of each repeated sample as having the same household incomes. Further examples are considered later in this chapter; some later chapters are devoted exclusively to specific examples of random regressors. Also, there will be many situations, other than the random regressor one, where large sample theory is needed.

Our objectives in this chapter are the following:

1. To describe in more detail the property of consistency and the related concept of a probability limit. Random regressor models are used to illustrate the relevance of these concepts (Section 14.1).

2. To summarize some of the possible random regressor models (Section 14.2).

3. To describe large sample approximate distributions and large sample efficiency. Three commonly used large sample test statistics, the Wald, the Lagrange multiplier, and the likelihood ratio, are introduced as examples (Section 14.3).

4. To use a measurement error model to introduce instrumental variables estimation. This estimation procedure yields consistent estimators and is motivated by the method of moments. We introduce a way to test for the existence of correlation between the regressors and the error (Section 14.4).

5. To provide a general matrix algebra formulation for examining consistency, estimating instrumental variability, and testing in the general random regressor model (Appendix 14A).

The next step on the road ahead is to describe consistency and how it relates to random regressor models.

14.1   Consistency and Probability Limits

The property of *consistency* ensures that an estimation rule will produce an estimate that is *close* to the true parameter value with high probability if the sample size is large enough. More precisely, let $\hat{\theta}_T$ be an estimator of θ based on a sample of size T. Then $\hat{\theta}_T$ is a *consistent* estimator of θ if

$$\lim_{T \to \infty} P\left(\left|\hat{\theta}_T - \theta\right| < \varepsilon\right) = 1 \qquad (14.1.1)$$

where ε is an arbitrarily small positive number. This means that the probability that the value of $\hat{\theta}_T$ falls in the interval $[\theta - \varepsilon, \theta + \varepsilon]$ can be made arbitrarily close to 1 given a large enough sample size, *no matter how small ε is*. If equation 14.1.1 is true, then the sequence of random variables $\hat{\theta}_T$ is said to *converge in probability* to the constant θ; and θ is said to be the *probability limit* of the sequence $\hat{\theta}_T$. This is usually abbreviated as

$$\text{plim } \hat{\theta}_T = \theta \qquad (14.1.2)$$

Thus, the estimator $\hat{\theta}_T$ is consistent for θ if equation 14.1.1 is true or, equivalently, when plim $\hat{\theta}_T = \theta$.

The meaning of equation 14.1.1 was discussed in Section 3.4.3 of Chapter 3 in conjunction with the estimator $b = \Sigma_{i=1}^T Y_i / T$ calculated from a random sample $Y_1, Y_2, \ldots, Y_T$ from a $N(\beta, \sigma^2)$ population. In this case b is a consistent estimator for β. Let us see why. We know that $b \sim N\left(\beta, \sigma^2 / T\right)$. If we consider three sample sizes, $T_3 > T_2 > T_1$, the sampling distributions of b might appear as in Figure 14.1. We see that the probability mass in the interval $[\beta - \varepsilon, \beta + \varepsilon]$ is getting large as the sample size increases from T_1 to T_2 to T_3, and the sampling distribution of b is collapsing about the true parameter β. In fact, since $\lim_{T \to \infty} \text{var}(b) = \lim_{T \to \infty} \sigma^2 / T = 0$, the sampling distribution of b becomes degenerate at the true parameter value in the limit, so that all its probability mass occurs at β.

Given the foregoing discussion, it should be intuitively reasonable that sufficient, but not necessary, conditions for an estimator $\hat{\theta}_T$ to be consistent for θ are

$$\lim_{T \to \infty} E\left[\hat{\theta}_T\right] = \theta \qquad (14.1.3a)$$

$$\lim_{T \to \infty} \text{var}\left(\hat{\theta}_T\right) = 0 \qquad (14.1.3b)$$

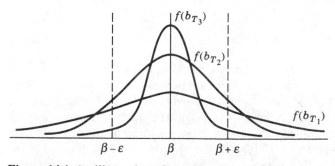

Figure 14.1 An illustration of consistency.

If both the conditions in equation 14.1.3 are satisfied then the sampling distribution of $\hat{\theta}_T$ will "collapse" on the true parameter value as depicted in Figure 14.1. Since these conditions are sufficient but not necessary, however, there are some cases where estimators are consistent without the conditions in equation 14.1.3 holding true.

14.1.1 Consistency, Random Regressors, and the Least Squares Estimator

Let us consider how the concept of consistency relates to the least squares estimator for the linear statistical model with random regressors. First, consider the "simple" model with one (possibly random) regressor x_t

$$y_t = \beta_1 + \beta_2 x_t + e_t \tag{14.1.4}$$

We continue to assume the e_t are independent random variables with $e_t \sim (0, \sigma^2)$. The least squares estimator for β_2 is given by

$$
\begin{aligned}
b_2 &= \frac{T\Sigma x_t y_t - \Sigma x_t \Sigma y_t}{T\Sigma x_t^2 - \left(\Sigma x_t\right)^2} \\
&= \beta_2 + \frac{\Sigma(x_t - \bar{x})e_t}{\Sigma(x_t - \bar{x})^2}
\end{aligned}
\tag{14.1.5}
$$

Derivation of the second line in equation 14.1.5 is left as an exercise (Exercise 14.1).

If we attempt to prove that b_2 is unbiased, we do so by taking expectations of both sides of equation 14.1.5. This yields

$$E[b_2] = \beta_2 + E\left[\frac{\Sigma(x_t - \bar{x})e_t}{\Sigma(x_t - \bar{x})^2}\right] \tag{14.1.6}$$

Since we are assuming that both x_t and e_t are random variables, the expectation of the last term in equation 14.1.6 depends on the nature of the joint probability distribution for x_t and e_t. If all the regressors $x_1, x_2, \ldots, x_T$ are fully independent of all the errors $e_1, e_2, \ldots, e_T$, then

$$
\begin{aligned}
E\left[\frac{\Sigma(x_t - \bar{x})e_t}{\Sigma(x_t - \bar{x})^2}\right] &= \Sigma\left[E\left\{\left(\frac{x_t - \bar{x}}{\Sigma(x_t - \bar{x})^2}\right)e_t\right\}\right] \\
&= \Sigma\left[E\left(\frac{x_t - \bar{x}}{\Sigma(x_t - \bar{x})^2}\right)E[e_t]\right]
\end{aligned}
\tag{14.1.7}
$$

To convince yourself of the validity of interchanging E and Σ in the first equality in equation 14.1.7, you should write out in full a number of terms in the summation. Providing $E\left[(x_t - \bar{x})/\Sigma(x_t - \bar{x})^2\right]$ is finite, the quantity in equation 14.1.7 will be zero because $E[e_t] = 0$. Thus, when the x_t and the e_t are fully independent, the least squares estimator is unbiased. If, however, some of the x_t are correlated with some of the e_t, we cannot proceed as we did in equation 14.1.7 to write the expectation of the product as the product of two expectations. In this instance the least squares estimator will be biased.

Thus, whether the presence of a random regressor leads to the least squares estimator being biased depends heavily on whether that regressor is correlated with the error term. The concepts of consistency and probability limits become relevant when we recognize that there are often circumstances where the least squares estimator, although biased, is still consistent.

To investigate the consistency of b_2 we first need to present results pertaining to the probability limits of functions of random variables.

Rules for Working with Probability Limits

1. The probability limit of a constant, say β, is equal to that constant.

$$\text{plim} \, \beta = \beta \tag{14.1.8a}$$

2. The probability limit of the sum (or difference) of two random variables, say Y_1 and Y_2, is equal to the sum (or difference) of the probability limits of Y_1 and Y_2.

$$\text{plim}(Y_1 \pm Y_2) = \text{plim}(Y_1) \pm \text{plim}(Y_2) \tag{14.1.8b}$$

3. The probability limit of the product (or quotient) of two random variables is equal to the product (or quotient) of the probability limits of those random variables.

$$\text{plim}(Y_1 Y_2) = \text{plim}(Y_1)\text{plim}(Y_2) \qquad \text{plim}\left(\frac{Y_1}{Y_2}\right) = \frac{\text{plim}(Y_1)}{\text{plim}(Y_2)} \tag{14.1.8c}$$

4. Slutsky's theorem: The probability limit of a continuous function g of a random variable Y is equal to the same function of the probability limit.

$$\text{plim}[g(Y)] = g(\text{plim} \, Y) \tag{14.1.8d}$$

Examples of applications of these rules will be given shortly. Note at this point that rules 1 and 2 still hold true if plim is replaced by the expectation operator, E, but rules 3 and 4 do not. That is,

$$E[\beta] = \beta$$

$$E[Y_1 \pm Y_2] = E[Y_1] \pm E[Y_2]$$

$$E[Y_1 Y_2] \neq E[Y_1]E[Y_2] \qquad \text{unless } Y_1 \text{ and } Y_2 \text{ are independent}$$

$$E\left[\frac{Y_1}{Y_2}\right] \neq \frac{E[Y_1]}{E[Y_2]}$$

$$E[g(Y)] \neq g(E[Y])$$

The fact that rules 3 and 4 hold when taking probability limits, but not when taking expectations, means that we have greater flexibility when working with probability limits. For this reason it is often easier to establish consistency than to establish unbiasedness.

Returning to the problem of investigating the consistency of b_2, we take the probability limit of both sides of equation 14.1.5 and obtain

$$\text{plim} \, b_2 = \text{plim} \, \beta_2 + \text{plim}\left[\frac{\Sigma(x_t - \bar{x})e_t}{\Sigma(x_t - \bar{x})^2}\right] \qquad \text{(from rule 2)}$$

$$= \beta_2 + \frac{\text{plim}\left[\dfrac{1}{T}\Sigma(x_t - \bar{x})e_t\right]}{\text{plim}\left[\dfrac{1}{T}\Sigma(x_t - \bar{x})^2\right]} \qquad \text{(from rules 1 and 3)}$$

$$\tag{14.1.9}$$

In the last line of equation 14.1.9 we included $1/T$ in both the numerator and the denominator. This inclusion is designed to turn these quantities into a sample variance and a sample covariance. In Section 3.5 we learned that it is usual to use $(T - 1)$ rather than T in the denominator for a sample variance, so as to make that quantity an unbiased estimator. We use T here since, when we examine properties as $T \rightarrow \infty$, there is no practical difference between T and $(T - 1)$.

Thus, we treat the denominator term $\frac{1}{T}\Sigma(x_t - \bar{x})^2$ as the sample variance of x_t. This sample variance is a consistent estimator of the population variance of x_t, say σ_{xx}. We can write this result as

$$\text{plim}\left[\frac{1}{T}\Sigma(x_t - \bar{x})^2\right] = \sigma_{xx} \qquad (14.1.10a)$$

The numerator term $\frac{1}{T}\Sigma(x_t - \bar{x})e_t$ is the sample covariance between x_t and e_t; this sample covariance is a consistent estimator of the population covariance between x_t and e_t. If the population covariance between x_t and e_t is zero, then $\frac{1}{T}\Sigma(x_t - \bar{x})e_t$ is a consistent estimator of zero, and we write

$$\text{plim}\left[\frac{1}{T}\Sigma(x_t - \bar{x})e_t\right] = 0 \qquad (14.1.10b)$$

Substituting equations 14.1.10a and 14.1.10b into 14.1.9 gives

$$\text{plim}\,b_2 = \beta_2 + \frac{0}{\sigma_{xx}} = \beta_2$$
$$(14.1.11)$$

Hence, when x_t and e_t are uncorrelated, and therefore have a covariance of zero, the least squares estimator b_2 is consistent. The converse is also true. If x_t and e_t are correlated and hence have a nonzero covariance, the probability limit of the numerator in equation 14.1.9 will be nonzero and b_2 will not be consistent.

There is an important difference between what we had to assume to establish that the least squares estimator is unbiased (equations 14.1.6 and 14.1.7) and what we had to assume to establish the consistency of the least squares estimator (equations 14.1.9–14.1.11). To prove unbiasedness we had to assume that all the x_t (for all observations) were independent of all the e_t. To prove consistency we assumed only that x_t and e_t were *contemporaneously* uncorrelated. That is, we assumed only that x_t and e_t are uncorrelated for a given observation or a given time period. Consistency still holds when x_t is correlated with past values of the errors $e_{t-1}, e_{t-2},\ldots$.

An example that makes this distinction clear is where the regressor is the dependent variable lagged one period. That is, $x_t = y_{t-1}$ and we have the model

$$y_t = \beta_1 + \beta_2 y_{t-1} + e_t \qquad (14.1.12)$$

This model is studied in detail in Chapter 20. What we emphasize here is that, because e_t is realized after y_{t-1}, e_t and y_{t-1} will be uncorrelated. However, because $y_{t-1} = \beta_1 + \beta_2 y_{t-2} + e_{t-1}$, it follows that y_{t-1} will be correlated with $e_{t-1}, e_{t-2},\ldots$. In the context of this model, equation 14.1.5 becomes

$$b_2 = \beta_2 + \frac{\Sigma(y_{t-1} - \bar{y}_{-1})e_t}{\Sigma(y_{t-1} - \bar{y}_{-1})^2}$$
$$(14.1.13)$$

where $\bar{y}_{-1}$ is the sample mean of the y_{t-1}. If we take expectations of both sides of equation 14.1.13 the term

$$E\left[\frac{\Sigma(y_{t-1}-\bar{y}_{-1})e_t}{\Sigma(y_{t-1}-\bar{y}_{-1})^2}\right] = \Sigma\left[E\left\{\left(\frac{y_{t-1}-\bar{y}_{-1}}{\Sigma(y_{t-1}-\bar{y}_{-1})^2}\right)e_t\right\}\right]$$

does not go to zero because $(y_{t-1}-\bar{y}_{-1})/\Sigma(y_{t-1}-\bar{y}_{-1})^2$ and e_t are correlated. The terms $\bar{y}_{-1}$ and $\Sigma(y_{t-1}-\bar{y}_{-1})^2$ involve $y_0, y_1, y_2, \ldots$, which are not fully independent of e_t. Thus, b_2 is biased. However, providing $|\beta_2| < 1$, we can show that b_2 is consistent. The requirement that $|\beta_2| < 1$ is discussed further in Chapter 20. Consistency follows because the probability limit of a sample variance or covariance is equal to the population variance or covariance, and we have

$$\frac{\text{plim}\left[\dfrac{1}{T}\Sigma(y_{t-1}-\bar{y}_{-1})e_t\right]}{\text{plim}\left[\dfrac{1}{T}\Sigma(y_{t-1}-\bar{y}_{-1})^2\right]} = \frac{0}{\sigma_{yy}} = 0$$

(14.1.14)

where σ_{yy} is the variance of y and the covariance between y_{t-1} and e_t is zero. A more general matrix algebra representation of consistency in random regressor models is developed in Appendix 14A.

14.2 Random-Regressor Models

We have discovered that the consequences of relaxing the assumption that the regressors are nonstochastic and fixed in repeated samples, and assuming instead that they are random, depends on the nature of the random regressors. The least squares estimator can be *(i)* unbiased and consistent, *(ii)* biased, but consistent, or *(iii)* biased and inconsistent. In this section we summarize the models that lead to these different outcomes and describe particular examples that get more detailed attention in the pages ahead. In each instance it should be kept in mind that as well as making an assumption about the correlation between the regressors and the errors, we need to make assumptions about the behavior of the random regressors. For example, in equation 14.1.9 we assumed that σ_{xx} exists and is nonzero.

We can distinguish the following cases:

1. The random regressors are totally independent of all errors. In this situation the least squares estimator is unbiased and consistent.

2. The random regressors are contemporaneously uncorrelated with the error term. In this situation the least squares estimator is biased in finite samples but it is nevertheless consistent. A common example is a model where one of the regressors is the dependent variable lagged one period. That is,

$$y_t = \beta_1 + \beta_2 y_{t-1} + e_t$$

(14.2.1)

This model is studied in more depth in Chapter 20.

3. The random regressors are contemporaneously correlated with the error term. Under these circumstances the least squares estimator is both biased and inconsistent. Let us consider some examples.

Lagged Dependent Variable and Correlated Error Consider the model

$$y_t = \beta_1 + \beta_2 x_t + \beta_3 y_{t-1} + e_t - \lambda e_{t-1} \qquad (14.2.2)$$

where the e_t are independent and distributed according to $e_t \sim (0, \sigma^2)$. This model is studied in more detail in Chapter 21. The point to note here is that the error term $v_t = e_t - \lambda e_{t-1}$ is correlated with the regressor y_{t-1}. This correlation arises because the error term has two components, one of which is e_{t-1}, and because y_{t-1} depends directly on e_{t-1}, as can be seen by lagging equation 14.2.2 by one period. This model is called a correlated error model because v_t is correlated with v_{t-1}; both v_t and v_{t-1} contain the component e_{t-1}. In general, the least squares estimator is inconsistent when it is applied to a model with a lagged dependent variable and a correlated error term.

Measurement Error A second example of random regressors that are correlated with the error term is where one or more of the explanatory variables is measured with error. Explicit details of such a model appear in Section 14.4. What happens in this model is that the measurement error from the random regressor forms part of the equation error and, consequently, the equation error is correlated with the regressor. The least squares rule is again inconsistent.

Simultaneous Equations In Chapters 18 and 19 we study simultaneous equation models where the values of a number of variables are jointly determined. A simple simultaneous equation model is one consisting of a consumption function

$$c_t = \beta + \gamma y_t + e_t \qquad (14.2.3a)$$

and a national income identity

$$y_t = c_t + i_t \qquad (14.2.3b)$$

In this model consumption (c_t) and income (y_t) are determined jointly by the two equations; investment (i_t) is assumed determined exogenously. The least squares estimation of β and γ is inconsistent, with the inconsistency arising because y_t and e_t are correlated. The variable y_t depends on c_t through equation 14.2.3b; but, since c_t depends on e_t through equation 14.2.3a, it follows that y_t depends on e_t and, hence, they are correlated.

4. The random regressors are "nonstationary." The concept of stationarity is discussed in Chapter 20. For the moment we note that, with a nonstationary random regressor, the assumption that the sample variance of x approaches a finite limit is violated. Under these circumstances the least squares estimator may no longer be consistent, and the usual large sample approximate distribution is no longer appropriate, and hence our conventional confidence intervals and hypothesis tests are not valid. To solve the problem, we need to model the process generating the observations on the random regressor, and possibly other variables, and the relationships between them. This material comes under the general headings of inference for nonstationary time series and cointegration; it is considered in Chapter 21.

In instances where the regressors and the error term are contemporaneously correlated, an alternative estimation technique to least squares is needed. One such technique is instrumental variable estimation, which we study in Section 14.4 and Appendix 14A. Other, related techniques are considered for specific cases in Chapters 19 and 21.

14.3   Large-Sample Probability Distributions

We learned in Chapters 2 to 4 that when we have a random sample $Y_1, Y_2, \ldots, Y_T$ drawn from a (β, σ^2) distribution, then, from a Central Limit Theorem, the following result holds approximately for large T

$$\frac{\overline{Y} - \beta}{\sigma / \sqrt{T}} \sim N(0, 1)$$

(14.3.1)

This result holds true irrespective of the nature of the original distribution from which the Y_i were drawn. It also holds if the unknown parameter σ is replaced by the sample standard deviation $\hat{\sigma}$. The distribution in equation 14.3.1 is known as a *large sample distribution*. Other names it is given are a *limiting distribution* and an *asymptotic distribution*. This distribution is used to construct interval estimates and test hypotheses about the population mean β. In general, large sample approximate distribution results are used when the mathematics is too difficult, or we have insufficient information to derive exact distributions that hold in small samples.

Turning to the general linear statistical model $\mathbf{y} = X\beta + \mathbf{e}$, we have seen in previous chapters that the least squares estimator $\mathbf{b} = (X'X)^{-1}X'\mathbf{y}$ can be written as

$$\mathbf{b} = \beta + \left(X'X\right)^{-1} X'\mathbf{e}$$

(14.3.2)

Clearly, the probability distribution for $\mathbf{b}$ depends on that for $\mathbf{e}$ and, if the regressor matrix X is random, it will also depend on the probability distribution for X. When X is nonrandom and $\mathbf{e}$ is normally distributed, the exact result $\mathbf{b} \sim N[\beta, \sigma^2(X'X)^{-1}]$ is used for interval estimation and hypothesis testing. Details of test statistics based on this result were given in Chapters 10 and 11.

When $\mathbf{e}$ is not normally distributed, or X is random, or both, we have to resort to large sample distributions. We assume that $X'X/T$ converges to a finite nonsingular matrix Σ_{XX}, and that X, if it is random, is at least contemporaneously uncorrelated with $\mathbf{e}$. Let b_k and β_k represent single elements (the kth elements) from $\mathbf{b}$ and β, respectively. The first useful result is that, approximately for large T,

$$\frac{b_k - \beta_k}{\sqrt{\hat{\text{var}}(b_k)}} \sim N(0, 1)$$

(14.3.3)

In other words, for hypothesis tests and interval estimates for single elements from β, we can use the normal distribution in the usual way. The only differences between this result and the earlier one given in equation 10.1.12 of Chapter 10 are *(i)* the result in equation 14.3.3 is approximate not exact, and *(ii)* the large sample theory suggests that the normal distribution not the t-distribution should be used. In practice, however, it may be true that the t-distribution provides a more accurate *finite sample* approximation. For this reason the t distribution is frequently used despite the fact that the large sample theory is in terms of the normal distribution.

When we move from testing a hypothesis about a single coefficient to testing one or more linear combinations of the elements in β, we move from the normal distribution to the chi-square distribution. Along the lines of Appendix 10C, let us assume that we wish to test

$$H_0: R\beta = \mathbf{r} \quad \text{against} \quad H_1: R\beta \neq \mathbf{r}$$

(14.3.4)

where R is a $(J \times K)$ matrix that selects the appropriate elements from β so as to specify the linear combinations of β that are of interest; $\mathbf{r}$ is a $(J \times 1)$ vector of values to which we hypothesize that the linear combinations are equal. The number of rows in R and $\mathbf{r}$ is equal to the number of single linear combinations or single hypotheses that comprises the joint hypothesis in equation 14.3.4. We denote this number by J. We can use the following large sample result:

$$\lambda_W = \frac{(R\mathbf{b}-\mathbf{r})'\left[R(X'X)^{-1}R'\right]^{-1}(R\mathbf{b}-\mathbf{r})}{\hat{\sigma}^2}$$

$$= \frac{\text{SSE}_R - \text{SSE}_U}{\hat{\sigma}^2} \sim \chi^2_{(J)} \tag{14.3.5}$$

The first line in equation 14.3.5 is the formulation that is in line with the discussion in Appendix 10C of Chapter 10. The second line involves the sum of squared errors from estimation under H_0, where the restrictions are true (SSE_R) and the sum of squared errors from the unrestricted model, where H_1 is true (SSE_U); this alternative formulation is more in line with the discussion in Section 11.6.2 of Chapter 11. The null hypothesis is rejected for large values of λ_W. Thus, at the 5% level of significance, we reject H_0 if $\lambda_W > \chi^2_c$, where the critical value χ^2_c is chosen such that $P\left[\chi^2_{(J)} > \chi^2_c\right] = 0.05$.

This test procedure is known as the *Wald test*. A related test that is also sometimes used is the LM or *Lagrange multiplier test*. To describe the difference between the Wald and LM tests, first note that $\hat{\sigma}^2$ is the estimated variance we get from estimating the unrestricted model. That is, $\hat{\sigma}^2 = \text{SSE}_U / (T - K)$. When we estimate the restricted model, we get another estimator for the variance that is given by $\hat{\sigma}^2_* = \text{SSE}_R / (T - K + J)$. The LM test is obtained by replacing $\hat{\sigma}^2$ in equation 14.3.5 by $\hat{\sigma}^2_*$. Also, instead of using the divisors $(T - K)$ and $(T - K + J)$ that are needed, respectively, to make $\hat{\sigma}^2$ and $\hat{\sigma}^2_*$ unbiased estimators, the divisor T is often used in both instances. That is, the alternative definitions $\hat{\sigma}^2 = \text{SSE}_U / T$ and $\hat{\sigma}^2_* = \text{SSE}_R / T$ are often used. Whether we use T or $(T - K)$ or $(T - K + J)$ does not make any difference when we are considering approximate results for large T. Also, the fact that there are a number of slight variations of equation 14.3.5 that all have the same approximate $\chi^2_{(J)}$ distribution emphasizes the approximate nature of the testing procedure. The different variations could lead to different test outcomes. For any given problem, one variation is likely to be a better finite sample approximation than the others. But which one is better will depend on the problem, and we have no way of making a general recommendation for choice.

When we discussed the approximate large sample distribution for testing a hypothesis about a single element β_k, we indicated that the large sample distribution specified by the theory was the normal distribution, but that the t distribution is often used instead in the hope that it might provide a more accurate finite sample approximation. For the case of testing a joint hypothesis involving more than one coefficient or linear combinations of coefficients, the same can be said about the χ^2- and F-distributions. The χ^2-distribution is the relevant one suggested by the large sample theory, but the F-distribution might provide a better finite sample approximation in some circumstances. Using the sum of squared errors formulation, we can see from equations 11.6.5 and 14.3.5 that

$$F = \frac{\lambda_W}{J} = \frac{(\text{SSE}_R - \text{SSE}_U)/J}{\hat{\sigma}^2} \tag{14.3.6}$$

If this statistic is used, we reject H_0 if $F > F_c$, where F_c is a critical value from the F-distribution for $[J, (T - K)]$ degrees of freedom and a specified significance level.

There is one further large sample approximate test that can be used for testing restrictions on parameters. This test is based on the principle of maximum likelihood estimation that was introduced in Chapters 3 and 5. It compares the values of the maximized likelihood functions under H_0 and H_1. We proceed as follows. Two sets of maximum likelihood estimates of the parameters are obtained, one under the assumption that H_0 is true, and the other under the assumption that H_1 is true. Substituting these estimates into their respective likelihood functions gives the maximized values of the likelihoods. If the maximum value of the restricted likelihood (under H_0) is "not much less" than the maximum value of the unrestricted likelihood (under H_1), then there is no evidence in the data to refute H_0. If the restricted maximum is "much less" than the unrestricted maximum or, in other words, the data have a strong preference for H_1, this constitutes evidence against H_0. To decide what is "not much less" and what is "much less," we need a test statistic that makes allowance for the maximum difference that can be attributable to chance. Let $L(H_0)$ and $L(H_1)$ be the maximized values of the log-likelihood functions under H_0 and H_1, respectively. The *likelihood ratio test* that compares these values is based on the statistic

$$\lambda_{LR} = 2[L(H_1) - L(H_0)]$$

(14.3.7)

Given that the null hypothesis is true, λ_{LR} has an approximate $\chi^2_{(J)}$-distribution, where J is the number of restrictions under H_0. We reject H_0 when $\lambda_{LR} > \chi^2_c$, where χ^2_c is a chosen critical value from the $\chi^2_{(J)}$-distribution.

For the null and alternative hypotheses in equation 14.3.4 and normally distributed errors, it can be shown that equation 14.3.7 simplifies to

$$\lambda_{LR} = T(\ln SSE_R - \ln SSE_U)$$

(14.3.8)

Thus, like the Wald and Lagrange multiplier test statistics, the likelihood ratio test statistic can be written in terms of the restricted and unrestricted sums of squared errors. Also, the likelihood ratio principle adds to the list another statistic that has a large sample approximate $\chi^2_{(J)}$-distribution.

Before proceeding to an example, it is worth pointing out that the Wald, LM, and likelihood ratio tests can be utilized for a far wider and more general range of testing problems than that considered here. The principles of all these test procedures can be applied, for example, to testing nonlinear functions of the elements in β, or to testing parameter restrictions in a more general error covariance matrix. Some examples will be encountered later in the book. A more general description can be found in Judge et al. (1988, pp. 541–551).

14.3.1   An Example

Let us revisit the demand-for-beer equation introduced in Chapter 11. We specified a log-linear demand equation where the quantity of beer demanded (q) depended on the price of beer (p_B), the price of other liquor (p_L), the price of remaining goods and services (p_R), and income (m). We wrote the equation as

$$\ln q_t = \beta_1 + \beta_2 \ln p_{Bt} + \beta_3 \ln p_{Lt} + \beta_4 \ln p_{Rt} + \beta_5 \ln m_t + e_t$$

(14.3.9)

In Section 11.6 we estimated a restricted version of this model and tested the validity of the restrictions. These restrictions were

$$\beta_2 + \beta_3 + \beta_4 + \beta_5 = 0$$

(14.3.10a)

$$\beta_3 - \beta_4 = 0 \qquad (14.3.10b)$$

$$\beta_5 = 1 \qquad (14.3.10c)$$

The information that we need to implement the Wald, LM, F, or likelihood ratio (LR) tests is

$$SSE_R = 0.09899 \qquad SSE_U = 0.08992$$

$$J = 3 \qquad T = 30 \qquad K = 5$$

Results from the different test variations that were discussed are given in Table 14.1. Students should verify the test value entries. Note that all tests lead to the same outcome—a failure to reject the null hypothesis. However, the differences in the values of the test statistics are far from negligible. It is easy to imagine circumstances where the different variations could lead to different outcomes.

In practice, we usually compute the value of just one test statistic and go with the decision that results from that statistic. The one that is computed is usually the one that is most convenient—the one automatically computed by our computer software. The purpose of our example is to illustrate the approximate nature of large sample tests. Of course, the approximation becomes better, and the differences between the tests disappear, as the sample size T becomes larger. A natural question is: What sample size is needed for a large sample distribution to be a reasonable approximation? Unfortunately, there is no definite answer to this question. For some models $T = 30$ or 40 may be sufficient; in other instances $T = 100$ might be required.

Finally, let us emphasize that if the errors are normally distributed and the explanatory variables are treated as nonstochastic, the F-statistic provides us with an *exact* finite sample test. The χ^2 large sample approximations, and treating the F-test as an approximation, become relevant only if the errors are nonnormal or the regressors are random.

14.3.2 Large-Sample Efficiency and Maximum Likelihood Estimation

When the mathematics is not too difficult to derive exact finite sample results, we prefer estimators that are minimum variance (best) unbiased estimators. A minimum variance unbiased estimator is an unbiased estimator that has a lower variance than all other unbiased estimators. We also say that such an estimator is *efficient*. One estimator is said to be *more efficient* than another estimator if they are both unbiased and if the variance of the former is less than that of the latter.

Table 14.1 Results from Alternative Large Sample Tests

Test	Distribution	Divisor Used for Estimate of σ^2	Test Value	5% Critical Value	Reject H_0
Wald	$\chi^2_{(3)}$	$T - K = 25$	2.52	7.81	No
Wald	$\chi^2_{(3)}$	$T = 30$	3.03	7.81	No
LM	$\chi^2_{(3)}$	$T - K + J = 28$	2.57	7.81	No
LM	$\chi^2_{(3)}$	$T = 30$	2.75	7.81	No
F	$F_{[3,25]}$	$T - K = 25$	0.84	2.76	No
LR	$\chi^2_{(3)}$	—	2.88	7.81	No

When the mathematics is too difficult to establish the superiority of an estimator in terms of its finite sample efficiency, we must look for ways of comparing estimators in terms of their large sample or approximate properties. Instead of restricting ourselves to unbiased estimators, we begin by restricting ourselves to consistent estimators. Then, we say one consistent estimator has greater large sample efficiency, or is *asymptotically more efficient*, than another, if the variance of its approximate large sample distribution is less. An estimator is said to be *asymptotically efficient* (or *efficient in large samples*) if the variance of its approximate large sample distribution is less than that of all other consistent estimators. Naturally, when finite sample properties of estimators cannot be established, it is desirable to use an estimator that is efficient in large samples.

Many of the estimators suggested in subsequent chapters of this text are consistent and asymptotically efficient. As we have indicated, estimators with these properties are used when the superiority of one estimator, in terms of finite sample efficiency, cannot be established. In Chapters 3 and 5 we introduced a principle for obtaining estimators known as the *maximum likelihood* principle. This principle is a general one that can be applied to a wide range of models and problems. One of its great advantages is that it produces estimators (maximum likelihood estimators) that are known to be consistent and asymptotically efficient. Furthermore, the large sample approximate distribution for maximum likelihood estimators is normal. Thus, when we use a maximum likelihood estimator, we do so with the assurance that, in terms of large sample properties, a better estimator cannot be found. Also, we have the added convenience of knowing that the normal distribution, or test statistics derived from it, can be used to implement approximate large sample tests.

In Chapters 3 and 5 the maximum likelihood principle was unnecessary in the sense that we had a least squares estimator with desirable finite sample properties. In other models, however, where derivation of finite sample properties is not possible, the maximum likelihood principle is an extremely valuable one.

14.3.3   Method of Moments Estimators

Another principle that can be used to produce estimators is the so-called *method of moments*. This principle produces estimators that are always consistent, but not necessarily asymptotically efficient. To follow the method of moments principle, we use estimators that result from equating sample moments with population moments. Means, variances, and covariances are examples of moments. We will illustrate the technique by using the simple regression model

$$y_t = \beta_1 + \beta_2 x_t + e_t \tag{14.3.11}$$

Two assumptions we make about population moments are

(i) $E[e_t] = 0$, the population mean of the e_t is zero;

(ii) $E[x_t e_t] = 0$, the population contemporaneous covariance between the error e_t and a possibly stochastic regressor x_t is zero.

Let $\hat{\beta}_1$ and $\hat{\beta}_2$ be method of moments estimators for β_1 and β_2, and let $\hat{e}_t = y_t - \hat{\beta}_1 - \hat{\beta}_2 x_t$ be the sample counterpart of the unobserved errors e_t. The sample moment counterparts of assumptions *(i)* and *(ii)* are

$$\frac{1}{T}\Sigma\hat{e}_t = 0 \tag{14.3.12a}$$

$$\frac{1}{T}\Sigma x_t \hat{e}_t = 0 \tag{14.3.12b}$$

Substituting for $\hat{e}_t$, these two conditions are equivalent to

$$\Sigma y_t - T\hat{\beta}_1 - \hat{\beta}_2 \Sigma x_t = 0$$

$$\Sigma x_t y_t - \hat{\beta}_1 \Sigma x_t - \hat{\beta}_2 \Sigma x_t^2 = 0$$

or

$$T\hat{\beta}_1 + \Sigma x_t \hat{\beta}_2 = \Sigma y_t \tag{14.3.13a}$$

$$\Sigma x_t \hat{\beta}_1 + \Sigma x_t^2 \hat{\beta}_2 = \Sigma x_t y_t \tag{14.3.13b}$$

These two equations are identical to the normal equations given in equation 5.3.8 of Chapter 5, where expressions for the least squares estimator were being derived. Thus, for this particular example, the least squares, maximum likelihood, and method of moments principles all lead to exactly the same estimator. This result is not true in general, however. In many more complex situations, the method of moments provides a simple, convenient means for obtaining a consistent estimator.

14.4   Unobservables, Measurement Error, and Instrumental Variable Estimation

In Section 14.2 we indicated that a model where one or more of the explanatory variables is measured with error leads to contemporaneous correlation between random regressors and the error term and that, as a consequence, the least squares estimator is inconsistent. This model is discussed in more detail in this section; also, instrumental variable estimation, which is an alternative estimation technique that has the property of consistency, is introduced.

Models constructed for many areas of scientific inquiry include theoretical or abstract variables, for which measures are known to be imperfect or for which scales of measurement do not exist. Under these circumstances we are often forced to deal with unobservable or erroneously observed economic variables. Examples of such variables are utility, ability, achievement, ambition, and political attitudes. For example, although measures of ability are imperfect, they are often used in explaining an individual's earning or status attainment. Observable measures of an individual's success, such as income and occupational standing, may depend on schooling and an unobservable ability variable. In another model, permanent change in the earnings of individuals during any time period is modeled as the sum of an unobserved initial human capital level and the previously accumulated permanent change in earnings.

Another example of unobserved variables arises with Friedman's permanent income hypothesis. In his consumption function model, unobserved permanent consumption c_p is proportional to unobserved permanent income y_p, that is, $c_p = \beta y_p$. The actual observable measured income in any period, for any individual or economy, consists of the sum of unobserved permanent and transitory components y_p, y_T, that is, $y = y_p + y_T$. Also, actual measured consumption is viewed as consisting of a basic permanent component plus a random transitory component, that is, $c = c_p + c_T$.

There are many other examples where the variables we measure are not really what we want to measure and, consequently, measurement errors occur. Observed test scores may be used as a proxy for years of education. Proxy variables may, therefore, be subject to large random measurement errors. Even for theoretically observable variables, the data may be subject to a variety of errors. For example, errors may be introduced by the wording of survey questionnaires, where words such as "weak" or "strong" may imply different things to different respondents. These errors in supposedly observable variables arise because *(i)* in economics the data producers and data analyzers are separate, *(ii)* there is fuzziness about what it is we would like to observe, and *(iii)* the phenomena that we are trying to measure are complex. It is clear that the *unobservable variable* problem is inseparable from the *measurement error* or *errors in variables* problem, and that we need a statistical framework for dealing with these problems.

14.4.1   Statistical Consequences of Errors in Variables

One way to conceptualize the errors in variables problem is to treat the true, or theoretically desired, measure as one variable and the actual observations as another variable. The difference between the two may then be defined as a random error variable. In the two-variable case, let us assume that z_t and y_t are the observed or measured values of the true unobservable variables z_t^* and y_t^*, respectively. Thus,

$$z_t = z_t^* + u_t \tag{14.4.1}$$

$$y_t = y_t^* + v_t \tag{14.4.2}$$

where u_t and v_t are random errors representing the measurement errors for the tth observation. Let us assume that these errors have zero means and constant variances, and are uncorrelated, both with each other and from observation to observation. That is,

$$E[u_t] = 0 \quad \text{and} \quad E[v_t] = 0 \tag{14.4.3}$$

$$\text{var}(u_t) = E[u_t^2] = \sigma_u^2 \quad \text{and} \quad \text{var}(v_t) = E[v_t^2] = \sigma_v^2 \tag{14.4.4}$$

$$\text{cov}(u_t, u_s) = E[u_t u_s] = 0 \quad \text{and} \quad \text{cov}(v_t, v_s) = E[v_t v_s] = 0 \quad \text{for } t \neq s \tag{14.4.5}$$

$$\text{cov}(u_t, v_s) = E[u_t v_s] = 0 \quad \text{for all } t, s \tag{14.4.6}$$

Furthermore, we assume that the measurement errors u_t and v_t are independent of the true values z_t^* and y_t^*.

The unobservable variable or measurement error problem emerges in estimation when a researcher specifies, in terms of the true variables, that y_t^* is a function of z_t^*, and would like to measure the parameters of an exact linear relation such as

$$y_t^* = \beta_1 + \beta_2 z_t^* \tag{14.4.7}$$

where β_1 and β_2 are unknown scalar parameters to be estimated. Since the variables y_t^* and z_t^* are unobservable, and only z_t and y_t can be observed, to make progress toward estimation of β_1 and β_2, we must transform the model 14.4.7 into one that involves z_t and y_t. Substituting equations 14.4.1 and 14.4.2 into equation 14.4.7 yields the statistical model

$$y_t - v_t = \beta_1 + \beta_2 (z_t - u_t) \tag{14.4.8}$$

or

$$y_t = \beta_1 + \beta_2 z_t + v_t - \beta_2 u_t$$
$$= \beta_1 + \beta_2 z_t + e_t \tag{14.4.9}$$

where $e_t = v_t - \beta_2 u_t$. This statistical model involves the observable variables y_t and z_t, but we need to investigate the properties of e_t to discover whether the least squares estimation rule is appropriate. Working in this direction, we have

$$E[e_t] = E[v_t] - \beta_2 E[u_t] = 0 \tag{14.4.10a}$$

and

$$\text{var}(e_t) = \text{var}(v_t) + \beta_2^2 \text{ var}(u_t) - 2\beta_2 \text{ cov}(v_t, u_t)$$
$$= \sigma_v^2 + \beta_2^2 \sigma_u^2 \tag{14.4.10b}$$

Thus, e_t has a zero mean and constant variance. It further follows that the e_t are uncorrelated over observations because u_t and v_t are uncorrelated over observations. On the surface, one might suspect that the least squares rule is appropriate. However, it turns out that the random error e_t and the random regressor z_t are correlated and, hence, as we indicated in Section 14.1, the least squares estimator is biased and inconsistent.

To prove that e_t and z_t are correlated, we find the covariance between these random variables as

$$\text{cov}(z_t, e_t) = E\big[(z_t - E[z_t])(e_t - E[e_t])\big]$$
$$= E\big[u_t(v_t - u_t\beta_2)\big]$$
$$= E[u_t v_t] - \beta_2 E[u_t^2]$$
$$= -\beta_2 \sigma_u^2$$

To prove the inconsistency of the least squares estimator, we use equation 14.1.9 which, in this context, is

$$\text{plim } b_2 = \beta_2 + \frac{\text{plim}\left[\dfrac{1}{T}\Sigma(z_t - \bar{z})e_t\right]}{\text{plim}\left[\dfrac{1}{T}\Sigma(z_t - \bar{z})^2\right]}$$

$$= \beta_2 - \frac{\beta_2 \sigma_u^2}{\sigma_{zz}}$$

$$= \beta_2\left(1 - \frac{\sigma_u^2}{\sigma_{zz}}\right) \tag{14.4.11}$$

In deriving equation 14.4.11 we have used the results that $\Sigma(z_t - \bar{z})e_t / T$ is a consistent estimator of $\text{cov}(z_t, e_t)$ and $\Sigma(z_t - \bar{z})^2 / T$ is a consistent estimator of $\text{var}(z_t) = \sigma_{zz}$. Equation 14.4.11 demonstrates the inconsistency of the least squares estimator and tells us that the inconsistency will depend on the magnitude of the variance of the measurement error relative to the variance of z_t.

14.4.2   Instrumental Variable Estimation

In Section 14.3 we discussed the method of moments as a possible estimation principle that would lead to a consistent estimator. The population moment criteria that we used were $E[e_t] = 0$ and $\text{cov}(x_t, e_t) = 0$ where x_t was a (possibly) random regressor and e_t was the equation error. In the measurement error model we are considering, z_t is the random regressor, and $\text{cov}(z_t, e_t) \neq 0$. Thus, we cannot employ the condition $\text{cov}(z_t, e_t) = 0$. However, if we can find another variable x_t that is uncorrelated with e_t, then it is possible that application of the method of moments to the condition $\text{cov}(x_t, e_t) = 0$ might prove fruitful.

Let us examine this question in terms of the Friedman permanent consumption–income hypothesis. In this context $y_t^* = c_{Pt} = $ permanent consumption and $z_t^* = y_{Pt} = $ permanent income, and the errors $v_t = y_t - y_t^*$ and $u_t = z_t - z_t^*$ represent the differences between observed and permanent consumption and observed and permanent income, respectively. Another macroeconomic variable that is closely related to income and consumption is investment. Also, we would not expect the errors v_t and u_t to be related to investment. Thus, if we denote investment by x_t, then reasonable population moment conditions are $E[e_t] = 0$ and $\text{cov}(x_t, e_t) = 0$. The corresponding sample moment conditions are

$$\frac{1}{T}\Sigma \hat{e}_t = 0 \quad \text{and} \quad \frac{1}{T}\Sigma x_t \hat{e}_t = 0 \tag{14.4.12}$$

or

$$\Sigma\left(y_t - \hat{\beta}_{1(iv)} - \hat{\beta}_{2(iv)} z_t\right) = 0 \tag{14.4.13a}$$

$$\Sigma x_t \left(y_t - \hat{\beta}_{1(iv)} - \hat{\beta}_{2(iv)} z_t\right) = 0 \tag{14.4.13b}$$

The significance of the (iv) subscript notation will become clear in due course. Simplifying, we have

$$T\hat{\beta}_{1(iv)} + \Sigma z_t \hat{\beta}_{2(iv)} = \Sigma y_t \tag{14.4.14a}$$

$$\Sigma x_t \hat{\beta}_{1(iv)} + \Sigma x_t z_t \hat{\beta}_{2(iv)} = \Sigma x_t y_t \tag{14.4.14b}$$

Solving these two equations for $\hat{\beta}_{1(iv)}$ and $\hat{\beta}_{2(iv)}$ yields (see Exercise 14.2)

$$\hat{\beta}_{2(iv)} = \frac{\Sigma(x_t - \bar{x})(y_t - \bar{y})}{\Sigma(x_t - \bar{x})(z_t - \bar{z})} \tag{14.4.15a}$$

$$\hat{\beta}_{1(iv)} = \bar{y} - \hat{\beta}_{2(iv)} \bar{z} \tag{14.4.15b}$$

To investigate the consistency of these estimators, we will consider $\hat{\beta}_{2(iv)}$. Note that we can write (Exercise 14.3)

$$\hat{\beta}_{2(iv)} = \beta_2 + \frac{\Sigma(x_t - \bar{x})e_t}{\Sigma(x_t - \bar{x})(z_t - \bar{z})} \tag{14.4.16}$$

and so

$$\text{plim}\,\hat{\beta}_{2(iv)} = \beta_2 + \frac{\text{plim}\left[\frac{1}{T}\Sigma(x_t - \bar{x})e_t\right]}{\text{plim}\left[\frac{1}{T}\Sigma(x_t - \bar{x})(z_t - \bar{z})\right]} \tag{14.4.17}$$

Because $\Sigma(x_t - \bar{x})e_t / T$ is a consistent estimator of $\text{cov}(x_t, e_t)$, the numerator of the right-hand-side term is zero. The denominator is the plim of the sample covariance between x_t and z_t; it is equal to the population covariance, say σ_{xz}. Providing that σ_{xz} is nonzero, we have

$$\text{plim}\,\hat{\beta}_{2(iv)} = \beta_2 + \frac{0}{\sigma_{xz}} = \beta_2 \qquad (14.4.18)$$

Hence, $\hat{\beta}_{2(iv)}$ is a consistent estimator for β_2 if x_t is uncorrelated with e_t, but correlated with z_t. Note that these conditions are indeed likely to be satisfied. Measurement errors for consumption and income are unlikely to be correlated with investment, but investment is likely to be correlated with income. It also follows that $\hat{\beta}_{1(iv)}$ is a consistent estimator for β_1. See Exercise 14.4.

The estimation procedure we have described is known as *instrumental variable estimation* and the variable x_t is known as an *instrumental variable* or, more simply, as an *instrument*. The object of instrumental variable estimation is to use the method of moments to generate a consistent estimator by finding an instrument x_t that is correlated with the random regressor z_t, but uncorrelated with the random error e_t. Of course, in any given situation, a number of possible instruments could be chosen. Each choice of instrument leads to an alternative consistent estimator. Consequently, we cannot say that an instrumental variable estimator is efficient. Note that when we say "efficiency" in this case, we mean large sample efficiency. What we can say, however, is that the greater the correlation between x_t and z_t, the more efficient will be the instrumental variable estimator. We can see this result by noting the variance of the approximate large sample distribution for $\hat{\beta}_{2(iv)}$. In large samples it is approximately true that

$$\hat{\beta}_{2(iv)} \sim N\left(\beta_2, \text{var}\left(\hat{\beta}_{2(iv)}\right)\right) \qquad (14.4.19)$$

where

$$\hat{\text{var}}\left(\hat{\beta}_{2(iv)}\right) = \frac{\hat{\sigma}^2 \Sigma\left(x_t - \bar{x}\right)^2}{\left[\Sigma\left(x_t - \bar{x}\right)\left(z_t - \bar{z}\right)\right]^2} \qquad (14.4.20)$$

$$\hat{\sigma}^2 = \frac{1}{T}\Sigma\hat{e}_t^2 \qquad (14.4.21)$$

and the instrumental variable residual is given by

$$\hat{e}_t = y_t - \hat{\beta}_{1(iv)} - \hat{\beta}_{2(iv)}z_t \qquad (14.4.22)$$

The higher the correlation between x_t and z_t, the larger will be the denominator in equation 14.4.20 and the smaller the variance of $\hat{\beta}_{2(iv)}$.

A more general, elegant, and compact representation of instrumental variable estimation is possible when we use matrix algebra. Such a representation is given in Appendix 14A for the general case of any number of random regressors and corresponding instruments.

14.4.3   Testing for Correlation Between a Regressor and the Error

Consider again the model

$$y_t = \beta_1 + \beta_2 z_t + e_t \qquad (14.4.23)$$

but suppose there is doubt concerning whether or not z_t is contemporaneously correlated with e_t. We may be in doubt about whether measurement error exists, or there may be some other reason for suspecting that z_t is correlated with e_t. In Chapter 18 we learn that if z_t is an "endogenous" variable, it will be correlated with e_t. Since the existence or nonexistence of correlation between z_t and e_t has a large bearing on whether the least squares estimator is consistent, it is important to have a testing mechanism to help establish the presence or absence of such correlation. For example, it is important to test for the existence of measurement error or to test whether a regressor variable is endogenous. The relevant null and alternative hypotheses are

$$H_0 : \text{plim} \frac{1}{T} \Sigma (z_t - \bar{z}) e_t = 0 \qquad H_1 : \text{plim} \frac{1}{T} \Sigma (z_t - \bar{z}) e_t \neq 0 \tag{14.4.24}$$

One possibility for testing H_0 against the alternative H_1 is a test known as Hausman's specification test. This test is designed to test whether the least squares estimator b_2 yields a value that is significantly different from that produced by the instrumental variables estimator $\hat{\beta}_{2(iv)}$. If H_0 is true, then both are consistent estimators for β_2. We would not expect the two estimators to produce estimates that are vastly different. On the other hand, if H_1 is true, then b_2 is inconsistent, and we would expect some difference between the estimates b_2 and $\hat{\beta}_{2(iv)}$. The following statistic has a large sample chi-square distribution with one degree of freedom when the null hypothesis is true.

$$m = \frac{\left(\hat{\beta}_{2(iv)} - b_2 \right)^2}{\text{vâr}\left(\hat{\beta}_{2(iv)} \right) - \text{vâr}(b_2)} \tag{14.4.25}$$

We reject H_0 and conclude that contemporaneous correlation between z_t and e_t does exist if $m > \chi_c^2$, where, for a 5% significance level, $\chi_c^2 = 3.84$.

When computing $\text{vâr}\left(\hat{\beta}_{2(iv)} \right)$ and $\text{vâr}(b_2)$ the same estimate of σ^2 should be used in each instance. This estimate could be the usual least squares one, relevant when H_0 is true, or it could be the one that results from the instrumental variables procedure, relevant when H_1 is true. The fact that we can use either estimate illustrates again the approximate nature of large sample tests.

Our test description has only been in terms of the single coefficient β_2. In some cases it is possible to employ a more general version of the test that is described in Appendix 14A.

14.4.4   An Example

Consider the data on investment (x), consumption (y), and income (z) given in Table 14.2. To apply the instrumental variable estimator to the model

$$y_t = \beta_1 + \beta_2 z_t + e_t$$

with x_t as the instrument, we carry out the following preliminary calculations:

$$\begin{aligned} \Sigma (x_t - \bar{x})(z_t - \bar{z}) &= \Sigma x_t z_t - \Sigma x_t \Sigma z_t / T \\ &= 1461.174 - (58)(492.78)/20 \\ &= 32.112 \end{aligned}$$

Table 14.2 Data for x, y, and z

Observation	x	y	z
1	2.0	15.30	17.30
2	2.0	19.91	21.91
3	2.2	20.94	22.96
4	2.2	19.66	21.86
5	2.4	21.32	23.72
6	2.4	18.33	20.73
7	2.6	19.59	22.19
8	2.6	21.30	23.90
9	2.8	20.93	23.73
10	2.8	21.64	24.44
11	3.0	21.90	24.90
12	3.0	20.50	23.50
13	3.2	22.83	26.05
14	3.2	23.49	26.69
15	3.4	24.20	27.60
16	3.4	23.05	26.45
17	3.6	24.01	27.61
18	3.6	25.83	29.43
19	3.8	25.15	28.95
20	3.8	25.06	28.86

$$\Sigma(x_t - \bar{x})(y_t - \bar{y}) = \Sigma x_t y_t - \Sigma x_t \Sigma y_t / T$$
$$= 1286.706 - (58)(434.94)/20$$
$$= 25.38$$

$$\Sigma(x_t - \bar{x})^2 = \Sigma x_t^2 - (\Sigma x_t)^2 / T$$
$$= 174.8 - (58)^2 / 20$$
$$= 6.6$$

In line with equation 14.4.15, the instrumental variable estimates are

$$\hat{\beta}_{2(iv)} = \frac{\Sigma(x_t - \bar{x})(y_t - \bar{y})}{\Sigma(x_t - \bar{x})(z_t - \bar{z})} = \frac{25.38}{32.112} = 0.7904$$

$$\hat{\beta}_{1(iv)} = \bar{y} - \hat{\beta}_{2(iv)}\bar{z} = 21.747 - (0.79036)(24.639) = 2.273$$

The sum of squared residuals is 1.3435, which yields $\hat{\sigma}^2 = 0.0672$. The estimated variance of the approximate large sample distribution for $\hat{\beta}_{2(iv)}$ is

$$\text{vâr}(\hat{\beta}_{2(iv)}) = \frac{\hat{\sigma}^2 \Sigma(x_t - \bar{x})^2}{[\Sigma(x_t - \bar{x})(z_t - \bar{z})]^2} = \frac{(0.0672)(6.6)}{(32.112)^2} = 0.00043$$

and the corresponding standard error is 0.0207. The ratio of $\hat{\beta}_{2(iv)}$ to its standard error is therefore 38.12. Using this number as an *approximate* t-value shows that $\hat{\beta}_{2(iv)}$ is significant at the 1% level.

To test whether the data suggest that correlation between z_t and e_t does exist, and hence to test whether it is necessary to employ the instrumental variable procedure, we compute the least squares estimate and then the value for Hausman's test statistic. The least squares estimate for β_2 is

$$b_2 = \frac{\Sigma(z_t - \bar{z})(y_t - \bar{y})}{\Sigma(z_t - \bar{z})^2} = \frac{150.734}{183.176} = 0.8229$$

Using the error variance estimate $\hat{\sigma}^2 = 0.0672$ obtained from instrumental variable estimation, the estimated variance of b_2 is

$$\text{vâr}(b_2) = \frac{\hat{\sigma}^2}{\Sigma(z_t - \bar{z})^2} = \frac{0.0672}{183.176} = 0.0003667$$

Thus, the value for Hausman's test statistic is

$$m = \frac{\left(\hat{\beta}_{2(iv)} - b_2\right)^2}{\text{vâr}\left(\hat{\beta}_{2(iv)}\right) - \text{vâr}(b_2)} = \frac{(0.7904 - 0.8229)^2}{0.0004299 - 0.0003667} = 16.7$$

Since this value is greater than 3.84, the 5% critical value from a $\chi^2_{(1)}$-distribution, we reject H_0 and conclude that the least squares estimator is inconsistent. Contemporaneous correlation between z_t and e_t does exist.

14.5 Summary

In a random regressor statistical model, the sampling properties of the least squares estimator depend on the relationship between the stochastic regressors and the equation errors. If the stochastic regressors are not contemporaneously correlated with the equation errors, least squares procedures have desirable properties in large samples. In particular, the least squares estimator is consistent. Its distribution collapses around the true parameter value as the sample size increases. Unfortunately, in many statistical models involving economic variables, the assumption of stochastic regressors that are contemporaneously uncorrelated with the equation error vector is hard to justify. Under these circumstances the least squares estimator is inconsistent. Examples of random regressor models where contemporaneous correlation between regressors and errors exists, and where the least squares estimator is inconsistent, are *(i)* models where the dependent variable lagged is a regressor and the errors are correlated over time, *(ii)* measurement error models, and *(iii)* simultaneous equation models. In a model with a lagged dependent variable and an error that is not correlated over time, the lagged dependent variable is not totally uncorrelated with the error vector, but it is contemporaneously uncorrelated and the least squares estimator is consistent.

In random regressor models, as well as other models that are encountered later in the book, it is not mathematically possible to derive the exact probability distribution of the least squares estimator and associated test statistics. As an alternative we use limiting or asymptotic distributions that can be derived by letting the sample size T approach infinity. Such distributions are approximately valid in large samples, and for this reason we have referred to them as large sample approximate distributions. Central Limit Theorems are usually the basis for large sample distributions. In the random regressor model with no contemporaneous correlation between the regressor and the error term, approximate normal and chi-square distributions can be used to test hypotheses about the coefficient vector β. The normal distribution is relevant when testing a single null hypothesis; the chi-square distribution is relevant for a null hypothesis that comprises joint hypotheses (one or more) about the elements in β. There are several variations of the chi-square statistic, depending on which estimator is used for the error variance. Although all of these variations have the same large sample distribution, they produce different results in finite samples. The chi-square test based on an estimate of σ^2 when H_1 is true is called the Wald test; when σ^2 is estimated assuming H_0 is true, the test is a Lagrange multiplier test. Sometimes t- and F-distributions are used instead of the normal and χ^2-distributions, respectively. Some practitioners argue that the usual t- and F-tests, and their associated critical values, are likely to be better finite sample approximations than the normal and χ^2-tests that are dictated by the asymptotic theory.

One estimator is more efficient in large samples than another if the variance of its large sample probability distribution is smaller. The maximum likelihood principle leads to estimators with the property of large sample efficiency. A further large sample test that can be used for testing hypotheses is the likelihood ratio test. This test compares the maximized likelihood function values under H_0 and H_1. Another principle of estimation that can be employed is the method of moments; this principle can be used to find a consistent estimator.

An example of a model where the regressors are contemporaneously correlated with the error is an errors in variables or measurement error model. Since the least squares estimator is inconsistent for this model, we need an alternative estimator. The method of moments can be used to suggest a consistent estimator known as the instrumental variables estimator. This estimator uses instrument variables that are uncorrelated with the error, but are as highly correlated as possible with the random regressors. One possible strategy for using the instrumental variable estimator is to use one instrument for each regressor that is correlated with the error. However, as we discover in Appendix 14A, if we have a greater number of suitable instruments than we do offending regressors, we can improve the (large sample) efficiency of the instrumental variable estimator by using all instruments in a more general estimator. This more general instrumental variables estimator is also known as the two-stage least squares estimator.

If there is uncertainty about whether some of the regressors are correlated with the error term, we can test for the existence of such correlation by using a specification test suggested by Hausman. This test examines whether or not the difference between the least squares estimator and an instrumental variables estimator is significant.

14.6 Exercises

14.1 For the simple regression model $y_t = \beta_1 + \beta_2 x_t + e_t$, prove that the least squares estimator for β_2 can be written as

$$b_2 = \beta_2 + \frac{\Sigma(x_t - \bar{x})e_t}{\Sigma(x_t - \bar{x})^2}$$

14.2 Show that

$$\hat{\beta}_{1(iv)} = \bar{y} - \hat{\beta}_{2(iv)}\bar{z}$$

and

$$\hat{\beta}_{2(iv)} = \frac{\Sigma(x_t - \bar{x})(y_t - \bar{y})}{\Sigma(x_t - \bar{x})(z_t - \bar{z})}$$

are the solutions to the two simultaneous equations

$$T\hat{\beta}_{1(iv)} + \Sigma z_t \hat{\beta}_{2(iv)} = \Sigma y_t$$

$$\Sigma x_t \hat{\beta}_{1(iv)} + \Sigma x_t z_t \hat{\beta}_{2(iv)} = \Sigma x_t y_t$$

14.3 For the model $y_t = \beta_1 + \beta_2 z_t + e_t$, prove that

$$\frac{\Sigma(x_t - \bar{x})(y_t - \bar{y})}{\Sigma(x_t - \bar{x})(z_t - \bar{z})} = \beta_2 + \frac{\Sigma(x_t - \bar{x})e_t}{\Sigma(x_t - \bar{x})(z_t - \bar{z})}$$

14.4 Given the assumptions utilized in Section 14.4.2, prove that $\hat{\beta}_{1(iv)}$ is a consistent estimator for β_1.

14.5 Consider the general instrumental variables estimator

$$\hat{\boldsymbol{\beta}}_{(iv)} = \left[Z'X(X'X)^{-1} X'Z \right]^{-1} Z'X(X'X)^{-1} X'\mathbf{y}$$

that is given in equation 14A.17 of Appendix 14A.3.
(a) In what sense can $\hat{\boldsymbol{\beta}}_{(iv)}$ be viewed as a method of moments estimator?
(b) Prove that $\hat{\boldsymbol{\beta}}_{(iv)}$ is a consistent estimator for $\boldsymbol{\beta}$.

14.6 Given that $\mathbf{z}_1$ is a $(T \times 1)$ vector with all of its elements equal to unity, and X is a $(T \times K)$ matrix whose first column is equal to $\mathbf{z}_1$, prove that

$$\mathbf{z}_1 = X(X'X)^{-1} X'\mathbf{z}_1$$

14.7 For the linear model $\mathbf{y} = X\boldsymbol{\beta} + \mathbf{e}$, with normally distributed errors, and the hypotheses $H_0: R\boldsymbol{\beta} = \mathbf{r}$ and $H_1: R\boldsymbol{\beta} \neq \mathbf{r}$, show that the two expressions for the likelihood ratio test statistic in equations 14.3.7 and 14.3.8 are identical. That is, show that

$$2\left[L(H_1) - L(H_0)\right] = T\left[\ln \mathrm{SSE}_R - \ln \mathrm{SSE}_U\right]$$

14.8 Suppose that we want to estimate the consumption function

$$c_t^* = \beta_1 + \beta_2 y_t^*$$

where c_t^* and y_t^* are true but unobservable consumption and income, respectively. The observable values c_t and y_t are subject to errors of measurement and are related to the true values as follows:

$$c_t = c_t^* + v_t, \quad y_t = y_t^* + u_t$$

where v_t and u_t are each independent and identically distributed random variables with $N(0, \sigma_v^2)$ and $N(0, \sigma_u^2)$ distributions, respectively. Data on c_t, y_t, and two potential instrumental variables, i_t (investment) and g_t (government expenditure), appear in Table 14.3.
(a) Find least squares estimates of β_1 and β_2.

Table 14.3 Hypothetical Data for i, g, c, and y

Observation	i	g	c	y
1	1.5	0.5	15.30	17.30
2	1.4	0.6	19.91	21.91
3	1.5	0.7	20.94	22.96
4	1.4	0.8	19.66	21.86
5	1.5	0.9	21.32	23.72
6	1.4	1.0	18.33	20.73
7	1.6	1.0	19.59	22.19
8	1.5	1.1	21.30	23.90
9	1.6	1.2	20.93	23.73
10	1.6	1.2	21.64	24.44
11	1.7	1.3	21.90	24.90
12	1.6	1.4	20.50	23.50
13	1.8	1.4	22.83	26.05
14	1.7	1.5	23.49	26.69
15	1.9	1.5	24.20	27.60
16	1.8	1.6	23.05	26.45
17	2.0	1.6	24.01	27.61
18	1.9	1.7	25.83	29.43
19	2.0	1.8	25.15	28.95
20	2.0	1.8	25.06	28.86

(b) Find instrumental variables estimates for β_1 and β_2 by using the following instruments:

(i) i_t (ii) g_t (iii) $x_t = i_t + g_t$ (iv) i_t and g_t

Comment on the alternative estimates and their standard errors.

(c) A number of variations of Hausman's specification test for testing for contemporaneous correlation between y_t and the composite error $v_t - \beta_2 u_t$ are possible. These variations depend on (i) the instrumental variable (IV) estimator that is used, and (ii) whether the error variance $\text{var}(v_t - \beta_2 u_t) = \sigma^2$ is estimated from least squares procedures or instrumental variables procedures. Using estimates for β_2, carry out Hausman's test for the following cases. Comment on the outcome.

Case	IV Estimator	Choice of $\hat{\sigma}^2$
1	Uses i_t	IV
2	Uses g_t	IV
3	Uses x_t	Least squares
4	Uses x_t	IV
5	Uses i_t and g_t	IV

14.9 Consider the following log-linear production function, where output (y) is related to a composite input index (x) through the equation

$$\ln y_t = \beta_1 + \beta_2 \ln x_t + e_t$$

The error term e_t consists of two components; one is a random completely unpredictable component, whereas the other is a measure of the managerial or technical efficiency of the tth firm. It is believed that the input level of a firm x_t could depend on, and hence be correlated with, the component of e_t that represents technical efficiency. To test this hypothesis the input price p_t facing the tth firm is used as an instrumental variable. Given that price is exogenously determined, it is assumed that price is uncorrelated with technical efficiency. However, x_t and p_t are likely to be correlated because the choice of the level of input will depend on its price.

(a) Use the data on 40 firms given in Table 14.4 to find least squares and instrumental variable estimators for β_1 and β_2. Comment on the two sets of estimates.

(b) Use Hausman's specification test on the estimates for β_2 to test whether the input and technical efficiency are correlated.

14.10 In an attempt to explain annual income of a cross section of 45 people, a researcher sets up the model

$$y_t = \beta_1 + \beta_2 a_t + \beta_3 g_t + \beta_4 m_t + e_t$$

where y_t is income (in thousands of dollars), a_t is age, g_t is gender (0 for male and 1 for female), and m_t is a measure of the ability of the tth individual. Data on these variables, as well as on the number of years of schooling after high school s_t, appear in Table 14.5.

(a) Use least squares to estimate $\beta = (\beta_1, \beta_2, \beta_3, \beta_4)'$.

(b) Use the Wald, LM, LR, and F tests to test (i) the hypothesis that gender does not influence income, and (ii) the hypothesis that gender and ability do not influence income.

(c) Using s_t as an instrument for m_t, find the instrumental variables estimate $\hat{\beta}_{(iv)}$ for β. Comment on the results relative to those in part (a).

(d) Using b and $\hat{\beta}_{(iv)}$, test whether contemporaneous correlation between the regressors and the error exists.

(e) Suggest and carry through a Wald test that uses the instrumental variables estimator to test whether gender and ability do not influence income.

14.7 References

For a more complete discussion of stochastic regressors and unobservable variables see
JUDGE, G. G., R. C. HILL, W. E. GRIFFITHS, H. LÜTKEPOHL, and T. C. LEE (1988) *Introduction to the Theory and Practice of Econometrics*, New York: John Wiley & Sons, Inc., pp. 571–599 and the references contained therein.

For other treatments of large sample theory and testing see
DORAN, H. E. (1989) *Applied Regression Analysis in Econometrics*, New York: Marcel Dekker, Inc., Chapter 11 and pp.356–360.
MADDALA, G. S. (1989) *Introduction to Econometrics*, New York: Macmillan, Publishing Co., pp. 33–35, 137–139, 435–441.

Table 14.4   Data for Exercise 14.9

y	x	p
31.18	91.19	50.51
32.08	112.70	38.56
30.46	120.67	43.42
28.28	93.65	59.89
30.34	116.00	46.24
32.29	104.97	59.33
31.54	104.17	51.00
34.35	92.60	49.14
36.26	98.87	45.66
31.40	93.16	47.73
27.82	74.37	56.01
30.24	109.03	46.68
32.92	122.50	43.17
28.33	92.55	54.82
27.54	88.13	51.02
32.72	106.68	52.28
27.43	80.47	54.34
27.86	97.08	50.21
28.00	84.85	49.33
33.63	86.26	55.39
33.85	103.04	48.64
26.25	78.95	56.25
35.33	114.84	46.58
36.54	100.38	53.78
32.77	118.93	44.04
33.95	107.54	54.44
38.59	128.48	45.49
26.14	83.95	54.31
31.09	112.76	47.17
33.51	102.94	48.01
33.81	105.27	28.74
31.74	97.70	49.84
31.66	88.20	55.74
29.97	101.91	44.47
30.41	82.86	42.69
28.51	76.39	59.50
28.39	79.86	59.99
30.69	92.26	48.56
25.57	78.40	58.62
31.04	115.37	61.56

Table 14.5   Data for Exercise 14.10

y	a	g	m	s
44.886	42	1	132	10
42.344	46	1	123	6
34.187	27	1	140	10
48.218	53	1	146	7
16.733	23	0	52	0
42.449	27	0	110	9
44.889	55	0	86	5
35.093	30	1	113	8
45.678	60	0	131	7
31.859	23	0	118	6
37.042	35	0	136	9
28.689	22	1	112	5
41.501	35	0	113	3
40.280	48	0	112	7
35.071	27	1	70	8
35.715	36	1	105	3
29.268	28	1	76	0
33.863	43	1	53	0
49.412	55	0	119	6
44.609	41	0	153	10
29.894	24	1	97	6
58.527	62	1	107	3
40.462	29	1	113	10
38.146	29	1	155	8
53.980	62	1	105	4
29.367	34	1	62	2
48.261	54	0	88	4
42.150	42	0	95	4
55.936	57	1	121	5
33.843	22	0	155	10
31.660	26	0	84	9
36.031	29	0	117	4
42.419	43	1	129	4
40.439	43	1	76	3
57.956	59	0	110	6
34.545	36	0	90	6
23.945	28	1	87	9
41.485	32	1	143	7
27.188	31	1	100	5
50.725	53	1	118	8
26.699	33	0	86	2
36.571	22	0	80	5
40.716	31	1	116	6
56.298	62	0	99	7
49.707	61	0	113	6

APPENDIX 14A   Consistency, Random Regressors and Instrumental Variable Estimation in the General Linear Statistical Model

In this section we use matrix algebra notation to describe the general linear statistical model with random regressors. We are concerned with *(i)* consistency, *(ii)* a general formulation of instrumental variable estimation, and *(iii)* a more general version of Hausman's specification test.

14A.1   Consistency in the General Random Regressor Model

Consider the general model

$$\mathbf{y} = X\boldsymbol{\beta} + \mathbf{e}$$

where $\mathbf{e} \sim (\mathbf{0}, \sigma^2 I_T)$ and where X can contain one or more random regressors. The probability limit of the least squares estimator

$$\mathbf{b} = \left(X'X\right)^{-1} X'\mathbf{y} = \boldsymbol{\beta} + \left(X'X\right)^{-1} X'\mathbf{e}$$

$$= \boldsymbol{\beta} + \left(\frac{X'X}{T}\right)^{-1} \frac{X'\mathbf{e}}{T} \tag{14A.1}$$

is given by

$$\text{plim } \mathbf{b} = \boldsymbol{\beta} + \left(\text{plim}\frac{X'X}{T}\right)^{-1} \text{plim}\frac{X'\mathbf{e}}{T} \tag{14A.2}$$

In going from equation 14A.1 to equation 14A.2 we have used the results given in equation 14.1.8.

Typical terms in the matrix $X'X/T$ are $\Sigma x_{t2}^2 /T$ and $\Sigma x_{t2}x_{t3} /T$. We will assume that such terms have a finite probability limit. This assumption is satisfied if the random regressors have finite variances and covariances. Let us denote the finite probability limit of $X'X/T$ by $\text{plim } X'X/T = \Sigma_{XX}$ and let us also assume this matrix is nonsingular.

A typical term in the vector $X'\mathbf{e}/T$ is $\Sigma x_{t2}e_t /T$. This term is a consistent estimator of the covariance between x_{t2} and e_t. Thus, if this, and the other regressors, are contemporaneously uncorrelated with e_t, the term $X'\mathbf{e}/T$ will be a consistent estimator of zero; and we have $\text{plim } X'\mathbf{e}/T = \mathbf{0}$. Inserting these results into equation 14A.2 yields

$$\text{plim } \mathbf{b} = \boldsymbol{\beta} + \Sigma_{XX}^{-1} \cdot \mathbf{0} = \boldsymbol{\beta} \tag{14A.3}$$

Thus, we have shown that the least squares estimator is consistent when the regressors are contemporaneously uncorrelated with the error term. It also follows that if the regressors are correlated with the error term, then $\text{plim } X'\mathbf{e}/T \neq \mathbf{0}$ and the least squares estimator is inconsistent.

14A.2 Instrumental Variable Estimation in the General Random-Regressor Model

Consider the *general* stochastic linear regression model

$$\mathbf{y} = Z\boldsymbol{\beta} + \mathbf{e} \tag{14A.4}$$

where $\mathbf{y}$ is a $(T \times 1)$ vector of observations, $\boldsymbol{\beta}$ is a $(K \times 1)$ vector of unknown parameters, the $(T \times K)$ regressor matrix Z contains one or more stochastic variables, and $\mathbf{e}$ is a $(T \times 1)$ vector of random errors with the properties $E[\mathbf{e}] = \mathbf{0}$, and $E[\mathbf{ee'}] = \sigma^2 I_T$. We denote the stochastic regressor matrix as Z rather than the usual X to emphasize that *we are also assuming that one or more of the stochastic regressors is contemporaneously correlated with the error vector* $\mathbf{e}$. The inconsistency of the least squares estimator under this set of assumptions was demonstrated in the previous section. We can cure the problem, and find a consistent estimator, by applying the method of moments to

$$\text{plim} \frac{X'\mathbf{e}}{T} = \mathbf{0} \tag{14A.5}$$

where X is a $(T \times K)$ matrix of instruments that is uncorrelated with $\mathbf{e}$, and hence satisfies equation 14A.5. We also assume that X is correlated, and preferably *highly correlated*, with Z. The existence of correlation between X and Z means that we can write

$$\text{plim} \frac{X'Z}{T} = \Sigma_{xz} \tag{14A.6}$$

where Σ_{xz} is finite and nonsingular. Under these assumptions, $\text{plim}\, X'\mathbf{y}/T$ also exists, and we write this limit as

$$\text{plim} \frac{X'\mathbf{y}}{T} = \Sigma_{xy} \tag{14A.7}$$

It is convenient to use X' to premultiply the original equation, equation 14A.4 to obtain

$$X'\mathbf{y} = X'Z\boldsymbol{\beta} + X'\mathbf{e} \tag{14A.8}$$

Dividing both sides of equation 14A.8 by T and taking the probability limit, we have

$$\text{plim} \frac{X'\mathbf{y}}{T} = \text{plim} \frac{X'Z}{T}\boldsymbol{\beta} + \text{plim} \frac{X'\mathbf{e}}{T} \tag{14A.9}$$

Since $\text{plim}\, X'\mathbf{e}/T = \mathbf{0}$, if we make use of equations 14A.6 and 14A.7, solving for $\boldsymbol{\beta}$ yields

$$\boldsymbol{\beta} = \Sigma_{xz}^{-1}\Sigma_{xy} \tag{14A.10}$$

To apply the method of moments to this equation, we replace the population moments Σ_{xz} and Σ_{xy} by their sample counterparts $X'Z/T$ and $X'\mathbf{y}/T$. This replacement yields the *instrumental variables estimator*

$$\hat{\boldsymbol{\beta}}_{(iv)} = \left(\frac{X'Z}{T}\right)^{-1} \frac{X'\mathbf{y}}{T} = (X'Z)^{-1} X'\mathbf{y} \tag{14A.11}$$

The variables $\mathbf{x}_1, \mathbf{x}_2, \ldots, \mathbf{x}_K$ that make up the $(T \times K)$ matrix X are called *instrumental variables*.

Noting that

$$\hat{\beta}_{(iv)} = (X'Z)^{-1} X'y = (X'Z)^{-1} X'(Z\beta + e) = \beta + (X'Z)^{-1} X'e \qquad (14A.12)$$

we can establish the consistency of the instrumental variables estimator as follows

$$\text{plim}\,\hat{\beta}_{(iv)} = \beta + \left(\text{plim}\,\frac{X'Z}{T} \right)^{-1} \text{plim}\left(\frac{X'e}{T} \right)$$

$$= \beta + \Sigma_{XZ}^{-1} \cdot \mathbf{0}$$

$$= \beta \qquad (14A.13)$$

It is clearly crucial that X *be uncorrelated with* **e** *but correlated with the explanatory variables Z* so that the second-order moment matrix Σ_{XZ} exists and is nonsingular.

For large samples $\hat{\beta}_{(iv)}$ has a covariance matrix that can be estimated by

$$\hat{\text{cov}}\left(\hat{\beta}_{(iv)}\right) = \hat{\sigma}^2 (X'Z)^{-1} (X'X)(Z'X)^{-1} \qquad (14A.14)$$

where $\hat{\sigma}^2 = \left(\mathbf{y} - Z\hat{\beta}_{(iv)}\right)' \left(\mathbf{y} - Z\hat{\beta}_{(iv)}\right) \Big/ T$. However, the variance of $\hat{\beta}_{(iv)}$ is *not necessarily a minimum large sample variance,* since there may be many sets of instrumental variables that fulfill the requirement of being uncorrelated with the stochastic term and correlated with the stochastic regressors. The more correlated the instruments are with the stochastic regressors Z, the smaller is the large sample covariance matrix. Despite its lack of efficiency, the instrumental variable estimator provides at least a consistent estimator, in a world of biased alternatives.

14A.3 A More General Instrumental Variables Estimator

The instrumental variables approach developed in the previous section implicitly assumed that we have one instrument for each of the variables in Z. That is, it assumed that X and Z are of the same dimension, both $(T \times K)$. If some of the variables in Z are nonstochastic, say z_1 and z_2, then it is usual for these variables to be instruments for themselves. That is, we choose, $x_1 = z_1$ and $x_2 = z_2$. Since the first variable z_1 will almost always be a column of ones (and, hence, nonstochastic), the first instrument x_1 will almost always be a column of ones. It is only for the stochastic regressors that are correlated with the error that we need to choose instruments different from the regressors themselves.

The question that we address in this section is: Is there a way to proceed if we have available more instruments than there are stochastic regressors that require instruments? Intuitively, we would expect that more instruments may give us more information and, hence, greater efficiency. To answer this question consider again the model $\mathbf{y} = Z\beta + \mathbf{e}$, but let us assume that Z is of dimension $(T \times 2)$, comprising z_1, which is a column of ones, and one stochastic regressor z_2. Assume also that there is available a $(T \times K)$ matrix of possible instruments X. Multiplying both sides of the original equation by X' yields

$$X'\mathbf{y} = X'Z\beta + X'\mathbf{e} \qquad (14A.15)$$

A rough way of describing our earlier steps to obtain the instrumental variables estimator is to say we ignore $X'\mathbf{e}$, and then premultiply both sides of equation 14A.15 by

$(X'Z)^{-1}$ to yield $\hat{\boldsymbol{\beta}}_{(iv)} = \left(X'Z\right)^{-1} X'\mathbf{y}$. However, with our current set of assumptions, this is not possible. It is impossible because $X'Z$ is of dimension $(K \times 2)$; a matrix that is not square cannot be inverted. We overcome this problem by multiplying both sides of the original equation by $Z'X(X'X)^{-1}X'$ to obtain

$$Z'X\left(X'X\right)^{-1} X'\mathbf{y} = Z'X\left(X'X\right)^{-1} X'Z\boldsymbol{\beta} + Z'X\left(X'X\right)^{-1} X'\mathbf{e} \tag{14A.16}$$

Ignoring the last term and premultiplying by the (2×2) matrix, $[Z'X(X'X)^{-1}X'Z]^{-1}$ yields the more general instrumental variables estimator

$$\hat{\boldsymbol{\beta}}_{(iv)} = \left[Z'X\left(X'X\right)^{-1} X'Z\right]^{-1} Z'X\left(X'X\right)^{-1} X'\mathbf{y} \tag{14A.17}$$

In Exercise 14.5 you are asked to show how this estimator can be viewed as a method of moments estimator and to prove that it is consistent. The covariance matrix of its approximate large sample distribution can be estimated from

$$\hat{\text{cov}}\left(\hat{\boldsymbol{\beta}}_{(iv)}\right) = \hat{\sigma}^2 \left[Z'X\left(X'X\right)^{-1} X'Z\right]^{-1} \tag{14A.18}$$

The instrumental variables estimator in equation 14A.17 provides a convenient way of utilizing the information from all K instruments in the matrix X. It can also be given an interpretation as a *two-stage least squares estimator*. This estimator is discussed in more depth in the context of simultaneous equations models in Chapter 19. In the context of this chapter, we can explain the two-stage interpretation as follows: Given that the stochastic regressor $\mathbf{z}_2$ is correlated with the variables in X, it seems reasonable to create a linear statistical model where $\mathbf{z}_2$ depends on X. We can write such a model as

$$\mathbf{z}_2 = X\boldsymbol{\pi} + \mathbf{u} \tag{14A.19}$$

The least squares estimator for $\boldsymbol{\pi}$ from this equation is

$$\hat{\boldsymbol{\pi}} = \left(X'X\right)^{-1} X'\mathbf{z}_2 \tag{14A.20}$$

This estimator represents the first stage of our two-stage least squares procedure.

Now consider our original equation in terms of the two vectors $\mathbf{z}_1$ and $\mathbf{z}_2$; it can be written as

$$\mathbf{y} = \mathbf{z}_1\beta_1 + \mathbf{z}_2\beta_2 + \mathbf{e} \tag{14A.21}$$

The second least squares stage is to estimate this model with the offending random regressor $\mathbf{z}_2$ replaced by the predictions from equation 14A.19. These predictions are given by

$$\hat{\mathbf{z}}_2 = X\hat{\boldsymbol{\pi}} = X\left(X'X\right)^{-1} X'\mathbf{z}_2 \tag{14A.22}$$

If $\hat{\mathbf{u}} = \mathbf{z}_2 - \hat{\mathbf{z}}_2$, then, substituting this result into equation 14A.21 yields

$$\begin{aligned}
\mathbf{y} &= \mathbf{z}_1\beta_1 + (\hat{\mathbf{z}}_2 + \hat{\mathbf{u}})\beta_2 + \mathbf{e} \\
&= \mathbf{z}_1\beta_1 + \hat{\mathbf{z}}_2\beta_2 + \hat{\mathbf{u}}\beta_2 + \mathbf{e}
\end{aligned} \tag{14A.23}$$

Application of least squares to this equation yields the consistent estimator in equation 14A.17. It is for this reason the instrumental variables estimator in equation 14A.17 is often called the two-stage least squares estimator.

To prove that equation 14A.17 is identical to least squares applied to equation 14A.23, we first note, from Exercise 14.6, that

$$\mathbf{z}_1 = X(X'X)^{-1} X'\mathbf{z}_1 \tag{14A.24}$$

Substituting equations 14A.22 and 14A.24 into equation 14A.23 yields

$$\mathbf{y} = X(X'X)^{-1} X'\mathbf{z}_1\beta_1 + X(X'X)^{-1} X'\mathbf{z}_2\beta_2 + \hat{\mathbf{u}}\beta_2 + \mathbf{e}$$

$$= X(X'X)^{-1} X'[\mathbf{z}_1 \quad \mathbf{z}_2]\begin{pmatrix} \beta_1 \\ \beta_2 \end{pmatrix} + \hat{\mathbf{u}}\beta_2 + \mathbf{e}$$

$$= X(X'X)^{-1} X'Z\boldsymbol{\beta} + \hat{\mathbf{u}}\beta_2 + \mathbf{e}$$

$$= W\boldsymbol{\beta} + \hat{\mathbf{u}}\beta_2 + \mathbf{e} \tag{14A.25}$$

where $W = X(X'X)^{-1}X'Z$. Now, applying least squares to this equation gives

$$\hat{\boldsymbol{\beta}}_{(iv)} = (W'W)^{-1} W'\mathbf{y}$$

$$= \left[Z'X(X'X)^{-1} X'X(X'X)^{-1} X'Z \right]^{-1} Z'X(X'X)^{-1} X'\mathbf{y}$$

$$= \left[Z'X(X'X)^{-1} X'Z \right]^{-1} Z'X(X'X)^{-1} X'\mathbf{y} \tag{14A.26}$$

A comparison of equation 14A.2 with equation 14A.17 shows the equivalence of the two procedures.

Although our results have been described in terms of a regressor matrix Z that is of dimension $(T \times 2)$, they are equally true for models where Z has more than 2 columns, providing that the number of instruments (columns) in X is greater than or equal to the number of columns in Z.

14A.4   Hausman's Specification Test

The test statistic given in Section 14.4.3 for testing whether a random regressor z_t is correlated with an error e_t was based on the difference between the least squares estimate and the instrumental variable estimate of the coefficient of z_t. The associated test can also be performed in the more general context of the general linear random regressor model.

Let $\mathbf{y} = Z\boldsymbol{\beta} + \mathbf{e}$ be the general random regressor model, where Z is of dimension $(T \times J)$, and let X be a $(T \times K)$ matrix of instruments with $K \ge J$. The relevant least squares and instrumental variables estimators, and their respective approximate covariance matrices, are given by

$$\mathbf{b} = (Z'Z)^{-1} Z'\mathbf{y} \qquad\qquad \text{cov}(\mathbf{b}) = \sigma^2 (Z'Z)^{-1}$$

$$\hat{\boldsymbol{\beta}}_{(iv)} = \left[Z'X(X'X)^{-1} X'Z \right]^{-1} Z'X(X'X)^{-1} X'\mathbf{y} \qquad \text{cov}\left(\hat{\boldsymbol{\beta}}_{(iv)}\right) = \sigma^2 \left[Z'X(X'X)^{-1} X'Z \right]^{-1}$$

If Z and $\mathbf{e}$ are contemporaneously uncorrelated, both $\mathbf{b}$ and $\hat{\boldsymbol{\beta}}_{(iv)}$ are consistent estimators for $\boldsymbol{\beta}$; if correlation exists, $\mathbf{b}$ is inconsistent. We test for the existence of regressor–error correlation by testing whether $\mathbf{b}$ and $\hat{\boldsymbol{\beta}}_{(iv)}$ are significantly different. The Hausman test statistic for this purpose is

$$m = \left[\hat{\boldsymbol{\beta}}_{(iv)} - \mathbf{b}\right]' \left[\hat{\text{cov}}\left(\hat{\boldsymbol{\beta}}_{(iv)}\right) - \hat{\text{cov}}(\mathbf{b})\right]^{-1} \left[\hat{\boldsymbol{\beta}}_{(iv)} - \mathbf{b}\right] \qquad (14A.27)$$

When H_0 is true (there is no regressor–error correlation), m has a large sample approximate $\chi^2_{(J)}$-distribution. We reject H_0 if m is greater than a chosen critical value from the $\chi^2_{(J)}$ distribution. Note that, for computation of $\hat{\text{cov}}\left(\hat{\boldsymbol{\beta}}_{(iv)}\right)$ and $\hat{\text{cov}}(\mathbf{b})$, the same estimate of σ^2 should be used; it could be the estimate obtained from least squares procedures or that produced by the instrumental variables technique. Also, the statistic 14A.27 assumes that X and Z have no columns in common. Where there are common columns, the various components in equation 14A.27 should be replaced by the subvectors and submatrices that correspond to the columns of Z not also in X.

Part V

Linear Statistical Models with a General Error Covariance Matrix

In Part III we specified and analyzed a general linear statistical model that relates a sample of observations for a dependent or outcome variable to two or more explanatory variables. The least squares rule was used to estimate the unknown coefficients that describe this relationship. The properties of the least squares rule, when applied to this statistical model, were evaluated, and we investigated how to obtain further information in the form of interval estimates and hypothesis tests. Our results depended on a number of assumptions. Namely, we assumed that we had an appropriate model in the sense that the functional form of the relationship was correct, that all relevant explanatory variables were included, that the explanatory variables were nonstochastic, and that the stochastic assumptions we made about the random error term were true. The consequences of relaxing some of these assumptions have been investigated. In Chapter 9 we considered the consequences of omitting relevant explanatory variables. In Chapter 14 we relaxed the assumption that the regressors are nonstochastic. It is now time to question some of the statistical assumptions about the random error term. In particular, what happens if the error variance is not constant for each observation? Can we detect a changing variance, and do we need to adjust our estimation procedure if such detection occurs? Similarly, what are the consequences of correlated errors? How do we handle detection and mitigation in this case? These and other questions, such as pooling samples of data, are tackled in Chapters 15, 16, and 17.

V.1 Nonscalar Identity Error Covariance

In the empirical examples we have encountered, two types of data have been used and discussed. One type, known as *cross-sectional data,* refers to having data on a number of economic units such as firms or households, *at a given point in time*. The household data on income and food expenditure utilized in Chapters 5–8 fall into this category. Other possible examples include data on costs, outputs, and inputs for a number of firms, and data on quantities purchased and prices for some commodity, or commodities, in a number of retail establishments. The other type of data, known as *time-series data,* refers to having data *over time* on *one* economic unit, such as a firm, a household, or even a whole economy. The aggregate consumption and income data on the U. S. economy, utilized in Chapter 8, fall into this category. The macroeconomic data on investment, population, unemployment, money supply, and so on presented in Chapter 2 are also examples of time-series data.

Whatever the nature of the data on economic variables of interest, to describe relationships between such variables, we have used the linear statistical model

$$y_t = \beta_1 + \beta_2 x_{t2} + \beta_3 x_{t3} + \ldots + \beta_K x_{tK} + e_t$$

or, in matrix notation,

$$\mathbf{y} = X\boldsymbol{\beta} + \mathbf{e}$$

where the error terms e_t are assumed to be uncorrelated random variables, each with zero mean and identical (constant) variance σ^2. In matrix algebra notation we have written these assumptions in terms of the error vector $\mathbf{e}$ as

$$E[\mathbf{e}] = \mathbf{0} \quad \text{and} \quad \text{cov}(\mathbf{e}) = E[\mathbf{e}\mathbf{e}'] = \sigma^2 I_T$$

or

$$\mathbf{e} \sim \left(\mathbf{0}, \sigma^2 I_T\right)$$

In the three chapters that compose this part of the book, we question and examine the alternatives to the assumption that $\text{cov}(\mathbf{e}) = \sigma^2 I_T$. In other words, we ask under what circumstances is the assumption of uncorrelated, identically distributed random errors likely to be violated; and we examine the consequences and implications of such violation. Two different ways in which the assumption $\text{cov}(\mathbf{e}) = \sigma^2 I_T$ can be violated are explained in Chapters 15 and 16. In Chapter 15 models where the error variance is not constant for each observation are examined. Nonconstancy of the error variance is a characteristic or property known as _heteroskedasticity_; it is a property that frequently exists when we use cross-sectional data. The other violation of the assumption $\text{cov}(\mathbf{e}) = \sigma^2 I_T$, the one that is examined in Chapter 16, occurs when the errors corresponding to different observations are correlated. This property is known as _autocorrelation_; its existence is always a possibility when time-series data are used. When we combine both time-series and cross-sectional data, in the form of a set of economic relations, both heteroskedasticity and autocorrelation can be present. This topic is examined in Chapter 17.

Before proceeding to Chapters 15, 16, and 17, and discussing heteroskedasticity and autocorrelation in depth, let us get an overview of the economic circumstances that might lead to each of these characteristics. Cross-sectional data invariably involve data on economic units of varying sizes. For example, data on households will involve households with varying numbers of household members and different levels of household income. With data on a number of firms, we might measure the size of the firm by the quantity of output it produces. Frequently, the larger the firm, or the larger the household, the more difficult it is to explain the variation in some outcome variable $\mathbf{y}$ by the variation in a set of explanatory variables X. Larger firms and households are likely to be more diverse and flexible with respect to the way in which values for $\mathbf{y}$ are determined. What this means for the linear model $\mathbf{y} = X\boldsymbol{\beta} + \mathbf{e}$ is that, as the size of the economic unit becomes larger, larger absolute values in the error vector $\mathbf{e}$ are possible, and so the proportion of variation in $\mathbf{y}$ attributable to $\mathbf{e}$ becomes larger. For our linear statistical model to describe a data-generation process with this property, the variance of the error term has to be larger, the larger the size of the economic unit. Thus, we need to specify a model where the error variance is not constant; that is, a model where heteroskedasticity exists. In Section 15.1 of Chapter 15, we revisit the household food expenditure–income relationship, which is an example of a model with these characteristics.

Heteroskedasticity is not a property that is necessarily restricted to cross-sectional data. With time-series data it is possible that the error variance will change. This would be true if there was an external shock or change in circumstances that made the "explainable" part of y proportionately smaller. An example that fits into this category is the supply response example that we consider in Section 15.2.

Let us consider autocorrelation and ask why the errors are likely to be correlated when we have time-series data. The error term can be viewed as the effect on the outcome variable y of various external shocks to the model. For example, suppose we were relating the aggregate demand for money in the economy to national income, interest rate expectations and inflationary expectations. The error term does, of course, represent a multitude of different factors. However, suppose that an interest rate realization was different from what was expected. The effect of this difference would be felt through the error term. Some of the effect is likely to be on money demanded in the current period, but it is also likely that there will be an effect on money demanded in the next period, and possibly the period after that, and so on. Such a phenomenon is characteristic of many models that utilize time-series data, not just a demand for money model. What it means is that, in any one period, the current error term contains not only the effects of current shocks but also the partial carryover from shocks in previous periods. A shock that is a partial carryover from a previous period will be related to, or *correlated with*, the original shock in the previous period. Consequently, the error terms that contain these different components will also be correlated, and we say that autocorrelation exists. For these reasons the possibility of autocorrelation should always be entertained when we are dealing with time-series data. How we entertain the possibility, and the appropriate course of action, are dealt with in the context of an area response model in Chapter 16.

Often we are interested in estimating a set of economic relationships such as demand curves for a number of commodities, cost functions for a number of firms, or supply functions for a number of geographical regions. In such circumstances the error terms from different relationships can be correlated and heteroskedastic. In Chapter 17 we outline how we can take advantage of these properties to develop a more efficient estimation procedure.

Our discussion about error characteristics raises several questions.

1. Suppose that the assumption $\operatorname{cov}(\mathbf{e}) = \sigma^2 I_T$ is violated because of the existence of heteroskedasticity or autocorrelation. What are the sampling properties of our least squares estimation and inference procedures under these circumstances?

2. How do we detect the existence of heteroskedasticity or autocorrelation?

3. Is there an alternative estimation procedure that should be used if heteroskedasticity or autocorrelation is present?

We continue this introduction with an examination of the first of these questions in a general context where the errors could be heteroskedastic or autocorrelated. The other two questions are examined in Chapters 15 and 16, where we focus on identifying and mitigating *heteroskedastic* and *autocorrelated errors*.

V.2 Properties of Least Squares Under Heteroskedastic or Autocorrelated Errors

Suppose that we are unaware of the possible existence of heteroskedasticity or autocorrelation, or that we simply ignore their possible presence, and we proceed to use the least squares estimator and associated inference procedures that have been utilized thus far in the text. What are the consequences? If there are no adverse consequences, then there is little cause for concern. If there are some difficulties, however, then it is important for us to learn how to detect heteroskedasticity and autocorrelation and to learn what alternative estimation procedures might be preferable.

The first step toward examining the sampling properties of our least squares procedures when $\operatorname{cov}(\mathbf{e}) \neq \sigma^2 I_T$ is to find an alternative expression for the error covariance matrix $\operatorname{cov}(\mathbf{e})$. Recall that the components of this matrix are

$$
\operatorname{cov}(\mathbf{e}) = E[\mathbf{ee}'] =
\begin{bmatrix}
\operatorname{var}(e_1) & \operatorname{cov}(e_1, e_2) & \cdots & \operatorname{cov}(e_1, e_T) \\
\operatorname{cov}(e_2, e_1) & \operatorname{var}(e_2) & \cdots & \operatorname{cov}(e_2, e_T) \\
\vdots & \vdots & \ddots & \vdots \\
\operatorname{cov}(e_T, e_1) & \operatorname{cov}(e_T, e_2) & \cdots & \operatorname{var}(e_T)
\end{bmatrix}
$$

$$
=
\begin{bmatrix}
E[e_1^2] & E[e_1 e_2] & \cdots & E[e_1 e_T] \\
E[e_2 e_1] & E[e_2^2] & \cdots & E[e_2 e_T] \\
\vdots & \vdots & \ddots & \vdots \\
E[e_T e_1] & E[e_T e_2] & \cdots & E[e_T^2]
\end{bmatrix}
\tag{V.2.1}
$$

When the variances for all errors are equal to the same constant σ^2, we have

$$
E[e_1^2] = E[e_2^2] = \ldots = E[e_T^2] = \sigma^2
\tag{V.2.2}
$$

That is, all the diagonal elements in equation V.2.1 are the same and equal to σ^2. We say the errors are *homoskedastic*.

When the errors are not correlated (autocorrelation does not exist), then

$$
E[e_t e_s] = 0
\tag{V.2.3}
$$

for all pairs of errors ($t \neq s$). In other words, all the off-diagonal elements in equation V.2.1 are zero. Substituting equations V.2.2 and V.2.3 into equation V.2.1 yields the familiar expression

$$
\operatorname{cov}(\mathbf{e}) = E[\mathbf{ee}'] =
\begin{bmatrix}
\sigma^2 & 0 & \cdots & 0 \\
0 & \sigma^2 & \cdots & 0 \\
\vdots & \vdots & \ddots & \vdots \\
0 & 0 & \cdots & \sigma^2
\end{bmatrix}
= \sigma^2
\begin{bmatrix}
1 & 0 & \cdots & 0 \\
0 & 1 & \cdots & 0 \\
\vdots & \vdots & \ddots & \vdots \\
0 & 0 & \cdots & 1
\end{bmatrix}
= \sigma^2 I_T \tag{V.2.4}
$$

Now suppose that equation V.2.2 or equation V.2.3 or both are not true. That is, heteroskedasticity or autocorrelation or both are present. In this instance it is impossible to simplify equation V.2.1 without any further information. The diagonal elements could be all different, and the off-diagonal elements could be all nonzero. At this stage we are saying nothing about their possible values or how they are related. The best we can do under these circumstances is to write the error covariance matrix as some general $(T \times T)$ matrix W. We cannot know the precise components of W without making further assumptions. Thus, we assume that

$$\text{cov}(\mathbf{e}) = E[\mathbf{e}\mathbf{e}'] = W \tag{V.2.5}$$

If the errors are homoskedastic and uncorrelated, then we know that $W = \sigma^2 I_T$. With heteroskedasticity and/or autocorrelation, we can say nothing further about W, at least, at this time.

Under these circumstances our complete statistical model can be summarized as

$$\mathbf{y} = X\boldsymbol{\beta} + \mathbf{e} \qquad E[\mathbf{e}] = \mathbf{0} \qquad \text{cov}(\mathbf{e}) = E[\mathbf{e}\mathbf{e}'] = W \tag{V.2.6}$$

or,

$$\mathbf{e} \sim (\mathbf{0}, W) \tag{V.2.7}$$

The question that we want to ask is: What are the sampling properties of the least squares estimator $\mathbf{b} = (X'X)^{-1}X'\mathbf{y}$ under this set of assumptions?

The first sampling theory result is that *the least squares estimator remains unbiased.* This result is proved as follows:

$$
\begin{aligned}
E[\mathbf{b}] &= E\left[(X'X)^{-1} X'\mathbf{y} \right] \\
&= E\left[\boldsymbol{\beta} + (X'X)^{-1} X'\mathbf{e} \right] \\
&= \boldsymbol{\beta} + (X'X)^{-1} X'E[\mathbf{e}] \\
&= \boldsymbol{\beta} \qquad \text{since } E[\mathbf{e}] = \mathbf{0}
\end{aligned}
\tag{V.2.8}
$$

Since this proof uses only the information that the mean of $\mathbf{e}$ is zero, not information on the covariance matrix of $\mathbf{e}$, the unbiasedness property is retained despite the presence of heteroskedasticity or autocorrelation.

To obtain the covariance matrix for $\mathbf{b}$, we begin by noting that

$$\mathbf{b} - \boldsymbol{\beta} = (X'X)^{-1} X'\mathbf{e}$$

so that

$$(\mathbf{b} - \boldsymbol{\beta})(\mathbf{b} - \boldsymbol{\beta})' = (X'X)^{-1} X'\mathbf{e}\mathbf{e}'X(X'X)^{-1}$$

and

$$
\begin{aligned}
\text{cov}(\mathbf{b}) &= E\left[(\mathbf{b} - \boldsymbol{\beta})(\mathbf{b} - \boldsymbol{\beta})' \right] \\
&= (X'X)^{-1} X'E[\mathbf{e}\mathbf{e}']X(X'X)^{-1} \tag{V.2.9} \\
&= (X'X)^{-1} X'WX(X'X)^{-1}
\end{aligned}
$$

Thus,

$$\text{cov}(\mathbf{b}) = (X'X)^{-1} X'WX(X'X)^{-1} \qquad \text{when} \qquad \text{cov}(\mathbf{e}) = W$$

compared with

$$\text{cov}(\mathbf{b}) = \sigma^2 (X'X)^{-1} \qquad \text{when} \qquad \text{cov}(\mathbf{e}) = \sigma^2 I_T$$

That is, when autocorrelation or heteroskedasticity or both exist, and we consequently represent the error covariance matrix by W, the covariance matrix for the least squares estimator $\mathbf{b}$ is $(X'X)^{-1}X'WX(X'X)^{-1}$, *not* $\sigma^2(X'X)^{-1}$. If we are unaware that $\text{cov}(\mathbf{e}) = W$, and instead use inference procedures that assume that $\text{cov}(\mathbf{e}) = \sigma^2 I$, we will be basing our inferences on the *wrong* covariance matrix for $\mathbf{b}$. We would mistakenly compute

$$\hat{\sigma}_0^2 = \frac{(\mathbf{y} - X\mathbf{b})'(\mathbf{y} - X\mathbf{b})}{T - K} \tag{V.2.10}$$

and then find standard errors as the square roots of the diagonal elements of $\hat{\sigma}_0^2 (X'X)^{-1}$, when the sampling variability of the estimates should be described by the matrix $(X'X)^{-1} X'WX(X'X)^{-1}$. Depending on the nature of the matrix W (the nature of the heteroskedasticity or autocorrelation) and the values of the explanatory variables X, these standard errors may overstate or understate the true sampling variability of the elements in $\mathbf{b}$. Correspondingly, confidence intervals may be too wide or too narrow, and hypothesis tests may reject a correct null hypothesis less often or more often than is suggested by the significance level of the test.

Another consequence of using the least squares estimator $\mathbf{b} = (X'X)^{-1}X'\mathbf{y}$ when $\text{cov}(\mathbf{e}) = W$ is that we are not using the most efficient estimator that is available to us. The minimum variance property of the least squares estimator depends critically on the assumption $\text{cov}(\mathbf{e}) = \sigma^2 I_T$. As we will soon see, when this assumption is violated, the least squares estimator is no longer minimum variance; another, more efficient estimator is preferable.

In summary, the consequences of using the least squares estimator $\mathbf{b} = (X'X)^{-1}X'\mathbf{y}$ when the errors are heteroskedastic or autocorrelated and hence have covariance matrix $\text{cov}(\mathbf{e}) = W$ are as follows:

1. The least squares estimator is still unbiased, but it is no longer efficient. It is not the *best* linear unbiased estimator for β.

2. The standard errors usually computed for the least squares estimator are no longer appropriate, and hence confidence intervals and hypothesis tests that use these standard errors may be misleading.

Given these consequences, it is important to be able to detect the existence of heteroskedasticity or autocorrelation, and to develop alternative inference and estimation procedures. Let us turn now to these problems.

Chapter 15

Heteroskedastic Errors

New Key Words, Concepts and Models

Heteroskedasticity,   **Weighted Least Squares**
Generalized Least Squares   **Estimated Generalized Least Squares**
Goldfeld–Quandt Test   **Breusch–Pagan Test**
Model Transformation

Having demonstrated in the introduction to Part V that, under the existence of heteroskedasticity or autocorrelation, our least squares techniques no longer have all the desired sampling properties, in this chapter we analyze the heteroskedastic error model in detail. To begin, we examine heteroskedasticity in the context of the food expenditure–income model that was developed in Chapters 5 to 7. Sections 15.1 to 15.3 provide an introduction to the heteroskedasticity problem and how we can mitigate its negative impacts.

15.1 Heteroskedastic Errors in an Expenditure Function

15.1.1 The Economic Model

In Chapter 5 we introduced the linear model

$$y = \beta_1 + \beta_2 x \tag{15.1.1}$$

to explain household expenditure on food (y) as a function of household income (x). In this function β_1 and β_2 are unknown parameters that convey information about the expenditure function. The response parameter β_2 describes how household food expenditure changes when household income increases by one unit. The intercept parameter β_1 measures expenditure on food for a zero income level. Knowledge of these parameters aids planning by institutions like government agencies or food retail chains.

Following the discussion in the introduction to Part V, in this section we ask whether a function such as $y = \beta_1 + \beta_2 x$ might be better at explaining expenditure on food for low-income households than it would be for high-income households. Low-income households do not have the option of extravagant food tastes; comparatively, they have few choices and are almost forced to spend a particular portion of their income on food. High-income households, on the other hand, could have simple food tastes or extravagant food tastes. Income by itself is likely to be relatively less important as an explanatory variable for food expenditure of high-income families.

This type of effect can be captured by a statistical model that exhibits hetero-skedasticity. To discover how, let us return to the statistical model for the food expen-diture–income relationship that we analyzed in Chapter 5.

15.1.2   The Statistical Model

Given $T = 40$ cross-sectional household observations on food expenditure and income, the statistical model specified in Chapter 5 was given by

$$y_t = \beta_1 + \beta_2 x_t + e_t \qquad (15.1.2)$$

where y_t represents weekly food expenditure for the tth household, x_t represents weekly household income for the tth household, β_1 and β_2 are unknown parameters to estimate, and the e_t are uncorrelated random error terms with mean zero and constant variance σ^2. That is,

$$E[e_t] = 0 \qquad \mathrm{var}(e_t) = E[e_t^2] = \sigma^2 \qquad \mathrm{cov}[e_t, e_s] = 0 \qquad (15.1.3)$$

Using the least squares procedure and the data in Table 5.2, we went on to find estimates $b_1 = 7.3832$ and $b_2 = 0.2323$ for the unknown parameters β_1 and β_2. Including the stan-dard errors for b_1 and b_2, the estimated mean function was

$$\hat{y}_t = 7.3832 + 0.2323 x_t$$
$$(4.008) \quad (0.0553) \qquad (\text{s.e.}) \qquad\qquad (15.1.4)$$

A graph of this estimated function, along with all the observed expenditure–income points (y_t, x_t), appears in Figure 15.1. One thing that can be noticed from this figure is that, as income (x_t) grows, the observed data points (y_t, x_t) have a tendency to deviate more and more from the estimated mean function. Another way of describing this feature is to say that the least squares residuals, defined by

$$\hat{e}_t = y_t - b_1 - b_2 x_t \qquad (15.1.5)$$

increase in absolute value as income grows.

The observable least squares residuals $(\hat{e}_t)$ can be viewed as estimates of the unob-servable errors (e_t) that are given by

$$e_t = y_t - \beta_1 - \beta_2 x_t \qquad (15.1.6)$$

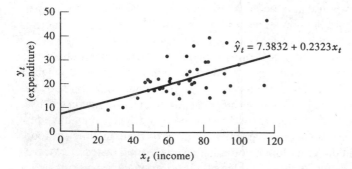

Figure 15.1 The least squares estimated relationship between expenditure on food and income.

Thus, if the $\hat{e}_t$ accurately reflect the behavior of the e_t, the information in Figure 15.1 suggests that the unobservable errors also increase in absolute value as income (x_t) increases. That is, the variation of food expenditure y_t around mean food expenditure $E[y_t]$ increases as income x_t increases. This type of behavior is not consistent with the constant variance assumption of our model. The parameter that controls the spread of y_t around the mean function is the variance σ^2. If this spread increases as x_t increases, then we have evidence to suggest the existence of heteroskedasticity—the variance changes as x_t increases. A variance σ^2 that is constant for all income levels implies that the errors are not more likely to be larger for some values of x_t than for others; in other words, the spread of y_t around $E[y_t]$ does not depend on x_t. In our situation, the large estimated errors that we found for large values of x_t could be attributable to chance, but a more plausible explanation is that the variance of y_t around $E[y_t]$ is not constant, but increases as x_t increases.

Before we can estimate β_1 and β_2, or investigate the best way to estimate β_1 and β_2, we need a way to model the error process. Given that our inspection of the least squares residuals suggests that the error variance increases as income increases, a reasonable model for the variance relationship is

$$\mathrm{var}(e_t) = \sigma_t^2 = \sigma^2 x_t \qquad (15.1.7)$$

That is, we denote the variance of the tth error term by σ_t^2, and we assume that this variance is given by a positive unknown constant parameter σ^2 multiplied by the positive income variable x_t. In economic terms this assumption implies that for low levels of income (x_t), food expenditure (y_t) will be clustered close to the mean function $E[y_t]$ $= \beta_1 + \beta_2 x_t$; expenditure on food for low-income households will be almost totally explained by the level of income. At high levels of income, food expenditures can deviate much more from the mean function. This means that there are likely to be many other factors, such as specific tastes and preferences, that reside in the error term and that lead to a greater variation in food expenditure for high-income households. Thus, the assumption of heteroskedastic errors seems a reasonable one for this economic model. In any given practical setting, it is important to think not only about whether the residuals from the data exhibit heteroskedasticity, but also about whether such heteroskedasticity is a likely phenomenon from an economic standpoint.

As we have mentioned, errors whose variances are not constant for all observations because they follow an assumption such as that in equation 15.1.7 are called heteroskedastic. Conversely, errors that do have the same variance for all observations are called homoskedastic. We learned in the earlier chapters that, when the errors are homoskedastic (and the other least squares assumptions hold), then the error covariance matrix is equal to a scalar (σ^2) multiplied by the identity matrix, and the least squares estimator is the best linear unbiased estimator for β_1 and β_2. However, from the introduction to Part V, we know that when the errors are heteroskedastic, and the error covariance matrix is of the more general form $E[\mathbf{ee}'] = W$, the least squares estimator is no longer minimum variance. Also, under these circumstances, the standard errors produced by least squares procedures are inappropriate. How, then, should we proceed? This is the question to which we now turn.

15.1.2a Summary of the Heteroskedastic Error Model   Let us begin by summarizing our new heteroskedastic statistical model that describes the food expenditure–income relationship. It is given by

$$y_t = \beta_1 + \beta_2 x_t + e_t \qquad (15.1.8)$$

with the new variance assumption

$$\text{var}(e_t) = E[e_t^2] = \sigma_t^2 = \sigma^2 x_t$$

(15.1.9)

Alternatively, we write

$$e_t \sim (0, \sigma^2 x_t)$$

(15.1.10)

The errors are also assumed to be uncorrelated; thus, $E[e_t e_s] = 0$ for $t \neq s$. Furthermore, we assume that the explanatory variable income (x_t) is nonstochastic.

As we have discussed, the least squares estimator is not the best linear unbiased estimator under these circumstances. One way of overcoming this dilemma is *to change or transform our new statistical model into one with homoskedastic errors*. If it is possible to turn our heteroskedastic error model into a homoskedastic error model, through some kind of transformation, then we might be able to work on the transformed model that has the advantage that it possesses more familiar homoskedastic errors. Let us explore this idea further.

15.1.2b Transforming the Statistical Model

To introduce a transformed model that will lead to an estimator with more precision than the least squares estimator, as well as appropriate hypothesis testing procedures, we note that

$$\text{var}\left(\frac{e_t}{x_t^{1/2}}\right) = \frac{1}{x_t}\text{var}(e_t) = \frac{1}{x_t}\sigma^2 x_t = \sigma^2$$

(15.1.11)

That is, if the tth error term (e_t) is divided by the square root of the corresponding observation for the explanatory variable, then the variance of this quotient is equal to the constant σ^2. This result suggests a method for transforming our model into one with a constant variance. Dividing both sides of the original equation 15.1.8 by $x_t^{1/2}$ yields

$$\frac{y_t}{x_t^{1/2}} = \beta_1\left(\frac{1}{x_t^{1/2}}\right) + \beta_2\left(\frac{x_t}{x_t^{1/2}}\right) + \frac{e_t}{x_t^{1/2}}$$

(15.1.12a)

where, from equation 15.1.11

$$\frac{e_t}{x_t^{1/2}} \sim (0, \sigma^2)$$

(15.1.12b)

Now, define the following transformed variables

$$y_t^* = \frac{y_t}{x_t^{1/2}} \qquad x_{t1}^* = \frac{1}{x_t^{1/2}} \qquad x_{t2}^* = \frac{x_t}{x_t^{1/2}} = x_t^{1/2} \qquad e_t^* = \frac{e_t}{x_t^{1/2}}$$

(15.1.13)

so that equation 15.1.12a can be rewritten as

$$y_t^* = \beta_1 x_{t1}^* + \beta_2 x_{t2}^* + e_t^*$$

(15.1.14a)

where

$$e_t^* \sim (0, \sigma^2)$$

(15.1.14b)

Let us note some important characteristics of this transformed model. First, from equation 15.1.11, the transformed error term e_t^* has a constant variance. Second, the transformed variables y_t^*, x_{t1}^*, and x_{t2}^* are all observable; it is a straightforward matter to compute "the observations" on these variables. Third, the transformed model is linear in the unknown parameters β_1 and β_2. These are the original parameters that we are interested in estimating. They have not been affected by the transformation. In short, the transformed model is a linear statistical model to which we can apply procedures developed earlier in the text.

15.1.3   Estimation

Because the error term e_t^* is homoskedastic and also satisfies the other assumptions of zero mean, $E[e_t^*] = 0$, and being uncorrelated with other errors, $E[e_t^* e_s^*] = 0$ for $t \neq s$, the least squares estimator applied to the model in equation 15.1.14 will be the best linear unbiased estimator for β_1 and β_2. Thus, it is straightforward to "correct" for heteroskedasticity of the type specified in equation 15.1.9. We simply do the following:

1.   Calculate the transformed variables given in equation 15.1.13.
2.   Use least squares to estimate the transformed model given in equation 15.1.14a.

It is instructive to examine the nature of the least squares estimator that used transformed observations. Toward this end, note that the matrix of transformed explanatory variables and the vector of the transformed dependent variable are given by

$$X^* = \begin{bmatrix} x_{11}^* & x_{12}^* \\ x_{21}^* & x_{22}^* \\ \vdots & \vdots \\ x_{T1}^* & x_{T2}^* \end{bmatrix} = \begin{bmatrix} x_1^{-1/2} & x_1^{1/2} \\ x_2^{-1/2} & x_2^{1/2} \\ \vdots & \vdots \\ x_T^{-1/2} & x_T^{1/2} \end{bmatrix} \qquad y^* = \begin{bmatrix} y_1^* \\ y_2^* \\ \vdots \\ y_T^* \end{bmatrix} = \begin{bmatrix} y_1 / x_1^{1/2} \\ y_2 / x_2^{1/2} \\ \vdots \\ y_T / x_T^{1/2} \end{bmatrix}$$

$$(15.1.15)$$

The vector of transformed error terms is

$$e^* = \begin{bmatrix} e_1 / x_1^{1/2} \\ e_2 / x_2^{1/2} \\ \vdots \\ e_T / x_T^{1/2} \end{bmatrix}$$

and the transformed model in matrix notation can be written as

$$y^* = X^* \beta + e^* \qquad (15.1.16a)$$

where $E[e^*] = 0$, $cov(e^*) = E[e^* e^{*\prime}] = \sigma^2 I$, and

$$e^* \sim \left(0, \sigma^2 I_T\right) \qquad (15.1.16b)$$

The transformed model is a little unusual in the sense that the first column in X^* is not a column of ones. However, this is not a characteristic that has any consequence for the important properties of least squares estimation. All that is required is an observable matrix X whose columns are not linearly dependent.

Given that the linear statistical model in equation 15.1.16 is the conventional one that we have been studying thus far, we can use the least squares estimator $\hat{\beta} = \left(X^{*\prime} X^*\right)^{-1} X^{*\prime} y^*$ as a basis for estimating $\beta = (\beta_1, \beta_2)'$. In our current example this estimator is given by

$$\hat{\beta} = \left(X*' X* \right)^{-1} X*' y*$$

$$= \begin{bmatrix} \Sigma x_{t1}^{*2} & \Sigma x_{t1}^{*} \Sigma x_{t2}^{*} \\ \Sigma x_{t1}^{*} \Sigma x_{t2}^{*} & \Sigma x_{t2}^{*2} \end{bmatrix}^{-1} \begin{bmatrix} \Sigma x_{t1}^{*} y_{t}^{*} \\ \Sigma x_{t2}^{*} y_{t}^{*} \end{bmatrix}$$

$$= \begin{bmatrix} \Sigma x_{t}^{-1} & T \\ T & \Sigma x_{t} \end{bmatrix}^{-1} \begin{bmatrix} \Sigma y_{t} x_{t}^{-1} \\ \Sigma y_{t} \end{bmatrix} \tag{15.1.17}$$

One way of viewing this estimator is as a *weighted least squares estimator*. Recall that the least squares estimator is that value of β that minimizes the sum of squared errors. In this case, $\hat{\beta}$ minimizes

$$\sum_{t=1}^{T} e_{t}^{*2} = \sum_{t=1}^{T} \frac{e_{t}^{2}}{x_{t}}$$

The errors are *weighted* by the inverse of x_{t}. When x_{t} is large and income is relatively less important in explaining food expenditure, the observations are less reliable and are weighted lightly. When x_{t} is small and income is more important as an explanatory variable, the observations are more reliable and are weighted more heavily.

Application of equation 15.1.17 to our household expenditure data yields

$$\hat{\beta} = \begin{bmatrix} \hat{\beta}_{1} \\ \hat{\beta}_{2} \end{bmatrix} = \begin{bmatrix} 0.62895 & 40 \\ 40 & 2792 \end{bmatrix}^{-1} \begin{bmatrix} 13.844 \\ 943.78 \end{bmatrix}$$

$$= \begin{bmatrix} 17.893 & -0.25635 \\ -0.25635 & 0.00403 \end{bmatrix} \begin{bmatrix} 13.844 \\ 943.78 \end{bmatrix}$$

$$= \begin{bmatrix} 5.782 \\ 0.2552 \end{bmatrix}$$

That is, we estimate the intercept term as $\hat{\beta}_{1} = 5.782$ and the slope coefficient that shows the response of food expenditure to a change in income as $\hat{\beta}_{2} = 0.2552$. These estimates are somewhat different from the least squares estimates $b_{1} = 7.3832$ and $b_{2} = 0.2323$ that did not allow for the existence of heteroskedasticity. It is important to recognize that the interpretations for β_{1} and β_{2} are the same in the transformed model in equation 15.1.14 as they are in the untransformed model in equation 15.1.8. *Transformation of the variables should be regarded as a device for converting a heteroskedastic error model into a homoskedastic error model, not as something that changes the meaning of the coefficients.*

What about the covariance matrix of the coefficient estimates? And their standard errors? Since the transformed model that involves $y*$ and $X*$ satisfies our earlier set of assumptions, all our earlier formulas are still valid, providing that we replace y by $y*$ and X by $X*$. Thus, the covariance matrix for $\hat{\beta}$ is given by

$$\text{cov}\left(\hat{\beta} \right) = \sigma^{2} \left(X*' X* \right)^{-1} \tag{15.1.18}$$

To estimate σ^{2}, we can compute the residuals

$$\hat{e}* = y* - X* \hat{\beta} \tag{15.1.19}$$

and use the unbiased estimator

$$\hat{\sigma}^2 = \frac{\hat{e}*'\hat{e}*}{T-K}$$

(15.1.20)

If we use values from the household expenditure data

$$\hat{\sigma}^2 = \frac{22.523}{38} = 0.5927$$

and the estimated covariance matrix for $\hat{\beta}$ is given by

$$\hat{cov}\left(\hat{\beta}\right) = \hat{\sigma}^2 \left(X*'X*\right)^{-1}$$

$$= \begin{bmatrix} 10.605 & -0.1519 \\ -0.1519 & 0.00239 \end{bmatrix}$$

The standard errors for $\hat{\beta}_1$ and $\hat{\beta}_2$ are given by the square roots of the diagonal elements of this matrix. Thus, the estimated equation, with standard errors in parentheses below the estimated coefficients, can be written as

$$\hat{y}_t = 5.782 + 0.2552 x_t$$

$$(3.257)\ (0.0489) \qquad \text{(s.e.)}$$

(15.1.21)

Both the coefficients and their standard errors differ somewhat from those obtained from the least squares estimator applied to the untransformed variables. (See equation 15.1.4.) The natural question to ask is: Do we have a basis for choosing one set of estimates over another? One set of estimates is obtained from $\mathbf{b} = (X'X)^{-1}X'\mathbf{y}$, the least squares estimator applied to the untransformed variables; the other set of estimates is obtained from $\hat{\beta} = \left(X*'X*\right)^{-1} X*'\mathbf{y}*$, the least squares estimator applied to the transformed variables. The errors in the untransformed model are heteroskedastic. The errors in the transformed model are homoskedastic.

Because the errors in the transformed model are homoskedastic, the least squares estimator $\hat{\beta} = \left(X*'X*\right)^{-1} X*'\mathbf{y}*$, which uses the transformed variables, is necessarily the minimum variance linear unbiased estimator for β. It must, therefore, have lower sampling variability than the least squares estimator $\mathbf{b} = \left(X'X\right)^{-1} X'\mathbf{y}$ that uses the untransformed variables. On the basis of precision the estimator $\hat{\beta} = \left(X*'X*\right)^{-1} X*'\mathbf{y}*$ is preferred.

Furthermore, we learned in the introduction to Part V that hypothesis tests and interval estimates derived from the estimator $\mathbf{b} = \left(X'X\right)^{-1} X'\mathbf{y}$ will be inappropriate because they will typically be based on standard errors computed from the matrix $\hat{\sigma}_0^2 \left(X'X\right)^{-1}$. This matrix is not appropriate under heteroskedasticity because, then, the covariance matrix for $\mathbf{b}$ is given by $(X'X)^{-1}X'WX(X'X)^{-1}$, not by $\sigma^2(X'X)^{-1}$. On the other hand, the estimated covariance matrix $\hat{\sigma}^2 \left(X*'X*\right)^{-1}$, which is computed in conjunction with the estimator $\hat{\beta} = \left(X*'X*\right)^{-1} X*'\mathbf{y}*$, will be an appropriate reflection of that estimator's sampling variability; confidence intervals and hypothesis tests that use $\hat{\beta}$, and standard errors from $\hat{\sigma}^2 \left(X*'X*\right)^{-1}$, will be valid.

To summarize, the least squares estimator $\hat{\beta} = \left(X*'X*\right)^{-1} X*'\mathbf{y}*$ that uses transformed variables is better than the least squares estimator $\mathbf{b} = \left(X'X\right)^{-1} X'\mathbf{y}$ that uses untransformed variables. It is more efficient and it leads to valid standard errors, confidence intervals, and hypothesis tests.

The estimator $\hat{\beta} = \left(X*'X*\right)^{-1} X*'\mathbf{y}*$ is also known as the *generalized least squares* (GLS) estimator. In the introduction to Part V we talked about a general form of the error covariance matrix that we wrote as $\text{cov}(\mathbf{e}) = W$. In its most general context, the generalized least squares estimator is relevant for all linear statistical models that have an error covariance matrix of the general form $\text{cov}(\mathbf{e}) = W$. Later in this chapter (Section 15.4) we discover how the generalized least squares estimator can be written not only in terms of transformed variables but also in terms of the error covariance matrix W.

The food expenditure example is an example of how heteroskedasticity can arise in a cross-sectional sample of observations. In the example in the next section, another form of heteroskedasticity that has arisen in the context of time series data is considered.

15.2   A Sample With a Heteroskedastic Partition

15.2.1   Economic and Statistical Model

Let us consider modeling the supply of wheat in a particular wheat-growing area in Australia. In the supply function for such a task, the quantity of wheat supplied will typically depend on the production technology of the firm, on the price of wheat or expectations about the price of wheat, and on weather conditions. We can depict this supply function as

$$\text{Quantity} = f(\text{Price, Technology, Weather}) \qquad (15.2.1)$$

Information on the response of quantity supplied to price is important for government policy purposes. If the government is to pay a guaranteed price to wheat growers, or to support the price in any other way, it needs an idea of the wheat supply that a given price will bring forth; a large proportion of this wheat needs to be sold on the international market.

To estimate how the quantity supplied responds to price and other variables, we need to move from the economic model in equation 15.2.1 to a statistical model that we can estimate. The choice of statistical model will depend on the nature of the data. If we have cross-sectional data on a number of wheat farms at a given point in time, then the effective prices that different farmers receive will need to take into account any differences in farm costs such as transportation costs and input prices. Also, at a single point in time, all farmers are likely to be using similar production technologies; there would be no need to include a variable to try to capture technology differences. Similarly, the weather effect in any given year would be similar for all farms. If we have a sample of time-series data, aggregated over all farms, the situation is somewhat different. There will be price variation from year to year, variation that can be used to estimate the response of quantity to price. Also, production technology will improve over time, meaning that a greater supply can become profitable at the same level of output price. Finally, a large part of the year-to-year variation in supply could be attributable to weather conditions.

The data we have available from the Australian wheat-growing district consist of 26 years of aggregate time-series data on quantity supplied and price. Because there is no obvious index of production technology, some kind of proxy needs to be used for this variable. As a proxy to represent changes in technology, we will use a simple linear trend, a variable that takes the value 1 in year 1, 2 in year 2, and so on, up to 26 in year 26. An obvious weather variable is also unavailable; thus, in our statistical model, weather effects will form part of the random error term. Using these considerations, we specify the linear supply function

$$q_t = \beta_1 + \beta_2 p_t + \beta_3 t + e_t \qquad t = 1, 2, \ldots, 26 \qquad (15.2.2)$$

where

q_t is the quantity of wheat produced in year t,

p_t is the price of wheat guaranteed for year t,

$t = 1, 2, \ldots, 26$ is a trend variable introduced to capture changes in production technology, and

e_t is a random error term that includes, among other things, the influence of weather.

As previously, β_1, β_2, and β_3 are unknown parameters that we wish to estimate. The data on q, p, and t are given in Table 15.1. Although we have specified just a *linear* function of p and t, other functional forms might be appropriate.

To complete the statistical model in equation 15.2.2 some statistical assumptions for the random error term e_t are needed. One possibility is to assume the e_t are independent identically distributed random variables with zero mean and constant variance. This assumption is in line with those made in earlier chapters. In this instance,

Table 15.1 Data on Quantity, Price, and Trend for an Australian Wheat-Growing District

q	p	t
197.6	1.47	1
140.1	1.30	2
162.3	1.59	3
166.5	1.44	4
159.5	1.89	5
195.6	1.49	6
207.0	1.94	7
218.4	1.52	8
239.0	2.15	9
208.2	2.09	10
253.4	1.74	11
278.7	2.51	12
221.1	2.14	13
240.0	2.42	14
236.1	2.45	15
234.5	2.44	16
239.0	2.26	17
258.4	2.50	18
247.9	2.41	19
272.2	2.83	20
266.2	2.79	21
284.1	3.17	22
283.4	2.83	23
277.4	2.69	24
301.0	3.65	25
281.4	3.36	26

however, we have additional information that makes an alternative assumption more realistic. We know that, after the thirteenth year, new wheat varieties whose yields are less susceptible to variations in weather conditions were introduced. These new varieties do not have a mean yield that is higher than that of the old varieties, but the variance of their yields is lower because yield is less dependent on weather conditions. Since the weather effect is a major component of the random error term e_t, we can model the reduced weather effect of the last 13 years by assuming that the error variance in those years is different from the error variance in the first 13 years. Thus, we assume that

$$E[e_t] = 0 \qquad\qquad t = 1, 2, \ldots, 26$$

$$\text{var}(e_t) = E[e_t^2] = \sigma_1^2 \qquad\qquad t = 1, 2, \ldots, 13$$

$$\text{var}(e_t) = E[e_t^2] = \sigma_2^2 \qquad\qquad t = 14, 15, \ldots, 26 \qquad (15.2.3)$$

From the above argument, we expect that $\sigma_2^2 < \sigma_1^2$.

Since the error variance in equation 15.2.3 is not constant for all observations, this model describes another form of heteroskedasticity. It is a form that partitions the sample into two subsets, one subset where the error variance is σ_1^2 and one where the error variance is σ_2^2. It is convenient to describe this partition in matrix algebra notation as follows. Let

$\mathbf{e}_1$ be a (13×1) vector containing the first 13 errors, whose variance is σ_1^2,

$\mathbf{y}_1$ be a (13×1) vector containing the observations on quantity for the first 13 years,

X_1 be a (13×3) nonstochastic regressor matrix containing a column of ones and observations on price and the trend variable for the first 13 years,

$\mathbf{e}_2$ be a (13×1) vector containing the last 13 errors, whose variance is σ_2^2,

$\mathbf{y}_2$ be a (13×1) vector containing the observations on quantity for the last 13 years, and

X_2 be a (13×3) nonstochastic regressor matrix containing a column of ones and observations on price and the trend variable for the last 13 years,

Thus, we have

$$\mathbf{e}_1 = \begin{bmatrix} e_1 \\ e_2 \\ \vdots \\ e_{13} \end{bmatrix} \qquad \mathbf{y}_1 = \begin{bmatrix} q_1 \\ q_2 \\ \vdots \\ q_{13} \end{bmatrix} \qquad X_1 = \begin{bmatrix} 1 & p_1 & 1 \\ 1 & p_2 & 2 \\ \vdots & \vdots & \vdots \\ 1 & p_{13} & 13 \end{bmatrix} \qquad (15.2.4)$$

$$\mathbf{e}_2 = \begin{bmatrix} e_{14} \\ e_{15} \\ \vdots \\ e_{26} \end{bmatrix} \qquad \mathbf{y}_2 = \begin{bmatrix} q_{14} \\ q_{15} \\ \vdots \\ q_{26} \end{bmatrix} \qquad X_2 = \begin{bmatrix} 1 & p_{14} & 14 \\ 1 & p_{15} & 15 \\ \vdots & \vdots & \vdots \\ 1 & p_{26} & 26 \end{bmatrix} \qquad (15.2.5)$$

Assuming that all the errors are independent, we have

$$\text{cov}(e_t, e_s) = E[e_t e_s] = 0 \qquad\quad \text{for } t \neq s \qquad (15.2.6)$$

Using this result and those results in equation 15.2.3, and defining $\beta = (\beta_1, \beta_2, \beta_3)'$ as the unknown coefficient vector, the statistical model and assumptions can be written in matrix algebra notation as the following two partitions:

$$\mathbf{y}_1 = X_1\boldsymbol{\beta} + \mathbf{e}_1 \qquad E[\mathbf{e}_1] = \mathbf{0} \qquad \text{cov}(\mathbf{e}_1) = E[\mathbf{e}_1\mathbf{e}_1'] = \sigma_1^2 I_{13}$$

$$\mathbf{y}_2 = X_2\boldsymbol{\beta} + \mathbf{e}_2 \qquad E[\mathbf{e}_2] = \mathbf{0} \qquad \text{cov}(\mathbf{e}_2) = E[\mathbf{e}_2\mathbf{e}_2'] = \sigma_2^2 I_{13} \qquad (15.2.7)$$

Thus, we can view the model as two separate equations where the coefficient vector β is the same in each equation, but the error variances in each equation, σ_1^2 and σ_2^2, are different. When each equation is viewed in isolation from the other one, there is no heteroskedasticity problem. The least squares technique can be legitimately applied to each equation to estimate β and to obtain corresponding estimates for σ_1^2 and σ_2^2. Let us proceed in this direction first. Then, we will see how estimation can be improved by taking into account the heteroskedasticity and the fact that the same coefficient vector β is common to both equations.

15.2.2   Separate Least Squares Estimation of Each Partition

Treating each of the equations in equation 15.2.7 separately, two least squares estimators for β can be used, one from each equation. They are

$$\mathbf{b}_1 = (X_1'X_1)^{-1}X_1'\mathbf{y}_1 \quad \text{and} \quad \mathbf{b}_2 = (X_2'X_2)^{-1}X_2'\mathbf{y}_2 \qquad (15.2.8)$$

Each of these estimators is best linear unbiased when viewed by itself, with the other 13 observations ignored. Soon we will see how to optimally combine all 26 observations.

The least squares residuals from each subset of observations are

$$\hat{\mathbf{e}}_1 = \mathbf{y}_1 - X_1\mathbf{b}_1 \quad \text{and} \quad \hat{\mathbf{e}}_2 = \mathbf{y}_2 - X_2\mathbf{b}_2 \qquad (15.2.9)$$

If T_1 and T_2 represent the numbers of observations in the first and second subsets of observations, respectively, both 13 in our example, then the variance estimators for each subset are

$$\hat{\sigma}_1^2 = \frac{\hat{\mathbf{e}}_1'\hat{\mathbf{e}}_1}{T_1 - K} \quad \text{and} \quad \hat{\sigma}_2^2 = \frac{\hat{\mathbf{e}}_2'\hat{\mathbf{e}}_2}{T_2 - K} \qquad (15.2.10)$$

The corresponding estimated covariance matrices for $\mathbf{b}_1$ and $\mathbf{b}_2$ are

$$\hat{\text{cov}}(\mathbf{b}_1) = \hat{\sigma}_1^2(X_1'X_1)^{-1} \quad \text{and} \quad \hat{\text{cov}}(\mathbf{b}_2) = \hat{\sigma}_2^2(X_2'X_2)^{-1} \qquad (15.2.11)$$

Applying these procedures to the data in Table 15.1 yields the following results. Standard errors appear in parentheses below the estimated coefficients and are computed from the square roots of the diagonal elements of $\hat{\sigma}_1^2(X_1'X_1)^{-1}$ and $\hat{\sigma}_2^2(X_2'X_2)^{-1}$.

$$\text{1st subset: } \hat{q}_t = 121.2 + 19.15p_t + 6.885t \qquad \hat{\sigma}_1^2 = 641.64$$
$$\qquad\qquad (44.2) \quad (32.42) \quad (3.005) \qquad \text{(s.e)}$$

$$\text{2nd subset: } \hat{q}_t = 137.3 + 22.06p_t + 3.257t \qquad \hat{\sigma}_2^2 = 57.76$$
$$\qquad\qquad (14.7) \quad (9.28) \quad (0.994) \qquad \text{(s.e)} \qquad\qquad (15.2.12)$$

Each subset of observations yields a different set of estimates for the same coefficient vector β. In terms of the variances, we hypothesized that the error variances were different with $\sigma_1^2 > \sigma_2^2$.

Since $\hat{\sigma}_1^2$ is more than 10 times greater than $\hat{\sigma}_2^2$, it appears that our a priori ideas about different variances are well founded. To establish whether the different magnitudes for $\hat{\sigma}_1^2$ and $\hat{\sigma}_2^2$ could be due to chance, or whether there is indeed statistical evidence to suggest $\sigma_1^2 > \sigma_2^2$, we can employ a test known as the Goldfeld–Quandt test.

15.2.3   Testing for Heteroskedasticity

As we have mentioned, the estimates $\hat{\sigma}_1^2 = 641.64$ and $\hat{\sigma}_2^2 = 57.76$ certainly suggest that the introduction of the new varieties has reduced the error variance and hence also the variance of the supply of wheat. But it remains to be established whether this difference can be attributable to chance or whether the data support the hypothesis that $\sigma_2^2 < \sigma_1^2$. If the variances are equal, then we can combine both subsets of observations, and least squares applied to the combined data will yield the minimum variance unbiased estimator for β. If the variances are not equal, we need to investigate how to improve on both combined and separate least squares estimation.

15.2.3a The Goldfeld–Quandt Test   One test we can use to establish whether $\sigma_1^2 > \sigma_2^2$ is a test suggested by Goldfeld and Quandt. We begin by setting up the null and alternative hypotheses

$$H_0 : \sigma_1^2 = \sigma_2^2$$
$$H_1 : \sigma_2^2 < \sigma_1^2 \tag{15.2.13}$$

Providing that we make the additional assumption that the equation errors are normally distributed, Goldfeld and Quandt have noted that, when H_0 is true, the statistic

$$GQ = \frac{\hat{\sigma}_1^2}{\hat{\sigma}_2^2} \sim F_{[(T_1 - K_1), (T_2 - K_2)]} \tag{15.2.14}$$

That is, under H_0, the ratio of the two variance estimators follows an F-distribution with $[(T_1 - K_1), (T_2 - K_2)]$ degrees of freedom. Here, T_1, T_2, K_1, and K_2 refer to the number of observations and number of coefficients in each of the subsets of observations. Thus, $(T_1 - K_1)$ is the degrees of freedom for the first subset and $(T_2 - K_2)$ is the degrees of freedom for the second subset. It is important that $\hat{\sigma}_2^2$ and $\hat{\sigma}_1^2$ be independent random variables, as will be guaranteed when they are estimates from two separate least squares regressions. If GQ is sufficiently large, H_0 is rejected in favor of H_1.

In our example we have

$$GQ = \frac{641.64}{57.76} = 11.11$$

Also, $T_1 = T_2 = 13$ and $K_1 = K_2 = 3$; thus, if H_0 is true, 11.11 is an observed value from an F distribution with (10, 10) degrees of freedom. The corresponding 5% critical value is $F_c = 2.98$. Since GQ = 11.11 > F_c = 2.98, we reject H_0 and conclude that the observed difference between $\hat{\sigma}_1^2$ and $\hat{\sigma}_2^2$ could not reasonably be attributable to chance. There is evidence to suggest that the new varieties have reduced the variance in the supply of wheat.

The Goldfeld–Quandt test is also useful for detecting forms of heteroskedasticity other than the sample partition case. In the example on household food expenditure, we postulated that

$$\sigma_t^2 = \sigma^2 x_t \tag{15.2.15}$$

If there is no heteroskedasticity, $\sigma_t^2 = \sigma^2$ and separate least squares estimation on two halves of the data will yield independent variance estimates $\hat{\sigma}_1^2$ and $\hat{\sigma}_2^2$; the ratio of these estimates will follow an F-distribution. If the null hypothesis is not true, but instead equation 15.2.15 holds true, then GQ $= \hat{\sigma}_1^2 / \hat{\sigma}_2^2$ will tend to be large if $\hat{\sigma}_1^2$ is estimated from that one half of the sample where x_t is large, and $\hat{\sigma}_2^2$ is estimated from that one half of the sample where x_t is small. Thus, to employ the Goldfeld–Quandt test where the suspected form of heteroskedasticity is like that in equation 15.2.15, we should begin by ordering all observations according to the magnitude of x_t, from the largest value of x_t to the smallest value of x_t. Following this procedure for the household expenditure data, with a partition of 20 observations in each subset of data, we find $\hat{\sigma}_2^2$ $= 22.377$ and $\hat{\sigma}_1^2 = 74.933$. Hence, the value of the Goldfeld–Quandt statistic is

$$\text{GQ} = \frac{74.933}{22.377} = 3.349$$

The 5% critical value for $(18, 18)$ degrees of freedom is $F_c = 2.22$. Thus, because GQ $= 3.349 > F_c = 2.22$, we reject H_0 and conclude that heteroskedasticity does exist, and that the error variance does depend on the level of income.

In some formulations of the GQ test, some "middle observations" are omitted when computing the estimates $\hat{\sigma}_1^2$ and $\hat{\sigma}_2^2$. The idea is that this omission may improve the power of the test. For an example, see Exercise 15.2.

Both of the Goldfeld–Quandt tests that we have performed in this section are one-sided tests; the alternative hypothesis suggests which sample partition will have the larger variance. If we suspect that two sample partitions could have different variances, but we do not know which variance is potentially larger, then a two-sided test with alternative hypothesis H_1: $\sigma_1^2 \neq \sigma_2^2$ is more appropriate than H_1: $\sigma_2^2 < \sigma_1^2$. To perform a two-sided test at the 5% significance level, we put the larger variance estimate in the numerator and use a critical value F_c such that $P[F > F_c] = 0.025$.

15.2.3b The Breusch–Pagan Test

The Goldfeld–Quandt test is a satisfactory test when, given that the alternative hypothesis of heteroskedasticity is true, we can unambiguously split the sample into two parts, one part with high error variance(s) and the other part with low error variance(s). Such a split can be carried out if, under H_1, the observations can be ordered according to increasing or decreasing variances.

Suppose, however, that we have an error variance that is related to more than one variable, as is true in the heteroskedastic specification

$$\sigma_t^2 = \alpha_1 + \alpha_2 z_{t2} + \alpha_3 z_{t3} \tag{15.2.16a}$$

The variables z_{t2} and z_{t3} are any observable variables on which we believe the variance could depend. They may include all or some of the variables in the mean function $E[y_t]$ $= \beta_1 + \beta_2 x_{t2} + \ldots + \beta_K x_{tK}$. The coefficients α_1, α_2, α_3 are unknown parameters. Because it is impossible to order the observations according to both z_{t2} and z_{t3}, the Goldfeld–Quandt test may lack power in this situation. A satisfactory alternative test is one proposed by Breusch and Pagan. In the context of equation 15.2.16a, the Breusch–Pagan test is a test of the null hypothesis H_0: $\alpha_2 = \alpha_3 = 0$ against the alternative H_1: α_2 or α_3 or both are nonzero. If H_0 is true, the errors are homoskedastic because, in this case, $\sigma_t^2 = \alpha_1$ where α_1 is a constant.

To perform the Breusch–Pagan test we carry out the following steps:

1.   Estimate the original equation using least squares and obtain the least squares residuals $\hat{\mathbf{e}} = \mathbf{y} - X\mathbf{b}$.

2. Replace the unknown σ_t^2 in equation 15.2.16a with the squared least squares residuals $\hat{e}_t^2$, so that we have the "artificial regression equation"

$$\hat{e}_t^2 = \alpha_1 + \alpha_2 z_{t2} + \alpha_3 z_{t3} + v_t \tag{15.2.16b}$$

The error $v_t = \hat{e}_t^2 - \sigma_t^2$ arises because $\hat{e}_t^2 \neq \sigma_t^2$.

3. Compute *(i)* SSR = regression sum of squares or explained variation (see Sections 9.2.4 and 10.6) from application of least squares to equation 15.2.16b and *(ii)* $\tilde{\sigma}^2 = \Sigma \hat{e}_t^2 / T$.

4. Compute the Breusch–Pagan statistic that is given by

$$BP = \frac{SSR}{2\tilde{\sigma}^4} \tag{15.2.17}$$

If σ_t^2 depends on z_{t2} and z_{t3} (heteroskedasticity exists), then it is likely that z_{t2} and z_{t3} will help explain variations in the magnitude of the squared residuals $\hat{e}_t^2$, and hence equation 15.2.16b will be a good explanatory model. If equation 15.2.16b is a good explanatory model, SSR, and hence BP, will be large. Thus, we reject H_0 for large values of BP.

5. When the null hypothesis of homoskedasticity is true, BP has a large sample approximate $\chi_{(S)}^2$-distribution, with the number of degrees of freedom S being equal to the number of variables in equation 15.2.16b. In our particular case S = 2. The null hypothesis is rejected, and hence we conclude that heteroskedasticity exists, if $BP > \chi_c^2$ where χ_c^2 is a critical value from the $\chi_{(S)}^2$-distribution for a given significance level.

There are several points worth noting about this test. First, S, the number of variables upon which σ_t^2 depends, does not have to be equal to 2 as we have specified in equation 15.2.16. Second, the variance function in equation 15.2.16a does not have to be linear for the test to be valid. We can still proceed with equations 15.2.16b and 15.2.17 even if equation 15.2.16a is some other function of z_{t2} and z_{t3}, such as $\sigma_t^2 = \exp(\alpha_1 + \alpha_2 z_{t2} + \alpha_3 z_{t3})$. Third, the equation errors **e** must be normally distributed for the test to be valid. However, when the errors are not normal, an alternative test statistic is TR^2, where R^2 is the coefficient of determination from least squares estimation of equation 15.2.16b. This test statistic has the same large sample approximate $\chi_{(S)}^2$ distribution.

For examples of applications of the Breusch–Pagan test, see Exercises 15.7 and 15.8.

15.2.4   Generalized Least Squares Through Model Transformation

It is time now to return to our wheat supply example. Given that the Goldfeld–Quandt test has rejected the null hypothesis of homoskedastic errors and has suggested that the errors in our wheat example are heteroskedastic ($\sigma_2^2 < \sigma_1^2$), it is time to ask whether we can improve on estimates obtained through either least squares applied to the whole sample or least squares applied to each subset of observations. In the first instance, when using the complete set of data, we would be ignoring the existence of heteroskedasticity and, hence, we know that least squares is inefficient. In the second instance, heteroskedasticity *does not exist in each of the separate subsets*. However, each subset yields a different estimate for β and an estimate from one subset does not, by itself, utilize all the information in the data. A preferable direction in which to proceed is to find a transformed model with a homoskedastic transformed error term, as we did for the household food expenditure example. Least squares applied to the transformed model will be the minimum variance linear unbiased estimator.

Reconsidering equations 15.2.2 and 15.2.3, we can write the model corresponding to the two subsets of observations as

$$q_t = \beta_1 + \beta_2 p_t + \beta_3 t + e_t, \quad \mathrm{var}(e_t) = \sigma_1^2 \quad \text{for } t = 1, 2,\dots, 13$$

$$q_t = \beta_1 + \beta_2 p_t + \beta_3 t + e_t, \quad \mathrm{var}(e_t) = \sigma_2^2 \quad \text{for } t = 14, 15,\dots, 26 \quad (15.2.18)$$

Dividing each variable by σ_1 for the first 13 observations and by σ_2 for the last 13 observations yields

$$\frac{q_t}{\sigma_1} = \beta_1 \left(\frac{1}{\sigma_1} \right) + \beta_2 \left(\frac{p_t}{\sigma_1} \right) + \beta_3 \left(\frac{t}{\sigma_1} \right) + \frac{e_t}{\sigma_1} \qquad \text{for } t = 1, 2,\dots, 13$$

$$\frac{q_t}{\sigma_2} = \beta_1 \left(\frac{1}{\sigma_2} \right) + \beta_2 \left(\frac{p_t}{\sigma_2} \right) + \beta_3 \left(\frac{t}{\sigma_2} \right) + \frac{e_t}{\sigma_2} \qquad \text{for } t = 14, 15,\dots, 26$$

$$(15.2.19)$$

This transformation yields transformed error terms that have the same variance for all observations. Specifically, the transformed error variances are all equal to 1 because

$$\mathrm{var}\left(\frac{e_t}{\sigma_1} \right) = \frac{1}{\sigma_1^2} \mathrm{var}(e_t) = \frac{\sigma_1^2}{\sigma_1^2} = 1 \qquad \text{for } t = 1, 2,\dots, 13$$

$$\mathrm{var}\left(\frac{e_t}{\sigma_2} \right) = \frac{1}{\sigma_2^2} \mathrm{var}(e_t) = \frac{\sigma_2^2}{\sigma_2^2} = 1 \qquad \text{for } t = 14, 15,\dots, 26$$

Providing σ_1 and σ_2 are known, the transformed model in equation 15.2.19 provides a set of new transformed variables to which we can apply the least squares principle to obtain a minimum variance linear unbiased estimator for β. Assuming for the moment that σ_1 and σ_2 are known, the transformed variables in matrix notation are

$$\mathbf{y}^* = \begin{bmatrix} q_1 / \sigma_1 \\ \vdots \\ q_{13} / \sigma_1 \\ q_{14} / \sigma_2 \\ \vdots \\ q_{26} / \sigma_2 \end{bmatrix} \qquad X^* = \begin{bmatrix} 1/\sigma_1 & p_1 / \sigma_1 & 1/\sigma_1 \\ \vdots & \vdots & \vdots \\ 1/\sigma_1 & p_{13} / \sigma_1 & 13/\sigma_1 \\ 1/\sigma_2 & p_{14} / \sigma_2 & 14/\sigma_2 \\ \vdots & \vdots & \vdots \\ 1/\sigma_2 & p_{26} / \sigma_2 & 26/\sigma_2 \end{bmatrix} \qquad \mathbf{e}^* = \begin{bmatrix} e_1 / \sigma_1 \\ \vdots \\ e_{13} / \sigma_1 \\ e_{14} / \sigma_2 \\ \vdots \\ e_{26} / \sigma_2 \end{bmatrix}$$

$$(15.2.20)$$

The transformed equations 15.2.19 can now be written in the familiar matrix algebra notation

$$\mathbf{y}^* = X^* \boldsymbol{\beta} + \mathbf{e}^* \qquad (15.2.21)$$

Furthermore, because the elements in $\mathbf{e}^*$ all have a variance of one and are uncorrelated, the covariance matrix for $\mathbf{e}^*$ can be written as

$$\mathrm{cov}(\mathbf{e}^*) = E[\mathbf{e}^* \mathbf{e}^{*\prime}] = I_{26} \qquad (15.2.22)$$

This error variance matrix can be viewed as a special case of the scalar times an identity matrix form of $\sigma^2 I_T$, where $\sigma^2 = 1$. The least squares estimator applied to the transformed observations

$$\hat{\beta} = \left(X^{*\prime} X^* \right)^{-1} X^{*\prime} y^* \qquad (15.2.23)$$

is the minimum variance linear unbiased generalized least squares estimator. Its covariance matrix is given by

$$\mathrm{cov}\!\left(\hat{\beta}\right) = \left(X^{*\prime} X^* \right)^{-1} \qquad (15.2.24)$$

15.2.4a Estimated Generalized Least Squares

An important difference between the generalized least squares estimator in equation 15.2.23 and the one we used for the earlier heteroskedastic error model is that the estimator in equation 15.2.23 depends on the unknown variance parameters σ_1^2 and σ_2^2, through the transformed variables in equation 15.2.20. Thus, as it stands, this estimator is not a feasible one that can be employed. To overcome this difficulty, we use estimates of σ_1^2 and σ_2^2 and transform the variables as if the estimates were the true variances. Estimates that can be used are those defined by equation 15.2.10. They are obtained through separate estimation of each subset of observations.

When we transform the variables by $\hat{\sigma}_1$ and $\hat{\sigma}_2$ instead of σ_1 and σ_2, and then apply the rule $\hat{\beta} = \left(X^{*\prime} X^* \right)^{-1} X^{*\prime} y^*$, we are changing the precise definition of the generalized least squares estimator. The new estimator is known as an *estimated generalized least squares estimator* (EGLS) or a *feasible* generalized least squares estimator. To distinguish it from the generalized least squares estimator, we describe it by using the notation $\hat{\hat{\beta}}$, or "beta hat-hat." The use of $\hat{\sigma}_1$ and $\hat{\sigma}_2$ in place of σ_1 and σ_2 in this estimator means that its sampling properties will not necessarily be the same as those of the generalized least squares estimator. Any derivation of the sampling properties of the EGLS estimator must recognize that, in addition to y_1 and y_2, the EGLS estimator also depends on the random variables $\hat{\sigma}_1$ and $\hat{\sigma}_2$. Because the matrix of transformed explanatory variables X^* depends on $\hat{\sigma}_1$ and $\hat{\sigma}_2$, it can be viewed as a matrix of random regressors. When we encountered models with random regressors in Chapter 14, we discovered that, in general, finite sample properties of estimators were too difficult to derive, and we had to be content with approximate large sample or asymptotic properties. The same is true for the EGLS estimator $\hat{\hat{\beta}}$ that depends on $\hat{\sigma}_1$ and $\hat{\sigma}_2$ through the random regressors X^* and the transformed dependent variable y^*. It can be shown that the EGLS estimator is unbiased, but this is the only finite sample property that we can retain. We cannot say $\hat{\hat{\beta}}$ is minimum variance because it is mathematically too difficult to derive the exact covariance matrix for $\hat{\hat{\beta}}$. Also, $\hat{\hat{\beta}}$ is no longer a linear function of y because $\hat{\sigma}_1$ and $\hat{\sigma}_2$ depend on y.

We can, however, say quite a bit about the large sample approximate properties of the EGLS estimator. Under appropriate assumptions about X, it can be shown that the EGLS estimator is consistent and that its approximate (large sample) sampling distribution is the same as that of the generalized least squares estimator. Thus, our usual interval estimates and hypothesis tests are valid in large samples. As discussed in Section 14.3 of Chapter 14, theoretically some of our hypotheses that previously were tested with t and F distributions should now be tested in conjunction with the normal and χ^2 distributions. However, many practitioners argue that the usual t- and F-tests, and their associated critical values, are likely to be better finite sample approximations than the normal and χ^2-tests, which are dictated by the asymptotic theory.

To return to our example, the estimates for σ_1^2 and σ_2^2 that were obtained earlier through separate least squares estimation of the two subsets of observations are

$$\hat{\sigma}_1^2 = 641.64 \quad \text{and} \quad \hat{\sigma}_2^2 = 57.76$$

Using the square roots of these quantities ($\hat{\sigma}_1 = 25.33$ and $\hat{\sigma}_2 = 7.587$) to transform the variables, followed by application of the EGLS estimator $\hat{\hat{\beta}} = \left(X^{*\prime} X^{*}\right)^{-1} X^{*\prime} y^{*}$ yields the following results. The standard errors that appear in parentheses are taken from the diagonal elements of $\left(X^{*\prime} X^{*}\right)^{-1}$.

$$\hat{q}_t = \quad 138.1 + 21.72 p_t + 3.283 t$$
$$\quad\quad (12.7) \ (8.81) \quad\quad (0.812) \quad\quad \text{(s.e.)} \quad\quad\quad\quad (15.2.25)$$

These estimates suggest that an increase in price of 1 unit will bring about an increase in supply of 21.72 units. The coefficient of the trend variable suggests that, each year, technological advances will mean that an additional 3.283 units will be supplied, given price remains constant. Also, the estimates in equation 15.2.25 are closer to the least squares estimates from the second subset of observations than they are to the least squares estimates from the first subset. This outcome can be attributed to the weighted least squares nature of the estimator. The larger error variance associated with the first subset means that those observations are less reliable than those in the second subset and, therefore, they are weighted less heavily in the estimation procedure. Finally, note that the standard errors are all less than those from a separate estimation using each subset of data, reflecting the added precision of the estimated generalized least squares estimator.

A matrix formulation for the generalized least squares estimator used in this section is given in Section 15.4. Section 15.4 will be valuable for students who work their way through Chapter 17.

15.2.5   What If the Error Variances Are Assumed Equal?

Finally, it is useful to ask what would have happened if we had ignored the reduced error variance that was attributable to the new varieties and had applied least squares techniques to the complete sample of 26 observations. In the introduction to Part V we learned that the least squares estimator would be less efficient (less precise) than the generalized least squares estimator and that, when using least squares, the usual techniques for estimating standard errors and obtaining interval estimates and hypothesis tests could yield misleading results. Let us examine both these questions. The least squares estimates that do not utilize the information that $\sigma_1^2 \neq \sigma_2^2$ are given from the rule $\mathbf{b} = (X'X)^{-1}X'\mathbf{y}$. From equation V.9 the estimated variances for $\mathbf{b}$ are given by the diagonal elements of

$$\text{c\^{o}v}(\mathbf{b}) = \left(X'X\right)^{-1} X'\hat{W}X\left(X'X\right)^{-1} \quad\quad\quad\quad (15.2.26)$$

We will define the precise nature of $\hat{W}$ in Section 15.4. Using the square roots of the diagonal elements of $\text{c\^{o}v}(\mathbf{b})$ as standard errors, we can report the least squares estimated equation as

$$\hat{q}_t = \quad 139.9 + 19.54 p_t + 3.639 t$$
$$\quad\quad (21.6) \ (15.85) \quad\quad (1.321) \quad\quad \text{(s.e.)} \quad\quad\quad\quad (15.2.27)$$

We find that the standard errors in this equation are uniformly larger than those in equation 15.2.25, reflecting the lower precision of least squares relative to generalized least squares.

In practice it is unlikely that the results in equation 15.2.27 would be reported. If we use least squares and not generalized least squares, and hence ignore heteroskedasticity when computing estimates for β, it is likely that we will also ignore the heteroskedasticity when we compute the estimated covariance matrix for $\mathbf{b} = (X'X)^{-1}X'\mathbf{y}$. Thus, the inappropriate estimate

$$\hat{cov}_0(\mathbf{b}) = \hat{\sigma}_0^2(X'X)^{-1} \tag{15.2.28}$$

is likely to be computed. Please refer back to the discussion in the introduction to Part V.

The least squares estimated equation with inappropriate standard errors is

$$\hat{q}_t = 139.9 + 19.54 p_t + 3.639t$$
$$(23.2) \quad (17.42) \quad (1.418) \quad (\text{s.e.}) \tag{15.2.29}$$

These standard errors are slightly larger than those in equation 15.2.27, meaning that confidence intervals would be too wide and that the estimates appear to be less reliable than they really are.

15.3   Summary of Results on Heteroskedastic Error Models

When the economic data-generation process is such that error variance for the general linear statistical model $\mathbf{y} = X\beta + \mathbf{e}$ is not constant for all observations, we say the errors are *heteroskedastic*. Under these circumstances the error covariance matrix $\text{cov}(\mathbf{e}) = E[\mathbf{ee}']$ can no longer be written as $\sigma^2 I_T$ (a scalar times the identity matrix). All the diagonal elements in $\text{cov}(\mathbf{e})$ will not be equal. The heteroskedastic error assumption is often a reasonable one for cross-sectional data where the sample involves a number of firms or households. In such instances the error variance could be related to variables like household income or firm output. Heteroskedastic errors can also arise with aggregate time-series data, and a natural basis for partitioning the sample of data may exist. The two examples we studied fit into these categories. In the first model the error variance was related to household income as

$$\text{var}(e_t) = \sigma^2 x_t \tag{15.3.1}$$

In the second example the error variance assumption was

$$\text{var}(e_t) = \sigma_1^2 \qquad t = 1, 2, \ldots, T_1$$
$$\text{var}(e_t) = \sigma_2^2 \qquad t = T_1 + 1, \ldots, T_1 + T_2 \tag{15.3.2}$$

Under both these specifications the generalized least squares estimator is the minimum variance linear unbiased estimator.

One way to compute the generalized least squares estimator is to transform the model so that it has a new transformed error term that is homoskedastic, and to then apply least squares to the transformed model. For the error specification in equation 15.3.1, the model is transformed by dividing the tth observation by $x_t^{1/2}$. For the error specification in equation 15.3.2, the tth observation is divided by σ_1 if it is one of the first T_1 observations, and by σ_2 if it is one of the last T_2 observations. In both cases the transformed observations can be written in terms of matrices X^* and $\mathbf{y}^*$ and the generalized least squares estimator is given by $\hat{\beta} = (X^{*'}X^*)^{-1}X^{*'}\mathbf{y}^*$.

In the second model, where the variables are transformed by using the standard deviations σ_1 and σ_2, there is the added complication of σ_1 and σ_2 being unknown. If we transform the variables using the estimates $\hat{\sigma}_1$ and $\hat{\sigma}_2$ in place of σ_1 and σ_2, and then apply least squares to the resulting transformed variables, we call the estimator an estimated generalized least squares estimator. We denote it by $\hat{\hat{\beta}}$; its sampling properties in large samples are approximately the same as those of the generalized least squares estimator.

If we ignore or are unaware of heteroskedasticity, and the least squares estimator $\mathbf{b} = (X'X)^{-1}X'\mathbf{y}$ is used instead of the generalized least squares estimator $\hat{\beta} = \left(X*'X* \right)^{-1} X*'\mathbf{y}*$, we will be using an estimator with less efficiency than could be achieved and we will compute inappropriate standard errors. Interval estimates and hypothesis tests will not be valid.

To test for heteroskedasticity the Goldfeld–Quandt statistic

$$ GQ = \frac{\hat{\sigma}_1^2}{\hat{\sigma}_2^2} \sim F_{[(T_1 - K_1),(T_2 - K_2)]} $$

can be employed. Here we assume that the observations have been ordered according to potentially decreasing variance magnitudes and that $\hat{\sigma}_2^2$ and $\hat{\sigma}_1^2$ are independent variance estimates from two subsamples. If we cannot order the observations according to potentially decreasing or potentially increasing variance magnitudes, but we can hypothesize a variance relationship where the error variance depends on one or more "explanatory variables," we can use the Breusch–Pagan statistic

$$ BP = \frac{SSR}{2\tilde{\sigma}^4} \sim \chi^2_{(S)} $$

to test for heteroskedasticity. In this equation SSR is the regression sum of squares in the regression of the squared least squares residuals on the explanatory variables in the variance function and $\tilde{\sigma}^2$ is the sample average of the squares of the least squares residuals.

There are, of course, many other ways to represent the incidence of heteroskedasticity. For example, a more general assumption than $\text{var}(e_t) = \sigma^2 x_t$ is to specify $\text{var}(e_t) = \sigma^2 x_t^p$ where p is an unknown parameter to be estimated. As another alternative, sometimes it is reasonable to model the variance as proportional to the square of the expectation of y_t. That is, $\text{var}(e_t) = \sigma^2(E[y_t])^2 = \sigma^2(\beta_1 + \beta_2 x_t)^2$. Procedures for coping with these and other possibilities can be found in Judge et al. (1985, Chapter 11) and Judge et al. (1988, Chapter 8).

15.4   Generalized Least Squares

In Sections 15.1 and 15.2 we developed the estimator $\hat{\beta} = \left(X*'X* \right)^{-1} X*'\mathbf{y}*$ by transforming a model with heteroskedastic errors into one with homoskedastic errors and applying the least squares technique. We noted that this estimator is called the *generalized least squares* (GLS) *estimator*. It is convenient for later models, particularly in Chapter 17, if we write the generalized least squares estimator in an alternative form that involves the error covariance matrix rather than the transformed variables. To develop this alternative form we begin by specifying our linear statistical model as

$$ \mathbf{y} = X\beta + \mathbf{e} \qquad (15.4.1) $$

where X is of dimension $(T \times K)$,

$$ E[\mathbf{e}] = \mathbf{0} \qquad \text{and} \qquad \text{cov}(\mathbf{e}) = E[\mathbf{e}\mathbf{e}'] = W = \sigma^2 V \qquad (15.4.2) $$

The results that we derive are results that hold for any general linear statistical model where $E[ee'] \neq \sigma^2 I_T$. Thus, W in equation 15.4.2 can be any nonsingular covariance matrix where $W \neq \sigma^2 I_T$. By writing $W = \sigma^2 V$, we are saying that sometimes it is convenient to factor a constant σ^2 out of the matrix W and write it in the alternative form $\sigma^2 V$. For example, for the model considered in Section 15.1, we define V and W as follows

$$\text{cov}(\mathbf{e}) = E[\mathbf{ee'}] = W = \begin{bmatrix} \sigma^2 x_1 & 0 & \cdots & 0 \\ 0 & \sigma^2 x_2 & \cdots & 0 \\ \vdots & \vdots & \ddots & \vdots \\ 0 & 0 & \cdots & \sigma^2 x_T \end{bmatrix} = \sigma^2 \begin{bmatrix} x_1 & 0 & \cdots & 0 \\ 0 & x_2 & \cdots & 0 \\ \vdots & \vdots & \ddots & \vdots \\ 0 & 0 & \cdots & x_T \end{bmatrix} = \sigma^2 V$$

(15.4.3)

From a theorem in matrix algebra, it is always possible to find what is called a *transformation matrix* P such that the transformed error vector defined by

$$\mathbf{e}^* = P\mathbf{e} \tag{15.4.4}$$

has covariance matrix

$$\text{cov}(\mathbf{e}^*) = E[\mathbf{e}^*\mathbf{e}^{*\prime}] = \sigma^2 I_T \tag{15.4.5}$$

The P transformation matrix is of dimension $(T \times T)$. Its precise nature—the elements that it contains—depends on the elements in the error covariance matrix $W = \sigma^2 V$. We will consider some examples of P transformation matrices shortly. For the moment, it is sufficient to be aware that a matrix P with the properties in equations 15.4.4 and 15.4.5 *does exist.*

We examine the consequences of using P to transform not just the error vector $\mathbf{e}$, but the complete model in equation 15.4.1. Premultiplying this model by the matrix P yields

$$P\mathbf{y} = PX\boldsymbol{\beta} + P\mathbf{e} \tag{15.4.6}$$

or

$$\mathbf{y}^* = X^*\boldsymbol{\beta} + \mathbf{e}^* \tag{15.4.7}$$

where $\mathbf{y}^* = P\mathbf{y}$ is the vector of transformed observations on the dependent variable, $X^* = PX$ is the matrix of transformed explanatory variables, and $\mathbf{e}^* = P\mathbf{e}$ is the transformed error vector. From equation 15.4.4, our transformed model 15.4.7 has errors that are homoskedastic and uncorrelated. The presence of the "well-behaved" errors means that the least squares estimator $\hat{\boldsymbol{\beta}} = (X^{*\prime} X^*)^{-1} X^{*\prime} \mathbf{y}^*$, which uses the transformed observations $\mathbf{y}^*$ and X^*, will be the best linear unbiased estimator for $\boldsymbol{\beta}$. As we illustrate later in this section, the transformed variables $\mathbf{y}^*$ and X^* that we obtained in Sections 15.1 and 15.2 can be defined in terms of specific P transformation matrices.

In addition, a *matrix P that yields a homoskedastic uncorrelated error vector* $\mathbf{e}^*$ *always has the property that*

$$P'P = V^{-1} \tag{15.4.8}$$

Consequently, the best linear unbiased estimator $\hat{\boldsymbol{\beta}} = (X^{*\prime} X^*)^{-1} X^{*\prime} \mathbf{y}^*$ can also be written as

$$\hat{\boldsymbol{\beta}} = (X^{*\prime} X^*)^{-1} X^{*\prime} \mathbf{y}^* = (X'P'PX)^{-1} X'P'P\mathbf{y} = (X'V^{-1}X)^{-1} X'V^{-1}\mathbf{y} \tag{15.4.9}$$

The right side of this equation is an alternative convenient form for writing the generalized least squares estimator. Apart from the constant σ^2, it is written in terms of the error covariance matrix V, rather than the transformed variables. In later formulations another expression for the generalized least squares estimator will also prove to be useful. From equation 15.4.2, $E[\mathbf{ee'}] = W = \sigma^2 V$ and, hence,

$$W^{-1} = \frac{1}{\sigma^2} V^{-1} \quad \text{and} \quad V^{-1} = \sigma^2 W^{-1} \tag{15.4.10}$$

Making this substitution into equation 15.4.9 yields

$$\hat{\boldsymbol{\beta}} = \left(X'\sigma^2 W^{-1} X\right)^{-1} X'\sigma^2 W^{-1} \mathbf{y}$$

$$= \frac{1}{\sigma^2}\left(X'W^{-1} X\right)^{-1} X'\sigma^2 W^{-1} \mathbf{y}$$

$$= \left(X'W^{-1} X\right)^{-1} X'W^{-1} \mathbf{y}$$

Thus, we have three different, but numerically identical, expressions for the generalized least squares estimator. They are

$$\hat{\boldsymbol{\beta}} = \left(X*'X*\right)^{-1} X*'\mathbf{y}* = \left(X'V^{-1} X\right)^{-1} X'V^{-1}\mathbf{y} = \left(X'W^{-1} X\right)^{-1} X'W^{-1}\mathbf{y}$$

$$\tag{15.4.11}$$

Correspondingly, three alternative expressions for the covariance matrix of the generalized least squares estimator are

$$\text{cov}\left(\hat{\boldsymbol{\beta}}\right) - \sigma^2\left(X*'X*\right)^{-1} = \sigma^2\left(X'V^{-1} X\right)^{-1} = \left(X'W^{-1} X\right)^{-1}$$

$$\tag{15.4.12}$$

The generalized least squares estimator is the minimum variance linear unbiased estimator under any general error covariance specification that could reflect heteroskedasticity or autocorrelation or both. As we have discussed, as such, it will be better than the least squares estimator $\mathbf{b} = (X'X)^{-1}X'\mathbf{y}$. In other words, the diagonal elements of the matrix $\text{cov}(\mathbf{b}) = \left(X'X\right)^{-1} X'WX\left(X'X\right)^{-1}$ will be greater than the corresponding diagonal elements of $\text{cov}\left(\hat{\boldsymbol{\beta}}\right) = \left(X'W^{-1}X\right)^{-1}$.

The heteroskedastic error assumption $E[e_t^2] = \sigma^2 x_t$ is one particular example where the error covariance matrix is of the more general form $\sigma^2 V$. Also, from equation 15.4.3 we can see that it is an example where the matrix V is known or observable. The sample with a heteroskedastic partition is an example where the matrix W depends on more than one unknown parameter. Under these circumstances it is necessary to estimate W before we can proceed with the generalized least squares estimator $\hat{\boldsymbol{\beta}} = \left(X'W^{-1}X\right)^{-1} X'W^{-1}\mathbf{y}$ or its covariance matrix $(X'W^{-1}X)^{-1}$. In the next two subsections we return to these two examples and, for these cases, consider the nature of the generalized least squares estimator written in terms of the error covariance matrix.

15.4.1   GLS Estimation of the Expenditure Function: Further Details

Consider the heteroskedastic error model of Section 15.1, where the error variance was given by

$$E[e_t^2] = \sigma^2 x_t$$

and where the first step toward computing the estimator $\hat{\boldsymbol{\beta}} = \left(X*'X*\right)^{-1} X*'\mathbf{y}*$ was to divide all the original observations by $x_t^{1/2}$. The transformed variables X^* and $\mathbf{y}^*$ that appear in this estimator, and that were defined in equation 15.1.15, can be written in terms of the untransformed variables X and $\mathbf{y}$ as follows

$$
\mathbf{y}^* = \begin{bmatrix} y_1^* \\ y_2^* \\ \vdots \\ y_T^* \end{bmatrix} = \begin{bmatrix} x_1^{-1/2} & 0 & \cdots & 0 \\ 0 & x_2^{-1/2} & \cdots & 0 \\ \vdots & \vdots & \ddots & \vdots \\ 0 & 0 & \cdots & x_T^{-1/2} \end{bmatrix} \begin{bmatrix} y_1 \\ y_2 \\ \vdots \\ y_T \end{bmatrix} = \begin{bmatrix} y_1/x_1^{1/2} \\ y_2/x_2^{1/2} \\ \vdots \\ y_T/x_T^{1/2} \end{bmatrix} \quad (15.4.13)
$$

$$
X^* = \begin{bmatrix} x_{11}^* & x_{12}^* \\ x_{21}^* & x_{22}^* \\ \vdots & \vdots \\ x_{T1}^* & x_{T2}^* \end{bmatrix} = \begin{bmatrix} x_1^{-1/2} & 0 & \cdots & 0 \\ 0 & x_2^{-1/2} & \cdots & 0 \\ \vdots & \vdots & \ddots & \vdots \\ 0 & 0 & \cdots & x_T^{-1/2} \end{bmatrix} \begin{bmatrix} 1 & x_1 \\ 1 & x_2 \\ \vdots & \vdots \\ 1 & x_T \end{bmatrix} = \begin{bmatrix} x_1^{-1/2} & x_1^{1/2} \\ x_2^{-1/2} & x_2^{1/2} \\ \vdots & \vdots \\ x_T^{-1/2} & x_T^{1/2} \end{bmatrix}
$$

$$(15.4.14)$$

If we use the symbol P to denote the diagonal matrix

$$
P = \begin{bmatrix} x_1^{-1/2} & 0 & \cdots & 0 \\ 0 & x_2^{-1/2} & \cdots & 0 \\ \vdots & \vdots & \ddots & \vdots \\ 0 & 0 & \cdots & x_T^{-1/2} \end{bmatrix} \quad (15.4.15)
$$

then equations 15.4.13 and 15.4.14 can be written in matrix notation as

$$\mathbf{y}^* = P\mathbf{y} \qquad \text{and} \qquad X^* = PX \qquad (15.4.16)$$

Now let us consider how we can write the estimator $\hat{\boldsymbol{\beta}} = \left(X^{*\prime}X^*\right)^{-1}X^{*\prime}\mathbf{y}^*$ in terms of the original observations $\mathbf{y}$ and X. From equation 15.4.16 we have

$$
\hat{\boldsymbol{\beta}} = \left(X^{*\prime}X^*\right)^{-1}X^{*\prime}\mathbf{y}^*
$$
$$
= \left(X'P'PX\right)^{-1}X'P'P\mathbf{y} \qquad (15.4.17)
$$

where, using equation 15.4.3,

$$
P'P = \begin{bmatrix} x_1^{-1} & 0 & \cdots & 0 \\ 0 & x_2^{-1} & \cdots & 0 \\ \vdots & \vdots & \ddots & \vdots \\ 0 & 0 & \cdots & x_T^{-1} \end{bmatrix} = \begin{bmatrix} x_1 & 0 & \cdots & 0 \\ 0 & x_2 & \cdots & 0 \\ \vdots & \vdots & \ddots & \vdots \\ 0 & 0 & \cdots & x_T \end{bmatrix}^{-1} = V^{-1}
$$

$$(15.4.18)$$

Hence, the estimator $\hat{\boldsymbol{\beta}}$ in equation 15.4.17 can be written, using the known matrix V, as the generalized least squares estimator

$$\hat{\boldsymbol{\beta}} = \left(X'V^{-1}X\right)^{-1}X'V^{-1}\mathbf{y} \qquad (15.4.19)$$

Let us now turn to the second example and examine the nature of the generalized least squares estimator for this case.

15.4.2   GLS Estimation of the Wheat Supply Function: Further Details

In Section 15.2 we considered the linear statistical model

$$q_t = \beta_1 + \beta_2 p_t + \beta_3 t + e_t, \quad E[e_t] = 0 \quad \text{var}(e_t) = \sigma_1^2 \quad \text{for } t = 1, 2, \ldots, 13$$

$$q_t = \beta_1 + \beta_2 p_t + \beta_3 t + e_t, \quad E[e_t] = 0 \quad \text{var}(e_t) = \sigma_2^2 \quad \text{for } t = 14, 15, \ldots, 26$$

$$(15.4.20)$$

and $E[e_t e_s] = 0$ for $t \neq s$. Returning to the definitions of $\mathbf{y}_1$, $\mathbf{y}_2$, X_1, X_2, $\mathbf{e}_1$ and $\mathbf{e}_2$ given in equations 15.2.4 and 15.2.5, we can write the complete model that contains all 26 observations in the form $\mathbf{y} = X\beta + \mathbf{e}$ by defining $\mathbf{y}$, X, and $\mathbf{e}$ as follows:

$$\mathbf{y} = \begin{bmatrix} \mathbf{y}_1 \\ \mathbf{y}_2 \end{bmatrix} = \begin{bmatrix} q_1 \\ q_2 \\ \vdots \\ q_{26} \end{bmatrix} \qquad X = \begin{bmatrix} X_1 \\ X_2 \end{bmatrix} = \begin{bmatrix} 1 & p_1 & 1 \\ 1 & p_2 & 2 \\ \vdots & \vdots & \vdots \\ 1 & p_{26} & 26 \end{bmatrix} \qquad \mathbf{e} = \begin{bmatrix} \mathbf{e}_1 \\ \mathbf{e}_2 \end{bmatrix} = \begin{bmatrix} e_1 \\ e_2 \\ \vdots \\ e_{26} \end{bmatrix}$$

$$(15.4.21)$$

To find the covariance matrix W of the error vector $\mathbf{e}$, we note that

$$\text{cov}(\mathbf{e}_1) = E[\mathbf{e}_1 \mathbf{e}_1'] = \sigma_1^2 I_{13} \quad \text{cov}(\mathbf{e}_2) = E[\mathbf{e}_2 \mathbf{e}_2'] = \sigma_2^2 I_{13} \quad \text{cov}(\mathbf{e}_1, \mathbf{e}_2) = E[\mathbf{e}_1 \mathbf{e}_2'] = 0$$

$$(15.4.22)$$

and so

$$W = \text{cov}(\mathbf{e}) = E[\mathbf{e}\mathbf{e}'] = E\left[\begin{pmatrix} \mathbf{e}_1 \\ \mathbf{e}_2 \end{pmatrix} (\mathbf{e}_1' \quad \mathbf{e}_2') \right] = \begin{bmatrix} E[\mathbf{e}_1 \mathbf{e}_1'] & E[\mathbf{e}_1 \mathbf{e}_2'] \\ E[\mathbf{e}_2 \mathbf{e}_1'] & E[\mathbf{e}_2 \mathbf{e}_2'] \end{bmatrix}$$

$$= \begin{bmatrix} \sigma_1^2 I_{13} & 0 \\ 0 & \sigma_2^2 I_{13} \end{bmatrix} \qquad (15.4.23)$$

Alternatively, we can write

$$\mathbf{e} \sim \left[\begin{pmatrix} \mathbf{0} \\ \mathbf{0} \end{pmatrix}, \begin{pmatrix} \sigma_1^2 I_{13} & 0 \\ 0 & \sigma_2^2 I_{13} \end{pmatrix} \right] \qquad (15.4.24)$$

Thus, we can think of the (26×26) covariance matrix W as consisting of 4 (13×13) blocks. The two diagonal blocks are $\sigma_1^2 I_{13}$ and $\sigma_2^2 I_{13}$. The blocks off the diagonal are (13×13) matrices containing all zeros. The inverse of the matrix W is given by

$$W^{-1} = \begin{bmatrix} \dfrac{1}{\sigma_1^2} I_{13} & 0 \\ 0 & \dfrac{1}{\sigma_2^2} I_{13} \end{bmatrix}$$

$$(15.4.25)$$

By using this result and the partitions of $\mathbf{y}$ and X given in equation 15.4.21, we can write the generalized least squares estimator $\hat{\boldsymbol{\beta}} = \left(X'W^{-1}X\right)^{-1}X'W^{-1}\mathbf{y}$ as

$$\hat{\boldsymbol{\beta}} = \left(X'W^{-1}X\right)^{-1}X'W^{-1}\mathbf{y}$$

$$= \left[\left(X_1' \quad X_2'\right) \begin{pmatrix} \dfrac{1}{\sigma_1^2}I_{13} & 0 \\ 0 & \dfrac{1}{\sigma_2^2}I_{13} \end{pmatrix} \begin{pmatrix} X_1 \\ X_2 \end{pmatrix} \right]^{-1} \left[X_1' \quad X_2'\right] \begin{pmatrix} \dfrac{1}{\sigma_1^2}I_{13} & 0 \\ 0 & \dfrac{1}{\sigma_2^2}I_{13} \end{pmatrix} \begin{pmatrix} \mathbf{y}_1 \\ \mathbf{y}_2 \end{pmatrix}$$

$$= \left[\dfrac{X_1'X_1}{\sigma_1^2} + \dfrac{X_2'X_2}{\sigma_2^2} \right]^{-1} \left[\dfrac{X_1'\mathbf{y}_1}{\sigma_1^2} + \dfrac{X_2'\mathbf{y}_2}{\sigma_2^2} \right] \qquad (15.4.26)$$

In going from the second to the last line in equation 15.4.26 we can multiply the blocks of partitioned matrices together as if they were single matrix elements, provided the various blocks are conformable for multiplication. The covariance matrix for this estimator is given by

$$\operatorname{cov}\!\left(\hat{\boldsymbol{\beta}}\right) = \left(X'W^{-1}X\right)^{-1}$$

$$= \left[\left(X_1' \quad X_2'\right) \begin{pmatrix} \dfrac{1}{\sigma_1^2}I_{13} & 0 \\ 0 & \dfrac{1}{\sigma_2^2}I_{13} \end{pmatrix} \begin{pmatrix} X_1 \\ X_2 \end{pmatrix} \right]^{-1}$$

$$= \left[\dfrac{X_1'X_1}{\sigma_1^2} + \dfrac{X_2'X_2}{\sigma_2^2} \right]^{-1} \qquad (15.4.27)$$

In equations 15.4.26 and 15.4.27, we can think of X_1 and $\mathbf{y}_1$ as being weighted by σ_1^{-1}, and X_2 and $\mathbf{y}_2$ as being weighted by σ_2^{-1}. The observations with the lower variance get weighted more heavily because they are more reliable. As in the previous model, the generalized least squares estimator can be viewed as a weighted least squares estimator. Higher weights are given to the observations that correspond to the lower error variance. It makes sense to give these observations greater weight because the more likely it is that the errors are small, the more likely the observations will be close to the mean function that we are trying to estimate.

The generalized least squares estimator $\hat{\boldsymbol{\beta}}$ defined in equation 15.4.26 is identical to $\hat{\boldsymbol{\beta}} = \left(X*'X*\right)^{-1}X*'\mathbf{y}*$ that we developed in Section 15.2, using the transformed variables $\mathbf{y}*$ and $X*$. See Exercise 15.1.

What happens when we move from the generalized least squares estimator to the estimated generalized least squares estimator that utilizes variance estimates $\hat{\sigma}_1^2$ and $\hat{\sigma}_2^2$ instead of the true values σ_1^2 and σ_2^2? In this situation we recognize that the error covariance matrix W has been estimated by writing $\hat{W}$. The estimated generalized least squares estimator that utilizes $\hat{W}$ and that we write as $\hat{\hat{\boldsymbol{\beta}}}$ is given by

$$\hat{\hat{\boldsymbol{\beta}}} = \left(X'\hat{W}^{-1}X\right)^{-1}X'\hat{W}^{-1}\mathbf{y}$$

$$= \left[\dfrac{X_1'X_1}{\hat{\sigma}_1^2} + \dfrac{X_2'X_2}{\hat{\sigma}_2^2} \right]^{-1} \left[\dfrac{X_1'\mathbf{y}_1}{\hat{\sigma}_1^2} + \dfrac{X_2'\mathbf{y}_2}{\hat{\sigma}_2^2} \right] \qquad (15.4.28)$$

As we mentioned previously, in large samples this estimator has approximately the same properties as the generalized least squares estimator.

15.4.3   A Summary

The matrix algebra results we have developed for the generalized least squares estimator in the context of two heteroskedastic error models are summarized in Table 15.2. In practice, we usually compute the generalized least squares estimator by transforming the variables as described in Sections 15.1 and 15.2. However, the formulations given in Table 15.2 provide a greater depth of understanding as well as a basis for models and results considered later in the book. It is important to remember that, for the linear model

$$\mathbf{y} = X\boldsymbol{\beta} + \mathbf{e}$$

where

$$E[\mathbf{e}] = 0 \qquad \text{and} \qquad E[\mathbf{ee}'] = W = \sigma^2 V$$

the best linear unbiased estimator is the generalized least squares rule

$$\hat{\boldsymbol{\beta}} = \left(X'V^{-1}X\right)^{-1} X'V^{-1}\mathbf{y} = \left(X'W^{-1}X\right)^{-1} X'W^{-1}\mathbf{y}$$

When V and W are unknown, the operational version of this rule is the estimated generalized least squares estimator

$$\hat{\hat{\boldsymbol{\beta}}} = \left(X'\hat{V}^{-1}X\right)^{-1} X'\hat{V}^{-1}\mathbf{y} = \left(X'\hat{W}^{-1}X\right)^{-1} X'\hat{W}^{-1}\mathbf{y}$$

where $\hat{V}$ and $\hat{W}$ are estimators for V and W, respectively. The estimated generalized least squares estimator is not best linear unbiased, but its approximate large sample properties are the same as those of the generalized least squares estimator.

15.5   Exercises

15.1 Consider the model outlined in Section 15.4.2, namely

$$\mathbf{y} = X\boldsymbol{\beta} + \mathbf{e}$$

where

$$\mathrm{cov}(\mathbf{e}) = E[\mathbf{ee}'] = W = \begin{bmatrix} \sigma_1^2 I_{T_1} & 0 \\ 0 & \sigma_2^2 I_{T_2} \end{bmatrix}$$

(a) Find a matrix P such that

$$\hat{\boldsymbol{\beta}} = \left(X*'X*\right)^{-1} X*'\mathbf{y}* = \left(X'W^{-1}X\right)^{-1} X'W^{-1}\mathbf{y}$$

where $\mathbf{y}* = P\mathbf{y}$ and $X* = PX$.

(b) Give details of the missing step in the matrix multiplication in equations 15.4.26 and 15.4.27.

15.2 When the Goldfeld–Quandt test (discussed in Section 15.2.3a) is used to test for heteroskedasticity of the form $\sigma_i^2 = \sigma^2 x_i$, it is often modified by omitting some "central observations" where the error variances are moderate in

Table 15.2 A Summary of Results for Two Heteroskedastic Error Models

	Food Expenditure	Wheat Supply
Error Variance	$\text{var}(e_t) = \sigma^2 x_t$	$\begin{aligned}\text{var}(e_t) &= \sigma_1^2 & t &= 1,2,\ldots,T_1 \\ &= \sigma_2^2 & t &= T_1+1,\ldots,T_1+T_2\end{aligned}$
Error Covariance Matrix	$\text{cov}(\mathbf{e}) = \sigma^2 V = \sigma^2 \begin{bmatrix} x_1 & 0 & \cdots & 0 \\ 0 & x_2 & \cdots & 0 \\ \vdots & \vdots & \ddots & \vdots \\ 0 & 0 & \cdots & x_T \end{bmatrix}$	$\text{cov}(\mathbf{e}) = W = \begin{bmatrix} \sigma_1^2 I_{T_1} & 0 \\ 0 & \sigma_2^2 I_{T_2} \end{bmatrix}$
Generalized Least Squares Estimator	$\begin{aligned}\hat{\boldsymbol{\beta}} &= (X^{*\prime}X^*)^{-1}X^{*\prime}\mathbf{y}^* \\ &= (X'V^{-1}X)^{-1}X'V^{-1}\mathbf{y}\end{aligned}$	$\begin{aligned}\hat{\boldsymbol{\beta}} &= (X^{*\prime}X^*)^{-1}X^{*\prime}\mathbf{y}^* \\ &= (X'W^{-1}X)^{-1}X'W^{-1}\mathbf{y}\end{aligned}$
Estimator Covariance Matrix	$\begin{aligned}\text{cov}(\hat{\boldsymbol{\beta}}) &= \sigma^2(X^{*\prime}X^*)^{-1} \\ &= \sigma^2(X'V^{-1}X)^{-1}\end{aligned}$	$\begin{aligned}\text{cov}(\hat{\boldsymbol{\beta}}) &= (X^{*\prime}X^*)^{-1} \\ &= (X'W^{-1}X)^{-1}\end{aligned}$
Estimating σ^2, or σ_1^2 and σ_2^2	$\begin{aligned}\hat{\sigma}^2 &= \frac{(\mathbf{y}^* - X^*\hat{\boldsymbol{\beta}})'(\mathbf{y}^* - X^*\hat{\boldsymbol{\beta}})}{T-K} \\ &= \frac{(\mathbf{y}-X\hat{\boldsymbol{\beta}})'V^{-1}(\mathbf{y}-X\hat{\boldsymbol{\beta}})}{T-K}\end{aligned}$	$\begin{aligned}\hat{\sigma}_1^2 &= \frac{(\mathbf{y}_1 - X_1\mathbf{b}_1)'(\mathbf{y}_1 - X_1\mathbf{b}_1)}{T_1 - K} \\ \hat{\sigma}_2^2 &= \frac{(\mathbf{y}_2 - X_2\mathbf{b}_2)'(\mathbf{y}_2 - X_2\mathbf{b}_2)}{T_2 - K}\end{aligned}$
Estimated Generalized Least Squares	Not Applicable	$\hat{\hat{\boldsymbol{\beta}}} = (X'\hat{W}^{-1}X)^{-1}X'\hat{W}^{-1}\mathbf{y}$

magnitude relative to those corresponding to small x_ts and relative to those corresponding to large x_ts. The idea is that this practice will increase the probability of getting a large F-value, should the null hypothesis of homoskedasticity be false. Redo the Goldfeld–Quandt test that was performed in the text on the household expenditure data, but with the middle 10 observations omitted. That is, use 15 observations to estimate each of the variances. Comment on the test results.

15.3 Reconsider the household expenditure model that appears in the text, the data for which appear in Table 5.2. That is, we have the model

$$y_t = \beta_1 + \beta_2 x_t + e_t$$

where y_t is food expenditure for the tth household and x_t is income.
(a) Find generalized least squares estimates for β_1 and β_2 under the assumption that $\text{var}(e_t) = \sigma_t^2 = \sigma^2 x_t^2$.
(b) Now suppose

$$\text{var}(e_t) = \sigma_t^2 = \sigma^2 x_t^\gamma$$

where γ is an unknown parameter.
(i) Show that we can write

$$\sigma_t^2 = \exp\{\alpha + \gamma \ln x_t\} = \sigma^2 x_t^\gamma$$

where $\alpha = \ln \sigma^2$.
(ii) Find least squares estimates for β_1 and β_2 and the corresponding least squares residuals $(\hat{e}_t)$.
(iii) Estimate α and γ through application of least squares to the equation

$$\ln \hat{e}_t^2 = \alpha + \gamma \ln x_t + v_t$$

where v_t is an error term. Using the standard error for the least squares estimate of γ, construct a 95% confidence interval for γ. Would null hypotheses of the form H_0: $\gamma = 1$ and H_0: $\gamma = 2$ be rejected? Comment.
(iv) Denote the least squares estimates of α and γ by $\hat{\alpha}$ and $\hat{\gamma}$. Compute the variance estimates

$$\hat{\sigma}_t^2 = \exp\{\hat{\alpha} + \hat{\gamma} \ln x_t\}$$

(v) Use the variance estimates obtained in part (iv) to find estimated generalized least squares estimates for β_1 and β_2. Report the results in the usual way. Based on your results in this part and part (a), and the results recorded in the text, do you think the estimates for β_1 and β_2, and their standard errors are very sensitive to the assumed form of heteroskedasticity?

15.4 In Table 15.3 there are time series data on total cost (C) and output (Q) for two firms. It is hypothesized that both firms' cost functions are cubic and can be written as

$$\text{firm 1: } C_{1t} = \beta_1 + \beta_2 Q_{1t} + \beta_3 Q_{1t}^2 + \beta_4 Q_{1t}^3 + e_{1t}$$
$$\text{firm 2: } C_{2t} = \gamma_1 + \gamma_2 Q_{2t} + \gamma_3 Q_{2t}^2 + \gamma_4 Q_{2t}^3 + e_{2t}$$

Table 15.3 Time Series Data on Total Cost (C) and Output (Q) for Two Firms

C_1	Q_1	C_2	Q_2
232	3.65	353	6.99
293	4.32	240	4.43
564	9.02	271	4.78
549	8.79	323	5.81
313	5.11	332	5.39
217	2.38	256	2.68
420	7.19	140	1.35
204	2.08	221	3.17
733	9.87	418	7.02
169	1.30	292	4.33
550	9.09	582	9.34
221	2.75	193	1.57
278	4.93	282	3.68
374	6.53	163	1.04
497	8.28	326	4.89
234	2.72	763	9.93
326	5.36	464	7.87
252	3.74	350	5.84
183	2.09	272	4.33
207	3.10	208	1.93
280	4.70	192	1.41
459	8.04	262	5.49
214	2.32	219	3.30
373	6.78	208	2.34
393	7.42	289	4.13
237	3.23	340	6.82
445	7.44	132	1.48
482	7.99	434	7.49

where

$$E[e_{1t}] = E[e_{2t}] = 0 \qquad E[e_{1t}^2] = \sigma_1^2 \qquad E[e_{2t}^2] = \sigma_2^2$$

and e_{1t} and e_{2t} are independent of each other and over time.

(a) Estimate each function using least squares. Report and comment on the results.

(b) Test the hypothesis that H_0: $\sigma_1^2 = \sigma_2^2$ against the alternative that H_1: $\sigma_1^2 \neq \sigma_2^2$. Use a 10% significance level and note that this is a two-tailed test.

(c) Estimate both equations jointly assuming that $\beta_1 = \gamma_1$, $\beta_2 = \gamma_2$, $\beta_3 = \gamma_3$, and $\beta_4 = \gamma_4$. Get two sets of estimates, one assuming $\sigma_1^2 = \sigma_2^2$, and one assuming $\sigma_1^2 \neq \sigma_2^2$. Report and comment on the results.

(d) Test the hypothesis

$$H_0: \beta_1 = \gamma_1 \qquad \beta_2 = \gamma_2 \qquad \beta_3 = \gamma_3 \qquad \beta_4 = \gamma_4$$

against

$$H_1: \text{at least one of the equalities in } H_0 \text{ does not hold}$$

Do this test twice. First assuming $\sigma_1^2 = \sigma_2^2$ and then assuming $\sigma_1^2 \neq \sigma_2^2$. Comment on the test outcomes.

15.5 In Section 15.1.3 the generalized least squares estimates of the household expenditure function, and the corresponding error variance estimate, were found to be

$$\hat{y}_t = 5.782 + 0.2552 x_t, \qquad \hat{\sigma}^2 = 0.5927$$

where it was assumed that $\mathrm{var}(e_t) = \sigma_t^2 = \sigma^2 x_t$. Assuming that these values are the true parameters, and using the observations on x_t in Table 5.2, carry out a Monte Carlo sampling experiment with 500 samples of size 40 to answer the following questions:

(a) Are the least squares estimator $\mathbf{b} = (X'X)^{-1} X'\mathbf{y}$ and the generalized least squares estimator $\hat{\boldsymbol{\beta}} = (X*'X*)^{-1} X*'\mathbf{y}*$ unbiased?

(b) Which estimator is more efficient, the least squares estimator $\mathbf{b} = (X'X)^{-1} X'\mathbf{y}$ or the generalized least squares estimator $\hat{\boldsymbol{\beta}} = (X*'X*)^{-1} X*'\mathbf{y}*$?

(c) Compare the variances of $\mathbf{b}$ and $\hat{\boldsymbol{\beta}}$ that were estimated from the 500 samples with the diagonal elements of $(X'X)^{-1} X'WX(X'X)^{-1}$ and $\sigma^2 (X*'X*)^{-1}$.

15.6 Consider the cost function for firm 1 in Exercise 15.4, but assume that $\mathrm{var}(e_{1t}) = \sigma^2 Q_{1t}$.

(a) Find generalized least squares estimates of β_1, β_2, β_3, and β_4 under this assumption.

(b) Test the hypothesis $\beta_1 = \beta_4 = 0$.

(c) What can you say about the nature of the average cost function if the hypothesis in (b) is true?

15.7 Table 15.4 contains observations on food expenditure (y_t), income (x_t), and number of persons in each household (n_t) from a random sample of 38 households in a large U. S. city. Food expenditure and income are measured in terms of thousands of dollars. Consider the statistical model

$$y_t = \beta_1 + \beta_2 x_t + \beta_3 n_t + e_t \tag{15.5.1}$$

where the e_t are independent normal random errors with zero mean and variances

$$\sigma_t^2 = \alpha_1 + \alpha_2 x_t + \alpha_3 n_t \tag{15.5.2}$$

(a) Test for heteroskedasticity in the errors e_t using
   (i) a Goldfeld–Quandt test with the observations ordered according to decreasing values of x_t, and
   (ii) the Breusch–Pagan test with equation 15.5.2 as the alternative hypothesis.
   Comment on the outcomes.

(b) In part (a)(ii) you would have obtained least squares estimates $\hat{\alpha}_1$, $\hat{\alpha}_2$, and $\hat{\alpha}_3$. What goes wrong if you try to compute estimated variances $\hat{\sigma}_t^2$ from

$$\hat{\sigma}_t^2 = \hat{\alpha}_1 + \hat{\alpha}_2 x_t + \hat{\alpha}_3 n_t$$

   Discuss this problem.

(c) Find generalized least squares estimates of β_1, β_2, and β_3 under the assumption that $\sigma_t^2 = 0.25(0.01 x_t + 0.25 n_t + 0.1 x_t n_t)$ and compare the results with those from least squares.

(d) Repeat part (a) of this question with equation 15.5.1 replaced by

$$\ln y_t = \gamma_1 + \gamma_2 x_t + \gamma_3 n_t + e_t$$

Table 15.4   Data for Exercise 15.7

y_t	x_t	n_t
15.998	62.476	1
16.652	82.304	5
21.741	74.679	3
7.431	39.151	3
10.481	64.724	5
13.548	36.786	3
23.256	83.052	4
17.976	86.935	1
14.161	88.233	2
8.825	38.695	2
14.184	73.831	7
19.604	77.122	3
13.728	45.519	2
21.141	82.251	2
17.446	59.862	3
9.629	26.563	3
14.005	61.818	2
9.160	29.682	1
18.831	50.825	5
7.641	71.062	4
13.882	41.990	4
9.670	37.324	3
21.604	86.352	5
10.866	45.506	2
28.980	69.929	6
10.882	61.041	2
18.561	82.469	1
11.629	44.208	2
18.067	49.467	5
14.539	25.905	5
19.192	79.178	5
25.918	75.811	3
28.833	82.718	6
15.869	48.311	4
14.910	42.494	5
9.550	40.573	4
23.066	44.872	6
14.751	27.167	7

15.8 By defining an appropriate dummy variable, use the Breusch–Pagan test to test for heteroskedasticity in the wheat-supply example that was considered in Section 15.2.

15.9 In Appendix 14A of Chapter 14, we considered the random regressor model $\mathbf{y} = Z\boldsymbol{\beta} + \mathbf{e}$, where $\mathbf{e} \sim (\mathbf{0}, \sigma^2 I_T)$ and Z is a matrix of random regressors that are contemporaneously correlated with the error vector $\mathbf{e}$. In equation 14A.15 we considered the transformed equation

$$X'\mathbf{y} = X'Z\boldsymbol{\beta} + X'\mathbf{e}$$

where X is a matrix of instrumental variables. Show that the generalized least squares estimator for β in the transformed equation is

$$\hat{\beta} = \left[Z'X(X'X)^{-1} X'Z \right]^{-1} Z'X(X'X)^{-1} X'\mathbf{y}$$

Compare this result with Equation 14A.17.

15.6   References

More details on the procedures and models discussed in this chapter can be found in

JUDGE, G. G., R. C. HILL, W. E. GRIFFITHS, H. LÜTKEPOHL, and T. C. LEE (1988) *Introduction to the Theory and Practice of Econometrics*, 2nd Edition, New York: John Wiley & Sons Inc., Chapters 8 and 9.

Other error processes for modeling heteroskedasticity can be found in

JUDGE, G. G., W. E. GRIFFITHS, R. C. HILL, H. LÜTKEPOHL, and T. C. LEE (1985) *The Theory and Practice of Econometrics*, New York: John Wiley & Sons, Inc., Chapter 8.

Other treatments of heteroskedasticity, at a less advanced level, can be found in

DORAN, H. E. (1989) *Applied Regression Analysis in Econometrics*, New York: Marcel Dekker, Inc., Chapter 8.

KENNEDY, P. (1992) *A Guide to Econometrics*, 3rd Edition, Oxford: Basil Blackwell, Chapter 8.

MADDALA, G. S. (1989) *Introduction to Econometrics*, New York: Macmillan Publishing Co., Chapter 5.

Chapter 16

An Autocorrelated Error Model

New Key Words, Concepts and Models

Autocorrelation	Durbin–Watson Test
First-Order Autoregressive Process	AR(1) Errors
Autocorrelated Error Models	Stationary Process
Nonlinear Least Squares	Durbin–Watson Bounds Test

The heteroskedastic error model studied in Chapter 15 is one example of how the error covariance matrix assumption $\text{cov}(\mathbf{e}) = \sigma^2 I_T$, for the general linear model $\mathbf{y} = X\beta + \mathbf{e}$, can be violated. We learned that, if the errors corresponding to different observations have different variances, the error covariance matrix can no longer be written as a scalar times the identity matrix. Instead, it becomes a more general diagonal matrix that we can write as $\text{cov}(\mathbf{e}) = \sigma^2 V$ or, sometimes, as just $\text{cov}(\mathbf{e}) = W$. Another way in which the assumption $\text{cov}(\mathbf{e}) = \sigma^2 I_T$ can be violated is for errors corresponding to different observations to be correlated. When such correlation exists, the error covariance W takes on a different form and we say the errors are *autocorrelated*. Under these circumstances the error covariance matrix is no longer diagonal; that is, the off-diagonal elements are no longer all zero. We begin a discussion of autocorrelated errors by introducing an economic model and a corresponding statistical model, where autocorrelated errors are potentially a problem. As part of this discussion we introduce a particular kind of autocorrelated error process and examine its properties.

In this context, we address the following questions:

1. How does correlation in the errors affect the statistical properties of the least squares estimator $\mathbf{b} = (X'X)^{-1}X'\mathbf{y}$?

2. How can we test whether or not the equation errors in an econometric model are correlated?

3. For efficient estimation of the coefficient vector β, can we follow a similar general procedure to that adopted for estimation under heteroskedastic errors? Specifically, is it possible to find a transformed model such that the new or transformed error term has the nice properties of being homoskedastic and uncorrelated? What is the nature of the least squares estimator applied to the transformed observations?

16.1 An Economic Model and Data

One way of modeling supply response for an agricultural crop is to specify quantity produced or output as the dependent variable and to relate this variable to price and other relevant supply determining variables. This was the approach used previously for modeling wheat supply in a given region of Australia. Another approach is to model area (acres) sown as the dependent variable. Quantity produced is equal to area sown multiplied by yield. Area sown is that component of quantity that is completely controlled by the firm. The decision to sow a given area will largely depend on the firm's desired output at the beginning of the season. Price or expected price is a major determinant of desired output. After a given area has been sown, it is yield that determines quantity produced. Yield will depend on the effects of weather, pests, and diseases and so is less controllable by the firm. Some control on yield can be exerted, however, possibly through irrigation, pesticides, weed control, and the like.

In this section we are concerned with modeling the response of area of sugarcane sown in a region of Bangladesh. By using area sown, not quantity, as the dependent variable, we are eliminating yield uncertainty and concentrating on the firm's main decision variable. Also, since improvements in technology over time are likely to have their effect on yield, not on area, there is no need, as we did for wheat, to include a proxy for technological change as an explanatory variable. The main product that competes with sugarcane is jute. Thus, when farmers decide on an area for sugarcane production (A), it is likely to be largely determined by the relative price of sugarcane (P_S) to that of jute (P_J). An appropriate economic model is $A = f(P_S/P_J)$. Assuming a log-linear (constant elasticity) functional form, this economic model can be written as

$$\ln(A) = \beta_1 + \beta_2 \ln(P_S / P_J) \tag{16.1.1}$$

In this model β_2 is the elasticity of area with respect to the sugar price and $-\beta_2$ is the elasticity of area with respect to the jute price. Building on the calculus material in Appendix 10A, we prove this result as follows. Differentiating both sides of this equation with respect to P_S yields

$$\frac{1}{A}\frac{\partial A}{\partial P_S} = \beta_2 \frac{P_J}{P_S}\frac{1}{P_J}$$

Hence, the elasticity of area with respect to a change in the sugarcane price is

$$\frac{P_S}{A}\frac{\partial A}{\partial P_S} = \beta_2 \tag{16.1.2}$$

Similarly, differentiating equation 16.1.1 with respect to P_J yields

$$\frac{1}{A}\frac{\partial A}{\partial P_J} = \beta_2 \frac{P_J}{P_S}\left(-\frac{P_S}{P_J^2}\right)$$

This result leads to an elasticity of area sown with respect to jute price of

$$\frac{P_J}{A}\frac{\partial A}{\partial P_J} = -\beta_2 \tag{16.1.3}$$

Thus, with the model specified in equation 16.1.1, the elasticity with respect to jute price is of the same magnitude, but of opposite sign, to the elasticity with respect to sugar price. This elasticity assumption that is built into the model may be unrealistic, and later on we will examine how it might be tested.

Information on the area elasticities is useful for government planning. It is important to know whether existing sugar-processing mills are likely to be able to handle predicted output, whether there is likely to be excess milling capacity, and whether a pricing policy linking production, processing, and consumption is desirable.

Data comprising 34 annual observations on area (thousands of hectares), sugarcane price (taka/tonne), and jute price (taka/tonne) are given in Table 16.1. After we specify a statistical model corresponding to equation 16.1.1, we will use these data to estimate the parameters β_1 and β_2.

Table 16.1   Data for Area Response for Sugarcane in Bangladesh

Area (1000 of hectares)	Price of Sugarcane (taka/tonne)	Price of Jute (taka/tonne)
29	73	970
71	108	940
42	94	930
90	107	970
72	110	1004
57	146	1102
44	132	931
61	171	816
42	186	988
26	174	888
88	182	805
80	183	1257
125	208	1072
232	239	884
125	237	1005
99	246	1114
250	240	630
91	297	1446
121	269	1006
162	297	1289
143	333	903
138	319	1119
230	347	963
128	343	1062
87	357	1185
124	388	1348
97	391	974
152	414	1023
197	421	1192
220	441	1075
171	448	1243
208	483	1043
237	457	1138
235	479	1223

16.2 Statistical Model

Using the subscript t to describe area and prices in year t, and adding a random error term e_t to the area response equation 16.1.1, yields

$$\ln(A_t) = \beta_1 + \beta_2 \ln\left(\frac{P_{St}}{P_{Jt}}\right) + e_t \qquad (16.2.1)$$

To complete the specification of this statistical model, we need to make assumptions about the random error term e_t.

It is common for time-series observations on economic variables to be correlated over time. A large value of a variable in one period often means that there is a high probability that that variable will be high again next period. Similarly, if a variable takes a low value, there is a high probability that it will be low in the following period. When we specify equations such as equation 16.2.1, the error term e_t contains effects on the dependent variable that have not been explicitly modeled by the explanatory variables on the right-hand side of the equation. If these effects come from variables that are correlated over time, then the error e_t will be correlated over time. Furthermore, the effects of variables collected into the error term may not all be felt instantaneously; there could be some delayed effect that is felt in the next and subsequent periods. If so, this characteristic can be captured through errors that are autocorrelated.

For the model in equation 16.2.1, it is likely that farmers' decisions about area of sugarcane sown will depend on their perceptions about future prices and about government policies on prices and the establishment of processing mills. Since variables for these perceptions are not explicitly included in the model, their effect on area sown will be felt through the error term e_t. Also, if perceptions change slowly over time, or at least not in a completely random manner, the e_t will be correlated over time.

16.2.1 A First-Order Autoregressive Process

Given the likely existence of correlated errors, the next question is: How should we model this correlation? Is there some way to describe how the e_t are correlated? If we are going to allow for autocorrelation when estimating β_1 and β_2, then we need some way of modeling this autocorrelation. There are a number of time-series patterns or processes that can be used to model correlated errors. By far the most common is what is known as a first-order autoregressive process or, more simply, an AR(1) process. In this process e_t depends on its lagged value e_{t-1} plus another random component that is independent and identically distributed with zero mean and constant variance. That is,

$$e_t = \rho e_{t-1} + \varepsilon_t \qquad (16.2.2)$$

where ρ (rho) is a parameter that determines the properties of e_t, and the ε_t are independent with a constant variance σ_ε^2. Thus, ε_t has the statistical properties that we assumed about e_t in the earlier chapters:

$$E[\varepsilon_t] = 0 \qquad \mathrm{var}(\varepsilon_t) = E[\varepsilon_t^2] = \sigma_\varepsilon^2 \qquad \mathrm{cov}(\varepsilon_t, \varepsilon_s) = E[\varepsilon_t \varepsilon_s] = 0 \qquad (t \neq s)$$

$$(16.2.3)$$

The rationale for the autoregressive model in equation 16.2.2 is a simple one. It is that the random component e_t in time period t is composed of two parts: *(i)* ρe_{t-1} is a carryover from the random error in the previous period, because of the inertia in economic systems, with the magnitude of the parameter ρ determining how much carryover there is, and *(ii)* ε_t is a "new" shock to the level of the economic variable. In our example the "carryover" might be farmers' perceptions of government policies on pricing and the establishment of mills. A new shock could be the announcement of a new policy or information on sugar cane shortages or excesses. The autoregressive model asserts that shocks to an economic variable do not work themselves out in one period. The parameter ρ in equation 16.2.2 is the autoregressive parameter that determines how quickly the effect of a shock dissipates. The larger the magnitude of ρ, the greater the carryover from one period to another and the more slowly the shock spreads over time.

Figure 16.1 illustrates some errors e_t generated from an AR(1) process with $\rho = 0.9$, and plotted against time. It is, of course, not universally true, but note how positive errors tend to follow positive errors and negative errors tend to follow negative errors.

16.2.2   Statistical Properties of an AR(1) Error

Our next task is to examine the implications of the AR(1) error model in equation 16.2.2 for the statistical properties (mean, variance, and correlations) of the e_t. Further details of these statistical properties, and their derivation, can be found in Chapter 20, which focuses on time-series analysis. For the e_t to have properties that do not change from year to year, we assume that ρ is less than one in absolute value. That is,

$$-1 < \rho < 1 \qquad (16.2.4)$$

If we did not make this assumption, then, through the relationship $e_t = \rho e_{t-1} + \varepsilon_t$, the e_t would tend to become larger and larger through time, eventually becoming infinite. When an AR(1) process satisfies equation 16.2.4, it is called a *stationary* process and its mean, variance, and correlations do not change over time. Looking first at the mean, this result implies that $E[e_t] = E[e_{t-1}]$ and, hence, from equations 16.2.2 and 16.2.3, we have

$$E[e_t] = \rho E[e_{t-1}] + E[\varepsilon_t]$$
$$= \rho E[e_t] + 0$$

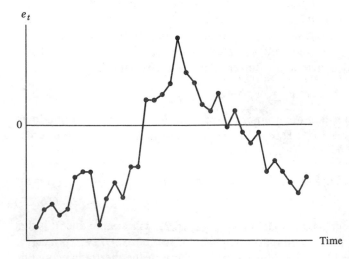

Figure 16.1 Error generated from an AR(1) process with $e_t = 0.9 e_{t-1} + \varepsilon_t$.

Bringing $\rho E[e_t]$ to the left side of the equation yields

$$(1-\rho)E[e_t] = 0$$

and, hence,

$$E[e_t] = 0 \qquad (16.2.5)$$

Thus, when the equation errors follow an AR(1) process, they continue to have a zero mean.

For the variance of e_t we use the symbol σ_e^2 and the fact that $\mathrm{var}(e_t) = \mathrm{var}(e_{t-1}) = \sigma_e^2$. Taking the variance of both sides of $e_t = \rho e_{t-1} + \varepsilon_t$ gives

$$\mathrm{var}(e_t) = \rho^2 \, \mathrm{var}(e_{t-1}) + \mathrm{var}(\varepsilon_t) + 2\rho \, \mathrm{cov}(e_{t-1}, \varepsilon_t)$$
$$= \rho^2 \, \mathrm{var}(e_t) + \sigma_\varepsilon^2 + 0$$

Thus,

$$(1-\rho^2)\sigma_e^2 = \sigma_\varepsilon^2$$
$$\sigma_e^2 = \frac{\sigma_\varepsilon^2}{1-\rho^2} \qquad (16.2.6)$$

In the derivation of equation 16.2.6, $\mathrm{cov}(e_{t-1}, \varepsilon_t) = 0$ because the ε_t are independent random shocks that do not depend on past observations, in general, and the last period error e_{t-1}, in particular. Equation 16.2.6 shows the relationship between the variance (σ_e^2) of the equation error e and the variance (σ_ε^2) of the independent homoskedastic error ε_t.

To find the correlations between e_t and lagged values of itself, we begin with the covariance between e_t and e_{t-1}. From the definition of covariance we have

$$\mathrm{cov}(e_t, e_{t-1}) = E[(e_t - E(e_t))(e_{t-1} - E(e_{t-1}))]$$
$$= E[e_t e_{t-1}]$$
$$= E[(\rho e_{t-1} + \varepsilon_t)e_{t-1}] \qquad (16.2.7)$$
$$= \rho E[e_{t-1}^2] + E[\varepsilon_t e_{t-1}]$$
$$= \rho \sigma_e^2$$

The correlation between e_t and e_{t-1} is given by

$$\mathrm{corr}(e_t, e_{t-1}) = \frac{\mathrm{cov}(e_t, e_{t-1})}{\sqrt{\mathrm{var}(e_t)\,\mathrm{var}(e_{t-1})}}$$
$$= \frac{\mathrm{cov}(e_t, e_{t-1})}{\mathrm{var}(e_t)} = \frac{\rho \sigma_e^2}{\sigma_e^2} = \rho \qquad (16.2.8)$$

Thus, the parameter ρ describes the correlation between errors that are one period apart in time. For $\rho > 0$, successive errors are positively correlated; for $\rho < 0$, successive errors are negatively correlated. Extending the algebraic tools in equations 16.2.7 and 16.2.8, we can show that the covariance between errors that are k periods apart in time is given by

$$\text{cov}(e_t, e_{t-k}) = \rho^k \sigma_e^2 \qquad k = 1, 2, 3, \ldots \qquad (16.2.9)$$

and the corresponding correlation is

$$\text{corr}(e_t, e_{t-k}) = \rho^k \qquad k = 1, 2, 3, \ldots \qquad (16.2.10)$$

Thus, there is always some correlation between the random errors e_t no matter how far apart they are. However, because $-1 < \rho < 1$, this correlation declines in absolute value as the errors become further apart.

16.2.3   The Reformulated Statistical Model

We are now in a position to summarize the assumptions and properties of our linear statistical model. This model is given by

$$\ln(A_t) = \beta_1 + \beta_2 \ln\left(\frac{P_{St}}{P_{Jt}}\right) + e_t \qquad (16.2.11)$$

where

$$e_t = \rho e_{t-1} + \varepsilon_t, \quad -1 < \rho < 1 \qquad (16.2.12)$$

and

$$E[\varepsilon_t] = 0 \qquad \text{var}(\varepsilon_t) = E[\varepsilon_t^2] = \sigma_\varepsilon^2 \qquad \text{cov}(\varepsilon_t, \varepsilon_{t-k}) = E[\varepsilon_t \varepsilon_{t-k}] = 0, \qquad k \neq 0$$
$$(16.2.13)$$

These assumptions imply that

$$E[e_t] = 0 \qquad E[e_t^2] = \sigma_e^2 = \frac{\sigma_\varepsilon^2}{1 - \rho^2} \qquad t = 1.2, \ldots, T$$

$$\text{cov}(e_t, e_{t-k}) = E[e_t e_{t-k}] = \rho^k \sigma_e^2 \qquad \text{corr}(e_t, e_{t-k}) = \rho^k \qquad k = 1, 2, 3, \ldots$$
$$(16.2.14)$$

The errors e_t are autocorrelated because $\text{cov}(e_t, e_{t-k}) \neq 0$. They are, however, homoskedastic because $\text{var}(e_t) = \sigma_\varepsilon^2 / (1 - \rho^2)$ is the same for all observations.

Defining $y_t = \ln(A_t)$ and $x_{t2} = \ln(P_{St}/P_{Jt})$, we can write equation 16.2.11 as

$$y_t = \beta_1 + x_{t2}\beta_2 + e_t \qquad (16.2.15a)$$

or in the familiar matrix algebra notation

$$y = X\beta + e \qquad (16.2.15b)$$

where

$$y = \begin{bmatrix} y_1 \\ y_2 \\ \vdots \\ y_T \end{bmatrix} = \begin{bmatrix} \ln(A_1) \\ \ln(A_2) \\ \vdots \\ \ln(A_T) \end{bmatrix} \qquad X = \begin{bmatrix} 1 & x_{12} \\ 1 & x_{22} \\ \vdots & \vdots \\ 1 & x_{T2} \end{bmatrix} = \begin{bmatrix} 1 & \ln(P_{S1}/P_{J1}) \\ 1 & \ln(P_{S2}/P_{J2}) \\ \vdots & \vdots \\ 1 & \ln(P_{ST}/P_{JT}) \end{bmatrix} \qquad (16.2.16)$$

$$\beta = \begin{bmatrix} \beta_1 \\ \beta_2 \end{bmatrix} \qquad \text{and} \qquad e = \begin{bmatrix} e_1 \\ e_2 \\ \vdots \\ e_T \end{bmatrix}$$

Since we are representing the error process as $e_t = \rho e_{t-1} + \varepsilon_t$, what about the error covariance matrix $\text{cov}(\mathbf{e}) = E[\mathbf{ee'}]$? Because the e_t are correlated, we know the off-diagonal elements of this matrix will no longer be zero and, hence, that this matrix cannot be written as $\sigma^2 I_T$. Instead, we write it as the general form $\text{cov}(\mathbf{e}) = E[\mathbf{ee'}] = W = \sigma_\varepsilon^2 V$. For details of the nature of the matrices V and W in this case, see Exercise 16.1.

Given that $\text{cov}(\mathbf{e}) = W \neq \sigma^2 I_T$, the results in the introduction to Part V on the properties of the least squares estimator are relevant. Let us briefly review these results.

16.2.4   Properties of the Least Squares Rule Under Autocorrelation

If, because of the existence of autocorrelation, $\text{cov}(\mathbf{e}) \neq \sigma^2 I_T$, the least squares estimator $\mathbf{b} = (X'X)^{-1}X'\mathbf{y}$ will be unbiased, but not efficient. It is possible to find an alternative estimator, the generalized least squares estimator, that is also unbiased and has lower variance. Furthermore, ignoring the existence of autocorrelation means that the reported covariance matrix for the least squares estimator will be biased. Standard errors and consequent interval estimates and hypothesis tests will be invalid. The details provided in the introduction to Part V are relevant, just as they were under the existence of heteroskedasticity. It is important, therefore, to have a valid set of tools for estimating β, and making inferences about β, in the presence of autocorrelation. We turn now to this subject. After discussing these tools we move on to testing for autocorrelation. Testing is important because it helps us decide whether the assumption of a first-order autoregressive process should be entertained and, hence, whether the new tools should be employed.

16.3   Generalized Least Squares Estimation of an Autocorrelated Error Model

In Section 16.2.3 the statistical model with errors that follow an AR(1) process was outlined. The next question is, given this model: How should we proceed to estimate the parameter vector β? In Section 16.2.4 we noted that the least squares estimator $\mathbf{b}$ $= (X'X)^{-1}X'\mathbf{y}$ will no longer be efficient and that the usual estimator for the covariance matrix will be biased. Having a biased covariance matrix estimator means that confidence intervals and hypothesis tests are no longer soundly based procedures. We can do better than the least squares estimator by using the generalized least squares estimator introduced in Chapter 15. In that chapter we learned that the generalized least squares estimator can be computed *(i)* through the formula $\hat{\beta} = \left(X'V^{-1}X \right)^{-1} X'V^{-1}\mathbf{y}$, or *(ii)* by transforming the model so that it has a new uncorrelated homoskedastic error term, and applying least squares to the transformed model. It is this transformation approach that we will now pursue. The equivalence of this approach with the generalized least squares approach will be made evident and reviewed in Exercise 16.1.

16.3.1 The Transformed Model

Using the more general notation introduced in equations 16.2.15 and 16.2.16, our model in scalar notation is

$$y_t = \beta_1 + x_{t2}\beta_2 + e_t \tag{16.3.1}$$

where

$$e_t = \rho e_{t-1} + \varepsilon_t \tag{16.3.2}$$

and the ε_t are independent, identically distributed random errors. Since the ε_t have "nice" properties, if we can transform the equation so that the error for the new transformed equation is ε_t, not e_t, then least squares estimates from the transformed equation will not suffer the ill effects that result from autocorrelated errors. Working in this direction, we substitute equation 16.3.2 into equation 16.3.1 to obtain

$$y_t = \beta_1 + x_{t2}\beta_2 + \rho e_{t-1} + \varepsilon_t \tag{16.3.3}$$

Now, since equation 16.3.1 holds for every single observation, in terms of the previous period's observation we have

$$y_{t-1} = \beta_1 + x_{t-1,2}\beta_2 + e_{t-1} \tag{16.3.4a}$$

or

$$e_{t-1} = y_{t-1} - \beta_1 - x_{t-1,2}\beta_2 \tag{16.3.4b}$$

Multiplying equation 16.3.4b by the autoregressive parameter ρ, and substituting into equation 16.3.3, yields

$$y_t = \beta_1 + x_{t2}\beta_2 + \rho y_{t-1} - \rho\beta_1 - \rho x_{t-1,2}\beta_2 + \varepsilon_t$$

or

$$y_t - \rho y_{t-1} = (1-\rho)\beta_1 + (x_{t2} - \rho x_{t-1,2})\beta_2 + \varepsilon_t \tag{16.3.5}$$

This is the transformed equation that we seek. The transformed dependent variable is

$$y_t^* = y_t - \rho y_{t-1} \quad t = 2, 3, \ldots, T \tag{16.3.6a}$$

The transformed explanatory variable is

$$x_{t2}^* = x_{t2} - \rho x_{t-1,2} \qquad t = 2, 3, \ldots, T \tag{16.3.6b}$$

and the new constant term is

$$x_{t1}^* = 1 - \rho \qquad t = 2, 3, \ldots, T \tag{16.3.6c}$$

Making the substitutions we have

$$y_t^* = x_{t1}^*\beta_1 + x_{t2}^*\beta_2 + \varepsilon_t \tag{16.3.7a}$$

where

$$\varepsilon_t \sim (0, \sigma_\varepsilon^2) \tag{16.3.7b}$$

Thus we have formed a new transformed statistical model with transformed variables y_t^*, x_{t1}^*, and x_{t2}^* and, *importantly*, with an error term that is *not* the correlated e_t, but the uncorrelated ε_t that we have assumed to be distributed $(0, \sigma_\varepsilon^2)$. We would expect application of least squares to equation 16.3.7 to yield a best linear unbiased estimator for β_1 and β_2.

There are two additional problems that we need to solve, however:

1. Because lagged values of y_t and x_{t2} had to be formed, only $(T-1)$ new observations were created by the transformation in equation 16.3.6. We have values

$(y_2{}^*, y_3{}^*,\ldots, y_T{}^*)$ and $(x_{22}{}^*, x_{32}{}^*,\ldots, x_{T2}{}^*)$, but no $y_1{}^*$ and $x_{12}{}^*$.

2. The value of the autoregressive parameter ρ is typically not known. Since $y_t{}^*$, $x_{t1}{}^*$, and $x_{t2}{}^*$ depend on ρ, we cannot compute these transformed observations, or estimates of them, without estimating ρ.

16.3.2 The Generalized Least Squares Estimator

One way to tackle the first problem, where we have only $(T-1)$ instead of T transformed observations, is to simply ignore the problem and to proceed with estimation on the basis of $(T-1)$ transformed observations. If T is large, this strategy might be a reasonable one. However, the resulting estimator is not the best linear unbiased generalized least squares estimator. To get the generalized least squares estimator we need to transform the first observation in a way that yields a transformed error term that has the same properties as the errors $(\varepsilon_2, \varepsilon_3,\ldots, \varepsilon_T)$.

The first observation is modeled as

$$y_1 = \beta_1 + x_{12}\beta_2 + e_1 \tag{16.3.8}$$

We transform this equation by multiplying by $\sqrt{1-\rho^2}$

$$\sqrt{1-\rho^2}\, y_1 = \sqrt{1-\rho^2}\,\beta_1 + \sqrt{1-\rho^2}\, x_{12}\beta_2 + \sqrt{1-\rho^2}\, e_1 \tag{16.3.9}$$

or

$$y_1^* = x_{11}^*\beta_1 + x_{12}^*\beta_2 + e_1^* \tag{16.3.10a}$$

where

$$
\begin{aligned}
y_1^* &= \sqrt{1-\rho^2}\, y_1 \qquad x_{11}^* = \sqrt{1-\rho^2} \\
x_{12}^* &= \sqrt{1-\rho^2}\, x_{12} \qquad\qquad e_1^* = \sqrt{1-\rho^2}\, e_1
\end{aligned}
\tag{16.3.10b}
$$

This transformation will be an appropriate one providing e_1^* has the same properties as the ε_t. Note that e_1^* has a zero mean

$$E[e_1^*] = \sqrt{1-\rho^2}\, E[e_1] = 0$$

Its variance is σ_ε^2 because

$$\mathrm{var}(e_1^*) = (1-\rho^2)\,\mathrm{var}(e_1) = (1-\rho^2)\frac{\sigma_\varepsilon^2}{1-\rho^2} = \sigma_\varepsilon^2$$

The remaining desired property is that e_1^* be uncorrelated with $(\varepsilon_2, \varepsilon_3,\ldots, \varepsilon_T)$. This result will hold true because each of the ε_t does not depend on any past values for e_t. Thus, the transformed first observation defined in equation 16.3.10 has the desired properties.

The complete transformed model is obtained by combining the first transformed observation in equation 16.3.10 with the remaining $(T-1)$ transformed observations in equations 16.3.6 and 16.3.7. Collecting all these observations into convenient matrices, we have

$$
\mathbf{y^*} = \begin{bmatrix} y_1^* \\ y_2^* \\ y_3^* \\ \vdots \\ y_T^* \end{bmatrix} = \begin{bmatrix} \sqrt{1-\rho^2}\, y_1 \\ y_2 - \rho y_1 \\ y_3 - \rho y_2 \\ \vdots \\ y_T - \rho y_{T-1} \end{bmatrix} \qquad \boldsymbol{\varepsilon} = \begin{bmatrix} e_1^* \\ \varepsilon_2 \\ \varepsilon_3 \\ \vdots \\ \varepsilon_T \end{bmatrix}
$$

$$
X^* = \begin{bmatrix} x_{11}^* & x_{12}^* \\ x_{21}^* & x_{22}^* \\ x_{31}^* & x_{32}^* \\ \vdots & \vdots \\ x_{T1}^* & x_{T2}^* \end{bmatrix} = \begin{bmatrix} \sqrt{1-\rho^2} & \sqrt{1-\rho^2}\, x_{12} \\ 1-\rho & x_{22} - \rho x_{12} \\ 1-\rho & x_{32} - \rho x_{22} \\ \vdots & \vdots \\ 1-\rho & x_{T2} - \rho x_{T-1,2} \end{bmatrix} \tag{16.3.11}
$$

The transformed model is

$$
\mathbf{y^*} = X^* \boldsymbol{\beta} + \boldsymbol{\varepsilon} \tag{16.3.12}
$$

where

$$
E[\boldsymbol{\varepsilon}] = \mathbf{0} \qquad \text{and} \qquad \text{cov}(\boldsymbol{\varepsilon}) = E[\boldsymbol{\varepsilon}\boldsymbol{\varepsilon}'] = \sigma_\varepsilon^2 I_T \tag{16.3.13}
$$

The generalized least squares estimator for β that is best linear unbiased is given by

$$
\hat{\boldsymbol{\beta}} = \left(X^{*\prime} X^* \right)^{-1} X^{*\prime} \mathbf{y} \tag{16.3.14}
$$

Its covariance matrix is

$$
\text{cov}\left(\hat{\boldsymbol{\beta}} \right) = \sigma_\varepsilon^2 \left(X^{*\prime} X^* \right)^{-1} \tag{16.3.15}
$$

where σ_ε^2 can be estimated from

$$
\hat{\sigma}_\varepsilon^2 = \frac{\left(\mathbf{y^*} - X^* \hat{\boldsymbol{\beta}} \right)' \left(\mathbf{y^*} - X^* \hat{\boldsymbol{\beta}} \right)}{T - K} \tag{16.3.16}
$$

We can summarize the results in equations 16.3.12 to 16.3.16 by saying that, *providing ρ is known, we can find the best linear unbiased estimator for β by replacing $\mathbf{y}$ with $\mathbf{y^*}$ and X with X^*, and applying usual least squares procedures. Furthermore, all the procedures you have learned for testing hypotheses and constructing interval estimators still hold true for the current case as long as the transformed model (and data) is used and the generalized least squares estimators $\hat{\boldsymbol{\beta}}$ and $\hat{\sigma}_\varepsilon^2$ are used for β and σ_ε^2.* Our caveat to this statement is that the interpretation of "R^2" no longer holds in the usual way, and its use should probably be avoided in econometric models with correlated errors. When you study econometrics at a more advanced level, you will learn alternative ways of calculating summary goodness-of-fit statistics for this and similar models.

16.3.3   An Estimated Generalized Least Squares Estimator

The remaining problem is the fact that the transformed variables $\mathbf{y^*}$ and X^* cannot be calculated without knowledge of the parameter ρ. We overcome this problem by using instead an estimate of ρ. As a method for estimating ρ consider the equation

$$e_t = \rho e_{t-1} + \varepsilon_t \qquad (16.3.17)$$

If the e_t values were observable, we could treat this equation as a linear statistical model and estimate ρ by least squares. However, the e_t are not observable because they depend on the unknown parameters β_1 and β_2 through the equation

$$e_t = y_t - E[y_t] = y_t - \beta_1 - \beta_2 x_{t2} \qquad (16.3.18)$$

As an approximation to the e_t we use instead the least squares residuals

$$\hat{e}_t = y_t - b_1 - b_2 x_{t2} \qquad (16.3.19)$$

where b_1 and b_2 are the elements in the least squares vector $\mathbf{b} = (X'X)^{-1}X'\mathbf{y}$. Substituting the $\hat{e}_t$ for the e_t in equation 16.3.17 is justified providing the sample size T is large. Making this substitution yields the model

$$\hat{e}_t = \rho \hat{e}_{t-1} + v_t \qquad (16.3.20)$$

where v_t is an error term.

The least squares estimator of ρ from equation 16.3.20 has good statistical properties if the sample size T is large; it is given by

$$\hat{\rho} = \frac{\sum\limits_{t=2}^{T} \hat{e}_t \hat{e}_{t-1}}{\sum\limits_{t=2}^{T} \hat{e}_{t-1}^2} \qquad (16.3.21)$$

Thus, in practice, the transformed data that are defined in equations 16.3.6 and 16.3.10, and in matrix notation in equation 16.3.11, are computed using the estimated value of $\hat{\rho}$ from equation 16.3.21. In line with the heteroskedastic error model of Section 15.2, the estimator $\hat{\boldsymbol{\beta}} = (X^{*\prime}X^*)^{-1}X^{*\prime}\mathbf{y}^*$ that uses $\hat{\rho}$ instead of the true value ρ is called the *estimated* generalized least squares estimator for β. As was discussed in Section 15.2.4a of Chapter 15, the properties of the estimated generalized least squares estimator are approximately the same as those of the generalized least squares estimator, providing the sample size is large. If the sample is not large, then great care must be taken when making claims about the results of hypothesis tests and interval estimations, so as *not* to overstate the importance of the results obtained.

16.3.4   The Sugarcane Example

Let us return to the area response function for sugarcane in Bangladesh. Using the data in Table 16.1, and the least squares rule $\mathbf{b} = (X'X)^{-1}X'\mathbf{y}$, our estimated equation is

$$\ln\left(\hat{A}_t\right) = 6.120 + 1.004\ln\left(P_{St} / P_{Jt}\right)$$

$$(0.214) \ (0.141) \ \text{(s.e.)} \qquad (16.3.22)$$

$$(28.54) \ (7.136) \ (t) \qquad R^2 = 0.614$$

These results suggest that the elasticity of area with respect to the sugarcane–jute price ratio is approximately one. Also, based on equation 16.3.22, a 95% confidence interval for the elasticity (β_2) is

$$\left[1.004 - (2.037)(0.141), \ 1.004 + (2.037)(0.141)\right]$$

or

$$\left[0.717, 1.291\right] \tag{16.3.23}$$

If the errors in the equation are autocorrelated, however, as we suggested when specifying the statistical model, the least squares rule is not the best rule that we could use; furthermore, the standard errors will not be an accurate reflection of the reliability of the estimates, meaning that the interval estimate in equation 16.3.23 is unlikely to be a true "95%" confidence interval. Later, we will see how to test whether autocorrelation might be present but, for now, let us proceed with estimation and inference under the assumption that the errors do follow an AR(1) error process.

After using equation 16.3.22 to compute the least squares residuals ($\hat{e}_t$), we estimate ρ as

$$\hat{\rho} = \frac{\displaystyle\sum_{t=2}^{T} \hat{e}_t \hat{e}_{t-1}}{\displaystyle\sum_{t=2}^{T} \hat{e}_{t-1}^2} = 0.4501 \tag{16.3.24}$$

The next step toward finding estimated generalized least squares estimates is to transform the data as shown in equation 16.3.11. To illustrate we give the first four observations in **y**, **y***, X, and $X*$

$$\mathbf{y}[1:4] = \begin{bmatrix} 3.3673 \\ 4.2627 \\ 3.7377 \\ 4.4998 \end{bmatrix} \qquad \mathbf{y}*[1:4] = \begin{bmatrix} 3.0070 \\ 2.7472 \\ 1.5759 \\ 2.0259 \end{bmatrix}$$

$$X[1:4] = \begin{bmatrix} 1 & -2.5868 \\ 1 & -2.1637 \\ 1 & -2.2919 \\ 1 & -2.2045 \end{bmatrix} \qquad X*[1:4] = \begin{bmatrix} 0.8930 & -2.3100 \\ 0.5499 & -0.9995 \\ 0.5499 & -1.3181 \\ 0.5499 & -1.1730 \end{bmatrix}$$

As examples, note that

$$\begin{aligned} y_1^* &= \sqrt{1 - \hat{\rho}^2} \, y_1 \\ &= \sqrt{1 - (0.4501)^2} \, (3.3673) \\ &= 3.0070 \end{aligned}$$

and

$$\begin{aligned} x_{32}^* &= x_{32} - \hat{\rho} x_{22} \\ &= -2.2919 - (0.4501)(-2.1637) \\ &= -1.3181 \end{aligned}$$

The reader is encouraged to verify some of the other entries. Computations such as these are usually done automatically on the computer, but, nevertheless, it is instructive to understand their nature.

Using the estimated generalized least squares rule $\hat{\boldsymbol{\beta}} = (X^{*\prime}X^*)^{-1}X^{*\prime}\mathbf{y}^*$ yields the following results

$$\ln\left(\hat{A}_t\right) = 6.205 + 1.060\ln\left(P_{St} \,/\, P_{Jt}\right)$$

$$(0.286)\ (0.181) \qquad\quad (\text{s.e.})$$

$$(21.72)\ (5.848) \qquad\quad (t) \qquad\qquad\qquad (16.3.25)$$

Comparing these estimates with the least squares estimates in equation 16.3.22, we observe that there has been little change in the estimates for β_1 and β_2 and that there has been a slight increase in the standard errors. The corresponding 95% confidence interval for β_2 is thus slightly wider than before, namely,

$$[0.691, 1.429] \qquad\qquad\qquad (16.3.26)$$

Because the least squares standard errors are less than the generalized least squares standard errors, one might be tempted to conclude that the precision of generalized least squares is worse, a contradiction of our earlier claim. It must be remembered, however, that the least squares standard errors given in equation 16.3.22 are inappropriate because they ignore the presence of autocorrelation. Along the lines of the introduction to Part V, an appropriate measure of the precision of the least squares estimates is given by the covariance matrix $(X'X)^{-1}X'WX(X'X)^{-1}$, or its corresponding standard errors. After estimating W and using these "more appropriate" standard errors with the least squares estimates in equation 16.3.22, we obtain

$$\ln\left(\hat{A}_t\right) = 6.120 + 1.004\ln\left(P_{St} \,/\, P_{Jt}\right)$$

$$(0.319)\ (0.206)\ (\text{s.e.}) \qquad\qquad (16.3.27)$$

$$(19.18)\ (4.874)\ (t)$$

with a corresponding 95% confidence interval for β_2 as

$$[0.584, 1.424] \qquad\qquad\qquad (16.3.28)$$

This interval is noticeably wider than both *(i)* the least squares interval based on inappropriate standard errors, and *(ii)* the generalized least squares interval. The comparison with *(i)* indicates that using least squares in the presence of autocorrelation will lead one to believe that the estimates are more precise or reliable than they really are. The comparison with *(ii)* suggests that the generalized least squares estimates are more efficient or reliable than the least squares estimates.

16.3.4a Testing the Elasticity Assumption

When introducing the economic model for area response of sugarcane in Bangladesh, we showed that using the price ratio variable $\ln(P_S/P_J)$ implied that the elasticity of area response with respect to the price of jute was the same as the elasticity of area response with respect to sugarcane, but with a negative sign. A more general model that does not impose this restriction is

$$\ln\left(A_t\right) = \beta_1 + \beta_2\ln\left(P_{St}\right) + \beta_3\ln\left(P_{Jt}\right) + e_t \qquad (16.3.29)$$

Here the elasticities with respect to P_S and P_J are β_2, and β_3, respectively. Thus, if we wished to test the restriction implied by our earlier model, we could write the relevant null and alternative hypotheses as

$$H_0: \beta_2 = -\beta_3$$

$$H_1: \beta_2 \neq -\beta_3$$

If we use the same value for $\hat{\rho}$, namely $\hat{\rho} = 0.4501$, the estimated generalized least squares estimate of equation 16.3.29 is

$$\ln\left(\hat{A}_t\right) = 5.423 + 1.083\ln\left(P_{St}\right) - 0.966\ln\left(P_{Jt}\right)$$

$$
\begin{array}{cccl}
(2.322)\ (0.196) & (0.334) & \text{(s.e.)} & \\
(2.336)\ (5.530) & (-2.894) & (t) & (16.3.30)
\end{array}
$$

These estimates suggest that $\beta_2 \approx -\beta_3$, but to properly ascertain whether the difference between $\hat{\beta}_2$ and $-\hat{\beta}_3$ could be attributable to chance, a hypothesis test is necessary. For this purpose the F-test that compares the restricted and unrestricted sums of squared errors can be employed, remembering that the residuals must be computed from the transformed variables. For example, if $\hat{\beta} = (X^{*\prime}X^*)^{-1}X^{*\prime}y^*$ is the estimated generalized least squares estimator for the original restricted model, where $\ln(P_{St}/P_{Jt})$ is the explanatory variable, then the corresponding sum of squared errors is

$$\text{SSE}_R = \hat{e}^{*\prime}\hat{e}^* = \left(y^* - X^*\hat{\beta}\right)^{\prime}\left(y^* - X^*\hat{\beta}\right) \qquad (16.3.31)$$

The F-statistic for testing H_0: $\beta_2 = -\beta_3$ against H_1: $\beta_2 \neq -\beta_3$ is given by

$$
\begin{aligned}
F &= \frac{\left(\text{SSE}_R - \text{SSE}_U\right)/J}{\text{SSE}_U/(T-K)} \\
&= \frac{(3.9352 - 3.9206)/1}{3.9206/(34-3)} \\
&= 0.115
\end{aligned}
$$

The 5% critical value from the $F_{(1,31)}$-distribution is $F_c = 4.16$. Since $0.115 < 4.16$, there is no sample evidence to suggest that $\beta_2 \neq -\beta_3$. Our original specification is not rejected by the data.

In this section we have suggested and used just one method for estimating ρ. You may discover that the computer package that you use gives several alternative methods or estimators for ρ. Some of these are discussed in the next section.

16.4   Other Estimators for an AR(1) Error Model

Early work on the AR(1) error model was done more than 40 years ago by two authors named Cochrane and Orcutt. The model has been subsequently analyzed by an enormous number of researchers, many of whom have suggested alternative estimators for ρ and β. Let us very briefly examine some of these alternatives. First, it is usually a better practice to estimate ρ and β *at the same time* rather than to estimate ρ first, then β, then stop. There are a variety of ways to find joint estimates of β and ρ. To introduce one of these ways, consider equation 16.3.5, rearranged so that ρy_{t-1} is on the right-hand side. That is,

$$y_t = (1-\rho)\beta_1 + \rho y_{t-1} + x_{t2}\beta_2 - x_{t-1,2}\rho\beta_2 + \varepsilon_t \qquad t = 2, 3,\ldots, T \quad (16.4.1)$$

This equation is unlike any you have seen to date because on the right-hand side you have terms like $(1 - \rho)\beta_1$ and $\rho\beta_2$, where parameters are multiplied together. Equation

16.4.1 is called a nonlinear model because of this fact. It can be estimated by using a rule called *nonlinear least squares*. Using equation 16.4.1, this rule or technique jointly finds estimates for ρ, β_1, and β_2 by minimizing the sum of squared errors

$$S*(\beta_1,\beta_2,\rho) = \sum_{t=2}^{T}\left(y_t -(1-\rho)\beta_1 -\rho y_{t-1} -x_{t2}\beta_2 +x_{t-1,2}\rho\beta_2\right)^2 \quad (16.4.2)$$

This principle is the same as that employed for other least squares estimates found throughout this book but, because the parameters enter in a nonlinear way, it is impossible to find simple complete algebraic formulas for the estimators. This inability to find appropriate formulas might seem to be a big problem, but it is not. It is straightforward for modern statistical computer programs, like SAS and SHAZAM, to numerically find values for ρ, β_1, and β_2 that minimize equation 16.4.2. More details about nonlinear least squares can be found in Chapter 22.

A slight modification of the nonlinear least squares estimator that minimizes equation 16.4.2 can be found by recognizing, as we did before, that equation 16.4.1 essentially uses only $(T-1)$ transformed observations. A little more information can be injected into the minimization process by adding the squared error from the first transformed observation

$$\sqrt{1-\rho^2}\, y_1 = \sqrt{1-\rho^2}\,\beta_1 +x_{12}\sqrt{1-\rho^2}\,\beta_1 +\sqrt{1-\rho^2}\,e_1 \quad (16.4.3)$$

Making this injection yields the nonlinear least squares estimator that jointly finds ρ, β_1, and β_2 that minimize

$$S(\beta_1,\beta_2,\rho) = S*(\beta_1,\beta_2,\rho)+\left(y_1 -\beta_1 -x_{12}\beta_2\right)^2\left(1-\rho^2\right) \quad (16.4.4)$$

Finally, if the maximum likelihood (ML) rule that makes use of the information that the errors are normally distributed is used, we get estimators for ρ, β_1, and β_2 that are equivalent to minimizing

$$S_{\mathrm{ML}} = S(\beta_1,\beta_2,\rho)\left(1-\rho^2\right)^{-1/T} \quad (16.4.5)$$

Table 16.2 contains estimates for (ρ, β_1, and β_2) that were obtained using these three nonlinear (NL) techniques, as well as the estimated generalized least squares (EGLS) results obtained previously. In this particular example (Bangladesh sugarcane response), there is little difference between the estimates from the different estimation rules.

Table 16.2   Estimates of Sugarcane Response
Parameters Using Alternative Estimators

Estimator	ρ	β_1	β_2
EGLS	0.4501	6.205	1.060
NL, min $S*$	0.4529	6.166	1.026
NL, min S	0.4574	6.207	1.062
ML, min S_{ML}	0.4448	6.204	1.059

16.5   Testing for Autocorrelated Errors

The next task that we face is to test for the presence of autocorrelated errors. Such testing is necessary because in real-world problems we are uncertain as to whether the errors in our econometric model are correlated. If the errors are correlated, the generalized least squares (or nonlinear least squares) procedures are needed for estimation and inference.

16.5.1   A Test Statistic

The most popular and powerful tool for detecting AR(1) errors in a linear model is a test developed by Durbin and Watson (1950). This test is based on the "Durbin–Watson statistic"

$$d = \frac{\sum_{t=2}^{T} \left(\hat{e}_t - \hat{e}_{t-1} \right)^2}{\sum_{t=1}^{T} \hat{e}_t^2} \tag{16.5.1}$$

where the $\hat{e}_t$ are the least squares residuals from the vector

$$\hat{\mathbf{e}} = \mathbf{y} - X\mathbf{b} \tag{16.5.2}$$

To see why d might be a reasonable statistic for testing for autocorrelation, let us expand equation 16.5.1 as

$$d = \frac{\sum_{t=2}^{T} \hat{e}_t^2 + \sum_{t=2}^{T} \hat{e}_{t-1}^2 - 2 \sum_{t=2}^{T} \hat{e}_t \hat{e}_{t-1}}{\sum_{t=1}^{T} \hat{e}_t^2}$$

$$= \frac{\sum_{t=2}^{T} \hat{e}_t^2}{\sum_{t=1}^{T} \hat{e}_t^2} + \frac{\sum_{t=2}^{T} \hat{e}_{t-1}^2}{\sum_{t=1}^{T} \hat{e}_t^2} - 2 \frac{\sum_{t=2}^{T} \hat{e}_t \hat{e}_{t-1}}{\sum_{t=1}^{T} \hat{e}_t^2} \tag{16.5.3}$$

$$\approx 1 + 1 - 2\hat{\rho}$$

The last line in equation 16.5.3 holds only approximately. The first two terms differ from one through the exclusion of $\hat{e}_1^2$ and $\hat{e}_T^2$ from the first and second numerator summations, respectively. The last term differs from $2\hat{\rho}$ through the inclusion of $\hat{e}_T^2$ in the denominator summation. Thus, we have

$$d \approx 2(1 - \hat{\rho}) \tag{16.5.4}$$

If the estimated value of ρ is $\hat{\rho} = 0$, then the Durbin–Watson statistic $d \approx 2$, which is taken as an indication that the model errors are not autocorrelated. If the estimate of ρ happened to be $\hat{\rho} = 1$, then $d \approx 0$, and thus a low value for the Durbin–Watson test statistic implies that the model errors are correlated, and $\rho > 0$. Similarly, for $\hat{\rho} = -1$, $d \approx 4$, and hence a value of d close to 4 is suggestive of negatively correlated errors where $\rho < 0$.

16.5.2   The Test Mechanism

Let us examine how the statistic d can be used to test the null hypothesis of no autocorrelation against the alternative that positive autocorrelation exists. We are considering the linear statistical model

$$y_t = \beta_1 + x_{t2}\beta_2 + e_t \tag{16.5.5}$$

where

$$e_t = \rho e_{t-1} + \varepsilon_t \tag{16.5.6}$$

and the ε_t are independent random errors with distribution $N(0, \sigma_\varepsilon^2)$. We have added the assumption of *normally* distributed random errors because this assumption is needed to obtain the probability distribution of d. The null and alternative hypotheses are

$$\begin{aligned} H_0 &: \rho = 0 \\ H_1 &: \rho > 0 \end{aligned} \tag{16.5.7}$$

Since a value of d close to zero suggests H_1: $\rho > 0$ is true, the question we need to answer is: How close to zero does the value of the test statistic have to be before we conclude that the errors are correlated? In other words, what is a critical value d_c such that we reject H_0 when

$$d < d_c$$

As we discussed in Chapter 4, determination of critical values for conventional statistical tests requires knowledge of the probability distribution of the test statistic under the assumption that the "null" hypothesis, which here is H_0: $\rho = 0$, is true. If a 5% significance level is required, knowledge of the probability distribution $f(d)$ under H_0 allows us to find d_c such that $P(d < d_c) = .05$. Then, as illustrated in Figure 16.2, we reject H_0 if $d < d_c$ and fail to reject H_0 if $d > d_c$. Alternatively, we can state the test procedure in terms of the p-value of the test. The p-value is given by the area under $f(d)$ to the left of the calculated value of d. Thus, if the p-value is less than .05, it follows that $d < d_c$ and H_0 is rejected. If the p-value is greater than .05, then $d > d_c$, and H_0 is accepted.

In any event, whether the test result is found by comparing d with d_c, or by computing the p-value, the probability distribution $f(d)$ is required. A difficulty associated with

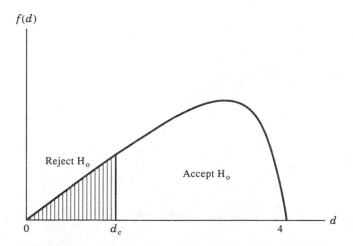

Figure 16.2 Testing for positive autocorrelation.

$f(d)$, and one that we have not previously encountered when using other test statistics, is that this probability distribution depends on the matrix X. Different sets of explanatory variables (as represented by X) lead to different distributions for d. Because $f(d)$ depends on X, the critical value d_c for any given problem will also depend on X. This property means that it is impossible to tabulate critical values that can be used for every possible X matrix that might arise in practice. With other test statistics, such as t, F, and χ^2, the tabulated critical values are relevant for all models.

This problem can be readily overcome if an appropriate specialized computer program is available. For example, the program SHAZAM can compute the Durbin–Watson p-value for any problem being considered. As we have mentioned, if this p-value is less than the specified significance level, H_0: $\rho = 0$ is rejected and we conclude that autocorrelation does exist.

16.5.3 The Bounds Test

Forty years ago, when Durbin and Watson suggested a test based on d, computing capabilities were very primitive; it was out of the question to compute a p-value for each model or problem under consideration. They partially overcame this problem by considering two other statistics d_L and d_U, whose probability distributions do not depend on X and which have the property that

$$d_L < d < d_U \qquad (16.5.8)$$

That is, irrespective of the X matrix for the problem under consideration, d will be bounded by an upper bound d_U and a lower bound d_L. The relationship between the probability distributions $f(d_L)$, $f(d)$, and $f(d_U)$ is depicted in Figure 16.3. Let d_{Lc} be the 5% critical value from the probability distribution for d_L. That is, d_{Lc} is such that $P(d_L < d_{Lc}) = .05$. Similarly, let d_{Uc} be such that $P(d_U < d_{Uc}) = .05$. Since the probability distributions $f(d_L)$ and $f(d_U)$ do not depend on X, it is possible to tabulate the critical values d_{Lc} and d_{Uc}. These values do depend on T and K, but it is possible to tabulate the alternative values for different T and K. See Table 5 at the end of this book.

Thus, in Figure 16.3 we have three critical values. The values d_{Lc} and d_{Uc} can be readily obtained from the tables. The value d_c, the one in which we are really interested for testing purposes, cannot be found without a specialized computer program. However,

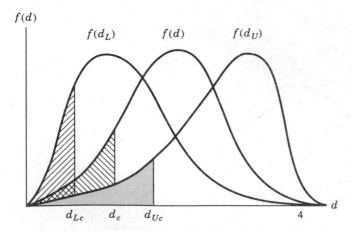

Figure 16.3 Upper and lower critical value bounds for the Durbin–Watson test.

it is clear from the figure that if the calculated value d is such that $d < d_{Lc}$, then it must follow that $d < d_c$, and H_0 is rejected. Also, if $d > d_{Uc}$, then it follows that $d > d_c$, and H_0 is accepted. If it turns out that $d_{Lc} < d < d_{Uc}$, then, because we do not know the location of d_c, we cannot be sure whether to accept or reject. These considerations led Durbin and Watson to suggest the following decision rules, which are known collectively as the Durbin–Watson *bounds test*.

If $d < d_{Lc}$, reject H_0: $\rho = 0$ and accept H_1: $\rho > 0$;

if $d > d_{Uc}$, do not reject H_0: $\rho = 0$;

if $d_{Lc} < d < d_{Uc}$, the test is inconclusive.

The presence of a range of values where no conclusion can be reached is an obvious disadvantage of the test. If the value of d falls in this "indeterminate" region, and an exact p-value cannot be computed, then one may pursue alternative tests, some of which are described in Judge et al. (1988, Chapter 9, Section 5).

16.5.4   The Example

For our sugarcane area response model, we find that

$$d = \frac{\sum_{t=2}^{T}(\hat{e}_t - \hat{e}_{t-1})^2}{\sum_{t=1}^{T}\hat{e}^2} = 1.093$$

The critical value bounds for a 5% significance level are found in Table 5 at the end of the book and, for $T = 34$ and $K = 2$, these values are

$$d_{Lc} = 1.393 \qquad d_{Uc} = 1.514$$

Since $d < d_{Lc}$ we conclude that $d < d_c$, and hence we reject H_0; there is evidence to suggest that autocorrelation exists. The relevant p-value is given by the area under $f(d)$ to the left of 1.093. That is,

$$p - \text{value} = P(d < 1.093) = 0.00132$$

This value is much less than .05 and, hence, leads us to the same conclusion. The data suggest the existence of a first-order autoregressive error.

16.5.5   Testing for Negatively Correlated Errors

Thus far we have concentrated on testing when the alternative hypothesis is H_1: $\rho > 0$. This is the most common alternative in practice. However, the alternative of negatively autocorrelated errors can be entertained, particularly if differenced data are being used. In these circumstances the null and alternative hypotheses are

$$H_0 : \rho = 0$$
$$H_1 : \rho < 0$$

At the 5% significance level we reject H_0 in favor of H_1 if $P(d > d_{\text{calc}}) < .05$ where we have used d_{calc} as the calculated value of the Durbin–Watson statistic to distinguish it from the random variable d. If the computing software needed to calculate this p-value is unavailable, we can proceed with the following bounds test:

If $d < 4 - d_{Uc}$, we do not reject H_0;

if $d > 4 - d_{Lc}$, we reject H_0 and accept H_1;

if $4 - d_{Uc} < d < 4 - d_{Lc}$, the test is inconclusive.

16.6   Forecasting in the AR(1) Correlated Error Model

In Chapters 7 and 11 we considered the problem of forecasting or predicting a future observation y_0 that we assumed would be generated from the linear statistical model

$$
\begin{aligned}
y_0 &= \beta_1 + x_{02}\beta_2 + \dots + x_{0K}\beta_K + e_0 \\
&= \mathbf{x}_0'\boldsymbol{\beta} + e_0
\end{aligned}
\tag{16.6.1}
$$

where $\mathbf{x}_0 = (1, x_{02}, \dots, x_{0K})'$ was a vector of future observations on the explanatory variables and e_0 was a future error term. To solve this problem we used the past sample information $\mathbf{y}$ and X where the corresponding variables were assumed to be related through the linear model

$$
\mathbf{y} = X\boldsymbol{\beta} + \mathbf{e}
\tag{16.6.2}
$$

The best linear unbiased predictor for y_0 was

$$
\hat{y}_0 = \mathbf{x}_0'\mathbf{b}
\tag{16.6.3}
$$

where $\mathbf{b} = (X'X)^{-1}X'\mathbf{y}$ was the least squares estimator for $\boldsymbol{\beta}$.

There are two important differences between this forecasting problem and the forecasting problem that involves a linear model with AR(1) errors. The first difference relates to the best way to estimate $\boldsymbol{\beta}$. In Chapters 7 and 11 where the errors were uncorrelated identically distributed random variables [that is, $\text{cov}(\mathbf{e}) = \sigma^2 I_T$], the least squares estimator $\mathbf{b} = (X'X)^{-1}X'\mathbf{y}$ was the best linear unbiased estimator for $\boldsymbol{\beta}$. Correspondingly, $\mathbf{x}_0'\mathbf{b}$ was the best linear unbiased estimator for $\mathbf{x}_0'\boldsymbol{\beta}$. Thus, it was natural to use $\mathbf{x}_0'\mathbf{b}$ as a predictor for $\mathbf{x}_0'\boldsymbol{\beta}$.

When we have a model with autocorrelated errors, the generalized least squares estimator $\hat{\boldsymbol{\beta}} = (X^{*\prime}X^*)^{-1}X^{*\prime}\mathbf{y}^*$ is the best linear unbiased estimator for $\boldsymbol{\beta}$. Hence, in these circumstances, $\mathbf{x}_0'\hat{\boldsymbol{\beta}}$ is the best linear unbiased estimator for $\mathbf{x}_0'\boldsymbol{\beta}$ and it is natural to use $\mathbf{x}_0'\hat{\boldsymbol{\beta}}$ as a predictor for $\mathbf{x}_0'\boldsymbol{\beta}$.

The term $\mathbf{x}_0'\boldsymbol{\beta}$ represents only one component of the future observation y_0, however. The other component is e_0. The second difference between the forecasting problem in Chapters 7 and 11 and that for the AR(1) error model relates to the best forecast for the future error e_0. When e_0 is uncorrelated with the past error vector $\mathbf{e}$, as was assumed in Chapters 7 and 11, the best forecast of e_0 is its mean value of zero. When e_0 is correlated with $\mathbf{e}$, as it will be in the AR(1) error model, we can use information contained in the past errors $\mathbf{e}$ to improve on zero as a forecast for e_0.

To understand how such an improvement can be made, and to collect all of the results mentioned thus far, let us begin with a formal statement of the problem. We are considering the model

$$
\begin{aligned}
y_t &= \beta_1 + x_{t2}\beta_2 + \dots + x_{tK}\beta_K + e_t \\
&= \mathbf{x}_t'\boldsymbol{\beta} + e_t, \qquad t = 1, 2, \dots, T
\end{aligned}
\tag{16.6.4}
$$

where $\mathbf{x}_t = (1, x_{t2}, \ldots, x_{tK})'$, the random errors e_t are AR(1)

$$e_t = \rho e_{t-1} + \varepsilon_t \tag{16.6.5}$$

the random errors ε_t are independent and identically distributed, and $|\rho| < 1$. Our first objective is to forecast the next period's observation on y that is given by

$$
\begin{aligned}
y_{T+1} &= \beta_1 + x_{T+1,2}\beta_2 + \ldots + x_{T+1,K}\beta_K + e_{T+1} \\
&= \mathbf{x}'_{T+1}\boldsymbol{\beta} + e_{T+1} \\
&= \mathbf{x}'_{T+1}\boldsymbol{\beta} + \rho e_T + \varepsilon_{T+1}
\end{aligned}
\tag{16.6.6}
$$

where we have used $e_{T+1} = \rho e_T + \varepsilon_{T+1}$. Let us consider each of the three components of equation 16.6.6 in turn.

As we have mentioned, given the explanatory variable values $\mathbf{x}_{T+1}$, the best linear unbiased predictor for $\mathbf{x}'_{T+1}\boldsymbol{\beta}$ is $\mathbf{x}'_{T+1}\hat{\boldsymbol{\beta}}$, where $\hat{\boldsymbol{\beta}}$ is the generalized least squares estimator.

To predict the second component ρe_T, we need estimates for both ρ and e_T. For ρ we can use the estimator $\hat{\rho}$ specified in equation 16.3.21. To estimate e_T we use the generalized least squares residual defined as

$$\tilde{e}_T = y_T - \mathbf{x}'_T\hat{\boldsymbol{\beta}} \tag{16.6.7}$$

The best forecast of the third component ε_{T+1} is zero because this component is uncorrelated with past values $\varepsilon_1, \varepsilon_2, \ldots, \varepsilon_T$.

Collecting all these results *our predictor for y_{T+1} is given by*

$$\hat{y}_{T+1} = \mathbf{x}'_{T+1}\hat{\boldsymbol{\beta}} + \hat{\rho}\tilde{e}_T \tag{16.6.8}$$

In practice, because ρ is unknown, we use the estimated generalized least squares estimator $\hat{\boldsymbol{\beta}}$ in both equations 16.6.7 and 16.6.8.

A comparison of equations 16.6.6 and 16.6.8 shows that we are using $\hat{\rho}\tilde{e}_T$ to predict the future error e_{T+1}. That is, we are using information on the Tth error e_T, and our knowledge that e_T and e_{T+1} are correlated, to improve on zero as a predictor for e_{T+1}.

What about forecasting more than one period into the future? For two periods ahead we have

$$e_{T+2} = \rho e_{T+1} + \varepsilon_{T+2} = \rho^2 e_T + \rho\varepsilon_{T+1} + \varepsilon_{T+2} \tag{16.6.9}$$

and, in general, for h periods ahead

$$e_{T+h} = \rho^h e_T + \rho^{h-1}\varepsilon_{T+1} + \rho^{h-2}\varepsilon_{T+2} + \ldots + \varepsilon_{T+h} \tag{16.6.10}$$

In equation 16.6.10 the best forecast for the future uncorrelated errors $\varepsilon_{T+1}, \varepsilon_{T+2}, \ldots, \varepsilon_{T+h}$ is zero. Thus, to forecast e_{T+h} we use

$$\hat{e}_{T+h} = \hat{\rho}^h \tilde{e}_T \tag{16.6.11}$$

Correspondingly, to predict y, h periods ahead, we use

$$\hat{y}_{T+h} = \mathbf{x}'_{T+h}\hat{\boldsymbol{\beta}} + \hat{\rho}^h \tilde{e}_T \tag{16.6.12}$$

Assuming $|\hat{\rho}| < 1$ (as it should be since $|\rho| < 1$), the influence of the term $\hat{\rho}^h \tilde{e}_T$ diminishes the further we go into the future (the larger h becomes).

16.6.1   An Example

In the Bangladesh sugarcane example

$$\hat{\hat{\beta}} = (6.205, \ 1.060)' \qquad \hat{\rho} = 0.4501$$

and

$$\tilde{e}_T = y_T - \hat{\hat{\beta}}_1 - \hat{\hat{\beta}}_2 + x_{T2}$$
$$= \ln(A_T) - \hat{\hat{\beta}}_1 - \hat{\hat{\beta}}_2 \ln(P_{ST} \ / \ P_{JT})$$
$$= 5.4596 - 6.205 - (1.060)(-0.9374)$$
$$= .248$$

To predict y_{T+1} and y_{T+2} for a sugarcane–jute price ratio of 0.4, in both periods $(T + 1)$ and $(T + 2)$, we have

$$y_{T+1} = \mathbf{x}'_{T+1}\hat{\hat{\beta}} + \hat{\rho}\tilde{e}_T$$
$$= 6.205 + 1.060 \ln(0.4) + (0.4501)(0.2483)$$
$$= 5.345$$

$$y_{T+2} = \mathbf{x}'_{T+2}\hat{\hat{\beta}} + \hat{\rho}\tilde{e}_T$$
$$= 6.205 + 1.060 \ln(0.4) + (0.4501)^2 (0.2483)$$
$$= 5.284$$

16.7   Summary of Results on Autocorrelated Error Models

This chapter has been concerned with the linear statistical model $\mathbf{y} = X\beta + \mathbf{e}$ and with the implications of having an error vector $\mathbf{e}$ whose elements are autocorrelated. Under these circumstances the off-diagonal elements of the error covariance matrix $\text{cov}(\mathbf{e}) = W$ are nonzero.

The existence of autocorrelated errors is always a real possibility and is worth investigating when we have a sample of time-series observations. If a model possesses autocorrelated errors, but we ignore or are unaware of the correlation and hence use the least squares estimator $\mathbf{b} = (X'X)^{-1}X'\mathbf{y}$, we will be using an estimator that is inefficient relative to the generalized least squares estimator, and we will be using standard errors that are not a proper reflection of the precision of the least squares estimates.

There are many "time-series processes" that can be used to model autocorrelated errors. For a review of alternatives see Judge et al. (1985, pp. 283–315). The most common, and the one considered in this chapter, is the first-order autoregressive process

$$e_t = \rho e_{t-1} + \varepsilon_t \tag{16.7.1}$$

where the ε_t are independent identically distributed errors. Assuming that $-1 < \rho < 1$ implies that the process is stationary with

$$E[e_t] = 0 \qquad \text{var}[e_t] = \frac{\sigma_\varepsilon^2}{1-\rho^2} \qquad \text{corr}(e_t, e_{t-k}) = \rho^k \tag{16.7.2}$$

To detect the presence of autocorrelated errors of the form given in equation 16.7.1, we use the Durbin–Watson test to test the null hypothesis $\rho = 0$ against an alternative that $\rho > 0$ or $\rho < 0$. Because of the impossibility of producing Durbin–Watson critical values relevant for all possible problems, the Durbin–Watson test uses a so-called bounds test, or computer software that can automatically compute the relevant p-value. Many alternatives to the Durbin–Watson test have appeared in the literature. For a summary of these alternatives see Judge et al. (1985, pp. 319–330).

If $\rho \neq 0$, a generalized least squares (or nonlinear least squares) estimation technique is called for. The first step toward finding (estimated) generalized least squares estimates is to estimate ρ from the least squares residuals as

$$\hat{\rho} = \sum_{t=2}^{T} \hat{e}_t \hat{e}_{t-1} \Bigg/ \sum_{t=2}^{T} \hat{e}_{t-1}^2$$

Then, using the dependent variable y_t as an example, the observations are transformed as

$$
\begin{aligned}
y_t^* &= y_t - \hat{\rho} y_{t-1} \quad t = 2, 3, \ldots, T \\
y_1^* &= \sqrt{1 - \hat{\rho}^2}\, y_1
\end{aligned}
\tag{16.7.3}
$$

The estimated generalized least squares estimator is equivalent to least squares applied to the transformed observations, and thus is given by

$$\hat{\hat{\boldsymbol{\beta}}} = \left(X^{*\prime} X^* \right)^{-1} X^{*\prime} \mathbf{y}^* \tag{16.7.4}$$

Its estimated covariance matrix is

$$\hat{\text{cov}}\left(\hat{\hat{\boldsymbol{\beta}}} \right) = \hat{\sigma}_\varepsilon^2 \left(X^{*\prime} X^* \right)^{-1} \tag{16.7.5}$$

where

$$\hat{\sigma}_\varepsilon^2 = \frac{\left(\mathbf{y}^* - X^* \hat{\hat{\boldsymbol{\beta}}} \right)^{\prime} \left(\mathbf{y}^* - X^* \hat{\hat{\boldsymbol{\beta}}} \right)}{T - K} \tag{16.7.6}$$

The expressions 16.7.4 to 16.7.6 are general ones that hold true for any model where the error covariance matrix is not equal to a scalar times the identity matrix. The only thing that changes is the way in which the variables (observations) are transformed. Other estimation techniques, which are nonlinear in nature and which estimate β and ρ simultaneously, can also be employed.

A future observation, h periods ahead, is defined as

$$y_{T+h} = \mathbf{x}_{T+h}^{\prime} \boldsymbol{\beta} + e_{T+h} \tag{16.7.7}$$

To predict y_{T+h} when the errors follow an AR(1) process, we use the predictor

$$\hat{y}_{T+h} = \mathbf{x}_{T+h}^{\prime} \hat{\hat{\boldsymbol{\beta}}} + \hat{\rho}^h \tilde{e}_T \tag{16.7.8}$$

where $\tilde{e}_T$ is the most recent generalized least squares residual.

Finally, it should be emphasized that the range of economic models where autocorrelated errors might exist is much broader than our example might suggest. Routine checking for the presence of autocorrelated errors is advisable in all economic models that utilize time-series data.

16.8 Exercises

16.1 Suppose that a general linear statistical model has the AR(1) error model

$$e_t = \rho e_{t-1} + \varepsilon_t$$

where $E[\varepsilon_t] = 0$, $E[\varepsilon_t \varepsilon_s] = 0$ for $t \neq s$, and $\mathrm{var}(\varepsilon_t) = E[\varepsilon_t^2] = \sigma_\varepsilon^2$. Suppose (unrealistically) that $T = 4$.

(a) Using the notation in the text show that $E[\mathbf{ee'}] = \sigma_\varepsilon^2 V$ where

$$V = \frac{1}{1-\rho^2} \begin{bmatrix} 1 & \rho & \rho^2 & \rho^3 \\ \rho & 1 & \rho & \rho^2 \\ \rho^2 & \rho & 1 & \rho \\ \rho^3 & \rho^2 & \rho & 1 \end{bmatrix}$$

(b) Show that $VV^{-1} = I$ where

$$V^{-1} = \begin{bmatrix} 1 & -\rho & 0 & 0 \\ -\rho & 1+\rho^2 & -\rho & 0 \\ 0 & -\rho & 1+\rho^2 & -\rho \\ 0 & 0 & -\rho & 1 \end{bmatrix}$$

(c) Show that $P'P = V^{-1}$ where

$$P = \begin{bmatrix} \sqrt{1-\rho^2} & 0 & 0 & 0 \\ -\rho & 1 & 0 & 0 \\ 0 & -\rho & 1 & 0 \\ 0 & 0 & -\rho & 1 \end{bmatrix}$$

(d) Let $\mathbf{y^*} = P\mathbf{y}$ where

$$\mathbf{y^*} = \begin{bmatrix} y_1^* \\ y_2^* \\ y_3^* \\ y_4^* \end{bmatrix} \quad \text{and} \quad \mathbf{y} = \begin{bmatrix} y_1 \\ y_2 \\ y_3 \\ y_4 \end{bmatrix}$$

Find each of the y_t^* in terms of the y_t.

(e) Explain why the results in parts (a), (b), (c), and (d) imply that the generalized least squares estimator $\hat{\boldsymbol{\beta}} = \left(X'V^{-1}X\right)^{-1}X'V^{-1}\mathbf{y}$ can be computed using the transformations in equation 16.7.11.

16.2 Consider the investment function

$$I_t = \beta_1 + \beta_2 Y_t + \beta_3 R_t + e_t$$

where

I_t = investment in year t,

Y_t = GNP in year t,

R_t = interest rate in year t.

Thirty observations on I, Y, and R are given in Table 16.3. Use these data to answer the following questions.

(a) Find least squares estimates of β_1, β_2, and β_3 and report the results in the usual way. Comment.

(b) Use the Durbin–Watson test to test for autocorrelation.

(c) Reestimate the model after correcting for autocorrelation. Report the results. Note any differences between these results and those obtained in part (a). Suggest how the results obtained in part (a) could be misleading.

(d) Forecast next year's level of investment given that next year's values for Y and R are $Y = 36$ and $R = 14$.

16.3 To investigate the relationship between job vacancies (JV) and the unemployment rate (U), a researcher sets up the model

$$\ln(JV_t) = \beta_1 + \beta_2 \ln U_t + e_t$$

and assumes that the e_t are independent $N(0, \sigma_e^2)$ random variables.

(a) Use the data in Table 16.4 to find least squares estimates for β_1 and β_2. Construct a 95% confidence interval for β_2.

(b) Find the value of the Durbin–Watson statistic. In light of this value, what can you say about the original assumptions for the error e_t; what can you say about the confidence interval for β_2 found in (a)?

(c) R-estimate the model assuming the errors follow an AR(1) error process. Find a new 95% confidence interval for β_2 and comment on the results, particularly in relation to your answers for part (a).

16.4 Data for a monopolist's total revenue (tr), total cost (tc), and output (q), for 48 consecutive months, appear in Table 16.5. Suppose that the monopolist's economic models for total revenue and total cost are given, respectively, by

$$tr = \beta_1 q + \beta_2 q^2$$
$$tc = \alpha_1 + \alpha_2 q + \alpha_3 q^2$$

(a) Find the profit-maximizing level of output as a function of the unknown parameters β_1, β_2, α_2, and α_3.

(b) Use the least squares estimator to estimate the total revenue and total cost functions. For what statistical models are these estimates appropriate? What do the least squares estimates suggest is the profit-maximizing level of output?

(c) Separately test the errors for each of the functions to see if these errors might be autocorrelated.

(d) Where autocorrelation has been suggested by the tests in part (c), find estimated generalized least squares estimates of the relevant function(s).

(e) What is the profit-maximizing level of output suggested by the results in part (d)?

(f) Given the output level found in part (e), forecast total revenue, total cost, and hence profit for the next few months. Comment.

Table 16.3 Thirty Observations on I, Y, and R

I	Y	R
11.53	8.58	18.12
13.25	10.47	11.07
10.87	8.34	8.98
10.46	10.64	17.01
15.09	9.65	16.26
17.49	12.01	13.78
17.77	13.45	19.95
16.11	14.20	18.73
10.66	13.83	9.53
10.59	14.45	13.79
9.32	16.57	19.31
11.00	18.02	15.19
15.03	18.38	12.40
15.09	20.42	16.48
22.70	20.99	5.93
21.96	23.74	17.51
23.07	25.74	16.42
25.67	24.21	7.42
26.15	25.21	15.47
25.56	26.21	19.16
28.12	28.60	5.47
24.21	30.58	9.51
21.51	25.98	7.44
22.93	26.86	19.91
32.30	31.32	7.94
24.60	32.93	21.35
30.44	32.10	8.65
32.51	33.29	11.12
29.49	35.59	21.68
31.18	33.86	15.82

Table 16.4 Observations for Exercise 16.3

JV	U
0.74	9.66
0.93	5.80
3.07	3.69
4.16	3.65
2.54	3.57
0.70	9.09
0.93	9.81
1.55	6.53
4.08	3.87
1.79	6.27
3.45	4.31
2.20	6.47
1.24	7.83
1.09	9.27
2.38	4.44
1.12	8.76
2.15	5.72
0.90	8.48
1.28	7.23
5.14	3.64
1.10	9.58
7.36	3.59
1.72	7.28
5.12	3.72

16.9 References

Three important early articles on estimation and testing with autocorrelated error models are

COCHRANE, D., and G. H. ORCUTT (1949) "Application of Least Squares Regressions to Relationships Containing Autocorrelated Error Terms," *Journal of the American Statistical Association*, 44, 32–61.

DURBIN, J., and G. S. WATSON (1950) "Testing for Serial Correlation in Least Squares Regression I," *Biometrika*, 37, 409–428.

DURBIN, J., and G. S. WATSON (1951) "Testing for Serial Correlation in Least Squares Regression II," *Biometrika*, 38, 159–178.

More details on the procedures and models discussed in this chapter can be found in

JUDGE, G. G., R. C. HILL, W. E. GRIFFITHS, H. LÜTKEPOHL and T. C. LEE (1988) *Introduction to the Theory and Practice of Econometrics*, 2nd Edition, New York: John Wiley & Sons, Inc., Chapters 8 and 9.

Table 16.5 Data on Total Revenue, Total Cost, and Output

Month	tr	tc	q	Month	tr	tc	q
1	13536	11790	206	25	14564	10501	196
2	12205	14503	231	26	14878	6246	138
3	12881	15323	245	27	16298	9419	180
4	12837	3276	96	28	14304	5053	115
5	13477	13523	228	29	16074	8791	173
6	14524	5337	133	30	12859	15690	248
7	15041	8431	178	31	13076	3633	91
8	14938	8960	183	32	15912	9230	177
9	14278	12207	220	33	14041	13459	225
10	12480	14756	244	34	16268	8026	158
11	14708	5923	134	35	17028	7375	151
12	13950	13297	223	36	16203	10517	190
13	15564	8342	161	37	16516	7685	155
14	13414	4593	108	38	14864	5900	129
15	15360	10851	198	39	12096	4393	91
16	14371	5746	138	40	14772	10066	184
17	14030	4925	126	41	9396	3525	73
18	13974	10087	196	42	13055	5580	128
19	13450	13007	226	43	12590	5217	123
20	12753	3449	95	44	12497	6513	141
21	13342	3930	101	45	11656	5638	130
22	15447	9281	183	46	8743	2839	86
23	15245	9463	184	47	11421	8692	187
24	15299	7005	153	48	8435	2151	83

Other error processes for modelling autocorrelation can be found in

JUDGE, G. G., W. E. GRIFFITHS, R. C. HILL, H. LÜTKEPOHL and T. C. LEE (1985) *The Theory and Practice of Econometrics*, New York: John Wiley & Sons, Inc., Chapter 8.

Other treatments of autocorrelation, at a less advanced level, can be found in

DORAN, H. E. (1989), *Applied Regression Analysis in Econometrics*, New York: Marcel Dekker, Inc., Chapter 8.

KENNEDY, P. (1992) *A Guide to Econometrics*, 3rd Edition, Oxford: Basil Blackwell, Chapter 8.

MADDALA, G. S. (1989) *Introduction to Econometrics*, New York: Macmillan Publishing Co., Chapter 6.

Chapter 17

Estimating the Parameters of a Set of Error Related Economic Relations

New Key Words and Concepts

Pooling of Sample Observations
Contemporaneously Correlated
   Equation Errors
Estimated Generalized Least Squares
Sampling Precision
Firm Investment Relations
Time-Series–Cross-Section Data
Error Component Models

Seemingly Unrelated Regression
   Equations
Generalized Least Squares
   Estimation
Aggregation Test
A Set of Demand Relations
Dummy Variables,

Up to this point we have considered estimation and inference procedures for a single relation and one sample of data. In this chapter we extend our analysis to consider two or more sets of economic and statistical relations and, correspondingly, two or more samples of data. For example, many sets of economic data consist of the same cross-sectional sample and possibly reflect the outcomes of economic relations that exist at different points in time. In addition to time, geographical areas, economic commodities, and individual decision makers are other examples of entities that provide a basis for partitioning sample observations and thus defining a set of economic relations. Because economic relations may, for example, have parameters that vary over time (months, quarters, years) and space (regions, countries), this property needs to be recognized when specifying the economic and statistical models and developing methods of estimation and inference.

In developing a basis for estimation and inference when considering a set of economic-regression equations we will, as in previous chapters, start with the economic model and identify the corresponding economic data. We then specify a statistical-econometric model that we believe is consistent with the sampling process by which the data are generated and then go on to identify appropriate estimating procedures and the corresponding basis for inference. As before, the tools we develop will be applicable for a broad range of economic-statistical models. In the process of completing this analysis, we will add a new set of statistical models and econometric tools. Chapters 14 to 16 have provided the basis for the statistical tools that we need to analyze the problems encountered in this chapter. When working with a set of economic relations, a way to organize the specification of the pieces of sample information will be proposed that permits us to make use of a variation of the normal linear statistical model that was introduced in Chapters 5 and 12.

The organization of the chapter is as follows: Economic and statistical models involving investment relations for the two firms are specified and corresponding estimation and hypothesis testing procedures are proposed. Next estimation and inference relevant for handling a set of three demand relations are considered. Finally in Appendices 17A and 17B a general formulation involving a set of M relations is specified and analyzed and variants of the set of equations model are used as a basis for analyzing the problem of pooling time series and cross section data.

Sections 17.2 and 17.3 provide a good introduction to the theory and practice of particular economic problems that may be cast in the sets of regression equations framework. Appendices 17A and 17B, which require a more complete understanding of linear algebra and statistical machinery, provide a general framework for specifying and carrying through a range of economic problems within the context of the seemingly unrelated regressions statistical model.

17.1   Firm Investment Relations

To motivate the specification and analysis of the multiple equation model, we focus on the firm and investigate the spending by firms on new plant and equipment and maintenance and repairs. We use firm data and econometric procedures to determine if we can identify, for two U. S. firms, what determines net annual investment and why it changes dramatically from year to year.

17.1.1   The Economic Model

Investment demand is the purchase of durable goods by both households and firms. In terms of total spending, investment spending is the volatile component. Therefore, understanding what determines investment is crucial to understanding the sources of fluctuations in aggregate demand. In addition, a firm's net fixed investment, which is the flow of additions to capital stock or replacements for worn-out capital, is important because it determines the future value of the capital stock and thus affects future labor productivity and aggregate supply.

There are several interesting and elaborate theories that seek to describe the determinants of the investment process for the firm. Most of these theories evolve to the conclusion that perceived profit opportunities (expected profits or present discounted value of future earnings) and desired capital stock are two important determinants of a firm's fixed business investment. Unfortunately, neither of these variables is directly observable. Therefore, in formulating our economic model, the question we face is whether or not viable observable proxies for these variables exist.

In terms of expected profits, one alternative is to identify the present discounted value of future earnings as the market value of the firm's securities. The price of a firm's stock represents and contains information about these expected profits. Consequently, if one follows this line of thought, the stock market value of the firm at the beginning of the year, denoted by v_t, may be used as a proxy for expected profits.

In terms of desired capital stock, expectations play a definite role. To catch these expectational effects, one possibility is to use a model that recognizes that actual capital stock in any period is the sum of a large number of past desired capital stocks. One possible way of capturing this is to use the beginning of the year actual capital stock k_t as a proxy for permanent desired capital stock.

Focusing on these explanatory variables, for the tth time period, the economic model for describing gross firm investment i_t may be expressed as

$$i_t = f(v_t, k_t; \boldsymbol{\beta})$$

(17.1.1)

where $\boldsymbol{\beta}$ is an unknown coefficient vector linking v_t and k_t to i_t. Given the economic model 17.1.1, what we desire is a basis for estimating the unknown parameters $\boldsymbol{\beta}$ that connect i_t with v_t and k_t and a means for evaluating the validity of this economic model.

In order to have a basis for analyzing the conjecture that v_t and k_t condition the outcome for i_t, let us consider the gross investment patterns for two U. S. firms, General Electric and Westinghouse. These large-scale firms are engaged in some similar business activities and thus should have many things in common relative to their investment decisions. Annual data, taken from an article by Boot and Dewitt, for i_t, v_t, and k_t, and as tabulated by Theil, are given in Table 17.1. The (20×1) vectors $\mathbf{i}_1$, $\mathbf{v}_1$, and $\mathbf{k}_1$ contain the relevant observations for General Electric; the corresponding observations for Westinghouse are contained in the vectors $\mathbf{i}_2$, $\mathbf{v}_2$, and $\mathbf{k}_2$.

17.1.2 The Statistical Model

Given the economic model 17.1.1, we focus attention on specifying a statistical model that may be consistent with the sampling process underlying the two samples of investment data given in Table 17.1. In line with previous chapters, we initially assume that the General Electric (GE) sample of data can be described by the following statistical model:

$$i_{1t} = \beta_{11} + v_{1t}\beta_{12} + k_{1t}\beta_{13} + e_{1t}$$

(17.1.2a)

Table 17.1 Time Series Data on **i**, **v**, and **k** in Millions of Constant Dollars for General Electric and Westinghouse

Year	General Electric			Westinghouse		
	$\mathbf{i}_1$	$\mathbf{v}_1$	$\mathbf{k}_1$	$\mathbf{i}_2$	$\mathbf{v}_2$	$\mathbf{k}_2$
1	33.1	1170.6	97.8	12.93	191.5	1.8
2	45.0	2015.8	104.4	25.90	516.0	0.8
3	77.2	2803.3	118.0	35.05	729.0	7.4
4	44.6	2039.7	156.2	22.89	560.4	18.1
5	48.1	2256.2	172.6	18.84	519.9	23.5
6	74.4	2132.2	186.6	28.57	628.5	26.5
7	113.0	1834.1	220.9	48.51	537.1	36.2
8	91.9	1588.0	287.8	43.34	561.2	60.8
9	61.3	1749.4	319.9	37.02	617.2	84.4
10	56.8	1687.2	321.3	37.81	626.7	91.2
11	93.6	2007.7	319.6	39.27	737.2	92.4
12	159.9	2208.3	346.0	53.46	760.5	86.0
13	147.2	1656.7	456.4	55.56	581.4	111.1
14	146.3	1604.4	543.4	49.56	662.3	130.6
15	98.3	1431.8	618.3	32.04	583.8	141.8
16	93.5	1610.5	647.4	32.24	635.2	136.7
17	135.2	1819.4	671.3	54.38	723.8	129.7
18	157.3	2079.7	726.1	71.78	864.1	145.5
19	179.5	2371.6	800.3	90.08	1193.5	174.8
20	189.6	2759.9	888.9	68.60	1188.9	213.5

which we write for the whole data sample as

$$\mathbf{i}_1 = \mathbf{j}\beta_{11} + \mathbf{v}_1\beta_{12} + \mathbf{k}_1\beta_{13} + \mathbf{e}_1 \tag{17.1.2b}$$

where $\mathbf{i}_1$, $\mathbf{j}$, $\mathbf{v}_1$, $\mathbf{k}_1$, and $\mathbf{e}_1$ are $(T \times 1)$ vectors. If we let $\mathbf{j} = \mathbf{x}_{11}$, $\mathbf{v}_1 = \mathbf{x}_{12}$, and $\mathbf{k}_1 = \mathbf{x}_{13}$, we may specify the statistical model for GE in a conventional context as

$$\mathbf{y}_1 = \begin{bmatrix} \mathbf{x}_{11} & \mathbf{x}_{12} & \mathbf{x}_{13} \end{bmatrix} \begin{bmatrix} \beta_{11} \\ \beta_{12} \\ \beta_{13} \end{bmatrix} + \mathbf{e}_1$$

$$= \mathbf{x}_{11}\beta_{11} + \mathbf{x}_{12}\beta_{12} + \mathbf{x}_{13}\beta_{13} + \mathbf{e}_1$$

$$= X_1\boldsymbol{\beta}_1 + \mathbf{e}_1 \tag{17.1.2c}$$

where

$$\mathbf{y}_1 = \begin{bmatrix} i_{11} \\ i_{12} \\ \vdots \\ i_{1T} \end{bmatrix}, \qquad X_1 = \begin{bmatrix} 1 & v_{11} & k_{11} \\ 1 & v_{12} & k_{12} \\ \vdots & \vdots & \vdots \\ 1 & v_{1T} & k_{1T} \end{bmatrix}, \qquad \boldsymbol{\beta}_1 = \begin{bmatrix} \beta_{11} \\ \beta_{12} \\ \beta_{13} \end{bmatrix} \quad \text{and} \quad \mathbf{e} = \begin{bmatrix} e_{11} \\ e_{12} \\ \vdots \\ e_{1T} \end{bmatrix}$$

Thus, $\mathbf{y}_1$ is a (20×1) vector of observed values for General Electric investment, X_1 is a (20×3) matrix that contains the constant unit vector $\mathbf{j}$ and the explanatory variables $\mathbf{v}_1$ and $\mathbf{k}_1$, $\boldsymbol{\beta}_1$ is a (3×1) dimensional vector of unknown coefficients. We assume that the (20×1) dimensional random error vector $\mathbf{e}_1 \sim N(\mathbf{0}, \sigma_1^2 I_T)$ with unknown scale (variance) parameter σ_1^2.

Likewise, under the same assumptions, we may write the statistical model for Westinghouse as

$$i_{2t} = \beta_{21} + v_{2t}\beta_{22} + k_{2t}\beta_{23} + e_{2t} \tag{17.1.3a}$$

or in terms of the complete set of sample observations

$$\mathbf{i}_2 = \mathbf{j}\beta_{21} + \mathbf{v}_2\beta_{22} + \mathbf{k}_2\beta_{23} + \mathbf{e}_2 \tag{17.1.3b}$$

If we let $\mathbf{j} = \mathbf{x}_{21}$, $\mathbf{v}_2 = \mathbf{x}_{22}$, and $\mathbf{k}_2 = \mathbf{x}_{23}$, we may rewrite the statistical model for Westinghouse as

$$\mathbf{y}_2 = \begin{bmatrix} \mathbf{x}_{21} & \mathbf{x}_{22} & \mathbf{x}_{23} \end{bmatrix} \begin{bmatrix} \beta_{21} \\ \beta_{22} \\ \beta_{23} \end{bmatrix} + \mathbf{e}_2$$

$$= \mathbf{x}_{21}\beta_{21} + \mathbf{x}_{22}\beta_{22} + \mathbf{x}_{23}\beta_{23} + \mathbf{e}_2$$

$$= X_2\boldsymbol{\beta}_2 + \mathbf{e}_2 \tag{17.1.3c}$$

where the definitions and dimensions of $\mathbf{y}_2$, X_2, $\boldsymbol{\beta}_2$ are the same as for equation 17.1.2b, except that they are now related to Westinghouse and carry the subscript 2. The (20×1) dimensional random vector $\mathbf{e}_2 \sim N(\mathbf{0}, \sigma_2^2 I_T)$ and again σ_2^2 is unknown.

17.1.3   The Least Squares Estimation Rule for Each Equation

Given these two statistical models, which are of the same standard sampling theory form that we used in Chapters 9 to 11, and given that we have two samples of data, let us continue to treat each equation separately and use the least squares rules $\mathbf{b}_1 = \left(X_1'X_1\right)^{-1} X_1'\mathbf{y}_1$ and $\mathbf{b}_2 = \left(X_2'X_2\right)^{-1} X_2'\mathbf{y}_2$ to obtain estimates of the unknown parameter vectors β_1 and β_2. In this context the results for both firms are

General Electric $\hat{\mathbf{y}}_1 = -9.956\mathbf{x}_{11} + 0.0265\mathbf{x}_{12} + 0.1517\mathbf{x}_{13}$ $R_1^2 = 0.705$

$\qquad\qquad\qquad$ (31.37)   (0.015)   (0.026) $se(b_i)$

$\qquad\qquad\qquad$ (−0.32)   (1.71)   (5.90) t (17.1.4)

Westinghouse $\hat{\mathbf{y}}_2 = -0.509\mathbf{x}_{21} + 0.0529\mathbf{x}_{22} + 0.0924\mathbf{x}_{23}$ $R_2^2 = 0.744$

$\qquad\qquad\qquad$ (8.02)   (0.0157)   (0.0501) $se(b_i)$

$\qquad\qquad\qquad$ (−0.06)   (3.37)   (1.65) t (17.1.5)

The numbers in parenthesis below the coefficients are the corresponding standard errors and $t_{(17)}$-values. The t-values and standard errors for the estimated coefficients indicate that, with the exception of β_{13} and β_{22}, all estimated coefficients are measured with limited sampling precision. In both the General Electric and Westinghouse estimated relations, the signs of the coefficients of expected profits $\mathbf{x}_{i2}$ and capital stock $\mathbf{x}_{i3}$ variables are positive and thus consistent with expectations. In each case the squared multiple correlation coefficient R_i^2 is in excess of 0.70, indicating that the two explanatory variables $\mathbf{x}_{i2}$ and $\mathbf{x}_{i3}$ have been successful in reducing the unexplained variability of the investment variables about their means. From a positive economic standpoint, these estimated relations help us to understand how certain economic variables condition the levels of firm investment and put us in a position to make predictions about investment levels. From an economic policy or prescriptive standpoint, the estimated coefficients provide some information as to the potential investment consequences of changes in government control variables such as taxes that might affect expected profits $\mathbf{x}_{i2}$ and interest rates that might affect changes in capital stock $\mathbf{x}_{i3}$.

17.2   A New Statistical Model

As indicated by their estimated standard errors, some of the coefficients in the estimated relations 17.1.4 and 17.1.5 exhibit a good deal of sampling variability and thus may lack the precision necessary for the use or uses for which they are intended. Thus, to improve precision it is useful to investigate whether it is possible to reformulate the statistical model to make use of additional sample information that may be at our disposal.

Thus far we have considered the firm investment relations separately. Since General Electric and Westinghouse are firms that have many things in common, perhaps we should consider ways of pooling the sample information and possibly modeling them as a set of relations so that we can take account of this information explicitly. To achieve this we may write the statistical models

$$\begin{aligned} \mathbf{y}_1 &= \mathbf{x}_{11}\beta_{11} + \mathbf{x}_{12}\beta_{12} + \mathbf{x}_{13}\beta_{13} + \mathbf{e}_1 \\ \mathbf{y}_2 &= \mathbf{x}_{21}\beta_{21} + \mathbf{x}_{22}\beta_{22} + \mathbf{x}_{23}\beta_{23} + \mathbf{e}_2 \end{aligned} \qquad (17.2.1a)$$

as a single linear statistical model

$$\begin{bmatrix} \mathbf{y}_1 \\ \mathbf{y}_2 \end{bmatrix} = \begin{bmatrix} \mathbf{x}_{11} & \mathbf{x}_{12} & \mathbf{x}_{13} & 0 & 0 & 0 \\ 0 & 0 & 0 & \mathbf{x}_{21} & \mathbf{x}_{22} & \mathbf{x}_{23} \end{bmatrix} \begin{bmatrix} \beta_{11} \\ \beta_{12} \\ \beta_{13} \\ \beta_{21} \\ \beta_{22} \\ \beta_{23} \end{bmatrix} + \begin{bmatrix} \mathbf{e}_1 \\ \mathbf{e}_2 \end{bmatrix}$$

(17.2.1b)

In turn, equation 17.2.1 may be rewritten in compact form, using equation 17.1.2c and equation 17.1.3c, as

$$\begin{bmatrix} \mathbf{y}_1 \\ \mathbf{y}_2 \end{bmatrix} = \begin{bmatrix} X_1 & 0 \\ 0 & X_2 \end{bmatrix} \begin{bmatrix} \boldsymbol{\beta}_1 \\ \boldsymbol{\beta}_2 \end{bmatrix} + \begin{bmatrix} \mathbf{e}_1 \\ \mathbf{e}_2 \end{bmatrix}$$

(17.2.2)

where $X_1 = [\mathbf{x}_{11}\ \mathbf{x}_{12}\ \mathbf{x}_{13}]$ and $X_2 = [\mathbf{x}_{21}\ \mathbf{x}_{22}\ \mathbf{x}_{23}]$ are matrices of dimension $(T \times 3) = (20 \times 3)$. Consistent with Section 17.1 the corresponding error vectors may be specified as

$$\begin{bmatrix} \mathbf{e}_1 \\ \mathbf{e}_2 \end{bmatrix} \sim N\left(\begin{pmatrix} \mathbf{0} \\ \mathbf{0} \end{pmatrix}, \begin{pmatrix} \sigma_1^2 I_T & 0 \\ 0 & \sigma_2^2 I_T \end{pmatrix} \right)$$

(17.2.3)

where the covariance matrix for the error vector containing both $\mathbf{e}_1$ and $\mathbf{e}_2$ is given by

$$W = E\left[\begin{pmatrix} \mathbf{e}_1 \\ \mathbf{e}_2 \end{pmatrix} \begin{pmatrix} \mathbf{e}_1' & \mathbf{e}_2' \end{pmatrix} \right] = E\begin{bmatrix} E[\mathbf{e}_1\mathbf{e}_1'] & E[\mathbf{e}_1\mathbf{e}_2'] \\ E[\mathbf{e}_2\mathbf{e}_1'] & E[\mathbf{e}_2\mathbf{e}_2'] \end{bmatrix} = \begin{bmatrix} \sigma_1^2 I_T & 0 \\ 0 & \sigma_2^2 I_T \end{bmatrix}$$

This specification assumes $E[\mathbf{e}_1\mathbf{e}_2'] = 0$. That is, the Westinghouse equation errors are uncorrelated with the General Electric equation errors.

Writing the two equations in this way produces a single model that is similar in nature to one sample with a heteroskedastic partition that we studied in Sections 15.2 and 15.4.2 of Chapter 15. However, the difference in this instance is that each firm (partition) has a different coefficient vector $\boldsymbol{\beta}$. Nevertheless, we can still proceed to write the two equations in a single equation framework. If we let

$$\begin{bmatrix} y_{11} \\ y_{12} \\ \vdots \\ y_{1T} \\ y_{21} \\ y_{22} \\ \vdots \\ y_{2T} \end{bmatrix} = \begin{bmatrix} \mathbf{y}_1 \\ \mathbf{y}_2 \end{bmatrix} = \mathbf{y} \qquad \begin{bmatrix} \begin{pmatrix} x_{11} & x_{12} & x_{13} \\ x_{21} & x_{22} & x_{23} \\ \vdots & \vdots & \vdots \\ x_{T1} & x_{T2} & x_{T3} \end{pmatrix} & 0 \\ 0 & \begin{pmatrix} x_{11} & x_{12} & x_{13} \\ x_{21} & x_{22} & x_{23} \\ \vdots & \vdots & \vdots \\ x_{T1} & x_{T2} & x_{T3} \end{pmatrix} \end{bmatrix} = \begin{bmatrix} X_1 & 0 \\ 0 & X_2 \end{bmatrix} = X$$

$$\begin{bmatrix} \beta_{11} \\ \beta_{12} \\ \beta_{13} \\ \beta_{21} \\ \beta_{22} \\ \beta_{23} \end{bmatrix} = \begin{bmatrix} \boldsymbol{\beta}_1 \\ \boldsymbol{\beta}_2 \end{bmatrix} = \boldsymbol{\beta} \qquad \text{and} \qquad \begin{bmatrix} e_{11} \\ e_{12} \\ \vdots \\ e_{1T} \\ e_{21} \\ e_{22} \\ \vdots \\ e_{2T} \end{bmatrix} = \begin{bmatrix} \mathbf{e}_1 \\ \mathbf{e}_2 \end{bmatrix} = \mathbf{e}$$

then we may write the joint equations statistical model 17.2.2 in the single linear statistical model form of Chapter 15 as

$$\mathbf{y} = X\boldsymbol{\beta} + \mathbf{e} \tag{17.2.4a}$$

where

$$\mathbf{e} \sim N\left(\mathbf{0}, \begin{pmatrix} \sigma_1^2 I_T & 0 \\ 0 & \sigma_2^2 I_T \end{pmatrix} \right) \tag{17.2.5b}$$

In equation 17.2.4 $\mathbf{y}$ is a (40×1) dimensional vector of observed investments for General Electric and Westinghouse, and $\mathbf{e}$ is a (40×1) dimensional vector of unobservable normal random variables. Formulating the sampling model in this way permits us to specify a single linear statistical model with one coefficient vector and a single error covariance matrix. From an estimation viewpoint the error covariance matrix involves the variances σ_1^2 and σ_2^2, and thus suggests that if $\sigma_1^2 \neq \sigma_2^2$ the generalized least squares rule of Chapter 15 may be appropriate.

However, it turns out that, because of the block-diagonal nature of X and W, the generalized least squares estimator for this model is identical to applying the least squares rule separately to each equation. Specifically, X and W are called block diagonal matrices because their off-diagonal blocks consist of zeros. Following equation 15.4.26 of Chapter 15, the GLS estimator is given by

$$\hat{\boldsymbol{\beta}} = \left(X'W^{-1}X \right)^{-1} X'W^{-1}\mathbf{y}$$

$$= \left[\begin{pmatrix} X_1 & 0 \\ 0 & X_2 \end{pmatrix}' \begin{bmatrix} \sigma_1^2 I_T & 0 \\ 0 & \sigma_2^2 I_T \end{bmatrix}^{-1} \begin{pmatrix} X_1 & 0 \\ 0 & X_2 \end{pmatrix} \right]^{-1} \begin{pmatrix} X_1 & 0 \\ 0 & X_2 \end{pmatrix}' \begin{bmatrix} \sigma_1^2 I_T & 0 \\ 0 & \sigma_2^2 I_T \end{bmatrix}^{-1} \begin{pmatrix} \mathbf{y}_1 \\ \mathbf{y}_2 \end{pmatrix}$$

$$= \begin{bmatrix} \dfrac{1}{\sigma_1^2} X_1'X_1 & 0 \\ 0 & \dfrac{1}{\sigma_2^2} X_2'X_2 \end{bmatrix}^{-1} \begin{bmatrix} \dfrac{1}{\sigma_1^2} X_1'\mathbf{y}_1 \\ \dfrac{1}{\sigma_2^2} X_2'\mathbf{y}_2 \end{bmatrix}$$

$$= \begin{bmatrix} \left(X_1'X_1 \right)^{-1} X_1'\mathbf{y}_1 \\ \left(X_2'X_2 \right)^{-1} X_2'\mathbf{y}_2 \end{bmatrix} = \begin{bmatrix} \mathbf{b}_1 \\ \mathbf{b}_2 \end{bmatrix} = \mathbf{b}$$

$$\tag{17.2.5}$$

That is, it yields the same result as estimating each of the equations individually by least squares. Consequently, the pooled statistical model in equations 17.2.2 and 17.2.3 does not lead to a more efficient way of using the sample information. However, it does provide a convenient and useful framework in which to view a set of economic relations. As we will discover, with a more general set of assumptions, it is possible to use this framework to demonstrate how efficiency gains may be achieved.

17.2.1   A General Statistical Model

To this point we have searched for ways to reformulate the statistical model for the General Electric and Westinghouse investment relations that would make use of our sample information and possibly lead to improved sampling precision. We started this search by pooling the sample observations and allowing for different error variances. We found that this led back to least squares estimates for the individual equations and thus to no change in our estimates or their estimated sampling precision. Given this result, we should ask ourselves whether we have overlooked any sample information that we may use to increase the sampling precision with which the unknown parameters of the investment relation may be estimated.

The answer is "perhaps." Since General Electric and Westinghouse operate in the same industry, perhaps formulating the statistical model in the form of equation 17.2.2 may have raised the following "what-if" question in your mind: *"What if the errors in different equations, e_1 and e_2, are correlated and hence the zero covariance assumption in equation 17.2.3 is violated?"* Let us pursue this question.

One way to increase sampling precision is to efficiently use all of the sample and so-called nonsample information that is available. As we learned in Chapter 11, nonsample information may take the form of restrictions that are implied by economic theory, and imposition of these restrictions when estimating the model leads to efficiency gains. Thus far in estimating the unknown coefficient vector(s), we have made use of the sample observations y_1 and y_2. One bit of additional information that we might include is the following: We have used only two explanatory variables x_{i2} and x_{i3} to explain the outcomes of investment decisions. Undoubtedly there are other factors such as utilization of capacity, current and past interest rates, and a measure of liquidity that could have affected investment decisions and, thus, the observed outcomes for the sample observations on investments y_1 and y_2. Since these other factors were omitted from the individual investment relations, they become a part of the unobservable error processes e_1 and e_2. Because both General Electric and Westinghouse operate to some extent in the same branch of industry, the information contained in these omitted variables will be included in both error terms. Also the state of the economy, whose influence is felt through e_1 and e_2, is likely to have similar effects on each of the firms. Consequently, it is natural to assume that the equation errors e_1 for General Electric may be related to (correlated with) the equation errors e_2 for Westinghouse.

To identify this type of situation we follow Zellner and label the firm investment relations that contain correlated equation errors as seemingly unrelated regressions (SUR). Note that the SUR label arises because separate estimation of each of the relations ignores the possible relatedness of the equation errors. Given the possibility of cross-equation error correlation, the question before us is how to take account of this information. In equation 17.2.5 we *assumed*, in terms of the equation errors, that

$$e = \begin{bmatrix} e_1 \\ e_2 \end{bmatrix} \sim N\left[\begin{pmatrix} 0 \\ 0 \end{pmatrix}, E\begin{pmatrix} e_1 e_1' & e_1 e_2' \\ e_2 e_1' & e_2 e_2' \end{pmatrix} = \begin{pmatrix} \sigma_1^2 I_T & 0 \\ 0 & \sigma_2^2 I_T \end{pmatrix} \right] \qquad (17.2.6)$$

That is, we assumed that e_1 and e_2 are uncorrelated and thus the off-diagonal blocks of the covariance matrix were zero. We now want to take account of the fact that the errors for the two equations *may* be *contemporaneously* (same time period) correlated and thus the off-diagonal blocks in equation 17.2.6 may not be equal to zero. Consider the off-diagonal block $E[e_1 e_2']$. In full it is given by

$$E[e_1 e_2'] = E\left[\begin{pmatrix} e_{11} \\ e_{12} \\ \vdots \\ e_{1T} \end{pmatrix} \begin{pmatrix} e_{21} & e_{22} & \cdots & e_{2T} \end{pmatrix} \right] = E\begin{bmatrix} e_{11}e_{21} & e_{11}e_{22} & \cdots & e_{11}e_{2T} \\ e_{12}e_{21} & e_{12}e_{22} & \cdots & e_{12}e_{2T} \\ \vdots & \vdots & \ddots & \vdots \\ e_{1T}e_{21} & e_{1T}e_{22} & \cdots & e_{1T}e_{2T} \end{bmatrix} \quad (17.2.7)$$

The elements on the diagonal of this matrix are *contemporaneous covariances*. That is, they represent the covariance between the errors from the different equations in *the same time period*. We will denote this covariance by σ_{12}. That is,

$$\text{cov}(e_{1t}, e_{2t}) = E[e_{1t}e_{2t}] = \sigma_{12} \qquad t = 1, 2, ..., T \qquad (17.2.8a)$$

The off-diagonal elements in the above matrix involve covariances between the errors from the two different equations in *different time periods*. Since we assume such covariances are zero, we write

$$\text{cov}(e_{1t}, e_{2s}) = E[e_{1t}e_{2s}] = 0 \qquad (t \neq s) \qquad (17.2.8b)$$

Substituting these results into equation 17.2.7 yields

$$E[\mathbf{e}_1 \mathbf{e}_2'] = \begin{bmatrix} \sigma_{12} & 0 & \cdots & 0 \\ 0 & \sigma_{12} & \cdots & 0 \\ \vdots & \vdots & \ddots & \vdots \\ 0 & 0 & \cdots & \sigma_{12} \end{bmatrix} = \sigma_{12} I_T \qquad (17.2.9)$$

If for notational convenience we let $\sigma_1^2 = \sigma_{11}$ and $\sigma_2^2 = \sigma_{22}$, including equation 17.2.9 leads to our *new* error specification for the joint error vector of the two firms as

$$\mathbf{e} = \begin{bmatrix} \mathbf{e}_1 \\ \mathbf{e}_2 \end{bmatrix} \sim N\left[\begin{pmatrix} \mathbf{0} \\ \mathbf{0} \end{pmatrix}, \begin{pmatrix} \sigma_{11}I_T & \sigma_{12}I_T \\ \sigma_{21}I_T & \sigma_{22}I_T \end{pmatrix} = W \right] \qquad (17.2.10)$$

where $\sigma_{12} = \sigma_{21}$ are the error covariances that reflect the *contemporaneous* correlation (correlated across equation errors in the same time period) between the General Electric and Westinghouse individual equation errors $\mathbf{e}_1$ and $\mathbf{e}_2$. If equation 17.2.10 is the correct specification, and we follow the first procedure in Section 17.2, where we use only information on the diagonal elements, then for estimation purposes we have neglected the information contained in the covariances $\sigma_{12} = \sigma_{21}$.

17.2.2   A Seemingly Unrelated Regressions (SUR) Statistical Model and Estimator

Given an error covariance matrix structure that recognizes that contemporaneous correlation between $\mathbf{e}_1$ and $\mathbf{e}_2$ may exist, what we desire is a statistical model that will accommodate this new covariance specification and an estimation rule that will provide, at increased levels of sampling precision, estimates of the coefficients of the *investment relations*. In other words, we need an estimation rule consistent with the following statistical model

$$\begin{bmatrix} \mathbf{y}_1 \\ \mathbf{y}_2 \end{bmatrix} = \begin{bmatrix} X_1 & 0 \\ 0 & X_2 \end{bmatrix} \begin{bmatrix} \boldsymbol{\beta}_1 \\ \boldsymbol{\beta}_2 \end{bmatrix} + \begin{bmatrix} \mathbf{e}_1 \\ \mathbf{e}_2 \end{bmatrix} \qquad (17.2.11)$$

or

$$\mathbf{y} = X\boldsymbol{\beta} + \mathbf{e} \qquad (17.2.12)$$

where

$$\begin{bmatrix} \mathbf{e}_1 \\ \mathbf{e}_2 \end{bmatrix} = \mathbf{e} \sim N\left[\begin{pmatrix} \mathbf{0} \\ \mathbf{0} \end{pmatrix}, \begin{pmatrix} \sigma_{11}I_T & \sigma_{12}I_T \\ \sigma_{21}I_T & \sigma_{22}I_T \end{pmatrix} = W \right] \qquad (17.2.13a)$$

or

$$\mathbf{e} \sim N(\mathbf{0}, W) \tag{17.2.13b}$$

In terms of the tth observation, we may write the statistical model of equations 17.2.12 and equation 17.2.13 as

$$\begin{bmatrix} y_{1t} \\ y_{2t} \end{bmatrix} = \begin{bmatrix} \mathbf{x}_{1t}' & \mathbf{0} \\ \mathbf{0} & \mathbf{x}_{2t}' \end{bmatrix} \begin{bmatrix} \boldsymbol{\beta}_1 \\ \boldsymbol{\beta}_2 \end{bmatrix} + \begin{bmatrix} e_{1t} \\ e_{2t} \end{bmatrix}$$

or

$$\mathbf{y}_t = X_t \boldsymbol{\beta} + \mathbf{e}_t \tag{17.2.14a}$$

where $\mathbf{y}_t$ is a (2×1) vector, X_t is a (2×6) matrix, $\boldsymbol{\beta}$ is a (6×1) vector of unknown coefficients, and $\mathbf{e}_t$ is a (2×1) random error vector with the characteristics

$$\mathbf{e}_t \sim N(\mathbf{0}, \Sigma) \tag{17.2.14b}$$

where

$$\Sigma = \begin{bmatrix} \sigma_{11} & \sigma_{12} \\ \sigma_{21} & \sigma_{22} \end{bmatrix}$$

Zellner has given this type of statistical model the name of *seemingly unrelated regressions* (SUR) or error related regression equations. This is just another form of the general error covariance statistical model introduced in the introduction to Part V and Chapters 15 and 16, involving a special form of heteroskedasticity and autocorrelation that appears jointly. Thus, if we want to use all of the information at our disposal, the generalized least squares estimator developed in Chapter 15 is the appropriate rule:

$$\hat{\boldsymbol{\beta}} = \left(X'W^{-1}X \right)^{-1} X'W^{-1}\mathbf{y}$$

$$= \left[\begin{bmatrix} X_1 & 0 \\ 0 & X_2 \end{bmatrix}' \begin{bmatrix} \sigma_{11}I_T & \sigma_{12}I_T \\ \sigma_{21}I_T & \sigma_{22}I_T \end{bmatrix}^{-1} \begin{bmatrix} X_1 & 0 \\ 0 & X_2 \end{bmatrix} \right]^{-1} \begin{bmatrix} X_1 & 0 \\ 0 & X_2 \end{bmatrix}' \begin{bmatrix} \sigma_{11}I_T & \sigma_{12}I_T \\ \sigma_{21}I_T & \sigma_{22}I_T \end{bmatrix}^{-1} \begin{bmatrix} \mathbf{y}_1 \\ \mathbf{y}_2 \end{bmatrix}$$

$$\tag{17.2.15}$$

and is the *best unbiased estimator*. The corresponding covariance matrix for $\hat{\boldsymbol{\beta}}$ is

$$\text{cov}\left(\hat{\boldsymbol{\beta}} \right) = \left(X'W^{-1}X \right)^{-1} \tag{17.2.16}$$

Like the generalized least squares estimator encountered in Section 15.4.2 of Chapter 15, this generalized least squares estimator is not a feasible one because the error covariance matrix W is unknown. One way to overcome this problem is to replace the unknown σ_{ij} with consistent estimates

$$\hat{\sigma}_{ij} = \left(\mathbf{y}_i - X_i \mathbf{b}_i \right)' \left(\mathbf{y}_j - X_j \mathbf{b}_j \right) / T \tag{17.2.17}$$

This covariance estimator is similar to that used to estimate the error variance in the single equation models studied in Chapters 5 to 11. One difference is that T not $(T - K)$ appears in the denominator. In this case we use T because $(T - K)$ is not unambiguously defined if the number of columns in X_i and X_j are different. Although $\hat{\sigma}_{ij}$ is a biased estimator, it is consistent (see Section 14.1 of Chapter 14) and consistency is sufficient for our purposes. If we use $\hat{\sigma}_{ij}$ as defined in equation 17.2.17, the corresponding estimated covariance matrix $\hat{W}$ is given by

$$\hat{W} = \begin{bmatrix} \hat{\sigma}_{11}I_T & \hat{\sigma}_{12}I_T \\ \hat{\sigma}_{21}I_T & \hat{\sigma}_{22}I_T \end{bmatrix} = \frac{1}{20}\begin{bmatrix} \hat{e}'_1\hat{e}_1 I_{20} & \hat{e}'_1\hat{e}_2 I_{20} \\ \hat{e}'_2\hat{e}_1 I_{20} & \hat{e}'_2\hat{e}_2 I_{20} \end{bmatrix} \qquad (17.2.18)$$

where use is made of the least squares residuals $\hat{e}_1$ and $\hat{e}_2$ for the individual equations. For the General Electric and Westinghouse data, the *estimated* covariance matrix is

$$\hat{W} = \begin{bmatrix} 660.83I_{20} & 176.45I_{20} \\ 176.45I_{20} & 88.662I_{20} \end{bmatrix} \qquad (17.2.19)$$

and the squared contemporaneous correlation between e_1 and e_2 is

$$r_{12}^2 = \frac{(\hat{\sigma}_{12})^2}{\hat{\sigma}_1^2\hat{\sigma}_2^2} = \frac{(176.45)^2}{(660.83)(88.662)} = 0.7290 \qquad (17.2.20)$$

To check the statistical significance of r_{12}^2, we test the null hypothesis H_0: $\sigma_{12} = 0$. For this purpose we note that Tr_{12}^2 is a test statistic that, in large samples and if $\sigma_{12} = 0$, is distributed as a $\chi_{(1)}^2$ random variable. The 5% critical value of a χ^2 distribution with one degree of freedom is 3.84. The value of the test statistic from our data is $Tr_{12}^2 = 10.628$. Hence, we reject the null hypothesis of no correlation between the random vectors e_1 and e_2 and conclude that contemporaneous correlation between the equation errors does exist.

Since a nonzero covariance σ_{12} seems appropriate, we use statistical model 17.2.11, the estimated covariance matrix $\hat{W}$ equation 17.2.19, and the following *estimated* generalized least squares estimator:

$$\hat{\hat{\beta}} = \left(X'\hat{W}^{-1}X\right)^{-1} X'\hat{W}^{-1}y$$

$$= \left[\begin{bmatrix} X_1 & 0 \\ 0 & X_2 \end{bmatrix}'\begin{bmatrix} \hat{\sigma}_{11}I_T & \hat{\sigma}_{12}I_T \\ \hat{\sigma}_{21}I_T & \hat{\sigma}_{22}I_T \end{bmatrix}^{-1}\begin{bmatrix} X_1 & 0 \\ 0 & X_2 \end{bmatrix}\right]^{-1}\begin{bmatrix} X_1 & 0 \\ 0 & X_2 \end{bmatrix}'\begin{bmatrix} \hat{\sigma}_{11}I_T & \hat{\sigma}_{12}I_T \\ \hat{\sigma}_{21}I_T & \hat{\sigma}_{22}I_T \end{bmatrix}^{-1}\begin{bmatrix} y_1 \\ y_2 \end{bmatrix}$$

$$(17.2.21)$$

with

$$\hat{cov}\left(\hat{\hat{\beta}}\right) = \left(X'\hat{W}^{-1}X\right)^{-1}$$

$$= \left[\begin{bmatrix} X_1 & 0 \\ 0 & X_2 \end{bmatrix}'\begin{bmatrix} \hat{\sigma}_{11}I_T & \hat{\sigma}_{12}I_T \\ \hat{\sigma}_{21}I_T & \hat{\sigma}_{22}I_T \end{bmatrix}^{-1}\begin{bmatrix} X_1 & 0 \\ 0 & X_2 \end{bmatrix}\right]^{-1} \qquad (17.2.22)$$

The properties of estimated generalized least squares estimators such as $\hat{\hat{\beta}}$ were discussed in Chapter 15. Although the estimated generalized least squares estimator is unbiased, we can no longer say it is best unbiased. However, in large samples it does have properties approximately the same as those of the generalized least squares estimator, that is, we can say that $\hat{\hat{\beta}}$ has an asymptotic normal distribution with mean β and covariance $(X'W^{-1}X)^{-1}$ and that the usual test statistics hold true in large samples.

For the General Electric and Westinghouse data, the estimated generalized least squares estimator yields the following estimated investment relations

$$\hat{\boldsymbol{\beta}} = \begin{bmatrix} \hat{\boldsymbol{\beta}}_1 \\ \hat{\boldsymbol{\beta}}_2 \end{bmatrix} = \begin{bmatrix} -27.7193 \\ 0.0383 \\ 0.1390 \\ -1.2520 \\ 0.0576 \\ 0.0640 \end{bmatrix} \qquad (17.2.23)$$

with estimated sampling precision (variances)

$$\hat{\text{var}}\left(\hat{\beta}_{11}\right) = 730.7738 \quad \hat{\text{var}}\left(\hat{\beta}_{12}\right) = 0.0002 \quad \hat{\text{var}}\left(\hat{\beta}_{13}\right) = 0.0005$$

$$\hat{\text{var}}\left(\hat{\beta}_{21}\right) = 48.3908 \quad \hat{\text{var}}\left(\hat{\beta}_{22}\right) = 0.0002 \quad \hat{\text{var}}\left(\hat{\beta}_{23}\right) = 0.0024$$

$$(17.2.24)$$

These estimated variances should be compared with the results for the incompletely specified statistical model, where each equation was treated separately as in equations 17.1.4 and 17.1.7. The information in equations 17.2.22 and 17.2.23 for the individual investment relations may be summarized as follows:

$$(GE) \qquad \hat{\mathbf{y}}_1 = -27.7193\mathbf{x}_{11} + 0.0383\mathbf{x}_{12} + 0.1390\mathbf{x}_{13}$$
$$(27.0328) \qquad (0.0133) \qquad (0.0230) \qquad \text{se}\left(\hat{\boldsymbol{\beta}}_1\right)$$
$$(-1.025) \qquad (2.883) \qquad (6.036) \qquad t \qquad (17.2.25)$$

and

$$(WEST) \qquad \hat{\mathbf{y}}_2 = -1.2520\mathbf{x}_{21} + 0.0576\mathbf{x}_{22} + 0.0640\mathbf{x}_{23}$$
$$(6.9563) \qquad (0.0134) \qquad (0.0489) \qquad \text{se}\left(\hat{\boldsymbol{\beta}}_2\right)$$
$$(-0.180) \qquad (4.297) \qquad (1.308) \qquad t \qquad (17.2.26)$$

Since the generalized least squares estimator is the best unbiased estimator for our joint statistical model, it is necessarily better than least squares applied separately to each equation. By including information on the error covariance and using the SUR statistical model and the estimated generalized least squares estimation rule, we have, relative to individual relations with their corresponding least squares estimates of the unknown parameters, been able to improve the estimated sampling precision with which we can estimate the unknown coefficient vectors β_1 and β_2. For the General Electric investment relation, both expected profits $\mathbf{x}_{i2}$ and capital stock $\mathbf{x}_{i3}$ appear to be statistically significant. In the Westinghouse investment relation, the capital stock variable continues to be estimated with limited precision (low t-value). In fact, the standard error may be greater than the corresponding least squares error. Such a result does not contradict our claim of improved precision on the average. Although, as we have noted before, the true (on the average) sampling variability will go down in large samples, *for an individual small sample* the estimated sampling variability may go up.

17.2.3 Do the Investment Relations Have a Common Coefficient Vector?

Thus far we have assumed that the coefficient vectors for the two relations are different. Since General Electric and Westinghouse have many things in common perhaps the relations can be aggregated and represented with a common coefficient vector, that is, in terms of equation 17.2.13a $\beta_1 = \beta_2 = \gamma$. If so, this would reduce the number of parameters to be estimated from the $2T$ observations and possibly increase the precision with which they are estimated. In this context, the statistical model could be written in the restricted form

$$y = \begin{bmatrix} \mathbf{y}_1 \\ \mathbf{y}_2 \end{bmatrix} = \begin{bmatrix} X_1 & 0 \\ 0 & X_2 \end{bmatrix} \begin{bmatrix} \boldsymbol{\beta}_1 \\ \boldsymbol{\beta}_2 \end{bmatrix} + \begin{bmatrix} \mathbf{e}_1 \\ \mathbf{e}_2 \end{bmatrix} = X\boldsymbol{\beta} + \mathbf{e} \qquad (17.2.11)$$

with the restriction

$$\boldsymbol{\beta}_1 = \boldsymbol{\beta}_2 \quad \text{or} \quad \boldsymbol{\beta}_1 - \boldsymbol{\beta}_2 = 0 \qquad (17.2.27)$$

In the notation of Chapters 10 and 11, where we discussed the aggregation or combining of one or more of the right-hand-side variables, we may specify the aggregation over statistical models (equations) as

$$R\boldsymbol{\beta} = 0 \qquad (17.2.28)$$

where

$$R\boldsymbol{\beta} = R\begin{bmatrix} \boldsymbol{\beta}_1 \\ \boldsymbol{\beta}_2 \end{bmatrix} = \begin{bmatrix} 1 & 0 & 0 & -1 & 0 & 0 \\ 0 & 1 & 0 & 0 & -1 & 0 \\ 0 & 0 & 1 & 0 & 0 & -1 \end{bmatrix} \begin{bmatrix} \beta_{11} \\ \beta_{12} \\ \beta_{13} \\ \beta_{21} \\ \beta_{22} \\ \beta_{23} \end{bmatrix} = \begin{bmatrix} 0 \\ 0 \\ 0 \end{bmatrix} \qquad (17.2.29)$$

To take account of the conjecture (coefficient restriction) that $\beta_1 = \beta_2$, we may also formulate the "restricted" statistical model as

$$y = \begin{bmatrix} \mathbf{y}_1 \\ \mathbf{y}_2 \end{bmatrix} = \begin{bmatrix} X_1 \\ X_2 \end{bmatrix} \boldsymbol{\gamma} + \begin{bmatrix} \mathbf{e}_1 \\ \mathbf{e}_2 \end{bmatrix} = Z\boldsymbol{\gamma} + \mathbf{e} \qquad (17.2.30)$$

where γ is the coefficient vector under the condition that $\gamma = \beta_1 = \beta_2$. Also, the error covariance matrix is of the form of equation 17.2.10 or 17.2.13a. Under the nondiagonal covariance matrix formulation, and equation 17.2.30, we would use the following estimated generalized least squares estimator

$$\hat{\boldsymbol{\gamma}} = \left[Z' \hat{W}^{-1} Z \right]^{-1} Z' \hat{W}^{-1} \mathbf{y} \qquad (17.2.31)$$

to compute a value for the restricted estimator. Using the SHAZAM or SAS computer program for the GLS rule results in the following estimate for γ :

$$\hat{\boldsymbol{\gamma}} = \begin{bmatrix} 19.1578 \\ 0.0227 \\ 0.1091 \end{bmatrix} \qquad (17.2.32)$$

and

$$\text{vâr}\left(\hat{\hat{\gamma}}_1\right) = 6.4653 \quad \text{vâr}\left(\hat{\hat{\gamma}}_2\right) = 0.00003 \quad \text{vâr}\left(\hat{\hat{\gamma}}_3\right) = 0.00036 \quad (17.2.33)$$

This information may be summarized in terms of standard errors and $t_{(37)}$ values as follows:

$$\hat{y}_t = \begin{array}{llll} 19.1578 + & 0.0227v_t & +0.1091k_t & \\ (2.5427) & (0.0050) & (0.0190) & \text{se} \\ (7.535) & (4.512) & (5.725) & t_{(37)} \end{array} \quad (17.2.34)$$

For the restricted estimator $\hat{\hat{\gamma}}$ the signs of the explanatory variables $\mathbf{v}$ ($\mathbf{x}_2$) and $\mathbf{k}$ ($\mathbf{x}_3$) are positive, as we would expect. Also, based on the results for the t-statistics, all of the estimated coefficients are statistically significant at or above the $\alpha = .05$ level. Note that adding the information that $\beta_1 = \beta_2$ along with that of the off-diagonal error covariances has improved the estimated sampling precision (smaller standard errors relative to equations 17.2.26 and 17.2.27) with which the unknown coefficients of the investment relation have been estimated. It is important to note that the standard errors are only *estimates* of the square roots of the true variances. Nevertheless, the standard errors do provide a guide with respect to the estimation precision.

At this point we have unconstrained SUR estimates $\hat{\boldsymbol{\beta}}$ of the investment relations 17.2.22 and the constrained estimates $\hat{\hat{\boldsymbol{\gamma}}}$ given in equation 17.2.32. Next we wish to check the compatibility of the estimators $\hat{\boldsymbol{\beta}}$ and $\hat{\hat{\boldsymbol{\gamma}}}$. In other words, we want to check the compatibility of the sample information with the hypothesis H_0: $\beta_1 = \beta_2$ to determine whether from a statistical point of view it makes sense for the relations to be aggregated. To do this we use hypothesis testing procedures similar to those developed in Chapters 10 and 11. Such tests cany be performed automatically by most econometric computer programs. To outline the test framework, we start by setting up the null hypothesis H_0: $\beta_1 = \beta_2$ as

$$H_0 : R\boldsymbol{\beta} = \mathbf{0} \quad (17.2.28)$$

or

$$H_0 : R\boldsymbol{\beta} = R\begin{bmatrix} \boldsymbol{\beta}_1 \\ \boldsymbol{\beta}_2 \end{bmatrix} = \begin{bmatrix} 1 & 0 & 0 & -1 & 0 & 0 \\ 0 & 1 & 0 & 0 & -1 & 0 \\ 0 & 0 & 1 & 0 & 0 & -1 \end{bmatrix} \begin{bmatrix} \beta_{11} \\ \beta_{12} \\ \beta_{13} \\ \beta_{21} \\ \beta_{22} \\ \beta_{23} \end{bmatrix} = \begin{bmatrix} 0 \\ 0 \\ 0 \end{bmatrix} \quad (17.2.29)$$

and make use of the following generalized error covariance version of the test statistic that was discussed in Chapters 10 and 11:

$$q = \left(R\hat{\boldsymbol{\beta}} \right)' \left[R\left(X'\hat{W}^{-1}X \right)^{-1} R' \right]^{-1} R\hat{\boldsymbol{\beta}} \Big/ J \quad (17.2.35)$$

If T is large, it is approximately distributed as an F random variable with $J = K$ and $2(T - K)$ degrees of freedom. In our case

$$F = \frac{10.31379}{3} = 3.438 \quad (17.2.36)$$

The 5% critical value for an F with 3 and 34 degrees of freedom is 2.88. Since the empirical test value $3.438 > 2.88$, we reject the null hypothesis $\beta_1 = \beta_2$ at the 5% significance level. Thus, the use of one coefficient vector for both samples of data is of questionable validity. As we discussed in regard to the restricted least squares estimator in Section 11.5 of Chapter 11, under the restriction $\beta_1 = \beta_2$, improved sampling precision might still occur. However, if the restriction is not appropriate, the estimation rule is biased and the standard errors are not appropriate.

17.2.4   Critique of Models, Estimators, and Results

In this chapter we have focused on how to make the best use of the information in two samples of data when estimating the unknown parameters of investment functions of the firms General Electric and Westinghouse. In this search process we faced the following questions:

1.   Should we use each sample of data separately and estimate individual investment functions? (Section 17.1)

2.   Since the firms have many things in common, are the equation errors for each of the firm's samples contemporaneously correlated and, if so, what is the appropriate statistical model and estimation rule that will let us make use of this information? (Sections 17.2.1 and 17.2.2)

3.   Should the samples for the two firms be aggregated and a combined investment function, which makes use of the generalized least squares estimator, be estimated? (Section 17.2.3)

Fortunately, we have been able to obtain answers for each of these questions by respecifying the statistical model and demonstrating an appropriate corresponding estimation rule and test statistic. In the process we have greatly increased the range of operational statistical models and estimation rules that may be used to learn from a sample or samples of economic data. As one basis for summarizing the empirical results of this chapter, the alternative sets of estimates that we have developed along with their estimated measures of precision are tabulated in Table 17.2.

As suggested by our theory, if we compare our least squares and SUR estimates in Table 17.2, the estimates that make use of information about the unknown error covariance matrix are more efficient (smaller standard errors) if the true error covariance matrix is known. Remember that these are only estimates of the square roots of the true variances but they do provide a guide with respect to on-average changes in sampling precision. The restricted generalized least squares estimates when $\sigma_{ij} = 0$ are obtained by completing Exercise 17.3.

In specifying the alternative statistical models and their corresponding basis for estimation and inference, we focused on samples of investment data for two firms. The questions and the general approach would not have been changed if we had samples of data from three or more firms. Also, since contemporaneous correlation in economic data seems to be the rule and not the exception, the questions and the general approach would have been the same if we were analyzing, for example, samples of data underlying two or more demand relations, two or more supply relations, the production functions of two or more firms or two or more industries, or the consumption functions of two or more regions or countries or time periods. Thus, any time we face questions regarding the analysis or two or more samples of data, the econometric tools acquired in this chapter may provide an efficient basis for squeezing information out of the samples concerning the appropriate statistical model and corresponding estimation rule. To reinforce

Table 17.2 Investment Relation(s) Estimates

Parameter	Least Squares	SUR	Generalized Least Squares (Restricted)	
			$\sigma_{ij} = 0$	$\sigma_{ij} \neq 0$
β_{11}	−9.956	−27.7193		
	(31.37)	(27.0328)		
β_{12}	0.0265	0.0383		
	(0.016)	(0.0133)		
β_{13}	0.1517	0.1390		
	(0.026)	(0.0230)		
β_{21}	−0.509	−1.2520		
	(8.02)	(6.9563)		
β_{22}	0.0529	0.0576		
	(0.0157)	(0.0134)		
β_{23}	0.0924	0.0640		
	(0.0561)	(0.0489)		
$\gamma_1(\beta_{11} = \beta_{21})$			16.7468	19.1578
			(4.1369)	(2.543)
$\gamma_2(\beta_{12} = \beta_{22})$			0.0204	0.0227
			(0.0063)	(0.0050)
$\gamma_3(\beta_{13} = \beta_{23})$			0.1337	0.1091
			(0.0209)	(0.0190)

this idea and to summarize the concepts already developed, in the next section we carry through an example involving a set of demand relations.

17.3   An Example Involving a Set of Demand Equations

To fix more securely the idea of introducing and making use of contemporaneously correlated equation errors to improve on separate least squares estimation when several equations are involved, consider the following economic model for a set of three demand equations:

$$\ln q_{1t} = \beta_{11} + \beta_{12} \ln p_{1t} + \beta_{13} \ln y_t$$
$$\ln q_{2t} = \beta_{21} + \beta_{22} \ln p_{2t} + \beta_{23} \ln y_t$$
$$\ln q_{3t} = \beta_{31} + \beta_{32} \ln p_{3t} + \beta_{33} \ln y_t \qquad (17.3.1)$$

where q_{it} is the quantity consumed of the ith commodity, $i = 1, 2, 3$, in the tth time period, $t = 1, 2, \ldots, T$, p_{it} is the price of the ith commodity in time t, and y_t is disposable income in period t. If, for example, we were concerned with food, the three commodities could be (1) meat, (2) fruits and vegetables, and (3) cereals and bakery products. Given this set of demand relations, let's carry through the steps of statistical model specification and identify appropriate estimation and inference procedures.

17.3.1   The Statistical Model

Following procedures used in the preceding sections, if we add equation errors e_{it}, we may write the statistical model for the set of demand relations 17.3.1, in the following form:

$$\mathbf{y}_1 = X_1 \boldsymbol{\beta}_1 + \mathbf{e}_1$$
$$\mathbf{y}_2 = X_2 \boldsymbol{\beta}_2 + \mathbf{e}_2$$
$$\mathbf{y}_3 = X_3 \boldsymbol{\beta}_3 + \mathbf{e}_3 \qquad (17.3.2)$$

where, for $i = 1, 2, 3$

$$\mathbf{y}_i = \begin{bmatrix} \ln q_{i1} \\ \ln q_{i2} \\ \vdots \\ \ln q_{iT} \end{bmatrix} \qquad X_i = \begin{bmatrix} 1 & \ln p_{i1} & \ln y_1 \\ 1 & \ln p_{i2} & \ln y_2 \\ \vdots & \vdots & \vdots \\ 1 & \ln p_{iT} & \ln y_T \end{bmatrix} \qquad (17.3.3)$$

and

$$\boldsymbol{\beta}_1 = \begin{bmatrix} \beta_{11} \\ \beta_{12} \\ \beta_{13} \end{bmatrix} \qquad \boldsymbol{\beta}_2 = \begin{bmatrix} \beta_{21} \\ \beta_{22} \\ \beta_{23} \end{bmatrix} \qquad \boldsymbol{\beta}_3 = \begin{bmatrix} \beta_{31} \\ \beta_{32} \\ \beta_{33} \end{bmatrix} \qquad \mathbf{e}_i = \begin{bmatrix} e_{i1} \\ e_{i2} \\ \vdots \\ e_{iT} \end{bmatrix} \qquad (17.3.4)$$

Thus, $\mathbf{y}_1$ and X_1 contain all T observations on the dependent and explanatory variables in the demand equation for commodity one, $\mathbf{y}_2$ and X_2 contain all T observations on the dependent and explanatory variables in the demand equation for commodity two, and $\mathbf{y}_3$ and X_3 contain all T observations on the dependent and explanatory variables in the demand equation for commodity three. Similarly, $\boldsymbol{\beta}_1$, $\boldsymbol{\beta}_2$, and $\boldsymbol{\beta}_3$ are the (3×1) unknown coefficient vectors for each of the demand equations and $\mathbf{e}_1$, $\mathbf{e}_2$, and $\mathbf{e}_3$ are the corresponding $(T \times 1)$ equation error vectors.

Given this notation we may use the seemingly unrelated regression framework of equation 17.2.15 to rewrite the set of demand equations as the single linear statistical model

$$\begin{bmatrix} \mathbf{y}_1 \\ \mathbf{y}_2 \\ \mathbf{y}_3 \end{bmatrix} = \begin{bmatrix} X_1 & 0 & 0 \\ 0 & X_2 & 0 \\ 0 & 0 & X_3 \end{bmatrix} \begin{bmatrix} \boldsymbol{\beta}_1 \\ \boldsymbol{\beta}_2 \\ \boldsymbol{\beta}_3 \end{bmatrix} + \begin{bmatrix} \mathbf{e}_1 \\ \mathbf{e}_2 \\ \mathbf{e}_3 \end{bmatrix} \qquad (17.3.5a)$$

or

$$\mathbf{y} = X\boldsymbol{\beta} + \mathbf{e} \qquad (17.3.5b)$$

where X_i, $\mathbf{y}_i$, and $\mathbf{e}_i$ are given in equations 17.3.3 and 17.3.4.

In terms of the equation errors $\mathbf{e}_1$, $\mathbf{e}_2$, and $\mathbf{e}_3$, the assumptions we employ are as follows:

1. All errors have a zero mean:

$$E[e_{it}] = 0; \quad \text{for } i = 1, 2, 3; t = 1, 2, \dots, T \qquad (17.3.6)$$

2. In a given equation the error variance is constant over time, but each equation can have a different variance:

$$\left. \begin{aligned} \text{var}(e_{1t}) &= E[e_{1t}^2] = \sigma_1^2 = \sigma_{11} \\ \text{var}(e_{2t}) &= E[e_{2t}^2] = \sigma_2^2 = \sigma_{22} \\ \text{var}(e_{3t}) &= E[e_{3t}^2] = \sigma_3^2 = \sigma_{33} \end{aligned} \right\}; \quad \text{for } t = 1, 2, \dots, T$$

$$(17.3.7)$$

3. Two errors in different equations but corresponding to the same time period are correlated (contemporaneous correlation):

$$\text{cov}\left(e_{it}, e_{jt}\right) = E\left[e_{it} e_{jt}\right] = \sigma_{ij}; \qquad \text{for } i, j = 1, 2, 3 \tag{17.3.8}$$

4. Errors in different time periods, whether they are in the same equation or not, are uncorrelated (autocorrelation does not exist):

$$\text{cov}\left(e_{it}, e_{js}\right) = E\left[e_{it} e_{js}\right] = 0; \qquad \text{for } t \neq s \text{ and } i, j = 1, 2, 3 \tag{17.3.9}$$

In matrix notation these assumptions may be written compactly as

$$E[\mathbf{e}_i] = 0 \quad \text{and} \quad E[\mathbf{e}_i \mathbf{e}_j'] = \sigma_{ij} I; \qquad \text{for } i, j = 1, 2, 3 \tag{17.3.10a}$$

where

$$E[\mathbf{ee}'] = E\left[\begin{bmatrix} \mathbf{e}_1 \\ \mathbf{e}_2 \\ \mathbf{e}_3 \end{bmatrix}\begin{bmatrix} \mathbf{e}_1' & \mathbf{e}_2' & \mathbf{e}_3' \end{bmatrix}\right] = \begin{bmatrix} E[\mathbf{e}_1 \mathbf{e}_1'] & E[\mathbf{e}_1 \mathbf{e}_2'] & E[\mathbf{e}_1 \mathbf{e}_3'] \\ E[\mathbf{e}_2 \mathbf{e}_1'] & E[\mathbf{e}_2 \mathbf{e}_2'] & E[\mathbf{e}_2 \mathbf{e}_3'] \\ E[\mathbf{e}_3 \mathbf{e}_1'] & E[\mathbf{e}_3 \mathbf{e}_2'] & E[\mathbf{e}_3 \mathbf{e}_3'] \end{bmatrix}$$

$$= \begin{bmatrix} \sigma_{11} I_T & \sigma_{12} I_T & \sigma_{13} I_T \\ \sigma_{12} I_T & \sigma_{22} I_T & \sigma_{23} I_T \\ \sigma_{13} I_T & \sigma_{23} I_T & \sigma_{33} I_T \end{bmatrix} = W$$

$$\tag{17.3.10b}$$

which is a matrix of dimension $(3T \times 3T)$ with each $(T \times T)$ submatrix being equal to a scalar multiplied by a T-dimensional identity matrix.

Therefore, in terms of equation 17.3.5b we may compactly express the equation error assumptions for $\mathbf{e}$ as

$$\mathbf{e} \sim N(0, W) \tag{17.3.11}$$

Note that we have been able to write *the set of equations within the framework of a single linear statistical model*. The change from earlier chapters such as Chapter 5 or 9 is that the covariance matrix W is not in scalar identity form, but rather now it is a symmetric matrix of the form given in equation 17.3.10b which is a special case of the general form discussed in Chapters 15 and 16.

17.3.2 Estimation

The next question we face is how to estimate the unknown coefficient vector β. One way to proceed is to *assume that W is of the scalar identity form $\sigma^2 I_{3T}$* and apply the least squares rule $\mathbf{b} = (X'X)^{-1}X'\mathbf{y}$ to equation 17.3.5b. Also, as we learned in regard to equation 17.2.9, if W is diagonal, applying the least squares rule to the set of equations is identical to applying the least squares rule separately to each of the three equations. Either assumption, however, ignores the fact that W contains information on the contemporaneous correlation between the errors in the different equations. To take account of all the information in equation 17.3.10b, we use the generalized least squares rule

$$\hat{\beta} = \left(X'W^{-1}X\right)^{-1} X'W^{-1}\mathbf{y} \tag{17.3.12}$$

which we know from Chapter 15 is best unbiased when either or both heteroskedastic and autocorrelated errors are present. In the case of the linear statistical model for the demand equations, the reader should, using the definitions for X, W, and $\mathbf{y}$ given in equations 17.3.5 and 17.3.10, write down the estimator.

At this point let us note that *there are two cases when the generalized least squares (GLS) and least squares estimators applied to the set of equations 17.3.5 are equal,* that is,

$$\hat{\boldsymbol{\beta}} = \mathbf{b} = \left(X'W^{-1}X \right)^{-1} X'W^{-1}\mathbf{y} = \left(X'X \right)^{-1} X'\mathbf{y} \qquad (17.3.13)$$

One case is when the contemporaneous correlations are zero, that is, $\sigma_{12} = \sigma_{13} = \sigma_{23} = 0$ *and thus W is a diagonal matrix. Another case is when the data for the explanatory variables are identical, that is,* $X_1 = X_2 = X_3$. Note that in our investment problem the X_i variables had the same definition but the data representing X_i were different. The same is true for the demand equations and consequently neither of these conditions (diagonal covariance or identical Xs) holds. Thus using the generalized least squares rule equation 17.3.12 is more efficient (on the average has more precision) than applying the least squares rule to equations 17.3.5 and 17.3.10.

In practice in estimating economic relations, the variances and covariances (σ_{ij}s) are unknown and must be estimated. To obtain these estimates we first estimate each equation by least squares

$$\mathbf{b}_i = \left(X_i'X_i \right)^{-1} X_i'\mathbf{y}_i ; \qquad \text{for } i = 1, 2, 3 \qquad (17.3.14)$$

and obtain the least squares residuals

$$\hat{\mathbf{e}}_i = \mathbf{y}_i - X_i\mathbf{b}_i ; \qquad \text{for } i = 1, 2, 3 \qquad (17.3.15)$$

Consistent estimates of the variances and covariances are then given by

$$\hat{\sigma}_{ij} = \frac{1}{T}\hat{\mathbf{e}}_i'\hat{\mathbf{e}}_j = \frac{1}{T}\sum_{t=1}^{T} \hat{e}_{it}\hat{e}_{jt} ; \qquad \text{for } i, j = 1, 2, 3 \qquad (17.3.16)$$

If we define $\hat{W}$ as the matrix W with the unknown σ_{ij} replaced by the estimates $\hat{\sigma}_{ij}$, then we can write the estimated generalized least squares estimator for β as

$$\hat{\boldsymbol{\beta}} = \left(X'\hat{W}^{-1}X \right)^{-1} X'\hat{W}^{-1}\mathbf{y}$$

$$= \left[\begin{pmatrix} X_1 & 0 & 0 \\ 0 & X_2 & 0 \\ 0 & 0 & X_3 \end{pmatrix}' \begin{bmatrix} \hat{\sigma}_{11}I_T & \hat{\sigma}_{12}I_T & \hat{\sigma}_{13}I_T \\ \hat{\sigma}_{21}I_T & \hat{\sigma}_{22}I_T & \hat{\sigma}_{23}I_T \\ \hat{\sigma}_{31}I_T & \hat{\sigma}_{32}I_T & \hat{\sigma}_{33}I_T \end{bmatrix}^{-1} \begin{pmatrix} X_1 & 0 & 0 \\ 0 & X_2 & 0 \\ 0 & 0 & X_3 \end{pmatrix} \right]^{-1}$$

$$\times \begin{pmatrix} X_1 & 0 & 0 \\ 0 & X_2 & 0 \\ 0 & 0 & X_3 \end{pmatrix}' \begin{bmatrix} \hat{\sigma}_{11}I_T & \hat{\sigma}_{12}I_T & \hat{\sigma}_{13}I_T \\ \hat{\sigma}_{21}I_T & \hat{\sigma}_{22}I_T & \hat{\sigma}_{23}I_T \\ \hat{\sigma}_{31}I_T & \hat{\sigma}_{32}I_T & \hat{\sigma}_{33}I_T \end{bmatrix}^{-1} \begin{pmatrix} \mathbf{y}_1 \\ \mathbf{y}_2 \\ \mathbf{y}_3 \end{pmatrix}$$

$$(17.3.17)$$

with estimated covariance (precision) matrix

$$\hat{\text{cov}}\left(\hat{\boldsymbol{\beta}} \right) = \left(X'\hat{W}^{-1}X \right)^{-1} \qquad (17.3.18)$$

This is the estimator that is generally used in practice and that is often referred to as Zellner's seemingly unrelated regression (SUR) estimator.

Most econometric computer packages, such as SHAZAM and SAS, have straight-forward instructions for computing the SUR estimator $\hat{\beta}$ and related statistics. These packages will automatically go through the steps of first obtaining least squares estimates, estimating the variances and covariances, and then computing the estimated GLS estimator $\hat{\beta}$ and related test statistics. In Exercise 17.4 you will be given a sample of data and asked to carry through the estimation and inference phases for the economic and statistical model discussed in this section.

17.3.3   Testing for Contemporaneous Correlation

If contemporaneous correlation does not exist, the least squares rule applied separately to each equation is fully efficient and there is no need to employ the SUR estimator to the set of equations. Thus, if there is uncertainty concerning this proposition, it is useful to test whether the contemporaneous covariances are zero. In the context of our three commodity demand example, the null and alternative hypotheses for this test are

$$H_0 : \sigma_{12} = \sigma_{13} = \sigma_{23} = 0$$

$$H_1 : \text{at least one covariance is non - zero}$$

An appropriate test statistic, under the normal linear model, is given by

$$\lambda = T\left(r_{21}^2 + r_{31}^2 + r_{32}^2\right) \tag{17.3.19}$$

where r_{ij}^2 is the squared correlation $r_{ij}^2 = \hat{\sigma}_{ij}^2 / \hat{\sigma}_{ii}\hat{\sigma}_{jj}$ and $\hat{\sigma}_{ij} = \left(\mathbf{y}_i - X_i\mathbf{b}_i\right)'\left(\mathbf{y}_j - X_j\mathbf{b}_j\right)\big/T$. Under H_0, the test statistic λ has an asymptotic χ^2-distribution with $M(M-1)/2 = 3$ degrees of freedom, where M is the number of equations and the estimated error correlations are used in the computation of λ. The null hypothesis is rejected if λ is greater than the critical value for a $\chi^2_{(3)}$-distribution at a prespecified significance level.

17.3.4   An Aggregation Test

Given the estimated relations and the corresponding estimated covariance matrix, the usual hypotheses can be tested relative to individual coefficients and two or more coefficients in each of the demand equations. Since we have written the statistical model for the three demand equations in the form of one equation, we may also test hypotheses about the coefficients across equations. For example, possibly all three commodities have the same price elasticities of demand, that is, $\beta_{12} = \beta_{22} = \beta_{32}$. We may write this in the form of linear hypotheses

$$\beta_{12} - \beta_{22} = 0$$
$$\beta_{12} - \beta_{32} = 0 \tag{17.3.20a}$$

or, from Chapter 10, in the form of a general linear hypothesis

$$R\beta = \begin{bmatrix} 0 & 1 & 0 & 0 & -1 & 0 & 0 & 0 & 0 \\ 0 & 1 & 0 & 0 & 0 & 0 & 0 & -1 & 0 \end{bmatrix} \begin{bmatrix} \beta_{11} \\ \beta_{12} \\ \beta_{13} \\ \beta_{21} \\ \beta_{22} \\ \beta_{23} \\ \beta_{31} \\ \beta_{32} \\ \beta_{33} \end{bmatrix} = \begin{bmatrix} 0 \\ 0 \end{bmatrix}$$

(17.3.20b)

The F-test given in equation 17.2.36 may then be used to check whether the statistical model 17.3.10 or

$$\begin{bmatrix} \mathbf{y}_1 \\ \mathbf{y}_2 \\ \mathbf{y}_3 \end{bmatrix} = \begin{bmatrix} \mathbf{x}_{11}\beta_{11} + \mathbf{x}_{13}\beta_{13} & & +\mathbf{x}_{12}\beta_2 \\ & \mathbf{x}_{21}\beta_{2i} + \mathbf{x}_{23}\beta_{23} & +\mathbf{x}_{22}\beta_2 \\ & & \mathbf{x}_{31}\beta_{31} + \mathbf{x}_{33}\beta_{33} \quad +\mathbf{x}_{32}\beta_2 \end{bmatrix} + \begin{bmatrix} \mathbf{e}_1 \\ \mathbf{e}_2 \\ \mathbf{e}_3 \end{bmatrix}$$

(17.3.21)

is appropriate. This F-test statistic in equation 17.2.36 can be computed by using software packages such as SHAZAM and SAS. Alternatively, the hypothesis that all of the income elasticities are the same, that is, $\beta_{13} = \beta_{23} = \beta_{33}$, or that both the price and income elasticities are the same for the three demand relations, could be tested.

17.4 Combining Time-Series and Cross-Sectional Data

In many applications $\mathbf{y}_i$ and X_i, for $i = 1, 2,\ldots, M$, will contain observations on variables for T different time periods, where the subscript i corresponds to a particular economic or geographic unit, such as a household, a firm, or a region within a country. Consequently, the SUR model for a set of equations provides a framework for specifying a statistical model reflecting how time-series and cross-sectional data can be combined. Two variants of the SUR model in this context are discussed in Appendix 17B.

17.5 Statistical Implications of Using Sets of Regression Equations

In Chapters 15 and 16 we considered the incidence of heteroskedastic and autocorrelated equation errors and devised an estimation rule to make use of this type of information. In this chapter we extended these concepts and have considered sets of regression equations that are error related. When we write the set of equations as a single linear statistical model, the new error vector may be both heteroskedastic and correlated. To take account of this information we demonstrated a variant of the generalized least squares estimation rule that was introduced in Chapters 15 and 16.

Relative to using the least squares rule on each equation individually, we noted that, under many conditions normally fulfilled in practice, when the equations are combined and the equation error information is used, we have an improvement in terms of the precision with which the unknown parameters are estimated. Given the estimated co-efficients and the estimated covariance matrix, it was possible to test individual and cross-equations hypotheses regarding the unknown coefficients.

The significant idea in this chapter revolves around *(i)* writing two or more linear statistical models as a single linear statistical model, and *(ii)* recognizing that if the cross-equation errors are correlated, making use of this information in a generalized least squares estimator context results in an increase in estimation precision.

This is another example of a two-stage estimation procedure that we first encountered in Chapters 15 and 16. The first stage involves least squares estimates of the individual equation coefficients $\mathbf{b}_i$ and equation errors $\hat{\mathbf{e}}_i$. The estimated equation errors $\hat{\mathbf{e}}_i$ are then used to construct an estimated error covariance matrix for the single linear statistical model representing the set of equations. The second stage consists of using the estimated covariance matrix and the generalized least squares rule to estimate the unknown parameters and to conduct relevant tests of hypotheses.

The statistical inference machine runs on information and in this seemingly unrelated regressions (SUR) chapter we have focused on how to make use of the additional information concerning cross correlations among equation errors. When equations are estimated individually, this potential information is omitted. In the next two chapters we will again be analyzing a set of regression equations that have equation errors that are interrelated. However, in these chapters we will also note for each equation a special relationship between the left-hand-side $\mathbf{y}_i$ variable and some of the right-hand-side X variables. Given the new statistical model, we then sort out how to deal with this new information or to ascertain what the statistical consequences are if we neglect it.

Before going on to the next chapter, you should make sure you understand the meaning of the items listed under new key words and concepts that appear at the beginning of this chapter.

17.6   Exercises

17.1 Consider the SUR statistical model

$$
\begin{bmatrix} \mathbf{y}_1 \\ \mathbf{y}_2 \end{bmatrix} = \begin{bmatrix} X_1 & 0 \\ 0 & X_2 \end{bmatrix} \begin{bmatrix} \boldsymbol{\beta}_1 \\ \boldsymbol{\beta}_2 \end{bmatrix} + \begin{bmatrix} \mathbf{e}_1 \\ \mathbf{e}_2 \end{bmatrix}
$$

or

$$
\mathbf{y} = X\boldsymbol{\beta} + \mathbf{e} \quad \text{where} \quad \mathbf{e} \sim N\left(\mathbf{0}, \begin{bmatrix} \sigma_{11} I_T & \sigma_{12} I_T \\ \sigma_{21} I_T & \sigma_{22} I_T \end{bmatrix} = W \right)
$$

(a) Show that if $\sigma_{12} = \sigma_{21} = 0$, the least squares estimator $\mathbf{b} = (X'X)^{-1}X'\mathbf{y} = (X'W^{-1}X)^{-1}X'W^{-1}\mathbf{y} = \hat{\boldsymbol{\beta}}$, the generalized least squares estimator. In other words, show that equation 17.2.16 is correct and provide the necessary intermediate steps for the proof given in equation 17.2.16.

(b) Demonstrate that the generalized least squares-SUR estimator $\hat{\boldsymbol{\beta}}$ is an unbiased estimator of $\boldsymbol{\beta}$.

(c) How would you go about demonstrating for the SUR statistical model that the generalized least squares estimator $\hat{\boldsymbol{\beta}}$ has a sampling precision superior to the least squares estimator $\mathbf{b} = (X'X)^{-1}X'\mathbf{y}$?

(d) We have indicated for the SUR statistical model that $\hat{\boldsymbol{\beta}} = \mathbf{b}$ when $X_1 = X_2$. Demonstrate that this is a correct conclusion.

17.2 We know that in large samples the estimated generalized least squares estimator $\hat{\boldsymbol{\beta}}$ is superior, or at least not inferior, to the least squares estimator **b**. However, this is not necessarily true in small samples. Since in the analysis presented in the previous sections of this chapter we had the results from only one sample, it may be interesting to investigate the small sample properties of **b** and $\hat{\boldsymbol{\beta}}$ in a Monte Carlo experiment. By using procedures described in the *Computer Handbooks*, generate 100 samples of $\mathbf{y}_1$ and $\mathbf{y}_2$, each of size 20, from the statistical model

$$\mathbf{y}_1 = -28\mathbf{x}_{11} + 0.04\mathbf{x}_{12} + 0.14\mathbf{x}_{13} + \mathbf{e}_1$$
$$\mathbf{y}_2 = -1.3\mathbf{x}_{21} + 0.06\mathbf{x}_{22} + 0.06\mathbf{x}_{23} + \mathbf{e}_2$$

where the regressors x_{i2} and x_{i3} correspond to the vectors $\mathbf{v}_i$ and $\mathbf{k}_i$ given in Table 17.1 and $\mathbf{e}_1, \mathbf{e}_2$ are normal random vectors with mean zero and joint variance-covariance matrix:

$$E\left[\binom{\mathbf{e}_1}{\mathbf{e}_2}\left(\mathbf{e}_1' \quad \mathbf{e}_2'\right)\right] = \begin{bmatrix} 660I_{20} & 175I_{20} \\ 175I_{20} & 90I_{20} \end{bmatrix} = W$$

Methods for generating bivariate normal random variables are given in the *Computer Handbooks*.

(a) Use five samples of the data to estimate the model with
   (*i*) the least squares rule, **b**,
   (*ii*) generalized least squares (known error covariance matrix), $\hat{\boldsymbol{\beta}}$,
   (*iii*) estimated generalized least squares (estimated error covariance matrix), $\hat{\boldsymbol{\beta}}$.
   Comment on the various estimates from the different samples.

(b) Using all 100 samples of data, calculate the sample mean and variance for each of the parameter estimates obtained by using the estimators specified in part (a). Comment on the results.

17.3 Under the assumption $\sigma_{12} = \sigma_{21} = 0$, specify the statistical model and compute the restricted estimated generalized least squares results given in Table 17.2.

17.4 Consider the three demand equations outlined in equation 17.3.1, namely,

$$\ln q_{it} = \beta_{i1} + \beta_{i2} \ln p_{it} + \beta_{i3} \ln y_t + e_{it} \qquad i = 1,2,3 \qquad (17.7.1)$$

Thirty observations on prices, quantities, and income are given in Table 17.3. Use the demand specification 17.7.1 with statistical models 17.3.10 and 17.3.11 and data in Table 17.3 to:

(a) Estimate each equation by least squares and compute the corresponding estimated precision (covariance) matrix for the least squares estimates of each equation.

(b) Compute the estimated error covariance matrix

$$\begin{bmatrix} \hat{\sigma}_{11}I_T & \hat{\sigma}_{12}I_T & \hat{\sigma}_{13}I_T \\ \hat{\sigma}_{21}I_T & \hat{\sigma}_{22}I_T & \hat{\sigma}_{23}I_T \\ \hat{\sigma}_{31}I_T & \hat{\sigma}_{32}I_T & \hat{\sigma}_{33}I_T \end{bmatrix}$$

(c) Test for contemporaneous correlation between the equation errors.

(d) Estimate the unknown coefficients for the set of relations using the seemingly unrelated regression (SUR) estimator and compute the corresponding precision (covariance) matrices for each equation.

Table 17.3 Data for Demand Model

p_1	p_2	p_3	y	q_1	q_2	q_3
10.763	4.474	6.629	487.648	11.632	13.194	45.770
13.033	10.836	13.774	364.877	12.029	2.181	13.393
9.244	5.856	4.063	541.037	8.916	5.586	104.819
4.605	14.010	3.868	760.343	33.908	5.231	137.269
13.045	11.417	14.922	421.746	4.561	10.930	15.914
7.706	8.755	14.318	578.214	17.594	11.854	23.667
7.405	7.317	4.794	561.734	18.842	17.045	62.057
7.519	6.360	3.768	301.470	11.637	2.682	52.262
8.764	4.188	8.089	379.636	7.645	13.008	31.916
13.511	1.996	2.708	478.855	7.881	19.623	123.026
4.943	7.268	12.901	433.741	9.614	6.534	26.255
8.360	5.839	11.115	525.702	9.067	9.397	35.540
5.721	5.160	11.220	513.067	14.070	13.188	32.487
7.225	9.145	5.810	408.666	15.474	3.340	45.838
6.617	5.034	5.516	192.061	3.041	4.716	26.867
14.219	5.926	3.707	462.621	14.096	17.141	43.325
6.769	8.187	10.125	312.659	4.118	4.695	24.330
7.769	7.193	2.471	400.848	10.489	7.639	107.017
9.804	13.315	8.976	392.215	6.231	9.089	23.407
11.063	6.874	12.883	377.724	6.458	10.346	18.254
6.535	15.533	4.115	343.552	8.736	3.901	54.895
11.063	4.477	4.962	301.599	5.158	4.350	45.360
4.016	9.231	6.294	294.112	16.618	7.371	25.318
4.759	5.907	8.298	365.032	11.342	6.507	32.852
5.483	7.077	9.638	256.125	2.903	3.770	22.154
7.890	9.942	7.122	184.798	3.138	1.360	20.575
8.460	7.043	4.157	359.084	15.315	6.497	44.205
6.195	4.142	10.040	629.378	22.240	10.963	44.443
6.743	3.369	15.459	306.527	10.012	10.140	13.251
11.977	4.806	6.172	347.488	3.982	8.637	41.845

(e) Compare the corresponding diagonal elements from the estimated covariance matrices in (a) and (d) and comment on the relative sampling efficiencies of estimators **b** and $\hat{\boldsymbol{\beta}}$.

(f) Give economic interpretations to the price and income coefficients.

(g) Using SUR results, compute 95% interval estimates for the price coefficients and interpret.

(h) Suppose you knew that the price coefficients were identical. Under this restriction obtain estimates of the unknown coefficients and contrast your results with those estimates obtained in (a) and (d).

(i) Test the hypothesis that the price elasticity coefficients over all equations are identical, that is, $\beta_{12} = \beta_{22} = \beta_{32}$.

17.5 Consider within the SUR framework the reformulated three-equation demand system

$$\ln q_{it} = \beta_{i0} + \beta_{i1} \ln p_{1t} + \beta_{i2} \ln p_{2t} + \beta_{i3} \ln p_{3t} + \beta_{i4} \ln y_t + e_{it}$$

for $i = 1, 2, 3$, and the data given in Table 17.3. Note we now assume the cross-elasticities β_{ij}, for $i \neq j$, may not be zero. Note also under this specification that $X_1 = X_2 = X_3$ and thus there would be no gain in efficiency in estimating the unknown coefficients from the *set* of equations. However, this does not hold true if we make cross equation restrictions. Therefore, let us assume we know that the following cross equation conditions hold:

$$\beta_{12} = \beta_{21}, \qquad \beta_{13} = \beta_{31} \qquad \text{and} \qquad \beta_{23} = \beta_{32}$$

(a) Estimate the coefficients of the three equations using least squares applied separately to each equation.

(b) Estimate the three equations using restricted least squares (diagonal error covariance and estimator from Chapter 11).

(c) Test for contemporaneous correlation among the errors.

(d) Write the constraints in the form $R\beta = \mathbf{r}$ and make use of the following *restricted seemingly unrelated regression* estimator:

$$\hat{\boldsymbol{\beta}}* = \hat{\boldsymbol{\beta}} + \left(X'\hat{W}^{-1}X\right)^{-1} R'\left[R\left(X'\hat{W}^{-1}X\right)^{-1} R'\right]^{-1}\left(\mathbf{r} - R\hat{\boldsymbol{\beta}}\right)$$

that is computed by programs such as SHAZAM or SAS, to estimate the coefficients of the three equations.

(e) Comment on the three sets of estimated coefficients and their standard errors.

(f) Test the validity of the symmetry constraint imposed in (d).

17.6 The U. S. Secretary of Agriculture asks one of his economists to provide him with a basis for determining cattle inventories in the Midwest, Southwest, and West regions. Let $i = 1, 2, 3$ denote the three regions. The economist hypothesizes that in each region cattle numbers at the end of the year (c_{it}) depend on average price during the year (p_{it}), rainfall during the year (r_{it}), and cattle numbers at the end of the previous year (c_{it-1}). Because growing conditions are quite different in the three regions, he wants to try three separate equations, one for each region, that he writes as

$$c_{1t} = \beta_{11} + \beta_{12} p_{1t} + \beta_{13} r_{1t} + \beta_{14} c_{1,t-1} + e_{1t}$$
$$c_{2t} = \beta_{21} + \beta_{22} p_{2t} + \beta_{23} r_{2t} + \beta_{24} c_{2,t-1} + e_{2t}$$
$$c_{3t} = \beta_{31} + \beta_{32} p_{3t} + \beta_{33} r_{3t} + \beta_{34} c_{3,t-1} + e_{3t}$$

(a) What signs would you expect on the various coefficients? Why?

(b) Under what assumptions about the e_{it} should the three equations be estimated jointly as a set rather than individually?

(c) Use the data that appear in Table 17.4 to find separate least squares estimates for each equation, and the corresponding standard errors and t-values.

(d) Test for the existence of contemporaneous correlation between the e_{it}.

(e) Estimate the three equations jointly using the seemingly unrelated regression technique. Compare these results with those obtained in (c) in terms of reliability and economic feasibility.

(f) Reestimate the three equations assuming that the coefficients in the three equations are identical and assuming there is
(i) no contemporaneous correlation between the e_{it}.
(ii) contemporaneous correlation between the e_{it}.
Comment on the economic and statistical significance of the results.

17.7 Consider the production function

$$Q_t = f\left(K_t, L_t\right)$$

Table 17.4 Data for Beef Cattle Inventory Model

Region 1			Region 2			Region 3		
Cattle Numbers (thousands)	Price (cents/ pound)	Rainfall (inches)	Cattle Numbers (thousands)	Price (cents/ pound)	Rainfall (inches)	Cattle Numbers (thousands)	Price (cents/ pound)	Rainfall (inches)
244	43	25.8	157	43	24.5	335	43	29.7
226	27	19.4	150	26	18.1	291	31	23.4
227	43	15.8	157	44	13.1	267	42	20.4
213	18	27.2	147	14	26.3	240	17	28.6
246	48	21.8	174	48	19.0	288	47	22.6
272	41	27.8	191	45	24.6	319	41	27.9
274	43	16.1	188	45	16.1	309	41	19.4
271	27	19.3	174	28	18.0	316	25	23.4
254	17	27.3	161	10	26.5	312	17	32.3
246	38	19.9	167	40	16.4	294	39	26.2
272	38	20.2	169	36	16.7	326	39	23.1
230	34	23.7	159	32	19.0	292	32	24.1
236	41	17.7	165	39	15.8	292	41	20.4
218	26	10.3	141	25	5.5	256	26	10.6
238	25	20.8	153	25	20.1	279	25	26.0
234	39	19.1	161	44	15.3	280	41	21.2
235	29	27.3	166	29	26.5	287	32	32.3
232	43	25.6	164	35	24.1	296	45	29.3
200	36	11.6	140	32	9.9	256	37	18.3
193	28	18.1	135	27	13.9	236	28	19.4
204	46	13.8	156	49	12.8	246	46	18.6
220	27	29.2	166	27	29.1	262	27	32.3
210	26	20.2	152	27	16.8	249	24	23.2
238	34	23.4	166	35	21.2	276	37	25.4
222	17	27.8	155	17	27.2	257	14	33.3
228	25	20.8	155	26	17.6	255	26	27.8
225	42	17.0	159	42	14.8	256	40	19.2

where Q_t is output, K_t is capital, and L_t is labor, all for the tth firm. Suppose the function $f(\cdot)$ is a CES or constant elasticity of substitution production function (see Section 22.3.2 of Chapter 22). The elasticity of substitution which we denote by η measures the degree to which capital and labor are substituted when the factor price ratio changes. Let P_t be the price of output, R_t be the price of capital, and W_t the price of labor. If the function $f(\cdot)$ is a CES production function, then the conditions for profit maximization with additive errors are

$$\ln\left(\frac{Q_t}{L_t}\right) = \gamma_1 + \eta\ln\left(\frac{W_t}{P_t}\right) + e_{1t}, \text{ where } e_{1t} \sim N(0, \sigma_{11}I_T)$$

$$\ln\left(\frac{Q_t}{K_t}\right) = \gamma_2 + \eta\ln\left(\frac{R_t}{P_t}\right) + e_{2t}, \text{ where } e_{2t} \sim N(0, \sigma_{22}I_T)$$

Since these equations (statistical models) are linear in γ_1, γ_2, and η, some version(s) of least squares can be used to estimate these parameters. Data on 20 firms appear in Table 17.5.

Table 17.5 Data for Estimation of CES Production Function

K	L	Q	R	W	P
11.33	23.81	25.07	6.50	3.09	3.37
25.92	75.83	23.82	9.33	2.85	8.29
7.03	9.46	7.59	8.66	7.03	9.15
29.68	5.71	8.07	1.32	7.77	9.68
21.81	85.78	24.01	5.99	1.27	4.92
0.57	0.37	3.14	6.16	9.36	1.31
11.25	8.82	15.05	4.93	6.18	8.71
19.01	8.99	12.37	4.30	9.18	7.04
75.25	37.65	18.32	1.95	4.71	7.17
8.40	8.43	8.03	5.28	5.27	4.88
30.30	16.10	13.48	4.00	8.28	9.22
21.06	33.66	14.80	8.97	5.87	7.96
11.86	15.72	12.88	6.97	4.25	6.18
14.53	8.44	8.58	3.60	8.34	7.17
34.20	30.20	17.89	4.21	4.96	5.91
8.68	8.89	10.82	7.22	6.32	7.37
2.84	5.14	8.94	6.95	3.66	2.07
1.20	0.64	3.45	3.79	6.22	1.53
70.18	30.40	10.10	1.79	4.26	8.69
6.93	5.28	5.93	8.32	9.40	7.36

(a) Find separate least squares estimates of each of the first-order conditions. Compare the two estimates of the elasticity of substitution.

(b) Test for contemporaneous correlation between e_{1t} and e_{2t}.

(c) Estimate the two equations using generalized least squares, allowing for the existence of contemporaneous correlation.

(d) Repeat part (c), but impose a restriction so that only one estimate of the elasticity of substitution is obtained. Comment on the results.

(e) Compare the standard errors obtained in parts (a), (c), and (d). Do they reflect the efficiency gains that you would expect?

(f) If $\eta = 1$, the CES production function becomes a Cobb–Douglas production function. Use the results in (d) to test whether a Cobb–Douglas production function is adequate.

17.8 Identify and discuss a real-world problem where the SUR model may be appropriate.

17.7 A Guide to Further Reading

For a more complete discussion of the generalized least squares framework and seemingly unrelated regression, refer to Chapters 8, 9 and 11 of the Second Edition of *Introduction to the Theory and Practice of Econometrics* by G. G. Judge, R. C. Hill, W. E. Griffiths, H. Lütkepohl and T.C. Lee (John Wiley & Sons, Inc., 1988) and the references it contains, such as *Seemingly Related Regression Equation Models: Estimation and Inference*, by V. K. Srivastava and D. E. Giles (Marcel Dekker, Inc., 1988).

For a more complete writeup of combining cross section and time-series data see *Analysis of Panel Data* by C. Hsaio (Cambridge University Press, 1986) and Chapter 10 and Sections 11.4 to 11.6 of Chapter 11 in *Introduction to the Theory and Practice of Econometrics*.

APPENDIX 17A A General SUR Formulation

Since the previous sections have considered special cases, before concluding this chapter let us consider a general formulation for the SUR statistical model. In a general specification of M seemingly unrelated regression equations the ith equation is given by

$$\mathbf{y}_i = X_i\boldsymbol{\beta}_i + \mathbf{e}_i \qquad\qquad i = 1, 2, \ldots, M \tag{17A.1}$$

where $\mathbf{y}_i$ and $\mathbf{e}_i$ are of dimension $(T \times 1)$, X_i is $(T \times K_i)$, and $\boldsymbol{\beta}_i$ is $(K_i \times 1)$. Note that each equation does not have to have the same number of explanatory variables. Combining all equations into one big model yields

$$\begin{bmatrix} \mathbf{y}_1 \\ \mathbf{y}_2 \\ \vdots \\ \mathbf{y}_M \end{bmatrix} = \begin{bmatrix} X_1 & & & \\ & X_2 & & \\ & & \ddots & \\ & & & X_M \end{bmatrix} \begin{bmatrix} \boldsymbol{\beta}_1 \\ \boldsymbol{\beta}_2 \\ \vdots \\ \boldsymbol{\beta}_M \end{bmatrix} + \begin{bmatrix} \mathbf{e}_1 \\ \mathbf{e}_2 \\ \vdots \\ \mathbf{e}_M \end{bmatrix} \tag{17A.2}$$

or, alternatively,

$$\mathbf{y} = X\boldsymbol{\beta} + \mathbf{e} \tag{17A.3}$$

where the definitions of $\mathbf{y}$, X, $\boldsymbol{\beta}$ and $\mathbf{e}$ are obvious from equation 17A.2 and their dimensions are, respectively, $(MT \times 1)$, $(MT \times K)$, $(K \times 1)$, and $(MT \times 1)$, with $K = \sum_{i=1}^{M} K_i$. Thus, the specification 17A.3 has precisely the form of the linear statistical model considered in earlier chapters.

Given that e_{it} is the error for the ith equation in the tth time period, the assumption of contemporaneous disturbance correlation, but not correlation over time, implies that the covariance matrix for the complete error vector can be written as

$$W = E[\mathbf{ee}'] = \begin{bmatrix} \sigma_{11}I_T & \sigma_{12}I_T & \cdots & \sigma_{1M}I_T \\ \sigma_{21}I_T & \sigma_{22}I_T & \cdots & \sigma_{2M}I_T \\ \vdots & \vdots & & \vdots \\ \sigma_{M1}I_T & \sigma_{M2}I_T & \cdots & \sigma_{MM}I_T \end{bmatrix} = \Sigma \otimes I_T \tag{17A.4}$$

where

$$\Sigma = \begin{bmatrix} \sigma_{11} & \sigma_{12} & \cdots & \sigma_{1M} \\ \sigma_{21} & \sigma_{22} & \cdots & \sigma_{2M} \\ \vdots & \vdots & & \vdots \\ \sigma_{M1} & \sigma_{M2} & \cdots & \sigma_{MM} \end{bmatrix} \tag{17A.5}$$

and $\otimes$ indicates each element of Σ is multiplied by an identity matrix. The matrix Σ is symmetric, so that $\sigma_{ij} = \sigma_{ji}$, and it is nonsingular and thus has an inverse.

17A.1 Estimation with a Known and Unknown Covariance Matrix

When the system of equation 17A.2 is viewed as the single equation 17A.3, we can estimate $\boldsymbol{\beta}$ and hence all the $\boldsymbol{\beta}_i$ by the generalized least squares procedures that were discussed in Chapters 15 and 16. Thus, using the results of Chapters 15 and 16, the generalized least squares estimator

$$\hat{\boldsymbol{\beta}} = \left(X'W^{-1}X\right)^{-1} X'W^{-1}\mathbf{y} = \left[X'\left(\Sigma^{-1} \otimes I\right)X\right]^{-1} X'\left(\Sigma^{-1} \otimes I\right)\mathbf{y} \tag{17A.6}$$

is best linear unbiased. The covariance matrix for $\hat{\boldsymbol{\beta}}$ is given by $\left(X'W^{-1}X\right)^{-1} = [X'\left(\Sigma^{-1} \otimes I\right)X]^{-1}$. In these expressions we have used the result $W^{-1} = \left(\Sigma \otimes I\right)^{-1} = \Sigma^{-1} \otimes I$.

In practice the variances and covariances (σ_{ij}s) are unknown and must be estimated, with their estimates being used in equation 17A.1 to form an estimated generalized least squares estimator. To estimate the σ_{ij} we first estimate each equation by least squares $\mathbf{b}_i = \left(X'_i X_i\right)^{-1} X'_i \mathbf{y}_i$ and obtain the least squares residuals $\hat{\mathbf{e}}_i = \mathbf{y}_i - X_i \mathbf{b}_i$. Consistent estimates of the variances and covariances are then given by

$$\hat{\sigma}_{ij} = \frac{1}{T}\hat{\mathbf{e}}'_i\hat{\mathbf{e}}_j = \frac{1}{T}\sum_{t=1}^{T}\hat{e}_{it}\hat{e}_{jt} \tag{17A.7}$$

If we define $\hat{\Sigma}$ as the matrix Σ with the unknown σ_{ij} replaced by $\hat{\sigma}_{ij}$, then the estimated generalized least squares estimator for β corresponding to equation 17A.6 can be written as

$$\hat{\hat{\boldsymbol{\beta}}} = \left[X'\left(\hat{\Sigma}^{-1} \otimes I\right)X\right]^{-1} X'\left(\hat{\Sigma}^{-1} \otimes I\right)\mathbf{y} \tag{17A.8}$$

This estimator is the one that is generally used in practice and is the general version of Zellner's *seemingly unrelated regression (SUR) estimator*.

17A.2 Hypothesis Testing

17A.2a Testing for Contemporaneous Correlation

If contemporaneous correlation does not exist, least squares applied separately to each equation is fully efficient and there is no need to employ the seemingly unrelated regression estimator. Thus, it is useful to test whether

H_0: the contemporaneous covariances σ_{ij} are zero, for $i \neq j$

H_1: at least one covariance is nonzero

For the general case of M equations, the statistic discussed in Section 17.3.3 is given by

$$\lambda = T\sum_{i=2}^{M}\sum_{j=1}^{i-1}r_{ij}^2 \tag{17A.9}$$

Under H_0, λ has an asymptotic χ^2 distribution with $M(M-1)/2$ degrees of freedom.

17A.2b Linear Restrictions on the Coefficients

Consider a set of linear restrictions of the form $R\beta = \mathbf{r}$, where R and $\mathbf{r}$ are known matrices of dimensions $(J \times K)$ and $(J \times 1)$, respectively. It is possible to extend the analysis in Section 11.5 of Chapter 11 to construct a test statistic for testing the null hypothesis H_0: $R\beta = \mathbf{r}$. There are two main differences between the earlier procedures and those adopted in this section. First, the relevant test statistic will now depend on Σ which, because it is unknown, needs to be replaced by the estimator $\hat{\Sigma}$. This replacement means that estimator properties and test statistics are based on asymptotic rather than finite sample distributions. Second, it is now possible to test and impose restrictions that relate the coefficients in one equation with the coefficients in other equations. This possibility is of particular interest in economics. For example, if the coefficient vectors for each equation are all equal, $\beta_1 = \beta_2 = \ldots = \beta_M$, the use of data aggregated over microunits does not lead to aggregation bias. Also, some aspects of economic theory often suggest symmetric and other linear relationships between coefficients in different equations. For this purpose, a generalized version of the F-test for a set of linear restrictions, developed in Chapter 10, may be used.

Turning to the question of testing $H_0: R\beta = \mathbf{r}$ against the alternative $R\beta \neq \mathbf{r}$, we note that, when H_0 is true,

$$R\hat{\beta} \sim N\left(\mathbf{r}, RCR'\right) \tag{17A.10}$$

where $C = \left[X'\left(\Sigma^{-1} \otimes I\right)X\right]^{-1}$. Thus

$$g = \left(R\hat{\beta} - \mathbf{r}\right)'\left(RCR'\right)^{-1}\left(R\hat{\beta} - \mathbf{r}\right) \sim \chi^2_{(J)} \tag{17A.11}$$

This result is a finite sample one (providing the errors are normally distributed), but it is not operational because it depends on the unknown covariance matrix Σ. When Σ is replaced by $\hat{\Sigma}$, we have the asymptotic result

$$\hat{g} = \left(R\hat{\hat{\beta}} - \mathbf{r}\right)'\left(R\hat{C}R'\right)^{-1}\left(R\hat{\hat{\beta}} - \mathbf{r}\right) \xrightarrow{d} \chi^2_{(J)} \tag{17A.12}$$

Since equation 17A.12 holds only when H_0 is true, we reject H_0 if a calculated value for $\hat{g}$ exceeds the appropriate critical value from a $\chi^2_{(J)}$ distribution.

APPENDIX 17B   Combining Cross-Sectional and Time-Series Data

Estimation of economic relationships by using data on a set of economic units (a cross section) that are observed at more than one point in time (a time series) is a problem frequently encountered in econometrics. For example, if we are studying the economic behavior of electric utility firms, we may observe costs, inputs, and outputs for a number of firms across the United States every year for a number of years. On the aggregate level, if we are studying the international usage of oil and coal, we may observe usage, and the corresponding explanatory variables, for a number of countries every quarter or every year for a number of years. In these examples an investigator will possess a time series of data on a cross section of economic units. The problem is how to specify a statistical model that will capture individual differences in behavior so that we may combine or *pool all* the data (information) for estimation and inference purposes.

In this chapter we have considered one statistical model that may be used to combine time series and cross-sectional data, and an example was given about the investment behavior of firms. We will use that example introduced in Section 17.1 as a framework for introducing ideas in this appendix. Let us consider the investment behavior of $N = 10$ firms, over the $T = 20$ years 1935 to 1954, using the data in Table 17B.1, which was contained in a recent book by Vinod and Ullah.

Table 17B.1   Data on Investment **i**, Expected Profits **v** and Desired
Capital Stock **k** for 10 Firms and 20 Years

	i	v	k	i	v	k	i	v	k
	General Motors			**Atlantic Richfield**			**Westinghouse**		
1935	317.6	3078.5	2.8	39.68	157.7	183.2	12.93	191.5	1.8
1936	391.8	4661.7	52.6	50.73	167.9	204.0	25.90	516.0	.8
1937	410.6	5387.1	156.9	74.24	192.9	236.0	35.05	729.0	7.4
1938	257.7	2792.2	209.2	53.51	156.7	291.7	22.89	560.4	18.1
1939	330.8	4313.2	203.4	42.65	191.4	323.1	18.84	519.9	23.5
1940	461.2	4643.9	207.2	46.48	185.5	344.0	28.57	628.5	26.5
1941	512.0	4551.2	255.2	61.40	199.6	367.7	48.51	537.1	36.2
1942	448.0	3244.1	303.7	39.67	189.5	407.2	43.34	561.2	60.8
1943	499.6	4053.7	264.1	62.24	151.2	426.6	37.02	617.2	84.4
1944	547.5	4379.3	201.6	52.32	187.7	470.0	37.81	626.7	91.2
1945	561.2	4840.9	265.0	63.21	214.7	499.2	39.27	737.2	92.4
1946	688.1	4900.9	402.2	59.37	232.9	534.6	53.46	760.5	86.0
1947	568.9	3526.5	761.5	58.02	249.0	566.6	55.56	581.4	111.1
1948	529.2	3254.7	922.4	70.34	224.5	595.3	49.56	662.3	130.6
1949	555.1	3700.2	1020.1	67.42	237.3	631.4	32.04	583.8	141.8
1950	642.9	3755.6	1099.0	55.74	240.1	662.3	32.24	635.2	136.7
1951	755.9	4833.0	1207.7	80.30	327.3	683.9	54.38	723.8	129.7
1952	891.2	4924.9	1430.5	85.40	359.4	729.3	71.78	864.1	145.5
1953	1304.4	6241.7	1777.3	81.90	398.4	774.3	90.08	1193.5	174.8
1954	1486.7	5593.6	2226.3	81.43	365.7	804.9	68.60	1188.9	213.5
	US Steel			**IBM**			**Goodyear**		
1935	209.9	1362.4	53.8	20.36	197.0	6.5	26.63	290.6	162
1936	355.3	1807.1	50.5	25.98	210.3	15.8	23.39	291.1	174
1937	469.9	2676.3	118.1	25.94	223.1	27.7	30.65	335.0	183
1938	262.3	1801.9	260.2	27.53	216.7	39.2	20.89	246.0	198
1939	230.4	1957.3	312.7	24.60	286.4	48.6	28.78	356.2	208
1940	361.6	2202.9	254.2	28.54	298.0	52.5	26.93	289.8	223
1941	472.8	2380.5	261.4	43.41	276.9	61.5	32.08	268.2	234
1942	445.6	2168.6	298.7	42.81	272.6	80.5	32.21	213.3	248
1943	361.6	1985.1	301.8	27.84	287.4	94.4	35.69	348.2	274
1944	288.2	1813.9	279.1	32.60	330.3	92.6	62.47	374.2	282
1945	258.7	1850.2	213.8	39.03	324.4	92.3	52.32	387.2	316
1946	420.3	2067.7	232.6	50.17	401.9	94.2	56.95	347.4	302
1947	420.5	1796.7	264.8	51.85	407.4	111.4	54.32	291.9	333
1948	494.5	1625.8	306.9	64.03	409.2	127.4	40.53	297.2	359
1949	405.1	1667.0	351.1	68.16	482.2	149.3	32.54	276.9	370
1950	418.8	1677.4	357.8	77.34	673.8	164.4	43.48	274.6	376
1951	588.2	2289.5	342.1	95.30	676.9	177.2	56.49	339.9	391
1952	645.2	2159.4	444.2	99.49	702.0	200.0	65.98	474.8	414
1953	641.0	2031.3	623.6	127.52	793.5	211.5	66.11	496.0	443
1954	459.3	2115.5	669.7	135.72	927.3	238.7	49.34	474.5	468

continued

Using the economic model developed earlier in this chapter and the corresponding
statistical model for this appendix, we let y_{it} = investment (**i**) by the ith firm in year t,
x_{2it} = profit measure (**v**) for the ith firm in year t, x_{3it} = capital stock measure (**k**) for the

Table 17B.1 Continued

i	v	k	i	v	k	i	v	k
	General Electric			Union Oil			Diamond Match	
1935	33.1	1170.6	97.8	24.43	138.0	100.2	2.54	70.91	4.50
1936	45.0	2015.8	104.4	23.21	200.1	125.0	2.00	87.94	4.71
1937	77.2	2803.3	118.0	32.78	210.1	142.4	2.19	82.20	4.57
1938	44.6	2039.7	156.2	32.54	161.2	165.1	1.99	58.72	4.56
1939	48.1	2256.2	172.6	26.65	161.7	194.8	2.03	80.54	4.38
1940	74.4	2132.2	186.6	33.71	145.1	222.9	1.81	86.47	4.21
1941	113.0	1834.1	220.9	43.50	110.6	252.1	2.14	77.68	4.12
1942	91.9	1588.0	287.8	34.46	98.1	276.3	1.86	62.16	3.83
1943	61.3	1749.4	319.9	44.28	108.8	300.3	.93	62.24	3.58
1944	56.8	1687.2	321.3	70.80	118.2	318.2	1.18	61.82	3.41
1945	93.6	2007.7	319.6	44.12	126.5	336.2	1.36	65.85	3.31
1946	159.9	2208.3	346.0	48.98	156.7	351.2	2.24	69.54	3.23
1947	147.2	1656.7	456.4	48.51	119.4	373.6	3.81	64.97	3.90
1948	146.3	1604.4	543.4	50.00	129.1	389.4	5.66	68.00	5.38
1949	98.3	1431.8	618.3	50.59	134.8	406.7	4.21	71.24	7.39
1950	93.5	1610.5	647.4	42.53	140.8	429.5	3.42	69.05	8.74
1951	135.2	1819.4	671.3	64.77	179.0	450.6	4.67	83.04	9.07
1952	157.3	2079.7	726.1	72.68	178.1	466.9	6.00	74.42	9.93
1953	179.5	2371.6	800.3	73.86	186.8	486.2	6.53	63.51	11.68
1954	189.6	2759.9	888.9	89.51	192.7	511.3	5.12	58.12	14.33
	Chrysler								
1935	40.29	417.5	10.5						
1936	72.76	837.8	10.2						
1937	66.26	883.9	34.7						
1938	51.60	437.9	51.8						
1939	52.41	679.7	64.3						
1940	69.41	727.8	67.1						
1941	68.35	643.6	75.2						
1942	46.80	410.9	71.4						
1943	47.40	588.4	67.1						
1944	59.57	698.4	60.5						
1945	88.78	846.4	54.6						
1946	74.12	893.8	84.8						
1947	62.68	579.0	96.8						
1948	89.36	694.6	110.2						
1949	78.98	590.3	147.4						
1950	100.66	693.5	163.2						
1951	160.62	809.0	203.5						
1952	145.00	727.0	290.6						
1953	174.93	1001.5	346.1						
1954	172.49	703.2	414.9						

ith firm in year t, e_{it} = error term for the ith firm in year t, and specify the flexible statistical model

$$y_{it} = \beta_{1it} + \beta_{2it} x_{2it} + \beta_{3it} x_{3it} + e_{it}$$

$$i = 1,\ldots, N = 10$$

$$t = 1,\ldots, T = 20 \tag{17B.1}$$

In this general model the intercepts and response parameters are permitted to differ for each firm in every time period. This model is intractable in its current form, as there are more unknown parameters than data points. *There are many types of simplifying assumptions that can be made to make the model operational. The challenge is to specify a statistical model that is consistent with the data-generation process.*

As one possibility the seemingly unrelated regression (SUR) equation model is obtained if we assume the errors e_{it} are contemporaneously correlated. Under the SUR specification

$$\beta_{1it} = \beta_{1i}$$
$$\beta_{2it} = \beta_{2i}$$
$$\beta_{3it} = \beta_{3i} \tag{17B.2}$$

That is, the parameters of the investment function differ across firms (note that the "i" subscript remains) but are constant across time.

Other possible ways of simplifying the statistical model 17B.1 are considered in this appendix. Specifically, we consider the frequently used dummy variable and error components models for pooling time series and cross-sectional data. For both of these models, we will make the assumption that the errors e_{it} are independent and distributed $N(0, \sigma_e^2)$ for all individuals and in all time periods.

17B.1   A Dummy Variable Model

The first model we consider for pooling time-series and cross-sectional data uses dummy variables. Specifically, within the context of the investment model 17B.1, we assume that

$$\beta_{1it} = \beta_{1i}$$
$$\beta_{2it} = \beta_{2}$$
$$\beta_{3it} = \beta_{3} \tag{17B.3}$$

This model of parameter variation specifies that *only* the intercept parameter varies, and the intercept varies only across firms and not over time. *We say that all behavioral differences between individual firms and over time are captured by the intercept.* The resulting statistical model is

$$y_{it} = \beta_{1i} + \beta_{2}x_{2it} + \beta_{3}x_{3it} + e_{it} \tag{17B.4}$$

This model is more conventionally written if we define dummy variables for each firm; for example,

$$D_{1i} = \begin{cases} 1 & i = 1 \\ 0 & \text{otherwise} \end{cases} \quad \text{and} \quad D_{2i} = \begin{cases} 1 & i = 2 \\ 0 & \text{otherwise} \end{cases} \quad \text{and} \quad D_{3i} = \begin{cases} 1 & i = 3 \\ 0 & \text{otherwise} \end{cases} \tag{17B.5}$$

Under this specification equation 17B.4 becomes

$$y_{it} = \beta_{11}D_{1i} + \beta_{12}D_{2i} + \dots + \beta_{1,10}D_{10i} + \beta_{2}x_{2it} + \beta_{3}x_{3it} + e_{it} \tag{17B.6a}$$

$$= \sum_{j=1}^{N}\beta_{1j}D_{ji} + \sum_{k=2}^{K}\beta_{k}x_{kit} + e_{it} \tag{17B.6b}$$

where expression 17B.6b generalizes the example we are considering to the case where there are N cross-sections and $K - 1$ nonconstant explanatory variables.

If we let $\mathbf{x}_1$ be a $(T \times 1)$ vector of ones, we may write the statistical model 17B.6a for the ith firm as

$$
\begin{bmatrix} y_{i1} \\ y_{i2} \\ \vdots \\ y_{iT} \end{bmatrix} = \begin{bmatrix} 1 \\ 1 \\ \vdots \\ 1 \end{bmatrix} \beta_{1i} + \begin{bmatrix} x_{2i1} & x_{3i2} \\ \vdots & \vdots \\ x_{2iT} & x_{3iT} \end{bmatrix} \begin{bmatrix} \beta_2 \\ \beta_3 \end{bmatrix} + \begin{bmatrix} e_{i1} \\ \vdots \\ e_{iT} \end{bmatrix} \tag{17B.7a}
$$

or

$$
\mathbf{y}_i = \mathbf{x}_1 \beta_{1i} + X_{si} \boldsymbol{\beta}_s + \mathbf{e}_i \quad i = 1, \ldots, N \tag{17B.7b}
$$

where X_{si} is the $T \times 2$ $(= K - 1)$ matrix of observations on the nonconstant explanatory variables, and $\boldsymbol{\beta}_s$ is the corresponding vector of slope parameters for the ith individual (firm).

To write all $NT = 10T$ observations for the investment example, we "stack" the vectors and matrices in equation 17B.7b as

$$
\begin{bmatrix} \mathbf{y}_1 \\ \mathbf{y}_2 \\ \vdots \\ \mathbf{y}_N \end{bmatrix} = \begin{bmatrix} \mathbf{x}_1 & \mathbf{0} & \mathbf{0} & X_{s1} \\ \mathbf{0} & \mathbf{x}_1 & \mathbf{0} & X_{s2} \\ \vdots & \vdots & \vdots & \vdots \\ \mathbf{0} & \mathbf{0} & \mathbf{x}_1 & X_{sN} \end{bmatrix} \begin{bmatrix} \beta_{11} \\ \beta_{12} \\ \vdots \\ \beta_{1N} \\ \boldsymbol{\beta}_s \end{bmatrix} + \begin{bmatrix} \mathbf{e}_1 \\ \mathbf{e}_2 \\ \vdots \\ \mathbf{e}_N \end{bmatrix} \tag{17B.8}
$$

where $\mathbf{0}$ denotes a $(T \times 1)$ vector of zeroes. Finally, we can write the stacked system 17B.8 as

$$
\mathbf{y} = X\boldsymbol{\beta} + \mathbf{e} \tag{17B.9}
$$

which is the usual linear statistical model. Note the following about the stacked equations represented by equations 17B.8 and 17B.9. First, there is no overall constant term, or column of ones, in the X matrix. Instead, the $N = 10$ dummy variables, as in equation 17B.5, define separate intercept variables for each of the firms with intercept parameters $\beta_{11}, \beta_{12}, \ldots, \beta_{1N}$. See Exercise 12.9. Second, under the simple error assumptions made (that the e_{it} are independent and $N(0, \sigma_e^2)$ for all observations], the best linear unbiased estimator of equation 17B.9 is the usual least squares estimator.

Given an estimator for the unknown parameters in equation 17B.9, a natural question to ask is whether there is evidence to suggest that different individuals (firms) have different intercepts, or would the model be adequate if we simply assumed that all the parameters are equal for the N cross-sectional units? If all parameters are the same, and other assumptions of the model continue to hold true, then there are no behavioral differences across individuals or time and, for estimation and inference purposes, the data can be treated as *one* sample of NT observations.

To check this question the relevant hypotheses are

$$
H_0 : \beta_{1i} = \beta_{12} = \ldots = \beta_{1N}
$$
$$
H_1 : \text{the } \beta_{1i} \text{ are not all equal} \tag{17B.10}
$$

These $(N - 1)$ joint null hypotheses may be tested jointly by using the usual F- test statistic and software packages exist (see the *Computer Handbooks*) for carrying through the computations.

17B.2   Error Components

In the previous section we modeled differences in firm investment behavior by permitting each firm to have a different intercept parameter. In this section we offer an alternative model that is useful *if the individual firms (or cross-sectional units) appearing in the sample were randomly chosen and taken to be "representative" of a larger population of firms*. In this instance, where the firms examined are randomly selected, the individual differences we observe are *random*, and a result of the sampling process. Thus, within equation 17B.4

$$y_{it} = \beta_{1i} + \beta_2 x_{2it} + \beta_3 x_{3it} + e_{it} \qquad (17B.4)$$

we take β_{1i} to be *random* and modeled as

$$\beta_{1i} = \overline{\beta}_1 + \mu_i \qquad i = 1, ..., N \qquad (17B.11)$$

$\overline{\beta}_1$ is an unknown parameter that represents the *population mean intercept*, and μ_i is an unobservable random disturbance that accounts for individual differences in firm behavior. We assume that the μ_i are independent of each other and e_{it}, and that

$$E(\mu_i) = 0$$

$$\text{var}(\mu_i) = \sigma_\mu^2$$

Consequently, $E[\beta_{1i}] = \overline{\beta}_1$ and $\text{var}(\beta_{1i}) = \sigma_\mu^2$.

As with systematically varying parameter models (Section 12.7), the model of parameter variation equation 17B.11 is substituted into the statistical model 17B.4 to obtain

$$y_{it} = (\overline{\beta}_1 + \mu_i) + \beta_2 x_{2it} + \beta_3 x_{3it} + e_{it} \qquad (17B.12a)$$

$$= \overline{\beta}_1 + \sum_{k=2}^{K} \beta_k x_{kit} + (e_{it} + \mu_i) \qquad (17B.12b)$$

where expression 17B.12b is the general expression for the error components model. The phrase "error components" comes from the fact that term $(e_{it} + \mu_i)$ is the disturbance term for expression 17B.12b and consists of two components: the overall disturbance e_{it} and the individual specific error μ_i that reflects individual differences and varies across individual, but is constant across time.

In matrix terms the observations for the ith individual in the sample are written

$$\mathbf{y}_i = X_i \boldsymbol{\beta} + \mu_i \mathbf{x}_1 + \mathbf{e}_i \qquad (17B.13)$$

where $\mathbf{y}_i$, $\mathbf{x}_1$, and $\mathbf{e}_i$ were defined in the previous section in respect to equation 17B.7b, $X_i = (\mathbf{x}_1 \ X_{si})$ is a $(T \times K)$ matrix of observations on the explanatory variables (including the constant term) for the ith individual, and $\boldsymbol{\beta}' = (\overline{\beta}_1, \beta_2, ..., \beta_K)$. In equation 17B.13 the term $(\mu_i \mathbf{x}_1 + \mathbf{e}_i)$ can be regarded as a composite disturbance vector that has mean $\mathbf{0}$ and covariance matrix

$$V = E\left[\left(\mu_i \mathbf{x}_1 + \mathbf{e}_i\right)\left(\mu_i \mathbf{x}_1 + \mathbf{e}_i\right)'\right]$$

$$= \begin{bmatrix} \sigma_\mu^2 + \sigma_e^2 & \sigma_\mu^2 & \cdots & \sigma_\mu^2 \\ \sigma_\mu^2 & \sigma_\mu^2 + \sigma_e^2 & \cdots & \sigma_\mu^2 \\ \vdots & \vdots & \ddots & \vdots \\ \sigma_\mu^2 & \sigma_\mu^2 & \cdots & \sigma_\mu^2 + \sigma_e^2 \end{bmatrix}$$

(17B.14)

The structure of this covariance matrix is such that, for a given individual, the correlation between any two disturbances in different time periods is the same. Thus, in contrast to the first-order autoregressive model discussed in Chapter 16, the correlation is constant and does not decline as the disturbances become farther apart in time. Another feature of this matrix is that V does not depend on i, which implies that, not only is the correlation constant over time, it is identical for all individuals.

The complete set of NT observations can be written as

$$\begin{bmatrix} \mathbf{y}_1 \\ \mathbf{y}_2 \\ \vdots \\ \mathbf{y}_N \end{bmatrix} = \begin{bmatrix} X_1 \\ X_2 \\ \vdots \\ X_N \end{bmatrix} \boldsymbol{\beta} + \begin{bmatrix} \mu_1 \mathbf{x}_1 \\ \mu_2 \mathbf{x}_1 \\ \vdots \\ \mu_N \mathbf{x}_1 \end{bmatrix} + \begin{bmatrix} \mathbf{e}_1 \\ \mathbf{e}_2 \\ \vdots \\ \mathbf{e}_N \end{bmatrix}$$

(17B.15)

The covariance matrix W for the complete ($NT \times 1$) disturbance vector $\mathbf{e}$ is block diagonal with each block given by equation 17B.14. That is

$$W = \begin{bmatrix} V & 0 & \cdots & 0 \\ 0 & V & \cdots & 0 \\ \vdots & \vdots & \ddots & \vdots \\ 0 & 0 & \cdots & V \end{bmatrix}$$

The block-diagonal property arises because the disturbance vectors corresponding to different individuals are uncorrelated.

17B.2a   Estimation

Now let us turn to the problem of estimating $\boldsymbol{\beta}$. The covariance matrix W for the error components model is not of the $\sigma^2 I$ type, and, consequently, the model and generalized least squares (GLS) estimation framework examined in Chapters 15 to 17 is appropriate. If σ_μ^2 and σ_e^2 (and, consequently, V and W) are known, then the generalized least squares estimator

$$\hat{\boldsymbol{\beta}} = \left(X'W^{-1}X\right)^{-1} X'W^{-1}\mathbf{y}$$

(17B.16)

is best linear unbiased. In practice, the generalized least squares estimator $\hat{\boldsymbol{\beta}}$ cannot be used because the variance components σ_μ^2 and σ_e^2 are unknown. Following the practice established in many of the earlier chapters, however, it is possible to replace σ_μ^2 and σ_e^2 with estimates $\hat{\sigma}_\mu^2$ and $\hat{\sigma}_e^2$. When this is done the covariance matrix W is replaced with its estimate $\hat{W}$, and the resulting estimator for $\boldsymbol{\beta}$ is an estimated generalized least squares estimator

$$\hat{\boldsymbol{\beta}} = \left(X'\hat{W}^{-1}X\right)^{-1} X'\hat{W}^{-1}\mathbf{y}$$

(17B.17)

Many estimators for σ_μ^2 and σ_e^2 have been suggested in the literature. As one alternative we present unbiased estimators that are developed in Judge et al. (1988, pp. 484–485).

To estimate σ_e^2 we use the least squares residuals $\hat{\mathbf{e}}$, obtained by estimating the dummy variable model described in Section 17B.1. The unbiased estimator of σ_e^2 is

$$\hat{\sigma}_e^2 = \frac{\hat{\mathbf{e}}'\hat{\mathbf{e}}}{NT - N - K'}$$

(17B.18)

where $K' = K - 1$ is the number of nonconstant explanatory variables, $\hat{\mathbf{e}} = \mathbf{y} - X\mathbf{b}$, where $\mathbf{b}$ is the least squares estimator of β in equation 17B.9, and $\mathbf{y}$ and X are as in equation 17B.8.

To obtain an estimator of σ_μ^2, we must obtain the *average* over time of the individual models, given in equation 17B.12. That is

$$\bar{y}_i = \sum_{t=1}^{T} y_{it}/T \qquad \bar{x}_{ki} = \sum_{t=1}^{T} x_{kit}/T \qquad \bar{e}_i = \sum_{t=1}^{T} e_{it}/T$$

Then we may write

$$\bar{y}_i = \bar{\beta}_1 + \sum_{k=2}^{K} \beta_k \bar{x}_{ki} + \left(\mu_i + \bar{e}_i\right) \qquad i = 1,\dots, N$$

(17B.19)

The variance of the disturbance term $\left(\mu_i + \bar{e}_i\right)$ in equation 17B.19 is

$$\text{var}\left(\mu_i + \bar{e}_i\right) = \sigma_\mu^2 + \frac{\sigma_e^2}{T} = \sigma_1^2/T$$

(17B.20)

where $\sigma_1^2 = T\sigma_\mu^2 + \sigma_e^2$. The errors in equation 17B.19 are uncorrelated, and we may use least squares to estimate the parameters. If we write equation 17B.19 in matrix terms

$$\bar{\mathbf{y}} = \bar{X}\beta + \mathbf{v}$$

(17B.21)

where $\bar{\mathbf{y}}$ is $(N \times 1)$, $\bar{X}$ is $(N \times K)$, and $\mathbf{v}$ is $(N \times 1)$, then the least squares estimator of β is

$$\beta^* = \left(\bar{X}'\bar{X}\right)^{-1}\bar{X}'\bar{\mathbf{y}}$$

(17B.22)

An unbiased estimator of the variance equation 17B.20 is

$$\frac{\hat{\sigma}_1^2}{T} = \frac{\hat{\mathbf{v}}'\hat{\mathbf{v}}}{N - K}$$

(17B.23)

where $\hat{\mathbf{v}} = \bar{\mathbf{y}} - \bar{X}\beta^*$ are the least squares residuals. An unbiased estimator of σ_μ^2 is then

$$\hat{\sigma}_\mu^2 = \frac{\hat{\sigma}_1^2 - \hat{\sigma}_e^2}{T}$$

(17B.24)

Given these estimates of σ_μ^2 and σ_e^2, we can implement the estimated generalized least squares estimator in equation 17B.17. Like many estimated generalized least squares estimation rules, it is possible to obtain the EGLS estimates by transforming the data and applying the usual least squares estimator. The data transformation is described in Judge et al. (1988, p. 483) and in the *Computer Handbook* that accompanies this book.

17B.3   An Example

Let us illustrate the dummy variable and error components models by using the data in Table 17B.1. First, the results of least squares estimation of the dummy variable model given in equation 17B.6a appear in Table 17B.2. We note that the estimated intercept

Table 17B.2 Dummy Variable Results

Variable	Parameter Estimate	Standard Error	t-Statistic
D_1	−69.14	49.68	−1.39
D_2	100.86	24.91	4.05
D_3	−235.12	24.42	−9.63
D_4	−27.63	14.07	−1.96
D_5	−115.32	14.16	−8.14
D_6	−23.07	12.66	−1.82
D_7	−66.68	12.84	−5.19
D_8	−57.36	13.99	−4.10
D_9	−87.28	12.89	−6.77
D_{10}	−6.55	11.82	−0.55
F	0.11	0.01	9.26
C	0.31	0.02	17.88

parameters of the $N = 10$ firms, given by the coefficients of the dummy variables D_{ji} vary substantially. The hypothesis 17B.10 is tested by computing the test statistic

$$u = \frac{\left(\text{SSE}_R - \text{SSE}_U\right)/J}{\text{SSE}_U /\left(NT - N - K'\right)}$$

$$= \frac{(1749127 - 522855)/9}{522855/(200 - 10 - 2)}$$

$$= 48.99$$

If the null hypothesis is true, then $u \sim F_{9,\,188}$. The value of the test statistic $u = 48.99$ yields a p-value of less than .0001, and we reject the null hypothesis that the intercept parameters for all firms are equal. We note, for future reference, that the estimated error variance is

$$\hat{\sigma}_e^2 = \frac{\hat{e}'\hat{e}}{NT - N - K'} = \frac{522855}{188} = 2781.14$$

To estimate the error components model, we must obtain the estimate of σ_μ^2 given in equation 17B.24. To do so we must first obtain the least squares estimates of the "averaged model" given in equation 17B.21. Doing so, and calculating the sum of squared errors, we estimate that

$$\hat{\sigma}_1^2 = \frac{T(\hat{v}'\hat{v})}{N - K} = 144365$$

Then the estimate of σ_μ^2 is

$$\hat{\sigma}_\mu^2 = \frac{\hat{\sigma}_1^2 - \hat{\sigma}_e^2}{T}$$

$$= \frac{144365 - 2781}{20} = 7079$$

The corresponding estimated error components model using equation 17B.16 is

$$\hat{I} = -57.87 \quad +0.11v \quad +0.31k$$
$$(28.65) \quad (.01) \quad (.02) \quad se$$
$$(-2.02) \quad (10.52) \quad (18.09) \quad t$$

It is interesting to note that in this example the effects of firm value (v) and capital stock (k) increases are virtually identical for the dummy variable and error components models.

Part VI

Specifying and Estimating Economic and Statistical Models with Feedback Mechanisms

Much of the economic data that we observe comes from an economic system that can be described by a set of economic relations that are stochastic (random), dynamic, and simultaneous. In the previous chapters we have focused on the random nature of economic relations. In Part VI we consider the simultaneous and interdependent nature of economic variables and the implications this has for data generation, estimation and inference. To introduce the simultaneous, interdependent data-generation characteristic into our economic and statistical models, and the corresponding estimation and inference procedures, we will need several new words and concepts. Therefore, let us use this part introduction to get started along this road.

VI.1   Examples of Endogenous Economic Variables

VI.1.1   A Demand and Supply Model

In the previous chapters we have viewed, from economic and statistical standpoints, individual or sets of relations where the outcome value of an observable economic variable is a function of (determined-explained by) other economic variables. For a particular economic relationship we viewed changes in the right-hand-side variables X as affecting the outcome for the left-hand-side variable y. Thus, for example, in a demand and supply context, price and other variables were viewed as having an impact on the quantity demanded and on the quantity supplied. We did not consider, however, the possibility of a reverse impact, or feedback, where the quantity supplied or demanded had an impact on price, that is, that price and quantity were jointly or interdependently determined outcome variables.

In this context we have not considered, as you did in an introductory economics course, a single market where the outcomes for the economic variables, price and quantity, are determined by the following *system* of demand and supply functions:

$$y_t^d = f_1(p_t)$$
$$y_t^s = f_2(p_t)$$
(VI.1.1)

In this system, equilibrium for the market is defined by a price p_t that makes $y_t^s = y_t^d = y_t$, the equilibrium quantity. In this system, y_t^d is the quantity demanded, y_t^s is the quantity supplied, and p_t is the price observed in time period t. Viewed as a *system*, this set of demand and supply equations reflects a situation where the observables y_t^d, , and p_t are all jointly and interdependently determined. That is, the economic variables in the system are simultaneously determined, and there is an equilibrating feedback mechanism operating on price and quantity to determine the equilibrium outcomes for the price and quantity variables. Both the demand and supply equations are needed to define the equilibrium values that are the observed values of the economic variables. *Thus each economic variable is determined not by a single supply or demand equation, but simultaneously by the complete system.* Considering only the demand equation or the supply equation in isolation and not taking into account the equilibrium condition ignores a great deal of information about how the outcome values of the economic variables y and p are determined.

To illustrate what we mean by "instantaneous feedback," suppose that, for some external reason, there was an increase in demand such that $y_t^d > y_t^s$ at the existing price level. This inequality would bring forth an increase in price that would then decrease y_t^d and increase y_t^s until such time as the system is in equilibrium, $y_t^d = y_t^s$. In fact, it is assumed that we are always in equilibrium, and hence these adjustments are called *feedback* because a change in quantity changes price, which then feeds back to quantity and then to price, and so on.

To recognize the random and interdependent nature of the data-generating process for quantity and price, and to provide a probability approach to economic systems, a statistical model for the system VI.1.1 may be specified as

$$y_t^d = f(p_t) + e_{t1} = \beta_{11} + \beta_{12}p_t + e_{t1}$$
$$y_t^s = f(p_t) + e_{t2} = \beta_{21} + \beta_{22}p_t + e_{t2}$$
(VI.1.2)

where e_{t1} and e_{t2} are random equation errors. To make clear the idea of the simultaneous and interdependent nature of the variables in the economic and statistical models, let us make use of an "influence diagram", which is a graphical representation of relationships between relevant random quantities. *In the previous chapters we have modeled demand and supply relations separately as follows:*

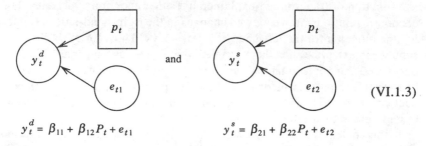

and   (VI.1.3)

$$y_t^d = \beta_{11} + \beta_{12}P_t + e_{t1} \qquad\qquad y_t^s = \beta_{21} + \beta_{22}P_t + e_{t2}$$

where circled nodes denote random quantities, square nodes represent fixed or non-random quantities, and the arrows denote the direction of presumed dependence. Note that in equation VI.1.3 we assumed that the equation errors e_{ti} and p_t are statistically independent.

Alternatively, we now recognize that to determine the observed equilibrium values $y_t^d = y_t^s = y_t$ and p_t, an economic model involving a system of demand and supply relations such as equation VI.1.2 is needed. The graphical representation of this equilibrium system, where y and p are jointly determined, appears as

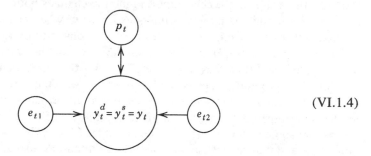

(VI.1.4)

Since the error term e_{t1} in the demand function equation VI.2 indicates a shift in the demand function, a shift in the demand function changes both y_t and p_t. Thus the right-hand-side variables p_t and e_{t1} in equation VI.1.2 are correlated. Consequently, in the influence diagram VI.1.4 both y_t and p_t are random quantities, and an instantaneous feedback mechanism between the two random quantities is implied. Because of the joint determination of y_t and p_t and thus e_{t1} and e_{t2}, the *random variables e_{t1} and p_t are no longer uncorrelated*. This violates the regressor-error *independence assumption* we have been using and raises the question as to whether the least squares procedure, applied directly to either the demand or supply function, is an appropriate (for example, unbiased or consistent) estimator for the unknown parameters (see Section 14.2 of Chapter 14).

VI.1.2   An Aggregate Economic Model

To take this matter of jointly determined variables a bit further, let's move to the area of aggregative economics and consider the simple Keynesian model

$$c_t = f(y_t)$$
$$y_t = c_t + i_t$$

(VI.1.5)

with a statistical model counterpart

$$c_t = f(y_t) + e_t = \beta + \gamma y_t + e_t$$
$$y_t = c_t + i_t$$

(VI.1.6)

where, in time period t, c_t is consumption, y_t is income, i_t is investment, and e_t is a random equation error. In this model c_t and y_t are jointly and interdependently determined variables and both equations are necessary to describe how the outcome values are determined. The influence diagram for this system of relations is as follows:

$$e_t \longrightarrow c_t \longleftrightarrow y_t \longleftarrow i_t$$

(VI.1.7)

In this simple but elegant model, the random quantities c_t *and y_t are jointly and inter-dependently determined*, and i_t is a variable that affects c_t and y_t but is not reciprocally affected. The jointly determined random quantities such as c_t and y_t we will call *endogenous* variables. Quantities such as i_t, whose values are determined outside the system and independently of c_t, y_t and e_t, we will call *exogenous* variables. The random shock or disturbance quantity e_t we will call a *random error* variable. As in the demand and supply model, in equation VI.1.6 e_t represents shifts in the consumption function and a shift in the consumption function changes both c_t and y_t. Thus, y_t *and* e_t *are correlated* and again there is the question as to whether the least squares rule is applicable for estimating the parameters of the consumption function.

These economic models envision economic data that are generated from a simultaneous system and thus they have characteristics that are much different from those considered in previous chapters. To be consistent with the way the data are generated, the statistical models imply an experimental design consistent with an interdependent, jointly determined data-generation process for some of the economic variables. This means that some of the right-hand-side variables may not be independent of the equation errors and thus the statistical models and estimation rules that we have used in the past may be inadequate or inappropriate for a range of economic models. Given this setting, in the two chapters ahead, we specify a statistical model consistent with the stochastic and simultaneous nature of many economic models and sets of economic data, and we demonstrate corresponding estimation rules that have good sampling properties. We also investigate how one can make use of the corresponding system of relation's econometric results for economic policy and forecasting purposes.

Chapter 18

An Introduction to Simultaneous Equation Econometric Models

New Key Words and Concepts

Instantaneous Feedback Mechanism	Endogenous Variable
Exogenous Variable	System of Economic Relations
Structural Equations	Structural Parameters
Least Squares Bias	Identification,
Reduced Form Equations	Consistent Estimator
Consistent Estimator	Indirect Least Squares Estimator
Instrumental Variable Estimator	Order Condition of Identification

18.1 A Macro Econometric Model

To give a taste of the economic and statistical ingredients of simultaneous equation models discussed in the introduction to Part VI, let us continue to consider the simple macroeconomic model VI.1.5 and pursue the econometric ingredients of the determinants of aggregate equilibrium income. If your knowledge of this area of aggregative economics is a bit incomplete, you may want to refer to an introductory macroeconomics book.

18.1.1 The Economic Model

In the simple income–consumption macroeconomic model introduced in the introduction to Part VI we assume, among other things, that

(*i*) consumption expenditures c_t are a stable function of income y_t,

(*ii*) aggregate expenditures (which is equal to income y_t) consists of the two components, consumption c_t and investment i_t, with investment taken to include both autonomous planned investment and total government expenditures on goods and services, and

(*iii*) investment expenditures i_t are assumed to be independent of income levels y_t.

These assumptions may be translated into the following simple macro model:

$$c_t = \beta + \gamma y_t \tag{18.1.1a}$$

$$y_t = c_t + i_t \tag{18.1.1b}$$

In this simple equilibrium model we visualize income y and consumption c to be jointly determined *within* the system, and we designate c_t and y_t as *endogenous* (jointly determined) variables. There is a feedback mechanism between the endogenous variables because c "depends on" y through equation 18.1.1a and y "depends on" c through equation 18.1.1b. In contrast, we visualize i (planned investment and government expenditures) as being an *exogenous* variable whose values are determined by forces outside of our simple macroeconomic system equation 18.1.1. The equilibrium values of c and y are determined by simultaneously solving equtaions 18.1.1, as we do later in equation 18.1.3.

In the economic model 18.1.1, there are two unknown parameters β and γ. The parameter β is consumption that occurs independent of income. The particularly interesting parameter is γ, the marginal propensity to consume. This coefficient is very important if we want to consider the multiplier effect on income, following an increase in planned investment or government expenditures. In the economic model, equation 18.1.1a is considered a *behavioral equation* and equation 18.1.1b is an *identity*. An identity in economic terms is a economic relation with no unknown parameters and no error term. Given this economic model, which involves a system of two equations that contain two endogenous variables and one exogenous variable, the next task is to consider an appropriate corresponding statistical model.

18.1.2   The Statistical Model

To convert the economic model 18.1.1 to a statistical model, we need to recognize that the behavioral relation is an incomplete specification and hence include a random unknown equation error or disturbance e. Recognizing this and letting t represent the observed values of the economic variables in time period t, we may rewrite the economic model and specify the sampling process described by the statistical model as

$$c_t = \beta + \gamma y_t + e_t \qquad (18.1.2a)$$

$$y_t = c_t + i_t \qquad (18.1.2b)$$

and

$$e_t \sim N\!\left(0, \sigma^2\right) \qquad (18.1.2c)$$

where e_t is an independent unobserved normal random variable with mean zero and variance σ^2. The random quantity e_t is, in line with influence diagram VI.1.7, uncorrelated with i_t but not uncorrelated with c_t and y_t. In the context of equation 18.1.2, imagine a positive outcome for the random error e_t and consider the repercussions back through the system. A positive outcome for e_t causes direct change in c_t, from equation 18.1.2a, and then a change in y_t, from equation 18.1.2b. Therefore, every change in e_t will cause a change in y_t. Thus, the random variables e_t and y_t are positively correlated. *Consequently, for equation 18.1.2a the usual assumption, that the right-hand-side variable y_t is fixed and uncorrelated with e_t, no longer holds true.*

18.1.3   Estimating the Marginal Propensity to Consume

To grasp the estimation implications of y_t and e_t being correlated let us simplify statistical model 18.1.2 and assume in equation 18.1.2a that $\beta = 0$ and that γ is the only unknown parameter in the system. Therefore, the revised statistical model is

$$c_t = \gamma y_t + e_t \qquad (18.1.3a)$$

$$y_t = c_t + i_t \qquad (18.1.3b)$$

18.1.3a A Least Squares Estimator   Looking at the system 18.1.3, your first impulse may be to consider *only* equation 18.1.3a and to ignore the simultaneous data-generation process. If we go in this direction and apply the least squares rule to estimate γ in equation 18.1.3a, the result is

$$
\hat{\gamma} = \frac{\Sigma c_t y_t}{\Sigma y_t^2}
$$

$$
= \frac{\Sigma(\gamma y_t + e_t)y_t}{\Sigma y_t^2} \qquad \text{(substituting for } c_t\text{)}
$$

$$
= \gamma + \frac{\Sigma e_t y_t}{\Sigma y_t^2} \tag{18.1.4}
$$

To gauge the sampling properties of the direct least squares estimator of γ, one approach is to take the expectations of both sides of equation 18.1.4. However, as we learned in Section 14.1 of Chapter 14, when e_t and y_t are correlated random variables, it is not very useful to take expectations of both sides of equation 18.1.4. Evaluation of $E[\Sigma y_t e_t / \Sigma y_t^2]$ is a difficult task. The difficulty arises because

$$
E\left[\frac{\Sigma y_t e_t}{\Sigma y_t^2}\right] \neq \frac{E[\Sigma y_t e_t]}{E[y_t^2]} \tag{18.1.5}
$$

We could separately evaluate the expectations $E[\Sigma y_t e_t]$ and $E[y_t^2]$ but, because of the inequality in equation 18.1.5, such an evaluation would not give us the required information.

As we did in Chapter 14, we overcome this problem by considering instead the *probability limit* of $\Sigma y_t e_t / \Sigma y_t^2$. In Section 14.1 of Chapter 14, we defined a *consistent estimator* in the following way. Suppose that $\hat{\theta}$ is an estimator for the unknown parameter θ, and let $P(|\hat{\theta} - \theta| > \varepsilon)$ be the probability that the estimator $\hat{\theta}$ yields an estimate that differs from θ by more than an arbitrarily small amount ε. The estimator $\hat{\theta}$ is said to be a consistent estimator for θ if this probability goes to zero as $T \to \infty$. We also say that $\hat{\theta}$ converges in probability to θ or that the *probability limit* of $\hat{\theta}$ is θ. The latter we write as

$$
\text{plim}\left(\hat{\theta}\right) = \theta
$$

If an estimator is *not consistent*, then it converges in probability to something other than the corresponding unknown parameter. Supposing $\hat{\gamma}$ is the estimator, then $\text{plim}(\hat{\gamma}) - \gamma$ reflects its *inconsistency*. In the simultaneous equation framework we often talk of the difference $\text{plim}(\hat{\gamma}) - \gamma$ as the simultaneous equation or least squares bias from direct application of least squares to a structural equation. Strictly speaking, "inconsistency" is not the same thing as "large sample bias." See Judge et al. (1985, Chapter 5) for details. However, for our purposes it is convenient to continue to use what is common terminology, and therefore we will refer to the inconsistency as large sample bias.

How then, do we use equation 18.1.4 to evaluate the least squares bias of $\hat{\gamma}$? We begin by taking probability limits. That is,

$$
\text{plim}\left(\hat{\gamma}\right) = \gamma + \frac{\text{plim}\left(\Sigma y_t e_t / T\right)}{\text{plim}\left(\Sigma y_t^2 / T\right)} \tag{18.1.6}
$$

On the right-hand side of this equation we have written the probability limit of a ratio as the ratio of the probability limits. This is a legitimate operation, unlike the problem we had with taking expectations in equation 18.1.5. We have also included the sample size T in the numerator and denominator in equation 18.1.6. The reason for doing so will become clear shortly. Let us consider each probability limit separately. First, if we solve for y_t in equation 18.1.3 we have

$$y_t = \frac{1}{1-\gamma} i_t + \frac{1}{1-\gamma} e_t$$

Consequently,

$$\text{plim}\left(\frac{\Sigma y_t e_t}{T}\right) = \text{plim}\left(\frac{\Sigma\left[(1-\gamma)^{-1} i_t + (1-\gamma)^{-1} e_t\right] e_t}{T}\right)$$

$$= (1-\gamma)^{-1}\left[\text{plim}\left(\frac{\Sigma i_t e_t}{T}\right) + \text{plim}\left(\frac{\Sigma e_t^2}{T}\right)\right]$$

Now $\Sigma i_t e_t / T$ is a consistent estimator of the covariance between i_t and e_t. Since i_t is an exogenous variable, it is assumed uncorrelated with e_t, and their covariance is zero. Thus, $\Sigma i_t e_t / T$ is a consistent estimator of zero; its probability limit is zero. Similarly, $\Sigma e_t^2 / T$ is a consistent estimator of σ_e^2 or, in other words, $\text{plim}(\Sigma e_t^2 / T) = \sigma_e^2$. Hence, we can write

$$\text{plim}\left(\frac{\Sigma y_t e_t}{T}\right) = (1-\gamma)^{-1} \sigma_e^2 \qquad (18.1.7)$$

For the denominator in equation 18.1.6, it is sufficient to note that, under usual assumptions, the average of the squares of the ys converges in probability to some positive quantity that we denote by m_{yy}. Thus, we write

$$\text{plim}\left(\frac{\Sigma y_t^2}{T}\right) = m_{yy} \qquad (18.1.8)$$

Substituting equations 18.1.7 and 18.1.8 into equation 18.1.6 we have

$$\text{plim}\,\hat{\gamma} = \gamma + \frac{(1-\gamma)^{-1} \sigma_e^2}{m_{yy}} > \gamma \qquad (18.1.9)$$

Since the second term on the right-hand side of the equality is not equal to zero, the least squares estimator applied directly to equation 18.1.3a is not consistent. Given that $0 \le \gamma < 1$, the effect of y_t on c_t is overstated when the least squares estimator is used for γ, the marginal propensity to consume. The size of the bias will vary from one empirical situation to another. *Let us note that this bias problem is a general one that we will encounter in simultaneous equation models whenever one or more endogenous variables occurs on the right-hand side of an equation in a statistical model.* Also you may wish to review the random regressor–least squares bias problem that was discussed in Section 14.2 of Chapter 14.

18.1.4 Respecifying the Statistical Model

Since it is inappropriate to use our old friend the least squares estimator to estimate the unknowns in the consumption function 18.1.2a, let us consider another approach. In this simultaneous equations system, there are two equations and two endogenous variables. Therefore, we can use the two equations to solve for the equilibrium quantities c_t and y_t. Returning to the model where $\beta \neq 0$, if we substitute the equilibrium condition $y_t = c_t + i_t$ into the consumption function, we may rewrite the statistical model as

$$c_t = \beta + \gamma\left(c_t + i_t\right) + e_t$$

Solving for c_t in terms of i_t, we have

$$c_t = \frac{\beta}{1-\gamma} + \frac{\gamma}{1-\gamma}i_t + \frac{1}{1-\gamma}e_t$$
$$= \pi_{10} + \pi_{11}i_t + v_t \tag{18.1.10a}$$

where

$$\pi_{10} = \frac{\beta}{1-\gamma} \qquad \pi_{11} = \frac{\gamma}{1-\gamma} \qquad \text{and} \qquad v_t = \frac{1}{1-\gamma}e_t \sim N\left(0, \frac{\sigma^2}{\left(1-\gamma\right)^2}\right)$$
$$\tag{18.1.10b}$$

Alternatively, if we substitute for c_t into equation 18.1.2b, we have

$$y_t = \beta + \gamma y_t + e_t + i_t$$

Solving this equation for y_t yields

$$y_t = \frac{\beta}{1-\gamma} + \frac{1}{1-\gamma}i_t + \frac{1}{1-\gamma}e_t$$
$$= \pi_{20} + \pi_{21}i_t + v_t \tag{18.1.10c}$$

where

$$\pi_{20} = \frac{\beta}{1-\gamma} \qquad \pi_{21} = \frac{1}{1-\gamma} \qquad \text{and} \qquad v_t = \frac{1}{1-\gamma}e_t \sim N\left(0, \sigma^2/\left(1-\gamma\right)^2\right)$$
$$\tag{18.1.10d}$$

The specification equation 18.1.10, which is an equivalent probability model, yields an alternative statistical model called the *reduced form* statistical model. In the reduced form model, the *jointly determined random variables* c_t and y_t are expressed as linear functions of the exogenous variable i_t and a random error $v_t = \left(1/\left(1-\gamma\right)\right)e_t$, where $v_t \sim N\left(0, \sigma^2/\left(1-\gamma\right)^2\right)$. Only the exogenous variable i_t appears on the right-hand side of the equation.

For the endogenous variables c_t and y_t this means that

$$c_t \sim N\left(\frac{\beta}{1-\gamma} + \frac{\gamma}{1-\gamma}i_t, \left(\frac{\sigma^2}{\left(1-\gamma\right)^2}\right)\right) \tag{18.1.11a}$$

and

$$y_t \sim N\left(\frac{\beta}{1-\gamma} + \frac{1}{1-\gamma}i_t, \left(\frac{\sigma^2}{\left(1-\gamma\right)^2}\right)\right) \tag{18.1.11b}$$

The covariances between c_t and e_t and y_t and e_t are

$$E\left[(c_t - E[c_t])e_t\right] = \frac{\gamma}{1-\gamma} E[e_t^2] = \frac{\gamma}{1-\gamma} \sigma_e^2 \tag{18.1.11c}$$

$$E\left[(y_t - E[y_t])e_t\right] = \frac{1}{1-\gamma} E[e_t^2] = \frac{1}{1-\gamma} \sigma_e^2 \tag{18.1.11d}$$

Equations 18.1.10 and 18.1.11 make clear the dependence of both c_t and y_t on the random error e_t. When we have a system of equations involving jointly determined economic variables, the foregoing equations show that there are two ways to specify the statistical model. We will call equation 18.1.2 the *statistical model for the structural equations,* and β and γ we call structural parameters. Alternatively, we will denote equations 18.1.10 and 18.1.11 as the *statistical model for the reduced form equations* and the πs as the reduced form parameters. It should be clear from equations 18.1.10b and 18.1.10d that the reduced form πs are functions of the structural parameters.

In this reduced form model, the reduced form parameters π show the effect on the equilibrium values of c and y from a change in i after all feedbacks have taken place. In this respect $\pi_{21} = 1/(1 - \gamma)$ is the investment multiplier effect on y and $\pi_{11} = \gamma/(1 - \gamma)$ is the multiplier effect on c from a change in i.

In describing the economic and statistical models we have added to our vocabulary the terms endogenous (determined inside the system) variables, exogenous (determined outside the system) variables, disturbances or shocks (equation errors), structural parameters (β, γ), reduced form equations (18.1.10 and 18.1.11), and reduced form parameters (πs).

18.1.5   Estimation of the Reduced Form Parameters

Given the reduced form statistical model that describes the sampling process by which the economic variables c_t and y_t are generated, the next question we face is how to use economic data to estimate the unknown reduced form parameters, the π_{ij}.

In pursuing this estimation goal consider the reduced form statistical model 18.1.10:

$$c_t = \left(\frac{\beta}{1-\gamma}\right) + \left(\frac{\gamma}{1-\gamma}\right)i_t + \left(\frac{1}{1-\gamma}\right)e_t = \pi_{10} + \pi_{11}i_t + v_t \tag{18.1.12a}$$

$$y_t = \left(\frac{\beta}{1-\gamma}\right) + \left(\frac{1}{1-\gamma}\right)i_t + \left(\frac{1}{1-\gamma}\right)e_t = \pi_{20} + \pi_{21}i_t + v_t \tag{18.1.12b}$$

where $(1 - \gamma)^{-1}e_t = v_t \sim N(0, \sigma^2/(1 - \gamma)^2)$. Since investment i_t is exogenous to the system, it is not correlated with the error e_t and we can write $E[i_t e_t] = 0$. Therefore, $E[i_t e_t] = 0$, and assuming i_t is nonstochastic, the statistical models 18.1.12 satisfy all of the assumptions necessary for the least squares estimators of π_{10} and π_{11}, π_{20} and π_{21} to be best (minimum variance) unbiased. If investment i_t is treated as stochastic, the least squares estimator is still consistent. Consequently, we may proceed to use the least squares estimator and estimate the unknown reduced form parameters.

The estimated reduced form equations provide estimates (see equation 18.1.12) of the multipliers for c and y for changes in i. Perhaps at this point we should reiterate the distinction between a structural econometric model and its corresponding reduced form. The structural model represents the economist's conception of how current values of endogenous economic variables are related to other endogenous, exogenous, and random error variables, and thus it describes how a particular reduced form came about. Many different structural models can give rise to the same reduced form. However, when a structural model implies certain restrictions on the reduced form, distinction between the structural models can be made and economic theory may be tested.

18.1.6   An Indirect Least Squares Estimator

Since we learned in Section 18.1.3 that it is not appropriate to estimate β and γ by direct least squares, we need to search for another rule that has "good" sampling properties. In this regard remember in the reduced form equations that the reduced form parameters, the πs, are functions of β and γ. In this model, if we *knew* the πs we could solve for the structural parameters γ and β in the following way:

$$\hat{\pi}_{11} / \hat{\pi}_{21} = \left(\frac{\tilde{\gamma}}{1-\tilde{\gamma}} \right) \Big/ \left(\frac{1}{1-\tilde{\gamma}} \right) = \tilde{\gamma} \qquad (18.1.13a)$$

and

$$\pi_{20} / \pi_{21} = \left(\frac{\beta}{1-\gamma} \right) \Big/ \left(\frac{1}{1-\gamma} \right) = \beta \qquad (18.1.13b)$$

Unfortunately, the πs are unknown and we cannot solve for γ and β. However, we know that, if the least squares estimator is used with equation 18.1.12, a best unbiased estimator of the πs results. Therefore, one possibility is to use the least squares estimates for the πs to obtain the following estimates for γ and β:

$$\hat{\pi}_{11} / \hat{\pi}_{21} = \left(\frac{\tilde{\gamma}}{1-\tilde{\gamma}} \right) \Big/ \left(\frac{1}{1-\tilde{\gamma}} \right) = \tilde{\gamma} \qquad (18.1.14a)$$

and

$$\hat{\pi}_{20} / \hat{\pi}_{21} = \left(\frac{\tilde{\beta}}{1-\tilde{\gamma}} \right) \Big/ \left(\frac{1}{1-\tilde{\gamma}} \right) = \tilde{\beta} \qquad (18.1.14b)$$

These rules (equations 18.1.14a and 18.1.14b) are known as *indirect least squares estimators* of β and γ. They are indirect estimators in the sense that they are obtained from the estimators of the reduced form parameters. The estimators $\tilde{\beta}$ and $\tilde{\gamma}$ are distributed as the ratio of two normal (but not independent) random variables, and their distribution, even for this simple case, is difficult to derive. However, it is possible, in the spirit of Chapter 14, to show that the estimators are consistent and that each has a large sample approximate normal distribution. Recall that a consistent estimator has an increasingly large probability of being close to the true parameter value as the sample size $T \to \infty$. Thus, in large samples, consistent estimators yield estimates that are likely to be near the true parameter values. You should note the indirect least squares estimator 18.1.14 is not unbiased, and it is not a linear function of the endogenous variables. However, *no unbiased estimator of β and γ exists*, and by going this route we have at least obtained a consistent estimator of the structural parameters.

For the macroeconomic model 18.1.2, we have just enough information to let us go from an estimate of the reduced form parameters back to an estimate of the structural parameters. If we had treated planned investment and government expenditures as two *separate* exogenous variables, i_{1t} and i_{2t}, as we do in Exercise 18.3, then we would not have been able, by the indirect least squares route, to obtain *unique* estimates of β and

γ. This creates a problem of how to use the information from both i_{1t} and i_{2t} and we return to this topic later in this chapter and in Chapter 19.

18.1.7   Some Empirical Estimates

Now that we have some of the economic and statistical theory outlined, let us see what this translates to in terms of estimates for the 1965–1986 sample of data for consumption, income, and investment given in Table 18.1.

18.1.7a Indirect Least Squares   If we make use of the sample of data in Table 18.1, the least squares estimates of the reduced form equations 18.1.12 are

Table 18.1 Consumption, Income, and Investment and Government Expenditures, 1955–1986, in Billions of 1982 Dollars

	c Consumption Expenditures	y Disposable Personal Income	i Investment and Government Expenditures
1955	873.8	944.5	70.70
1956	899.8	989.4	89.60
1957	919.7	1,012.1	92.40
1958	932.9	1,028.8	95.90
1959	979.4	1,067.2	87.80
1960	1,005.1	1,091.1	86.00
1961	1,025.2	1,123.2	98.00
1962	1,069.0	1,170.2	101.20
1963	1,108.4	1,207.3	98.90
1964	1,170.6	1,291.0	120.40
1965	1,236.4	1,365.7	129.30
1966	1,298.9	1,431.3	132.40
1967	1,337.7	1,493.2	155.50
1968	1,405.9	1,551.3	145.40
1969	1,456.7	1,599.8	143.10
1970	1,492.0	1,668.1	176.10
1971	1,538.8	1,728.4	189.60
1972	1,621.9	1,797.4	175.50
1973	1,689.6	1,916.3	226.70
1974	1,674.0	1,896.6	222.60
1975	1,711.9	1,931.7	219.80
1976	1,803.0	2,001.0	198.00
1977	1,883.8	2,066.6	182.80
1978	1,961.0	2,167.4	206.40
1979	2,004.4	2,212.6	208.20
1980	2,000.4	2,214.3	213.90
1981	2,024.2	2,248.6	224.40
1982	2,050.7	2,261.5	210.80
1983	2,146.0	2,331.9	185.90
1984	2,246.3	2,470.6	224.30
1985	2,324.5	2,528.0	203.50
1986	2,418.6	2,603.7	185.10

Source: Economic Report of the President, 1987.

$$\hat{c}_t = \hat{\pi}_{10} + \hat{\pi}_{11}i_t$$
$$= 394.52 + 7.368i_t$$

$$(352.70)\ (1.84) \qquad \text{s.e.}$$

$$(1.12) \quad (4.00) \qquad t \qquad\qquad (18.1.15a)$$

and

$$\hat{y}_t = \hat{\pi}_{20} + \hat{\pi}_{21}i_t$$
$$= 394.52 + 8.368i_t$$

$$(352.70)\ (1.84) \qquad \text{s.e.}$$

$$(1.12) \quad (4.54) \qquad t \qquad\qquad (18.1.15b)$$

where the numbers in parentheses are standard errors and t-values, respectively. From equation 18.1.12 we know that

$$\pi_{10} = \pi_{20} = \left(\frac{\beta}{1-\gamma}\right) \qquad \pi_{11} = \left(\frac{\gamma}{1-\gamma}\right) \qquad \pi_{21} = \left(\frac{1}{1-\gamma}\right)$$

and from equation 18.1.15

$$\hat{\pi}_{10} = 394.52 \qquad\qquad \hat{\pi}_{11} = 7.368 \qquad\qquad \hat{\pi}_{21} = 8.368$$

Therefore, if we use these estimated reduced form coefficients and the indirect least squares rule 18.1.14, we have the result that

$$\tilde{\gamma} = \hat{\pi}_{11} / \hat{\pi}_{21} = 0.8805 \qquad\qquad (18.1.16a)$$

and

$$\tilde{\beta} = \hat{\pi}_{10} / \hat{\pi}_{21} = 47.144 \qquad\qquad (18.1.16b)$$

Thus the estimated marginal propensity to consume is $\tilde{\gamma} = 0.88$ and the corresponding estimated multiplier is $\tilde{\lambda} = 1/(1 - .8805) = 8.368$. This estimated value of λ suggests the impact on equilibrium income of a one-unit increase in investment. Note that the multiplier λ is equal to the reduced form coefficient π_{21}.

At this point let us review the indirect least squares approach.

1. We first established a relationship between the structural and reduced form equations and parameters.
2. We then estimated the reduced form parameters using the least squares estimation rule.
3. We then derived estimates of the structural parameters from the estimated reduced form parameters.
4. We noted that while the *direct* least squares estimator used to estimate β and γ was biased and inconsistent, the *indirect* least squares estimator, using the estimated reduced form parameters, had the statistical property of consistency.

18.1.7b Direct Least Squares Estimates

What if we had not written equation 18.1.2a or 18.1.2b as a system of equations but, instead, had focused only on the consumption relation:

$$c_t = \beta + \gamma y_t + e_t \qquad\qquad (18.1.2a)$$

Under this scenario it might seem natural to use the least squares rule to estimate β and γ. If we had followed this route, the least squares estimates of β and γ are

$$c_t = -69.090 + 0.939 y_t \qquad (18.1.17)$$

Using the *biased* least squares estimator, our estimate of γ, the marginal propensity to consume, is .939 and the corresponding estimated income multiplier $\hat{\lambda} = 1/(1 - \hat{\gamma}) = 16.39$. Note that this is a much higher estimate of λ than we obtained with the consistent estimator in equation 18.1.16a. Also note the negative intercept estimate of β, which suggests that the estimate of γ may be overstated.

A graph (Figure 18.1) may help to visualize how this result may happen. Let c_1, c_2 and c_3 represent three levels of the consumption function consistent with three error outcomes e_t in equation 18.1.2a and let y_1, y_2, and y_3 represent three levels of the income relations ($y - i = c$), for three levels of investment i_1, i_2, i_3. If all observations fall within these levels, the outcome data that would result from the equilibrium values of the system would be contained within and around the parallelogram $abd f$. The estimates of β and γ that will result when, for example, a least squares line is fitted through the equilibrium points a, h, and d will overstate the magnitude of γ and understate β. The smaller the fluctuation in investment, the more the parallelogram is tilted in a counterclockwise direction and the more we would tend to incorrectly estimate γ, the marginal propensity to consume. From a policy standpoint, this would mean that we would also overstate the income multiplier $1/(1 - \gamma)$, and therefore the economic policy prescriptions may be too timid.

18.1.8 Summary

In this section we formulated economic and statistical models that are consistent with the simultaneous-interdependent way that we visualize how many samples of economic data are generated. We then investigated estimation rules for the structural and reduced form parameters and found that there was no way to obtain an unbiased rule for the structural parameters β and γ. However, for the reduced form parameters π, the least squares rule was unbiased. Since the structural parameters are functions of the reduced form parameters, for the aggregate consumption model it was possible to use the estimated πs to devise an estimator of the structural parameters that had the statistical property of consistency. There are some similarities between the model and estimator considered here and that considered in Section 14.4 of Chapter 14. With the consump-

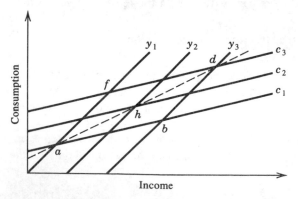

Figure 18.1 Hypothetical representation of the equilibrium c_t and y_t in a simple Keynesian model.

tion function model in Chapter 14, the correlation between y_t and e_t was a consequence of measurement error in y_t, and an instrumental variable was used to obtain a consistent estimator. In the current chapter the correlation between y_t and e_t is a consequence of the endogenous nature of y_t, and indirect least squares was suggested for obtaining a consistent estimator. Later we see that indirect least squares is in fact a type of instrumental variable estimator.

To tie down a little more firmly some of the ideas associated with economic and statistical models when an instantaneous feedback mechanism is working, let us consider another economic and statistical model. Investigating how we might cope with the estimation and inference problems for this model will lead to more new concepts and additional implications for the specification and analysis of simultaneous equations models.

18.2   Specifying and Estimating Models Involving Equilibrium Prices and Quantities

In competitive equilibrium theory, commodity prices and quantities are viewed as determined by sets of demand and supply relations. For example, in a partial equilibrium situation involving a single commodity, we visualize the quantity demanded q_t^d, the quantity supplied q_t^s, and price p_t as being determined by a demand relation, a supply relation, and an equilibrium condition that would close the system, or in some instances a disequilibrium relation that would specify the equilibrium adjustment process. These relations act jointly to simultaneously determine q_t^d, q_t^s, and p_t. To give these propositions content, let us consider some simple economic models that describe this type of interdependent data-generation process.

18.2.1   An Economic Model

As a basis for determining the demand and supply quantities for a particular commodity, the micro theories of the firm and the household might suggest the following system of relations:

demand: $p_t = f\left(q_t^d, ps_t, di_t\right) = \beta_{11} + \gamma_{12} q_t^d + \beta_{12} ps_t + \beta_{13} di_t$

supply: $q_t^s = f\left(p_t, pf_t\right) = \beta_{21} + \gamma_{21} p_t + \beta_{24} pf_t$ (18.2.1)

or given the equilibrium condition that $q_t^d = q_t^s = q_t$

$$p_t = \beta_{11} + \gamma_{12} q_t + \beta_{12} ps_t + \beta_{13} di_t$$
$$q_t = \beta_{21} + \gamma_{21} p_t + \beta_{24} pf_t$$ (18.2.2)

In this system, quantity q_t and price p_t are the jointly determined–endogenous variables, and the price of a substitute good ps_t, disposable income di_t, and the price of a factor of production pf_t are exogenous variables. Thus, the system 18.2.2 visualizes a situation where the equilibrium values of q_t and p_t are determined within the system and the observed values of ps_t, di_t, and pf_t are determined outside of the system. Graphically, we think of p_t and q_t as being determined by the intersection of a demand and supply function. Changes in ps_t or di_t cause shifts in the demand function and changes in pf_t cause shifts in the supply function. Again both equations in equation 18.2.2 are necessary to describe the data-generation process.

Given this economic model that seeks to describe how observed prices and quantities may be generated, let us turn to the corresponding statistical model.

18.2.2 The Statistical Model

The economic model depicting demand and supply as a system of equations defines the sampling process that we use to describe how the economic data were generated. To convert the equilibrium economic model to a statistical model that reflects this underlying data-generation process we need to be specific about *(i)* the classification of the endogenous and exogenous economic variables and the leads or lags that may be involved, *(ii)* the functional or algebraic form of the relations, and *(iii)* the assumptions underlying the equation error processes. To lay the groundwork for this and future simultaneous equation model specifications, let's consider economic model 18.2.2, which, if we add unobservable equation errors is

$$p_t = \beta_{11} + \gamma_{12} q_t + \beta_{12} ps_t + \beta_{13} di_t + e_{1t} \tag{18.2.3a}$$

and

$$q_t = \beta_{21} + \gamma_{21} p_t + \beta_{24} pf_t + e_{2t} \tag{18.2.3b}$$

As mentioned above, q_t and p_t are endogenous (jointly determined) random variables and ps_t, di_t, and pf_t are exogenous (determined outside the system) variables. In terms of an influence diagram, this system may be represented as

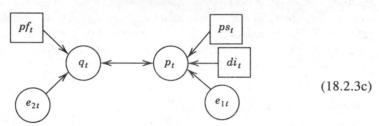

$$(18.2.3c)$$

where the circles represent random quantities, the squares represent conditioning (non-random) quantities determined outside the system (exogenous variables), and the arrows give the presumed direction of dependence.

The unobservable normal random equation errors are assumed to be related across equations and generated as follows:

$$E[e_{it}] = 0 \qquad \text{for } i = 1, 2 \tag{18.2.4a}$$

$$\text{var}(e_{it}) = E[e_{it}^2] = \sigma_{ii} = \sigma_i^2 \qquad \text{for } i = 1, 2 \tag{18.2.4b}$$

and

$$\text{cov}(e_{it}, e_{jt}) = E[e_{it} e_{jt}] = \sigma_{ij} \neq 0 \qquad \text{for } i, j = 1, 2 \tag{18.2.4c}$$

These variances and covariances may be compactly written as

$$\text{cov}\begin{pmatrix} e_{1t} \\ e_{2t} \end{pmatrix} = \begin{bmatrix} \sigma_{11} & \sigma_{12} \\ \sigma_{21} & \sigma_{22} \end{bmatrix} \tag{18.2.4d}$$

where

$$\begin{bmatrix} e_{1t} \\ e_{2t} \end{bmatrix} \sim N\left[\begin{pmatrix} 0 \\ 0 \end{pmatrix}, \begin{pmatrix} \sigma_{11} & \sigma_{12} \\ \sigma_{21} & \sigma_{22} \end{pmatrix} \right] \tag{18.2.4e}$$

As in Chapter 17 when we were working with a set of regression equations, we are assuming that the errors in different equations, e_{1t}, e_{2t}, have different variances and across equations are contemporaneously correlated.

As we learned in Section 18.1.3a, since each of the equations in the statistical model 18.2.3 contains endogenous right-hand-side variables that are correlated with the e_{it}, application of the least squares rule in estimating the βs and γs for each equation leads to a biased estimator. To devise a way around this problem, let us follow our strategy of Sections 18.1.4 and 18.1.6 and respecify (develop the corresponding reduced form) statistical model and consider estimation of the reduced form parameters.

18.2.2a The Reduced Form Statistical Model

In developing another parametric form for the structural equations 18.2.3, we begin by deriving the statistical model for the reduced form equation for p_t. We substitute equation 18.2.3b into equation 18.2.3a and rearrange the terms as follows:

$$p_t = \beta_{11} + \gamma_{12}\left(\beta_{21} + \gamma_{21}p_t + \beta_{24}pf_t + e_{2t}\right) + \beta_{12}ps_t + \beta_{13}di_t + e_{1t}$$

$$\left(1 - \gamma_{12}\gamma_{21}\right)p_t = \beta_{11} + \gamma_{12}\beta_{21} + \gamma_{12}\beta_{24}pf_t + \beta_{12}ps_t + \beta_{13}di_t + \gamma_{12}e_{2t} + e_{1t}$$

$$p_t = \frac{\beta_{11} + \gamma_{12}\beta_{21}}{1 - \gamma_{12}\gamma_{21}} + \frac{\beta_{12}}{1 - \gamma_{12}\gamma_{21}}ps_t + \frac{\beta_{13}}{1 - \gamma_{12}\gamma_{21}}di_t + \frac{\gamma_{12}\beta_{24}}{1 - \gamma_{12}\gamma_{21}}pf_t$$

$$+ \frac{\gamma_{12}e_{2t} + e_{1t}}{1 - \gamma_{12}\gamma_{21}}$$

$$= \pi_{11} + \pi_{12}ps_t + \pi_{13}di_t + \pi_{14}pf_t + v_{1t} \qquad \text{(by rewriting)}$$

(18.2.5a)

where

$$v_{1t} \sim N\!\left(0, \sigma_{v_1}^2\right)$$

Substituting equation 18.2.5a into equation 18.2.3b gives the following reduced form statistical model for q_t:

$$q_t = \beta_{21} + \gamma_{21}\left[\frac{\beta_{11} + \gamma_{12}\beta_{21}}{1 - \gamma_{12}\gamma_{21}} + \frac{\beta_{12}}{1 - \gamma_{12}\gamma_{21}}ps_t + \frac{\beta_{13}}{1 - \gamma_{12}\gamma_{21}}di_t + \frac{\gamma_{12}\beta_{24}}{1 - \gamma_{12}\gamma_{21}}pf_t + \frac{\gamma_{12}e_{2t} + e_{1t}}{1 - \gamma_{12}\gamma_{21}}\right] + \beta_{24}pf_t + e_{2t}$$

$$= \frac{\gamma_{21}\beta_{11} + \beta_{21}}{1 - \gamma_{12}\gamma_{21}} + \frac{\gamma_{21}\beta_{12}}{1 - \gamma_{12}\gamma_{21}}ps_t + \frac{\gamma_{21}\beta_{13}}{1 - \gamma_{12}\gamma_{21}}di_t + \frac{\beta_{24}}{1 - \gamma_{12}\gamma_{21}}pf_t + \frac{\gamma_{21}e_{1t} + e_{2t}}{1 - \gamma_{12}\gamma_{21}}$$

$$= \pi_{21} + \pi_{22}ps_t + \pi_{23}di_t + \pi_{24}pf_t + v_{2t}$$

(18.2.5b)

where

$$v_{2t} \sim N\!\left(0, \sigma_{v_2}^2\right)$$

Consequently, from equation 18.2.5, the reduced form coefficients (πs) in the terms of the structural coefficients (γs and βs) are

$$\pi_{11} = \frac{\beta_{11} + \gamma_{12}\beta_{21}}{1 - \gamma_{12}\gamma_{21}} \qquad \pi_{12} = \frac{\beta_{12}}{1 - \gamma_{12}\gamma_{21}} \qquad \pi_{13} = \frac{\beta_{13}}{1 - \gamma_{12}\gamma_{21}} \qquad \pi_{14} = \frac{\gamma_{12}\beta_{24}}{1 - \gamma_{12}\gamma_{21}}$$

$$\pi_{21} = \frac{\gamma_{21}\beta_{11} + \beta_{21}}{1 - \gamma_{12}\gamma_{21}} \qquad \pi_{22} = \frac{\gamma_{21}\beta_{12}}{1 - \gamma_{12}\gamma_{21}} \qquad \pi_{23} = \frac{\gamma_{21}\beta_{13}}{1 - \gamma_{12}\gamma_{21}} \qquad \pi_{24} = \frac{\beta_{24}}{1 - \gamma_{12}\gamma_{21}}$$

(18.2.6)

and the reduced form equation errors in terms of the structural equation errors are

$$v_{1t} = \frac{e_{1t} + \gamma_{12} e_{2t}}{1 - \gamma_{12} \gamma_{21}} \quad \text{and} \quad v_{2t} = \frac{\gamma_{21} e_{1t} + e_{2t}}{1 - \gamma_{12} \gamma_{21}} \tag{18.2.7}$$

The reduced form model 18.2.5 expresses the stochastic characteristics of the equilibrium values of the endogenous variables q_t and p_t. For example, if we knew the γs and βs in equation 18.2.5 and the σ_{ij} in equation 18.2.4e, we could use the reduced form equations to generate, for the observed values of the exogenous variables, equilibrium outcomes for the random variables q_t and p_t. The instantaneous feedback nature of q_t and p_t are reflected in the πs and the v_ts given in equations 18.2.6 and 18.2.7. The γs and βs describe the usual price and income responses and the πs reflect the basis for reaching equilibrium values of q_t and p_t.

Considering the reduced form equations 18.2.5, note that each equation contains all of the exogenous variables in the complete model. This is a general result, so that having classified the variables in the complete model as endogenous or exogenous, it is possible to write down the reduced form equations in π notation without deriving the relationships between the πs and the βs and γs. That is, we could have written down the equations in expression 18.2.5b without knowledge of the relationships in equation 18.2.6.

18.2.3   Estimation

In the macro model of Section 18.1, we were able to use estimates of the reduced form parameters to obtain an estimate of the structural (marginal propensity to consume) parameter. Since we were able to obtain estimates of the reduced form parameters by using the least squares rule, no new estimation rules were required for this special case of an economic and statistical model. The case for the economic model 18.2.2 and the corresponding statistical model 18.2.3 is different. For example, if we use the reduced form coefficients to derive the structural parameter γ_{21} in the supply equation as a function of the reduced form parameters, we have from equation 18.2.6 the result

$$\gamma_{21} = \frac{\pi_{22}}{\pi_{12}} \quad \text{and} \quad \gamma_{21} = \frac{\pi_{23}}{\pi_{13}} \tag{18.2.8a}$$

Thus $\pi_{22} / \pi_{12} = \pi_{23} / \pi_{13}$. This means that knowledge of the structural form leads to restrictions on the parameters of the reduced form. However, if we use *estimates* of the reduced form parameters, then we should not be surprised if $\hat{\pi}_{22} / \hat{\pi}_{12} \neq \hat{\pi}_{23} / \hat{\pi}_{13}$. There is nothing in the least squares procedure that makes the reduced form *estimates* satisfy the restriction. Consequently, if we use least squares estimates of the reduced form parameters, the two expressions in equation 18.2.8a give two ways of estimating γ_{21}. This means indirect least squares does not yield a *unique* estimator of γ_{21}, and instead we are faced with a choice between two estimators, both of which are consistent. In this case we have more information in the system than the indirect least squares rule used to estimate γ_{21}. If we want to use all the information in the system concerning the exogenous variables when we estimate the parameters of the supply relation, a new estimation procedure is required. An estimation procedure to cope with this problem is developed in Chapter 19.

Alternatively with the demand equation 18.2.3, we have just enough information to uniquely estimate γ_{12}, that is, making use of equation 18.2.6

$$\gamma_{12} = \frac{\pi_{14}}{\pi_{24}}$$
$$(18.2.8b)$$

For each equation, once estimates of the γs are found, the estimates of the βs (the coefficients of the exogenous variables) can then be obtained by making use of equation 18.2.6.

18.2.3a An Instrumental Variable Estimator
For the macro model 18.1.2 and the demand equation 18.2.3a or 18.2.5a, we had just enough information, in the form of exogenous variables in the system, to use the indirect least squares estimator to obtain consistent estimators of the structural parameters. At this point it may be useful to ask: "In the case of the macro model and the demand equation 18.2.3a, is there another estimation procedure that leads to a consistent estimator for the structural parameters?" The answer to this question is yes.

To develop this alternative estimation procedure, let us use the statistical model for demand and supply equation 18.2.3:

$$p_t = \beta_{11} + \gamma_{12} q_t + \beta_{12} ps_t + \beta_{13} di_t + e_{1t} \qquad (18.2.3a)$$

$$q_t = \beta_{21} + \gamma_{21} p_t + \beta_{24} pf_t + e_{2t} \qquad (18.2.3b)$$

For notational simplicity we denote the endogenous variables as ys and the exogenous variables as xs. Thus, in equation 18.2.3 we let $p_t = y_{1t}$, $q_t = y_{2t}$, $ps_t = x_{2t}$, $di_t = x_{3t}$, and $pf_t = x_{4t}$, and we use x_{1t} to denote the intercept variable (vector of unit values) in each equation. Under these definitions we may rewrite the statistical model 18.2.3 as

$$y_{1t} = y_{2t} \gamma_{12} + x_{1t} \beta_{11} + x_{2t} \beta_{12} + x_{3t} \beta_{13} + e_{1t} \qquad (18.2.9a)$$

$$y_{2t} = y_{1t} \gamma_{21} + x_{1t} \beta_{21} + x_{4t} \beta_{24} + e_{2t} \qquad (18.2.9b)$$

where the e_{it} are distributed as in equation 18.2.4e. If we assume a sample of T observations on each economic variable, then the vectors that contain all T observations on these variables are $\mathbf{p} = \mathbf{y}_1$, $\mathbf{q} = \mathbf{y}_2$, $\mathbf{x}_1$ is a T-dimensional vector of unit values, $\mathbf{ps} = \mathbf{x}_2$, $\mathbf{di} = \mathbf{x}_3$, and $\mathbf{pf} = \mathbf{x}_4$. To represent the complete sample of data, we may rewrite equation 18.2.9 in vector form as

$$\mathbf{y}_1 = \mathbf{y}_2 \gamma_{12} + \mathbf{x}_1 \beta_{11} + \mathbf{x}_2 \beta_{12} + \mathbf{x}_3 \beta_{13} + \mathbf{e}_1 \qquad (18.2.10a)$$

$$\mathbf{y}_2 = \mathbf{y}_1 \gamma_{21} + \mathbf{x}_1 \beta_{21} + \mathbf{x}_4 \beta_{24} + \mathbf{e}_2 \qquad (18.2.10b)$$

where, in line with Chapter 17, the error assumptions 18.2.4 may be compactly expressed as

$$\mathbf{e} = \begin{bmatrix} \mathbf{e}_1 \\ \mathbf{e}_2 \end{bmatrix} \sim N\left[\begin{pmatrix} \mathbf{0} \\ \mathbf{0} \end{pmatrix}, \begin{pmatrix} \sigma_{11} I_T & \sigma_{12} I_T \\ \sigma_{21} I_T & \sigma_{22} I_T \end{pmatrix} \right] \qquad (18.2.10c)$$

We now rewrite the demand and supply equations 18.2.10 as

$$\mathbf{y}_1 = \mathbf{y}_2 \gamma_{12} + \mathbf{x}_1 \beta_{11} + \mathbf{x}_2 \beta_{12} + \mathbf{x}_3 \beta_{13} + \mathbf{e}_1$$

$$= \begin{bmatrix} \mathbf{y}_2 & \mathbf{x}_1 & \mathbf{x}_2 & \mathbf{x}_3 \end{bmatrix} \begin{bmatrix} \gamma_{12} \\ \beta_{11} \\ \beta_{12} \\ \beta_{13} \end{bmatrix} + \mathbf{e}_1 = Z_1 \delta_1 + \mathbf{e}_1$$
$$(18.2.11a)$$

and

$$\mathbf{y}_2 = \mathbf{y}_1 \gamma_{21} + \mathbf{x}_1 \beta_{21} + \mathbf{x}_4 \beta_{24} + \mathbf{e}_2$$

$$= \begin{bmatrix} \mathbf{y}_1 & \mathbf{x}_1 & \mathbf{x}_4 \end{bmatrix} \begin{bmatrix} \gamma_{21} \\ \beta_{21} \\ \beta_{24} \end{bmatrix} + \mathbf{e}_2 = Z_2 \boldsymbol{\delta}_2 + \mathbf{e}_2$$

$$(18.2.11\text{b})$$

where $\boldsymbol{\delta}_1' = (\gamma_{12} \quad \beta_{11} \quad \beta_{12} \quad \beta_{13})$, $\boldsymbol{\delta}_2' = (\gamma_{21} \quad \beta_{21} \quad \beta_{24})$, $Z_1 = \begin{bmatrix} \mathbf{y}_2 & \mathbf{x}_1 & \mathbf{x}_2 & \mathbf{x}_3 \end{bmatrix}$, $Z_2 = \begin{bmatrix} \mathbf{y}_1 & \mathbf{x}_1 & \mathbf{x}_4 \end{bmatrix}$, and, for future reference, $X = \begin{bmatrix} \mathbf{x}_1 & \mathbf{x}_2 & \mathbf{x}_3 & \mathbf{x}_4 \end{bmatrix}$. In developing the new estimation procedure, let's concentrate on the demand equation 18.2.11a:

$$\mathbf{y}_1 = Z_1 \boldsymbol{\delta}_1 + \mathbf{e}_1; \qquad \mathbf{e}_1 \sim N(\mathbf{0}, \sigma_{11} I_T) \qquad (18.2.12)$$

where in Section 18.2.3, when using the indirect least squares method, we obtained *unique* estimates of the structural parameters $\boldsymbol{\delta}_1' = (\gamma_{12} \quad \beta_{11} \quad \beta_{12} \quad \beta_{13})$.

Of course, in terms of estimation one possibility is to use the least squares rule to estimate $\boldsymbol{\delta}_1$. If we make use of the least squares rule then

$$\overline{\boldsymbol{\delta}}_1 = \begin{bmatrix} Z_1' Z_1 \end{bmatrix}^{-1} Z_1' \mathbf{y}_1 \qquad (18.2.13)$$

The mean of the random vector $\overline{\boldsymbol{\delta}}_1$ is

$$E[\overline{\boldsymbol{\delta}}_1] = E[(Z_1'Z_1)^{-1} Z_1'(Z_1 \boldsymbol{\delta}_1 + \mathbf{e}_1)] = \boldsymbol{\delta}_1 + E[(Z_1'Z_1)^{-1} Z_1' \mathbf{e}_1] \quad (18.2.14)$$

Since the endogenous variable $\mathbf{y}_2$ in Z_1, is correlated with $\mathbf{e}_1$, the last term in equation 18.2.14 does not vanish and $E[\overline{\boldsymbol{\delta}}_1] \neq \boldsymbol{\delta}_1$. Consequently, since Z_1 contains the endogenous variable $\mathbf{y}_1$, the direct least squares estimator $\overline{\boldsymbol{\delta}}_1$ is biased. It is also inconsistent because this result continues to hold true as sample size increases.

As you may remember from the appendix to Chapter 14, when we had a problem with the right-hand-side Xs being correlated with the equation error e, we developed an instrumental variable method to obtain a consistent estimator. If we follow this lead, this suggests in terms of equation 18.2.12 that we should search for a matrix X of variables that are uncorrelated with $\mathbf{e}$ and highly correlated with the stochastic regressor $\mathbf{y}_2$. In the demand and supply system 18.2.11 the exogenous variables $X = \begin{bmatrix} \mathbf{x}_1 & \mathbf{x}_2 & \mathbf{x}_3 & \mathbf{x}_4 \end{bmatrix}$ should be highly correlated with $\mathbf{y}_2$ and, by assumption, are uncorrelated with $\mathbf{e}_1$. This latter result means that $\operatorname{plim} X' \mathbf{e}/T = \mathbf{0}$, a condition necessary for X to be used as a matrix of instrumental variables. Thus, if we use X' to premultiply the original demand equation 18.2.11, we obtain

$$X' \mathbf{y}_1 = X' Z_1 \boldsymbol{\delta}_1 + X' \mathbf{e}_1 \qquad (18.2.15)$$

Dividing both sides by T and taking the probability limit (Appendix 14A of Chapter 14), we have

$$\operatorname{plim} \frac{X' \mathbf{y}_1}{T} = \operatorname{plim} \frac{X' Z_1}{T} \boldsymbol{\delta}_1 + \operatorname{plim} \frac{X' \mathbf{e}_1}{T} \qquad (18.2.16)$$

where $\operatorname{plim} X' \mathbf{e}_1 / T = \mathbf{0}$, $\operatorname{plim} X' \mathbf{y}_1 = \Sigma_{xy_1}$ exists and $\operatorname{plim} X' Z_1 / T = \Sigma_{xz_1}$ exists and is nonsingular. Thus if we solve for $\boldsymbol{\delta}_1$, we have

$$\boldsymbol{\delta}_1 = \Sigma_{xz_1}^{-1} \Sigma_{xy_1} \qquad (18.2.17)$$

If we use our *sample* quantities $X'Z_1/T$ and $X'\mathbf{y}_1/T$ for the population quantities Σ_{xz_1} and Σ_{xy_1} as substitutions in equation 18.2.17 we obtain the *instrumental variable estimator*

$$\hat{\hat{\boldsymbol{\delta}}} = \left(X'Z_1\right)^{-1} X'\mathbf{y}_1 \qquad (18.2.18)$$

The variables $X = \begin{bmatrix} \mathbf{x}_1 & \mathbf{x}_2 & \mathbf{x}_3 & \mathbf{x}_4 \end{bmatrix}$ that make up the $(T \times K)$ matrix X are called instrumental variables. In addition to the exogenous variables in the demand equation that we are estimating, the exogenous variable $\mathbf{x}_4$ that appears in the supply equation serves as an instrumental variable. The estimator is consistent because

$$
\begin{aligned}
\text{plim}\,\hat{\hat{\boldsymbol{\delta}}} &= \text{plim}\left[\left(\frac{X'Z_1}{T}\right)^{-1}\frac{X'\mathbf{y}_1}{T}\right] = \text{plim}\left[\left(\frac{X'Z_1}{T}\right)^{-1}\frac{X'(Z_1\boldsymbol{\delta}_1 + \mathbf{e}_1)}{T}\right] \\
&= \text{plim}\left[\boldsymbol{\delta}_1 + \left(\frac{X'Z_1}{T}\right)^{-1}\frac{X'\mathbf{e}_1}{T}\right] = \boldsymbol{\delta}_1 + \text{plim}\left(\frac{X'Z_1}{T}\right)^{-1}\text{plim}\left(\frac{X'\mathbf{e}_1}{T}\right) \\
&= \boldsymbol{\delta}_1 + \Sigma_{xz_1}^{-1}\,\mathbf{0} = \boldsymbol{\delta}_1
\end{aligned}
$$

$$(18.2.19)$$

As we will demonstrate in Chapter 19, for large samples, $\hat{\hat{\boldsymbol{\delta}}}_1$ has a covariance matrix that can be consistently estimated by

$$\hat{\sigma}^2 \left(X'Z_1\right)^{-1} X'X \left(Z_1'X\right)^{-1} \qquad (18.2.20)$$

where

$$\hat{\sigma}^2 = \left(\mathbf{y}_1 - Z_1\hat{\hat{\boldsymbol{\delta}}}_1\right)'\left(\mathbf{y}_1 - Z_1\hat{\hat{\boldsymbol{\delta}}}_1\right)\Big/T \qquad (18.2.21)$$

In terms of the supply equation 18.2.11b, note that $X'Z_2$ is not a square matrix, and thus this version of the instrumental variable estimator cannot be used as an estimator of $\boldsymbol{\delta}_2$ unless a choice between the exogenous variables $\mathbf{x}_2$, $\mathbf{x}_3$ is made. As we will demonstrate in Chapter 19, when $X'Z_i$ is square and nonsingular, the instrumental variable and indirect least squares estimators are *identical*.

Before closing this section, let us apply the instrumental variable estimator to the macro model 18.1.2

$$
\begin{aligned}
c_t &= \beta + \gamma y_t + e_t \\
y_t &= c_t + i_t
\end{aligned}
\qquad (18.1.2)
$$

where, with a sample of T observations, we write it as

$$
\begin{aligned}
\mathbf{c} &= \mathbf{y}\gamma + \mathbf{x}_1\beta + \mathbf{e} \\
\mathbf{y} &= \mathbf{c} + \mathbf{i}
\end{aligned}
\qquad (18.2.22)
$$

or

$$
\begin{aligned}
\mathbf{y}_1 &= \mathbf{y}_2\gamma + \mathbf{x}_1\beta + \mathbf{e} = \begin{bmatrix} \mathbf{y}_2 & \mathbf{x}_1 \end{bmatrix}\begin{bmatrix} \gamma \\ \beta \end{bmatrix} + \mathbf{e} = Z\boldsymbol{\delta} + \mathbf{e} \\
\mathbf{y}_2 &= \mathbf{y}_1 + \mathbf{x}_2
\end{aligned}
\qquad (18.2.23)
$$

where $y_1 = c$, $y_2 = y$, $i = x_2$, x_1 is a $(T \times 1)$ vector of ones, and $X = [x_1 \ x_2]$. The instrumental variable estimator for $\delta = (\gamma, \beta)'$ is

$$\hat{\delta} = \left[X'Z \right]^{-1} X'y_1 = \begin{bmatrix} x_1'y_2 & x_1'x_1 \\ x_2'y_2 & x_2'x_1 \end{bmatrix}^{-1} \begin{bmatrix} x_1'y_1 \\ x_2'y_1 \end{bmatrix} \qquad (18.2.24)$$

By making use of the data in Table 18.1, we find that

$$\hat{\delta} = \begin{bmatrix} 43486 & 22 \\ 8391853.5 & 4159.3 \end{bmatrix}^{-1} \begin{bmatrix} 39326.7 \\ 7585134.2 \end{bmatrix} = \begin{bmatrix} 0.8805 \\ 47.144 \end{bmatrix} \qquad (18.2.25)$$

which is the same as obtained with the indirect least squares estimator 18.1.16.

18.2.4   Exogenous and Predetermined Variables

Often the structural equations contain lagged endogenous variables. When this happens, for estimation purposes, the critical distinction is between endogenous and predetermined variables, where predetermined variables include both exogenous and lagged endogenous variables. For example, consider the following variant of the macro model 18.1.2:

$$c_t = \beta_1 + \gamma y_t + \beta_2 y_{t-1} + e_t \qquad (18.2.26a)$$

$$y_t = c_t + i_t \qquad (18.2.26b)$$

where c_t and y_t are current endogenous variables, and i_t and y_{t-1} are the predetermined variables where i_t is an exogenous variable and y_{t-1} is a lagged endogenous variable. Lagged endogenous variables have the characteristics of exogenous variables in that they may affect current endogenous variables but are not reciprocally affected. Under this designation the corresponding reduced form equations 18.2.26 are

$$c_t = \pi_{11} + \pi_{12}i_t + \pi_{13}y_{t-1} + v_{1t} \qquad (18.2.27a)$$

$$y_t = \pi_{21} + \pi_{22}i_t + \pi_{23}y_{t-1} + v_{2t} \qquad (18.2.27b)$$

and the πs are the reduced form parameters.

18.3   Identification

In each of the statistical models we have analyzed, the reduced form relations contained enough information to permit us to estimate the structural parameters γ and β by indirect least squares. There may be other cases where we do not have enough information in the reduced form to permit estimation of the structural parameters, in one or more of the equations within the system. In this context, before proceeding, let us look at another case that is reflected by the statistical model for the partial equilibrium market situation:

$$p_t = \gamma_{12}q_t + \beta_{11} + e_{1t} \qquad (18.3.1a)$$

$$q_t = \gamma_{21}p_t + \beta_{21} + e_{2t} \qquad (18.3.1b)$$

and the $e_{it} \sim N(0, \sigma_i^2)$ for $i = 1, 2$. This model arises from two behavioral equations and an identity representing market clearing in the context of static equilibrium. Substituting from equations 18.3.1a and 18.3.1b yields the following reduced form equations for the price and quantity p_t and q_t

$$p_t = \frac{\gamma_{12}\beta_{21} + \beta_{11}}{1 - \gamma_{12}\gamma_{21}} + \frac{e_{1t} + \gamma_{12}e_{2t}}{1 - \gamma_{12}\gamma_{21}}$$
$$= \mu_p + v_{1t} \qquad \qquad (18.3.1c)$$

$$q_t = \frac{\gamma_{21}\beta_{11} + \beta_{21}}{1 - \gamma_{12}\gamma_{21}} + \frac{\gamma_{21}e_{1t} + e_{2t}}{1 - \gamma_{12}\gamma_{21}}$$
$$= \mu_q + v_{2t} \qquad \qquad (18.3.1d)$$

where μ_p and μ_q are the mean values of p and q, respectively, and $E[v_{1t}^2] = \sigma_{v_1}^2$, $E[v_{2t}^2] = \sigma_{v_2}^2$, and $\text{cov}(v_{1t}, v_{2t}) = \sigma_{v_1 v_2}$. Writing the reduced form equations in terms of these parameters helps us to illustrate the amount of information contained in the variables p_t and q_t. This information is such that we can identify and estimate only the five parameters μ_p, μ_q, $\sigma_{v_1}^2$, $\sigma_{v_2}^2$, and $\sigma_{v_1 v_2}$. However, we would like to estimate the seven parameters γ_{12}, γ_{21}, β_{11}, β_{21}, σ_1^2, σ_2^2, and σ_{12}. Graphically, we can think of the problem as follows: The reduced forms show that, on average, both price and quantity have equilibrium values μ_p and μ_q. The realized values for p_t and q_t vary about the equilibrium values according to the variation in e_{1t} and e_{2t} over time. Thus the reduced form indicates that both price and quantity in the market simply vary randomly about the equilibrium point over time. Since all observations represent random variation about the equilibrium point, they do not provide information on the supply and demand equations and it is *impossible* to estimate the structural parameters of either of the behavioral equations 18.3.1c and 18.3.1d. This characteristic is known as observational equivalence and is typical of *underidentified* equations in a simultaneous system. In such cases there is *no way* of relating the set of structural parameters to the set of reduced form parameters. Another way to look at this is as follows: There are four structural parameters (γ_{12}, γ_{21}, β_{11}, and β_{21}) of the model 18.3.1 and μ_p and μ_q are the reduced form parameters. Given μ_p and μ_q can we say anything about γ_{12}, γ_{21}, β_{11}, and β_{21}? The intuition that you have gathered about solving for unknowns should suggest that in general two equations involving four unknowns do not result in unique solutions. In fact, in this case there are an infinite number of possible sets of γ_{12}, γ_{21}, β_{11}, and β_{21} that satisfy μ_p and μ_q. The equilibrium values for p_t and q_t are given in Figure 18.2. Note that there are an infinite number of possible sets of the structural parameters or ways that one may pass a demand or supply function through these observations and *no way* to isolate the demand and supply functions that may have generated these equilibrium values. Thus, without additional information it is not possible to identify and estimate results from either equation as a demand or a supply relation.

18.3.1   Observationally Equivalent Relations

In Section 18.3 we investigated, for a demand and supply system, whether we had enough information to estimate the unknown structural parameters. This problem is known as the identification problem. In this section, as a basis for determining identification status, we look at whether two or more equations in a system are observationally equivalent. To do this we consider whether a particular equation can be distinguished from a *linear* combination of all equations in the system. In this context let us return to the world of demand and supply functions. Consider first the following demand and

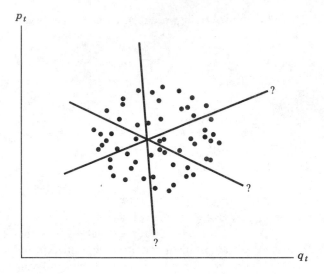

Figure 18.2 Equilibrium values for p_t and q_t for statistical model 18.3.1.

supply system:

$$\text{Demand} \qquad q_t = \beta_{11} + \gamma_{11} p_t + e_{1t} \qquad \qquad (18.3.2a)$$

$$\text{Supply} \qquad q_t = \beta_{21} + \gamma_{21} p_t + e_{2t} \qquad \qquad (18.3.2b)$$

$$e_{it} \sim N\left(0, \sigma_i^2\right) \qquad \text{for } i = 1, 2 \qquad (18.3.2c)$$

In contrast to equation 18.3.1, in this case we have written quantity as the left-hand-side variable in both equations. The question we ask is the following: If we use equilibrium outcome data for q_t and p_t to estimate the demand relation, how can we be sure that we are estimating a demand or supply relation or perhaps some combination of the two? To sort this out, let's take a linear combination of the two equations with weights λ and $(1 - \lambda)$. This yields

$$q_t = \lambda\left(\beta_{11} + \gamma_{11} p_t + e_{1t}\right) + (1 - \lambda)\left(\beta_{21} + \gamma_{21} p_t + e_{2t}\right) \qquad (18.3.3a)$$

$$= \left(\lambda\beta_{11} + (1 - \lambda)\beta_{21}\right) + \left(\lambda\gamma_{11} + (1 - \lambda)\gamma_{21}\right)p_t + \left(\lambda e_{1t} + (1 - \lambda)e_{2t}\right) \quad (18.3.3b)$$

$$= \alpha + \delta p_t + e_t^* \qquad \qquad (18.3.3c)$$

where $\alpha = \lambda\beta_{11} + (1 - \lambda)\beta_{21}$, $\delta = \lambda\gamma_{11} + (1 - \lambda)\gamma_{21}$ and $e_t^* = \lambda e_{1t} + (1 - \lambda)e_{2t}$. The resulting equation 18.3.3c cannot be distinguished in form from either equation 18.3.2a or equation 18.3.2b. Thus, we do not know whether we are estimating the parameters of equation 18.3.2a or equation 18.3.2b or some mixture of the two (see Figure 18.2). In this case the *demand and supply relations are observationally equivalent* and neither equation is identified. Thus, as we found in Section 18.3, we have no consistent basis for estimating the βs and γs for either equation.

Alternatively, let us reformulate the statistical model 18.3.2 as follows:

$$q_t = \beta_{11} + \gamma_{11} p_t + \beta_{12} di_t + e_{1t} \qquad \qquad (18.3.4a)$$

$$q_t = \beta_{21} + \gamma_{21} p_t + e_{2t} \qquad \qquad (18.3.4b)$$

$$e_{it} \sim N\left(0, \sigma_i^2\right) \qquad \text{for } i = 1, 2 \tag{18.3.4c}$$

where di, disposable income, is an exogenous variable and uncorrelated with e_{it}. If as before we take a weighted average of the two equations, using λ and $(1 - \lambda)$ as weights, we have

$$
\begin{aligned}
q_t &= \lambda\left(\beta_{11} + \gamma_{11} p_t + \beta_{12} di_t + e_{1t}\right) + (1 - \lambda)\left(\beta_{21} + \gamma_{21} p_t + e_{2t}\right) \\
&= \left(\lambda\beta_{11} + (1 - \lambda)\beta_{21}\right) + \left(\lambda\gamma_{11} + (1 - \lambda)\gamma_{21}\right) p_t + \lambda\beta_{12} di_t + \left(\lambda e_{1t} + (1 - \lambda)e_{2t}\right) \\
&= \alpha + \delta p_t + \lambda\beta_{12} di_t + e_t^*
\end{aligned}
\tag{18.3.5}
$$

In this case the mixture of equations 18.3.5 cannot be distinguished from equation 18.3.4a, and thus is observationally equivalent to it. Therefore, the demand relation is not identified, and we have no consistent basis for estimating β_{11}, β_{12}, and γ_{11}.

On the other hand, mixture equation 18.3.5 can be made to look like supply equation 18.3.4b only if $\lambda = 0$. Furthermore, if we set $\lambda = 0$ in equation 18.3.5, we get exactly equation 18.3.4b. Consequently, the supply equation is identified, and we can use the indirect least squares estimator to obtain estimates of β_{21} and γ_{21}.

If you make use of these procedures with the demand and supply model in Section 18.2.2, you will find that neither equation is observationally equivalent to the mixture equation and thus that both equations are identified as particular economic relations.

18.3.2 Counting Rules (Order Conditions) for Identification

Before we complete this section, let us see if we can devise some simple rules for determining the identifiability of each of the structural equations. In equations 18.2.3 and 18.2.9 we wrote our demand and supply equations model in the form

$$p_t = \beta_{11} + \gamma_{12} q_t + \beta_{12} ps_t + \beta_{13} di_t + e_{1t} \tag{18.2.3a}$$

$$q_t = \beta_{21} + \gamma_{21} p_t + \beta_{24} pf_t + e_{2t} \tag{18.2.3b}$$

or when denoting the endogenous variables as ys and the exogenous variables as xs, and letting $p_t = y_{1t}$, $q_t = y_{2t}$, $ps_t = x_{2t}$, $di_t = x_{3t}$, $pf_t = x_{4t}$, and x_{1t} as an intercept variable

$$y_{1t} = y_{2t}\gamma_{12} + x_{1t}\beta_{11} + x_{2t}\beta_{12} + x_{3t}\beta_{13} + e_{1t} \tag{18.2.9a}$$

$$y_{2t} = y_{1t}\gamma_{21} + x_{1t}\beta_{21} + x_{4t}\beta_{24} + e_{2t} \tag{18.2.9b}$$

Instead of using the procedures developed in Section 18.3.1 to show that these relations are not observationally equivalent, let's develop a simple counting rule to accomplish the same purpose. If, for the ith equation, we let

g^* be the number of endogenous variables present in the ith equation (for example, equation 18.2.9a has two endogenous variables y_1 and y_2)

k^* be the number of exogenous variables present in the ith equation (for example, equation 18.2.9a has three exogenous variables x_1, x_2, and x_3)

K be the total number of exogenous variables in the system (for example, x_1, x_2, x_3, and x_4 for the system 18.2.9)

then we may use the following counting rules to summarize the *order conditions* for identifying an equation in a system of equations:

1. When the number of endogenous and exogenous variables in the equation minus one ($g^* + k^* - 1$) is less than the total number of exogenous variables in the system K, then the equation is said to be overidentified, that is, $g^* + k^* - 1 < K$ or $g^* - 1 < K - k^*$. If we apply this counting rule to supply equation 18.2.9b, we have the result $g^* - 1 = 1 < K - k^* = 4 - 2$. Consequently, the equation is overidentified and the indirect least squares procedure is neither efficient nor unique. As we have learned, in this case the indirect least squares and instrumental variable estimators do not yield a unique estimate of the structural parameters.

2. When the number of endogenous and exogenous variables in the equation minus one is *equal* to the total number of exogenous variables in the system, which implies $g^* + k^* - 1 = K$, then the equation is said to be just identified. If we apply this rule to demand equation 18.2.9b, then we have the result $2 + 3 - 1 = 4$. Consequently, by the counting rule this equation is just identified and the indirect least squares and the instrumental variable estimators provide estimates of the structural parameters.

3. When the number of endogenous and exogenous variables minus one is *greater* than the total number of exogenous variables in the system, which implies $g^* + k^* - 1 > K$, then the equation is said to be *underidentified and estimation is not possible*. Equation 18.2.4a is an example of an underidentified equation in a simultaneous system of equations.

In summary, if

$$g^* + k^* - 1 < K \text{ or } g^* - 1 < K - k^*, \text{ then the equation is overidentified}$$
$$g^* + k^* - 1 = K \text{ or } g^* - 1 = K - k^*, \text{ then the equation is just-identified}$$
$$g^* + k^* - 1 > K \text{ or } g^* - 1 > K - k^*, \text{ then the equation is underidentified}$$

Thus, to achieve identification for each stochastic equation in the system, the number of right-hand-side variables in an equation must be equal to or less than $K - k^*$, the number of exogenous variables excluded from the ith equation.

When a system contains lagged endogenous variables, these variables are treated as exogenous for the purpose of identification. Hence, the counting rules should be in terms of both predetermined and exogenous variables. Also, the counting rules are only necessary conditions for identification. Sufficient (rank) conditions for identification also exist. These require an addition to the counting rules that no linear combination of the *other* equations in the system can produce the ith structural equation.

18.3.3   Summary

We have demonstrated that, as we attempt to estimate the unknown parameters of a simultaneous system of equations, we may face the following three situations:

(*i*) a statistical model such as equation 18.3.1 or equation 18.3.2, where it is not possible to estimate the unknown parameters,

(*ii*) a situation such as that for the consumption function in the macro model in Section 18.1 or the demand equation 18.2.3a, where an exogenous variable in the other equation gave us just enough information to go directly and uniquely from the reduced form parameters (πs) to the structural coefficients (γs and βs), and

(iii) a situation such as the supply equation 18.2.3b, where exogenous variables in the demand equation resulted in estimated reduced form coefficients that yielded multiple estimates of the structural parameters.

In Section 18.3.2 we developed a rule that you may use to determine when an equation within a system of equations is *(i)* underidentified, *(ii)* just identified, or *(iii)* overidentified. Since estimation of an underidentified equation in a system of equations is not possible, in Chapter 19 we concentrate on developing estimation rules for the just- and overidentified situations *(ii)* and *(iii)*.

18.4   Why Are We Interested in Estimating the Parameters of the Structural Equations?

After going through the preceding sections of this chapter, you may still be led to ask why there is this great emphasis on being able to identify and to estimate the parameters of structural economic equations. After all, the reduced form equations and their coefficients tell us all we need to know about the economic process under examination, since they determine the set of outcomes for the current endogenous variables, given any set of values for the predetermined variables. Surely, this is enough for the purposes of prediction and policy?

In framing an answer to this question it is important to note that forecasting and policy analysis are not the only reasons for econometric analysis. In the longer term both of these purposes are dependent on the further development of economic theory through hypothesis testing as we attempt to discriminate among alternative explanations of the ways in which economic processes and institutions interact and behave. Theoretical specifications of these alternative explanations in econometric models are couched in terms of structural relations, and it is the testing of structural parameters for statistical significance that is involved in attempts to discriminate empirically among alternative admissible explanations (theories). The clarification of theoretical relationships is of value in its own right, but it also contributes to better forecasting and better policy analysis as well.

Structural equations have the autonomous characteristic that if any one equation is subjected to a change of specification, this need not affect the specification of any other structural equation. For example, a change in income tax rates will affect the institutional relationship that determines the level of income after tax. However, there is no reason to assume that such a change would affect the marginal propensity to consume out of post-tax income that appears in the consumption function. Knowing what has happened to the tax equation in a structural model, one may proceed to adjust the corresponding structural coefficients accordingly, while leaving all other structural coefficients unchanged.

By way of contrast, it is not possible to say how such a change in tax rates would affect the reduced form of a structural model, except by deriving a modified reduced form from the *structural form coefficient estimates*. Generally, *all* of the reduced form equations may be affected by changes in the parameters of *one* structural form equation. This result is particularly important if the parameter changes involve one or more endogenous variables in the particular structural form equation. Consequently, reduced form equations estimated from sample data can be safely used only for prediction purposes only if one is certain that *no changes* in economic structure have occurred between the sample time periods and the prediction time periods.

Particular structural changes that arise *during* the sample time periods may be allowed for by introducing appropriate dummy variables (Chapters 12 and 17) into structural equations. These dummy variables will, in turn, affect the estimated reduced form equations, but the problem of how to take further post-sample structural shifts directly into account in estimated reduced form equations remains. It is possible to do so only by using what are known as *derived* reduced form estimates that incorporate the shifts in structural parameters along with any nonsample information (restrictions) from the structural equations.

The assumed autonomous nature of structural relationships means that structural parameters are much more stable than composite reduced form coefficients. Structural parameters may therefore be much more readily the subject of a priori or nonsample knowledge (Chapter 11) concerning their signs and magnitudes. The reasonableness of structural parameters estimates is therefore much more easily judged by econometric intuition than is the acceptability of reduced form coefficient estimates. Similarly, shifts in structural parameters, when they arise, are much more readily the subject of rational explanation and interpretation than are the associated shifts in reduced form coefficients. Structural parameter estimates are also much more easily compared with accumulated empirical evidence, which invariably refers to economic structure rather than to reduced form equations.

18.5   Summary of Chapter

We started the chapter by noting that many sets of economic data are generated by a system of economic relations that are dynamic, stochastic, and simultaneous. To capture the simultaneous aspect of the data-generation process, we recognized the joint, interdependent, endogenous instantaneous feedback nature of some economic variables and noted the implications that this had for specifying a viable statistical model that was consistent with the sampling process generating the outcome data. Since endogenous variables that are correlated with the equation error may appear on both the right- and left-hand side of each economic relation, we recognized we could no longer use the least squares rule to obtain an unbiased estimator of the structural parameters for each structural equation. We then developed estimators for the βs and γs in the simultaneous equation statistical model, which made use of least squares estimates of the reduced form parameters and had the statistical property of consistency.

By considering systems of relations that we think are consistent with the way economic data are generated we have opened a very significant statistical-econometric door. From now on, each time you see an economic model involving only one equation, you may be led to question whether this specification is sufficient to describe how the economic data were generated. If not, perhaps you can easily spot the potential error in specifying the statistical model and corresponding errors in estimation and inference.

Many new concepts were introduced in this chapter. It is recommended that as a review you reread the chapter and at the same time write down the definitions or your understanding of the following terms:

simultaneous equation system	reduced form estimation
endogenous variable	indirect least squares
exogenous variable	jointly determined random variables
structural equations	structural error

reduced form equations
structural parameters
reduced form parameters
feedback mechanism
behavioral equation
identity
least squares bias

reduced form error
multiplier effect
consistency
statistical assumptions about errors
identification (under-, just-, and over-)
uses of: structural coefficient estimates
uses of: reduced form coefficient estimates

In the next chapter we focus on two questions that we have left unanswered in Chapter 18: how to determine the identification property of an equation in a system of equations and how to estimate the parameters of an overidentified equation.

18.6   Exercises

18.1 Consider the following simultaneous equation model of demand and supply:

$$\text{Demand:} \quad \mathbf{q} = \mathbf{p}\gamma_{12} + \mathbf{j}\beta_{11} + \mathbf{e}_1$$
$$\text{Supply:} \quad \mathbf{q} = \mathbf{p}\gamma_{22} + \mathbf{j}\beta_{21} + \mathbf{w}\beta_{22} + \mathbf{e}_2 \qquad (18.6.1)$$

or

$$\mathbf{y}_1 = \mathbf{y}_2\gamma_{12} + \mathbf{x}_1\beta_{11} + \mathbf{e}_1$$
$$\mathbf{y}_1 = \mathbf{y}_2\gamma_{22} + \mathbf{x}_1\beta_{21} + \mathbf{x}_2\beta_{22} + \mathbf{e}_2 \qquad (18.6.2)$$

where $\mathbf{q} = \mathbf{y}_1 =$ quantity and $\mathbf{p} = \mathbf{y}_2 =$ price are endogenous variables, and $\mathbf{w} = \mathbf{x}_2 =$ wage rate is an exogenous variable. We assume that $\mathbf{e}_i \sim N(\mathbf{0}, \sigma_i^2 I_T)$ for $i = 1, 2$ and $\mathbf{j} = \mathbf{x}_1 =$ vector of unit values (intercept variable).

Suppose the following observations are available:

q	p	w
4	2	2
6	4	3
9	3	1
3	5	1
3	8	3

Using a *hand calculator* and not a computer, answer the following questions:
(a) Given the reduced form equations:

$$\mathbf{p} = \mathbf{x}_1\pi_{11} + \mathbf{x}_2\pi_{12} + \mathbf{v}_1$$
$$\mathbf{q} = \mathbf{x}_1\pi_{21} + \mathbf{x}_2\pi_{22} + \mathbf{v}_2 \qquad (18.6.3)$$

derive the reduced form coefficients in terms of the structural coefficients and show that

$$\gamma_{12} = \frac{\pi_{22}}{\pi_{12}} \quad \text{and} \quad \beta_{11} = \pi_{21} - \gamma_{12}\pi_{11}$$

(b) Find least squares estimates of the reduced form coefficients.
(c) Are the signs of your estimates for π_{12} and π_{22} consistent with what you would expect from economic theory?

(d) Using the reduced form estimates find indirect least squares estimates of γ_{12} and β_{11}.

(e) Attempt to develop indirect least squares estimates of γ_{22}, β_{21}, and β_{22} and discuss your finding.

18.2 Repeat parts (b) and (d) using a computer package such as SHAZAM or SAS.

18.3 Assume that you have reformulated the income–consumption model to the following model of the U. S. economy:

$$c_t = \gamma_{12} y_t + \beta_{11} + e_{1t} \qquad (18.6.4a)$$

$$i_t = \beta_{21} + \beta_{22} r_t + e_{2t} \qquad (18.6.4b)$$

$$y_t = c_t + i_t + g_t \qquad (18.6.4c)$$

where

c_t is private consumption expenditure in year t,
i_t is private investment expenditure in year t,
y_t is gross national expenditure in year t,
r_t is a weighted average of interest rates in year t,
g_t is government expenditure in year t.

The variables c_t, i_t, and y_t are endogenous variables and g_t and r_t are considered to be exogenous.

(a) Briefly explain what signs you expect a priori for each of the coefficients and the theoretical basis for your expectations.

(b) Derive algebraically the following reduced form coefficients in terms of the structural coefficients:

$$y_t = \pi_{10} + \pi_{11} r_t + \pi_{12} g_t + v_{1t}$$
$$c_t = \pi_{20} + \pi_{21} r_t + \pi_{22} g_t + v_{2t}$$
$$i_t = \pi_{30} + \pi_{31} r_t + \pi_{32} g_t + v_{3t} \qquad (18.6.5)$$

(c) Determine the identifiability characteristics of each equation and develop an indirect least squares estimator for γ_{12} and β_{11}. Is this the only possible indirect least squares estimator of γ_{12} and β_{11}?

(d) Use the data in Table 18.2 on **y, c, i, r** and SHAZAM, SAS, or some other computer package to obtain
   (i) least squares estimates of the reduced form parameters in equation 18.6.5
   (ii) least squares estimates of the structural parameters of equations 18.6.4a and 18.6.4b
   (iii) indirect least squares estimates of the structural parameters of equations 18.6.4a and 18.6.4b and comment on their identification status.

(e) Report your results and comment on their statistical reliability and economic feasibility.

18.4 The reduced form equations, within the context of Chapter 17, may be written as a set of regression equations. Using the model 18.2.3
(a) Write out the statistical model for the set of regression equations.
(b) Comment on the statistical properties that result when estimating the reduced form parameters as a system versus estimating them one at a time using the least squares rule.

Table 18.2 Data for the Macro Model

y	c	i	r	g
43.517	30.217	9.727	19.042	3.572
50.931	45.836	1.571	18.292	3.523
56.334	37.275	13.798	16.054	5.262
67.660	42.143	20.915	9.384	4.602
63.977	47.028	12.943	10.470	4.005
77.357	45.185	27.917	18.189	4.255
67.304	54.270	8.088	12.248	4.946
59.548	47.004	7.338	11.278	5.206
51.849	33.955	12.102	14.229	5.792
48.479	25.830	17.161	19.755	5.488
21.570	9.218	6.622	15.420	5.729
27.341	24.947	0.067	14.035	5.461
30.031	18.331	4.649	8.587	7.051
48.359	42.881	0.995	14.138	6.473
59.483	27.637	25.084	6.118	6.761
43.698	25.700	11.169	15.916	6.828
52.686	31.062	13.707	15.224	7.917
61.496	49.972	4.797	7.613	6.727
110.467	68.655	33.136	10.880	8.675
99.937	54.229	38.376	10.524	7.332
89.862	58.498	24.137	19.236	7.228
93.716	51.197	34.591	16.802	7.927
88.036	67.538	11.692	12.662	8.806
124.089	73.149	41.889	15.625	9.050
94.129	55.661	30.305	18.114	8.164
59.892	31.469	20.079	16.087	8.344
53.502	25.717	18.426	17.452	9.359
45.677	20.876	15.847	15.106	8.954
72.337	52.665	9.264	18.039	10.408
93.513	46.519	36.723	7.722	10.271
80.490	51.252	18.324	17.670	10.914
80.070	53.369	16.585	19.447	10.116
77.235	53.343	14.104	15.462	9.788
76.731	47.003	19.509	12.870	10.219
78.813	36.451	30.691	5.484	11.671
112.207	64.928	35.950	7.195	11.329
140.327	85.949	42.423	11.959	11.956
137.900	77.820	48.019	7.105	12.061
132.317	75.999	43.845	5.694	12.473
149.423	93.575	42.962	8.258	12.885
135.115	77.400	44.942	16.949	12.774
132.813	68.397	51.086	17.793	13.330
123.915	78.177	33.111	18.676	12.626
143.804	84.703	46.529	12.672	12.571
128.086	82.504	33.466	7.897	12.116
124.524	62.217	48.958	9.705	13.349
122.158	75.356	32.716	7.719	14.086
115.744	56.283	45.937	7.976	13.524
116.275	72.794	29.626	19.810	13.855
139.871	70.840	54.401	12.817	14.630

(c) Using model 18.2.3 and the data in Table 19.1, estimate the parameters of the reduced form equations using *(i)* the least squares rule on each equation, and *(ii)* the generalized least squares estimator employed in Chapter 17 and comment on your results.

18.5 Write down your interpretation of the key words and concepts listed at the front of this chapter.

18.6 Review the set of questions noted in the first few pages of Chapter 1, choose one question area and develop an econometric model that you think might, when implemented, provide useful information for answering the question.

18.7 References

There is a vast literature on simultaneous equation models and the corresponding "appropriate" estimation procedures. Many think that econometrics started in the 1940s when we started to think about the experimental conditions that are envisioned when we write down an economic relation and what this implies about the corresponding statistical model and estimation rules. A bit of history in this area is captured in the following monograph:

HOOD, W., and T. KOOPMANS (eds.) (1953) *Studies in Econometric Method*, Cowles Foundation Monograph No.14, New York: John Wiley & Sons, Inc.

For an easy-to-read modern discussion of simultaneous equation models see:

ROTHENBERG, T. (1987) "Simultaneous Equation Models," in *The New Palgrave: A Dictionary of Economics*, edited by J. M. EATWELL, M. MILGATE, and P. NEWMAN, New York: Stockton Press, pp. 344–347.

For a more complete and formal presentation of the simultaneous equation model and corresponding estimation rules and their statistical properties see:

JUDGE, G. G., R.C. HILL, W. E. GRIFFITHS, H. LÜTKEPOHL and T. C. LEE (1988) *Introduction to the Theory and Practice of Econometrics*, 2nd Edition, New York: John Wiley & Sons, Inc., pp. 599–669.

JUDGE, G. G., W. E. GRIFFITHS, R .C. HILL, H. LÜTKEPOHL and T. C. LEE (1985) *The Theory and Practice of Econometrics*, New York: John Wiley & Sons, Inc., pp. 144–190, 563–640.

For an application of the simultaneous equations model see:

BERNDT, E. (1990) *The Practice of Econometrics*, New York: Addison-Wesley Publishing Co., pp. 361–380.

Chapter 19

Estimation and Inference for the Simultaneous Equations Model

New Keywords and Concepts

Two-Stage Least Squares (2SLS) Estimator

Static Model

Forecasting with a Simultaneous Equations Model

Three-Stage Least Squares (3SLS) Estimator

Dynamic Model

In Chapter 18 we introduced the idea of endogenous-jointly determined economic variables and noted the implications that this type of interdependent feedback mechanism had for economic and statistical model specification and estimation. We discovered that for certain equations in a system of structural equations, we could use indirect least squares or instrumental variable rules to obtain a *consistent* estimator of the unknown parameters. We further discovered that for some equations we did not have enough information to obtain estimates of the unknown parameters. For some other equations which, by the order condition or counting rule, we labeled as overidentified, we found we were *unable* to obtain unique estimates of the unknown parameters or, in other words, to use all of the information in the system of equations concerning the exogenous variables. In this chapter we want to pursue this question and consider how in general to deal with the problems of estimation and inference as they relate to simultaneous equation economic statistical models that contain equations that are just- or overidentified.

19.1 Estimation in Just- and Overidentified Equations

To pursue the question of estimating the structural parameters in just- and overidentified situations, let us return to the statistical model for demand and supply (equation 18.2.3) that was discussed in Chapter 18:

$$p_t = \beta_{11} + \gamma_{12} q_t + \beta_{12} ps_t + \beta_{13} di_t + e_{1t} \tag{18.2.3a}$$

$$q_t = \beta_{21} + \gamma_{21} p_t + \beta_{24} pf_t + e_{2t} \tag{18.2.3b}$$

If we let $p_t = y_{1t}$, $q_t = y_{2t}$, $ps_t = x_{2t}$, $di_t = x_{3t}$, $pf_t = x_{4t}$, and x_{1t} represent the intercept variable, we may, as we did in Chapter 18, rewrite the equations for a sample of T observations as

$$\mathbf{y}_1 = \mathbf{y}_2 \gamma_{12} + \mathbf{x}_1 \beta_{11} + \mathbf{x}_2 \beta_{12} + \mathbf{x}_3 \beta_{13} + \mathbf{e}_1$$

$$= \begin{bmatrix} \mathbf{y}_2 & \mathbf{x}_1 & \mathbf{x}_2 & \mathbf{x}_3 \end{bmatrix} \begin{bmatrix} \gamma_{12} \\ \beta_{11} \\ \beta_{12} \\ \beta_{13} \end{bmatrix} + \mathbf{e}_1 = Z_1 \boldsymbol{\delta}_1 + \mathbf{e}_1$$

$$(19.1.1a)$$

and

$$\mathbf{y}_2 = \mathbf{y}_1 \gamma_{21} + \mathbf{x}_1 \beta_{21} + \mathbf{x}_4 \beta_{24} + \mathbf{e}_2$$

$$= \begin{bmatrix} \mathbf{y}_1 & \mathbf{x}_1 & \mathbf{x}_4 \end{bmatrix} \begin{bmatrix} \gamma_{21} \\ \beta_{21} \\ \beta_{24} \end{bmatrix} + \mathbf{e}_2 = Z_2 \boldsymbol{\delta}_2 + \mathbf{e}_2$$

$$(19.1.1b)$$

where $\boldsymbol{\delta}_1' = \begin{pmatrix} \gamma_{12} & \beta_{11} & \beta_{12} & \beta_{13} \end{pmatrix}$, $\boldsymbol{\delta}_2' = \begin{pmatrix} \gamma_{21} & \beta_{21} & \beta_{24} \end{pmatrix}$, $Z_1 = \begin{bmatrix} \mathbf{y}_2 & \mathbf{x}_1 & \mathbf{x}_2 & \mathbf{x}_3 \end{bmatrix}$, $Z_2 = \begin{bmatrix} \mathbf{y}_1 & \mathbf{x}_1 & \mathbf{x}_4 \end{bmatrix}$, and $X = \begin{bmatrix} \mathbf{x}_1 & \mathbf{x}_2 & \mathbf{x}_3 & \mathbf{x}_4 \end{bmatrix}$. Writing the model in this form, let us concentrate on the supply equation 19.1.1b

$$\mathbf{y}_2 = Z_2 \boldsymbol{\delta}_2 + \mathbf{e}_2 \qquad \mathbf{e}_2 \sim N\big(\mathbf{0},\, \sigma_{22} I_T \big) \qquad (19.1.2)$$

where in Chapter 18, when using the indirect least squares method, we obtained *multiple* estimates of the structural parameters $\boldsymbol{\delta}_2' = \begin{pmatrix} \gamma_{21} & \beta_{21} & \beta_{24} \end{pmatrix}$ and when using the order condition we defined the equation as overidentified.

For estimation, one possibility is to use the least squares rule to estimate $\boldsymbol{\delta}_2$. However, as we learned in Chapter 18, since the endogenous variable $\mathbf{y}_1$ in Z_2 is correlated with $\mathbf{e}_2$, the direct least squares estimator $\overline{\boldsymbol{\delta}}_2$ is biased and inconsistent.

19.1.1 A Two-Stage Least Squares (2SLS) Estimator

Given this least squares bias result, is there some way to get, as we did for γ for the macro model in Chapter 18 and the parameters of the demand equation 18.2.3, an estimator that is consistent and uses all of the information in the system on the exogenous variables? Indirect least squares and the instrumental variable method are not totally satisfactory because they do not yield *unique* estimates of the unknown structural parameters. These estimators are consistent but not efficient since, to obtain an estimate, we must exclude one of the exogenous variables in the system. In Chapters 15 to 17, when, because of a nonscalar error covariance matrix, we had a problem with using the least squares rule, we were able to find a way of transforming the statistical model so that the least squares rule could be used and retain satisfactory sampling properties. As we will see, this is also the case when estimating the unknown parameters of an overidentified equation in a system of equations.

19.1.1a A Consistent Estimator of the Parameters of an Overidentified Supply Equation
To find out how we might cope with this problem of correlation between the random variables y and e in an overidentified equation, consider the statistical model for the supply equation

$$\mathbf{y}_2 = Z_2 \boldsymbol{\delta}_2 + \mathbf{e}_2 \qquad \mathbf{e}_2 \sim N\big(\mathbf{0},\, \sigma_{22} I_T \big) \qquad (19.1.2)$$

and the matrix of exogenous variables $X = \begin{bmatrix} \mathbf{x}_1 & \mathbf{x}_2 & \mathbf{x}_3 & \mathbf{x}_4 \end{bmatrix}$. This matrix represents the set of exogenous variables that are contained in the statistical model for the *complete* demand and supply system 19.1.1. Note that the nonrandom exogenous variables X, which influence the endogenous variables in the system, are assumed to be uncorrelated with the equation errors $\mathbf{e}_1$ and $\mathbf{e}_2$, and the means of the random vectors $E[X'\mathbf{e}_2]$ and $E[\mathbf{e}_2]$ are both equal to the zero vector. To exploit the fact that $E[X'\mathbf{e}_2] = \mathbf{0}$, one possibility is to make use of information on all of the exogenous variables in the system and use X through the reduced form equations to transform statistical model 19.1.2 as follows.

In equation 19.1.2 where $Z_2 = \begin{bmatrix} \mathbf{y}_1 & \mathbf{x}_1 & \mathbf{x}_4 \end{bmatrix}$, the endogenous variable $\mathbf{y}_1$ is correlated with $\mathbf{e}_2$ and thus is the offending variable when we make use of the least squares estimator to estimate δ_2. From the reduced form equation for $\mathbf{y}_1$, we can write

$$\mathbf{y}_1 = \mathbf{x}_1 \pi_{11} + \mathbf{x}_2 \pi_{12} + \mathbf{x}_3 \pi_{13} + \mathbf{x}_4 \pi_{14} + \mathbf{v}_1 = X\boldsymbol{\pi}_1 + \mathbf{v}_1 \qquad (19.1.3a)$$

and

$$\mathbf{y}_1 = X\hat{\boldsymbol{\pi}}_1 + \hat{\mathbf{v}}_1 = \hat{\mathbf{y}}_1 + \hat{\mathbf{v}}_1 \qquad (19.1.3b)$$

where $\hat{\boldsymbol{\pi}}_1$ is the least squares estimator of $\boldsymbol{\pi}_1$. Predictions of $\mathbf{y}_1$ are given by $\hat{\mathbf{y}}_1 = X\hat{\boldsymbol{\pi}}_1$ and $\hat{\mathbf{v}}_1 = \mathbf{y}_1 - X\hat{\boldsymbol{\pi}}_1$ are the least squares residuals.

If we replace $\mathbf{y}_1$ in $Z_2 = \begin{bmatrix} \mathbf{y}_1 & \mathbf{x}_1 & \mathbf{x}_4 \end{bmatrix}$ by $\hat{\mathbf{y}}_1 + \hat{\mathbf{v}}_1$, then $Z_2 = \begin{bmatrix} \hat{\mathbf{y}}_1 + \hat{\mathbf{v}}_1 & \mathbf{x}_1 & \mathbf{x}_4 \end{bmatrix}$ and we may rewrite the supply equation 19.1.2 as

$$\mathbf{y}_2 = \begin{bmatrix} \hat{\mathbf{y}}_1 + \hat{\mathbf{v}}_1 & \mathbf{x}_1 & \mathbf{x}_4 \end{bmatrix} \begin{bmatrix} \gamma_{21} \\ \beta_{21} \\ \beta_{24} \end{bmatrix} + \mathbf{e}_2 \qquad (19.1.4)$$

or

$$\mathbf{y}_2 = \begin{bmatrix} \hat{\mathbf{y}}_1 & \mathbf{x}_1 & \mathbf{x}_4 \end{bmatrix} \begin{bmatrix} \gamma_{21} \\ \beta_{21} \\ \beta_{24} \end{bmatrix} + \hat{\mathbf{v}}_1 \gamma_{21} + \mathbf{e}_2 \qquad (19.1.5)$$

or

$$\mathbf{y}_2 = \hat{Z}_2 \delta_2 + \bar{\mathbf{e}}_2 \qquad (19.1.6)$$

where $\bar{\mathbf{e}}_2 = \hat{\mathbf{v}}_1 \gamma_{21} + \mathbf{e}_2$. We have replaced the endogenous variable on the right-hand side, $\mathbf{y}_1$, by its predictions from the reduced form, $\hat{\mathbf{y}}_1$. The complete matrix of right-hand-side variables, where $\mathbf{y}_1$ has been replaced by $\hat{\mathbf{y}}_1$, we denote by $\hat{Z}_2$. The replacement process means that we now have a new error term $\bar{\mathbf{e}}_2$ that depends on the reduced form residuals $\hat{\mathbf{v}}_1$ and the original error $\mathbf{e}_2$.

The advantage of the new formulation in equation 19.1.6 is that, as $T \to \infty$, $\hat{Z}_2$ and $\bar{\mathbf{e}}_2$ become uncorrelated. Because $\hat{Z}_2$ depends on $\hat{\boldsymbol{\pi}}_1$, which in turn depends on $\mathbf{y}_1$, correlation between $\hat{Z}_2$ and $\bar{\mathbf{e}}_2$ will exist. However, in terms of the probability limit concept introduced in Chapters 14 and 18, it can be shown that this correlation disappears as sample size T becomes large. Consequently, the *least squares estimator* may be used with the statistical model 19.1.6 to provide a consistent estimator of δ_2. The least squares rule applied to equation 19.1.6 yields

$$\hat{\delta}_2 = \begin{bmatrix} \hat{Z}_2' \hat{Z}_2 \end{bmatrix}^{-1} \hat{Z}_2' \mathbf{y}_2 \qquad (19.1.7)$$

and provides a consistent estimator for δ_2, the unknown parameters of the supply equation. The covariance matrix $\text{cov}(\hat{\delta}_2)$ can be estimated by

$$\hat{\text{cov}}(\hat{\delta}_2) = \hat{\sigma}_2^2 \begin{bmatrix} \hat{Z}_2' \hat{Z}_2 \end{bmatrix}^{-1} \qquad (19.1.8)$$

with

$$\hat{\sigma}_{22}^2 = \left(\mathbf{y}_2 - Z_2\hat{\boldsymbol{\delta}}_2\right)'\left(\mathbf{y}_2 - Z_2\hat{\boldsymbol{\delta}}_2\right)\Big/T \qquad (19.1.9)$$

Note that the original right-hand-side variables Z_2, not those that involve the predictions $\hat{Z}_2$, are used for estimation of the error variance σ_{22}^2.

Thus, as an alternative to the indirect least squares estimator, which yields more than one possible estimator for an overidentified structural equation, we have from equation 19.1.7, the consistent estimator $\hat{\boldsymbol{\delta}}$ that makes use of all the information in the system concerning the exogenous variables. This estimator is known as the *two-stage least squares estimator*. For another discussion of this estimator see Section 14.3.3 of Chapter 14. Before exploring the origin of this title, let us consider the use of the corresponding estimator in estimating the unknown structural parameters of the demand equation.

19.1.1b A Consistent Estimator of the Demand Parameters   In terms of the demand equation 19.1.1a

$$\mathbf{y}_1 = \begin{bmatrix} \mathbf{y}_2 & \mathbf{x}_1 & \mathbf{x}_2 & \mathbf{x}_3 \end{bmatrix}\begin{bmatrix} \gamma_{12} \\ \beta_{11} \\ \beta_{12} \\ \beta_{13} \end{bmatrix} + \mathbf{e}_1$$

$$= Z_1\boldsymbol{\delta}_1 + \mathbf{e}_1 \qquad (19.1.1a)$$

and $\mathbf{y}_2$ is the offending right-hand-side variable. Again, if we replace $\mathbf{y}_2 = X\hat{\boldsymbol{\pi}}_2 + \hat{\mathbf{v}}_2 = \hat{\mathbf{y}}_2 + \hat{\mathbf{v}}_2$ in Z_1, we have

$$\mathbf{y}_1 = \begin{bmatrix} \hat{\mathbf{y}}_2 + \hat{\mathbf{v}}_2 & \mathbf{x}_1 & \mathbf{x}_2 & \mathbf{x}_3 \end{bmatrix}\begin{bmatrix} \gamma_{12} \\ \beta_{11} \\ \beta_{12} \\ \beta_{13} \end{bmatrix} + \mathbf{e}_1$$

or

$$\mathbf{y}_1 = \begin{bmatrix} \mathbf{y}_2 & \mathbf{x}_1 & \mathbf{x}_2 & \mathbf{x}_3 \end{bmatrix}\begin{bmatrix} \gamma_{12} \\ \beta_{11} \\ \beta_{12} \\ \beta_{13} \end{bmatrix} + \gamma_{12}\hat{\mathbf{v}}_2 + \mathbf{e}_1$$

$$= \hat{Z}_1\boldsymbol{\delta}_1 + \bar{\mathbf{e}}_1 \qquad (19.1.10)$$

As in the supply equation, as sample size gets larger, the correlation between $\hat{Z}_1$ and $\bar{\mathbf{e}}_1$ disappears. Consequently, we may apply to the statistical model 19.1.10 the least squares rule

$$\hat{\boldsymbol{\delta}}_1 = \left(\hat{Z}_1'\hat{Z}_1\right)^{-1}\hat{Z}_1\mathbf{y}_1 \qquad (19.1.11)$$

to obtain a consistent estimator of the unknown parameters of the demand equation $\boldsymbol{\delta}_1$. It turns out that this estimation is identical to the indirect least squares and instrumental variable estimators developed in Chapter 18. Again,

$$\hat{\text{cov}}\left(\hat{\boldsymbol{\delta}}_1\right) = \hat{\sigma}_{11}^2\left[\hat{Z}_1'\hat{Z}_1\right]^{-1} \qquad (19.1.12)$$

where $\hat{\sigma}_{11}^2 = \left(\mathbf{y}_1 - Z_1 \hat{\boldsymbol{\delta}}_1 \right)' \left(\mathbf{y}_1 - Z_1 \hat{\boldsymbol{\delta}}_1 \right) / T$. Equation 19.1.12 provides an estimator of the covariance matrix and a basis for interval estimation and hypothesis testing.

19.1.1c Estimation Procedure   To summarize, a consistent estimator of the structural parameters of an identified equation in a simultaneous system can be found as follows:

> ***Stage 1***   Estimate the reduced form parameters, $\boldsymbol{\pi}_i$ for each endogenous variable by $\hat{\boldsymbol{\pi}}_i = (X'X)^{-1} X' \mathbf{y}_i$. Use the estimates of the reduced form parameters to predict the sample values $\hat{\mathbf{y}}_i$, where $\hat{\mathbf{y}}_i = X(X'X)^{-1} X' \mathbf{y}_i = X \hat{\boldsymbol{\pi}}_i$. Replace the right-hand-side endogenous variables by $\hat{\mathbf{y}}_i$ and specify the statistical model as $\mathbf{y}_i = \hat{Z}_i \boldsymbol{\delta}_i + \overline{\mathbf{e}}_i$.
>
> ***Stage 2***   Given the statistical model $\mathbf{y}_i = \hat{Z}_i \boldsymbol{\delta}_i + \overline{\mathbf{e}}_i$, where the correlation between $\hat{Z}_i$ and $\overline{\mathbf{e}}_i$ disappears as $T \to \infty$, use the least squares rule to obtain estimates of the structural parameters $\boldsymbol{\delta}_i$ and then compute the covariance matrix $\hat{\mathrm{cov}}(\hat{\boldsymbol{\delta}}_i) = \hat{\sigma}_{ii}^2 [\hat{Z}_i' \hat{Z}_i]^{-1}$, where $\hat{\sigma}_{ii}^2 = (\mathbf{y}_i - Z_i \hat{\boldsymbol{\delta}}_i)' (\mathbf{y}_i - Z_i \hat{\boldsymbol{\delta}}_i) / T$.

Estimates for the parameters of each equation in the system may be obtained by repeating this procedure for each equation. In the econometrics literature the estimator $\hat{\boldsymbol{\delta}}_i$ is called a *two-stage least squares* (2SLS) estimator, and computer programs, which are discussed in the SHAZAM and SAS *Computer Handbooks*, exist for its use in applied problems.

In practice, it is the two-stage least squares estimator, not the indirect least squares estimator, that is used to estimate the structural parameters in both just-identified and overidentified equations. In overidentified equations the two-stage least squares estimator has the advantage of being a unique consistent estimator. For just-identified equations it can be shown that the two-stage least squares estimator is identical to the indirect least squares estimator. However, the two-stage least squares estimator is more convenient; it does not require explicit solution for the structural parameters (the βs and γs) in terms of the reduced form parameters.

19.2   Estimation of the Parameters in a Demand and Supply Model

Given the two-stage least squares (2SLS) rule, which is a consistent estimator of the unknown parameters of a just- or overidentified equation in a system of equations, let us make use of it to estimate the parameters of the demand and supply model discussed in Sections 18.2.1 of Chapter 18 and 19.1 of this chapter. In these sections we wrote the model as

$$p_t = \beta_{11} + \gamma_{12} q_t + \beta_{12} ps_t + \beta_{13} di_t + e_{1t} \tag{19.2.1a}$$

$$q_t = \beta_{21} + \gamma_{21} p_t + \beta_{24} pf_t + e_{2t} \tag{19.2.1b}$$

or

$$\mathbf{y}_1 = \mathbf{y}_2 \gamma_{12} + \mathbf{x}_1 \beta_{11} + \mathbf{x}_2 \beta_{12} + \mathbf{x}_3 \beta_{13} + \mathbf{e}_1 \tag{19.2.2a}$$

$$\mathbf{y}_2 = \mathbf{y}_1 \gamma_{21} + \mathbf{x}_1 \beta_{21} + \mathbf{x}_4 \beta_{24} + \mathbf{e}_2 \tag{19.2.2b}$$

19.2.1   A Sample of Data

Corresponding to this model a sample of quantity, price, and income data is given in

Table 19.1. These data were obtained from a randomly generated sample based on the following values for the parameters of the demand and supply equations:

$$\gamma_{12} = -1.0 \qquad \beta_{11} = 0 \qquad \beta_{12} = 1.0 \qquad \beta_{13} = 0.5 \qquad (19.2.3a)$$

$$\gamma_{21} = 1.0 \qquad \beta_{21} = 20.0 \qquad \beta_{24} = -1.0 \qquad (19.2.3b)$$

$$\text{cov}(e_1) = 38.25 I_{30} \qquad \text{cov}(e_2) = 2.25 I_{30} \qquad E[e_1 e_2'] = 2.25 I_{30} \quad (19.2.3c)$$

The corresponding parameters of the reduced form equations are, from equation 18.2.5

$$\pi_{11} = -10.00 \qquad \pi_{12} = 0.5 \qquad \pi_{13} = 0.25 \qquad \pi_{14} = 0.5 \qquad (19.2.3d)$$

$$\pi_{21} = 10.00 \qquad \pi_{22} = 0.5 \qquad \pi_{23} = 0.25 \qquad \pi_{24} = -0.5 \qquad (19.2.3e)$$

$$\text{cov}(v_1) = 9 I_{30} \qquad \text{cov}(v_2) = 11.25 I_{30} \qquad E[v_1 v_2'] = 9 I_{30}$$

Table 19.1 Price, Quantity, and Income Data for Model 19.2.1

p	q	ps	di	pf
9.88	19.89	19.97	21.03	10.52
13.41	13.04	18.04	20.43	19.67
11.57	19.61	22.36	18.70	13.74
13.81	17.13	20.87	15.25	17.95
17.79	22.55	19.79	27.09	13.71
12.84	6.37	15.98	24.89	24.95
18.11	15.02	17.94	22.94	24.17
13.52	10.22	17.09	21.96	23.61
22.45	23.64	22.72	38.85	19.52
16.55	16.12	15.74	31.69	20.03
19.39	24.55	24.64	26.23	15.38
22.29	18.92	23.70	30.07	22.98
16.65	11.94	15.93	33.67	25.76
21.65	18.93	23.34	32.90	25.17
17.56	12.60	15.21	37.46	25.82
20.40	20.49	26.04	35.18	19.31
26.85	22.94	22.95	43.81	26.02
29.98	21.08	27.10	41.21	29.65
23.59	16.68	23.65	38.20	27.45
19.11	17.61	20.06	43.98	18.00
15.41	16.62	26.38	37.64	18.87
25.81	20.99	24.28	45.24	24.58
27.67	24.53	26.64	48.15	25.25
23.57	19.67	22.65	36.70	24.24
22.25	23.29	19.68	43.92	22.63
25.60	16.64	23.82	46.03	27.35
27.90	20.81	28.98	46.32	27.80
27.00	14.95	18.52	48.94	30.34
29.48	26.27	28.16	51.25	24.12
35.15	20.65	28.43	48.36	34.01

19.2.2   Parameter Estimates

First, to provide a basis of comparison, let us suppose we had ignored the endogenous nature of the price and quantity variables y_1 and y_2 and had used the *biased* least squares estimator to estimate the unknown parameters in the demand equation 19.2.1a. For the demand relations 19.2.1a we have the following result for p_t:

$$p_t = -4.5398 + 0.0504q_t + 0.4536ps_t + 0.4119di_t \qquad (19.2.4)$$

One thing to note in equation 19.2.4 is the positive coefficient connecting price and quantity in the demand relation. Since we are analyzing a normal good, we would expect this coefficient to be negative. Also, when compared with the true parameters equation 19.2.3, the other parameter estimates miss the mark quite badly.

The reduced form estimated parameters corresponding to statistical model 19.2.1 are

$$p_t = -10.837 + 0.5694ps_t + 0.2534di_t + 0.4513pf_t$$
$$\quad (2.6614)\ (0.1170) \qquad (0.0575) \qquad (0.0995) \qquad \text{s.e.} \qquad (19.2.5a)$$

$$q_t = 7.8951 + 0.6564ps_t + 0.2167di_t - 0.5070pf_t$$
$$\quad (3.2437)\ (0.1425) \qquad (0.0700) \qquad (0.1213) \qquad \text{s.e.} \qquad (19.2.5b)$$

These estimated reduced form equations, which agree quite well with the true reduced form parameters equations 19.2.3d and 19.2.3e, form the basis for computing equilibrium values of p_t and q_t. Since the demand equation 19.2.1a is by the counting rule just- or overidentified, these estimated reduced form coefficients also form the basis for formulating the statistical model that is to be used with the 2SLS rule.

When we reformulate the statistical models as equations 19.1.8 and 19.1.12, using the reduced form equations to respecify Z_1 as $\hat{Z}_1$ and Z_2 as $\hat{Z}_2$, the 2SLS estimator results in the following estimated demand and supply equations:

$$p_t = -3.8095 - 0.8902q_t + 1.1537ps_t + 0.4463di_t$$
$$\quad (4.2177)\ (0.3646) \quad (0.3462) \qquad (0.0852) \qquad \text{s.e.} \qquad (19.2.6a)$$

$$q_t = 20.033 + 1.0139p_t - 1.0009pf_t$$
$$\quad (1.1603)\ (0.0709) \quad (0.0783) \qquad \text{s.e.} \qquad (19.2.6b)$$

All of the coefficients of the prices, quantities and income have the expected sign and agree quite well with the true parameters in equation 19.2.3. Note especially, relative to equation 19.2.4, the sign change of the parameter connecting the price and quantity variables in the demand equation 19.2.6a.

19.3   Another Look at Estimating the Structural Parameters in the Aggregate Macro Model

Given the estimation and identification results for the demand and supply equations, let us make use of this type of information to rewrite the statistical model and to develop an estimator for the aggregate consumption model 18.1.3 of Chapter 18. If we let consumption $= y_1$, income $= y_2$, investment $= x_2$, and x_1 be the intercept variable, we may rewrite the aggregate consumption model, for a sample of T observations, as

$$\mathbf{y}_1 = \mathbf{y}_2\gamma + \mathbf{x}_1\beta + \mathbf{e} = \begin{bmatrix} \mathbf{y}_2 & \mathbf{x}_1 \end{bmatrix}\begin{bmatrix} \gamma \\ \beta \end{bmatrix} + \mathbf{e} = Z\boldsymbol{\delta} + \mathbf{e} \qquad (19.3.1a)$$

and

$$\mathbf{y}_2 = \mathbf{y}_1 + \mathbf{x}_2 \tag{19.3.1b}$$

where $Z = \begin{bmatrix} \mathbf{y}_2 & \mathbf{x}_1 \end{bmatrix}$ and $\mathbf{e} \sim N(\mathbf{0}, \sigma^2 I_T)$. If we let $X = \begin{bmatrix} \mathbf{x}_1 & \mathbf{x}_2 \end{bmatrix}$, we can write the reduced form equation for $\mathbf{y}_2$ as

$$\mathbf{y}_2 = \mathbf{x}_1 \pi_{21} + \mathbf{x}_2 \pi_{22} + \mathbf{v}_2 = X\boldsymbol{\pi} + \mathbf{v}_2 \tag{19.3.2a}$$

or

$$\mathbf{y}_2 = X\hat{\boldsymbol{\pi}} + \hat{\mathbf{v}}_2 \tag{19.3.2b}$$

where $\hat{\boldsymbol{\pi}}$ is the least squares estimator of $\boldsymbol{\pi}$, $\hat{\mathbf{y}}_2 = X\hat{\boldsymbol{\pi}}$ is the estimated value of $\mathbf{y}_2$, and $\hat{\mathbf{v}}_2$ is the estimated equation error. If we replace $\mathbf{y}_2$ in $Z = \begin{bmatrix} \mathbf{y}_2 & \mathbf{x}_1 \end{bmatrix}$ by $Z = \begin{bmatrix} \hat{\mathbf{y}}_2 + \hat{\mathbf{v}}_2 & \mathbf{x}_1 \end{bmatrix}$, we may rewrite equation 19.3.1a as

$$
\begin{aligned}
\mathbf{y}_1 &= \begin{bmatrix} \hat{\mathbf{y}}_2 + \hat{\mathbf{v}}_2 & \mathbf{x}_1 \end{bmatrix} \begin{bmatrix} \gamma \\ \beta \end{bmatrix} + \mathbf{e} \\
&= \begin{bmatrix} \hat{\mathbf{y}}_2 & \mathbf{x}_1 \end{bmatrix} \begin{bmatrix} \gamma \\ \beta \end{bmatrix} + \gamma\hat{\mathbf{v}}_2 + \mathbf{e} \\
&= \hat{Z}\boldsymbol{\delta} + \bar{\mathbf{e}}
\end{aligned}
\tag{19.3.3}
$$

where $\hat{Z} = \begin{bmatrix} \hat{\mathbf{y}}_2 & \mathbf{x}_1 \end{bmatrix}$ and $\bar{\mathbf{e}} = \gamma\mathbf{v}_2 + \mathbf{e}$. In this case the 2SLS estimator reduces to the least squares estimator applied to equation 19.3.3. With the consumption data in Table 18.1, the estimate of $\boldsymbol{\delta} = \begin{bmatrix} \gamma \\ \beta \end{bmatrix}$ is

$$\hat{\boldsymbol{\delta}} = \begin{bmatrix} \hat{Z}'\hat{Z} \end{bmatrix}^{-1} \hat{Z}'\mathbf{y}_1 = \begin{bmatrix} 0.881 \\ 47.144 \end{bmatrix} \tag{19.3.4}$$

and, since the equation is by our counting rule just-identified, it yields the same result that we obtained in equation 18.1.16 when the indirect least squares estimation rule 18.1.14a was used in Chapter 18. Writing the results in the traditional form and making use of the estimated covariance $\hat{\mathrm{cov}}(\boldsymbol{\delta}) = \hat{\sigma}^2 \begin{bmatrix} \hat{Z}'\hat{Z} \end{bmatrix}^{-1}$, we have the following for the estimated relation and corresponding statistics:

$$
\begin{aligned}
\hat{\mathbf{c}} = \hat{\mathbf{y}}_1 &= 47.144\mathbf{x}_1 + 0.881\mathbf{y}_2 \\
&\quad (49.98) \quad\ (0.025) \qquad \text{s.e.} \\
&\quad (0.94) \quad\ (35.11) \qquad t
\end{aligned}
\tag{19.3.5}
$$

19.4   Another Method for Estimating the Unknown Parameters of an Overidentified Equation

In Section 18.3.2a we were able to use, for a just-identified equation, an instrumental variable estimator to obtain a consistent estimator of the unknown parameters of a structural equation. An interesting question is whether the instrumental variable approach can be used to provide a consistent estimator in the case of an overidentified equation. Fortunately, the answer is yes, and it can be shown to be identical to the two-stage least squares estimator.

To develop as we did in Chapter 14 a general variant of the instrumental variable estimator, consider again the statistical model for the supply equation

$$\mathbf{y}_2 = Z_2\boldsymbol{\delta}_2 + \mathbf{e}_2 \qquad \mathbf{e}_2 \sim N\big(\mathbf{0}, \sigma_{22} I_T\big) \tag{19.1.2}$$

and the matrix of exogenous variables $X = [\mathbf{x}_1 \ \mathbf{x}_2 \ \mathbf{x}_3 \ \mathbf{x}_4]$ that is contained in the statistical model for the *complete* demand and supply system 19.1.1. Note that the nonrandom exogenous variables X, which influence the endogenous variables in the system, are assumed to be uncorrelated with the equation errors $\mathbf{e}_1$ and $\mathbf{e}_2$ and the means of the random vectors $E[X'\mathbf{e}_2]$ and $E[\mathbf{e}_2]$ equal a zero vector. One possibility is to utilize information on all of the exogenous variables in the system through the instrumental variable approach and use X to transform statistical model 19.1.2 in the following way:

$$X'\mathbf{y}_2 = X'Z_2\boldsymbol{\delta}_2 + X'\mathbf{e}_2 \qquad X'\mathbf{e}_2 \sim N\big(\mathbf{0}, \sigma_{22}\big[X'X\big]\big) \tag{19.4.1}$$

where $\text{cov}\big(X'\mathbf{e}_2\big) = E\big[X'\mathbf{e}_2\mathbf{e}_2'X\big] = \sigma_{22}X'X$.

If we let $\mathbf{y}_2^* = X'\mathbf{y}_2$, $Z_2^* = X'Z_2$, and $\mathbf{e}^* = X'\mathbf{e}_2$, then we may rewrite equation 19.4.1 as

$$\mathbf{y}^* = Z_2^*\boldsymbol{\delta}_2 + \mathbf{e}_2^* \tag{19.4.2}$$

where in the notation of Chapter 15, $E[\mathbf{e}_2^*\mathbf{e}_2^{*'}] = \sigma_{22}X'X = \sigma_{22}W$.

If we then apply the least squares rule to this linear statistical model, we have

$$
\begin{aligned}
\hat{\boldsymbol{\delta}}_2 &= \Big[Z_2^{*'}Z_2^*\Big]^{-1} Z_2^{*'}\mathbf{y}_2 \\
&= \Big[Z_2'XX'Z_2\Big]^{-1} Z_2'XX'\mathbf{y}_2
\end{aligned} \tag{19.4.3a}
$$

whose expectations can be rewritten as

$$
\begin{aligned}
E[\hat{\boldsymbol{\delta}}_2] &= E\Big[Z_2'XX'Z_2\Big]^{-1} Z_2'X\big(X'Z_2\boldsymbol{\delta}_2 + X'\mathbf{e}_2\big) \\
&= \boldsymbol{\delta}_2 + E\Big[Z_2'XX'Z_2\Big]^{-1} Z_2'XX'\mathbf{e}_2
\end{aligned} \tag{19.4.3b}
$$

In this case as the sample size $T \to \infty$, $T^{-1}Z_2^* = T^{-1}X'Z_2$ converges to a fixed matrix that is independent of $\mathbf{e}_2^* = X'\mathbf{e}_2$, and $\mathbf{e}_2^* = X'\mathbf{e}_2$ converges to zero. Consequently, in terms of the probability limit concept introduced in Chapter 14, the last right-hand term vanishes and $\hat{\boldsymbol{\delta}}_2$ converges to $\boldsymbol{\delta}_2$ and is a consistent estimator. However, note that the *covariance* matrix for the equation error $X'\mathbf{e}_2$ in equation 19.4.1 is not a scalar identity. Therefore, as in Chapters 15 and 16, this means the estimator $\hat{\boldsymbol{\delta}}_2$ may not be efficient. In line with Chapters 15 and 16, to attain statistical efficiency the generalized least squares (GLS) estimator should be used. Noting that $\text{cov}(X'\mathbf{e}_2) = \sigma_{22}X'X = \sigma_{22}W$, and that $W = X'X$ is known, the GLS estimator is

$$
\begin{aligned}
\hat{\hat{\boldsymbol{\delta}}}_2 &= \Big[Z_2^{*'}W^{-1}Z_2^*\Big]^{-1} Z_2^{*'}W^{-1}\mathbf{y}_2 \\
&= \Big[Z_2'X(X'X)^{-1}X'Z_2\Big]^{-1} Z_2'X(X'X)^{-1}X'\mathbf{y}_2
\end{aligned} \tag{19.4.4}
$$

In *large* samples

$$\hat{\hat{\boldsymbol{\delta}}}_2 \sim N\Big(\boldsymbol{\delta}_2, \sigma_{22}\Big[Z_2'X(X'X)^{-1}X'Z_2\Big]^{-1}\Big) \tag{19.4.5}$$

The covariance matrix may be estimated by

$$\hat{\mathrm{cov}}\left[\hat{\hat{\boldsymbol{\delta}}}_2\right] = \hat{\sigma}_{22}\left[Z_2^{*'}W^{-1}Z_2^*\right]^{-1}$$

$$= \hat{\sigma}_{22}\left[Z_2'X(X'X)^{-1}X'Z_2\right]^{-1} \tag{19.4.6}$$

where

$$\hat{\sigma}_{22} = \left(\mathbf{y}_2 - Z_2\hat{\hat{\boldsymbol{\delta}}}_2\right)'\left(\mathbf{y}_2 - Z_2\hat{\hat{\boldsymbol{\delta}}}_2\right)\Big/T \tag{19.4.7}$$

The estimated covariance matrix provides a basis for computing approximate standard errors and for carrying out hypothesis tests.

19.4.1   Another Estimator for a Just-Identified Equation

Now turn to the demand equation

$$\mathbf{y}_1 = \begin{bmatrix} \mathbf{y}_2 & \mathbf{x}_1 & \mathbf{x}_2 & \mathbf{x}_3 \end{bmatrix}\begin{bmatrix} \gamma_{12} \\ \beta_{11} \\ \beta_{12} \\ \beta_{13} \end{bmatrix} + \mathbf{e}_1 = Z_1\boldsymbol{\delta}_1 + \mathbf{e}_1 \tag{19.4.8}$$

where $Z_1 = \begin{bmatrix} \mathbf{y}_2 & \mathbf{x}_1 & \mathbf{x}_2 & \mathbf{x}_3 \end{bmatrix}$ and $\boldsymbol{\delta}_1' = \begin{bmatrix} \gamma_{12} & \beta_{11} & \beta_{12} & \beta_{13} \end{bmatrix}$. Using all the information on the exogenous variables in the system and the X transformation, we have

$$X'\mathbf{y}_1 = X'Z_1\boldsymbol{\delta}_1 + X'\mathbf{e}_1 \tag{19.4.9a}$$

or

$$\mathbf{y}_1^* = Z_1^*\boldsymbol{\delta}_1 + \mathbf{e}_1^* \tag{19.4.9b}$$

where $\mathbf{e}_1^* = X'\mathbf{e}_1 \sim N\left(\mathbf{0}, \sigma_{11}\left[X'X\right]\right)$. Therefore, if we let $X'X = W$ the generalized least squares estimator for equation 19.4.9 is

$$\hat{\hat{\boldsymbol{\delta}}}_1 = \left[Z_1^{*'}W^{-1}Z_1^*\right]^{-1}Z_1^{*'}W^{-1}\mathbf{y}_1$$

$$= \left[Z_1'X(X'X)^{-1}X'Z_1\right]^{-1}Z_1'X(X'X)^{-1}X'\mathbf{y}_1 \tag{19.4.10}$$

In *large* samples

$$\hat{\hat{\boldsymbol{\delta}}}_1 \sim N\left(\boldsymbol{\delta}_1, \sigma_{11}\left[Z_1'X(X'X)^{-1}X'Z_1\right]^{-1}\right) \tag{19.4.11}$$

The covariance matrix of $\hat{\hat{\boldsymbol{\delta}}}_1$ may be estimated by

$$\hat{\mathrm{cov}}\left(\hat{\hat{\boldsymbol{\delta}}}_1\right) = \hat{\sigma}_{11}\left[Z_1'X(X'X)^{-1}X'Z_1\right]^{-1} \tag{19.4.12}$$

where

$$\hat{\sigma}_{11} = \left(\mathbf{y}_1 - Z_1\hat{\hat{\boldsymbol{\delta}}}_1\right)'\left(\mathbf{y}_1 - Z_1\hat{\hat{\boldsymbol{\delta}}}_1\right)\Big/T \tag{19.4.13}$$

Note that in this just-identified case, the matrices Z_1 and X have the same column dimension and thus $Z_1'X$ is a *square nonsingular matrix* that has an inverse. If we use the matrix algebra result that $[ABC]^{-1} = C^{-1}B^{-1}A^{-1}$, this means that the generalized least squares (GLS) estimator 19.4.10 may be rewritten as

$$\hat{\hat{\boldsymbol{\delta}}}_1 = \left(X'Z_1 \right)^{-1} X'X \left(Z_1'X \right)^{-1} Z_1'X \left(X'X \right)^{-1} X'\mathbf{y}_1$$

$$= \left(X'Z_1 \right)^{-1} X'\mathbf{y}_1 = \hat{\boldsymbol{\delta}}_1 \tag{19.4.14}$$

This is exactly what we get if we use the least squares rule $\hat{\boldsymbol{\delta}}_1 = \left[Z_1'XX'Z_1 \right]^{-1} Z_1'XX'\mathbf{y}_1$ directly on equation 19.4.9. Therefore, when X and Z have the same column dimension, the least squares estimator may be applied directly to the transformed model (19.4.9). Note, in terms of the supply equation 19.1.2, that the column dimension of X (all of the exogenous variables in the system) is greater than the column dimension of Z_2, and to get an efficient estimator we had to use the GLS estimator in equation 19.4.4. In the econometrics literature the estimator $\hat{\hat{\boldsymbol{\delta}}}_i$ is equivalent to the *two-stage least squares* (2SLS) estimator developed in Section 19.1. Computer programs, which are discussed in the *Computer Handbook*, exist for the use of the GLS estimator in applied problems. Note that the estimator in equations 19.4.10 and 19.4.14 is the same as the instrumental variable estimator demonstrated in Section 18.2.3a of Chapter 18.

19.4.2   A "More Efficient" Estimation Rule

In the demand and supply model 19.1.1, by considering *individual* structural equations and a two-stage least squares rule or a generalized instrumental variable rule, we have been able to obtain consistent estimators for the structural parameters δ_1 and δ_2. Is there any way that we might be able to improve on this estimation rule and get an estimator that has greater efficiency? In Chapter 17 when we had two or more regression equations we found that, if the equation errors between equations were correlated, we could improve the efficiency of our estimator if we estimated them as a system, rather than estimating each equation separately. Since in the simultaneous equations models we have considered, the equation errors are assumed correlated, the idea of using a variant of the SUR statistical model is developed in Appendix 19A of this chapter.

19.5   Forecasting with an Econometric Model

Given our ability to specify (*i*) economic and statistical models reflecting endogenous-feedback mechanisms for variables in a system of equations, and (*ii*) estimators that permit us to use a sample of data to capture the unknown parameters of the structural and reduced form equations, the next question to be faced is how to make use of the results for forecasting and multiplier analysis purposes. Forecasting is useful for the following three main purposes: (*i*) to predict what will happen in the future, (*ii*) to determine the effect of changing various policy instruments, and (*iii*) for validation of models. Prediction of the future has obvious practical value. *Ex ante* forecasting is distinguished from other types of forecasts that are generated primarily to help with the analysis of forecast error and, hence, with the validation process. For purposes of economic and statistical model specification and estimation, it has been important in this chapter to distinguish between endogenous and exogenous or predetermined (lagged endogenous) variables. As we turn to forecasting, it becomes important also to identify within the class of predetermined variables those that are lagged endogenous.

A static model is one in which there are no lagged endogenous (predetermined) variables. As a result the model is always in equilibrium, since the influence of a change in an exogenous variable is experienced instantaneously. This can be contrasted with a dynamic model, where lagged endogenous variables exist and where the model takes more than one period to reach equilibrium. Static models provide us with a simple framework for examining the effect of a change in one variable on the values of the others. They indicate both the direction of change and the point toward which the endogenous variables are moving.

In the real world, economic conditions very seldom appear to be in equilibrium. At best they are tending to particular equilibria, from which they are disturbed by random shocks such as weather effects, political events, strikes, shifts in taste, and changes in the technological conditions of production. When one fits a particular econometric structure using real-world data, important elements of interest in the results obtained are the structural dynamics of the fitted equations and the stability conditions inherent in them. One wants to know whether the fitted structure would itself quickly tend to equilibrium if it were not subjected to further random shocks, and what time paths the endogenous variables tend to follow in adjusting to particular exogenous disturbances. Dynamic behavior is an important aspect of the validation process for any fitted structure. If the structural dynamics differ markedly from those inherent in empirical observation of an actual economy or sector or economic entity, this suggests that the specification of the basic model may not have correctly captured the real mechanisms by which the economy or sector economic agent adjusts.

Multipliers indicate how endogenous variables in a model respond to changes in exogenous variables. In a static model all multipliers are instantaneous (impact multipliers) and are given by the reduced form coefficients. With a dynamic model, where there are delayed effects from changes in exogenous variables, the concepts of delayed and interim multipliers become important. Definitions and methods for learning about these multipliers are part of the subject matter of this section.

In a static model, forecasting and tracing the paths of endogenous variables for given values of the exogenous variables can be carried out by using the reduced form. With a dynamic model, it is convenient to derive what is known as the fundamental dynamic equation for an endogenous variable.

In the section that follows we make the above ideas more concrete and provide some explicit definitions that are related to a simple dynamic model. However, we will begin by considering a static model, so that the differences between static and dynamic models will be more apparent.

19.5.1   A Static Model

Suppose that the aggregate demand and supply for food can be modeled as

$$p_t = \beta_{11} + \gamma_1 q_t^d + \beta_{12} i_t + e_{1t} \tag{19.5.1}$$

$$q_t^s = \beta_{21} + \gamma_2 p_t + \beta_{23} r_t + e_{2t} \tag{19.5.2}$$

where $q_t^d = q_t^s = q_t$ and p_t (price of food) and q_t (quantity of food) are the endogenous variables, i_t (the disposable income), and r_t (rainfall) are the exogenous variables, the subscript t refers to observations in year t, and β_{11}, γ_1, β_{12}, β_{21}, γ_2, and β_{23} are the structural coefficients. This is a static model because there are no lagged endogenous variables; only current values of p and q appear.

To derive the reduced form equation for p_t we substitute equation 19.5.2 into equation 19.5.1 and rearrange the terms appropriately. The steps are

$$p_t = \beta_{11} + \gamma_1 \left(\beta_{21} + \gamma_2 p_t + \beta_{23} r_t + e_{2t} \right) + \beta_{12} i_t + e_{1t}$$

$$(1 - \gamma_1 \gamma_2) p_t = \beta_{11} + \gamma_1 \beta_{21} + \gamma_1 \beta_{23} r_t + \beta_{12} i_t + e_{1t} + \gamma_1 e_{2t}$$

$$p_t = \frac{\beta_{11} + \gamma_1 \beta_{21}}{1 - \gamma_1 \gamma_2} + \frac{\gamma_1 \beta_{23}}{1 - \gamma_1 \gamma_2} r_t + \frac{\beta_{12}}{1 - \gamma_1 \gamma_2} i_t + \frac{e_{1t} + \gamma_1 e_{2t}}{1 - \gamma_1 \gamma_2}$$

$$(19.5.3a)$$

or

$$p_t = \pi_{11} + \pi_{12} r_t + \pi_{13} i_t + v_{1t} \qquad (19.5.3b)$$

Substituting this equation into equation 19.5.2 gives the reduced form equation for quantity, namely,

$$q_t = \beta_{21} + \gamma_2 \left[\frac{\beta_{11} + \gamma_1 \beta_{21}}{1 - \gamma_1 \gamma_2} + \frac{\gamma_1 \beta_{23}}{1 - \gamma_1 \gamma_2} r_t + \frac{\beta_{12}}{1 - \gamma_1 \gamma_2} i_t + \frac{e_{1t} + \gamma_1 e_{2t}}{1 - \gamma_1 \gamma_2} \right] + \beta_{23} r_t + e_{2t}$$

$$q_t = \frac{\beta_{21} + \gamma_2 \beta_{11}}{1 - \gamma_1 \gamma_2} + \frac{\beta_{23}}{1 - \gamma_1 \gamma_2} r_t + \frac{\gamma_2 \beta_{12}}{1 - \gamma_1 \gamma_2} i_t + \frac{\gamma_2 e_{1t} + e_{2t}}{1 - \gamma_1 \gamma_2}$$

$$(19.5.4a)$$

or

$$q_t = \pi_{21} + \pi_{22} r_t + \pi_{23} i_t + v_{2t} \qquad (19.5.4b)$$

The first implication of the static nature of this model is that, for given values of r and i, the system will always be in equilibrium, and the equilibrium values for p and q are those values that would be computed by using equations 19.5.3 and 19.5.4. For example, if there is an increase in r, the supply curve shifts to the right ($\beta_{23} > 0$) and a new equilibrium price and quantity given by the intersection of the demand curve and shifted supply curve are obtained. Since there are no lags in the system, the new price and quantity are realized instantaneously, that is, in the same period as the increase in rainfall. A "one-unit increase in rainfall" will decrease price by π_{12} units and increase quantity by π_{22} units (providing $\gamma_1 < 0$ and $\gamma_2 > 0$). The reduced form coefficient π_{12} gives the multiplier effect of a change in rainfall on price, and the reduced form coefficient π_{22} gives the multiplier effect of a change in rainfall on quantity. When the multiplier effects are instantaneous as they are here, they are called impact multipliers. The effect of a change in income can be similarly analyzed by using a shift in the demand curve.

Another implication of the static nature of the model is that the reduced form equations are satisfactory for forecasting the endogenous variables and for tracking the paths of endogenous variables for given values of the exogenous variables. Values of p and q that are designed for either of these purposes are simply calculated from equations 19.5.3 and 19.5.4 and specified values for i and r.

19.5.2   Relaxing the Static Assumption

To contrast static and dynamic models and to introduce dynamic model concepts, we now alter the above model by making *quantity supplied* a function of lagged instead of current price. Thus, we are hypothesizing that producers make plans for next year's food supply on the basis of this year's price. When next year arrives, supply has already been determined from the previous year's price and, through the demand curve, price adjusts to a new level so as to clear the predetermined supply.

The new model is

$$p_t = \beta_{11} + \gamma_1 q_t + \beta_{12} i_t + e_{1t} \qquad (19.5.5)$$

$$q_t = \beta_{21} + \beta_{22} p_{t-1} + \beta_{23} r_t + e_{2t} \qquad (19.5.6)$$

The choice of notation is not critical, but we have changed the structural coefficient γ_2 to β_{22}, since the endogenous variable p_t has been changed to the lagged endogenous (predetermined) variable p_{t-1}.

Since there are no longer any current endogenous variables on the right-hand side of the supply function, the least squares estimation rule will yield consistent estimates of the coefficients of this function. Also, providing that there is no contemporaneous correlation in the errors (e_{1t} and e_{2t} are uncorrelated), q_t will be uncorrelated with e_{1t}, and the least squares rule will also yield consistent estimates of the parameters of the demand equation. Thus in this special case, called a recursive statistical model, the simultaneous equation estimation procedures are not necessary. We now examine questions more directly associated with the dynamic nature of the model.

Consider the reduced form equations for the structural model in equations 19.5.5 and 19.5.6. Since there are no current endogenous variables on the right-hand side of the supply function, the reduced form equation for quantity is identical to the structural supply function. The reduced form equation for price can be obtained by substituting q_t into demand. Thus, the reduced form equations are

$$q_t = \beta_{21} + \beta_{22} p_{t-1} + \beta_{23} r_t + e_{2t} \qquad (19.5.7)$$

$$p_t = (\beta_{11} + \gamma_1 \beta_{21}) + \gamma_1 \beta_{22} p_{t-1} + \gamma_1 \beta_{23} r_t + \beta_{12} i_t + e_{1t} + \gamma_1 e_{2t} \qquad (19.5.8)$$

Let us now rewrite the reduced form equation for price as

$$p_t = \theta_1 + \delta p_{t-1} + \omega_{11} r_t + \omega_{12} i_t + \varepsilon_{1t} \qquad (19.5.9)$$

where $\theta_1 = \beta_{11} + \gamma_1 \beta_{21}$, $\omega_{11} = \gamma_1 \beta_{23}$, $\delta = \gamma_1 \beta_{22}$, $\omega_{12} = \beta_{12}$, and $\varepsilon_{1t} = e_{1t} + \gamma_1 e_{2t}$. Thus, in this equation the current value of an endogenous variable is expressed in terms of lagged values of itself (predetermined variable) and in terms of current and lagged values of the exogenous variables in the system. Lagged values of *other endogenous* variables (q in this case) do not appear in the equation.

This fundamental dynamic equation is convenient for tracing or predicting the time-path of p for given values of r and i. It is straightforward to use the equation recursively, substituting past values of p, or past predicted values, into the equation to predict future values. The fundamental dynamic equation is also useful for examining the stability of the system and is a first step toward deriving the final form for an endogenous variable. Multipliers can be derived from the final form, as can an equilibrium equation.

19.6   Exercises

19.1. Using the economic-statistical model 19.2.1, the data sample given in Table 19.1, and a computer package such as SHAZAM or SAS, reproduce the empirical results reported in Section 19.2.

19.2. Given the parameters in equation 19.2.3 for the econometric model discussed in Section 19.2, along with the values of the exogenous variables in Table

19.1, indicate how you would go about setting up a Monte Carlo experiment to generate a sample of 30 observations for y_1 and y_2.

19.3. Assume that you have constructed the following aggregate econometric model of the U. S. economy:

$$c_t = \gamma_{12} y_t + \beta_{11} + \beta_{12} c_{t-1} + e_{1t} \tag{19.6.1a}$$

$$i_t = \gamma_{22} y_t + \beta_{21} + \beta_{22} r_t + e_{2t} \tag{19.6.1b}$$

$$y_t = c_t + i_t + g_t \tag{19.6.1c}$$

where

c_t is private consumption expenditure in year t,
i_t is private investment expenditure in year t,
y_t is gross national expenditure in year t,
g_t is government expenditure in year t, and
r_t is a weighted average of interest rates in year t.

The variables c_t, i_t, and y_t are endogenous variables and g_t and r_t are considered to be exogenous.

(a) What are the predetermined variables in the model? Briefly explain what signs you expect a priori for each of the coefficients and the theoretical basis for your expectations.

(b) Examine equations 19.6.1a and 19.6.1b and use the order condition to determine their identification status.

(c) Derive algebraically the following reduced form coefficients in terms of the structural coefficients.

$$y_t = \pi_{10} + \pi_{11} c_{t-1} + \pi_{12} r_t + \pi_{13} g_t + v_{1t}$$
$$c_t = \pi_{20} + \pi_{21} c_{t-1} + \pi_{22} r_t + \pi_{23} g_t + v_{2t}$$
$$i_t = \pi_{30} + \pi_{31} c_{t-1} + \pi_{32} r_t + \pi_{33} g_t + v_{3t} \tag{19.6.2}$$

(d) Use the data in Table 18.2 of Chapter 18 on **y, c, i, g, r,** and SHAZAM, SAS or some other computer package to obtain

    (*i*) Least squares estimates of the reduced form parameters in equation 19.6.2;

    (*ii*) Least squares estimates of the structural parameters of equations 19.6.1a and 19.6.1b;

    (*iii*) 2SLS estimates of the structural parameters of equations 19.6.1a and 19.6.1b along with measures of precision (standard errors).

(e) Report your results and comment on their statistical reliability and economic feasibility.

(f) Use the 2SLS estimates obtained in (d)(*iii*) and the expressions derived in part (c) to obtain reduced form estimates. Do any of these estimates differ markedly from the unrestricted ones obtained in (d)(*i*)? Which estimates would you expect to be the most statistically efficient?

19.4. Reconsider the econometric model in Exercise 19.3 with c_{t-1} omitted from the consumption function and y_t omitted from the investment function.

(a) What is the identification status of each of the new equations?

(b) Use SHAZAM, SAS or some other computer package to obtain

    (*i*) reduced form estimates for each reduced form equation;

    (*ii*) least squares and 2SLS estimates of the structural parameters.

    (c) Are there any close similarities between the least squares and 2SLS estimates? Can you explain these similarities?

    (d) Contrast the problem of forecasting with the two statistical models considered in Exercises 19.3 and 19.4.

19.5. In the model of the meat sector (Appendix 19B) *assume* that, in addition to the prices p_b, p_p, and p_c, the quantities q_b, q_p, and q_c are also endogenous variables whose values are determined within the system. Under this assumption specify what you consider to be an economic and statistical model and discuss the identification and estimation implications.

19.6. If, indeed, economic data are generated by a set of economic relations that are stochastic, dynamic, and simultaneous:

    (a) Briefly summarize and contrast how the sampling theory simultaneous statistical model differs from the statistical models considered in previous chapters.

    (b) Explain why direct application of the least squares rule may not be appropriate.

    (c) Discuss why structural estimation may be important.

    (d) How would you make use of the results of model 19.6.1?

19.7. If you *knew* the parameters for the equations in model 19.6.1, along with the covariance matrix for the equation errors and the values of the exogenous variables, how would you go about developing observations on c_t, y_t, and i_t that might be used in Monte Carlo sampling experiments when contrasting the statistical performance of the least squares and 2SLS estimators *for small samples of data*?

19.8. If you worked through Appendix 19B, use the data in Table 19.1 to obtain, using a computer package, 3SLS estimates of the unknown structural and reduced form parameters. Contrast these results to those obtained in Exercise 19.1.

19.7 References

There is a vast literature on simultaneous equation models and the corresponding "appropriate" estimation procedures. Many think that econometrics started in the 1940s, when we started to think about the experimental conditions that are envisioned when we write down an economic relation and what this implies about the corresponding statistical model and estimation rules. A bit of history in this area is captured in the following monograph:

HOOD, W., and T. KOOPMANS (eds.) (1953) *Studies in Econometric Method*, Cowles Foundation Monograph No.14, New York: John Wiley & Sons, Inc.

For an easy-to-read modern discussion of simultaneous equation models refer to:

ROTHENBERG, T. (1987) "Simultaneous Equation Models," in *The New Palgrave: A Dictionary of Economics*, edited by J. M. EATWELL, M. MILGATE, and P. NEWMAN, New York: Stockton Press, pp. 344–347.

For a more complete and formal presentation of the simultaneous equation model and corresponding estimation rules and their statistical properties see:

JUDGE, G. G., R. C. HILL, W. E. GRIFFITHS, H. LÜTKEPOHL, and T. C. LEE (1988) *Introduction to the Theory and Practice of Econometrics*, 2nd Edition, New York: John Wiley & Sons, Inc., pp. 599–669.

JUDGE, G. G., W. E. GRIFFITHS, R. C. HILL, H. LÜTKEPOHL, and T. C. LEE (1985) *The Theory and Practice of Econometrics*, 2nd Edition, New York: John Wiley & Sons, Inc., pp. 144–190, 563–640.

APPENDIX 19A   A More Efficient Estimator?

19A.1   The Statistical Model

Although the two-stage least squares estimator is available for use with just- and overidentified equations, for completeness let us consider another formulation and estimation procedure for the simultaneous equations statistical model that makes use of the generalized least squares (Chapter 15) and seemingly unrelated regressions (Chapter 17) frameworks. In the context of the demand and supply model discussed in Section 19.1, let us specify the statistical model 19.1.1 in the two-equation linear form as

$$\mathbf{y}_1 = \begin{bmatrix} \mathbf{y}_2 & \mathbf{x}_1 & \mathbf{x}_2 & \mathbf{x}_3 \end{bmatrix} \begin{bmatrix} \gamma_{12} \\ \beta_{11} \\ \beta_{12} \\ \beta_{13} \end{bmatrix} + \mathbf{e}_1 = Z_1 \boldsymbol{\delta}_1 + \mathbf{e}_1$$

(19A.1a)

and

$$\mathbf{y}_2 = \begin{bmatrix} \mathbf{y}_1 & \mathbf{x}_1 & \mathbf{x}_4 \end{bmatrix} \begin{bmatrix} \gamma_{21} \\ \beta_{21} \\ \beta_{24} \end{bmatrix} + \mathbf{e}_2 = Z_2 \boldsymbol{\delta}_2 + \mathbf{e}_2$$

(19A.1b)

or in the seemingly unrelated framework of Chapter 14 as

$$\begin{bmatrix} \mathbf{y}_1 \\ \mathbf{y}_2 \end{bmatrix} = \begin{bmatrix} Z_1 & \\ & Z_2 \end{bmatrix} \begin{bmatrix} \boldsymbol{\delta}_1 \\ \boldsymbol{\delta}_2 \end{bmatrix} + \begin{bmatrix} \mathbf{e}_1 \\ \mathbf{e}_2 \end{bmatrix}$$

(19A.2a)

where

$$\mathbf{e} = \begin{bmatrix} \mathbf{e}_1 \\ \mathbf{e}_2 \end{bmatrix} \sim N \left[\begin{pmatrix} \mathbf{0} \\ \mathbf{0} \end{pmatrix}, \begin{pmatrix} \sigma_{11} I_T & \sigma_{12} I_T \\ \sigma_{21} I_T & \sigma_{22} I_T \end{pmatrix} \right]$$

(19A.2b)

which recognizes that the contemporaneous correlation between the equation errors may *not* be zero. At first glance, in this form the statistical model looks very much like the seemingly unrelated regression (SUR) equation models analyzed in Chapter 17. The difference is that now the right-hand-side matrices Z_1 and Z_2 contain both endogenous and exogenous variables and the endogenous variables are *not* assumed to be uncorrelated with $\mathbf{e}$. If we use the least squares rule on each individual equation, this estimator will not be consistent (simultaneous least squares bias). If we apply the generalized least squares estimator directly to the *set* of equations, as we did with two or more regressions in the SUR chapter, the resulting estimator will not be consistent.

In Chapter 17 when we had two or more regression equations *we found that if the equation errors between equations were correlated, we could improve the efficiency of our estimator* if we estimated them as a system, rather than estimating each equation separately. Now, if we write the system of equations as in equation 19A.2a and apply this idea in our demand and supply problem, we note the covariance matrix for the equation errors in equation 19A.2b is

$$\text{cov} \begin{bmatrix} \mathbf{e}_1 \\ \mathbf{e}_2 \end{bmatrix} = \begin{bmatrix} \sigma_{11} I_T & \sigma_{12} I_T \\ \sigma_{21} I_T & \sigma_{22} I_T \end{bmatrix}$$

(19A.2c)

and thus has the same error covariance structure as the SUR model in Chapter 17. Therefore, if we organize our statistical model 19A.1 in a seemingly unrelated regression (SUR) form, we have

$$\begin{bmatrix} \mathbf{y}_1 \\ \mathbf{y}_2 \end{bmatrix} = \begin{bmatrix} Z_1 & 0 \\ 0 & Z_2 \end{bmatrix} \begin{pmatrix} \boldsymbol{\delta}_1 \\ \boldsymbol{\delta}_2 \end{pmatrix} = \begin{bmatrix} \mathbf{e}_1 \\ \mathbf{e}_2 \end{bmatrix} \tag{19A.2a}$$

or

$$\mathbf{y} = Z\boldsymbol{\delta} + \mathbf{e} \tag{19A.3}$$

where

$$\mathbf{y} = \begin{bmatrix} \mathbf{y}_1 \\ \mathbf{y}_2 \end{bmatrix} \qquad Z = \begin{bmatrix} Z_1 & 0 \\ 0 & Z_2 \end{bmatrix} \qquad \boldsymbol{\delta} = \begin{bmatrix} \boldsymbol{\delta}_1 \\ \boldsymbol{\delta}_2 \end{bmatrix}$$

and

$$\mathbf{e} = \begin{pmatrix} \mathbf{e}_1 \\ \mathbf{e}_2 \end{pmatrix} \sim N\left(\mathbf{0}, \begin{pmatrix} \sigma_{11} I_T & \sigma_{12} I_T \\ \sigma_{21} I_T & \sigma_{22} I_T \end{pmatrix} = W_1 \right) \tag{19A.4}$$

Because the Z_i contain endogenous variables, to get a consistent estimator of $\boldsymbol{\delta}$ we use the matrix of exogenous variables X to transform the statistical model 19A.3, and this yields

$$\begin{bmatrix} X' & 0 \\ 0 & X' \end{bmatrix} \begin{bmatrix} \mathbf{y}_1 \\ \mathbf{y}_2 \end{bmatrix} = \begin{bmatrix} X' & 0 \\ 0 & X' \end{bmatrix} \begin{bmatrix} Z_1 & 0 \\ 0 & Z_2 \end{bmatrix} \begin{bmatrix} \boldsymbol{\delta}_1 \\ \boldsymbol{\delta}_2 \end{bmatrix} + \begin{bmatrix} X' & 0 \\ 0 & X' \end{bmatrix} \begin{bmatrix} \mathbf{e}_1 \\ \mathbf{e}_2 \end{bmatrix}$$

$$\begin{bmatrix} X'\mathbf{y}_1 \\ X'\mathbf{y}_2 \end{bmatrix} = \begin{bmatrix} X'Z_1 & 0 \\ 0 & X'Z_2 \end{bmatrix} \begin{bmatrix} \boldsymbol{\delta}_1 \\ \boldsymbol{\delta}_2 \end{bmatrix} + \begin{bmatrix} X'\mathbf{e}_1 \\ X'\mathbf{e}_2 \end{bmatrix} \tag{19A.5}$$

which is in terms of equation 19A.3, with $X_1 = \begin{bmatrix} X & 0 \\ 0 & X \end{bmatrix}$,

$$X_1' \mathbf{y} = X_1' Z\boldsymbol{\delta} + X_1' \mathbf{e} \tag{19A.6}$$

or

$$\mathbf{y}* = Z*\boldsymbol{\delta} + \mathbf{e}*$$

where

$$\mathbf{e}* = X_1' \mathbf{e} \sim N\left(\mathbf{0}, \begin{bmatrix} \sigma_{11} X'X & \sigma_{12} X'X \\ \sigma_{21} X'X & \sigma_{22} X'X \end{bmatrix} = W_1^* \right)$$

If

$$W_1^* = \begin{bmatrix} \sigma_{11} X'X & \sigma_{12} X'X \\ \sigma_{21} X'X & \sigma_{22} X'X \end{bmatrix}$$

is known, then as in Chapter 17 the efficient estimator is the GLS estimator

$$\tilde{\boldsymbol{\delta}} = \left[Z*' W_1^{*-1} Z* \right]^{-1} Z* W_1^{*-1} \mathbf{y}*$$

$$= \left[Z'X_1 W_1^{*-1} X_1' Z \right]^{-1} Z'X_1 W_1^{*-1} X_1' \mathbf{y} \tag{19A.7}$$

In *large* samples

$$\tilde{\boldsymbol{\delta}} \sim N\left(\boldsymbol{\delta}, \left[Z'X_1 \hat{W}_1^{*-1} X_1' Z \right]^{-1} \right) \tag{19A.8}$$

As was true with the SUR model, in practice,

$$\begin{bmatrix} \sigma_{11} & \sigma_{12} \\ \sigma_{21} & \sigma_{22} \end{bmatrix}$$

and thus W_1^* is not known. However, a consistent estimator $\hat{W}_1^*$ of W_1^* may be computed by using the estimated errors $(\mathbf{y}_i - Z_i \hat{\boldsymbol{\delta}}_i) = \hat{\mathbf{e}}_i$ in the following way to compute estimates of the variances and covariance:

$$\hat{\sigma}_{ij} = \left(\mathbf{y}_i - Z_i \hat{\boldsymbol{\delta}}_i \right)'\left(\mathbf{y}_j - Z_j \hat{\boldsymbol{\delta}}_j \right)\Big/ T \tag{19A.9}$$

Thus from the GLS format the operational estimator for estimating the two equations jointly is

$$\tilde{\tilde{\boldsymbol{\delta}}} = \left[Z'X_1 \hat{W}_1^{*-1} X_1' Z \right]^{-1} Z'X_1 \hat{W}_1^{*-1} X_1' \mathbf{y} \tag{19A.10}$$

with

$$\hat{\text{cov}}(\tilde{\tilde{\boldsymbol{\delta}}}) = \left[Z'X_1 \hat{W}_1^{*-1} X_1' Z \right]^{-1} \tag{19A.11}$$

Given the estimated covariance matrix 19A.11, *approximate* standard errors of $\tilde{\tilde{\boldsymbol{\delta}}}$ can be computed and hypothesis tests may be carried out.

The estimator $\tilde{\tilde{\boldsymbol{\delta}}}$ is referred to in the econometrics literature as the three-stage least squares (3SLS) estimator, and computer programs given in the *Computer Handbooks* exist for use in applied work. The three stages in the life of this estimator are to

(i) transform the system by multiplying each equation by the matrix of all exogenous variables X and count to determine that the column dimension of X is equal to or greater than the column dimension of Z_i the matrix of endogenous and exogenous variables in each equation;

(ii) use the 2SLS estimator to estimate each of the equations individually and estimate for each equation the errors $\mathbf{e}_i$;

(iii) use the estimated errors $\hat{\mathbf{e}}_i$ to compute, for the system of equations, the estimated error covariance matrix

$$\hat{W}_1^* = \begin{bmatrix} \hat{\sigma}_{11} X'X & \hat{\sigma}_{12} X'X \\ \hat{\sigma}_{21} X'X & \hat{\sigma}_{22} X'X \end{bmatrix}$$

and then use the SUR (GLS) procedure to estimate the unknown parameters and sampling errors.

For a more complete discussion of the 3SLS estimator see Section 15.2 of Judge et al. (1988). At this stage your intuition should be that you are applying the SUR procedure to the transformed simultaneous statistical model 19A.5.

APPENDIX 19B An Application of a Simultaneous Equations Model

In Section 18.2 we reviewed a simple economic demand and supply equilibrium model, and in Section 19.1 we discussed the possibilities for estimating the corresponding unknown parameters. At this point let us consider a particular model involving questions concerning the demand for meat. For this analysis we consider the disaggregated meat components, beef, pork, and chicken.

19B.1 The Economic Model

From the micro theory of the household, we expect the level of consumption of each of these meat components to be a function of the price of the commodity, the price of substitutes, and the level of income. Under this general specification we might specify the price-dependent demand relations as follows:

$$p_{bt} = f_1\left(p_{pt}, p_{ct}, q_{bt}, di_t\right)$$ (19B.1a)

$$p_{ct} = f_2\left(p_{bt}, p_{pt}, q_{ct}, di_t\right)$$ (19B.1b)

$$p_{pt} = f_3\left(p_{bt}, p_{ct}, q_{pt}, di_t\right)$$ (19B.1c)

where in time period t, q_b is the per capita consumption of beef, q_p is the per capita consumption of pork, q_c is the per capita consumption of chicken, p_b, p_p, and p_c are the prices of beef, pork, and chicken, and di is per capita disposable income. The sample observations underlying these economic variables are quarterly for the period 1973:1 to 1984:4. All prices and disposable income are given in real terms.

Since the observations are *quarterly*, the quantities of beef, pork, and chicken produced and marketed are predetermined by decisions taken in previous quarters. Thus, prices in a particular quarter t are assumed to have little or no effect on the production in that quarter t and the supply of each meat is fixed. Consequently, in each period the market clearing price for each meat is determined by fixed supply, competing prices and income. Therefore, we will assume in this static equilibrium model 19B.1 that the per capita quantities consumed q_{bt}, q_{pt}, and q_{ct}, along with per capita disposable income, are economic variables whose values are determined outside of the system in time t and are thus exogenous variables. Since beef, pork, and chicken are substitutes for each other as the consumer allocates purchases, subject to the budget constraint, we assume that the observed prices are determined jointly within the system and thus that they are endogenous variables. The prices simultaneously adjust to clear the market given the exogenous supplies q_b, q_p, and q_c. Consequently, we have a system of price-dependent demand relations that involve three endogenous variables p_b, p_p, and p_c and four exogenous variables q_b, q_p, q_c and d_i.

Many realistic choices exist for extending and making more complete the economic model 19B.1. Other food and nonfood prices could be included. Since consumption patterns adjust over time, disposable income lagged one or more time periods might also be included. Although there may be little adjustment in production to current prices, some price effect may exist. Therefore, it may be reasonable to specify supply relations that spell out the dynamics of production as affected by current and lagged product and factor prices. Although each of these possibilities may add a bit of realism, the model specified in equation 19B.1 has enough real-world content to be sufficient for our purposes. Extensions or variations of the model 19B.1 are included as Exercise 19.5.

In terms of the economic rationale underlying equation 19B.1, we would expect (*i*) a negative relationship between the own price and quantity in each demand relation, and (*ii*) positive relationships betweeen prices of substitutes and income. If we are correct about the direction of the relations, the tricky question remaining concerns the magnitudes involved. For example, if the level of income is constant and if there is a certain change in the quantities of the three meats that are available for consumption and consumed, how much do the beef, pork, and chicken prices change and what are their equilibrium values? To provide a basis for answering some of these questions, we need next to consider a statistical model corresponding to the economic model 19B.1.

19B.2   The Statistical Model

To convert the economic model 19B.1 to a statistical model, define the vectors of observations on the endogenous variables p_b, p_c and p_p as $\mathbf{y}_1$, $\mathbf{y}_2$ and $\mathbf{y}_3$ respectively. Also, redefine the vectors of observations on the exogenous variables q_b, q_c, q_p, and di as $\mathbf{x}_2$, $\mathbf{x}_3$, $\mathbf{x}_4$, and $\mathbf{x}_5$, respectively. We will let the vector of unit values $\mathbf{x}_1$ denote the intercept variable in each demand equation. Assuming a specification linear in the variables and letting $\mathbf{e}_1$, $\mathbf{e}_2$, and $\mathbf{e}_3$ represent the unobservable equation errors, we may write the statistical model as

$$\mathbf{y}_1 = \mathbf{y}_2\gamma_{12} + \mathbf{y}_3\gamma_{13} + \mathbf{x}_1\beta_{11} + \mathbf{x}_2\beta_{12} + \mathbf{x}_5\beta_{15} + \mathbf{e}_1 \qquad (19B.2a)$$

$$\mathbf{y}_2 = \mathbf{y}_1\gamma_{21} + \mathbf{y}_3\gamma_{23} + \mathbf{x}_1\beta_{21} + \mathbf{x}_3\beta_{23} + \mathbf{x}_5\beta_{25} + \mathbf{e}_2 \qquad (19B.2b)$$

$$\mathbf{y}_3 = \mathbf{y}_1\gamma_{31} + \mathbf{y}_2\gamma_{32} + \mathbf{x}_1\beta_{31} + \mathbf{x}_4\beta_{34} + \mathbf{x}_5\beta_{35} + \mathbf{e}_3 \qquad (19B.2c)$$

where, in line with stochastic assumptions of Section 19A.4 of Appendix 19A, the equation-dependent random errors are

$$\mathbf{e} = \begin{bmatrix} \mathbf{e}_1 \\ \mathbf{e}_2 \\ \mathbf{e}_3 \end{bmatrix} \sim N\left[\begin{pmatrix} \mathbf{0} \\ \mathbf{0} \\ \mathbf{0} \end{pmatrix}, \begin{bmatrix} \sigma_{11}I_T & \sigma_{12}I_T & \sigma_{13}I_T \\ \sigma_{21}I_T & \sigma_{22}I_T & \sigma_{23}I_T \\ \sigma_{31}I_T & \sigma_{32}I_T & \sigma_{33}I_T \end{bmatrix} \right] \qquad (19B.3)$$

In terms of the statistical model for the structural equations 19B.2, each equation has five unknown parameters and there are five exogenous variables in the system; of the five, two do not appear in each equation. Using the counting rule, each equation is just-identified and thus may be estimated as a system or individually. In the context of Section 19.4, the transformed statistical model for the *i*th equation is

$$X'\mathbf{y}_i = X'Z_i\boldsymbol{\delta}_i + X'\mathbf{e}_i \qquad (19B.4)$$

Since $X'Z_i$ is a square matrix, following the results developed in Section 19.4, we may apply the least squares rule to 19B.4 to estimate δ_i:

$$\hat{\boldsymbol{\delta}}_i = \left(X'Z_i \right)^{-1} X'\mathbf{y}_i \qquad (19B.5)$$

An approximate estimator of the covariance matrix for $\hat{\boldsymbol{\delta}}_i$ is

$$\hat{\text{cov}}\left(\hat{\boldsymbol{\delta}}_i \right) = \hat{\sigma}_{ii}\left[X'Z_i \right]^{-1} \qquad (19B.6)$$

and the resulting estimates may be used to compute standard errors and make tests of hypotheses.

19B.3   Some Empirical Results

Using the quarterly sample observations for the period 1973:1 to 1984:4, and the statistical model for the structural equations 19B.2 and the simultaneous equation estimator 19B.5, the empirical results for the demand relations for meat are as follows:

$$\hat{y}_1 = 0.250y_2 + 1.477y_3 + 57.727x_1 - 2.587x_2 + 11.570x_5$$

(0.311)	(0.637)	(21.208)	(0.373)	(5.932)	s.e.	
(0.802)	(2.320)	(2.722)	(−6.937)	(1.951)	t	
(0.195)	(0.573)		(−0.775)	(0.393)	ε	(19B.7)

$$\hat{y}_2 = 0.087y_1 + 0.332y_3 + 19.825x_1 - 1.460x_3 - 0.142x_5$$

(0.067)	(0.072)	(5.431)	(0.401)	(2.603)	s.e.	
(1.312)	(4.620)	(3.651)	(−3.637)	(−0.054)	t	
(0.225)	(0.668)		(−0.425)	(−0.012)	ε	(19B.8)

$$\hat{y}_3 = 0.224y_1 + 1.338y_2 + 7.940x_1 - 1.647x_4 + 7.147x_5$$

(0.117)	(0.248)	(18.618)	(0.444)	(3.780)	s.e.	
(1.914)	(5.403)	(0.426)	(−3.711)	(1.891)	t	
(0.287)	(0.664)		(−0.369)	(0.311)	ε	(19B.9)

The standard errors, the t-statistics, and ε (the elasticities computed at the mean), $(\partial y_i / \partial y_j)(\bar{y}_j / \bar{y}_i)$ and $(\partial y_i / \partial x_j)(\bar{x}_j / \bar{y}_i)$, are given in parenthesis below the estimates of the structural coefficients. The coefficients connecting the price and quantity of a particular meat are, as expected, negative, and in each instance the estimated coefficient is statistically significant at or above the .05 level. All of the estimated structural coefficients have the expected sign except the income coefficient for chicken, which is negative. In this case the unknown coefficient is measured imprecisely and carries a t-statistic that approaches zero. In each equation the coefficients of price are positive, thus reflecting competitive relationships among the meats in consumption. As expected the income coefficients for beef and pork are positive and are estimated with satisfactory sampling precision. The income–price elasticities for beef and pork are 0.39 and 0.31, respectively. Seldom in econometric analyses do all of the estimated coefficients have the expected signs. The income–price coefficient for chicken fails into that category in this analysis. Because of its place in a low-fat diet, the level of consumption of chicken is also affected by noneconomic factors.

If, in the context of previous chapters, we had been willing to ignore the interdependent relations among meat prices, one alternative would have been to estimate each demand relation in equation 19B.2 using the least squares estimator 19B.5. If, for example, we had done this for pork, we would have obtained the following estimated relationship:

$$\hat{y}_3 = 0.293y_1 + 1.136y_2 + 20.537x_1 - 1.860x_4 + 4.585x_5$$

(0.073)	(0.162)	(14.052)	(0.387)	(3.021)	s.e.
(4.032)	(7.004)	(1.462)	(−4.80)	(1.518)	t
(0.374)	(0.564)		(−0.417)	(0.199)	ε (19B.9)

If this result is considered relative to equation 19B.6, it is qualitatively not different, but some differences in the estimated coefficients and elasticities and thus differences in policy actions are evident.

The corresponding estimated reduced form equations for the simultaneous meats demand model are

$$\hat{y}_1 = 318.00x_1 - 6.1936x_2 - 5.2435x_3 - 11.3750x_4 + 49.3500x_5$$

(52.02)	(1.2026)	(1.1758)	(2.1139)	(14.5210)	s.e.
(6.11)	(−5.15)	(−4.46)	(−5.38)	(3.40)	t

(19B.10)

$$\hat{y}_2 = 256.83x_1 - 3.7958x_2 - 6.1746x_3 - 10.4800x_4 + 42.7520x_5$$

(42.69)	(0.9869)	(0.9649)	(1.7347)	(11.9160)	s.e.
(6.02)	(−3.85)	(−6.40)	(−6.04)	(3.59)	t

(19B.11)

$$\hat{y}_3 = 132.80x_1 - 1.800x_2 - 2.5063x_3 - 5.9297x_4 + 18.3510x_5$$

(22.62)	(.5229)	(.5112)	(.9191)	(6.3139)	s.e.
(5.87)	(−3.44)	(−4.90)	(−6.45)	(2.91)	t

(19B.12)

The corresponding R^2 for the reduced form equations are 0.40, 0.53, and 0.56, respectively. The standard errors and the t values appear in the parentheses below the coefficients.

The reduced form equations reflect the estimated relationships between the endogenous variables y_1, y_2, and y_3 and the exogenous variables x_2, x_3, x_4, and x_5 after all interaction or feedbacks in the system have taken place. Since in this system, if q changes, p changes, it could be argued that estimates of own price elasticities should come from these reduced form equations. The reduced form coefficients are without exception statistically significant at or above the .05 level. All the reduced form coefficients have a priori the correct signs, which means the quantity variables have negative coefficients and the income variable has a positive coefficient. The moderate size R^2's indicates the simplified nature of our model as well as the presence of many other factors influencing the variation in the prices.

The potential use of the estimated reduced form equations was discussed in Section 19.5. In this static model, forecasting and tracing the path of the endogenous price variables for given values of the exogenous variables can be carried out by using the reduced forms. For given values of the quantities of the meats x_2, x_3, x_4 and the income x_5, the subsystem will always be in equilibrium. The equilibrium values for the prices y_1, y_2, and y_3 are those values that would result from using the reduced form equations. Changes in the quantities and the level of income cause changes in the equilibrium prices. For example, a one-unit increase in disposable income will increase the prices y_1, y_2, and

y_3 by 49, 43, and 18 units, respectively. The impact on prices of changes in the quantity produced and consumed for one or more of the meats can be similarly obtained. By constructing an economic and statistical model for the meat sector that reflects an endogenous, instantaneous feedback mechanism between the meat prices, we are able to obtain estimates of both the structural and reduced form parameters for the system of relations. Thus, our information is tailored for the particular decision purpose and action at hand.

Part VII

Time-Series and Dynamic Economic Models

In Chapter 19 we observed that economic behavior contains a *dynamic* component, and many economic shocks and decisions may take many months for their impact to be felt throughout the system. The dynamic and interrelated nature of the economy means that the impact of shocks and decisions in time t_0 will have an effect on the level of the endogenous variable y_t not only in period t_0, but also for many time periods $t_0 + 1$, $t_0 + 2$, $t_0 + 3$, ...

In Chapter 16 we noted that in the context of time-series data, random disturbances may be autocorrelated. The model of first-order autocorrelation, proposed in Chapter 16, related the current disturbance, e_t, to e_{t-1}. In general, the dynamic relationship by which disturbances affect the current value of an economic variable y_t may be complicated and involve, not only e_t and e_{t-1}, but also e_{t-2}, e_{t-3}, and higher lags of the disturbance term. The dynamic behavior of an economy can reveal itself through a dependence of the current value of an economic variable depending on its own past values. Specifically, models of how decisionmakers' expectations are formed, and how they react to changes in the economy, result in the value of y_t depending on y_{t-1}. More generally the current value of an economic variable may depend, not only on its value in the previous period, but also on its values in many periods before.

In Chapter 20, a univariate time-series model is introduced that relates the current and future values of y to its own past values, and the values of current and past values of a random disturbance term. This univariate time-series model neglects any relationship between y_t and other economic variables, which leads to the dynamic model

$$y_t = f\left(y_{t-1}, y_{t-2}, y_{t-3}, \ldots; e_t, e_{t-1}, e_{t-2}, e_{t-3}, \ldots\right)$$

Univariate time-series models of this type are used for short-run economic forecasting and are an alternative to traditional types of econometric models for this purpose.

In Chapter 21 bivariate and multivariate time-series analysis is introduced, and two (or more) economic time series, x_t and y_t, are jointly considered. First, distributed lag models of the form

$$y_t = f\left(x_t, x_{t-1}, \ldots; e_t\right)$$

are described. In these models x_t is considered predetermined (before y_t) and changes Δx_t have effects that are distributed over future values of y_t. The effects may last a finite or infinite number of periods, and models for both of these cases are considered. Next, we treat the pair (y_t, x_t) as random and jointly determined by their own past values in a dynamic reduced form equation called a vector autoregression. These models are useful for forecasting values of the endogenous variables, in the near future, *without* building a structural equation model. Finally, we consider the topics of spurious regressions, unit root tests, and cointegration. These issues relate to the question of whether structural models involving economic time series should be specified as levels or first differences and bear on the problem of deducing information on long-run relationships from time-series data.

Chapter 20

Univariate Time-Series Analysis and Forecasting

New Key Words and Concepts

Forecasting	Time-Series Models
Moving Average Process	Autoregressive Models
ARMA Models	ARIMA Models
Invertible Process	

20.1 Introduction

One objective of analyzing economic data is to predict or forecast the future values of economic variables. In the preceding chapters the econometric model-building approach that we have used for obtaining forecasts is to *(i)* formulate an economic model involving economic variables that explain the behavior of the economic outcome variable in question; *(ii)* construct a statistical model that is thought to be consistent with the sampling process by which the data were generated; and *(iii)* use a sample of data, and an appropriate estimation procedure, to estimate the unknown parameters of the statistical model and use them as a basis for forecasting and inference.

In this chapter we focus on a different technique that may be useful in short-term forecasting situations. Instead of building an economic and statistical model that relates the values of an economic variable to a set of explanatory or control variables, the *time-series approach* that we discuss in this chapter relates current values of an economic variable *only* to its past values and to the values of current and past random disturbances. The statistical model that results from this idea is called a "time-series model." Time-series models differ from traditional econometric models in that they do not begin with a conceptual framework, provided by economic theory, that specifies a relationship between economic variables. Thus, behavioral or technical equations, like those specified in Chapters 18 and 19, are not considered. Instead, the emphasis is on making use of the information in the past values of a variable for forecasting its future values by using what amounts to a sophisticated extrapolation procedure. Time-series methods offer the possibility of making accurate forecasts, even when the underlying structural model is unknown, by replacing the structural restrictions needed to reduce the sampling error and improve forecasts, with restrictions determined by the data. The use of a time-series model for forecasting may be attractive, from a cost-benefit perspective, when *(i)* the (only) objective is a *short-run* forecast, *(ii)* the development of an econometric model explaining the behavior of the variable to be forecast would require significant amounts of time and energy, and *(iii)* there is a sufficiently large amount of data on the variable to be forecast, that is, a long enough time series, so that an effective time-series model can be built.

Given this framework, the purpose of this chapter is to *(i)* discuss alternative ways of specifying time-series statistical models; *(ii)* develop procedures for estimating the parameters of the resulting statistical model; and *(iii)* demonstrate how the resulting estimated univariate time-series model may be used to forecast future values of an economic variable.

The plan of the chapter is as follows: In Section 20.2 we discuss the characteristics of statistical models that are designed to represent the sampling process by which time-series data are obtained. In Sections 20.3 and 20.4 we present autoregressive (AR) and moving average (MA) statistical models, analyze their statistical properties, and discuss issues relating to specification and estimation. In Section 20.5 we combine AR and MA models to obtain an autoregressive-moving average (ARMA) statistical model. In Section 20.6 we recognize that time series representing economic variables may not be generated by a stationary process. The Box–Jenkins approach to model building is summarized in Section 20.7, and forecasting is the main focus of Section 20.8.

20.2   The Characteristics of Univariate Time-Series Statistical Models

To introduce time-series analysis and to illustrate the nature of the problem of forecasting future values of an economic variable on the basis of the information in its past values, consider Figures 20.1, 20.2, and 20.3. These figures are plots of values of three economic variables over time. Let us consider each in turn.

1. The yearly price of U. S. corn, from 1867 to 1948, is plotted in Figure 20.1. As you can see, the corn price varies considerably over the period with peaks followed by valleys, or cycles, appearing in the series. Our objective is, based on these data alone, to forecast the values of corn price one, two, or three or more years beyond the end of the sample of data.

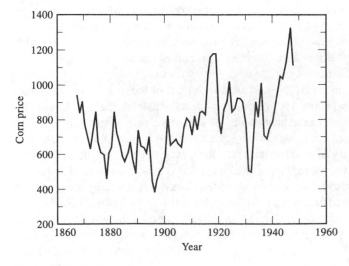

Figure 20.1 U. S. corn prices.

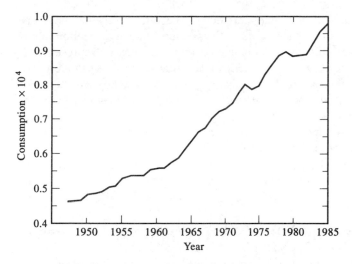

Figure 20.2 U. S. personal consumption expenditures.

2.   Annual U. S. personal consumption (billions of 1982 dollars) is plotted for 1947 to 1985 in Figure 20.2. Though there are "bumps" in the series, these data exhibit a strong upward trend. Given these characteristics can future values of consumption be predicted?

3.   In Figure 20.3 monthly U. S. residential construction (millions of current dollars and seasonally unadjusted) is plotted for 1947 to 1970. Note that there is a seasonal pattern with peaks and valleys at time multiples of 12. Can this seasonal pattern be taken into account using time-series model, and be used to assist forecasting performance of future monthly residential construction?

These time-series of observations, which reflect the dynamic characteristics of economic variables, are typical ones. As a basis for forecasting, we need to specify a

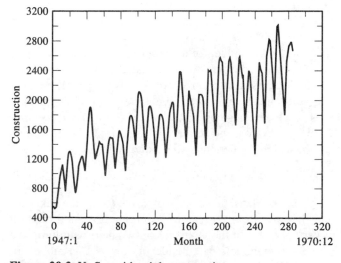

Figure 20.3 U. S. residential construction.

statistical model consistent with the characteristics of these time-series data. To begin, we note that time-series models are based on the assumption that an economic variable, say y_t, is a random variable whose outcome possibilities may be represented by a probability density function $f(y_t)$. A time series is a sequence of these random variables that are observed at regular time intervals, $y_1, y_2, \ldots, y_T$. The key assumption in the specification of a statistical model of time-series data is that the value of a random economic variable y_t depends only on its own past values $y_{t-1}, y_{t-2}, \ldots$, and current and past values of random disturbances $e_t, e_{t-1}, e_{t-2}, \ldots$. In a univariate time-series model, the values of no other economic variables are considered.

In the following section we propose a simple time-series statistical model, for a single observable economic variable y_t, that serves as a basis for forecasting its future values.

20.3   Statistical Models for Autoregressive Processes

In time-series modeling the notion that information contained in past values of an economic variable y_t is useful for forecasting future values of an economic variable is a key one. To make this idea operational, we develop a statistical model that reflects this characteristic.

One example of a statistical model representing this type of lagged dependence is given by the following autoregressive process of order 1:

$$y_t = \delta + \theta_1 y_{t-1} + e_t \qquad t = 1, 2, \ldots, T \qquad (20.3.1)$$

In this first-order autoregressive statistical model, δ is an intercept parameter, θ_1 is an unknown parameter that is assumed to take a value between -1 and 1, and e_t is an uncorrelated random error with mean zero, and constant variance σ_e^2. Equation 20.3.1 is an autoregressive time-series model of the first order, since y_t depends only on its value in the previous period, y_{t-1}, plus a random disturbance. This statistical model specification is denoted as an AR(1) time-series model, or AR(1) *process*.

This is not the first time we have discussed the first-order autoregressive process. In Chapter 16 we dealt with the problem of serial correlation, or autocorrelation, in the context of the linear regression model. The first-order autocorrelation structure for the equation errors that was examined there is a special case of the AR(1) process in equation 20.3.1. In the model of serially correlated random errors, the parameter $\delta = 0$, and the random variables involved were the unobservable equation random errors e_t. Here, on the other hand, *the random variable y_t is observable*.

When specifying a time-series statistical model for an economic variable, the exact nature of the process generating the time series $y_1, y_2, \ldots, y_T$ is usually not known. Even if we are willing to assume that the process is autoregressive, it may very well be more complicated than the first-order autoregressive process given in equation 20.3.1. Specifically y_t may not only depend on y_{t-1}, but also on y_{t-2}, y_{t-3}, and so on. To accommodate these more general dependencies, we introduce the statistical model of an autoregressive process of order p, which we denote AR(p), and write as

$$y_t = \delta + \theta_1 y_{t-1} + \theta_2 y_{t-2} + \ldots + \theta_p y_{t-p} + e_t \qquad (20.3.2)$$

where δ is an "intercept parameter" that is related to the mean of y_t, the θ_is are the unknown autoregressive parameters, and the errors e_t are assumed to be uncorrelated random variables with zero mean and variance σ_e^2. In the next section we begin studying the properties of autoregressive time-series models by considering the AR(1) model. In subsequent sections we consider more general AR(p) models.

20.3.1   Statistical Properties of First-Order Autoregressive Models

In Chapter 3 we stressed that knowledge of the joint probability density function of a set of random variables, including the means of the random variables, as well as their variances and covariances, is an informative way to characterize their sampling behavior. In the time-series context, the set of random variables we consider is $y_1, y_2, \ldots, y_T$. As *we analyze alternative time-series models, calculation of the means, variances, and co-variances of the time series variables y_t is an important first step.*

As a starting point, time-series models are based on the assumption that the time-series process that generates the outcomes y_t began in the infinite past and continues into the infinite future. Furthermore, it is assumed that past and future random variables follow the *same* probability density function $f(y_t)$ as that of the sample observations $y_1, y_2, \ldots, y_T$. Thus, all the random variables y_t, whether they represent past, present, or future values of an economic variable, are assumed to have the same mean and the same variance. Furthermore, covariances between any two of the random variables, say, y_t and y_{t+s}, are assumed not to depend on time, but only on the lead or lag s between the two random variables. This is an important assumption if we seek to predict the future on the basis of the past. If the data-generation process that produced the observed sample does not hold for future values of the random variable, then forecasts based on the sample of data will not be reliable.

We now compute the mean, variance, and covariances for an AR(1) process. As we proceed, note the similarities between the expressions we derive here, and those found in Chapter 16.

20.3.1a   The Mean of an AR(1) Process   If the observable outcomes y_t of a time series have the same probability density function for all time periods, then the mean of y_t, and its variance, must be the same in all time periods. In terms of the mean, this implies that $E[y_t] = E[y_{t-1}] = \ldots = \mu$. Taking the expected value of y_t in equation 20.3.1, we obtain

$$E[y_t] = E[\delta + \theta_1 y_{t-1} + e_t]$$

or

$$\mu = \delta + \theta_1 \mu \tag{20.3.3}$$

Solving for the mean μ gives

$$E[y_t] = \mu = \delta/(1-\theta_1) \tag{20.3.4}$$

For convenience in determining other properties of an AR(1) process, we assume that the intercept parameter $\delta = 0$, so that the mean of the time-series variables y_t is $\mu = 0$. Setting $\delta = 0$ is equivalent to measuring the series y_t in terms of deviations about its mean, or $(y_t - \mu)$. That this adjustment in the mean does not affect the variances or covariances of the time series is demonstrated in Exercise 20.1.

20.3.1b   The Variance and Covariances of an AR(1) Process   To find the variance of y_t in the AR(1) statistical model, we use the assumption that this variance is the same in all time periods. Taking the variance of both sides of equation 20.3.1, we obtain

$$\text{var}(y_t) = \sigma_y^2 = \text{var}(\theta_1 y_{t-1} + e_t)$$
$$= \theta_1^2 \text{var}(y_{t-1}) + \text{var}(e_t) \quad \text{(since } y_{t-1} \text{ and } e_t \text{ are independent)}$$
$$= \theta_1^2 \sigma_y^2 + \sigma_e^2$$

Solving for σ_y^2 we obtain

$$\sigma_y^2 = \frac{\sigma_e^2}{1 - \theta_1^2} \qquad (20.3.5a)$$

In addition to the mean and variance of y_t being identical for all time periods, time-series variables are assumed to have covariances that are constant over time. For example,

$$
\begin{aligned}
\mathrm{cov}(y_t, y_{t-1}) &= E\big[y_t - E(y_t)\big]\big[y_{t-1} - E(y_{t-1})\big] \\
&= E\big[y_t y_{t-1}\big] \qquad \text{(since } E[y_t] = 0\text{)} \\
&= E\big[(\theta_1 y_{t-1} + e_t) y_{t-1}\big] \\
&= \theta_1 E\big[y_{t-1}^2\big] + E\big[e_t y_{t-1}\big] \\
&= \theta_1 \sigma_y^2 \qquad \text{(since } e_t \text{ and } y_{t-1} \text{ are uncorrelated)} \quad (20.3.5b)
\end{aligned}
$$

This covariance is the same for all random variables that are one period apart. The reader may verify that

$$
\begin{aligned}
\mathrm{cov}(y_{t-1}, y_{t-2}) &= E\big[y_{t-1} y_{t-2}\big] = \theta_1 \sigma_y^2 \\
\mathrm{cov}(y_{t-2}, y_{t-3}) &= E\big[y_{t-2} y_{t-3}\big] = \theta_1 \sigma_y^2
\end{aligned}
$$

and so on. The covariance for all random variables that are two periods apart is given by

$$
\begin{aligned}
\mathrm{cov}(y_t, y_{t-2}) &= E\big[y_t - E(y_t)\big]\big[y_{t-2} - E(y_{t-2})\big] \\
&= E\big[y_t y_{t-2}\big] \\
&= E\big[(\theta_1 y_{t-1} + e_t) y_{t-2}\big] \\
&= \theta_1 E\big[y_{t-1} y_{t-2}\big] + E\big[e_t y_{t-1}\big] \\
&= \theta_1 \big(\theta_1 \sigma_y^2\big) = \theta_1^2 \sigma_y^2 \qquad (20.3.5c)
\end{aligned}
$$

The covariances $\mathrm{cov}(y_t, y_{t-1})$ and $\mathrm{cov}(y_t, y_{t-2})$ are for pairs of random variables that are 1 or 2 periods apart, respectively, no matter where they appear in the time series. Similarly, the covariance between y_t and y_{t-k}, which we denote γ_k, does not depend on t and is given by

$$\gamma_k = \mathrm{cov}(y_t, y_{t-k}) = \theta_1^k \sigma_y^2 \qquad k = 0, 1, 2,\dots \qquad (20.3.5d)$$

In this general notation the variance of y_t is $\gamma_0 = \sigma_y^2 = \sigma_e^2 / (1 - \theta_1^2)$, and the k-lag covariance is

$$\gamma_k = \theta_1^k \sigma_y^2 = \theta_1^k \gamma_0 \qquad (20.3.5e)$$

20.3.1c The Autocorrelation Function of an AR(1) Process

One difficulty with examining the covariances γ_k for a time series is that they are dependent on the units of measurement of the variable y_t. One way to circumvent this problem is to consider the correlation between y_t and y_{t-k}. The correlation between y_t and y_{t-k} is defined as

$$\mathrm{corr}(y_t, y_{t-k}) = \frac{\mathrm{cov}(y_t, y_{t-k})}{\sqrt{\mathrm{var}(y_t)}\sqrt{\mathrm{var}(y_{t-k})}}$$

The covariance between y_t and y_{t-k} is γ_k given in equation 20.3.5e, and the variances of y_t and y_{t-k} are $\gamma_0 = \sigma_y^2$. Consequently, we divide each covariance γ_k by the variance $\gamma_0 = \sigma_y^2$ to obtain the correlation, or as it is called in the time-series literature, the *autocorrelation function*

$$\rho_k = \frac{\gamma_k}{\gamma_0} \qquad k = 0, \pm 1, \pm 2,\ldots \qquad (20.3.6)$$

From the definition of covariance we know that the autocorrelation function is symmetric, so that $\rho_{-k} = \rho_k$. Consequently, when examining autocorrelation functions of time series, we need consider only values of $k \geq 1$, since $\rho_0 = 1$. Thus, using equations 20.3.5a and 20.3.5e, the autocorrelation function for a first-order autoregressive process is

$$\rho_k = \gamma_k / \gamma_0 = \theta_1^k \qquad (20.3.7)$$

20.3.1d   Some Sample AR(1) Time-Series and Autocorrelation Functions
When we examine a time series of data for an observable economic variable, we want to identify the type of process that it follows. One tool that we use is the autocorrelation function. Consequently, it is important to have an idea of what autocorrelation functions look like for the basic types of time-series processes. With that in mind, let us examine some typical AR(1) processes and their autocorrelation functions. In Figure 20.4a we show a typical realization from the AR(1) time-series process

$$y_t = \delta + \theta_1 y_{t-1} + e_t = 0.8 y_{t-1} + e_t$$

where the random error e_t has mean zero and variance 1, and in Figure 20.4b we depict its autocorrelation function. Note that the autocorrelation function declines geometrically toward zero. In Figure 20.4c we depict an AR(1) time series with the same intercept and variance parameters, but with $\theta_1 = -0.8$. Its autocorrelation function appears in Figure 20.4d. The negative value of the parameter θ_1 tends to cause the value of the outcome variable y_t to be the opposite sign of y_{t-1}. On the other hand, a positive value of θ_1 tends to cause the sign of y_t to be the same as y_{t-1}.

Note that in both cases the autocorrelation function dies off, toward zero, as the value of the lag k increases. That is, $\theta_1^k \to 0$ as $k \to \infty$. This occurs because the value of the parameter θ_1 of the AR(1) time-series model falls between -1 and 1, or $|\theta_1| < 1$. *Autoregressive time-series models with this property, that is, whose autocorrelation functions taper off to zero as the lag k increases, are said to be stationary.*

Stationarity, or the lack of it, is an important property of time-series processes. In general, we say that a time series y_t is stationary if:

(i) the mean of the series is a finite constant,

$$E[y_t] = \mu \qquad \text{for all } t \qquad (20.3.8a)$$

so that $E[y_t] = E[y_{t+k}]$ for any t and k.

(ii) the variance of the series is a finite constant

$$\text{var}(y_t) = \sigma_y^2 \qquad \text{for all } t \qquad (20.3.8b)$$

so that $\text{var}(y_t) = \text{var}(y_{t+k})$ for any t and k.

(iii) the covariance of the series, for random variables k periods apart, is a finite constant

$$\text{cov}(y_t, y_{t+k}) = E\big[(y_t - \mu)(y_{t+k} - \mu)\big] = \gamma_k \qquad (20.3.8c)$$

so that $\text{cov}(y_t, y_{t+k}) = \text{cov}(y_{t+m}, y_{t+k+m})$ for any t, k, or m.

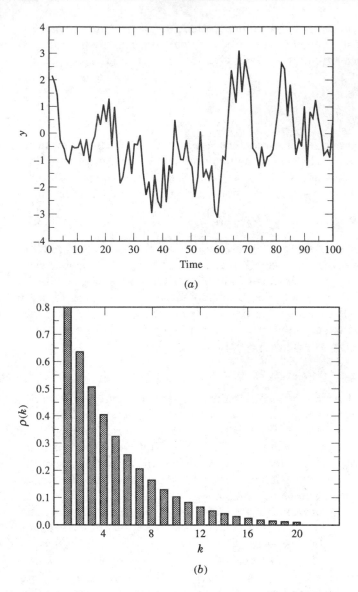

Figure 20.4 AR(1) time-series and autocorrelation functions. *(a)* Sample realization of $y_t = .8y_{t-1} + e_t$. *(b)* Autocorrelation function for $y_t = .8y_{t-1} + e_t$.

This last property ensures that two random variables from a time series that are k periods apart have the same covariance as any two other random variables that are k periods apart, irrespective of their position. Since all time series may not be stationary, in Section 20.6 we consider *nonstationary* time series and indicate how to work with them.

20.3.2   Properties of Second-Order Autoregressive Processes

First-order autoregressive time-series models adequately describe many economic time series. However, more general autoregressive processes may be required for other series.

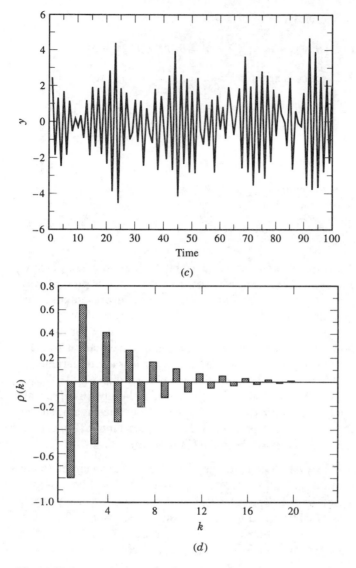

Figure 20.4 *(c)* Sample realization of $y_t = -.8y_{t-1} + e_t$. *(d)* Autocorrelation function of $y_t = -.8y_{t-1} + e_t$.

One possibility is a second-order autoregressive model, or AR(2), given by

$$y_t = \delta + \theta_1 y_{t-1} + \theta_2 y_{t-2} + e_t \qquad (20.3.9)$$

We again assume that the random disturbance is an uncorrelated random variable with mean zero and variance σ_e^2. The mean of the random variable y_t in the AR(2) process is

$$E[y_t] = E[\delta + \theta_1 y_{t-1} + \theta_2 y_{t-2} + e_t]$$
$$= \delta + \theta_1 \mu + \theta_2 \mu$$

or

$$E[y_t] = \mu = \delta / (1 - \theta_1 - \theta_2)$$

For the AR(2) process to be stationary, the parameters θ_1 and θ_2 must take values so that *(i)* $\theta_2 + \theta_1 < 1$, *(ii)* $\theta_2 - \theta_1 < 1$ and $|\theta_2| < 1$.

Assuming that $\delta = \mu = 0$, the variance of y_t is

$$\gamma_0 = E\left[y_t^2\right] = E\left[y_t\left(\theta_1 y_{t-1} + \theta_2 y_{t-2} + e_t\right)\right] = \theta_1 \gamma_1 + \theta_2 \gamma_2 + \sigma_e^2$$

The covariances for an AR(2) process are, for $k > 0$,

$$\gamma_k = E\left[y_{t-k} y_t\right] = E\left[y_{t-k}\left(\theta_1 y_{t-1} + \theta_2 y_{t-2} + e_t\right)\right] = \theta_1 \gamma_{k-1} + \theta_2 \gamma_{k-2}$$

Dividing this equation by γ_0 yields

$$\rho_k = \theta_1 \rho_{k-1} + \theta_2 \rho_{k-2} \qquad k > 0 \tag{20.3.10a}$$

Since $\rho_k = \rho_{-k}$, and $\rho_0 = 1$, from equation 20.3.10a we can compute

$$\rho_1 = \frac{\theta_1}{1 - \theta_2} \qquad \rho_2 = \theta_2 + \frac{\theta_1^2}{1 - \theta_2} \tag{20.3.10b}$$

Some samples of AR(2) processes and their autocorrelation functions are given in Figure 20.5. In Figure 20.5a a typical realization of an AR(2) time-series process with parameters $\delta = 0$, $\theta_1 = 0.5$, $\theta_2 = 0.3$, and an error variance $\sigma_e^2 = 1.0$ is presented. Since the two θ_1 parameters are positive, the value of y_t tends to be the same as in the previous periods. Examining, in Figure 20.5b, the autocorrelation function for this process, we see that as the lag k, increases the autocorrelations, given in equation 20.3.10, taper off to zero. The time series in Figure 20.5c is an AR(2) process with parameters that differ only in that $\theta_1 = -0.5$. Because θ_1 is negative, and larger than θ_2, the sign of y_t tends to be opposite that of y_{t-1}. The autocorrelation function in Figure 20.5d reveals this tendency as the autocorrelations alternate in sign as well. Note once again that the autocorrelation functions for each of the depicted AR(2) processes taper off to zero as k increases. This reflects the stationarity of these AR(2) processes.

20.3.2a A Summary Statement   Let us summarize what we have learned to this point. Univariate time-series statistical models are designed to be used in short-run forecasting problems and are based on the dependence of an economic variable y_t on its past values y_{t-i} and the values of current and past disturbances e_{t-i}, $i = 0, 1, 2, \ldots$. Unlike traditional econometric models, the mean of the values y_t do not depend on other economic variables. Nor is the process consistent with an optimizing or choice framework provided by economic theory. In autoregressive time series models the value of an economic outcome variable y_t is related to its values in the past $1, 2, \ldots, p$ periods, plus a disturbance, that is assumed to be uncorrelated random variables with mean zero and constant variance σ_e^2. With these assumptions we derived the means, variances, covariances, and autocorrelations of AR(1) and AR(2) statistical models. We have observed that for stationary AR processes the autocorrelation function tapers off to zero. Given this foundation, in the following section we consider the estimation of the unknown parameters of AR(p) models.

20.3.3 Estimation of AR(p) Processes

Assuming that the observed sample values of the economic variable y_t are generated by an AR process, in a real-world context there is usually uncertainty about its order. Given the general AR(p) model in equation 20.3.2

$$y_t = \delta + \theta_1 y_{t-1} + \theta_2 y_{t-2} + \ldots + \theta_p y_{t-p} + e_t \tag{20.3.2}$$

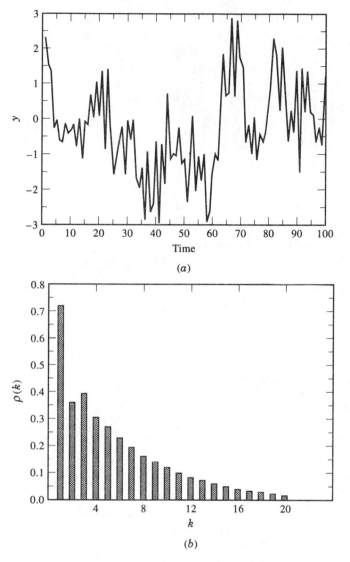

Figure 20.5 AR(2) time-series and autocorrelation functions. *(a)* Sample realization of $y_t = .5y_{t-1} + .3y_{t-2} + e_t$. *(b)* Autocorrelation function for $y_t = .5y_{t-1} + .3y_{t-2} + e_t$.

we face the problems of determining its order p and estimating the corresponding parameters θ_1, θ_2,..., θ_p and δ.

Assume for the moment that we know p, the order of the AR process. Equation 20.3.2 is in the form of a linear statistical model involving the unknown parameters θ_i and δ. One difference between the linear model in equation 20.3.2 and those considered in Chapters 5 to 11 is that the right-hand-side variables in this model are *random*, since they are lagged values of the random dependent variable y_t. If the error terms e_t are uncorrelated random variables, then they are not correlated with the lagged values of y_t on the right-hand side of equation 20.3.2. Consequently, lagged values of y_t depend *only on lagged values of e_t*, which are not correlated with the current disturbance e_t. Thus use of the least squares estimator in this instance yields an estimation rule that is consistent. The general basis for this result is discussed in Chapter 14, where we consider the linear statistical models with stochastic (random) explanatory variables.

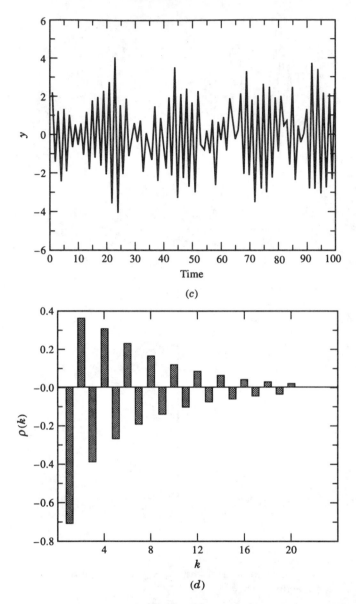

Figure 20.5 *(c)* Sample realization of $y_t = -.5y_{t-1} + .3y_{t-2} + e_t$. *(d)* Autocorrelation function of $y_t = -.5y_{t-1} + .3y_{t-2} + e_t$.

If we write out equation 20.3.2 for the observed values of the time series process, we obtain

$$y_{p+1} = \delta + \theta_1 y_p + \theta_2 y_{p-1} + ... + \theta_p y_1 + e_{p+1}$$
$$y_{p+2} = \delta + \theta_1 y_{p+1} + \theta_2 y_p + ... + \theta_p y_2 + e_{p+2}$$
$$\vdots$$
$$y_T = \delta + \theta_1 y_{T-1} + \theta_2 y_{T-2} + ... + \theta_p y_{T-p} + e_T \qquad (20.3.11a)$$

In matrix notation, equations 20.3.11a may be written

$$\mathbf{y} = X\boldsymbol{\beta} + \mathbf{e} \qquad (20.3.11b)$$

where $\mathbf{y}' = (y_{p+1}, y_{p+2}, \ldots, y_T)$, $\mathbf{e}' = (e_{p+1}, e_{p+2}, \ldots, e_T)$, $\boldsymbol{\beta}' = (\delta, \theta_1, \theta_2, \ldots, \theta_p)$, and

$$
X = \begin{bmatrix}
1 & y_p & y_{p-1} & \cdots & y_1 \\
1 & y_{p+1} & y_p & \cdots & y_2 \\
& & \vdots & & \\
1 & y_{T-1} & y_{T-2} & \cdots & y_{T-p}
\end{bmatrix}
$$

For the linear statistical model 20.3.11b, the least squares estimator of $\boldsymbol{\beta}$ is

$$
\hat{\boldsymbol{\beta}} = (X'X)^{-1} X'\mathbf{y} \tag{20.3.12a}
$$

Under the assumptions that we have made, the least squares estimator $\hat{\boldsymbol{\beta}}$ is a consistent estimator of $\boldsymbol{\beta}$ and approximately normally distributed in large samples. The estimated covariance matrix of $\hat{\boldsymbol{\beta}}$ is

$$
\hat{\mathrm{cov}}(\hat{\boldsymbol{\beta}}) = \hat{\sigma}_e^2 (X'X)^{-1} \tag{20.3.12b}
$$

where

$$
\hat{\sigma}_e^2 = (\mathbf{y} - X\hat{\boldsymbol{\beta}})'(\mathbf{y} - X\hat{\boldsymbol{\beta}}) \big/ (T - 2p - 1) \tag{20.3.12c}
$$

Although the divisor of the sum of squared errors appears unusual, it is equal to the number of observations less the number of parameters. The quantity $(T - 2p - 1)$ results, since there are only $(T - p)$ complete observations with which to estimate the $(p + 1)$ parameters in $\boldsymbol{\beta}$. An estimator of the mean μ of an AR(p) process is

$$
\hat{\mu} = \frac{\hat{\delta}}{1 - \hat{\theta}_1 - \hat{\theta}_2 - \ldots - \hat{\theta}_p}
$$

20.3.3a An Example   To illustrate the estimation procedure, consider the data that are represented by Figure 20.5a. The data consist of $T = 100$ values of y_t that were artificially generated from the AR(2) model

$$
y_t = 0.5y_{t-1} + 0.3y_{t-2} + e_t
$$

with the random disturbance $e_t \sim (0, \sigma_e^2 = 1)$. With the AR(2) version of the linear statistical model given in equations 20.3.11, the fitted equation is

$$
\hat{y}_t = -0.114 + 0.212y_{t-1} + 0.493y_{t-2} \qquad \hat{\sigma}_e^2 = 0.937
$$
$$
\quad (.101) \quad (.089) \qquad (.087) \qquad s.e.
$$
$$
\quad (-1.13) \quad (2.37) \qquad (5.65) \qquad t
$$

On the basis of the t-values we conclude that the AR parameters θ_1 and θ_2 are significantly different from zero, but that the intercept δ is not significantly different from zero. Note that, relative to the true underlying model, the estimated values of the parameters θ_i have the correct sign and that the estimated error variance is close to the true value.

20.3.4   Partial Autocorrelations

We have assumed thus far that the order of the AR process p is known. In practice this will not be true. One strategy is to choose a value for p that is an upper bound of what the actual order is thought to be. Unfortunately, this procedure is inefficient as extra and unnecessary parameters are estimated. It is analogous to including irrelevant explanatory variables in a linear regression model which, as we discussed in Chapters 9 and 10, leads to a decrease in sampling precision. A procedure based on *partial autocorrelations* is often used to determine the order p of the AR process, and it is to this topic that we now turn.

One way to identify the order of an AR process for a given set of data is to estimate AR processes of increasing order $p = 1, 2,...$ and test the significance of the newly added parameter θ_p in each case. We denote the pth coefficient of the AR process of order p as θ_{pp}, and call it the *pth partial autocorrelation coefficient*. This coefficient measures the correlation between y_t and y_{t-p} after the effects of $y_{t-1}, y_{t-2},..., y_{t-p+1}$ have been taken into account. Specifically, we first estimate the model 20.3.2 with $p = 1$:

$$y_t = \delta + \theta_1 y_{t-1} + e_t \qquad (20.3.13)$$

The parameter θ_1 in this model is the first partial autocorrelation θ_{11}, and its least squares estimate is $\hat{\theta}_{11}$. We then estimate the model 20.3.2 with $p = 2$:

$$y_t = \delta + \theta_1 y_{t-1} + \theta_2 y_{t-2} + e_t \qquad (20.3.14)$$

The parameter θ_2 in this model is the second partial autocorrelation θ_{22}. Its estimate $\hat{\theta}_{22}$ measures the linear association between y_t and y_{t-2}, with the effect of y_{t-1} "removed." The sequence of partial autocorrelations $\theta_{11}, \theta_{22},...$, formed by adding one lag at a time, is called the *partial autocorrelation function*.

The order p of the AR process is chosen so that θ_{kk} is not equal to zero for $k = p$, but $\theta_{kk} = 0$ for $k > p$. Since the true partial autocorrelations are not known, we test their significance using the estimated values, $\hat{\theta}_{kk}$. The test is based on the fact that for lags k that are greater than the order p of an AR(p) process, the estimated partial autocorrelations $\hat{\theta}_{kk}$ are approximately normally distributed with means zero and variances $1/T$ in large samples. Consequently, we can use the test statistic

$$t_k = \frac{\hat{\theta}_{kk}}{(1/T)^{1/2}} = \sqrt{T}\hat{\theta}_{kk} \qquad (20.3.15)$$

to calculate a "t"-value. To test the significance of the partial autocorrelation θ_{kk}, we compare the value of this test statistic to the rough critical value $t_c = 2$, which is the approximate $\alpha = .05$ critical value from the standard normal distribution. As we examine the sequence of values t_k, $k = 1, 2,...$, we choose the order of the AR process to be the p corresponding to the *last* significant value of t_k.

To understand the use of the partial autocorrelation function in determining the order of an AR time series process once again consider the data underlying Figure 20.5a. We now operate under the assumption that the process generating the data can be modeled as an autoregressive process, but that we do not know the order of the AR process, or the parameter values. We estimate the partial autocorrelations to use as a basis for determining the order of the AR process, p, and in Table 20.1 we report the least squares

Table 20.1 Least Squares Parameter Estimates of AR(p) Models

$p = 1$: $\hat{y}_t = -0.166 + 0.464 y_{t-1}$

$p = 2$: $\hat{y}_t = -0.114 + 0.212 y_{t-1} + 0.493 y_{t-2}$

$p = 3$: $\hat{y}_t = -0.115 + 0.221 y_{t-1} + 0.498 y_{t-2} - 0.017 y_{t-3}$

Table 20.2 Estimated Partial
Autocorrelations

k	$\hat{\theta}_{kk}$	t_k
1	0.464	4.64
2	0.493	4.93
3	−0.017	−0.17
4	−0.047	−0.47
5	−0.136	−1.36
6	−0.188	−1.88
7	0.106	1.06
8	0.162	1.62
9	−0.061	−0.61
10	0.062	0.62

parameter estimates of models with $p = 1, 2$, and 3. The model with $p = 2$ we have already considered at the end of the previous section.

The estimated partial autocorrelations are the estimated coefficients of the last term in each least squares regression. The estimated partial autocorrelations for up to $k = 10$ lags are given in Table 20.2.

The t-statistic t_k, given in equation 20.3.15, is reported in the last column of Table 20.2. Based on the rough critical values ±2 for the $\alpha = .05$ level of significance, we would conclude that the lag length of the AR time-series process was $p = 2$, which, in this instance, is correct.

20.3.5   Another Representation of a Stationary AR(p) Time Series

An important property of all stationary AR processes is that they can be rewritten as functions only of the random disturbance e_t. To illustrate, assume $\delta = 0$ and consider the AR(1) process

$$y_t = \theta_1 y_{t-1} + e_t \tag{20.3.16}$$

This relation holds true for all values of t, so that

$$y_{t-1} = \theta_1 y_{t-2} + e_{t-1} \tag{20.3.17}$$

Substituting equation 20.3.17 into equation 20.3.16, we obtain

$$y_t = \theta_1 \left(\theta_1 y_{t-2} + e_{t-1} \right) + e_t$$
$$= \theta_1^2 y_{t-2} + e_t + \theta_1 e_{t-1}$$

If we repeat this process an infinite number of times we obtain

$$y_t = \sum_{i=0}^{\infty} \theta_1^i e_{t-i} \tag{20.3.18}$$

since the term $\theta_1^i y_{t-i}$ converges to the limit 0 when $|\theta_1| < 1$. In equation 20.3.18 we represent y_t as an infinite weighted sum of the uncorrelated random disturbance e_t and its lagged values e_{t-i}. This is called the *moving average* representation of the AR(1) process equation 20.3.16 and illustrates that *any* stationary AR process can be represented, as in equation 20.3.18, as an infinite weighted sum of the uncorrelated random errors e_t.

20.4 Moving Average Processes

In Section 20.3 we considered the AR(p) statistical model for time series data. In the AR(p) model the observed value of an economic variable is related to its own past values and the value of a random disturbance. Relationships of the type represented by the AR(p) model are encountered frequently in economics. However, there are several economic hypotheses that lead to another form of a time-series structure, called a *moving average process*. As an example, many students of the stock market have found that the *change* in the price of a stock from one day to the next behaves as a series of uncorrelated random variables with mean zero and constant variance. If P_t is the price of a stock on day t, then the change in price from one day to the next is

$$y_t = P_t - P_{t-1} = e_t, \quad t = 1,\ldots, T,$$

where the errors e_t are uncorrelated random variables. The random component e_t reflects unexpected news items, such as new information about the financial health of the corporation, the popularity of the product suddenly rising or falling (as might happen if the firm's products are reported to cause desirable or undesirable side effects), the emergence of a new and effective competitor, the announcement of a technical breakthrough, or the revelation of a management scandal. But suppose that the *full* impact of any unexpected news is *not completely* absorbed by the market in *one* day. Then the price change the next day might be

$$y_{t+1} = e_{t+1} + \alpha e_t \qquad (20.4.1a)$$

where e_{t+1} is the effect of the new information received during day $t + 1$, and αe_t reflects the continuing assessment of yesterday's news.

The statistical model in equation 20.4.1a is a *moving average process*. The value of the economic variable y_{t+1} is a *weighted average of a current and a past random disturbance*. It is a model in which random shocks require more than one period to work themselves through the system. In general, a moving average process represents time-series observations on the economic variable y_t as a weighted average of random disturbances e_t going back 1, 2, or more periods. We represent the statistical model for a general MA(q) process as

$$y_t = \mu + e_t + \alpha_1 e_{t-1} + \alpha_2 e_{t-2} + \ldots + \alpha_q e_{t-q} \qquad (20.4.1b)$$

where the uncorrelated random disturbances e_t have mean zero and variance σ_e^2 and the α_i are unknown parameters. Note that in equation 20.4.1b the "intercept" parameter is denoted as μ, rather than δ as in the AR(p) model. This specification reflects the fact that the MA(q) process has mean

$$E[y_t] = \mu$$

and variance

$$
\begin{aligned}
\operatorname{var}(y_t) = \gamma_0 &= E\left[(y_t - \mu)^2\right] \\
&= E\left[e_t^2 + \alpha_1^2 e_{t-1}^2 + \ldots + \alpha_q^2 e_{t-q}^2 + 2\alpha_1 \alpha_2 e_{t-1} e_{t-2} + \ldots\right] \\
&= \sigma_e^2 + \alpha_1^2 \sigma_e^2 + \ldots + \alpha_q^2 \sigma_e^2 \\
&= \sigma_e^2 \left(1 + \alpha_1^2 + \ldots + \alpha_q^2\right)
\end{aligned}
\qquad (20.4.2)
$$

The expected value of all the cross-product terms is zero, since the random disturbances e_t are assumed to be independent, and thus uncorrelated.

It is important to examine the properties of specific moving average processes, and in particular calculate their covariances and autocorrelation function. When examining sample data, these characteristics will enable us to identify the order, q, of a moving average model.

20.4.1   Properties of the MA(1) Process

Consider the MA(1) process

$$y_t = \mu + e_t + \alpha_1 e_{t-1} \tag{20.4.3a}$$

This process has mean $E[y_t] = \mu$ and variance

$$\text{var}(y_t) = \gamma_0 = E[y_t - \mu]^2 = \sigma_e^2 (1 + \alpha_1^2) \tag{20.4.3b}$$

The covariance between y_t and y_{t-1} is

$$\begin{aligned}
\text{cov}(y_t, y_{t-1}) = \gamma_1 &= E[(y_t - \mu)(y_{t-1} - \mu)] \\
&= E[(e_t + \alpha_1 e_{t-1})(e_{t-1} + \alpha_1 e_{t-2})] \\
&= \alpha_1 \sigma_e^2
\end{aligned} \tag{20.4.3c}$$

The covariance between y_t and y_{t-2} is

$$\begin{aligned}
\text{cov}(y_t, y_{t-2}) = \gamma_2 &= E[(y_t - \mu)(y_{t-2} - \mu)] \\
&= E[(e_t + \alpha_1 e_{t-1})(e_{t-2} + \alpha_1 e_{t-3})] \\
&= 0
\end{aligned} \tag{20.4.3d}$$

It can be shown in the same way that for *all* lags $k > 1$, the covariances γ_k of the MA(1) time-series process are *zero*. Thus, the autocorrelation function for the MA(1) process is

$$\rho_k = \frac{\gamma_k}{\gamma_0} = \begin{cases} \dfrac{\alpha_1}{1 + \alpha_1^2} & k = 1 \\ 0 & k > 1 \end{cases} \tag{20.4.3e}$$

The autocorrelation function for the MA(1) process "cuts off" after lag $k = 1$. Thus, one way to characterize the MA(1) process is that it has a "memory" of one period. In contrast, this is not true for *stationary AR processes*, which have autocorrelations that die out gradually as k increases.

In Figure 20.6 we plot typical realizations of MA(1) processes

$$y_t = \mu + e_t + \alpha_1 e_{t-1} = e_t + \alpha_1 e_{t-1}$$

In Figure 20.6a the parameter $\alpha_1 = .8$ and in Figure 20.6b $\alpha_1 = -.8$. In both cases the random errors have mean zero and variance $\sigma_e^2 = 1$. By using equation 20.4.3e, we can calculate the theoretical autocorrelations ρ_1 for various values of α_1. These are given for selected values in Table 20.3. Note that the autocorrelations approach the limiting value .50 as α_1 approaches 1.

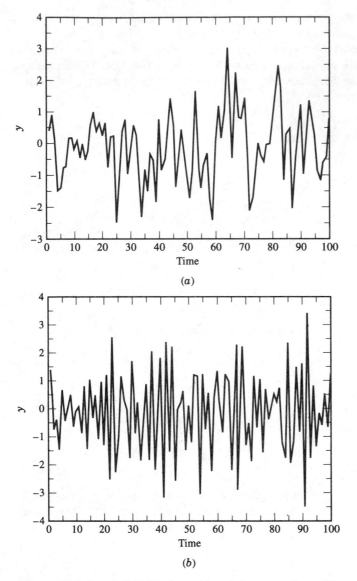

Figure 20.6 Sample MA(1) time series. *(a)* $y_t = e_t + .8e_{t-1}$. *(b)* $y_t = e_t - .8e_{t-1}$.

Table 20.3 Theoretical
Autocorrelations for
MA(1) Processes

α_1	ρ_1
0.1	0.10
0.2	0.19
0.3	0.28
0.4	0.34
0.5	0.40
0.6	0.44
0.7	0.47
0.8	0.48
0.9	0.50

20.4.2   Properties of the MA(2) Process

Let us now examine the properties of a MA(2) statistical model, which is given by

$$y_t = \mu + e_t + \alpha_1 e_{t-1} + \alpha_2 e_{t-2} \tag{20.4.4a}$$

This time series process has mean $E[y_t] = \mu$ and variance

$$\text{var}(y_t) = \gamma_0 = \sigma_e^2 \left(1 + \alpha_1^2 + \alpha_2^2\right) \tag{20.4.4b}$$

The one-period lag covariance is

$$\begin{aligned}
\text{cov}(y_t, y_{t-1}) = \gamma_1 &= E\left[\left(e_t + \alpha_1 e_{t-1} + \alpha_2 e_{t-2}\right)\left(e_{t-1} + \alpha_1 e_{t-2} + \alpha_2 e_{t-3}\right)\right] \\
&= \alpha_1 \sigma_e^2 + \alpha_1 \alpha_2 \sigma_e^2 = \sigma_e^2 \left(\alpha_1 + \alpha_1 \alpha_2\right)
\end{aligned} \tag{20.4.4c}$$

The two-period lag covariance is

$$\begin{aligned}
\text{cov}(y_t, y_{t-2}) = \gamma_2 &= E\left[\left(e_t + \alpha_1 e_{t-1} + \alpha_2 e_{t-2}\right)\left(e_{t-2} + \alpha_1 e_{t-3} + \alpha_2 e_{t-4}\right)\right] \\
&= \alpha_2 \sigma_e^2
\end{aligned} \tag{20.4.4d}$$

The three-period covariance is

$$\begin{aligned}
\text{cov}(y_t, y_{t-3}) = \gamma_3 &= E\left[\left(e_t + \alpha_1 e_{t-1} + \alpha_2 e_{t-2}\right)\left(e_{t-3} + \alpha_1 e_{t-4} + \alpha_2 e_{t-5}\right)\right] \\
&= 0
\end{aligned} \tag{20.4.4e}$$

It can be shown, in the same way as in Section 20.4.1, that the covariances at lags of more than two periods are all zero. Thus $\gamma_k = 0$ for all $k > 2$. The corresponding autocorrelation function for the MA(2) process is

$$\rho_1 = \frac{\alpha_1 \left(1 + \alpha_2\right)}{1 + \alpha_1^2 + \alpha_2^2}$$

$$\rho_2 = \frac{\alpha_1}{1 + \alpha_1^2 + \alpha_2^2} \tag{20.4.4f}$$

and

$$\rho_k = 0 \qquad \text{for } k > 2$$

Thus, the MA(2) process has a memory that is two periods long, and y_t is affected by e_{t-1} and e_{t-2} and is not affected by any higher lagged values.

In Figure 20.7 two MA(2) processes, of the form

$$y_t = \mu + e_t + \alpha_1 e_{t-1} + \alpha_2 e_{t-2} = e_t + \alpha_1 e_{t-1} + \alpha_2 e_{t-2}$$

are illustrated. The process in Figure 20.7a is generated by the MA(2) model with $\alpha_1 = .5$ and $\alpha_2 = .3$ with error term $e_t \sim N(0, 1)$. The process in Figure 20.7b is the same, except $\alpha_1 = -.5$.

It is clear that the MA(1) and MA(2) processes that we have used as illustrations are *stationary, because the means, variances, and covariances are finite and invariant with respect to time.* Such is always the case for stationary finite-order MA processes.

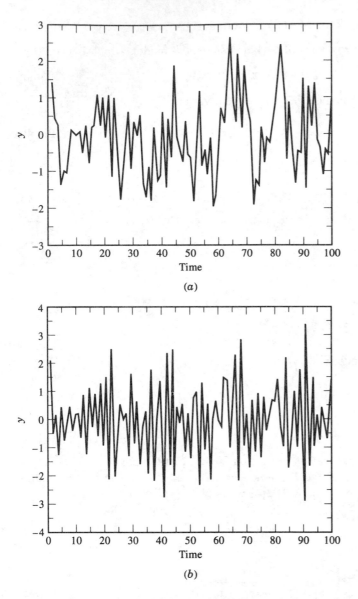

Figure 20.7 Sample MA(2) time series. *(a)* $y_t = e_t + .5e_{t-1} + .3e_{t-2}$. *(b)* $y_t = e_t - .5e_{t-1} + .3y_{t-2}$.

The autocorrelation function for the general MA(q) process is given by

$$\rho_k = \begin{cases} \dfrac{\displaystyle\sum_{i=0}^{q-k} \alpha_i \alpha_{i+k}}{\displaystyle\sum_{i=0}^{q} \alpha_i^2} & \text{for } k = 0, 1, 2, \ldots, q \\ 0 & k > q \end{cases} \tag{20.4.5}$$

Thus the order of an MA process corresponds to the maximum k for which the autocorrelation ρ_k is nonzero.

20.4.3   The Sample Autocorrelation Function

Because the autocorrelation function of a MA(q) process is zero after q lags, we can identify the order q of a MA process by determining the lag at which the autocorrelations no longer differ from zero. In practice we use an estimated autocorrelation function, based on a time series of data, to determine the order q of an MA process. An estimator for the mean μ of the time series is the sample mean

$$\hat{\mu} = \bar{y} = \sum_{t=1}^{T} y_t / T \qquad (20.4.6)$$

The sample autocorrelation function is

$$r_k = \frac{\sum_{t=1}^{T-k}(y_t - \bar{y})(y_{t+k} - \bar{y})}{\sum_{t=1}^{T}(y_t - \bar{y})^2} \qquad (20.4.7)$$

The significance of the autocorrelations is frequently checked by relying on a test based on the fact that if a time series is made up of uncorrelated random variables with zero means and constant variances, then the sample autocorrelations r_k, for $k > 0$, are approximately normally distributed with mean zero and standard deviation $1/\sqrt{T}$ in large samples. Consequently, we can test, at the $\alpha = .05$ level of significance, the null hypothesis H_0: $\rho_k = 0$ against the alternative H_1: $\rho_k \neq 0$, by comparing the sample autocorrelation r_k to the rough bound $\pm 2/\sqrt{T}$. If the 95% confidence interval $\left(r_k \pm 2/\sqrt{T}\right)$ does not include the value 0, then the null hypothesis that $\rho_k = 0$ is rejected.

When examining a time series that is MA(q), we anticipate that the autocorrelations for lags $k \le q$, will be significantly different from zero and that autocorrelations corresponding to lags $k > q$ will not be significantly different from zero. Although the use of this procedure is common, a word of warning is due. *The test is valid only if the sample size T is large.* If the sample size is not large, then the test can be quite misleading. Also, when carrying out a number of tests of individual hypotheses, the probability that one or more gives an incorrect conclusion can be quite high.

To illustrate the use of this test consider the $T = 100$ values of y_t that were used to generate Figure 20.7a. The sample autocorrelations, using equation 20.4.7, and lags $k = 1, 2, \ldots, 10$, are computed and plotted in Figure 20.8. Note that only the first two

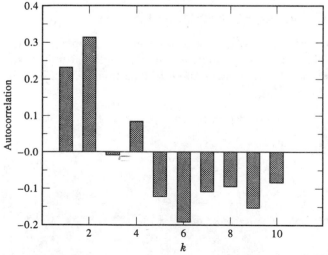

Figure 20.8 An estimated autocorrelation function of a MA(2) time series.

autocorrelations differ significantly from zero, if we use the approximate $\alpha = .05$ critical values $\pm 2/\sqrt{T} = \pm 0.2$. Consequently, in this case, the test correctly identifies the data series in Figure 20.7*a* as an MA(2) process.

20.4.4   Estimation of the Parameters of an MA(*q*) Process

Given a basis for determining the order *q* of the MA process, the next task is to estimate the unknown parameters α_i. One estimation alternative is to use the least squares principle. For example, if we assume that the mean of a MA(1) process is zero, then an estimate of α_1 may be obtained by minimizing the sum of squares

$$S(\alpha_1) = \sum_{t=1}^{T} e_t^2 = \sum_{t=1}^{T} (y_t - \alpha_1 e_{t-1})^2 \qquad (20.4.8)$$

Unfortunately, as is shown in Exercise 20.10, this sum of squares function is one that is nonlinear in the parameter α_1, and a nonlinear optimization technique must be used to obtain the minimizing value. Fortunately, specialized computer programs are available to estimate the parameters of MA(*q*) time-series models. The problem of estimating models that are nonlinear in the parameters is discussed in Chapter 22, with MA(*q*) models discussed in Appendix 22A of that chapter.

As an example consider the data series represented by Figure 20.7*a*, which was generated by the MA(2) process

$$y_t = e_t + .5e_{t-1} + .3e_{t-2}$$

with the uncorrelated errors $e_t \sim N(0, 1)$. In the previous section we identified the order of this MA time series process as $q = 2$. Using the SHAZAM or SAS software packages, as described in the *Computer Handbooks* accompanying this book, we find that the nonlinear least squares parameter estimates for the MA(2) model are

$$\hat{y}_t = -0.11 + e_t + 0.23e_{t-1} + 0.28e_{t-2}$$
$$(.77) \qquad (2.36) \qquad (2.87) \qquad t\text{-values}$$

Note that the estimated intercept is small and not significantly different from zero on the basis of its small *t*-value. The estimated values of α_1 and α_2 are of the correct sign and significantly different from zero at the .05 level of significance.

20.4.5   Another Way to Represent the MA(*q*) Process

Just as stationary AR processes have infinite moving average representations, some MA processes, which are called "invertible" MA processes, have infinite AR representations. For example, consider the MA(1) process given in equation 20.4.3a with its mean $\mu = 0$:

$$y_t = e_t + \alpha_1 e_{t-1} \qquad (20.4.9)$$

Solving equation 20.4.9 for e_t we have

$$e_t = y_t - \alpha_1 e_{t-1} \qquad (20.4.10)$$

This expression holds true for all *t*, so that

$$e_{t-1} = y_{t-1} - \alpha_1 e_{t-2} \qquad (20.4.11)$$

Substitute equation 20.4.11 into equation 20.4.9 to obtain

$$
\begin{aligned}
y_t &= e_t + \alpha_1 e_{t-1} \\
&= \alpha_1 \left(y_{t-1} - \alpha_1 e_{t-2} \right) + e_t \\
&= \alpha_1 y_{t-1} - \alpha_1^2 e_{t-2} + e_t
\end{aligned}
\tag{20.4.12}
$$

If we proceed to substitute for e_{t-2}, e_{t-3}, and so on, an infinite AR process is generated, if the term $\alpha_1^i e_{t-i}$ converges to zero. This occurs if $|\alpha_1| < 1$. Thus, *if $|\alpha_1| < 1$, the MA(1) process is said to be invertible.* This fact is useful when specifying and using time-series models for forecasting purposes, as we shall see in the following sections.

20.5   Autoregressive-Moving Average Models

In Sections 20.3 and 20.4 we discussed two important classes of time-series statistical models, the autoregressive (AR) and moving average (MA) processes. In empirical work, one of the tasks facing an investigator is to identify a representation of the data-generation process and then to specify the corresponding statistical model that may be used with a given sample of time-series data. We have seen that AR and MA processes have certain characteristics that are revealed by examining their autocorrelation and partial autocorrelation functions. *A MA(q) process is indicated if the autocorrelations ρ_k have a "cutoff" point.* That is, they are zero for all lags k greater than the value q. Since invertible MA(q) processes can be written as infinite AR processes, the partial autocorrelation function will taper off to zero.

However, *if the autocorrelations taper off toward zero at higher lags, and if the partial autocorrelations have a cutoff point, then an autoregressive process is favored.* There are many instances, however, when a time series of data does not have a cutoff point for either the autocorrelation or partial autocorrelation functions, or where the autocorrelations taper off very slowly toward zero. In these cases it may be advantageous to construct a time-series model that has both autoregressive and moving average components.

Moving in this direction, we denote a time-series model that contains both AR and MA components as an ARMA(p, q) model, where p and q are the orders of the AR and MA components, respectively. The algebraic representation of the statistical model is

$$
y_t = \delta + \theta_1 y_{t-1} + \theta_2 y_{t-2} + \ldots + \theta_p y_{t-p} + e_t + \alpha_1 e_{t-1} + \alpha_2 e_{t-2} + \ldots + \alpha_q e_{t-q}
\tag{20.5.1}
$$

where the intercept parameter δ is related to the mean of y_t, and the errors e_t are assumed to be uncorrelated random variables, with $E[e_t] = 0$ and $\mathrm{var}(e_t) = \sigma_e^2$.

If this process is stationary, then it must have a constant mean μ for all time periods. Taking the expectation of equation 20.5.1, we have

$$
E[y_t] = \mu = \delta + \theta_1 \mu + \theta_2 \mu + \ldots + \theta_p \mu + 0 + \alpha_1 0 + \alpha_2 0 + \ldots + \alpha_q 0
$$

so that

$$
\mu = \frac{\delta}{1 - \theta_1 - \ldots - \theta_p}
$$

20.5.1   Properties of ARMA Processes

To illustrate the properties of ARMA processes consider the ARMA(1, 1) model given by

$$y_t = \delta + \theta_1 y_{t-1} + e_t + \alpha_1 e_{t-1} \tag{20.5.2}$$

If $\delta = 0$, or equivalently the series y_t is in deviation from the mean form, then the variances and covariances of the process are

$$
\begin{aligned}
\gamma_0 = \text{var}(y_t) &= E\left[(y_t - \mu)^2\right] \\
&= E\left[(\theta_1 y_{t-1} + e_t + \alpha_1 e_{t-1})^2\right] \\
&= \theta_1^2 \gamma_0 + 2\theta_1 \alpha_1 E[y_{t-1} e_{t-1}] + \sigma_e^2 + \alpha_1^2 \sigma_e^2
\end{aligned}
$$

but

$$
\begin{aligned}
E[y_{t-1} e_{t-1}] &= E\left[(\theta_1 y_{t-2} + e_{t-1} + \alpha_1 e_{t-2})e_{t-1}\right] \\
&= E[e_{t-1}^2] = \sigma_e^2
\end{aligned}
$$

where we have used the fact that e_{t-1} is not correlated with y_{t-2} or e_{t-2}. Thus, if $|\theta_1| < 1$,

$$\gamma_0 = \left(\frac{1 + \alpha_1^2 + 2\theta_1 \alpha_1}{1 - \theta_1^2}\right)\sigma_e^2$$

The covariances are given by

$$
\begin{aligned}
\gamma_1 = E[y_{t-1} y_t] &= E\left[y_{t-1}(\theta_1 y_{t-1} + e_t + \alpha_1 e_{t-1})\right] \\
&= \left(\frac{(1 + \theta_1 \alpha_1)(\theta_1 + \alpha_1)}{1 - \theta_1^2}\right)\sigma_e^2 \\
&= \theta_1 \gamma_0 + \alpha_1 \sigma_e^2
\end{aligned}
$$

and

$$\gamma_k = \theta_1 \gamma_{k-1}, \qquad k \geq 2$$

Therefore, the autocorrelation function is given by

$$
\begin{aligned}
\rho_1 = \frac{\gamma_1}{\gamma_0} &= \frac{(1 + \theta_1 \alpha_1)(\theta_1 + \alpha_1)}{1 + \alpha_1^2 + 2\theta_1 \alpha_1} \\
\rho_k &= \theta_1 \rho_{k-1} \qquad \text{for } k > 1
\end{aligned}
\tag{20.5.3}
$$

Since the ARMA(1, 1) process is a combination of AR and MA components, the autocorrelation function should exhibit the characteristics of both AR and MA processes. The MA component has a memory of only one period, and thus we expect its contribution to the autocorrelation function to cut off after one period. The AR component has geometrically declining autocorrelations, and we expect this behavior for lags greater than one. The autocorrelation function in equation 20.5.3 begins at its starting value ρ_1, which depends on both the autocorrelation and moving average parameters, and then decays geometrically for lags $k = 2, 3, ...$ as anticipated. Several sample autocorrelation functions for ARMA(1, 1) statistical models are shown in Figure 20.9.

For higher order ARMA processes, the variance and covariances are complicated, as they are solutions to high-order difference equations. However, it can be shown that for an ARMA(p, q) process

$$\rho_k = \theta_1 \rho_{k-1} + \theta_2 \rho_{k-2} + \ldots + \theta_p \rho_{k-p}, \quad \text{for } k > q$$

For lags $k > q$ the autocorrelations behave like a purely autoregressive process, and thus will taper off to zero if the ARMA(p, q) process is stationary. This means that the moving average component contributes nothing to the autocorrelation function after q lags, which reflects the fact that the MA component of the ARMA process has a memory of only q periods.

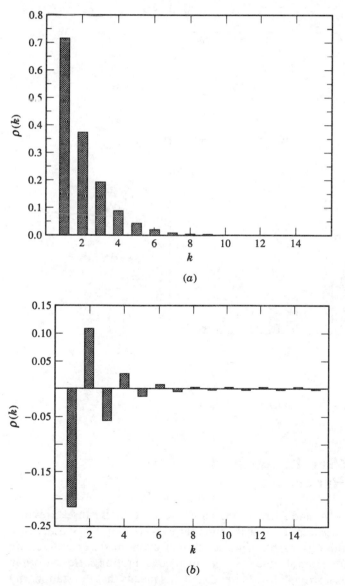

Figure 20.9 Sample autocorrelation functions for ARMA(1, 1) models. *(a)* $\theta_1 = .5$, $\alpha_1 = .5$. *(b)* $\theta_1 = -.5$, $\alpha_1 = .3$.

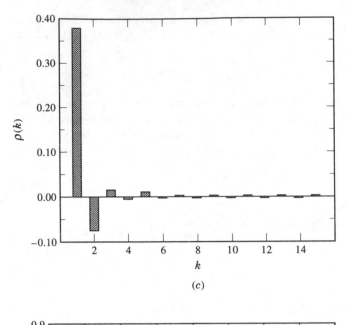

(c)

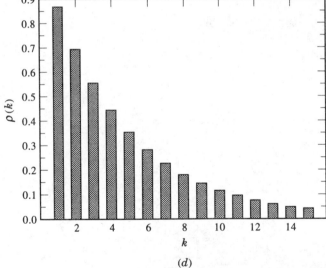

(d)

Figure 20.9 (c) $\Theta_1 = -.2$, $\alpha_1 = .8$. (d) $\Theta_1 = .8$, $\alpha_1 = .3$.

20.6 Autoregressive Integrated Moving Average Processes

The discussion of the AR, MA, and ARMA time series processes in the three previous sections was based on the assumption that the time series were stationary processes. Unfortunately, many of the observable time series that economists encounter are nonstationary. Consider, for example, the U. S. personal consumption series shown in Figure 20.2. This series has a strong upward trend, and this means that the stationarity condition in equation 20.3.8a, the assumption that the time-series process has a constant mean, is violated.

As a second example consider a first-order autoregressive process with parameter $\theta_1 = 1$, given by

$$y_t = y_{t-1} + e_t \qquad (20.6.1)$$

This process, with e_t being an uncorrelated random disturbance term, is known as a *random walk*. In Figure 20.10 a typical realization of this time series is given.

Many economic and financial (stock prices) series have been found to display the characteristics of a random walk time-series process. The random walk process is, however, a nonstationary process. Granger and Newbold (1986, p. 40) show that the variance of the process is infinite, violating the stationarity conditions in equation 20.3.8. Thus, the random walk model, which may be consistent with many economic variables, is a nonstationary time-series process.

Fortunately, many nonstationary time-series processes can be transformed, by differencing the series one or more times, to make them stationary. Such time series are called *integrated processes*. The number of times d that the integrated process must be differenced to be stationary is said to be the *order* of the integrated process. Consequently, if y_t is an integrated process of order 1, then the series

$$x_t = y_t - y_{t-1} \qquad (20.6.2)$$

is stationary. The series x_t results from differencing the series y_t once. If y_t is an integrated process of order 2, then we must difference again, to obtain

$$w_t = x_t - x_{t-1} = \left(y_t - y_{t-1}\right) - \left(y_{t-1} - y_{t-2}\right) \qquad (20.6.3)$$

which is stationary.

The random walk process is an example of an integrated process of order 1. This follows since the first difference of the series

$$x_t = y_t - y_{t-1} = e_t \qquad (20.6.4)$$

forms a stationary time-series process.

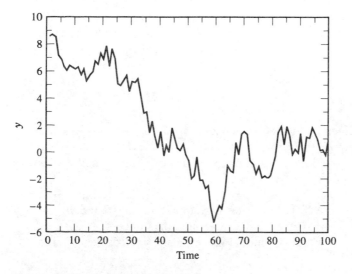

Figure 20.10 A random walk process.

Because we knew exactly the nature of the random walk process, we were able to transform it into a stationary process. However, when examining a time series of observations, as in Figures 20.1 to 20.3, the exact nature of the process is not known. Given the conditions for stationarity, however, it is sometimes clear when a series is *not* stationary. As we noted, the U. S. personal consumption series, in Figure 20.2, has a strong upward trend, and it is likely that the consumption series will have to be differenced one or more times to achieve stationarity. But how many times must we difference a series to achieve stationarity?

We can begin to answer this question by examining the sample autocorrelation function for the time-series process. *The autocorrelation function for a stationary series drops off to zero quickly as k, the length of the lag, increases. However, for integrated processes this will not occur.* The statistical significance of the autocorrelations can be checked by comparing them to the bounds $\pm 2/\sqrt{T}$ developed in Section 20.4.3.

To illustrate these ideas we consider the U. S. corn price series and U. S. personal consumption series in Figures 20.1 and 20.2, respectively. In Figure 20.11 the sample autocorrelation functions for the corn price and personal consumption data are plotted. In examining the sample autocorrelation functions, note that the corn price data show one large autocorrelation, but then the autocorrelations quickly taper to zero. Thus differencing the data does not appear to be necessary for the corn price data. On the other hand, the autocorrelations for the U. S. personal consumption data exhibit large autocorrelations that slowly decline. Thus, differencing appears to be necessary for the consumption data. In Exercise 20.6 that choice is examined.

If x_t is a time series that has been made stationary by differencing the original series y_t one or more times, then we can represent x_t using an ARMA(p, q) model and estimate the underlying parameters, just as we have discussed in the preceding sections. In this case the series y_t is called an autoregressive-*integrated*-moving average process of order p, d, q where d is the number of times the series has been differenced to achieve stationarity. We denote this ARIMA(p, d, q).

20.7 The Box–Jenkins Approach to Time-Series Model Building

The Box–Jenkins (1976) approach to time-series model building is a method of finding, for a given sample of data, an ARIMA model that may adequately represent the data-generation process. The method consists of three steps: *(i) identification, (ii) estimation,* and *(iii) diagnostic checking.*

20.7.1 Identification

In the identification step a tentative ARIMA model is specified for a given sample of data on the basis of the estimated autocorrelation and partial autocorrelation functions. The relationships that we have identified in the previous sections are summarized as follows:

1. If the autocorrelations taper off slowly, or do not die out, nonstationarity is indicated. This may be removed by differencing the data once or twice until stationarity is achieved. An ARMA model is then identified for the differenced series.

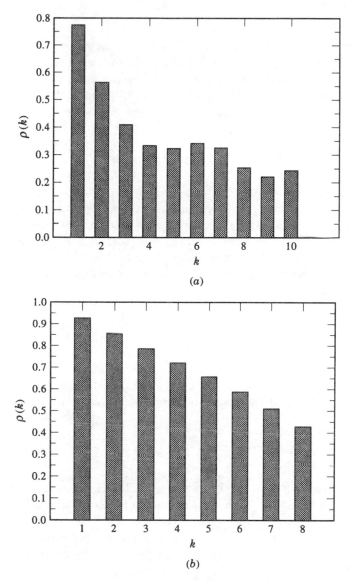

Figure 20.11 (a) Sample autocorrelation function of U. S. corn price series. (b) Sample autocorrelation function of U. S. personal consumption series.

2. For an MA(q) process, the autocorrelations $\rho_k = 0$ for $k > q$, and the partial autocorrelations taper off. To determine a cutoff point for the autocorrelation function, the sample autocorrelations are compared to $\pm 2/\sqrt{T}$.

3. For an AR(p) process the partial autocorrelations $\theta_{kk} = 0$ for $k > p$, and the autocorrelations taper off. A cutoff point for the partial autocorrelation function may be determined by comparing the estimates to $\pm 2/\sqrt{T}$.

4. If neither the autocorrelations nor the partial autocorrelations have a cutoff point, then an ARMA model may be appropriate. The order of the MA and AR components may be inferred from the pattern of autocorrelations and partial autocorrelations.

20.7.2 Estimation

Once a tentative specification of the ARIMA model has been made, the parameters of the process are estimated. If a pure AR process is identified then the parameters can be estimated by using least squares. If any MA terms are identified then maximum likelihood or least squares estimation, both of which require nonlinear optimization methods, may be used. These methods are discussed in the *Computer Handbook* accompanying this text and in Chapter 22.

20.7.3 Diagnostic Checking

The third step in Box–Jenkins model building is to check the model adequacy using diagnostic tests. The suggested tests include residual analysis and model overfitting. By overfitting we mean that if an ARIMA(p, d, q) model is specified and estimated, then we could estimate an ARIMA($p + 1$, d, q) model and an ARIMA(p, d, $q + 1$) model and check the significance of the additional parameters. If the model is ARIMA(p, d, q), then the additional parameters introduced by the larger models should not be significantly different from zero.

A residual analysis is based on the fact that if an ARIMA(p, d, q) model is an adequate representation of the data-generation process, then the residuals should be uncorrelated random disturbances. Thus, a plot of the residuals should show no patterns, and there should be no "unusual" values, or outliers. Furthermore, an autocorrelation function fit to the residuals should reveal no significant autocorrelations. Residual autocorrelations may be checked for significance by comparing them to $\pm 2 / \sqrt{T}$.

To check the overall acceptability of the residual autocorrelations, we can use the test statistic

$$Q = T(T+2)\sum_{k=1}^{K} \frac{1}{T-k} r_k^2 \qquad (20.7.1)$$

which was developed by Ljung and Box (1978). In equation 20.7.1 the r_k are the autocorrelations of the estimated residuals and K is the number of autocorrelations that are included in the test statistic. Values of Q for various values of K may be computed during the residual analysis. If the ARIMA(p, d, q) model is correctly specified, then the statistic Q, computed from the calculated residuals, is approximately χ^2-distributed with $K - p - q$ degrees of freedom.

20.7.4 An Example

By using these ideas let us build a time-series model for the U. S. corn price data illustrated in Figure 20.1. In Figure 20.11a we presented the sample autocorrelation function for the original corn price data. On the basis of the geometrically declining sample autocorrelations, we concluded that the data do not require differencing to achieve stationarity. Furthermore, since the sample autocorrelations do not cut off, when compared with the bound $2 / \sqrt{T} = 0.22$, we conclude that the corn price data do not follow a pure MA process.

The partial autocorrelation function for the corn price data is given in Figure 20.12. Compared with the bound $2 / \sqrt{T} = 0.22$ these partial autocorrelations clearly cut off, that is, they are not significantly different from zero, after $k = 1$. Thus, based on the facts that the sample autocorrelation function tapers off, and the partial autocorrelation function cuts off after lag $k = 1$, we tentatively conclude that the corn price data can be adequately modeled by an AR(1) process.

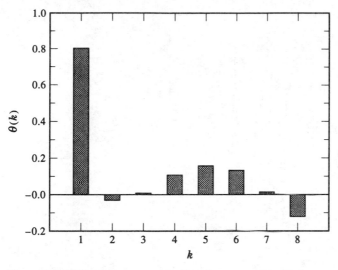

Figure 20.12 Partial autocorrelations for corn price data.

Given that we have tentatively identified an AR(1) process for the corn price data, we now estimate the unknown parameters of that model as we have written it in equation 20.3.1. In Section 20.3.3 we noted that the unknown parameters of AR models can be estimated by least squares. The resulting fitted model is

$$\hat{y}_t = 155.29 + 0.80 y_{t-1} \qquad \hat{\sigma}_e^2 = 14631.52$$
$$\quad (55.63) \ (0.07) \qquad\quad s.e.$$

The third step in the Box–Jenkins model-building procedure is to check for model adequacy by "overfitting" the model and checking that the calculated residuals exhibit no patterns or unusual or large values. For the corn price data no moving average component is indicated, so we overfit by estimating an AR(2) model, which yields

$$\hat{y}_t = 158.87 + 0.828 y_{t-1} - 0.0308 y_{t-2}$$
$$\quad\quad\ (.11) \quad (.12) \qquad\quad s.e.$$
$$\quad\quad\ (7.24) \ (-.25) \qquad\quad (t)$$

The coefficient on y_{t-2} is insignificant, based on its t-statistic, which suggests that the AR(1) specification is correct.

The least squares residuals from the estimated AR(1) model are calculated as

$$\hat{e}_t = y_t - 155.29 - 0.80 y_{t-1}$$

and are plotted in Figure 20.13. There are no particular patterns visible. The estimated residual autocorrelations are given in Table 20.4 They are small and also reveal no pattern.

Table 20.4   Residual Autocorrelations from AR(1) Model of U.S. Corn Price

k	r_k	k	r_k	k	r_k
1	0.026	6	0.118	11	0.201
2	−0.015	7	0.172	12	−0.070
3	−0.077	8	−0.013	13	−0.010
4	−0.074	9	−0.073	14	−0.130
5	0.004	10	0.140	15	−0.130

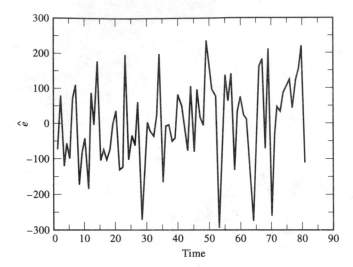

Figure 20.13 Least squares residuals from AR(1) model of corn price.

The value of the Ljung–Box test statistic, based on $K = 15$, is $Q = 15.13$, which we compare to the $\alpha = .05$ critical value of the $\chi^2_{(K-p=14)}$ distribution, which is 23.68. We conclude that the AR(1) model for the U. S. corn price series appears to be adequate.

20.8   Forecasting with Time-Series Models

Once a time-series model has been specified, estimated, and checked, it can be used for forecasting. In this section we discuss how an ARMA(p, q) model, estimated from information gathered up to time T, may be used to forecast the value of the random variable y_t in period $T + h$, y_{T+h}.

A general reason for wanting to forecast the value of y_{T+h} is that a decision must be made at time T, and the optimal decision depends on the future value of the random variable, given by y_{T+h}. We assume that there is a cost to an incorrect decision, and that the cost of an incorrect decision increases the further the forecast, which we denote as $\hat{y}_{T+h}$, is from the actual future value y_{T+h}. Consequently, our objective is to obtain a forecast that is "close" to the true future value. One way to characterize this objective is to say that we seek to minimize the average squared error between the true and predicted value, or the mean squared error (MSE), based on the information available to us at time T. Specifically, we seek to minimize the expectation

$$E_T \left[\left(\hat{y}_{T+h} - y_{T+h} \right)^2 \right] \qquad (20.8.1)$$

where the expectation operator E with the subscript T denotes that the expectation is a conditional one that assumes the information up to time T as given. *The optimal forecast of y_{T+h}, made at time T, is the conditional expectation of y_{T+h}, given the information up to time period T.* That is, the optimal forecast is

$$\hat{y}_{T+h} = E_T \left[y_{T+h} \right] \qquad (20.8.2)$$

The proof of this result is available in many books that emphasize time–series analysis. For example, see Pindyck and Rubinfeld (1991, pp. 516–518).

20.8.1 Computing the Forecast, Forecast Error, and Forecast Error Variance

In this section we demonstrate *(i)* how to use simple ARMA(p, q) models to obtain forecasts, *(ii)* how to compute the forecast error, and *(iii)* how to obtain the variance of the forecast error. As illustrations we consider the AR(1), MA(1), and ARMA(1,1) models. In the next section these results are used as a basis for constructing forecast confidence intervals.

20.8.1a *Forecasting with AR(1) Models*   The AR(1) time-series model is

$$y_t = \delta + \theta_1 y_{t-1} + e_t$$

Assume that the unknown parameters δ, θ_1, and the error variance σ_e^2 are known or that they have been estimated. In either instance we will treat them as if they are known and nonstochastic. We wish to forecast the value of y_t in period $T + h$ given the sample information at time T. We develop this forecast recursively, first obtaining the $h = 1$ period ahead forecast, then the $h = 2$ period ahead forecast, and so on.

1. Forecasting $h = 1$ period ahead: The value of y_{T+1}, assuming that the AR(1) representation is correct, is

    $$y_{T+1} = \delta + \theta_1 y_T + e_{T+1}$$

    The minimum mean squared error forecast of y_{T+1}, denoted $\hat{y}_{T+1}$, is its conditional expectation $E_T[y_{T+1}]$. To find this conditional expectation, we use the idea that at time $t = T$, every term with a time subscript $t \leq T$ is known. Thus, for time $t \leq T$,

    $$E_T[y_t] = y_t$$

    and

    $$E_T[e_t] = e_t$$

    and for time $t > T$

    $$E_T[e_t] = E[e_t] = 0$$

    Using these results, the minimum mean squared error forecast of y_{T+1} is

    $$\hat{y}_{T+1} = E_T[y_{T+1}] = E_T[\delta + \theta_1 y_T + e_{T+1}] = \delta + \theta_1 y_T$$

    The forecast error, denoted $\hat{e}_{T+1}$, is the difference between the value of y_t in period $T + 1$ and its forecasted value. That is

    $$\hat{e}_{T+1} = y_{T+1} - \hat{y}_{T+1} = \delta + \theta_1 y_T + e_{T+1} - (\delta + \theta_1 y_T) = e_{T+1}$$

    Then the variance of the forecast error is

    $$\mathrm{var}(\hat{e}_{T+1}) = \mathrm{var}(e_{T+1}) = \sigma_e^2$$

2. Forecasting $h = 2$ periods ahead: Given the AR(1) model the value of y_{T+2} is

    $$y_{T+2} = \delta + \theta_1 y_{T+1} + e_{T+2}$$

    The minimum mean squared error forecast of y_{T+2} is

    $$\hat{y}_{T+2} = E_T[y_{T+2}] = \delta + \theta_1 E_T[y_{T+1}] = \delta + \theta_1 \hat{y}_{T+1}$$

where we have replaced $E_T[y_{T+1}]$ by $\hat{y}_{T+1}$ and $E_T[e_{T+1}]$ by zero. The forecast error is

$$
\begin{aligned}
\hat{e}_{T+2} = y_{T+2} - \hat{y}_{T+2} &= \delta + \theta_1 y_{T+1} + e_{T+2} - \left(\delta + \theta_1 \hat{y}_{T+1}\right) \\
&= e_{T+2} + \theta_1\left(y_{T+1} - \hat{y}_{T+1}\right) \\
&= e_{T+2} + \theta_1 \hat{e}_{T+1} = e_{T+2} + \theta_1 e_{T+1}
\end{aligned}
$$

where in the last step we used the result that $\hat{e}_{T+1} = e_{T+1}$ derived in (1). The forecast error variance is

$$
\operatorname{var}\left(\hat{e}_{T+2}\right) = \operatorname{var}\left(e_{T+2} + \theta_1 e_{T+1}\right) = \sigma_e^2 + \theta_1^2 \sigma_e^2 = \sigma_e^2\left(1 + \theta_1^2\right)
$$

3. Forecasting h periods ahead: This process is continued until the h-step-ahead forecast is obtained,

$$
\hat{y}_{T+h} = \delta + \theta_1 E_T[y_{T+h-1}] = \delta + \theta_1 \hat{y}_{T+h-1}
$$

with forecast error variance

$$
\operatorname{var}\left(\hat{e}_{T+h}\right) = \sigma_e^2\left(1 + \theta_1^2 + \theta_1^4 + \ldots + \theta_1^{2(h-1)}\right)
$$

20.8.1b Forecasting with MA(1) Models

Given the ideas developed in the previous section, we can easily establish the forecasts, forecast errors, and forecast error variances for the MA(1) process. The MA(1) model is

$$
y_t = \mu + e_t + \alpha_1 e_{t-1}
$$

Once again we develop the h-period-ahead forecast recursively, one period at a time.

1. Forecasting $h = 1$ period ahead: The value of y_{T+1}, assuming that the MA(1) representation is correct, is

$$
y_{T+1} = \mu + e_{T+1} + \alpha_1 e_T
$$

The minimum mean squared error forecast is

$$
\hat{y}_{T+1} = E_T[y_{T+1}] = E_T[\mu + e_{T+1} + \alpha_1 e_T] = \mu + \alpha_1 e_T
$$

The forecast error is

$$
\hat{e}_{T+1} = y_{T+1} - \hat{y}_{T+1} = \mu + e_{T+1} + \alpha_1 e_T - \left(\mu + \alpha_1 e_T\right) = e_{T+1}
$$

Hence, the forecast error variance is

$$
\operatorname{var}\left(\hat{e}_{T+1}\right) = \operatorname{var}\left(e_{T+1}\right) = \sigma_e^2
$$

2. Forecasting $h = 2$ periods ahead: The value of y_{T+2} is

$$
y_{T+2} = \mu + e_{T+2} + \alpha_1 e_{T+1}
$$

Its minimum mean square error forecast is

$$
\hat{y}_{T+2} = E_T[y_{T+2}] = \mu
$$

and the forecast error variance is

$$\operatorname{var}(\hat{e}_{T+2}) = \operatorname{var}(e_{T+2} + \alpha_1 e_{T+1}) = \sigma_e^2 + \alpha_1^2 \sigma_e^2 = \sigma_e^2(1 + \alpha_1^2)$$

3. Forecasting h periods ahead: From the results in (2) it is easy to show that the h-period-ahead minimum mean squared error forecast for the MA(1) model is $\hat{y}_{T+h} = \mu$, and that the forecast error variance is $\operatorname{var}(\hat{e}_{T+h}) = \sigma_e^2(1 + \alpha_1^2)$.

Note that the $h = 1$ period ahead forecast $\hat{y}_{T+1}$ depends on e_t the random error in time T. Although this value is not actually known, it can be consistently estimated. We have shown that $e_{T+1} = y_{T+1} - \hat{y}_{T+1}$. That is, the error e_{T+1} is simply the forecast error resulting from predicting y_{T+1} using its minimum mean squared error forecast $\hat{y}_{T+1}$, based on all information available at time $t = T$. Consequently, the value e_T that enters the minimum mean squared error forecast can be calculated from past forecast errors.

To see how this is done, we continue to suppose that the parameter values are known. Starting at time $t = 0$, what is the optimal forecast of y_1? The value of y_1, given the MA(1) model, is

$$y_1 = \mu + e_1 + \alpha_1 e_0$$

Its forecast is

$$\hat{y}_1 = E_0[y_1] = \mu + \alpha_1 e_0$$

The presample value e_0 is usually not known and can be replaced by its unconditional expectation, which is zero. In that case the best forecast of y_1, at time $t = 0$, is $\hat{y}_1 = \mu$. Then we can calculate

$$\hat{e}_1 = y_1 - \hat{y}_1 = y_1 - \mu$$

Now forecast y_2 from time $t = 1$:

$$\hat{y}_2 = \mu + \alpha_1 \hat{e}_1$$

where we have replaced e_1 by $\hat{e}_1$. Then we calculate

$$\hat{e}_2 = y_2 - \hat{y}_2$$

which allows us to forecast y_3. Thus we can continue, recursively, to calculate estimates $\hat{e}_3, \dots, \hat{e}_T$. In practice, the unknown parameters are replaced by their estimated values, which is justifiable if the sample size T is large, so that the estimated parameters have a high probability of being near their true values.

20.8.1c Forecasting with ARMA(1, 1) Models   The ARMA(1, 1) model is given by

$$y_t = \delta + \theta_1 y_{t-1} + e_t + \alpha_1 e_{t-1}$$

It is a combination of an AR(1) and a MA(1) process, and therefore what we have learned in the previous two sections can be applied to the forecasting problem.

1. Forecasting $h = 1$ period ahead: The value of y_t in period $T + 1$ is

$$y_{T+1} = \delta + \theta_1 y_T + e_{T+1} + \alpha_1 e_T$$

The minimum mean squared error forecast for y_{T+1} is

$$\hat{y}_{T+1} = E_T[\delta + \theta_1 y_T + e_{T+1} + \alpha_1 e_T] = \delta + \theta_1 y_T + \alpha_1 e_T$$

The forecast error is

$$\hat{e}_{T+1} = y_{T+1} - \hat{y}_{T+1} = e_{T+1}$$

Hence, the forecast error variance is

$$\mathrm{var}\!\left(\hat{e}_{T+1}\right) = \mathrm{var}\!\left(e_{T+1}\right) = \sigma_e^2$$

2. Forecasting $h = 2$ periods ahead: The minimum mean squared error forecast for y_{T+2} is

$$
\begin{aligned}
\hat{y}_{T+2} &= E_T\!\left[\delta + \theta_1 y_{T+1} + e_{T+2} + \alpha_1 e_{T+1}\right] \\
&= \delta + \theta_1 E_T\!\left[y_{T+1}\right] = \delta + \theta_1 \hat{y}_{T+1}
\end{aligned}
$$

The forecast error is

$$
\begin{aligned}
\hat{e}_{T+2} &= y_{T+2} - \hat{y}_{T+2} = \theta_1\!\left(y_{T+1} - \hat{y}_{T+1}\right) + e_{T+2} + \alpha_1 e_{T+1} \\
&= \left(\theta_1 + \alpha_1\right) e_{T+1} + e_{T+2}
\end{aligned}
$$

where we have used the fact that the $h = 1$ period forecast error is e_{T+1}. Consequently, the forecast error variance is

$$\mathrm{var}\!\left(\hat{e}_{T+2}\right) = \sigma_e^2\!\left[\left(\theta_1 + \alpha_1\right)^2 + 1\right]$$

3. Forecasting $h = 3$ periods ahead: The $h = 3$ periods ahead forecast for the ARMA(1, 1) model is

$$\hat{y}_{T+3} = \delta + \theta_1 \hat{y}_{T+2}$$

and the forecast error variance is

$$\mathrm{var}\!\left(\hat{e}_{T+3}\right) = \sigma_e^2\!\left[1 + \left(\theta_1 + \alpha_1\right)^2 + \left(\theta_1^2 + \theta_1 \alpha_1\right)^2\right]$$

20.8.1d Forecasting with ARMA(p, q) Models   As we have demonstrated, the calculation of h-period-ahead minimum mean squared error forecasts is a relatively simple task, involving only the computation of a conditional expectation. It is straightforward to show that the h-period-ahead forecast for a general ARMA(p, q) model is

$$\hat{y}_{T+h} = \delta + \theta_1 \hat{y}_{T+h-1} + \ldots + \theta_{h-1}\hat{y}_{T+1} + \theta_h y_T + \ldots + \theta_p y_{T-p+h} + \alpha_h e_T + \ldots + \alpha_q e_{T-q+h}$$

Calculation of the forecast error variances is, however, somewhat more tedious. In Exercise 20.8 a general formula for forecast error variances is given that holds for any h-period-ahead forecast from an ARMA(p, q) model. This general result greatly eases the burden of computing forecast error variances, which we use in the following section to construct forecast intervals.

20.8.2   Forecast Confidence Intervals

The final step in our analysis of forecasting using ARMA(p, q) models addresses the fact that users of forecasts often want not only a "point" forecast $\hat{y}_{T+h}$ but also some measure of forecast reliability, such as a forecast confidence interval. A $(1 - \alpha) \times 100\%$ forecast interval will have the form

$$\hat{y}_{T+h} \pm z_c \left(\text{forecast error variance}\right)^{1/2}$$

where z_c is the upper $\alpha/2$ critical value for the standard normal $N(0, 1)$ distribution. One caveat is in order here, and that is that the forecast error variances that we have derived were obtained under the assumption that the parameter values are *known* rather than estimated. Consequently, the forecast intervals based on them will *overstate* the level of confidence that one should have in the intervals. The hope is that in large samples the intervals will not be too far off their proper size.

20.8.3   An Example

We conclude this section by constructing forecasts and forecast intervals for the U. S. corn price data. The estimated AR(1) model is

$$\hat{y}_t = 155.29 + 0.80 y_{t-1}$$

The value y_T for that sample is $y_{1948} = 1114$. Point forecasts for corn price in 1949 to 1953 are, using the results in Section 20.8.1a,

$$\hat{y}_{1949} = \hat{y}_{T+1} = \hat{\delta} + \hat{\theta}_1 y_T = 155.29 + 0.80(1114) = 1048.04$$

$$\hat{y}_{1950} = \hat{y}_{T+2} = \hat{\delta} + \hat{\theta}_1 \hat{y}_{T+1} = 155.29 + 0.80(1048.04) = 995.19$$

$$\hat{y}_{1951} = \hat{y}_{T+3} = \hat{\delta} + \hat{\theta}_1 \hat{y}_{T+2} = 155.29 + 0.80(995.52) = 952.84$$

$$\hat{y}_{1952} = \hat{y}_{T+4} = \hat{\delta} + \hat{\theta}_1 \hat{y}_{T+3} = 155.29 + 0.80(952.84) = 918.89$$

$$\hat{y}_{1953} = \hat{y}_{T+5} = \hat{\delta} + \hat{\theta}_1 \hat{y}_{T+4} = 155.29 + 0.80(918.89) = 891.69$$

Using the general expression for the forecast error variance of an AR(1) process derived in Section 20.8.1a, we report the forecast error variance, which we denote $\hat{\sigma}_h^2$, and the 95% forecast intervals, which are based on the critical value $z_c = 1.96$, in Table 20.5.

The predicted values and forecast intervals are shown in Figure 20.14. As expected, the further into the future one wishes to forecast, the wider the forecast interval, though terms like θ_1^{2h-2} have little impact when h is large.

20.9   Summary and Guide to Further Reading

This chapter has been devoted to the study of forecasting future values of individual economic variables using time-series models. We have developed the univarate time-series model and outlined the Box–Jenkins approach to fitting ARIMA models. It is broken into three steps: *(i)* identification, in which the data series is differenced to achieve stationarity, if necessary, and AR and MA components are specified on the basis of sample autocorrelation and partial autocorrelation functions; *(ii)* estimation; and *(iii)*

Table 20.5   Forecast Error Variances and Confidence Intervals

t	$\hat{y}_t$	$\hat{\sigma}_h^2$	95% Forecast Interval
1949	1048.04	14631.52	[810.96, 1285.13]
1950	995.19	24028.38	[691.37, 1299.01]
1951	952.84	30063.37	[613.00, 1292.68]
1952	918.89	33939.24	[557.81, 1279.98]
1953	891.69	36428.47	[517.60, 1265.78]

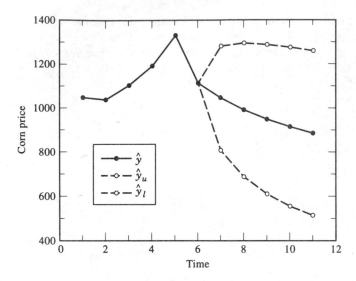

Figure 20.14 Forecasts and forecast intervals for corn price.

diagnostic checking. Given the estimated time-series model, forecasts can be generated for future values of the economic variable.

Time-series analysis has a fundamental weakness which, ironically, is also a source of its attraction. The models we have considered use *only* the data on a *single* observable economic variable. Consequently, subsequent analysis is inexpensive, not time consuming, and serves well in many cases as a basis of *short-run* forecasting. A problem arises for pure time-series models *(i)* when the systematic component of the economic variable is *not* easily removed by differencing the data, or fitting a simple time trend [as discussed, for example, in Pindyck and Rubinfeld (1991, Chapter 14)]; *(ii)* when forecasts substantially into the future are desired; or *(iii)* when we need to isolate the impact of changes in instrument variables on y_t, the economic variable in question. In these instances the systematic component of the economic variable might be better explained by a specification resulting from economic theory. This brings us back to the specification of an *econometric model* to explain the behavior of an economic variable, that is

$$y_t = f(x_1, ..., x_K, \beta_1, ..., \beta_n) + e_t \tag{20.9.1a}$$

$$= \beta_1 + x_{t2}\beta_2 + ... + x_{tK}\beta_K + e_t \tag{20.9.1b}$$

where y_t is an economic variable whose behavior we wish to predict or explain. In equation 20.9.1a $f(\cdot)$ is a function of the explanatory variables x_k and the unknown parameters thought to represent the systematic part of y_t, which in this case is $E[y_t]$, the mathematical expectation, or expected value, of the economic variable. In equation 20.9.1b the function $f(\cdot)$ is taken to be linear in the parameters, as we have assumed thus far in this book.

The random component in equations 20.9.1 *still* may be well represented by an ARMA model, even though the systematic part of y_t is based on a model arising from economic theory. In Chapter 16 an example of this nature was given, where the random disturbance in a linear model followed a first-order autocorrelation process.

Our discussion of time series is incomplete in several regards. First, we used differencing the data as the only way that nonstationary time series may be transformed to stationarity. Other approaches are available, for example, fitting time trends and taking logarithms. Second, we did not treat the problem of seasonality in the data. Seasonality imparts another pattern into the time series that can be accounted for and used to aid forecasts. Third, we presented time series techniques for single economic variables. Techniques are also available to treat multiple time series, in which covariation between time series is used to assist not only in forecasting but also to test economic hypotheses about causality. These models are introduced in Chapter 21. Fourth, when discussing forecasting with time-series models, we did not deal with the problem of forecasting series that had been differenced to achieve stationarity. This, however, is covered in the computer handbooks accompanying this book.

For further discussion of time series models and their uses, see Judge et al. (1988, Chapters 17–19), Pindyck and Rubinfeld (1991, Chapters 14–19), Newbold and Bos (1990), Vandaele (1983), Granger (1989), Pankratz (1983), and Nazem (1988).

Also, it should be noted that many standard statistical and econometric software packages incorporate special functions and programs for identification, estimation, diagnostic checking, and forecasting by using Box–Jenkins models. Relevant software packages include SAS, SHAZAM, TSP, RATS, and SORTITEC. This list is representative rather than exhaustive.

20.10   Exercises

20.1   Consider the AR(1) process in equation 20.3.1. Define a new random variable $y_t^* = y_t - \mu$, and show that y_t and y_t^* have the same variances, covariances, and autocorrelations.

20.2   Show that the autocorrelation function of the MA(2) statistical model of equation 20.4.4a is given by equation 20.4.5.

20.3   Derive the covariances γ_k of the ARMA(1, 1) statistical model given in equation 20.5.2 and show that the autocorrelation function is given by equation 20.5.3.

20.4   Consider the random walk process in equation 20.6.1. Using your computer software, and guided by the examples in your computer manual, construct and plot $T = 1000$ values of y_t, assuming $y_1 = 0$. Repeat this process several times using different sets of random disturbances.

20.5   Show that the time series e_t formed of independent and identically distributed $N(0, \sigma_e^2)$ random variables is stationary.

20.6   Consider the U. S. personal consumption data illustrated in Figure 20.2. Construct the sample autocorrelation functions for the first and second differences of the data. What order of differencing appears appropriate? Explain. (*Hint:* Plot the differenced series.)

20.7   Define each of the following terms: (*a*) stationary process, (*b*) invertible process, (*c*) random walk, (*d*) integrated process.

20.8   For the general ARMA(p, q) model, the forecast error variance can be constructed as follows. Define the parameters ϕ_i as

$$\phi_1 = \alpha_1 + \theta_1$$

$$\phi_n = \begin{cases} \alpha_n + \displaystyle\sum_{i=1}^{\min(n,\,p)} \theta_i \phi_{n-1} & \text{for } n = 1, 2, \ldots, q \\[2em] \displaystyle\sum_{i=1}^{\min(n,\,p)} \theta_i \phi_{n-1} & \text{for } n > q \end{cases}$$

Then the h-period-ahead forecast variance for an ARMA(p, q) model is

$$\sigma_h^2 = \sigma_e^2 \sum_{i=0}^{h-1} \phi_i^2$$

where $\phi_0 = 1$. Use this result to verify the forecast error variances for $h = 1$ and 2 periods ahead forecasts for the AR(1), MA(1), and ARMA(1, 1) models given in Section 20.8.1.

20.9 Assume that the MA(1) model in equation 20.4.9 is invertible, or $|\alpha_1| < 1$. Carry out the repeated substitutions, begun in equation 20.4.12, to illustrate that the MA(1) process has an infinite AR representation.

20.10 Use the infinite AR representation for an invertible MA(1) process, derived in Exercise 20.9, to rewrite the sum of squares in equation 20.4.8 in terms of the observable random variables y_t, y_{t-1},..., y_1. Why is it justifiable, in large samples, to delete terms involving the presample values y_0, y_{-1},...?

20.11 In Table 20.6 three data series of 100 observations each are given. For *each* of the series do the following:
   (a) Plot the observations against time.
   (b) Use the first $T = 90$ observations to identify, estimate, and check the adequacy of a Box–Jenkins time series model fitting the data.
   (c) Use the model developed in part (b) to construct forecast intervals for observations $T = 91$,..., 100.

20.11   References

GRANGER, C. W. J. (1980) *Forecasting in Business and Economics*. New York: Academic Press, Inc.

GRANGER, C. W. J., and P. NEWBOLD (1986) *Forecasting Economic Time Series*, 2nd Edition, New York: Academic Press, Inc.

JUDGE, G. G., R. C. HILL, W. E. GRIFFITHS, H. LÜTKEPOHL, and T. C. LEE (1988) *Introduction to the Theory and Practice of Econometrics*, 2nd Edition, New York: John Wiley & Sons, Inc.

NAZEM, S. (1988) *Applied Time Series Analysis for Business and Economic Forecasting*, New York: Marcel Dekker, Inc.

NEWBOLD, P., and T. BOS (1990) *Introductory Business Forecasting*. Cincinnati, OH: South-Western Publishing Co.

PANKRATZ, A. (1983) *Forecasting with Univariate Box-Jenkins Models*, New York: John Wiley & Sons, Inc.

PINDYCK, R. S., and D. L. RUBINFELD (1991) *Econometric Models and Economic Forecasts*, 3rd Edition, New York: McGraw-Hill, Inc.

VANDAELE, W. (1983) *Applied Time Series and Box-Jenkins Models*, New York: Academic Press, Inc.

Table 20.6 Sample Time Series

Observation	y_1	y_2	y_3	Observation	y_1	y_2	y_3
1	3.6877	12.6893	37.9928	51	0.5894	10.4447	34.3592
2	3.1978	12.4573	37.7335	52	1.6616	11.7054	35.0558
3	2.6961	11.9171	37.0559	53	3.4887	13.5458	37.2654
4	1.1523	10.5487	35.3283	54	1.2313	10.7827	35.6734
5	1.4623	11.2104	35.0744	55	1.7742	11.3608	35.4077
6	1.3849	11.3701	35.0995	56	1.4506	11.3688	35.2749
7	1.5414	11.4815	35.2242	57	2.1189	11.9896	35.8253
8	2.3574	12.2858	36.0946	58	0.3378	10.1575	34.2849
9	2.2112	11.9740	36.2442	59	0.4433	10.4354	33.7464
10	2.2126	11.8472	36.1966	60	2.1517	12.4593	35.4849
11	2.4576	12.1193	36.4435	61	2.8130	12.8156	36.7626
12	1.8156	11.4361	35.8912	62	2.3421	11.9147	36.5389
13	2.5679	12.2498	36.4121	63	3.5527	13.0802	37.5858
14	1.5885	11.2649	35.7033	64	5.0817	14.4951	39.5556
15	2.4723	12.1715	36.2342	65	3.4327	12.3644	38.4688
16	2.6411	12.3759	36.7201	66	2.7956	11.7166	37.2451
17	3.3363	12.8777	37.4793	67	4.9430	14.2789	39.1588
18	2.6057	11.9994	37.0034	68	2.6851	11.7816	37.6757
19	3.3782	12.7638	37.5156	69	4.1909	13.2627	38.3708
20	2.4452	11.8384	36.8617	70	3.4817	12.7244	38.2010
21	3.4366	12.8412	37.5179	71	2.7207	11.8002	37.1867
22	1.3704	10.7839	35.8084	72	0.6415	9.9807	34.8296
23	3.3068	12.8799	36.9984	73	1.2354	11.0642	34.6639
24	1.9206	11.5569	36.3061	74	1.0539	11.1724	34.6843
25	0.4035	9.9091	34.2913	75	2.3040	12.3418	35.8645
26	1.2626	11.2808	34.5952	76	1.4617	11.3247	35.4728
27	2.2011	12.3597	35.8351	77	2.0539	11.8237	35.7643
28	2.7095	12.5506	36.6832	78	2.1073	11.9357	36.0308
29	1.2696	10.8502	35.4323	79	2.3208	12.0295	36.2659
30	2.6394	12.3654	36.2845	80	3.0989	12.7620	37.1229
31	2.4200	12.1866	36.5574	81	3.7457	13.2389	38.0541
32	2.7197	12.2667	36.7821	82	4.7940	14.0336	39.3423
33	1.1103	10.6483	35.2828	83	3.9746	12.9182	38.9096
34	0.5919	10.3426	34.1825	84	1.8554	10.7397	36.5018
35	1.5634	11.7017	34.9584	85	3.5450	12.9365	37.4225
36	0.3653	10.4384	34.1063	86	2.3365	11.8423	36.8162
37	2.2665	12.3579	35.5743	87	0.8858	10.2773	34.9299
38	1.0188	11.0168	35.0112	88	2.0603	11.9201	35.5730
39	0.8937	10.7445	34.4404	89	1.8923	11.8274	35.8211
40	2.9799	13.0850	36.4784	90	3.6376	13.3810	37.5062
41	0.7530	10.5330	35.0066	91	0.8915	10.3749	35.3932
42	2.5037	12.2653	35.9588	92	3.4920	13.1076	37.0059
43	1.8408	11.7267	35.9249	93	2.8432	12.5382	37.2913
44	3.9846	13.6537	37.8339	94	3.4943	12.8111	37.7155
45	2.2941	11.7292	36.9212	95	2.4369	11.7663	36.8955
46	1.7179	11.0343	35.7425	96	2.0078	11.3921	36.0867
47	1.8324	11.5612	35.6448	97	1.3989	11.0526	35.3186
48	2.7033	12.5208	36.5525	98	1.9590	11.7947	35.6535
49	1.7075	11.3582	35.8710	99	1.7216	11.5777	35.6140
50	1.6179	11.2720	35.4236	100	3.2881	13.0790	37.0945

Chapter 21

Bivariate and Multivariate
Time Series Models

New Key Words and Concepts

Finite Distributed Lags   Infinite Distributed Lags

Polynomial Lags   Geometric Lag

Koyck Transformation   Vector Autoregressive Models

Causality   Cointegration

Spurious Regressions   Unit Roots

21.1 Introduction

As we have stated in previous chapters, economic data are generated by systems of economic relations that are dynamic, stochastic (random), and simultaneous. In Chapter 20 we considered *univariate* time series forecasting models in which a *single* economic variable was written as a function of its own lagged values and current and lagged values of a random disturbance, or

$$y_t = f\left(y_{t-1}, y_{t-2}, \ldots, y_{t-p}, e_t, e_{t-1}, \ldots, e_{t-q}\right)$$

In this chapter we introduce another time series of data on an economic variable, say x_t, and jointly consider the *bivariate time series* (y_t, x_t). Introduction of additional time-series variables produces a *multivariate time series*.

Bivariate time-series models fall into two general categories. First, *distributed lag models*, in which variations in y_t are determined by current and lagged values of x_t, plus a random disturbance, are written

$$y_t = f\left(x_t, x_{t-1}, x_{t-2}, \ldots\right) + e_t$$

As in the linear statistical models considered in Chapters 5 to 11, distributed lag models treat the x_t variable as exogenous, or predetermined, and treat y_t as the outcome variable. In these models, the objective is to understand how changes in x_t at one point in time influence values of y_t in the current and subsequent periods. If we denote a change in x_t by Δx_t, the situation where a change Δx_t affects the outcome variable y_t in the current period (Δy_t) and in the succeeding n periods ($\Delta y_{t+1}, \Delta y_{t+2}, \ldots, \Delta y_{t+n}$) is shown diagrammatically in Figure 21.1.

A second type of bivariate time series model is the *vector autoregressive model* in which random variables y_t and x_t are placed into a vector $\mathbf{z}_t = (y_t, x_t)'$, and the random vector $\mathbf{z}_t$ is assumed to be a (vector valued) function of its own lagged values plus a

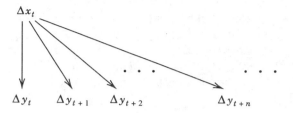

Figure 21.1 The lag effects of a change in x_t

vector of random disturbances, or

$$\mathbf{z}_t = \mathbf{f}\left(\mathbf{z}_{t-1}, \mathbf{z}_{t-2}, \ldots, \mathbf{z}_{t-p}\right) + \mathbf{e}_t$$

The vector autoregressive model, like the univariate time series models of Chapter 20, is useful primarily for short-run forecasting. However, it is also used to examine certain economic hypotheses about the lead-lag relationship between the two (or more) variables.

The plan of the chapter is as follows: in Section 21.2 we introduce distributed lag models and discuss the popular Almon polynomial version of the finite distributed lag. Section 21.3 contains a description of infinite distributed lag models in general and the geometric distributed lag model in particular. In Section 21.4 we introduce vector autoregressive models and discuss their estimation and use. Finally, in Section 21.5 we briefly introduce some special topics: cointegration, spurious regressions, and "unit roots."

21.2   The Finite Distributed Lag Model: The Almon Polynomial Distributed Lag

In this section we consider a *finite distributed lag model* in which the change in an independent variable has an effect on the outcome variable that is "distributed" over several future periods. The lagged effects on the outcome variable may arise from factors such as habit persistence or institutional or technological constraints. Lagged effects may also be the consequence of how individual decision maker's expectations are linked with experience. The problem of explaining quarterly capital expenditures by manufacturing industries is an example, so let us turn our attention in this direction.

21.2.1 An Economic Model

Quarterly capital expenditures by manufacturing firms arise from appropriations decisions in prior periods. The appropriations decisions themselves are based on projections of the profitability of alternative investment projects, and comparison of the marginal efficiency of investments to the cost of capital funds. Once an investment project is decided on, funds for it are "appropriated," or approved for expenditure. The actual expenditures arising from any appropriation decision are observed over subsequent quarters as plans are finalized, materials and labor engaged in the project, and construction carried out. Thus, if x_t is the amount of capital appropriations observed at a particular time, we can be sure that the effects of that decision, in the form of capital expenditures y_t, will be "distributed" over periods t, $t + 1$, $t + 2$, and so on until the projects are completed. Furthermore, since a certain amount of "start-up" time is required for any investment project, we would not be surprised to see the major effects of the appropriation decision delayed for several quarters. Furthermore, as the work on the investment projects draws to a close, we expect to observe the expenditures related to the appropriation x_t declining.

Since capital appropriations at time t, designated by x_t, affect capital expenditures in the current and future periods $(y_t, y_{t+1}, \ldots)$, until the appropriated projects are completed, we may say equivalently that current expenditures y_t are a function of current and past appropriations $x_t, x_{t-1}, \ldots$. Furthermore, let us assert that after n quarters, where n is an unknown integer called the lag length, the effect of any appropriation decision on capital expenditure is exhausted, so

$$y_t = f(x_t, x_{t-1}, \ldots, x_{t-n}) \tag{21.2.1}$$

Equation 21.2.1 is an economic framework for a distributed lag model. It is *finite* as the duration of the lag effects is a finite period of time, namely, n periods. If we specify the functional form in the finite lag model to be linear in the parameters, we have

$$y_t = \delta + \beta_0 x_t + \beta_1 x_{t-1} + \ldots + \beta_n x_{t-n} \tag{21.2.2}$$

where δ is the intercept parameter, and β_i is the parameter, called a *distributed lag weight*, reflecting the effect of the level of appropriation in period $t - i$, $i = 0, 1, \ldots, n$, on current expenditures y_t. This is our economic model of the relationship between capital appropriations and expenditures.

21.2.2 The Statistical Model

To convert equation 21.2.2 into a statistical model, we add a random disturbance e_t and specify its properties. For the present let us assume that e_t has zero mean, has constant variance σ^2, and is not autocorrelated. In this context the finite distributed lag statistical model is

$$y_t = \delta + \beta_0 x_t + \beta_1 x_{t-1} + \ldots + \beta_n x_{t-n} + e_t, \quad t = n+1, \ldots, T \tag{21.2.3a}$$

and

$$e_t \sim (0, \sigma^2) \tag{21.2.3b}$$

Note that in this statistical model, if T bivariate observations are available on (y_t, x_t), only $(T - n)$ *complete* observations may be used for estimation purposes since n observations are "lost" creating $x_{t-1}, \ldots, x_{t-n}$.

We can write equation 21.2.3 in matrix terms as

$$\mathbf{y} = \delta \mathbf{x}_1 + X_s \boldsymbol{\beta}_s + \mathbf{e}$$

$$= \begin{bmatrix} \mathbf{x}_1 & X_s \end{bmatrix} \begin{bmatrix} \delta \\ \boldsymbol{\beta}_s \end{bmatrix} + \mathbf{e}$$

$$= X\boldsymbol{\beta} + \mathbf{e} \tag{21.2.4}$$

where

$$\mathbf{y} = \begin{bmatrix} y_{n+1} \\ y_{n+2} \\ \vdots \\ y_T \end{bmatrix}, \quad X_s = \begin{bmatrix} x_{n+1} & x_n & \cdots & x_1 \\ x_{n+2} & x_{n+1} & \cdots & x_2 \\ \vdots & \vdots & \ddots & \vdots \\ x_T & x_{T-1} & \cdots & x_{T-n} \end{bmatrix}, \quad \boldsymbol{\beta}_s = \begin{bmatrix} \beta_0 \\ \beta_1 \\ \vdots \\ \beta_n \end{bmatrix}, \quad \mathbf{e} = \begin{bmatrix} e_{n+1} \\ e_{n+2} \\ \vdots \\ e_T \end{bmatrix}$$

$$X = \begin{bmatrix} \mathbf{x}_1 & X_s \end{bmatrix}, \quad \boldsymbol{\beta} = \begin{bmatrix} \delta \\ \boldsymbol{\beta}_s \end{bmatrix}$$

and x_1 is a $(T - n) \times 1$ vector of ones. We assume that the error vector $\mathbf{e}$ has expectation $E[\mathbf{e}] = \mathbf{0}$ and covariance matrix $\text{cov}(\mathbf{e}) = \sigma^2 I_{T-n}$, and thus $\mathbf{y} \sim \left(X\boldsymbol{\beta}, \sigma^2 I_{T-n} \right)$.

Since this is a conventional linear statistical model, of the type considered in Chapters 9 to 11, the intercept and distributed lag weight parameters in equation 21.2.3 may be estimated by using the least squares estimation rule. It is clear, however, that multicollinearity (Chapter 13) may be a *severe* problem in this model, since the explanatory variables in X_s are current and n lagged values of capital appropriations x_t.

To give an empirical illustration of this type of model, consider the data in Table 21.1 on quarterly capital expenditures and appropriations for U. S. manufacturing firms. We assume that $n = 8$ periods are required to exhaust the expenditure effects of a capital appropriation in manufacturing. The basis for this choice is investigated in Exercise 21.2, since the lag length n is actually an unknown constant. The least squares parameter estimates, using the statistical model 21.2.3 and data in Table 21.1, are

$$\hat{y}_t = 33.4 + 0.04x_t + 0.07x_{t-1} + 0.18x_{t-2} + 0.19x_{t-3} + 0.17x_{t-4}$$
$$+ 0.05x_{t-5} + 0.05x_{t-6} + 0.06x_{t-7} + 0.13x_{t-8} \tag{21.2.5}$$

The corresponding standard errors, t-statistics, and p-values of the estimated parameters are given in Table 21.2. The R^2 for the estimated relation is 0.99 and the overall F-test value is 1174.8. The statistical model "fits" the data well and the F-test of the joint hypothesis—that all distributed lag weights $\beta_i = 0$, $i = 0, \ldots, n$—is rejected at the $\alpha = .01$ level of significance. Examining the parameter estimates themselves, we notice several disquieting facts. First, only the lag weights β_2, β_3, β_4, and β_8 appear to be statistically significantly different from zero based on individual t-tests. Second, the estimated lag weights b_7 and b_8 are *larger* than the estimated lag weights for lags of 5 and 6 periods. This does not agree with our anticipations that the lag effects of appropriations should decrease with time and in the most distant periods should be small and approaching zero.

As discussed in Chapter 13, these characteristics are symptomatic of multicollinearity in the data. Following procedures developed in Chapter 13, let us examine the data for this problem. The simple correlations among the current and lagged values of capital appropriations are given in Table 21.3 and are all very large. The results of an auxiliary regression of x_t on the intercept variable and $x_{t-1}, \ldots, x_{t-n}$ yields an $R^2 = .96$. The R^2 values for other auxiliary regressions range from .96 to .99. Consequently, a high level of *linear* dependence is indicated among the explanatory variables. Thus, we conclude that the least squares estimates in Table 21.2 are subject to great sampling variability and are unreliable owing to the limited independent information provided by each explanatory variable x_{t-i}.

21.2.3   Polynomial Distributed Lags

In the context of the finite distributed lag model, it is typically not possible to "solve" the multicollinearity problem by obtaining more data. We expect new quarterly observations on capital appropriations, as they become available, to exhibit the same or similar linear associations as the previous appropriations data, and thus not to provide much new information about the lag weights.

The other alternative is to use nonsample information, and following Almon (1965) we use *nonsample* information about the distributed lag weights to improve the precision of estimation. In keeping with the discussion of Section 21.2.1, we wish to impose constraints on the parameters β_i that conform to the notion that capital appropriations have their peak effect on capital expenditures after several quarters and then have slowly

Table 21.1 Quarterly Capital Expenditures (y_t) and Appropriations (x_t) for U. S. Manufacturing Firms

t	y_t	x_t	t	y_t	x_t
1	2072	1767	45	3136	4123
2	2077	2061	46	3299	4656
3	2078	2289	47	3514	4906
4	2043	2047	48	3815	4344
5	2062	1856	49	4040	5080
6	2067	1842	50	4274	5539
7	1964	1866	51	4565	5583
8	1981	2279	52	4838	6147
9	1914	2688	53	5222	6545
10	1991	3264	54	5406	6770
11	2129	3896	55	5705	5955
12	2309	4014	56	5871	6015
13	2614	4041	57	5953	6029
14	2896	3710	58	5868	5975
15	3058	3383	59	5573	5894
16	3309	3431	60	5672	5951
17	3446	3613	61	5543	5952
18	3466	3205	62	5526	5723
19	3435	2426	63	5750	6351
20	3183	2330	64	5761	6636
21	2697	1954	65	5943	6799
22	2338	1936	66	6212	7753
23	2140	2201	67	6631	7595
24	2012	2233	68	6828	7436
25	2071	2690	69	6645	6679
26	2192	2940	70	6703	6475
27	2240	3127	71	6659	6319
28	2421	3131	72	6337	5860
29	2639	2872	73	6165	5705
30	2733	2515	74	5875	5521
31	2721	2271	75	5798	5920
32	2640	2711	76	5921	5937
33	2513	2394	77	5772	6570
34	2448	2457	78	5874	7087
35	2429	2720	79	5872	7206
36	2516	2703	80	6159	8431
37	2534	2992	81	6583	9718
38	2494	2516	82	6961	10921
39	2596	2817	83	7449	11672
40	2572	3153	84	8093	12199
41	2601	2756	85	9013	12865
42	2648	3269	86	9752	14985
43	2840	3657	87	10704	16378
44	2937	3941	88	11597	12680

diminishing effects, finally disappearing at a lag of $n + 1$ periods ($\beta_{n+1} = 0$). Almon's insight was that a smooth pattern of lag weights could be approximated by a polynomial of relatively low order. We assume that a polynomial of degree $q = 2$ is sufficiently

Table 21.2   Standard Errors, t-Statistics, and p-Values for the Estimated Distributed Lag Model

Variable	Coefficients	Standard Errors	t-Statistics	p-Values
Const.	33.42	53.71	0.62	0.54
x_t	0.04	0.03	1.11	0.27
x_{t-1}	0.07	0.07	0.98	0.33
x_{t-2}	0.18	0.09	2.03	0.05
x_{t-3}	0.19	0.09	2.10	0.04
x_{t-4}	0.17	0.09	1.82	0.07
x_{t-5}	0.05	0.09	0.57	0.57
x_{t-6}	0.05	0.09	0.56	0.58
x_{t-7}	0.06	0.09	0.60	0.55
x_{t-8}	0.13	0.06	2.12	0.04

flexible to represent the smooth pattern of lag weights we envision. Consequently, we express the lag weights as a polynomial function of the lag index-variable i,

$$\beta_i = \alpha_0 + \alpha_1 i + \alpha_2 i^2 \qquad i = 0, 1, ..., n \tag{21.2.6}$$

In the context of Chapter 12, on dummy and varying parameter models, we have expressed each of the lag weights β_i as a parameter that varies systematically with the lag index i. The $n + 1$ auxiliary relations 21.2.6 may be substituted into the finite lag model 21.2.3, creating interaction variables between x_{t-i}, i and i^2.

The substitution is much simplified if we use matrix notation to write equation 21.2.6 as

$$\boldsymbol{\beta}_s = \begin{bmatrix} \beta_0 \\ \beta_1 \\ \beta_2 \\ \vdots \\ \beta_n \end{bmatrix}_{(n+1)\times 1} = \begin{bmatrix} 1 & 0 & 0 \\ 1 & 1 & 1 \\ 1 & 2 & 4 \\ & \vdots & \\ 1 & n & n^2 \end{bmatrix}_{(n+1)\times 3} \begin{bmatrix} \alpha_0 \\ \alpha_1 \\ \alpha_2 \end{bmatrix}_{(3\times 1)} = H\boldsymbol{\alpha}_s \tag{21.2.7}$$

Table 21.3   Correlation Matrix for Variables $x_{t-1}, x_{t-2}, ..., x_{t-8}$

	x_{t-1}	x_{t-2}	x_{t-3}	x_{t-4}	x_{t-5}	x_{t-6}	x_{t-7}	x_{t-8}
x_{t-1}	1.00	0.99	0.97	0.94	0.90	0.86	0.81	0.76
x_{t-2}	0.99	1.00	0.99	0.96	0.93	0.89	0.84	0.79
x_{t-3}	0.97	0.99	1.00	0.99	0.96	0.92	0.87	0.82
x_{t-4}	0.94	0.96	0.99	1.00	0.98	0.95	0.91	0.86
x_{t-5}	0.90	0.93	0.96	0.98	1.00	0.98	0.95	0.91
x_{t-6}	0.86	0.89	0.92	0.95	0.98	1.00	0.98	0.94
x_{t-7}	0.81	0.84	0.87	0.91	0.95	0.98	1.00	0.98
x_{t-8}	0.76	0.79	0.82	0.86	0.91	0.94	0.98	1.00

so that the linear statistical model may be written

$$\begin{aligned}
\mathbf{y} &= \delta\mathbf{x}_1 + X_s\boldsymbol{\beta}_s + \mathbf{e} \\
&= \delta\mathbf{x}_1 + X_s H\boldsymbol{\alpha}_s + \mathbf{e} \\
&= \begin{bmatrix} \mathbf{x}_1 & X_s H \end{bmatrix} \begin{bmatrix} \delta \\ \boldsymbol{\alpha}_s \end{bmatrix} + \mathbf{e} \\
&= Z\boldsymbol{\alpha} + \mathbf{e}
\end{aligned}$$

(21.2.8)

where $Z = \begin{bmatrix} \mathbf{x}_1 & X_s H \end{bmatrix}$ is a $(T - n) \times (q + 2)$ matrix of constants.

What has this substitution accomplished? The finite lag model 21.2.4 requires estimation of $(n + 2)$ parameters ($n + 1$ distributed lag weights plus an intercept) using the collinear $(T - n) \times (n + 2)$ data matrix X. By assuming that the distributed lag weights fall on a polynomial of degree $q = 2$, we can reduce the number of parameters that we estimate to $q + 2 = 4$ (3 polynomial coefficients plus an intercept). By imposing the *exact linear constraints* (equation 21.2.6) on the $(n + 1)$ distributed lag weights, we reduce the number of parameters to estimate by $J = n - q$, which is the number of exact linear constraints implicit in the polynomial relations 21.2.6. In Chapter 11 exact linear restrictions were shown to increase the precision of estimation and reduce estimator variance, which is exactly the objective we pursue when data are collinear.

Although the constraints in equation 21.2.7 are *not* in the form $R\boldsymbol{\beta} = \mathbf{r}$ presented in Chapter 11, they are $J = n - q$ exact linear parameter restrictions. Any time a *larger* set of parameters ($\boldsymbol{\beta}_s$) is expressed exactly in terms of a *smaller* set of parameters ($\boldsymbol{\alpha}_s$), then the larger set ($\boldsymbol{\beta}_s$) obeys J restrictions, where J is the difference between the number of parameters in the larger set and the number of parameters in the smaller set. Since $\boldsymbol{\beta}_s$ has $n + 1$ elements and $\boldsymbol{\alpha}_s$ has $q + 1$ elements, then $J = n - q$.

The parameters $\boldsymbol{\alpha}$ in equation 21.2.8 can be estimated by least squares to obtain

$$\hat{\boldsymbol{\alpha}} = \begin{bmatrix} \hat{\delta} \\ \hat{\boldsymbol{\alpha}}_s \end{bmatrix} = (Z'Z)^{-1} Z'\mathbf{y}$$

(21.2.9)

If we estimate the error variance σ^2 as

$$\hat{\sigma}^2 = \frac{(\mathbf{y} - Z\hat{\boldsymbol{\alpha}})'(\mathbf{y} - Z\hat{\boldsymbol{\alpha}})}{(T - n) - (q + 2)}$$

(21.2.10)

then

$$\text{côv}(\hat{\boldsymbol{\alpha}}) = \hat{\sigma}^2 (Z'Z)^{-1}$$

(21.2.11)

and

$$\text{côv}(\hat{\boldsymbol{\alpha}}_s) = \hat{\sigma}^2 D$$

(21.2.12)

where D is the $(q + 1) \times (q + 1)$ matrix obtained by deleting the first row and first column of $(Z'Z)^{-1}$.

Using the data in Table 21.1, the least squares estimates of the parameters in equation 21.2.9 are given in Table 21.4. Estimates of the distributed lag weights $\boldsymbol{\beta}_s$ are then obtained by using the relation $\boldsymbol{\beta}_s = H\boldsymbol{\alpha}_s$, hence,

$$\hat{\boldsymbol{\beta}}_s = H\hat{\boldsymbol{\alpha}}_s$$

(21.2.13)

The estimates $\hat{\boldsymbol{\beta}}_s$ are *restricted least squares estimates* of the distributed lag weights,

Table 21.4 Estimated (Almon) Polynomial Coefficients

Variable	Coefficients	Standard Errors	t-Statistics	p-Value
Const.	51.57	53.16	0.97	0.34
α_0	0.07	0.02	4.41	2.53 E-05
α_1	0.04	0.01	2.98	0.004
α_2	−0.005	0.002	−3.16	0.002

and are constrained to fall on a polynomial of degree $q = 2$. The sampling variability of $\hat{\beta}_s$ is derived from that of $\hat{\alpha}_s$, and is estimated as

$$\text{côv}\left(\hat{\beta}_s\right) = H\,\text{côv}\left(\hat{\alpha}_s\right)H' \qquad (21.2.14)$$

where $\text{côv}\left(\hat{\alpha}_s\right)$ is given by equation 21.2.12. The restricted estimates of the distributed lag weights and their (restricted) standard errors are given in Table 21.5.

Notice that the standard errors of the estimates for these restricted estimates $\hat{\beta}_s$ are smaller than the standard errors of the unrestricted estimates, given in Table 21.2, reflecting the increased precision of estimation obtained by imposing polynomial constraints on the lag parameters.

In Figure 21.2 we plot the unrestricted estimates of lag weights and the restricted estimates. Note that the restricted estimates display the increasing then decreasing "humped" shape that economic reasoning led us to expect.

We have demonstrated the effect of placing polynomial restrictions on the parameters of a finite distributed lag model. Parameter restrictions reduce the sampling variability of the estimation rule, relative to (unrestricted) least squares, and can provide a pattern of lag weights that is consistent with our expectations.

21.3   Infinite Distributed Lags

In the previous section we assumed that the lagged effects of a change in an explanatory variable x_t on the outcome y_t persisted only for a finite number of periods, n, and thus wrote the distributed lag model as equation 21.2.2. In the absence of any information about *how long* the effect of a change in an explanatory variable persists,

Table 21.5 Restricted Least Squares Estimates of Distributed Lag Weights

Parameters	Estimates	s.e.	t	p-Value
β_0	0.067	0.015	4.411	2.54 E-05
β_1	0.100	0.005	19.597	1.92 E-31
β_2	0.123	0.005	22.741	1.20 E-35
β_3	0.136	0.009	14.401	2.02 E-23
β_4	0.138	0.011	12.857	9.40 E-21
β_5	0.130	0.009	14.306	2.93 E-23
β_6	0.112	0.005	20.919	2.88 E-33
β_7	0.083	0.007	11.323	5.57 E-18
β_8	0.044	0.018	2.473	0.0156

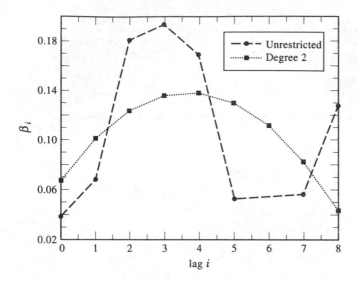

Figure 21.2 Restricted and unrestricted distributed lag weights.

however, we may consider the *general infinite distributed lag model*

$$y_t = \delta + \beta_0 x_t + \beta_1 x_{t-1} + \beta_2 x_{t-2} + \ldots + e_t$$

$$= \delta + \sum_{i=0}^{\infty} \beta_i x_{t-i} + e_t \qquad (21.3.1)$$

One difficulty with this model is readily apparent. It has an infinite number of unknown parameters and cannot be estimated with a finite amount of data. Restrictions of some sort must be placed on the parameters β_i, to reduce the number of unknowns to a manageable number. The finite distributed lag model 21.2.2 can be thought of as arising from equation 21.3.1 under the restrictions

$$\beta_{n+j} = 0 \qquad j = 1, 2, \ldots \qquad (21.3.2)$$

In this section we assume that the distributed lag weights β_i *decline geometrically* and discuss estimation and inference in the resulting geometric distributed lag.

21.3.1 A Geometric Lag Statistical Model

When specifying an infinite distributed lag, it is convenient to *normalize* the lag weights by writing

$$y_t = \delta + \sum_{i=0}^{\infty} \beta_i x_{t-i} + e_t$$

$$= \delta + \beta \sum_{i=0}^{\infty} w_i x_{t-i} + e_t \qquad (21.3.3)$$

where $\beta = \Sigma_{i=0}^{\infty} w_i$ is the total lag effect (or the long-run multiplier of a change in x_t) and the normalized lag weights $w_i = \beta_i / \beta$, sum to unity, $\Sigma_{i=0}^{\infty} w_1 = 1$. The *geometric lag model* specifies

$$\beta_i = \beta w_i = \beta(1-\lambda)\lambda^i \qquad i = 0, 1, \ldots \qquad (21.3.4)$$

where $0 < (1 - \lambda) < 1$ so that

$$y_t = \delta + \beta \sum_{i=0}^{\infty} (1-\lambda)\lambda^i x_{t-1} + e_t$$

$$= \delta + \beta(1-\lambda)\left(x_t + \lambda x_{t-1} + \lambda^2 x_{t-2} + \ldots\right) + e_t \qquad (21.3.5)$$

The lag weights β_i, as the name implies, decline geometrically as illustrated in Figure 21.3.

The economic assumption embodied in the geometric lag model is that a change in the explanatory variable x_t has its greatest effect on the outcome y_t in the current period, the impact multiplier being $\beta(1 - \lambda)$, and that the effect diminishes in each succeeding period. Also, note that by using the nonsample, or a priori, information that the lag weights are positive and decline with time, we have been able to reduce the infinite parameter specification equation 21.3.1 to one involving only δ, β, and λ.

One particular version of the geometric lag model arises naturally through a model known as the *adaptive expectations model*. Such a model is relevant, for example, when a firm must make decisions concerning what output y_t to produce this period, before it knows the price x_{t+1} at which the output can be sold next period. Because this price is unknown at the time the decision is made, it is assumed that the decision is based on an anticipated (or expected) price x_{t+1}^*. Thus, current output y_t is related to *expected* price x_{t+1}^*, in the following way

$$y_t = \alpha_0 + \alpha_1 x_{t+1}^* + e_t \qquad (21.3.6)$$

where α_0 and α_1 are unknown parameters and the independent random error $e_t \sim (0, \sigma^2)$. This model would pose no new problem if observations on x_{t+1}^* were available. However, since the expected price is unobservable, it is necessary to find some mechanism for relating anticipated price to actual price before we can make any progress toward the estimation of α_1 and α_2. The *adaptive expectations hypothesis* postulates that the change in expectations $x_{t+1}^* - x_t^*$ is equal to the proportion $(1 - \lambda)$ of last period's error in expectations $(x_t - x_t^*)$. That is,

$$x_{t+1}^* - x_t^* = (1-\lambda)\left(x_t - x_t^*\right) \qquad (21.3.7a)$$

where $0 < (1 - \lambda) < 1$ and x_t is the actual price in period t. Expectations are changed

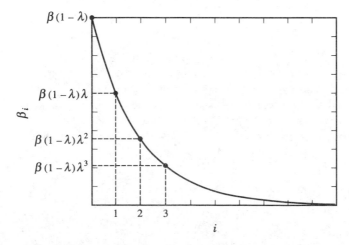

Figure 21.3 The geometric distributed lag.

adaptively depending on how wrong these expectations were in the previous period. Alternatively,

$$x_{t+1}^* = (1-\lambda)x_t + \lambda x_t^* \tag{21.3.7b}$$

Writing the adaptive expectations hypothesis in this way suggests that the expected level of price x_{t+1}^* is a weighted linear combination of the actual price x and expected price x^* in period t.

To replace the unobservable expected price in equation 21.3.6 with an observable variable, we repeatedly lag and substitute equation 21.3.7b to obtain

$$x_{t+1}^* = (1-\lambda)\left(x_t + \lambda x_{t-1} + \lambda^2 x_{t-2} + \ldots\right) \tag{21.3.8}$$

which means that x_{t+1}^* is a linear function of observable variables x_{t-i}, $i = 0, 1, \ldots$. If we substitute equation 21.3.8 into equation 21.3.6, we have

$$y_t = \alpha_0 + \alpha_1(1-\lambda)\left(x_t + \lambda x_{t-1} + \lambda^2 x_{t-2} + \ldots\right) + e_t \tag{21.3.9}$$

so that the weights $\alpha_1(1-\lambda)$, $\alpha_1(1-\lambda)\lambda$, $\alpha_1(1-\lambda)\lambda^2, \ldots$ decline geometrically as given by equation 21.3.4. Thus, the adaptive expectations formulation results in a geometric lag model. It is in the form of equation 21.3.5, where $\delta = \alpha_0$, $\beta = \alpha_1$ and $w_i = (1-\lambda)\lambda^i$. Under this formulation we have reduced the unknown parameters to α_0, α_1, and λ.

21.3.2   The Koyck Transformation: A Moving Average Error Formulation of the Geometric Lag

Given the geometric lag models 21.3.5 and 21.3.9, let us concentrate on specifying a statistical model that would permit us to use a finite sample of data to estimate the three unknown parameters. To do this let's return to the geometric lag model 21.3.5. If we lag this relation by one period we have

$$y_{t-1} = \delta + \beta(1-\lambda)\left(x_{t-1} + \lambda x_{t-2} + \lambda^2 x_{t-3} + \ldots\right) + e_{t-1} \tag{21.3.10}$$

If we then subtract λy_{t-1} from y_t, which is given by equation 21.3.5, we have

$$y_t - \lambda y_{t-1} = \delta(1-\lambda) + \beta(1-\lambda)x_t + e_t - \lambda e_{t-1} \tag{21.3.11a}$$

or

$$y_t = \delta_0 + \delta_1 x_t + \lambda y_{t-1} + v_t \tag{21.3.11b}$$

where $\delta_0 = \delta(1-\lambda)$, $\delta_1 = \beta(1-\lambda)$ and in the context of the univariate time-series models studied in Chapter 20, $v_t = e_t - \lambda e_{t-1}$ is a MA(1) error. Rewriting equation 21.3.5 as equation 21.3.11 is known as the *Koyck transformation*. The statistical model 21.3.11 specifies the stochastic data-generation process by which we visualize y_t is determined and identifies the three unknown parameters δ_0, δ_1, and λ. In this context the short-run impact multiplier of a change in price is measured by $\delta_1 = \beta(1-\lambda)$ and the long-run total multiplier is β.

21.3.3   Estimation of the Geometric Lag–Adaptive Expectations Statistical Model

Given the geometric lag statistical model

$$y_t = \delta + \beta(1-\lambda)\left[x_t + \lambda x_{t-1} + \lambda^2 x_{t-2} + \ldots +\right] + e_t \tag{21.3.5}$$

with independent random errors $e_t \sim (0, \sigma^2)$, and the corresponding Koyck transformation

$$y_t = \delta(1-\lambda) + \lambda y_{t-1} + \beta(1-\lambda)x_t + e_t - \lambda e_{t-1}$$
$$= \delta_0 + \lambda y_{t-1} + \delta_1 x_t + v_t \qquad (21.3.11)$$

where $v_t = (e_t - \lambda e_{t-1}) \sim (0, (1+\lambda^2)\sigma^2)$, let us consider the problem of estimating the unknown parameters δ_0, δ_1, and λ. Since this equation contains y_{t-1} as a random regressor on the right-hand side, and the random disturbance v_t is autocorrelated, it follows from Section 14.2 of Chapter 14 (see equation 14.2.2) that the least squares estimators of the parameters δ_0, δ_1, and λ are *inconsistent*. Specifically, since the random disturbances v_t are autocorrelated, the current error v_t depends on v_{t-1}. Furthermore, y_{t-1} depends directly on v_{t-1}. Consequently the lagged dependent variable y_{t-1}, which is a random regressor, is contemporaneously correlated with the error v_t, which makes the least squares estimator of equation 21.3.11 both biased and inconsistent, since the bias does not disappear in large samples.

Fortunately it is straightforward to construct a consistent estimator of the lagged dependent variable model in equation 21.3.11 by using the instrumental variable estimation procedure discussed in the appendix of Chapter 14. To develop that estimator let us rewrite equation 21.3.11 in vector notation. Let

$$\mathbf{y} = \begin{bmatrix} y_2 \\ y_3 \\ \vdots \\ y_T \end{bmatrix} \qquad Z = \begin{bmatrix} 1 & x_2 & y_1 \\ 1 & x_3 & y_2 \\ \vdots & \vdots & \vdots \\ 1 & x_T & y_{T-1} \end{bmatrix} \qquad \text{and} \qquad \mathbf{v} = \begin{bmatrix} v_2 \\ v_3 \\ \vdots \\ v_T \end{bmatrix} = \begin{bmatrix} e_2 - \lambda e_1 \\ e_3 - \lambda e_2 \\ \vdots \\ e_T - \lambda e_{T-1} \end{bmatrix} = \mathbf{e} - \lambda \mathbf{e}_{-1}$$

so that

$$\mathbf{y} = Z\boldsymbol{\delta} + \mathbf{v} \qquad (21.3.12)$$

where $\boldsymbol{\delta} = \left(\delta_0 = \delta(1-\lambda), \ \delta_1 = \beta(1-\lambda), \ \lambda\right)'$. We will use the matrix Z, instead of X, in this statistical model to indicate that it contains one or more random regressors.

One candidate for an instrumental variable for y_{t-1} is x_{t-1}, since, for example, last year's output y_{t-1} and last year's price x_{t-1} should be highly correlated. Also x_t is uncorrelated with the equation error and thus it seems reasonable to assume the same for the variable x_{t-1}. Consequently, x_{t-1} should qualify as an instrument variable for y_{t-1}. Therefore, the matrix

$$X = \begin{bmatrix} 1 & x_2 & x_1 \\ 1 & x_3 & x_2 \\ \vdots & \vdots & \vdots \\ 1 & x_T & x_{T-1} \end{bmatrix}$$

should fulfill the requirements of being uncorrelated with the equation error $\mathbf{v}$ and highly correlated with Z, so that we can use the instrumental variable estimator

$$\hat{\boldsymbol{\delta}}_{IV} = \left(X'Z\right)^{-1} X'\mathbf{y} \qquad (21.3.13)$$

Recall from Chapter 14 that while instrumental variable estimators are not necessarily efficient, in the sense of having a minimum variance, they are, in large samples, approximately normally distributed. Furthermore, their covariance matrix is consistently estimated by

$$\operatorname{cov}\left(\hat{\boldsymbol{\delta}}_{IV}\right) = \hat{\sigma}^2 \left(X'Z\right)^{-1} X'X \left(Z'X\right)^{-1} \tag{21.3.14}$$

where $\hat{\sigma}^2 = \left(\mathbf{y} - Z\hat{\boldsymbol{\delta}}_{IV}\right)'\left(\mathbf{y} - Z\hat{\boldsymbol{\delta}}_{IV}\right)\big/T.$

We mention in passing that it is possible to estimate the model 21.3.11 by nonlinear least squares. This procedure is described in Chapter 22. For an example of the use of the instrumental variable estimator 21.3.13 to estimate a geometric lag-adaptive expectations model, see Exercise 21.4.

21.4   Vector Autoregressive (VAR) Models

In the preceding section we considered a pair of economic variables y_t and x_t that were observed over time. The variable x_t was treated as predetermined, or exogenous, and its variation was used to help explain the variation in the outcome (endogenous) variable y_t. We now consider the possibility that *both* time series variables are random and jointly determined (endogenous) and develop a forecasting model that captures their dynamic and interdependent relationship. The model we develop is an extension of the univariate time series models of Chapter 20 and follows from the discussion of simultaneous equations models in Chapters 18 and 19. In Chapter 18 we learned that the reduced form of a simultaneous equations system formed a basis for forecasting the values of the endogenous variables, and this result is a key one for the models we present in this section.

21.4.1   An Economic Example

As an example let us consider the macroeconomic time-series variables consumption expenditures (y_{t1}) and disposable income (y_{t2}). We denote these variables as y_{t1} and y_{t2} to emphasize that they are both endogenous. Since these variables are jointly determined, we may wish to build a structural simultaneous equations model to explain their behavior. For pedagogic purposes we ignore exogenous variables and assume that current consumption (y_{t1}) depends on current income (y_{t2}) and, owing to habit persistence, lagged consumption $(y_{t-1,1})$, so that we can write

$$y_{t1} = \alpha_1 + \alpha_2 y_{t2} + \alpha_3 y_{t-1,1} + e_{t1} \tag{21.4.1}$$

Current income (y_{t2}) may depend on lagged income $(y_{t-1,2})$ and, since increased consumption may stimulate growth and thus income, lagged consumption $(y_{t-1,1})$, so that

$$y_{t2} = \beta_1 + \beta_2 y_{t-1,1} + \beta_3 y_{t-1,2} + e_{t2} \tag{21.4.2}$$

Taken together, equations 21.4.1 and 21.4.2 constitute a system of simultaneous equations that describe the dynamic relationship between the two variables. As discussed in Chapter 19, the unknown parameters α_i and β_i could be estimated, for example, by two-stage least squares.

However, if the primary objective of building the model is forecasting, then we can consider the *reduced form* equations

$$y_{t1} = \pi_{11} + \pi_{12} y_{t-1,1} + \pi_{13} y_{t-1,2} + v_{t1} \tag{21.4.3}$$

$$y_{t2} = \pi_{21} + \pi_{22} y_{t-1,1} + \pi_{23} y_{t-1,2} + v_{t2} \qquad (21.4.4)$$

The reduced form equations express current endogenous variables in terms of exogenous and predetermined, lagged endogenous variables. If we are *only* interested in forecasting, then we skip from the structural equations (which need not be actually estimated) to the reduced form equations, whose form is easy to specify once endogenous and exogenous variables, appearing in the structural model, are specified.

The reduced form equations 21.4.3 and 21.4.4 are a *vector autoregressive* model, of order 1, and denoted VAR(1). In general a vector autoregressive model expresses the current values of the endogenous variables *solely* as a function of an intercept variable and lagged values of the endogenous variables. No other exogenous variables are considered. The number of lagged values determines the order of the VAR model, and as the terminology implies, the VAR model is an extension of the univariate AR(p) models considered in Chapter 20. This is clearly seen by forming the vector equation

$$\mathbf{y}_t = \boldsymbol{\delta} + \boldsymbol{\Theta} \mathbf{y}_{t-1} + \mathbf{v}_t \qquad (21.4.5)$$

where

$$\mathbf{y}_t = \begin{bmatrix} y_{t1} \\ y_{t2} \end{bmatrix} \qquad \boldsymbol{\delta} = \begin{bmatrix} \pi_{11} \\ \pi_{21} \end{bmatrix} \qquad \boldsymbol{\Theta} = \begin{bmatrix} \pi_{12} & \pi_{13} \\ \pi_{22} & \pi_{23} \end{bmatrix} \qquad \mathbf{v}_t = \begin{bmatrix} v_{t1} \\ v_{t2} \end{bmatrix} \qquad (21.4.6)$$

Equation 21.4.5 is an AR(1) model for the *bivariate* observation (y_{t1}, y_{t2}), hence the name *vector* autoregression.

Examining equation 21.4.5 we can easily see that the model can be extended to more than two endogenous variables. Furthermore, we may wish to consider more than a single lag. The VAR(p) model includes p lags and is written

$$\mathbf{y}_t = \boldsymbol{\delta} + \boldsymbol{\Theta}_1 \mathbf{y}_{t-1} + \boldsymbol{\Theta}_2 \mathbf{y}_{t-2} + \dots + \boldsymbol{\Theta}_p \mathbf{y}_{t-p} + \mathbf{v}_t \qquad (21.4.7)$$

In the following section we consider the assumptions of the statistical model 21.4.7.

21.4.2   VAR(p) Model Assumptions

To consistently estimate the model 21.4.5, or in general equation 21.4.7, we must make some strong assumptions. Since the VAR model is a reduced form, its error assumptions follow from the structural equation error properties. Following the discussion in Chapter 18 we assume that $E[\mathbf{v}_t] = \mathbf{0}$ and

$$\text{cov}(\mathbf{v}_t) = \Omega = \begin{bmatrix} w_{11} & w_{12} \\ w_{21} & w_{22} \end{bmatrix} = \begin{bmatrix} \text{var}(v_{t1}) & \text{cov}(v_{t1}, v_{t2}) \\ \text{cov}(v_{t2}, v_{t1}) & \text{var}(v_{t2}) \end{bmatrix} \qquad (21.4.8)$$

where w_{12} is the contemporaneous covariance between the reduced form errors. We will assume that there is no serial correlation in the reduced form errors so $\mathbf{v}_t$ and $\mathbf{v}_s$ are uncorrelated.

In addition to these now standard error assumptions, we must also assume that the VAR process is *stationary*, in the same sense as in Section 20.3 of Chapter 20. Specifically, this means that the random vector $\mathbf{y}_t$ has mean $E[\mathbf{y}_t] = \mu$ that is constant over time and that the covariance matrices between $\mathbf{y}_t$ and $\mathbf{y}_{t+k}$ depend only on k and not on t, for $k = 0, 1, 2, \dots$. The latter assumption, for $k = 0$, means that $\text{cov}(\mathbf{y}_t)$ does not change over time.

In practice, these assumptions mean that the time series may not have trends, nor seasonal patterns, nor variances that change over time. To achieve these conditions some transformations of the data may be required. There are conditions on the parameter matrices Θ_i that can be checked to verify stationarity. These conditions are discussed in Judge, et al. (1988, p. 754).

21.4.3   Estimation of VAR Models

Given that the assumptions in the previous section hold true, the least squares estimator of the VAR equations is consistent and approximately normally distributed in large samples. To illustrate, consider the VAR(1) model in equation 21.4.5, which represents the reduced form equations 21.4.3 and 21.4.4. Let the $(T \times 3)$ matrix X be

$$X = \begin{bmatrix} \mathbf{x}_1 & \mathbf{y}_{t-1,1} & \mathbf{y}_{t-1,2} \end{bmatrix}$$

and denote

$$\mathbf{y}_1 = (y_{11}, y_{21}, \ldots, y_{T1})' \qquad \mathbf{y}_2 = (y_{12}, y_{22}, \ldots, y_{T2})'$$

$$\boldsymbol{\pi}_1 = (\pi_{11}, \pi_{12}, \pi_{13})' \qquad \boldsymbol{\pi}_2 = (\pi_{21}, \pi_{22}, \pi_{23})'$$

then

$$\hat{\boldsymbol{\pi}}_i = (X'X)^{-1} X'\mathbf{y}_i \overset{asy}{\sim} N\left(\boldsymbol{\pi}_i, w_{ii}(X'X)^{-1}\right) \tag{21.4.9}$$

where " $\overset{asy}{\sim}$ " means "asymptotically distributed as." Consistent estimators of the elements w_{ij} of Ω in equation 21.4.8 are

$$\hat{w}_{ij} = (\mathbf{y}_i - X\hat{\boldsymbol{\pi}}_i)'(\mathbf{y}_j - X\hat{\boldsymbol{\pi}}_j)/T \qquad i, j = 1, 2 \tag{21.4.10}$$

These estimation results follow from the fact that equations 21.4.3 and 21.4.4 are random regressor models, as we have studied in Chapter 14. The large sample or asymptotic properties of $\hat{\boldsymbol{\pi}}_i$ in equation 21.4.9 are based on the assumptions that the random regressors are contemporaneously uncorrelated with the errors, and the stationarity assumption ensures that $X'X/T$ converges to a finite, nonsingular matrix. These consistent estimators form a basis for statistical inference in the VAR model and forecasting postsample values of the endogenous variables. We did not use a joint estimation technique, like seemingly unrelated regressions, since X is the same for both equations, and least squares is efficient in this case. We illustrate these results in the following section.

21.4.4   Estimation Results

In Table 21.6 are quarterly observations on U. S. consumption and income. The data have been seasonally adjusted and differenced to achieve stationarity. Using these data we estimate the VAR(1) model by least squares to obtain

$$\hat{y}_{t1} = 7.038 + .019 y_{t-1,1} + .440 y_{t-1,2}$$
$$\quad\;\; (2.37)\; (.10) \qquad\;\; (.10) \tag{21.4.11a}$$

$$\hat{y}_{t2} = 7.657 + .241 y_{t-1,1} + .283 y_{t-1,2}$$
$$\quad\;\; (2.87)\; (.12) \qquad\;\; (.12) \tag{21.4.11b}$$

where asymptotic standard errors are given in parentheses.

Table 21.6 Changes of Quarterly, Seasonally Adjusted U. S. Per Capita Personal Consumption Expenditures (y_1) and Disposable Income (y_2) in 1972 Dollars at Annual Rates: 1951.II–1969.IV

t	y_1	y_2	t	y_1	y_2	t	y_1	y_2
1	−61	42	26	5	1	51	8	30
2	8	−1	27	−6	−20	52	39	47
3	−1	−11	28	−37	−35	53	38	75
4	−4	−12	29	12	6	54	35	27
5	30	16	30	25	45	55	−3	23
6	−1	41	31	16	25	56	46	22
7	45	14	32	39	6	57	17	32
8	17	17	33	23	32	58	35	76
9	2	26	34	9	−30	59	65	47
10	−17	−20	35	−5	10	60	29	17
11	−16	−10	36	1	6	61	−2	6
12	−4	−11	37	24	6	62	22	27
13	8	−23	38	−19	−12	63	0	21
14	23	29	39	−9	−23	64	15	38
15	31	36	40	−5	13	65	31	21
16	31	8	41	23	28	66	7	16
17	33	43	42	−3	17	67	6	17
18	14	31	43	37	38	68	54	36
19	26	29	44	13	14	69	30	43
20	−7	8	45	21	16	70	54	−7
21	−6	9	46	10	3	71	8	9
22	−4	2	47	23	1	72	21	−2
23	13	20	48	8	15	73	9	19
24	4	−10	49	15	17	74	9	47
25	−6	5	50	24	19	75	16	10

As with univariate time series, there are questions concerning the adequacy of the statistical model. Are the residuals autocorrelated? Should lags larger than $p = 1$ be included? Is the estimated model stationary? Some of these issues are discussed in Judge et al. (1988, pp. 761–764). The estimated reduced form equations in equation 21.4.11 can be used to forecast values of the endogenous variables. See Exercise 21.5. In Judge et al. (1988, pp. 764–767) forecast error variances are derived and used as a basis for constructing forecast interval estimates.

21.4.5 Granger Causality

One question concerning model specification is whether one variable is causally related to another. To provide a basis for addressing this question, Granger (1969) introduced a concept of causality that has come to be known as "Granger" causality. Broadly speaking, a variable y_{t1} is said to be *Granger-caused* by y_{t2} if current and past information on y_{t2} *help* improve the forecasts of y_{t1}. In the context of VAR models, this is rather easily tested. For example, in equation 21.4.3, y_2 *does not* Granger-cause y_1 if, and only if, $\pi_{13} = 0$. If we considered a VAR(2) model

$$y_{t1} = \pi_{11} + \pi_{12} y_{t-1,1} + \pi_{13} y_{t-1,2} + \pi_{14} y_{t-2,1} + \pi_{15} y_{t-2,2} + v_{t1}$$

then y_2 *does not* Granger-cause y_1 if, and only if, $\pi_{13} = \pi_{15} = 0$. In other words y_2 *does not* Granger-cause y_1 if, and only if, lagged values of y_2 do not appear in the reduced form equation for y_1. Based on the asymptotic normality of the least squares estimator, in equation 21.4.9, the appropriate *t*- (for a single hypothesis) or *F*-test (for joint hypotheses) can be carried out in the usual way to check these conjectures. It should be noted that Granger's concept of causality does *not* imply a cause–effect relationship, but rather is based only on "predictability." Based on the empirical results in equation 21.4.11b, we can *reject* the null hypothesis that consumption does not cause income at the $\alpha = .05$ level, but not at the $\alpha = .01$ level. Thus, consumption does help predict income. See Exercise 21.6.

21.5   Spurious Regressions, Unit Root Tests, and Cointegration

In the vector autoregressive models in the previous section, and in the univariate time series models of Chapter 20, we assumed that the economic time series used in the construction of the forecasting models were *stationary*. We noted that nonstationary time series are frequently transformed to stationarity by differencing. As we shall see in this section, the assumption of stationarity is an important one for many reasons. We begin the section by discussing the problem of "spurious" regressions, a term describing the artificial and misleading results that least squares regression can produce when one trended, nonstationary, economic time series is regressed on another one. Then, we present a simple test, called a "unit root" test, to determine if a time series is stationary or not. We then discuss the concept of cointegration when a regression involving nonstationary variables not only is *not spurious*, but very informative about the long-run equilibrium behavior of economic variables.

21.5.1   Spurious Regressions

Granger and Newbold (1974) coined the phrase "spurious regressions" to describe regression results, involving economic time series, that "look good," in the sense of have high R^2 values and significant *t*-statistics, but which, in fact, have *no real meaning*. This outcome can occur when a regression model is specified, say

$$y_t = \beta_1 + \beta_2 x_t + e_t \qquad (21.5.1)$$

involving economic time series y_t and x_t that are *trended or nonstationary* random processes. Equation 21.5.1 is a regression model with a random regressor x_t. In this model, however, contrary to the random regressor model considered in Section 14.2 of Chapter 14, the time series x_t is *not* a stationary process. Consequently, the $X'X/T$ matrix does *not* converge to any limiting value, the least squares estimator is not consistent, and the usual inference procedures do not hold true. To illustrate the problem Granger and Newbold carried out a Monte Carlo experiment in which the nonstationary series y_t and x_t were generated as *independent* random walks. Recall from Chapter 20 that an economic time series, z_t is called a random walk if

$$z_t = z_{t-1} + \varepsilon_t \qquad (21.5.2)$$

where $\varepsilon_t \sim (0, \sigma^2)$ and is uncorrelated. As illustrated in Figure 20.10 a random walk is a rather smooth series that changes slowly. *Many* economic time series have the characteristics of a random walk. Nelson and Plosser (1982), for example, found, by using a unit root test we describe in Section 21.5.2, that they *could not reject the null hy-*

pothesis that many macroeconomic variables, such as GNP (real, nominal, or real per capita), industrial production, employment, consumer prices, wages, common stock prices, *followed a random walk process*. Only for the unemployment rate was the random walk model rejected.

Returning to Granger and Newbold, in their Monte Carlo experiment they created samples of $T = 50$ observations on y_t and x_t, which were, to repeat, *independent* random walks. When they estimated the regression model 21.5.1, however, they found that the usual t-test of the null hypothesis H_0: $\beta_2 = 0$ was rejected (*wrongly*) 75% of the time when testing at the $\alpha = .05$ level of significance. Hence a "significant" relationship was found, *where none existed*, in three-quarters of the cases. Granger and Newbold concluded that when regression equations like equation 21.5.1 are specified between the levels of economic time series that are "like" random walks, (*i*) such regression equations frequently have high R^2 values, and (*ii*) at the same time they have *low* Durbin–Watson statistics indicating highly autocorrelated disturbance terms. Granger and Newbold contended that in situations like this, the usual t-tests of statistical significance can be *very* misleading because they reject the null hypothesis of "no relationship" much too frequently and, thus, accept as significant relationships that are spurious far too often.

Granger and Newbold suggested that when a least squares regression leads to a *high* R^2 but *low* Durbin–Watson statistic, then the relationship should be estimated in first differences of the variables rather than the levels; that is, estimate

$$\Delta y_t = \beta_1 + \beta_2 \Delta x_t + v_t \qquad (21.5.3)$$

If the errors in equation 21.5.1 are uncorrelated and $e_t \sim (0, \sigma^2)$ then $v_t = e_t - e_{t-1}$ will be serially correlated [as MA(1)], but the least squares estimator of β_2 in equation 21.5.3 is still consistent, even though it is biased and is inefficient related to the generalized least squares estimator. In this sense it is safer to estimate equation 21.5.3 by least squares than equation 21.5.1. The Monte Carlo results of Granger and Newbold indicate that the estimation of equation 21.5.3 does not lead to overacceptance of spurious relationships as significant ones.

The findings of Granger and Newbold have subsequently been theoretically explained. For regressions between *integrated* time series (that is, time series that must be differenced once or more to be stationary), distributions of conventional test statistics (e.g., t, F) do *not* have distributions anything like the t- and F-distributions that we expect to hold when a null hypothesis is true. Consequently, critical values normally used are inappropriate. Furthermore the least squares estimators of the intercept and slope are not consistent, and the Durbin–Watson statistic converges to zero. In a nutshell, the usual properties of least squares estimators in equation 21.5.1 *do not hold* when y_t and x_t are integrated economic time series that require differencing to achieve stationarity.

21.5.2 Unit Root Tests

The findings discussed in the previous section argue strongly for exercising great care when using economic time series stated in *levels* rather than *differences*. The usual statistical properties of least squares hold *only* when the time series variables involved are stationary. Nonstationary time series must be detrended before the analysis, and as stated in Chapter 20 there are two common approaches: (*i*) estimation of time-trend regressions and (*ii*) differencing the series once or more.

The time trend regression approach specifies that the trended time series z_t can be expressed as

$$z_t = f(t) + \varepsilon_t \qquad (21.5.4a)$$

where $f(t)$ is a function of time and $\varepsilon_t \sim (0, \sigma^2)$ is a stationary error process. If z_t follows a linear trend, for example, we specify

$$z_t = \alpha + \beta t + \varepsilon_t \qquad (21.5.4b)$$

If we estimate equation 21.5.4b by least squares, then the least squares residuals $\hat{\varepsilon}_t = z_t - \hat{\alpha} - \hat{\beta}t$ form a detrended, stationary series that can be used in a regression analysis. Time series that can be detrended in this way are called *trend stationary* processes (TSP).

On the other hand, suppose z_t is generated by a random walk with a trend or drift

$$z_t = z_{t-1} + \beta + \varepsilon_t \qquad (21.5.5)$$

where $\varepsilon_t \sim (0, \sigma^2)$ is a stationary error process and β is a constant. Then z_t is made stationary by differencing once, since

$$\Delta z_t = z_t - z_{t-1} = \beta + \varepsilon_t \qquad (21.5.6)$$

is stationary. Series like equation 21.5.5 are called *difference stationary* processes (DSP).

The difficulty is that the two types of processes, TSP and DSP, can behave in similar ways, yet require different detrending methods. To show their similarity assume that at time $t = 0$ the value of z_t is z_0. Then successive values of the DSP in equation 21.5.5 are

$$z_1 = z_0 + \beta + \varepsilon_1$$
$$z_2 = z_1 + \beta + \varepsilon_2 = z_0 + \beta(2) + (\varepsilon_1 + \varepsilon_2)$$
$$\vdots$$
$$z_t = z_0 + \beta t + v_t \qquad (21.5.7)$$

where $v_t = \Sigma_{j=0}^{t} \varepsilon_j$. Note that equations 21.5.7 and 21.5.4 look just alike, *except* that the error term v_t in equation 21.5.7 is *not stationary*, since var$(v_t) = \sigma^2 t$, which is not constant over time. Thus, if we estimate equation 21.5.7 by least squares, to remove its trend, we encounter the "spurious regression" problem, since z_t and t are nonstationary. The residuals from this regression will not be stationary and subsequent analysis will be impaired.

Nelson and Plosser (1982) used a test developed by Dickey and Fuller (1979, 1981) to determine if a time series is difference stationary or trend stationary. The test is based on the model

$$z_t = \alpha + \beta t + \rho z_{t-1} + \varepsilon_t \qquad (21.5.8)$$

If $\rho = 1$ *and* $\beta = 0$ in this model, then $z_t = \alpha + z_{t-1} + \varepsilon_t$ is difference stationary as in equation 21.5.5. However, if the autoregressive parameter has $|\rho| < 1$, then z_t is trend stationary. The contribution of Dickey and Fuller was to determine the distribution of the usual F-statistic for the joint null hypothesis H_0: $\rho = 1$, $\beta = 0$ *when the null hypothesis is true*. This is *not* an easy problem because if $\rho = 1$, then z_t is *not* stationary and least squares estimation of equation 21.5.8 and the corresponding tests do not have the usual properties.

To implement the test we subtract z_{t-1} from both sides of equation 21.5.8, to obtain

$$\Delta z_t = z_t - z_{t-1} = \alpha + \beta t + (\rho - 1)z_{t-1} + \varepsilon_t$$

Then, to protect against the possibility that z_t follows a higher order autoregressive process we add more Δz_{t-j} terms to the right-hand side, so that

$$\Delta z_t = \alpha + \beta t + (\rho - 1)z_{t-1} + \sum_{j=1}^{n} \rho_j \Delta z_{t-j} + \varepsilon_t \qquad (21.5.9)$$

If the n extra terms are not needed, then they can be omitted without affecting the test. The test statistic for the joint null hypothesis H_0: $\beta = 0$, $\rho = 1$ is the usual F-statistic

$$u = \frac{\text{SSE}_R - \text{SSE}_U}{J(\text{SSE}_U)/df} \qquad (21.5.10)$$

where SSE_U is the unrestricted sum of squared errors from the least squares regression equation 21.5.9, J is the number of hypotheses, $df = T - 3 - n$, and SSE_R is the sum of squared errors from the restricted model

$$\Delta z_t = \alpha + \sum_{j=1}^{n} \rho_j \Delta z_{t-j} + \varepsilon_t \qquad (21.5.11)$$

which holds if the null hypothesis is true. While the test statistic 21.5.10 is the usual one, the critical values are *not* from the usual $F_{(J,df)}$ distribution. The $\alpha = .05$ critical values for u, for alternative sample sizes, are presented in Table 21.7. For comparison we show the $\alpha = .05$ critical values from an $F_{(2,T)}$ distribution, which would be (approximately) the usual critical values for u.

Dickey and Fuller (1981) illustrate the use of the test by studying the logarithm of the quarterly Federal Reserve Board industrial production index (1950.1 to 1977.4). They assume that the time series is adequately modeled by

$$z_t = \alpha + \beta t + \rho z_{t-1} + \rho_1 (z_{t-1} - z_{t-2}) + \varepsilon_t \qquad (21.5.12)$$

The unrestricted and restricted regressions 21.5.9 and 21.5.11 are

$$\Delta \hat{z}_t = 0.52 + 0.00120t - 0.119 z_{t-1} + 0.498 \Delta z_{t-1}$$
$$\quad (0.15)\ (0.00034)\ (0.033)\qquad (0.081)\qquad \text{s.e.}$$
$$\text{SSE}_U = 0.056448$$

$$\Delta \hat{z}_t = 0.0054 + 0.447 \Delta z_{t-1}$$
$$\quad (0.0025)\ (0.083)\qquad \text{s.e.}$$
$$\text{SSE}_R = 0.063211$$

Thus

$$u = \frac{\text{SSE}_R - \text{SSE}_U}{J\,\text{SSE}_U/df} = \frac{0.063211 - 0.056448}{2(0.056448)/(110 - 4)}$$
$$= 5.95$$

Table 21.7 Critical Values for Dickey–Fuller Test

Sample Size T	$\alpha = .05$ Critical Value for u	$\alpha = .05$ Critical Value for $F_{(2,T)}$
25	7.24	3.38
50	6.73	3.18
100	6.49	3.09
∞	6.25	2.99

Source: Dickey and Fuller (1981, p. 1063, Table VI).

From Table 21.7, when T = 100, the α = .05 critical value is 6.49; thus we do *not* reject the null hypothesis that $\beta = 0$ and $\rho = 1$, and thus *do not* reject the hypothesis that the logarithm of the industrial production index is a difference stationary process. Consequently, trying to detrend this time series by using a time trend regression like equation 21.5.4, or using its *undifferenced* value in a regression, may lead to spurious results. Remember, however, just because we do not reject the null hypothesis that H_0: $\beta = 0$, $\rho = 1$ does not mean that it is true. There is a chance of a Type II error of an unknown magnitude. Nevertheless, this suggests that it is "prudent" to use differencing to remove the trend in this variable before further analysis.

21.5.3 Cointegration

The foregoing results would seem to suggest that economists should analyze differences of economic time series to obtain estimates of important parameters. However, there are some basic concepts to which economists cling, one being the existence of long-run, steady-state equilibrium. In steady-state equilibrium, economic variables take the same values from period to period, so $z_t = z_{t-1} = z_{t-2} = \dots = z^*$, until the system is disturbed. Furthermore, in equilibrium there are relationships between economic variables, like consumption and income, that economists would like to understand. In this context, consider an example given by Mills (1990, p. 269). Let the time series y_t and x_t be related by

$$y_t = \alpha + \beta x_t + \gamma x_{t-1} + \delta y_{t-1} + \varepsilon_t$$

In steady-state equilibrium the relationship becomes

$$y^* = \alpha + \beta x^* + \gamma x^* + \delta y^*$$

so that we have the steady-state solution

$$y^* = \frac{\alpha}{1-\delta} + \frac{\beta + \gamma}{1-\delta} x^*$$

However, if the differenced model is considered,

$$\Delta y_t = \beta \Delta x_t + \gamma \Delta x_{t-1} + \delta \Delta y_{t-1} + v_t$$

all steady-state differences are zero and there is no solution. This example illustrates, contrary to earlier advice, that if we wish to study long-run relationships between variables then it is important to consider their *levels* rather than their differences.

A remarkable link between nonstationary processes and the concept of long-run equilibrium was introduced by Granger (1981). The link is the concept of *cointegration*. Although the concept is a very general one, for this discussion we will consider its simplest form. If an economic time series y_t follows a random walk, as in equation 21.5.5, its first differences form a stationary series. In this case y_t is said to be an integrated process of order 1 and denoted I(1). On the other hand, if y_t is stationary, then it is integrated of order zero and denoted I(0). Granger and Newbold warned of regressing one I(1) variable on another I(1) variable and called these regressions "spurious," since the least squares estimator, it turns out, breaks down in this case. Granger, however, identified a situation when the regression of an I(1) process on an I(1) process was not spurious. In fact in a situation where the variables are cointegrated, the least squares estimator works better, in that it converges to the true parameter value faster than usual.

If two time series y_t and x_t are I(1) then, in general, the linear combination

$$y_t - \alpha - \beta x_t = \varepsilon_t \tag{21.5.13}$$

is also I(1). However, it is *possible* that ε_t is *stationary*, or I(0). In order for this to happen the "trends" in y_t and x_t must cancel out when $\varepsilon_t = y_t - \alpha - \beta x_t$ is formed. In this case y_t and x_t are said to be *cointegrated*, and β is called the *cointegrating parameter*. Thus a pair of series y_t, x_t are defined as cointegrated if they are each I(1) but there exists a linear combination of them, $\varepsilon_t = y_t - \alpha - \beta x_t$, that is I(0).

The concept of cointegration relates to, or in a sense mimics, the concept of long-run equilibrium in the following way. Suppose a long-run equilibrium relationship was defined by $y_t = \alpha + \beta x_t$, or $y_t - \alpha - \beta x_t = 0$. In that case, ε_t in equation 21.5.13 would represent how far y_t and x_t were away from equilibrium and could be called the "equilibrium error." If y_t and x_t are cointegrated and the error ε_t is *stationary* with mean 0, then

$$y_t = \alpha + \beta x_t + \varepsilon_t \qquad (21.5.14)$$

Since $\varepsilon_t \sim (0, \sigma^2)$ is stationary, the variables y_t and x_t obey a stable, long-run relationship. In *this* case, where y_t and x_t are cointegrated, least squares estimation of equation 21.5.14 provides in large samples an *excellent* (super consistent) estimator of β, which describes the long-run, steady-state equilibrium relationship between y_t and x_t.

Once we have an economic model involving y_t and x_t, an important question is: How can we tell if two variables are cointegrated? One answer is derived from equation 21.5.14. If y_t and x_t are cointegrated, then $\varepsilon_t \sim$ I(0) and is stationary. If y_t and x_t are *not* cointegrated, then $\varepsilon_t \sim$ I(1) is *not* stationary. Thus we can estimate equation 21.5.14, which is called the *cointegrating regression*, by least squares and test whether or not the residuals $\hat{\varepsilon}_t$ are stationary using a modified Dickey–Fuller unit root test. The test must be modified, since it is based on calculated least squares residuals.

Let $\hat{\varepsilon}_t$ be the least squares residuals from the cointegrating regression in equation 21.5.14. Form the first-order autoregressive model

$$\hat{\varepsilon}_t = \rho \hat{\varepsilon}_{t-1} + v_t \qquad (21.5.15a)$$

In this AR(1) model $\hat{\varepsilon}_t$ is stationary if $|\rho| < 1$. But if $\rho = 1$, then the errors are nonstationary. To carry out a test of the null hypothesis $H_0: \rho = 1$, subtract $\hat{\varepsilon}_{t-1}$ from both sides of equation 21.5.15a to form

$$\Delta \hat{\varepsilon}_t = \hat{\varepsilon}_t - \hat{\varepsilon}_{t-1} = (\rho - 1)\hat{\varepsilon}_{t-1} + v_t$$
$$= \rho^* \hat{\varepsilon}_{t-1} + v_t \qquad (21.5.15b)$$

The null hypothesis is $H_0: \rho = 1$ or $\rho^* = 0$. The null hypothesis is rejected, on the basis of a one-tailed t-test, if $t \le t_c^*$, where the critical values t_c^* are given in Table 21.8. The last row shows the critical values from the standard normal for a test of the same size.

Table 21.8   Critical Values for the Cointegration Test When the Cointegrating Regression Contains Two Parameters

Sample Size T	α		
	.01	.05	.10
50	−4.32	−3.67	−3.28
100	−4.07	−3.37	−3.03
200	−4.00	−3.37	−3.02
$N(0,1)$	−2.32	−1.64	−1.28

Source: Engle and Yoo (1987, p. 157, Table 2, minus signs added).

Granger (1986) cites support for the conclusions that the following variables are apparently cointegrated: U. S. national income and consumption, production and sales of U. S. nondurables, U. S. short- and long-term interest rates. On the other hand, U. S. wages and prices, production and sales of U. S. durables, and U. S. money stock and prices are apparently not cointegrated.

To illustrate let us examine whether U. S. consumption and income are cointegrated. In Table 21.9 are U.S. quarterly data on real per capita consumption and disposable income from 1947.I to 1980.IV. The estimated cointegrating equation 21.5.14 is

$$\hat{c}_t = 326 + .862 y_t$$

$$(9.91) \ (189.45) \qquad s.e. \qquad\qquad (21.5.16)$$

where the usual least squares t-statistics are given in parentheses. Estimating equation 21.5.15b by least squares we obtain

$$\Delta\hat{\varepsilon}_t = -.317\hat{\varepsilon}_{t-1}$$

$$(-5.03) \qquad\qquad\qquad (21.5.17)$$

Using the critical values t_c^* for $T = 100$ (since our sample size is 136), we find that

$$t = -5.03 \le -4.07 = t_c^* \,(\alpha = .01)$$

Thus, we *(i) reject* the null hypothesis that the least squares residuals are not stationary and therefore *(ii) do not* reject the null hypothesis that real per capita consumption and disposable income are cointegrated and *(iii)* accept that .862 is a valid estimate of the long-run marginal propensity to consume. Unfortunately, the t-statistics in equation 21.5.16 do *not* indicate the precision of the least squares estimator in the cointegrating equation, since if c_t and y_t are I(1), the usual least squares sampling results do not hold. Specifically, Stock (1987) has shown that the least squares estimator of the cointegrating regression is "super" consistent, converging to the true parameter at a rate faster than the least squares estimator converges in the usual case where y_t and x_t are not integrated. However, the large sample distributions are *not* normal, so usual inference procedures do not hold. Thus, while we reported "t"-values in equation 21.5.16, they cannot be used to make inferences about population parameters.

21.6 Summary

In this chapter we have considered economic models relating two, or more, time series. Distributed lag models treat one time series x_t as predetermined and explain variations in y_t with variations in current and lagged values of x_t. Finite distributed lag models assume that a change in x_t will have an effect on y_t for only a finite number of time periods. The resulting regression model is typically plagued by multicollinearity, so that the least squares estimator is imprecise and unreliable. Restrictions are frequently placed on the regression parameters, called distributed lag weights, that impose a smooth structure. Almon's (1965) polynomial distributed lag is one example, though there are many others. For further discussion of finite distributed lag models, see Judge et al. (1988, pp. 722–734), Greene (1990, pp. 553–558), Maddala (1992, pp. 423–429), or Gujarati (1988, pp. 534–541).

In contrast to a finite lag model, when a change in x_t has an effect on y_t in *all* succeeding time periods, then an infinite lag model is generated. Once again structure must

Table 21.9 U. S. Quarterly Data on Real Per Capita Consumption and Disposable Income, 1947.I–1980.IV (1982 Dollars)

Year	Consumption				Disposable Income			
	I	II	III	IV	I	II	III	IV
1947	4596	4655	4637	4609	4886	4766	4855	4774
1948	4627	4658	4646	4660	4869	4993	5070	5059
1949	4644	4681	4651	4665	4938	4916	4903	4897
1950	4718	4794	4966	4849	5228	5183	5184	5275
1951	4921	4810	4834	4841	5215	5333	5347	5332
1952	4838	4905	4912	5000	5305	5335	5427	5441
1953	5043	5048	5019	4998	5486	5546	5510	5507
1954	5001	5027	5082	5149	5489	5440	5502	5581
1955	5206	5270	5299	5362	5590	5679	5751	5827
1956	5354	5339	5330	5359	5851	5871	5874	5917
1957	5372	5361	5374	5366	5902	5918	5923	5888
1958	5294	5328	5385	5416	5827	5848	5948	6000
1959	5479	5530	5557	5550	5991	6066	6010	6034
1960	5549	5601	5553	5540	6051	6064	6036	5994
1961	5528	5584	5565	5641	6028	6097	6124	6203
1962	5677	5712	5740	5785	6243	6272	6285	6286
1963	5810	5824	5883	5901	6324	6343	6385	6458
1964	5996	6077	6101	6159	6566	6722	6783	6834
1965	6244	6298	6384	6519	6859	6942	7106	7199
1966	6576	6587	6630	6631	7224	7247	7301	7348
1967	6664	6733	6750	6771	7446	7498	7538	7570
1968	6891	6966	7072	7082	7653	7756	7737	7766
1969	7143	7172	7192	7230	7756	7829	7969	8009
1970	7259	7270	7308	7264	8026	8139	8208	8160
1971	7354	7392	7409	7479	8261	8352	8337	8338
1972	7565	7671	7755	7916	8372	8432	8571	8871
1973	8002	7970	7986	7930	8965	9013	9059	9130
1974	7825	7852	7878	7754	8948	8840	8866	8814
1975	7797	7909	7970	8028	8707	9115	8947	9007
1976	8179	8220	8291	8395	9125	9151	9187	9237
1977	8495	8495	8558	8654	9237	9318	9461	9506
1978	8673	8821	8839	8899	9599	9730	9763	9849
1979	8909	8874	8907	8925	9889	9819	9820	9790
1980	8890	8681	8752	8809	9816	9611	9676	9786

Source: Citibase.

be placed on the model prior to estimation. The geometric model arises from several economic hypotheses about expectation formulation. The model can be transformed for estimation by using the Koyck transformation, which produces a linear regression model with a lagged dependent variable as a regressor and MA(1) serial correlation. Consequently, the least squares estimator of this random regressor model is biased and inconsistent. An instrumental variable estimator for this model is easy to construct, however, and is consistent, although not efficient. Infinite lag models are discussed by Judge et al. (1988, pp. 735–745), Greene (1990, pp. 559–577), Maddala (1992, pp. 3405–423), and Gujarati (1988, pp. 505–534).

When y_t and x_t are jointly determined endogenous random variables then, as in Chapters 18 and 19, we may construct a simultaneous equations model for them. Alternatively, if our primary objective is short-run forecasting, we can use a multiple time-series model.

In these models the pair (y_t, x_t) is explained by its lagged values. Estimation can be carried out by using least squares and the resulting model used to forecast values of (y_t, x_t). These models are fully discussed in Judge et al. (1988, Chapter 18).

The final topics in Chapter 21 are spurious regressions, unit root tests, and cointegration. Spurious regressions describe exercises in which one nonstationary variable is regressed on another nonstationary variable. In such a random regressor model the least squares estimator is not consistent nor does it have the usual asymptotic distribution. Unit root tests are used to check whether an economic time series is stationary. An exception to the spurious results yielded by the regression of one nonstationary variable on another occurs when the economic time series are cointegrated. That is, when the series themselves are nonstationary but a linear combination of them *is* stationary. A test for this property is carried out by testing whether the least squares residuals from the regression of y_t on x_t are stationary using a modified unit root test. Further discussion of these topics may be found in Maddala (1988, Chapter 14), in an excellent survey article by Dickey, Jansen, and Thornton (1991), and Mills (1990, pp. 267–276) and references cited therein.

21.7 Exercises

21.1 Plot the data on capital appropriations and expenditures in Table 21.1 against time $t = 1,..., 88$. Which series appears to be the leading one?

21.2 Following on from Exercise 21.1, assume that the expenditures y_t depend on the lag appropiations x_t and that the lag length n is an unknown parameter. Assume a maximum lag of $n_{max} = 12$ quarters. Using the Almon data, estimate the unrestricted model

$$y_t = \delta + \sum_{i=0}^{n_{max}} \beta_i x_{t-i} + e_t$$

Then test the following hypotheses using an appropriate test
(a) $H_0 : \beta_{12} = 0$
(b) $H_0 : \beta_{11} = \beta_{12} = 0$
(c) $H_0 : \beta_{10} = \beta_{11} = \beta_{12} = 0$
(d) $H_0 : \beta_9 = \beta_{10} = \beta_{11} = \beta_{12} = 0$
(e) $H_0 : \beta_8 = \beta_9 = \beta_{10} = \beta_{11} = \beta_{12} = 0$
(f) $H_0 : \beta_7 = \beta_8 = \beta_9 = \beta_{10} = \beta_{11} = \beta_{12} = 0$

What do you conclude about the length of the lag?

21.3 Continuing from Exercise 21.2, assume that the length of the finite lag for the capital expenditure data is $n = 8$. Estimate the lag weights assuming that they fall on polynomials of degree $q = 2, 3, 4, 5$ and 6. Test the following hypotheses.
(a) that $q = 5$ against $q = 6$
(b) that $q = 4$ against $q = 5$
(c) that $q = 3$ against $q = 4$
(d) that $q = 2$ against $q = 3$

What do you conclude about the degree of the polynomial, given that $n = 8$?

21.4 Consider the consumption function

$$c_t = \alpha_0 + \alpha_1 y_t^* + e_t, \qquad t = 1, 2,..., T$$

where c_t is measured consumption, y_t^* is "normal" real income, and e_t is a random disturbance. Assume that "normal" income is unobservable but satisfies the adaptive expectations hypothesis so that

$$y_t^* - y_{t-1}^* = (1 - \lambda)(y_t - y_{t-1}^*)$$

(a) Derive the infinite geometric lag representation of this consumption, as in equation 21.3.9.

(b) Obtain a moving average error formulation of the geometric lag via the Koyck transformation explained in Section 21.3.2.

(c) Use the consumption and income data given in Table 21.10 to obtain instrumental variable estimates of the model derived in (b). These data span the period 1947.I–1960.IV and are taken from Griliches et al. (1962, pp. 499–400). c_t and y_t are in billions of 1954 dollars, seasonally adjusted.

(d) Discuss the results. What is the estimate of the short run marginal propensity to consume? What is the estimate of the long run marginal propensity to consume?

21.5 Use the estimated VAR equations in equations 21.4.11 to generate forecasts of y_{t1} and y_{t2} in periods $t = T + 1,\ldots, T + 5$. Note that after forecasting into period $t = T + 1$, the "X" matrix must be composed of forecasted values from the previous period. Speculate on how this affects forecast precision and justify, intuitively, your answer.

21.6 (a) Reestimate the VAR model in equations 21.4.3 and 21.4.4 by using the data in Table 21.6 but only with observations $t = 1,\ldots, 70$.

(b) Compare the estimates in (a) to those in equations 21.4.11.

(c) Use the results from (a) to test for Granger causality.

(d) Use the results from (a) and only data values $t = 1,\ldots, 70$ to forecast values of y_{t1} and y_{t2} for periods $t = 71,\ldots, 75$. (See Exercise 21.5.) Compare the forecasted to actual values.

21.7 Use the data on disposable income in Table 21.9 and the data on consumption of nondurables in Table 21.11 to test whether disposable income and nondurable consumption are cointegrated.

Table 21.10

Year	Consumption				Income			
	I	II	III	IV	I	II	III	IV
1947	192.5	196.1	196.9	197.0	202.3	197.1	202.9	202.2
1948	198.1	199.0	199.4	200.6	203.5	211.7	215.3	215.1
1949	199.9	203.6	204.8	209.0	212.9	213.9	214.0	214.9
1950	210.7	214.2	225.6	217.0	228.0	227.3	232.0	236.1
1951	223.3	214.5	217.5	219.8	230.9	236.3	239.1	240.8
1952	220.0	227.7	223.8	230.2	231.1	240.9	245.8	248.8
1953	234.0	236.2	236.0	234.1	253.3	256.1	255.9	255.9
1954	233.4	236.4	239.0	243.2	254.4	254.8	257.0	260.9
1955	248.7	253.7	259.9	261.8	263.0	271.5	276.5	281.4
1956	263.2	263.7	263.4	266.9	282.0	286.2	287.7	291.0
1957	268.9	270.4	273.4	272.1	291.1	294.6	296.1	293.3
1958	268.9	270.9	274.4	278.7	291.3	292.6	299.9	302.1
1959	283.8	289.7	290.8	292.8	305.9	312.5	311.3	313.2
1960	295.4	299.5	298.6	299.6	315.4	320.3	321.0	320.1

Table 21.11

	Nondurable Consumption			
Year	I	II	III	IV
1947	2323	2364	2358	2317
1948	2312	2325	2292	2305
1949	2305	2301	2278	2293
1950	2310	2330	2359	2301
1951	2352	2319	2358	2376
1952	2351	2393	2416	2435
1953	2451	2446	2420	2411
1954	2418	2401	2425	2453
1955	2461	2492	2502	2541
1956	2556	2537	2522	2530
1957	2531	2530	2555	2534
1958	2497	2507	2540	2558
1959	2570	2572	2575	2576
1960	2564	2584	2557	2548
1961	2548	2566	2549	2572
1962	2587	2585	2599	2609
1963	2615	2606	2616	2608
1964	2645	2686	2727	2727
1965	2745	2763	2799	2871
1966	2877	2897	2913	2894
1967	2911	2917	2908	2919
1968	2971	2989	3028	3015
1969	3037	3044	3043	3052
1970	3079	3076	3088	3094
1971	3092	3090	3072	3077
1972	3097	3157	3190	3238
1973	3257	3216	3226	3194
1974	3120	3115	3130	3092
1975	3100	3142	3143	3143
1976	3204	3237	3262	3297
1977	3322	3306	3301	3349
1978	3364	3370	3380	3427
1979	3417	3392	3398	3415
1980	3387	3346	3331	3328

Source: Citibase. Data are in 1982 dollars per capita..

21.8 Use the Dickey–Fuller test and the data in Tables 21.9 and 21.11 to test the null hypothesis that the real, per capita series on consumption, nondurable consumption, and disposable income are difference stationary processes.

21.8 References

ALMON, S. (1965) "The Distributed Lag Between Capital Appropriations and Expectations," *Econometrica*, 33, 178–196.

Dickey, D. A., and W. A. Fuller (1979) "Distribution of the Estimates for Autoregressive Time Series with Unit Root," *Journal of American Statistical Assocation*, 74, 427–431.

DICKEY, D. A., and W. A. FULLER (1981) "Likelihood Ratio Statistics for Autoregressive Time-Series with a Unit Root," *Econometrica*, 49, 1057–1072.

DICKEY, D. A., D. W. JANSEN, and D. L. THORNTON (1991) "A Primer on Cointegration with an Application to Money and Income," *Federal Reserve Bank of St. Louis Review*, 73, 58–78.

ENGLE, R. F., and C. W. J. GRANGER (1987) "Co-integration and Error Correction: Representation, Estimation and Testing," *Econometrica*, 55, 251–276.

ENGLE, R. F., and B. S. YOO (1987) "Forecasting and Testing in Co-integrated Systems," *Journal of Econometrics*, 35, 143–150.

GRANGER, C. W. J. (1981) "Some Properties of Time Series Data and Their Use in Econometric Model Specification," *Journal of Econometrics*, 16, 121–130.

GRANGER, C. W. J. (1986) "Developments in the Study of Cointegrated Economic Variables," *Oxford Bulletin of Economics and Statistics*, 48, 213–228.

GRANGER, C. W. J. and P. NEWBOLD (1974) "Spurious Regressions in Econometrics," *Journal of Econometrics*, 2, 111–120.

GREENE, W. H. (1990) *Econometric Analysis*, New York: Macmillan Publishing Co..

GRILICHES, Z., G. S. MADDALA, R. LUCAS, and N. WALLACE (1962) "Notes on Estimated Aggregate Quarterly Consumption Functions," *Econometrica*, 30, 491–500.

GUJARATI, D. N. (1988) *Basic Econometrics*, 2nd Edition, New York: McGraw-Hill.

JUDGE, G. G., R. C. HILL, W. E. GRIFFITHS, H. LÜTKEPOHL, and T. C. LEE (1988) *Introduction to the Theory and Practice of Econometrics*, 2nd Edition, New York: John Wiley & Sons, Inc.

KLEIN, L. R., and A. S. GOLDBERGER (1955) *An Econometric Model of the United States, 1929–1952*. Amsterdam: North-Holland.

MADDALA, G. S. (1992) *Introduction to Econometrics*, 2nd Edition, New York: Macmillan Publishing Co.

MILLS, T. C. (1990) *Time Series Techniques for Economists*, Cambridge: Cambridge University Press.

NELSON, C. R., and C. I. PLOSSER (1982) "Trends and Random Walks in Macroeconomic Time Series," *Journal of Monetary Economics*, 10, 139–162.

STOCK, J. H. (1987) "Asymptotic Properties of Least Squares Estimators of Cointegrating Vectors," *Econometrica*, 55, 1035–1056.

Part VIII

Econometric Topics II

A common feature of most of the statistical models that we have considered is that they are linear functions of the unknown parameters $\beta_1, \beta_2, \ldots, \beta_K$. In practice, there are many economic and statistical models that are not linear functions of the unknown parameters. Consequently, the first chapter in this part is concerned with the basic concepts underlying nonlinear least squares estimation. Several examples are given to indicate the procedures to be followed with single- and multiple-parameter models. In the second chapter in this part, we recognize there are many situations when choice alternatives are limited, and thus the outcomes of economic variables appear in discrete or dummy variable form. The probit and logit statistical models are nonlinear models designed to provide a basis for inference in these cases.

Chapter 22

Nonlinear Least Squares

New Key Words and Concepts

Parameter Nonlinearities   Nonlinear Estimation

Local Minimum   Global Minimum

Sum of Squares Function   Iteration

Gauss–Newton Algorithm

22.1 Nonlinear Models

Throughout this text we have been concerned with relating values of an outcome, response, or dependent variable y_t to values of a number of explanatory variables $\mathbf{x}'_t = (x_{t1}, x_{t2}, \ldots, x_{tK})$. A general relationship of this type can be described by a function f and a vector of unknown parameters $\boldsymbol{\beta}$, and written as

$$y_t = f(\mathbf{x}_t, \boldsymbol{\beta}) \tag{22.1.1}$$

The most common functional specification for equation 22.1.1 has been the linear one

$$y_t = x_{t1}\beta_1 + x_{t2}\beta_2 + \ldots + x_{tK}\beta_K \tag{22.1.2}$$

However, we have also encountered the nonlinear function (for example, Section 11.8 of Chapter 11)

$$y_t = \alpha x_{t2}^{\beta_2} x_{t3}^{\beta_3} \ldots x_{tK}^{\beta_K} \tag{22.1.3}$$

that can be written in terms of logarithms as

$$\ln y_t = \beta_1 + \beta_2 \ln x_{t2} + \beta_3 \ln x_{t3} + \ldots + \beta_K \ln x_{tK} \tag{22.1.4}$$

where $\beta_1 = \ln \alpha$. Another example of equation 22.1.1 that we have discussed is that where y_t is a quadratic function of a single explanatory variable x_t; that case can be written as

$$y_t = \beta_1 + \beta_2 x_t + \beta_3 x_t^2 \tag{22.1.5}$$

A common feature of these examples of models, and the many other examples that were outlined in Chapter 8, is that they are *linear functions of the unknown parameters* $\beta_1, \beta_2, \ldots, \beta_K$. Some of the models, such as equations 22.1.4 and 22.1.5, are nonlinear functions of the variables $(y_t, x_{t1}, x_{t2}, \ldots, x_{tK})$, but they are all linear functions of the unknown parameters.

A consequence of the parameter linearity in models such as equations 22.1.2, 22.1.4, and 22.1.5 is that, after specifying a statistical model that includes a random independent and identically distributed error term e_t, we can estimate the parameters using the least squares rule. Furthermore, for this statistical model, the least squares estimator has the advantage of being best linear unbiased.

In practice, however, *there are many economic and corresponding statistical models that are not linear functions of the unknown parameters.* For example, in terms of production theory, a statistical model for the Cobb–Douglas production function where output y_t is related to two inputs, say, capital x_{t2} and labor x_{t3}, can be specified as

$$y_t = \alpha x_{t2}^{\beta_2} x_{t3}^{\beta_3} + e_t \tag{22.1.6}$$

Because the random error in this model has been added to the power function form (equation 22.1.3) and not the logarithmic form (equation 22.1.4), equation 22.1.6 is nonlinear in the parameters β_2 and β_3. Also, taking logarithms will not make it linear. For least squares estimation it is clearly crucial how the random error e_t appears.

Another example of a function that is nonlinear in the parameters is the relationship between consumption (c_t) and income (y_t) that is given by the consumption function

$$c_t = \beta_1 + \beta_2 y_t^{\beta_3} + e_t \tag{22.1.7}$$

This function would be a reasonable and general functional form to estimate if we believed that functions such as

$$c_t = \beta_1 + \beta_2 y_t^{1/2} + e_t \quad \text{or} \quad c_t = \beta_1 + \beta_2 y_t^2 + e_t \quad \text{or} \quad c_t = \beta_1 + \beta_2 y_t^{-1} + e_t \tag{22.1.8}$$

were all plausible. By estimating equation 22.1.7 we would be letting the data suggest a value for the exponent of y_t.

The nonlinearity in the parameters in the consumption function in equation 22.1.7 arises because of the assumed nature of the economic model. Often assumptions in a *statistical* model are such that they lead to a transformed version of the statistical model that is nonlinear. For example, in Section 16.4 of Chapter 16, where we were concerned with estimation of a linear statistical model $y_t = \beta_1 + x_t\beta_2 + e_t$ with first-order autoregressive errors $e_t = \rho e_{t-1} + \varepsilon_t$, we discovered that a transformed nonlinear version of the statistical model is

$$y_t = (1-\rho)\beta_1 + \rho y_{t-1} + x_{t2}\beta_2 - x_{t-1,2}\rho\beta_2 + \varepsilon_t \tag{22.1.9}$$

This model is a linear function of the *variables* y_{t-1}, x_{t2}, $x_{t-1,2}$, but it is a *nonlinear* function of the mean function parameters β_1 and β_2 and the autoregressive parameter ρ.

Given the many examples of economic and statistical models that lead to functions that are nonlinear in the parameters, we need to ask whether these functions introduce any special problems. Can we proceed with our least squares rule and develop an estimator with good statistical properties? The answer is yes, but computation of the least squares estimator, which in this instance we call the *nonlinear least squares estimator*, is more difficult. This chapter is concerned with nonlinear least squares estimation. In Section 22.2, we explain the essential ingredients of nonlinear least squares using a simple one-parameter model. This model is an artificial one, and introducing it at this stage deviates from our normal practice of beginning with an economic model. However, it is convenient and important to introduce a number of concepts in terms of the simple one-parameter model. These concepts generalize in a natural way to more realistic multiparameter models such as the CES production function that is considered in Section 22.3. As another example of a nonlinear estimation problem, estimation of a moving average process is considered in Appendix 22A.

22.2   Principles of Nonlinear Least Squares Estimation

To introduce nonlinear least squares estimation, let us begin by considering the following linear statistical model:

$$y_t = \beta_1 x_{t1} + \beta_2 x_{t2} + e_t \tag{22.2.1}$$

where the e_t are independent and identically distributed random errors with mean 0 and variance σ^2. Now suppose that we have nonsample information that suggests $\beta_2 = \beta_1^2$, so that our model can be written as

$$y_t = \beta_1 x_{t1} + \beta_1^2 x_{t2} + e_t \tag{22.2.2}$$

That is, we have a model that is linear in the variables x_{t1} and x_{t2}, but nonlinear in the single parameter β_1. For ease of notation we will drop the subscript 1 from β_1 and rewrite equation 22.2.2 as

$$y_t = \beta x_{t1} + \beta^2 x_{t2} + e_t \tag{22.2.3}$$

Consistent with this sampling process, 20 observations on y_t, x_{t1}, and x_{t2} are given in Table 22.1.

The first question that we will ask is: Given the model in equation 22.2.3 and the data in Table 22.1, how can we use the least squares criterion to find an estimate for β? To answer this question, first consider how we would have used the least squares principles outlined in Chapters 3 and 5 to find the least squares estimate for β in the more simple *linear* model

$$y_t = \beta x_t + e_t \tag{22.2.4}$$

Table 22.1 Data for Single-Parameter Example

y	x_1	x_2
3.284	.286	.645
3.149	.973	.585
2.877	.384	.310
−.467	.276	.058
1.211	.973	.455
1.389	.543	.779
1.145	.957	.259
2.321	.948	.202
.998	.543	.028
.379	.797	.099
1.106	.936	.142
.428	.889	.296
.011	.006	.175
1.179	.828	.180
1.858	.399	.842
.388	.617	.039
.651	.939	.103
.593	.784	.620
.046	.072	.158
1.152	.889	.704

In this case we would find that value of β that minimizes

$$S(\beta) = \sum_{t=1}^{T} (y_t - \beta x_t)^2$$

$$= \sum_{t=1}^{T} y_t^2 + \beta^2 \sum_{t=1}^{T} x_t^2 - 2\beta \sum_{t=1}^{T} x_t y_t \qquad (22.2.5)$$

The minimizing value for β occurs where the derivative $dS/d\beta = 0$. Since this derivative is given by

$$\frac{dS}{d\beta} = 2\beta \Sigma x_t^2 - 2\Sigma x_t y_t \qquad (22.2.6)$$

the minimizing value (the least squares estimate), which we denote by b, must satisfy the equation

$$2b\Sigma x_t^2 - 2\Sigma x_t y_t = 0 \qquad (22.2.7)$$

That is,

$$b = \frac{\Sigma x_t y_t}{\Sigma x_t^2} \qquad (22.2.8)$$

When equation 22.2.8 is viewed as a formula or rule for estimating β we call it the least squares *estimator*. When values for the summations $\Sigma x_t y_t$ and Σx_t^2 are inserted into equation 22.2.8, we call it the least squares *estimate*.

What happens if we apply this least squares procedure to our *nonlinear* model

$$y_t = \beta x_{t1} + \beta^2 x_{t2} + e_t \qquad (22.2.9)$$

That is, we want to find that value of β that minimizes

$$S(\beta) = \sum_{t=1}^{T} \left(y_t - \beta x_{t1} - \beta^2 x_{t2} \right)^2$$

$$= \Sigma y_t^2 + \beta^2 \Sigma x_{t1}^2 + \beta^4 \Sigma x_{t2}^2 - 2\beta \Sigma x_{t1} y_t - 2\beta^2 \Sigma x_{t2} y_t + 2\beta^3 \Sigma x_{t1} x_{t2}$$

$$(22.2.10)$$

As previously, we can look for that value of β where the derivative $dS/d\beta = 0$. Working in this direction, we have

$$\frac{dS}{d\beta} = 4\beta^3 \Sigma x_{t2}^2 + 6\beta^2 \Sigma x_{t1} x_{t2} + 2\beta \left(\Sigma x_{t1}^2 - 2\Sigma x_{t2} y_t \right) - 2\Sigma x_{t1} y_t \qquad (22.2.11)$$

Setting this derivative equal to zero, we find that the least squares estimate b must satisfy

$$2b^3 \Sigma x_{t2}^2 + 3b^2 \Sigma x_{t1} x_{t2} + b \left(\Sigma x_{t1}^2 - 2\Sigma x_{t2} y_t \right) - \Sigma x_{t1} y_t = 0 \qquad (22.2.12)$$

It is at this stage that we run into difficulties. The corresponding stage for the simple linear model was equation 22.2.7. Because this latter equation was linear in b, it was a simple matter to solve for b to get the result in equation 22.2.8. In contrast, equation 22.2.12 is a cubic equation in β. There are two immediate implications. The first is that it is harder to obtain the least squares estimate b, because solving a cubic equation is harder than solving a linear equation. The second difficulty is that a cubic equation will have three solutions for b. How do we determine which one is the nonlinear least squares estimate?

Before we explore these issues further, it is worth emphasizing that these difficulties arise with almost all nonlinear least squares problems. That is, *nonlinear least squares estimation is characterized by (i) an inability to solve the equation $dS/d\beta = 0$ to obtain an analytical expression or formula for the least squares estimator b, and (ii) the possibility of more than one estimate (or set of estimates) that will satisfy the equation $dS/d\beta = 0$.*

We can gain some insights into these problems, and how we solve them, by graphing the sum of squares function $S(\beta)$ that appears in equation 22.2.10. The graph of this function, using the data in Table 22.1, is given in Figure 22.1. There are three points where the slope of this function $dS/d\beta$ is equal to zero. They are, approximately, $\beta = -2$, $\beta = -1$, and $\beta = 1.2$. In other words, these are the three solutions to the cubic equation 22.2.12. However, only one of them, namely $b = 1.2$, is the nonlinear least squares estimate. This value is the nonlinear least squares estimate because it is at this point that the sum of squares function $S(b)$ is smallest. The smallest value of $S(\beta)$ is called its *global minimum*. The nonlinear least squares estimate $b = 1.2$ is the point at which $S(\beta)$ achieves its global minimum.

The point where $\beta = -2$ is known as a *local minimum*. It is a local minimum in the sense that $S(\beta)$ is smaller at $\beta = -2$ than it is at any of the surrounding points that are close to $\beta = -2$. Similarly, $\beta = -1$ is called a local maximum. The function $S(\beta)$ is greater at $\beta = -1$ than it is at any of the surrounding points that are close to $\beta = -1$.

Let us pause and summarize what we have learned thus far. The objective in least squares estimation is to locate the global minimum of the function $S(\beta)$. That is, we wish to find that value of β where $S(\beta)$ is smallest. With a linear-in-the-parameters model we can do so by finding that value of β for which $dS/d\beta = 0$. In this case setting the derivative $dS/d\beta$ to zero leads to a formula for the least squares estimator b. With a nonlinear-in-the-parameters model, the complexity of the required algebra makes it impossible to use the result $dS/d\beta = 0$ to find a formula for the nonlinear least squares estimator. In addition, there may be more than one point where $dS/d\beta = 0$.

In our nonlinear example we have located the global minimum by drawing a complete graph of the function $S(\beta)$. Drawing such a graph is not always practical, however,

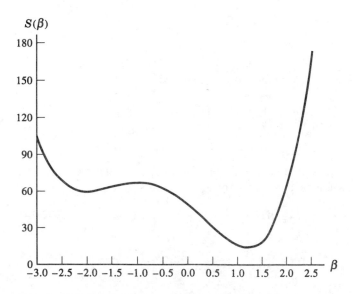

Figure 22.1 Sum of squares function for single-parameter example

particularly if we have more than one parameter. Nor is it a very efficient way to find the nonlinear least squares estimate. Thus, we need to explore other methods.

22.2.1   Finding the Least Squares Estimate Numerically

Most statistical and econometric computer software packages have procedures for finding nonlinear least squares estimates. These procedures are not all the same, although they do follow the same general principles. In this section we provide an intuitive feel for the general principles. Details of some of the different procedures can be found in Judge et al. (1988), Chapter 12. Our discussion will be in terms of finding a single nonlinear least squares estimate b for a single parameter β. The same principles hold when searching for a vector of estimates $\mathbf{b}$ for a vector of parameters β.

Procedures, or algorithms, for finding the nonlinear least squares estimate b for a parameter β begin with some initial value for β. This value may be a guess, it may be suggested by nonsample information about the problem, or it could come from estimating an approximate linear model. The sum of squares function $S(\beta)$ is computed for this initial value. The next step is to change the initial parameter value in a direction that leads to a decrease in $S(\beta)$. A new parameter value is found and the process is repeated. Eventually a point is reached where a change in the parameter value will not lead to a decrease in $S(\beta)$. At this point the algorithm is said to have converged. Because a small change in β will not decrease $S(\beta)$ further, we must have reached either a local or the global minimum of $S(\beta)$. Assuming for the moment that we have found the global minimum, the value of b at this point is the nonlinear least squares estimate. Because numerical procedures or algorithms "search" for a minimum, they are often called *search procedures*.

As an example of one procedure, we consider the steps taken by the *Gauss–Newton algorithm* in its search for the global minimum. Each step at which the value of β is changed so as to decrease $S(\beta)$ is called an *iteration*. If β_n is the nth value of β for which a value of $S(\beta)$ is computed, then the change in β that takes place at the nth iteration can be written as

$$\beta_{n+1} = \beta_n - p_n d_n \tag{22.2.13}$$

where

$$d_n = \frac{dS}{d\beta}\bigg|_{\beta_n}$$

is the value of the derivative $dS/d\beta$ evaluated at β_n, and where

$$p_n = \frac{1}{2}\left[\sum_{t=1}^{T}\left(\frac{df_t}{d\beta}\right)^2\right]^{-1}$$

with the derivative $df_t/d\beta$ being evaluated at β_n and $f_t = f(\mathbf{x}_t, \beta)$ being the nonrandom component of the statistical model. In the example we are considering

$$y_t = f_t + e_t = f(\mathbf{x}_t, \beta) + e_t = \beta x_{t1} + \beta^2 x_{t2} + e_t \tag{22.2.14}$$

and

$$\frac{df_t}{d\beta} = x_{t1} + 2\beta x_{t2} \tag{22.2.15}$$

The derivative $dS/d\beta$ is given in equation 22.2.11.

At the first iteration β_1 is the initial value or guess for β, d_1 is the slope of the sum of squares function at β_1, p_1 is also evaluated at β_1, and β_2 is the new value of β. When a minimum is reached, the slope $d_n = 0$ and so $\beta_{n+1} = \beta_n$. Further iterations do not lead to a change in the value for β. See Exercise 22.1 for further details on the Gauss–Newton algorithm for our example problem.

The Gauss–Newton algorithm was used to find the nonlinear least squares estimate b that, by plotting the sum of squares function, we noted was approximately equal to 1.2. The procedure was applied twice, using a different initial value for β in each case. The results at each iteration are given in Table 22.2. In one case $\beta_1 = 4$ was used as the initial value; in the other case $\beta_1 = -0.9$ was used. Note that the nonlinear least squares estimate is given by 1.1612 and the global minimum of $S(\beta)$ is 16.308.

A point that needs further discussion is that the Gauss–Newton algorithm may lead to a local minimum rather than the global minimum. As equation 22.2.13 indicates, algorithms converge when the slope of the function $dS/d\beta$ equals zero. This slope will be zero at local minima as well as at the global minimum. Since it is the global minimum that yields the nonlinear least squares estimate, it is desirable to avoid local minima. Table 22.3 illustrates how the Gauss–Newton algorithm can reach the local minimum at $\beta = -2$ when initial values of $\beta_1 = -3$ or $\beta_1 = -1.05$ are used. How, then, can we ensure that an answer, produced by our computer program, is the global not a local minimum? The answer is that you can never be absolutely sure. However, the chances of choosing a local minimum can be minimized if the procedure is followed for a number of different initial values. If convergence to the same point occurs each time, there is a good chance that the global minimum has been reached. If convergence to different points occurs, then that point with the lowest residual or error sum of squares should be chosen, and further checks should be carried out to ensure that this point is not a local minimum.

Another possible problem is that the procedure may not converge at all. The shapes of some sum-of-squares functions are such that many algorithms have difficulty finding the minimum. Under these circumstances you should again try different initial parameter values and, if this strategy proves unsuccessful, investigate the use of alternative algorithms.

Details of how computer programs can be used to find nonlinear least squares estimates can be found in the SAS and SHAZAM *Computer Handbooks*. Usually the only information that must be provided is the function to be estimated and some initial values for the unknown parameters. The program will usually compute the necessary derivatives and automatically carry out the iterations.

Table 22.2 Iterations of the Gauss–Newton Algorithm Using Two Different Initial Values for β

n	β_n	$S(\beta_n)$	n	β_n	$S(\beta_n)$
1	4.000000	1226.89912	1	−0.900000	65.84007
2	2.032239	72.36060	2	−0.689307	64.49820
3	1.308562	17.45425	3	0.322688	37.47599
4	1.169699	16.31152	4	1.367249	18.61578
5	1.161445	16.30797	5	1.175455	16.31798
6	1.161213	16.30797	6	1.161625	16.30798
7	1.161207	16.30797	7	1.161218	16.30797
8	1.161207	16.30797	8	1.161207	16.30797
			9	1.161207	16.30797

Table 22.3 Iterations of the Gauss–Newton Algorithm that Lead to a Local Minimum

n	β_n	$S(\beta_n)$	n	β_n	$S(\beta_n)$
1	−3.000000	102.93069	1	−1.050000	65.85713
2	−2.323290	61.14292	2	−1.196026	65.23206
3	−2.112326	58.70033	3	−1.509215	62.44607
4	−2.052903	58.53688	4	−1.831210	59.31742
5	−2.036150	58.52450	5	−1.969877	58.60475
6	−2.031391	58.52352	6	−2.012307	58.53044
7	−2.030035	58.52344	7	−2.024579	58.52401
8	−2.029649	58.52343	8	−2.028091	58.52348
9	−2.029538	58.52343	9	−2.029094	58.52343
10	−2.029507	58.52343	10	−2.029380	58.52343
11	−2.029498	58.52343	11	−2.029462	58.52343
12	−2.029495	58.52343	12	−2.029485	58.52343
13	−2.029495	58.52343	13	−2.029492	58.52343
			14	−2.029494	58.52343
			15	−2.029494	58.52343

22.2.2 Properties of the Nonlinear Least Squares Estimator

With the linear least squares estimator $\mathbf{b} = (X'X)^{-1}X'\mathbf{y}$, we were able to demonstrate that it has the desirable properties of being best linear unbiased, and we were able to derive its mean and covariance matrix. What about the nonlinear least squares estimator? What can we say about its properties? In general, any nonlinear least squares estimator will be a complicated function of $\mathbf{y}$ and, as a result, it is impossible to establish its finite sample properties. It is possible, however, to establish asymptotic, or approximate large sample properties. Under appropriate conditions, *the nonlinear least squares estimator is consistent, it is approximately normally distributed, and it is possible to estimate its approximate covariance matrix.*

Let us consider an expression for the variance of the nonlinear least squares estimator in a single parameter problem. To introduce this expression, we first discuss the two nonlinear least squares minima in Figure 22.2. In Figure 22.2a the sum-of-squares function is relatively flat around the nonlinear least squares value b_A; on the other hand, in Figure 22.2b the sum-of-squares function is steep near the estimate b_B. In the flat case we are unlikely to be confident about the reliability of the estimate b_A. Because the sum-of-squares function is flat, there are many other values of β for which this function is only slightly greater than its minimum. In the steep case we are likely to be confident about the reliability of b_B. A small change in β away from b_B leads to a dramatic increase in the sum-of-squares function. Since the reliability of an estimator is described by its variance, this discussion suggests that the variance of the nonlinear least squares estimator should depend on how flat or steep the sum-of-squares function is at the point b. How do we measure flatness or steepness? We do so with the rate of change of the slope of the sum-of-squares function. The rate of change of the slope at b_B is greater than it is at b_A. Also, this rate of change in the slope is given by the second derivative $d^2S/d\beta^2$. Consequently, if the value of $d^2S/d\beta^2$, calculated at b, is relatively low [$S(\beta)$ is flat], we expect the variance of the nonlinear least squares estimator to be relatively large. Conversely, if $d^2S/d\beta^2$ is relatively large, $S(\beta)$ is steep, and we expect the variance of the nonlinear least squares estimator to be relatively small.

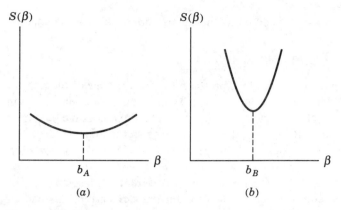

Figure 22.2 Two examples of nonlinear least squares estimates: other things being equal, the estimated variance of b_A is greater than that of b_B.

It should, therefore, come as no surprise that the variance of the nonlinear least squares estimator is a function of $d^2 S/d\beta^2$. The appropriate expression is

$$\text{var}(b) \approx 2\sigma^2 \left(\frac{d^2 S}{d\beta^2}\right)^{-1} \tag{22.2.16}$$

We can estimate this quantity by evaluating $d^2 S/d\beta^2$ at the nonlinear least squares estimate b and by estimating the error variance σ^2 by way of the consistent estimator

$$\hat{\sigma}^2 = \frac{S(b)}{T} = \frac{\sum\limits_{t=1}^{T}\left[y_t - f(\mathbf{x}_t, b)\right]^2}{T} \tag{22.2.17}$$

In our example we have (see Exercise 22.2)

$$\frac{d^2 S}{d\beta^2} = 12\beta^2 \Sigma x_{t2}^2 + 12\beta\Sigma x_{t1} x_{t2} + 2\left(\Sigma x_{t1}^2 - 2\Sigma x_{t2} y_t\right) \tag{22.2.18}$$

Replacing β by $b = 1.1612$ and evaluating this expression yields

$$\frac{d^2 S}{d\beta^2} = 97.914 \tag{22.2.19}$$

Our estimate for σ^2 is given by

$$\hat{\sigma}^2 = \frac{1}{T}\Sigma\left[y_t - f(\mathbf{x}_t, b)\right]^2$$

$$= \frac{1}{T}\Sigma\left(y_t - bx_{t1} - b^2 x_{t2}\right)^2$$

$$= \frac{16.30797}{20} = 0.8154 \tag{22.2.20}$$

Collecting all these results we have as an estimate of the variance of b

$$\hat{\text{var}}(b) = 2 \times 0.8154 \times (97.914)^{-1} = 0.01666 \tag{22.2.21}$$

An approximate standard error for b is given by the square root of this estimated variance, namely

$$\text{s.e.}(b) = \sqrt{0.016655} = 0.129 \tag{22.2.22}$$

Equation 22.2.16 is not the only possible expression for the variance of the nonlinear least squares estimator. This expression is an approximate one, the approximation being better, the larger the sample size. However, it is important to recognize that other approximations exist and that different computer programs frequently use different approximations. Consequently, although *all programs should yield the same nonlinear least squares estimate, different programs can yield different standard errors.* Such differences can occur not only through the use of different expressions for the variance, but also because some programs use numerical derivatives instead of analytical derivatives.

Summarizing the results for our nonlinear model

$$y_t = \beta x_{t1} + \beta^2 x_{t2} + e_t \tag{22.2.23}$$

we have found the nonlinear squares estimate for β and its standard error are given by

$$b = 1.1612 \qquad \text{s.e.}(b) = 0.129$$

In conjunction with the normal distribution, these results can be used to construct confidence intervals for β or test hypotheses about β in the usual way.

22.2.3   Summary and Extensions

For a statistical model that is nonlinear in a single parameter β, we have discovered that a numerical algorithm, implemented by a computer, can be used to find a nonlinear least squares estimate b. This estimate is that value that minimizes the sum of squared errors function $S(\beta)$, and it satisfies the equation $dS/d\beta = 0$. Because other values of β that yield local minima can also satisfy the equation $dS/d\beta = 0$, it is advisable to execute the program for a number of different initial values for β. An estimate of the variance of the nonlinear least squares estimator can be found from an estimate of the error variance and from the rate of change of the slope of the function $S(\beta)$ at the nonlinear least squares estimate b.

The single parameter nonlinear-in-the-parameters model is a convenient one for presenting the principles of nonlinear least squares estimation. However, it is unrealistic in the sense that very few economic and corresponding statistical models have only one parameter. We must ask, therefore, whether our principles naturally extend to nonlinear models with more than one parameter. Although the situation is more complicated, the answer is yes. We must provide initial values for each of the parameters, or, in other words, for the complete parameter vector β. At each iteration the value of every parameter is changed so as to decrease the sum of squares function $S(\beta)$. The algorithm converges when all partial derivatives of S with respect to each of the elements in β is equal to zero. That is, the following vector, known as the *gradient vector,* must equal the zero vector.

$$\frac{\partial S}{\partial \boldsymbol{\beta}} = \left(\frac{\partial S}{\partial \beta_1}, \frac{\partial S}{\partial \beta_2}, \ldots, \frac{\partial S}{\partial \beta_K} \right)' \tag{22.2.24}$$

Finally, an estimate of the covariance matrix of the nonlinear least squares estimator can be found by considering the rates of change of the slope of $S(\beta)$ in all possible directions. Interval estimation and hypothesis testing are based on the result that the nonlinear least squares estimator **b** is approximately normally distributed with mean β and with the covariance matrix that is estimated through the nonlinear least squares algorithm. Building on this base, let us now turn our attention to a nonlinear economic model involving more than one unknown parameter.

22.3 The CES Production Function

In Section 11.8 of Chapter 11 we introduced a Cobb–Douglas production function so that we could measure the response of corn output to the level of the fertilizer inputs nitrogen and phosphate. The properties of the function were discussed, the function was estimated, and the results were analyzed. In this section we introduce a more general function known as the constant elasticity of substitution (CES) production function. We begin by revising properties of the economic model corresponding to the Cobb–Douglas production function. The CES production function is introduced and its properties contrasted with those of the Cobb–Douglas. Then, the statistical model is introduced and applied to some aggregate data on output, labor and capital.

22.3.1 Properties of the Cobb–Douglas Production Function

Suppose that we are interested in estimating the relationship between aggregate output in an industry y and the two inputs labor (l) and capital (k). If we used a Cobb–Douglas production function to describe this relationship we could write it as

$$y = \alpha l^{\beta_2} k^{\beta_3} \tag{22.3.1}$$

Various properties of this function were described in Chapter 11. Of particular interest at the moment are the marginal products, the marginal rate of substitution, and the elasticity of substitution of this function.

The marginal products are given by

$$\text{MP}_l = \frac{\partial y}{\partial l} = \frac{\beta_2 y}{l} \qquad \text{MP}_k = \frac{\partial y}{\partial k} = \frac{\beta_3 y}{k} \tag{22.3.2}$$

An *isoquant* is a curve that describes those combinations of labor and capital that produce a given level of output. The slope of the isoquant measures the rate at which capital can substitute for labor (or vice versa) while maintaining a constant output. This slope is called the *marginal rate of substitution* (MRS) and is given by the ratio of marginal products. That is

$$\text{MRS} = \frac{\text{MP}_k}{\text{MP}_l} = \frac{\partial y / \partial k}{\partial y / \partial l} = \frac{\beta_3 y / k}{\beta_2 y / l} = \frac{\beta_3 l}{\beta_2 k} \tag{22.3.3}$$

One difficulty with the marginal rate of substitution as a measure of how much capital can substitute for labor is that it depends on the units of measurement of capital and labor. It is not meaningful to compare the marginal rates of substitution from two industries that use different units of measurement. To overcome this problem, the concept of *elasticity of substitution* was introduced. The elasticity of substitution ES is defined as

$$\text{ES} = \frac{d \ln(l / k)}{d \ln(\text{MRS})} \tag{22.3.4}$$

When a small change in the slope (the MRS) is associated with a large change in the labor–capital ratio (l/k), the isoquant is flat, as in Figure 22.3a, and a large degree of substitution is possible; the value of ES is large. When a large change in the slope is associated with a small change in the labor–capital ratio, the isoquant is well-rounded, as in Figure 22.3b, and little substitution is possible; the value of ES is small. In general $0 < ES < \infty$, and it does not depend on the units of measurement of capital and labor.

To find the elasticity of substitution of the Cobb–Douglas production function, we take logarithms of both sides of equation 22.3.3 and rearrange it to obtain

$$\ln(l/k) = -\ln(\beta_3/\beta_2) + \ln(\text{MRS})$$

Finding the elasticity of substitution from this equation is like finding the derivative dy/dx in the equation $y = a + x$. It is given by

$$\text{ES} = \frac{d \ln(l/k)}{d \ln(\text{MRS})} = 1 \tag{22.3.5}$$

That is, the elasticity of substitution for the Cobb–Douglas production function is always equal to unity.

This result implies that the Cobb–Douglas production function is quite restrictive; by specifying a Cobb–Douglas production function, we are automatically specifying the rate at which the two inputs capital and labor can substitute for each other to achieve a given level of output. Under many circumstances it would be more satisfying if this question were an empirical one. That is, it would be more appropriate if we could specify a function where we could estimate the elasticity of substitution from the data. The CES production function was developed with these ideas in mind.

22.3.2 Properties of the CES Production Function

The constant elasticity of substitution (CES) production function is a more general function than the Cobb–Douglas. It is specified as

$$y = \alpha\left[\delta l^{-\rho} + (1-\delta)k^{-\rho}\right]^{-\eta/\rho} \tag{22.3.6}$$

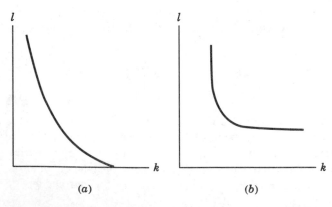

(a) (b)

Figure 23.3 Two isoquants with large and small elasticities of substitution. (a) Flat isoquant, large ES. (b) Well-rounded isoquant, small ES.

The unknown parameters in this function are the efficiency parameter ($\alpha > 0$), the returns to scale parameter ($\eta > 0$), the substitution parameter ($\rho > -1$), and the distribution parameter ($0 < \delta < 1$) that relates the share of output to the two inputs. Let us give the marginal products, the marginal rate of substitution, and the elasticity of substitution, for this function. We will also see how the elasticity of substitution is related to the substitution parameter ρ and indicate how the Cobb–Douglas can be viewed as a special case of the CES production function. Only results will be given. Proofs are left as an exercise (Exercise 22.3).

The marginal products for the CES production function are given by

$$\text{MP}_l = \frac{\partial y}{\partial l} = \eta \alpha^{-\rho/\eta} \delta l^{-(1+\rho)} y^{(1+\rho/\eta)} \tag{22.3.7}$$

$$\text{MP}_k = \frac{\partial y}{\partial k} = \eta \alpha^{-\rho/\eta} (1-\delta) k^{-(1+\rho)} y^{(1+\rho/\eta)} \tag{22.3.8}$$

Taking the ratio of these marginal products to get the marginal rate of substitution we obtain

$$\text{MRS} = \frac{\partial y / \partial k}{\partial y / \partial l} = \frac{1-\delta}{\delta}\left(\frac{l}{k}\right)^{1+\rho} \tag{22.3.9}$$

Taking logarithms of both sides of this equation, rearranging and differentiating gives, for the elasticity of substitution,

$$\text{ES} = \frac{d\ln(l/k)}{d\ln(\text{MRS})} = \frac{1}{1+\rho} \tag{22.3.10}$$

Thus, for the CES production function, the elasticity of substitution depends on the unknown parameter ρ. By estimating ρ we are letting the data suggest a value for the elasticity of substitution. This result is in contrast to that for the Cobb–Douglas production function where the elasticity of substitution is always equal to unity. Note that

$$\text{ES} \rightarrow 0 \text{ as } \rho \rightarrow \infty$$
$$\text{ES} = 1 \text{ when } \rho = 0$$
$$\text{ES} \rightarrow \infty \text{ as } \rho \rightarrow -1$$

Thus, the larger the value of ρ, the smaller the elasticity of substitution. Also, using a limiting process, it can be shown that as $\rho \rightarrow 0$, the CES production function approaches a Cobb–Douglas production function with elasticity of substitution equal to unity. In this sense the Cobb–Douglas function can be viewed as a special case of the CES function, and we can test the adequacy of the Cobb–Douglas function by testing whether ρ is significantly different from zero.

22.3.3   Statistical Model and Data

To turn the economic model in equation 22.3.6 into a statistical model, we denote the tth observation on output, labor, and capital by adding a subscript t to those variables, and we also include a random error term e_t. For the Cobb–Douglas function in Chapter 11, the random error was included so that, after taking logarithms, it appeared additively. Following that same practice here, we write the statistical model as

$$y_t = \alpha \left[\delta l_t^{-\rho} + (1-\delta) k_t^{-\rho} \right]^{-\eta/\rho} \exp\{e_t\} \tag{22.3.11}$$

Taking logarithms yields

$$\ln y_t = \beta - \frac{\eta}{\rho}\ln\left[\delta l_t^{-\rho} + (1-\delta)k_t^{-\rho}\right] + e_t \tag{22.3.12}$$

where $\beta = \ln \alpha$. We assume the e_t are independent identically distributed random variables with zero mean and constant variance σ^2.

Thirty cross-sectional observations on firms in a manufacturing industry appear in Table 22.4. We now consider the problem of using these data to estimate the unknown parameters β, η, ρ and δ.

22.3.4   Estimation of the CES Production Function

To find least squares estimates of the parameters β, η, ρ, and δ, we find the values of those parameters that minimize

$$S(\beta, \eta, \rho, \delta) = \sum_{t=1}^{T} e_t^2 = \sum_{t=1}^{T}\left\{\ln y_t - \beta + \frac{\eta}{\rho}\ln\left[\delta l_t^{-\rho} + (1-\delta)k_t^{-\rho}\right]\right\}^2 \tag{22.3.13}$$

Table 22.4 Data for CES
Production Function Example

l_t	k_t	y_t
.228	.802	.256918
.258	.249	.183599
.821	.771	1.212883
.767	.511	.522568
.495	.758	.847894
.487	.425	.763379
.678	.452	.623130
.748	.817	1.031485
.727	.845	.569498
.695	.958	.882497
.458	.084	.108827
.981	.021	.026437
.002	.295	.003750
.429	.277	.461626
.231	.546	.268474
.664	.129	.186747
.631	.017	.020671
.059	.906	.100159
.811	.223	.252334
.758	.145	.103312
.050	.161	.078945
.823	.006	.005799
.483	.836	.723250
.682	.521	.776468
.116	.930	.216536
.440	.495	.541182
.456	.185	.316320
.342	.092	.123811
.358	.485	.386354
.162	.934	.279431

If we take partial derivatives of this sum of squares function with respect to each of the unknown parameters, and set these partial derivatives equal to zero, we obtain a set of four equations in the four unknown parameters. See Exercise 22.7. The least squares estimates will be a solution to this set of equations. Unfortunately, the four equations turn out to be very nonlinear and cannot be readily solved. As a consequence, we use a multiparameter equivalent of the nonlinear least squares procedure described in Section 22.2. The nonlinear least squares estimates are found by starting with a set of initial parameter values and by continually changing these values so as to decrease the function in equation 22.3.13 until the minimum is reached. Standard errors are found by estimating the error variance and by measuring the rates of change of the slope of the function at its minimum. The results we obtain are

$$\hat{\beta} = 0.1245 \qquad \hat{\eta} = 1.0126 \qquad \hat{\rho} = 3.0109 \qquad \hat{\delta} = 0.3367$$

$$\text{s.e.}\left(\hat{\beta}\right) = 0.0692 \quad \text{s.e.}\left(\hat{\eta}\right) = 0.0459 \quad \text{s.e.}\left(\hat{\rho}\right) = 2.0165 \quad \text{s.e.}\left(\hat{\delta}\right) = 0.0988$$

$$\hat{\sigma}^2 = 0.0587$$

The estimate of η is close to unity, suggesting that the industry may be operating at constant returns to scale. From the estimate of ρ, an estimate of the elasticity of substitution can be found as

$$\hat{ES} = \frac{1}{1+\hat{\rho}} = \frac{1}{1+3.0109} = 0.249$$

This value is quite a bit different from unity, suggesting that the Cobb–Douglas production function would not be an adequate specification. However, when we take into account the uncertainty associated with estimation of ρ, as reflected by its standard error, we find that $\hat{\rho}$ is not significantly different from zero. Specifically, for testing H_0: $\rho = 0$ against the alternative H_1: $\rho \neq 0$, we compute

$$z = \frac{3.0109}{2.0165} = 1.493$$

Using a 5% significance level, we compare this value with the critical value 1.96 from the standard normal distribution. Since $-1.96 < 1.493 < 1.96$, we do not have sufficient evidence to reject H_0. There is not sufficient evidence from the data to suggest that the Cobb–Douglas function is inadequate.

Other tests of hypotheses for other coefficients can be performed in a similar manner. For example, to test an hypothesis about η, we use the approximate result that

$$\frac{\hat{\eta}-\eta}{\text{s.e.}\left(\hat{\eta}\right)} \sim N(0,1) \tag{22.3.14}$$

Similarly, if **b** represents the nonlinear least squares estimator for all coefficients, and β is the corresponding vector of unknown parameters, then a general linear hypothesis of the form $R\beta = \mathbf{r}$, which was developed in Chapter 10, can be tested using the statistic

$$\lambda = (R\mathbf{b}-\mathbf{r})'\left[\hat{\text{cov}}(R\mathbf{b})\right]^{-1}(R\mathbf{b}-\mathbf{r}) \sim \chi^2_{(J)} \tag{22.3.15}$$

where J is the row dimension of R. As an alternative to this approximate chi-square test, the F-statistic that is computed from restricted and unrestricted sums of squared errors and that was defined in Section 11.6.2 of Chapter 11 can also be used. In this case the associated F-test is only an approximate large sample one, but it can be used for testing nonlinear as well as linear hypotheses about β. See Exercise 22.6 for an example.

22.4   Summary

Many economic models that we encounter are nonlinear in the unknown parameters. Under these circumstances it is no longer possible to derive a formula for the least squares estimator. The equations that are obtained by setting the first-order partial derivatives of the error sum-of-squares function equal to zero are too difficult to solve. We can overcome this problem, however, by using a computer algorithm that numerically searches the sum-of-squares function, in an efficient, organized way, until the minimum is found. The point at which the error sum-of-squares function is a minimum is the nonlinear least squares estimate. An approximate covariance matrix for the nonlinear least squares estimator can be found from the rate of change of the sum-of-squares function at its minimum. It is not always straightforward to obtain nonlinear least squares estimates. Sometimes computer algorithms do not converge. Sometimes they converge to local minima instead of the global minimum. These difficulties can often be reduced by using different initial values for the minimization process.

As an example of a model that is nonlinear in the parameters, we used the CES production function. Two other examples, a first-order moving-average process, and a geometric lag (adaptive expectations) model appear in Appendix 22A. There are, of course, many other models where nonlinearities in the parameters exist.

22.5   Exercises

22.1 Show that the Gauss–Newton iterations for the example problem in Section 22.2 can be written as

$$\beta_{n+1} = \beta_n + \frac{\displaystyle\sum_{t=1}^{T}\left(x_{t1} + 2\beta_n x_{t2}\right)\left(y_t - \beta_n x_{t1} - \beta_n^2 x_{t2}\right)}{\displaystyle\sum_{t=1}^{T}\left(x_{t1} + 2\beta_n x_{t2}\right)^2}$$

22.2 For the example problem in Section 22.2, show that

$$\frac{d^2 S}{d\beta^2} = 12\beta^2 \Sigma x_{t2}^2 + 12\beta\Sigma x_{t1} x_{t2} + 2\left(\Sigma x_{t1}^2 - 2\Sigma x_{t2} y_t\right)$$

and that when β is replaced by $b = 1.1612$ we obtain

$$\frac{d^2 S}{d\beta^2} = 97.914$$

22.3 Derive the properties of the CES production function that are given in equations 22.3.7–22.3.10.

22.4 Consider the following equation, where the quantity of wool demanded q depends on the price of wool p and the price of synthetics s:

$$q_t = \beta_1 + \frac{\beta_2\left(p_t^\lambda - 1\right)}{\lambda} + \frac{\beta_3\left(s_t^\lambda - 1\right)}{\lambda} + e_t$$

(22.5.1)

where β_1, β_2, β_3, and λ are unknown parameters and e_t is an independent identically distributed random error with mean zero and variance σ^2.

(a) Find, in terms of the unknown parameters, the elasticity of demand for wool with respect to
  (i) its own price
  (ii) the price of synthetics.

(b) Show that equation 22.5.1 is
  (i) a linear function of p and s if $\lambda = 1$,
  (ii) a linear function of $\ln p$ and $\ln s$ if $\lambda = 0$.
  [*Hint:* Use L'Hôpital's rule to show that $\lim_{\lambda \to 0}\left[\left(z^\lambda - 1\right)/\lambda\right] = \ln z$.]

(c) Use the 45 observations given in Table 22.5 and nonlinear least squares to estimate the unknown parameters. Find corresponding elasticity estimates at the means of the sample data. Comment.

(d) Test the hypotheses
  (i) $\lambda = 0$
  (ii) $\lambda = 1$
  What is the relevance of these tests?

(e) Test the hypothesis that $\beta_2 = -\beta_3$.

22.5 Use nonlinear least squares and the data in Table 22.6 to estimate a CES production function.

(a) Test for constant returns to scale.
(b) Test whether a Cobb–Douglas production function would be adequate.
(c) Predict the level of output for $k = l = 10$.
(d) Find the marginal products of labor and capital, and the marginal rate of substitution for $k = l = 10$.

22.6 Consider the following consumption function where consumption c_t depends on income y_t through the model:

$$c_t = \beta_1 + \beta_2 y_t + e_t$$
$$e_t = \theta_1 e_{t-1} + \theta_2 e_{t-2} + v_t$$

where the v_t are independent identically distributed random errors with mean 0 and variance σ_v^2. The error e_t is known as a second-order autoregressive error [or AR(2) error].

(a) Show that the model can also be written as

$$c_t = \beta_1(1 - \theta_1 - \theta_2) + \theta_1 c_{t-1} + \theta_2 c_{t-2} + \beta_2 y_t - \beta_2 \theta_1 y_{t-1} - \beta_2 \theta_2 y_{t-2} + v_t$$

(b) Use the 38 observations that appear in Table 22.7 and nonlinear least squares to estimate β_1, β_2, θ_1, and θ_2.

(c) Test the hypothesis that the marginal propensity to consume equals 0.85 against the alternative that it does not.

(d) Test whether an AR(1) error model would have been adequate.

(e) Use the last 36 observations and linear least squares to estimate β_1 and β_2 under the assumption that the e_t are independent and identically distributed random errors with zero mean and variance σ_e^2.

Table 22.5 Wool Demand Data for Exercise 22.4

q	p	s
580	184	230
690	116	154
460	228	220
340	281	219
221	286	120
791	106	233
651	133	159
239	304	164
182	334	173
353	260	181
74	348	104
233	305	155
196	309	140
279	294	184
325	303	243
169	337	162
727	108	166
500	190	162
167	362	230
178	363	216
609	176	242
167	377	247
296	309	230
123	358	165
80	357	129
148	350	171
694	139	225
174	328	157
601	130	121
411	262	248
530	182	174
205	324	172
668	145	227
377	253	188
539	148	105
355	253	168
183	363	231
26	381	121
563	146	119
601	140	142
628	162	226
572	149	137
67	398	184
641	141	178
570	169	184

Table 22.6 Production Function Data for Exercise 22.5

l	k	q
23.81	11.33	22.76
75.83	25.92	76.73
9.46	7.03	8.62
5.71	29.68	10.98
85.78	21.81	86.77
0.37	0.57	0.97
8.82	11.25	11.82
8.99	19.01	16.63
37.65	75.25	67.40
8.43	8.40	8.81
16.10	30.30	21.54
0.64	1.20	1.34
5.28	6.93	12.38
30.40	70.18	58.37
33.66	21.06	29.90
15.72	11.86	14.54
8.44	14.53	17.54
30.20	34.20	29.43
8.89	8.68	11.41
5.14	2.84	5.45

Table 22.7 Consumption Function Data for
Exercise 22.6

t	c_t	y_t	t	c_t	y_t
1	25.00	31.61	20	38.72	49.52
2	28.00	28.67	21	31.44	46.45
3	30.42	27.67	22	46.91	50.87
4	47.96	42.28	23	49.29	49.72
5	28.24	28.83	24	62.03	66.47
6	30.88	42.31	25	56.10	53.66
7	27.43	36.54	26	64.75	57.76
8	33.73	36.67	27	57.47	53.67
9	39.38	37.30	28	60.16	62.66
10	43.07	40.94	29	47.48	60.74
11	46.70	44.30	30	46.48	56.61
12	24.33	43.06	31	60.19	62.21
13	21.12	34.49	32	56.64	62.33
14	34.75	32.11	33	56.31	63.73
15	52.44	46.53	34	52.12	65.29
16	57.22	52.08	35	41.14	57.76
17	52.52	48.07	36	58.20	66.48
18	49.45	47.49	37	69.06	68.98
19	51.37	51.58	38	75.85	65.49

(f) Use an F-test and the sums of squared errors in parts (b) and (e) to test the null hypothesis H_0: $\theta_1 = \theta_2 = 0$.

(g) Use linear least squares to estimate the πs in the equation

$$c_t = \pi_1 + \pi_2 c_{t-1} + \pi_3 c_{t-2} + \pi_4 y_t + \pi_5 y_{t-1} + \pi_6 y_{t-2} + e_t$$

What restrictions on the πs will give a model that is equivalent to that in part (a)? Use an F-test to test the validity of these restrictions.

22.7 Differentiate the sum of squares function in equation 22.3.13 with respect to β, η, ρ, and δ. Show that the equations that result from setting these derivatives equal to zero are nonlinear in β, η, ρ, and δ.

22.8 An important ingredient underlying firm cost theory is the learning curve. The idea behind the learning curve is that, as more items are produced, workers become more experienced, and the average cost of production falls. If AC_X represents the average cost of producing X items, then one learning curve model is

$$AC_X = \gamma X^\delta$$

where γ and δ are unknown parameters. The total cost of producing X items is

$$TC_X = X \cdot AC_X = \gamma X^{\delta+1}$$

For estimation of γ and δ, cost data usually takes the form of the time taken to produce a given *lot* of items. To accommodate this type of data let

c_i = time taken to produce the ith lot,

x_i = number of items produced in the ith lot, and

$X_i = \Sigma_{j=1}^{i} x_j$ = total number of items produced after i lots have been completed.

Then,

$$c_i = TC_{X_i} - TC_{X_{i-1}} = \gamma X_i^{\delta+1} - \gamma X_{i-1}^{\delta+1}$$

Converting this equation into a statistical model to which we can apply nonlinear least squares, we have

$$c_i = \gamma \left[X_i^{\delta+1} - X_{i-1}^{\delta+1} \right] + e_i$$

Tables 22.8 to 22.10 report relevant data taken from N. K. Warner and J. Wayne Patterson (1983). These data relate to production of aircraft parts (Table 22.8), doffing of spinning frames in the yarn industry (Table 22.9), and output in the printing industry (Table 22.10).

(a) (i) Use the aircraft data to estimate γ and δ.
   (ii) Compare predicted average cost (in terms of thousands of hours) after producing 50, 100, 150, and 200 units.
(b) (i) Use the yarn industry data to estimate γ and δ.
   (ii) Graph the average cost learning curve.
   (iii) Reestimate the model assuming the errors follow an AR(1) process.
   (iv) Compare and comment on 95% interval estimates for γ and δ obtained from the results in parts (b)(i) and (b)(iii).
(c) (i) Use the printing industry data to estimate γ and δ.
   (ii) Compare and comment on the rate of change of average cost (in terms of time) after 100, 500, and 1000 units have been produced.
(d) Compare the learning processes that occur in each of the three industries.

22.6   References

Further details about nonlinear least squares can be found in
   JUDGE, G. G., R. C. HILL, W. E. GRIFFITHS, H. LÜTKEPOHL, and T. C. LEE (1988) *Introduction to the Theory and Practice of Econometrics*, 2nd Edition, New York: John Wiley & Sons, Inc., Chapter 12.
   JUDGE, G. G., W. E. GRIFFITHS, R. C. HILL, H. LÜTKEPOHL, and T. C. LEE (1985) *The Theory and Practice of Econometrics*, 2nd Edition, New York: John Wiley & Sons, Inc., Chapter 6 and Appendix B.

Table 22.8   Cost Data for Aircraft Production

Lot (i)	Time (c_i) (thousands of hours)	Units Produced in Each Lot (x_i)	Total Units Produced (X_i)
1	2116	5	5
2	1812	6	11
3	2212	10	21
4	2510	15	36
5	3798	30	66
6	2954	28	94
7	2478	28	122
8	2296	28	150
9	2741	34	184
10	2556	33	217
11	2435	33	250
12	2850	34	284

Table 22.9   Cost Data for Doffing Frames in the Yarn Industry

Lot (i)	Time (c_i) (min.)	Total Frames (X_i)	Lot (i)	Time (c_i) (min.)	Total Frames (X_i)
1	154.8	3	31	167.7	313
2	210.0	9	32	134.1	328
3	107.0	13	33	193.1	346
4	84.9	16	34	177.1	364
5	60.0	19	35	174.1	382
6	45.0	22	36	183.7	401
7	137.0	31	37	175.0	419
8	172.0	43	38	185.4	438
9	186.6	56	39	160.6	456
10	73.0	61	40	146.2	473
11	141.9	72	41	108.7	485
12	110.8	81	42	146.5	501
13	92.4	88	43	55.7	507
14	85.3	95	44	128.2	521
15	97.0	102	45	178.9	542
16	96.5	109	46	174.6	562
17	67.6	115	47	158.0	580
18	125.0	126	48	190.3	602
19	120.5	136	49	150.8	619
20	131.8	148	50	187.5	640
21	139.8	161	51	151.6	657
22	103.2	171	52	190.5	678
23	154.0	185	53	217.0	703
24	159.0	199	54	194.5	725
25	176.0	215	55	194.3	747
26	127.3	226	56	116.6	761
27	173.5	244	57	159.3	779
28	197.4	264	58	203.3	802
29	221.8	284	59	177.5	824
30	132.1	297	60	187.2	847

Table 22.10   Cost Data for Printing Firm

Lot (i)	Time (c_i) (hours)	Output (x_i)	Cumulative Output (X_i)
1	41.56	101	101
2	40.81	103	204
3	31.51	82	286
4	33.77	90	376
5	31.01	84	460
6	44.28	122	582
7	35.91	100	682
8	29.72	85	767
9	29.06	85	852
10	35.19	104	956
11	30.29	90	1046
12	24.71	74	1120

A specialist book on nonlinear estimation is

NASH, J. C., and M. WALKER-SMITH (1987) *Nonlinear Parameter Estimation*, New York: Marcel Dekker Inc.

Further information on learning curves can be found in

WARNER, N. K., and J. WAYNE PATTERSON, "Estimation and Testing of Learning Curves," *Journal of Business and Economic Statistics*, 1, 265–272.

APPENDIX 22A   Estimation of Moving Average Models

22A.1   A Moving Average Process

The CES production function that we considered in Section 22.3 is, of course, just one of many possible examples of nonlinear models that could have been examined. In this appendix we are concerned with estimation of a nonlinear model that arises in time-series analysis, the moving average process. In Chapter 20, the first-order moving average process, or MA(1), was specified as

$$y_t = e_t + \alpha e_{t-1} \tag{22A.1}$$

where the e_t are unobservable independent random errors with mean zero and variance σ^2, α is an unknown parameter, and y_t are observable random variables that are said to follow an MA(1) process. Our problem is to use the T observations $(y_1, y_2, \ldots, y_T)$ to estimate α. Information on α is needed if we wish to forecast future values of y.

What happens if we set out to obtain a *least squares estimate* of α? Recall that we find least squares estimates by finding those values of the parameters that minimize the sum of squares of T independent identically distributed random errors. In this particular case, the e_t are the independent identically distributed random errors. Thus, the least squares principle tells us we should find that value of α that minimizes

$$S(\alpha) = \sum_{t=1}^{T} e_t^2 = \sum_{t=1}^{T} \left(y_t - \alpha e_{t-1} \right)^2 \tag{22A.2}$$

A characteristic of equation 22A.2 that we have not encountered in previous examples is the appearance of the lagged errors on the right side of this equation. Let us examine the consequences of this characteristic.

When finding least squares estimates from an error sum-of-squares function like $S(\alpha)$, we must be able to compute a value for this function for any given set of values of the parameters. We then choose those parameters for which the computed value of the sum-of-squares function is a minimum. Thus, for the MA(1) model, we need to be able to compute $S(\alpha)$ for any given value of α. To compute $S(\alpha)$ we need to be able to compute values for the errors $e_1, e_2, \ldots, e_T$. Note that values of these errors are given by

$$e_1 = y_1 - \alpha e_0$$

$$e_2 = y_2 - \alpha e_1 = y_2 - \alpha y_1 + \alpha^2 e_0$$

$$e_3 = y_3 - \alpha e_2 = y_3 - \alpha y_2 + \alpha^2 y_1 - \alpha^3 e_0$$

$$\vdots$$

$$e_T = y_T - \alpha e_{T-1} = y_T - \alpha y_{T-1} + \alpha^2 y_{T-2} + \ldots - \alpha^{T-1} y_1 + \alpha^T e_0 \tag{22A.3}$$

The signs in the last expression assume that T, the sample size, is an even number. Providing that the presample error e_0 is known or given, it is possible to use the equations 22A.3 to compute each of the $e_1, e_2, \ldots, e_T$ for a given value of α. It then becomes possible to compute $S(\alpha) = \Sigma_{t=1}^{T} e_t^2$ for a given value of α. The easiest way to make the calculations is recursively through the relationship that is given by the first set of equalities in equation 22A.3, namely,

$$e_t = y_t - \alpha e_{t-1} \qquad t = 1, 2, \ldots, T \qquad (22A.4)$$

The right sides of the equations 22A.3 illustrate the highly nonlinear way in which α appears in the calculations. It is the nonlinearity in α that makes this problem a nonlinear least squares one.

Thus, it is possible to compute $S(\alpha)$ for a given value of α and, hence, to find a nonlinear least squares estimate for α, providing we have some way of specifying e_0 to initiate the computations in equation 22A.3. Two approaches to the specification of e_0 are often used. One approach is to simply set $e_0 = 0$, its mean value. The other approach is to treat e_0 as an unknown parameter to be estimated. In this latter case both α and e_0 would be the unknown parameters for which we seek nonlinear least squares estimates.

If the e_t and hence the y_t are normally distributed, then the maximum likelihood principle provides a further method for estimation of α. In this case, it can be shown that the function that is maximized is equivalent to

$$L(\alpha) = -\left(\frac{1 - \alpha^{2T+2}}{1 - \alpha^2}\right)^{1/T} S(\alpha)$$

$$(22A.5)$$

See Judge et al. (1985, p. 301) for details.

22A.1.1   Some Empirical Results

Table 22A.1 contains 50 observations artificially generated from the moving average process

$$y_t = e_t - 0.7e_{t-1} \qquad (22A.6)$$

where $e_t \sim N(0, 1)$. Thus, $\alpha = -0.7$, but in reality the true underlying value of α is unknown and we must use the 50 observations on y_t to estimate it.

Table 22A.1   Fifty Artificially Generated Observations on a MA(1) Process

t	y_t	t	y_t	t	y_t	t	y_t
1	0.7952	14	-0.2190	27	1.1328	40	-0.3676
2	-1.3608	15	1.3207	28	-0.7450	41	0.9614
3	0.1879	16	-0.1733	29	0.9094	42	-0.8113
4	0.5588	17	-1.0408	30	-0.2014	43	-0.0302
5	-0.4941	18	0.8710	31	-0.8137	44	-0.2626
6	0.8917	19	1.3849	32	0.5080	45	-0.0951
7	-0.1328	20	-1.8708	33	-0.7009	46	-0.7859
8	-0.5121	21	1.2562	34	1.4931	47	0.7503
9	1.3496	22	-1.0840	35	-0.4453	48	-1.6776
10	-1.5235	23	-0.5215	36	-0.1492	49	-0.4252
11	1.1426	24	-0.9199	37	0.8779	50	1.9604
12	-0.6834	25	1.4652	38	0.1348		
13	0.5006	26	-1.9822	39	0.6418		

Table 22A.2   Results from Three Different Estimators for α

	$\hat{\alpha}$	s.e.$(\hat{\alpha})$	$\hat{\sigma}^2$
Nonlinear least squares, $e_0 = 0$	− 0.5749	0.1018	0.6321
Nonlinear least squares, e_0 estimated	− 0.5733	0.1042	0.6312
Maximum likelihood	− 0.5741	0.1153	0.6316

The two nonlinear least squares estimators and the maximum likelihood estimator were used to estimate α. The results from using these three estimators are given in Table 22A.2. All three methods produce similar results. The estimate $\hat{\alpha} = -0.57$ is somewhat lower than the true value of $\alpha = -0.7$ but, in all cases, a 95% confidence interval for α would include the true value of $\alpha = -0.7$.

22A.2 Nonlinear Least Squares Estimation of the Geometric Lag Model

In Chapter 21 we considered the geometric lag model that was given by (see equation 21.3.5)

$$y_t = \delta + \beta(1 - \lambda)(x_t + \lambda x_{t-1} + \lambda^2 x_{t-2} + \ldots) + e_t \qquad (22A.7)$$

where δ, β, and $0 < \lambda < 1$ are unknown parameters that we wish to estimate and the e_t are independent and identically distributed random variables with zero mean and variance σ^2. With reference to Chapter 14, it was pointed out that least squares estimation of a transformed version of equation 22A.7 that involved y_{t-1} as a random regressor would lead to biased and inconsistent estimates of the unknown parameters, and that one way of obtaining consistent estimates is to use instrumental variable estimation. In this section we explore how the nonlinear least squares technique can be used to obtain consistent estimates. We use a transformed equation that has y_{t-1} as a regressor and a moving-average error term.

In Chapter 21, equation 21.3.11, we showed that the geometric lag model in equation 22A.7 can be written alternatively as

$$\begin{aligned} y_t &= \delta(1 - \lambda) + \lambda y_{t-1} + \beta(1 - \lambda)x_t + e_t - \lambda e_{t-1} \\ &= \delta_0 + \lambda y_{t-1} + \delta_1 x_t + v_t \end{aligned} \qquad (22A.8)$$

where $\delta_0 = \delta(1 - \lambda)$, $\delta_1 = \beta(1 - \lambda)$, and $v_t = e_t - \lambda e_{t-1}$. When written in this way, the model no longer contains an infinite series of lagged xs, but it does contain a first-order moving-average error term with a parameter λ that is identical to the coefficient of y_{t-1}. For estimation we can follow a procedure similar to that prescribed in the previous section for estimation of the MA(1) model. Specifically, we can use a nonlinear least squares algorithm to find the values of δ_0, δ_1, and λ that minimize the sum of squares function

$$S(\delta_0, \delta_1, \lambda) = \sum_{t=2}^{T} e_t^2 = \sum_{t=2}^{T} [y_t - \delta_0 - \lambda y_{t-1} - \delta_1 x_t + \lambda e_{t-1}]^2 \qquad (22A.9)$$

Because y_{t-1} appears on the right-hand side, and because y_1 is the first available observation, the summation in this expression begins at 2. Also, providing the first error e_1

is specified so as to initiate the procedure, for a given set of parameters each e_t can be calculated recursively from

$$e_t = y_t - \delta_0 - \lambda y_{t-1} - \delta_1 x_t + \lambda e_{t-1} \qquad (22A.10)$$

As with the MA(1) process, we can "specify" e_1 by treating it as an unknown parameter to be estimated or by setting it equal to zero. Equations 22A.8 and 22A.10 might, at first glance, appear to be linear in the unknown parameters. However, as with the MA(1) model, nonlinearities become evident if equation 22A.10 is repeatedly lagged and e_{t-1}, e_{t-2}, etc., are substituted out of the expression.

Chapter 23

Models with Discrete Dependent Variables

New Key Words and Concepts

Random Utility Models   Choice Probability Models
Likelihood Function   Logit
Probit   Numerical Optimization
Wald Test Statistic   Likelihood Ratio Test

Individuals, firms, and governments must make *choices* about what, how, and for whom. For example, within a market economy individuals and households must choose *how much* of alternative goods to purchase; firms must choose *how much* of alternative resources to employ and *how much* of alternative outputs to produce. Such choices of "how much" usually involve quantities that are continuous variables, and throughout the book we have focused on economic and statistical models to explain economic outcome variables that are *continuous* in nature.

Many choices, however, are *discrete* in nature, and involve "either–or" situations, in which one alternative or another must be chosen. For example, we face questions like the following: Why do some high school graduates decide to attend college and others not? Why do some married women enter the labor force and others not? Why did some states in the United States pass the equal rights amendment and others not? Why do some individuals drive themselves to work while others take public transportation? In each of these situations a decision maker must choose between two alternatives. In this chapter, to reflect this type of situation, we specify and analyze economic and statistical models where the outcome or dependent variable y_i is a dummy variable that takes the value 1 if one choice is made and 0 if the other is chosen. These specialized economic and statistical models for explaining discrete outcomes lead us to new estimation and inference techniques that are appropriate for describing discrete choice behavior.

23.1 The Economic Model

Consider an individual decision maker, faced with choosing between two alternatives. If we assume that the individual derives a certain amount of *utility* from each of the outcomes, then it follows that the individual will choose the alternative that provides the greater utility. So that we may be specific, let us focus on the example of an individual i who must choose to drive to work (alternative 1) or take public transportation (alternative 0). For any individual we can *observe* the alternative chosen and define a discrete (dummy) economic variable y as the outcome,

$$y_i = \begin{cases} 1 & \text{if individual } i \text{ drives to work} \\ 0 & \text{if individual } i \text{ choses public transportation} \end{cases} \qquad (23.1.1)$$

Since we assume that in their choices individuals act to maximize their utility, alternative 1 will be chosen if driving yields the individual more utility than taking public transportation. That is, if

U_{i1} = utility that individual i derives from driving to work

U_{i0} = utility that individual i derives from taking public transportation to work

then,

$$y_i = \begin{cases} 1 & \text{if } U_{i1} \geq U_{i0} \\ 0 & \text{if } U_{i0} > U_{i1} \end{cases} \qquad (23.1.2)$$

where we have given the "tie" to alternative 1.

As economists we want to understand, explain, and predict the choices that are made. To do so we create an economic model of the utility derived from the choice of each alternative. We may, in general, think of the utility derived from the selection of alternative j ($j = 1$ or 0) by individual i ($i = 1,\dots, T$) as a function of *(i)* the attributes (e.g., cost, convenience, quality) of that alternative to the individual, and *(ii)* the characteristics (e.g., income, educational attainment, profession) of the individual.

For example, the utility received by an individual from driving to work depends on, among other things, the time that the commute takes. When choosing between driving and using public transportation the *difference* in time spent commuting via the alternatives is a key factor. If each mode of transportation requires the *same* commuting time, then the time factor alone provides no basis for choice. Let us define

x_i = (commuting time for the ith individual via public transportation) −
(commuting time for the ith individual via auto)

If $x_i > 0$, then using public transportation takes more time than driving and, other things held constant, the opportunity cost of using public transportation is greater than the opportunity cost of driving. The greater the value of x_i, the greater the relative cost of using public transportation, and thus the more likely an individual is to drive.

Of course, many other economic factors affect the choice of mode of transportation, such as the price of public transportation, the price of gasoline, the price of parking, and so on. The logic behind the potential importance of, and thus including, these and other variables is clear. In the next section, however, for expository purposes, we will focus only on the explanatory factor x_i, the difference in commuting time, and build a statistical model that relates the choice of transportation mode to the magnitude of x_i.

23.2   The Statistical Model

Building a statistical model that is consistent with the discrete choice data-generation process begins with recognizing that the observable choice variable y_i in equation 23.1.1, is a *discrete random variable*. The outcome of the choice is random, since we cannot predict with *certainty* the choice that a randomly selected individual will make. These choices depend on both observable and unobservable characteristics of the individual *and* the alternatives that are available to the individual. The probability density function for a discrete random variable, like y_i in equation 23.1.1, is discussed in Section 2.4.2 of Chapter 2 and is the basis of a statistical model of choice. Let P_i be the probability that individual i chooses alternative 1 (driving) and $(1 - P_i)$ be the probability that alternative 0 (public transportation) is chosen. In this choice situation the probability density function of y_i is

$$g(y_i) = P_i^{y_i} \left(1 - P_i\right)^{1-y_i} \qquad y_i = 1, 0 \qquad (23.2.1)$$

For the discrete random variable y_i, the resulting probability density function yields the *probability* of each of the alternatives. Therefore, given equation 23.2.1 the probability of driving is

$$g(1) = P[y_i = 1] = P_i \qquad (23.2.2a)$$

and the probability of taking public transportation is

$$g(0) = P[y_i = 0] = 1 - P_i \qquad (23.2.2b)$$

The mean and variance of the discrete random variable y_i (see Exercise 2.9 in Chapter 2) are

$$E[y_i] = P_i \qquad (23.2.3a)$$

$$\text{var}(y_i) = P_i(1 - P_i) \qquad (23.2.3b)$$

The probability distribution of y_i is completely determined by P_i, which is the probability of the individual choosing alternative 1, and which is also the expected value of y_i. As economists we are interested in "explaining" the variation in y_i. To do so we "explain" the choice probability P_i (the probability that individual i chooses alternative 1), by relating it to characteristics of alternatives facing an individual and the characteristics of the individual. For example, we have indicated that the probability of driving a car to work, P_i, will depend on factors such as the time difference between driving and public transportation and the opportunity cost of time for the individual. Several statistical models may be used to relate the choice probability P_i to various explanatory variables. In this chapter we present the *linear probability model*, the *probit model*, and the *logit model*.

As we noted in Section 23.1, the statistical models we present have an intimate relationship to economic *utility theory*. The link between the models we present and the underlying economic principles is developed more completely in Appendix 23A.

23.3   The Linear Probability Model

Consistent with the way in which we have modeled continuous outcome variables, the linear probability model treats the task of modeling the variation of the random variable y_i as a regression problem. Specifically, we assume that y_i consists of a systematic component $E[y_i] = P_i$ and a random component e_i that has mean $E[e_i] = 0$. Consequently

$$y_i = E[y_i] + e_i \qquad (23.3.1)$$

Furthermore, just as we did in Chapters 5 to 11, we assume that the systematic component $E[y_i] = P_i$ is a linear (in the parameters) function of a set of explanatory variables, including an intercept. Thus, we write

$$E[y_i] = P_i = \beta_1 + \beta_2 x_{i2} + \ldots + \beta_K x_{iK} \qquad (23.3.2)$$

This allows us to use a linear model to relate the *probability* that y_i takes the value 1 to a set of economic factors that reflect the characteristics of the alternatives available to the individual and the characteristics of the individual decision maker. This is the heart of the logic underlying the linear probability model.

Substituting equation 23.3.2 into equation 23.3.1 we have

$$y_i = \beta_1 + \beta_2 x_{i2} + \ldots + \beta_K x_{iK} + e_i \qquad (23.3.3)$$

which is the *linear probability statistical model* for the discrete random variable y_i.

The linear probability model, which follows from our experience and is reassuringly familiar, is flawed as a statistical model for discrete choice behavior. First, although we may assume that the random errors e_i have a zero mean, we obviously cannot assume that they are normal. Since y_i is discrete, the errors $e_i = y_i - P_i$ are discrete as well. Furthermore, the variance of e_i is

$$\text{var}(e_i) = \text{var}(y_i) = P_i(1 - P_i) \qquad (23.3.4)$$

which is *not* a constant (like σ^2) for all individuals. The variance of each random error depends on the choice probability P_i for the ith individual, which *varies* across individuals, as shown by equation 23.3.2. In Chapter 15 we learned that when error variances differ over observations, the problem of heteroskedasticity exists, and the least squares estimation rule is no longer best linear unbiased. In Exercise 23.1 you are asked to construct a feasible generalized least squares estimator for this model.

The fact that the least squares estimator for the linear probability model is not best linear unbiased is *not* the model's most serious flaw. Another flaw with the linear probability model is that by representing the choice probability P_i as a function like equation 23.3.2 that is *linear in the parameters*, when the explanatory variables x_{ik} vary, there is *nothing to keep the probability P_i in the* [0, 1] *interval*.

To make this flaw clear, let us continue with the example suggested previously in the chapter. Let the discrete random variable y_i reflect the choice between driving to work ($y_i = 1$) and using public transportation ($y_i = 0$), and let x_i be the time difference between commuting via public transportation and driving. The primary linear probability model assumption is that

$$E[y_i] = P_i = \beta_1 + \beta_2 x_i \qquad (23.3.5)$$

As x_i increases, the opportunity cost of using public transportation rises relative to that of driving, and we expect an increase in the probability of an individual choosing to drive. Consequently, we expect that the parameter β_2 is positive. The intercept parameter β_1 is the probability that an individual drives when there is no time difference between the two modes of transportation. Thus, β_1 must lie in the [0, 1] interval and reflects attitudes about driving and public transportation that are independent of time and other cost factors. It may be described as a "taste" factor. In Figure 23.1 we depict the linear probability model 23.3.5. Each value of x_i corresponds to a different probability P_i. When $x_i = x_1$, the probability that $y_i = 1$ is P_1. Since x_i is unbounded, and since there are no constraints on the parameters β_1 and β_2, there are ranges of the explanatory variable x_i where the probability P_i is outside the [0, 1] interval. If $x_i = x_2$ then $P[y_i = 1] = P_2 > 1$. *A probability measure greater than one is clearly not satisfactory* and, as a consequence, the linear probability model, even when correctly estimated via generalized least squares, is generally not recommended for use in practice.

The problem with this probability model is that it is *linear* in the parameters. In the

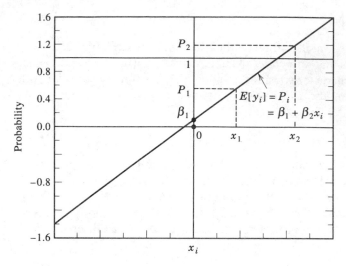

Figure 23.1 The linear probability model.

next section we present the *probit statistical model*, which is a statistical model for discrete choice that is *not* linear in the parameters and does not result in choice probabilities that fall outside the [0, 1] interval.

23.4   The Probit Statistical Model for Discrete Choice

The probit model is a *nonlinear* (in the parameters) statistical model that achieves the objective of relating the choice probability P_i to explanatory factors in such a way that the probability remains in the [0, 1] interval. To develop the probit model for a discrete choice, as in equation 23.1.1, let us define the "utility index" I_i for the ith individual as

$$I_i = \beta_1 + \beta_2 x_{i2} + \ldots + \beta_K x_{iK} \tag{23.4.1a}$$

By using vector notation to let $\beta = (\beta_1, \beta_2, \ldots, \beta_K)'$ and $\mathbf{x}_i' = \begin{pmatrix} 1 & x_{i2} \ldots x_{iK} \end{pmatrix}$, the utility index is

$$I_i = \mathbf{x}_i'\beta \tag{23.4.1b}$$

As the value of the explanatory variables x_{ik} change, the value of the index I_i varies over the real number line. The larger the value of I_i, the greater the utility individual i receives from choosing the option $y_i = 1$. Thus, the greater the value of I_i, the greater will be P_i, the probability that individual i chooses the option where $y_i = 1$. To capture this type of relationship between I_i and P_i, we need a function that depicts how the probability P_i varies between zero and one as I_i varies between $-\infty$ and $+\infty$ *and* that is strictly increasing, or *monotonic*.

As an example, consider the driving versus public transportation choice, in which the utility index is

$$I_i = \beta_1 + \beta_2 x_i \tag{23.4.2}$$

Since we assume that $\beta_2 > 0$, as the difference x_i between commuting time via public transportation and driving time increases, so does the utility index I_i. The larger the value of the index, the greater the probability that an individual will choose to drive. Thus the utility index measures an individual's "propensity" to drive. However, the index I_i that measures the propensity to drive can lie between $-\infty$ and $+\infty$, while the probability of driving must lie between zero and one. The cumulative distribution function is a probability transformation of I_i that achieves our objectives of keeping P_i between zero and one and yields a monotonic relationship between the utility index I_i and P_i. One specification, which is called a *probit model*, represents the choice probability P_i as

$$P_i = F\left(I_i\right) = F\left(\beta_1 + \beta_2 x_{i2} + \ldots + \beta_K x_{iK}\right) = F\left(\mathbf{x}_i'\boldsymbol{\beta}\right) \qquad (23.4.3)$$

where $F(I_i)$ is the cumulative distribution function of the standard normal $N(0, 1)$ random variable evaluated at I_i. The cumulative distribution function is given by

$$P_i = F\left(I_i\right) = P\left[z \le I_i\right] = \int_{-\infty}^{I_i} (2\pi)^{-1/2} e^{-z^2/2} dz \qquad (23.4.4)$$

where z is a standard normal random variable. An *economic* rationale for choosing the normal cumulative distribution function transformation is developed in the appendix to this chapter. Note that with this probability model, the probability P_i that $y_i = 1$ varies between zero and one, since it is the probability that the standard normal random variable z is less than or equal to $I_i = \mathbf{x}_i'\boldsymbol{\beta}$. As the utility index I_i increases from $-\infty$ to $+\infty$, the probability P_i that $y_i = 1$ increases monotonically, as we desire. Building on this base, let us examine the probit model in greater detail.

23.4.1 Interpreting the Probit Model

Since the cumulative distribution function $F(\cdot)$ is nondecreasing, the probit choice probability model in equation 23.4.3 is consistent with the intuitive principle that the larger the utility index (an index of how much alternative 1 is "better" than the alternative 0), the larger the probability that alternative 1 will be chosen.

In Figure 23.2a we depict the cumulative distribution function $F(I)$ of the standard normal random variable and the associated probabilities as given by the probit choice probability model 23.4.3. The horizontal axis of the figure is the utility index I and the vertical axis is the probability P_i that alternative 1 is chosen. For example, if the utility index of an individual is given by the value I_i in Figure 23.2a, then the corresponding probability of choosing alternative 1 is given by $P_i = F(I_i)$ as shown. When the utility index $I_i = 0$ then the probability $P_i = .5$, indicating that the alternatives are equally likely to be chosen. As the value of the utility index increases, the probability that an individual chooses alternative 1 increases. The increases in the probability are not constant, however, for equal increases in the utility index. Examine the increase in the probability of choosing alternative 1 for two equal increases in the utility index in Figure 23.2a. When the utility index increases from I_1 to I_2, and then from I_3 to I_4, the increase in probability $P_4 - P_3$ is smaller than the increase $P_2 - P_1$.

To understand why this is so we must consider the choice probability P_i in greater detail. In the probability model 23.4.3 the parameters β_k relate the changes in the explanatory variables x_k, which represent characteristics of the alternatives and the individual decision maker, to changes in the probability of alternative 1 being chosen. Specifically, using the "chain-rule" from calculus (see Appendix 8A of Chapter 8), the rate of change in the probability that alternative 1 is chosen, given a change in the kth explanatory variable is

$$\frac{\partial P_i}{\partial x_{ik}} = \frac{\partial F(\mathbf{x}_i'\boldsymbol{\beta})}{\partial x_{ik}} = F'(\mathbf{x}_i'\boldsymbol{\beta})\frac{\partial(\mathbf{x}_i'\boldsymbol{\beta})}{\partial x_{ik}} = f(\mathbf{x}_i'\boldsymbol{\beta})\beta_k \tag{23.4.5}$$

where $f(\mathbf{x}_i'\boldsymbol{\beta})$ is the standard normal probability density function evaluated at the point $I_i = \mathbf{x}_i'\boldsymbol{\beta}$ (depicted in Figure 23.2b) and β_k is the kth parameter in the vector $\boldsymbol{\beta}$.

In the probit model, unlike the usual linear statistical models that we have considered (including the linear probability model), the parameter value β_k is *not* directly interpretable as the effect of a change in an explanatory variable on the mean, or expected value, of the dependent variable. From equation 23.4.5 we observe that:

1. Since the value of the probability density function $f(\mathbf{x}_i'\boldsymbol{\beta})$ is *always* positive, the *sign* of β_k indicates the direction of the relationship between the explanatory

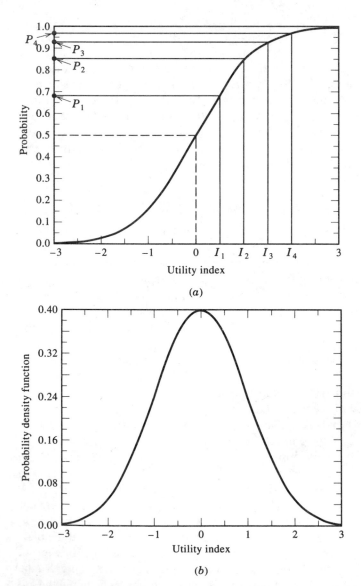

(a)

(b)

Figure 23.2 (a) Standard normal cumulative distribution function. (b) Standard normal probability density function.

variable and the probability P_i. If $\beta_k > 0$ then an increase in x_{ik} increases the probability that $y_i = 1$; and if $\beta_k < 0$ an increase in x_{ik} reduces the probability that $y_i = 1$.

2. The magnitude of the change in the probability, given a change in x_{ik}, is determined by the magnitude of β_k *and* the magnitude of $f\left(\mathbf{x}_i'\boldsymbol{\beta}\right)$.

Let us elaborate on the second point. Given $\boldsymbol{\beta}$, think of the values of the explanatory variables $\mathbf{x}_i$ as describing the "conditions" that affect the choice between two alternatives. From Figure 23.2a we know that the larger the value of I_i, the greater the probability $P_i = F(I_i)$ that $y_i = 1$. In Figure 23.2b we plot the standard normal probability density function values $f(I_i) = f\left(\mathbf{x}_i'\boldsymbol{\beta}\right)$. The maximum value of $f\left(\mathbf{x}_i'\boldsymbol{\beta}\right)$ occurs where $I_i = 0$ and $P_i = F(I_i = 0) = .5$.

Thus, a change in the conditions (x_{ik}) that affects the choice of alternatives has its greatest effect when $I_i = \mathbf{x}_i'\boldsymbol{\beta} = 0$ and $P_i = F(I_i = 0) = 0.5$. The closer $P_i = F(I_i)$ is to zero or one, the smaller $f\left(\mathbf{x}_i'\boldsymbol{\beta}\right)$ becomes and the less effect a change in x_{ik} has. Intuitively, a change in the conditions surrounding a choice has its greatest effect for those individuals on the "borderline" and less of an effect for those who are "set" in their ways (P_i near one or zero).

23.4.2   A Summary Statement

In Section 23.4.3 we discuss procedures for estimating the unknown parameters $\boldsymbol{\beta}$ in the probit model. Before proceeding, however, let us summarize what we have done thus far. Probabilistic models of discrete choice are characterized by a binary outcome variable y_i that takes the values 1 and 0 with probabilities P_i and $1 - P_i$, respectively. The probability density function of y_i, say $g(y_i)$, can be written

$$
\begin{array}{cc}
y_i & g(y_i) \\
\hline
1 & P_i \\
0 & 1 - P_i
\end{array}
\tag{23.4.6}
$$

or algebraically as

$$
g\left(y_i\right) = P_i^{y_i}\left(1 - P_i\right)^{1 - y_i}, \qquad y_i = 1, 0
\tag{23.4.7}
$$

To study how the choice probability P_i is affected by characteristics and alternatives of individual decision makers, we have specified both the linear probability and the probit model. With the linear probability model, the choice probability is

$$
P_i = \mathbf{x}_i'\boldsymbol{\beta} = \beta_1 + \beta_2 x_{i2} + \ldots + \beta_K x_{iK}
\tag{23.4.8}
$$

and

$$
\frac{\partial P_i}{\partial x_{ik}} = \beta_k
\tag{23.4.9}
$$

The linear probability model has the disadvantage that P_i can be outside the interval [0, 1].

The probit model specifies the choice probability to be

$$
P_i = F\left(\mathbf{x}_i'\boldsymbol{\beta}\right) = P\left(z \leq \mathbf{x}_i'\boldsymbol{\beta}\right)
\tag{23.4.10}
$$

where $F(\cdot)$ is the standard normal cumulative distribution function, z is a standard normal random variable, and $I_i = \mathbf{x}_i'\boldsymbol{\beta}$ is a utility index. For the probit model

$$\frac{\partial P_i}{\partial x_{ik}} = f\left(\mathbf{x}_i'\boldsymbol{\beta}\right)\cdot\beta_k$$

$$(23.4.11)$$

where $f\left(\mathbf{x}_i'\boldsymbol{\beta}\right)$ is the standard normal probability density function.

23.4.3 Estimation of the Unknown Parameters of Probit Models

In this section we will consider estimation of the unknown parameters $\boldsymbol{\beta}$ for the probit model of discrete choice. In the estimation of the probit model, we will assume that the data are specific observations on individuals. We focus on data that are in the form of choices made by individual decision makers and use the method of maximum likelihood, introduced in Section 3.5.3 of Chapter 3, to estimate the unknown parameters $\boldsymbol{\beta}$. We use maximum likelihood estimation for this problem because of the discrete nature of the outcome variable, and the nonlinear, in the parameters, functional relation between the choice probability P_i and the explanatory variables x_k.

Given a sample of T independent observations on individual choices y_i, the first step toward maximum likelihood estimation of the unknown parameters $\boldsymbol{\beta}$ of the probit model is to specify the probability density functions of the observable random variables y_i. They are

$$g\left(y_i\right) = P_i^{y_i}\left(1 - P_i\right)^{1-y_i}$$

Maximum likelihood estimation is based on the fact that the *joint probability density function* of the sample of *T independent* observations is the product of the T probability density functions $g(y_i)$. That is,

$$g\left(y_1, y_2, \ldots, y_T\right) = \prod_{i=1}^{T} g\left(y_i\right)$$

$$= \prod_{i=1}^{T} P_i^{y_i}\left(1 - P_i\right)^{1-y_i}$$

$$= \prod_{i=1}^{T} F\left(\mathbf{x}_i'\boldsymbol{\beta}\right)^{y_i}\left[1 - F\left(\mathbf{x}_i'\boldsymbol{\beta}\right)\right]^{1-y_i}$$

$$(23.4.12)$$

where

$$\prod_{i=1}^{T} a_i = a_1 a_2 \ldots a_T$$

is the "product" operator, analogous to the summation operator Σ.

If the parameters $\boldsymbol{\beta}$ were known, this joint probability density function could be used to calculate the probability that any set of T choice outcomes occurs. However, $\boldsymbol{\beta}$ is not known, and after the sample is collected only the T values of y_i and $\mathbf{x}_i$ are known. The idea of maximum likelihood estimation is to choose, as estimates of $\boldsymbol{\beta}$, the values of $\boldsymbol{\beta}$ that *maximize* the probability of obtaining the sample that is actually observed. The resulting maximum likelihood estimates of the probit model are obtained by considering the joint probability density function in equation 23.4.12 to be a function of the unknown parameters $\boldsymbol{\beta}$, assuming that the sample outcomes y_i and $\mathbf{x}_i$ are known. Interpreted in this way, the joint probability density function is known as the *likelihood function* and written

$$l(\boldsymbol{\beta}) = \prod_{i=1}^{T}\left[F\left(\mathbf{x}_i'\boldsymbol{\beta}\right)\right]^{y_i}\left[1 - F\left(\mathbf{x}_i'\boldsymbol{\beta}\right)\right]^{1-y_i}$$

$$(23.4.13)$$

where $F(x_i'\beta)$ is the standard normal cumulative distribution function evaluated at $x_i'\beta$.

The maximum likelihood estimates of β are those values that maximize $l(\beta)$ in equation 23.4.13. In this case, the actual maximization of the likelihood function $l(\beta)$ is a complicated problem, and one that does not have an easy algebraic representation. That is, maximizing the likelihood function with respect to β does not lead to a nice formula like the least squares rule. Modern computer software uses *numerical optimization* methods to find the values of β that maximize the likelihood function, or more generally the natural logarithm of the likelihood function, $\ln(l)$, which is an equivalent and somewhat easier problem. The details of numerical optimization methods for the probit model are given in Judge et al. (1988, pp. 791–793) and need not concern us here. Many computer software packages have routines that are easy to use to obtain maximum likelihood estimates for the probit model and that are similar in spirit to the nonlinear techniques discussed in Chapter 22.

As a basis for bringing these models and methods to life, data from Ben-Akiva and Lerman (1985) on automobile and public transportation travel times and the alternative chosen for $T = 21$ individuals are given in Table 23.1, in which the variable $x_i =$ (transit time – auto time) and the outcome variable $y_i = 1$ if automobile transportation is chosen.

Within the context of the general probit statistical model, given in equations 23.4.3 and 23.4.4, and the data in Table 23.1, if we use a numerical optimization program for the probit model, the maximum likelihood estimates of the parameters are

$$\hat{I}_i = \hat{\beta}_1 + \hat{\beta}_2 x_i = -0.0644 + 0.0299 x_i$$

The negative sign of $\hat{\beta}_1$ implies that individuals have a bias against driving to work, relative to public transportation. The positive sign of $\hat{\beta}_2$ indicates that an increase in

Table 23.1   Data for Transportation Example

Auto Time	Transit Time	x_i	y_i
52.9	4.4	−48.5	0
4.1	28.5	24.4	0
4.1	86.9	82.8	1
56.2	31.6	−24.6	0
51.8	20.2	−31.6	0
0.2	91.2	91.0	1
27.6	79.7	52.1	1
89.9	2.2	−87.7	0
41.5	24.5	−17.0	0
95.0	43.5	−51.5	0
99.1	8.4	−90.7	0
18.5	84.0	65.5	1
82.0	38.0	−44.0	1
8.6	1.6	−7.0	0
22.5	74.1	51.6	1
51.4	83.8	32.4	1
81.0	19.2	−61.8	0
51.0	85.0	34.0	1
62.2	90.1	27.9	1
95.1	22.2	−72.9	0
41.6	91.5	49.9	1

public transportation travel time increases the probability that an individual will choose to drive to work.

The natural logarithm of the likelihood function, $\ln(l)$ in equation 23.4.13, for the data in Table 23.1, is plotted as a function of the parameters β_1 and β_2 in Figure 23.3. The specialized computer programs that carry out maximum likelihood estimation use numerical procedures to find the maximum of this surface and use the resulting values of the parameters as estimates of the true values. This point is identified in Figure 23.3.

23.4.4 Properties of the Maximum Likelihood Estimators for the Probit Model

Given a procedure for obtaining estimates of the unknown parameters β of the probit model, the question we must address now is whether the maximum likelihood estimation method has good statistical properties in repeated sampling situations. The properties of the maximum likelihood rule cannot, in general, be determined unless the sample size T is large. The resulting sampling properties are "asymptotic" ones and have characteristics that were introduced in Section 14.3 of Chapter 14. When T is large, the maximum likelihood estimator $\hat{\beta}$ for the probit model has a sampling distribution that is approximately normal with mean β and covariance matrix

$$\text{cov}\left(\hat{\beta}\right) = \left(X'DX\right)^{-1} \tag{23.4.14}$$

where X is the usual $(T \times K)$ design matrix of observations on K explanatory variables for T individuals, and $D = \text{diag}(d_1, d_2, \ldots, d_T)$ is a diagonal matrix with elements

$$d_i = \frac{\left[f\left(x_i'\beta\right)\right]^2}{F\left(x_i'\beta\right)\left[1 - F\left(x_i'\beta\right)\right]} \tag{23.4.15}$$

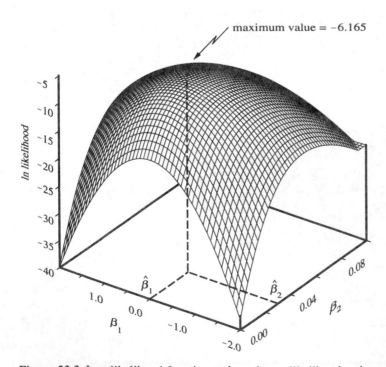

Figure 23.3 Log-likelihood function and maximum likelihood estimates.

where $f(\mathbf{x}_i'\boldsymbol{\beta})$ and $F(\mathbf{x}_i'\boldsymbol{\beta})$ are the probability density function and cumulative distribution function of the standard normal random variable, respectively, evaluated at $\mathbf{x}_i'\boldsymbol{\beta}$.

The probit model results for the driving/public transportation example can be reported in the usual way, with approximate standard errors and t-statistics that are valid in sufficiently large samples. Estimated standard errors of the maximum likelihood estimator $\hat{\boldsymbol{\beta}}$ are obtained by taking the square roots of the diagonal elements of $\operatorname{cov}(\hat{\boldsymbol{\beta}}) = (X'DX)^{-1}$, after replacing $\boldsymbol{\beta}$ by $\hat{\boldsymbol{\beta}}$ in D. The t-statistics are asymptotic ones and are calculated by dividing each parameter estimate by the estimated standard error. The use of the t-statistics will be examined in the subsequent section.

Probit Model Results:

$$\hat{I}_i = -0.0644 + 0.0299 x_i$$

$$
\begin{array}{llll}
(.399) & (.010) & \text{(standard errors)} & \\
-.161 & 2.915 & (t\text{-ratios}) & (23.4.16)
\end{array}
$$

Based on the positive sign on the estimated coefficient $\hat{\beta}_2$, we infer that an increase in public transportation time relative to auto travel increases the probability of auto travel. Suppose that we wish to make a judgment about the magnitude of the effect of increased public transportation time given that travel via public transportation currently takes 20 minutes longer than auto travel. Thus, the "current" values of the explanatory variables are $\mathbf{x}_i^{*\prime} = \begin{bmatrix} 1 & 20 \end{bmatrix}$. The values of the utility index and derivatives, using equation 23.4.5 are

$$\hat{I} = \mathbf{x}_i^{*\prime}\hat{\boldsymbol{\beta}} = -0.0644 + 0.0299(20) = 0.5355$$

$$\frac{\partial \hat{P}_i}{\partial x_{i2}} = f\left(\mathbf{x}_i^{*\prime}\hat{\boldsymbol{\beta}}\right)\hat{\beta}_2 = f(0.54)(0.0299) = (0.3456)(0.0299) = 0.0104$$

For the probit probability model, an incremental (one-minute) increase in the travel time via public transportation increases the probability of travel via auto by approximately 0.01.

The estimated parameters of the probit model can also be used to "predict" the behavior of an individual who must choose between auto and public transportation to travel to work. If an individual is faced with the situation that it takes 30 minutes longer to take public transportation than to drive to work, then the estimated probability that auto transportation will be selected is based on $\mathbf{x}_i^{*\prime} = \begin{bmatrix} 1 & 30 \end{bmatrix}$. The estimated probability is calculated from the probability model in equation 23.4.3, with the maximum likelihood estimates of the parameters $\hat{\boldsymbol{\beta}}$ replacing the true values $\boldsymbol{\beta}$, and is

$$\hat{P} = F\left(\mathbf{x}_i^{*\prime}\hat{\boldsymbol{\beta}}\right) = F(0.835) = .798$$

Since the estimated probability that the individual will choose to drive to work is greater than 0.5, we "predict" that when public transportation takes 30 minutes longer than driving to work, the individual will choose to drive.

23.5 Hypothesis Tests in the Probit Model

Another aspect of evaluation and interpretation of probit model results concerns hypothesis tests. Hypothesis tests are carried out in probability models of discrete choice because we may want to ask (*i*) whether the explanatory factors that we have included have a significant effect, individually or jointly, on the probability of choice, or *(ii)* whether an increase in an explanatory variable significantly increases or decreases the probability that an alternative will be chosen. The approximate $N[\beta, (X'DX)^{-1}]$ sampling distribution of the maximum likelihood estimator $\hat{\beta}$ forms the statistical basis for tests of hypotheses in the probit model. This sampling distribution holds true in large samples, and the tests we develop for our small sample of observations are *approximate* and are strictly appropriate only in large samples.

23.5.1   Testing the Significance of Individual Parameters

Tests of the significance of individual parameters are based on the fact that in large samples the maximum likelihood estimator $\hat{\beta}$ from the probit model has the distribution

$$\hat{\beta} \sim N\left[\beta, \text{cov}\left(\hat{\beta}\right)\right]$$

where $\text{cov}\left(\hat{\beta}\right)$ is given by equation 23.4.14. Consequently,

$$t = \frac{\hat{\beta}_k - \beta_k}{\text{se}\left(\hat{\beta}_k\right)} \sim N(0, 1)$$ (23.5.1)

Given the null and alternative hypotheses

$$H_0 : \beta_k = 0$$
$$H_1 : \beta_k \neq 0$$

the *t*-ratio is

$$t = \frac{\hat{\beta}_k}{\text{se}\left(\hat{\beta}_k\right)}$$

If the null hypothesis is true, the *t*-ratio has a normal distribution (approximately) in large samples, and the critical values for the test may be taken from the standard normal distribution (if the sample is large) or the $t_{(T-K)}$-distribution if the sample is not large.

To illustrate the tests of significance, let us test, as separate hypotheses, whether the "taste" factor for automobile transportation and the variable measuring difference in travel time have significant explanatory effects on the probability of choosing to drive to work. To answer those questions we test the individual null hypotheses

$$H_0 : \beta_1 = 0 \qquad H_0 : \beta_2 = 0$$
$$H_1 : \beta_1 \neq 0 \qquad H_1 : \beta_2 \neq 0$$

The "usual" *t*-statistics, reported below the estimated utility index for the probit probability model in equation 23.4.16, may be used to test these null hypotheses. The degrees of freedom are $(T - K) = 19$ and the $\alpha = .05$ critical value from the $t_{(19)}$-distribution (chosen since the sample is not large) is 2.093. Considering β_2 first, using the *t*-ratio in equation 23.4.16, the test leads us to reject the null hypothesis that travel time does not affect the probability of an individual choosing to drive to work; but the null hypothesis concerning β_1, that there is no taste factor affecting the probability of choice, is not rejected at the $\alpha = .05$ level of significance.

23.5.2   Tests of General Hypotheses

Within the framework of maximum likelihood estimation, general and joint hypotheses about the parameter values may be tested several ways. Let the null and alternative hypotheses be stated as

$$H_0 : R\beta = r$$
$$H_1 : R\beta \neq r \tag{23.5.2}$$

These linear equations represent J independent hypotheses about the parameters β and are constructed exactly as in Chapters 10 and 11. When testing the significance of a single parameter, the basis for testing the null hypothesis in equation 23.5.2 is the sampling distribution of the maximum likelihood estimator for the probit probability model, $\hat{\beta} \sim N[\beta, \text{cov}(\hat{\beta})]$. Consequently,

$$\left(R\hat{\beta} - r \right) \sim N\left[(R\beta - r), R\,\text{cov}(\hat{\beta})R' \right]$$

and if the hypotheses are true

$$\lambda_W = \left(R\hat{\beta} - r \right)' \left[R\,\text{cov}(\hat{\beta})R' \right]^{-1} \left(R\hat{\beta} - r \right) \sim \chi^2_{(J)} \tag{23.5.3}$$

where J is the number of independent restrictions being tested. This chi-square test statistic, introduced in equation 14.3.5 of Chapter 14 and known as the "Wald" test statistic, becomes large if the data do not support the null hypothesis, which is rejected if $\lambda_W \geq \chi^2_{(J)}$.

The chi-square test statistic is appropriate for tests of joint hypotheses in the nonlinear probit model rather than the usual F-statistic presented in Chapters 10 and 11, as there is no "σ^2" term to deal with in the probit model. In small samples, however, the test statistic λ_W / J is sometimes advocated as a superior test statistic in nonlinear models. If the null hypothesis is true, λ_W / J is approximately distributed as $F_{(J, T-K)}$, and the F-test can be carried out in the usual way using this test statistic.

We illustrate the use of the chi-square test by testing the "overall" significance of the probit statistical model used to explain the choice between driving and taking public transportation to work. That is, we wish to test the joint null and alternative hypotheses

$$H_0 : \beta_1 = \beta_2 = 0$$
$$H_1 : \beta_1 \neq 0 \text{ and / or } \beta_2 \neq 0 \tag{23.5.4}$$

In order to write the null hypothesis in equation 23.5.4 as a general linear restriction, we define

$$R\beta = \begin{bmatrix} 1 & 0 \\ 0 & 1 \end{bmatrix} \begin{bmatrix} \beta_1 \\ \beta_2 \end{bmatrix} = \begin{bmatrix} \beta_1 \\ \beta_2 \end{bmatrix}$$

and

$$r = \begin{bmatrix} 0 \\ 0 \end{bmatrix}$$

The chi-square statistic, using the probit maximum likelihood estimates, is

$$\lambda_w = \left(R\hat{\boldsymbol{\beta}} - \mathbf{r}\right)' \left[R\operatorname{cov}\left(\hat{\boldsymbol{\beta}}\right)R'\right]^{-1}\left(R\hat{\boldsymbol{\beta}} - \mathbf{r}\right)$$

$$= \hat{\boldsymbol{\beta}}'\left[\operatorname{cov}\left(\hat{\boldsymbol{\beta}}\right)\right]^{-1}\hat{\boldsymbol{\beta}}$$

$$= \begin{bmatrix} -.0644 & 0.0299 \end{bmatrix} \begin{bmatrix} .1594 & -3.261 \times 10^{-5} \\ -3.261 \times 10^{-5} & 1.06 \times 10^{-4} \end{bmatrix}^{-1} \begin{bmatrix} -.0644 \\ 0.0299 \end{bmatrix}$$

$$= 8.506$$

The appropriate large sample critical value comes from the $\chi^2_{(2)}$-distribution. For the $\alpha = .05$ level of significance, this value is 5.99; thus, on the basis of the chi-square test, we reject the null hypothesis that taste and travel time have no effect on the probability of choosing to drive to work.

23.5.2a The Likelihood Ratio Test   An alternative, and in large samples an equivalent, test procedure is the likelihood ratio test that compares the value of the log-likelihood function, ln l, evaluated at the maximum likelihood estimator ($\hat{\boldsymbol{\beta}}$) to the *restricted maximum likelihood estimator* ($\hat{\boldsymbol{\beta}}*$) that results when the log-likelihood function is maximized subject to the restrictions $R\beta = \mathbf{r}$ being true. Depending on the software that is available and the generality of the hypothesis to be tested, the likelihood ratio test is often easier to use than the chi-square procedure. *If the hypotheses to be tested can be substituted easily into the model to obtain a restricted model, then the restricted value of the log-likelihood function is obtained by reestimating the restricted version of the probit model.* The likelihood ratio test statistic

$$\lambda_{LR} = 2\left[\ln l\left(\hat{\boldsymbol{\beta}}\right) - \ln l\left(\hat{\boldsymbol{\beta}}*\right)\right] \tag{23.5.5}$$

has a $\chi^2_{(J)}$ distribution if the joint null hypothesis is true. If the data do not support the null hypotheses then the value of the test statistic becomes large, and the null hypothesis is rejected if $\lambda_{LR} \geq \chi^2_{(J)}$.

On most probit software printouts, there appears a likelihood ratio test statistic for the null hypothesis that all the parameters in the model are zero. In the context of this hypothesis, the restricted estimator and the corresponding value of the log-likelihood function are easily computed. To carry out a likelihood ratio test of the null hypothesis in equation 23.5.4 we must calculate the value of the log-likelihood function, assuming that the null hypothesis is true, $\ln l(\hat{\boldsymbol{\beta}}*)$, and compare that value to the unrestricted maximum of the log-likelihood function $\ln l(\hat{\boldsymbol{\beta}})$. To calculate $\ln l(\hat{\boldsymbol{\beta}}*)$ we estimate the probit model under the assumption that the null hypothesis is true. If the null hypothesis is true, then the parameter vector $\beta = \mathbf{0}$, and the restricted maximum likelihood estimates of β are $\hat{\boldsymbol{\beta}}* = \mathbf{0}$ and no reestimation is required. Consequently, the utility index $I* = \mathbf{x}'\hat{\boldsymbol{\beta}}* = 0$, and the probability that an individual chooses to drive to work is $P* = F(I*) = .5$. The value of the restricted log-likelihood function (see Exercise 23.5) for our transportation example is

$$\ln l\left(\hat{\boldsymbol{\beta}}*\right) = \ln \prod_{i=1}^{T}\left[F\left(\mathbf{x}_i'\hat{\boldsymbol{\beta}}*\right)\right]^{y_i}\left[1 - F\left(\mathbf{x}_i'\hat{\boldsymbol{\beta}}*\right)\right]^{1-y_i}$$

$$= 21\ln(0.5) = -14.556$$

The value of the unrestricted log-likelihood function is provided by the probit software and is

$$\ln l\left(\hat{\boldsymbol{\beta}}\right) = -6.165$$

The value of the likelihood ratio test statistic is

$$
\begin{aligned}
\lambda_{LR} &= 2\left[\ln l\left(\hat{\boldsymbol{\beta}}\right) - \ln l\left(\hat{\boldsymbol{\beta}}*\right)\right] \\
&= 2\left[-6.165 - (-14.556)\right] \\
&= 16.782
\end{aligned}
\tag{23.5.6}
$$

At the $\alpha = 0.05$ level of significance the test critical value is $\chi^2_{(2)} = 5.99$, and thus we reject the hypothesis that taste and travel time have no significant impact on the probability of an individual driving to work.

23.6   The Logit Model

The probit model is one statistical model that is used for discrete or binary choice models. A popular alternative to the probit statistical model is the *logit statistical model*. The logit model differs from the probit model only in the *cumulative distribution function* that is used to define choice probabilities. For the logit model the choice probabilities are given by

$$
P_i = F\left(\mathbf{x}_i'\boldsymbol{\beta}\right) = F\left(I_i\right)
\tag{23.6.1}
$$

where $F(\cdot)$ is the cumulative distribution of a logistic random variable and given by

$$
\begin{aligned}
P_i &= F\left(\mathbf{x}_i'\boldsymbol{\beta}\right) \\
&= \frac{1}{1 + e^{-\mathbf{x}_i'\boldsymbol{\beta}}} \qquad \text{(logit)}
\end{aligned}
\tag{23.6.2}
$$

If you compare the logit model to the probit model given in equation 23.4.4, you will notice that the cumulative distribution function for the logit model is not in integral form. This change makes the logit model somewhat easier to work with. The logistic probability density function is smooth, symmetric about zero and bell-shaped, like the standard normal probability density function, but has slightly thicker tails, somewhat like a t random variable with low degrees of freedom. This is depicted in Figure 23A.1 in the appendix.

Maximum likelihood estimation of the logit model is carried out in exactly the same way as in the probit model. The likelihood function of the logit model is written exactly as in equation 23.4.13, with the cumulative distribution function $F(\cdot)$ being given by equation 23.6.2. Using a specialized computer program to obtain the maximum likelihood estimates of the parameters of the logit model for the automobile versus public transportation example, we have the estimated utility index

$$
\hat{I}_i = -0.2376 + 0.0531 x_i \qquad \text{(logit)}
$$

The maximum likelihood estimator of the logit model parameters also has an approximate normal distribution, in large samples, with mean $\boldsymbol{\beta}$ and a covariance matrix given by equation 23.4.14 with $d_i = F(I_i)[1 - F(I_i)]$, where $F(\cdot)$ is the logistic cumulative distribution function in equation 23.6.2. The complete logit model results are:

Logit Model Results:

$$\hat{I}_i = -0.2376 + 0.0531 x_i$$

$$\quad (.750) \quad (.021) \qquad \text{(standard errors)}$$

$$\quad -.316 \quad 2.573 \qquad (t\text{-ratio}) \qquad\qquad (23.6.3)$$

If we compare the logit results to those from the probit model by examining equations 23.4.16 and 23.6.3, we observe that the signs of the estimated parameters are the same, but the magnitudes and t-ratios are slightly different. To make a judgment about the magnitude of the effect of an increase in public transportation commuting time, consider the effect of this change given that public transportation time currently takes 20 minutes longer than auto travel. Thus, the "current" values of the explanatory variables are $\mathbf{x}_i^{*'} = \begin{bmatrix} 1 & 20 \end{bmatrix}$ and the values of the utility index and derivatives, using equation 23.4.5 with $f(\mathbf{x}_i'\boldsymbol{\beta})$ representing the probability density function of a logistic random variable (derived in Exercise 23.2), are

$$\hat{I} = \mathbf{x}_i^{*'}\hat{\boldsymbol{\beta}} = -0.2376 + 0.0531(20) = 0.8246$$

$$\frac{\partial \hat{P}_i}{\partial x_{i2}} = f\left(\mathbf{x}_i^{*'}\hat{\boldsymbol{\beta}}\right)\hat{\beta}_2 = f(0.8246)(0.0531) = (0.2119)(0.0531) = 0.0113$$

Thus, both the logit *and* probit models yield an increase in the probability of driving of 1%, given a one minute increase in the travel time via public transportation and the same initial values $\mathbf{x}_i^{*'} = \begin{bmatrix} 1 & 20 \end{bmatrix}$.

To predict the probability that an individual will drive given that it takes 30 minutes longer to take public transportation than it does to drive to work, we calculate

$$\hat{P} = F\left(\mathbf{x}_i^{*'}\hat{\boldsymbol{\beta}}\right) = F(-0.2376 + 0.0531(30))$$

$$= F(1.3557) = 0.7950$$

where I is the logistic cumulative distribution function. Based on these results we would conclude that there is little difference between the probit and logit models.

As a final comparison we calculate the log-likelihoods for the alternative models. For the probit model the maximum value of the log-likelihood function is -6.165; for the logit model the maximum value is -6.166, and thus there is little basis for choosing between probit and logit models in this problem.

23.7 Examples of Alternative Economic Models for Which the Probit and Logit Models May Be Useful

The list of economic models in which probit or logit statistical models may be useful is a long one. These statistical models are useful in *any* economic setting in which an agent must choose one of two alternatives. Examples include the following:

1. An economic model explaining why some states in the United States ratified the Equal Rights Amendment and others did not.

2. An economic model explaining why some individuals take a second, or third, job and engage in "moonlighting."

3. An economic model of why some legislators in the U. S. House of Representatives vote for a particular bill and others do not.

4. An economic model of why the federal government awards development grants to some large cities and not others.

5. An economic model explaining why some loan applications are accepted and others not at a large metropolitan bank.

6. An economic model explaining why some individuals vote "yes" in a school board election for increased spending and others vote "no."

7. An economic model explaining why some female college students decide to study engineering and others do not.

This list illustrates the great variety of circumstances in which a probit or logit model of discrete choice may be used. In each case an economic decision maker chooses between two mutually exclusive outcomes. Other examples can be found in Pindyck and Rubinfeld (1991, Chapter 10).

23.8 Summary

In this chapter we have extended the use of econometric models to study economic choices in either–or situations. Economic theory provides the base for probit and logit models; individuals make choices so as to maximize utility. Although the utility value associated with the choices is known to the individual decision maker, they are unobservable by economic investigators. Consequently, in the process of building economic and statistical models to explain choice behavior, we consider utility to be a function of the characteristics of the individual and the alternatives. The linear probability model is a linear statistical model designed to explain choices. However, it is unsatisfactory as a probability model because it can lead to predicted probabilities outside the interval [0, 1]. The probit and logit models do not have this failing. They are alternative, but very similar, statistical models that relate observed choices to the observed characteristics of the alternatives and the individuals. The unknown parameters of these models can be estimated by maximum likelihood procedures, and inferences follow from the fact that in large samples the maximum likelihood estimators have approximate normal distributions. The sampling distribution results provide a basis for interval estimation and individual and joint hypothesis tests about the parameters of the model.

In this chapter we have focused on economic and statistical models that explain either–or choices. There are many closely related "choice" situations that require methods similar to probit or logistic regression. One extension is to allow choices between *more* than two alternatives. For example, a commuter may choose between the three alternatives of driving alone, using public transportation, or joining a car pool. Probit and logit can be extended to such *multinomial* or *polychotomous* choice situations.

The standard multinomial choice model deals with alternatives that are not ordered in any way. In the commuting example there is no natural ranking of the alternatives. Suppose, however, that we wished to explain the bond ratings (AAA, AA, A, etc.) received by issuing bodies. These outcomes are ordered and reflect the economic health of the bond issuer. The *ordinal* probit regression model is designed for this type of outcome variable.

For a discussion of these and other discrete choice models see Judge et al. (1985, Chapter 18), Maddala (1983, Chapters 2–5), Greene (1990, Chapter 20), and Maddala (1992, Chapter 8).

The probit and logit models can also be estimated when the data are *proportions* based on repeated observations on the individual decision makers. Under these circumstances, the estimation of the probit model can be carried out by generalized least squares, with the transformation being similar to the heteroskedasticity transformations of Chapter 15. We will not consider data in the form of proportions, as it is a less common case. See Judge et al. (1988, pp. 788–791), Gujarati (1988, Chapter 15), and Greene (1990, pp. 666–671) for a discussion of how to estimate linear probability, probit, and logit models with proportion or grouped data.

Closely related to discrete choice models are models for dependent variables that are continuous, but *limited* or *constrained* in some way. For example, suppose we wished to explain the number of times an individual goes fishing during a year. Responses from a random sample of individuals will vary from zero to as many as several hundred. This outcome variable is *truncated* since its value cannot be negative. As a second example, perhaps we wish to explain expenditures on a consumer durable, such as a refrigerator, during a year. Randomly selected individuals will have expenditures varying from zero up to substantial amounts, but once again there will be no negative values.

Models like these, which have outcome variables constrained to be nonnegative ($y_t \geq 0$), were first analyzed by Tobin (1958), and the resulting statistical model is dubbed the *tobit* model in his honor, or sometimes a *censored* regression model. Methods for estimating the tobit model and its variations are described in Maddala (1983, Chapter 6), Maddala (1992, pp. 338–345), Greene (1990, Chapter 21), and Judge et al. (1988, pp. 795–801).

23.9 Exercises

23.1 In the linear probability model 23.3.3, the error variance is

$$\text{var}(e_i) = P_i[1 - P_i] = E[y_i](1 - E[y_i])$$
$$= (\mathbf{x}_i'\boldsymbol{\beta})(1 - \mathbf{x}_i'\boldsymbol{\beta})$$

(a) Use the data in Table 23.1 to estimate the parameters of the linear probability model for the auto/public transportation choice described in the chapter.

(b) Plot the fitted regression line $\hat{y}_i = b_1 + b_2 x_i$.

(c) Use the least squares estimates **b** of $\boldsymbol{\beta}$ to estimate the error variance for each observation. Comment on these estimates. What difficulties do you encounter if you attempt to obtain feasible generalized least squares estimates of $\boldsymbol{\beta}$?

(d) Plot the fitted GLS regression function and comment.

23.2 The cumulative distribution function of a logistic random variable is

$$F(t) = \frac{1}{1 + e^{-t}}$$

(a) Use the fact that $F'(t) = f(t)$ to show that the probability density function of a logistic random variable is

$$f(t) = \frac{e^{-t}}{\left(1 + e^{-t}\right)^2}$$

(b) Show that $f(t) = F(t)[1 - F(t)]$.

23.3 Use the data in Table 23.1, and your computer software, to obtain maximum likelihood estimates of the probit and logit models for the auto/public transportation example.

23.4 Within the context of the auto/public transportation example, what is the probability of choosing to drive to work, and what is the effect of an incremental increase in public transportation travel time on the probability of auto travel, if it currently takes
   (a) Exactly the same amount of time to travel to work via car and public transportation?
   (b) If the auto takes 15 minutes less?
   (c) If the auto takes 60 minutes less?

23.5 Verify that the value of the log-likelihood function for *either* the probit or logit model takes the value $T \ln (.5)$ under the condition that $\beta = \mathbf{0}$.

23.6 In Table 23.2 are data (Greene, 1990, p. 672) on the voting outcome, by state, in the 1976 U. S. presidential election. The outcome variable y takes the value of 1 if the popular vote favored the Democratic candidate (Jimmy Carter) and 0 if the vote favored the Republican candidate (Gerry Ford). The other variables are

Income = 1975 median income

School = median number of years of school completed by persons 18 years of age or older

Urban = percentage of population living in an urban area

Region = 1 for Northeast, 2 for Southeast, 3 for Midwest and Middle South, 4 for West and Mountain regions.

   (a) Estimate a probit model for the vote outcome using the explanatory variables income, school, urban, and dummy variables for the Midwest and West. Discuss the fitted model.
   (b) Calculate the effect on the probability of the state voting Democratic, given an increase in income of $1000, in the states of Louisiana, Oklahoma, and California.
   (c) What is the estimated probability that Oregon would favor the Democratic candidate?
   (d) Use the likelihood ratio test to test that there are no regional effects.
   (e) Use the likelihood ratio test statistic to test the joint hypothesis that income, school, and urban variables have no effect on the vote outcome.

23.7 Repeat Exercise 23.6 using the logit statistical model rather than probit.

23.8 Write short paragraphs defining the new key words and concepts introduced in this chapter.

23.10   References

BEN-AKIVA, M., and S. LERMAN (1985) *Discrete Choice Analysis*, Cambridge, MA: MIT Press.

GREENE, WILLIAM H. (1990) *Econometric Analysis*, New York: Macmillan Publishing Co., Chapters 20, 21.

GUJARATI, D. N. (1988) *Basic Econometrics*, 2nd Edition, New York: McGraw-Hill, Inc., Chapter 15.

Table 23.2 Voting Data

State	Dem.	Rep.	Income	School	Urban	Region
Alabama	659	504	11785	12.2	61.8	2
Alaska	44	72	22432	12.7	43.7	4
Arizona	296	419	13569	12.6	74.7	4
Arkansas	499	268	10106	12.2	38.4	3
California	3742	3882	15069	12.7	92.7	4
Colorado	460	584	14992	12.8	80.6	4
Connecticut	684	719	16244	12.6	88.2	1
Delaware	123	110	15732	12.5	68.5	1
District of Columbia	138	28	15002	12.6	100.0	1
Florida	1636	1470	12205	12.4	85.9	2
Georgia	979	484	12441	12.3	56.8	2
Hawaii	147	140	17770	12.7	80.5	4
Idaho	127	204	12844	12.6	16.9	4
Illinois	2271	2364	16032	12.5	81.3	3
Indiana	1015	1184	14411	12.4	67.8	3
Iowa	620	663	14464	12.5	37.4	3
Kansas	430	503	13412	12.6	46.2	3
Kentucky	616	532	11019	12.1	45.1	3
Louisiana	661	587	12576	12.3	63.2	2
Maine	232	236	11839	12.5	23.3	1
Maryland	760	673	17556	12.6	84.8	1
Massachusetts	1429	1030	15531	12.6	86.1	1
Michigan	1697	1894	15385	12.5	81.3	3
Minnesota	1070	819	14740	12.5	63.9	3
Mississippi	381	367	9999	12.1	26.6	2
Missouri	998	927	13011	12.4	63.5	3
Montana	149	174	13608	12.6	24.4	4
Nebraska	234	360	14209	12.6	44.6	3
Nevada	92	101	14961	12.6	81.3	4
New Hampshire	148	186	14258	12.6	36.6	1
New Jersey	1445	1510	16432	12.4	92.1	1
New Mexico	201	211	11798	12.5	33.6	4
New York	3390	3101	15288	12.5	88.4	1
North Carolina	927	742	11834	12.2	45.2	2
North Dakota	136	153	13626	12.5	22.7	4
Ohio	2012	2001	14822	12.4	79.8	3
Oklahoma	532	546	12172	12.4	55.6	4
Oregon	490	492	13854	12.7	59.9	4
Pennsylvania	2329	2206	14153	12.4	80.4	1
Rhode Island	228	181	14530	12.4	92.2	1
South Carolina	451	346	12188	12.2	48.3	2
South Dakota	147	152	12051	12.5	27.9	4
Tennessee	826	634	11341	12.2	63.0	3
Texas	2082	1953	12672	12.4	79.4	4
Utah	182	338	14329	12.8	78.7	4
Vermont	81	102	12415	12.5	0.0	1
Virginia	814	837	14579	12.4	65.6	1
Washington	717	778	14962	12.7	71.1	4
West Virginia	436	315	12007	12.1	36.1	1
Wisconsin	1040	1005	15064	12.5	63.0	3
Wyoming	62	93	14784	12.6	0.0	4

JUDGE, G. G., R. C. HILL, W. E. GRIFFITHS, H. LÜTKEPOHL, and T. C. LEE (1985) *Theory and Practice of Econometrics*, 2nd Edition, New York: John Wiley & Sons.

JUDGE, G. G., R. C. HILL, W. E. GRIFFITHS, H. LÜTKEPOHL, and T. C. LEE (1988) *Introduction to the Theory and Practice of Econometrics*, 2nd Edition, New York: John Wiley & Sons, Chapter 19.

MADDALA, G. S. (1983) *Limited-Dependent and Qualitative Variables in Economics*, Cambridge, UK: Cambridge University Press.

MADDALA, G. S. (1992) *Introduction to Econometrics*, 2nd Edition, New York: Macmillan Publishing Co.

PINDYCK, R., and D. RUBINFELD (1991) *Econometric Models and Economic Forecasts*, 3rd Edition. New York: McGraw-Hill, Inc., Chapter 10.

TOBIN, J. (1958) "Estimation of Relationships for Limited Dependent Variables," *Econometrica*, 26, 24–36.

APPENDIX 23A   A Statistical Model of Choice

Building a statistical model that is consistent with the discrete choice data-generation process described in Section 23.1 involves, as a first step, modeling, at least conceptually, the unobservable utilities U_{ij}, where U_{ij} is the utility received by the ith individual from the jth alternative. Since the utility U_{ij} in unobservable, we represent it as random quantity and assume that it is composed of a systematic part, $\overline{U}_{ij}$, and a random part, ε_{ij}. That is, given a random sample of T individuals, we express the random utility U_{ij} of alternative $j(= 1$ or $0)$ to individual i as

$$U_{ij} = \overline{U}_{ij} + \varepsilon_{ij} \quad i = 1,\ldots, T; j = 1, 0 \tag{23A.1}$$

We wish to express the utilities U_{ij} as a function of *(i)* the attributes (e.g., cost, convenience, quality) of the alternative to the individual, and *(ii)* the characteristics (e.g., income, educational attainment, profession) of the individual. We denote the vector of attributes of alternative j to individual i as $\mathbf{z}_{ij}$, and the vector of individual characteristics as $\mathbf{c}_i$. Writing the systematic portion of random utility as a function of the attributes $\mathbf{z}_{ij}$ and the characteristics $\mathbf{c}_i$, we have the model

$$\overline{U}_{ij} = \mathbf{z}'_{ij}\boldsymbol{\alpha} + \mathbf{c}'_i\boldsymbol{\beta}_j \tag{23A.2}$$

where $\boldsymbol{\alpha}$ and $\boldsymbol{\beta}_j$ $(j = 1, 0)$ are vectors of unknown parameters. Note that the parameters with the attributes $\mathbf{z}_{ij}$, $\boldsymbol{\alpha}$ have no subscript, whereas the parameters with the characteristics are indexed by alternative, $\boldsymbol{\beta}_j$. This implies that characteristics of the individual affect the utility of alternatives differently. The reason for this assumption will become clear in Section 23A.1.2.

Thus, we have expressed the systematic portion of utility as a function that is linear in the parameters $\boldsymbol{\alpha}$ and $\boldsymbol{\beta}_j$. Combining equations 23A.1 and 23A.2 we have a "random utility" model for U_{ij}, the unobservable economic variable utility,

$$U_{ij} = \mathbf{z}'_{ij}\boldsymbol{\alpha} + \mathbf{c}'_i\boldsymbol{\beta}_j + \varepsilon_{ij} \tag{23A.3}$$

where we assume that the errors ε_{ij} are independent for each individual and alternative, and normally distributed with zero means and variances σ_j^2 $(j = 1, 0)$. The independence assumptions imply that the utility derived by one individual is not related to the utility derived by any other individual, and that the utility that an individual derives from the choice of one alternative is not related to the utility provided by the other alternative.

23A.1 Modeling Choice Probabilities

Our assumption that utility is random leads to a probabilistic representation of individual choice behavior. As the values of the variables reflecting the characteristics of the alternatives change, so do the utilities yielded by the alternative choices. But given any set of characteristics, since utility is random, we cannot be *certain* which alternative will be chosen. *We can only make statements concerning the probability that one outcome or the other will occur.*

23A.1.1 A Random Utility Model

For example, suppose that an individual must choose between driving to work and taking public transportation and that the systematic portions of utility from the alternatives are

$$\overline{U}_{i1} = -14 \qquad \text{(driving to work)}$$

$$\overline{U}_{i0} = -17 \qquad \text{(taking public transportation to work)}$$

The utilities are negative to indicate that both driving and taking public transportation to work yield disutility. *If utility were not random*, then we could assert that the individual would choose to drive to work, as driving yields less disutility. When the random errors are added to the systematic portions of utility to obtain the utility of the alternatives, we have

$$U_{i1} = \overline{U}_{i1} + \varepsilon_{i1} = -14 + \varepsilon_{i1} \qquad \text{(driving to work)}$$

$$U_{i0} = \overline{U}_{i0} + \varepsilon_{i0} = -17 + \varepsilon_{i0} \qquad \text{(taking public transportation to work)}$$

Thus, even if we know the systematic portions of utility, the utilities of the alternatives, which determine the choice that is made, are unknown, since the random errors are unobservable. Consequently, we cannot be certain which choice the individual will make, although we can make a probability statement about it. Specifically, we may represent the probability that individual i chooses each alternative as

$$P_i = \Pr[y_i = 1] = \Pr[U_{i1} \geq U_{i0}]$$

$$1 - P_i = \Pr[y_i = 0] = \Pr[U_{i1} < U_{i0}] \qquad (23A.4)$$

Given the random utility model in equation 23A.3, we can express the ith individual's probability of choosing alternative 1 (automobile transportation to work) as

$$P_i = \Pr[U_{i1} \geq U_{i0}]$$

$$= \Pr[\overline{U}_{i1} + \varepsilon_{i1} \geq \overline{U}_{i0} + \varepsilon_{i0}]$$

$$= \Pr[\varepsilon_{i0} - \varepsilon_{i1} \leq \overline{U}_{i1} - \overline{U}_{i0}] \qquad (23A.5)$$

23A.1.2 The Probit Statistical Model

Given this utility theory base, to specify a statistical model of a choice probability, we substitute equation 23A.3 into equation 23A.4 and specify the probability distribution of the difference in random utility errors, $\varepsilon_{i0} - \varepsilon_{i1}$. First, the difference in the systematic portion of utility, which we define to be a utility "index" I_i, on the right-hand side of equation 23A.5, is

$$I_i = \overline{U}_{i1} - \overline{U}_{i0} = (\mathbf{z}'_{i1} - \mathbf{z}'_{i0})\boldsymbol{\alpha} + \mathbf{c}'_i(\boldsymbol{\beta}_1 - \boldsymbol{\beta}_0)$$

$$= \left[(\mathbf{z}'_{i1} - \mathbf{z}'_{i0})\quad \mathbf{c}'_i\right]\left[\begin{array}{c}\boldsymbol{\alpha}\\ \boldsymbol{\beta}_1 - \boldsymbol{\beta}_0\end{array}\right]$$

$$= \mathbf{x}'_i\boldsymbol{\gamma} \qquad\qquad (23A.6)$$

Note that if the parameters β_1 and β_0 had originally been assumed to be *equal*, and simply denoted β, then individual characteristics would contribute nothing to the difference in utilities. The utility index is the difference between the systematic utility of alternative 1 and the systematic utility of alternative 0. The larger the value of the index the more the systematic utility of alternative 1 exceeds that of alternative 0, and thus the greater the utility index I_i and the greater the probability that alternative 1 will be chosen over alternative 0. Substituting equation 23A.5 into equation 23A.6, we have

$$P_i = \Pr\left[U_{i1} \geq U_{i0}\right]$$

$$= \Pr\left[\varepsilon_{i0} - \varepsilon_{i1} \leq \overline{U}_{i1} - \overline{U}_{i0}\right]$$

$$= \Pr\left[\varepsilon_{i0} - \varepsilon_{i1} \leq \mathbf{x}'_i\boldsymbol{\gamma}\right] \qquad\qquad (23A.7)$$

Thus, the probability that alternative 1 is chosen is the probability that the difference in the random errors, which we will denote as $e_i = \varepsilon_{i0} - \varepsilon_{i1}$, is less than or equal to the utility index $I_i = \mathbf{x}'_i\boldsymbol{\gamma}$. Since the errors ε_{ij} are independent normal random variables with zero means and variances σ_j^2, their difference $e_i \sim N(0, \sigma^2 = \sigma_0^2 + \sigma_1^2)$. We convert the choice probability to one involving a standard normal random variable by scaling the random variable and utility index by the standard deviation σ,

$$P_i = \Pr\left[e_i \leq \mathbf{x}'_i\boldsymbol{\gamma}\right]$$

$$= \Pr\left[e_i/\sigma \leq \mathbf{x}'_i\boldsymbol{\gamma}/\sigma\right]$$

$$= \Pr\left[z_i \leq \mathbf{x}'_i\boldsymbol{\beta}\right]$$

where $z_i = e_i/\sigma$ and $\beta = \gamma/\sigma$. The random variable z_i has the $N(0, 1)$ or standard normal distribution. The probability that a random variable is less than or equal to a given value is provided by the *cumulative distribution function* of the random variable. Thus, the probability that alternative 1 is selected is

$$P_{i1} = \Pr\left[z_i \leq \mathbf{x}'_i\boldsymbol{\beta}\right]$$

$$= F(\mathbf{x}'_i\boldsymbol{\beta})$$

where $F(\cdot)$ is the cumulative distribution function of the standard random variable.

In choice probability models, when only the choices of individuals are made and not their utilities, the variance parameter σ^2 is not *identified*, in the spirit of Chapter 18, and cannot be estimated. Consequently its value is assigned to be $\sigma^2 = 1$ or, equivalently, the parameters γ are assumed to be scaled by the standard deviation σ, which is why we have denoted $\beta = \gamma/\sigma$. The resulting probability model is called the *probit model*, and the choice probabilities can be summarized as

$$P_i = F(x_i'\beta) = F(I_i)$$ (23A.8)

where $F(x_i'\beta)$ is the value of cumulative distribution function of the standard normal random variable and is given by

$$F(x_i'\beta) = \int_{-\infty}^{x_i'\beta} (2\pi)^{-1/2} e^{-z^2/2} dz$$

23A.2 The Logit Statistical Model

The logit statistical model introduced in Section 23.6 is obtained by *exactly* the same logical process used in developing the probit mode. The *only* difference is that the random error $e_i = \varepsilon_{i0} - \varepsilon_{i1}$ in equation 23A.7 is assumed to have a *logistic* distribution, so that the cumulative distribution function $F(I_i)$ in equation 23A.8 is

$$F(I_i) = \frac{1}{1 + e^{-I_i}}$$ (23A.9)

The logistic and standard normal probability density functions are depicted in Figure 23A.1. The distributions differ in the thickness of the tails of the distribution, with the logistic distribution being similar to a *t*-distribution with low degrees of freedom.

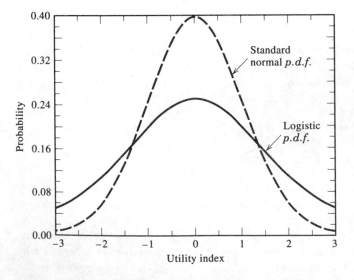

Figure 23A.1 Standard normal and logistic probability density functions.

Part IX

Bayesian Estimation and Inference

To cope with the implications of scarcity, economics is to a large extent concerned with the problem of making decisions. The fuel for the decision machine is information. With an eye to providing an improved basis for choice, in the first 23 chapters of this book we have been concerned with procedures for obtaining statistical information that may be used in a decision context.

In developing statistical information, the classical sampling theory approach to inference, which has occupied our thoughts until now, is focused toward the use of *sample information* in making inferences about unknown quantities such as the βs and σ^2. Under this approach, the resulting inferences are for the most part developed without regard to the use to which they are to be put and do not consider the possible consequences of alternative decisions. For example, for the linear statistical model considered in Chapters 5 to 11, economic examples illustrated how estimates of the βs could be used, but these uses had no bearing on the chosen estimation and inference techniques. The least squares criterion was used to obtain point estimates, and associated interval estimates were developed, without reference to the uses of these estimates. These considerations point up that, as an aid in decision making, perhaps we should identify the particular choice context and consider how the loss or gain for various values of the unknown parameters might influence the choice of a point estimate. Moving in this direction, statisticians, being pessimistic characters, have labeled the decision-parameter space a loss function whose coordinates show the loss $L(a_1, \beta_1)$ if the action or point estimate a_1 is taken and β_1 turns out to be the unknown parameter. Thus, when we become specific in terms of the use of statistical information, a loss function may be a useful aid in making a decision.

Interval estimates, in the form of confidence intervals, provide one way of representing uncertainty about unknown parameters. Since, as statisticians, we are used to using probability and probability distributions to describe uncertainty, perhaps it might be convenient and useful to use probability distributions to describe our uncertainty about the βs.

Finally, if we are interested in making the best decision, then in addition to the sample information perhaps we should take account of any other *nonsample* or *prior information* that may be relevant. Economists usually think they have a good deal of nonsample information as it relates to economic processes and institutions. If this information does not arise from the statistical investigation that is available, then the question is how to make the best use of it.

One approach to inference, which seeks to provide a systematic way to utilize sample and nonsample information and which uses probability distributions to express uncertainty about unknown parameters and finds point estimates within the context of a loss function, is called Bayesian statistics. In the next two chapters we develop the basic concepts for this Bayesian decision-theoretic approach to inference and contrast it to its sampling theory counterpart for a range of problems.

Chapter 24

The Bayesian Approach to Estimation and Inference: Some Basic Definitions, Concepts and Applications

New Key Words and Concepts

Expressing Uncertainty	Prior Information
Accumulating Information	Prior and Post-sample Density
Bayes' Rule	Functions
Expected Loss	Odds Ratio

In Chapters 3 and 4, by using a sample of household expenditure data for food, we explored methods for summarizing the statistical evidence from the data and methods for making inferences about β, the mean or average expenditure of the population. We used the data or sample information to learn about the unknown parameter β, using a repeated sampling context to evaluate point and interval estimates and hypothesis tests. We were able to make probability statements concerning sample outcomes, *before* the sample information was collected. Indeed, it was our ability to make probability statements about *future sample outcomes* that influenced our choice of techniques and governed the way in which we expressed our limited information or uncertainty about the unknown parameter β. For example, the least squares estimator was chosen as a point estimator because of its properties of unbiasedness and minimum variance. These properties refer to outcomes that will occur from future samples. A second example is an interval estimate, such as a 95% confidence interval, that was used to express the precision or reliability of our information about β. This expression of reliability is based on a probability statement that says, *before* we sample, there is a .95 probability of getting a sample outcome, and a consequent interval, that contains β. A third example is a hypothesis-testing procedure chosen such that the probability of a Type I error is .05. This refers to the probability of getting a sample outcome such that the corresponding value of the test statistic leads to rejection of a correct null hypothesis. *In all of these cases, probability statements are reserved for future sample outcomes.*

In this chapter and the following one we are concerned with an alternative approach to making inferences and expressing uncertainty about the unknown parameter β. A distinguishing feature of this alternative approach, known as the Bayesian approach, is that *we use probability statements about the unknown parameter β in expressing uncertainty about that parameter*. In the frequentist approach to inference that we employed in the earlier chapters, parameters such as β were regarded as fixed numbers about which we cannot make probability statements. Probability statements were made for random variables (sample outcomes) only, not fixed numbers. In the Bayesian approach that we begin describing in this chapter, probability statements are used, not only for sample outcomes, but also for fixed unknown parameters. As we will see, we can use probability density functions of different types to (*i*) express uncertainty about a parameter before a sample is taken (prior probability density function), (*ii*) describe the likelihood of particular sample outcomes, and (*iii*) express uncertainty about a parameter *after* a sample is taken (*post-sample* probability density function). Also, within this framework, it is possible to include uncertain nonsample information about a parameter and to take into account any losses that might occur from making incorrect decisions. In Chapters 3 and 4 we used only sample information to make inferences about β. Nonsample information in the form of *exact* linear restrictions on the parameters in the general linear statistical model was considered in Chapter 11. The nonsample information considered in Chapters 24 and 25 is *inexact* or *uncertain*. Also, in preceding chapters, although we did indicate that information about parameters is useful for making decisions, estimates and inferences concerning these parameters were largely obtained without regard for the uses to which they were to be put. The framework of this chapter provides a formal basis for including possible losses from incorrect inferences.

Thus, in this chapter we broaden our approach to estimation and inference and within the context of an economic problem we consider the following questions:

1. Can we express uncertainty with respect to parameters or hypotheses before and after a sample is taken?

2. How do we combine sample information with prior, nonsample, or experimental information?

3. Is there a framework for considering the consequences of decisions? In particular, when we obtain a point estimate for a parameter, is there a way of considering the losses that are incurred from an incorrect decision?

These questions are investigated within the context of a sample of household expenditure data similar to that introduced in Chapter 3. The techniques that are introduced to answer the questions have general applicability and can be used for data on many different economic variables.

Let us elaborate on the three questions. Suppose that, before we collect a sample, we have absolutely no idea about what the mean expenditure on food might be. We would say we are completely uncertain about the value of β. Then, we collect a sample of observations, say 40 of them ($y_1, y_2, \ldots, y_{40}$), and use the sample mean $\bar{y}$ as a point estimate for β. Our uncertainty about β has been reduced. We do not know the value of β with total certainty; we have observed only one sample of size 40, not the whole population. Nevertheless, we are "more certain" or at least "less uncertain" than we were before we observed the sample. The first question that we wish to address in this chapter is: *Do we have some means for expressing our uncertainty (or what we know) about β before and after the sample is taken*? How do we express our state of knowledge at a given point in time? What can we use as a basis for inference at a given point in time?

The second and related question is concerned with including information about β, other than that provided by the sample. Suppose that, at the outset, before a sample is taken, we are *not* completely uncertain about mean expenditure on food per week and that we have at least some vague idea about its value. This idea may come from previous samples others have taken, it may be from our own experience about how much we spend on food each week, or it might come from talking to "experts" such as supermarket managers. We refer to this kind of information as *prior information*. It is information (possibly nonsample information) that we have *prior* to the sampling process. Our second set of questions is concerned with describing and using this prior information. *How can we represent prior information?* After we take a sample and hence obtain additional information about β, *how do we update our state of knowledge (or level of uncertainty) about β?* How do we describe and make operational the process of accumulating information?

In connection with this second question, note that economic principles provide us with many kinds of implied prior information. In demand equations the response of quantity demanded to a change in price is negative; in supply equations the response of quantity supplied to a change in price is positive. For consumption functions the marginal propensity to consume lies between zero and one. There is a negative relationship between investment and the interest rate. The list goes on and on. More general problems of this type, where we have prior information on the relationship between economic variables, will be considered in Chapter 25. In this chapter we are concerned with prior information on the mean of a single random variable, and we use as our example the observed economic variable, household expenditure on food.

The third question relates to methods for incorporating the costs and benefits of using point estimates as a basis for decision making. Suppose a supermarket chain is interested in mean expenditure on food. What are the consequences of overestimating β? The supermarket chain will build a bigger supermarket than is necessary; it will stock more food than is necessary. Consequently, it will have certain costs or losses associated with overstating mean expenditure. Similarly, there will be costs and losses associated with underestimating mean expenditure. If the supermarket is too small, the food stocks are inadequate, and there are insufficient employees, then the supermarket will be forgoing profits it could have made; disgruntled customers, sick of waiting in long lines for inadequate supplies, are likely to go elsewhere. Thus, the third question we consider in this chapter is: *When we obtain a point estimate, can we do so within a framework that allows for losses or costs from over- or underestimation?* In other words, can we allow for the economic consequences of not knowing the parameter and having to estimate it?

Because they have their origin in the work of the eighteenth century mathematician the Reverend Thomas Bayes, the techniques introduced in this chapter come under the general title of *Bayesian inference*. These Bayesian inference techniques are relatively modern, despite their early beginnings. We will begin our study of Bayesian inference by considering the question: If we begin with no information, how do we represent uncertainty about mean expenditure before and after a sample is taken?

24.1 Expressing Uncertainty About Mean Expenditure

Let us begin by formally restating our model from Chapter 3. We represent the statistical model or sampling process for the data on household expenditure for food, given in Table 24.1, by the model

$$y_t = \beta + e_t \qquad t = 1, 2, \ldots, T \tag{24.1.1}$$

In this model y_t is the observed expenditure on food for the tth household; β is an unknown parameter representing the mean of the distribution for y (mean expenditure for the population); e_t is an unobservable random variable (or error) defined as the difference $(y_t - \beta)$ between each observed value and the mean. The mean of e_t is zero and its variance, denoted by σ^2, is the same as that of the random variable y_t. Also, because we are assuming our sample is a random one, each drawing of y_t is independent of the other drawings and the covariance between any two drawings (say y_t and y_s) is zero. Similarly, the covariance between e_t and e_s is zero. These assumptions are neatly summarized in matrix algebra notation by writing the model as

$$\mathbf{y} = \mathbf{x}\beta + \mathbf{e} \qquad E[\mathbf{e}] = \mathbf{0} \qquad E[\mathbf{e}\mathbf{e}'] = \sigma^2 I_T \qquad (24.1.2)$$

where $\mathbf{y}$ is a T-dimensional vector containing the expenditure observations, $\mathbf{x} = (1,1,...,1)'$ is a T-dimensional vector with all of its elements equal to unity, $\mathbf{e}$ is T-dimensional vector of errors, and I_T is the identity matrix of order T. Throughout this chapter we assume that the observations are drawings from a normal distribution, and write the model as

$$\mathbf{y} \sim N(\mathbf{x}\beta, \sigma^2 I_T) \qquad \text{or} \qquad \mathbf{e} \sim N(\mathbf{0}, \sigma^2 I_T) \qquad (24.1.3)$$

To focus on the basic concepts of Bayesian inference we assume that the variance parameter σ^2 is known. Familiarity with the concepts to be introduced provides a basis for analysis when this assumption is eliminated.

24.1.1 Post-sample Information

Suppose that we have no knowledge whatsoever about β—we are completely uncertain—and thus we draw a random sample of 40 households and observe their weekly expenditures on food, $(y_1, y_2,..., y_{40})$. We summarize this information with the sample mean $\bar{y}$. Using the observations in Table 24.1, we find that $\bar{y} = 23.5945$. *Given that we have observed this sample information, how do we express our current state of uncertainty about β?*

To answer this question, let us back up for a minute and ask how we usually express uncertainty about anything. Being students of statistics, we would undoubtedly use the concept of probability. For example, if you are uncertain about tomorrow's weather, you might say there is a .4 probability that it will rain. If a friend is seldom on time for a date, you might say there is a .05 probability of that friend turning up on time. When we built our statistical model for household expenditure on food, we specified a probability density function that describes our uncertainty about y_t, weekly food expenditure. If the parameters (β and σ^2) of this probability density function were known, it would tell us, *before a sample is taken*, the probability that food expenditure for a household lies within some range. Given these conventional methods for expressing uncertainty, it seems reasonable to express uncertainty about mean food expenditure β in terms of a probability density function for β. If we have such a density function, we can make probability statements about where the value for β is likely (or unlikely) to lie.

Table 24.1 Sample of Weekly Household Expenditures on Food

9.46	10.56	14.81	21.71	22.79	18.19	22.00	18.12
23.13	19.00	19.46	17.83	32.81	22.13	23.46	16.81
21.35	14.87	33.00	25.19	17.77	22.44	22.87	26.52
21.00	37.52	21.69	27.40	30.69	19.56	30.58	41.12
15.38	17.87	25.54	39.00	20.44	30.10	20.90	48.71

Let us try to find a probability density function for β. In Chapter 3 we learned that, *before* a sample is taken, the sample mean $\bar{y}$ is an estimator with probability density function

$$\bar{y} \sim N\left(\beta, \sigma^2/T\right) \tag{24.1.4}$$

With knowledge of β and σ^2, this density function describes the probability of the sample mean lying within any specified range. That is, it gives the probability of collecting a sample such that the mean of that sample lies within a range. From equation 24.1.4 we know that $(\bar{y} - \beta) \sim N(0, \sigma^2/T)$ and thus

$$z = \frac{\bar{y} - \beta}{\sigma/\sqrt{T}} \sim N(0,1) \tag{24.1.5}$$

In Chapter 4 we viewed z as a random variable because $\bar{y}$ was a random variable. Probability statements about future values of z or $\bar{y}$ were used to construct confidence intervals for β or to test hypotheses about β. *The parameter β was treated as a constant.*

To find a probability density function for β, it is again convenient to begin with equation 24.1.5. However, instead of treating $\bar{y}$ as a random variable and β as fixed, we treat $\bar{y}$ as fixed and β as a random variable. We treat $\bar{y}$ as fixed because we are interested in an expression of uncertainty about β *after $\bar{y}$ has been observed*—after we know that $\bar{y} = 23.5945$. Now if it is true that $z \sim N(0, 1)$, and that β (but not $\bar{y}$) is a random variable, then, to find the probability density function of β from that for z, we can begin by rewriting equation 24.1.5 as

$$\beta = \bar{y} - \frac{\sigma}{\sqrt{T}} z$$

where $\bar{y}$ and $\sigma/\sqrt{T}$ are constants. Since β is a linear function of z and linear functions of normal random variables are normal random variables, the first thing we can say is that β has a normal distribution. Second, its mean is given by

$$E[\beta] = \bar{y} - \frac{\sigma}{\sqrt{T}} E[z] = \bar{y}$$

That is, adding $\bar{y}$ to a multiple of z changes the mean from zero to $\bar{y}$. Also, multiplying z by a constant $\sigma/\sqrt{T}$ changes the variance from one to σ^2/T. That is,

$$\text{var}(\beta) = \frac{\sigma^2}{T} \text{var}(z) = \frac{\sigma^2}{T}$$

Thus, we can write

$$\beta \sim N\left(\bar{y}, \sigma^2/T\right) \tag{24.1.6}$$

This is the probability density function for β that we will use to express our *uncertainty* about β after the sample has been observed. Since it is a normal probability density function, its equation is given by

$$f(\beta|\mathbf{y}) = \left(\frac{T}{2\pi\sigma^2}\right)^{1/2} \exp\left\{-\frac{T}{2\sigma^2}(\beta - \bar{y})^2\right\} \tag{24.1.7}$$

We use the notation $f(\beta \mid \mathbf{y})$ rather than just $f(\beta)$ to denote that $\mathbf{y}$ is given; $f(\beta \mid \mathbf{y})$ is an expression of uncertainty about β after the sample information $\mathbf{y}$ has been observed.

We will soon discover the various uses to which $f(\beta \mid \mathbf{y})$ can be put. First, some explanatory remarks are in order. We do not really believe that the mean of our population is a random variable. It is not some value that depends on chance and varies from experiment to experiment (or sample to sample). The parameter β is a constant but unknown quantity. However, *we treat β as a random variable in the sense that we are uncertain about its value and we assign to it a probability density function that expresses our beliefs about what are likely and unlikely values for β*. To distinguish probability density functions for unknown parameters from those for random variables that depend on chance outcomes, we refer to probability density functions that express uncertainty about parameters as *subjective probability density functions*.

24.1.2   Updating Prior Information

Let us return to the argument surrounding equations 24.1.5 and 24.1.6. We have said that if $\sqrt{T}(\bar{y} - \beta)/\sigma \sim N(0, 1)$, and if we *treat* $\bar{y}$ as fixed and β as random, then it follows that $\beta \sim N(\bar{y}, \sigma^2/T)$ and that this density function for β can be used to express uncertainty about β. The missing link in this argument is the presumption that $\sqrt{T}(\bar{y} - \beta)/\sigma \sim N(0, 1)$. Certainly, we know this result is true when $\bar{y}$ is random and β is fixed; but are we justified in assuming it is true after we observe the sample, when $\bar{y}$ is fixed and β is treated as random? Furthermore, what do we use for an expression of uncertainty about β before the sample is taken? If $f(\beta \mid y)$ expresses uncertainty about β after the sample, and $f(\beta)$ expresses uncertainty about β before the sample, how do we specify $f(\beta)$ when we are completely uncertain (or totally ignorant) about β?

These questions are taken up more fully in Appendix 24A.2 of this chapter. A distribution for $f(\beta)$ known as a *noninformative prior density function* is the specification chosen to represent ignorance about β. This density function is a uniform density function on the interval from $-\infty$ to ∞; it represents ignorance in the sense that all values of β are equally likely. Then, a rule, originally due to the Reverend Thomas Bayes (*Bayes' rule*), is used to update $f(\beta)$ with the information provided by the sample. The updated distribution $f(\beta \mid y)$ is called a *post-sample density function* and is the normal probability density function that we have specified in equation 24.1.7.

This post-sample normal density function is a complete statement of our knowledge (or uncertainty) about β, after the sample has been taken. Given that $\bar{y} = 23.5945$ and given a known value for σ^2, we can specify this distribution precisely. Let us assume we know that $\sigma^2 = 57.6$, so that $\sigma^2/T = 57.6/40 = 1.44$, then we express our information about β by saying

$$\beta \sim N(23.5945, 1.44) \qquad (24.1.8)$$

Graphing this density function, as we have done in Figure 24.1, is another way of expressing the information.

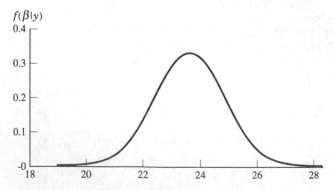

Figure 24.1 Post-sample density function for β.

Both equation 24.1.8 and the graph in Figure 24.1 mean something to trained statisticians. Suppose, however, that you have been employed by a supermarket chain to carry out the survey of households. What would happen if, when giving your results to the chief executive officer (CEO) of the supermarket chain, you said: "Beta has a normal post-sample density function with mean 23.5945 and variance 1.44." The CEO is unlikely to be impressed. It would be more useful to him if we could use equation 24.1.8 to derive some summary measures that can be readily interpreted by nonstatisticians. We will describe three such summary measures—probability statements about β, interval estimation, and comparison of hypotheses.

24.1.3   Probability Statements for Mean Expenditure

From just a visual inspection of Figure 24.1 we can see that we are almost certain that mean expenditure β lies between \$21 and \$26. Since, before we took a sample, we assumed we had no knowledge of what mean expenditure might be, the sample has provided us with a considerable amount of information. The CEO might be quite happy with the statement, "We are almost certain β lies between \$21 and \$26." However, it can be made more precise for him by computing the probability

$$P(21 < \beta < 26) = P\left(\frac{21 - 23.5945}{\sqrt{1.44}} < z < \frac{26 - 23.5945}{\sqrt{1.44}} \right)$$
$$= P(-2.1621 < z < 2.0046)$$
$$= 0.962$$

Thus, one way of reporting your findings to the CEO, and a way that he is likely to understand, is to say there is a 96% probability that mean expenditure on food lies between \$21 and \$26 per week.

Other useful probabilities that could be used in a decision context could also be computed. For example, the probability that mean expenditure lies between \$22 and \$24 is given by

$$P(22 < \beta < 24) = P\left(\frac{22 - 23.5945}{\sqrt{1.44}} < z < \frac{24 - 23.5945}{\sqrt{1.44}} \right)$$
$$= P(-1.3288 < z < 0.3379)$$
$$= 0.540$$

This is another result that could be reported to the CEO.

Note that probability statements such as these could not have been made within the context of the repeated-sample or frequentist approach to inference that we used in the earlier chapters. In the frequentist approach we make probability statements about $\bar{y}$ and we use these statements to construct interval estimates for β. A 95% (frequentist) confidence interval does not mean that a *given interval* contains β with a .95 probability. It refers to the probability of getting a $\bar{y}$ such that a *future interval* will include β. In many ways probability statements such as $P(21 < \beta < 26) = .962$ and $P(22 < \beta < 24) = .540$ are more natural measures of our uncertainty about β. Let us examine this distinction further by considering interval estimation from a Bayesian inference point of view.

24.1.4   Interval Estimation

We have just learned that one way to report information about a parameter to nonstatisticians is to use the post-sample density function to calculate the probability that our unknown parameter β lies in a specified interval. Often it is useful to turn this question around and to ask: What is an interval that contains β with a specified probability? For example, we might be interested in an interval (a_1, a_2) such that $P(a_1 < \beta < a_2) = .95$. The provision of such an interval gives us a good indication of where β is likely to lie and hence is a convenient expression of our state of knowledge about β. There are many intervals that satisfy the requirement that $P(a_1 < \beta < a_2) = .95$. Which .95 interval should we choose? *The interval that conveys the most information is the narrowest one.* It tells us more about where the value β lies. In Figure 24.2 three alternative .95 intervals, (a_1, a_2), (b_1, b_2), and (c_1, c_2) are drawn. Note that the narrowest (a_1, a_2) is in the center of the post-sample density function, that it is symmetric about the mean, and that the heights of the density at the endpoints are equal. That is, $f(a_1 \mid \mathbf{y}) = f(a_2 \mid \mathbf{y})$. These characteristics generally hold for symmetric post-sample density functions with a single mode.

We compute the narrowest .95 interval as follows. From knowledge of the standard normal distribution we know that

$$P\left(-1.96 < \frac{\beta - 23.5945}{\sqrt{1.44}} < 1.96\right) = .95$$

or

$$P\left(23.5945 - 1.96\sqrt{1.44} < \beta < 23.5945 + 1.96\sqrt{1.44}\right) = .95$$

Carrying out the necessary calculations leads to

$$P(21.24 < \beta < 25.95) = .95$$

Thus, our .95 interval estimate for expressing our state of knowledge about β is (21.24, 25.95). We could tell the CEO that there is a .95 probability that mean expenditure on food lies between \$21.24 and \$25.95 per week. He would readily understand this statement; it is just like the probability statements in Section 24.1.3. In this case, however, instead of beginning with an interval for mean expenditure and computing the corresponding probability, we began with the probability and found the corresponding interval.

The .95 interval estimate (21.24, 25.95) is identical to a 95% confidence interval that would be obtained using the repeated sample theory discussed in Chapter 4. However, we have given it a different interpretation in this chapter. The interpretation in this chapter

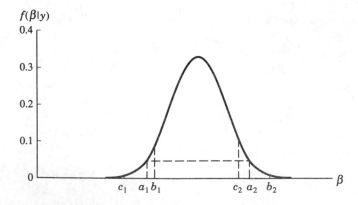

Figure 24.2 Some alternative .95 interval estimates.

is: *Given that the sample has been observed*, and given that we express uncertainty about β in terms of a probability density function, what is an interval that contains β with .95 probability? The endpoints of the interval are given, and we are uncertain about β. In Chapter 4 we were concerned with making probability statements about the endpoints of the interval $(\bar{y} \pm 1.96\,\sigma/\sqrt{T})$ *before the sample is taken*. We say that there is a .95 probability of obtaining a sample (and a $\bar{y}$) that leads to an interval that contains β. In one case we are making probability statements about characteristics of the sample before the sample is taken; in the other we are making subjective probability statements about the parameter, after the sample has been taken. Another way of viewing the distinction is to say that, in this chapter, we are *expressing our results in terms of a probability statement*; with confidence intervals we are using a *probability statement to justify use of a technique*.

Note that, in other cases, .95 interval estimates from post-sample density functions can differ from 95% confidence intervals in *magnitude* as well as in interpretation. Their equivalence in this case results from prior ignorance about β and from the model being studied.

24.1.5   Comparing Hypotheses

As a third way of presenting information about mean expenditure on food to someone not trained in statistics, we consider the problem of comparing hypotheses. Suppose that the CEO has collected relevant information on the costs and income from the establishment and running of a new supermarket. He has decided that it will be worthwhile opening a new supermarket if average expenditure on food is at least $22 per week. Under these circumstances we set up two hypotheses

$$H_0 : \beta < 22$$
$$H_1 : \beta \geq 22 \tag{24.1.9}$$

and examine the evidence in favor of each hypothesis.

Given that the sample has been observed, the post-sample density function $\beta \sim N(23.5945, 1.44)$ can be used to compute the probability of each hypothesis being correct. We have for each of the hypotheses

$$P(H_0) = P(\beta < 22) = P\left(z < \frac{22 - 23.5945}{\sqrt{1.44}} \right)$$
$$= P(z < -1.3288)$$
$$= .092$$
$$P(H_1) = P(\beta \geq 22) = 1 - P(\beta < 22)$$
$$= .908$$

Thus, we could report to the CEO that the probability of mean expenditure being at least $22 is 0.908. An alternative way to present this information is in terms of the *odds ratio K_{10}*, defined as

$$K_{10} = \frac{P(H_1)}{P(H_0)} = \frac{0.908}{0.092} = 9.87 \tag{24.1.10}$$

A value $K_{10} = 9.87$ says that the odds in favor of H_1 relative to H_0 are 9.87. The hypothesis H_1 is nearly 10 times more likely to be true than the hypothesis H_0. Whether or not this value is sufficiently high for the CEO to go ahead with his supermarket will depend on a comparison of the costs associated with incorrectly setting up a supermarket when H_0 is true, with the opportunity cost of not setting up a supermarket when H_1 is true. Courses in statistical decision theory deal with methods for choosing H_0 or H_1 based on the odds ratio in equation 24.1.10 and on the losses associated with making the wrong decision. Some of the issues involved in the setting up of a loss function are discussed in Section 24.2. If our objective is to learn about hypotheses without a need for acceptance or rejection of either, then the odds ratio in equation 24.1.10 is sufficient.

In Chapter 4 we described a rule for accepting or rejecting the null hypothesis H_0 depending on whether or not the sample mean $\bar{y}$ is "compatible" with the null hypothesis. This approach does not explicitly allow for the losses associated with a wrong decision. However, some recognition of these losses is implicit in the choice of a significance level α. This raises an interesting question for the techniques used in Chapter 4—what is the optimal level α for a test? In Exercise 24.1 you are asked to make a comparison of the significance-test approach with the "odds-ratio approach."

24.1.6   A Summary

Our first objective in this chapter was to show how to express uncertainty about a parameter (mean expenditure), before and after a sample has been taken, *given that we know nothing about the parameter at the outset*. Taking the situation where the variance of expenditure on food is known, we described how the normal post-sample density function $\beta \sim N(\bar{y}, \sigma^2/T)$ can be used to express uncertainty about β after a sample has been taken. This post-sample density function was used to make probability statements, to obtain an interval estimate, and to compare hypotheses—three ways of reporting information or results to nonstatisticians. Details on how to express uncertainty before the sample is taken, and the updating procedure that is used when the sample information becomes available, are given in Appendix Section 24A.2.1. When the variance σ^2 is unknown the post-sample t-distribution becomes relevant. To retrace the steps when σ^2 is unknown see Judge et al. (1988, pp. 140–152).

24.2   Point Estimation

In the first section of this chapter we summarized post-sample information about mean expenditure on food in terms of probability statements of one form or another. In addition to direct probability statements about β, we examined interval estimation and odds ratios, both of which are indirect ways of making probability statements about β. In this section, rather than make probability statements, we are concerned with summarizing our information about β with just a *single point estimate*. We wish to address another question raised in the introduction to this chapter. How do we choose a single point estimate for β so as to minimize in some sense the losses that occur from over- or underestimation?

Let $\hat{\beta}$ be an estimate for β. In the context of one supermarket in the chain, overestimation of β ($\hat{\beta} > \beta$) will mean that some unnecessary costs or losses are incurred. Too many employees will be hired, too much stock will be purchased, and perishable stocks may go bad. On the other hand, with underestimation of mean expenditure ($\hat{\beta} < \beta$), losses will take the form of forgone profits that could have been realized had supermarket stocks and facilities been adequate for the demand. *The function that describes what losses will be incurred if mean expenditure is β, which we estimate by $\hat{\beta}$, is called a loss function.* The notation we use for this function is $L(\hat{\beta}, \beta)$.

It is customary to measure loss in a relative sense, so we assume that $L(\hat{\beta}, \beta) = 0$ when $\hat{\beta} = \beta$. That is, if our estimate is right on the mark, there is no relative loss (or profit). Thus, the function $L(\hat{\beta}, \beta)$ measures how much worse off we are relative to the ideal situation, where we can estimate β exactly. What other properties are reasonable for the loss function? We would expect the loss to be larger the larger is the error in estimating β. In other words, we would expect $L(\hat{\beta}, \beta)$ to be an increasing function of $|\hat{\beta} - \beta|$. Furthermore, the loss from overestimating might be different from the loss from underestimating; that is, the loss from a given difference $(\hat{\beta} - \beta) = a(a > 0)$, might be different from that for $(\hat{\beta} - \beta) = a(a < 0)$. In this case we say that loss is asymmetric.

To give life to these ideas, we first consider point estimation from the symmetric quadratic loss function

$$L(\hat{\beta}, \beta) = c(\beta - \hat{\beta})^2$$

(24.2.1)

where c is a constant. This function is symmetric in the sense that the losses from overestimation are identical to the losses from underestimation; it is quadratic because loss is a quadratic function of the estimation error $|\beta - \hat{\beta}|$. In the case of the supermarket, the constant c translates the units of the squared estimation error into the relevant dollar units for loss. A detailed examination of supermarket costs and profits would be needed to determine whether such a function is suitable.

As a basis for obtaining a point estimate for β, it seems natural to consider minimizing loss in some sense. The value for $\hat{\beta}$ that minimizes equation 24.2.1 is clearly $\hat{\beta} = \beta$. However, because β is unknown, it is not a feasible estimate. To overcome this problem we find a weighted average of the losses associated with all values that β could take and choose that $\hat{\beta}$ that minimizes the average loss. What should we use to weight all the different possible values for β in this averaging process? The post-sample density function $f(\beta \mid \mathbf{y})$ serves as a suitable weighting function since it weights more likely values of β more heavily and less likely values less heavily. Let us investigate how this process works. Suppose the point b in Figure 24.3 is chosen as an estimate for β. The loss function corresponding to this choice also appears in Figure 24.3. It is equal to zero when $\beta = b$ and gets larger as $|\beta - b|$ gets larger. To obtain an expression for *average* loss for the choice $\hat{\beta} = b$, we take the following expectation

$$E[L(\beta, b)] = E[c(\beta - b)^2] = \int c(\beta - b)^2 f(\beta \mid \mathbf{y}) \, d\beta$$

(24.2.2)

Recall from Chapter 2 that the expected value of a random variable can be viewed as a weighted average of all possible values of that random variable, with the probability density function of the random variable providing the weights. The expected value of a *function* of a random variable is a weighted average of that *function*. When we have a continuous random variable, the appropriate way of representing the expectation (or the weighted average) is via an integral. In equation 24.2.2 we are treating β as our random variable and $f(\beta \mid \mathbf{y})$ as its probability density function. We are interested in the expectation or average of a function of β, namely, the function $c(\beta - b)^2$. Thus, we think of equation 24.2.2 as being computed in the following way: For each value of β, we find the loss $c(\beta - b)^2$. Then, we weight each loss with the corresponding point from the post-sample density $f(\beta \mid \mathbf{y})$. See Figure 24.3, where the loss at β_1 is weighted by $f(\beta_1 \mid \mathbf{y})$. The weighted losses $c(\beta - b)^2 f(\beta \mid \mathbf{y})$ are then averaged over all possible values of β.

These steps lead to a value of expected loss for the choice of estimate $\hat{\beta} = b$. Of course, there are many other choices we could make, each one leading to a different expected loss. As the optimal choice of an estimate we take the one that minimizes expected loss. *It can be shown that, when loss is quadratic, the mean of the post-sample density func-*

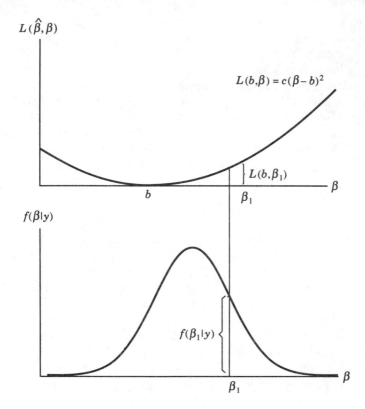

Figure 24.3 An example of average loss.

tion is always that value of $\hat{\beta}$ that minimizes expected loss. The post-sample density function that we have considered thus far, which is the normal when σ is known, has as its mean the sample mean $\bar{y}$. Thus, for the post-sample density function, the point estimate that minimizes expected loss, when loss is quadratic, is $\bar{y} = 23.5945$. Note that this is the same estimate as that obtained by using the sampling theory least squares procedure outlined in Chapter 3. In Chapter 3 we discovered, in the sampling theory repeated sampling context, that the *estimator* $\bar{y}$ is a minimum variance unbiased estimator. Now we have an additional property of $\bar{y}$. If we have available loss information on the consequences of over- or underestimating β, and if this information can be expressed in terms of a quadratic loss function, then $\bar{y}$ is the estimator that *minimizes expected (average) loss.*

Let us now consider an example of an asymmetric loss function, one where the losses from overestimating β are greater than the losses from underestimating β. Thus, we envisage a situation where overexpansion in the food industry (building and enlarging supermarkets unnecessarily) is more costly than underexpansion (having existing supermarkets unable to cope with demand). A possible loss function to describe these circumstances is

$$L\left(\hat{\beta}, \beta\right) = c\left[\exp\left\{a\left(\hat{\beta} - \beta\right)\right\} - a\left(\hat{\beta} - \beta\right) - 1\right] \qquad c > 0, a > 0 \qquad (24.2.3)$$

The constant c is a scale factor that depends on the units of measurement of β and the units of measurement of loss. The value of the constant a determines the shape of the loss function. Overestimation is penalized more heavily than underestimation because the term $\exp\{a(\hat{\beta} - \beta)\}$ dominates the linear term $a(\hat{\beta} - \beta)$ when $\hat{\beta} - \beta > 0$, but the linear term is dominant when $\hat{\beta} - \beta < 0$. The greater the value for a, the more asymmetric is the loss function.

Let β have a normal postsample density function with mean $E[\beta]$ and variance $\text{var}(\beta)$. Then, the optimal point estimate that minimizes expected loss for the loss function in equation 24.2.3 is

$$\hat{\beta} = E[\beta] - \frac{a\,\text{var}(\beta)}{2} \qquad (24.2.4)$$

Thus, the post-sample mean $E[\beta]$ is no longer optimal. Because underestimation is less risky than overestimation, an amount equal to $a.\text{var}(\beta)/2$ is subtracted from $E[\beta]$.

Suppose that $a = 2$, then from the post-sample density function derived in Section 24.1, where $E[\beta] = \bar{y} = 23.5945$ and $\text{var}(\beta) = \sigma^2/T = 1.44$, the optimal point estimate for mean food expenditure is

$$\hat{\beta} = 23.5945 - \frac{2 \times 1.44}{2} = 22.1545$$

The reduction in this estimate relative to that from the symmetric quadratic loss function is not large. This reduction is greater the larger the value of a and the larger the variance of the post-sample probability density function (p.d.f).

In this section we have illustrated how loss information can be used to find point estimates for a symmetric quadratic loss function and for an asymmetric loss function with a linear and an exponential term. We now turn to the last question posed in the introduction.

24.3 Accumulating Information

The remaining question that we posed in the introduction, and that we have not yet tackled, concerns a situation where we have some prior, presample, or nonsample information about mean food expenditure. Our previous analysis was based on the assumption that, before we took a sample, we were totally ignorant or totally uncertain about β. What happens if other information is available? Our intuition would suggest that, in decision problems under uncertainty, we should accumulate and make use of all information that is available. For instance, the results from a previous sample might be available, you might have some idea of mean expenditure based simply on how much *you* spend on food each week, or you might get some information by talking to an expert such as a supermarket manager. How do we represent this state of knowledge or level of uncertainty about β before a sample is taken? After we observe a sample, how do we update our information, or describe the "reduction" in the level of our uncertainty? In other words, what information processing rule do we employ?

24.3.1 Including Prior Information

We continue to be interested in learning about mean expenditure on food β by using observations from the statistical model $y_t = \beta + e_t$, where the e_t are independent and $e_t \sim N(0, \sigma^2)$ with σ^2 known. As we discussed in the introduction, initial or *prior information* about β could be from a previous sample, from our own knowledge, or from the opinion of experts. We will investigate the case where we have information from a previous sample. For another case where prior information from your own knowledge of weekly expenditure on food is available, you are invited to trace through Exercise 24.3.

Suppose that before our major sample of size 40 was taken, a small pilot survey involving just six households was carried out. The average weekly food expenditure for these six households is given in Table 24.2.

The sample mean and sample variance from these 6 observations are

$$\bar{y}_0 = \frac{1}{6}\sum_{t=1}^{6} y_t = 25.475 \qquad \hat{\sigma}_0^2 = \frac{1}{5}\sum_{t=1}^{6}(y_t - \bar{y}_0)^2 = 53.27187 \qquad (24.3.1)$$

A "0" subscript has been attached to $\bar{y}$ and $\hat{\sigma}^2$ to indicate that they are from the pilot survey. A subscript "1" will be used to denote the same sample quantities from the major sample of 40 observations. Thus, we have

$$\bar{y}_1 = 23.5945 \qquad \hat{\sigma}_1^2 = 66.84738 \qquad (24.3.2)$$

Suppose now that we are at a point where the pilot survey has been taken and these observations are available, but the major sample has not yet been drawn. How will we summarize the information from the pilot survey? The natural device to use is the post-sample density function derived from this survey. Let us introduce T_0 as notation for the sample size of the pilot survey (to distinguish it from T_1 that we will later use for the sample size for the major sample). From our analysis in Section 24.1, we know that, if we assume σ^2 known, our information from the pilot survey is represented by the post-sample density function

$$\beta \sim N\left(\bar{y}_0, \frac{\sigma^2}{T_0}\right) \qquad \text{or} \qquad \beta \sim N(25.475, 9.6) \qquad (24.3.3)$$

Given this statement of our knowledge about β, the next step is to take the larger sample of 40 households. With respect to the larger sample, the information in equation 24.3.3 becomes prior information or a prior density function. That is, *the post-sample density function from the first sample becomes a prior density function with respect to the second sample.*

Having established the prior representation of our state of knowledge in equation 24.3.3, we are ready to collect and use the 40 new sample observations so as to update our state of knowledge. Suppose then that we have the new sample observations and we know that $\bar{y}_1 = 23.5945$. If we ignore the prior information, we know we represent the new sample information by the density function

$$\beta \sim N\left(\bar{y}_1, \frac{\sigma^2}{T_1}\right) \qquad \text{or} \qquad \beta \sim N(23.5945, 1.44) \qquad (24.3.4)$$

Thus, the question becomes: How do we combine the two pieces of information, that given in equation 24.3.3 and that given in equation 24.3.4?

Table 24.2 Weekly Expenditure on Food from a Pilot Survey of Six Households

30.00	23.69	29.04
11.48	30.83	27.81

Before we investigate this question, it is instructive to compare the two pieces of information. Both normal distributions are graphed in Figure 24.4. Note that $f(\beta \mid \mathbf{y}_0)$, the density function from the pilot survey, is much more dispersed or spread out than $f(\beta \mid \mathbf{y}_1)$, the density function from the second sample. The additional dispersion reflects additional uncertainty about β. After we take a sample of size 6, we are going to be much less certain about the value of β than after we take a sample of size 40. A comparison of 95% interval estimates from each of the density functions makes this fact more evident. From $f(\beta \mid \mathbf{y}_0)$ we can show that

$$P(19.40 < \beta < 31.55) = .95 \tag{24.3.5}$$

whereas from $f(\beta \mid \mathbf{y}_1)$ we have already observed in Section 24.1.4 that

$$P(21.24 < \beta < 25.95) = .95 \tag{24.3.6}$$

The first interval is much wider than the second.

We turn now to the question of combining the information in equation 24.3.3 with that in equation 24.3.4. The formal rule for this procedure is known as Bayes' rule; its application to this problem is discussed in Appendix 24A.2. Here we rely on an intuitive argument. We seek a post-sample density function for β, one that is obtained by updating equation 24.3.3 with the information in equation 24.3.4. Let us use the notation $f(\beta \mid \mathbf{y}_0, \mathbf{y}_1)$ for the post-sample density function and $\overline{\overline{\beta}}$ and $\overline{\overline{\sigma}}_\beta^2$ for its mean and variance. It can be shown that $f(\beta \mid \mathbf{y}_0, \mathbf{y}_1)$ is a normal distribution. That is,

$$\beta \sim N\left(\overline{\overline{\beta}}, \overline{\overline{\sigma}}_\beta^2\right) \tag{24.3.7}$$

How do we find $\overline{\overline{\beta}}$ and $\overline{\overline{\sigma}}_\beta^2$ from $\overline{y}_0$, $\overline{y}_1$, σ^2, T_0, and T_1? It seems reasonable that the post-sample mean $\overline{\overline{\beta}}$ should depend on the means $\overline{y}_0$ and $\overline{y}_1$ from each source of information. It also seems reasonable that each source of information should be weighted according to its reliability. We can measure the reliability of information on β by its *precision*, which is the inverse of the variance of the density function that provides the information. The *precisions* of each source of information are given by

$$h_0 = \left(\frac{\sigma^2}{T_0}\right)^{-1} = \frac{T_0}{\sigma^2} = 0.10417 = \text{precision of information in equation 24.3.3}$$

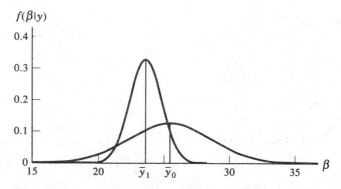

$f(\beta \mid y)$

Figure 24.4 Density functions for β from two samples, σ^2 known.

$$h_1 = \left(\frac{\sigma^2}{T_1}\right)^{-1} = \frac{T_1}{\sigma^2} = 0.69444 = \text{precision of information in equation 24.3.4}$$

The larger sample yields the greater precision.

The post-sample mean $\overline{\overline{\beta}}$ that combines information from both sources is a weighted average of $\overline{y}_0$ and $\overline{y}_1$, with the respective precisions h_0 and h_1 as the weights. That is,

$$\overline{\overline{\beta}} = \frac{h_0 \overline{y}_0 + h_1 \overline{y}_1}{h_0 + h_1} = \frac{T_0 \overline{y}_0 + T_1 \overline{y}_1}{T_0 + T_1}$$

$$= \frac{(6)(25.475) + (40)(23.5945)}{6 + 40} = 23.8398 \qquad (24.3.8)$$

Note that $\overline{\overline{\beta}}$ lies between $\overline{y}_0$ and $\overline{y}_1$, but it is much closer to $\overline{y}_1$ because the reliability of information associated with $\overline{y}_1$ is greater than that associated with $\overline{y}_0$.

Let us now consider $\overline{\overline{\sigma}}_\beta^2$. The precision of the combined information $\overline{\overline{h}}$ is simply the sum of the precision of each source of information. That is,

$$\overline{\overline{h}} = h_0 + h_1 = 0.10417 + 0.69444 = 0.79861 \qquad (24.3.9)$$

where $\overline{\overline{h}}$ is the precision, or the inverse of the variance, of the normal post-sample density function. Thus, any change in the precision of one source of information changes the precision in the total information by the same amount. For $\overline{\overline{\sigma}}_\beta^2$, we have

$$\overline{\overline{\sigma}}_\beta^2 = \frac{1}{\overline{\overline{h}}} = \frac{1}{h_0 + h_1} = \frac{1}{\dfrac{T_0}{\sigma^2} + \dfrac{T_1}{\sigma^2}} = \frac{\sigma^2}{T_0 + T_1} = \frac{57.6}{40 + 6} = 1.25217 \qquad (24.3.10)$$

The information provided by our post-sample density function is

$$\beta \sim N(23.8398, 1.25217) \qquad (24.3.11)$$

This density function is graphed in Figure 24.5, alongside the density functions from each source of information, $f(\beta \mid y_0)$ and $f(\beta \mid y_1)$. Note that it has less variance or dis-

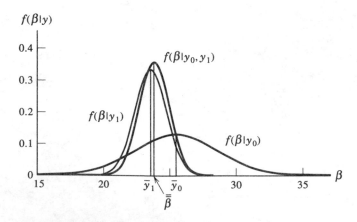

Figure 24.5 Combining information from two sources, σ known.

persion than both the other density functions. In particular, a comparison of $f(\beta \mid \mathbf{y}_1)$ with $f(\beta \mid \mathbf{y}_0, \mathbf{y}_1)$ indicates how the additional information provided by the pilot survey has changed our views about β. A new 95% interval estimate is one way of summarizing the combined information. Proceeding as before we have

$$P(21.65 < \beta < 26.03) = .95 \tag{24.3.12}$$

Comparing this interval with (21.24, 25.95), the one obtained from just the sample information, we see that the upper limit has increased slightly but the overall interval is narrower, reflecting the increased precision from inclusion of prior information.

Finally, note that the results we have obtained for the post-sample density function are exactly the same as those that we would have obtained if we had pooled both samples into one bigger sample of 46 observations. We can see this result by rewriting equation 24.3.8 as

$$\overline{\overline{\beta}} = \frac{T_0 \overline{y}_0 + T_1 \overline{y}_1}{T_0 + T_1} = \frac{\sum\limits_{t=1}^{T_0} y_t + \sum\limits_{s=1}^{T_1} y_s}{T_0 + T_1} \tag{24.3.13}$$

Also, note that the variance of the post-sample density function from a combined sample of size $(T_0 + T_1)$ will be $\sigma^2/(T_0 + T_1)$, the same as that in equation 24.3.10. Since it seems intuitively obvious to combine both samples into one bigger one of size 46, the reader may ask why we have concentrated on representing information at different points in time, and on how to formally adjust our state of knowledge as we accumulate more information. We have followed this strategy because, in practice, we are continually gathering more information and using this additional information to update our state of knowledge. Furthermore, as we'll learn in Section 24.4 and in Exercise 24.3, prior information does not always come in the form of a previous (pilot) sample. Under these circumstances it is still convenient to think of it as arising from a hypothetical previous sample.

Our main result in this section can be summarized as follows: Suppose we are interested in learning about the mean of a normal population β when the variance of that population σ^2 is known. If we have prior sample or nonsample information on β in the form of a normal density function with mean $\overline{y}_0$ and variance σ^2/T_0, and we collect sample information represented by a normal density function with mean $\overline{y}_1$ and variance σ^2/T_1, then the post-sample density function for β will be normal with mean $\overline{\overline{\beta}} = (T_0 \overline{y}_0 + T_1 \overline{y}_1)/(T_0 + T_1)$ and variance $\sigma^2/(T_0 + T_1)$. When σ^2 is unknown the t-distribution is relevant; this case is discussed in Judge et al. (1988, pp. 140--52).

24.3.2   A Summary

In many instances when we wish to learn about a parameter such as the mean of household expenditure on food, we have some kind of beginning or *prior* information about that parameter. A convenient way to express our knowledge or level of uncertainty about the parameter is through a probability density function. We examined a normal prior probability density function (σ known) for the case where our prior information comes from a pilot survey. We then showed how our prior information is updated as additional sample information becomes available. The post-sample probability density function shows the effect of this accumulation of knowledge; it indicates how our expression of uncertainty about mean food expenditure has changed after the new sample information has been included. The results that we derived are summarized in Table 24.3.

Table 24.3 Summary of Bayes and Sampling Theory Results, σ Known

	Bayes Results			
Prior	**Post-Sample**	**General Result**	**Sampling Theory Result**	

Noninformative

Uniform density function $\qquad \beta \sim N\left(\bar{y}, \dfrac{\sigma^2}{T}\right) \qquad \dfrac{\sqrt{T}(\bar{y}-\beta)}{\sigma} \sim N(0,1) \qquad \bar{y} \sim N\left(\beta, \dfrac{\sigma^2}{T}\right)$

Previous sample

$$\beta \sim N\left(\bar{y}_0, \frac{\sigma^2}{T_0}\right) \qquad \beta \sim N\left(\bar{\bar{\beta}}, \frac{\sigma^2}{T_0 + T_1}\right) \qquad \frac{\sqrt{T_0 + T_1}\left(\bar{\bar{\beta}} - \beta\right)}{\sigma} \sim N(0,1)$$

$$\bar{\bar{\beta}} \sim N\left(\beta, \frac{\sigma^2}{T_0 + T_1}\right)$$

In Section 24.1 we described the normal post-sample density function as a "technical" way of presenting information to trained statisticians. The same remarks are valid in our current section, Section 24.3. To present our results to nonstatisticians, less technical ways of summarizing the density functions, such as probability statements, interval estimates, or hypotheses comparisons can be used; these are introduced in Exercise 24.3.

24.4 Bayesian Inference for a Second Problem

To help you become more comfortable with the concepts and approach of Bayesian inference, consider, in a somewhat different context, the following problem. Suppose that weekly receipts (in thousands of dollars) at a Louisiana Fried Chicken (LFC) outlet are normally distributed with a mean of β and variance $\sigma^2 = 4$. Denoting weekly receipts by y, we have $y \sim N(\beta, \sigma^2 = 4)$. Assume that you are interested in purchasing the LFC outlet and, therefore, that you are interested in gathering information about mean weekly receipts β. In the sampling theory approach you would begin by taking a sample of weekly receipts. Suppose that a sample of size 10 is taken and that it yields these observations.

$$\mathbf{y}' = \left(y_1, y_2, ..., y_{10}\right)$$
$$= (4.74,\ 7.11,\ 5.31,\ 6.28,\ 6.09,\ 8.52,\ 2.78,\ 7.38,\ 5.44,\ 5.72)$$

Using any of the estimation rules outlined in Chapter 3, the sample mean would be used as a point estimate, and, in this case, it is given by

$$\bar{y} = \sum_{t=1}^{10} y_t / 10 = 5.937 \tag{24.4.1}$$

For an interval estimate, say a 95% confidence interval, we have

$$\bar{y} \pm 1.96\sigma / \sqrt{T} = 5.937 \pm 1.96 \times 2 / \sqrt{10}$$

or

$$(4.697,\ 7.177) \tag{24.4.2}$$

Thus, roughly speaking, our sample information suggests that mean weekly receipts are about \$5900 but that this mean could be as low as \$4700 or as high as \$7200.

24.4.1   Prior Information

In the Bayesian approach we tackle the problem by first asking whether we have any prior information about β and by expressing this information in terms of a subjective prior density function (p.d.f.), denoted by $f(\beta)$. Suppose that, from our previous experience in fast-food chicken outlets, we believe that there is a .95 probability that mean weekly receipts lie between \$5000 and \$11,000. That is, in thousands of dollars,

$$P(5 < \beta < 11) = .95 \tag{24.4.3}$$

Suppose also that the subjective p.d.f. about likely values of β can be adequately represented by a normal distribution with mean $\bar{\beta}$ and variance $\bar{\sigma}_\beta^2$. That is,

$$\beta \sim N\left(\bar{\beta}, \bar{\sigma}_\beta^2\right) \tag{24.4.4}$$

How do we use our prior information, expressed in probability form in equation 24.4.3, to find values for $\bar{\beta}$ and variance $\bar{\sigma}_\beta^2$, so that we can also express it in terms of the normal p.d.f.? Using properties of the normal distribution, we have from equation 24.4.3

$$P(5 < \beta < 11) = P\left(\frac{5-\bar{\beta}}{\bar{\sigma}_\beta} < \frac{\beta-\bar{\beta}}{\bar{\sigma}_\beta} < \frac{11-\bar{\beta}}{\bar{\sigma}_\beta}\right) = .95 \tag{24.4.5}$$

where $z = \left(\beta - \bar{\beta}\right)/\bar{\sigma}_\beta$ is a standard normal [$N(0, 1)$] random variable. We also know that

$$P\left(-1.96 < \frac{\beta-\bar{\beta}}{\bar{\sigma}_\beta} < 1.96\right) = .95 \tag{24.4.6}$$

Because equations 24.4.5 and 24.4.6 are equivalent probability statements, a suitable pair of values for the prior parameters $\bar{\beta}$ and $\bar{\sigma}_\beta$ can be obtained by solving the two equations

$$-1.96 = \frac{5-\bar{\beta}}{\bar{\sigma}_\beta} \qquad \text{and} \qquad 1.96 = \frac{11-\bar{\beta}}{\bar{\sigma}_\beta}$$

Solving these two equations for $\bar{\beta}$ and $\bar{\sigma}_\beta$ yields

$$\bar{\beta} = 8 \qquad \bar{\sigma}_\beta = 1.5306 \qquad \text{and} \qquad \bar{\sigma}_\beta^2 = 2.3427$$

Thus, if a normal distribution is appropriate to represent prior views about β, and you believe that $P(5 < \beta < 11) = .95$, then a suitable prior p.d.f. $f(\beta)$ is such that $\beta \sim N(8, 2.3427)$. Note that, in addition to equation 24.4.3, the assumption of a normal distribution implies other probability statements about β. For example,

$$P(\beta > 8) = P(\beta < 8) = .5$$
$$P(6 < \beta < 10) = .81$$

and

$$P(4 < \beta < 12) = .99$$

In Section 24.3 where we had prior information in the form of a pilot survey, we wrote the prior information as

$$\beta \sim N\left(\bar{y}_0, \frac{\sigma^2}{T_0}\right)$$

$$(24.4.7)$$

In the LFC example of this section we are representing our prior information in the form

$$\beta \sim N\left(\bar{\beta}, \sigma_\beta^2\right)$$

$$(24.4.8)$$

No pilot survey exists in this case. However, we can nevertheless treat information in equation 24.4.8 *as if it comes from a previous hypothetical sample*. In other words, we can pretend that

$$\bar{\beta} = \bar{y}_0 \quad \text{and} \quad \sigma_\beta^2 = \frac{\sigma^2}{T_0}$$

If we follow this pretense, then the same rules and formulas that we introduced in Section 24.3 are relevant. All that we need to·do is to find values for $\bar{y}_0$ and T_0. For $\bar{y}_0$ we have

$$\bar{y}_0 = \bar{\beta} = 8$$

$$(24.4.9)$$

For T_0 we use

$$\frac{\sigma^2}{T_0} = \frac{4}{T_0} = \sigma_\beta^2 = 2.3427$$

or

$$T_0 = \frac{4}{2.3427} = 1.7074$$

$$(24.4.10)$$

Thus, we act as if the "size" of our hypothetical sample is 1.7074. The fact that this value is not an integer does not invalidate our procedures.

You could decide whether or not to purchase the LFC outlet simply on the basis of the prior information. However, you are likely to make a more informed decision if you can collect additional information in the form of a sample of weekly receipts and combine this sample information with the prior information. Let us examine, then, the nature of the post-sample information after we combine the prior information in equations 24.4.9 and 24.4.10 with the sample information in equation 24.4.1.

24.4.2   Updating the Prior Information

In Section 24.3 we learned that when we combine prior information expressed in the form of a normal p.d.f., with sample information from a normal p.d.f. with known variance, the result is a normal post-sample p.d.f. with mean and variance given, respectively, by

$$\bar{\bar{\beta}} = \frac{T_0 \bar{y}_0 + T_1 \bar{y}_1}{T_0 + T_1} \quad \text{and} \quad \bar{\bar{\sigma}}_\beta^2 = \frac{\sigma^2}{T_0 + T_1}$$

In our case we have

$$T_0 = 1.7074 \qquad T_1 = 10 \qquad \bar{y}_0 = 8 \qquad \bar{y}_1 = 5.937 \qquad \sigma^2 = 4$$

Thus,

$$\overline{\overline{\beta}} = \frac{(1.7074)(8)+(10)(5.937)}{1.7074+10} = 6.238$$

and

$$\overline{\overline{\sigma}}_{\beta}^2 = \frac{4}{1.7074+10} = 0.3417$$

The post-sample p.d.f. for mean weekly receipts β is the normal distribution

$$\beta \sim N(6.238, 0.3417)$$

A comparison of the prior and post-sample p.d.f.s for β, which are graphed in Figure 24.6, clearly shows the effect of the sample information. The sample information has moved the distribution to the left and made it much sharper, reflecting the improved precision in our information.

24.4.3   Interval Estimation

To develop an interval estimate for mean weekly receipts β from the post-sample density function $\beta \sim N(6.238, 0.3417)$, we begin with the result

$$\frac{\beta-6.238}{\sqrt{0.3417}} \sim N(0, 1)$$

and, for an interval estimate with probability content .95,

$$P\left(-1.96 < \frac{\beta-6.238}{\sqrt{0.3417}} < 1.96\right) = .95$$

or

$$P(5.092 < \beta < 7.384) = .95 \qquad (24.4.11)$$

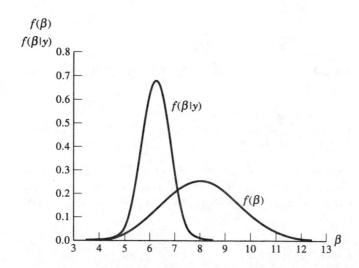

Figure 24.6 Prior and post-sample densities for β when σ is known.

Thus, the .95 interval estimate for β is (5.092, 7.384). After observing the sample, there is .95 probability that β lies between 5.092 to 7.384. Note the effect of the sample information. Based only on prior information, there was a .95 probability that β lies between 5.0 and 11.0.

24.4.4 Hypothesis Testing

Let us compare two one-sided hypotheses of the form

$$H_0 : \beta \le 5 \tag{24.4.12a}$$

$$H_1 : \beta > 5 \tag{24.4.12b}$$

In the context of the LFC example, such hypotheses might be relevant for a decision concerning whether or not to purchase the chicken outlet. Let us suppose that it is profitable to purchase the outlet if H_1 is true (average weekly earnings are greater than $5000); otherwise, it is not profitable (H_0 is true). Using the sampling theory procedures outlined in Chapter 4, the first step toward carrying out this test is to calculate a value of the relevant test statistic, namely,

$$z = \frac{\hat{\beta} - 5}{\sigma / \sqrt{T}} = \frac{5.937 - 5}{2 / \sqrt{10}} = 1.482 \tag{24.4.13}$$

Using a 5% significance level (or a maximum Type I error of .05), the critical value for the test is $z_{(0.05)} = 1.645$. Since $z = 1.482 < 1.645$, the sampling theory approach leads us to accept H_0 and to not purchase the outlet.

To compute the odds in favor of H_0, we use the post-sample p.d.f. $\beta \sim N(6.238, 0.3417)$. We have

$$P(H_0) = P(\beta \le 5)$$

$$= P\left(z \le \frac{5 - 6.238}{\sqrt{0.3417}} \right)$$

$$= P(z \le -2.12)$$

$$= .017$$

$$P(H_1) = P(\beta > 5) = .983$$

Thus, the odds in favor of H_0 are $K_{01} = P(H_0)/P(H_1) = .017/.983 = .0173$. Alternatively, the posterior odds in favor of H_1 are

$$K_{10} = \frac{P(H_1)}{P(H_0)} = \frac{.983}{.017} = 57.8 \tag{24.4.14}$$

Thus, within the Bayesian framework, we conclude that H_1 is more than 57 times more likely to be true than is H_0. This example clearly demonstrates how vastly different the outcomes of the two inference procedures can be. Note also that this result depends on the prior information for β.

24.4.5 Prediction

Suppose that, after purchasing the LFC outlet, we are interested in obtaining information about receipts in some future week, say $(T + 1)$. In the Bayesian framework such information is summarized by using a predictive p.d.f. for y_{T+1}. This predictive p.d.f. can tell us the probability of a future week's receipts lying within some specified range.

To derive the predictive p.d.f. for y_{T+1}, it is convenient to write the model generating this observation as

$$y_{T+1} = \beta + e_{T+1} \qquad (24.4.15)$$

where $e_{T+1} \sim N(0,\ \sigma^2 = 4)$. Using all the information on β that was outlined in Section 24.4.2, the post-sample p.d.f. derived in that section is relevant and is

$$\beta \sim N(6.238, 0.3417) \qquad (24.4.16)$$

Since in equation 24.4.16 both β and e_{T+1} are normally distributed, it follows that the predictive p.d.f. for y_{T+1} will be normal. Furthermore, e_{T+1} and β can be treated as independent because the post-sample p.d.f. for β is based only on past observations (y_1, y_2,...,y_T), which are assumed to be independent of the future observation y_{T+1} (and the future error term e_{T+1}). Thus

$$E[y_{T+1}] = E[\beta] + E[e_{T+1}] = 6.238$$
$$\mathrm{var}(y_{T+1}) = \mathrm{var}(\beta) + \mathrm{var}(e_{T+1}) = 4.3417$$

The predictive p.d.f. for y_{T+1} is, therefore,

$$y_{T+1} \sim N(6.238, 4.3417)$$

and this p.d.f. can be used to make probability statements about likely future values of weekly receipts.

24.4.6   Unknown Variance

If the assumption of known variance is relaxed, Bayesian inference procedures must be developed for both the mean β and the standard deviation σ of the normal distribution. To handle this situation, a joint prior p.d.f. for (β, σ) and the corresponding joint post-sample p.d.f. are developed in Judge et al. (1988, pp. 140–152).

24.5   Critique of Concepts

In this chapter we began with three main objectives:

1.   To provide a framework for expressing uncertainty about the mean of a normal population before and after a sample of data has been collected.

2.   To provide a framework for introducing additional information about a parameter other than that provided by the sample.

3.   To provide a framework for including information on potential losses when obtaining point estimates.

We showed that we can express uncertainty about a parameter by treating it or thinking about it as a random variable. We assign to it a probability density function that expresses our state of knowledge concerning what are likely and unlikely values for the parameter. The density function expressing uncertainty before a sample is taken is called a prior density function; that which expresses uncertainty after a sample is taken is called a post-sample density function. Bayes' information processing rule provides a formal framework for updating a prior density function with sample information to give a post-sample density function.

We examined the results from updating from a prior position of no information about the population mean, and from a prior position where information from a pilot survey is available. The latter case is an example of how to achieve our second objective— how to introduce additional information about a parameter other than that provided by the sample. A further example, where prior information exists in the form of a subjective p.d.f., was also introduced. A normal probability density function was used to express uncertainty about the mean β when the population variance σ^2 was known. For those not trained in statistics, the information contained in a probability density function can be summarized by using probability statements, interval estimates and hypothesis comparisons. If the losses from over- or underestimation of β can be expressed in terms of a symmetric quadratic loss function, then $\bar{y}$, the sample mean, is the estimator that minimizes expected loss. This example of a loss function showed how loss information can be included in the framework for choosing a point estimate, and thus it let us achieve our third objective.

The approach taken in this chapter was different from that in Chapters 3 and 4. In Chapters 3 and 4 the emphasis was on developing techniques because of their properties *before* a sample was taken. An estimator $\bar{y}$ was used because of its anticipated performance (minimum variance unbiasedness) in future samples. The probability statements that we could make about $\bar{y}$ before taking any observations led to our choice of estimator and to our choice of method for constructing confidence intervals. When we constructed a 95% confidence interval, we noted that, before the sample is taken, there is a .95 probability of observing $\bar{y}$ such that the constructed interval contains β. With respect to hypothesis testing, critical values for hypothesis tests were based on a fixed significance level (given Type I error) and were found by considering the probability of getting a $\bar{y}$ such that we reject an incorrect null hypothesis.

In contrast, in this chapter we were concerned with making probability statements *after* the sample and $\bar{y}$ have been observed. We make probability statements that express our uncertainty about β given what has been observed up to this point in time. To compare the two approaches, you should ask yourself what method of presenting information is more comfortable for you. Do you present information by saying: These point and interval estimates come from techniques that I know will yield "good" results if I use them over and over again. Or, do you say: Based on the information I have to date, I can make these probability statements about the unknown parameter. If you succeed in getting the ideas from both the sampling theory and Bayes' approaches to inference in your head, both inference procedures will serve you well. Rather than choose one approach over the other, you should ask: How can I make both approaches work for me?

Finally, we need to recognize that, although we have applied the techniques of this chapter to a sample of household expenditure data, there are many other economic variables and economic data sets where the concepts are equally relevant. Data on income, investment, production, wage rates and unemployment, for example, could be analyzed by using the approach in this chapter. Also, the techniques of this chapter can be extended to analyze relationships between economic variables, such as investment and interest rates, consumption and income, or quantity demanded and price. We begin an investigation of such extensions in Chapter 25. For further reading on the techniques outlined here and in Chapter 25, see Hey (1983), Press (1989), and Judge et al. (1988, pp. 117–153). Appendix 24A that follows describes in more detail how Bayes' rule is used to update or process information.

24.6 Exercises

24.1. Consider the problem of testing or comparing the two hypotheses H_0: $\beta < 22$ and H_1: $\beta \geq 22$ given in Section 24.1.5. Assume that we have available the information $\bar{y} = 23.5945$, $T = 40$, and $\sigma^2 = 57.6$. Using the sampling theory hypothesis testing procedure described in Chapter 4, would you reject H_0 at (a) the 5% significance level, (b) the 10% significance level? What value of $\bar{y}$ would be necessary for you to reject H_0 at the 5% significance level? If $\bar{y}$ was equal to this value, what would be the odds ratio in favor of H_1?

24.2. The average weekly *total* expenditure by the same 40 households whose food expenditure we have been investigating is given in Table 24.4. Suppose that you have no prior information about β, mean total expenditure for the whole population of households. However, assume that the population variance is known to be $\sigma^2 = 200$.
   (a) How would you represent your state of knowledge about β after the data in Table 24.4 have been observed?
   (b) Find $P(67 < \beta < 73)$ and $P(65 < \beta < 75)$.
   (c) Find a 95% interval estimate for β.
   (d) Find the odds ratio in favor of H_0: $\beta < 70$ relative to the alternative H_1: $\beta \geq 70$.

24.3. Consider the example carried through in the chapter, that of estimating β, mean household expenditure on food. However, presume that, at the outset, you have some idea of the value of β. You say there is a 50–50 chance that β is below or above 21. That is, $P(\beta > 21) = P(\beta < 21) = .5$. Also, you believe there is a 1 in 10 chance that β is above 30. That is, $P(\beta > 30) = .1$.
   (a) Find a normal distribution that describes your prior information.
   (b) Suppose that you know $\sigma^2 = 57.6$. Your prior information is equivalent to prior information from a pilot survey. What sample size T_0 is necessary for this equivalence to hold? (*Hint: T_0 does not have to be an integer.*) What sample mean $\bar{y}_0$ is necessary for the equivalence?
   (c) Given the sample information used in the chapter, namely $\beta \sim N(23.5945, 1.44)$, find the post-sample density function for β.
   (d) Find 90% and 95% interval estimates from both the prior density function and the post-sample density function. Comment on the results.
   (e) Assuming a quadratic loss function, what is your best point estimate for β before the sample is taken? After the sample is taken?

Table 24.4 Average Weekly Total Expenditure of 40 Households

Sample Number	Expenditure	Sample Number	Expenditure	Sample Number	Expenditure	Sample Number	Expenditure
1	25.83	11	56.46	21	71.98	31	82.56
2	34.31	12	58.83	22	72.00	32	83.33
3	42.50	13	59.13	23	72.23	33	83.40
4	46.75	14	60.73	24	72.23	34	91.81
5	48.29	15	61.12	25	73.44	35	91.81
6	48.77	16	63.10	26	74.25	36	92.96
7	49.65	17	65.96	27	74.77	37	95.17
8	51.94	18	66.40	28	76.33	38	101.40
9	54.33	19	70.42	29	81.02	39	114.13
10	54.87	20	70.48	30	81.85	40	115.46

24.4. Consider the probability density functions given in Table 24.3 of the text. Using their empirical counterparts derived in Section 24.3, find the following for each of the density functions:
(a) $P(23 < \beta < 24)$
(b) A 90% interval estimate
(c) The odds ratio

$$\frac{P(22.5 < \beta < 24)}{P\left[(\beta < 22.5) \text{ or } (\beta > 24)\right]}$$

Comment on the results.

24.5. Redo Exercise 24.2 given that you have prior information available from a pilot survey of 4 households whose average weekly total expenditures were 50.19, 51.25, 73.15, and 181.13.

24.6. Consider the sample (3, 4, 5, 6) of size $T = 4$ from a normal distribution with unknown mean β and known variance $\sigma^2 = 16$.
(a) Assuming no prior information about β, find the postsample density function for β.
(b) Given that one more observation, namely 12, becomes available, update your postsample density function.
(c) Compare and comment on the variances of the two density functions (the one before and the one after the extra observation).

24.7 References

HEY, J. D. (1983) *Data in Doubt*, Oxford: Basil Blackwell.

JUDGE, G. G., R. C. HILL, W. E. GRIFFITHS, H. LÜTKEPOHL, and T. C. LEE (1988) *Introduction to the Theory and Practice of Econometrics*, 2nd Edition, New York: John Wiley & Sons, Inc., pp. 117–153.

PRESS, S. J. (1989) *Bayesian Statistics: Principles, Models and Applications*, New York: John Wiley & Sons, Inc.

APPENDIX 24A Bayes' Rule

24A.1 Bayes' Rule for Discrete Events

One of the topics often covered in the probability section of introductory statistics courses is Bayes' rule for discrete events. We begin this appendix by revising Bayes' rule in this context, as a lead into Bayes' rule for continuous probability density functions. Consider the following example. Let us suppose that the population of the United States can be classified into three categories: those who are healthy, those who have asthma, and those who have TB (tuberculosis). It is known that 90% of the population are healthy, 9% have asthma, and 1% have TB. A person we will identify as Fred is chosen at random from the population. Let:

A_1: the event that Fred is healthy,

A_2: the event that Fred has asthma, and

A_3: the event that Fred has TB.

We can say

$$P(A_1) = .9 \qquad P(A_2) = .09 \qquad P(A_3) = .01 \qquad (24A.1.1)$$

Fred decides to go for a chest X-ray to see if he might have TB. From medical records we know that the probability of a healthy person getting an X-ray report that suggests TB is .03. The probability that somebody with asthma will yield such an X-ray report is .2. If somebody has TB, the probability that an X-ray report will suggest TB is .95. Let B be the event that Fred's X-ray report is positive—it suggests that he has TB. We have

$$P(B|A_1) = .03 \qquad P(B|A_2) = .2 \qquad P(B|A_3) = .95 \qquad (24A.1.2)$$

These probabilities are *conditional probabilities*. The probability of Fred's X-ray being positive, given he is healthy, is .03. The probability of the positive X-ray, given Fred has asthma, is .2, and the probability of Fred's X-ray being positive, given he has TB, is .95. Note that we can give these probabilities *before* Fred goes for his X-ray, before we know the X-ray outcome.

Fred is not interested in the conditional probabilities in equation 24A.1.2; he wants to know the probability of having TB. Before the X-ray is taken this probability is $P(A_3) = .01$. It can be viewed as a *prior* probability, prior to the information that the X-ray will provide. The results of the X-ray can be viewed as sample information that Fred can use to update the probability statement expressing his chances of having TB.

Let us suppose now that Fred's chest X-ray is positive. The event B has occurred. Fred is now interested in $P(A_3|B)$. How can he calculate this quantity? From rules about conditional probability we know that

$$P(A_3 \cap B) = P(B|A_3) \cdot P(A_3)$$
$$= P(A_3|B) \cdot P(B) \qquad (24A.1.3)$$

Thus, we have the following expression for $P(A_3|B)$

$$P(A_3|B) = \frac{P(B|A_3) \cdot P(A_3)}{P(B)} \qquad (24A.1.4)$$

This result is known as *Bayes' rule*. It shows how Fred can update his prior probability about TB, $P(A_3)$, to the post-sample (or post-X-ray) probability $P(A_3|B)$.

Let us compute $P(A_3|B)$ to see if Fred should be worried. Examining the right-hand side of equation 24A.1.4, we see that we have values for $P(B|A_3)$ and $P(A_3)$ that appear in the numerator, but we do not have a value for the denominator $P(B)$. To calculate $P(B)$, consider Figure 24A.1. The whole population can be placed in either A_1, A_2, or A_3. The ellipse B represents all those who have positive chest X-rays. The shaded portion represents those who have positive X-rays *and* have TB, the set $(A_3 \cap B)$. The shaded portion relative to A_3 gives $P(B|A_3)$; the shaded portion relative to B gives $P(A_3|B)$, the quantity we seek. To find $P(B)$ we sum the three sections inside the ellipse; that is,

$$P(B) = P(B \cap A_1) + P(B \cap A_2) + P(B \cap A_3)$$
$$= P(B|A_1) \cdot P(A_1) + P(B|A_2) \cdot P(A_2) + P(B|A_3) \cdot P(A_3)$$
$$= (.03)(.9) + (.2)(.09) + (.95)(.01)$$
$$= .0545$$

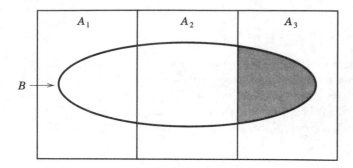

Figure 24A.1 An illustration of Bayes' rule for discrete events.

We can now use Bayes' rule to update Fred's probability. We have

$$P(A_3 \mid B) = \frac{(.95)(.01)}{.0545} = .17 \qquad (24A.1.5)$$

Thus, the probability that Fred has TB, after a chest X-ray has suggested he has TB, is .17. Fred should be more worried than he was before. The probability that he has TB has increased from .01 to .17. However, he should not get too uptight. There is still an 83% chance he does not have TB.

24A.2   Bayes' Rule for Continuous Distributions: Known Variance

We now return to the central model of this chapter, that where household observations on food expenditure are generated from the model

$$y_t = \beta + e_t \qquad e_t \sim N(0, \sigma^2) \qquad (24A.2.1)$$

where β is mean food expenditure, the parameter about which we wish to learn. Rather than make probability statements about whether or not Fred has TB, we want to make probability statements about possible values for β. We will assume that σ^2 is known. Any prior information that we might have about β, from a previous sample, from our own opinions and experience, or from that of experts, we summarize using a *prior probability density function* for β, $f(\beta)$. This density function represents our views about β *before* a sample is taken.

We will return to two different expressions (or different types of prior information) for $f(\beta)$ shortly. First, let us examine how we express the sample information. In the X-ray example we used $P(B \mid A_i)$, the probability of getting a positive X-ray, given the characteristics of the population. Here the characteristics of the population are summarized through β, and we want the probability density function for a sample of data on food expenditures, given β. This density function we write as $f(\mathbf{y} \mid \beta)$. It is the joint density function or likelihood function for the sample. We obtain it in the following way. The probability density function for one observation y_t is

$$f(y_t \mid \beta) = (2\pi\sigma^2)^{-\frac{1}{2}} \exp\left\{ -\frac{1}{2\sigma^2}(y_t - \beta)^2 \right\} \qquad (24A.2.2)$$

Given β, this function can be used to find the probability of observing household expenditure on food within some range. We use the notation $f(y_t \mid \beta)$ rather than just $f(y_t)$ to emphasize that, in the sampling process for y_t, we treat β as fixed. The joint density function for all observations when β is regarded as fixed is given by

$$
\begin{aligned}
f(\mathbf{y}\mid\beta) &= f(y_1, y_2, \ldots, y_T \mid \beta) \\
&= f(y_1 \mid \beta) \cdot f(y_2 \mid \beta) \ldots f(y_T \mid \beta) \\
&= \left(2\pi\sigma^2\right)^{-T/2} \exp\left\{ -\frac{1}{2\sigma^2} \sum_{t=1}^{T} (y_t - \beta)^2 \right\}
\end{aligned}
\qquad (24A.2.3)
$$

The second line in this expression uses the fact that the sample is a random one and hence $y_1, y_2, \ldots, y_T$ are independent.

We need to distinguish between the density function for the sampling process where β is treated as fixed, and the density functions that express our uncertainty about β and, hence, treat this parameter as random. The two density functions that express uncertainty about β are the prior density function $f(\beta)$ and the post-sample density function $f(\beta \mid \mathbf{y})$. Having expressed our prior information through the probability density function $f(\beta)$, and our sample information through the joint density function $f(\mathbf{y} \mid \beta)$, the next question is: How do we obtain $f(\beta \mid \mathbf{y})$, the post-sample density function that represents our *revised* prior views, revised on the basis of the information contained in the sample? Note that $f(\beta \mid \mathbf{y})$ is like $P(A_3 \mid B)$ in the X-ray example; in that example B represented the sample information, and A_3 was an unknown (has Fred got TB) in which we were interested. To find $f(\beta \mid \mathbf{y})$ we use the continuous probability density function form of Bayes' rule. It is given by

$$
\begin{aligned}
f(\beta \mid \mathbf{y}) &= \frac{f(\mathbf{y}\mid\beta)f(\beta)}{f(\mathbf{y})} \\
&= \kappa f(\mathbf{y}\mid\beta)f(\beta) \\
&= \kappa \times \text{sample information} \times \text{prior information}
\end{aligned}
\qquad (24A.2.4)
$$

The new ingredient in equation 24A.2.4 is the density function $f(\mathbf{y})$. However, once the sample $\mathbf{y}$ has been observed, the function $f(\mathbf{y})$ is not a function at all; it is simply a given number or constant. Hence, we have written $\kappa = [f(\mathbf{y})]^{-1}$. When equation 24A.2.4 is implemented, the first step is to multiply together the two density functions $f(\mathbf{y} \mid \beta)$ and $f(\beta)$. The result of this operation tells you the shape of the post-sample density function $f(\beta \mid \mathbf{y})$. The constant κ is then chosen to ensure that the total area under the probability density function $f(\beta \mid \mathbf{y})$ is equal to one.

Let us turn now to the results from application of Bayes' rule. We will consider two cases. The first is where $f(\beta)$ is chosen to represent ignorance; this was the scenario examined in Section 24.1, where we assumed we had no idea at all about the value for β. The second is where $f(\beta)$ comes from the results of a pilot survey. This case was considered in Section 24.3.1.

24A.2a   Noninformative Prior

Let us suppose that we have no prior information about mean expenditure β. We believe that it could be any value on the real line between $-\infty$ and $+\infty$. There is probably no one this ignorant. We all know that mean expenditure could not be negative; and we could undoubtedly set an upper limit for its value, well short of $+\infty$. However, at this stage, we want a density function that expresses complete ignorance. Later, in Chapter 19, we will see how to include information that restricts the range of a parameter. To represent complete uncertainty about β, we use a *uniform* prior density function that we write as

$$f(\beta) = 1 \qquad -\infty < \beta < \infty \qquad (24A.2.5)$$

This prior is depicted in Figure 24A.2. It is appropriate for expressing a lack of information because it suggests all values of β are equally likely. There are no values of β that are more likely to be the "true value" than are others. However, one question that might bother the reader is: What about the area under this density function? The area will be infinite rather than equal to 1 as is the case for conventional or *proper* density functions. It so happens that *improper* density functions, whose areas are infinite, are commonly used to represent a lack of substantial prior information. They serve this purpose well, and it turns out that, after we collect some sample information, and hence we are no longer ignorant, we end up with a proper post-sample density function to describe our views about β.

To apply Bayes' rule to equations 24A.2.5 and 24A.2.3, we substitute these into equation 24A.2.4, to obtain

$$f(\beta|\mathbf{y}) = \kappa f(\mathbf{y}|\beta) f(\beta)$$

$$= \kappa \left(2\pi\sigma^2\right)^{-T/2} \exp\left\{-\frac{1}{2\sigma^2}\sum_{t=1}^{T}(y_t - \beta)^2\right\} \cdot 1 \qquad (24A.2.6)$$

The next step is to rewrite this function as a density function for β. Working in this direction we write the term in the exponent as

$$\sum_{t=1}^{T}(y_t - \beta)^2 = \sum_{t=1}^{T}\left[(y_t - \bar{y}) - (\beta - \bar{y})\right]^2$$

$$= \sum_{t=1}^{T}(y_t - \bar{y})^2 + \sum_{t=1}^{T}(\beta - \bar{y})^2 - 2(\beta - \bar{y})\sum_{t=1}^{T}(y_t - \bar{y})$$

$$= \sum_{t=1}^{T}(y_t - \bar{y})^2 + T(\beta - \bar{y})^2 \qquad (24A.2.7)$$

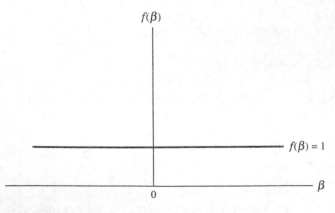

Figure 24A.2 Uniform prior density function for β.

Substituting this expression into $f(\beta \mid y)$ in equation 24A.2.6 yields

$$f(\beta|\mathbf{y}) = \kappa \left(2\pi\sigma^2\right)^{-T/2} \exp\left\{-\frac{1}{2\sigma^2}\left[\sum_{t=1}^{T}(y_t - \bar{y})^2 + T(\beta - \bar{y})^2\right]\right\}$$

$$= \kappa \left(2\pi\sigma^2\right)^{-T/2} \exp\left\{-\frac{1}{2\sigma^2}\sum_{t=1}^{T}(y_t - \bar{y})^2\right\}\exp\left\{-\frac{T}{2\sigma^2}(\beta - \bar{y})^2\right\}$$

$$= c_1 \exp\left\{-\frac{T}{2\sigma^2}(\beta - \bar{y})^2\right\} \tag{24A.2.8}$$

where

$$c_1 = \kappa \left(2\pi\sigma^2\right)^{-T/2} \exp\left\{-\frac{1}{2\sigma^2}\sum_{t=1}^{T}(y_t - \bar{y})^2\right\} \tag{24A.2.9}$$

What kind of density function is that in equation 24A.2.8? First, note that c_1 does not depend on β. Thus, because $f(\beta \mid y)$ is a probability density function *for* β, its shape is determined by the term

$$\exp\left\{-\frac{T}{2\sigma^2}(\beta - \bar{y}^2)\right\} \tag{24A.2.10}$$

The density function described by this term is a normal distribution with mean $\bar{y}$ and variance σ^2/T. Thus, we have

$$\beta \sim N\left(\bar{y}, \frac{\sigma^2}{T}\right) \tag{24A.2.11}$$

the result we used in Section 24.1. The constant c_1 is a scaling constant necessary to make the area under the density function equal to one. It therefore follows that $c_1 = (2\pi\sigma^2/T)^{-1/2}$ and the complete post-sample density function for β is

$$f(\beta|\mathbf{y}) = \left(2\pi\sigma^2/T\right)^{-\frac{1}{2}} \exp\left\{-\frac{T}{2\sigma^2}(\beta - \bar{y})^2\right\} \tag{24A.2.12}$$

One of the objectives of this chapter was to find a way of representing uncertainty about the mean of a normal distribution before and after a sample is taken. We began in Section 24.1, where we were completely uncertain about the mean β, but we knew the variance σ^2; we wanted a method of representing complete uncertainty about β and a method for changing our expression of uncertainty as sample information became available. In Section 24.1 we relied on an intuitive approach to describe the post-sample representation of uncertainty provided by $f(\beta \mid y)$ given in equation 24A.2.12. Now, in this part of the appendix, we have filled in the missing gaps. We have learned that the uniform density $f(\beta) = 1$ can be used to represent total uncertainty, and that the formal procedure for combining information, Bayes' rule, leads to the result in equation 24A.2.12.

24A.2b   An Informative Prior

We now turn to the application of Bayes' rule where prior information in the form of a pilot survey is available. We continue to assume that the variance σ^2 is known. In Section 24.3.1 we learned that such prior information is expressed through the normal density function

$$\beta \sim N\!\left(\overline{y}_0, \frac{\sigma^2}{T_0} \right)$$

(24A.2.13)

where $\overline{y}_0$ is the sample mean and T_0 is the sample size from the pilot survey. Treating equation 24A.2.1 as prior information that depends on $\mathbf{y}_0$, we can write its density function as

$$f(\beta) = f(\beta | \mathbf{y}_0) = \left(2\pi\sigma^2 / T_0\right)^{-\frac{1}{2}} \exp\!\left\{ -\frac{T_0}{2\sigma^2}(\beta - \overline{y}_0)^2 \right\}$$

(24A.2.14)

To derive a post-sample density function from this prior density function, we substitute equation 24A.2.14 and the sample information $f(\mathbf{y} \mid \beta)$ given in equation 24A.2.3 into the Bayes' rule formula in equation 24A.2.4. This process leads to

$$
\begin{aligned}
f(\beta | \mathbf{y}) = f(\beta | \mathbf{y}_0, \mathbf{y}_1) &= \kappa f(\mathbf{y} | \beta) f(\beta) \\
&= \kappa \left(2\pi\sigma^2\right)^{-T/2} \exp\!\left\{ -\frac{1}{2\sigma^2} \sum_{t=1}^{T}(y_t - \beta)^2 \right\} \\
&\quad \times \left(2\pi\sigma^2 / T_0\right)^{-\frac{1}{2}} \exp\!\left\{ -\frac{T_0}{2\sigma^2}(\beta - \overline{y}_0)^2 \right\} \\
&= \left[2\pi\sigma^2 / (T_0 + T_1)\right]^{-1} \exp\!\left\{ -\frac{T_0 + T_1}{2\sigma^2}\left(\beta - \overline{\overline{\beta}}\right)^2 \right\}
\end{aligned}
$$

(24A.2.15)

This is the post-sample density function that we derived from an intuitive standpoint in Section 24.3.1, namely,

$$\beta \sim N\!\left(\overline{\overline{\beta}}, \frac{\sigma^2}{T_0 + T_1} \right)$$

(24A.2.16)

Some tedious algebra is required to get from the second to the last line in equation 24A.2.15. Interested readers should consult Judge et al. (1988, p. 123). The intuitive argument that we used to derive equation 24A.2.16 in Section 24.3.1 relied on a "reasonable" scheme for weighting the information from the pilot survey with that from the main sample. A formal derivation of the result in equation 24A.2.16 is obtained by filling in between the lines in equation 24A.2.15.

24A.3   Bayes' Rule for Continuous Distributions: Unknown Variance

When we move from the world of known variance to the more realistic world of unknown variance, we can no longer write Bayes' rule in terms of just the unknown mean β. The fact that σ^2 is also unknown means that it too must be included in the expression for Bayes' rule. Specifically, in this case we write Bayes' rule as

$$
\begin{aligned}
f(\beta, \sigma^2 | \mathbf{y}) &= \frac{f(\mathbf{y} | \beta, \sigma^2) f(\beta, \sigma^2)}{f(\mathbf{y})} \\
&= \kappa f(\mathbf{y} | \beta, \sigma^2) f(\beta, \sigma^2)
\end{aligned}
$$

(24A.3.1)

Let us briefly comment on each of the components. First, $f(\beta, \sigma^2)$ represents a prior probability density function for β *and* σ^2. We assume that our state of knowledge about β and σ^2, before the sample is taken, can be captured by this prior density function. How, you ask, can we have prior information on σ^2? Remember that the value of σ^2 determines the *practical range* in which household expenditures on food will lie. Most observations from a normal distribution will lie within 3σ from the mean. Thus, if you have some idea of the range of weekly expenditures on food, and you are willing to assume a normal distribution, you have some idea of the variance σ^2. For an example of how to express such ideas in terms of a prior probability density function for σ, see Judge et al. (1988, p. 143).

Given a prior representation of $f(\beta, \sigma^2)$, the next step is an expression for the sample information $f(\mathbf{y} \mid \beta, \sigma^2)$. Such an expression is identical to that in equation 24A.2.3. The only difference is that we write $f(\mathbf{y} \mid \beta, \sigma^2)$ instead of $f(\mathbf{y} \mid \beta)$ to emphasize that now the role of σ^2 is important. Thus, we have

$$f\left(\mathbf{y}|\beta,\sigma^2\right) = \left(2\pi\sigma^2\right)^{-T/2} \exp\left\{ -\frac{1}{2\sigma^2} \sum_{t=1}^{T} \left(y_t - \beta\right)^2 \right\} \qquad (24A.3.2)$$

The constant κ has the same meaning as before; it is the constant needed to make the total area (or volume in this case) under the post-sample density function equal to one. The final term in equation 24A.3.1 is $f(\beta, \sigma^2 \mid \mathbf{y})$. This function is a *joint* post-sample density function that expresses our state of knowledge about β *and* σ^2 after the sample has been observed.

If our major concern is to describe our information about β, not that about σ^2, then σ^2 must be "eliminated" from the joint post-sample density function so that we can obtain $f(\beta \mid \mathbf{y})$. This elimination process takes the form of integrating out σ^2 from the *joint* density function $f(\beta, \sigma^2 \mid \mathbf{y})$ to obtain what is known as the *marginal* density function $f(\beta \mid \mathbf{y})$. This procedure can be followed for both informative and noninformative prior p.d.f.s for β and σ. The marginal density function $f(\beta \mid \mathbf{y})$ turns out to be a t-distribution. Details and proofs are given in Judge et al. (1988, Chapter 4).

Chapter 25

The Bayesian Approach to Using Sample and Nonsample Information in the Estimation of Relationships Between Economic Variables

New Key Words and Concepts

Prior Inequality Information
Marginal Propensity to Consume
Postsample Density Functions
Bivariate Normal Distribution
Truncated Distributions

Consumption Function
Least Squares Estimates
Bayes' Rule
Generation of an Artificial Sample
Prediction

In many of the preceding chapters we were concerned with estimating the unknown parameters of a relationship between economic variables. For example, in Chapter 5, as a basis for identifying and interpreting the appropriate econometric tools, we considered food expenditure of individual households and how this expenditure depends on the level of household income. In this chapter we again focus on methods for learning about the parameters of relationships between two economic variables, and we do so within the context of the aggregate consumption function that was analyzed in Section 8.3 of Chapter 8. A major aspect of this chapter that distinguishes it from chapters such as 5, 8, or 9 is that we use the Bayesian framework to examine methods for including prior inequality information about the unknown parameters in the relationship.

From economic principles we know a great deal about the signs of parameters in economic relationships. For example, we know that when the price of a commodity increases, the quantity demanded will fall; when interest rates rise, the level of investment in the economy falls; when income rises, consumption rises; when the prices of factors of production increase, output declines. All of these examples tell us something about the *sign* of a parameter in a relationship between two economic variables. Consider the parameters β_1 and β_2 that describe the following relationship between a dependent variable y and an explanatory variable x:

$$y = \beta_1 + \beta_2 x + e$$

If an increase in x leads to an increase in y, the coefficient β_2 will be positive. If an increase in x leads to a decrease in y, the coefficient β_2 will be negative. Thus, knowing the direction of change in this economic relationship tells us the sign of the parameter β_2. Suppose, for example, that we know that increases in x cause decreases in y; in other words we know that β_2 is negative. Because we can express this information as $\beta_2 < 0$, it is called *inequality* information about β_2. Also, because it is information that we have prior to the sampling process, it is called *prior* or *nonsample* inequality information.

A major objective of this chapter is to formally incorporate prior inequality information into our inference procedures which are used to obtain information about the magnitude of β_2. In other words, given that we know $\beta_2 < 0$, how do we obtain and represent information about the magnitude of β_2? The framework that we use is the Bayesian approach introduced in Chapter 24. In this context, we use a prior probability density function to express our uncertainty about β_1 and β_2 before the sample is observed. The sample information is then used to update the prior information to form a post-sample density function. This density function is then used to express our state of uncertainty about β_1 and β_2 after the sample has been observed. Thus, in the sections to follow, we extend the techniques of Chapter 24 to handle a more general model that involves a relationship between two or more economic variables, and we examine the implications of prior inequality information in particular.

25.1 Economic Model for Aggregate Consumption

Consider, as we did in Section 8.4 of Chapter 8, the problem of estimating the parameters of an aggregate consumption function. One simple way to model aggregate consumption is to specify that it is linearly related to disposable income; that is,

$$C = \beta_1 + \beta_2 Y_D \tag{25.1.1}$$

where C represents aggregate consumption, Y_D represents disposable income (income less taxes or $Y_D = Y - T$), and β_1 and β_2 are the unknown parameters of the consumption function. The parameter β_1 is autonomous consumption, the quantity consumed when disposable income is zero, and the other parameter β_2 is the marginal propensity to consume. As we discussed in Chapter 8, the marginal propensity to consume is an important parameter because it has a direct bearing on the multiplier or income-generating effects of government policy and on the tax multiplier.

Because both multipliers depend on the unknown parameter β_2, it is important to learn something about the magnitude of β_2. Another problem is that of predicting future values of consumption for given levels of national income. For this prediction problem we need information on the autonomous consumption parameter β_1 as well as the marginal propensity to consume β_2. Thus, our objective in this chapter is to estimate, and make inferences about, the unknown parameters β_1 and β_2. The first step toward achieving this objective is to specify a statistical model that corresponds to equation 25.1.1 and that is consistent with an observed sample of data on C and Y_D.

The techniques that we use to provide information about β_1 and β_2 are based on both sampling theory and Bayesian approaches to inference. Following Section 8.4 of Chapter 8, the least squares estimator introduced in Chapter 5 is used to provide, within the framework of sampling theory, point estimates for β_1 and β_2; following the theory developed in Chapter 7, corresponding interval estimates are used as an indication of the reliability of the point estimates. Also, along the lines of the Bayesian approach to inference developed in Chapter 24, probability density functions are used to express uncertainty about β_1 and β_2 before and after the sample of data has been collected. Procedures are provided for including prior inequality information about the parameters into the learning process.

Our economic principles suggest that out of every additional dollar of disposable income, some of it will be consumed and some of it will be saved. The marginal propensity to consume is equal to the proportion consumed and must, therefore, lie between zero and one. Similarly, we would expect autonomous consumption to be positive. Thus, the prior inequality information suggested by economic principles is that $\beta_1 > 0$ and $0 < \beta_2 < 1$. What is needed is a systematic way of introducing this prior inequality information into the estimation and inference process.

25.2 Statistical Model and Data

To convert the economic model for consumption in equation 25.1.1 to a statistical model that we can use for estimation and inference, we specify our statistical model as

$$y_t = \beta_1 + \beta_2 x_t + e_t \qquad (25.2.1)$$

where y_t denotes aggregate consumption in period t, x_t denotes disposable income in period t, and the e_t, the T unobservable equation errors, represent independent drawings from a normal distribution with mean zero and variance σ^2. Thus, in line with previous chapters, we write

$$e_t \sim N\left(0, \sigma^2\right) \qquad (25.2.2)$$

Because the drawings are assumed independent, the covariance between any pair of errors is zero, $E[e_t e_s] = 0$ for $t \neq s$, and thus for the error vector $\mathbf{e}' = (e_1, e_2, \ldots, e_T)$ we can specify the error assumptions as

$$\mathbf{e} \sim N\left(\mathbf{0}, \sigma^2 I_T\right) \qquad (25.2.3)$$

For an empirical example of a consumption function, we use 10 observations on disposable personal income and personal consumption expenditures for the U. S. economy for the period 1969 to 1978. These data are measured on a per capita basis and are expressed in terms of 1982 dollars and they are given in Table 8.4 of Chapter 8.

25.3 Estimation and Inference
Based on Sampling Theory Procedures

The estimation and inference procedures that were introduced, for example, in Chapters 5 to 8, are considered desirable ones because of their properties in repeated samples. We were concerned with the *sampling characteristics* of point and interval estimators and of hypothesis testing procedures. Consequently, these procedures come under the general heading of *sampling theory* procedures. To provide a basis for comparing the alternative approaches to inference, in this section we summarize the results of applying sampling theory procedures to our general problem of learning about the consumption function parameters β_1 and β_2. We repeat some of the results and discussion found in Section 8.4 of Chapter 8. In Section 25.4 the Bayesian techniques, introduced in Chapter 24 for expressing uncertainty about a parameter *after* a sample has been observed, are extended and applied to our two-variable economic relationship. The effects of introducing the prior inequality information $\beta_1 > 0$ and $0 < \beta_2 < 1$ are taken up in Section 25.5.

25.3.1   Statistical Model and Estimates

Before presenting the sampling theory results to learn about β_1 and β_2, along the lines of Section 5.4, we rewrite the statistical model as

$$\mathbf{y} = \mathbf{x}_1\beta_1 + \mathbf{x}_2\beta_2 + \mathbf{e} = X\boldsymbol{\beta} + \mathbf{e} \tag{25.3.1}$$

and

$$\mathbf{e} \sim N\left(0,\, \sigma^2 I_T\right) \tag{25.3.2}$$

The first sampling theory results are the point estimates of β_1 and β_2 obtained from the least squares rule $\mathbf{b} = (X'X)^{-1}X'\mathbf{y}$. They are

$$\mathbf{b} = \begin{bmatrix} b_1 \\ b_2 \end{bmatrix} = \begin{bmatrix} -128.9411 \\ 0.91126 \end{bmatrix} \tag{25.3.3}$$

Using the unbiased estimator of σ^2, introduced in Chapter 6, we have

$$\hat{\sigma}^2 = \frac{(\mathbf{y} - X\mathbf{b})'(\mathbf{y} - X\mathbf{b})}{T-2} = \frac{\hat{\mathbf{e}}'\hat{\mathbf{e}}}{T-2} = \frac{87312.93}{8} = 10{,}914.12 \tag{25.3.4}$$

and this yields the estimated covariance matrix for $\mathbf{b}$

$$\hat{\text{cov}}(\mathbf{b}) = \hat{\sigma}^2 \left(X'X\right)^{-1} = \begin{bmatrix} 284020.3 & -32.132 \\ -32.132 & 0.0036491 \end{bmatrix} \tag{25.3.5}$$

The square roots of the diagonal elements of this matrix, which are the standard errors for b_1 and b_2, are

$$se(b_1) = \sqrt{284020.3} = 532.94 \tag{25.3.6a}$$

and

$$se(b_2) = \sqrt{0.0036491} = 0.060408 \tag{25.3.6b}$$

The information that we have collected thus far can be summarized by using a format introduced in Chapter 8 as

$$\hat{y}_t = -128.94 + 0.9113x_t$$
$$(532.94)\,(0.0604) \tag{25.3.7}$$

As in Chapter 8, the estimates in equation 25.3.7 can be used in conjunction with their standard errors to construct interval estimates for each of the parameters. For a 95% interval estimate, the appropriate critical value from the t-distribution with 8 degrees of freedom is $t_c = 2.306$. Thus, a 95% interval estimate for β_1 is

$$-128.94 - (2.306)(532.94) < \beta_1 < -128.94 + (2.306)(532.94)$$

or

$$-1358 < \beta_1 < 1100 \tag{25.3.8}$$

Our interval estimate for β_1 suggests that autonomous consumption could be as high as \$1100 and as low as –\$1358. For a 95% interval estimate for β_2 we obtain

$$0.9113 - (2.306)(0.0604) < \beta_2 < 0.9113 + (2.306)(0.0604)$$

or

$$0.772 < \beta_2 < 1.051 \qquad (25.3.9)$$

This interval suggests the marginal propensity to consume lies somewhere between 0.772 and 1.051.

Suppose, as in Chapter 8, that it is critical for the government to learn whether or not the government expenditure multiplier is greater than 10. A multiplier $1/(1 - \beta_2)$ = 10 arises when the marginal propensity to consume $\beta_2 = 0.9$. Thus, a pair of hypotheses relevant for the government's question is

$$H_0 : \beta_2 \leq 0.9 \qquad H_1 : \beta_2 > 0.9 \qquad (25.3.10)$$

Assuming that H_0 is true, and using the least favorable value for β_2 under H_0, the calculated value for the t-statistic is

$$t = \frac{0.91126 - 0.9}{0.060408} = 0.186 \qquad (25.3.11)$$

At a 5% significance level, the critical value for this one-tailed test is $t_c = 1.860$. Since $t = 0.186 < 1.860 = t_c$, we conclude that there is insufficient evidence in the sample to contradict H_0.

25.3.2   Interpreting the Sampling Theory Results

Given these sampling theory results, let us look closely at the point and interval estimates. Consider first the point estimate $b_1 = -128.94$ and interval estimate $(-1358 < \beta_1 < 1100)$ for autonomous consumption. What have we learned about autonomous consumption? The negative value of approximately −129 dollars is nonsensical; consumption cannot be negative, even at a zero level of income. Can we give an explanation for this seemingly weird estimate? One possibility is that we have a bad model. There could be some relevant explanatory variables, other than per capita income, that we have omitted from the function. We might have the wrong functional form. Our stochastic assumptions about the equation errors might be inappropriate. However, *even within the framework of the model we are using*, there are two possible explanations for a negative value. The first explanation is that the estimate might be imprecise or unreliable. The interval estimate (−1358, 1100) is a wide one that includes a considerable range of positive values. Thus, it is quite likely that autonomous consumption is indeed positive but, because of sampling error, our one sample has produced a negative point estimate. We are inclined to make this suggestion because we have prior nonsample information that $\beta_1 > 0$. If we use information from the sample alone, and not information from our economic principles, it is difficult to say whether β_1 is negative or positive.

The second possible explanation for a negative estimate for β_1 is that the model may be a reasonable approximation only in the region for which we have data. If there are no years when income is approximately zero, then perhaps it is asking too much to have the data tell us what the level of consumption will be at a zero income level. Under these circumstances we treat β_1 as a parameter that helps determine the position of the estimated line in the region of the data, and as such it is important for prediction, but we do not attempt to give β_1 an economic interpretation.

Next let us consider the point and interval estimate for β_2. The point estimate of approximately 0.91 for the marginal propensity to consume is a reasonable one, but the interval estimate of (0.772, 1.051) is not very informative. The lower limit of this interval is quite low; the upper limit of 1.051 is greater than one and, hence, is not a feasible value.

The fact that both of our interval estimates include infeasible parameter ranges raises an interesting question. If we treat negative values of β_1 as impossible, and values of β_2 greater than 1 are impossible, is it meaningful to present interval estimates that include such infeasible values? With β_1 we have the additional complication that the *point* estimate is an infeasible value. Unfortunately, when we use sampling theory procedures that make no provision for including prior inequality information, there is no way of avoiding the infeasible point and interval estimates that arise from our sample of data. What would be desirable is another way of using the data to construct point and interval estimates, a way that includes prior information and yields results consistent with our economic principles. Furthermore, it would be good if the injection of prior inequality information into our inference procedures could not only eliminate infeasible estimates, but also produce more informative feasible estimates. For example, it would be nice to be able to say more about the marginal propensity to consume, and hence more about the government expenditure multiplier.

To analyze these questions we return to the Bayesian framework introduced in Chapter 24. In that chapter we learned how to represent information about a single parameter (mean expenditure on food) in terms of a probability density function. Our task now is to extend this framework to our current model, where we are investigating the relationship between two economic variables and where we have prior nonsample information of the inequality form $\beta_1 > 0$ and $0 < \beta_2 < 1$. We begin by first ignoring the prior information and examining the nature of the post-sample density functions for β_1 and β_2 when, before sampling, we were in a position of complete uncertainty.

25.4 Expressing Uncertainty About the Consumption Function Parameters: Known Variance and No Prior Information

Before considering the prior inequality information that $\beta_1 > 0$ and $0 < \beta_2 < 1$, it is useful to obtain post-sample density functions for β_1 and β_2 under complete prior uncertainty. We can then examine how the introduction of the prior inequality information modifies these post-sample density functions. Since our focus is on concepts, for expository purposes, we use the assumption of a known error variance σ^2.

Thus, we begin with the case where there is complete prior uncertainty about the consumption function parameters, and where σ^2 is assumed known. For this case some relevant results from Chapter 7 are

$$z_1 = \frac{b_1 - \beta_1}{\sqrt{\text{var}(b_1)}} \sim N(0, 1) \quad \text{where} \quad \text{var}(b_1) = \frac{\sigma^2 \Sigma x_t^2}{T\Sigma(x_t - \bar{x})^2} \qquad (25.4.1)$$

and

$$z_2 = \frac{b_2 - \beta_2}{\sqrt{\text{var}(b_2)}} \sim N(0, 1) \quad \text{where} \quad \text{var}(b_2) = \frac{\sigma^2}{\Sigma(x_t - \bar{x})^2} \qquad (25.4.2)$$

Both z_1 and z_2 are standard normal random variables because b_1 and b_2 are normal random variables. Providing that σ^2 is known, the standard normal distribution can be used to make probability statements about z_1 and z_2 *before* the sample is taken. For example, suppose we are testing a true null hypothesis, H_0: $\beta_2 = 0$, against the alternative H_1: $\beta_2 \neq 0$. Then, *before* the sample is taken, we can say that, if H_0 is true, there is a .05 probability of obtaining b_2 such that $|b_2| / \sqrt{\text{var}(b_2)} \geq 1.96$. Similarly, we can use the normal distribution for z_2 to say that, before a sample is taken, there is a .95 probability of obtaining b_2 such that the interval estimator $[b_2 - 1.96\sqrt{\text{var}(b_2)}, b_2 + 1.96\sqrt{\text{var}(b_2)}]$ contains the parameter β_2.

To use probability density functions to express our uncertainty or information about β_1 and β_2 *after* the sample has been taken, we parallel the approach taken in Chapter 24. We continue to treat z_1 and z_2 as standard normal random variables, despite the fact that the sample has been observed and, hence, that b_1 and b_2 are fixed nonrandom numbers. Using β_2 as an example, let us consider the implications of this treatment. If σ^2 is known, var(b_2) is also known, and so treating b_2 as a fixed number implies that the only source of randomness for z_2 is uncertainty about the parameter β_2. Thus, if z_2 continues to have a standard normal distribution after the sample has been observed, then β_2 must be treated as if it is a random variable. Of course β_2 is not a random variable in the sense that it is the outcome of an experiment. We are not assuming that the long-run marginal propensity to consume varies from time period to time period. *We are treating β_2 as a random variable in the sense that we can assign to it a subjective probability distribution that describes our uncertainty about the actual value of β_2.* To find this subjective probability distribution we note that, from equation 25.4.2, we can write

$$\beta_2 = b_2 - z_2 \sqrt{\text{var}(b_2)} \tag{25.4.3}$$

Thus, the problem becomes, given the constants b_2 and $\sqrt{\text{var}(b_2)}$ and given the standard normal random variable z_2, how do we use equation 25.4.3 to find the probability distribution for β_2? Since β_2 is a *linear* function of z_2, and z_2 is normally distributed, it follows that β_2 is normally distributed. It is this normal distribution that is the post-sample density function for β_2. It has mean

$$E[\beta_2] = b_2 - \sqrt{\text{var}(b_2)}E[z_2] = b_2 \tag{25.4.4}$$

and variance

$$\text{var}(\beta_2) = \left(\sqrt{\text{var}(b_2)}\right)^2 \text{var}(z_2) = \text{var}(b_2) \tag{25.4.5}$$

Equation 25.4.5 says that the *expression* for the variance of the normal post-sample density function for β_2 is identical to the *expression* for the variance of the least squares estimator b_2. Using $\sigma_{\beta_2}^2$ as notation for the variance of the post-sample density function, we have

$$\sigma_{\beta_2}^2 = \text{var}(\beta_2) = \frac{\sigma^2}{\Sigma(x_t - \bar{x})^2} \tag{25.4.6}$$

For the complete post-sample density function for β_2, we write

$$\beta_2 \sim N(b_2, \sigma_{\beta_2}^2) \tag{25.4.7}$$

Similarly, for β_1 we have

$$\beta_1 \sim N(b_1, \sigma_{\beta_1}^2) \tag{25.4.8}$$

where

$$\sigma_{\beta_1}^2 = \frac{\sigma^2 \Sigma x_t^2}{T\Sigma(x_t - \bar{x})^2} \tag{25.4.9}$$

Equations 25.4.7 and 25.4.8 are the probability distributions that express our state of knowledge, and uncertainty, about the parameters after the sample has been taken. That is, they represent the *post-sample density functions* for β_1 and β_2. However, for these post-sample density functions to be meaningful, we must ask: What was our state of knowledge about β_1 and β_2 before the sample was taken? Post-sample density functions describe our information about the parameters *after our prior information has been updated using the sample information*. Diagrammatically, we write

$$\text{Prior Information} \times \text{Data} \rightarrow \text{Post - Sample Information} \qquad (25.4.10)$$

Thus, to complete the argument we need to know what kind of prior information leads to the post-sample density functions in equations 25.4.7 and 25.4.8. We will not give details here, but Bayes' rule, represented in equation 25.4.10, provides the answer to this question. If we assume that, before we sample, we are completely uncertain about the values of β_1 and β_2 and have no prior information whatsoever, then, as described in the appendix to Chapter 24, we can represent this lack of prior information by uniform (noninformative) prior density functions for β_1 and β_2. Using Bayes' rule to combine these prior density functions with the sample information yields the post-sample density functions in equations 25.4.7 and 25.4.8. As shown in equation 25.4.10, the principles involved in the application of Bayes' rule, and formally discussed in the appendix to Chapter 24, imply that post-sample information depends on both sample and nonsample (prior) information.

Let us now examine the post-sample density functions in equations 25.4.7 and 25.4.8 in the context of our consumption function example. We will assume that $\sigma^2 = 11,000$. Using the data from Table 8.3 and this assumption we have

$$b_1 = -128.94 \qquad b_2 = 0.9113$$

$$\sigma_{\beta_1} = \sqrt{\frac{(11,000)(778,239,650)}{(10)(2,990,884)}} = 535.03$$

and

$$\sigma_{\beta_2} = \sqrt{\frac{11,000}{2,990,884}} = 0.06065$$

Thus, the normal post-sample density functions for β_1 and β_2 are

$$\beta_1 \sim N\left[-128.94, (535.03)^2\right] \qquad \beta_2 \sim N\left[0.9113, (0.06065)^2\right] \qquad (25.4.11)$$

These density functions are graphed in Figure 25.1. Given a known error variance of $\sigma^2 = 11,000$, they describe our state of knowledge about β_1 and β_2 after the sample has been observed, assuming that, before the sample, we had no prior nonsample information about β_1 and β_2.

Note that the standard deviations $\sigma_{\beta_1} = 535.03$ and $\sigma_{\beta_2} = 0.06065$ correspond closely to the sampling theory standard errors $se(b_1) = 532.94$ and $se(b_2) = 0.06041$. This close correspondence occurs because the sampling theory variance estimate $\hat{\sigma}^2 = 10,914$ is close to the value $\sigma^2 = 11,000$ that we have assumed as given in this section. As a consequence, the post-sample density functions for β_1 and β_2 are similar in shape (although not in interpretation) to the *estimated* probability density functions for the least squares *estimators* b_1 and b_2. They have the same means (-128.94 and 0.9113) and, as described above, almost the same standard deviations. This correspondence means that we can make convenient comparisons between the sampling theory inferences in Section 25.3 and Bayesian inferences. We now consider some of the inferences that can be drawn from Bayesian post-sample density functions and, where appropriate, we compare these inferences with sampling theory results.

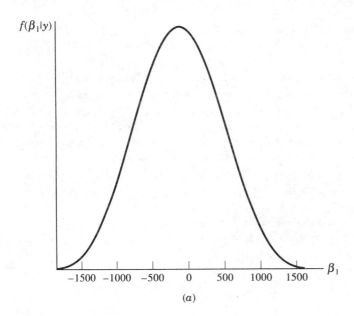

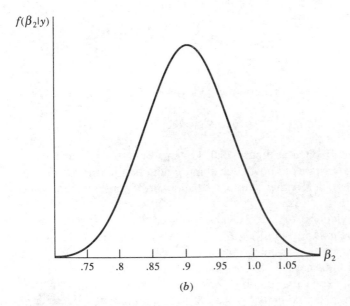

Figure 25.1 Normal post-sample density functions for consumption function parameters when no prior information exists and σ^2 is known. (a) Post-sample density function for β_1. (b) Post-sample density function for β_2.

25.4.1 Summarizing Information from the Post-Sample Density Functions

As indicated in Chapter 24, there are times when it is more convenient to report summary measures from a post-sample density function than to report the complete post-sample density function itself. This is particularly true when we are reporting results to people who are not trained statisticians. Three useful summary measures are probability statements about the parameters, interval estimates, and a comparison of hypotheses. Let us consider some examples of each.

Two interesting probability statements are $P(\beta_1 < 0)$ and $P(\beta_2 > 1)$. As we have indicated, it is unlikely that autonomous consumption is negative, and it is also unlikely that the marginal propensity to consume is greater than one. However, because our prior information did not preclude these ranges of values, the post-sample density functions attach positive probabilities to them. Specifically, by using tables at the end of this book, or instructions in the *Computer Handbooks*, we find that

$$P(\beta_1 < 0) = P\left(\frac{\beta_1 - b_1}{\sigma_{\beta_1}} < \frac{0 + 128.94}{535.03}\right) = P(z_1 < .241) = .595 \quad (25.4.12a)$$

$$P(\beta_2 > 1) = P\left(\frac{\beta_2 - b_2}{\sigma_{\beta_2}} > \frac{1 - .9113}{.06065}\right) = P(z_2 > 1.463) = .072 \quad (25.4.12b)$$

Thus, given our model and assumptions, there is some chance (approximately 7 in 100) that the marginal propensity to consume is greater than one. Similarly, there is about a 6 in 10 chance that autonomous consumption is negative. If you do not really believe these probabilities, then that is an indication that you are unhappy with the prior information that was specified. It suggests that, prior to sampling, you were not really completely uncertain about the values of the parameters β_1 and β_2.

To find 95% interval estimates, we follow the same procedure that was used in Section 25.3, where inference was based on a repeated sample context. However, in this case, because σ^2 is assumed known, we use the normal rather than the t-distribution. Also, with the post-sample density functions, the interpretation is different. We make probability statements about β_1 and β_2. Specifically,

$$P\left[b_2 - 1.96\sigma_{\beta_2} < \beta_2 < b_2 + 1.96\sigma_{\beta_2}\right] = .95$$

That is,

$$P(.792 < \beta_2 < 1.030) = .95$$

and, for β_1,

$$P(-1178 < \beta_1 < 920) = .95$$

As with the least squares results, our interval estimates include what might be considered infeasible regions ($\beta_2 > 1$ and $\beta_1 < 0$). It is the same problem as having positive probabilities assigned to these regions. It occurs because, when we specified our prior information, we assumed that we were completely uninformed and placed no conditions on β_1 and β_2.

Finally, let us compare the two hypotheses introduced in Section 25.3 on the basis of an odds ratio. Suppose that we are interested in whether or not $\beta_2 > .9$. A value $\beta_2 = .9$ implies a multiplier effect of $1/(1 - .9) = 10$, and hence we think of the government as wanting to collect information on whether the multiplier might be greater than 10. We set up the two hypotheses:

$$H_0 : \beta_2 \leq .9 \qquad H_1 : \beta_2 > .9$$

The odds ratio in favor of H_1 is given by

$$K_{10} = \frac{P(\beta_2 > .9)}{P(\beta_2 \leq .9)} = \frac{.57365}{.42635} = 1.35$$

The odds ratio in favor of H_0 is

$$K_{01} = \frac{1}{K_{10}} = \frac{1}{1.35} = .74$$

Thus, it is 1.35 times more likely for $\beta_2 > .9$ than it is for $\beta_2 < .9$. With the significance level approach to hypothesis testing, we did not reject $H_0 : \beta_2 \leq .9$. Interpreting this result within the odds-ratio framework, and given $\sigma^2 = 11,000$, we can say that the odds of 1.35 in favor of H_1 is not sufficiently strong evidence for the government to change its presumption that H_0 is true. As we shall see, this result is sensitive to how we specify our prior information.

25.5 Including Prior Information on the Consumption Function Parameters

Having examined the nature of the post-sample density functions for the consumption function parameters when only sample information contributes to these density functions, we turn now to the problem of including into the learning process both sample and prior inequality information. We continue to examine autonomous consumption β_1 and the marginal propensity to consume β_2 in the consumption function

$$y_t = \beta_1 + x_t \beta_2 + e_t \tag{25.5.1}$$

Also, we continue to assume that the error variance σ^2 is known. This assumption simplifies the introduction of a number of new concepts. At first we concentrate on the prior information that the marginal propensity to consume must lie between zero and one, $0 < \beta_2 < 1$, and we leave autonomous consumption β_1 unrestricted. The results under these circumstances are relevant when we regard the consumption function model as valid only around the region of the sample data and not around a zero income level. The inclusion of the additional information that autonomous consumption must be positive ($\beta_1 > 0$) is taken up in Section 25.5.4. In Sections 25.5.1 to 25.5.3, we investigate the following questions:

1. How can we express prior information that $0 < \beta_2 < 1$ in terms of a prior probability density function?

2. After we use Bayes' rule to combine the prior probability density function with the sample information, what is the nature of our post-sample density function for β_2? How do we express our information after the sample has been observed?

3. How do we use the new post-sample density function for β_2, which includes the prior inequality information, to make probability statements and to find point and interval estimates?

4.   Does prior inequality information on β_2 affect our post-sample information on β_1?

25.5.1   Prior Information on the Marginal Propensity to Consume

Let us examine the first question. How can prior inequality information of the form $0 < \beta_2 < 1$ be expressed in terms of a prior probability density function? If we know that $0 < \beta_2 < 1$, but we have no idea where within the interval $(0, 1)$ that β_2 might lie, then a probability density function that suggests all values between 0 and 1 are equally likely is a reasonable one. A probability density function with this property is the uniform density function:

$$f(\beta_2) = \begin{cases} 1 & \text{if } 0 < \beta_2 < 1 \\ 0 & \text{otherwise} \end{cases} \qquad (25.5.2)$$

It is graphed in Figure 25.2. With this function the probability of β_2 lying within any interval contained in $(0, 1)$ depends only on the length of that interval. For example, $P(.9 < \beta_2 < 1) = .1 = P(0.8 < \beta_2 < .9)$. Also, $P(0 < \beta_2 < .5) = P(.5 < \beta_2 < 1) = .5$. The reader might question this last probability statement. Most people would argue that it is much more likely for the marginal propensity to consume to be greater than .5, than it is to be less than .5. Some might say it cannot be less than .6 or .7. Other probability density functions on the interval $(0, 1)$ could be used to include this kind of information if we wish. However, we include only the prior information $0 < \beta_2 < 1$, without being specific about where in this interval β_2 is likely to lie; this is information that *everyone* can agree on. Other prior views such as $.6 < \beta_2 < 1$ or $.7 < \beta_2 < 1$ might be held by some people but not others.

How, then, does a prior probability density function like that in equation 25.5.2 change our post-sample density function for β_1 and β_2? This is the next question that we consider.

25.5.2   Post-Sample Density Function for β_2

In Section 25.4, when we examined the post-sample density function for β_2 corresponding to complete prior uncertainty and an assumed value of $\sigma^2 = 11,000$, we found that

$$\beta_2 \sim N\left(b_2, \sigma_{\beta_2}^2\right) \qquad (25.5.3)$$

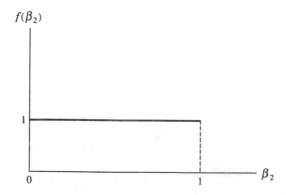

Figure 25.2 A uniform prior probability density function for β_2 on the interval $(0, 1)$.

where

$$b_2 = .9113 \qquad \text{and} \qquad \sigma_{\beta_2} = .06065 \qquad (25.5.4)$$

A 95% interval estimate was

$$P(.792 < \beta_2 < 1.030) = .95 \qquad (25.5.5)$$

and the probability of β_2 lying outside the interval (0, 1) was

$$P(\beta_2 > 1) = .072 \qquad (25.5.6)$$

Thus, with $\sigma^2 = 11,000$, the assumption of complete prior uncertainty yields a normal post-sample density function that suggests that the marginal propensity to consume can be greater than 1. The equation of the density function is

$$f_N(\beta_2 \mid y) = \frac{\left[\Sigma(x_t - \bar{x})^2\right]^{1/2}}{(2\pi\sigma^2)^{1/2}} \exp\left\{ -\frac{\Sigma(x_t - \bar{x})^2}{2\sigma^2}(\beta_2 - b_2)^2 \right\} \qquad (25.5.7)$$

In equation 25.5.7 the subscript N is used with $f(\beta_2 \mid y)$ to denote the normal distribution. Also, recall that the notation $\mid y$ means "conditional on the sample information." Thus, $f_N(\beta_2 \mid y)$ refers to a normal distribution that expresses our uncertainty or information about β_2 after the sample y has been observed. It is graphed in Figure 25.3.

If our prior density function $f(\beta_2)$ attaches zero probability to values of β_2 outside the range (0, 1), then the post-sample density function that includes this information, and the additional information provided by the sample, must also attach zero probability to values outside (0, 1). Let us investigate how we might modify $f_N(\beta_2 \mid y)$ in equation 25.5.7 so that $P(\beta_2 > 1) = P(\beta_2 < 0) = 0$. From $f_N(\beta_2 \mid y)$ in Figure 25.3 it is clear that, for all practical purposes, $P(\beta_2 < 0) = 0$. Thus, we only need to consider modifying $f_N(\beta_2 \mid y)$ to introduce the constraint $P(\beta_2 > 1) = 0$. Such a modification is to *truncate* the post-sample density function at one. To truncate the density function at one means that we take all of

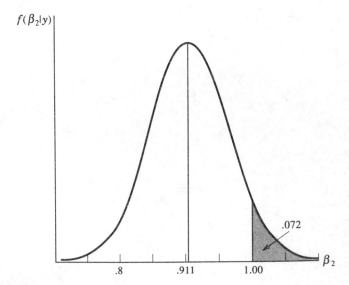

Figure 25.3 Normal post-sample density function $f_N(\beta_2 \mid y)$ (complete prior uncertainty).

the probability mass to the right of one (the shaded area under the density function in Figure 25.3) and *we distribute it proportionally over the remainder of the density function*. The resulting probability density function is called a *truncated normal distribution*. For this density function we use the notation $f_{TN}(\beta_2|\mathbf{y})$. It is pictured in Figure 25.4 alongside the regular normal distribution $f_N(\beta_2|\mathbf{y})$. Note how the new truncated normal density function has no area under its curve outside the interval (0, 1). Also, it is slightly higher than the old normal density function because the probability mass that was outside (0, 1) has been transferred to within (0, 1). That is, the shaded area outside (0, 1) equals the area that is inside (0, 1) and between the two density functions $f_N(\beta_2|\mathbf{y})$ and $f_{TN}(\beta_2|\mathbf{y})$.

The truncated normal distribution $f_{TN}(\beta_2|\mathbf{y})$ is the post-sample density function that is obtained when Bayes' rule is used to combine the uniform prior on (0, 1) with the sample information.

How do we obtain the equation of the density function $f_{TN}(\beta_2|\mathbf{y})$ from that for $f_N(\beta_2|\mathbf{y})$? Let us introduce the notation P_N to denote probabilities calculated from the normal distribution and P_{TN} for probabilities from the truncated normal distribution. Thus, so far, we have $P_N(\beta_2 > 1) = 0.072$ and $P_{TN}(\beta_2 > 1) = 0$. Inside the interval (0, 1) the density function for the truncated normal post-sample distribution is

$$f_{TN}(\beta_2|\mathbf{y}) = \frac{f_N(\beta_2|\mathbf{y})}{1 - P_N(\beta_2 > 1)} = \frac{f_N(\beta_2|\mathbf{y})}{P_N(\beta_2 < 1)} = \frac{f_N(\beta_2|\mathbf{y})}{0.928}$$

$$= \frac{\left[\Sigma(x_t - \bar{x})^2\right]^{1/2}}{0.928(2\pi\sigma^2)^{1/2}} \exp\left\{-\frac{\Sigma(x_t - \bar{x})^2}{2\sigma^2}(\beta_2 - b_2)^2\right\} \qquad (25.5.8)$$

Thus, inside the interval (0, 1), we obtain $f_{TN}(\beta_2|\mathbf{y})$ by dividing $f_N(\beta_2|\mathbf{y})$ by $[1 - P_N(\beta_2 > 1)]$. That is, we divide the equation for the normal distribution by the probability that β_2 lies within the feasible range. Since $[1 - P_N(\beta_2 > 1)]$ is less than one, dividing by this quantity increases the height of the density function. Also, note that

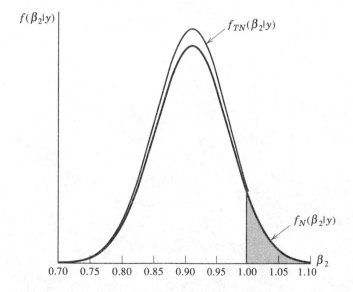

$f(\beta_2|y)$

$f_{TN}(\beta_2|y)$

$f_N(\beta_2|y)$

β_2

0.70   0.75   0.80   0.85   0.90   0.95   1.00   1.05   1.10

Figure 25.4 Normal and truncated normal post-sample density functions for β_2.

the smaller is $P_N(\beta_2 > 1)$, the smaller will be the change in the density function. In particular, if $P_N(\beta_2 > 1) \approx 0$, then $f_N(\beta_2|\mathbf{y})$ will remain unchanged; in this case the sample information alone suggests that $0 < \beta_2 < 1$ and so inclusion of this information as prior information has no additional influence. For values outside the interval $(0, 1)$, $f_{TN}(\beta_2|\mathbf{y}) = 0$.

Note that we have answered the second question posed in the introduction to Section 25.5. The truncated normal distribution in equation 25.5.8 is the post-sample density function that combines both prior inequality information and sample information on β_2. As was true with our previous post-sample density functions, the truncated normal density function represents all of our information about β_2 (prior and sample) after the sample has been observed. Because it is a complete statement of our knowledge about β_2, it is an appropriate way of reporting the results of our investigation into the marginal propensity to consume. However, it is often more meaningful, particularly to nonstatisticians, if we can report some summary measures derived from equation 25.5.8, such as probability statements and point and interval estimates. The question of how to compute such measures was the third question posed in the introduction. Let us investigate each of the measures in turn.

25.5.2a Probability Statements from the Truncated Normal Distribution
To compute probability statements from the truncated normal density we proceed as follows. If two points c and d lie *within* the range $(0, 1)$, then

$$P_{TN}\left(c < \beta_2 < d\right) = \frac{P_N\left(c < \beta_2 < d\right)}{1 - P_N\left(\beta_2 > 1\right)} \qquad (25.5.9)$$

That is, we divide the probability for the corresponding interval from the normal distribution by the same probability constant that is used to transform one density function to the other. For points c or d that lie *outside* $(0, 1)$, we must keep in mind that $P_{TN}(\beta_2 < 0) = 0$ and $P_{TN}(\beta_2 > 1) = 0$. As an example, suppose that, as in Section 25.4, we are interested in $P(\beta_2 \le 0.9)$ and $P(\beta_2 > 0.9)$. From the normal distribution we have

$$P_N\left(\beta_2 \le .9\right) = .426 \quad \text{and} \quad P_N\left(\beta_2 > .9\right) = .574 \qquad (25.5.10)$$

When we recognize that β_2 cannot be greater than 1 and, hence, use the truncated normal distribution, we have

$$
\begin{aligned}
P_{TN}\left(\beta_2 \le .9\right) &= P_{TN}\left(0 < \beta_2 \le .9\right) \\
&= \frac{P_N\left(0 < \beta_2 \le .9\right)}{1 - P_N\left(\beta_2 > 1\right)} \\
&= \frac{.426}{.928} = .459
\end{aligned}
\qquad (25.5.11)
$$

In going from $f_N(\beta_2|\mathbf{y})$ to $f_{TN}(\beta_2|\mathbf{y})$, the area under the density function to the left of .9 increases from .426 to .459. Now consider

$$
\begin{aligned}
P_{TN}\left(\beta_2 > .9\right) &= P_{TN}\left(.9 \le \beta_2 < 1\right) \\
&= \frac{P_N\left(.9 \le \beta_2 < 1\right)}{1 - P_N\left(\beta_2 > 1\right)} \\
&= \frac{.502}{.928} = .541
\end{aligned}
\qquad (25.5.12)
$$

As expected, the probabilities in equations 25.5.11 and 25.5.12 sum to unity. In the region to the right of .9, the probability of β_2 lying between .9 and 1 has increased from .502 to .541. Note the implications of this result for the probability value .072 that we transferred from the right tail of $f_N(\beta_2|\mathbf{y})$. The part of this probability that was transferred to the left of .9 is $(.459 - .426) = .033$. The part transferred to the right of .9 is $(.541 - .502) = .039$.

There is another way of obtaining, or *estimating*, probabilities such as these in equations 25.5.11 and 25.5.12. To introduce this method consider the general problem of estimating a proportion. Suppose we want to estimate the proportion of San Francisco households with an income greater than \$50,000. To estimate this proportion we would take a random sample of households and count the number with incomes in excess of \$50,000. Our estimate of the proportion is given by the number of sampled households with incomes in excess of \$50,000, divided by the total number of sampled households. Note that estimating this proportion is the same as estimating a probability. Specifically, it is estimating the probability that a San Francisco household, selected at random, will have an income greater than \$50,000.

A similar strategy can be adopted to estimate the probabilities in equations 25.5.11 and 25.5.12. This strategy uses a computer and is useful if we are unable to make calculations like those in equations 25.5.11 and 25.5.12. Using a computer-based random number generator, we can artificially generate a sample, as big as we like, from a normal distribution with mean $b_2 = .9113$ and standard deviation $\sigma_{\beta_2} = .06065$. Then, we can discard those observations that lie outside the range (0, 1). The remaining observations constitute a random sample from our truncated normal distribution. The proportion of these remaining observations that lie below .9 is an estimate of $P_{TN}(\beta_2 \leq .9)$. The proportion that lie above is an estimate for $P_{TN}(\beta_2 > .9)$. Note also, that the proportion of original observations that were thrown away is an estimate for $P_N(\beta_2 > 1)$. This approach may seem like an excessive amount of work when straightforward formulas like equation 25.5.9 are available. It will prove to be useful, however, for point estimation and when we have more complicated problems with more than one parameter and thus bivariate and multivariate distributions.

To illustrate the approach, 5000 normal random numbers were generated from a distribution with mean .9113 and standard deviation .06065. Instructions are given in the *Computer Handbooks*. The results we obtained appear in Table 25.1.

Note that the estimated probabilities are very close to the probabilities that we computed directly from the normal distribution. Our chances of getting closer estimates are increased if we take more than 5000 observations. See Exercise 25.6.

25.5.2b Point Estimation of β_2   In Chapter 24 we learned how to obtain a single point estimate or best guess for an unknown parameter by using both a loss function that reflects the consequences of a wrong decision and a post-sample density function for the unknown parameter. We indicated that, when the loss function is quadratic, the mean of the post-sample density function is the parameter estimate that minimizes expected loss. Suppose, now, that a quadratic loss function is again relevant, and thus we need the mean of the truncated normal distribution as a point estimate for β_2. This mean will *not* be the same as the mean from the regular distribution. To understand why, consider the definition of the mean of the normal distribution $f_N(\beta_2|\mathbf{y})$. It is given by

$$E_N[\beta_2] = \int_{-\infty}^{\infty} \beta_2 f_N(\beta_2|\mathbf{y})\, d\beta_2 \qquad (25.5.13)$$

We can think of this integral as a weighted average of all possible values for β_2, with weights given by the probability density function $f_N(\beta_2|\mathbf{y})$. All values of β_2, *including*

Table 25.1 Observations and Estimated Probabilities from Artificially Generated Sample

		Number of Observations	Estimated Probability	True Probability
Observations				
	Total	5000		
	Greater than 1	385		
	Less than 1	4615		
	Less than 0.9	2163		
	Between 0.9 and 1	2452		
Probabilities				
	$P_N(\beta_2 > 1)$		$\frac{385}{5000} = .077$	.072
	$P_{TN}(\beta_2 \leq .9)$		$\frac{2163}{4615} = .469$	.459
	$P_{TN}(\beta_2 > .9)$		$\frac{2452}{4615} = .531$	.541

those that are greater than 1, are weighted by $f_N(\beta_2|\mathbf{y})$. When we use the truncated normal distribution $f_{TN}(\beta_2|\mathbf{y})$, the weights outside the interval $(0, 1)$ are 0, and the weights inside are greater than those provided by the normal distribution. Also, in this particular example, the weights that both distributions assign to $\beta_2 < 0$ are effectively 0. Thus, when comparing the means of $f_N(\beta_2|\mathbf{y})$ and $f_{TN}(\beta_2|\mathbf{y})$, we need only consider the weights when β_2 is between 0 and 1 and the weights when β_2 is greater than 1. The important differences for the mean of $f_{TN}(\beta_2|\mathbf{y})$ are that values of β_2 greater than one no longer contribute to the mean, and values less than 1 make a greater contribution. Under these circumstances it follows that the mean for $f_{TN}(\beta_2|\mathbf{y})$ must be less than the mean of $f_N(\beta_2|\mathbf{y})$. It is defined by

$$E_{TN}[\beta_2] = \int_0^1 \beta_2 f_{TN}(\beta_2|\mathbf{y}) \, d\beta_2 \qquad (25.5.14)$$

How then do we compute the integral in equation 25.5.14 that defines the mean of the truncated normal distribution? One way is to use a computer-based numerical integration routine. Another way, and the way we consider, is to estimate the mean by using the artificially generated sample that we used in the previous section to estimate probabilities. In previous chapters when we were concerned with estimating the mean of a probability distribution, the procedure we followed was to take a random sample from the probability distribution (the population of household expenditures on food), and to use the sample mean as an estimate of the mean of the probability distribution. We can use the same procedure here. When discussing probability statements from the truncated normal distribution, we indicated how we could obtain an artificially generated random sample from that distribution. We use the computer to generate observations from $f_N(\beta_2|\mathbf{y})$, where $\beta_2 \sim N[.9113, (.06065)^2]$, and we discard those observations that are greater than one. The remaining observations constitute a random sample from the truncated normal distribution $f_{TN}(\beta_2|\mathbf{y})$. The sample mean from these remaining observations is an estimate of the mean of $f_{TN}(\beta_2|\mathbf{y})$, given in equation 25.5.14.

In the artificially generated sample we used to estimate probabilities, 4615 observations were retained (those where $\beta_2 < 1$) and 385 were discarded. We can use the same

4615 values to estimate $E_{TN}[\beta_2]$. Following this procedure we obtain

$$\hat{E}_{TN}[\beta_2] = \frac{\text{Sum of all "observations" on } \beta_2 \text{ that are less than 1}}{\text{Number of retained observations}}$$

$$= \frac{4160.86}{4615} = .9016 \qquad (25.5.15)$$

As expected, this estimate for the marginal propensity to consume is lower than the estimate of .9113 that did not take into account our prior information on the feasible range for β_2.

A measure of dispersion of the truncated normal distribution can also be obtained. The sample variance from the retained observations on β_2 is an estimate of the variance of $f_{TN}(\beta_2|\mathbf{y})$. Using the notation $\hat{\text{var}}_{TN}(\beta_2)$ for this estimated variance, from our 4615 observations we obtained

$$\hat{\text{var}}_{TN}(\beta_2) = (.05283)^2 \qquad (25.5.16)$$

The standard deviation of the truncated distribution, .05283, is less than that of .06065 from the normal distribution, reflecting the reduction in dispersion that occurs when prior information is used and only values of β_2 between 0 and 1 are possible. These results are summarized in Table 25.2.

25.5.2c Interval Estimation   The remaining summary measure from the truncated normal post-sample density function is that of an interval estimate. Assuming that an interval estimate with probability content of .95 is required, the interval estimation problem is one of finding values a_1 and a_2 such that

$$P_{TN}(a_1 < \beta_2 < a_2) = .95 \qquad (25.5.17)$$

Given that the interval estimate when no prior information was introduced was (.792, 1.030)—see equation 25.5.5—and given that most of the probability associated with $f_{TN}(\beta_2|\mathbf{y})$ is concentrated just below 1, it is reasonable to set the upper limit of the interval as $a_2 = 1$. Then our problem becomes one of obtaining a_1 such that

$$P_{TN}(a_1 < \beta_2 < 1) = .95 \qquad (25.5.18)$$

The value of a_1 can be found by using the relationship between probabilities from the truncated normal distribution and probabilities from the regular normal distribution. We have

$$P_{TN}(a_1 < \beta_2 < 1) = \frac{P_N(a_1 < \beta_2 < 1)}{1 - P_N(\beta_2 > 1)} = .95$$

Table 25.2   Means and Standard Deviations of Post-Sample Density Functions for β_2

	Uncertain Prior Information	Inequality Prior Information $0 < \beta_2 < 1$
Mean	.9113	.9016
Standard deviation	.06065	.05283

or

$$\frac{P_N\left(a_1 < \beta_2 < 1\right)}{.928} = .95$$

and

$$P_N\left(a_1 < \beta_2 < 1\right) = .882$$

Thus our problem of finding an interval estimate with probability content of .95 from the *truncated* normal distribution can be written in terms of finding an interval estimate with probability content of 0.882 from the regular normal distribution. Working in this direction we have

$$P_N\left(a_1 < \beta_2 < 1\right) = P_N\left(\beta_2 < 1\right) - P\left(\beta_2 < a_1\right) = .882$$

and thus

$$P_N\left(\beta_2 < a_1\right) = P_N\left(\beta_2 < 1\right) - .882 = .928 - .882 = .046$$

From this result we can use tables of probabilities from the standard normal distribution, or the instructions in the *Computer Handbooks*, to find $a_1 = .809$. Thus, our interval estimate with probability content of .95 is

$$P_{TN}\left(.809 < \beta_2 < 1\right) = .95 \tag{25.5.19}$$

Before introducing our prior information about the range of β_2 the corresponding interval estimate was (.793, 1.030). Thus, the introduction of prior information has resulted in a narrower, more informative interval estimate.

We could also use the artificially generated sample to obtain an interval estimate. If a frequency distribution or histogram for all the artificially generated observations is obtained, then we can find two values of β_2 between which 95% of the observations lie. Alternatively, if we do not wish to go to the extra trouble of constructing a frequency distribution, and we are prepared to live with an interval estimate whose probability content we do not know exactly before we generate the observations, we can pick two values of interest and find the proportion of observations that lie between these values. For example, suppose that we selected as our two endpoint values .82 and .95. In our artificially generated sample, 72.4% of the retained observations lay between these values. Thus, the interval (.82, .95) is an interval estimate with a probability content of .724.

25.5.3 How Is Information on β_1 and β_2 Related?

Thus far we have examined how prior inequality information on β_2 changes our post-sample density function for β_2. We have seen the implications for probability statements, point estimates, and interval estimates *for this parameter*. The question that we now wish to address—the fourth question posed in the introduction—is: Will prior inequality information about β_2 (the marginal propensity to consume) change the post-sample information about β_1 (autonomous consumption)? In general, the answer to this question is yes. Let us investigate how and why.

In Chapters 6 and 9 we examined properties of the least squares estimator $\mathbf{b} = (X'X)^{-1}X'\mathbf{y}$, and we summarized our results for this estimator by saying

$$\mathbf{b} \sim N\left[\boldsymbol{\beta}, \sigma^2\left(X'X\right)^{-1}\right] \tag{25.5.20}$$

That is, for our consumption problem, the estimator **b** has a bivariate normal distribution with mean vector β and covariance matrix $\sigma^2(X'X)^{-1}$. In the framework of this chapter, where we use a probability density function to express uncertainty about β after the sample has been observed, we say that

$$\beta \sim N\left[\mathbf{b}, \sigma^2 \left(X'X\right)^{-1}\right] \tag{25.5.21}$$

That is, the post-sample density function for β is a bivariate normal distribution with mean **b** and covariance matrix $\sigma^2(X'X)^{-1}$. This post-sample density function is a relevant one when σ^2 is known, and we have no prior information on β. To proceed with our investigation, it is convenient to write $\sigma^2(X'X)^{-1}$ out in full. Using notation that emphasizes that $\text{cov}(\beta) = \sigma^2(X'X)^{-1}$, and using some results from Chapter 6, we can write

$$\text{cov}(\beta) = \sigma^2 \left(X'X\right)^{-1} = \begin{bmatrix} \sigma^2_{\beta_1} & \sigma_{\beta_1 \beta_2} \\ \sigma_{\beta_1 \beta_2} & \sigma^2_{\beta_2} \end{bmatrix}$$

$$= \begin{bmatrix} \dfrac{\sigma^2 \Sigma x_t^2}{T\Sigma(x_t - \bar{x})^2} & \dfrac{-\bar{x}\sigma^2}{\Sigma(x_t - \bar{x})^2} \\ \dfrac{-\bar{x}\sigma^2}{\Sigma(x_t - \bar{x})^2} & \dfrac{\sigma^2}{\Sigma(x_t - \bar{x})^2} \end{bmatrix} \tag{25.5.22}$$

To summarize post-sample information about β_1 and β_2 *separately*, we say that $\beta_1 \sim N(b_1, \sigma^2_{\beta_1})$ and that $\beta_2 \sim N(b_2, \sigma^2_{\beta_2})$, where $\sigma^2_{\beta_1}$ is the first diagonal element of $\sigma^2(X'X)^{-1}$ and $\sigma^2_{\beta_2}$ is the second diagonal element of $\sigma^2(X'X)^{-1}$. What about the remaining term in $\sigma^2(X'X)^{-1}$? When is the covariance term

$$\sigma_{\beta_1 \beta_2} = \frac{-\bar{x}\sigma^2}{\Sigma(x_t - \bar{x})^2} \tag{25.5.23}$$

of interest? This term describes how our information about the two parameters β_1 and β_2 is related. When it is *nonzero*, knowing something about one parameter has a bearing on what we know about the other parameter. If we are just interested in β_1, or just β_2, then the separate density functions $\beta_1 \sim N(b_1, \sigma^2_{\beta_1})$ and $\beta_2 \sim N(b_2, \sigma^2_{\beta_2})$ are sufficient. However, to capture all the information that we have about β_1 and β_2 and, in particular, the way in which information about β_1 and β_2 is related, we need to specify the *joint* post-sample density function for both parameters. In other words, we need the post-sample density function for the vector $\beta = (\beta_1, \beta_2)'$. This joint post-sample density function is the bivariate normal distribution given in equation 25.5.21.

How then does the introduction of the information $0 < \beta_2 < 1$ change our knowledge about β_1? Because $\bar{x} > 0$, it follows that $\sigma_{\beta_1 \beta_2} < 0$. Consequently, we would expect that additional information that suggests a smaller value for β_2 would lead us to believe that β_1 is larger, and vice versa. If the slope of the line β_2 is to decrease, and the line with the new slope is to remain close to the data points, then the intercept β_1 must increase. Our inequality did, indeed, suggest that β_2 is smaller. Without the inequality, values for β_2 greater than 1 were possible. Thus, we would expect the joint post-sample density function that includes the information $0 < \beta_2 < 1$ to lead us to revise upward a point estimate for β_1. In addition, the probability that β_1 takes on larger values should increase. Note that this direction is a desirable one for revision of our knowledge. The negative value for autonomous consumption was of some concern, and it would be helpful if other information suggested it should be larger.

To discover more precisely how our information on β_1 has changed through the introduction of the prior inequality $0 < \beta_2 < 1$, we can use the computer to draw an artificially generated sample of observations from the bivariate distribution for β. In this case each observation that is generated comprises a pair of values, one value for β_1 and one for β_2. A random sample from the truncated bivariate normal distribution (the truncation again being outside $0 < \beta_2 < 1$) is obtained by discarding *each pair* of values where $\beta_2 > 1$ or $\beta_2 < 0$. The remaining observations can be used to estimate the mean and variance of β_1 as well as probability statements about β_1. Instructions for generating observations from the bivariate normal distribution are given in the *Computer Handbooks*. Using these instructions and an extension of the random sample of size 5000 considered in Section 25.5.2, we obtained the following information

Number of retained observations = 4615

Number of retained observations on β_1 that lie between 0 and 750 = 1832

Sample mean of retained observations on β_1 = −44.17

Sample standard deviation of retained observations on β_1 = 467.26

This information is presented in Table 25.3 alongside the corresponding information obtained without imposition of the inequality constraint. The reader is encouraged to confirm the results that arise when no prior information exists.

The changes that have resulted agree with our expectations. The probability that β_1 lies in the interval of positive values (0, 750) has increased slightly. The mean of the post-sample density (a point estimate for β_1 under quadratic loss) has increased, although it is still negative. And, the standard deviation of the post-sample density function has declined, reflecting the reduction in dispersion that occurs when the range of β_2 is restricted.

Thus, even though we might have prior inequality information on just one of the parameters that describe the economic relationship, we need to consider the effect of that prior information on the post-sample information for both parameters. We can summarize this post-sample information by using probability statements and point estimates obtained from a computer-based random sample generated from the truncated bivariate normal distribution. We have now supplied answers to the four questions posed in the introduction to this section. However, there are two remaining problems to be considered. We investigate the results that are obtained when inequality restrictions are imposed on *both* β_1 and β_2, and we examine the implications for prediction.

25.5.4   Including Prior Information on Both Parameters

Earlier in the chapter we indicated that there are two prior inequality restrictions that are reasonable for the parameters β_1 and β_2. One is the restriction that we have been considering, that the marginal propensity to consume lies between 0 and 1. The other

Table 25.3   Postsample Information on β_1

	Uncertain Prior Information	Inequality Prior Information $0 < \beta_2 < 1$
$P(0<\beta_1<750)$	.355	1832/4615 = .397
Mean	−128.94	−44.17
Standard deviation	535.03	467.26

restriction, that autonomous consumption β_1 is positive, is more controversial; with an aggregate consumption function income is never close to 0. Nevertheless, to illustrate the imposition of two restrictions, we also introduce the prior inequality that $\beta_1 > 0$.

When both inequalities $\beta_1 > 0$ *and* $0 < \beta_2 < 1$ are imposed, it is no longer possible to consider one of the parameters in isolation as we did in Sections 25.5.1 and 25.5.2. In these sections, where there was only a restriction on β_2, it was possible to consider the effect of that restriction on the post-sample density function for β_2, without examining β_1. However, we did need to consider both parameters together to see how the restriction on β_2 changed information about β_1. Where restrictions exist on both parameters, prior information on β_1 will influence post-sample information on β_2 and vice versa. Thus, both parameters need to be considered jointly, and we always need to draw an artificial sample from the bivariate normal distribution for $\beta = (\beta_1, \beta_2)'$. In this case, to obtain a random sample from the relevant *truncated* bivariate normal distribution, an observation pair is discarded if β_1 *or* β_2 *or* both do not satisfy their respective inequalities. The relevant *prior* probability density function for β_1 is a uniform one that is equal to 1 over positive values of β_1 and 0 over negative values. The procedure can be summarized as follows:

1.   Generate a number of observations (say, 5000) from a bivariate normal distribution with mean **b** and covariance matrix $\sigma^2(X'X)^{-1}$. These observations represent a random sample of observations on $\beta = (\beta_1, \beta_2)'$, taken from the post-sample density function *without* inequality prior information.

2.   Discard those observations on $(\beta_1, \beta_2)'$ where $\beta_1 < 0$, $\beta_2 < 0$ or $\beta_2 > 1$. The remaining observations on $\beta = (\beta_1, \beta_2)'$ constitute a random sample from the truncated bivariate normal distribution, that is, the post-sample density function that includes inequality prior information.

3.   Use the retained observations to estimate probabilities, means, and standard deviations associated with the truncated post-sample density function. For example, the proportion of retained observations on β_2 that lies within a given interval is an estimate of the probability that β_2 lies in that interval. Estimates of the means and standard deviations of β_1 and β_2 are given by the sample means and standard deviations from the retained observations.

This sampling procedure was followed for the same 5000 observations that were generated previously. The results, alongside some of those from previous sections, and some that were not previously reported, are summarized in Table 25.4.

There are a number of comments that can be made about Table 25.4. First, the standard deviations for β_1 and β_2 decrease as more prior information is added, reflecting the greater precision of the post-sample information as more prior information is included. Second, the two prior inequalities complement each other. The restriction $0 < \beta_2 < 1$ makes negative values of β_1 less likely and, conversely, the restriction $\beta_1 > 0$ makes values of β_2 that are greater than 1 less likely. This effect influences the results for the means and the probability statements. With both restrictions the point estimates are \$382.31 for autonomous consumption, and .85 for the marginal propensity to consume, compared with −44.17 and .90 with only the restriction $0 < \beta_2 < 1$. The dramatic effect from the restriction $\beta_1 > 0$ occurs because 2937 observations were discarded when this restriction was added. Only 385 were discarded for the single restriction $0 < \beta_2 < 1$. The odds in favor of $\beta_2 \leq .9$ relative to $\beta_2 > .9$ are extremely large and substantially different once all prior information is included. The difference occurs because, with both restrictions imposed, almost all the probability for β_2 is placed

Table 25.4 Summary Measures for Normal and Truncated Normal Post-Sample Density Functions for β_1 and β_2

	Complete Prior Uncertainty	$0 < \beta_2 < 1$	$0 < \beta_2 < 1$ and $\beta_1 > 0$
Number of discarded observations (out of 5000)	0	385	2937
$E[\beta_1]$	−128.94	−44.17	382.31
Standard deviation (β_1)	535.03	467.26	290.15
$P(0 < \beta_1 < 750)$	.355	.397	.888
$E[\beta_2]$	.9113	.9016	.8535
Standard deviation (β_2)	.06065	.05283	.03314
$P(.82 < \beta_2 < .95)$	.732	.724	.842
$P(.82 < \beta_2 < .9)$	.360	.398	.835
Odds in favor of $\beta_2 \leq .9$ against $\beta_2 > .9$	.74	.88	136.5

below .9. Otherwise, however, the proportion of probability greater than .9 is slightly greater than that below .9. The various *probability* statements in Table 25.4 reflect the same differences. Note also that the use of prior information has an effect on the estimate of the government expenditure multiplier. With no prior information this multiplier is approximately 11; when both restrictions are imposed, it is approximately 7.

In this section we have described how inequality constraints can be imposed on both the parameters in the consumption function. Also, we have illustrated how our post-sample information, summarized in terms of probability statements, point estimates, and interval estimates can be sensitive to the amount of prior information that is injected into the learning process. Since we often have inequality information about parameters in economic relationships, the techniques that we have illustrated are important ones for econometric practice.

25.5.5   Prediction

In Chapter 7 we examined how to predict the outcome of a dependent variable (household expenditure) for a given value of an explanatory variable (household income) and how to measure the reliability of the prediction through an estimate of the variance of the prediction error. The same techniques can be used in the context of the example in this chapter to predict consumption for a given level of disposable income. Such a prediction would not, however, make allowance for the prior information that we have concerning β_1 and β_2, namely, that $\beta_1 > 0$ and $0 < \beta_2 < 1$. It is possible to make predictions consistent with this additional information. It is this question that we now consider.

Let x_0 be the level of income for which we wish to predict the corresponding consumption, and let $\mathbf{x}_0 = (1, x_0)'$ be the two-dimensional vector containing the element 1 and the value of income. From Chapter 7, the corresponding predicted consumption level is

$$\hat{y}_0 = \mathbf{x}_0' \mathbf{b} \tag{25.5.24}$$

and the variance of the prediction error is

$$\text{var}(\hat{y}_0 - y_0) = \sigma^2 \left[1 + \mathbf{x}_0' (X'X)^{-1} \mathbf{x}_0 \right] \tag{25.5.25}$$

where $\mathbf{b} = (X'X)^{-1}X'\mathbf{y}$ is the least squares estimator and $\hat{\sigma}^2 = (\mathbf{y} - X\mathbf{b})'(\mathbf{y} - X\mathbf{b})/(T - 2)$ can be used as an unbiased estimator for the error variance. These results are valid *before* a sample of data is taken. They refer to a prediction rule and the variance of the error of that prediction rule. This prediction rule is: First, collect a sample of data, and estimate β. Second, use $\mathbf{b}$, the estimate for β, in the rule $\hat{y}_0 = \mathbf{x}_0'\mathbf{b}$. The variance of the prediction error includes variation attributable to estimation of β in repeated samples as well as variation in the error term e_0 if repeated predictions could be made.

We can also examine the problem *after* the sample has been observed, given that we have a post-sample density function that expresses our state of knowledge about β. Let us investigate how. The future observation that we wish to predict is given by

$$y_0 = \mathbf{x}_0'\boldsymbol{\beta} + e_0 \tag{25.5.26}$$

If we have the post-sample density function for β and we know that $e_0 \sim N(0, \sigma^2)$, then we should be able to use this information and equation 25.5.26 to derive a probability density function for y_0. This density function expresses our uncertainty about the future value y_0 and is called a *predictive density function*. Let us examine the mean and variance of the predictive density function. We have

$$E[y_0] = \mathbf{x}_0'E[\boldsymbol{\beta}] + E[e_0] = \mathbf{x}_0'E[\boldsymbol{\beta}] \tag{25.5.27}$$

If no prior information about β_1 and β_2 has been introduced (complete prior uncertainty), then the mean of the post-sample density function is identical to the least squares estimate $E[\beta] = \mathbf{b}$ and so

$$E[y_0] = \mathbf{x}_0'\mathbf{b} \tag{25.5.28}$$

In Chapter 24 we discovered that the mean of the post-sample density function minimizes expected loss when loss is quadratic. Similarly, the optimal point predictor under a quadratic loss function is the mean of the predictive density function. Thus, *if we have no prior information, considering the prediction problem after the sample of data has been observed leads to the same predictor as when we consider prediction before the sample has been observed.* However, if we have inequality prior information, then $E[\beta] \neq \mathbf{b}$, and our point predictor will be given by $E[y_0] = \mathbf{x}_0'E[\beta]$.

What about the variance of the predictive density function? From equation 25.5.26 we have

$$\mathrm{var}(y_0) = \mathrm{var}(\mathbf{x}_0'\boldsymbol{\beta}) + \mathrm{var}(e_0) + 2\,\mathrm{cov}(\mathbf{x}_0'\boldsymbol{\beta}, e_0)$$
$$= \mathbf{x}_0'\,\mathrm{cov}(\boldsymbol{\beta})\mathbf{x}_0 + \mathrm{var}(e_0) \tag{25.5.29}$$

where $\mathrm{cov}(\beta)$ is the covariance matrix of the joint post-sample density function for β and where $\mathrm{cov}(\mathbf{x}_0'\beta, e_0) = 0$ because our information about β depends only on past information, not the future e_0. Students who are uneasy about going from the first line to the second line in equation 25.5.29 should show the equivalence of $\mathrm{var}(\mathbf{x}_0'\beta)$ and $\mathbf{x}_0'\mathrm{cov}(\beta)\mathbf{x}_0$ by writing each expression out in full. When σ^2 is known, and we have no prior information about β_1 and β_2, then the predictive density function for β is a normal distribution, and $\mathrm{cov}(\beta) = \sigma^2(X'X)^{-1}$. Thus,

$$\mathrm{var}(y_0) = \sigma^2\left[\mathbf{x}_0'(X'X)^{-1}\mathbf{x}_0 + 1\right] \tag{25.5.30}$$

Note that these results are similar to those in Chapter 7. The difference is that here we used the post-sample density function for β to derive $\mathrm{var}(y_0)$. Hence we are talking about *information contained in a predictive density function after the sample has been observed*. In Chapter 7 we used the variance of the least squares estimator **b** to find the *prediction error variance* var($\hat{y}_0 - y_0$), *before the sample was observed*.

What happens if we introduce prior information in the form of inequality restrictions? In this case equation 25.5.29 does not simplify to equation 25.5.30 and cov(β) remains in equation 25.5.29 as the covariance matrix of the truncated post-sample density function for β. Under these circumstances, we need to estimate $E[y_0]$ and var(y_0). To do so the same artificially generated sample that we have employed throughout can be used again. Let β_{1i} and β_{2i} refer to the ith observations from the truncated bivariate normal distribution. That is, they represent the ith pair of retained observations that satisfy both inequality constraints $\beta_1 > 0$ and $0 < \beta_2 < 1$. Then, the sample mean from these observations is

$$\hat{E}_{TN}[\boldsymbol{\beta}] = \overline{\boldsymbol{\beta}} = \begin{bmatrix} \overline{\beta}_1 \\ \overline{\beta}_2 \end{bmatrix} = \frac{1}{n} \begin{bmatrix} \sum_{i=1}^{n} \beta_{1i} \\ \sum_{i=1}^{n} \beta_{2i} \end{bmatrix} \qquad (25.5.31)$$

where n is the number of retained observations. Similarly, for the estimated variances we have

$$\hat{\mathrm{var}}_{TN}(\beta_1) = \frac{1}{n-1} \sum_{i=1}^{n} (\beta_{1i} - \overline{\beta}_1)^2 \quad \text{and} \quad \hat{\mathrm{var}}_{TN}(\beta_2) = \frac{1}{n-1} \sum_{i=1}^{n} (\beta_{2i} - \overline{\beta}_2)^2 \qquad (25.5.32)$$

We need to use this information to estimate the mean

$$E_{TN}[y_0] = \mathbf{x}_0' E_{TN}[\boldsymbol{\beta}] \qquad (25.5.33)$$

and the variance

$$\mathrm{var}_{TN}(y_0) = \mathbf{x}_0' \, \mathrm{cov}_{TN}(\boldsymbol{\beta}) \mathbf{x}_0 + \sigma^2 \qquad (25.5.34)$$

of the predictive density function for y_0. For the mean we have

$$\hat{E}_{TN}[y_0] = \mathbf{x}_0' \hat{E}_{TN}[\boldsymbol{\beta}] = \mathbf{x}_0' \overline{\boldsymbol{\beta}} \qquad (25.5.35)$$

For the variance we need an estimate of the covariance matrix $\mathrm{cov}_{TN}(\boldsymbol{\beta})$. The diagonal elements of this matrix can be estimated using the variance terms in equation 25.5.32. The off-diagonal element that is the covariance term is estimated as follows:

$$\hat{\mathrm{cov}}_{TN}(\beta_1, \beta_2) = \frac{1}{n-1} \sum_{i=1}^{n} (\beta_{1i} - \overline{\beta}_1)(\beta_{2i} - \overline{\beta}_2) \qquad (25.5.36)$$

Thus, for the complete covariance matrix we have the estimator

$$\hat{\mathrm{cov}}_{TN}(\boldsymbol{\beta}) = \frac{1}{n-1} \begin{bmatrix} \sum_{i=1}^{n} (\beta_{1i} - \overline{\beta}_1)^2 & \sum_{i=1}^{n} (\beta_{1i} - \overline{\beta}_1)(\beta_{2i} - \overline{\beta}_2) \\ \sum_{i=1}^{n} (\beta_{1i} - \overline{\beta}_1)(\beta_{2i} - \overline{\beta}_2) & \sum_{i=1}^{n} (\beta_{2i} - \overline{\beta}_2)^2 \end{bmatrix} \qquad (25.5.37)$$

and an estimate of the variance of y_0 is

$$\hat{\text{var}}_{TN}\left(y_0\right) = \mathbf{x}_0'\,\hat{\text{cov}}_{TN}\left(\boldsymbol{\beta}\right)\mathbf{x}_0 + \sigma^2 \tag{25.5.38}$$

Since we are retaining the assumption of σ^2 known, this variance can be readily computed.

From the 2022 retained observations that we generated in Section 25.5.4 and that satisfied both $\beta_1 > 0$ and $0 < \beta_2 < 1$, we found

$$\hat{\text{cov}}_{TN}\left(\boldsymbol{\beta}\right) = \begin{bmatrix} 88673.83 & -10.05575 \\ -10.05575 & .00115427 \end{bmatrix} \tag{25.5.39}$$

If our prediction problem is one of predicting consumption for an income level of $10,000$, then $x_0 = 10{,}000$, $\mathbf{x}_0' = (1,\ 10000)$ and for equation 25.5.35 we have

$$\hat{E}_{TN}\left[y_0\right] = \begin{pmatrix} 1 & 10000 \end{pmatrix}\begin{pmatrix} 381.21 \\ 0.853587 \end{pmatrix} = 8917$$

Using $\hat{\text{cov}}_{TN}\left(\boldsymbol{\beta}\right)$ from equation 25.5.39 and the expression in equation 25.5.38, we obtain

$$\hat{\text{var}}_{TN}\left(y_0\right) = \begin{pmatrix} 1 & 10000 \end{pmatrix}\hat{\text{cov}}_{TN}\left(\boldsymbol{\beta}\right)\begin{pmatrix} 1 \\ 10000 \end{pmatrix} + 11000$$

$$= 13{,}985$$

When no prior information is introduced, the corresponding quantities are

$$E_N\left[y_0\right] = \begin{pmatrix} 1 & 10000 \end{pmatrix}\begin{pmatrix} -128.94 \\ .91126 \end{pmatrix} = 8984$$

and

$$\text{var}_N\left(y_0\right) = \sigma^2\left(1 + \mathbf{x}_0'\left(X'X\right)^{-1}\mathbf{x}_0\right)$$

$$= 11000\left[1 + \begin{pmatrix} 1 & 10000 \end{pmatrix}\begin{pmatrix} 26.0232 & -.2944\times10^{-2} \\ -.2944\times10^{-2} & .33435\times10^{-6} \end{pmatrix}\begin{pmatrix} 1 \\ 10000 \end{pmatrix}\right]$$

$$= 17{,}349$$

Thus, in our example the introduction of prior information has led to little change in the point prediction, but there is a noticeable reduction in the variance of the predictive density function.

In this section we have indicated how inequality prior information on the parameters can be introduced into the prediction problem. We do so by obtaining a predictive density function that depends on the truncated post-sample density function for the parameters. The mean and variance of the predictive density function can be found from the mean and covariance matrix of the truncated post-sample density function, with this mean and covariance matrix being estimated using a set of artificially generated observations.

If we were to continue this analysis, the next task would be to drop the assumption of a known variance and one explanatory variable and to reconsider the various concepts that have been introduced under this specification. A solution in this general case involves a modification of general concepts that have already been introduced, and readers who wish to pursue this objective are directed to Judge et al. (1988, pp. 275–318).

25.6 Summary and Critique of Concepts

Our objective in this chapter has been to show how the Bayesian approach to inference can be used to express uncertainty or knowledge about the parameters that describe the relationship between two economic variables. As an example of a relationship, we chose an aggregate consumption function that relates aggregate consumption to personal disposable income. The parameters that describe this relationship are the marginal propensity to consume and autonomous consumption (consumption at zero income). We have been interested in ways of expressing our knowledge about these two parameters before and after a sample has been observed. In particular, we examined how to express and include prior inequality information that the marginal propensity to consume must lie between 0 and 1 and autonomous consumption must be positive. We discovered that the methods and concepts introduced in Chapter 24 can be readily extended to this problem.

In this chapter there were two main extensions. First, now that we are considering the relationship between two economic variables rather than the mean of a single economic variable, there are two parameters rather than one to contend with. We examined post-sample density functions for each of the parameters. These density functions were normal distributions when the error variance was known. Although we did not pursue it, these density functions are t-distributions when the error variance is not known. When we consider the *joint* distribution of both parameters we move to a *bivariate* normal distribution. For a general economic relationship between more than two variables, and with more than two parameters, the bivariate distribution extends to a multivariate distribution. However, when no prior inequality information exists, a univariate normal distribution can be considered separately for each parameter.

The second extension of the methods of Chapter 24 was the introduction of prior inequality information and the consequent study of a truncated normal post-sample density function. We discovered that uniform prior density functions over the relevant range of the parameters can be used to describe prior inequality information. The post-sample density functions that result from combining the restricted uniform priors with the sample information are truncated normal when the variance is known and truncated t when the variance is unknown. When we have a single restriction on a given parameter, the univariate truncated post-sample distribution for that parameter can be considered separately. However, for information on the parameter that is not restricted, or if there is more than a single restriction, it is necessary to examine the truncated bivariate normal or, if the error variance is unknown, the truncated bivariate t-distribution.

In the univariate case probability statements from the truncated distributions can be obtained by using the relationships between truncated distributions and their nontruncated versions. Alternatively, probabilities of interest can be estimated by using the computer to artificially generate a sample from the relevant truncated distribution. In the bivariate case this alternative becomes essential. It is implemented by generating observations from the corresponding nontruncated distribution and discarding those that are infeasible.

Estimates of the mean and the variance of the truncated distribution are given by the sample mean and variance from the artificially generated observations. Interval estimates can also be found by using appropriate probability relationships, or the artificially generated observations. These summary measures are convenient ways of expressing post-sample information about the parameters consistent with prior inequality information.

The concept of a predictive density function can be used to express uncertainty about a future value for consumption with or without prior inequality information. The mean and variance of the predictive density function are convenient ways of summarizing information on the future value.

The relationship between the statistical techniques of this chapter and those of Chapters 5 to 7 is similar to the relationship between Chapter 24 and Chapters 3 and 4. In Chapters 5 to 7, estimation and inference techniques were chosen because of their properties before a sample is taken. We made probability statements about the least squares estimator, and about confidence intervals, before observing any data. In this chapter we are concerned with making subjective probability statements about parameters after the data have been observed. The techniques introduced in this chapter have wide applicability. Examples of inequality information are plentiful in economics. We know the response of quantity demanded to price is negative; the response of quantity supplied to price is positive; investment is negatively related to the rate of interest; for profit maximization a production function must have diminishing but positive marginal products. All of these examples can be handled within the framework of this chapter. Furthermore, the analysis extends in a straightforward way to relationships involving more than two economic variables. For further reading on the use of inequality information, consult Griffiths (1988) and Geweke (1986). More details about Bayesian inference in general linear models can be found in Judge et al. (1988, Chapter 7).

Finally, we note that there are (at least) two statistical assumptions that we could question that are the subject of earlier chapters in this book. When time-series data are used to estimate an economic relationship, it is possible for the error terms in different time periods to be correlated. Such correlation can occur because of the lagged effect of variables not included in the equation; this is known as autocorrelation. As we learned in Chapter 13, the presence of autocorrelation requires an adjustment to our estimation techniques. Second, the consumption function is just one of a number of functions that describe interrelationships within the economy. Not only does consumption depend on income but, through another relationship, income can depend on consumption. Techniques relevant for equations where such interrelationships exist were considered in Chapters 18 and 19.

25.7   Exercises

25.1. Let Z be a standard normal random variable such that $Z \sim N(0, 1)$ and let X be the truncated normal random variable obtained by truncating Z at .5 such that $P(X > .5) = 0$.
   (a) Find $P(Z > 0.5)$ and $P(-.5 < Z < .5)$.
   (b) Find $P(-.5 < X < .5)$.
   (c) Generate 1000 observations on a standard normal random variable and use these artificial observations to estimate $E(Z)$ and $E(X)$.
   (d) Suppose that Y was formed by truncating Z at .5 such that $P(Y < .5) = 0$. How would you use the artificial observations to estimate $E(Y)$?
   (e) Estimate the variances of the truncated distributions for X and Y.
   (f) Use the artificial observations to estimate $P(0 < X < 1)$ and $P(0 < Y < 1)$.

25.2. Table 25.5 contains data on per capita consumption and per capita disposable income for the U. S. economy for the period 1960 to 1986. These data are expressed in terms of 1982 dollars. Consider the consumption function

$$y_t = \beta_1 + x_t \beta_2 + e_t \tag{25.7.1}$$

where y_t is per capita consumption and x_t denotes per capita disposable income. Assume that the e_t are independent normal random variables with mean zero and *known variance* $\sigma^2 = 6000$. Using the last 10 observations (1977 to 1986) answer the following questions:

(a) Find least squares estimates for β_1 and β_2 and corresponding 95% confidence intervals. Note whether the confidence intervals include infeasible ranges of the parameters.

(b) Using the post-sample density functions for β_1 and β_2 under an assumption of complete prior uncertainty, find $P(\beta_1 < 0)$ and $P(\beta_2 > 1)$.

(c) From the same post-sample density functions, find the odds ratio in favor of H_0: $\beta_2 \geq .9$ relative to the alternative H_1: $\beta_2 < .9$.

(d) Generate 1000 observations from the bivariate normal post-sample density function for β_1 and β_2. Discard those observation pairs where $\beta_2 > 1$. Find the sample means and variances for β_1 and β_2 from the retained observations. Compare these values with those from the post-sample density functions used in parts (b) and (c).

(e) Using the same retained artificial observations, estimate the odds ratio in favor of H_0: $\beta_2 \geq .9$ relative to the alternative H_1: $\beta_2 < .9$.

(f) Repeat parts (d) and (e) but discard those observations where $\beta_2 > 1$ or $\beta_1 < 0$.

Table 25.5 U. S. Data on Consumption and Income

Year	Per Capita Disposable Personal Income in 1982 Dollars	Per Capita Consumption in 1982 Dollars
1960	6036	5561
1961	6113	5579
1962	6271	5729
1963	6378	5855
1964	6727	6099
1965	7027	6362
1966	7280	6607
1967	7513	6730
1968	7728	7003
1969	7891	7185
1970	8134	7275
1971	8322	7409
1972	8562	7726
1973	9042	7972
1974	8867	7826
1975	8944	7926
1976	9175	8272
1977	9381	8551
1978	9735	8808
1979	9829	8904
1980	9722	8783
1981	9769	8794
1982	9725	8818
1983	9930	9139
1984	10421	9475
1985	10563	9713
1986	10780	10014

25.3. Do Exercise 25.2 but use instead the first 10 observations for the period 1960 to 1969. Comment on the differences between these results and those obtained in Exercise 25.2.

25.4. The manager of a supermarket wishes to collect information on the elasticity of demand for tomatoes. The following model is set up

$$q_t = \beta_1 + p_t\beta_2 + e_t \qquad\qquad (25.7.2)$$

where q_t is the daily quantity of tomatoes purchased in kilograms, p_t is the price of tomatoes in cents/kilogram, β_1 and β_2 are unknown parameters, and the e_t are independent normal error terms with zero mean and constant known variance of $\sigma^2 = 64$. The manager decides to conduct an experiment. Each day for 25 days, a different price for tomatoes is set, and the quantity of tomatoes purchased at each price is observed. The prices and observed quantities are recorded in Table 25.6.

(a) Use the data in Table 25.6 to find least squares estimates of β_1 and β_2. What is an estimate of the elasticity of demand at the point $q = 125$, $p = 150$? What is a 95% confidence interval for the elasticity of demand at this point?

(b) Assuming no prior information on β_1 and β_2 exists, use the post-sample density function for β_2 to find $P(\beta_2 > 0)$.

(c) Let g be the elasticity of demand at the point $q = 125$, $p = 150$. Find $P(-1 < g < 0)$.

Table 25.6 Observations for Tomato Demand Equation

Quantity (kg)	Price (cents/kg)
115	190
138	173
130	175
119	176
109	170
121	144
118	143
120	125
127	154
119	187
133	178
132	154
137	140
127	155
132	138
124	122
131	166
137	152
115	136
122	140
129	157
129	104
133	138
115	141
116	174

(d) Repeat parts (b) and (c) using the truncated post-sample density function that arises under the prior inequality restriction $\beta_2 < 0$.
(e) Assuming that a quadratic loss function is relevant, find a point estimate for g when there is no prior information, and when we have the prior inequality information $\beta_2 < 0$.
(f) If the price is usually set at 150 cents, should the supermarket manager increase or decrease price to increase total revenue?

25.5. Consider again the consumption function model in equation 25.7.1. Using all the data in Table 25.5, find a point estimate (under quadratic loss) for the multiplier $1/(1 - \beta_2)$ given the inequality prior information $\beta_1 > 0$ and $0 < \beta_2 < 1$, and given that $\sigma^2 = 6000$.

25.6. Let $\hat{p}$ be a sample estimator for a population proportion p and let n be the sample size. From a central limit theorem, we have, approximately,

$$z = \frac{\hat{p} - p}{\sqrt{\dfrac{\hat{p}(1 - \hat{p})}{n}}} \sim N(0, 1)$$

(a) Given $\hat{p} = 0.077$ and $n = 5000$, construct a (sampling theory) 95% confidence interval for p.
(b) How large would n have to be to ensure that $|\hat{p} - p| < 0.003$ with a probability of .95?
(c) Discuss the relevance of parts (a) and (b) in relation to the entry for $P_N(\beta_2 > 1)$ in Table 25.1.

25.7. In Table 25.2 estimates of the mean and standard deviation of a truncated normal distribution were given as .9016 and .05283, respectively. These estimates were based on a sample size of 4615.
(a) Construct a 95% confidence interval for the mean of this truncated normal distribution.
(b) How large should the sample size be to ensure the maximum error when estimating the mean is .0005, with a probability of .95?

25.8 References

GEWEKE, J. (1986) "Exact Inference in the Inequality Constrained Normal Linear Regression Model," *Journal of Applied Econometrics*, 1, 127–141.

GRIFFITHS, W. E. (1988) "Bayesian Econometrics and How to Get Rid of Those Wrong Signs," *Review of Marketing and Agricultural Economics*, 56, 36–56.

JUDGE, G. G., R. C. HILL, W. E. GRIFFITHS, H. LÜTKEPOHL, and T. C. LEE (1988) *Introduction to the Theory and Practice of Econometrics*, 2nd Edition, New York: John Wiley & Sons, Inc., pp. 117–156, 275–318.

Part X

Economic Data Sources and the Writing Task

In applied econometrics there are some very important links in the econometric chain. One important link is the economic and statistical model. Another important link is the method of estimation and inference. A third link involves the sample observations or economic data that are used in the econometric analysis. A final link involves writing. This means the preparation of a research proposal or plan and/or the reporting of the results or both. The quality of an econometric analysis rests on the quality of each of these individual links. In Part X we emphasize the data and writing links in the econometric chain.

Chapter 26

Economic Data Sources, Guidelines for Choosing a Research Project, and the Writing of a Research Report

New Key Words and Concepts:

Data Collection Agencies	Stock Data
Observational Data	Qualitative Data
Controlled Experimental Data	Measurement Errors
Survey Data	Research Abstract
Flow Data	Research Report

In the preceding chapters we have emphasized the economic-statistical model and estimation and inference links in the econometric chain. In this chapter:

1. We discuss different types of economic data. Where the data have been collected, we identify a range of sources. Where the appropriate economic data do not exist we discuss the survey and controlled experiment routes to obtaining these data.

2. We offer some guidelines for choosing a research project and preparing an abstract that identifies the problem you have chosen, why you have chosen it, and how you intend to carry through your analysis.

3. In the writing link we suggest a format that may be used in preparing the post–econometric analysis research report.

26.1 Economic Data Samples

There are three primary sources or types of data that are used in econometric analyses. These sources or types of sample information include the following:

1. Economic outcome data that are generated from an experiment carried on by society. These observational data are sometimes called passively generated (nonexperimental) data, since society and not the researcher defines the treatments and the controls. This sample information includes data such as daily, monthly, and annual prices; outputs of final, intermediate, and primary commodities; the level of unemployment; total and per capita disposable income; and gross and net private investment.

2. Economic data that are generated from controlled experiments. In this context subjects are assigned so that the measured effects can be attributed directly to the treatments. Examples include the experimental data involving corn output and fertilizer inputs of Chapter 11 and public policy experiments such as income maintenance and the peak load pricing of electricity.

3. Economic data that are generated from surveys. In this context no treatments are applied, but the survey is designed to focus on the outcomes of particular variables of interest, such as level of income for a particular observational unit (individual), level of education, number of members of household, and the level of durable purchases.

Each of these data sources provides sample information that permits us to *describe* outcomes that are taking place at the micro and macro levels and permits us to investigate the relationships between economic variables so that this information can be used for decision or choice purposes. Let us look at each of the data sources in a little more detail.

26.1.1 Passively Generated Data

Much of the data that come out of the grand experiment of society are collected for administrative rather than research purposes. However, these data, over which the econometrician exercises no control, form the basis for a large proportion of applied econometric research. The data may be collected in these ways:

Time-series form—data collected over discrete intervals of time—for example, the annual price of wheat in the United States from 1880 to 1989 or the daily stock price of General Electric from 1980 to 1989.

Cross-section form—data collected over sample units in a particular time period—for example, income by counties in California during 1989.

The data may be collected at various levels of aggregation:

Micro—data collected on individual economic decision-making units such as individuals, households, or firms.

Macro—data resulting from a pooling or aggregating over individuals, households, or firms at the local, state, or national levels.

The data collected may also represent a flow or a stock:

Flow—outcome measures over a period of time such as the consumption of gasoline during the last quarter of 1989.

Stock—outcome measured at a particular point in time such as the quantity of crude oil held by Chevron in its U. S. storage tanks April 1, 1990, or the asset value of the Wells Fargo Bank on July 1, 1990.

The data collected may be quantitative or qualitative:

Quantitative—outcomes such as prices or income that may be expressed as numbers or some transformation of them such as real prices or per capita income.

Qualitative—outcomes that are of an "either–or" situation. For example, a consumer either did or did not make a purchase of a particular good, or a person is or is not married.

These are qualitative outcomes of the type, discussed in Chapters 12 and 23, where we represent discrete choices and qualitative forms of time and space, such as quarters or regions, or by dummy or qualitative variables.

These types of data are collected by various public agencies, and you will have ready access to them through your departmental, college, or university library. In your search for data sources you will find the library staff knowledgeable friends. A book by Daniels (1976), which is listed in the references, provides a guide to the vast and varied sources of economic and business data.

At the international level, macro data are published by agencies such as the International Monetary Fund (IMF), the European Economic Community (OECD), the United Nations (UN), and the Food and Agriculture Organization (FAO). Some examples of publications of these agencies that include a wide array of data include:

International Financial Statistics (IMF, monthly)

Basic Statistics of the Community (OECD, annual)

Consumer Price Indices in the European Community (OECD, annual)

World Statistics (UN, annual)

Yearbook of National Accounts Statistics (UN, annual)

FAO Trade Yearbook (annual)

At the national level some of the major sources of economic data are the Bureau of Economic Analysis (BEA), the Bureau of the Census (BC), the Bureau of Labor Statistics (BLS), the Federal Reserve (FR), and the Statistical Reporting Service of the Department of Agriculture (USDA). Some examples of publications of these U.S. agencies that include a wide array of macroeconomic data include:

Survey of Current Business (BEA, monthly)

Handbook of Basic Economic Statistics (Bureau of Economic Statistics, Inc., monthly)

Monthly Labor Review (BLS, monthly)

Federal Reserve Bulletin (FR, monthly)

Statistical Abstract of the US (BC, annual)

Economic Report of the President (annual)

Agricultural Statistics (USDA, annual)

Agricultural Situation Reports (USDA, monthly)

A table from the 1991 *Economic Report of the President* that is typical of how economic data are usually presented is given in Table 26.1. A book by Hoel et al. (1983), which is referenced at the end of this chapter, goes into considerable detail about how the main economic statistical series are compiled and discusses some of their strengths and weaknesses.

Data reported at the national level are often also available at the state, SMSA, county, and census tract levels. Some of these sources include:

State and Metropolitan Area Data Book (Commerce and BC, annual)

CPI Detailed Report (BLS, annual)

Census of Population and Housing (Commerce, BC, annual)

Table 26.1 A Table from the *Economic Report of the President*, Total and Per Capita Disposable Personal Income and Personal Consumption Expenditures in Current and 1982 Dollars, 1929-89

(Quarterly data at seasonally adjusted annual rates, except as noted)

| Year or Quarter | Disposable Personal Income | | | | Personal Consumption Expenditures | | | | Population (thousands)^a |
| | Total (billions of dollars) | | Per Capita (dollars) | | Total (billions of dollars) | | Per Capita (dollars) | | |
	Current Dollars	1982 Dollars	Current Dollars	1982 Dollars	Current Dollars	1982 Dollars	Current Dollars	1982 Dollars	
1929	81.7	498.6	671	4,091	77.3	471.4	634	3,868	121,878
1933	44.9	370.8	357	2,950	45.8	378.7	365	3,013	125,690
1939	69.7	499.5	532	3,812	67.0	480.5	511	3,667	131,028
1940	75.0	530.7	568	4,017	71.0	502.6	538	3,804	132,122
1941	91.9	604.1	689	4,528	80.8	531.1	606	3,981	133,402
1942	116.4	693.0	863	5,138	88.6	527.6	657	3,912	134,860
1943	132.9	721.4	972	5,276	99.5	539.9	727	3,949	136,739
1944	145.6	749.3	1.052	5,414	108.2	557.1	782	4,026	138,397
1945	149.2	739.5	1,066	5,285	119.6	592.7	855	4,236	139,928
1946	158.9	723.3	1,124	5,115	143.9	655.0	1,018	4,632	141,389
1947	168.8	694.8	1,171	4,820	161.9	666.6	1,123	4,625	144,126
1948	188.1	733.1	1,283	5,000	174.9	681.8	1,193	4,650	146,631
1949	187.9	733.2	1,260	4,915	178.3	695.4	1,195	4,661	149,188
1950	207.5	791.8	1,368	5,220	192.1	733.2	1,267	4,834	151,684
1951	227.6	819.0	1,475	5,308	208.1	748.7	1,349	4,853	154,287
1952	239.8	844.3	1,528	5,379	219.1	771.4	1,396	4,915	156,954
1953	255.1	880.0	1,599	5,515	232.6	802.5	1,458	5,029	159,565
1954	260.5	894.0	1,604	5,505	239.8	822.7	1,477	5,066	162,391
1955	278.8	944.5	1,687	5,714	257.9	873.8	1,560	5,287	165,275
1956	297.5	989.4	1,769	5,881	270.6	899.8	1,608	5,349	168,221
1957	313.9	1,012.1	1,833	5,909	285.3	919.7	1,666	5,370	171,274
1958	324.9	1,028.8	1,865	5,908	294.6	932.9	1,692	5,357	174,141
1959	344.6	1,067.2	1,946	6,027	316.3	979.4	1,786	5,531	177,073
1960	358.9	1,091.1	1,986	6,036	330.7	1,005.1	1,829	5,561	180,760
1961	373.8	1,123.2	2,034	6,113	341.1	1,025.2	1,857	5,579	183,742
1962	396.2	1,170.2	2,123	6,271	361.9	1,069.0	1,940	5,729	186,590
1963	415.8	1,207.3	2,197	6,378	381.7	1,108.4	2,017	5,855	189,300
1964	451.4	1,291.0	2,352	6,727	409.3	1,170.6	2,133	6,099	191,927
1965	486.8	1,365.7	2,505	7,027	440.7	1,236.4	2,268	6,362	194,347
1966	525.9	1,431.3	2,675	7,280	477.3	1,298.9	2,428	6,607	196,599
1967	562.1	1,493.2	2,828	7,513	503.6	1,337.7	2,534	6,730	198,752
1968	609.6	1,551.3	3,037	7,728	552.5	1,405.9	2,752	7,003	200,745
1969	656.7	1,599.8	3,239	7,891	597.9	1,456.7	2,949	7,185	202,736
1970	715.6	1,668.1	3,489	8,134	640.0	1,492.0	3,121	7,275	205,089
1971	776.8	1,728.4	3,740	8,322	691.6	1,538.8	3,330	7,409	207,692
1972	839.6	1,797.4	4,000	8,562	757.6	1,621.9	3,609	7,726	209,924
1973	949.8	1,916.3	4,481	9,042	837.2	1,689.6	3,950	7,972	211,939
1974	1,038.4	1,896.6	4,855	8,867	916.5	1,674.0	4,285	7,826	213,898
1975	1,142.8	1,931.7	5,291	8,944	1,012.8	1,711.9	4,689	7,926	215,981
1976	1,252.6	2,001.0	5,744	9,175	1,129.3	1,803.9	5,178	8,272	218,086
1977	1,379.3	2,066.6	6,262	9,381	1,257.2	1,883.8	5,707	8,551	220,289
1978	1,551.2	2,167.4	6,968	9,735	1,403.5	1,961.0	6,304	8,808	222,629
1979	1,729.3	2,212.6	7,682	9,829	1,566.8	2,004.4	6,960	8,904	225,106
1980	1,918.0	2,214.3	8,421	9,722	1,732.6	2,000.4	7,607	8,783	227,754
1981	2,127.6	2,248.6	9,243	9,769	1,915.1	2,024.2	8,320	8,794	230,182
1982	2,261.4	2,261.5	9,724	9,725	2,050.7	2,050.7	8,818	8,818	232,549
1983	2,428.1	2,331.9	10,340	9,930	2,234.5	2,146.0	9,516	9,139	234,829
1984	2,668.6	2,469.8	11,257	10,419	2,430.5	2,249.3	10,253	9,489	237,051
1985	2,838.7	2,542.8	11,861	10,625	2,629.0	2,354.8	10,985	9,840	239,322
1986	3,013.3	2,635.3	12,469	10,905	2,797.4	2,446.4	11,576	10,123	241,660
1987	3,194.7	2,670.7	13,094	10,946	3,009.4	2,515.8	12,334	10,311	243,982
1988	3,479.2	2,800.5	14,123	11,368	3,238.2	2,606.5	13,144	10,580	246,358
1989	3,725.5	2,869.0	14,973	11,531	3,450.1	2,656.8	13,866	10,678	248,810

Table 26.1 cont.

	(Quarterly data at seasonally adjusted annual rates, except as noted)								
	Disposable Personal Income				**Personal Consumption Expenditures**				
Year or Quarter	**Total (billions of dollars)**		**Per Capita (dollars)**		**Total (billions of dollars)**		**Per Capita (dollars)**		**Population (thousands)**[a]
	Current Dollars	**1982 Dollars**	**Current Dollars**	**1982 Dollars**	**Current Dollars**	**1982 Dollars**	**Current Dollars**	**1982 Dollars**	
1990	3,945.8	2,893.3	15,695	11,508	3,658.1	2,682.2	14,550	10,668	251,413
1982: IV	2,318.1	2,276.1	9,929	9,749	2,117.0	2,078.7	9,068	8,904	233,466
1983: IV	2,527.9	2,392.7	10,725	10,151	2,315.8	2,191.9	9,825	9,299	235,707
1984: IV	2,728.6	2,496.3	11,467	10,491	2,493.4	2,281.1	10,479	9,587	237,946
1985: IV	2,899.5	2,562.8	12,068	10,667	2,700.4	2,386.9	11,240	9,935	240,257
1986: IV	3,063.4	2,646.2	12,629	10,909	2,868.5	2,477.8	11,825	10,214	242,579
1987: IV	3,302.3	2,717.9	13,483	11,097	3,079.1	2,534.2	12,572	10,347	244,925
1988: I	3,378.6	2,765.9	13,765	11,268	3,147.7	2,576.8	12,824	10,498	245,453
II	3,439.4	2,784.4	13,982	11,320	3,204.3	2,594.1	13,027	10,546	245,981
III	3,520.1	2,818.0	14,271	11,424	3,268.2	2,616.4	13,249	10,607	246,667
IV	3,578.9	2,833.9	14,470	11,458	3,332.6	2,638.8	13,474	10,669	247,329
1989: I	3,661.7	2,863.5	14,773	11,553	3,371.7	2,636.7	13,603	10,638	247,863
II	3,697.3	2,854.9	14,883	11,492	3,425.9	2,645.3	13,790	10,648	248,431
III	3,743.4	2,874.3	15,026	11,538	3,484.3	2,675.3	13,986	10,739	249,127
IV	3,799.6	2,883.2	15,210	11,541	3,518.5	2,669.9	14,084	10,687	249,818
1990: I	3,887.7	2,900.9	15,527	11,586	3,588.1	2,677.3	14,330	10,693	250,392
II	3,925.7	2,902.8	15,639	11,564	3,622.7	2,678.8	14,432	10,671	251,026
III	3,969.1	2,898.0	15,703	11,511	3,093.4	2,696.0	14,670	10,711	251,767
IV	4,000.9	2,871.6	15,847	11,374	3,728.1	2,675.8	14,767	10,599	252,467

[a] Population of the United States including Armed Forces overseas; includes Alaska and Hawaii beginning 1960. Annual data are for July 1 through 1958 and are averages of quarterly data beginning 1959. Quarterly data are averages for the period.

Source: Department of Commerce (Bureau of Economic Analysis and Bureau of the Census).

Although public agencies are a major source of economic data, some private firms are also major players. For example, Standard and Poor (e.g. *Analyst's Handbook*), Dow Jones, Forbes, and Moody (e.g., *Handbook of Common Stocks*) offer a vast array of micro-oriented data. Much of this type of data is available on tapes such as Compustat.

26.1.2   Data from Surveys

A large amount of micro-oriented data, which also provides at the national level the foundation for the macro data counterparts, is obtained from surveys. For example, each month the Bureau of Labor Statistics analyzes and publishes statistics on the labor force, employment, unemployment, and persons not in the labor force classified by a variety of demographic, social, and economic characteristics. These data come from a survey that is conducted by the Bureau of the Census for the Bureau of Labor Statistics. This monthly survey is conducted by using a scientifically selected probability sample of 60,000 or more households that are representative of the noninstitutional population of the United States.

Although the above is an example of a national large-scale survey, the survey technique is useful anytime information is needed about a group or universe of objects, such as consumers or firms. The objective is to examine only a few objects, as we did in Chapters 3 and 4, and extend the finding to the whole group. In this process there are four major elements: *(i)* identifying the population of interest, *(ii)* designing the survey, determining the sample size, and selecting the sample, *(iii)* collecting the information, and *(iv)* reducing data, estimating, and making inferences about the population.

At many universities there are survey laboratories whose mission is to carry out these above data creation and analysis steps. There are also many private firms that perform the same function, and much of these data are in the public domain.

26.1.3 Controlled Experimental Data

One major problem faced by economists is how to obtain data that may be used to measure or predict the effect of changes in policy variables on the behavior of economic units. In this context, where appropriate data are not available, social experimentation in a controlled setting offers an attractive alternative. Through this process one seeks to generate data that may be used to measure the effects of changes in policy or instrument variables by applying "treatments" to human populations under conditions of controlled experimentation similar to that used in Chapter 11, where we tried to sort out the input–output mechanism for corn production. If a fundamental policy change is being considered, in many instances the way to obtain information on the effect of the policy is to put the policy into effect on a limited scale and to see what happens. In the past this approach has been used for the following type of policy questions:

1. How will labor force participation be influenced by a guaranteed minimum income? To get a handle on the work behavior of families receiving income supports (negative income tax), experiments were conducted in New Jersey and North Carolina.

2. What is the effect of a national program of cash housing allowances on the recipients of the allowances, on other households, on the market for housing, and on housing intermediaries? Specifically, the experimental housing allowance program sought to measure the effect of such a cash allowance program on the demand and supply of housing. Experiments were conducted in Pennsylvania, Arizona, Wisconsin, and Indiana.

3. A health insurance experiment was structured to ascertain how the use of medical care will change if a small fraction of the people in a given area have their medical costs reduced for a period of three to five years. Thus the experiment sought to provide information that would be useful in estimating the sensitivity of different income groups to price changes in the face of a fixed total supply of health services. Six thousand families in each of four sites were involved in the experiment.

4. During the 1970s and 1980s, national concern about the cost and availability of energy focused public attention on the pricing of electricity. The treatment of peak-load-pricing, where higher rates are charged during hours and seasons of higher demand was advocated as a way of lowering the overall social cost of energy. No satisfactory data base existed that would permit one to forecast the changes in load (demand) curves that would result from using various peak-load rate structures. Toward this end rate structure experiments were set up in Los Angeles and other areas to generate a data base on the daily pattern of electricity use by residential customers through systematic experimentation with a variety of peak-load tariffs. The objective was to provide information on the central policy questions concerning the peak-load pricing of electricity in the United States.

The preceding examples should be sufficient to indicate that social experiments offer unique opportunities for generating data bases that may be used for estimating response at the micro level to alternative economic policies. Social experimentation is a very useful addition to the economist-econometrician's set of tools. Each experiment carries with it a unique set of problems and much remains to be learned on how to best exploit this technique.

26.1.4   Some Characteristics of Economic Data

Economic relations are seldom free of shocks or disturbances, and economic data are seldom free of specification and/or measurement error. In an econometric analysis we can usually be quite precise, in our economic and statistical models, as to the definition of our variables and in regard to their timing, degree of aggregation, and the like. Unfortunately, there is seldom consistency between the theoretical models and the economic data that are used in an empirical analysis.

With passively generated data we must be content with whatever experimental design society decided to use. Out of this set of data, we are then restricted to whatever data the statistical agency decided to collect. Since the experimental design was not specified by the researcher, some of the variables of interest may not vary over a range that will let us identify their impact in the relation of interest. In other cases the variables (for example, prices) may move together over time in a collinear way, and thus again we may not be able to separate out their individual impacts. Some data may contain large measurement errors. For example, in one theory of the consumption function, the consumption data (c) that are usually available are viewed as made up of permanent (c_p) and transitory (c_t) components, that is, $c = c_p + c_t$. What is desired as a basis for estimating the consumption function are data in the form of c_p. Permanent consumption c_p is, however, unobservable. There are ways around this problem, but even so additional noise is introduced into our applied estimation and inference procedures. These and many other things concerning the data rear their ugly heads as we go from the theoretical model to the empirical counterpart.

As we have noted, much of the passively generated data are collected for administrative rather than research purposes. Thus, for any particular research problem, there may be considerable labor involved in transforming the data to a form that is usable for the problem at hand. It is impossible to overemphasize the importance of knowing how the data have been measured and making sure they are conformable over space, time and individuals. If data for a cross-country study are collected from national sources, they may need to be standardized. Alternatively, international agencies such as IMF and the World Bank use their own procedures for standardizing and cleaning data. Thus, before pushing the computer button, the researcher should be aware of how data may have been transformed or modified.

Even when the data are collected by the researcher, using the survey or controlled experiment routes, they may not be consistent with the specifications in the theoretical model. The survey or experimental design may have been inappropriate, the questionnaire may not have been correctly designed, the interviewer may not have recorded the actual response, or the experimenter may not have measured the outcome without error or held relevant factors constant.

All these pitfalls happen in the data search phase of an econometric analysis. How to handle them requires a good deal of creativity, patience, and experience. Just as you must be explicit in terms of the assumptions made in your economic and statistical models, you must also be explicit in terms of the data that you have used and any transformation that you have made. Several applied econometric journals now require that the data used in an econometric analysis be made available so that others may replicate and extend the results. For example, applied econometrics books by Berndt (1991), and Lott & Ray (1991) include a disk containing the data for the problems analyzed.

26.2   Some Guidelines for Choosing a Class Research Topic

As part of your course in econometrics, many of you will be asked to formulate and execute an empirical research project. In this regard you may be asked to pick a problem and analyze a set of data or perhaps critique and possibly redo a published applied econometric article. There are two basic questions to keep in mind:

(*i*) How should you go about choosing the topic or article on which to work?

(*ii*) How do you prepare an abstract that will permit you and your instructor to determine the potential payoff from your proposed investigation?

26.2.1   Choosing a Topic

The choice of a research topic should not be made in a cavalier way since choosing and identifying the question on which to work takes you a long way on the road toward a successful outcome. A good place to start the search is with the question, "What am I interested in?" If you are interested in a particular topic, then you increase your chances of being successful and possibly even enjoying the research effort. In choosing a general area of interest, the various subject areas of economics and business offer many alternatives. Areas such as public finance, international economics, labor economics, resource economics, environmental economics, industrial organization, and agricultural economics define some of the problem areas or requirements and informational content of economics and suggest general questions that need answers at the various micro and macro levels.

If you know your general area of interest but are uncertain of the question or questions to take on, a good strategy is to talk to one or more professors who have this as an area of specialization. They will be able to help you sort through a list of questions, to identify where relevant data may or may not exist, and to render a judgment as to whether a particular problem is researchable in the limited time you have to do your research and write up a report. Whether or not data exist is very important because you usually will not have the time to collect new data and also carry through the econometric analysis. Thus, it is important to choose a well-defined problem and be fairly secure you know how to put your hands on the corresponding data. A bit of time spent talking with a professor specializing in your area of interest can be very valuable in this regard and may save you a lot of time.

As an aid in choosing a research project it is important to:

(*i*) Identify a problem or question where there is uncertainty or a lack of information about an outcome, for example, a sign or magnitude of the coefficient of an economic variable;

(*ii*) Attempt to identify the payoff that might result if the uncertainty about the outcome were resolved or at least reduced; and

(*iii*) Choose a problem that lets you become more familiar with the econometric procedures you have covered or one that will permit you to learn about the theory and practice of a new procedure; that is, choose a topic that passes the tests of (*i*) and (*ii*) and lets you extend your econometric knowledge.

After a bit of homework do not be afraid to review the alternatives, make a choice, and plunge in. One benefit of research is that formulating and carrying through an investigation usually leads to other researchable and possibly more interesting questions or to a sharper formulation of the original question.

Alternatively, if you are going to do a critique of an applied econometric study that someone else has completed, there are a number of places to start. Journals such as the *Journal of Applied Econometrics*, the Applied Series of the *Journal of Econometrics*, *The Review of Economics and Statistics,* and *The Journal of the American Statistical Association* publish a wide range of econometric work. Subject area journals such as the *Journal of Finance*, *Journal of Economic Dynamics and Control,* and *American Journal of Agricultural Economics* publish applied econometric work in specific areas. Most economics departments and business schools publish working papers prepared by their faculties. These working papers are a rich source of applied studies, and many of these reports also contain the data on which the analyses are based. The guidelines presented for choosing a research topic should also be followed in identifying an applied study to critique.

26.2.2   Writing a Research Abstract

After you have chosen a specific topic, it is a good idea to write up for your econometrics instructor a brief abstract to see if you really understand what you want to do and how you should go about it. Your abstract should include:

(*i*) a concise statement of the problem;

(*ii*) comments on the information that is available, based on the contributions others may have made in this area;

(*iii*) a specification of the research design that includes:
  (a) the economic models relevant to providing information on the questions posed and the decision context in which the information may be used (economic model),
  (b) specification of the corresponding statistical model that specifies the sampling process by which you visualize that the underlying data should be or may have been generated,
  (c) suggestions for collecting or obtaining sample observations consistent with the statistical models, and
  (d) outlines of the estimation and hypothesis testing procedures and the corresponding sampling and power properties. It should be indicated whether or not point and interval estimates of the unknown parameters will be obtained along with point and interval forecasts; and

(*iv*) the potential economic and statistical implications of the results.

26.3   A Format for Writing a Research Report

Let us finally consider the writing link in the econometric chain. In a quantitative analysis the writing link is certainly different from the model, estimation, and data links, but it is nonetheless important. If the results of an econometric analysis are to have an impact, there must be a written report that presents what was discovered and how the new information may be used. In the section ahead we discuss the ingredients of such a research report.

26.3.1 Writing up the Research Results

If you have done a good job on your research abstract, you have gone a long way toward making the reporting of your results an easy task. It is important to recognize that the research has not been completed until this report is in the word processor.

Writing up the research results includes many of the items covered in the research abstract. Also, the format we have used throughout this book for learning from a sample of data will be very useful in this regard. However, now you will be reporting what you did instead of what you hope to do. To give the research reporting format an operational context, after sketching the ingredients of a research report, we will consider a writeup for a particular problem.

1. The place to start your research report is with the questions you have investigated, why they are important, who should be interested in the results, and how they relate to previous work done in this area. Identify some of the potential payoffs and state what is to be covered in each section.

2. Next, present the economic models you have used, define the economic variables, and state the assumptions that have been made and the hypotheses suggested.

3. Given the economic model, specify the corresponding statistical models, the variables to be included in each statistical model, the functional form(s), the stochastic characteristics of the equation errors, and any other relevant assumptions.

4. Next, identify the data you have used, state how they were generated or collected, discuss whether or not you believe that they are consistent with the sampling process specified in the statistical models, and make comments on their quality and the population(s) to which they apply.

5. Given the economic and statistical models, identify the estimation and inference procedures that you have used and be specific concerning the sampling properties of the estimation rules and the power of the tests. If alternative estimation rules or test statistics or both might have been appropriate, state why you made a particular choice.

6. Once you have carried through the econometric analysis, the next section should contain the empirical results. In this section you should present the estimated economic relations and the corresponding statistics and comment on their statistical significance (sampling precision, t-statistics, etc.). The statistical inferences that are appropriate should be summarized.

7. Now that you have reported the statistical findings, the next section should contain the economic implications or consequences of your results. These economic implications usually relate to a decision or choice. For the firm it might relate to pricing policy or scale. On an economic policy level, it might relate to Federal Reserve actions or taxing and spending alternatives.

8. Given the statistical and economic implications of your investigation, you should then comment on some of the shortcomings of your results. Have you used the correct economic and statistical models? Would an alternative statistical model have been more appropriate? What about possible measurement errors in your data? Have you used the most efficient estimation procedures and test statistics? Does the estimated sampling precision underlying your parameter estimates permit you to make economic decisions with the necessary level of confidence?

9. Finally, if you were going to carry on this research, what suggestions do you have for further study? What about the adequacy of the data sample? Should other economic and statistical models have been considered? Were the estimation procedures

appropriate, or should other estimation rules have been used? What new questions has the research suggested or, knowing what you know now, what would be the nature of your research proposal abstract?

26.3.2   Research Ingredients for a Particular Problem

Within the format suggested for organizing your research report, let's sketch out, by the numbers, a possible writeup for a particular problem. As a basis for choosing a problem, we recognize that many of the countries of Eastern Europe are moving toward market economies. In this setting, assume that you are the economist for a hamburger chain that is opening an outlet in Budapest, Hungary. Suppose this is the first outlet of its kind to operate in Hungary. In order to set up, staff, and operate the outlet certain information is needed.

1.   To identify the problem you would want to note that one piece of information that is needed as a basis for operating the outlet is the relationship between the price charged and the number of Budapest burgers sold per day. You would also want to note that another area about which there is uncertainty or a lack of information is the optimal scale of the outlet. Given the problems, you could indicate that the uncertainty about these outcomes could be resolved or, at least, reduced if the quantity demanded was known for each price. In this event the optimal supporting staff and the quantities of the meat, buns and other inputs could be determined. Furthermore, if the corresponding cost–quantity relationship were known, then the scale of the outlet and the price to charge to maximize net returns could be determined.

Next you would want to comment on the information that is available based on the contributions you and/or others may have made in this area. For hamburgers in general there may be a wealth of information about the price–quantity relationship in France and Germany. Will this information be useful and, if not, why not? For example, why are the consumers in Budapest unique or at least different from their French and German counterparts in terms of their price–quantity behavior? Alternatively, there may have been extensive research in France and Germany on the input–output relations for hamburger outlets, and this information may be directly useful in developing the cost–quantity relationship for the Budapest operation.

Having established the problem, identified the potential payoff of the new information, and determined what information does or does not exist, you next specify the research design.

2.   At this stage in the research report, the focus would turn to the economic models relevant to providing information on the questions posed and to suggesting a decision context in which the information may be used. In terms of the Budapest burgers and the corresponding price–quantity relationship, demand theory provides a basis for specifying the relationship and perhaps some information concerning its form and use. Thus, we may be led to specifying that q, the quantity of Budapest burgers sold each day, is a function of the price charged, p, that is, $q = f(p, \beta)$, where β is the unknown parameter connecting q and p. Our expectation is that β will be negative. We also might believe that q and possibly β might vary with the day of the week, and the economic model should reflect this possibility. On the cost side for the Budapest outlet, firm theory of the type covered in Chapter 11 provides a basis for specifying the production function for the outlet. For example, if we now let q be the quantity of Budapest burgers produced per day, we could specify the production function as $q = f(z_1, z_2, ..., z_p, \beta)$, where $\mathbf{z} = z_1, z_2, ..., z_p$ are the inputs of labor, capital, meat, and so on, and β is a vector of unknown coefficients connecting the inputs $\mathbf{z}$ and the output q. Given the production function and the prices of the inputs, a total cost function $c = f(q, \gamma)$ could be developed along with the corresponding average and marginal cost functions. Your writeup might then suggest how the demand relation $q = f(p, \beta)$ and the cost function $c = f(q, \gamma)$ might be used to make decisions concerning the optimal level of output and price and the corresponding mix of inputs.

3. The economic model provides a framework for identifying the relationship(s) investigated and how to make use of the resulting information. The next step is to specify a statistical model that is consistent with the sampling process by which underlying data were or may have been generated.

In the case of the Budapest burgers, for the demand relation we might write the statistical model in the general linear form as $\mathbf{y}_1 = X\beta + \mathbf{e}$, where $\mathbf{y}_1$ is a vector of quantities consumed, X is the design matrix that reflects the price, the day effect, and the functional form, β is the unknown coefficient vector, and $\mathbf{e}$ is an unobserved error vector reflecting the variability in $\mathbf{y}$ not accounted for in $X\beta$. The stochastic characteristics of the error vector must be specified. Is it reasonable to assume that $\mathbf{e}$ is made up of normal random variables that are independently and identically distributed? That is, $N(iid)$.

For the production function for the outlet, we could again use the linear statistical model framework and write $\mathbf{y}_2 = Z\beta + \mathbf{e}$, where $\mathbf{y}_2$ is the output of Budapest burgers and the design matrix Z reflects inputs such as capital and labor. The error vector $\mathbf{e}$ closes the model and, again, we state whether the $N(iid)$ assumption may or may not be appropriate and, if not, how the errors are to be modeled. Finally, a functional form for the input–output relation is specified or conjectured.

These statistical models describe the sampling process by which you visualized the outcomes for $\mathbf{y}_1$ and $\mathbf{y}_2$ to have been generated. Given these statistical models the focus of the writeup would turn to the sample data and the appropriate estimation and inference procedures.

4. The next step in the research design involves suggesting a basis for collecting sample observations consistent with the statistical models. Since, for the Budapest burgers, we are assuming that data for the price–quantity relationship do not exist, we must specify an experimental design that may be used as the basis for the sampling experiment and the sample outcome data. In the experimental design, price and days are the treatments. Thus, the composition and number of price-day combinations need to be specified and the number of observations devoted to each need to be noted. Possibly the randomization of the treatments would be used to guard against unseen and unanticipated influences. Given that parameter estimation and hypothesis testing are the purposes to which our data are to be put, you would note how you chose the number of observations after considering the precision of estimation and the power of the test.

The data for the production function and the cost function are provided by outlets operating in Germany and France. Perhaps an estimated production function from these data already exists. If not, the input classifications would need to be defined and you would note how the input–output data were collected. To convert the information contained in the production function to a cost function, the basis for determining the prices of the inputs in Budapest would need to be specified.

5. Given the statistical model and a plan for obtaining the sampling data, the estimation and hypothesis testing procedures must be outlined and the corresponding sampling and power properties must be discussed. It should be indicated whether or not point and interval estimates of the unknown parameters were obtained along with point and interval forecasts concerning $\mathbf{y}_1$ and $\mathbf{y}_2$. In the case of the Budapest burgers, the reason why the least squares estimation rule or some form of the generalized least squares rule was used must be discussed. For each estimated relation the hypotheses tested should be specified and the test statistic(s) should be identified.

6. Having laid out the economic and statistical frameworks on which your investigation was based, you would then present the empirical results. The demand, production function, and cost relations would be presented in the form we have employed starting with Chapter 8. The signs and magnitudes of the results would be discussed relative to consistency with theoretical expectations; the sampling variability and t-values of the individual coefficients would be noted. The major hypotheses would be specified and tested, and the corresponding inferences would be stated.

7. Given the empirical results and their statistical implications, the writeup would move on to drawing economic conclusions. Consequently, given the results, interest would focus on the pricing and scale recommendations. Comment on whether these economic decisions differ from those in use elsewhere. If they do differ, note why these differences exist.

8. Finally, assess your results and note any areas of incomplete information. Where your results are incomplete, note the direction of future research that could reduce these blind spots. At this point all that is left to do is to spend some time rewriting your research report so that it is clear what you did and did not do and what the reach and significance of your results are.

26.4   Some Concluding Remarks

In the pursuit of quantitative economic knowledge, this chapter has been concerned with economic data, choosing a research problem, and the writing of a research report. These are important items to have in your econometrician's tool chest.

In Chapter 2 we asked the question: Where do economic data come from? It is hoped that the material included in the first part of this chapter will give you a better appreciation of the collected and uncollected data space. Much of the data we need are collected for us. However, the data for many questions do not exist, and it is up to us to obtain them by survey or by controlled experiments. Experiments and surveys are costly, but it is also costly in many instances not to have the data. We hope that this book has helped to get you interested in choosing a research problem and has given you the tools you need to become involved in both the collection and analysis of economic data.

Writing up the research results is an important part of the research process. It is a very good way of ascertaining what you do and do not understand and what you did and did not find out as you attempted to learn from a sample of economic data and to become involved in the important process of producing and disseminating quantitative economic knowledge.

26.5   Exercises

26.1. Check out in your library the most recent *Economic Report of the President* and become acquainted with the aggregate income, employment, and production data and their sources that are reported therein and note how these data are used in the narrative portion of the report.

26.2. Describe the data provided by the Bureau of Labor Statistics and describe how some of these data are obtained.

26.3. From a research and statistical point of view, discuss some of the problems associated with data collected by national agencies.

26.4. Suppose you are interested in the feed-livestock economy. Specify a demand relationship for feed and obtain the corresponding annual or quarterly data for the period 1970 to 1990. Discuss the adequacy of these data for your problem.

26.5. Suppose you were interested in household food consumption and its relation to income and number in the household. Design a survey that could be used for obtaining data that could be used for estimation and hypothesis testing. If you obtained this information over the various food groups, what type of statistical model would you use in your statistical analysis?

26.6. Suppose you are the economist for a food chain and you want to devise an advertising and pricing policy for canned tuna. How would you go about designing an experiment that would generate data that could be used for your statistical analysis?

26.7. Write up a research report of the production function analysis carried through in Chapter 11 or the demand for meat analyzed in Chapter 17.

26.8. Suppose you were working for the Federal Trade Commission and you were asked to analyze the pricing policy of steel firms in the United States. Write up a research proposal that would portray how you would go about it.

26.9. Choose a journal article reporting an applied econometric study. Critique the format used in reporting the research results.

26.6   References

The following book provides a guide to the vast and varied sources or economic and business data:

DANIELS, L. M. (1976) *Business Information Sources*, Berkeley: University of California Press.

In the following book considerable detail is provided concerning how the main economic statistical series are compiled, with their strengths and weaknesses; the book provides an understanding of what they do and do not describe:

HOEL, A. A., K. W. CLARKSON, and R. M. MILLER (1983) *Economic Sourcebook of Government Statistics*, Lexington, MA: Lexington Books (D.C. Heath and Company).

The following books includes a disk that contains the data for a range of economic problems:

BERNDT, E. R. (1991) *The Practice of Econometrics*, Reading, MA: Addison-Wesley Publishing Company Inc.

LOTT, W. and C. R. SUBHASH (1991) Applied Econometrics: Problems with Data Sets, Fort Worth, TX: The Dryden Press.

Other very useful publications include:

FERBER, R. and W. Z. HIRSCH (1979) "Social Experiments in Economics," *Journal of Econometrics*, 11, 77–115.

FINK, ARLENE, and JACQUELINE KOSECOFF (1985) *How to Conduct Surveys: A Step-by-step Guide*, Newbury Park, CA: Sage Publications.

FOWLER, F. J. (1988) *Survey Research Methods*, Newbury Park, CA: Sage Publications.

KALTON, GRAHAM (1983) *Introduction to Survey Sampling*, Newbury Park, CA: Sage Publications.

MANNING, W. G., B. M. MITCHELL and J. P. ACTON (1979) "Design of the Los Angeles Peak Load Pricing Experiment for Electricity," *Journal of Econometrics*, 11, 131–193.

MORRIS, C., J. NEWHOUSE and R. ARCHIBALD (1977) "On the Theory and Practice of Obtaining Unbiased and Efficient Samples in Social Surveys and Experiments," Report No. R.2173-HEW, Santa Monica, CA: Rand Corporation.

Tables Included

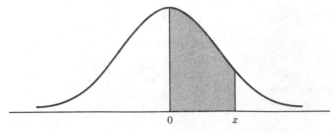

Example for $z = 0.64$
$P\{0 \leq N(0, 1) \leq 0.64\} = 0.2389$

Table 1 Area Under the Standard Normal Distribution

z	0.00	0.01	0.02	0.03	0.04	0.05	0.06	0.07	0.08	0.09
0.0	0.0000	0.0040	0.0080	0.0120	0.0160	0.0199	0.0239	0.0279	0.0319	0.0359
0.1	0.0398	0.0438	0.0478	0.0517	0.0557	0.0596	0.0636	0.0675	0.0714	0.0753
0.2	0.0793	0.0832	0.0871	0.0910	0.0948	0.0987	0.1026	0.1064	0.1103	0.1141
0.3	0.1179	0.1217	0.1255	0.1293	0.1331	0.1368	0.1406	0.1443	0.1480	0.1517
0.4	0.1554	0.1591	0.1628	0.1664	0.1700	0.1736	0.1772	0.1808	0.1844	0.1879
0.5	0.1915	0.1950	0.1985	0.2019	0.2054	0.2088	0.2123	0.2157	0.2190	0.2224
0.6	0.2257	0.2291	0.2324	0.2357	0.2389	0.2422	0.2454	0.2486	0.2517	0.2549
0.7	0.2580	0.2611	0.2642	0.2673	0.2704	0.2734	0.2764	0.2794	0.2823	0.2852
0.8	0.2881	0.2910	0.2939	0.2967	0.2995	0.3023	0.3051	0.3078	0.3106	0.3133
0.9	0.3159	0.3186	0.3212	0.3238	0.3264	0.3289	0.3315	0.3340	0.3365	0.3389
1.0	0.3413	0.3438	0.3461	0.3485	0.3508	0.3531	0.3554	0.3577	0.3599	0.3621
1.1	0.3643	0.3665	0.3686	0.3708	0.3729	0.3749	0.3770	0.3790	0.3810	0.3830
1.2	0.3849	0.3869	0.3888	0.3907	0.3925	0.3944	0.3962	0.3980	0.3997	0.4015
1.3	0.4032	0.4049	0.4066	0.4082	0.4099	0.4115	0.4131	0.4147	0.4162	0.4177
1.4	0.4192	0.4207	0.4222	0.4236	0.4251	0.4265	0.4279	0.4292	0.4306	0.4319
1.5	0.4332	0.4345	0.4357	0.4370	0.4382	0.4394	0.4406	0.4418	0.4429	0.4441
1.6	0.4452	0.4463	0.4474	0.4484	0.4495	0.4505	0.4515	0.4525	0.4535	0.4545
1.7	0.4554	0.4564	0.4573	0.4582	0.4591	0.4599	0.4608	0.4616	0.4625	0.4633
1.8	0.4641	0.4649	0.4656	0.4664	0.4671	0.4678	0.4686	0.4693	0.4699	0.4706
1.9	0.4713	0.4719	0.4726	0.4732	0.4738	0.4744	0.4750	0.4756	0.4761	0.4767
2.0	0.4772	0.4778	0.4783	0.4788	0.4793	0.4798	0.4803	0.4804	0.4812	0.4817
2.1	0.4821	0.4826	0.4830	0.4834	0.4838	0.4842	0.4846	0.4850	0.4854	0.4857
2.2	0.4861	0.4864	0.4868	0.4871	0.4875	0.4878	0.4881	0.4884	0.4887	0.4890
2.3	0.4893	0.4896	0.4898	0.4901	0.4904	0.4906	0.4909	0.4911	0.4913	0.4916
2.4	0.4918	0.4920	0.4922	0.4925	0.4927	0.4929	0.4931	0.4932	0.4934	0.4936
2.5	0.4938	0.4940	0.4941	0.4943	0.4945	0.4946	0.4948	0.4949	0.4951	0.4952
2.6	0.4953	0.4955	0.4956	0.4957	0.4959	0.4960	0.4961	0.4962	0.4963	0.4964
2.7	0.4965	0.4966	0.4967	0.4968	0.4969	0.4970	0.4971	0.4972	0.4973	0.4974
2.8	0.4974	0.4975	0.4976	0.4977	0.4977	0.4978	0.4979	0.4979	0.4980	0.4981
2.9	0.4981	0.4982	0.4982	0.4983	0.4984	0.4984	0.4985	0.4985	0.4986	0.4986
3.0	0.4987	0.4987	0.4987	0.4988	0.4988	0.4989	0.4989	0.4989	0.4990	0.4990

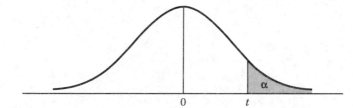

Table 2 Right-Tail Critical Values
for the t-Distribution

DF	$\alpha = 0.05$	$\alpha = 0.025$	$\alpha = 0.005$
1	6.314	12.706	63.657
2	2.920	4.303	9.925
3	2.353	3.182	5.841
4	2.132	2.776	4.604
5	2.015	2.571	4.032
6	1.943	2.447	3.707
7	1.895	2.365	3.499
8	1.860	2.306	3.355
9	1.833	2.262	3.250
10	1.812	2.228	3.169
11	1.796	2.201	3.106
12	1.782	2.179	3.055
13	1.771	2.160	3.012
14	1.761	2.145	2.977
15	1.753	2.131	2.947
16	1.746	2.120	2.921
17	1.740	2.110	2.898
18	1.734	2.101	2.878
19	1.729	2.093	2.861
20	1.725	2.086	2.845
21	1.721	2.080	2.831
22	1.717	2.074	2.819
23	1.714	2.069	2.807
24	1.711	2.064	2.797
25	1.708	2.060	2.787
26	1.706	2.056	2.779
27	1.703	2.052	2.771
28	1.701	2.048	2.763
29	1.699	2.045	2.756
30	1.697	2.042	2.750
40	1.684	2.021	2.704
60	1.671	2.000	2.660
120	1.658	1.980	2.617
∞	1.645	1.960	2.576

Source: This table is based on Table 12 of
Biometrika Tables for Statisticians. Vol. I,
edited by E. S. Pearson and H. O. Harley
(1970). By permission of the *Biometrika*
trustees.

Table 3 Right-Tail Critical Values for the χ^2 Distribution

DF	$\alpha = 0.995$	$\alpha = 0.975$	$\alpha = 0.950$	$\alpha = 0.500$	$\alpha = 0.100$	$\alpha = 0.050$	$\alpha = 0.025$	$\alpha = 0.010$	$\alpha = 0.005$
1	392704.10^{-10}	982069.10^{-9}	393214.10^{-8}	0.454936	2.70554	3.84146	5.02389	6.64390	7.87944
2	0.0100251	0.0506356	0.102587	1.38629	4.60517	5.99146	7.37776	9.21034	10.5966
3	0.0717218	0.215795	0.351846	2.36597	6.25139	7.81473	9.34840	11.3449	12.8382
4	0.206989	0.484419	0.710723	3.35669	7.77944	9.48773	11.1433	13.2767	14.8603
5	0.411742	0.831212	1.145476	4.35146	9.23635	11.0705	12.8325	15.0863	16.7496
6	0.675727	1.23734	1.63538	5.34812	10.6446	12.5916	14.4494	16.8119	18.5476
7	0.989256	1.68987	2.16735	6.34581	12.0170	14.0671	16.0128	18.4753	20.2777
8	1.34441	2.17973	2.73264	7.34412	13.3616	15.5073	17.5345	20.0902	21.9550
9	1.73493	2.70039	3.32511	8.34283	14.6837	16.9190	19.0228	21.6660	23.5894
10	2.15586	3.24697	3.94030	9.34182	15.9871	18.3070	20.4832	23.2093	25.1882
11	2.60322	3.81575	4.57481	10.3410	17.2750	19.6751	21.9200	24.7250	26.7568
12	3.07382	4.40379	5.22603	11.3403	18.5494	21.0261	23.3367	26.2170	28.2995
13	3.56503	5.00875	5.89186	12.3398	19.8119	22.3620	24.7356	27.6883	29.8195
14	4.07467	5.62873	6.57063	13.3393	21.0642	23.6848	26.1189	29.1413	31.3194
15	4.60092	6.26214	7.26094	14.3389	22.3072	24.9958	27.4884	30.5779	32.8013
16	5.14221	6.90766	7.96165	15.3385	23.5418	26.2962	28.8454	31.9999	34.2672
17	5.69722	7.56419	8.67176	16.3382	24.7690	27.5871	30.1910	33.4087	35.7185
18	6.26480	8.23075	9.39046	17.3379	25.9894	28.8693	31.5264	34.8053	37.1565
19	6.84397	8.90652	10.1170	18.3377	27.2036	30.1435	32.8523	36.1908	38.5823

Table 3 (continued)

DF	α = 0.995	α = 0.975	α = 0.950	α = 0.500	α = 0.100	α = 0.05	α = 0.025	α = 0.010	α = 0.005
20	7.43384	9.59078	10.8508	19.3374	28.4120	31.4104	34.1696	37.5662	39.9968
21	8.03365	10.28293	11.5913	20.3372	29.6151	32.6706	35.4789	38.9321	41.4011
22	8.64272	10.9823	12.3380	21.3370	30.8133	33.9244	36.7807	40.2984	42.7957
23	9.26043	11.6886	13.0905	22.3369	32.0069	35.1725	38.0756	41.6384	44.1813
24	9.88623	12.4012	13.8484	23.3367	33.1963	36.4150	39.3641	42.9798	45.5585
25	10.5197	13.1197	14.6114	24.3366	34.3816	37.6525	40.6465	44.3141	46.9279
26	11.1602	13.8439	15.3792	25.3365	35.5631	38.8851	41.9232	45.6417	48.2899
27	11.8076	14.5734	16.1514	26.3363	36.7412	40.1133	43.1945	46.9630	49.6449
28	12.4613	15.3079	16.9279	27.3362	37.9159	41.3371	44.4608	48.2782	50.9934
29	13.1211	16.0471	17.7084	28.3361	39.0875	42.5570	45.7223	49.5879	52.3356
30	13.7867	16.7908	18.4927	29.3360	40.2560	43.7730	46.9792	50.8922	53.6720
40	20.7065	24.4330	26.5093	39.3353	51.8050	55.7585	59.3417	63.6907	66.7660
50	27.9907	32.3574	34.7643	49.4439	63.1671	67.5048	71.4202	76.1539	79.4900
60	35.5345	40.4817	43.1880	59.3347	74.3970	79.0819	83.2977	88.3794	91.9517
70	43.2752	48.7576	51.7393	69.3345	85.5271	90.5312	95.0232	100.425	104.215
80	51.1719	57.1532	60.3915	79.3343	96.5782	101.879	106.629	116.329	116.321
90	59.1963	65.6446	69.1260	89.3342	107.565	113.145	118.136	124.116	128.299
100	67.3276	74.2219	77.9295	99.3341	118.494	124.342	129.561	135.807	140.169

Source: This table is based on Table 8 of *Biometrika Tables for Statisticians.* Vol., I, edited by E. S. Pearson and H. O. Hartley (1970). By permission of the *Biometrika* trustees.

Table 4   Right-Tailed Critical Values for the *F*-Distribution

Upper 1% Points

ν_2 \ ν_1	1	2	3	4	5	6	7	8	9	10	12	15	20	24	30	40	60	120	∞
1	4052	4999.5	5403	5625	5764	5859	5928	5981	6022	6056	6106	6157	6209	6235	6261	6287	6313	6339	6366
2	98.50	99.00	99.17	99.25	99.30	99.33	99.36	99.37	99.39	99.40	99.42	99.43	99.45	99.46	99.47	99.47	99.48	99.49	99.50
3	34.12	30.82	29.46	28.71	28.24	27.91	27.67	27.49	27.35	27.23	27.05	26.87	26.69	26.60	26.50	26.41	26.32	26.22	26.13
4	21.20	18.00	16.69	15.98	15.52	15.21	14.98	14.80	14.66	14.55	14.37	14.20	14.02	13.93	13.84	13.75	13.65	13.56	13.46
5	16.26	13.27	12.06	11.39	10.97	10.67	10.46	10.29	10.16	10.05	9.89	9.72	9.55	9.47	9.38	9.29	9.20	9.11	9.02
6	13.75	10.92	9.78	9.15	8.75	8.47	8.26	8.10	7.98	7.87	7.72	7.56	7.40	7.31	7.23	7.14	7.06	6.97	6.88
7	12.25	9.55	8.45	7.85	7.46	7.19	6.99	6.84	6.72	6.62	6.47	6.31	6.16	6.07	5.99	5.91	5.82	5.74	5.65
8	11.26	8.65	7.59	7.01	6.63	6.37	6.18	6.03	5.91	5.81	5.67	5.52	5.36	5.28	5.20	5.12	5.03	4.95	4.86
9	10.56	8.02	6.99	6.42	6.06	5.80	5.61	5.47	5.35	5.26	5.11	4.96	4.81	4.73	4.65	4.57	4.48	4.40	4.31
10	10.04	7.56	6.55	5.99	5.64	5.39	5.20	5.06	4.94	4.85	4.71	4.56	4.41	4.33	4.25	4.17	4.08	4.00	3.91
11	9.65	7.21	6.22	5.67	5.32	5.07	4.89	4.74	4.63	4.54	4.40	4.25	4.10	4.02	3.94	3.86	3.78	3.69	3.60
12	9.33	6.93	5.95	5.41	5.06	4.82	4.64	4.50	4.39	4.30	4.16	4.01	3.86	3.78	3.70	3.62	3.54	3.45	3.36
13	9.07	6.70	5.74	5.21	4.86	4.62	4.44	4.30	4.19	4.10	3.96	3.82	3.66	3.59	3.51	3.43	3.34	3.25	3.17
14	8.86	6.51	5.56	5.04	4.69	4.46	4.28	4.14	4.03	3.94	3.80	3.66	3.51	3.43	3.35	3.27	3.18	3.09	3.00
15	8.68	6.36	5.42	4.89	4.56	4.32	4.14	4.00	3.89	3.80	3.67	3.52	3.37	3.29	3.21	3.13	3.05	2.96	2.87
16	8.53	6.23	5.29	4.77	4.44	4.20	4.03	3.89	3.78	3.69	3.55	3.41	3.26	3.18	3.10	3.02	2.93	2.84	2.75
17	8.40	6.11	5.18	4.67	4.34	4.10	3.93	3.79	3.68	3.59	3.46	3.31	3.16	3.08	3.00	2.92	2.83	2.75	2.65
18	8.29	6.01	5.09	4.58	4.25	4.01	3.84	3.71	3.60	3.51	3.37	3.23	3.08	3.00	2.92	2.84	2.75	2.66	2.57
19	8.18	5.93	5.01	4.50	4.17	3.94	3.77	3.63	3.52	3.43	3.30	3.15	3.00	2.92	2.84	2.76	2.67	2.58	2.49
20	8.10	5.85	4.94	4.43	4.10	3.87	3.70	3.56	3.46	3.37	3.23	3.09	2.94	2.86	2.78	2.69	2.61	2.52	2.42
21	8.02	5.78	4.87	4.37	4.04	3.81	3.64	3.51	3.40	3.31	3.17	3.03	2.88	2.80	2.72	2.64	2.55	2.46	2.36
22	7.95	5.72	4.82	4.31	3.99	3.76	3.59	3.45	3.35	3.26	3.12	2.98	2.83	2.75	2.67	2.58	2.50	2.40	2.31
23	7.88	5.66	4.76	4.26	3.94	3.71	3.54	3.41	3.30	3.21	3.07	2.93	2.78	2.70	2.62	2.54	2.45	2.35	2.26
24	7.82	5.61	4.72	4.22	3.90	3.67	3.50	3.36	3.26	3.17	3.03	2.89	2.74	2.66	2.58	2.49	2.40	2.31	2.21
25	7.77	5.57	4.68	4.18	3.85	3.63	3.46	3.32	3.22	3.13	2.99	2.85	2.70	2.62	2.54	2.45	2.36	2.27	2.17
26	7.72	5.53	4.64	4.14	3.82	3.59	3.42	3.29	3.18	3.09	2.96	2.81	2.66	2.58	2.50	2.42	2.33	2.23	2.13
27	7.68	5.49	4.60	4.11	3.78	3.56	3.39	3.26	3.15	3.07	2.93	2.78	2.63	2.55	2.47	2.38	2.29	2.20	2.10
28	7.64	5.45	4.57	4.07	3.75	3.53	3.36	3.23	3.12	3.03	2.90	2.75	2.60	2.52	2.44	2.35	2.26	2.17	2.06
29	7.60	5.42	4.54	4.04	3.73	3.50	3.33	3.20	3.09	3.00	2.87	2.73	2.57	2.49	2.41	2.33	2.23	2.14	2.03
30	7.56	5.39	4.51	4.02	3.70	3.47	3.30	3.17	3.07	2.98	2.84	2.70	2.55	2.47	2.39	2.30	2.21	2.11	2.01
40	7.31	5.18	4.31	3.83	3.51	3.29	3.12	2.99	2.89	2.80	2.66	2.52	2.37	2.29	2.20	2.11	2.02	1.92	1.80
60	7.08	4.98	4.13	3.65	3.34	3.12	2.95	2.82	2.72	2.63	2.50	2.35	2.20	2.12	2.03	1.94	1.84	1.73	1.60
120	6.85	4.79	3.95	3.48	3.17	2.96	2.79	2.66	2.56	2.47	2.34	2.19	2.03	1.95	1.86	1.76	1.66	1.53	1.38
∞	6.63	4.61	3.78	3.32	3.02	2.80	2.64	2.51	2.41	2.32	2.18	2.04	1.88	1.79	1.70	1.59	1.47	1.32	1.00

Table 4 (continued)

Upper 5% Points

v_2 \ v_1	1	2	3	4	5	6	7	8	9	10	12	15	20	24	30	40	60	120	∞
1	161.4	199.5	215.7	224.6	230.2	235.0	236.8	238.9	240.5	251.9	243.9	245.9	248.0	249.1	250.1	251.1	252.2	253.3	254.3
2	18.51	19.00	19.16	19.25	19.30	19.33	19.35	19.37	19.38	19.40	19.41	19.43	19.45	19.45	19.46	19.47	19.48	19.49	19.50
3	10.13	9.55	9.28	2.12	9.01	8.94	8.89	8.85	8.81	8.79	8.74	8.70	8.66	8.64	8.62	8.59	8.57	8.55	8.53
4	7.71	6.94	6.59	5.39	6.26	6.16	6.09	6.04	6.00	5.96	5.91	5.86	5.80	5.77	5.75	5.72	5.69	5.66	5.63
5	6.61	5.79	5.41	5.19	5.05	4.95	4.88	4.82	4.77	4.74	4.68	4.62	4.56	4.53	4.50	4.46	4.43	4.40	4.36
6	5.99	5.14	4.76	4.43	4.39	4.28	4.21	4.15	4.10	4.06	4.00	3.94	3.87	3.84	3.81	3.77	3.74	3.70	3.67
7	5.59	4.74	4.35	4.12	3.97	3.87	3.79	3.73	3.68	3.64	3.57	3.51	3.44	3.41	3.38	3.34	3.30	3.27	3.23
8	5.32	4.46	4.07	3.84	3.69	3.58	3.50	3.44	3.39	3.35	3.28	3.22	3.15	3.12	3.08	3.04	3.01	2.97	2.93
9	5.12	4.26	3.86	3.63	3.48	3.37	3.29	3.23	3.18	3.14	3.07	3.01	2.94	2.90	2.896	2.83	22.79	2.75	2.71
10	4.96	4.10	3.71	3.48	3.33	3.22	3.14	3.07	3.02	2.98	2.91	2.85	2.77	2.74	2.70	2.66	2.62	2.58	2.54
11	4.84	3.98	3.59	3.36	3.20	3.09	3.01	2.95	2.90	2.85	2.79	2.72	2.65	2.61	21.57	2.53	2.49	2.45	2.40
12	4.75	3.89	3.49	3.26	3.11	3.00	2.91	2.85	2.80	2.75	2.69	2.62	2.54	2.51	2.47	2.43	2.38	2.34	2.30
13	4.67	3.81	3.41	3.18	3.03	2.92	2.83	2.77	2.71	2.67	2.60	2.53	2.46	2.42	2.38	2.34	2.30	2.25	2.21
14	4.60	3.74	3.34	3.11	2.96	2.85	2.76	2.70	2.65	2.60	2.53	2.46	2.39	2.35	2.31	2.27	2.22	2.18	2.13
15	4.54	3.68	3.29	3.06	2.90	2.79	2.71	2.64	2.59	2.54	2.48	2.40	2.33	2.29	2.25	2.20	2.16	2.11	2.07
16	4.49	3.63	3.24	3.01	2.85	2.74	2.66	2.59	2.54	2.49	2.42	2.35	2.28	2.24	2.19	2.15	2.11	2.06	2.01
17	4.45	3.59	3.20	2.96	2.81	2.70	2.61	2.55	2.49	2.45	2.38	2.31	2.23	2.19	2.15	2.10	2.06	2.01	1.96
18	4.41	3.55	3.16	2.93	2.77	2.66	2.58	2.51	2.46	2.41	2.34	2.27	2.19	2.15	2.11	2.06	2.02	1.97	1.92
19	4.38	3.52	3.13	2.90	2.74	2.63	2.54	2.48	2.42	2.38	2.31	2.23	2.16	2.11	2.07	2.03	1.98	1.93	1.88
20	4.35	3.49	3.10	2.87	2.71	2.60	2.51	2.45	2.39	2.35	2.28	2.20	2.12	2.08	2.04	1.99	1.95	1.90	1.84
21	4.32	3.47	3.07	2.84	2.68	2.57	2.49	2.42	2.37	2.32	2.25	2.18	2.10	2.05	2.01	1.96	1.92	1.87	1.81
22	4.30	3.44	3.05	2.82	2.66	2.55	2.46	2.40	2.34	2.30	2.23	2.15	2.07	2.03	1.98	1.94	1.89	1.84	1.78
23	4.28	3.42	3.03	2.80	2.64	2.53	2.44	2.37	2.32	2.27	2.20	2.12	2.05	2.01	1.96	1.91	1.86	1.81	1.76
24	4.26	3.40	3.01	2.78	2.62	2.51	2.42	2.36	2.30	2.25	2.18	2.11	2.03	1.98	1.94	1.89	1.84	1.79	1.73
25	4.24	3.39	2.99	2.76	2.60	2.49	2.40	2.34	2.28	2.24	2.16	2.09	2.01	1.96	1.92	1.87	1.82	1.77	1.71
26	4.23	3.37	2.98	2.74	2.59	2.47	2.39	2.32	2.27	2.22	2.15	2.07	2.99	1.95	1.90	1.85	1.80	1.75	1.69
27	4.21	3.35	2.96	2.73	2.57	2.46	2.37	2.31	2.25	2.20	2.13	2.06	1.96	1.93	1.88	1.84	1.79	1.73	1.67
28	4.20	3.34	2.95	2.71	2.56	2.45	2.36	2.29	2.24	2.19	2.12	2.04	1.96	1.91	1.87	1.82	1.77	1.71	1.65
29	4.18	3.33	2.93	2.70	2.55	2.43	2.35	2.28	2.22	2.18	2.10	2.03	1.94	1.90	1.85	1.81	1.75	1.70	1.64
30	4.17	3.32	2.92	2.69	2.53	2.42	2.33	2.27	2.21	2.16	2.09	2.01	1.93	1.89	1.84	1.79	1.74	1.68	1.62
40	4.08	3.23	2.84	2.61	2.45	2.34	2.25	2.18	2.12	2.08	2.00	1.92	1.84	1.79	1.74	1.69	1.64	1.58	1.51
60	4.00	3.15	2.76	2.53	2.37	2.25	2.17	2.10	2.04	1.99	1.92	1.84	1.75	1.70	1.65	1.59	1.53	1.47	1.39
120	3.92	3.07	2.68	2.45	2.29	2.17	2.09	2.02	1.96	1.91	1.83	1.75	1.66	1.61	1.55	1.50	1.43	1.35	1.25
∞	3.84	3.00	2.60	2.37	2.21	2.10	2.01	1.94	1.88	1.83	1.75	1.67	1.57	1.52	1.46	1.39	1.32	1.22	1.00

Source: This table is based on Table 18 of *Biometrika Tables for Statisticians*, Vol. I, edited by E.S. Pearson and H. O. Hartley (1970). By permission of the biometrika trustees. v_1 = numerator degrees of freedom; v_2 = denominator degrees of freedom.

Table 5 Critical Values for the Durbin–Watson Test: 5% Significance Level[a]

T	K=2 d_L	K=2 d_U	K=3 d_L	K=3 d_U	K=4 d_L	K=4 d_U	K=5 d_L	K=5 d_U	K=6 d_L	K=6 d_U	K=7 d_L	K=7 d_U	K=8 d_L	K=8 d_U	K=9 d_L	K=9 d_U	K=10 d_L	K=10 d_U	K=11 d_L	K=11 d_U
6	0.610	1.400																		
7	0.700	1.356	0.467	1.896																
8	0.763	1.332	0.559	1.777	0.368	2.287														
9	0.824	1.320	0.629	1.699	0.455	2.128	0.296	2.588												
10	0.879	1.320	0.697	1.641	0.525	2.016	0.376	2.414	0.243	2.822										
11	0.927	1.324	0.758	1.604	0.595	1.928	0.444	2.283	0.316	2.645	0.203	3.005								
12	0.971	1.331	0.812	1.579	0.658	1.864	0.512	2.177	0.379	2.506	0.268	2.832	0.171	3.149						
13	1.010	1.340	0.861	1.562	0.715	1.816	0.574	2.094	0.445	2.390	0.328	2.692	0.230	2.985	0.147	3.266				
14	1.045	1.350	0.905	1.551	0.767	1.779	0.632	2.030	0.505	2.296	0.389	2.572	0.286	2.848	0.200	3.111	0.127	3.360		
15	1.077	1.361	0.946	1.543	0.814	1.750	0.685	1.977	0.562	2.220	0.447	2.472	0.343	2.727	0.251	2.979	0.175	3.216	0.111	3.438
16	1.106	1.371	0.982	1.539	0.857	1.728	0.734	1.935	0.615	2.157	0.502	2.388	0.398	2.624	0.304	2.860	0.222	3.090	0.155	3.304
17	1.133	1.381	1.015	1.536	0.897	1.710	0.779	1.900	0.664	2.104	0.554	2.318	0.451	2.537	0.356	2.757	0.272	2.975	0.198	3.184
18	1.158	1.391	1.046	1.535	0.933	1.696	0.820	1.872	0.710	2.060	0.603	2.257	0.502	2.461	0.407	2.667	0.321	2.873	0.244	3.073
19	1.180	1.401	1.074	1.536	0.967	1.685	0.859	1.848	0.752	2.023	0.649	2.206	0.549	2.396	0.456	2.589	0.369	2.783	0.290	2.974
20	1.201	1.411	1.100	1.537	0.998	1.676	0.894	1.828	0.792	1.991	0.692	2.162	0.595	2.339	0.502	2.521	0.416	2.704	0.336	2.885
21	1.221	1.420	1.125	1.538	1.026	1.669	0.927	1.812	0.829	1.964	0.732	2.124	0.637	2.290	0.547	2.460	0.461	2.633	0.380	2.806
22	1.239	1.429	1.147	1.541	1.053	1.664	0.958	1.797	0.863	1.940	0.769	2.090	0.677	2.246	0.588	2.407	0.504	2.571	0.424	2.734
23	1.257	1.437	1.168	1.543	1.078	1.660	0.986	1.785	0.895	1.920	0.804	2.061	0.715	2.208	0.628	2.360	0.545	2.514	0.465	2.670
24	1.273	1.446	1.188	1.546	1.101	1.656	1.013	1.775	0.925	1.902	0.837	2.035	0.751	2.174	0.666	2.318	0.584	2.464	0.506	2.613
25	1.288	1.454	1.206	1.550	1.123	1.654	1.038	1.767	0.953	1.886	0.868	2.012	0.784	2.144	0.702	2.280	0.621	2.419	0.544	2.560
26	1.302	1.461	1.224	1.553	1.143	1.652	1.062	1.759	0.979	1.873	0.897	1.992	0.816	2.117	0.735	2.246	0.657	2.379	0.581	2.513
27	1.316	1.469	1.240	1.556	1.162	1.651	1.084	1.753	1.004	1.861	0.925	1.974	0.845	2.093	0.767	2.216	0.691	2.342	0.616	2.470
28	1.328	1.476	1.255	1.560	1.181	1.650	1.104	1.747	1.028	1.850	0.951	1.958	0.874	2.071	0.798	2.188	0.723	2.309	0.650	2.431
29	1.341	1.483	1.270	1.563	1.198	1.650	1.124	1.743	1.050	1.841	0.975	1.944	0.900	2.052	0.826	2.164	0.753	2.278	0.682	2.396
30	1.352	1.489	1.284	1.567	1.214	1.650	1.143	1.739	1.071	1.833	0.998	1.931	0.926	2.034	0.854	2.141	0.782	2.251	0.712	2.363
31	1.363	1.496	1.297	1.570	1.229	1.650	1.160	1.735	1.090	1.825	1.020	1.920	0.950	2.018	0.879	2.120	0.810	2.226	0.741	2.333

[a]K refers to the number of columns in X, including the constant term.

Table 5 (Continued)

T	K = 2		K = 3		K = 4		K = 5		K = 6		K = 7		K = 8		K = 9		K = 10		K = 11	
	d_L	d_U	d_L	d_U	d_L	d_U	d_L	d_U	d_L	d_U	d_L	d_U	d_L	d_U	d_L	d_U	d_L	d_U	d_L	d_U
32	1.373	1.502	1.309	1.574	1.244	1.650	1.177	1.732	1.109	1.819	1.041	1.909	0.972	2.004	0.904	2.102	0.836	2.203	0.769	2.306
33	1.383	1.508	1.321	1.577	1.258	1.651	1.193	1.730	1.127	1.813	1.061	1.900	0.994	1.991	0.927	2.085	0.861	2.181	0.795	2.281
34	1.393	1.514	1.333	1.580	1.271	1.652	1.208	1.728	1.144	1.808	1.080	1.891	1.015	1.979	0.950	2.069	0.885	2.162	0.821	2.257
35	1.402	1.519	1.343	1.584	1.283	1.653	1.222	1.726	1.160	1.803	1.097	1.884	1.034	1.967	0.971	2.054	0.908	2.144	0.845	2.236
36	1.411	1.525	1.354	1.587	1.295	1.654	1.236	1.724	1.175	1.799	1.114	1.877	1.053	1.957	0.991	2.041	0.930	2.127	0.868	2.216
37	1.419	1.530	1.364	1.590	1.307	1.655	1.249	1.723	1.190	1.795	1.131	1.870	1.071	1.948	1.011	2.029	0.951	2.112	0.891	2.198
38	1.427	1.535	1.373	1.594	1.318	1.656	1.261	1.722	1.204	1.792	1.146	1.864	1.088	1.939	1.029	2.017	0.970	2.098	0.912	2.180
39	1.435	1.540	1.382	1.597	1.328	1.658	1.273	1.722	1.218	1.789	1.161	1.859	1.104	1.932	1.047	2.007	0.990	2.085	0.932	2.164
40	1.442	1.544	1.391	1.600	1.338	1.659	1.285	1.720	1.230	1.786	1.175	1.854	1.120	1.924	1.064	1.997	1.008	2.072	0.945	2.149
45	1.475	1.566	1.430	1.615	1.383	1.666	1.336	1.721	1.287	1.776	1.238	1.835	1.189	1.895	1.139	1.958	1.089	2.022	1.038	2.088
50	1.503	1.585	1.462	1.628	1.421	1.674	1.378	1.724	1.335	1.771	1.291	1.822	1.246	1.875	1.201	1.930	1.156	1.986	1.110	2.044
55	1.528	1.601	1.490	1.641	1.452	1.681	1.414	1.727	1.374	1.768	1.334	1.814	1.294	1.861	1.253	1.909	1.212	1.959	1.170	2.010
60	1.549	1.616	1.514	1.652	1.480	1.689	1.444	1.731	1.408	1.767	1.372	1.808	1.335	1.850	1.298	1.894	1.260	1.939	1.222	1.984
65	1.567	1.629	1.536	1.662	1.503	1.696	1.471	1.735	1.438	1.767	1.404	1.805	1.370	1.843	1.336	1.882	1.301	1.923	1.266	1.964
70	1.583	1.641	1.554	1.672	1.525	1.703	1.494	1.739	1.464	1.768	1.433	1.802	1.401	1.837	1.369	1.873	1.337	1.910	1.305	1.948
75	1.598	1.652	1.571	1.680	1.543	1.709	1.515	1.743	1.487	1.770	1.458	1.801	1.428	1.834	1.399	1.867	1.369	1.901	1.339	1.935
80	1.611	1.662	1.586	1.688	1.560	1.715	1.534	1.747	1.507	1.772	1.480	1.801	1.453	1.831	1.425	1.861	1.397	1.893	1.369	1.925
85	1.624	1.671	1.600	1.696	1.575	1.721	1.550	1.751	1.525	1.774	1.500	1.801	1.474	1.829	1.448	1.857	1.422	1.886	1.396	1.916
90	1.635	1.679	1.612	1.703	1.589	1.726	1.566	1.755	1.542	1.776	1.518	1.801	1.494	1.827	1.469	1.854	1.445	1.881	1.420	1.909
95	1.645	1.687	1.623	1.709	1.602	1.732	1.579	1.758	1.557	1.778	1.535	1.802	1.512	1.827	1.489	1.852	1.465	1.877	1.442	1.903
100	1.654	1.694	1.634	1.715	1.613	1.736	1.592	1.758	1.571	1.780	1.550	1.803	1.528	1.826	1.506	1.850	1.484	1.874	1.462	1.898
150	1.720	1.746	1.706	1.760	1.693	1.774	1.679	1.788	1.665	1.802	1.651	1.817	1.637	1.832	1.622	1.847	1.608	1.862	1.594	1.877
200	1.758	1.778	1.748	1.789	1.738	1.799	1.728	1.810	1.718	1.820	1.707	1.831	1.697	1.841	1.686	1.852	1.675	1.863	1.665	1.874

Table 5 (Continued)

T	K=12 d_L	K=12 d_U	K=13 d_L	K=13 d_U	K=14 d_L	K=14 d_U	K=15 d_L	K=15 d_U	K=16 d_L	K=16 d_U	K=17 d_L	K=17 d_U	K=18 d_L	K=18 d_U	K=19 d_L	K=19 d_U	K=20 d_L	K=20 d_U	K=21 d_L	K=21 d_U
16	0.098	3.503																		
17	0.138	3.378	0.087	3.557																
18	0.177	3.265	0.123	3.441	0.078	3.603														
19	0.220	3.159	0.160	3.335	0.111	3.496	0.070	3.642												
20	0.263	3.063	0.200	3.234	0.145	3.395	0.100	3.542	0.063	3.676										
21	0.307	2.976	0.240	3.141	0.182	3.300	0.132	3.448	0.091	3.583	0.058	3.705								
22	0.349	2.897	0.281	3.057	0.220	3.211	0.166	3.358	0.120	3.495	0.083	3.619	0.052	3.731						
23	0.391	2.826	0.322	2.979	0.259	3.128	0.202	3.272	0.153	3.409	0.110	3.535	0.076	3.650	0.048	3.753				
24	0.431	2.761	0.362	2.908	0.297	3.053	0.239	3.193	0.186	3.327	0.141	3.454	0.101	3.572	0.070	3.678	0.044	3.773		
25	0.470	2.702	0.400	2.844	0.335	2.983	0.275	3.119	0.221	3.251	0.172	3.376	0.130	3.494	0.094	3.604	0.065	3.702	0.041	3.790
26	0.508	2.649	0.438	2.784	0.373	2.919	0.312	3.051	0.256	3.179	0.205	3.303	0.160	3.420	0.120	3.531	0.087	3.632	0.060	3.724
27	0.544	2.600	0.475	2.730	0.409	2.859	0.348	2.987	0.291	3.112	0.238	3.233	0.191	3.349	0.149	3.460	0.112	3.563	0.081	3.658
28	0.578	2.555	0.510	2.680	0.445	2.805	0.383	2.929	0.325	3.050	0.271	3.168	0.222	3.283	0.178	3.392	0.138	3.495	0.104	3.592
29	0.612	2.515	0.544	2.634	0.479	2.755	0.418	2.874	0.359	2.992	0.305	3.107	0.254	3.219	0.208	3.327	0.166	3.431	0.129	3.528
30	0.643	2.477	0.577	2.592	0.512	2.708	0.451	2.823	0.392	2.937	0.337	3.050	0.286	3.160	0.238	3.266	0.195	3.368	0.156	3.465
31	0.674	2.443	0.608	2.553	0.545	2.665	0.484	2.776	0.425	2.887	0.370	2.996	0.317	3.103	0.269	3.208	0.224	3.309	0.183	3.406
32	0.703	2.411	0.638	2.517	0.576	2.625	0.515	2.733	0.457	2.840	0.401	2.946	0.349	3.050	0.299	3.153	0.253	3.252	0.211	3.348
33	0.731	2.382	0.668	2.484	0.606	2.588	0.546	2.692	0.488	2.796	0.432	2.899	0.379	3.000	0.329	3.100	0.283	3.198	0.239	3.293
34	0.758	2.355	0.695	2.454	0.634	2.554	0.575	2.654	0.518	2.754	0.462	2.854	0.409	2.954	0.359	3.051	0.312	3.147	0.267	3.240
35	0.783	2.330	0.722	2.425	0.662	2.521	0.604	2.619	0.547	2.716	0.492	2.813	0.439	2.910	0.388	3.005	0.340	3.099	0.295	3.190
36	0.808	2.306	0.748	2.398	0.689	2.492	0.631	2.586	0.575	2.680	0.520	2.774	0.467	2.868	0.417	2.961	0.369	3.053	0.323	3.142
37	0.831	2.285	0.772	2.374	0.714	2.464	0.657	2.555	0.602	2.646	0.548	2.738	0.495	2.829	0.445	2.920	0.397	3.009	0.351	3.097
38	0.854	2.265	0.796	2.351	0.739	2.438	0.683	2.526	0.628	2.614	0.575	2.703	0.522	2.792	0.472	2.880	0.424	2.968	0.378	3.054

Table 5 (Continued)

T	K = 12 d_L	K = 12 d_U	K = 13 d_L	K = 13 d_U	K = 14 d_L	K = 14 d_U	K = 15 d_L	K = 15 d_U	K = 16 d_L	K = 16 d_U	K = 17 d_L	K = 17 d_U	K = 18 d_L	K = 18 d_U	K = 19 d_L	K = 19 d_U	K = 20 d_L	K = 20 d_U	K = 21 d_L	K = 21 d_U
39	0.875	2.246	0.819	2.329	0.763	2.413	0.707	2.499	0.653	2.585	0.600	2.671	0.549	2.757	0.499	2.843	0.451	2.929	0.404	3.013
40	0.896	2.228	0.840	2.309	0.785	2.391	0.731	2.473	0.678	2.557	0.626	2.641	0.575	2.724	0.525	2.808	0.477	2.892	0.430	2.974
45	0.988	2.156	0.938	2.225	0.887	2.296	0.838	2.367	0.788	2.439	0.740	2.512	0.692	2.586	0.644	2.659	0.598	2.733	0.553	2.807
50	1.064	2.103	1.019	2.163	0.973	2.225	0.927	2.287	0.882	2.350	0.836	2.414	0.792	2.479	0.747	2.544	0.703	2.610	0.660	2.675
55	1.129	2.062	1.087	2.116	1.045	2.170	1.003	2.225	0.961	2.281	0.919	2.338	0.877	2.396	0.836	2.454	0.795	2.512	0.754	2.571
60	1.184	2.031	1.145	2.079	1.106	2.127	1.068	2.177	1.029	2.227	0.990	2.278	0.951	2.330	0.913	2.382	0.874	2.434	0.836	2.487
65	1.231	2.006	1.195	2.049	1.160	2.093	1.124	2.138	1.088	2.183	1.052	2.229	1.016	2.276	0.980	2.323	0.944	3.371	0.908	2.419
70	1.272	1.986	1.239	2.026	1.206	2.066	1.172	2.106	1.139	2.148	1.105	2.189	1.072	2.232	1.038	2.275	1.005	2.318	0.971	2.362
75	1.308	1.970	1.277	2.006	1.247	2.043	1.215	2.080	1.184	2.118	1.153	2.156	1.121	2.195	1.090	2.235	1.058	2.275	1.027	2.315
80	1.340	1.957	1.311	1.991	1.283	2.024	1.253	2.059	1.224	2.093	1.195	2.129	1.165	2.165	1.136	2.201	1.106	2.238	1.076	2.275
85	1.369	1.946	1.342	1.977	1.315	2.009	1.287	2.040	1.260	2.073	1.232	2.105	1.205	2.139	1.177	2.172	1.149	2.206	1.121	2.241
90	1.395	1.937	1.369	1.966	1.344	1.995	1.318	2.025	1.292	2.055	1.266	2.085	1.240	2.116	1.213	2.148	1.187	2.179	1.160	2.211
95	1.418	1.929	1.394	1.956	1.370	2.984	1.345	2.012	1.321	2.040	1.296	2.068	1.271	2.097	1.247	2.126	1.222	2.156	1.197	2.186
100	1.439	1.923	1.416	1.948	1.393	1.974	1.371	2.000	1.347	2.026	1.324	2.053	1.301	2.080	1.277	2.108	1.253	2.135	1.229	2.164
150	1.579	1.892	1.564	1.908	1.550	1.924	1.535	1.940	1.519	1.956	1.504	1.972	1.489	1.989	1.474	2.006	1.458	2.023	1.443	2.040
200	1.654	1.885	1.643	1.896	1.632	1.908	1.621	1.919	1.610	1.931	1.599	1.943	1.588	1.955	1.576	1.967	1.565	1.979	1.554	1.991

Source: This table is reproduced from N. E. Savin, and K. J. White, "The Durbin–Watson Test for Serial Correlation with Extreme Sample Sizes or many Regressors." *Econometrica*, 45:1989–1996, 1977. With permission from The Econometric Society.

Index

INDEX NOTE

A list of econometric case studies is included under the main heading "Economic models"